Contributing authors

Dr Andrew Fabian, Institute of Astronomy, Cambridge, UK

Dr Vincent Icke, Institute of Astronomy, Cambridge, UK
  California Institute of Technology, Pasadena, California, USA

Dr Bernard Jones, Institute of Astronomy, Cambridge, UK

Dr Janet Jones, Institute of Astronomy, Cambridge, UK

Dr Craig Mackay, Institute of Astronomy, Cambridge, UK

Dr Barry Madore, Institute of Astronomy, Cambridge, UK

Katherine Madore, formerly University of Toronto, Canada

Dr Jacqueline Mitton, Institute of Astronomy, Cambridge, UK

Dr Simon Mitton, Institute of Astronomy, Cambridge, UK

Dr Peter Owen, Royal Military College of Science,
  Shrivenham, UK

Professor John R. Percy, David Dunlap Observatory, University
  of Toronto, Canada

Dr James Pringle, Institute of Astronomy, Cambridge, UK

Patricia Stewart, University Computer Laboratory,
  Cambridge, UK

Dr Adrian Webster, Institute of Astronomy, Cambridge, UK

Dr John Whelan, Institute of Astronomy, Cambridge, UK

Dr Gareth Wynn-Williams, Mullard Radio Astronomy
  Observatory, Cambridge, UK

The Cambridge Encyclopædia of Astronomy

Editor-in-Chief Simon Mitton MA PhD
University of Cambridge, Institute of Astronomy

Foreword by Sir Martin Ryle FRS
University of Cambridge, Department of Physics
Mullard Radio Astronomy Observatory

CROWN PUBLISHERS, INC., NEW YORK

First published in 1977 by Crown Publishers, Inc.,
One Park Avenue, New York, N.Y. 10016

Library of Congress Cataloging Publication Data

Main entry under title:

The Cambridge encyclopaedia of astronomy.

    Includes index.
    1. Astronomy.   I. Mitton, Simon, 1946–
QB43.2.C35   520   77–2766
ISBN 0–517–52806–1

Originated and produced for Crown Publishers, Inc. by
Trewin Copplestone Publishing Ltd, Advance House,
101–109 Ladbroke Grove, London W11

©Trewin Copplestone Publishing Ltd 1977

Editor: Ann Hill
Designer: Derek Birdsall AGI FSIA
Diagrams and graphs by Michael Robinson

Typesetting, monochrome and colour reproduction by
Westerham Press, Kent, England
Printed by Mohn Gordon in Italy

Contents

Foreword

The invention of the telescope in the seventeenth century led to the discovery that the Milky Way was composed of countless stars and its subsequent development eventually revealed that even the Milky Way system was itself but one of an immense number of similar star systems in a Universe of unimaginable extent. The last 30 years have seen a revolution in our knowledge of the Universe of no less significance which has developed from the extension of our observations outside the optical range, first to radio wavelengths and then, as spacecraft allowed telescopes to be carried above the absorption of the earth's atmosphere, to X-ray and gamma-ray wavelengths. The launching of deep-space probes has allowed the Moon and many of the planets to be investigated at close quarters.

The observations have revealed a remarkable range of unexpected phenomena: the existence of complex molecules in interstellar gas clouds; the conditions associated with star formation; the eventual collapse of stars to form the incredibly dense neutron stars and possibly the even more dramatic black holes; the discovery of distant galaxies where new sources of energy provide intense radio and X-ray emission, and the evidence from them and from the weak radio background radiation have given us new ways of exploring the earliest stages in the history of the Universe more than 10,000 million years ago.

These discoveries have changed the whole balance of astronomy; there are many phenomena which are still unexplained in the strange universe of high-energy astrophysics – the pulsars, the radio galaxies and quasars. But it is in just these objects, where the physical conditions are far beyond the reach of what we can attain in our terrestrial laboratories, that some of the most crucial tests of fundamental physical theory may be made.

The University of Cambridge has had a long association with astronomy. Here Newton developed the law of universal gravitation, and Eddington and Jeans worked on theories of the structure of stars. Large and active research groups are now established here in the fields of optical and radio astronomy and theoretical astrophysics. It is therefore appropriate perhaps that a major new reference work for a general readership should be compiled in Cambridge, where the editor has been able to call on the talents of astronomers whose research covers a very broad range of interests.

One person could scarcely hope to write a definitive survey of the whole of classical and modern astronomy. This *Cambridge Encyclopaedia of Astronomy* represents the combined efforts of a team of young astronomers, each qualified in the fields they write about. Close and continuous liaison between the writers has produced a uniformity of style and coverage that would be hard to achieve with a world-wide collaboration.

The Encyclopaedia draws together many remarkable discoveries and presents them in context through a series of themes rather than by a disjointed alphabetical listing. This book mirrors the interests of active astronomers without diminishing the achievements of classical astronomy. Its authoritative and lengthy text is complemented by finely-drawn diagrams and by new photographs contributed by many observatories. The authors have produced a reference work of lasting value by taking the difficult middle path between a too-simple popularisation and a textbook. It can be commended to all who have a keen interest in the world of modern science.

Martin Ryle

Introduction

In the last two decades a series of dramatic discoveries has transformed astronomy, the oldest of the sciences, and rolled back the frontiers of our Universe. The invention of new instruments, such as radio telescopes and X-ray satellites, has given us completely different views of the heavens. Man's own journeys into space have had a significant part to play, and probes have visited many other planets. Consequently the study of our Solar System has evolved from a quiet backwater to a raging torrent of information. In the realms of the stars, astronomers have made many fascinating discoveries of organic molecules, the precursors of life itself. Out in the far Universe, they have found entire galaxies that have suffered enormous explosions and that now emit prodigious quantities of high-energy rays. These are just a few highlights from an era that will unquestionably be looked upon as a golden age for astronomy. Our picture of the Universe has changed so much that most reference books have been completely overtaken by the onward rush of data. In addition to this, the direction of research has radically altered. In the circumstances only a totally new approach can give a comprehensive guide to modern astronomical knowledge.

It was against this background of new information that my colleagues and I worked out the specification for an entirely new astronomical reference book. The ideas crystallized during a summer school on galaxies held in Sicily in July 1974. After much planning we completed the text in early 1977. Our purpose is to present to you a broadly-based survey with an emphasis on firmly established new results. We have sought to create a reference work with a high scientific standard and of lasting value. Complementing the authoritative text are many photographs obtained from leading observatories and a large series of diagrams drawn exclusively for this book. Every section has been written by researchers active in the field concerned.

In this *Cambridge Encyclopaedia of Astronomy* an extensive index, together with the descriptive captions to the photographs and diagrams, provides you with a base from which to explore the main text. Where necessary, tables and appendices furnish supplementary information on measurements, symbols, and abbreviations. The computer-drawn star atlas shows all stars visible to the naked eye in both northern and southern skies. Our main text ranges over the whole of astronomy. There are descriptive sections on planets, our Sun, the stars, galaxies, life in the Universe, and cosmology. Practical aspects of astronomy are covered in depth in the chapters that describe professional and amateur instruments. Demanding topics such as binary stars, neutron stars, and black holes will challenge your growing knowledge as you are brought to the frontiers of research.

The *Cambridge Encyclopaedia* does not use the traditional alphabetical listing typical of most reference books. Instead the material has been gathered into cohesive themes in order to present a more accurate and understandable guide to the new Universe. Major descriptions and explanations are indicated by SMALL CAPITAL LETTERS; cross-references by *italic letters*. The extensive indexing system enables a particular topic to be located rapidly, where it will be discussed in context. This is an encyclopaedia which you can sit down and read in addition to using it as a reference book.

Simon Mitton

Abbreviations

Units

Throughout this book the international system of scientific units is used for specifying the magnitudes of physical quantities. This international system, based upon the metric system, was established in 1960 in the hope of securing world-wide uniformity. Although scientists have long used the metric system it is only recently that in English speaking countries the metric system has been adopted for everyday use. Since the international metric system is now widely used in educational institutions throughout the world we decided to adopt it for the Cambridge Encyclopaedia of Astronomy. This will ensure the long-term usefulness of the book when the present transitional period is over. In order to assist readers who may not be fully familiar with the international system we have gathered here the conversion factors for the principal units of that system.

As base units the international system has the **metre** for distance measurement, the **kilogram** for weight measurement, the **second** for the measurement of time, the **ampere** as the unit of electric current, and the **kelvin** as the unit of temperature. These units have internationally agreed definitions. The metre, for example, is defined in terms of the wavelength of light from a krypton-86 atom. From these basic units a whole system of derived units results : for example, the **watt** for measuring power, the **joule** for measuring energy, and the **newton** for measuring force.

In addition to the basic international system astronomers have agreed on certain special units which are of value when dealing with the large quantities often encountered in astronomy. A convenient unit for measuring distances within the Solar System, for example, is the **astronomical unit**, which is the average distance from the Earth to the Sun. Beyond the Solar System a convenient unit for the measurement of the distances of stars is the **parsec** (pc) ; this is the distance at which one astronomical unit subtends an angle of 1 second of arc. For larger distances the **kiloparsec** (kpc) and **megaparsec** (Mpc) are used. In popular literature the term light year is frequently encountered but this is not used either in professional work or in this book. The astronomical unit of mass is the mass of the Sun, and similarly the astronomical unit for luminosity is the luminosity of the Sun. Conversion factors for these units are given below.

Powers of ten or index notation

Astronomers deal with quantities ranging from the very large to the very small. The distance from Earth to Sun, for example, is 149,600,000,000 metres. These large numbers are not only hard to write but also they are difficult to visualize. To economize on writing time and to make comparison between numbers easier astronomers use the Powers of Ten or Index Notation. This mathematical shorthand is used throughout this book. Some examples will make the system clear.

$1000 = 10^3$; the number 3, called the power or index, tells us that the 1 is followed by 3 zeros written in full. Similarly $10^6 =$ one million, that is a 1 followed by 6 zeros.
The system can be extended to numbers smaller than 1 by use of a negative power. For example $10^{-1} = 0.1$, $10^{-3} = 0.001$, $10^{-6} = 0.000001$.

We can now consider the prefixes which are used in the metric system in order to extend the magnitude of the basic units.

mega- $= 10^6$
kilo- $= 10^3$
centi- $= 10^{-2}$
milli- $= 10^{-3}$
micro- $= 10^{-6}$
nano- $= 10^{-9}$

Chemical elements

H	hydrogen
He	helium
Li	lithium
Be	beryllium
B	boron
C	carbon
N	nitrogen
O	oxygen
Ne	neon
Mg	magnesium
Si	silicon
S	sulphur
A	argon
Fe	iron

Symbols

a	semi-major axis of ellipse
b	galactic longitude
c	speed of light
e	eccentricity of ellipse
G	gravitational constant
g	acceleration due to gravity
h	Planck's constant
i	angle of inclination
l	galactic latitude
m	mass
m_e	electron mass
m_p	proton mass
n	neutron
p	proton
PSR	pulsar
QSO	quasar
r	radius
t	time
v	velocity
γ	photon
ν	neutrino
☉	Sun
⊕	Earth
☾	Moon
☿	Mercury
♀	Venus
♆	Neptune
♅	Uranus
♂	Mars
♄	Saturn
♃	Jupiter
♇	Pluto
♈	First point of Aries
☊	Longitude of ascending node
☋	Longitude of descending node

Astronomical constants

Astronomical Distance Measurements

$$
\begin{aligned}
1 \text{ astronomical unit (AU)} &= 1.49598 \times 10^8 \text{ kilometres} \\
&= 9.29560 \times 10^7 \text{ miles} \\
1 \text{ parsec (pc)} &= 206264.8 \text{ AU} \\
&= 3.0856 \times 10^{13} \text{ kilometres} \\
&= 1.92 \times 10^{13} \text{ miles} \\
&= 3.2615 \text{ light years} \\
1 \text{ light year} &= 9.4605 \times 10^{15} \text{ metres} \\
&= 6.324 \times 10^4 \text{ AU} \\
&= 5.88 \times 10^{12} \text{ miles}
\end{aligned}
$$

Astronomical Measurement of Mass

$$
\begin{aligned}
\text{Solar mass } (M_\odot) &= 1.989 \times 10^{30} \text{ kilograms} \\
&= 1.989 \times 10^{27} \text{ tonnes} \\
\text{Earth mass } (M_\oplus) &= 5.977 \times 10^{24} \text{ kilograms} \\
&= 5.977 \times 10^{21} \text{ tonnes}
\end{aligned}
$$

Astronomical Measurement of Time

$$
\begin{aligned}
1 \text{ sidereal day} &= 23^h 56^m 04^s.098 \text{ mean solar time} \\
1 \text{ tropical year (equinox to equinox)} &= 365.2422 \text{ mean solar days} \\
1 \text{ sidereal year (fixed star to fixed star)} &= 365.2564 \text{ mean solar days}
\end{aligned}
$$

Other Astronomical Units

$$
\begin{aligned}
\text{Solar radius } (R_\odot) &= 6.96 \times 10^8 \text{ metres} \\
\text{Solar luminosity } (L_\odot) &= 3.9 \times 10^{26} \text{ watts} \\
\text{Solar mean density} &= 1.41 \times 10^3 \text{ kilogram per cubic metre} \\
\text{Earth mean radius} &= 6371.23 \text{ kilometres}
\end{aligned}
$$

Constants of Physics

$$
\begin{aligned}
\text{Velocity of light} &= 2.997925 \times 10^8 \text{ metres per second} \\
\text{Mass of electron} &= 9.10956 \times 10^{-31} \text{ kilograms} \\
\text{Mass of hydrogen atom} &= 1.67333 \times 10^{-27} \text{ kilograms} \\
\text{Ratio of proton to electron mass} &= 1836
\end{aligned}
$$

Electromagnetic spectrum

wavelength	frequency	equivalent energy
100 km	3 kHz	
1 km	300 kHz	
1 m	300 MHz	
1 cm	30 GHz	
1 mm	300 GHz	0.0012 eV
1 m	3×10^{14} Hz	1.24 eV
1 nm	3×10^{17} Hz	1.24 keV
1 Å	3×10^{18} Hz	12.4 keV
10^{-12} m	3×10^{20} Hz	1.24 Mev

Catalogue prefixes

M	Messier Catalogue of nebulae
IC	Index Catalogue of nebulae
NGC	New General Catalogue of nebulae
Arp	Arp Catalog of Peculiar Galaxies
PSR	pulsar
3C, 4C, etc	Third, Fourth Cambridge catalogues of radio sources
PKS	Parkes catalogue

Other conversion factors

length

$$
\begin{aligned}
1 \text{ metre (m)} &= 1.094 \text{ yards} \\
&= 39.37 \text{ inches} \\
1 \text{ centimetre (cm)} &= 0.394 \text{ inches} \\
1 \text{ kilometre (km)} &= 0.621 \text{ miles} \\
1 \text{ micrometre } (\mu m) &= 10^{-6} \text{ metres} \\
1 \text{ nanometre (nm)} &= 10^{-9} \text{ metres} \\
1 \text{ ångström (Å)} &= 0.1 \text{ nanometres} \\
&= 10^{-10} \text{ metres}
\end{aligned}
$$

volume

$$
\begin{aligned}
1 \text{ litre (l)} &= 0.131 \text{ cubic yards} \\
&= 0.220 \text{ UK gallons} \\
&= 0.264 \text{ US gallons} \\
1 \text{ cubic metre } (m^3) &= 1.308 \text{ cubic yards} \\
1 \text{ cubic parsec } (pc^3) &= 2.938 \times 10^{49} \text{ cubic metres}
\end{aligned}
$$

mass

$$
\begin{aligned}
1 \text{ tonne (t)} &= 1000 \text{ kilograms} \\
1 \text{ ton} &= 1016 \text{ kilograms} \\
&= 2240 \text{ pounds} \\
1 \text{ kilogram (kg)} &= 2.205 \text{ pounds} \\
1 \text{ pound} &= 454 \text{ grams} \\
1 \text{ solar mass } (M_\odot) &= 1.989 \times 10^{30} \text{ kg}
\end{aligned}
$$

density

$$
1 \text{ kilogram per cubic metre } (kg\,m^{-3}) = 0.062 \text{ pounds per cubic foot}
$$

velocity

$$
\begin{aligned}
1 \text{ metre per second } (m\,s^{-1}) &= 3.281 \text{ feet per second} \\
&= 0.911 \text{ kilometres per hour} \\
100 \text{ kilometres per hour} &= 62.1 \text{ miles per hour} \\
1000 \text{ kilometres per second } (1000\,km\,s^{-1}) &= 2.24 \text{ million miles per hour}
\end{aligned}
$$

force

$$
\begin{aligned}
1 \text{ newton (N)} &= 0.225 \text{ pounds-force} \\
1 \text{ dyne} &= 10 \text{ micronewtons}
\end{aligned}
$$

energy

$$
\begin{aligned}
1 \text{ joule (J)} &= 10^7 \text{ ergs} \\
&= 0.239 \text{ calories} \\
1 \text{ kilowatt-hour (kwh)} &= 3.6 \times 10^6 \text{ joules} \\
1 \text{ electron volt (eV)} &= 1.602 \times 10^{-19} \text{ joules} \\
1 \text{ million electron volts (MeV)} &= 1.602 \times 10^{-13} \text{ joules} \\
1 \text{ billion electron volts (GeV)} &= 1.602 \times 10^{-10} \text{ joules}
\end{aligned}
$$

power

$$
\begin{aligned}
1 \text{ watt (W)} &= 1 \text{ joule per second} \\
1 \text{ kilowatt (kw)} &= 10^3 \text{ watts} \\
&= 1.341 \text{ horsepower} \\
1 \text{ solar luminosity } (L_\odot) &= 3.9 \times 10^{26} \text{ watts}
\end{aligned}
$$

magnetism

$$
1 \text{ tesla (T)} = 10,000 \text{ gauss}
$$

Editorial acknowledgements

Many individuals and organizations have assisted in the preparation of this book, and it is impossible to thank all of them individually. We are grateful to all those who supported the project at the Institute of Astronomy, and especially to Professor D.Lynden-Bell for his encouragement. Credits are given below to several institutions that provided photographs. We would also like to thank the following individuals: William Baum (Lowell Observatory), Russell Cannon (UK Schmidt Telescope), Z.Ceplecha (Ondrejov Observatory), Richard Faller (Sacramento Peak Observatory), Leon Golub (American Science and Engineering), R.F.Griffin (Institute of Astronomy), S.Gull (Mullard Radio Astronomy Observatory), Guy Jackson (NASA), James Vette (NASA), Sarah Lee Lippincott (Sproul Observatory), David Malin (Anglo-Australian Observatory), S.Marx (Tautenberg Observatory), David Moore (Kitt Peak National Observatory), Gordon Newkirk (High Altitude Observatory), Donald Osterbrock (Lick Observatory), J.Weber (University of Maryland), R.M.West (European Southern Observatory), and Harold Zirin (Hale Observatories). The authors' manuscripts were expertly typed by J.Eagle, and other office assistance given by M.Jacobs and M.Lawrance.

It is my special pleasure to thank Trewin Copplestone, Derek Birdsall, Ann Hill and Michael Robinson for their enthusiastic support throughout the project.

The Apollo, Lunar Orbiter, and Mariner photography has been provided by the National Space Science Date Center through the World Data Center A for rockets and satellites; Goddard Space Flight Center, Maryland, USA.

Kitt Peak National Observatory and Cerro Tololo Inter-American Observatory photographs are © The Association of Universities for Research in Astronomy, Inc.

Hale Observatories photographs are © The Hale Observatories, Pasadena, California, USA.

Anglo-Australian Observatory photographs are © Anglo-Australian Observatory, Epping, NSW 2121, Australia.

UK Schmidt Telescope Unit Photographs are © UK Science Research Council.

University of Cambridge maps and photographs were originated at the Mullard Radio Astronomy Observatory and the Institute of Astronomy.

The Star Atlas was computed from copyrighted data kindly supplied by the Smithsonian Astrophysical Observatory, Cambridge, Massachusetts, USA on the IBM 370/165 computer at the University of Cambridge, UK.

S.M.

1. A survey of the Universe

Perspectives of astronomy

We are surrounded by the sounds and slowly fading images of a distant world. As each sound is recognized, each new sight put into perspective, we hopefully come to a clearer view of the Universe as a whole. In the present we find evidence of our origin and this evidence is not unintelligible to the methods of science. However, while we live in a world where news in many forms is still reaching us from the distant past, the future chapters of the world will not be read out to near generations of ours. In the time a thousand histories of the Universe have been written by man, the Universe itself has barely begun to turn another page. We must content ourselves with predicting how the story has progressed, and accepting how the chapters may proceed from here. Astronomy is one version of that story.

It is a difficult and ambiguous task to see the forest for the trees, to place the many aspects of astronomy in perspective. As in most disciplines, there are few absolutes and in many respects astronomy is still wondering about the relative ordering of things. Here, for example, the debate is at the level of deciding which of two objects is bigger or brighter or further away. These are obviously vital questions; certainly they are some of the simplest. Nonetheless, they can be amazingly difficult questions to answer. This is especially true in astronomy because we have quickly gone beyond the scales of common experience and are attempting to encompass parts of the Universe whose distances, sizes, energies and lifetimes are vastly different from anything we have previously encountered. And there lies a major part of the timeless appeal of astronomy.

Astronomers have produced a new vocabulary to describe the exotic objects that they have discovered and predicted; they have invented new names for the vast distances they have encountered; and, to place astronomy in a wider perspective, they have developed a new science. One of these, ASTROPHYSICS, is astronomy in an absolute context, the context of physical processes where the terminology and observations are reducible to accepted units of length, time and energy. These standard, absolute units link the laws of physics with common experience; astrophysics links the physical processes in stars with the experiences of the terrestrial laboratory.

We can gain a feeling for the Universe from observations of the relative properties of its constituents; but we only begin to have an understanding in terms of our own experience when the absolute properties of the Universe are revealed. The first absolute determinations of distances to planets, stars and galaxies, each heralded the birth of a new epoch of investigation. As we survey our Universe, we must take a series of bold steps away from home. We embark on a journey of incomparable proportions, a journey of changing perspectives and ever-widening horizons, a journey that is far from over.

Measurement

In everyday life, when we cannot directly pace off a distance, we confidently go beyond the metre stick and employ the tried-and-true methods of geometry and trigonometry. These become our new tools. But the way in which we use these tools is governed by a completely different, more subtle principle; our belief in the uniformity of nature. This belief allows us to draw parallels between the properties of objects near and far. In the context of the scale of the Universe we call this underlying principle, 'distance by analogy'.

Our methods are not foolproof and as such we must be prepared for a range of errors of many types. The methods and mathematics of surveying are well defined and can be modified to accommodate the measuring of a field, a city, a planet or distances to the stars. The methods of trigonometry are not concerned with the objects they measure, and the random errors we make in applying these methods of surveying depend strictly on how well we do our work. In astronomy this usually amounts to how accurately we can measure small angles. Analogy, on the other hand requires a new step, in fact, a leap. In it we assume that some critical quality (height or brightness, for example) of a distant object is the same as some nearby object. The nearby object is familiar to us and we have measured its properties directly. Subsequently, using these assumed properties, we can employ the principles of geometry to calculate an appropriate distance.

Our calculations may be well done, but if our assumptions are wrong, our answers will be systematically in error. While random errors in measurement quickly reach overwhelming proportions in frontier astronomy, where the limits of every experiment are pushed to their furthest, their effects are predictable (figure 1.1). However, systematic errors in our assumptions loom, unknown, at every turn. Astronomers must make many assumptions and draw many analogies about objects far outside our normal experience. To appreciate the consequences of this necessary fact is to understand a frailty of every model of the Universe.

1.1: *All observations of the physical world involve uncertainty and inaccuracy. These errors are frequently predictable and then the most likely value for a quantity may be calculated.*

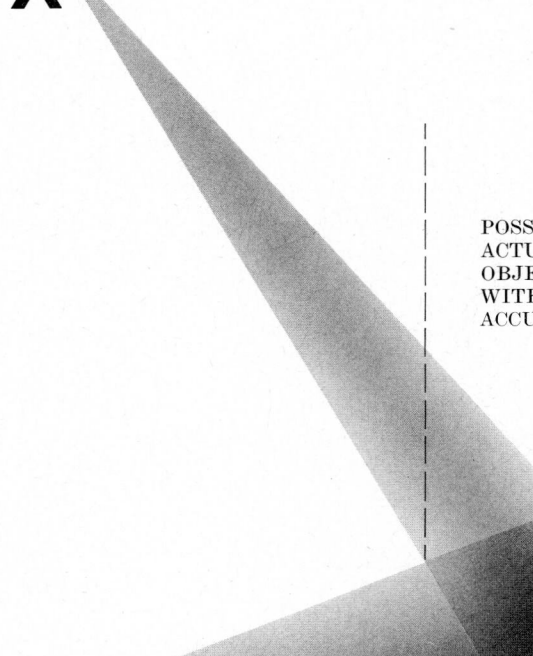

FIRST OBSERVATION

POSSIBLE RANGE IN ACTUAL POSITION OF OBJECT CONSISTENT WITH OBSERVATIONAL ACCURACY

ACCURACY OF MEASUREMENT

FORMAL CALCULATED POSITION OF OBJECT

SECOND OBSERVATION

Distances

Fundamental to the absolute determinations of distances in astronomy is the *trigonometrical parallax*. Although the name is not common outside of astronomy, the principle is in constant use by us all: we are walking in a field, the grass at our feet quickly brushes past us, a tree in the distance more slowly shifts its position, but a wooded hill on the horizon appears unmoved. Here we are playing tricks with our language. Neither the trees, nor the grass, nor the horizon has moved; we are the ones, the only ones, in motion. However, in realizing this we have stated the principle of parallax: as we change our position, objects around us appear to move. Moreover, if we want to keep an object in our view we must turn our head more quickly the closer it is to us. Here are the fundamentals of a relation between angles (the turn of our head) and distances (to the trees and the grass) which are the quantitative bases of trigonometrical parallax. It is again as true for trees and cities as it is for planets and stars (figure 1.2). Consciously or subconsciously, parallax is a natural method that we all use in judging distances as we move from place to place.

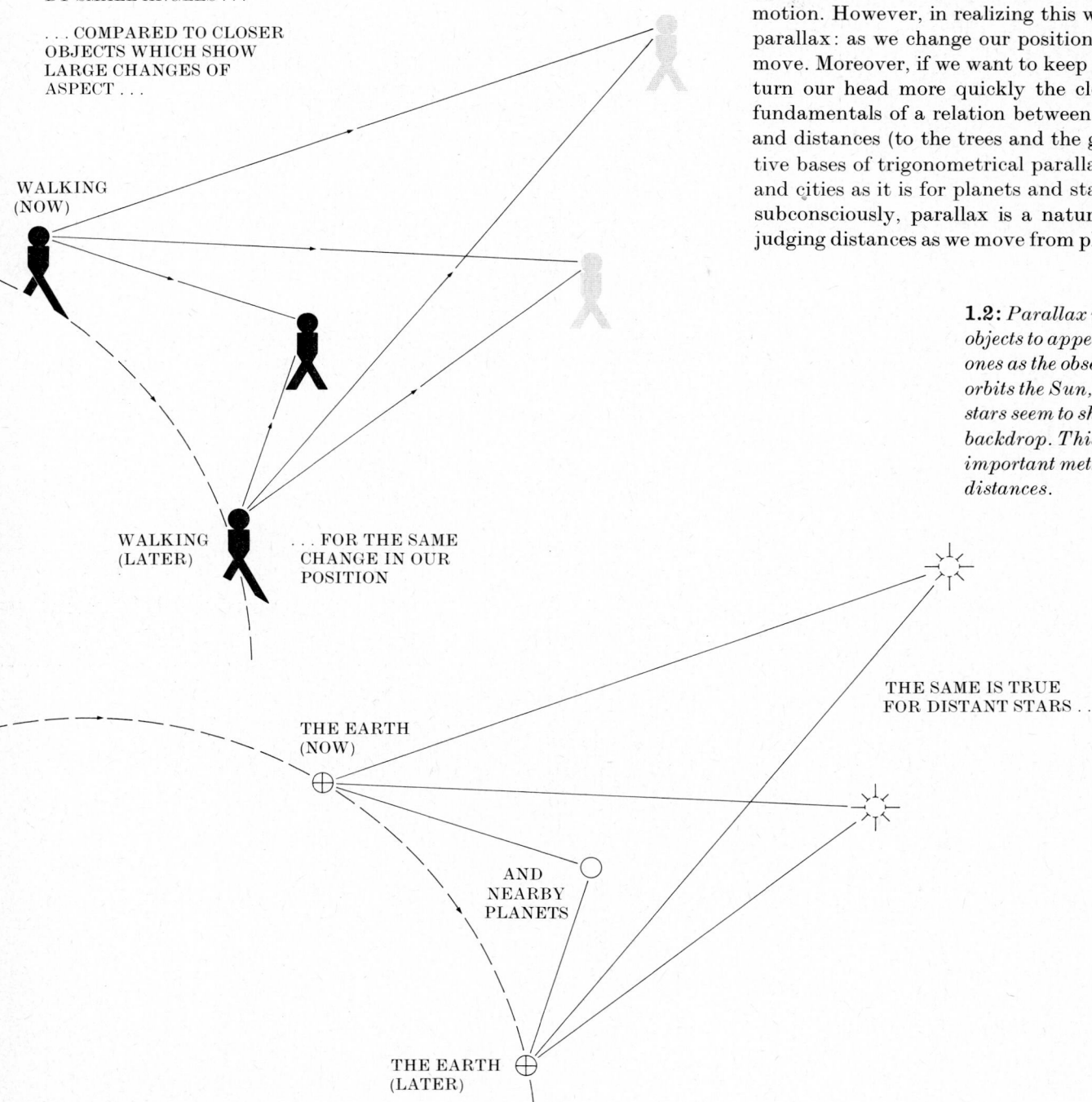

DISTANT OBJECTS SHIFT
THEIR APPARENT POSITIONS
BY SMALL ANGLES . . .

. . . COMPARED TO CLOSER
OBJECTS WHICH SHOW
LARGE CHANGES OF
ASPECT . . .

WALKING
(NOW)

WALKING
(LATER)

. . . FOR THE SAME
CHANGE IN OUR
POSITION

1.2: *Parallax is the effect which causes nearby objects to appear to move relative to distant ones as the observer moves. As the Earth orbits the Sun, planets and neighbouring stars seem to shift against the remote starry backdrop. This forms the basis of an important method for measuring astronomical distances.*

THE SAME IS TRUE
FOR DISTANT STARS . . .

THE EARTH
(NOW)

AND
NEARBY
PLANETS

THE EARTH
(LATER)

Nature has also provided us with another means of judging distance, but without our moving. Of course we have another name for it, but it is again the same principle. This time it is called stereo vision. Our visual sensation of depth is a direct consequence of our having two eyes; with it we have a natural ability to judge relative distances. Stereo vision, in fact, is so natural that we seldom have consciously to look out of one eye, remember how things are arranged, and then look out of the other to compare. Often it is amusing to stop and do just this, but the brain does such a fine job of assimilating the information for us that we rarely have to think about the process.

The relative distances of objects can be adequately judged over several hundred metres using stereo vision. Shifting our head back and forth can give us some additional depth and of course changing our position bodily is even more effective. In this process we have made the subtle transition between stereo vision and general parallax. Is there any limit? Can we see how far away the Moon is? Can we experience the depth of space? Surprisingly, perhaps, the answer is yes. We are forever changing our perspective: daily as the Earth rotates, yearly as we circle the Sun, over millennia as the stars proceed through space. All of the Universe is in motion and these motions can free us from our forest and actually allow us to see the depth of space.

Stars and planets constitute the first recognizable members of the Universe. The Sun itself is a star, shining by light produced deep in the hot reaches of its interior. Energized by reactions caused by the tremendous temperature and pressure exerted by its great mass, the Sun produces light by thermonuclear reactions. Many orders of magnitude smaller and less massive, the planets are found revolving around the Sun. Unable to produce temperatures in their interiors sufficient to start nuclear burning, the planets are without light of their own. The Earth, like the other planets that circle the Sun (and doubtlessly circle other similar stars) is dependent on its parent star for light. In the sky we see stars by their own light; the planets are visible only by reflection.

As a reminder of the initial whirl that existed when the Earth first formed, our planet is spinning. Drawn together by gravity and bound by molecular and atomic forces, it is a rocky sphere some six thousand kilometres in radius, formed in orbit round the Sun. It required a quarter of a million years of the evolution of man to discover this dimension of our Earth. For most of that time, six thousand kilometres was conceptually large enough to encompass most of the 'known Universe'. And yet soon after, the Earth itself gave man new eyes with which to look beyond.

Our planet turns in relative solitude in space, but it is neither unique nor totally alone in its travels around the Sun. The Earth is one of a system of planets of various sizes and distances from our star. By chance, one of these planets formed so close to us that we share the same orbit. Seen from afar, the Earth and Moon form a double planet, weaving their way carefully around the Sun, trading positions every 28 days or so.

Our satellite-planet, the Moon, is so close that in the course of an evening we can see the effects of its proximity. When the Moon appears to rise in the East as we turn with the surface of the Earth, a close inspection of its leading edge (or limb) will reveal features that slowly disappear as the evening progresses and the Earth moves us to a different point of view. This is known as daily or DIURNAL PARALLAX.

We may try the same test with the planets but to no avail. We must conclude that the planets are so much further away than the Moon that we cannot detect the effects of diurnal parallax on their images. And so the scale of our world must increase immensely as we progress beyond Earth. The discovery of horizons beyond horizons repeats over and over in the exploration of the Universe.

Let us now apply more fully our methods of geometry and analogy to the Solar System and in so doing highlight some dangers. For simplicity, let us assume (incorrectly) that all spherical objects in the Solar System are of the same diameter. This we boldly accept, for the moment, on the grounds of the uniformity of nature. Our simple assumption, right or wrong, allows us to go ahead and calculate distances to the Sun, the Moon and most of the planets. We don't even have to have the correct absolute sizes of any one of them in order to calculate their relative distances.

One immediate consequence of our assumption is that the Sun and Moon must be at the same distance, for in the sky they both appear to be of the same size. How confident can we be of our conclusion? We may repeat our measurements, but the result would be essentially the same. Alternatively, we may attempt a different experiment, such as looking for diurnal parallax of features on the surface of the Sun. But reconsiderations may be forced upon us from other directions. Having the Moon pass in front of the Sun would certainly demand that we abandon our conclusion and look again at our assumptions and this is the case in the simple illustration we give here. Unfortunately, in contemporary astronomy few tests of simple assumptions are as compelling as a total eclipse of the Sun!

Some assumptions about the uniformity of nature, as yet, have had no tests at all. Some of our crucial assumptions may be very wrong and the discovery of such systematic errors may result in a great restructuring of our thoughts. We have created a mental picture of the Universe based on our observations and our assumptions. Fuelled by new observations and different assumptions, revolutions of thought about the Universe have occurred many times in our recent past, and revolutions have occurred when many thought they understood the basic structure of the world; similarly, today, we believe we understand.

The neighbourhood of the Earth

From our vantage point on Earth, it is possible to observe the motions of the planets and to map out their relative distances from the Sun with great accuracy. This was first done over 300 years ago but it required most of the intervening centuries before the key to the absolute distance scale within the Solar System was found. Simple observations of the changing directions of the planets in the sky can give the ratios of their distances from the Sun; the absolute distance to any one member of the Solar System gives the distances to all others. Unfortunately, the major planets are too far away for our method of diurnal parallax to provide an absolute distance, and an alternative was slow in arriving.

Orbiting primarily in a region of space between Mars and Jupiter are the minor planets, known as *asteroids*. Some of these periodically swing close enough to the Earth for trigonometrical parallax to be employed to find their distances. At the turn of the twentieth century, the asteroid Eros passed within 40 million kilometres of Earth, sufficiently close to fix the absolute scale of the Solar System. The mean distance of the Earth to the Sun is well established and even the small variations about this mean are well studied. Today the fundamental place of the asteroids has been superseded by radar-ranging techniques using signals sent from Earth to Venus. Reflected from the surface of Venus and timed in their round-trip journey at the speed of light, these signals also measure the distance directly. With confidence we can write down that the mean distance from the Earth to the Sun is 149 597 893 km, the ASTRONOMICAL UNIT.

With centuries of technological expertise on our side, we have actually left the Earth. We have seen our planet from afar; we have followed our robot electronics to the Moon and have scraped at its surface; we have sent cameras in advance to study the atmospheres and surfaces of Mars, Mercury, Venus and Jupiter. We have landed spacecraft safely on the surfaces of Venus and Mars, and searched for traces of life in the Martian dust. While the Solar System was once the remote preserve of the astronomer, it is now fast becoming a conscious part of the daily experience of us all.

If we move away from the Sun, we pass its rocky companions, the inner planets and the asteroids, we pass beyond the giant outer planets of Jupiter and Saturn, still shrouded in their massive primordial atmospheres, and slowly we leave behind the icy comets which inhabit the outermost reaches of our Solar System. And then we face the seemingly limitless void of space. No sooner have we assimilated the duration of our lengthy journey as a measure of the size of our Solar System than the Galaxy looms beyond, even larger still.

The kingdom of the stars

The stars that form our Galaxy, the *Milky Way*, are still remote, but not untouched by our travels. Parallax has no theoretical limit in its application; the distances to all visible objects in the Universe could, in principle, be determined by this method. If our eyes could detect shifts in angles many times smaller than they can, it would be possible to experience the dimensions of our Galaxy immediately. To see how unrealistic this is is to receive another taste of the vastness of the Universe.

We can achieve the equivalent of stereo vision by taking successive photographs of a scene as we move relative to it. Our Earth is constantly moving with respect to the starry skies. We can photograph after moving a few centimetres, after moving 12 000 km, the distance the Earth will rotate us in half a day (diurnal parallax) or after 150 000 000 km, halfway across the orbit around the Sun (annual parallax). By measuring angles a thousand times smaller than can be detected by the human eye, by 'blinking' after our 'eyes' have separated a million million (10^{12}) times over, then and only then can we perceive the distance to the stars, but even then only the nearest ones.

On Earth, when the stereo effects of our vision fail us, we not uncommonly estimate a distance from the apparent size of distant objects such as large buildings or hills. For example, we can estimate the distance of an orchard by comparing the apparent size of its individual trees to the known sizes of trees around us. Of course we must be able to distinguish at a distance small saplings from their older, taller parents. Indeed, we must take care not to compare nearby cedars with distant oaks. In precisely the same way we may judge the distances to stars, individually or in groups. And like the sizes and types of trees we find that stars come in a variety of types with different intrinsic brightness and colours.

Like studying a forest, the study of a cluster of stars provides us with a group of objects all at a common distance. In a cluster we can discover the relative properties of many stars and later require that we know the true distance to only one of the stars in order to define the absolute properties of them all. It turns out that for the ordinary stars the intrinsic brightness of the star is determined by an easily-measurable quantity, the colour. So we can measure a colour, then calculate an intrinsic brightness and infer the distance from how bright a star appears. Here only distance is assumed to account for any difference between the intrinsic and apparent brightnesses.

Of great importance in the distance determination was the discovery of *interstellar dust*. Space is not devoid of matter between the stars. The environment in which a star is embedded and the dust in space through which its light must pass in reaching us can seriously affect the apparent luminosity of a star. This dimming, however, is quite independent of distance and special techniques had to be developed to detect it and remove its effects before distances were calculated. Fortunately *interstellar absorption*, as it is called, always makes stars appear redder in a very precise way.

1.3: *Great optical telescopes probe the kingdom of the stars and the far Universe beyond. The time-exposure of six hours shows circular trails of bright southern stars above the dome of the Anglo-Australian Telescope. Earth's rotation relative to the stars causes the trailing. Surveys of the southern sky are also conducted at the cluster of telescopes in the Chilean Andes, home of the Cerro Tololo Inter-American Observatory. (Anglo-Australian Observatory, Australia/Cerro Tololo Inter-American Observatory, Chile and USA)*

Furthermore, as the star is made fainter and redder by absorption, the details of its *spectrum* are still not affected, and thus it has been possible to separate the effects of reddening and distance independently.

Clusters of stars contain a wealth of information and their importance cannot be overstated. They have provided valuable keys in the understanding of *stellar evolution*, the structure of our Galaxy, and in the establishment of that amazing construct, the distance scale for objects beyond our Galaxy.

Within our Galaxy, supergiant stars of high luminosity can be used to peer out through the dust to great distances. Plotting the positions of these stars around us, we discover that we are living in a disc galaxy where stars are forming only in selected regions. When seen from afar, these regions form a two-armed spiral pattern which radiates out from the nucleus of our Galaxy and passes through the solar neighbourhood after several turns. Our optical picture soon runs out because of the obscuring effects of the dust, but the gas in these regions where stars are forming can be detected by other means.

The realm of the nebulae

Our Galaxy is some 5×10^{17} kilometres in radius, and our journey is still far from complete. Around us in space, far beyond the edge of our Galaxy, lie other spiral forms reminiscent of the Milky Way but still further away. The metre is not a convenient unit for astronomy, nor is the kilometre, for the numbers quickly become unmanageable. The distance from the Earth to the Sun, the astronomical unit (about 1.5×10^8 kilometres) is quickly dwarfed by the distances to stars. We must define new units in terms of the stars themselves. To this purpose we have the *parsec*, equal to 3×10^{13} kilometres. Suffice it to say that the nearest stars are a few parsecs distant, while our Galaxy sprawls over 30000 pc in diameter, containing some 100 000 000 000 stars.

Can we keep on going further? Such distances each time demand far bigger and far brighter objects to mark them out. Must we now say that all spiral objects have the same diameter and boldly gauge their distances on the uniformity of nature? Analogy has led us astray before. But even the demands of these distances are not yet too great, because in these distant forests there is still a recognizable flicker of light.

Seen in a handful of clusters in our Galaxy, and spread in greater numbers throughout the Milky Way, is an important class of stars, the *Cepheid variables*. The signal of their presence is their regular variation in brightness, and they have been found in the distant galaxies. These stars are so bright and their intrinsic properties are so well behaved, compared to other stars, that they dominate the survey of distances to local galaxies. Cepheids change their brightness and colour with precise repetition. We can in fact learn of a Cepheid's true luminosity by merely measuring its period of variation! Distances follow from a comparison of this true luminosity with the apparent luminosity.

Many secondary stellar distance indicators can be invoked to check the Cepheid distance scale in local galaxies, but each one carries its own list of uncertainties which far exceed the uncertainties involved in using Cepheids alone. All other regular variables, such as the *RR Lyrae* stars, are more uncertain in their intrinsic properties and, being much fainter than Cepheids, they can be seen only over shorter distances. Exploding stars are so rare and unpredictable that their properties have not been well determined: *novae* are too faint even at the peak of their explosion to be used much further than Cepheids, while *supernovae*, which sometimes rival entire galaxies in their brightness, are very rare. Finally, bright stable supergiants have a wide spread of intrinsic magnitudes and colours. The best that can be done with these secondary-distance indicators is to show that no tremendously great errors have been made so far.

Our LOCAL GROUP OF GALAXIES contains the Milky Way and its two irregular companions, the Magellanic Clouds, two other spirals in the constellations of Andromeda and Triangulum designated as M31 and M33 respectively, and finally a few dozen fainter systems of spherical, elliptical or irregular shape. Beyond the Local Group only one shaggy spiral galaxy NGC2403 has been studied for Cepheids. This galaxy is very similar to our nearer neighbour M33. While NGC2403 is our first step out of the Local Group, it is also the last step beyond which Cepheids, even at their maximum brightness, fall below the limits of detection of our most powerful telescopes. No sooner have we reached this realm of the

1.4: *Two star clusters in Perseus are examples of young star families. Cluster distances are often found by measuring the fluctuations of variable stars. (Royal Observatory, Edinburgh, UK)*

1.5: *The great globular cluster 47 Tucanae is a very ancient family of hundreds of thousands of stars. (Cerro Tololo Inter-American Observatory, Chile and USA)*

nebulae than we find ourselves again searching for new indicators of cosmic distance. Rapidly, too, our units of measure are becoming burdensome; the parsec has already been replaced by the kiloparsec, a thousand times larger but to cope with the galaxies we must use the megaparsec, a unit step one million parsecs long.

Our search for new distance indicators, the standard candles and standard metres of the Universe, must be conducted before other indicators have left off. We have the Local Group of galaxies, but it is NGC 2403 that holds an important key to further steps. Not far away in the sky from NGC 2403 is a grouping of several more galaxies, including the spiral M 81. If these now form a physical clustering in space with NGC 2403, the way is open for us to include this larger sample in our study. But first, how far is NGC 2403?

The cumulative efforts of many years of photography of NGC 2403, using the world's largest telescopes, revealed the stellar population of this galaxy. Viewing individual stars we can estimate its distance. As in the Local Group of galaxies, the best hope for an accurate distance lies with the Cepheids. Dozens of photographs have been taken to follow the Cepheids through their cycles, but the only result was barely to detect their presence as they reached their peak brightness every few weeks. Some seventeen Cepheids have been discovered in NGC 2403 but their properties leave the answer of the distance ambiguous. These Cepheids are not observed to be the same as local Cepheids; many of them are much too red. Does our assumption of the uniformity of nature fail with the Cepheids?

If we abandon Cepheids as standard candles to our nearby galaxies, then for some time to come we will have to relegate the extra-galactic distance scale to a realm of highly uncertain guesses, plagued by the vagaries of small samples. One hope still exists. The colours of the Cepheids in NGC 2403 may have been measured slightly wrong or interstellar reddening may be changing their light before it reaches us.

Meanwhile the possible effects of interstellar reddening are straightforward to evaluate. As for all stars, reddening makes us over-estimate the distance because we incorrectly associate its dimming effect with distance. Other luminous stars might also be affected by this dust, so they cannot be easily used to compare the results of the Cepheids. But a geometrical test is always welcome. Here, the discovery of objects with constant size would be of great benefit.

Great luminous regions of gas surround certain hot stars which have recently formed from the interstellar medium and which are responsible for energizing the surrounding gas. In galaxies where star formation is proceeding at about the same pace, the diameters of the largest excited gas clouds appear to be of about the same size. These regions are a few per cent of the diameters of galaxies themselves and they are both recognizable and measurable over cosmic distances. If we now assume that the largest gas clouds in each of the galaxies of the NGC 2403–M 81 group are identical in diameter to the clouds in other galaxies of similar type in the Local Group, then we can calculate a distance. The distance we find in this way is identical to the distance found to the Cepheids after correcting for reddening. This agreement increases our confidence, although the distances to the nearest groups of galaxies are still systematically uncertain by as much as 30 per cent.

The larger Virgo cluster of galaxies which can be seen stretching over ten degrees of our night-time sky is the next major step out. Here the last recognizable objects left, besides the gas clouds and the galaxies themselves, are the globular star clusters. In fact for galaxies where stars are no longer forming or where no gas exists, *globular clusters* are the last familiar objects for survey purposes. Smaller than the galaxies around which they orbit but larger than the loose galactic star clusters, the globular clusters can be seen by the combined light of their millions of members. But only if these systems are the same in age, constitution, and number as globular clusters around our Galaxy can we correctly judge the distances by them.

The expansion of the Universe

Before the brightest stars and globular clusters in distant galaxies fade below our limits of detection, and well before the hydrogen clouds can no longer be measured, we come face to face with one of the most amazing properties of our world: the Universe is expanding!

The space between galaxies is increasing. Smaller parts of the Universe may cling together but at increasing distances they fail to stop the outward motion; the Universe is proceeding on without them! If we cannot hold onto our neighbouring galaxies by gravity, the space between us and them will continue to increase. All galaxies around us are seen to be rushing away from us and we from them. Indeed when we measure the velocities of galaxies around us, the Universe is seen to be thinning out in all directions.

Bit by bit we are being left behind. The further we look out into space the greater volume we encompass. Greater distances mean greater velocities of expansion of one side relative to the other, so distant galaxies move away from us more quickly than near ones. However the rate of expansion is so small that we must go to cosmic distances before the general expansion is measurable. In the absence of any other forces, the change over the distance between the Sun and the nearest star would only be a few centimetres per second and the cumulative effect over a year would be to increase the distance by only one part in 30 000 000 000.

The combined light of millions upon millions of stars that form

1.6: *Special telescopes look at our nearest star, the Sun. This building houses the Kitt Peak solar telescope. (Kitt Peak National Observatory,* USA*)*

1.7: *The invisible Universe is probed by radio telescopes. This Jodrell Bank dish is the oldest of the large instruments. (University of Manchester,* UK*)*

individual galaxies is detectable long after the individual stars fail to be distinguishable in a telescope. Similarly, the composite spectrum of galaxies can be detected over vast distances. Bright and dark lines that appear in the spectra of galaxies provide our link to perhaps the most powerful distance indicator we can hope for at extragalactic distances. Lines in the spectra of distant galaxies show a systematic displacement in frequency when compared to reference lines observed in the laboratory. This change can be simply explained by a relative motion between us and the galaxies, a *Doppler shift*. Since the spectral lines are always found to shift towards the red end of the spectrum, we come to speak of the motions of galaxies in terms of their *redshifts*. For all intents and purposes the redshift and the expansion of the Universe are one and the same.

The general expansion continues out as far as we can see. But can it just continue forever? With distance, light dims and so our last sight is of the galaxies themselves, reduced to fading points of light. Our last chance now comes to learn about the distant void. Here we assume that all brightest galaxies of a given type are of the same intrinsic luminosity. With this assumption, the apparent luminosities of galaxies at the limit of detection become another measure of distance. We now have two independent measurements to the edge of the visible Universe (redshift and luminosity) and with them we have the makings of a grand experiment: to guess the fate of the Universe.

The distances to which we can see represent travel times, at the speed of light, which rival the age of the Universe as an entity in itself. On a simple view, the expansion could not have been going on for more than some 20 000 000 000 years in the past. Running the expansion backwards further than that would pass the time when all matter in the observable Universe was at a single point, the *big bang* or the beginning of the Universe.

The Universe, too, is a product of its past and so its fate will some day be judged by observations of its history up to now. That judgement is not in. The distant galaxies were younger when they shone with the light that reaches us today. Their images are from the past. The galaxies were different, but so too was the Universe around each galaxy. Comparing apparent brightnesses of galaxies with their redshifts may be telling us about the evolution of the Universe, and it may equally well be telling us about the evolution of galaxies. More likely it is telling us about both. As always, an inconsistency between our two distance indicators is a signal for change and a chance for discovery.

When we look at galaxies far in the past, it is like estimating the distance to a forest so remote in space and time that the trees whose heights we measure have long since died and their offspring have evolved a million times. Are these, indeed, the distant ancestors of more familiar sights? Our estimate of distances, based on unknown properties, must be very insecure. Each theory of evolution and each reasoned guess as to their environment carries factors of potential error. And, perhaps, these things we see became extinct and correspond to no object in our present experience!

In our race to see the extremes of the Universe, to predict its past, and to speculate on its future, astronomers have encountered galaxies of amazing variety: beautifully-formed spirals in massive clusters or adrift alone in space; radio galaxies, exploding systems alive with motion, radiation and activity; elliptical galaxies, slowly dying where star formation ended a billion years ago, and finally the *quasars*, points of light with redshifts indicating that they lived with fierce intensity in the most distant past. Our terrestrial laws of physics appear to be sufficient to explain most of what we want to see.

Every generation of astronomy has worked in this mixed aura of awe and confidence. We slowly change our views, with reluctance at first, which turns to fervour when we must. And so heresy can turn to dogma, dogma to history. Often in the past we may have missed the forest for the trees, but now what secrets await us in the sky and in the worlds beyond the forest?

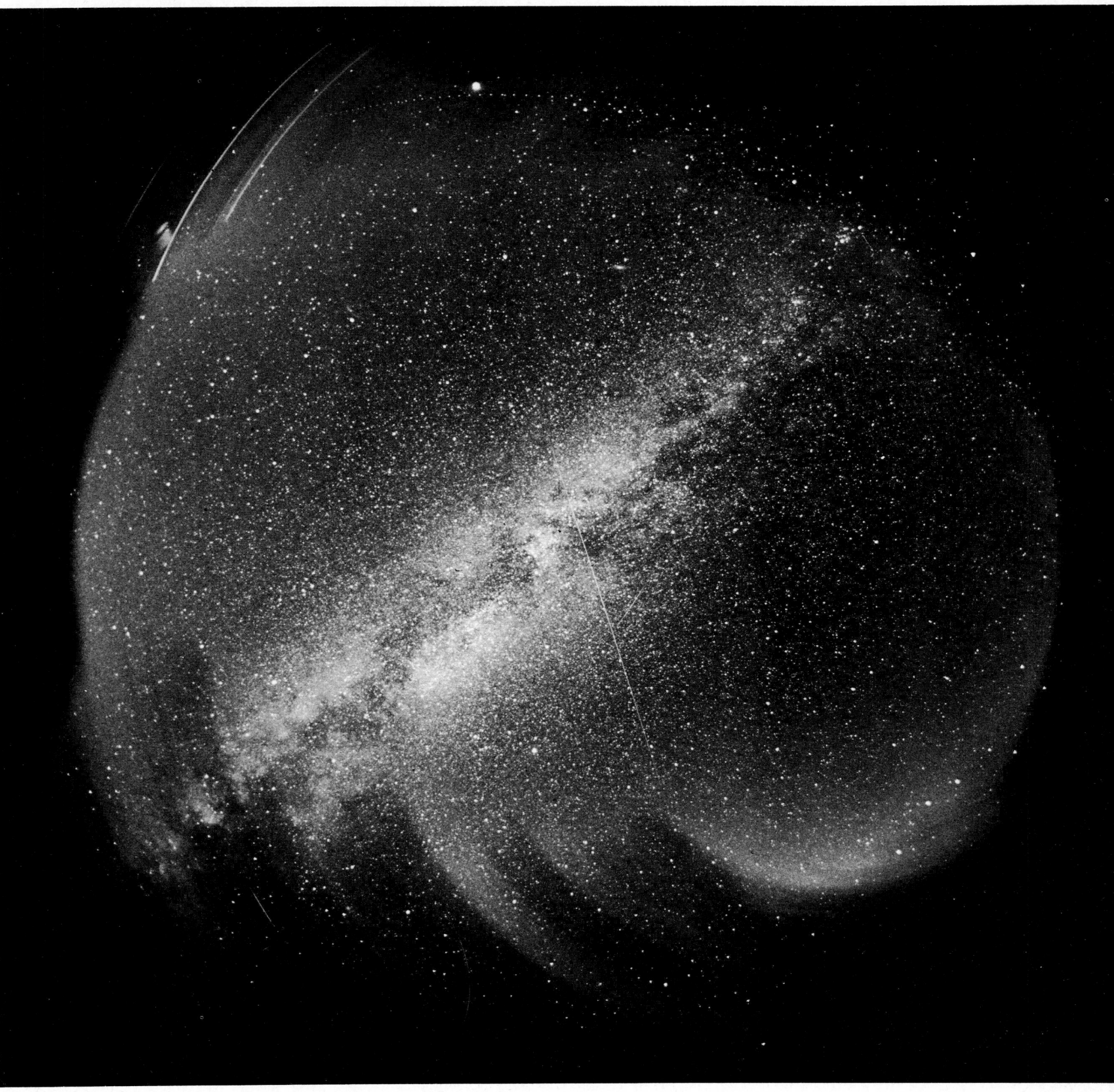

2. The stars observed

Introduction

This chapter describes the properties of stars that can be derived from observations. Stars may be the most important component of the Universe, and to illustrate this point we may note that life on Earth is sustained by light and heat from the nearest star, our Sun. The stars themselves make up the great galaxies, and are the principal source of galactic light, except in certain disturbed galaxies. On a clear moonless night you can see the faint band of light across the sky which is known as the *Milky Way* (figure 2.1). Galileo's telescope showed that the Milky Way is composed of millions of individual stars, and now we know that the entire Milky Way, our own Galaxy, contains about 10^{11} stars. Because the stars are a great distance from Earth it is not easy to observe all their properties. Although the energy output and temperature can both be found fairly readily, and the spectrum of the emitted light obtained, it is difficult or impossible to measure the mass and radius of the average star. Furthermore, no direct data whatever can be measured for the interiors of stars, with the possible exception of the Sun.

From careful analysis of the observed properties of stars, scientists have deduced how stars change with time. This triumph of astrophysics was largely possible because the behaviour of stars is controlled by relatively simple laws of physics. This contrasts with the evolution of galaxies, where a much more complicated situation, that has so far defied convincing explanation, exists. An understanding of the observational properties of stars provides an essential prelude to an astrophysical explanation of the life-styles of different stars, a theme we take up in chapter 3. Some of the properties of the nearest and brightest stars are given in tables 2.1 and 2.2.

Star distances and motions

If we are to understand the nature of heavenly bodies, it is essential to know how far away they are; only then can we calculate the sizes and energy outputs of planets, stars, and galaxies, and ultimately determine the scale of the Universe itself. So far as we can tell, mankind has always considered the stars to be further away than the Sun, Moon and planets, but the first measurement of a stellar distance was not until 1837, when Bessel determined the distance to 61 Cygni by TRIGONOMETRICAL PARALLAX.

The method of trigonometrical parallax is similar to the classical techniques used by surveyors, and it is based on the fact that the Earth circles the Sun on an orbit of about 300 million kilometres diameter. As Earth goes on its annual motion (figure 2.2), each of the nearest stars traces out a minute ellipse on the sky with respect to the faraway stars. In the course of a year the apparent position of a nearby star will vary by an angle that we shall here denote as 2p; one half of this angle, p, is termed the PARALLAX of the star, which is normally given in units of seconds of arc (arc sec). In practice the parallax is always less than 1 arc sec. The nearest star, Proxima Centauri, has a parallax of 0.765 arc sec, and 61 Cygni a parallax of 0.293 arc sec; these angles are far less than the smallest

2.1: *An all-sky panorama of the Milky Way taken with a camera that has a fish-eye lens. The Milky Way is the conspicuous band of light running from lower left to upper right. The circular streaks around the horizon are due to nearby trees and lights. The straight line near the centre is caused by sunlight reflected from the orbiting space laboratory, Skylab. (Ondrejov Observatory, Czechoslovakia)*

Table 2.1: The nearest 10 stars

Star		Apparent visual magnitude	Absolute visual magnitude	Spectral type	Proper motion (arc sec yr^{-1})	Distance (parsecs)	Radial velocity (km s^{-1})
Proxima Centauri		11.05	15.45	M5	3.85	1.31	−16
α Centauri	A	−0.01	4.35	G2V	3.68	1.34	−22
	B	1.33	5.69	K2V			
Barnard's Star		9.54	13.25	M5V	10.31	1.81	−108
Wolf 359		13.53	16.68	M8	4.71	2.33	+13
HD 95735		7.50	10.49	M2V	4.78	2.49	−84
Sirius	A	−1.45	1.42	A1V	1.33	2.65	−8
	B	8.68	11.56	WD			
UV Ceti	A	12.45	15.27	M5	3.36	2.72	+30
	B	12.95	15.8	M6			
Ross 154		10.6	13.3	M4	0.72	2.90	−4
Ross 248		12.29	14.80	M6	1.59	3.15	−81
ε Eridani		3.73	6.13	K2V	0.98	3.30	+16

Table 2.2: The brightest 14 stars

Star		Apparent visual magnitude	(B–V)	Absolute visual magnitude	Spectral type	Proper motion (arc sec yr^{-1})	Distance (parsecs)	Radial velocity (km s^{-1})
Sirius	α CMa	−1.45	0.00	+1.41	A1V	1.324	2.7	−8
Canopus	α Car	−0.73	+0.16	−4.7	F0Ib	0.025	60	+21
Rigil Kent	α Cen	−0.1	+0.7	+4.3	G2V	3.675	1.33	−24
Arcturus	α Boo	−0.06	+1.23	−0.2	K2III	2.285	11	−5
Vega	α Lyr	+0.04	0.00	+0.5	A0V	0.345	8.1	−14
Capella	α Aur	+0.08	+0.79	−0.6	G8	0.436	14	+30
Rigel	β Ori	+0.11	−0.03	−7.0	B8 Ia	0.001	250	+21
Procyon	α CMi	+0.35	0.41	+2.65	F5 IV	1.248	3.5	−3
Achernar	α Eri	+0.48	−0.18	−2.2	B5 IV	0.098	39	+19
Hadar	β Cen	+0.60	−0.23	−5.0	B1 II	0.035	120	−11
Altair	α Aql	+0.77	+0.22	+2.3	A7 V	0.658	5.0	−26
Betelgeuse	α Ori	+0.8	+1.86	−6	M2 I	0.029	200	+21
Aldebaran	α Tau	+0.85	+1.53	−0.7	K5 III	0.203	21	+54
Acrux	α Cru	+0.9	−0.26	−3.5	B2 IV	0.043	80	−7

discernible with the naked eye. The determination of trigono-metrical parallaxes is an exacting and tedious endeavour, requiring many photographs (up to 50) of each star field, spaced over several years. Only a few thousand stars have had their parallaxes measured by trigonometry, and only a few hundred are known correct to 10 per cent.

The method of trigonometrical parallax has given us the important unit of distance known as the PARSEC, abbreviated pc. This is the distance at which a star would have a parallax of 1 arc sec, and it is equal to 3.086×10^{13} km. In most popular writing the light year is used; there are 3.262 light years in a parsec. Actually there is no star within 1 pc; Proxima Centauri is 1.3 pc from us. To turn a parallax quoted in arc seconds into a distance in parsecs it is necessary to divide the quantity 1 by the parallax.

Star distances cannot be found by trigonometrical parallax beyond 300 pc as the angle is then immeasurably small, and accurate work is therefore restricted to about 30 pc from the Sun. Consequently if we had only this method at hand the task of surveying our Universe would be impossible. Fortunately we can keep track of distance by other methods.

2.2: *Stellar parallax. As the Earth orbits the Sun, a nearby star apparently moves relative to distant stars.*

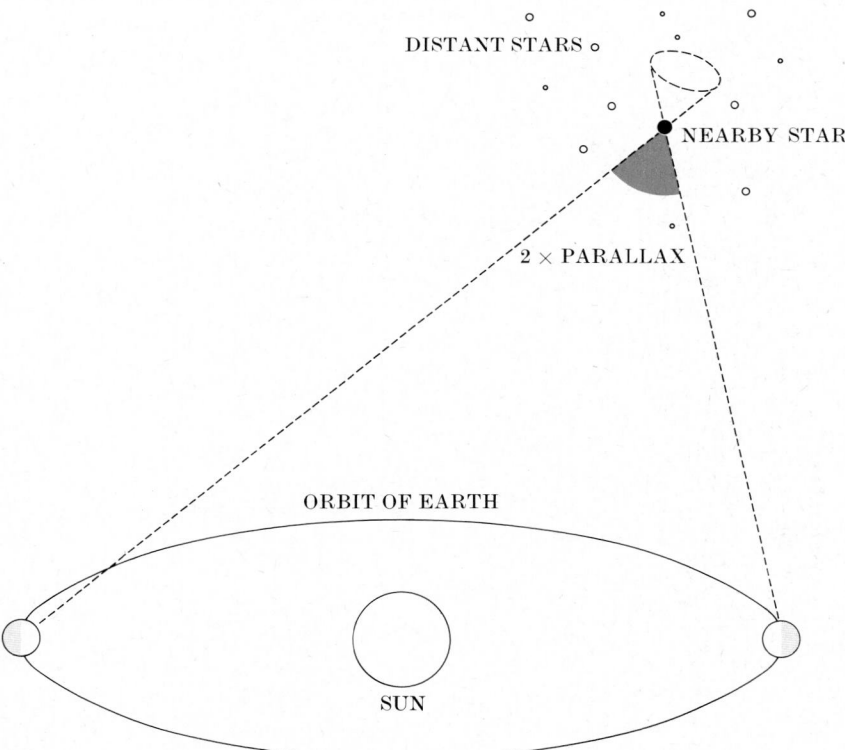

DISTANT STARS

NEARBY STAR

2 × PARALLAX

ORBIT OF EARTH

SUN

Another geometrical method exploits the observation that some of the local star clusters are moving relative to the Sun. All stars in such a cluster (or star family) are travelling on parallel tracks, which, due to perspective effects, appear to converge at one point in the sky. (Likewise the traffic on a straight road appears to converge in the distance.) The distance to a converging cluster is found by comparing its measured angular motion across the sky, in seconds of arc per year, with the true space velocity, in parsecs per year. The angular motion is found by taking several photographs over an interval of years and measuring the systematic changes. To find the true space velocity entails measuring the velocity component along the line of sight (*radial velocity*) and thence across the line of sight, by multiplying the radial velocity by the tangent of the angle between the cluster and the point of convergence. This moving-cluster method has been applied to give accurate results for the Hyades and Ursa Major star clusters, both of which are out of reach of direct surveying.

Apart from these essentially geometrical methods a whole series of distance-measuring techniques in astronomy is based on a simple but elegant principle. We can measure the apparent brightness of a star, and we know that this is determined by three factors: the intrinsic brightness, the distance, and complications such as the presence of dust in space. We will ignore the third while presenting the basic principle. Suppose we measure in magnitudes the apparent brightness m, and can deduce the actual brightness M. Then we can form the quantity (m−M) which, as we shall see in the next section, is linked to distance d (in parsecs) thus:

$$m - M = 5 \log_{10} d - 5$$
$$\text{or} \quad m - M = 5 \log_{10} (d/10),$$

where we are taking the actual brightness as the *absolute magnitude*. In fact there are several classes of stars as well as some galaxies for which we can find the absolute magnitude indirectly and so work out a distance.

The most important of the indirect distance measurements, at least historically, is the method of *Cepheid variables*. These stars rise and fall in brightness in a regular fashion, and the mean absolute magnitude depends on the time to go through one complete cycle of variability; the longer the period the greater the absolute magnitude. Therefore the distance to a Cepheid variable in a star cluster or another galaxy can be obtained from measurement of the period, which indicates the absolute magnitude, and from measurement of the apparent magnitude.

Another class of variable stars, that of the *RR Lyrae variables*, also has a link between the period of light variation and absolute magnitude, and so these also are used to map out our Galaxy and its neighbours. Astronomers have also found that for certain exploding stars, namely *novae* and *supernovae*, the absolute magnitude at maximum brightness can be deduced from the star's behaviour. Distances derived from novae and supernovae have an application in the determination of distances beyond the Milky Way.

A further indirect method is that of SPECTROSCOPIC PARALLAX. By means of standard techniques in *stellar spectroscopy* we can discover the physical conditions in a star's surface and atmosphere. Suppose that there exists another star with a similar spectrum and a known distance; we can then argue that both stars are comparable and probably have the same absolute magnitude. So, by relating the two measurable apparent magnitudes for these identical stars and the one known distance we can obtain the unknown distance or parallax.

It is important to realise that the measurement of star distances provides the key to the unfolding Universe. The most critical points are concerned with the two geometrical methods, applicable to the nearest stars and moving clusters, and the calibration of the period-luminosity relation for Cepheid variable stars. In the last analysis our ideas of the distances to galaxies and of the size of the Universe itself depend on these particular star-distance methods being right.

We are interested not only in where the stars are now, but also in how they are moving through space. A star's total space motion can be split into two components: the RADIAL VELOCITY along the line of sight, and the PROPER MOTION at right angles to the line of sight (figure 2.3).

The radial velocity is found by measuring the *Doppler shift* of lines in the star's spectrum. For certain types of star, this wavelength shift can be found semi-automatically by means of a radial velocity meter; one developed in England at the Cambridge Observatories compares the actual spectrum of a star with that of a similar star at rest and determines the wavelength shift necessary for bringing the two spectra into exact coincidence. From this wavelength shift the velocity is determined by application of the Doppler effect. For most stars it is necessary to measure the observed wavelengths of selected lines on a photographic plate of the spectrum. Radial velocities, which are now known for many thousands of stars, are taken as positive for stars moving away from us, and negative for those travelling towards us.

In principle a single observation of a star discloses the radial velocity, but this is not the case for proper motion. The systematic rate of change of a star's position against the distant background due to proper motion is usually less than a second of arc per year. Consequently it is necessary to take many photographs of the star field, separated by years or decades, in order to get accurate proper motions. It must be recalled that in general only the nearby stars will have measurable proper motions, and these are also the ones that exhibit trigonometrical parallax. A consequence of this is that the derivation of proper motion requires very precise measurement of star positions on photographic plates and computerized analysis of the data.

The star with the largest known proper motion was discovered by the great American observer E.E.Barnard (1857–1923). Now known as Barnard's star (figure 2.4), it has a proper motion of 10.3 arc sec per year and a parallax of 0.55 arc sec (1.83 pc).

By combining information on a star's distance with its proper motion we obtain the tangential velocity in kilometres per second. Taken in conjunction with the radial velocity, this establishes the true SPACE VELOCITY of the star relative to the Sun. In the solar neighbourhood, most of the space velocities are less than 50 km s^{-1}, but these are large enough to cause fundamental changes in the constellation patterns within a few thousand years. Our Sun is also moving along with the restless stars, and its motion through the nearby stars, the direction of the SOLAR APEX, was first worked out by William Herschel in 1783. Our Sun is travelling towards the constellation Hercules at a speed of 20 km s^{-1}.

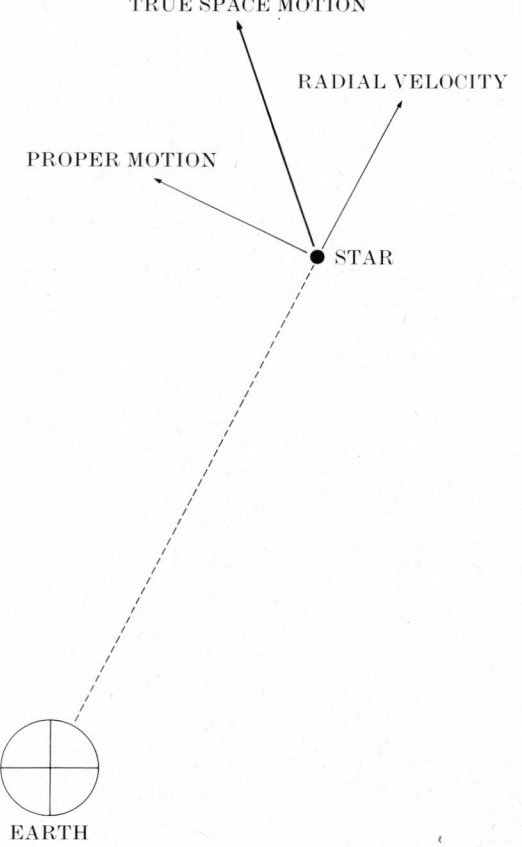

TRUE SPACE MOTION

RADIAL VELOCITY

PROPER MOTION

STAR

EARTH

2.3: *The true motion of a star in space, relative to the Earth can be described as a combination of a radial velocity along the observer's line of sight, and proper motion across the line of sight.*

2.4: *Barnard's Star has the highest known proper motion. Here, two photographs, taken at different times, have been superimposed with a small horizontal displacement between them. The proper motion stands out as a vertical shift. (Sproul Observatory, USA)*

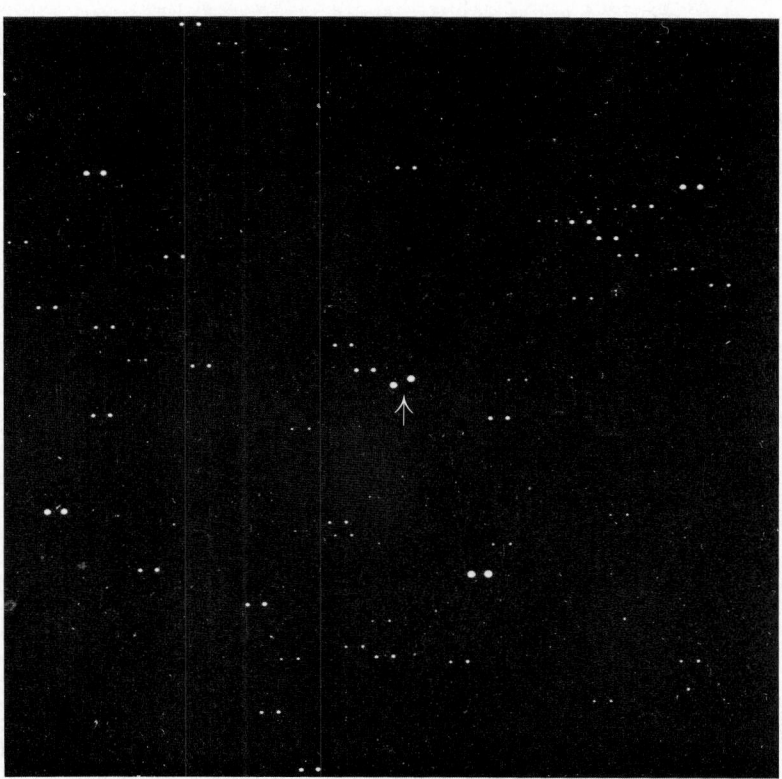

Brightnesses of the stars

The oldest quantitative observations of stars are connected with the determination of the apparent brightness of a star as seen from Earth. An unfortunate consequence of this is that the subject is even now laden with historical ballast. In particular, the unit given in antiquity, the MAGNITUDE, is still in regular use. Furthermore there is general confusion, even in professional literature over the terms brightness (a physical quantity) and the units in which it is measured (magnitude). Astronomers frequently speak of finding the magnitude of a star or galaxy, when in fact they have measured its brightness, in magnitudes. This section gives a short description of the several magnitude systems used to label stellar brightnesses; each has particular applications.

Apparent brightness or apparent magnitude
The nuclear powerhouse in the interior of a star is continuously sending energy up to the star's outer layers. Eventually, this energy is radiated into space, much of it in the form of light. The star's LUMINOSITY is the rate at which it emits radiant energy, and it depends chiefly on the size and surface temperature of the star. How bright a star looks in the sky depends on both its luminosity and its distance. Physicists measure the luminosity of an object in watts, but for historical and other reasons astronomers measure stellar luminosity in magnitudes. This magnitude system arose from the nature of the response of the human eye: what an observer judges to be equal increases in stimulus in the eye (that is equal increases in brightness) turn out to be approximately equal ratios of luminosity. This is because the physiological response to light is proportional to the logarithm of the stimulus. As an example, suppose there are three stars, all at the same distance from the Earth, whose light-energy outputs are in the ratios $1:10:100$. An observer would say that the brightness difference between the first two is about the same as that between the second and third, because the ratios of the luminosities are equal ($1/10$ and $10/100$, i.e. 0.1) in these two cases.

As far back as the second century BC, Hipparchus divided the stars that could be seen with the naked eye into six groups according to the sensation registered by the eye. The brightest were designated as first magnitude and the faintest as sixth magnitude. With advances in astronomy in more recent times, it became necessary to define a much more precise system, based on rational physical principles, and this was done by Pogson in 1856. He noted that a first-magnitude star was about one hundred times more luminous than one of the sixth magnitude, so he defined a magnitude difference of exactly 1.0 as corresponding to a ratio of luminosities of $\sqrt[5]{100} = 2.512$. A star seen to have magnitude 2 is emitting 2.512 times as much radiant energy as a star of magnitude 3 at the same distance. We use the term APPARENT BRIGHTNESS to refer to the brightness of a celestial object as measured by the observer (generally on Earth!), without regard for the effect of distance on the brightness. The more widely-used term APPARENT MAGNITUDE has the same meaning. Suppose two stars have apparent magnitudes m_1 and m_2, and their apparent luminosities are l_1 and l_2 (we say apparent because the effect of distance is being ignored for the moment), then the mathematical form of the relation between these quantities is expressed by the equation:

$$l_2/l_1 = 100^{-(m_2-m_1)/5} = 2.512^{(m_1-m_2)}$$

By taking logarithms (to base 10) this equation is written more simply:

$$\log(l_2/l_1) = -0.4(m_2-m_1)$$

To encompass very bright objects, the magnitude scale is extended to negative numbers. For example, the star Sirius has a magnitude of -1.4 and the full Moon -12.5. The faintest stars which can be photographed with the world's largest telescopes are about twenty-fifth magnitude; they have the same apparent brightness as a candle 300 000 km from an observer.

Brightnesses judged by the response of the human eye are called VISUAL MAGNITUDES, and they were the only magnitudes used prior to photography. However, many stars emit radiation in the ultraviolet and infrared regions of the spectrum. This radiation cannot be detected by the eye, and in fact some of these radiations in certain wavelength ranges never even reach the surface of Earth, as they are absorbed in the terrestrial atmosphere. A smaller magnitude (i.e. a smaller number in the magnitude scale and corresponding to greater brightness) than the visual one would be recorded if this unseen radiation were included, particularly for stars much hotter or cooler than the Sun, whose radiation falls primarily in the ultraviolet or infrared regions respectively. The brightness including radiation at all wavelengths is called the BOLOMETRIC MAGNITUDE. The bolometric correction (B.C.) is the correction which has to be applied to the visual magnitude: $\text{B.C.} = M_{bol} - M_v$. This correction is defined as zero for the Sun, whose radiation peaks in the visible region, so the bolometric correction is always a negative number. A BOLOMETER is an instrument for detecting electromagnetic radiation at all wavelengths. In practice bolometric magnitudes are difficult to measure directly owing to the atmospheric absorption.

A further complication arises if the brightnesses of stars are compared photographically. Many photographic emulsions are sensitive mainly to blue and violet light (hence the red safe-light used in dark rooms), whereas the eye's response peaks in the yellow-green spectral region. PHOTOGRAPHIC MAGNITUDES are, therefore, different again to visual or bolometric magnitudes. It is clearly important to specify the type of magnitude, which will depend on the technique used to find it, as well as its value.

Stellar magnitudes are determined by comparison with a few stars whose magnitudes have been measured very accurately by photoelectric techniques. The zero point of the magnitude scale is now fixed by means of frequently-measured standard stars. When the brightnesses of large numbers of stars are required, photography is the quickest way of finding the magnitudes. If visual magnitudes are required, it is possible to simulate the response of the eye by using a photographic emulsion that has been treated with a dye sensitive to green and yellow light, in conjunction with a yellow filter. Brightnesses measured in this way are described as PHOTOVISUAL MAGNITUDES.

The definition of magnitude can be extended to non-stellar and diffuse objects. The INTEGRATED MAGNITUDE is calculated by summing the light output over the entire object. In the case of an object whose luminosity decreases slowly towards the edges, it may be necessary to specify the area of sky which is included. For a very extended object, such as a nearby galaxy, the surface brightness, expressed in magnitudes per square second of arc may also be of interest.

Multicolour photometry

The values obtained for photographic and visual magnitudes depend on the range of wavelengths to which the detection equipment is sensitive. For the accurate, reproducible measurements of stellar light output required by modern astrophysics, it is necessary to define precisely the wavelength band used. The measurement of light intensity in particular wavelength regions for a star can be useful in establishing physical facts about the star, such as its temperature. To this end, several standard sets of magnitudes have been devised. The two sets most frequently used are the UBV SYSTEM of Johnson and Morgan and the UBVY SYSTEM of Strömgren. Such sets of magnitudes define what is called a PHOTOMETRIC SYSTEM, photometry meaning simply, the measurement of light. Each system is defined by the colour filters which are used to isolate the wavelength bands.

The UBV system, introduced in the 1950s, is now extensively used. The three magnitudes are measured using filters with the following characteristics:

magnitude name	wavelength range (nm)	wavelength of peak transmission (nm)
U (ultraviolet)	300–400	360
B (blue)	360–550	420
V (visual)	480–680	520

Figure 2.5 shows the transmissions of the filters, compared to the response of the human eye. Ordinary visual magnitudes correspond fairly closely with this precisely-defined V magnitude. Of particular use are the so-called COLOUR INDICES, (B–V) and (U–B) which are closely related to the star's temperature and luminosity. Colour index is defined as the difference between magnitudes measured at two different wavelengths. The UBV photometric system, based on wide wavelength bands, has been usefully extended by the introduction of two further magnitudes: R (red) and I (infrared), centred at 680 and 825 nm respectively.

The uvby system uses filters of narrower band width as follows:

magnitude name	band width (nm)	central wavelength (nm)
u (ultraviolet)	30	350
v (violet)	19	411
b (blue)	18	467
y (yellow)	23	547

Again, colour indices can be formed from combinations of these magnitudes. (b–y) is mainly a function of the star's temperature, and the index given by (u–v) — (v–b) depends on the star's luminosity. A further useful relation (v–b) — (b–y) is a good indicator of the relative proportion of elements heavier than hydrogen in the star's chemical composition. Multicolour photometry is therefore a very good way of deriving the physical parameters of large numbers of stars relatively quickly.

Absolute brightness or absolute magnitude

The apparent magnitude of a star is governed by the star's distance as well as its intrinsic luminosity. The apparent brightness of any source of light falls off at the square of the distance from the observer. The ABSOLUTE MAGNITUDE is defined as the brightness (in magnitudes) the star would have if it were at a standard distance from us, and by general agreement the unit distance is taken as 10 pc. Absolute magnitude is therefore a measure of the intrinsic energy output or absolute luminosity of the star.

We can form equations relating the apparent magnitude m and the absolute magnitude M. Suppose that a star is at a distance d parsecs, and denote the luminosity at d parsecs by l_d and at 10 parsecs by l_{10}. By applying the inverse square law we can write $l_{10}/l_d = d^2/10^2$. But we saw above that $l_2/l_1 = 100^{-(m_2 - m_1)/5}$, so:

$$\frac{l_{10}}{l_d} = \frac{d^2}{10^2} = 100^{-(M-m)/5},$$
$$= 100^{(m-M)/5},$$
$$= 10^{0.4\,(m-M)}.$$

Taking logarithms (to base 10) we obtain:
$$2\log_{10} d - 2 = 0.4\,(m-M).$$
Multiplying by 2.5 and rearranging gives us:
$$m-M = 5\log_{10} d - 5 = 5\log_{10}(d/10);$$
the quantity (m–M) is called the DISTANCE MODULUS.

The parallax of a star (measured in seconds of arc), p, is related to its distance in parsecs, d, by the simple expression d = 1/p, so the distance modulus is sometimes expressed in terms of p:
$$m-M = -(5 + 5\log p).$$

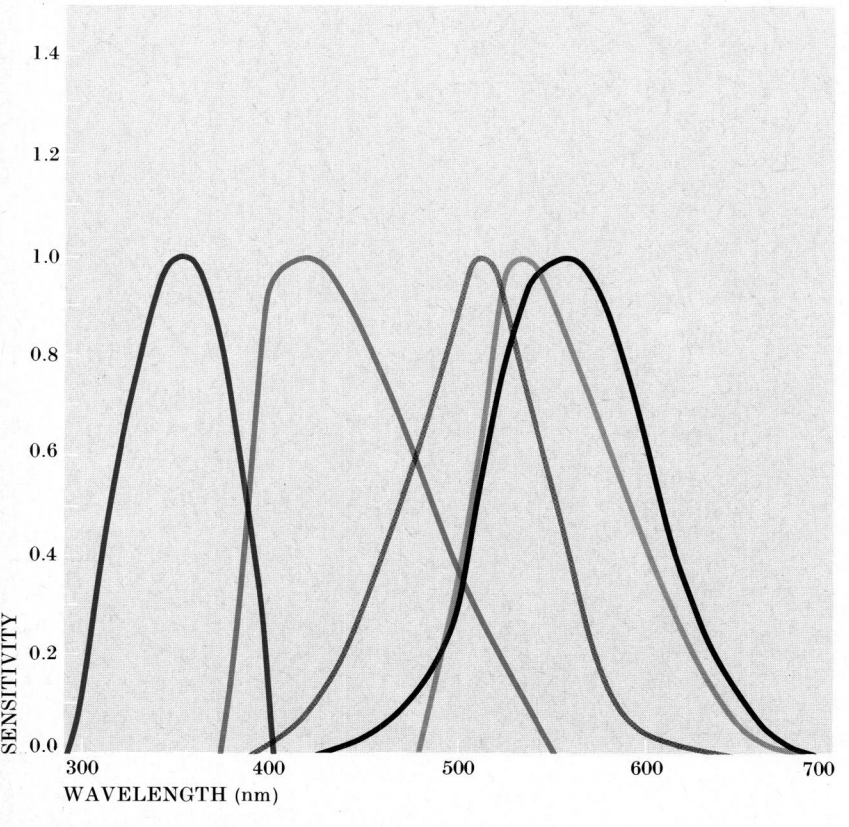

2.5: *The relative transmissions of the filters used in the UBV system of multicolour photometry, displayed as a function of wavelength. The responses of a normal, and a dark-adapted human eye are also given for comparison. Violet line (U); blue line (B); green line (V); grey line (normal vision); black line (dark-adapted vision).*

Stellar masses and radii

The mass of a star governs the physical nature of its interior, but masses are hard to determine: they can only be measured for stars in binary systems, and only then under favourable conditions.

The two stars in a *binary system* orbit around their common centre of mass. The properties of the orbit are connected with the masses of the stars by equations that are easily derived from the law of gravitation. These equations can be used to find the masses as long as several other quantities can be measured by means of independent observations.

Visual binaries have orbits that can be observed directly as ellipses traced out relative to the background of stars. If the linear dimensions of the orbits and the individual motions of the two components are known, then it is possible to deduce the masses of both stars. In practice this has only been achieved for a few dozen binary systems. If any data is missing – for example, if one of the two stars is too faint to be visible – then it may be possible to deduce the ratio of the masses, or perhaps the sum of the quantity but not the individual masses.

Spectroscopic binary stars cannot be resolved by any telescope, but the periodic *Doppler shift* of the spectrum lines gives away the orbital motion. In general, the angle i at which the orbital plane is inclined to the perpendicular to the line of sight is unknown, and in these cases the best data on the masses that can be obtained from the motion are $m_1 \sin^3 i$ and $m_2 \sin^3 i$, where m_1 and m_2 denote the two masses. This sets lower limits on the masses as $\sin^3 i$ has a maximum value of 1. If only one spectrum is visible, then only the quantity known as the MASS FUNCTION, $m_2{}^3 \sin^3 i/(m_1+m_2)^2$, can be deduced. However, if a spectroscopic binary is also eclipsing, the value of i must be close to $90°$ ($\sin^3 i$ about 1.0) and the values of m_1 and m_2 can be found.

There is another method of mass determination which has been applied to a handful of *white dwarfs*, but it is inapplicable to ordinary stars. White dwarfs are so dense that the spectrum lines suffer a gravitational *redshift*. The wavelength shift, $\Delta\lambda$, is related to the mass m_1 and the radius R of the star by the equation $\Delta\lambda/\lambda = Gm/c^2R$ and is of order 10^{-2} nm in the visible part of the spectrum. The results indicate that the masses of white dwarfs lie in the range 0.5 to 1.4 solar masses.

Masses are known for only a couple of hundred stars, but this data shows that their values cover a comparatively narrow range, between 0.1 and $50\,M_\odot$. Stars of low luminosity and low mass are very much more common than high mass stars. Examples of stellar masses and luminosities from visual binary systems are given in table 2.3, and figure 3.2 shows the important mass-luminosity relation. It can be expressed approximately by $L \propto M^3$ for main-sequence stars much more massive or much less massive than the Sun and $L \propto M^{4.5}$ for those similar to the Sun.

The stars are much too distant to show a measurable disc in conventional telescopes, and so several indirect methods have been developed for getting information on stellar diameters. The largest body of data comes from the *eclipsing binary stars*, which as we saw above, are so useful for giving us star masses. In the eclipsing binaries it is possible to work out the size of the star orbit in kilometres, and to measure what fraction of the orbit is taken up by an eclipse. The relative lengths of the eclipses depend on the diameters of the two stars concerned, and therefore the diameters in kilometres can be deduced.

It is also possible to measure the angular diameters of nearby giant stars by use of a *stellar interferometer* or *speckle interferometry*. For example, this has been accomplished for the red-giant star Betelgeuse, in Orion, for Aldebaran, and for Sirius. In the latter case, the angular size is 0.007 arc sec, and the parallax 0.377 arc sec (2.65 pc), which gives a diameter about twice that of the Sun. The masses and radii of stars on the main sequence are related as shown in figure 2.6, which illustrates the mass-radius relation for stars in binary systems.

We will mention one final method of deducing a star's surface area, and so being able to work out the radius. The spectrum of a star carries information on the temperature of the surface, and this temperature in turn governs the luminosity per unit area. If we can find the absolute brightness of the same star, then we know its total luminosity. Dividing this latter by the luminosity per unit area yields the area and hence the radius. Although this method is indirect it is of importance historically because it showed that giant and dwarf stars existed with roughly similar temperatures.

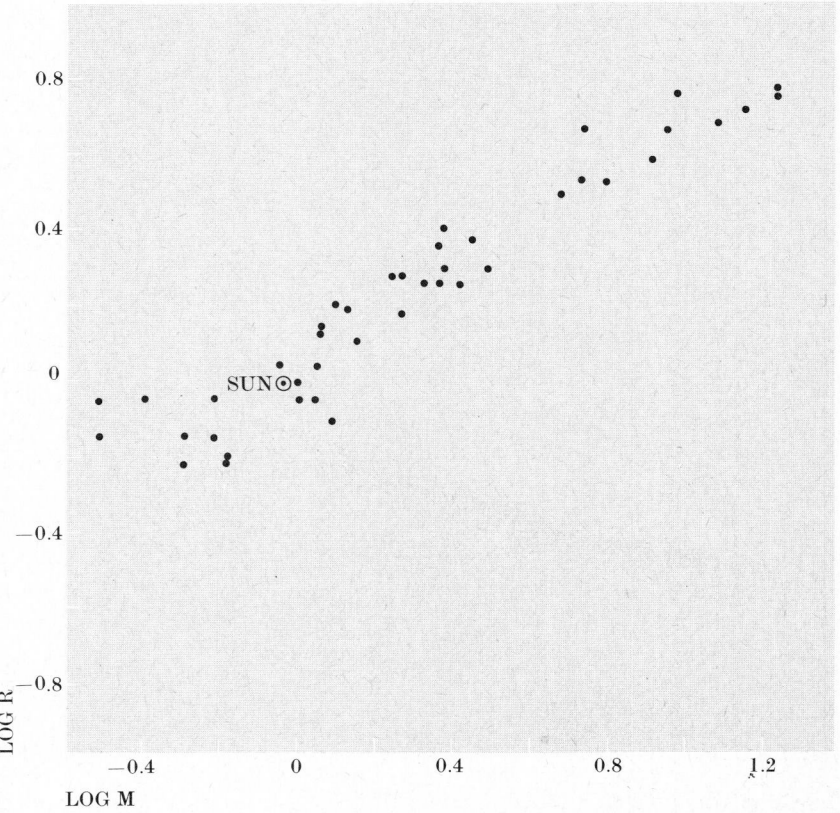

Table 2.3: Star masses for the members of some brighter visual binary systems

Name	Spectral types	Masses (solar masses)	Absolute bolometric magnitudes
η Cas	G0V	0.87	4.61
	M0V	0.54	7.35
ε Cet	F5 IV–V	0.34	4.6
	—	0.34	4.6
α Aur	G5 III	2.14	0.1
	G0 III	2.40	0.2
α CMa	A1V	2.14	1.22
	WD*	1.05	11.1
α CMi	F5 IV–V	1.78	2.63
	WD*	0.65	12.6
γ Vir	F0V	1.18	3.46
	F0V	1.12	3.48
α Com	F5V	1.41	3.66
	—	1.45	3.69
α Cen	G2V	1.05	4.29
	K5V	0.89	5.42
ζ Boo	G8V	0.83	5.39
	K4V	0.72	6.89
η CrB	G2V	0.66	4.62
	—	0.59	4.88
ζ Her	G0 IV	1.12	2.93
	K0 V	0.78	5.49
δ Equ	F7V	1.59	3.9
	—	1.51	4.0
τ Cyg	F0 IV	1.23	2.25
	—	0.87	4.75

*Note : *WD = White dwarf.*

2.6: *The observed relationship between stellar masses and radii for stars on the main sequence. The scales are logarithmic, and the units are solar masses and solar radii.*

Atmospheres of the stars
Formation of the spectrum

Most of the direct evidence we have on the physical conditions in stars is obtained from their spectra. The energy that finally reaches us from a star was originally created in the nuclear reactions in the star's deepest interior. This energy gradually filters out through the gas of which the star is composed; the light energy that finally leaves the surface has a spectrum which is governed by the temperature, density and chemical composition of only a thin layer of gas whose thickness is 10^{-3} or less of the star's radius.

Moving outwards from the centre of a star, there is a gradual decrease in temperature and density. A star has no sharply-defined surface because the density of gas just dwindles gradually until it is virtually zero. In general, as the density of the stellar material decreases, its opacity to light does too, so there is a region in the outer part of a star where the material becomes transparent to light. As this transition region is very thin compared with the size of the star as a whole, the visible disc is fairly sharply defined. This is obvious in the case of the Sun, which is the only star whose disc is resolvable by eye. The visible disc is called the *photosphere*, and it is precisely this layer in the star which is responsible for the characteristic spectrum. The decrease in opacity through the photosphere manifests itself as *limb darkening*, which is directly observed on the solar disc.

In the case of the Sun, it is possible to investigate the layers of more tenuous gas overlying the photosphere, the *chromosphere* and *corona* whose spectra can be obtained during total eclipse. It is reasonable to suppose that similar structures exist in the outermost parts of other stars. The photosphere and overlying regions of a star are known as the STELLAR ATMOSPHERE, but, there is no precise boundary between this atmosphere and the interior.

A typical stellar spectrum is an ABSORPTION-LINE SPECTRUM; that is, it consists of a continuous background of light crossed by dark absorption lines at particular wavelengths. In a simple approximation, the stellar atmosphere may be thought of as a layer of cool, transparent gas overlying the hotter region below. The region beneath the photosphere produces the continuous spectrum, while atoms and molecules in the cool atmosphere are responsible for the absorption lines. This picture is an over-simplification of the true state of affairs, for there is no dividing line between these regions. In fact, every part of the stellar gas both emits and absorbs light, but on the whole less light finally emerges at those precise wavelengths that are absorbed by the various atoms and molecules present in the atmosphere, and so absorption lines are formed.

Not surprisingly, the appearance of a star's spectrum depends strongly on the temperatures prevailing in the stellar atmosphere. As a star has no solid surface, and the temperature is different in different regions of the atmosphere, what exactly is meant by the TEMPERATURE of a star? It is necessary to choose a precise definition which is physically significant and can be used to compare one star with another. The EFFECTIVE TEMPERATURE (T_{eff}) of a star is taken as the temperature of a *black body* whose rate of energy radiation is equal to the star's. In practice, this temperature turns out to be the actual temperature somewhere in the middle of the photospheric layer.

Temperatures of normal stars cover a large range: between about 3000 and 40 000 K, but typically, the temperature in a stellar atmosphere is around several thousand degrees. At these temperatures many atoms are *ionized*, so the stellar material contains free electrons and positive ions as well as neutral atoms. The proportion of any particular element which is ionized depends on the temperature, the *ionization potential* of the element, and the density. At higher temperatures, more atoms will be stripped of electrons, but if the density is high, it is easier for the ions to re-capture their electrons, so that a high density limits ionization. The higher the ionization potential of an element, the more energy is required to produce ionization, so higher temperatures are re-quired. The degree of ionization in a star's atmosphere strongly influences the appearance of its spectrum. In physics the ioniza-tion state of an atom is conventionally represented by plus signs following the usual chemical symbol: thus H^0, Fe^0, Mg^0 represent neutral atoms of hydrogen, iron and magnesium respectively; Fe^+, Ti^+ represent singly ionized iron and titanium; N^{2+} means doubly-ionized nitrogen etc. In astronomy it has been traditional to use the chemical symbol followed by Roman numerals: e.g. HI, FeI, MgI for neutral atoms, FeII, TiII for singly-ionized atoms, NIII for doubly-ionized and so forth. In this book we often use the physics convention, not the astronomical tradition.

The classification of stellar spectra

The chief features of the appearance of a stellar spectrum are governed primarily by the star's effective temperature. An unusual chemical composition can alter the spectrum radically, but the vast majority of stars, those termed normal, have a composition closely resembling the Sun's, and it is only these that will be con-sidered here. The wide temperature range of stars means that there is also a wide variety in spectral appearance.

STELLAR SPECTRA are classified into seven main groups which form a temperature sequence. Each class is designated by a letter of the alphabet. From hottest to coolest they are: O, B, A, F, G, K, M. This rather odd sequence of letters arose from an empirical classification method, developed at Harvard in the early twen-tieth century, which was originally in alphabetical order. His-torically, the first classes chosen were absorption-line spectra in order of increasing strength of the hydrogen lines. Classes O and onwards were characterized by emission lines in the spectra and included the spectra of nebulae as well as stars. However, it later became clear that some classes were spurious, resulting from lack of uniformity in the photography, and that it would be better to order the classes as a temperature sequence. The classification of nebular spectra was also discarded. On revision, the original letter names for the remaining classes were kept. There is a well-known mnemonic which helps to recall the sequence: '*O Be A Fine Girl*,

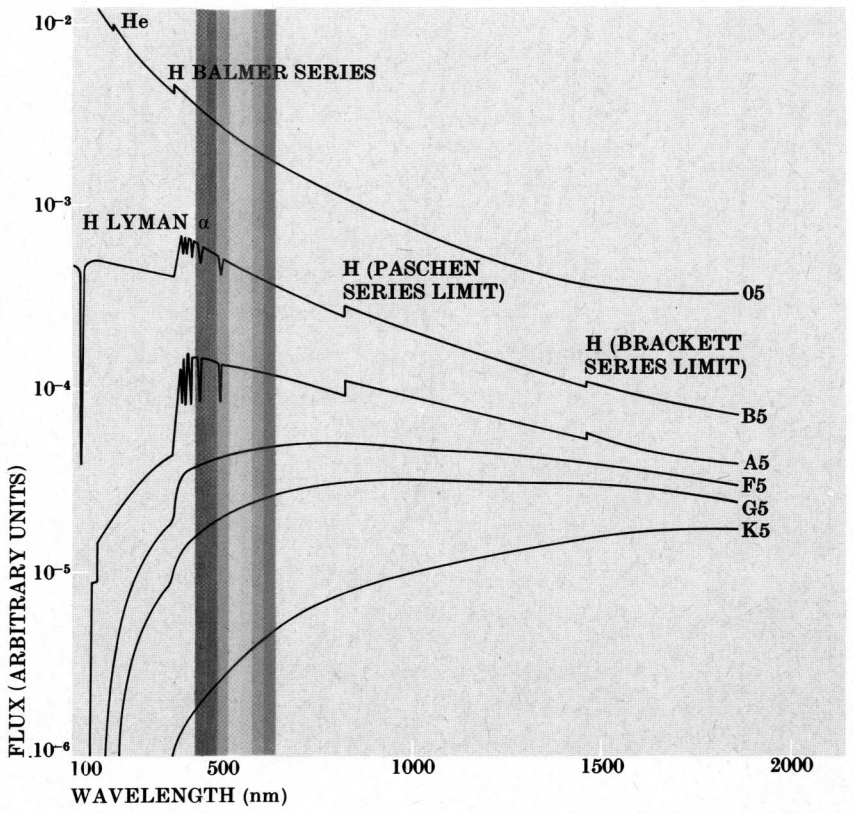

2.7: *A graphical representation of the continuous spectra of stars over a range of spectral classes. Note the strong ultraviolet emission of O and B stars.*

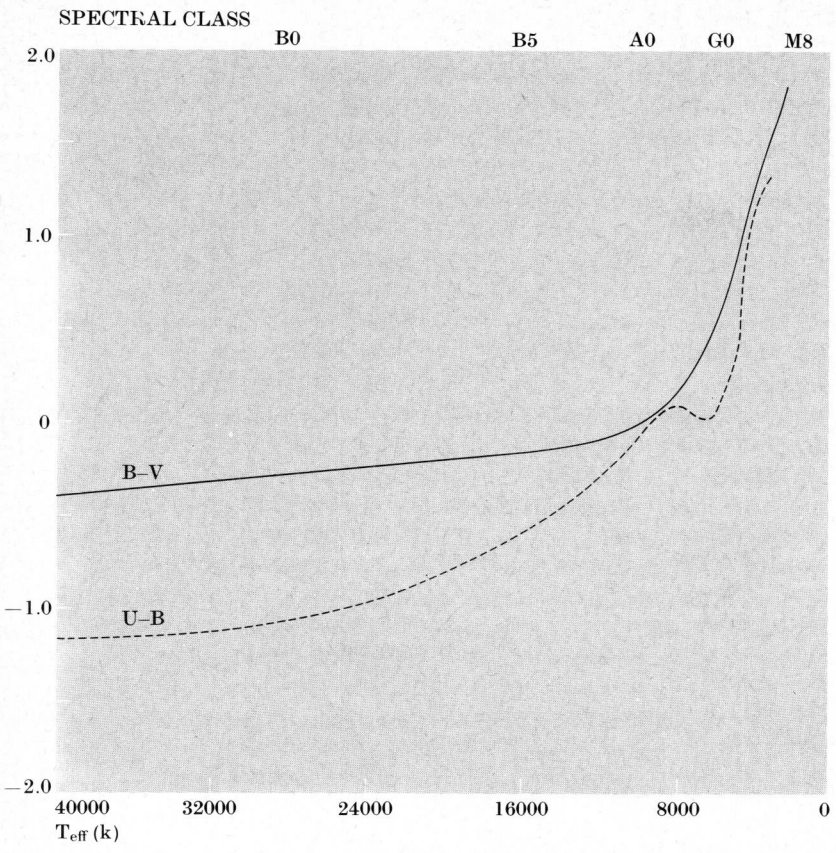

SPECTRAL CLASS

2.8 : *The correlation between the photometric indices (B–V) and (U–B), and temperature for normal, dwarf stars.*

2.9 : *A field of objective prism spectra. The image of each star is spread out into a spectrum from which the spectral type can be determined. In many of these spectra you can see the dark absorption lines. (University of Michigan,* USA *)*

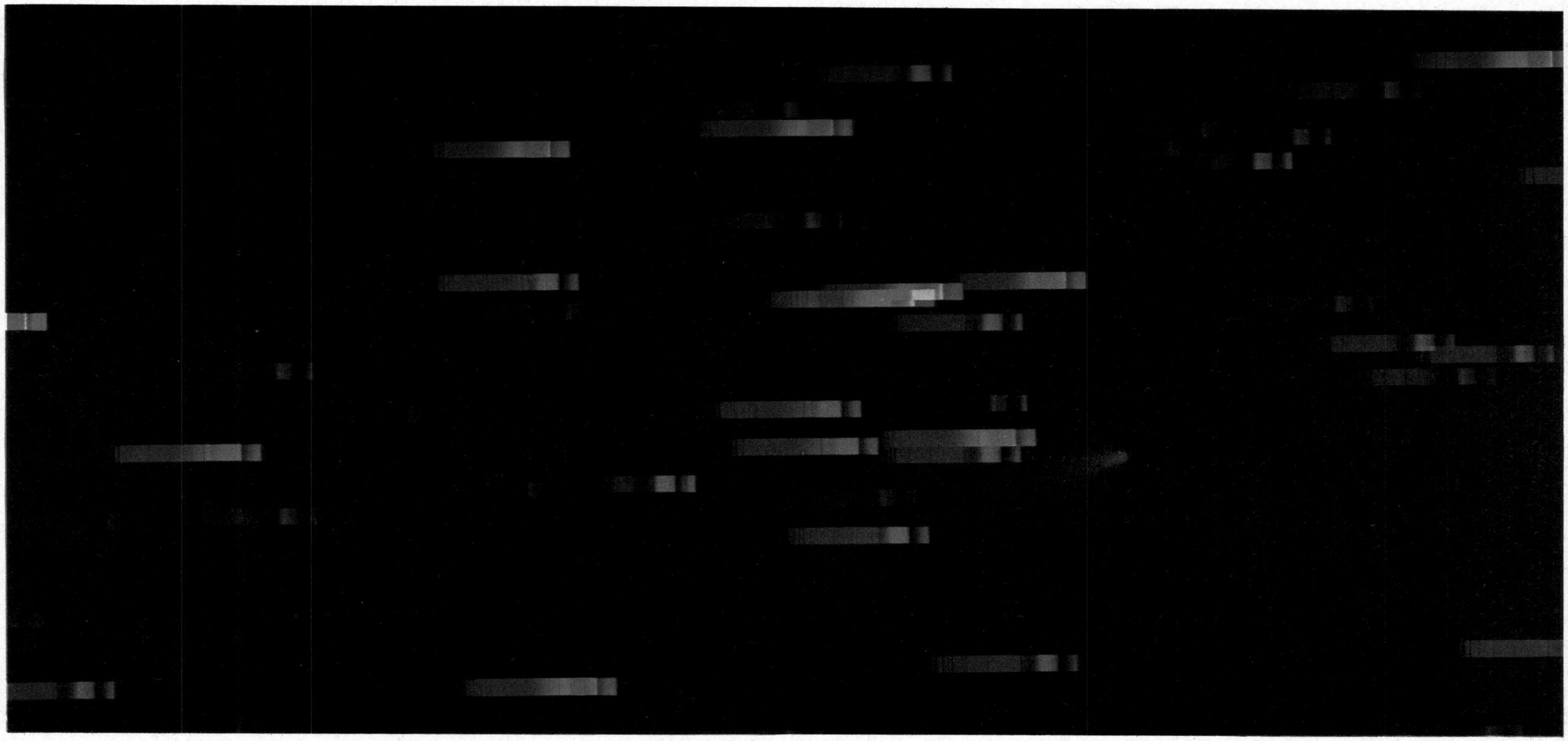

2.10: *The spectral sequence. Examples of stellar spectra that illustrate the chief features of the spectral classes O to M. (Royal Astronomical Society and University of Cambridge, UK)*

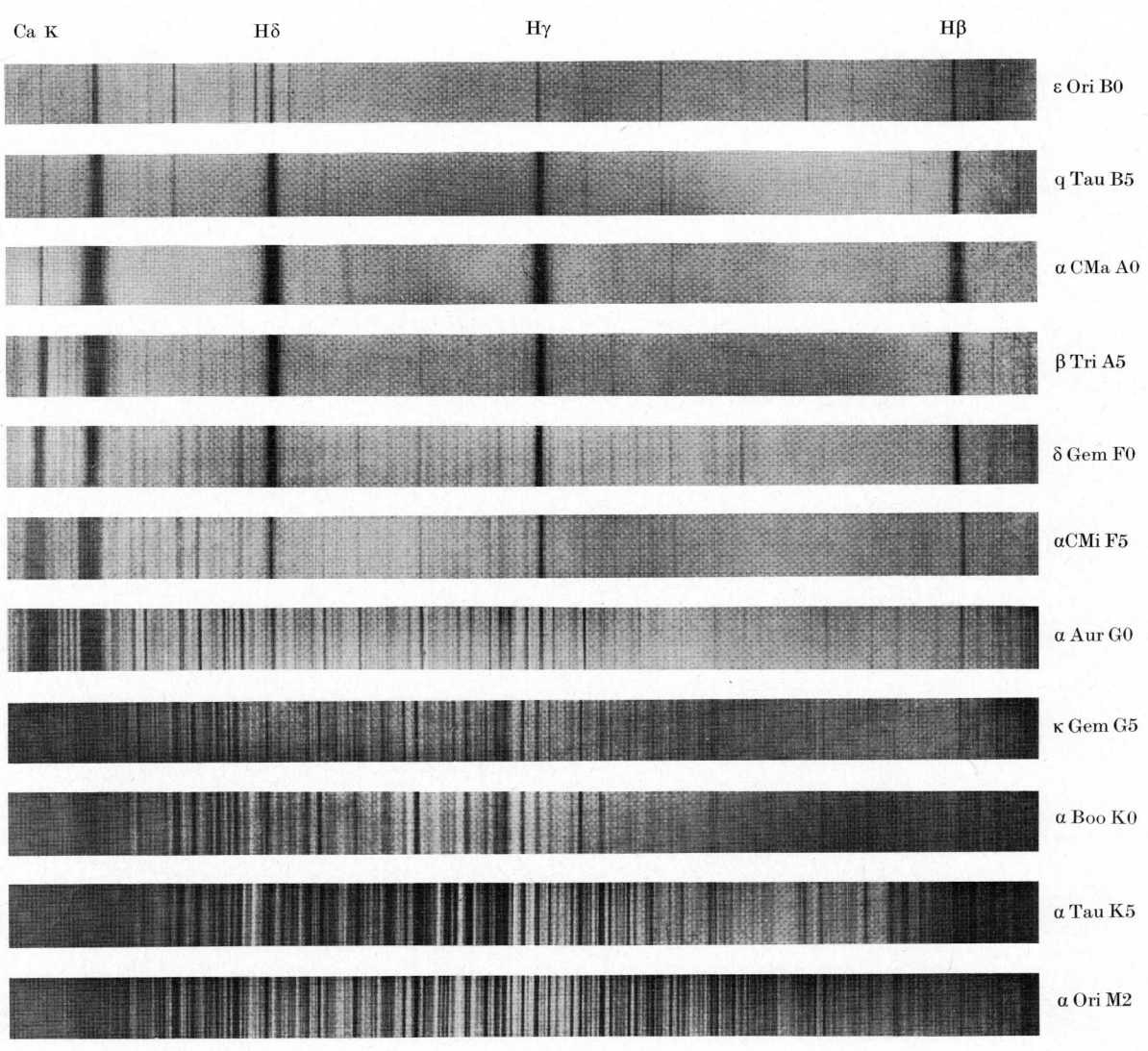

Ca κ   Hδ   Hγ   Hβ

ε Ori B0

q Tau B5

α CMa A0

β Tri A5

δ Gem F0

αCMi F5

α Aur G0

κ Gem G5

α Boo K0

α Tau K5

α Ori M2

Kiss Me!' Each class is further divided into 10 sub-classes numbered from 0 to 9. Examples of spectral classes are A0, F5, G2.

At one time it was supposed that the sequence of spectral classes might form an evolutionary sequence. This is now known to be entirely false but, unfortunately, the attendant terminology has never been dropped. As a result, O and B stars are referred to as EARLY-TYPE STARS and K and M stars as LATE-TYPE STARS. Where possible we avoid this misleading terminology.

The criteria by which spectral classes are judged are: the absence or presence of particular spectral lines, and/or the ratios of the intensities of certain spectral lines. These criteria have been proposed to enable classification from low-dispersion spectrograms without the necessity of determining the temperatures of stars from detailed analysis. W.W.Morgan and P.C.Keenan were largely responsible for the development of this system and their names are often linked with this classification scheme. The main features of each class are listed below and examples of spectra of each class are illustrated in figure 2.10.

O : lines of He^+, He^0, C^{2+}, Si^{3+} and other highly-ionized ions of the lighter elements.

B : He^+ disappears after B5. He^0 reaches a maximum at B2. O^+, N^+ etc. replace the more highly ionized atoms. Lines of H^0 become more prominent.

A : He^0 disappears and the spectrum is dominated by very strong lines of H^0 which reach their maximum in classes A0 to A3. Lines of Ca^+, Fe^+, Cr^+, Ti^+, Fe^0, Cr^0 and other neutral and singly-ionized heavier atoms gradually increase in strength through this class.

F : The spectrum is dominated by the many lines of neutral and singly-ionized metals and heavy atoms. The H^0 lines are much weaker than in class A, but the lines of Ca^+ become very strong.

G : Lines of neutral metals dominate. The molecular bands of CN and CH appear.

K : The lines of neutral metals and the molecular bands become even stronger than in class G. Bands of TiO appear about class K5.

M : The TiO bands intensify and many other molecular bands and lines of neutral metals are present.

No comment has been made so far on the way that the continuum radiation also varies through the sequence of spectral classes. The continuum radiation is distributed with wavelength in a way which closely resembles that emitted by a *black body* at the effective temperature of the star. Thus, the total amount of energy radiated is greatest for the hottest stars, and the hotter a star, the more radiation is emitted at shorter wavelengths.

The different ranges of continuous radiation emitted by stars of various temperatures result in their appearing different colours to the eye. Of course, the eye is taking in a mixture of light at many wavelengths simultaneously, so the sensation of colour depends on how the brain responds to the particular mixture of wavelengths. A fairly uniform mixture of light of all wavelengths gives the sensation of white. Sirius and Vega, both A stars, appear white. Hotter stars such as Spica may look bluish, as there is more blue light than red. The Sun is of spectral class G, and as all know, is distinctly yellow. Cooler stars, such as Betelgeuse and Antares are very red in colour.

Although the continuous spectra of stars resemble those of black bodies in general, the detailed shape of the curve is altered by the absorption by hydrogen and other atoms. As some 75 per cent of the material of which normal stars are made is hydrogen, it is not surprising that the chief spectral lines in the visible region, the *Balmer series*, are very prominent in the temperature range that gives rise to favourable physical conditions for hydrogen absorption. As many as 20 distinct lines in the Balmer series may commonly be detectable, but at shorter wavelengths the lines, which are getting closer together, all coalesce. This means that hydrogen is considerably more opaque to light of wavelengths less than about 365 nm than that of longer wavelength. This results in a sharp reduction in the level of continuum radiation output below 365 nm, a phenomenon called the Balmer discontinuity. The size of the discontinuity depends on spectral class, and may be used as a criterion for spectral classification. There are also discontinuities at the limits of the other series of hydrogen lines which lie outside the visible region. Less conspicuous discontinuities occur in the continuum owing to similar effects caused by other elements less abundant than hydrogen. Figure 2.7 shows graphically the continuous spectra of stars of various types.

The stellar spectra recorded on the surface of the Earth are further modified by the effects of Earth's atmosphere. Particularly in the infrared and ultraviolet, the atmosphere blocks much of the incident radiation. Observations at ultraviolet and shorter wavelengths have to be made outside the atmosphere. As water vapour is one of the chief absorbers in the infrared region, it is possible to make observations at these wavelengths in areas with very dry climates. In practice, it is not difficult to tell which spectral lines have been superposed on the true stellar spectrum by the atmosphere as they have a different shape, and usually a different *Doppler shift* in wavelength.

There are many ways in which the spectral classes of large numbers of stars can be determined without the necessity of taking high-dispersion spectrograms. For example, certain photometric indices, such as (B–V), are correlated with spectral class and temperature (figure 2.8). Alternatively, very low dispersion spectra of a whole field of stars can be obtained at one time by the objective prism technique: a narrow-angle prism placed over the telescope objective disperses each star image sufficiently to show up the chief spectral features (figure 2.9).

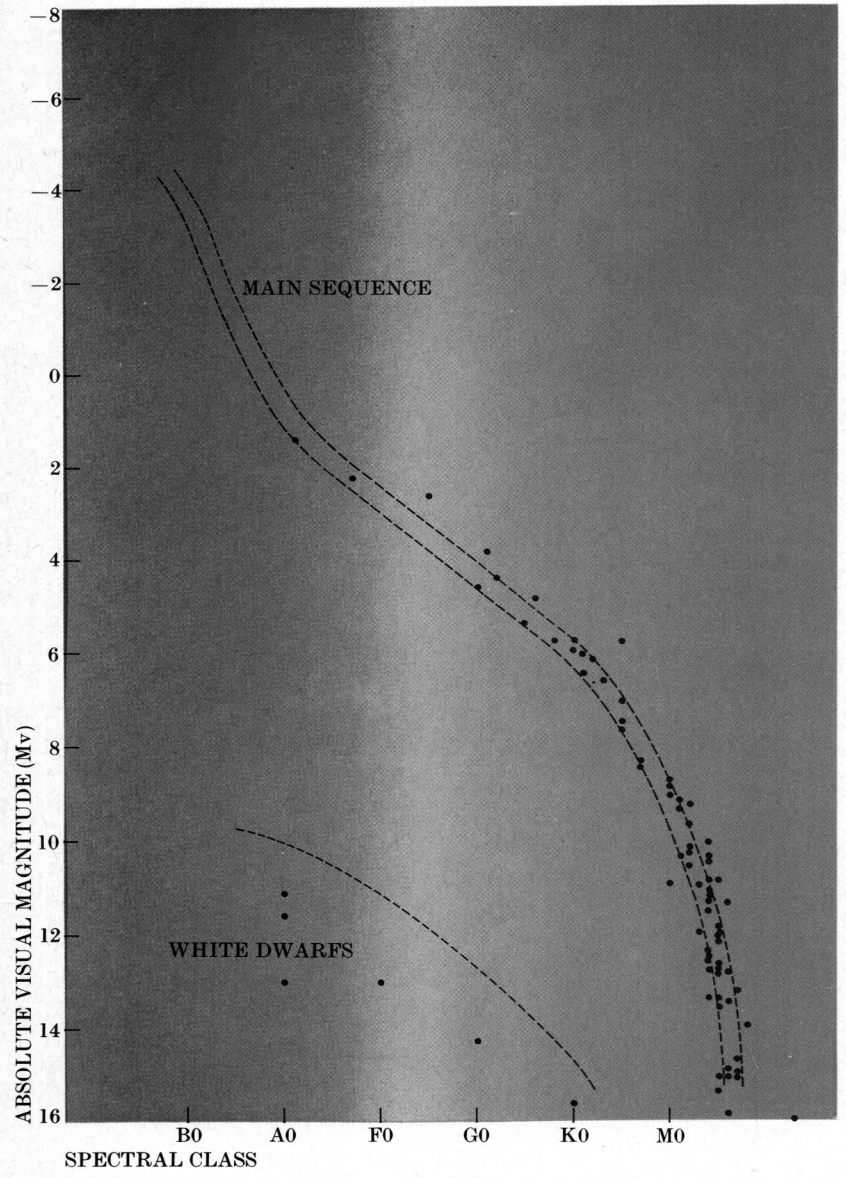

2.11: *The Hertzsprung-Russell diagram for the nearest 100 stars.*

MAIN SEQUENCE

WHITE DWARFS

ABSOLUTE VISUAL MAGNITUDE (Mv)

SPECTRAL CLASS

Luminosity classification

Figure 2.7 shows that the total flux of radiation leaving unit area of a star's surface increases with temperature. However, the total energy output of a star also depends on its size. A convenient measure of the energy output of a star is its *absolute magnitude*. A graph of absolute magnitude against temperature (or spectral class, which is virtually equivalent to temperature) for a large sample of stars in the solar neighbourhood shows that the vast majority lie in a narrow band stretching diagonally across the graph, with only a very few lying below this band. Certainly, the points are very far from being randomly distributed.

Such a graph is an example of a HERTZSPRUNG-RUSSELL (HR) DIAGRAM, named after the astronomers who first conceived this technique. The concentration of points in the narrow band, called the MAIN SEQUENCE is a result of the fact that the effective temperature that a star achieves increases with the mass of material it contains, and so also with size, in a clearly defined manner. Figure 2.11, which shows the HR diagram for the nearest 100 stars, also illustrates the fact that there are far more cool small stars than large hot ones in a sphere of space around the Sun. This suggests that there is probably a preponderance of small stars in the Galaxy as a whole, although as they are intrinsically so faint we can only see the nearby ones. The stars well below the main sequence are the *white dwarfs*, old stars whose origin is explained in chapter 3.

The HR diagram of the 100 brightest stars presents a very different picture, as shown in figure 2.12. This includes intrinsically bright stars from a large volume of space, but only the nearest of intrinsically faint stars. Only the top portion of the main sequence is represented, and there are a considerable number of points lying well above the main sequence. These stars are very much more luminous than main-sequence stars of the same spectral type because of their vastly larger size. This variation in the size and luminosity of stars can be interpreted in terms of the evolution of stars. It is sufficient to mention here that a star spends most of its life using up its hydrogen fuel, and, according to its mass, lies at some point on the main sequence in the HR diagram. Such a star is referred to as a DWARF. When a significant proportion of the hydrogen has been consumed and converted into other elements, changes occur in the structure of the star which cause it to expand greatly and move into the GIANT or SUPERGIANT class. Finally it may end up as a WHITE DWARF when all the possible nuclear fuels have been exhausted.

The atmosphere of a giant star is very much more tenuous than that of a dwarf. Table 2.4 indicates the differences in structure between the atmospheres of dwarf and giant stars at 5000 and 10 000 K. The much lower densities in the giants' atmospheres cause subtle differences in the appearance of giant spectra, and so stars of different luminosities can be recognized even if their absolute magnitudes cannot be determined directly.

Spectral classification has been extended to include luminosity classes as well as a temperature class. Morgan and Keenan have developed a system in which the luminosity is represented by a

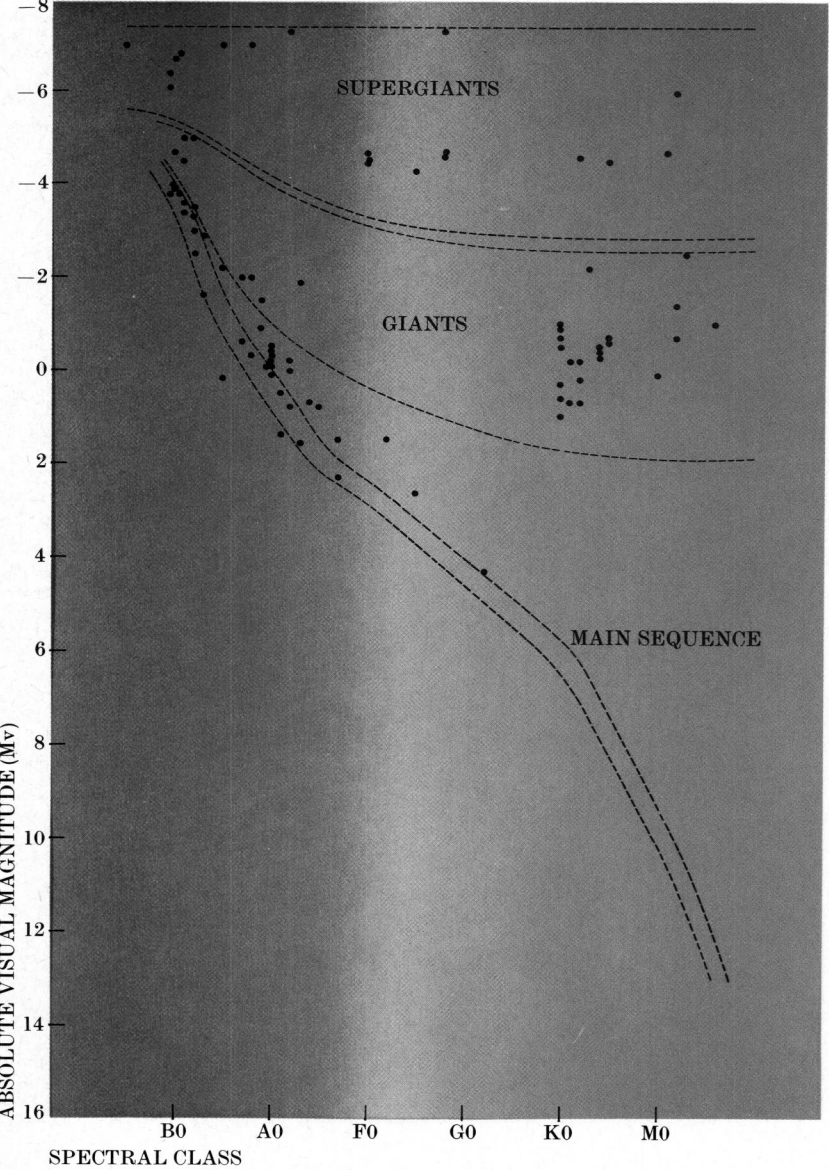

2.12: *The Hertzsprung-Russell diagram for the brightest 100 stars.*

Table 2.4: Stellar atmosphere data for models of dwarfs and giants with effective temperatures of 5 000 K and 10 000 K.

(Heights are measured above an arbitrary point defined from the opacity of the stellar material.)

(a) 5 000K (dwarf)

height (km)	temperature (K)	density (kg m^{-3})
120	7 900	3.4×10^{-10}
330	5 500	3.0×10^{-10}
710	4 460	1.1×10^{-10}
1 070	4 180	3.2×10^{-11}
1 400	4 070	8.7×10^{-12}

(b) 5 000K (giant)

height (km)	temperature (K)	density (kg m^{-3})
5 100	8 370	1.7×10^{-11}
16 300	5 580	2.1×10^{-11}
53 700	4 500	7.9×10^{-12}
9I 900	4 180	2.1×10^{-12}
131 000	4 070	5.0×10^{-13}

(c) 10 000K (dwarf)

height (km)	temperature (K)	density (kg m^{-3})
2 900	15 670	2.8×10^{-12}
5 000	11 390	1.2×10^{-12}
5 800	8 850	1.0×10^{-12}
6 600	8 030	3.1×10^{-13}
7 700	7 800	4.8×10^{-14}

(d) 10 000K (giant)

height (km)	temperature (K)	density (kg m^{-3})
433 000	15 960	2.1×10^{-13}
857 000	11 280	5.1×10^{-14}
1 110 000	8 700	1.7×10^{-14}
1 294 000	7 890	3.5×10^{-15}
1 500 000	7 770	3.9×10^{-16}

Roman numeral. The correspondence between these classes and actual absolute magnitudes for the different temperature classes is illustrated in figure 2.13. Supergiants are divided into classes Ia and Ib, giants into classes II and III. Members of class IV are called subgiants, and class V is the main sequence. A few slightly sub-luminous stars called subdwarfs are allotted to class VI and white dwarfs form class VII. Examples from among the brightest stars are shown in table 2.2.

The temperature classes O, B, A etc are based on the relative strengths of various spectral lines. As these strengths are also partially determined by the density, the spectral classes do not correspond to precisely the same effective temperature in giants and dwarfs. The effective temperature–spectral class relationships for dwarfs, giants and supergiants are given in table 2.5.

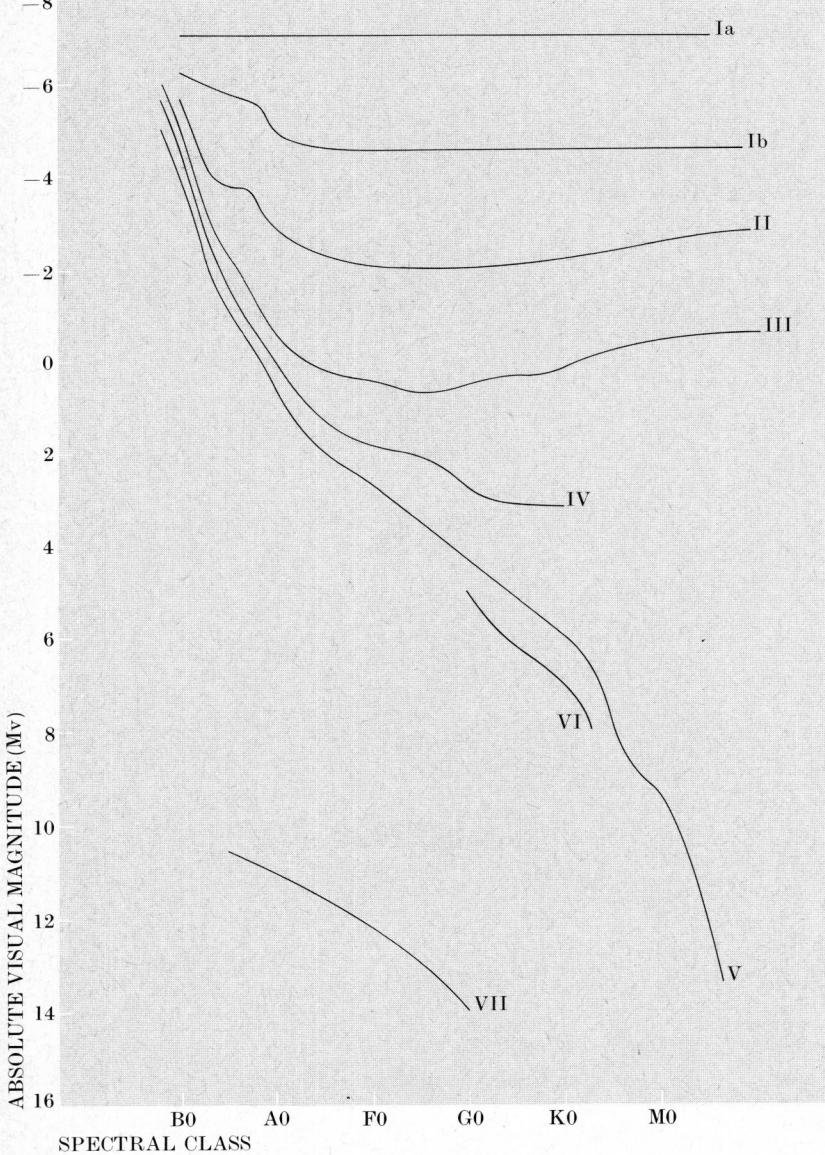

2.13: *Morgan and Keenan's two-dimensional classification of stellar spectra according to temperature and luminosity.*

Table 2.5 : Spectral class – effective temperature relationship

Spectral class	Dwarf (V)	Temperature (K) Giant (III)	Supergiant (I)
O5	40 000		30 000
B0	28 000		
B5	15 500		
A0	9 900		12 000
A5	8 500		
F0	7 400		7 000
F5	6 580		
G0	6 030	5 600	5 700
G5	5 520	5 000	4 850
K0	4 900	4 500	4 100
K5	4 130	3 800	3 500
M0	3 480	3 200	
M5	2 800		
M8	2 400		

The determination of the chemical composition of stars

The absorption-line spectra of stars allow astronomers to deduce the relative proportions or the ABUNDANCES of the various chemical elements in the stellar atmospheric layers where the absorption lines are formed. If the physical conditions in a stellar atmosphere can be discovered, then their effect on the appearance of the spectrum lines of an element can be calculated and eliminated. The remaining factor is then the abundance of the element. Of course, the process of finding the abundances is only possible for elements that actually have lines visible, and it cannot tell us the composition of the star's interior.

Many stellar spectra are still taken in the traditional way on photographic plates, but the use of direct photoelectric methods, in which the spectrum is produced as a graph of intensity against wavelength, is increasing. Photographic spectrograms have to be converted into intensity graphs, via a special instrument called a microphotometer. Figure 2.14 shows part of such an intensity tracing. On the original photographic spectrograms, a DISPERSION (wavelength per unit length of the final spectrum) between 1 and 0.1 nm wavelength per nm of plate is considered desirable in order to resolve the spectral features as well as possible. Spectra are widened at right angles to the spread of lines by trailing the star image back and forth across the entrance slit of the *spectrograph* because a wide spectrum improves the meaningful signal, relative to the noise, in the final tracing. However, the wider the spectrum and the higher the dispersion, the more the starlight is being spread out over the photographic plate and the longer the exposure that is required. Even with very large telescopes only stars visible to the naked eye are bright enough for investigation at high dispersion, and astronomers have to be content with poorer quality data for the fainter stars.

2.14: *A section of the absorption-line spectrum of the star Arcturus converted into a graph of light intensity against wavelength. The wavelength scale at the top is in Ångström's (0.1 nm). (University of Cambridge,* UK*)*

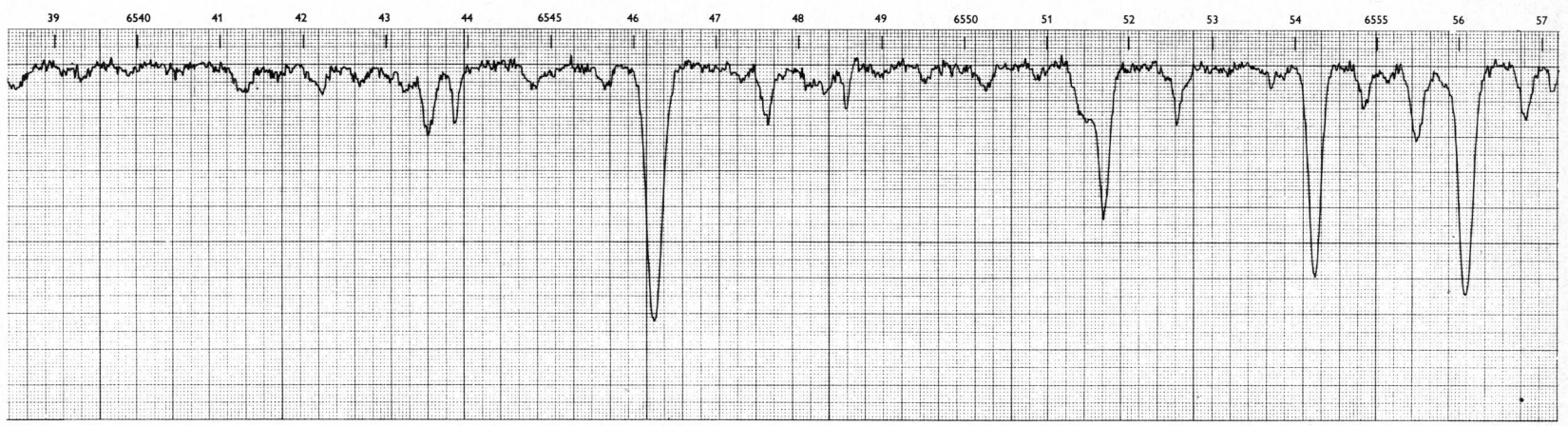

The absorption lines appear as inverted, bell-shaped dips in the level of the continuous spectrum. The actual shape of a spectral line is called the LINE PROFILE. However, more often than not, especially when the lines are narrow, the recorded profile is partly a result of instrumental factors, rather than a true record of the light leaving the star. What is much less affected is the total absorption caused by each line. The quantity measured is called the EQUIVALENT WIDTH. The definition of equivalent width is illustrated in figure 2.15. Essentially it is the width (in units of wavelength) that the line would have if the absorption-line profile were a completely black rectangle. When the profiles of spectrum lines can be obtained accurately, they provide valuable additional information. The profiles of the hydrogen lines, for example, are particularly useful in determining the stellar temperature and luminosity.

The spectral lines from stars are not especially sharp, chiefly because the atoms responsible for the absorption are in random motion. The hotter the star, the more energy of motion the atoms possess; thus the Doppler effect spreads the absorption in a given line over a corresponding larger range of wavelengths. Stellar lines are usually rather broader than might be expected, and this extra width is thought to be due to small-scale motions (up to $5\,\mathrm{km\,s^{-1}}$) of the gas as a whole, called MICROTURBULENCE. In giant and supergiant stars, the lines are often broadened in a way that indicates much larger-scale motion, that has come to be called MACROTURBULENCE (up to $50\,\mathrm{km\,s^{-1}}$). There are other reasons why spectral

2.15: *The definition of the equivalent width of an absorption line. The shaded parts have equal areas.*

2.16: *The profile of a very strong absorption line. This example is Hα in the spectrum of the K star, Arcturus. (University of Cambridge, UK)*

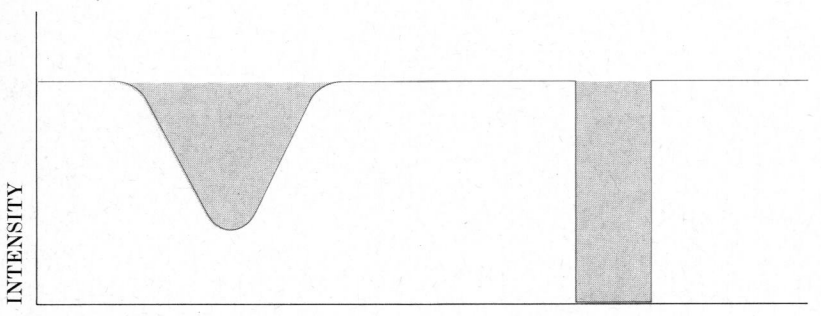

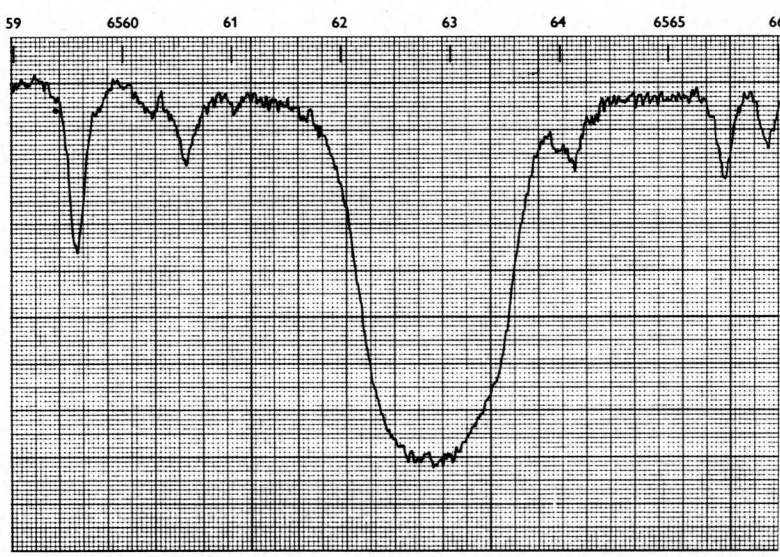

lines are broadened: for example, collisions between atoms that particularly affect the line further from the line centre. A very strong line has much of its absorption in broad wings far from the line centre (figure 2.16).

Figure 2.17 shows the effect on the profile of a spectral line of increasing the number of atoms that are effective at absorbing. Figure 2.18 shows the corresponding changes in the equivalent width, in a curve called the CURVE OF GROWTH. Now, in any one star, it is not possible to change the strength of one spectrum line, and so get the curve of growth experimentally. But if we assume that all the lines of one ion have similar curves of growth, then it is possible to construct the curve of growth for any given ion from the equivalent widths of several different lines of that ion. One problem encountered is that not all spectral lines have the same intrinsic strengths, so these latter have to be found experimentally in a laboratory or calculated. It is these quantities, properly weighted to account for the temperature effects, that are plotted on the horizontal axis. Then the number of absorbing atoms (i.e. the abundance) can be deduced from the relative position of the curve of growth along the horizontal axis.

The curve of growth method in its simplest form assumes that the stellar atmosphere can be represented by single values of temperature, pressure and so forth, but this is far from the truth. Fortunately, powerful computers make it possible to simulate stellar atmospheres by mathematical models which take account of the different physical conditions in different layers. Using these models, astrophysicists predict the appearance of spectra for trial values of the abundances of the elements and choose the ones that best fit the observations of a particular star. Results from this more sophisticated method have, however, largely vindicated the use of the curve of growth, which has the advantage of simplicity even if it does lack elegance!

2.17: *The profile of an absorption line depends on the number of atoms effective at absorbing that are present. Only half of each profile is shown, and each is labelled with the relative number of absorbing atoms.*

2.18: *The curve of growth shows how the equivalent width (W) of an absorption line increases as the number of absorbing atoms increases. It forms the basis of a method for determining the abundances of the chemical elements in stars.*

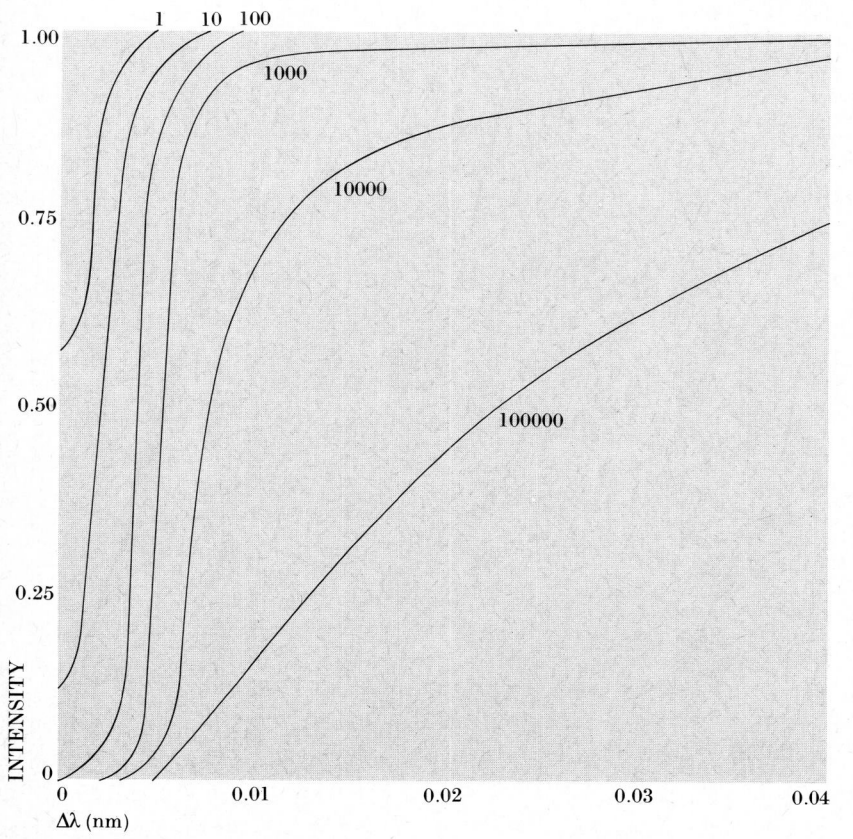

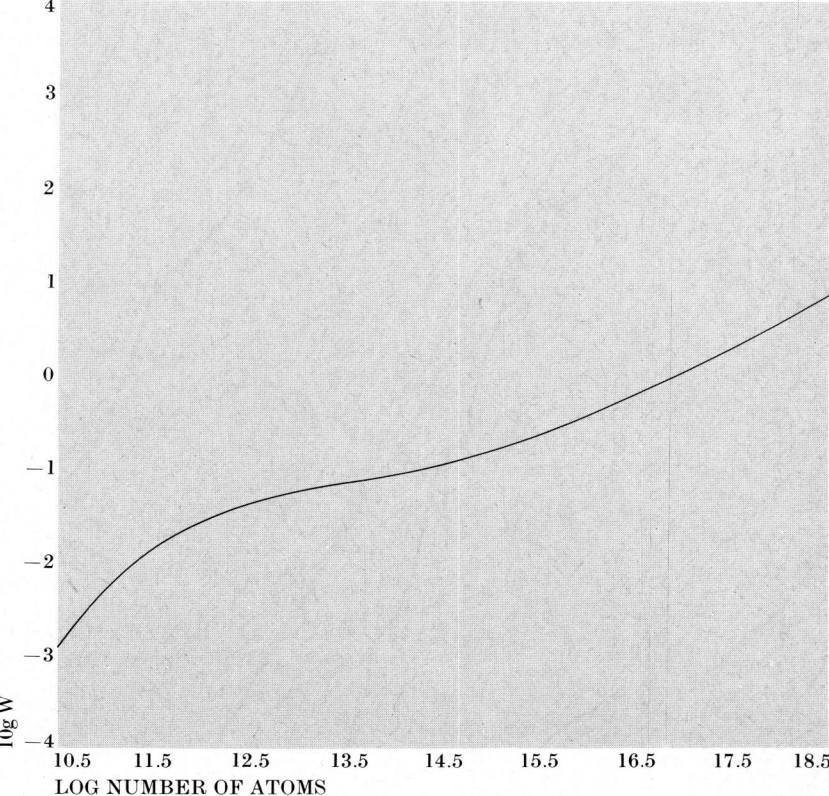

Stars with unusual spectra

We like to think of the Sun as a normal star. This idea is not un-justified, as there is not a great deal to distinguish its spectrum from those of most dwarf stars of the same temperature, and when due account is taken of the effects of temperature and luminosity differences, the solar composition seems fairly typical among stars with ages similar to the Sun's. Nevertheless, the more stellar spectra that are examined in detail, the more peculiarities seem to emerge.

There is a general tendency for stars that are known to be old, for example by their membership in *globular clusters*, to have comparatively weak absorption lines in their spectra. This is interpreted as a deficiency of metals, that is, everything heavier than helium, in the material from which these stars were formed. The other main types of unusual spectra fall broadly into three groups: hot stars with extended atmospheres, the peculiar and metallic-line A stars and cool giants of anomalous composition. Each will be discussed in turn.

Hot stars with extended atmospheres

In the terminology BE STAR, the 'e' in Be stands for emission; these stars are characterized by emission lines of hydrogen superimposed on a normal absorption spectrum. The first few members of the *Balmer series*, are usually affected and sometimes lines of ionized iron, titanium and silicon. The emission lines are sometimes split into two components.

2.19: *The spectrum of a hot star surrounded by a shell of gas shows the effects of light emission from the gas. The exact appearance of the spectrum depends on the relative orientation of the star and the observer.*

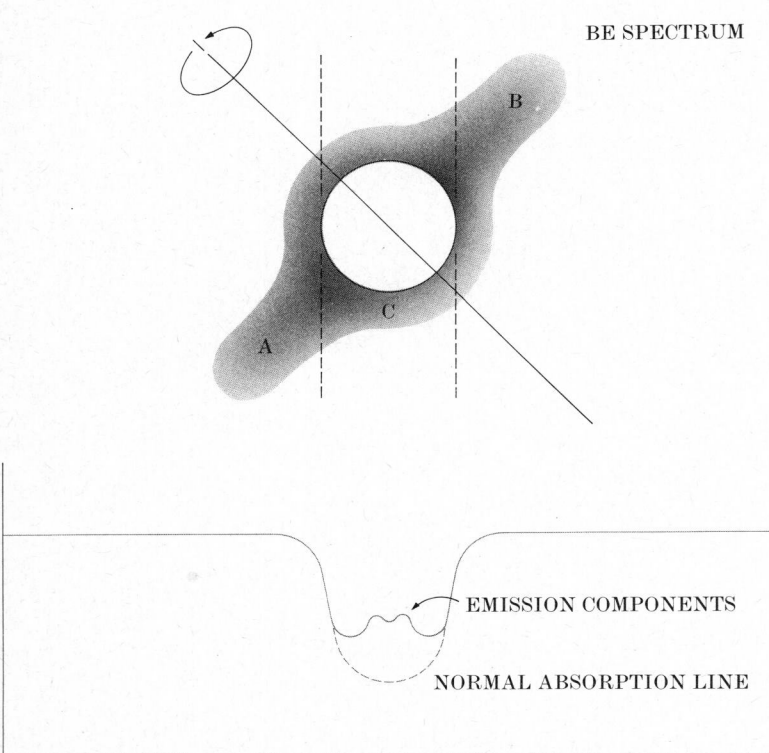

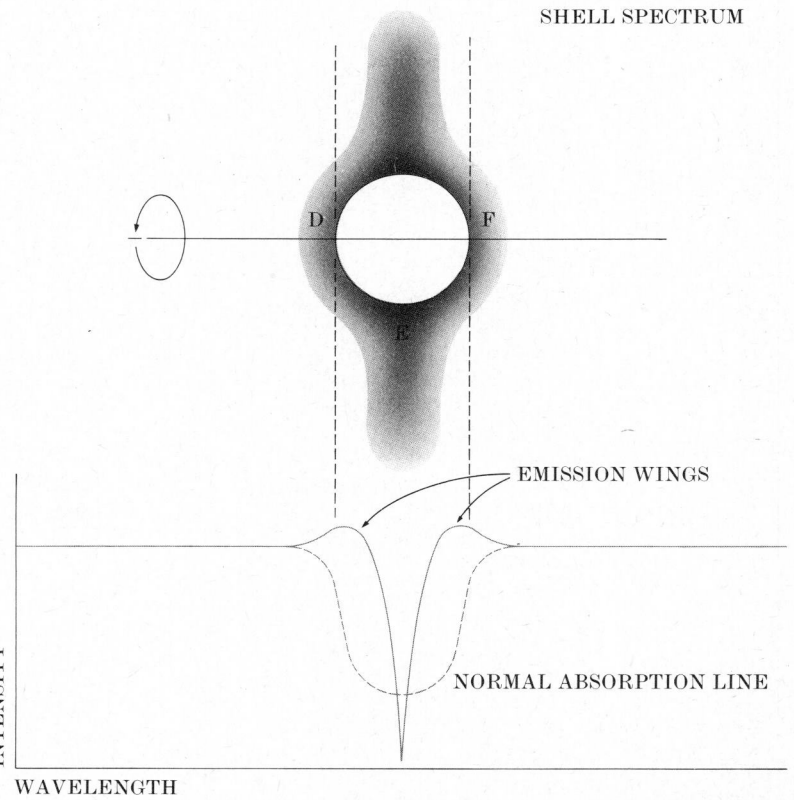

SHELL STARS have sharp, deep absorption lines with emission wings, superimposed on the normal absorption spectrum. Up to 35 members of the Balmer series may be visible, whereas normally only 20 would be detected.

It turns out that Be and shell stars are identical, the difference in appearance being due simply to the direction in which the stars are viewed, as figure 2.19 makes clear. The stars are surrounded by a distended envelope of gas, drawn out into a disc around the equator by rapid rotation. This gas is emitting light, but is cooler than the surface of the star. In case I, the observer sees the absorption spectrum of the star, the emission from the two parts A and B of the shell on either side of the star, and the absorption caused by the gas in region C against the background of the hot star. In case II, the observer sees the large amount of absorption by the extended shell (E) between him and the star, together with a small amount of emission from the thin shell layer near the poles, regions D and F.

Around 15 per cent of all O and B stars show emission and shell spectra of this kind. They are subject to irregular spectral and light variations, presumably as the shell structure changes. Two notable examples are Pleione in the Pleiades cluster and γ Cassiopeia; the latter was one of the first emission-line stars to be recognized when stellar spectroscopy started at the end of the nineteenth century, and at that time it appeared stable. In the period 1932–37 it underwent spectral changes, reaching a maximum brightness of 1.5 mag. Since 1940 it has stayed at 2.2 mag, with only minor fluctuations.

P CYGNI STARS occur in the temperature range 10 000 to 40 000 K. Their spectra include numerous emission lines. Associated with the emission lines, and always displaced to the violet, are sharp absorption lines. These features are attributed to expanding, extended atmospheres. P Cygni stars also experience random outbursts. For example, P Cygni itself rose from being invisible to the naked eye to 3 mag in the period AD 1600–1606, after which it declined to 6 mag. In 1655 it brightened again, reaching 3.5 mag for 4 years, after which it faded to 5.2 mag, to remain so ever since with only minor variations. The hydrogen lines Hα and Hβ, and other strong lines in the spectra of O- and B-type supergiants sometimes have profiles like P Cygni, with emission and absorption components.

WOLF-RAYET STARS, believed to be among the hottest visible stars known, were first noticed in 1867 by the French astronomers C.J.E.Wolf and G.Rayet. Their spectra are characterized by the broad emission lines of He^0, He^+, C^+, C^{2+}, C^{3+}, N^{2+}, N^{3+}, N^{4+}, O^+, O^{2+}, O^{3+}, O^{4+}, O^{5+}, and there are very few absorption lines. They are rare objects, with only around 100 brighter than 11 mag known; about half of these are known to be in binary systems. WR stars occur as the central stars in about one-fifth of the planetary nebulae.

Wolf-Rayet stars fall roughly into two categories: WC stars that have lines of He, C, and O, and WN stars that have the lines of He and N. There are also some intermediate between the two groups. It is difficult to determine their temperatures accurately because the energy distribution in their continuous spectra does not seem to correspond well with any one temperature. Estimates put the average effective temperatures at 50 000 K for the WN stars and 40 000 K for the WC stars.

The evolutionary status of Wolf-Rayet stars is unknown. One plausible theory accounts for the two types by assuming they are senile stars that have lost some mass, possibly to a companion in a binary system. According to the amount of material that has been lost, the new surface layer may be either an inner layer where all the carbon has been turned into nitrogen, or an outer layer still rich in carbon. Perhaps all Wolf-Rayet stars are binaries with undetected companions. If this supposition is right, then unless the companion were itself an O or B star, its spectrum would be too faint to see, and WR lines are so broad that a systematic velocity change would probably not be noticed either.

Certain O-type stars have some of the broad emission lines of the Wolf-Rayet spectra weakly present. However, there is no clear distinction between these and O supergiants, all of which probably have extended atmospheres. These O stars are designated Of to distinguish them from the hotter Be-type that are termed Oe stars.

The peculiar and metallic-line A stars

The term PECULIAR A STAR (Ap star) has come to encompass a whole range of oddities between spectral types B5 and F5. The chief feature that unites the group is the strong, and often variable, magnetic field that most of the members have. This magnetism was discovered by the pioneering work of the American, H.Babcock who detected the splitting of the spectrum lines (i.e. *Zeeman effect*) that it causes. Those Ap stars not known to be magnetic have spectral lines too broad for any splitting to be detectable.

Ap stars also have especially strong lines of certain elements, and can be broadly classified into groups according to which lines are enhanced. There is also some correlation of the spectral peculiarities with temperature. Thus, the manganese stars fall at the hot end of the range, the europium-chromium-strontium stars at the cool end, and silicon stars in the middle.

Those magnetic Ap stars that have been carefully observed seem to have cyclic variations in magnetic field, usually in a period of a few days. Associated with the magnetic variations, some of the spectrum lines change in intensity regularly, particularly those of chromium and europium. Typically, the chromium lines are at a maximum when the europium lines are at a minimum. This apparently strange behaviour of both magnetic field and spectrum can be explained reasonably well by a model called the OBLIQUE ROTATOR. The stellar magnetic poles are not close to poles of the rotation axis (unlike the situation on the Earth) and there are concentrations of different elements on different parts of the star's surface, perhaps near the magnetic poles. Then, as the star rotates, the N and S magnetic poles alternately come round to the observable side.

Some Ap stars have lines in their spectra that can only be explained by the excess of some very unusual elements. For example, some manganese stars have a strong spectral line for which the only identification seems to be ionized mercury. The very odd star, 3 Cen A has strong lines of phosphorus, gallium and krypton and the helium may be predominantly the isotope ^{3}He. The star HD 101065 seems only to have lines of rare earth elements (notably holmium) in its spectrum, and virtually none of iron and the more usual elements!

The Ap stars are not distinguished from normal stars in any other way apart from their spectroscopic appearance. They occur in clusters and in the general field of stars. They are definitely on or near the main sequence in the Hertzsprung-Russell diagram. The most plausible explanation put forward for the peculiarities is a DIFFUSION PROCESS in the atmospheres which brings certain ions to the surface and makes others sink. There is no observational support for any theories involving mass exchange or peculiar atmospheric structure.

AM STARS lie in the spectral-type range from A0 to F0. They are nothing like so peculiar as the Ap stars. Their chief characteristics are apparent under-abundances of calcium and scandium, slight over-abundances of the *iron-peak elements*, and over-abundances up to about a factor of 10 in the heavier elements and rare earths. None is known to vary or to have a measurable magnetic field. A large proportion seem to be in binary systems, sometimes with both members being Am stars, and none has so far been identified with anything more than a moderate rotation velocity (less than $100\,\mathrm{km\,s^{-1}}$). Like Ap stars, they are main-sequence stars, and it is difficult to explain the abundance anomalies. The diffusion theory looks the most promising explanation for the Am stars also.

Cool giants of unusual composition

The coolest stars of the spectral sequence are those classified as K and M, and their spectra are dominated by the bands of closely-spaced lines that originate from molecules rather than individual atoms. In these normal stars, the oxides of the metals titanium, scandium and vanadium are identified. However, there are some giant stars of the same temperature range, (table 2.6) whose spectra contain instead the lines of other molecules.

In the S STAR spectra, the oxides of titanium, scandium and vanadium are replaced by the oxides of the heavier metals zirconium, yttrium and barium. Also, in 1952, P.W.Merrill announced the discovery of lines of the element technetium in the spectra of some S stars. This discovery was remarkable because the longest-lived isotope of this unstable element has a half-life of only 2×10^6 years which is much shorter than the age of the stars. The implication is that we are seeing the results of *nuclear reactions* which are happening now or have taken place not very long ago in astronomical terms. Practically half of the known S stars are *irregular long-period variables*.

In the spectra of the C STARS (carbon stars), the metallic oxides are hardly observed, but instead there are strong bands of the molecules CN, C_2 and CH. It has been estimated that the ratio carbon/oxygen is four or five times greater in the C stars than in normal stars of the same temperature range (table 2.7). This class of stars is sometimes divided into R types that are hotter, and N types that are cooler examples.

Table 2.6: Effective temperatures of the different types of red giants

$T\mathit{eff}$ (K)	Normal types	Heavy metal types	Carbon types
4 500	G5		C0
4 000	K0–K1		C2
3 500	K5		C4
3 000	M3	S3	C5
2 500	M6	S5	C6
2 000	M8	S7	C7
1 500	M9–M10	S10	C9

Table 2.7: Possible abundances in red giants of different types

Type	Abundance ratios (no. of atoms) C/O	C/N	Zr/Ti
K–M	0.25	0.5	0.01
C	2	1	—
S	1	—	10

Among the giants of spectral type G and K are a number that have exceptionally strong lines of the elements strontium and barium and rare earths, and also the carbon compounds, CN, CH and C_2. It is noticeable that the enhanced elements in these BARIUM STARS are those which result from a particular nuclear process – called the *s-process*, which involves the capture of neutrons by lighter elements to form the heavier ones. It may be that the outer layers of these stars have undergone mixing with material from the interior.

Stellar rotation

The spectral lines of a rapidly rotating star are broadened by the Doppler effect, because one half of the disc is coming towards the observer, while the other half is moving away from him. The centre of the disc is travelling across the line of sight, so light from there suffers neither blue nor red shift, and figure 2.20 illustrates this point. Imagine the star's disc divided into strips, and that each strip contributes a spectral line of intensity proportional to its area, and shifted from its rest wavelength by $\Delta\lambda = \lambda v/c$ (where v is the strip's velocity along the line of sight of the observer); v is zero at the centre of the disc, and has its maximum value at the edges.

Rapid rotation makes it very difficult to measure the intensity of the spectral lines, as they are often so blurred as to be indistinguishable from the continuum. However, the shapes of stellar line profiles have revealed how rapidly stars rotate. Unfortunately, what is actually measured for an individual star is not the true rotational velocity at the star's equator, v, but v sin i where i is the angle between the star's rotation axis and the observer's line of sight. One consequence of this effect is that stars seen 'pole on' have unbroadened lines. We have every reason to suppose that the directions of stellar rotation axes are distributed randomly in space, so it is possible to apply statistics to find the average rotation velocities of various groups of stars. The results show that there is a general dependence of rotation velocity on spectral type: the hottest stars rotate most rapidly; O and B stars typically have rotational velocities of 200 to 250 km s^{-1}; G stars have values much lower, generally around 20 km s^{-1}. The extended clouds of gas surrounding *shell stars* are probably the result of extremely rapid rotation, up to 500 km s^{-1}.

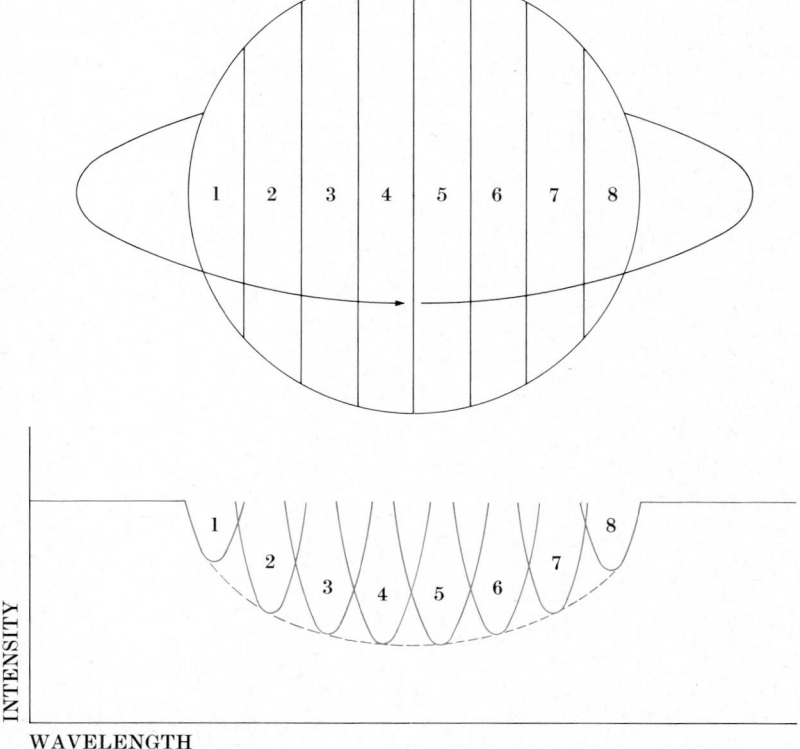

INTENSITY

WAVELENGTH

2.20: *The effect of a star's rotation on the appearance of its spectrum is to make the lines broader and shallower, the equivalent width being unaffected. Light from different parts of the star's visible disc are Doppler shifted by different amounts.*

Sociology of the stars

Even the philosophers of antiquity noted that some stars are grouped together to form clusters like the Pleiades. Photographs of the sky show that many stars are found arranged into a number of different groups. In addition to isolated stars in space, known as FIELD STARS, and to the *binary stars* and multiple stars, there are star clusters and associations.

OPEN CLUSTERS (or GALACTIC CLUSTERS, the terms are synonymous) are loose and irregular aggregations of stars containing a few hundred to a few thousand members. Individual stars in the cluster are easily resolved, and indeed their brighter members are visible to the naked eye in the cases of the Hyades, Pleiades, and κ Crucis (figure 2.21). About two dozen open clusters are visible to the unaided eye; over a thousand more are now catalogued as a result of systematic searches with telescopes. The open clusters are mainly located close to the galactic plane, or Milky Way, and most of the known ones are within 3 kpc of the Sun. Beyond this distance the clusters undoubtedly exist but they merge with the starry background.

GLOBULAR CLUSTERS are tightly-packed collections of hundreds of thousands, or even millions, of stars. They have a spherical shape and are distributed throughout a sphere surrounding the whole Galaxy. This sphere is often called the HALO. Figure 2.22 shows schematically the Galaxy and halo and the distribution of open and globular clusters. Many of the globular clusters are rather distant objects (3–60 kpc) of which just over a hundred are known in the Galaxy. The brightest globulars are ω Centauri and 47 Tucanae in the southern hemispheres, and M5 and M13 (Hercules) in the north. It is estimated that some globular clusters contain millions of stars. Their linear diameters are not large by astronomical standards: the range is 7–120 pc, and ω Cen at 20 pc is a typical example (figure 2.23). Globular clusters are known to contain large numbers of faint, evolved stars (e.g. *white dwarfs*), and the presence of these senile objects is an indication that the clusters are ancient.

There are also rather looser star families called ASSOCIATIONS, which lack any obvious structure. These are composed mainly of O and B stars, share a common motion through the Galaxy, and are expanding in total size. The signs are that associations are star groups of relatively recent origin.

Star clusters are of immense importance to observational and theoretical astrophysics because each cluster is a collection of objects that condensed from the matter between the stars at more or less the same time and with similar composition. Therefore the careful study of a cluster will show how the only remaining variable, the masses of the individual stars, affects its life history in relation to other stars. We return again to this important point in chapter 3 in our discussion of stellar evolution.

In addition to the families we must consider the STELLAR POPULATIONS into which stars can be categorized. In the 1940s, German-American observer Walter Baade resolved for the first time individual stars in the central regions of the *Andromeda Nebula*, or M31, a giant spiral galaxy 700 kpc from the Milky Way. This tech-

2.21: *The open star cluster* κ *Crucis.*
(Radcliffe Observatory, South Africa)

nical achievement led to an astronomical advance because Baade found that the stars in the central region of the M31 galaxy were quite unlike those in the *spiral arms* of M31. From this observation he developed the concept of stellar populations: that the properties of the broad range of observed stars differs from place to place in a galaxy. The young material in a galaxy tends to be found in the spiral arms and comprises hot, young stars, *gas nebulae* and dust; this is called POPULATION I, and it is distinguished chemically by a relatively high proportion of the heavier elements. Older material is found in globular clusters, galactic nuclei, and elliptical galaxies, and it is made up of old evolved stars (*red giants* and *white dwarfs*, for example); this is referred to as POPULATION II, and chemically it is matter that contains only a small amount of the heavier elements. Population I objects are made from interstellar gas that has been enriched by the debris from exploding stars, whereas Population II objects formed long ago from relatively unprocessed raw materials. The concept of stellar populations is particularly valuable to discussions of galactic structure.

2.22: *The distribution of open and globular clusters in the Galaxy, shown schematically. Open clusters are confined to the galactic plane, whereas globular clusters occur in a spherical halo surrounding the Galaxy.*

2.23: *The globular cluster ω Centauri. (Anglo-Australian Observatory, Australia)*

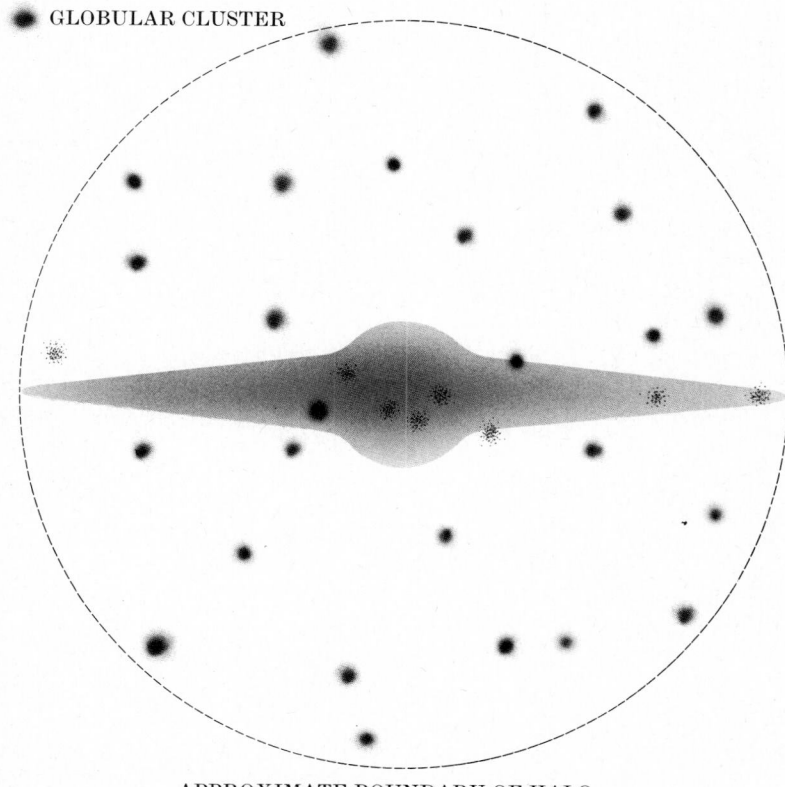

OPEN CLUSTER

GLOBULAR CLUSTER

APPROXIMATE BOUNDARY OF HALO

3. Inside the stars

3.1: *M13, the great globular cluster in the constellation Hercules. M13 is just visible to the naked eye in good sky conditions. Globular clusters have played an important role in helping astronomers to understand the life of the stars. (US Naval Observatory, USA)*

Introduction

In the previous chapter we gave an outline of the measurements that astronomers can make to find out the properties of stars. Most of the mass of a galaxy is in stars of one type or other. This chapter shows how mathematicians, physicists and theoretical astronomers have used the observations in order to deduce how stars work. One of the greatest achievements of astronomy in the first half of the twentieth century was the elucidation of the mechanisms that keep the Sun and other stars shining. We start our description of the workings of a star with an illuminating extract from the writings of the very distinguished Cambridge astrophysicist, Sir Arthur Stanley Eddington. He may fairly be said to have established the theory of stellar interiors. This extract from 'The Internal Constitution of the Stars' published in 1926 pre-dates modern nuclear physics, and yet it shows a remarkable grasp of the basic behaviour of atomic particles inside a star and the possible source of sub-atomic energy.

'The inside of a star is a hurly-burly of atoms, electrons and aether waves (photons). We have to call to aid the most recent discoveries of atomic physics to follow the intricacies of the dance. We started to explore the inside of a star; we soon find ourselves exploring the inside of an atom. Try to picture the tumult! Dishevelled atoms tear along at 50 miles a second with only a few tatters left of their elaborate cloaks of electrons torn from them in the scrimmage. The lost electrons are speeding a hundred times faster to find new resting-places. Look out! There is nearly a collision as an electron approaches an atomic nucleus; but putting on speed it sweeps round it in a sharp curve. A thousand narrow shaves happen to the electron in 10^{-10} of a second; sometimes there is a sideslip at the curve, but the electron still goes on with increased or decreased energy. Then comes a worse slip than usual; the electron is fairly caught and attached to the atom, and its career of freedom is at an end. But only for an instant. Barely has the atom arranged the new scalp on its girdle when a quantum of aether waves (a photon) runs into it. With a great explosion the electron is off again for further adventures. Elsewhere two of the atoms are meeting full tilt and rebounding, with further disaster to their scanty remains of vesture.'

'As we watch the scene we ask ourselves, can this be the stately drama of stellar evolution? It is more like the jolly crockery-smashing turn of a music hall. The knockabout comedy of atomic physics is not very considerate towards our aesthetic ideals; but it is all a question of time-scale. The motions of the electrons are as harmonious as those of the stars but in a different scale of space and time, and the music of the spheres is being played on a keyboard 50 octaves higher. To recover this elegance we must slow down the action, or alternatively accelerate our own wits; just as the slow-motion film resolves the lusty blows of the prize-fighter into movements of extreme grace and insipidity. And what is the result of all this bustle? Very little. Unless we have in mind an extremely long stretch of time the general state of a star remains steady. Just as many atoms are repaired as are smashed; just as many bundles of radiation are sent out as are absorbed; just as many electrons are captured as are exploded away. The atoms and the electrons for all their hurry never get anywhere; they only change places. The aether waves (photons) are the only part of the population which do actually accomplish something; although apparently darting about in all directions without purpose they do in spite of themselves make a slow general progress outwards. This flow would if uncompensated lead to a gradual change in the whole state of the star, very slow, but yet, we believe, too fast to accord with observational evidence. It is therefore necessary to assume that sub-atomic energy of some kind is liberated within the star, so as to replenish the store of radiant energy. This also involves a gradual transformation of the material of the star which, however, scarcely concerns the present discussion. The point which we wish here to explain is why this clash of atoms, electrons and aether waves is of practical concern to the astronomer, seeing that for each portion of radiation absorbed an equal quantity of radiation is being emitted?'

'We may think of the star as two bodies superimposed, a material body (atoms and electrons) and an aetherial body (radiation). The material body is in dynamical equilibrium, but the aetherial body is not; gravitation takes care that there is no outward flow of matter, but there is an outward flow of radiation. If there were no interaction between the two bodies, the whole store of radiation would diffuse away in a few minutes; it is because it is tied to the material body by the processes of absorption and emission that it is restrained to a slow rate of diffusion. Absorption followed by emission, although it leaves the quantity of radiation unaltered, has this effect: radiation with a slight outward bias is taken from the aetherial body; it is quickly restored again with the outward bias removed. The quicker the succession of these transformations the more strictly the outward flow is curbed. That is in accordance with the conclusion we had already reached that the factor which resists the outward flow of radiation is the absorption coefficient or opacity of the material of the star.'

In our reading of the writings of Eddington we must recall the stage of development of physics at that time. The Bohr theory of atomic structure, the old *quantum theory*, the theories of *special relativity* and *general relativity* and the theory of *black-body radiation* had all been recently developed. Eddington was able to bring together these new fields of physics for the first time in order to provide science with a unified picture of the structure of a star. With great insight he realized the importance of a sub-atomic source of energy about which little was then known. He rebuffed his critics, who suggested that stars were not hot enough for this sub-atomic process, with the retort 'go and find a hotter place'! Amazing as it may seem, Eddington was able to construct a detailed theory of how a star works, without knowledge of the exact nature of any nuclear energy processes. It remained for Hans Bethe and Carl von Weizsäcker to propose, in 1939, two possible nuclear fusion reactions to explain stellar energy production.

There has always been much interplay between physics and the theory of stellar structure. After the development in the nineteenth century of the theory of thermodynamics, which explains certain aspects of the behaviour of matter and heat energy, the work of J.H.Lane, A.Ritter, Lord Kelvin and R.Emden followed. These pioneers of stellar theory treated a star as a mass of gas that is held together by its own gravity. They investigated the mechanical properties, due to the balance of gravity and internal pressure forces, while also incorporating as much of the thermodynamic theory as possible. The thermal, or heat balance and heat flow aspects of stellar structure were developed by Karl Schwarzschild and Eddington himself, following in the wake of the momentous quantum theory. Eddington's 'The Internal Constitution of the Stars' in 1926 was a milestone in the development of astrophysics. It was later followed in 1939 by S.Chandrasekhar's detailed mathematical theory of the inside of stars, and the filling in of the nuclear physics details, also in 1939, by Bethe and von Weizsäcker.

More recent work on stellar structure theory has concentrated on the detailed physical process occurring inside stars and on the evolution of a star in time. This has been made possible both by a deeper understanding of the various branches of physics involved and also by the use of high-speed computers, which are capable of solving the complex mathematical equations that describe a star. The major reason, however, why so much progress has been made in studying the inside of a star, which has properties quite unlike that of ordinary matter, is that the laws governing its behaviour are the few basic laws and forces in nature. These fundamental laws, such as those of thermodynamics and the quantum theory, are now well understood. Indeed they form the backbone of any college-level course in basic physics. In other branches of astronomy, such as planetary theory or the structure of galaxies, many physical processes probably interact in a complex manner. For this reason it is not possible for us to describe the entire life history of a planet or a galaxy in anything like the detail which we can give for a star.

The observations that we must explain

Stars send out radiation over a wide range of frequencies, and the detection of such radiation gives information about their surface properties. For one star only, the Sun, there is additional information from the central regions, because there is the possibility of detecting certain sub-atomic particles, called *neutrinos* that are produced in the nuclear reactions. It is the task of stellar structure theory to explain, by means of the known laws of physics, the observed properties of a star and to fill in the gap between the inaccessible centre and the visible surface by theoretical deduction. The procedures for carrying out the necessary observations are described in chapter 2, and so we will simply draw attention to those results of particular relevance to stellar astrophysics.

The most significant observations for stellar structure theory are these:

(1) Stars radiate energy continuously.

(2) When we consider *main-sequence* stars, we find that the stars of a given mass have a given luminosity. This is the MASS-LUMINOSITY LAW; it implies that the energy which ultimately flows out of a star

is determined by how much matter the star is made up of (figure 3.2).

(3) In the *Hertzsprung-Russell diagram* stars are not scattered uniformly all over the place. Stars seem to occupy preferentially certain well-defined regions of the diagram. This teaches us that the surface temperature, or spectral type of a star is not independent of its absolute magnitude, or luminosity.

For the Sun, at least, we know from fossil remains on Earth, that it has continuously radiated energy at about the same rate as at present for about 4×10^9 years. Approximate ages can be inferred for other stars, and they run into billions of years. The most ancient stars in our Galaxy are thought to be around ten billion years old. This raises the important question of the source of stellar energy.

The mass-luminosity law is shown in figure 3.2. The main feature is the sharp dependence of luminosity (L) on mass (M); the rough relations are that L is proportional to M^3 for high masses (over about three solar masses) and for low masses (less than half the Sun) whereas L depends on $M^{4\cdot5}$ in between. The indices 3 and 4.5 are very approximate. To illustrate the relations, consider a star ten times as massive as the Sun (M = 10). This is about a thousand times as bright (i.e. $L = 10^3$), which corresponds to a difference of 7.5 mag. in the absolute magnitude. The magnitudes used in figure 3.2 are, of course, absolute ones; it would not make sense to compare apparent properties which are influenced by the distance of the individual stars from Earth. The masses in figure 3.2

were obtained from observations of *binary stars*, and the method of determining stellar masses is explained fully in chapter 5.

The main features of the Hertzsprung-Russell diagram are described in chapter 2. Figure 3.3 indicates schematically the features which we will need for our discussion. The figure shows the relationship of the various features to one another and where they are approximately in spectral type and absolute magnitude. In any given Hertzsprung-Russell diagram, many of the features may be absent. Of special importance to stellar evolution theory are the Hertzsprung-Russell diagrams of *clusters of stars*. The reason for this is as follows: the stars in a typical cluster are all at nearly the same distance from the Earth since the cluster diameter is very small compared to the cluster distance. Therefore it is not necessary to convert the measured apparent magnitudes into absolute ones because the conversion factor is the same for all the cluster members. We can therefore plot a Hertzsprung-Russell diagram for a given cluster with apparent magnitudes. Moreover it is reasonable to assume that the initial chemical compositions of all cluster members were similar, and that all the stars were born at almost the same time. Now, the observed properties of a star depend most strongly on its mass, age and chemical composition. Therefore a cluster gives an opportunity of isolating the evolutionary effects due to only one variable, the mass of a star, since the age and chemical composition are constant in a given cluster. Furthermore, different clusters at different ages, but with similar chemical

3.2: *The relationship between a star's luminosity (energy output) and mass, as deduced from observations of binary star systems. Visual binary stars that give data of high accuracy are shown by the black circles, and those of low accuracy by the blue circles. Eclipsing binary stars, which give the most reliable results, are indicated by red circles. The mass increases from right to left and is plotted in solar masses and the luminosity is expressed as an absolute magnitude. Two stars, Sirius B and Procyon B, do not lie on the main sequence of star masses; they are, in fact, white dwarfs, a class of underluminous dense stars.*

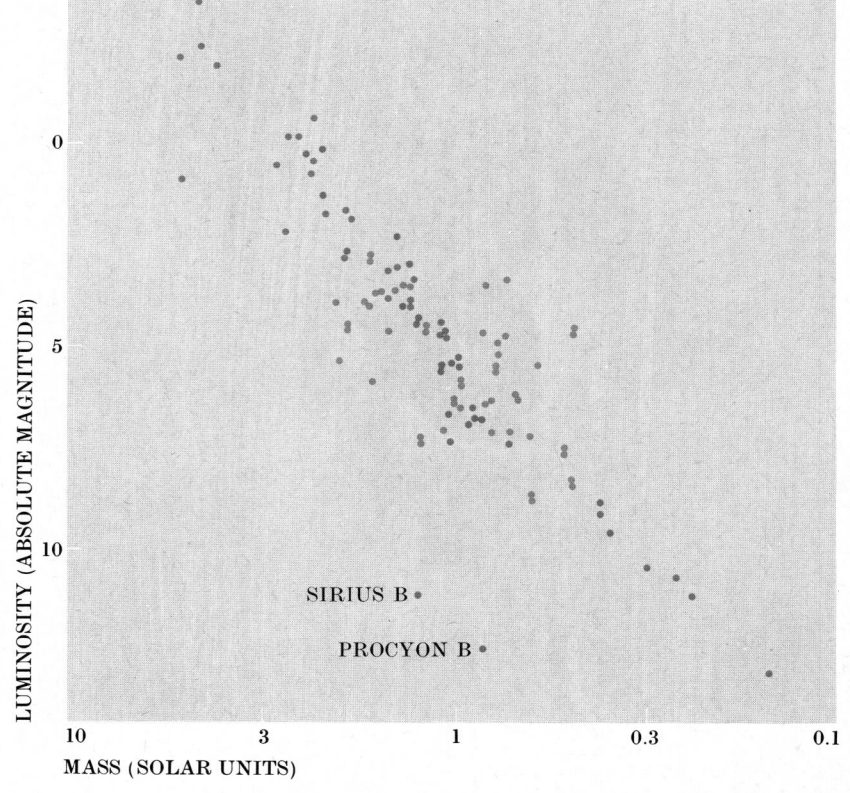

SIRIUS B

PROCYON B

LUMINOSITY (ABSOLUTE MAGNITUDE)

MASS (SOLAR UNITS)

10   3   1   0.3   0.1

0   5   10

compositions, enable us to investigate the effects of age. Figures 3.4 and 3.5 give typical examples of the Hertzsprung-Russell diagrams of a *galactic* (or open) *cluster* and of a *globular cluster*. It is one of the tasks of stellar evolution theory to explain how a star changes with time and the nature of the Hertzsprung-Russell diagrams of clusters.

The observed properties of stars cover a wide range which is given in table 3.1. The Sun, which is the only star whose shape can be seen easily, is spherical and we believe most stars to be so. Rapidly rotating stars and those in close binary systems are sometimes non-spherical in their outer layers; in a detailed theory the perturbing forces which cause these odd shapes would have to be considered. We shall concentrate here on spherical stars for simplicity.

The detailed chemical composition of stars is discussed in chapters 2 and 7. For our purposes the main results are that for stars like the Sun the composition by mass is about 70 per cent hydrogen, 28 per cent helium and 2 per cent for all the other elements together, the so-called HEAVY ELEMENTS. Very old stars of Population II appear to have a much smaller amount of the heavy elements, namely about 0.1 per cent by mass. The difference in the *stellar populations* is not confined to chemical composition alone, but includes variations of space distribution, age, and velocity dispersion. Typically Population I-type stars have small velocity dispersion of their space motion, show a space distribution

confined to the disc of the Galaxy and are relatively young. Population II objects have higher velocity dispersion, an almost spherical galactic distribution and are relatively old. The globular clusters in our Galaxy are examples of Population II objects, whereas young associations such as that in Orion are examples of Population I. The two populations are not always distinct: there is a continuum between. The origin of Population types is connected with the chemical and dynamical evolution of the galaxy (see chapter 17).

3.3: *A schematic version of the Hertzsprung-Russell diagram illustrating the approximate locations of several prominent features that are of interest to the theory of stellar evolution. The temperature and spectral type are shown on the horizontal axes, whereas luminosity and absolute magnitude are shown vertically.* ZAMS *denotes the zero-age main sequence, that is, the place in the diagram where newly-born stars settle to equilibrium and are hydrogen burning. The actual main sequence shows where a star will be after it has burnt a substantial amount of its hydrogen fuel.*

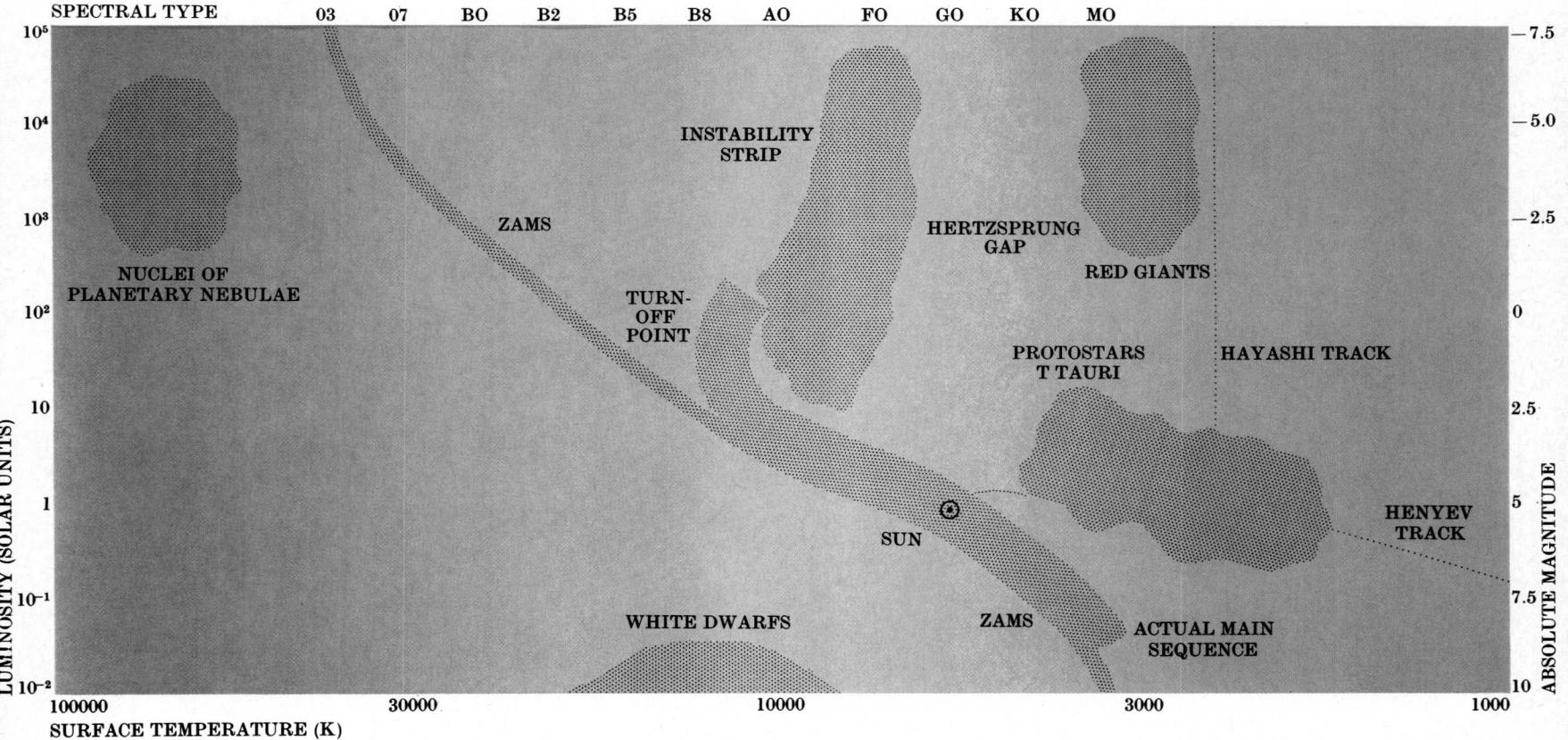

How a star holds itself together

The mass of gas in a star is held in place by gravity. A star is said to be self-gravitating, because it contains sufficient mass (typically about a million times that of the Earth) for its own gravitational force-field to be sufficiently strong to keep itself together. A star is also gaseous because, even despite large pressures, it is very hot throughout.

The material of a star is acted on by two main forces: the gravitational force, which tends to draw the stellar material inwards, and a pressure force which pushes outwards. In most stars these two forces are exactly balanced at every point of the star. An imbalance of the two forces leads to a net force which, by *Newton's second law of motion*, leads to a net acceleration or motion. The outsides of some variable stars, such as *Cepheid variable stars*, for example, are believed to be pulsating, inwards and outwards, as a consequence of a small imbalance between the gravitational and pressure forces. A large imbalance between the gravitational and pressure forces acting on the material of a star would have catastrophic consequences. Indeed this may be what happens in *supernovae* explosions. If the pressure support were removed from a star such as the Sun it would completely collapse under its own gravity in about half an hour! This has not been observed, and we believe that in most stars there is an extremely fine balance between the pressure and gravitational forces. Such stars are said to be in hydrostatic equilibrium which we write, at each point of the star:
Pressure Force = Gravitational Force.

The behaviour of stellar gas

The state of the gaseous material in a star can be described by various physical quantities such as its pressure, P, temperature, T, and density, ρ. These quantities do not vary independently. If we change the pressure at some point in a star we also alter the temperature and/or density. Clearly, if we are to give an account of how a star works, we must write an equation that tells us how pressure, temperature, and density interrelate. The relationship between these quantities is given by an EQUATION OF STATE. An example of one of these is the perfect gas law which can be written:
$$P = RT \rho / \mu$$
where R is the gas constant and μ is the mean molecular weight of stellar material. This relation is none other than the familiar $P = RT/V$ or $PV = RT$, in which the volume, V, has been replaced by μ/ρ; this substitution simply takes account of the fact that stellar material is composed of several different elements in different states of ionization. The perfect gas law holds reasonably well under the extreme densities and pressures in stars mainly because, at the high temperatures, ionization has stripped the atoms of their electrons so they have a much smaller size than usual. On Earth, for example, at a density of $10^3 \, \text{kg m}^{-3}$ (water) a material is a liquid at room temperature and the perfect gas law does not hold. In a star, however, at such density the temperature is about $10^6 \, \text{K}$ and the stellar material is highly ionized.

However, in stellar material the relatively simple equation of the perfect gas law may not always hold. Of special importance are the contributions of RADIATION PRESSURE and DEGENERACY. Radiation pressure is the pressure exerted by photons. It has a particularly simple form:
$$P_{rad} = (1/3) a T^4,$$
where a is the radiation density constant ($a = 7.56 \times 10^{-16} \, \text{J m}^{-3} \, \text{K}^{-4}$). It is clear that radiation pressure is very sensitive to temperature, since it depends on the fourth power, and it only becomes important at relatively high temperatures. For example, at the density of water the temperature must be over 10 million degrees Kelvin for radiation pressure to be greater than gas pressure. However in the interiors of many stars high enough temperatures are encountered for radiation pressure to be very important.

Degeneracy (see chapter 6) is a *quantum mechanical* effect whereby only two *electrons*, of opposite *spins* are permitted to be in the same very small volume of *phase-space*. The size of the small volume is set by the *Uncertainty Principle*. At a temperature of $10^6 \, \text{K}$ and at the density of ordinary matter (typical stellar quantities) the electrons can easily fit into the available space and degeneracy is of no consequence; at very high densities there are many more electrons per unit volume and degeneracy becomes important. The set of electrons is forced, by the constraints of the Uncertainty Principle, to take on a different distribution of velocities than it would have had at smaller densities. The different form of the distribution of velocity gives rise to a different pressure and hence a different (degenerate) equation of state. Typically degeneracy is important in stellar interiors at densities of order $10^7 \, \text{kg m}^{-3}$. Such densities are not usually encountered in ordinary stars but they are most important in very dense objects such as white dwarfs and neutron stars (chapter 6).

Energy transport inside stars

The pressure force, which opposes the self gravitation force, takes the form of a gradient of pressure; that is to say, the pressure is higher nearer the centre of the star than further out. The thermal structure of a star is related to the heat flowing through it in a complicated way. It turns out that for typical main-sequence stars, the temperature, density and pressure all increase towards the centre. Now we ask: what happens to the heat energy the star contains? The answer is that the heat must flow down the temperature gradient. This is the concept of energy transport in a star. The above argument is very simplified, but the same conclusion follows by saying that a star is hot inside and radiating away energy from its surface; energy must flow from inside to outside to replenish the loss. The energy must flow through the star by *conduction, convection* or *radiation*.

A simple argument shows that conduction is generally unimportant as a means of carrying energy in stars, compared with radiation. Conduction is a process in which electrons move the heat energy whereas in radiation photons carry the energy. Generally the amount of energy carried by the electrons may be higher than that carried by the photons, but the average distance an electron can travel before interaction with another particle (its MEAN FREE PATH) is much smaller than the mean free path of a photon. This means that the photons find it easier to take energy away from the hotter parts of the Star, even though an individual photon carries less energy than a typical electron. We can fix our ideas at a point half-way between the surface and centre of the Sun in order to give an example. In this locality the mean free path of a photon, its typical unimpeded travelling distance, is about 1 cm, whereas it is only about 10 nm (one million times less) for an electron. The large difference in mean free path demonstrates that, generally, conduction can be neglected as a means of carrying energy in stars. The main exception comes in degenerate conditions: then the density is high and the radiation is absorbed after only a small mean free path. Furthermore the peculiar momentum distribution of the electrons in the very dense parts of stars permits some electrons to have a rather long mean free path; in such a case conduction may be an important energy transport mechanism.

When energy moves by convection, the carrier of energy is a blob of material which rises bodily upwards from a hotter part of the star and deposits its heat in a cooler layer above. Cooler blobs also descend and a circulation motion is therefore set up. The motion has some similarity to that of a heavier liquid on top of a lighter one. The relative importances of convection and radiation as energy transporters in different parts of a star can be estimated by a mean free path argument similar to that used above for conduction and radiation. In general, once convection gets started it is a highly efficient way of moving heat through a star. Consequently we need only know whether convection will start or not, since if conditions are right for the onset of convection it will dominate the energy transport. Convection starts when the resistance to radiation is very high (that is to say when the stellar material is very opaque to radiation) such as is the case in the outer layers of a cool star. It can also begin when the amount of energy to be carried is so large that radiation cannot do so and mass motions become inevitable as the heat builds up; this happens near the centre of a very luminous star. Of course, the exact picture of energy transport is more complicated than we have sketched above and it includes thermodynamic effects; the theory becomes especially problematical when the efficiency of convection is low, which occurs in the very outer layers of cool stars.

Except in the special conditions noted above, the main transporter of energy in a star is radiation. The photons carrying this radiant energy are continually emitted and absorbed in the way described so aptly in the quotation from Eddington. While all the atomic processes are almost exactly in balance there is, nevertheless, a net diffusive outward flow of energy in response to the temperature gradient (about 10^{-2} degrees per metre) which alone dictates the direction along which the net flow of energy must occur.

Controlling the energy flow

The radiation does not leak out quickly because it is connected with the matter through the processes of absorption and emission. Indeed, as noted above, the typical mean free path of a photon is about 1 cm. A measure of the resistance to radiation is the *opacity* of the material; this quantity indicates how difficult the radiation finds it to get through the material. Any process which causes a photon to deviate from its path will contribute to the opacity. In simple terms we can see that the main sources of opacity are scattering and absorption. Scattering takes place when the photon is hindered in its chosen path by an interaction with a particle, usually an electron, but sometimes an atomic nucleus. In the scattering processes the photon maintains its identity; it is not destroyed, but its direction is altered. In an absorption process the photon is absorbed; it is destroyed and it gives its energy to an electron, which consequently changes its relationship with an atom. When an electron is orbiting an atom we call it a BOUND ELECTRON. If the electron is initially bound to the atom and, after absorption of the photon, it remains bound, but in a higher energy state, the process is called BOUND-BOUND ABSORPTION. Sometimes after absorption the previously-bound electron may be given enough energy by the absorbing photon to ionize the atom, that is, the electron frees itself from being tied to the parent atom; such a process is called BOUND-FREE ABSORPTION. The last main process is FREE-FREE ABSORPTION in which an electron not bound to an atom absorbs a photon and increases its energy still further while remaining free of an atom. All of these absorption processes may be followed by analogous emission processes which may return photons of the same or different energies to the energy transport pool. Scattering and absorption give opacity to the stellar material. Atomic physics and quantum mechanics enable us to estimate the total opacity.

Having outlined the physical processes that tend to slow the flow of energy from a star, it is interesting to ask ourselves how long it takes energy to move from the deep interior of a star, where it is created, to the surface, where it will journey through the Universe. We will therefore work out the transport time for solar energy. A rough estimate can be made of the time it takes radiation to leak out from the centre to the surface of the Sun, by remembering that the mean free path of a photon is typically 1 cm. The leaking process is similar to what mathematicians term a RANDOM WALK. In a random (or drunkard's) walk successive steps are taken in an arbitrary direction. The average effect is that after N steps of unit length the object is $\sqrt{N}$ distance units from the place where the walk commenced (figure 3.6). In a random walk of 100 paces of 1 metre each, the average drunkard would end up only 10 metres from the place where he gets drunk; after 10,000 paces he will have managed 100 metres! A step of 1 cm for a photon and a solar radius of about 10^9 m (10^{11} cm) means that $\sqrt{N} = 10^{11}$, or $N = 10^{22}$. Therefore 10^{22} steps of 1 cm each must be made by a photon in random walking its way out from the centre to surface of the Sun.

The total distance travelled is 10^{20} m (10^{22} cm). After the 10^{22} steps, or interactions, the average photon reaches the surface. Note

Table 3.1 : The range of the observed properties of normal stars

Property	Lowest	Sun	Highest
mass *(solar units)*	0.05	1	70
radius *(solar units)*	0.001	1	1500
luminosity *(solar units)*	10^{-6}	1	10^6
surface temperature *(degrees absolute)*	2000 K	5800 K	10^5 K

solar mass $= 1.99 \times 10^{30}\,\text{kg}$
solar radius $= 6.96 \times 10^8\,\text{m}$
solar luminosity $= 3.9 \times 10^{26}\,\text{w}$

3.4: *Stars in the open cluster M67 are plotted in accordance with their observed magnitudes and colours in this Hertzsprung-Russell diagram. The colour index (B–V) is frequently used by observational astronomers as a measure of a star's temperature. This star cluster has a well-defined main sequence, as well as a few red giant stars in the upper right corner of the diagram. This cluster is about 750 pc from the Sun.*

3.5: *For the ancient globular cluster M3 we see a heavily populated giant branch as well as a series of stars forming a horizontal branch. These features are typical of ancient star systems, in which many of the stars that were once on the main sequence have evolved.*

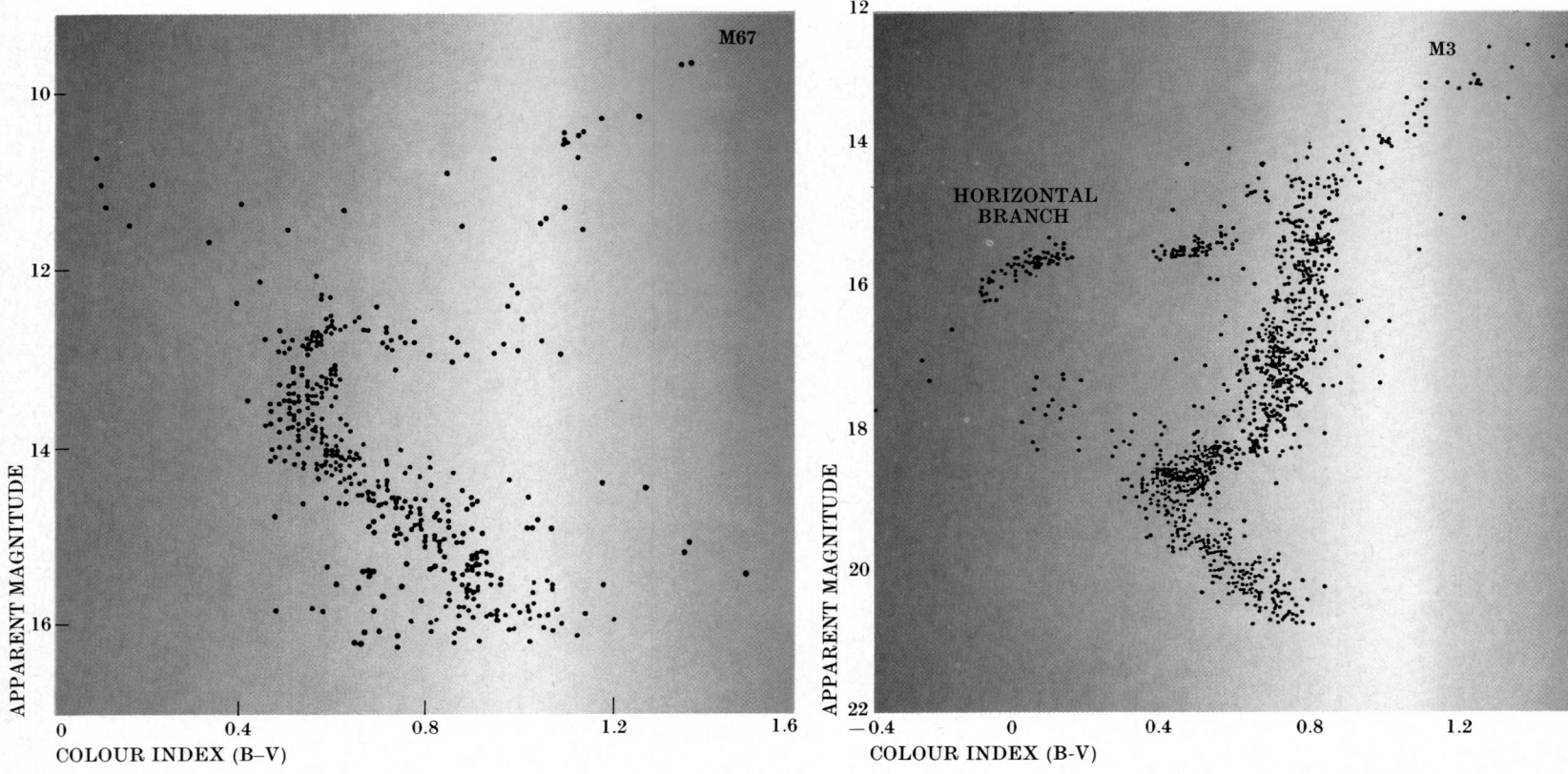

that in a random walk we cannot predict where on the surface a given packet of energy created in the star centre will finally emerge; this is the essence of the natural randomness of the process. Now that we have estimated statistically the distance that a photon has to travel aimlessly, we can work out correspondingly the length of time that it dallies on its journey. Since the speed of photons is that of light, $(c = 3 \times 10^8\,m\,s^{-1})$ we find a time of 10^4 years. This estimate is very approximate and only gives an idea of the order of magnitude of the quantity involved. However, it does imply that a long time elapses before the outside of a star is aware of any thermal changes in its deep interior. A more rigorous calculation would give a time of 10^7 years; the discrepancy is due to the assumption that the mean free path of the photon is always 1 cm.

Whatever the mode of heat transport in a star there is a mathematical equation that relates the flux of energy transported to the physical quantities (pressure, temperature, etc.) at every point of a star. This is called the ENERGY or HEAT TRANSPORT EQUATION.

There is one extra aspect which is important when energy transport is by convection, namely mixing. In convection, material is moving in order to carry the energy, so that layers of a star that are convective are mixed up. Within a short time the chemical structure becomes uniform throughout the stirred-up layer of a star. By contrast, in the radiative and conductive layers of a star the material is not moving significantly; therefore each layer retains its own chemical composition, which may be influenced by any nuclear transmutations taking place there.

We can summarize as follows the way in which a star works: the mass of the star supplies the strong self-gravitational force which in equilibrium must be checked by an opposing pressure force. The thermal structure of the star, which is related to the heat flow and the pressure structure, requires a temperature gradient. Energy flows from the interior and through the stellar surface and the star shines. Several disciplines of physics, including dynamics, thermodynamics, quantum mechanics and atomic physics, have been used to deduce this basic structure.

The source of stellar energy

The existence of the temperature gradient requires a flow and release of energy (luminosity) at the surface of the star. If the star is to remain stable the energy loss at the surface must be balanced by new energy from within. But what is the origin of this energy? For a simple model of the energy source we might suppose that the heat output occurs solely because the central regions of a star are hotter than the outer ones. However, a very important calculation shows that this cannot be sufficient, at least for the Sun. There is reliable geological evidence that the amount of solar radiation received at the Earth has changed only a little during the 4.5×10^9 years that the Earth has existed. Therefore we can legitimately use the present value for the solar luminosity in calculating an estimate of the total amount of energy radiated by the Sun during the lifetime of the Earth. Once the estimate is made, we may ask if the heat (or thermal) energy of the Sun, caused by the cooling of

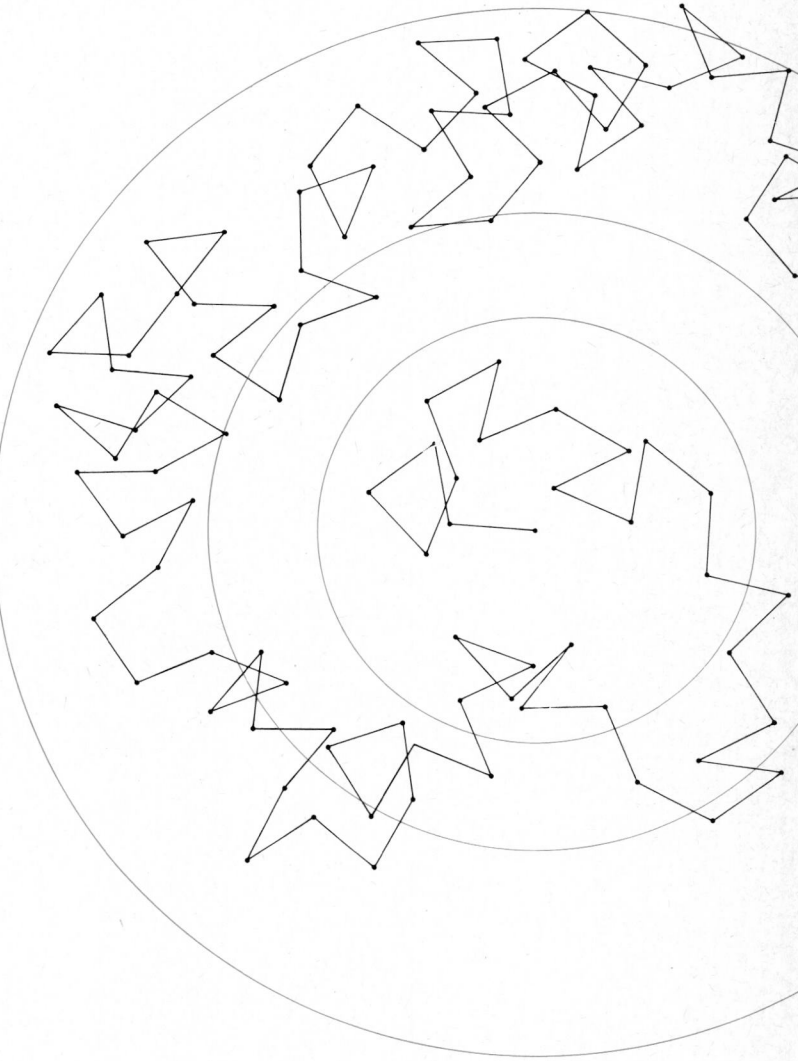

3.6: *This visualization of the random walk process shows how a series of random steps gradually takes a walker away from the starting point. Each step is of the same length, but the directions are entirely random. Random processes are of immense significance in the physical sciences, since many of the properties of atomic and nuclear matter are governed by the laws of chance. In a random walk the result of making N steps is to take the walker, on average, $N^{\frac{1}{2}}$ steps from the start. For example, 16 steps could be expected to take us about four paces from the origin, and 100 steps would achieve around ten paces. Radiation diffuses out from the centre of a star by the random walk method described here.*

the hot central regions is sufficient to account for the estimated output. To make this calculation we must remember that, as the central regions cool, the Sun will have to contract a little in order to keep up on the gas pressure. A cooler gas has to be compressed into a smaller volume if its pressure is to remain constant. Now it turns out that the total amount of heat energy that the Sun could have acquired in contracting to its present radius is given by its present gravitational potential energy. This latter quantity is roughly $GM_\odot^2/R_\odot$, where G is the universal gravitational constant, $M_\odot$ the solar mass and $R_\odot$ the present radius. This calculation was first made by Lord Kelvin and H.Helmholtz in the nineteenth century. The lifetime of this energy source radiating at the rate of the solar luminosity, $L_\odot$, is therefore roughly $GM_\odot^2/R_\odot L_\odot$, which turns out to be about ten million years. Hence we see that the thermal energy source in the Sun is sufficient to power it for only about 0.2 per cent of its known lifetime. Such a source is clearly insufficient, and this line of reasoning led Eddington to suggest that there should be another energy producing mechanism in stars, namely a nuclear energy source.

Before considering a nuclear source of energy, however, it is instructive to inquire if any known terrestrial sources of energy would be sufficient to power the Sun. Think, for example, of coal which still supplies a significant amount of the annual energy budget of Europe and North America, and let us suppose that the bulk of the Sun is made up of coal or of some similar source of chemical energy. A simple calculation shows that a coal-burning Sun might last for about 10 thousand years falling short of the observed requirements by a factor of nearly a million. The need for a sub-atomic nuclear source is therefore clear.

We stress in passing that the lack of a nuclear source does not mean a lack of energy for the star; it simply means lack of sufficient energy. There are indeed stages in the life of a star when no nuclear reactions are occurring. In such cases a star still radiates energy, but it draws it from its thermal energy account which is, in turn, derived ultimately from its gravitational potential energy. The star releases gravitational energy by contraction; some of the energy goes in radiation and some into heating up the whole star.

The question of whether stars are a suitable place for nuclear transmutations to occur was hotly debated in the 1920s. From the equations that describe the structure of a star it is possible to make order of magnitude estimates of the physical conditions near the centre of a star. These conditions turn out to be roughly: central temperature 10^7 K, central pressure 10^{16} Nm^{-2}, density 10^5 kg m^{-3}. Even at these high densities and pressures the high temperature ensures that the material is completely gaseous. The principle question facing physicists in the 1920s was simply whether or not nuclear reactions would work under such physical conditions. The main problem at the time was that since nuclear physics was in its infancy the exact reactions were unknown. However general arguments led scientists to believe that it would be difficult to conceive of a nuclear transmutation of elements occurring, simply because of the substantial amount of kinetic energy required to fuse four

hydrogen nuclei together. This is because of the strong electrical repulsion between the positive charges of the hydrogen nuclei. It was clear that a high temperature, with which high collision speeds would be associated was required. The question was how high, and it was this that persuaded Eddington to suggest ironically to his colleagues that they find a hotter place than the centres of the stars. New quantum mechanical calculations by G.Gamow on the probability of two nuclei penetrating their repulsive barriers and the proposal by H.Bethe and C.von Weizsäcker of specific reactions were the final ingredients in the story. Indeed we now know that in the Sun about one in 10^{22} collisions give rise to a nuclear reaction.

The nuclear powerhouse

The basic source of nuclear energy lies in the equivalence of mass and energy proposed by Einstein, and embodied in the relation:

$$E = Mc^2$$

If four hydrogen nuclei fuse together to form a helium nucleus there is a certain amount of mass converted into energy. If we write the small mass difference as Δm, then:

$$\Delta m = 4m_H - m_{He},$$

where m_H denotes the mass of the hydrogen nucleus (proton) and m_{He} denotes the mass of the helium nucleus. The mass of the nucleus is exceedingly small, and so nuclear masses are conventionally measured in atomic mass units (Amu) on a scale where the mass of the normal carbon nucleus (carbon-12) has the value 12.000. On this scale $m_H = 1.0081$ and $m_{He} = 4.0039$. (1 Amu $\sim$ 1.66×10^{-27} kg). The quoted numbers give $\Delta m = 0.0285$ atomic mass units from four hydrogen nuclei. In percentage terms, when four hydrogen nuclei unite to form a helium nucleus, 0.7 per cent of the mass vanishes. Multiplication by the velocity of the light squared ($c^2 = 9 \times 10^{16}$ m^2 s^{-2}) gives an energy release of 6×10^{14} joules per kilogram of hydrogen processed. This energy release of 2×10^8 kwH per kilogram vastly exceeds that of thermal cooling or coal. Indeed if the whole Sun were to be made of hydrogen and could convert it all to helium it would produce:

$$(6 \times 10^{14} \times (2 \times 10^{30})$$

(energy release per kg) $\times$ (mass in kilograms)
10^{45} joules in its lifetime. Radiation of this energy bank at the present rate ($L_\odot \sim 4 \times 10^{26}$ watts) gives a lifetime of 10^{11} years. Clearly nuclear energy production is a viable source of fuel for the Sun, since it can keep up the supply for considerably longer than the known age of the Solar System.

The mass difference mentioned above is essentially the difference in the energy that binds together the hydrogen nucleus and the helium nucleus. Figure 3.7 shows a plot of binding energy per nucleon against atomic mass number. A nucleon is a member of a nucleus, that is a proton or a neutron. A hydrogen nucleus (consisting of one proton) contains one nucleon; a helium nucleus (consisting of two protons and two neutrons) contains four nucleons. Figure 3.7 is only a rough guide and does not show fine structure. The peak of the binding energy curve occurs somewhere near atomic mass number 56, corresponding to iron (^{56}Fe). This means that the nuclei near iron have suffered the largest loss of mass per nucleon in their formation from separate protons and neutrons, since they are the most strongly bound nuclei. The two possible ways in which energy release by nuclear transmutation can occur now become clear from further consideration of figure 3.7. First let us look at the heaviest elements, such as uranium. Relative to iron these are loosely bound (low binding energy per nucleon). So if we can break uranium into smaller fragments they will be more tightly bound, and mass would be lost, releasing energy in the process. We call this means of gaining energy NUCLEAR FISSION. It is applied in atomic power stations and atomic bombs. Another way of gaining energy is to persuade the lightest elements such as hydrogen to team up and form heavier chunks of nuclear material, such as helium, carbon, oxygen and iron, because this also increases the binding of the nuclei and releases energy. This method, termed NUCLEAR FUSION, is applied in the hydrogen bomb; scientists and engineers hope that one day they will be able to control the reaction and produce cheap energy from nuclear fusion reactors.

In stars the most important nuclear process is the fusion of hydrogen to form helium. Further fusion to carbon and to iron and beyond may also occur. This is stellar alchemy! It is explained in more detail in chapter 7.

3.7: *This schematic illustration shows how the amount of energy needed to hold together the nucleus of an atom varies as the mass of the nucleus increases. In the relative scale used here, the binding energy per massive nuclear particle (nucleon) is plotted against the number of nucleons in the nucleus (atomic mass number). The binding energy is in units of millions of electron volts (1 MeV = 1.602×10^{-13} joules). The regions in which nuclear fusion and nuclear fission are possible are shown. Peak binding energy occurs in the neighbourhood of iron (^{56}Fe), and it is here that the most strongly-bound, or most stable substances are found. Inside stars, elements may be synthesized in controlled nuclear reactions.*

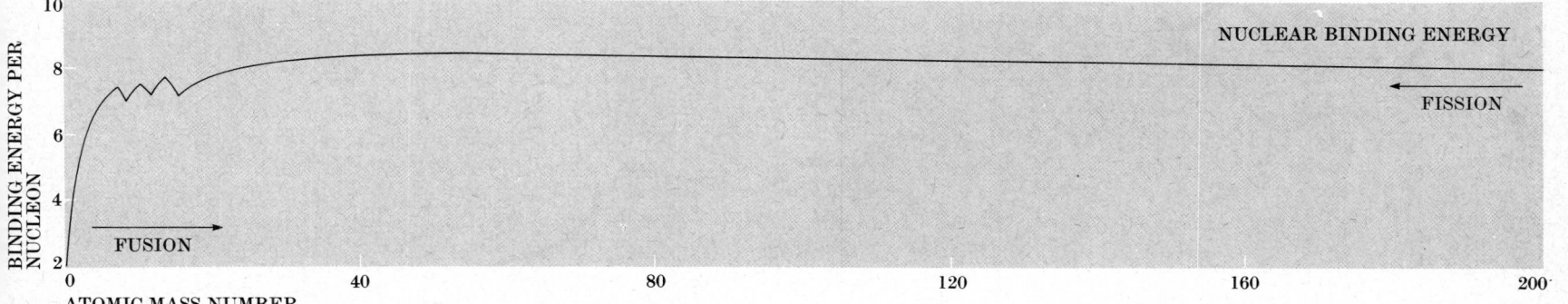

There are two important nuclear reactions for making helium from hydrogen: one is direct – the proton-proton chain; the other uses carbon as a catalyst and it is called the carbon-nitrogen cycle.

The PROTON-PROTON CHAIN (p-p chain) proceeds as follows:

$$^1\text{H} + {}^1\text{H} \rightarrow {}^2\text{H} + e^+ + \nu$$
$$^2\text{H} + {}^1\text{H} \rightarrow {}^3\text{He} + \gamma$$
$$^3\text{He} + {}^3\text{He} \rightarrow {}^4\text{He} + {}^1\text{H} + {}^1\text{H}$$

The reactions have been written in a nuclear physics shorthand which can easily be unravelled with a little effort. The number to the top left of an element is its atomic mass number, which indicates the number of nucleons: for example ^1H is a hydrogen nucleus or proton, ^2H is heavy hydrogen, a deuteron, consisting of a proton and neutron, ^3He is an isotope of helium consisting of two protons and one neutron and ^4He is the usual variety of helium nucleus consisting of two protons and two neutrons. e^+ denotes positive electron, or positron, which is released during the first stage of the reaction. It is an anti-matter particle and it interacts quickly with an electron; they annihilate one another producing two high-energy photons or gamma rays. ν symbolizes a neutrino, which is also produced in the first reaction. It is a fundamental particle without charge or rest mass and it rarely interacts with other particles; it leaves the star at the speed of light taking away with it some of the energy of the reaction. γ denotes a photon or high-energy gamma ray. The various reactions are shown schematically in figure 3.8. The proton-proton reaction may proceed slightly differently in some circumstances going through the reactions:

$$^1\text{H} + {}^1\text{H} \rightarrow {}^2\text{H} + e^+ + \nu$$
$$^2\text{H} + {}^1\text{H} \rightarrow {}^3\text{He} + \gamma$$
$$^3\text{He} + {}^4\text{He} \rightarrow {}^7\text{Be} + \gamma$$

and then either:

$$^7\text{Be} + e^- \rightarrow {}^7\text{Li} + \nu$$
$$^7\text{Li} + {}^1\text{H} \rightarrow {}^4\text{He} + {}^4\text{He} \quad \text{(figure 3.8)}$$

or:

$$^7\text{Be} + {}^1\text{H} \rightarrow {}^8\text{B} + \gamma$$
$$^8\text{B} \rightarrow {}^8\text{Be} + e^+ + \nu$$
$$^8\text{Be} \rightarrow {}^4\text{He} + {}^4\text{He}$$

3.8: *A schematic representation of one of the most important nuclear processes that occur in stars. In the proton-proton cycle protons fuse together in a series of reactions that ultimately lead to the production of helium nuclei, composed of two protons and two neutrons. During the sequence, energy, the source of starlight is produced, as well as a supply of neutrinos.*

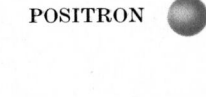

PROTON

NEUTRON

POSITRON

ELECTRON

PHOTON

NEUTRINO

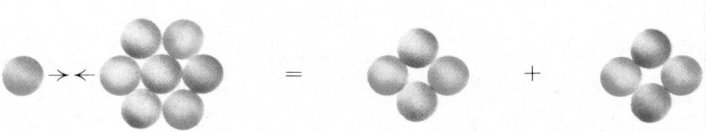

In these reactions the same notation is used for the nucleons as before; see also figure 3.8 and note that Li is lithium, B is boron, and Be is berylium. It is a matter of chance whether the newly produced ^{3}He nucleus interacts with a ^{3}He or a ^{4}He nucleus; the chance can be calculated however. Also if ^{7}Be, that is, berylium with seven nucleons (four protons and three neutrons), is made, it may either capture an electron and emit a neutrino to become ^{7}Li, or may interact with a further proton to make ^{8}B, boron-8. In all cases the net effect has been to convert four hydrogen nuclei (protons) into a helium nucleus.

In the CARBON-NITROGEN CYCLE REACTION (CN cycle) carbon (symbolized by C) is used as a catalyst and the main-line of the reaction is:

$$^{12}C + {}^1H \rightarrow {}^{13}N + \gamma$$
$$^{13}N \rightarrow {}^{13}C + e^+ + \nu$$
$$^{13}C + {}^1H \rightarrow {}^{14}N + \gamma$$
$$^{14}N + {}^1H \rightarrow {}^{15}O + \gamma$$
$$^{15}O \rightarrow {}^{15}N + e^+ + \nu$$
$$^{15}N + {}^1H \rightarrow {}^{12}C + {}^4He$$

In the final line of the reaction we see that the original carbon-12 atom is returned and the net effect is that four hydrogen nuclei have been turned into a ^{4}He one. The carbon-nitrogen cycle also has side chains; for example $^{15}N + {}^1H$ may go to $^{16}O + \gamma$ and then the reaction proceeds through stages that involve nuclei of oxygen and fluorine to produce eventually a ^{12}C nucleus and a ^{4}He one. The main reaction is shown in figure 3.9.

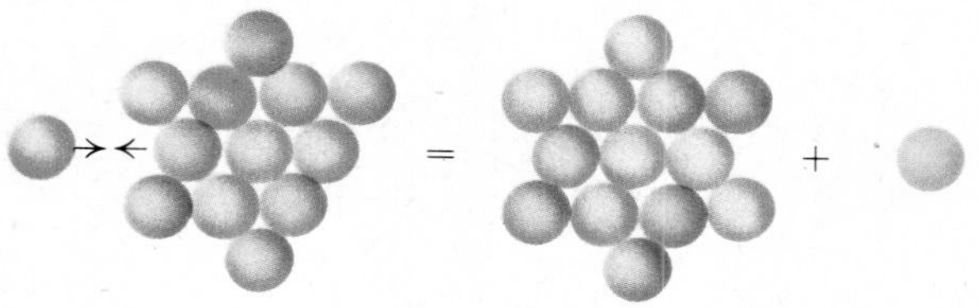

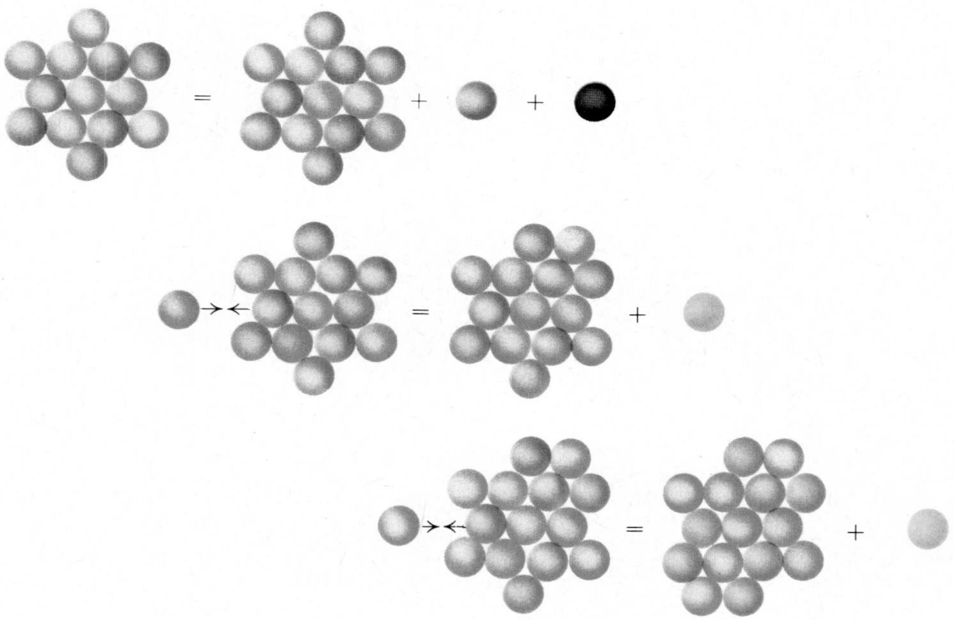

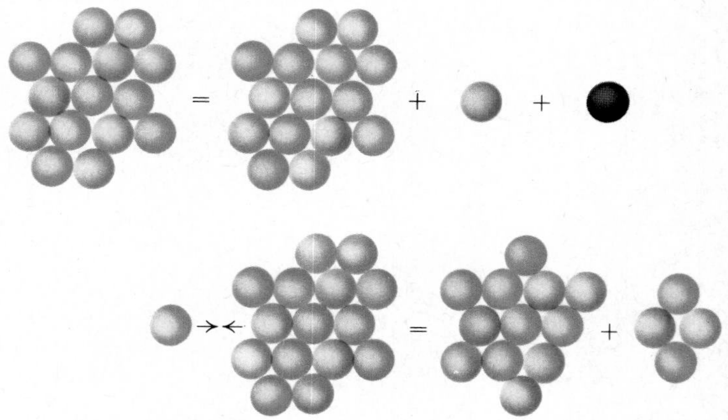

3.9: *In the carbon-nitrogen cycle the net effect is to convert four hydrogen nuclei (protons) into a helium nucleus. Carbon-12 (^{12}C) acts as a catalyst in this process; it is an essential ingredient that re-emerges as ^{12}C at the end, having been nitrogen-13, carbon-13, nitrogen-14, nitrogen-15 and oxygen-15 at various points in the cycle. This sequence of reactions is probably the major energy source in the more massive stars.*

The energy released in the hydrogen-helium fusion reactions is about 4×10^{-12} joules per helium atom formed or about 1×10^{-12} joules per hydrogen atom destroyed. (This number translates directly into the quantity 6×10^{14} joules per kg discussed previously). The effective energy release in the CN cycle is slightly less than the p-p chain because the neutrinos in the CN cycle reaction are more energetic and therefore remove a larger amount of the created energy.

The CN cycle is the dominant energy-producing mechanism at hotter temperatures (exceeding about 1.6×10^7 K), whereas the p-p chain dominates at cooler temperatures. Neither reaction produces significant energy at temperatures below about 7×10^6 K. It is important to note that all nuclear reactions are very sensitive to the exact temperature of the reacting material.

Many other nuclear reactions may occur in stars at various phases of their evolution. For example, helium may fuse to carbon through the TRIPLE-ALPHA REACTION, so called because an alpha particle is an alternative name for a helium nucleus. We may write the reaction thus:

$$3\,^4\text{He} \rightarrow {}^{12}\text{C} + 2\gamma$$

It releases 4×10^{-13} joules for each ^{4}He nucleus destroyed. The triple-alpha reaction occurs at temperatures near 2×10^8 K. There are further, more complicated reactions whereby carbon fuses to oxygen, sodium and magnesium, thence to silicon and so on up to iron. These reactions are discussed in chapter 7. Fusion reactions beyond iron are ENDOTHERMIC, that is to say they absorb energy when they take place. But they may occur in certain astrophysical situations especially in supernova explosions when a lot of neutrons are released which can build up elements in the periodic table beyond iron. The reactions after carbon contribute very little to the energy production; their main importance lies in synthesizing the chemical elements (see chapter 7). The main energy-producing reactions in stars are therefore hydrogen fusing to helium and helium fusing to carbon and oxygen.

The neutrinos produced by nuclear reactions travel directly out of the star and do not contribute to the measured photon luminosity. If they could be detected on Earth they would give direct information about the physical conditions at the centres of the stars. With present detection equipment the Sun is the only star close enough possibly to give a detectable neutrino flux and a detector has been placed 1.5 km underground in a gold mine to shield it from cosmic rays. The detector consists of an olympic-size swimming-pool full of perchloroethylene (C_2Cl_4). Neutrinos interact with heavy chlorine in the reaction:

$$\nu + {}^{37}\text{Cl} \rightarrow {}^{37}\text{Ar} + e^-$$

to produce ^{37}Ar (argon), and the ^{37}Ar is captured and measured. The experimental details are complicated. There may be a discrepancy between the observed and theoretically predicted flux of neutrinos. If so, several severe problems are posed for the usual interpretation of stellar structure; but until the experimental complexities are fully understood and the experiment has been shown to be repeatable it seems best to reserve judgement.

Now that we have outlined the nuclear reactions you should have some impression of the tremendous energy that is released deep inside the stars. We can pose the question: if the reactions are such prodigious suppliers of energy why are stars not blasted to pieces in gigantic explosions as soon as they form? How do stars tame the nuclear fury?

The answer is that an important feature of the nuclear processes is that they are self-stabilizing in the following sense. Consider a disturbance which causes the star to contract slightly. This causes a density and temperature increase in the nuclear reaction region, which speeds up the reactions that then produce energy more quickly. However the heating associated with the extra energy causes an extra outward pressure which tends to oppose the original contraction. Similarly a slight expansion causes a fall in the rate of energy generation and in the pressure. At most phases in the evolution of a star there is a perfect balance between the rate of energy radiated from the stellar surface and the rate of energy production in the central regions. If there is not a balance (suppose, for example, the energy production fell behind the surface demand), then the deficit would be made up by gravitational energy release through contraction. The contraction would, as above, lead to an enhancement of the nuclear energy production so that it could be brought into balance with the energy radiated at the surface.

The life of a star

STELLAR EVOLUTION is the study of how a star changes with time. There are three important distinct timescales on which a star may change. These are dynamical, thermal and nuclear timescales.

The DYNAMICAL TIMESCALE is the time it would take for the whole star to feel seriously and to react to an absence of pressure support. It is the time it takes a sound wave, or pressure wave moving at the speed of sound, to cross a star. We write this as:

$$t\,(\text{dynamical}) \simeq 1/(G\zeta)^{\frac{1}{2}} \simeq \text{about} \tfrac{1}{2}\,\text{hour for the Sun,}$$

where G is the gravitational constant and ζ is the average density of the star. For the Sun $\zeta \simeq 1.4 \times 10^3\,\text{kg m}^{-3}$.

The THERMAL TIMESCALE (or KELVIN-HELMHOLTZ TIMESCALE) is the time it takes for the whole star to feel seriously an absence of thermal equilibrium. It is the time it takes energy to diffuse from the centre to the surface, and it is equivalently the time it takes for the star to radiate away a significant amount of its thermal or heat energy. We write:

$$t\,(\text{thermal}) \simeq \frac{\frac{1}{2}GM^2}{RL} \simeq 10^7\,\text{yr for the Sun,}$$

where M, R, L are the mass, radius and luminosity of the star.

The NUCLEAR TIMESCALE is the time it takes for significant changes of chemical composition to occur in a star on account of nuclear transmutation, and the time for a significant amount of the nuclear fuel to be converted into energy. We write this as:

$$t\,(\text{nuclear}) \simeq \frac{(0.1\,\text{M})}{L}\varepsilon \simeq 10^{10}\,\text{yr for the Sun.}$$

In this equation one tenth of the total mass (0.1M) is usually taken for a significant amount of fuel, and ε is the energy release per kg (6×10^{14} joules kg^{-1} for conversion of hydrogen to helium).

These timescales are purposely left a little imprecise as they are designed only to give rough estimates. The important fact is that the three timescales are very different, and this is a useful feature when making computer simulations of stellar evolution. For example, when we consider the pulsations of a Cepheid variable star, which take place on a timescale of days, it is not necessary to worry about any nuclear evolution of the central regions as that only changes significantly on a much longer timescale. Conversely when considering the long-timescale nuclear evolution of the central regions of a Cepheid, the short-term outer layer pulsations can be averaged over, as a great many will occur while the interior changes only slightly.

When thinking about the evolution of stars one must keep in mind two factors: (i) the timescale on which physical conditions are changing and (ii) the source of the stellar energy.

The main part and the longest part of the life of nearly all stars is their MAIN-SEQUENCE PHASE, during which they convert hydrogen into helium on a nuclear timescale. Most stars spend a major part of their lives in the main-sequence phase; this fact accounts for the well-populated main-sequence band in the Hertzsprung-Russell diagram. The main-sequence lifetime of a star is essentially the time that it takes to process all the hydrogen in the core to helium. Only the core is hot enough for the occurrence of the nuclear reactions. The remainder of a star's life is relatively short in comparison to the main-sequence time, typically about 20 per cent. The actual lifetime of a star on the main sequence depends on the amount of its nuclear fuel and the rate at which it is consumed. The amount of fuel depends on M, the mass, and the rate of consumption on L, the luminosity. The lifetime therefore depends on the quantity M/L. From two forms of the mass-luminosity law we see that the lifetime is proportional to $1/M^2$ or $1/M^{3.5}$ on substituting M^3 or $M^{4.5}$ for L in M/L. Therefore higher-mass stars have shorter lives; to be sure, they have more nuclear fuel available but they consume it faster.

We have now reached the point in our story where we can explain a feature of the observed Hertzsprung-Russell diagram for star clusters. Let us consider a star cluster, in which initially all stars of different masses were burning hydrogen in their cores. The Hertzsprung-Russell diagram of such a cluster would then consist of a main sequence, with the more massive, more luminous stars at the top end. There would be no red-giant stars to start with. As time proceeds, the higher-mass, more luminous stars exhaust their central hydrogen. The adjustments that then take place in the star's structure cause it to move away from the main sequence. The stars peel off the top of the main sequence first. The point in the Hertzsprung-Russell diagram of a cluster where stars are just leaving the main sequence is called the TURN-OFF POINT of the cluster main sequence. Observations of where it is can be used as an estimate of the age of a star cluster; the age is such that stars of mass and luminosity above the turn-off have had time to evolve away. Figure 3.10 clearly shows the effect of age.

The birth of stars

The process of star formation is not well understood but we believe that *protostars* condense out of the tenuous interstellar gas. Without knowing the details we can only make a few general remarks. The material of a typical star smeared out to a typical interstellar density (10^{-21} kg m^{-3}) would occupy a spherical volume about one parsec in radius. Even a very small amount of rotation in a cloud this large would give it a very large angular momentum, so large in fact that during contraction, with angular momentum conservation, the protostar would rotate so fast that the centrifugal force would prevent further gravitational collapse. Since stars manifestly exist there must be some means of disposing of the excess angular momentum. The protostar presumably solves this angular momentum problem by losing angular momentum with a stellar wind or by forming a ring, a binary or multiple star system or a planetary system. Also, in order to become as tightly bound as a star, a protostar must lose a lot of gravitational potential energy. Some of this energy may be radiated away by various cooling processes and some of it may go into heating the protostar from interstellar-medium temperatures of 100 K to the much higher temperatures of stellar interiors.

An interstellar gas cloud may contain enough material to form several stars or even a star cluster and under certain conditions the cloud will fragment. The fragments will continue contracting, probably fairly rapidly while radiation can leak out easily. When the protostellar cloud becomes largely opaque to its own radiation collapse will proceed more slowly because the internal temperature and pressure start to build up. The cloud will be a dark cloud in the sense that very little optical radiation is emitted. The Ophiucus dark cloud and the Bok globules in Orion may be connected with this phase of evolution. Dust grains in the dark cloud may emit long-wave infrared radiation. *Interstellar molecules* such as OH, H_2O and formaldehyde may be formed by interactions with grains and these molecules may emit *maser* radiation. The ultimate source of this energy is the gravitational energy release by collapse. The study of protostar evolution is best made at infrared, millimetre and radio wavelengths.

The collapse of an interstellar cloud probably proceeds non-homologously; that is the central regions collapse faster than the surface ones. The central half of the cloud has contracted to stellar size in a thermal timescale, about 10^6 yr for a star like the Sun, whereas the outside regions have contracted only a little during this time. When the central region has contracted sufficiently it may become hot enough to commence hydrogen-burning nuclear reactions, the contraction stops, and a star is born. Even before the central nuclear reactions have started burning hydrogen, the protostar is producing a significant amount of energy from gravitational contraction. This energy is being radiated through the cooler infalling outer layers which absorb much of the blue radiation and reradiate it in the infrared. Indeed even some nuclear reactions occur, mostly of ^{2}H, Li, Be, B, the light elements, which contribute little to the energy but deplete the abundance of these elements.

The position that a protostar occupies in the Hertzsprung-Russell diagram is not certain partly because of theoretical problems associated with modifications to the spectrum of the radiation as it passes through the outer layers of the contracting object. After an uncertain rapid phase of evolution the protostar appears to the right of the main sequence as shown in figure 3.3, near the intersection of the Henyey and Hayashi tracks. Henyey and Hayashi were both important contributors to the theory of protostar or pre-main-sequence evolution. The Henyey track is the path that a completely radiative star would follow during protostellar contraction, while the Hayashi track is the same but for a star in which convection is occurring everywhere. At one time each of these tracks was thought to be the route protostars followed to the main sequence, but the realization that the central regions of the contracting protostar collapsed more quickly than the outer layers changed that view. In the latter stages of their contraction protostars probably follow the Henyey track. This is probably what is observed in young stellar clusters, such as NGC 2264, shown in figure 3.11, in which the fainter lower-mass stars above the main sequence are still contracting towards the main sequence. The age of this cluster, as estimated from its main sequence turn-off point, is about 2×10^6 yr. The massive stars whose nuclear lifetimes are about 3×10^6 yr have (thermal) contraction times of about 10^4 yr.

The contraction time is on the thermal timescale, which is much shorter than the nuclear timescale of a star. In general we do not expect to see a very large proportion of stars in their contracting phase since it is relatively short-lived. However one group of stars, the T Tauri stars, stand out. (See chapter 4 and figure 3.11.) For a variety of reasons these stars, which exhibit peculiar and active spectra including H emission, emit a lot of infrared radiation, and are thought to be in a pre-main-sequence phase. Detailed investigations of their properties may help to unravel the many mysteries remaining in this aspect of stellar evolution.

Beyond the main sequence

When hydrogen-burning nuclear reactions in the core are first fully supplying the radiating energy of the star it is said to be on the zero-age main sequence. The star stays in the main-sequence band of the Hertzsprung-Russell diagram as long as it has hydrogen nuclear reactions in its core. In general the layers of a star do not get mixed up (helium is heavier than hydrogen). In convective zones the layers are mixed, but only in the zone itself. As evolution proceeds the hydrogen nuclear fuel in the core is being depleted and the core is becoming rich in helium. With reduced fuel, nuclear energy output is not being maintained so the core contracts, which causes a raising of the temperature and a compensating enhancement of the nuclear reactions. For reasons not fully understood, but connected with the distribution of the total gravitational potential energy of the star, core contraction is accompanied by envelope expansion. The main-sequence phase of evolution is characterized by hydrogen depletion in the core and a slow expansion of the outer layers that occurs on the nuclear timescale. There is a slight

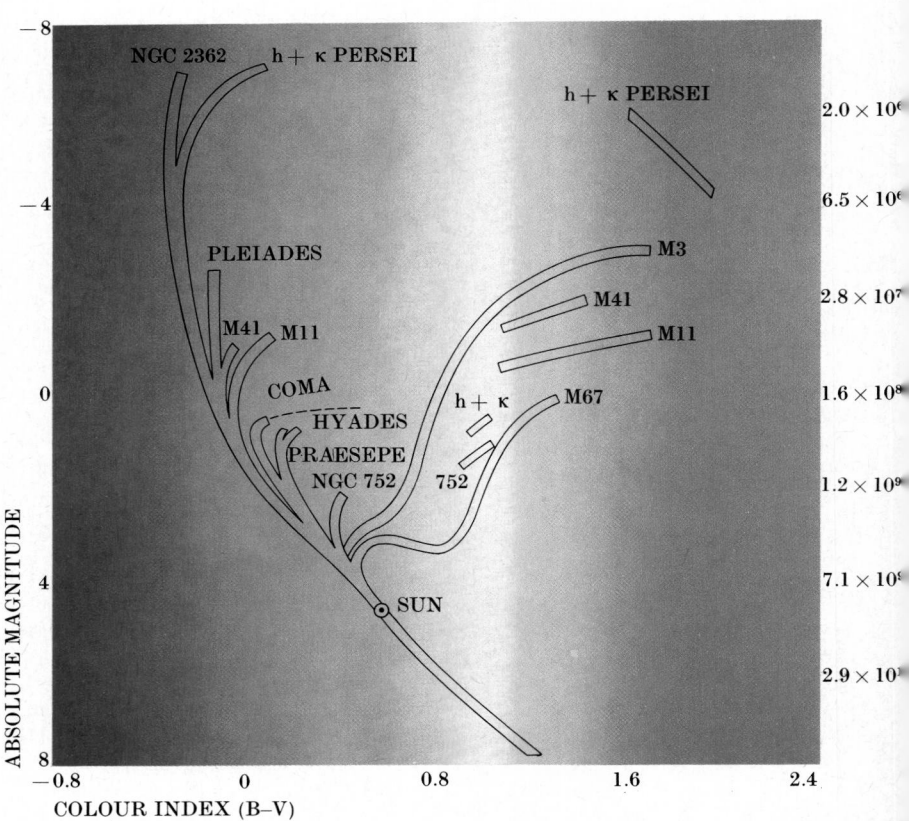

3.10: *The composite Hertzsprung-Russell diagram for ten open clusters and one globular cluster. (The data of figures 3.4 and 3.5 are indicated by the legends M67 and M3 respectively.) The deduced age of each cluster, which is calculated from the observed point at which the main sequence moves to the right (turn-off point) is shown on the right-hand vertical axis. This diagram provides convincing evidence that the stars we see in the sky formed at various times in the past and have evolved at various rates since their formation.*

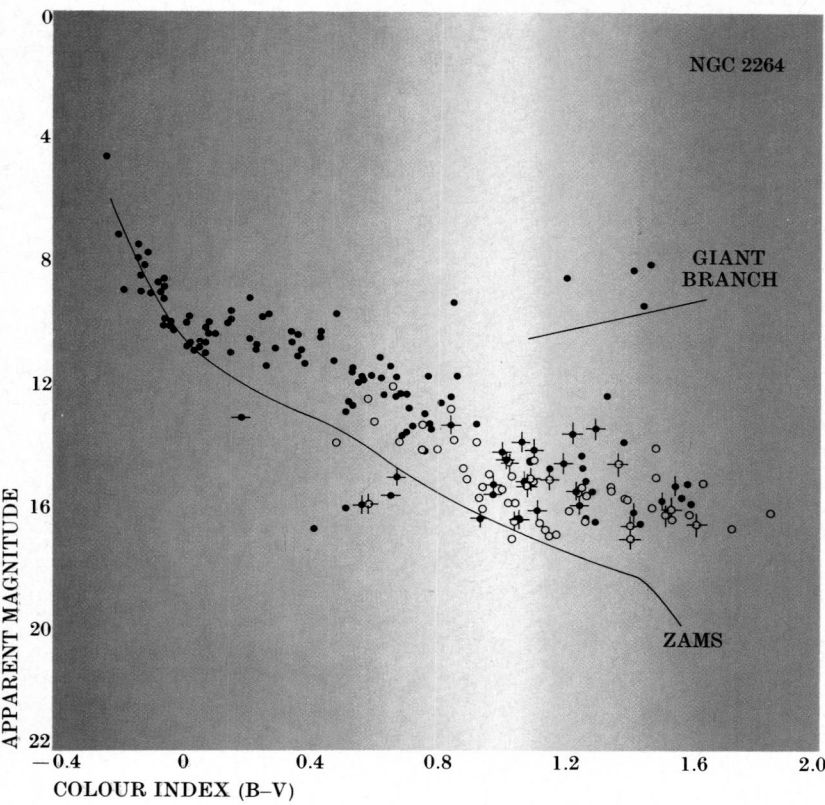

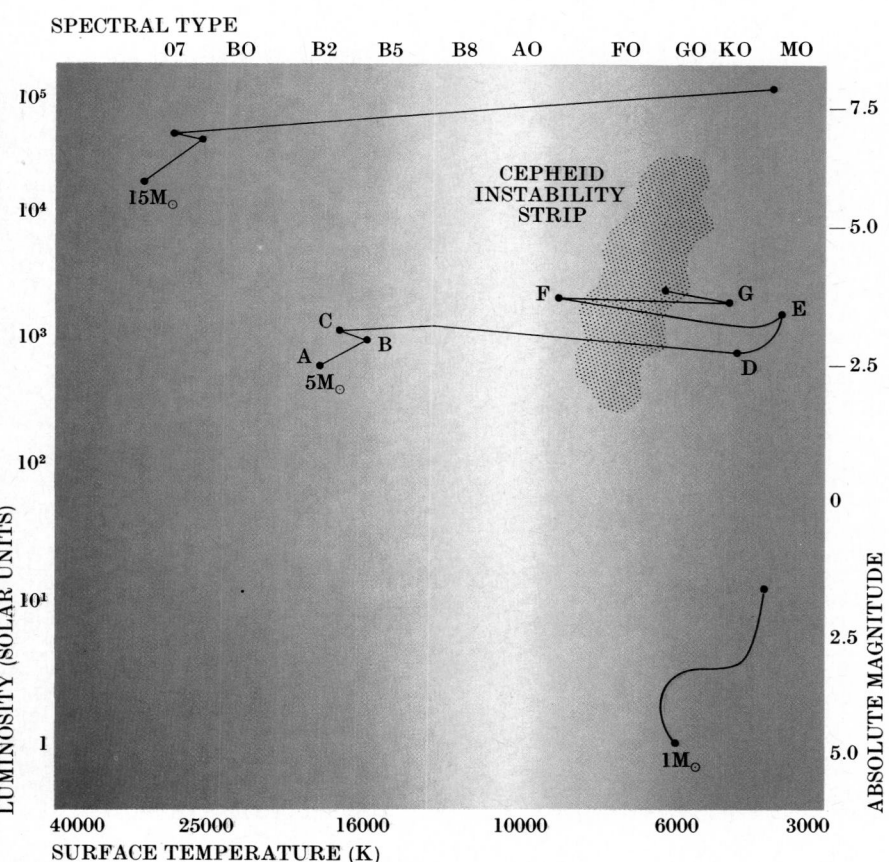

3.11: *The Hertzsprung-Russell, or colour-magnitude diagram for the young star cluster NGC 2264. The curves indicate the position of the zero-age main sequence and the giant branch, after correction for the effects of interstellar reddening. This cluster is about 800 pc from the Sun and is about 2×10^6 years old. This is a short time by astronomical standards, and there has not yet been sufficient time for stars with spectral type cooler than A0 to contract to the main sequence. Solid circles denote data collected by a photoelectric detector and open circles data derived from photographs. The horizontal bars represent stars that show emission lines in their spectra, an unusual occurrence, and vertical bars are the positions of variable stars.*

3.12: *The three tracks shown here are the theoretical evolutionary paths in the Hertzsprung-Russell diagram of stars with masses 1, 5, and 15 $M_\odot$. The exact shape depends on the mass of the star but the general features are similar for most masses. For the 5-$M_\odot$ star we can pick out the following significant phases in its evolution: A-B is the main sequence, when hydrogen burning is taking place in the central core; B-C, the star is contracting because the hydrogen in the core is exhausted; C-E, hydrogen burning in a shell around the core; E-F, helium burning in the core; F-G, helium in the core is running out. The Cepheid instability strip is crossed three times by a five-solar-mass star. The track C-D is very shortlived and corresponds to the Hertzsprung gap; very few stars are actually observed in that part of the Hertzsprung-Russell diagram.*

increase in energy output and the outer layers cool down somewhat (figure 3.12).

When all the hydrogen is exhausted in a stellar core, nuclear energy generation there stops. Without mixing, hydrogen-rich material cannot be brought down to the core. The outside of the star is still, however, radiating as before and it derives this energy from gravitational contraction of the whole star. This is the overall contraction phase of post-main-sequence stellar evolution. Half the energy from contraction goes into radiation and the other half heats up the whole star. This contraction phase continues until some part of the star becomes hot enough for nuclear reactions to work again. There is the possibility that the very central region, now made of helium will become hot enough (10^8 K) for helium to burn to carbon. In fact what happens first is that the layers of hydrogen outside the helium core become hot enough (10^7 K) for hydrogen to burn to helium. At this stage hydrogen burning starts to take place in a shell. The new release of energy halts the overall contraction and the energy radiated is now supplied by the nuclear energy liberated in the hydrogen-burning shell. The helium core is, however, still contracting while the envelope of the star is expanding slowly.

As successive shells of hydrogen are burnt the helium produced joins the core, which grows in mass. There is a maximum pressure that the inert helium core can exert. When its mass becomes too large it collapses under its own weight and the pressure of the overlying layers of the star. The critical mass of the core is about one tenth the mass of the star for a star of a few solar masses. The instability takes place on a thermal timescale, and core collapse is accompanied by envelope expansion. The star now increases rapidly in radius and moves to the right, lower temperature side of the Hertzsprung-Russell diagram. Stars spend only a little time in this phase of evolution, so in a cluster very few stars should be seen at this position in the Hertzsprung-Russell diagram; this region is called the Hertzsprung gap. The energy production at this phase is by hydrogen shell-burning.

The expansion and cooling of the outer layers of the star make them convective, and the star lies very near the Hayashi track in the Hertzsprung-Russell diagram. The helium core continues to contract until it becomes hot enough for the nuclear reactions of helium fusing to carbon to work. The core collapse is then stopped and there are now two energy sources: the nuclear burning of helium in the core and hydrogen in a shell further out. The star is now extremely luminous, extremely large and very cool; it is a RED GIANT.

The further evolution of a star may take it through further nuclear burnings, depending on its mass. These nuclear burnings do not produce very much energy because the changes in nuclear energy are rather small. The lifetime of a star in these phases of evolution is short. The main importance of these further reactions is the synthesis of heavy elements (see chapter 7). Much energy may be lost by neutrino emission; unfortunately no such star is close enough for these neutrinos to be detected.

Several times during its evolution after the main sequence, a star may be in the instability strip which is where its temperature and luminosity are such that its outer layers are pulsationally unstable. The star then appears as a Cepheid variable star, for example (see chapter 4). The time spent in the instability strip, while the star is crossing the Hertzsprung gap, is rather small. Much more time is spent there during the core-helium-burning phase, after the star has been a red giant. Cepheids are therefore core-helium-burning stars, at a late stage of evolution, whose outer layers are pulsationally unstable. A problem of stellar evolution theory has been to reconcile the mass of a Cepheid deduced from evolution with its mass deduced from pulsation theory. There is still controversy here. The instability strip has a limited width in the Hertzsprung-Russell diagram because if the star is too cool its outer layers are convective, which destroys pulsation; on the other hand, if the star is too hot the pulsation excitation mechanism does not operate.

Figure 3.12 gives the details of an evolutionary track, the path taken by an evolving star in the Hertzsprung-Russell diagram. The tracks are fairly similar for different masses and the various stages of evolution are indicated in the caption. The different initial direction of evolution for the 1.0 solar mass star occurs because it has a radiative core and is converting hydrogen to helium by the p-p chain. The higher mass stars have convective cores and convert hydrogen to helium by the CN cycle.

Two important observational quantities in the Hertzsprung-Russell diagram of a cluster are the number of red giants and Cepheids compared with the number of main-sequence stars. Roughly speaking the ratio of numbers of stars should be the ratio of their lifetimes in the appropriate phases of evolution. In general the observations of clusters confirm this theoretical expectation reasonably well. The range of observed stellar masses also may be explainable. For too small a mass, the temperature does not become hot enough for nuclear reactions, and the star becomes a BLACK DWARF, producing little luminosity. For too high a mass the luminosity is so high that radiation pressure blows the star apart or prevents its formation.

The exact details of a star's evolution depend primarily on its mass and initial chemical composition, but the general principles outlined above are broadly true. The radius of a star at the red-giant stage is roughly a hundred times its main-sequence radius. This is of special importance for the evolution of binary-star systems since, if the binary is a close binary, during certain stages of evolution mass may be exchanged between the two components.

A point that we have not yet mentioned concerns lower-mass stars. These might not ignite carbon, and when igniting helium might do so under degenerate conditions. Because of the peculiar equation of state of degenerate matter, the temperature and pressure are not strongly connected. Helium ignition causes an increase in energy production which increases the local temperature, which increases the reaction rate, but without a compensatory increase in pressure. A runaway therefore develops; this is known as the HELIUM-FLASH whose consequences are uncertain. Eventually there is so much energy that degeneracy is removed; the temperature is now connected through the equation of state to the pressure and expansion relieves the situation. At the peak of the flash the nuclear reactions inside one star may be producing as much energy as a whole galaxy of stars. Almost all this energy is probably absorbed by the outer layers of the star, which expand, and very little appears at the stellar surface to increase the observed luminosity.

The shape of a Population II star evolutionary track is different from that of a Population I star. The higher heavy-element abundance in the Population I stars strongly affects their opacities and alters the evolution. In our Galaxy the shapes of globular cluster (Population II) and galactic cluster (Population I) Hertzsprung-Russell diagrams are quite different, but this is largely caused by their different ages. The globular clusters in our Galaxy were probably formed during the early stages of the collapse of our galaxy and they are about 10^{10} yr old. Galactic or open clusters range in age from 10^6 to 10^{10} yr old. In globular clusters in our Galaxy, stars more massive than about a solar mass have already had time to evolve, whereas in an open cluster of age 10^7 yr a star of about ten solar masses is just evolving. An important feature of the Hertzsprung-Russell diagrams of globular clusters is the HORIZONTAL BRANCH (see figure 3.5). This consists of low-mass stars that have probably lost mass in the red-giant phase. The stars in the instability strip in globular clusters are also of low mass, they are the *RR Lyrae* stars (see chapter 4). In other galaxies such as the Magellanic Clouds, much younger globular clusters have been discovered which provide important tests for the theory of stellar evolution.

The death of stars

The timescale of stellar evolution is very long. The Sun, for example, took a few million years just to contract from an interstellar gas cloud to become a main-sequence star. Its lifetime as a main-sequence star is about ten thousand million years, of which it has used about four and a half thousand million years. In about five and a half thousand million years it will exhaust its central hydrogen and become a red giant. In agreement with popular expectation its further expansion will probably be sufficient to bring the Earth into its outer layers, and the Sun's large luminosity then will destroy organic life as we know it. The Sun will probably be a red giant or supergiant for a few million years.

There are many uncertainties in stellar evolution theory not least of which are the end points of stellar evolution or stellar death. Some stars, the more massive stars, probably die violently in a supernova explosion. After many stages of nuclear burning the core becomes unstable and implodes, while the outer layers of the star explode. There is a massive output of energy: a supernova often outshines the entire light output of its parent galaxy for a week or more. Neutrons created from the decomposition of the core move through the outer layers and nucleosynthesis of heavy elements may occur. The outer layers of gas are thrown off and become a supernova remnant which may shine and emit radio waves for 10^4 yr or more. The core implodes and may leave a remnant, such as a NEUTRON STAR, an object made largely of neutrons, of typical radius 10 km, at an average density of about 10^{16} kg m^{-3}. A cubic centimetre of such a star weighs over ten million tonnes! The neutron star rotates rapidly and may be observable as a radio *pulsar*. It is also possible that the remnant could be a *black hole*, but nobody knows for certain.

Since supernovae are rare events we must conclude that most stars die peacefully. Within our Galaxy they probably occur once every 50 years on average. Many stars probably end up as WHITE DWARFS. When nuclear burning has ceased they simply contract and radiate away their thermal energy. A typical white dwarf has a radius, similar to the Earth, of about 5000 km, an average density of about 10^9 kg m^{-3}, and a surface temperature of 10^4 K. At such high densities the stellar material is degenerate.

There is a maximum mass which a white dwarf is permitted to have. If it were to have a larger mass than this upper limit, it would collapse under its own weight, presumably to a neutron star or black hole. The critical mass is about 1.4 solar masses. However, observationally we know the important additional fact that stars can lose mass during their lifetime. Red giants lose mass in stellar winds. Radiation pressure blows away some of the outer layers at a rate as high as 10^{-6} to 10^{-7} solar masses a year. *Mira*, or long-period variables (see chapter 4), probably expel mass after each pulsation. There is also an instability in which a shell containing a large amount of mass is thrown off to expose the deeper regions of the star, producing a planetary nebula. A planetary nebula consists of a very hot (10^5 K) central star and a cool expanding envelope. Eventually the envelope fades away and the central star cools down to become a white dwarf. In this way stars more massive than the critical mass for a white dwarf may die peacefully.

In summary of the chapter we may say that many of the theoretical aspects of stellar evolution have found observational confirmation. Of special importance is the evolution to the red-giant stage: stars that were fully mixed chemically would not get to that stage, for example, and there is good agreement of theory and observations for clusters. We specially point out that the old theory of stellar evolution, that stars at the top of the main sequence evolved by losing mass and contracting down the main sequence can be ruled out. The mass-loss rates observed for main-sequence stars are too small to have any noticeable effect during a star's lifetime and the old theory fails to explain the number and properties of red giants. Nevertheless there are many uncertainties in the theory and the outlines given here are for the simple case of non-rotating single stars. Rotation, magnetic fields, mixing and mass loss must all eventually be considered in detail. The fundamental problems of what the mass of a Cepheid is, how convection really works and whether the solar neutrino experiment agrees with theory must be resolved by further painstaking research.

It is fitting to end where we started, by remarking, with Eddington, that 'It is reasonable to hope that in a not too distant future we shall be competent to understand so simple a thing as a star'.

4. Variable stars

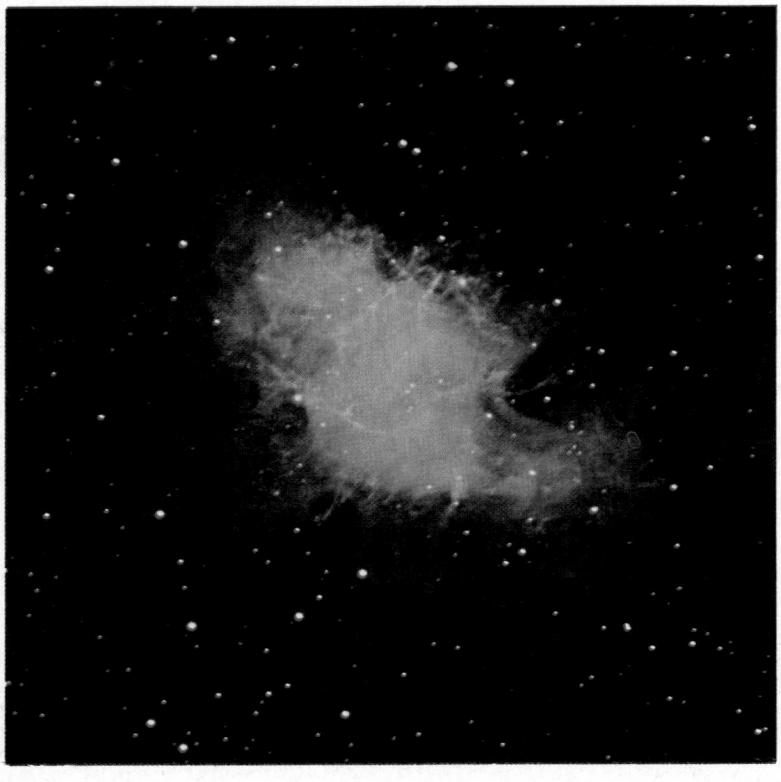

4.1: *The Crab Nebula is the relic of the most spectacular of all variable stars, a supernova, which exploded nine centuries ago. (Kitt Peak National Observatory,* USA*)*

Introduction

INTRINSIC VARIABLE STARS are stars that vary in brightness, or in other respects, for reasons that are internal to the star rather than external. Aside from their pathological interest, they provide important information about the structure, evolution and properties of the stars. For instance, the timescale of the variation may be correlated with the luminosity of the star. If so, observations of the variation can tell us the *luminosity*, and hence the distance of the star. Compared to constant stars, variable stars provide an extra dimension of interest and information.

The brightness variations in some stars can easily be seen by the unaided eye, yet the constancy of the stars was part of Aristotelian dogma, which persisted for centuries. Not until 1572 was a variable star recorded in Western literature. In that year, Tycho Brahe observed a 'new star' in the constellation of Cassiopeia. It rose rapidly in brightness to rival Venus, then slowly faded. Johannes Kepler observed another 'new star' in 1604. We now know that these 'new stars' (called *supernovae*) were actually old stars in the terminal stages of their evolution. Oriental astronomers had been recording such GUEST STARS since BC, and their catalogues provide a valuable record for astronomers today. The *Crab Nebula* (figure 4.1), for instance, has been identified as the remnant of a supernova observed by Oriental astronomers in AD 1054.

Some variable stars are more predictable than supernovae. In 1596, David Fabricius noted that o Ceti (subsequently called *Mira* – the wonderful) was sometimes visible, sometimes not; furthermore, the cycle of visibility repeated regularly every 11 months. By 1850, Friedrich Argelander could list an assortment of 22 variable stars (variables for short). Most of these had been discovered by accident: astronomers measuring the brightness of a star had found that their result differed from previous measurements. These discoveries probably mark the beginning of true astrophysics – the study of the nature of the stars as opposed to their positions and motions.

These early measurements were all made by eye. Despite the importance of cameras, spectrographs and photometers, there is still a place for the eye in astronomy. Amateur astronomers make hundreds of thousands of useful visual observations each year. These observations are co-ordinated, collected and analysed by such organizations as the British Astronomical Association, and the American Association of Variable Star Observers and they are circulated to professional astronomers around the world.

In the last few decades, new techniques have revolutionized variable star research and every other branch of astronomy. The camera, in a long time-exposure, can record thousands of faint star images on a single permanent photographic plate (figure 2.4). Astronomers then use a BLINK MICROSCOPE to compare this plate with a plate of the same field taken at a different time, to discover which stars have changed in brightness. They then use an IRIS PHOTOMETER to measure the size of the image, and hence the brightness of each star.

The PHOTOELECTRIC PHOTOMETER is a device that measures the

brightness of a star, through a telescope, using a photomultiplier. If used with care, it can measure brightness with an accuracy of 0.001 mag. This has permitted a detailed study of brightness and colour variations, and has resulted in the discovery of many micro-variables – including the Sun – whose variations could not be detected by visual or photographic techniques. At least a third of all bright stars turn out to be variables when examined carefully.

Spectroscopy provides detailed information about the spectrum of a variable. From the *absorption* or *emission* lines that are present, the astronomer can classify the star according to temperature, luminosity, chemical composition and other properties. From the *Doppler shift* of these lines, he can study the expansion and contraction which occur in the outer layers of variable stars.

Nomenclature and classification

Once a variable has been discovered and announced in an astronomical journal, it is catalogued and named according to the following system. Stars lacking a proper name (like Polaris) or a Greek letter name (like δ Cephei) are designated by one or two capital letters, followed by the genitive case of the constellation's Latin name. The letters are assigned in the order in which the variables are discovered, starting with R,S....Z, RR....RZ, SS....SZ through to ZZ, then AA....AS through to QZ, omitting J. This system provides 334 designations per constellation; subsequent variables are called V335, V336, etc., followed by the constellation name.

Millions of variables must still remain undiscovered. Of the 25 000 known variables listed in the General Catalogue of Variable Stars, only a small fraction has subsequently been studied in detail. The most basic property of a variable is its LIGHT CURVE – a graph of its brightness against time. The light curve can be described by its shape or form, its RANGE from maximum to minimum brightness, and (if the variation is regular) its PERIOD, the time for one complete cycle. Careful, repeated observations may reveal details or changes in the shape of the light curve, or changes in the range or period. Observations through colour filters reveal changes in the temperature of the outer layers of the variable. It is also particularly important to try to determine the 'normal' brightness and temperature of a variable – that is to say, the brightness and temperature which it would have if it were not variable. These can be compared with the brightness and temperature of non-variable stars.

The simplest classification scheme for variables is based on whether the light curve is PERIODIC or NON-PERIODIC. Periodic variables are subclassified according to cause into eclipsing, pulsating and rotating variables, and are further classified according to period, range and shape of light curve. The most numerous non-periodic variables are the eruptive variables, which suddenly brighten, then fade. These are further classified according to the magnitude and duration of the eruption.

The normal *absolute magnitude* and temperature of an intrinsic variable are usually correlated with the properties of the light curve. They therefore strengthen the classification scheme, and also provide clues to the cause of the variation. This leads finally to the most fundamental classification scheme: one based on the physical nature and cause of the variations.

Unfortunately, the understanding of variable stars has not yet reached this final exalted state. Through ignorance and historical accident, a cumbersome and sometimes misleading system of classification and terminology has arisen. In this chapter, for instance, we shall discuss pre-main-sequence variables separately, even though their light curves could be classified as eruptive. We shall also discuss flare stars as a subclass of eruptive variables, even though they are probably related to pre-main-sequence variables. There are some variables which still defy classification.

Variability may be environmental or genetic in origin. If a star has a companion in orbit around it, then its brightness may vary due to eclipse or tidal distortion by the companion. An eclipse occurs only if the observer is situated near the plane of the mutual orbit of the two stars. Hence, an eclipse is not an intrinsic property of the stars but is a property of the position of the observer. Occasionally, if the star and its companion are close, tidal forces may pull material from one star onto the other. If the star gaining the material is a compact star with a strong gravitational field, then the results of the transfer of material can be quite spectacular: the infalling material may generate X-rays, radio waves, rapid and irregular light variations and occasionally a full-scale eruption.

ROTATING VARIABLES are the least conspicuous of the intrinsic variables, but may possibly be the most numerous. Any star that rotates and has permanent or semi-permanent 'surface' features will appear to vary in brightness, unless the rotation axis points to the observer or unless the surface features are symmetrical about the axis. The *peculiar A stars*, are the best-known rotating variables. They have extremely strong magnetic fields, which may cause their peculiar chemical composition, and segregate different elements in patches on the star. As rotation carries different parts of the star under the observer's line of sight, the magnetic field, apparent composition, brightness and colour all vary in synchronism with the rotation (figure 4.2). Seen from a distance, these effects are quite small, but it is interesting to speculate on the appearance of these stars as seen by observers (if any) on planets (if any) in orbit around them. Even our own Sun – which is certainly spotty and rotating – varies slightly in brightness due to rotation. High-precision photoelectric photometry may eventually prove that every star is a rotating variable.

Gravitation can convert an innocuous rotating variable into an exotic one, by amplifying both the rotation and the magnetic field. Gravitation dominates the last phases of a star's evolution, converting it into a compact *white dwarf*, an even more compact *neutron star* or an infinitely compact *black hole*. Rotational variability has been observed in several white dwarfs and in the only visible neutron star – the one in the centre of the Crab Nebula. This latter object was first discovered because it was a pulsing radio source, or PULSAR. The term pulsar is another example of an

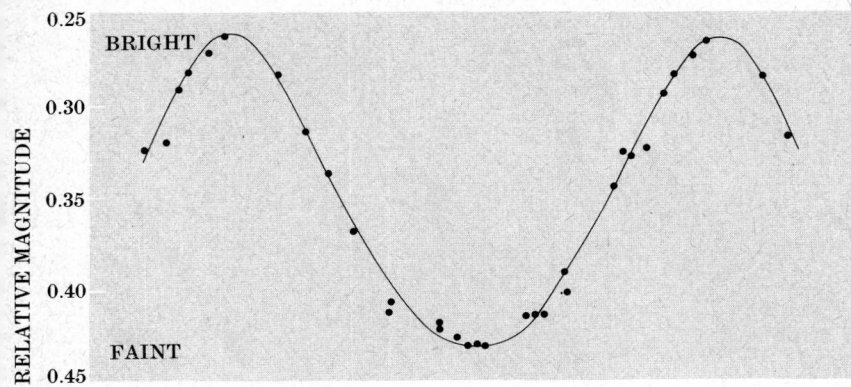

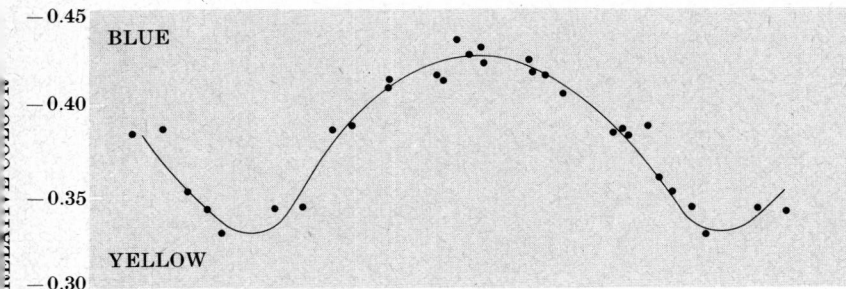

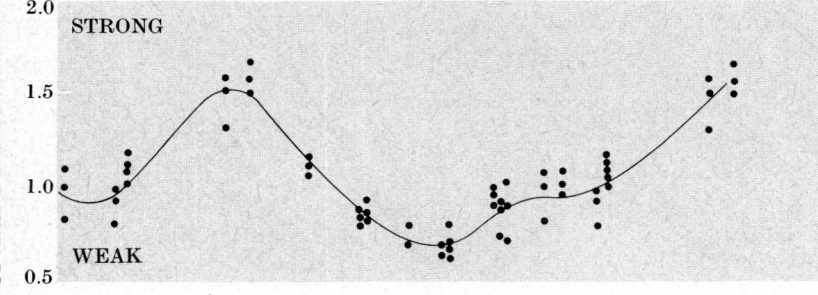

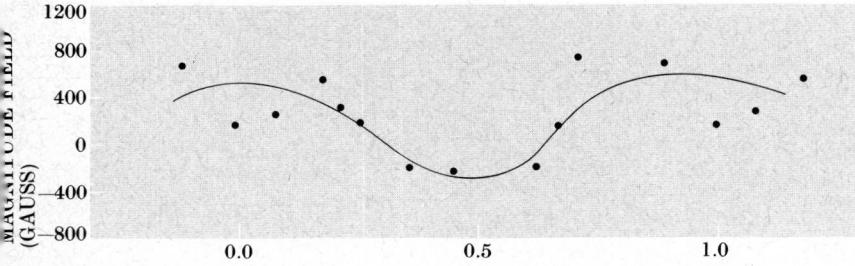

historical misnomer: pulsars rotate, and do not pulsate. It is also an example of our bias towards optical wavelengths. Many strong radio sources are variable; some of them are associated with eruptive (light) variables. In this chapter, however, we concentrate on stars that vary in light.

Pulsating and eruptive variability are examples of genetic variability. A star is born with certain properties, particularly the mass, that determine the future evolution of its luminosity and surface temperature. This evolution results from the finite nature of the star's energy supply. As the star radiates energy, it depletes, and eventually exhausts its thermonuclear energy supply. This causes changes in the internal chemical composition and structure, and in the luminosity and radius, which can make the star unstable against pulsations or eruptions. During its lifetime a star may become unstable several times, and thus exhibit different types of variability. However, evolution is so slow that we rarely see evolutionary changes take place. We see stars as in a snapshot, for a brief moment in their long lives.

Evolution, and its relation to variability, can best be illustrated in the *Hertzsprung-Russell* (HR) diagram, a graph of luminosity, or absolute magnitude, against effective surface temperature, or some measure thereof. Most stars lie on or near a narrow diagonal band called the MAIN SEQUENCE; variable stars lie in other specific areas of the HR diagram (figure 4.6). Most pulsating variables lie in a vertical band which merges into a broad region in the upper right. Pre-main-sequence variables lie in the lower right, supernovae in the upper right, novae in the lower left, and flare stars on the main sequence in the lower right.

4.2–4.5: *Synchronous variations in brightness, colour, apparent chemical composition (in particular, the rare earth elements) and magnetic field in the peculiar A star HD 51418.*

Pre-main-sequence variables

Variability begins as soon as a star forms by the gravitational contraction of an interstellar gas and dust cloud. Within the contracting cloud, a core of dense gas forms, heats up and begins to produce energy. This transition from a dark cloud to a self-luminous star would certainly be visible were it not for the veil of infalling material which still surrounds the star. The star may first appear when its light is able to penetrate the veil. Two possible examples of this process have been observed. In 1937, the star FU Orionis brightened by six magnitudes and it has remained bright since. This star has all the properties that would be expected of a very young star. It is located in a region thick with gas and dust. It is a giant *F-type star*, still much larger than a main-sequence star. It is rich in the element lithium, which is a strong indicator of youth. FU Orionis is also a strong source of infrared radiation, which presumably arises in the cloud of warm gas and dust which still surrounds the star. A second star, V1057 Cygni, brightened by six magnitudes in 1969, and has remained bright since; this star has properties similar to those of FU Orionis.

Elsewhere in Orion and along the Milky Way there are thousands of other very young stars. We can recognize them in many ways: by their association with gas and dust clouds, by their membership in short-lived *stellar associations*, or in young galactic clusters. NGC 2264 is one such cluster. Its colour-magnitude diagram (equivalent to an HR diagram) is shown in figure 2.11. There are many hot, bright *O- and B-type stars* on the main sequence, from which we can deduce that the cluster is only a few million years old. The fainter, less massive stars in the cluster have not yet had time to contract fully to the main sequence, hence they lie above and to the right of it. From such bona fide pre-main-sequence stars, we can learn some of the unique properties of this particular type of star.

T Tauri stars

The stars that vary irregularly in brightness are called T TAURI VARIABLES, after their prototype in the dark clouds of Taurus. The light curve of one such variable is shown in figure 4.7. T Tauri stars have absorption-line spectra typical of F, G or K giants, consistent with their location above the main sequence. The lines are broadened, probably due to fairly rapid rotation, or possibly due to some other large-scale atmospheric motion. Superimposed on the absorption-line spectra are strong emission lines due to hydrogen, calcium and other elements in the star. There is also an emission continuum in the violet portion of the spectrum, which may also be due to hydrogen. The emission lines and continuum are formed in the chromosphere – the middle and upper portion of the atmosphere of the star. The spectrum also contains FORBIDDEN LINES, which cannot arise in a dense stellar atmosphere, but must arise in a region of much lower density. These lines, and the strong infrared radiation from these stars, presumably come from the cloud of gas and dust which still surrounds the star.

Many T Tauri stars are observed to have their spectral lines systematically shifted to shorter wavelengths. This, according to the Doppler principle, means that the material in the atmosphere of the star is moving outward towards the observer. The amount of material leaving the star can be calculated from the velocity of motion (up to $300\,\mathrm{km\,s^{-1}}$) and from the strength of the lines; it amounts to about one ten-millionth of a solar mass per year. Since a star spends several million years in contracting to the main sequence, it may lose a significant amount of mass while it is a T Tauri star.

There is a subclass of the T Tauri stars, called the YY ORIONIS stars, in which the spectral lines are systematically shifted to the red, indicating that material is falling onto the star. These may be very young T Tauri stars, in which material is still contracting onto the star. In normal T Tauri stars, this inflow has been halted and reversed by some process that drives material away from the star. There are two subclasses of T Tauri stars called RW AURIGAE stars and T ORIONIS stars. Their observed light curves differ somewhat from those of normal T Tauri stars, and there is some evidence that they represent different evolutionary phases, but the evidence is rather weak.

What processes cause the emission lines, the light variations and the outflow of material in T Tauri stars? Our own Sun may provide a clue, because these phenomena all occur, to a minor extent, during a *solar flare*. A solar flare is a localized brightening of the Sun's surface, followed by the heating of the Sun's chromosphere and the ejection of matter. Solar flares are caused by a complex interaction between rotation, convection and the Sun's magnetic field. If T Tauri stars rotate fairly rapidly, and if convection is important in their outer layers (which it is in stars of F, G and K type) and if magnetic fields are strong in young stars, then it is not surprising that chromospheric activity is great in young stars.

4.6: *The Hertzsprung-Russell diagram, showing the location of several types of intrinsic variables. Also shown is the evolutionary track of a two-solar-mass star, contracting to the main sequence (red) and evolving away from the main sequence (blue).*

4.7: *The light curve of the pre-main-sequence variable T Tauri.*

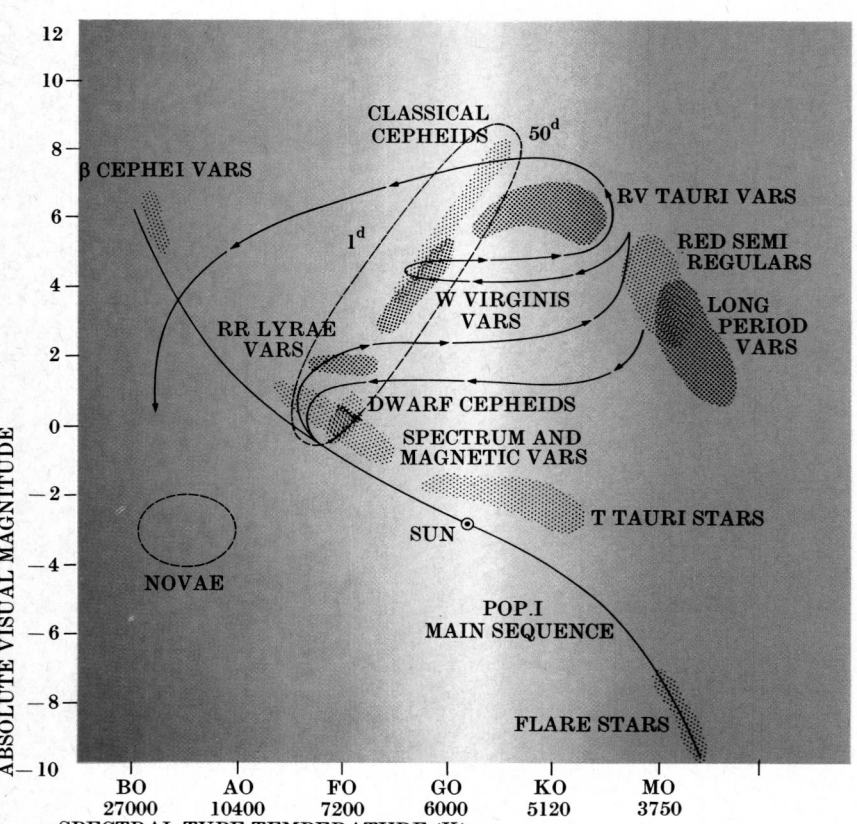

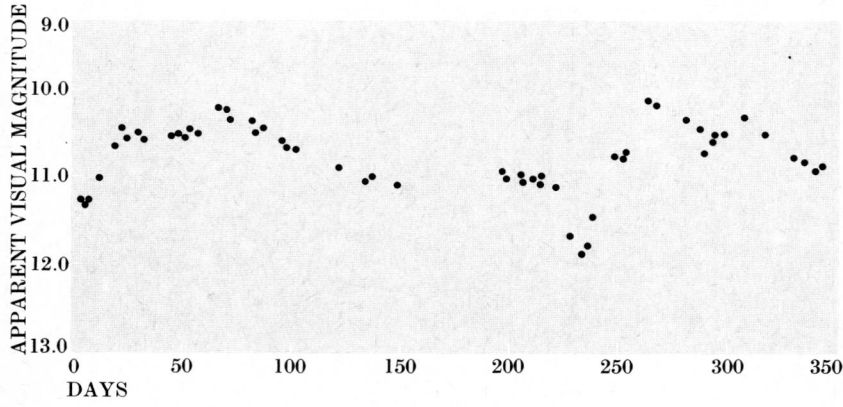

4.8–4.11: *The observed cycle of variations in brightness, temperature, radius and radial velocity of δ Cephei. This is the prototype of the important Cepheid variable stars.*

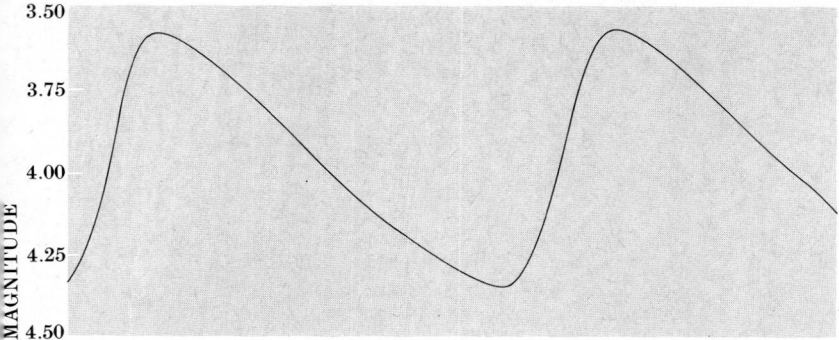

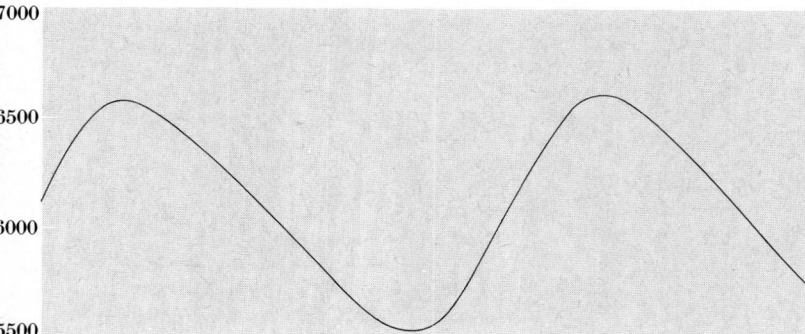

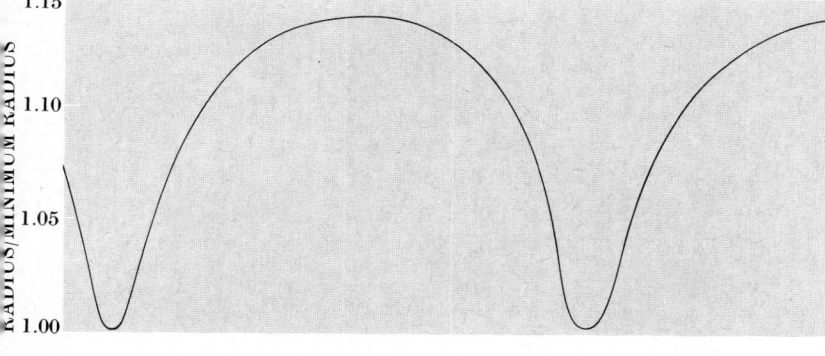

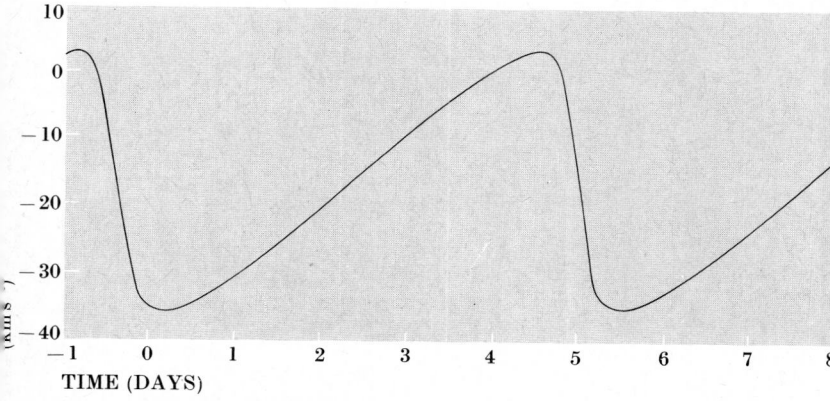

Pulsating variables

Pulsating variables brighten and fade because of a cyclic expansion and contraction of the whole star. As a result, the outer layers of the star alternately approach us and recede from us. These motions produce a periodic Doppler shift in the lines in the spectrum of the star. Using a spectrograph, the astronomer can measure this shift and plot a VELOCITY CURVE – a graph of *radial velocity* against time – for the star.

These velocity variations were first observed in the pulsating variable δ Cephei, by A.A.Belopolsky in 1894. At that time, the nature of the variations was unknown, and they were attributed to orbital motion of the star about an invisible companion. By 1914, Harlow Shapley had proved that the variations in brightness, velocity and temperature were not consistent with orbital motion, but could best be explained by the hypothesis of pulsation (figures 4.8–11).

When a star pulsates, it expands past its average size but is pulled back by gravity. Like a swinging pendulum, it overshoots again, and continues to contract. Gas pressure then pushes it back out again. Dissipative or frictional forces should eventually bring the pulsation to a stop; the fact that they do not tells us that some process is constantly feeding mechanical energy into the star. The pulsation motions are quite large in the outer layers of the star: typically $40 \, \mathrm{km \, s^{-1}}$ but as much as $200 \, \mathrm{km \, s^{-1}}$ in a few cases. In some stars, the expansion velocity may exceed the *escape velocity* from the star, and the outer layers may be ejected completely.

A star is a sphere of gas, confined in the centre and free at the surface. The pulsation of a star is similar to the vibration of the column of gas in an organ pipe, closed at one end and open at the other. In both cases, the gas can vibrate in one or more of several MODES. The simplest mode is called the FUNDAMENTAL MODE. In this mode, the amplitude of vibration decreases smoothly from the free end to the closed end. There are also HARMONIC MODES, which differ from the fundamental mode in that the periods are shorter and in that there are nodes or stationary points within the gas. The mode in which the star (or the organ pipe) vibrates depends on how and where the driving mechanism – the source of mechanical energy – is applied.

Pulsating variables are not distributed at random in the HR diagram; most lie in a vertical band called the CEPHEID INSTABILITY STRIP, or the GREAT SEQUENCE. This merges into a broad instability region in the upper right. Within these regions, many if not most stars pulsate. Furthermore, the period, range and shape of light curve are correlated with the position of the variable in the HR diagram. The largest, most luminous stars have the longest periods.

Cepheids

In the upper part of the Cepheid instability strip lie the CLASSICAL CEPHEIDS. These stars gave the instability strip its name; they are so called because they resemble the prototype δ Cephei. This star can be found on almost any star map, and its brightness variations can normally be seen easily by the unaided eye. Cepheids are supergiant yellow stars, with periods of one to 100 days and ranges of about one magnitude. A few – notably Polaris – have ranges which are much smaller. In fact, there may be many other microvariable Cepheids like Polaris, but the search for them has only just begun.

There is an important relation between the period of pulsation of a Cepheid and its luminosity, which is usually expressed as a relation between the logarithm of the period, and the absolute magnitude. The relation is then a linear one. The period also depends to a slight extent on the colour of the star, and this dependence introduces some of the scatter in the relation.

The Cepheid period-luminosity relation is a specific example of a much more general relation which applies to all pulsating variables. The physical explanation for this relation was determined in 1917 by Sir Arthur Eddington. He derived a wave equation, which like the wave equation that describes the vibration of a string, describes the vibration of the star. Roughly, the period of pulsation is the time required for a vibration to travel from the surface of the star to the centre and back again. The bigger the star, the longer this time will be. More precisely, the wave equation says that for a given class of pulsating variables, the period is inversely proportional to the square root of the average density of the star. Large, distended stars therefore have longer periods than small, compact stars. Since the luminosity of the star is also dependent on the size of the star, the period is related to the luminosity also. The fact that the luminosity of the star also depends on its temperature, or colour, explains why the period is furthermore slightly dependent on the colour. Stars with the same luminosity may have slightly different colours, and hence slightly different periods.

The period-luminosity relation for Cepheids was discovered in 1908 by Henrietta Leavitt, who noted that in the Small Magellanic Cloud (SMC), a nearby galaxy to our own, the brightest Cepheids had the longest periods. Since all the SMC Cepheids are at roughly the same distance, the apparently brightest ones are the most luminous. The route from this observation to the present period-luminosity relation was not an easy one. It required a detailed study of Cepheids whose distances were known: Cepheids in binary systems, in galactic star clusters and in nearby galaxies. Most of these studies were made in the 1960s.

From the period-luminosity relation, astronomers can determine the absolute magnitude, and hence the distance of any Cepheid for which period and apparent magnitude can be measured. Fortunately, Cepheids are extremely luminous, and can be seen at great distances. They have been used to establish the size and structure of our own Galaxy, and of nearby galaxies, and they are one of the fundamental tools of observational cosmology.

The understanding of Cepheids, and of the period-luminosity relation, became much clearer in the late 1940s when Walter Baade discovered that there were two POPULATIONS of Cepheids: the *classical Cepheids*, and the POPULATION II CEPHEIDS or W VIRGINIS STARS. Both populations share the same part of the HR diagram, and have similar light curves. Nevertheless, the two populations are fundamentally different: whereas the classical Cepheids are massive, young stars, the Population II Cepheids are very old stars with low masses. As a result, Population II Cepheids are two magnitudes fainter than classical Cepheids with the same period. The implications for the period-luminosity law are obvious!

Although Population II Cepheids are found throughout our Galaxy and other galaxies, they are particularly conspicuous in *globular clusters*. These enormous clusters which were formed billions of years ago consist entirely of Population II stars, of low mass. On a single photograph of a globular cluster, thousands of stars, including hundreds of variables, may be recorded.

Population II Cepheids are stars that have exhausted most of their supply of hydrogen fuel, and are now 'burning' helium. The shorter-period variables are in a relatively quiescent phase of evolution, but the longer-period variables are evolving rapidly through the instability strip, and are subject to abrupt changes in their period and range. The most bizarre case is RU Camelopardalis, which in the 1960s stopped pulsating completely! Several times, it made half-hearted attempts to recover its pulsation, but it has always stopped again.

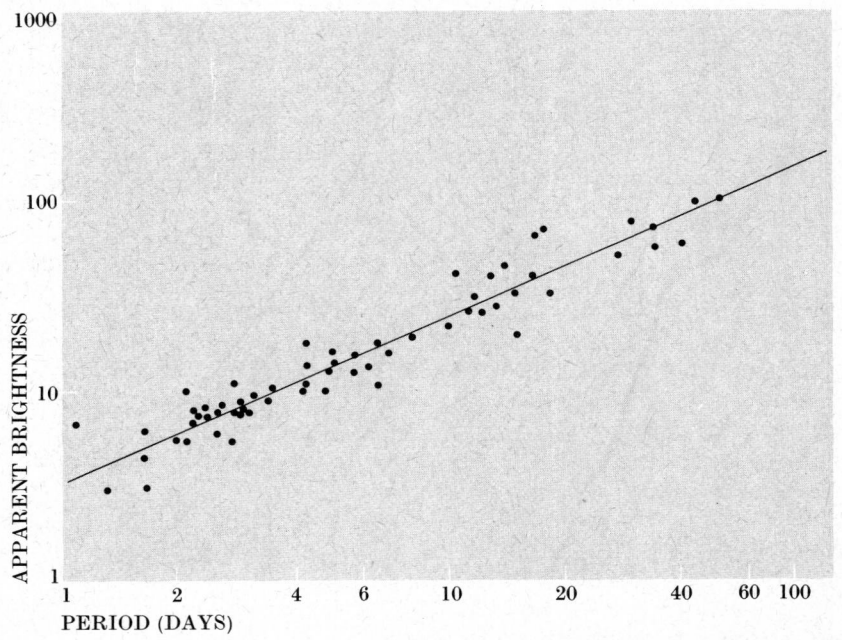

RR Lyrae stars

Even more conspicuous in globular star clusters are the RR LYRAE variables. Whereas a globular cluster may contain a handful of Population II Cepheids at the most, it may contain several hundred RR Lyrae variables. These variables are also found throughout our Galaxy, especially in the halo. RR Lyrae variables are giant stars, larger, hotter and more luminous than the Sun. They have periods from 0.3 to 1.0 day, ranges from 0.5 to 1.5 magnitude and light curves that, for the longer-period variables, brighten very quickly and fade more slowly. These longer-period variables are called type (a) and (b); the shorter-period variables, which have smaller ranges, smoother light curves, and higher temperatures, are called type (c) (figure 4.13). These types differ in that types (a) and (b) are pulsating in the *fundamental mode*, type (c) in the first *harmonic mode*.

Almost all RR Lyrae variables have an average absolute magnitude near +0.5, irrespective of their period. The astronomer can therefore determine their distances simply by measuring their average apparent magnitudes. RR Lyrae stars serve as yardsticks for old Population II stars in the same way that classical Cepheids serve as yardsticks for young Population I stars. The reason why all RR Lyrae stars have absolute magnitudes near +0.5 is because all RR Lyrae stars have about the same age, mass and helium content, and all are in the initial phases of 'burning' helium in their cores.

4.12: *The period-luminosity relation for classical Cepheid variable stars. When plotted as absolute magnitude against the logarithm of the period, the relation is linear. This relation is of fundamental importance to the determination of distance in astronomy.*

4.13: *Photographic light curves of three RR Lyrae variables in the globular star cluster omega Centauri: type* a *(top), type* b *(middle) and type* c *(bottom).*

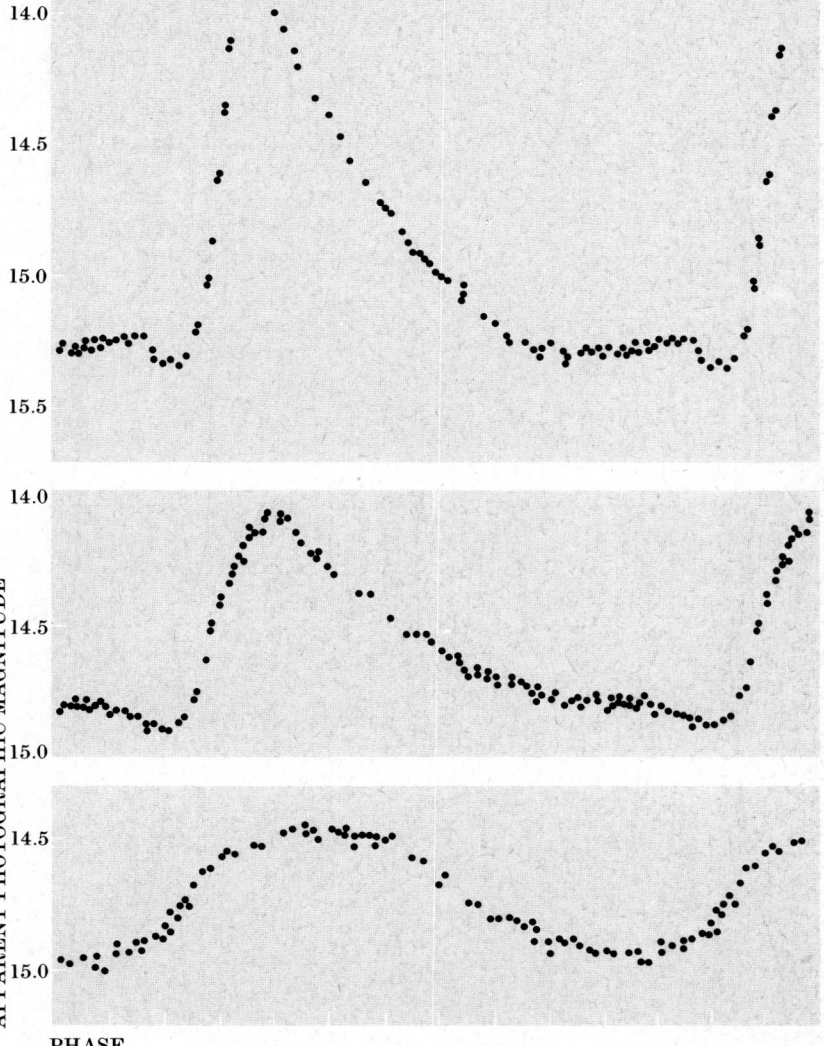

Dwarf Cepheid variables

Below the RR Lyrae variables in the Cepheid instability strip, we find the DWARF CEPHEID VARIABLES (sometimes called AI Velorum stars). As their name implies, they are smaller and fainter than Cepheids (or RR Lyrae stars). They have periods of 0.05 to 0.3 day, and ranges of 0.3 to 0.7 magnitude. Those with the larger ranges can be studied visually through a small telescope; a complete cycle lasts for only a few hours. Several dwarf Cepheids have light curves with slowly rising and falling range (figure 4.14). This phenomenon is called MODULATION, and arises because the star is pulsating simultaneously in two different modes, usually the fundamental and the first harmonic. We do not know whether the dwarf Cepheids are low-mass stars, slightly younger and richer in heavy elements than the RR Lyrae stars, or whether they are normal-mass young stars, closely related to the δ Scuti variables, which we will describe next.

The Cepheid instability strip intersects the richly-populated main sequence at a temperature corresponding to spectral type F0. Stars on and near the main sequence, with spectral types near F0, would be expected to pulsate – and they do. These are δ Scuti variables. However, the periods are only an hour or two, the ranges are as small as 0.01 magnitude, and the light curves are quite irregular.

4.14: *The light curve of the dwarf Cepheid variable SX Phoenicis. The slow modulation, or change in the amplitude, is due to an interference between the fundamental and first harmonic modes of pulsation.*

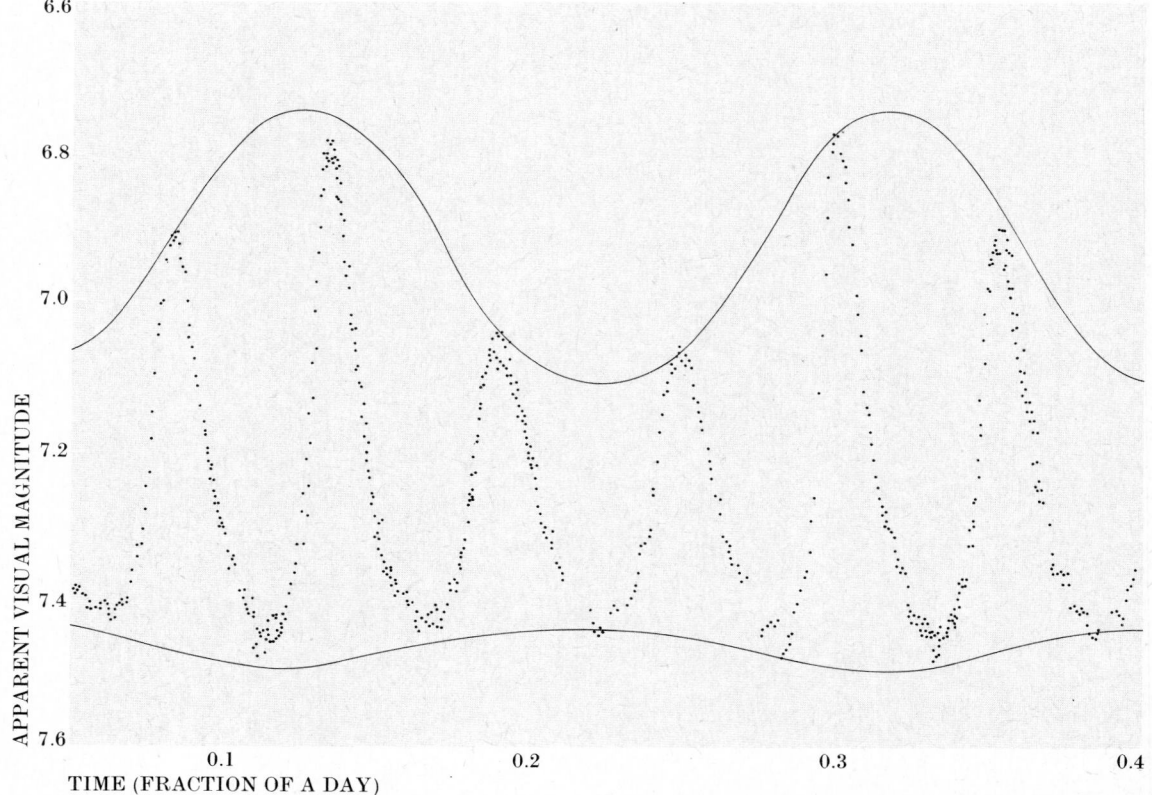

Beta Cephei and RV Tauri variables

There is one type of pulsating variable that lies nowhere near the Cepheid instability strip in the HR diagram: the β CEPHEI (or β Canis Majoris) stars. These hot, massive stars have periods of a few hours and ranges of a few hundredths of a magnitude in visible light. The ranges in ultraviolet light are much larger, because most of the energy of these hot stars is emitted in the ultraviolet, and the radial velocity variations in these stars are among the largest in any pulsating variables.

β Cephei stars are notable for several reasons. To begin with, they are the most numerous pulsating variables among the bright stars; they include α Virginis (Spica), β Crucis and β Centauri, among others. They exhibit several interesting pathological effects which have absorbed the efforts of astronomers for several decades. Yet despite this effort, the nature and cause of the pulsation are completely unknown!

The Cepheid instability strip merges, at its upper end, with a large instability region in the upper right portion of the HR diagram. The transition region is occupied by a group of rare, luminous stars of spectral type F, G and K, called RV TAURI VARIABLES. Their periods are 50 to 100 days and are weakly correlated with the luminosity. Their light curves have a unique feature – alternating shallow and deep minima – whose cause is completely unknown. They also emit strong infrared radiation, apparently from a shell of material which has been driven off the star by the pulsation.

Red variables

The last major instability region in the HR diagram is the one in the upper right. It is occupied by a variety of interesting objects, known collectively as RED VARIABLES. These occupants include numerous small-range variables with periods of a few weeks, conspicuous large-range variables with periods of a few months and rare supergiant variables with periods of several years.

The large-range variables in this region are known as MIRA STARS after the prototype o Ceti. Their periods are 100 to 500 days and their ranges can be as much as ten magnitudes, partly because at minimum brightness they are coolest, and most of their radiation is shifted from the visible portion of the spectrum into the infrared. The light variations are so large that they can easily be measured visually, and much of what we know about these stars has been learned from visual observations by amateur astronomers. Figure 4.15 shows the light curve of Mira itself, determined from visual observations by members of the American Association of Variable Star Observers. The period is 332 days and the range is about 8 magnitudes, but Mira can be as bright as 2 magnitudes at maximum or as faint as 4. Such irregularity is even more pronounced in some other red variables. Mira, at 3000 K, is one of the coolest stars known, and it is several hundred times larger than the Sun. However, the mass of material in this enormous volume is little greater than the mass of the Sun, so the density of the outer layers of Mira must be extremely low. When pulsation waves travel

4.15: *The light curve of the long-period variable star Mira during 1964–65, compiled from visual observations by members of the American Association of Variable Star Observers.*

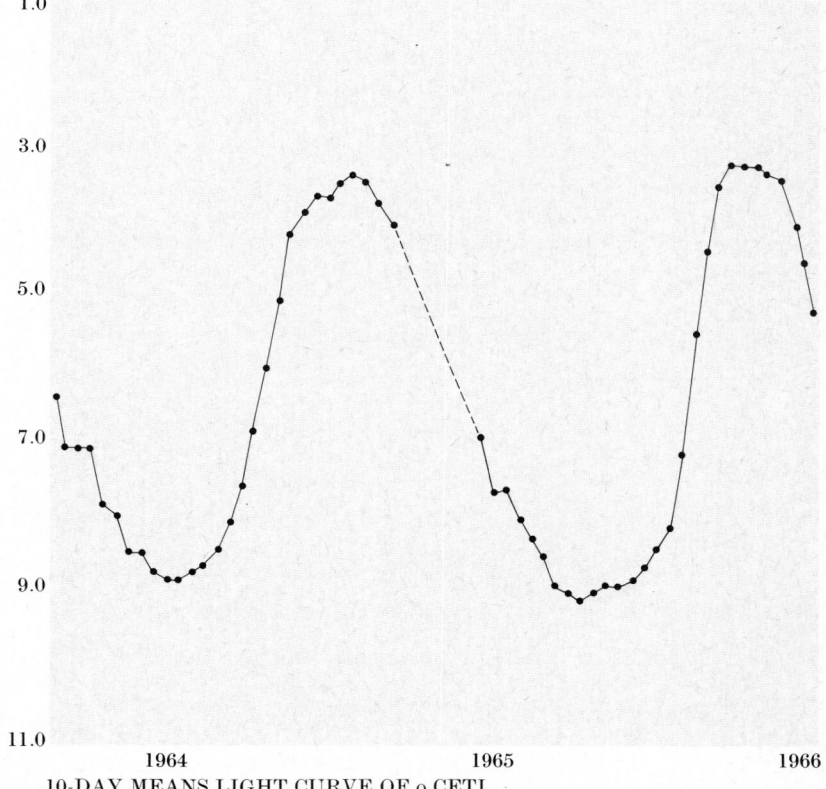

10-DAY MEANS LIGHT CURVE OF o CETI

through these layers, they produce *shock waves* (like a supersonic aircraft does) and a characteristic emission-line spectrum. Mira is classified as a cool giant star. Cool supergiant stars also vary in brightness, by as much as a magnitude on a timescale of several years, but the variation is quite irregular. If any periodicity is evident, the variable is called SEMI-REGULAR; if no periodicity is evident, it is called IRREGULAR.

α Orionis (Betelgeuse) is a prominent example of an irregular variable. It is not easy to detect periodicities in semi-regular variables. To begin with, we need many years of observations, and we also need sophisticated methods of mathematical analysis. μ Cephei is the best-studied, semi-regular variable; it has underlying periodicities of two and ten years. Incidentally, we have now met β, δ and μ Cephei; ε Cephei is a δ Scuti variable and γ, o and υ are suspected of small-range variations. This indicates how abundant variable stars are among the bright stars of a typical constellation.

Luminous variables like Betelgeuse are massive young stars, but less luminous variables like Mira are older, with ages and masses similar to those of our Sun. Some red variables are found in globular star clusters, and must therefore be among the oldest stars known. In the HR diagram, they lie at the tip of the *giant branch* which, according to our theoretical evolutionary tracks, means that they have almost exhausted the hydrogen fuel in their core. Other than that, we understand very little about the nature and cause of the pulsation in these stars. That is because their energy is transported outward, from the core to the surface, by *convection*, and convection is a poorly-understood process in astrophysics.

Convection refers to the transport of energy by material motions. Usually these motions occur in CELLS, in which hot material rises in the centre, cools and falls at the periphery. On the surface of the Sun, these cells are visible and are called granules; they are a few hundred kilometres in size. On a star like Betelgeuse, they may be much larger: almost as large as the star itself. The distinguished astrophysicist Martin Schwarzschild has suggested that there may only be about a dozen cells on the surface of Betelgeuse, giving it a faceted appearance. Observations of Betelgeuse, using the technique of *speckle interferometry*, have shown a hint of such faceting.

The cause of stellar pulsation

Why do stars pulsate? The fact that pulsating variables are not distributed randomly in the HR diagram strongly suggests that certain combinations of luminosity and effective surface temperature favour a state of pulsation as opposed to a state of rest. Sir Arthur Eddington made the first serious attempts to explain the cause of stellar pulsation. By 1917, he had derived the wave equation that described the mechanical (but not the thermodynamic) aspects of the pulsation. This equation provided an explanation for the period-luminosity relation. It also showed that the relative amplitude of pulsation decreased very rapidly from the surface of the star to the centre, because the density at the centre is so high. As a result, the centre of the star neither affects nor is affected by the pulsation.

This has two important consequences. It means that when we try to understand pulsation, we do not have to know about or to understand the complicated changes in chemical composition which may have occurred at the centre of the star, due to thermonuclear reactions. It also means that thermonuclear reactions at the centre are not likely to be the direct cause of pulsation. Eddington realized this and looked elsewhere for the cause of stellar pulsation. He reasoned that if a star pulsated then it must somehow have acquired mechanical energy, both to begin to pulsate and to maintain the pulsation against dissipative or frictional forces. The star must therefore function as a thermodynamic HEAT ENGINE, converting a small fraction of its abundant supply of radiant energy into motion. The basic requirement of a heat engine is that it must absorb excess heat when compressed (at high temperature); this heat is released as mechanical energy during the expansion phase of the pulsation. Eddington suggested that there might be a 'valve' near the surface of the star, where the relative pulsation amplitude was greatest. If the valve closed, trapping heat, when the star was hottest and most compressed, and opened, releasing heat, when the star was coolest and most expanded, then the requirements for a heat engine would be satisfied. Eddington considered that the natural *opacity* of the atoms in a star might provide the valve. Normally, they do not: they become more transparent when compressed, letting heat escape. Therefore, most stars do not pulsate. However, in a region of a star in which atoms of a particular element are *partially ionized* (called an IONIZATION ZONE), the atoms do become more opaque when compressed. Ionization zones are the direct cause of pulsation in stars. The most effective ionization zones are those of the abundant elements hydrogen and helium. In stars with an effective surface temperature of about 7000 K (those near the Cepheid instability strip), these ionization zones are close enough to the surface so that the relative pulsation amplitude is large, but deep enough in the star so that the density is high and the zones contain appreciable mass.

Eddington did not identify these ionization zones as the true cause of stellar pulsation because, in his time, it was believed (incorrectly) that hydrogen and helium were rather rare in stars.

In the last two decades, by use of better estimates of the chemical composition of the stars, astronomers have completely verified Eddington's ideas. Computers have figured prominently in this work. They have made it possible to calculate accurately the opacity of stellar material and to build mathematical models of pulsating stars. These models can duplicate most of the observed properties of stars in the Cepheid instability strip. They also provide clues about such properties as mass, absolute magnitude and helium content, that are difficult to observe directly. For example, the presence of helium and its ionization zones make pulsation possible in stars with effective surface temperatures of about 9000 K; without helium, this temperature would be about 6000 K. The fact that the oldest pulsating variables, the RR Lyrae and Population II Cepheid variables, have effective surface temperatures as high as 9000 K tells us that these stars contain 30 per cent helium by mass in their outer layers. Helium must therefore have been present when they were formed and must therefore be a primordial element from an earlier phase of the Universe. According to evolutionary cosmological theories, helium was synthesized in the *big bang*. We see that pulsating variables even provide information for cosmology!

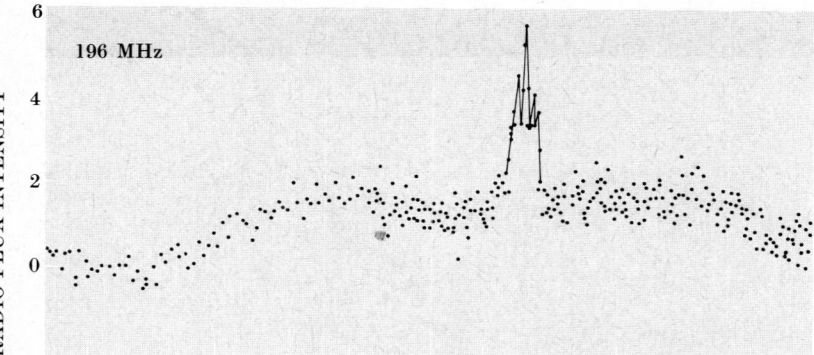

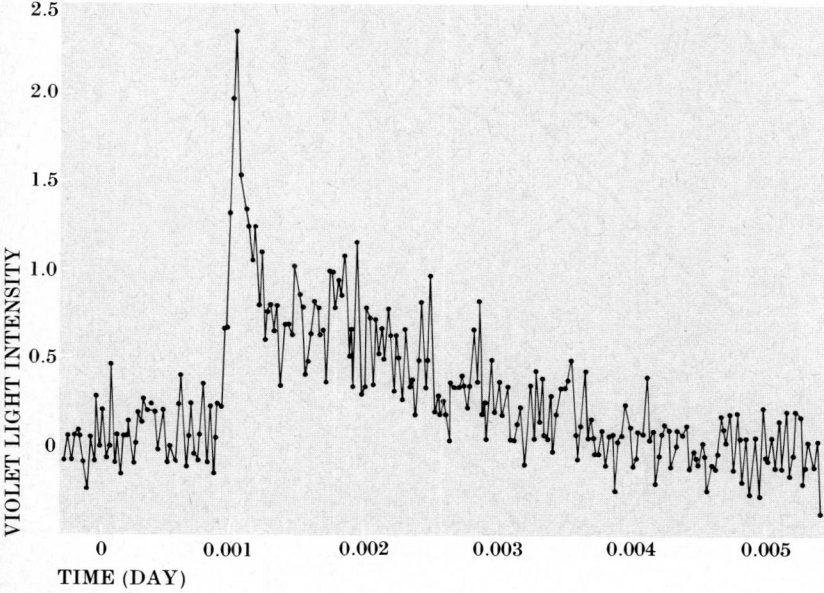

Evolution and pulsation

A star may become a pulsating variable several times during its lifetime, as evolution slowly changes its size, luminosity and internal structure. We can see this best by comparing theoretical evolutionary tracks with the positions of instability regions in the HR diagram (figure 4.6). We can determine which evolutionary track passes through the position of the star; hence we can determine how the star reached its present position, and what its mass must be. A star may pass through the Cepheid instability strip even before it reaches the main sequence. (Two pulsating pre-main-sequence stars have been found in NGC 2264.) When it reaches the main sequence, it will not pulsate unless its effective surface temperature is about 9000 K, in which case it will be a δ Scuti star. It may pass through the Cepheid instability strip one or more times before becoming a red variable, and one or more times thereafter before becoming a white dwarf.

Evolution affects pulsation in other ways, as well. We may occasionally see a star enter or leave an instability region, and then begin or cease to pulsate. The number of evolutionary tracks which cross an instability region, and the rate at which they cross, both affect the number of pulsating variables found in that region. Finally, the period and range of pulsation may slowly change as the star evolves through the region, because both the period and the range depend on the luminosity and effective surface temperature of the star. Evolution through a region usually takes millions of years, and the changes in the range are too small to detect. Changes in period can be detected, however, because they produce a cumulative discrepancy between the observed and expected times of maximum or minimum brightness. In the same way, small errors in the rate of a clock accumulate, and become readily apparent after several days. Period changes as small as one part in 10^{10} have been detected in this way, and provide a direct, observable confirmation of stellar evolution.

4.16: *Simultaneous radio (196 MHz) and optical (violet) observations of a flare on the star Wolf 424 AB on 30 January 1974. The flare begins almost simultaneously at the two wavelengths.*

Eruptive variables and flare stars

ERUPTIVE VARIABLE STARS are stars that brighten quickly and un-predictably, then fade. They may return to their previous, normal brightness or they may be so profoundly changed by the eruption that they could never return to their previous state. Some pre-main-sequence variables are eruptive by nature, and some Hubble-Sandage variables have properties in common with eruptive variables. No classification scheme is perfect, however, and we shall restrict our discussion here to those variables which are relatively quiescent before and after their eruptions.

FLARE STARS (also called UV Ceti stars) are cool, faint main-sequence stars which unpredictably brighten by up to four magnitudes in a few seconds then fade in a few minutes (figure 4.16). Only a few dozen of these variables are known, but that is because of the difficulty of detecting such faint stars much beyond the Sun's immediate neighbourhood. In fact, about 5 per cent of cool main-sequence stars are flare stars, and since 80 per cent of all stars are cool main-sequence stars, it follows that 4 per cent of all stars are flare stars, and that they are perhaps the most common variables known. A flare star may 'perform' several times in one night, and the flares are large enough to be observed visually by patient amateur astronomers. The spectra of flare stars are like those of normal K and M dwarfs, except that emission lines of hydrogen are present; these intensify considerably during a flare.

These stellar flares are quite similar to the flares which occur on the Sun. The amounts of energy released are comparable. This amount of energy is small, compared to the normal energy output of the Sun, but is large compared to the normal energy output of a K- or M-type dwarf. Therefore, solar flares would barely be detectable if the Sun were several parsecs away from us. Like solar flares, stellar flares are accompanied by bursts of radio waves. These were first observed by Sir Bernard Lovell at Jodrell Bank, England, and he has continued to study these bursts, in collaboration with observers using optical telescopes (figure 4.17). The flare and the burst arrive almost simultaneously – good evidence that light and radio waves travel at the same velocity! The small difference in arrival times is consistent with observations of solar flares, and suggests that the two kinds of flares are caused by a similar mechanism: a disruption of the magnetic field on the surface of the star sends a supersonic shock wave upward through the chromosphere and corona, accompanied by an expanding cloud of plasma and magnetic field.

A similar process, operating almost continuously, may cause the irregular light variations of the T Tauri stars. If that is the case, then the flare stars (and the Sun) are distant descendants of the pre-main-sequence variables, in more ways than one.

4.17: *Four successive exposures show the flare-up of the binary star Krüger 60 B (and a third distant companion) on 26 July 1939. (Sproul Observatory, USA)*

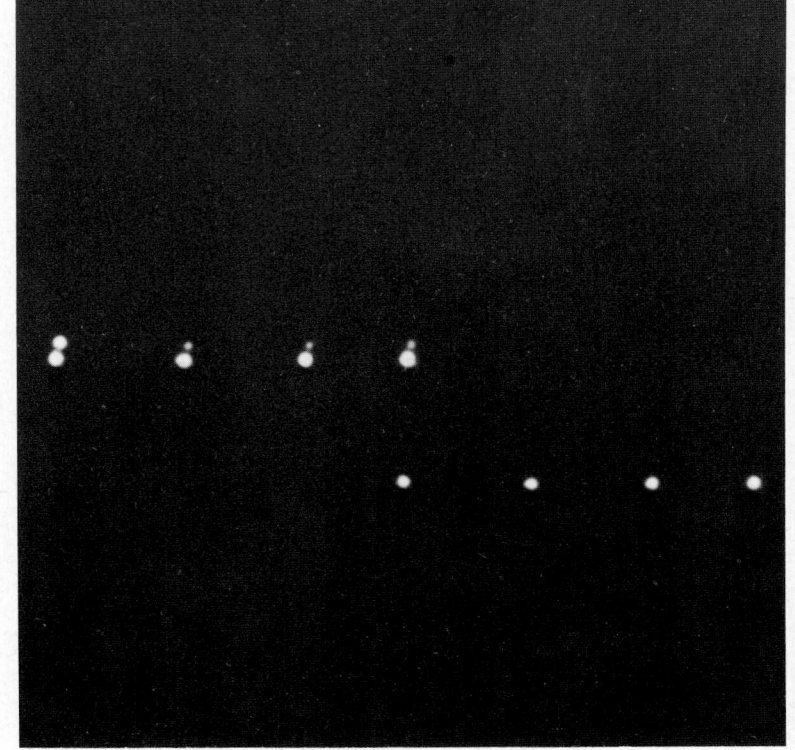

Hubble-Sandage variables

We have already noted that rare, luminous red stars like Betelgeuse vary irregularly in brightness. In 1953, Edwin Hubble and Allan Sandage reported that, in the nearby galaxies M 31 and M 33, the most luminous stars of all colours were variable in brightness. In most cases, the variations were slow, small and irregular, but in a few cases, the variations were quite the opposite. HUBBLE-SANDAGE VARIABLES have absolute magnitudes in excess of −9; in fact, were it not for their large variations in brightness, they would be useful distance indicators for nearby galaxies.

Their main interest, however, is the fact that they tell us something about the evolution of the most massive, luminous stars. Astronomers have always wondered why there are no stars with masses much greater than about 50 solar masses. They have suspected, from theoretical studies, that more massive stars would be unstable against the pressure of their own radiation, but the precise results of these studies are conflicting.

To get a better understanding of the nature of Hubble-Sandage variables, we should look for them in our own Galaxy. Unfortunately, they are likely to be hidden within the thick dust clouds in the Milky Way. However, there are at least two good candidates: P Cygni and η Carinae. P Cygni varied from magnitude 3 to below magnitude 6 several times during the 17th century, but has remained near magnitude 5 since. Its absolute magnitude is now − 9, but at maximum was − 11 – brighter than a million Suns. Its spectrum gives a clue to the nature of the light variations; it contains many sharp absorption lines, shifted to shorter wavelengths. These arise from an expanding shell of gas around the star. This suggests that the brightening episodes in the seventeenth century were caused by the expansion of the outer layers of the star and by the ejection of the shell of gas which we see today.

An even more exotic case is η Carinae. From 1600 to 1800, it rose in brightness until by 1840 it outshone every star except Sirius. It has now faded to magnitude 7 (figure 4.18). η Carinae is embedded in a dense, expanding cloud of dust and gas, even denser than the one around P Cygni. The dense cloud is itself situated in the complex nebulosity shown in figure 4.19. Much of the energy from η Carinae is absorbed by the dust cloud, and is re-emitted as infrared radiation; η Carinae is the strongest infrared source in the sky, outside the Solar System.

There is much controversy about the nature of the star within the cloud. Is it a massive young star in the last stages of birth? Is it a kind of slow supernova eruption, muffled by the cloud of material around it? Or is it a Hubble-Sandage variable: a massive young star trying to evolve normally but incapable of doing so in stable fashion? The key to this mystery lies buried within the obscuring cloud of dust, but modern astronomical techniques – particularly radio and infrared techniques – should uncover this key.

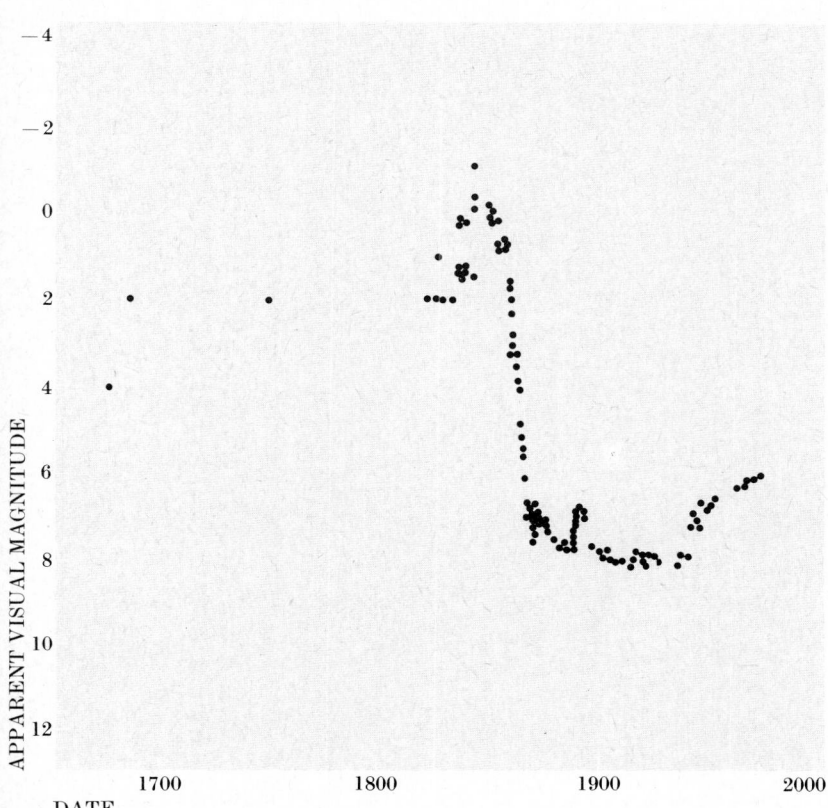

4.18: *The light curve of eta Carinae, one of the most luminous stars in our Galaxy.*

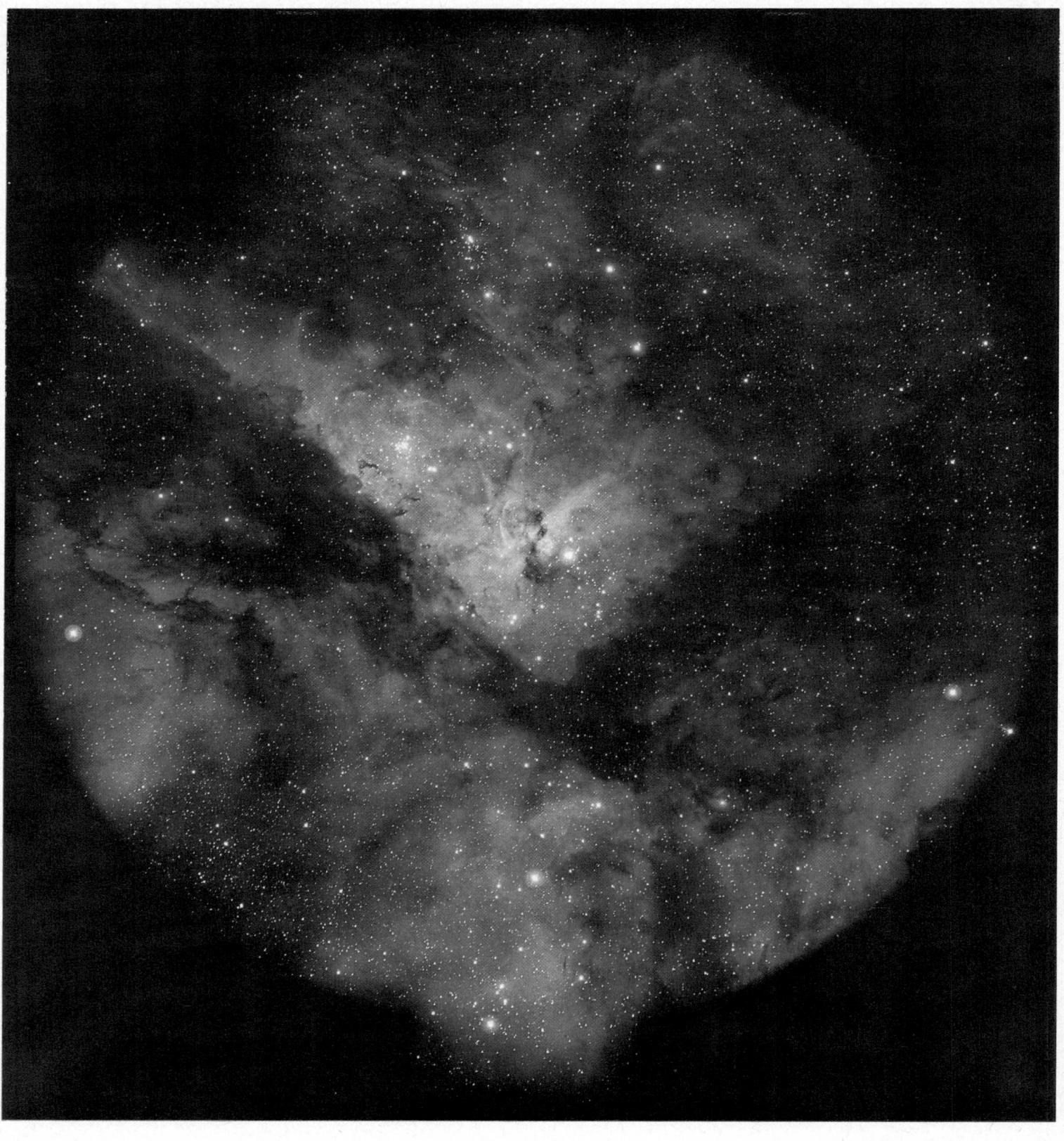

Novae and supernovae

NOVA is an example of picturesque but inaccurate terminology. The word means new, and refers to the appearance of a 'new' star which was apparently not present before. In fact, a nova is an eruption on a star in the last stages of its evolution. A nova, as we shall see, requires the presence of a companion in orbit around the old star. In this sense, a nova is an extrinsic rather than an intrinsic variable. The eruption occurs, however, because of an intrinsic instability which arises in the old star. This is yet another example of the difficulty of classifying variable stars.

Novae can be meaningfully subdivided into ORDINARY novae, RECURRENT novae and DWARF novae (also called U Geminorum stars). An ordinary nova brightens by as much as 18 magnitudes in a few days, then slowly fades (figure 4.20). A recurrent nova is an ordinary nova which erupts more than once. A dwarf nova brightens by only a few magnitudes, but does so repeatedly.

The behaviour of a typical nova can best be illustrated by a specific example – Nova Cygni 1975 – which rose suddenly to prominence on the night of 29 August 1975. Like many novae, it was seen first by amateur observers. Some amateurs make systematic searches for novae, scanning the skies with binoculars, looking for changes in carefully-memorized patterns of stars. One such amateur is the Englishman, G.D.Alcock, who searched patiently for many years before discovering a nova in Delphinus in 1967; a few months later, he discovered a second nova, in Vulpecula. Nova Cygni required considerably less effort. It was so conspicuous that it could be recognized by anyone reasonably familiar with the constellations.

The Japanese observer, Kentaro Osada, was officially credited with the discovery, and within an hour, dozens of other observers in Japan had confirmed the discovery. They immediately notified the director of the Tokyo Observatory, who in turn notified the International Astronomical Union's Central Bureau for Astronomical Telegrams, in Cambridge, USA; from there, the news was relayed by telegram to observatories all over the world. Intensive studies of the nova, using optical, radio, infrared and X-ray telescopes, began even before the nova had completed its rapid rise to maximum light.

The light curve shown in figure 4.20 has been assembled from hundreds of photoelectric and visual measurements. Novae can be classified as fast, medium and slow, according to how rapidly they fade from maximum light. Nova Cygni was a fast nova!

While some astronomers carried on the intensive study of Nova Cygni, others searched archival records for previous evidence of the nova. Routine patrol photographs, taken at the Harvard Observatory since 1898, showed no object brighter than magnitude 15.5 at the position of the nova at any time. Photographs in the Palomar Sky Survey (figure 4.21) showed no object brighter than magnitude 21. The total range of the nova outburst must have exceeded 19 magnitudes! The outburst apparently occurred in two steps, however, because on Russian patrol photographs taken earlier in August 1975, the nova appeared as an object of magnitude 16.

4.19: *The magnificent splendour of the Carina Nebula, one of the finest sights in southern skies. This dense expanding cloud surrounds the peculiar variable star eta Carinae. (Cerro Tololo Inter-American Observatory, Chile and USA)*

4.20: *The light curve of nova Cygni 1975, compiled from observations from many sources.*

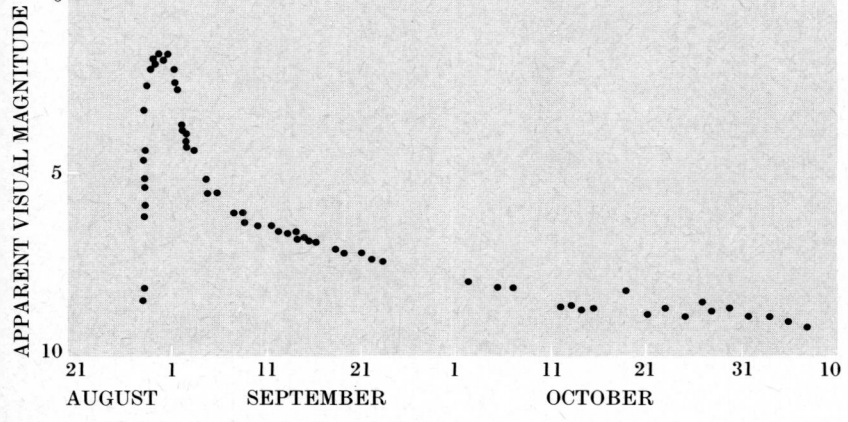

APPARENT VISUAL MAGNITUDE

0

5

10

21   1   11   21   1   11   21   31   10

AUGUST   SEPTEMBER   OCTOBER

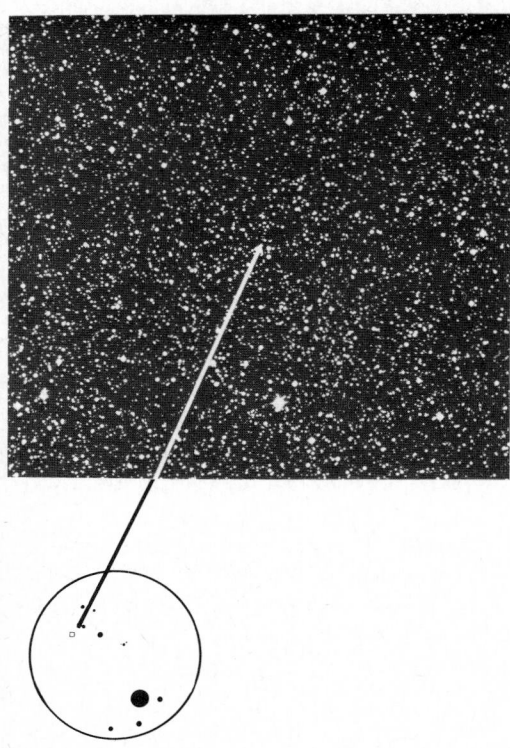

4.21: *The field of the spectacular nova Cygni 1975 before the outburst and at maximum. The nova is invisible at pre-outburst. (University of Toronto, Canada)*

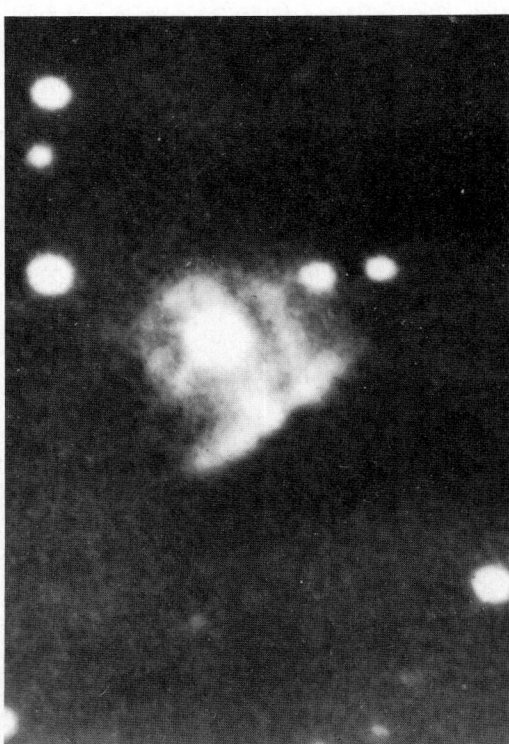
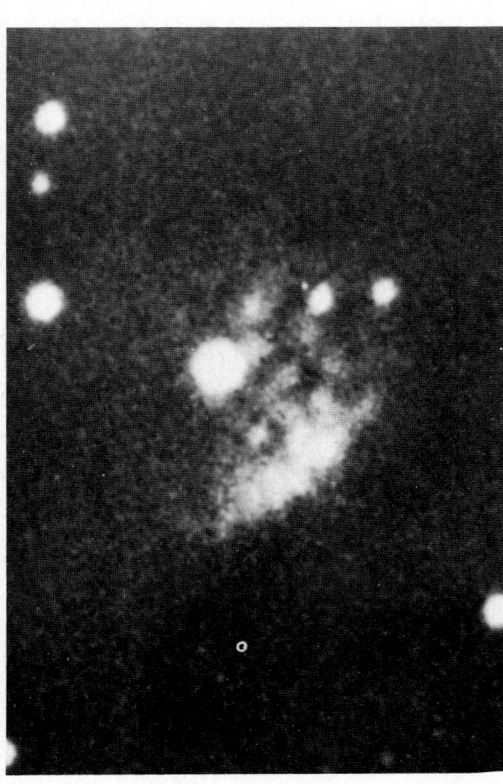

4.22: *Expanding nebulosity around nova Persei 1901. (Hale Observatories, USA)*

The spectacular changes in brightness were accompanied by equally spectacular changes in the spectrum (figure 4.23). Before maximum, the spectrum was that of a SUPERGIANT A-TYPE STAR, with broad, weak absorption lines greatly shifted to the violet. Soon thereafter, the spectrum developed strong emission and absorption lines of hydrogen and other elements; the emission lines were very broad, and the absorption lines were Doppler-shifted to shorter wavelengths by as much as $1000\,\mathrm{km\,s^{-1}}$. As the nova faded in brightness, the spectrum was dominated by these features. Additional sets of emission and absorption lines appeared, shifted by even greater amounts. Finally, the spectrum became that of a typical *emission nebula*, with emission lines of hydrogen, helium, oxygen, nitrogen and neon. Among these are *forbidden lines*, characteristic of a gas of very low density.

The light and spectrum variations are consistent with the following simple picture of the nova eruption. The star suddenly swells and ejects a spherical shell of material. The shell is small, but thick enough to mimic the distended atmosphere of a supergiant when the nova is at maximum. As the shell expands, we see Doppler-shifted absorption lines from the part of the shell between us and the star, and broad emission lines from the sides of the shell. Eventually, the shell dissipates, but is still faintly illuminated by the star. Figure 4.22 is a photograph of the shell ejected by a nova.

A dozen or more novae occur in our Galaxy each year, but most of them are never observed because of great distance, obscuration by dust, or both. In nearby galaxies, they can be seen more easily. From these novae, astronomers have discovered an interesting relationship between the absolute magnitude of a nova at maximum, and the time taken for the nova to decline in brightness by three magnitudes (figure 4.24). Fast novae are brightest at maximum. Nova Cygni, for instance, had an absolute magnitude of -10 at maximum. This relation, when 'calibrated' using novae of known distance and absolute magnitude, provides a useful tool for measuring distances to nearby galaxies.

DWARF NOVAE brighten by two to five magnitudes, at roughly constant intervals of ten to several hundred days (figure 4.25). Stars which have the largest eruptions tend to have the longest intervals between them; this tendency seems to extend to recurrent novae, which suggests that these two kinds of novae are closely related. There is a subclass of dwarf novae named after Z Camelopardalis; members of this subclass have long 'hesitations' in light, at levels intermediate between maximum and minimum. The cause of this phenomenon is not known.

The essential clue to the cause of the nova eruption was discovered in the 1950s by Robert Kraft and Merle Walker: every post-nova was a close binary system, consisting of a white dwarf and a relatively normal cool star. The two stars were so close that tidal forces exerted by the white dwarf pulled material from the outer layers of the cool star. This material formed a ring around the white dwarf. Astronomers already knew that a white dwarf was a dying star, which had exhausted its supply of nuclear fuel; it consists of a dense core of helium (or some heavier element) sur-

4.23: *The spectrum of nova Cygni 1975 shows emission lines of hydrogen. For comparison the absorption-line spectrum of an A star is shown below with the hydrogen lines visible. (University of Cambridge, UK)*

rounded by a thin layer of hydrogen-rich material. The addition of any more hydrogen-rich material to this layer (from the ring, for instance) creates a highly unstable situation, and an eruption can well occur.

Brian Warner and R.E.Nather have added many important details to this close binary model, using the technique of high-speed photometry which they developed at the University of Texas (figure 4.26). Kraft, Walker and others had already discovered that many post-novae were eclipsing variables. Warner and Nather showed that, in addition, there was rapid, irregular flickering, which disappeared during the eclipse. They attributed this to a HOT SPOT on the ring, at the place where material was flowing onto the ring from the cool star. Figure 4.26 shows the light curve of the dwarf nova Z Chamaeleontis. The flickering is quite intense, but disappears during the eclipse. The hump in the curve is due to the light from the hot spot when it faces the observer. The trough is the eclipse of the hot spot. In this system, the white dwarf supplies very little of the total light of the system (figure 4.27).

When Z Chamaeleontis undergoes an eruption, the nature of the light curve changes: the eclipse becomes shallower and wider,

4.24: *The relationship between the maximum absolute photographic magnitude of novae, and the logarithm of the time, in days, required for the nova to fade by two magnitudes from maximum light. The more luminous the nova, the more quickly it fades.*

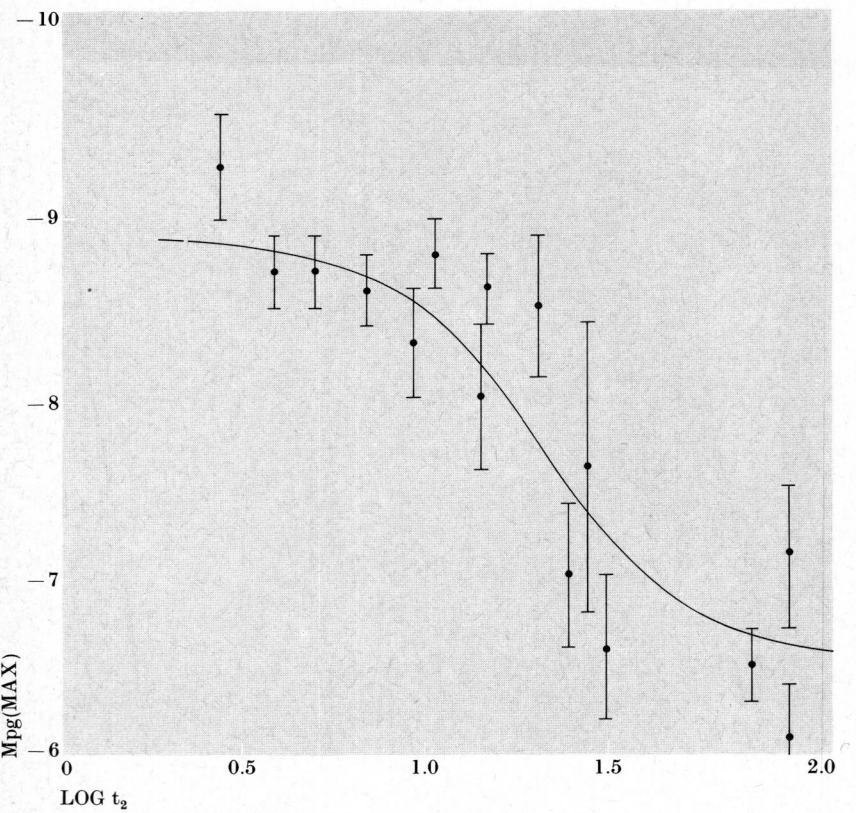

Mpg(MAX)

LOG t_2

4.25: *The light curve of the dwarf nova SS Cygni in 1974.*

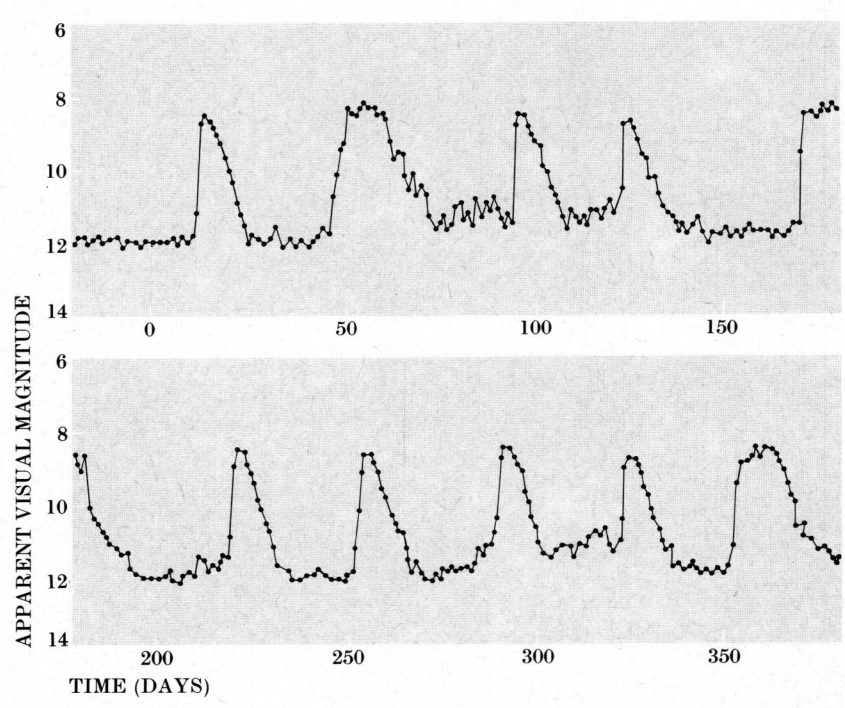

APPARENT VISUAL MAGNITUDE

TIME (DAYS)

indicating that the hot spot and/or the white dwarf have swelled. This is consistent with our simple picture of a nova eruption.

Astronomers have discovered a few stars that, although they have not been observed to erupt, have many properties in common with post-novae, such as emission lines (as from a gaseous ring) and intense flickering. Some of these NOVA-LIKE VARIABLES have other interesting properties. One such star is associated with Scorpio X1, a strong source of X-rays. These X-rays may be produced by material flowing from a normal star onto a ring, deep within the gravitational field of a compact white dwarf. Other X-ray sources have been identified with binary stars in which the compact member is a *neutron star* or even a *black hole*.

SUPERNOVAE are without doubt the most spectacular of all variable stars. In a supernova eruption, a single star brightens until it is as luminous as a billion suns. It ejects a shell of gas at velocities exceeding $10\,000\,km\,s^{-1}$, and in so doing, transforms itself irreversibly into a gaseous remnant and a tiny neutron star. In the course of this transformation, supernovae play a crucial role in the chemical evolution of a galaxy, because the gas which they eject into the interstellar medium has been enriched in heavy elements by thermonuclear reactions within the star.

4.27: *The 'close binary model' for the type of star system which produces a nova outburst.*

4.26: *The light curve of the dwarf nova Z Chamaeleontis at minimum light, observed by the technique of high-speed photometry developed at the University of Texas. The light curve shows intense flickering, a hump due to the light from the 'hot spot' and a trough due to the eclipse of the hot spot.*

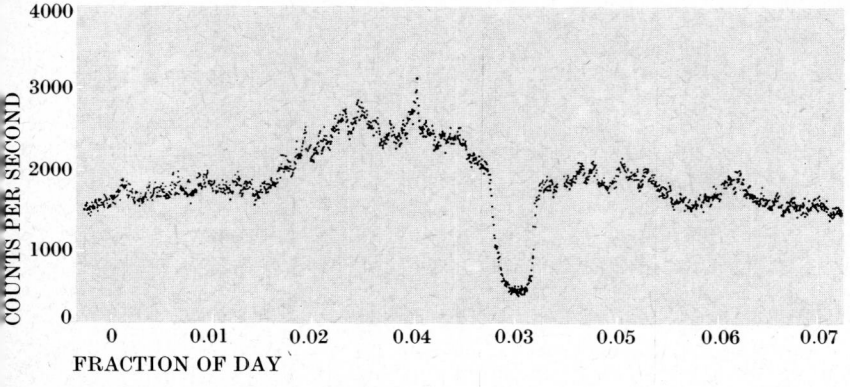

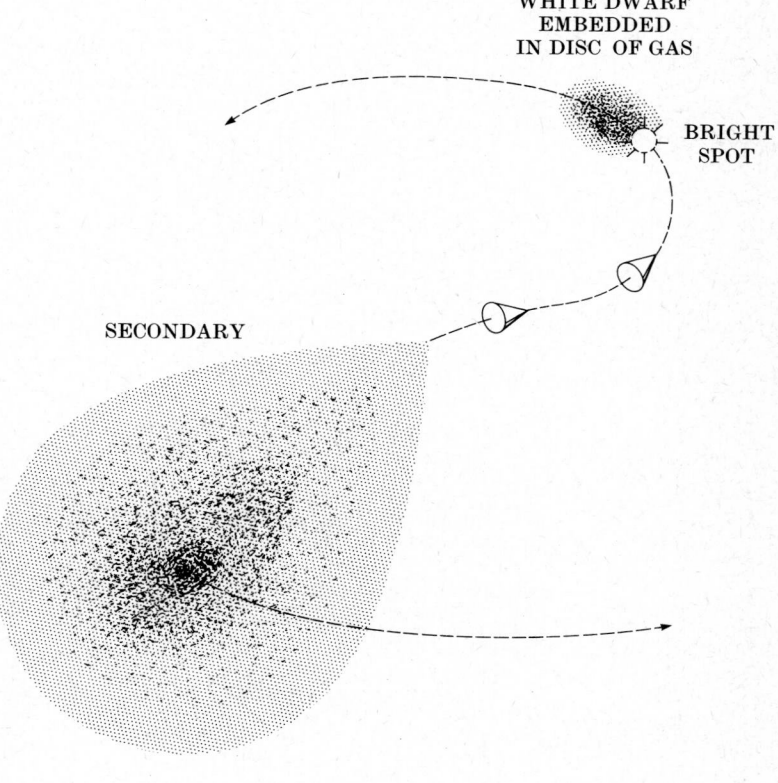

WHITE DWARF
EMBEDDED
IN DISC OF GAS

BRIGHT
SPOT

SECONDARY

Supernovae may perhaps occur as often as once a decade in our own Galaxy, but they are rarely detected, because they usually inhabit the regions of our Galaxy that are thick with obscuring dust. Supernovae were recorded in 1572 (by Tycho Brahe) and 1604 (by Johannes Kepler), but none has been recorded since. Astronomers therefore search for supernovae in other galaxies (figure 4.28). Several observatories carry out systematic surveys of a few hundred nearby galaxies, using wide-field *Schmidt telescopes*, and together they discover 10–20 supernovae each year. Most of these are fainter than magnitude ten, but even these can be studied in detail, using sensitive photoelectric photometers, spectrum scanners and image-tube spectrographs.

There are at least two, and possibly five different types of supernova. Type I occurs among old, low-mass stars of Population II; type II occurs among young, massive stars of Population I. (Again, note the problems of classification and terminology!) The light curve of a typical type-I supernova is shown in figure 4.29; note the characteristic hump at maximum, and the exactly linear decline in magnitude. The light curve of a type-II supernova is rather similar, except that the decline portion is more convex. Type-I supernovae attain an absolute magnitude of about -18.6 at maximum; type-II supernovae are about a magnitude fainter. Both types are useful for distance determination, because they can be seen in very distant galaxies.

The spectra of supernovae consist of very broad absorption and emission lines. In this respect, type-II supernovae are the better understood. Their spectra are similar to those of ordinary novae, but with expansion velocities of thousands rather than hundreds of $km\,s^{-1}$. From the expansion velocity and the strength of the lines, we can calculate the mass of material ejected by the supernova. We can check our calculation by measuring the mass of a supernova remnant such as the Crab Nebula. In each case, we arrive at a figure of between one and ten solar masses. Clearly, a star that ejects so much material will be profoundly changed.

The nuclear processes which precede a supernova eruption are described elsewhere, we only summarize them here. In the core of a highly-evolved star, there are several processes which can absorb energy, and therefore trigger a GRAVITATIONAL COLLAPSE; these processes were understood in the 1950s. The problem was to convert this collapse into the observed expansion of the supernova and its gaseous remnant. Clearly, Nature could effect this conversion, and the consequences for nucleosynthesis were discussed at length by E.M. and G.R.Burbidge, W.A.Fowler and Fred Hoyle in the late 1950s. At that time, astronomers assumed that the supernova eruption would leave no stellar remnant. This assumption was toppled in the late 1960s by the discovery of *pulsars*, and it soon became evident that pulsars must be rapidly-rotating neutron stars: collapsed stars with densities exceeding $10^{18}\,kg\,m^{-3}$. The only known way of producing such stars was in the collapse processes which had been implicated in the production of a supernova.

4.28: *Stages in a supernova explosion in a remote galaxy. At maximum (top) the apparent brightness rivals that of nearby stars in our Galaxy. (Hale Observatories, USA)*

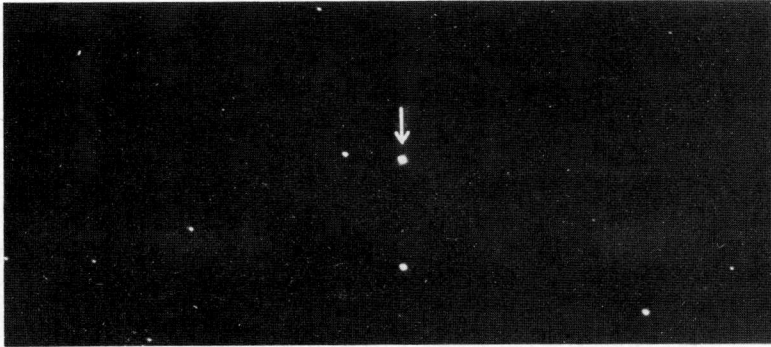

R Coronae Borealis stars

There remains one last class of intrinsic variable, which is like no other. The R CORONAE BOREALIS stars are novae in reverse: suddenly and unpredictably they decrease in brightness by up to ten magnitudes, then slowly they return to normal (figure 4.30). The two brightest members are the prototype (range 5.8 to 14.8 mag.) and RY Sagittarii (range 6.5 to 14.0 mag.).

As early as 1935, astronomers had observed that the atmosphere of R Coronae Borealis was rich in carbon and almost devoid of hydrogen. This suggested that the decreases in brightness might be caused by the occasional formation of solid carbon (soot!) in the cooler parts of the atmosphere. The star, thus enveloped in soot, would gradually disappear until the outward pressure of radiation and matter could blow the soot away. This hypothesis, with only minor modifications, is still accepted today. Soon after the soot begins to form, the absorption spectrum of the surface of the star fades, and is replaced by an emission-line spectrum from the top of the atmosphere. Soon, this spectrum also fades, as its source of energy (the surface of the star) is blocked from view. The light energy which is absorbed by the soot is re-emitted as infrared radiation, which can now be observed directly, using infrared detectors.

R Coronae Borealis stars are supergiant stars with effective surface temperatures similar to those of Cepheid variables. Not surprisingly, then, some R Coronae Borealis stars turn out to be pulsating variables. The pulsational light variations can be observed during the star's quiescent periods at maximum light. R Coronae Borealis itself has a period of 44 days and a small range; RY Sagittarii has a period of 38.6 days and a larger range.

The unusual chemical composition of these stars may arise in two possible ways: either they are the cores of stars that have previously ejected their outer, hydrogen-rich layers, or they are stars in which carbon, synthesized in the core, has been mixed outward to the surface by convection. In either case, the soot which is ejected by these stars may be an important source of replenishment of the interstellar dust.

The R Coronae Borealis stars aptly summarize the interest and importance of intrinsic variable stars. They are complex, a bit mysterious and never predictably the same from one day to the next. Most important, they represent an interesting and significant phase in the evolution of a star.

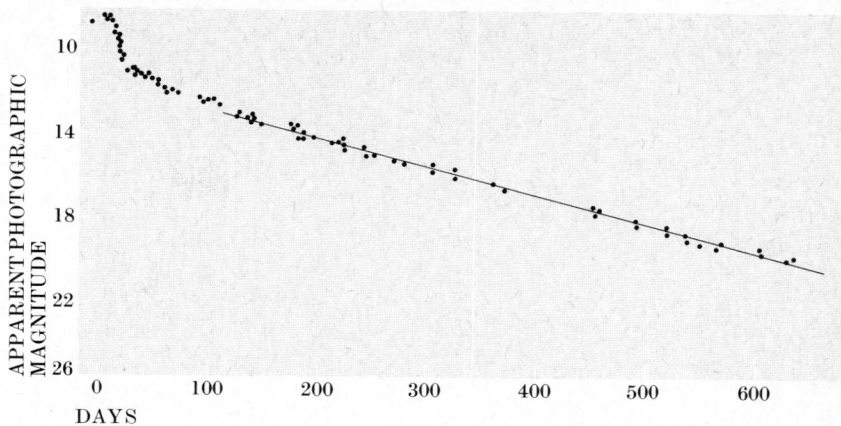

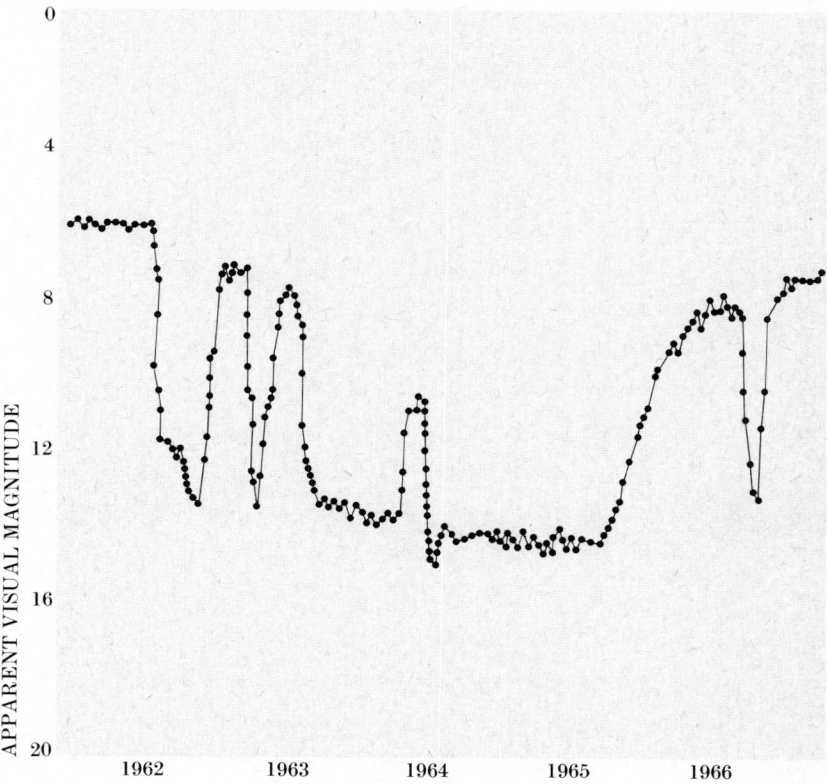

4.29: *The light curve of the supernova in the galaxy IC 4182.*

4.30: *The light curve of R Coronae Borealis during the especially deep prolonged minimum during the mid-1960s.*

5. Binary stars

Types of binary and multiple stars

Our Sun is a single star with a system of planets and other cold bodies as travelling companions. If we look around the sky we notice that some stars appear to be quite close to each other. For example, in the constellation Ursa Majoris the star ζ Ursae Majoris (Mizar) has a fainter star 80 Ursae Majoris (Alcor) near to it (figure 5.1). Note, however, that not all stars that appear to us as double (that is, which lie close to each other in the sky) are physically close to each other. Many just appear so because our line of sight to a more distant star just happens to pass very close to a nearby one. In fact, if we could watch such stars, known as optical doubles, for long enough we would see them drift apart.

Most stars in our Galaxy are not solitary, but are bound by the force of gravity to one, and sometimes many, companions. About a half of all star systems are BINARY or MULTIPLE SYSTEMS. In fact if you look at Mizar through a moderate-sized telescope you will find that it consists of two stars. These two stars are physically close to each other and if you were able to watch them for long enough (for much more than a thousand years) you would see them orbiting around one another in the same way that the Earth orbits around the Sun. A system of this type is known as a VISUAL BINARY (figure 5.2). If one star in such a system is too faint to be seen directly, we can sometimes infer its presence through the disturbances caused to the motion of the visible star. Stars with such inferred invisible companions are sometimes known as ASTROMETRIC BINARIES. The

5.1: *Seen from the Earth, both pairs of stars appear to lie equally close on the sky. The binary pair remain close, whereas the optical double slowly drifts apart.*

TRUE BINARY

DOUBLE STAR

EARTH

EARTH

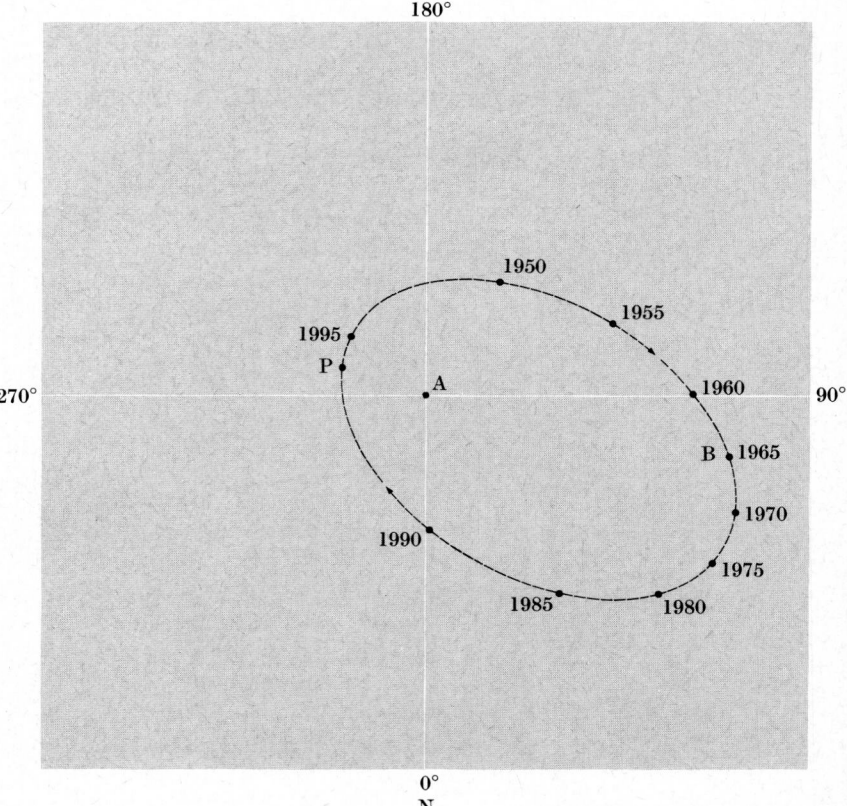

existence of the companion to Sirius (Sirius B) was inferred in this way long before techniques improved to the extent that it could be detected (figure 5.3). Similarly Barnard's star, is known to have a companion: analysis of the orbit indicates that the mass of the companion is not much larger than that of Jupiter (figure 2.4). Our Sun is not the only star to have a planet.

5.2: *The apparent orbit of the faint star Sirius B, relative to the bright star Sirius A.*

5.3: *The paths that Sirius A and B trace out on the sky. Upper right shows the apparent orbits of Sirius A and B, relative to their centre of mass.*

5.4: *This photograph, taken in December 1964, shows Sirius B as the faint image just to the right of the bright Sirius A. The peculiar shape of the image of Sirius A is produced by a hexagonal obscuring diaphragm designed to make Sirius B visible. (Sproul Observatory, USA)*

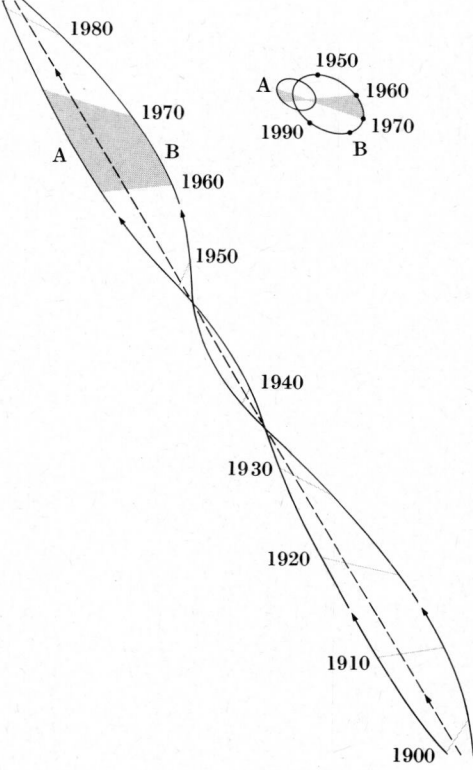

Importance of binary stars

From the spectrum of a single star we can obtain an estimate of its surface temperature and also, from the width of the spectral lines, a crude estimate of the surface gravity. If we know the distance to the star, we can deduce its luminosity from its apparent magnitude and hence, by applying Stefan's Radiation Law, an estimate of its radius. Having found the specific gravity and the radius, we can arrive at a crude estimate of the star's mass.

If the star is in a binary system, we are in a much stronger position and have many more possibilities open to us than in the case of solitary stars. It is possible to deduce from observations of binary stars the masses of individual stars and also their radii. It is, in fact, solely because of the study of binary stars, that astronomers feel that they know the masses and sizes of stars with some confidence. Theoretical studies based on these data, for example stellar evolution, which is of central importance to astrophysics, have reasonably solid foundations.

Most known binary systems appear to us as a single point of light because they are too far away for the two stars to be resolved separately. Such stars fall into two categories. For *spectroscopic binaries*, the binary nature is inferred from periodic shifts of the wavelengths of the spectral lines caused by the *Doppler effect* as the stars swing round each other. For *eclipsing binaries*, the duplicity is inferred from the regular variation of the brightness of the system which is interpreted as the eclipsing of one star by the other in each orbit.

It is sometimes found that one star of a binary system is, in fact, a binary system in its own right and the system as a whole is then called a TRIPLE SYSTEM. For example, the star Milburn 377 (also known as Vyssotsky 2) was originally thought to be just a visual binary consisting of a 10.5-mag M2 dwarf and a 12.5-mag M4 dwarf with a period of about 320 years. However it was found later that the brighter star is itself an astrometric binary and revolves around an unseen companion once every 15.9 years (figure 5.5).

The two components of Mizar are both spectroscopic binaries and there is evidence that the fainter one may be a triple system. Mizar itself may be a quintuple system! Alcor travels along a path parallel to that of Mizar. If Alcor and Mizar form a wide binary system, the system is at least quintuple and possibly sextuple. Multiple systems appear to be stable only when they are formed in a hierarchical structure of binary systems, with each binary pair acting as a single component in an even larger binary system. For this reason we now turn our attention to binary systems. These stars are of considerable importance in astrophysics because it is possible to determine many properties, especially sizes and masses, that cannot be found for single stars. In view of their value to astrophysics we shall first show how the orbits of binary stars are analysed in order to determine the physical properties.

The orbits of binary stars

Consider two stars orbiting around each other in space. Of course, the binary system itself orbits around the centre of our Galaxy, and so in general the paths along which the two stars move are intertwining spirals threading their way among the other stars. For simplicity, suppose that we are travelling through space with the same average speed as the two stars. From our new vantage point, the stars will appear to move continually around each other, with both stars remaining all the time in the same plane. We call this plane the ORBITAL PLANE. This plane in fact moves slowly through space, although for most binary systems it appears to move so slowly (because the stars are so far away) that it may be thought of as fixed. Within the orbital plane there is a point that corresponds to the centre of mass of the binary system. Remember that we are imagining that we are travelling the same course as the binary system. Therefore, from our viewpoint, the centre of mass of the binary system travels an exactly parallel path to our own, and is therefore a fixed point on the orbital plane. The two stars orbit about this point. In general their paths are ellipses with the centre of mass as one focus. At every instant in time, the two stars and the centre of mass all lie in a straight line. The centre of mass is the balance point. If the distances from the centre of mass to the two stars are denoted by r_1 and r_2, and the stars' masses are M_1 and M_2, then $M_1 r_1 = M_2 r_2$. Therefore the two stars trace out on the orbital plane two similar, but differently sized ellipses, with the lighter star tracing the larger ellipse (figure 5.6).

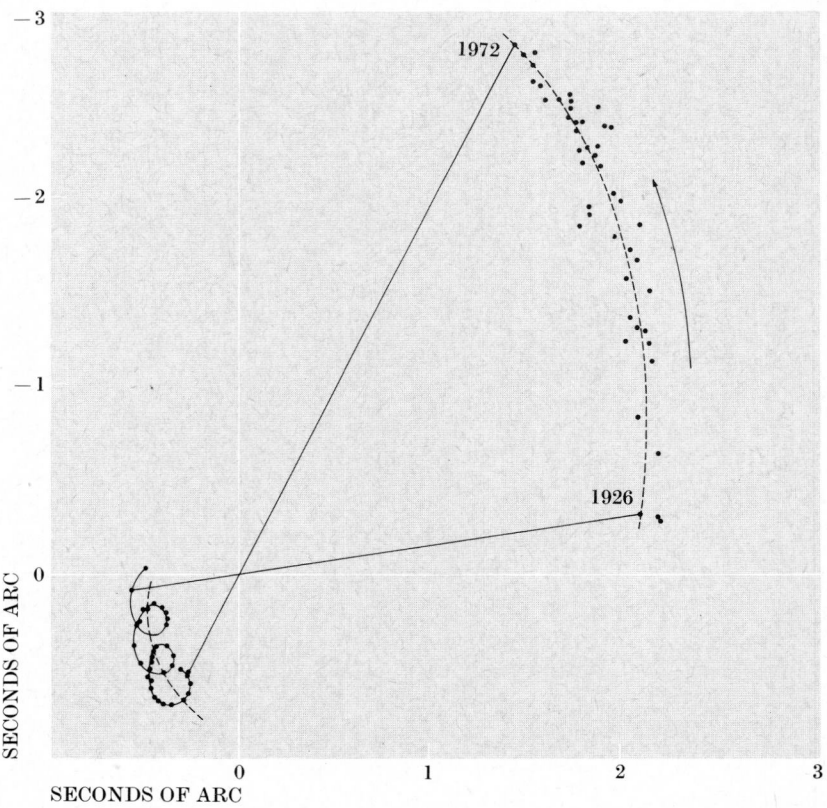

Orbital elements

When we have made observations of a binary system of stars, we wish to be able to deduce a set of numbers that describe completely the orbit of the stars in time and space. This set of parameters is known as the ORBITAL ELEMENTS of the binary system. As we shall see, it is not always possible to obtain a complete set of orbital elements. We often have to satisfy ourselves with merely a sub-set of them. It is these parameters which the observer of a binary system sets out to measure, and they are described in figure 5.7.

5.7: *The orbital plane and the tangent plane to the sky intersect in the line of nodes which passes through the centre of mass focus of the elliptical orbit. The ascending node occurs when the star passes through the plane of the sky in the direction away from the Earth. The other node is the descending node. Orbital elements shown are:*

i – inclination of orbital plane to plane of sky

Ω – position angle of line of nodes measured on the plane of the sky from North through East.

ω – longitude of periastron measured on the orbital plane from the ascending node to periastron.

Other orbital elements are

P – the period of the binary orbit

e – the eccentricity of the orbit

5.5: *The apparent orbital motion of the two visible stars in the triple system Milburn 377.*

5.6: *The orbits of stars in a binary system. The orbits are similar ellipses with a common focus at the centre of mass. Periastron occurs when the stars are closest and apastron when they are furthest apart.*

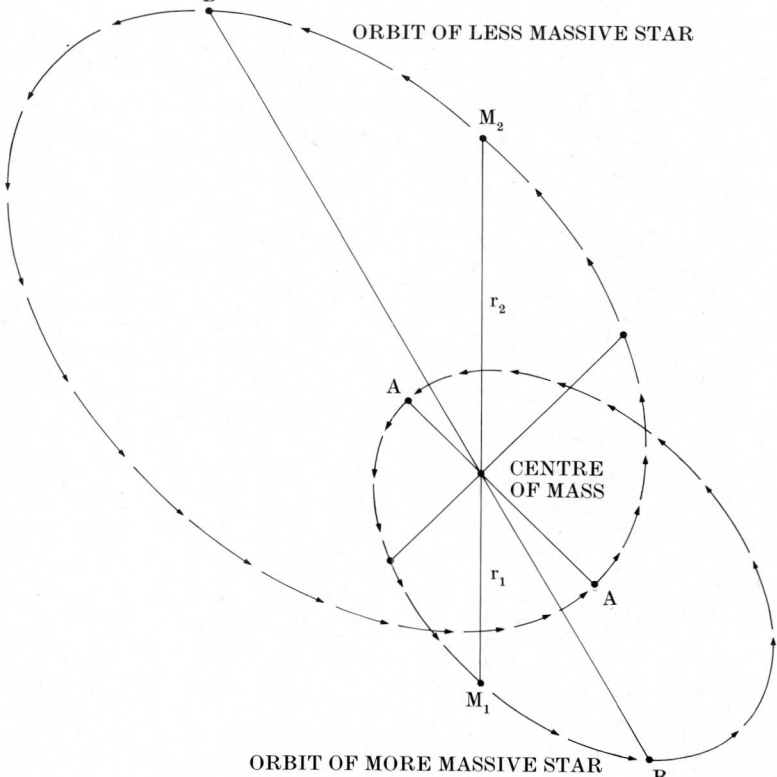

ORBIT OF LESS MASSIVE STAR

B

M_2

r_2

A

CENTRE OF MASS

r_1

A

M_1

B

ORBIT OF MORE MASSIVE STAR

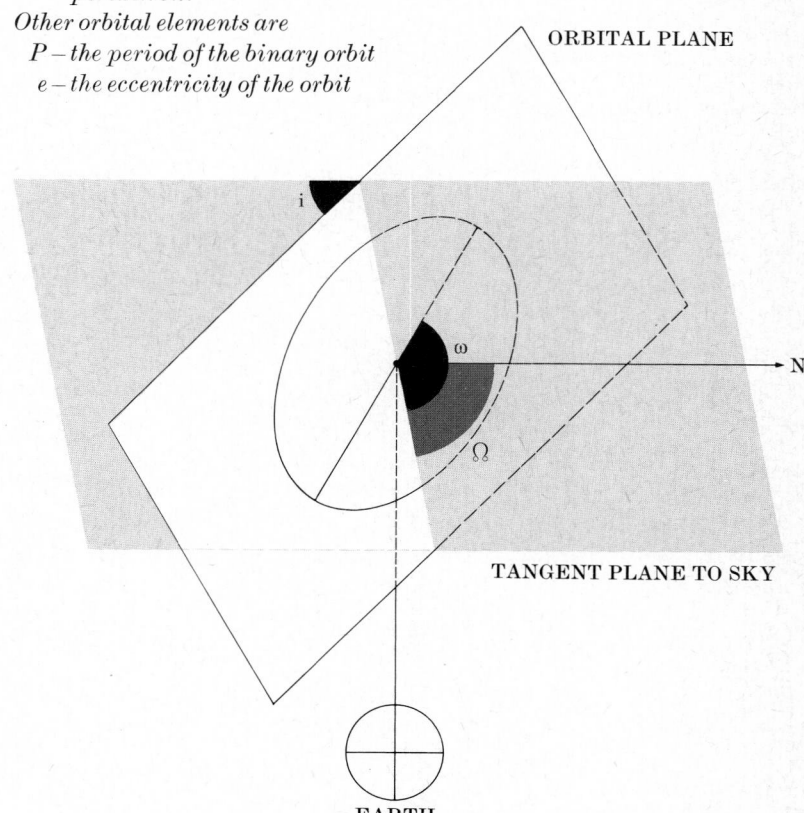

ORBITAL PLANE

i

ω

N

Ω

TANGENT PLANE TO SKY

EARTH

5.8: *The lower part of the diagram shows in black the actual elliptical orbit of a visual binary star and in red the auxiliary circle drawn round the ellipse. The major axis of the ellipse runs through A, the apastron, O, the centre, C, the focus at the centre of gravity and P the periastron. The minor axis is MON and the tangents to the ellipse at M and N are parallel to OC. The upper part of the diagram shows the orbit and auxiliary circle projected onto the sky as seen from the Earth. The apparent orbit is still an ellipse with centre O but the centre of mass C no longer lies at its focus. OC is therefore the projection of the major axis. The points, M and N, or the apparent ellipse at which the tangents are parallel to OC are the ends of the projected minor axes. From these the orbital elements e, i, Ω and w can be determined.*

Visual binaries

If a binary system is close enough to us, we can see each component as a separate point of light, each of which moves round the other in a regular manner. At each point in time we can plot the positions of each star in the sky. In time each star traces out a spiral projected on to the plane of the sky (figure 5.3). If we remove the motion along the spiral from our observations, we find that each star traces out a similar ellipse with apparent eccentricity e*, say. It is possible to find the orbital elements, as shown in figure 5.8. We can also measure the ratio of the angular distances of each star from the centre of mass (r_2/r_1), and this is the MASS RATIO $q = m_1/m_2$. This is as much as we can deduce without additional information: for example, we only know the apparent angular size of the system and do not know the physical size. However, if we have an independent estimate of the distance to the system, for example by *parallax*, we can deduce the physical size. Hence from *Kepler's law* we can deduce the total mass of the system, and knowing q, the mass of each star.

5.9: *The observed orbit of the visual binary α Centauri. Although the orbit is elliptical, the observed centre of mass does not lie at the focus of the ellipse because of projection effects. Ascending node Ω and descending node ℧ are also shown.*

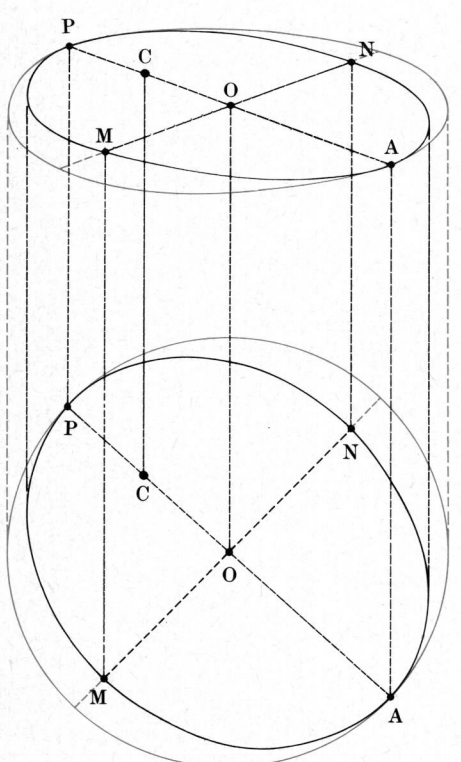

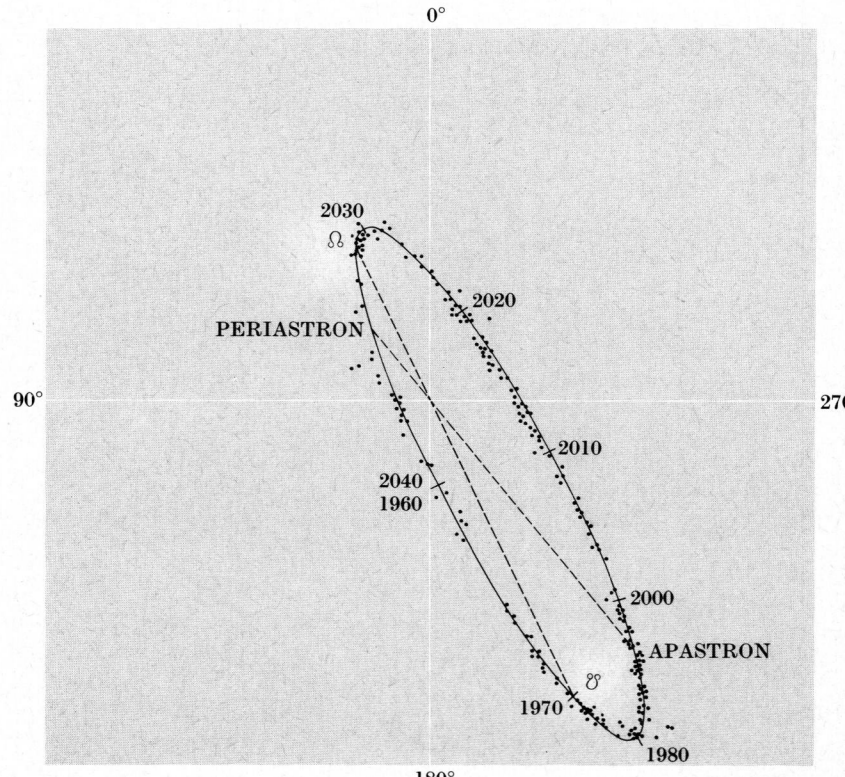

Spectroscopic binaries

Many stars that appear as a single pinpoint of light in the sky, when examined by means of a spectroscope produce a spectrum which appears to be the combination of the spectra from two separate stars. If the relative positions of features on the two spectra remain unaltered, the stars are known as a SPECTRUM BINARY and they constitute a widely-separated binary system; generally no more, and usually less, can be learnt from such a system than can be learnt from the spectra of a pair of single stars. Very often, however, positions of lines in the two separate spectra are seen to move relative to one another in a regular and periodic manner and these stars are known as SPECTROSCOPIC BINARIES (figure 5.10). Of course, a number of spectroscopic binaries are also visual binaries.

5.10: *Spectroscopic binary showing the combined spectra whose lines appear single when the stars are lined up with the Earth and are moving transversely to the line of sight but whose lines double because of the Doppler effect when the stars are at quadrature and are moving radially towards and away from us.*

5.11: *The radial velocity curve of the binary pulsar PSR 1913+16. Radial velocities are measured in units of kilometres per second with positive values indicating motion away from Earth. The orbital period is 0.323 days. The curve differs greatly from a simple sine curve because the orbit has an eccentricity $e = 0.6$.*

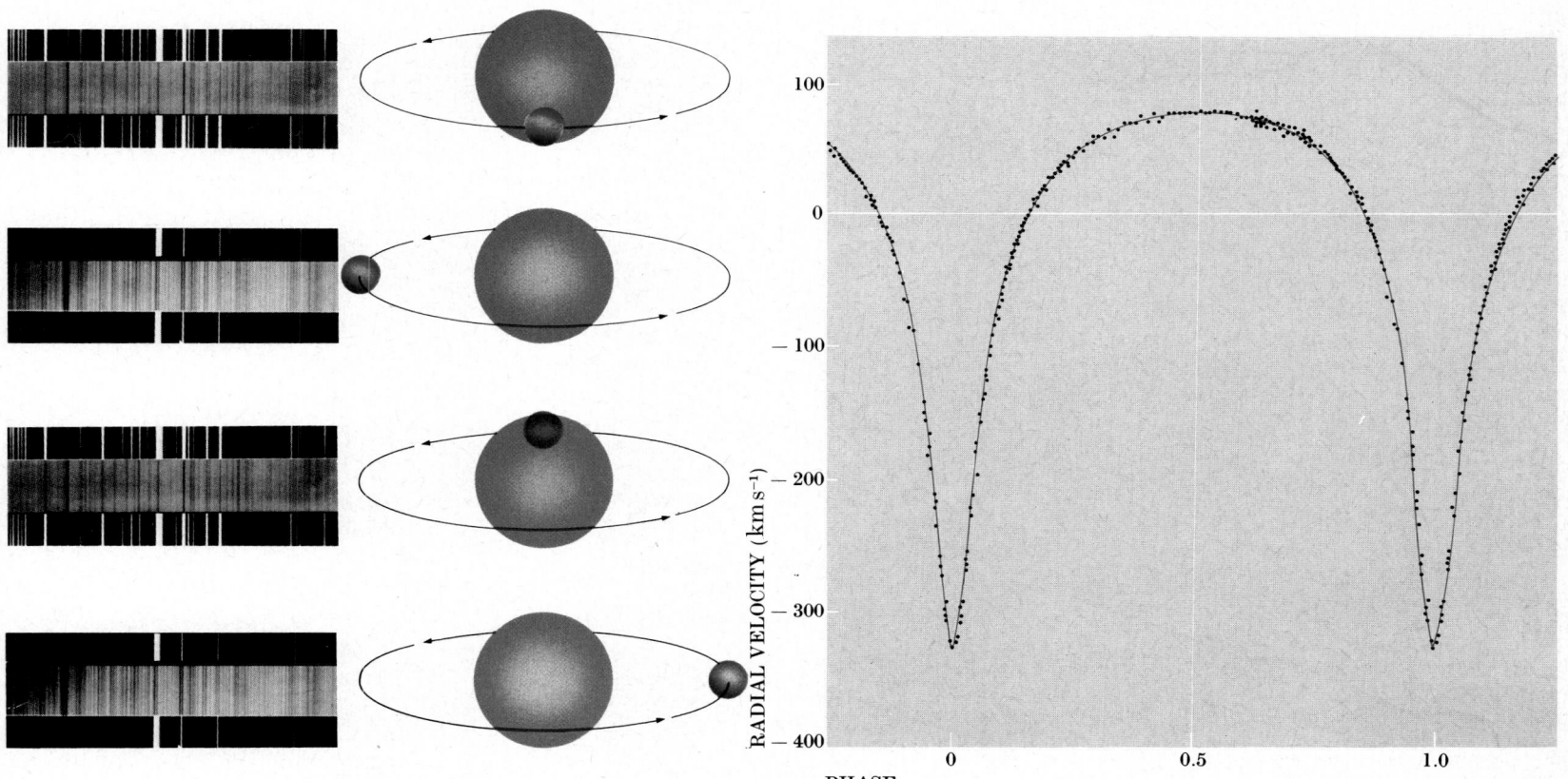

Let us consider each spectrum separately – in some stars all one can see is a single spectrum oscillating to and fro, since its inferred companion is too faint to be seen. At each moment in time the shift of the spectrum with respect to the laboratory frame of reference tells us the relative velocity of the Earth and the star along the line of sight – i.e. the *radial velocity*. It is necessary to make a large number of observations well separated in time. We must allow for the motion of the Earth around the Sun, to deduce the radial velocity of the star with respect to the Sun, as a function of time. Once the binary period has been established, observations are plotted relative to this period, to obtain the radial velocity through the orbit. The period of a spectroscopic binary is usually measured in days. An example of such a graph is shown in figure 5.11. From the velocity curves it is possible to deduce some of the orbital parameters.

The eccentricity e and longitude of periastron ω can be deduced from the shape of the velocity curve. Obviously the longitude of the node is indeterminate since the system could be rotated through an angle about our line of sight without affecting the radial velocities. However, since the orbital motion of the stars is always in the same plane, the actual velocities of the stars around the orbit can only be seen by the spectroscope as projected onto our line of sight. We only measure the radial, and not the actual, orbital velocities. Because of this, spectroscopic measurements alone do not allow us to determine the value of i. The magnitude of the velocity variation tells us, about the size of the system and hence, via *Kepler's Law*, about the mass. When the spectra of both stars are visible we can determine the masses of both stars, each multiplied by the unknown quantity $\sin^3 i$. We can, however, determine the mass ratio uniquely, being simply the inverse of the ratio of the magnitude of the velocity variations of each star. If only one spectrum is visible, the star is termed a single- rather than double-lined spectroscopic binary. In this case, we can only determine a relationship between the individual masses and the inclination angle known as the mass function.

Eclipsing binaries

When the orbital inclination i is sufficiently close to 90°, we can see the two components of a binary system eclipse each other. The graph of the apparent magnitude of the binary system against time is known as the LIGHT CURVE. In general the light curve of an eclipsing binary star displays two dips, or minima (the eclipses), in each orbital period – the deeper dip is called PRIMARY MINIMUM and the shallower one the SECONDARY MINIMUM. What information can we extract about the two stars from a study of the light curve alone? Often this is all the information we have available, although sometimes it is possible to see spectroscopic variability as well. Of course, just as for a spectroscopic binary, the longitude of the node is indeterminable, because we can rotate the picture of the eclipsing system on the sky about an axis along our line of sight and still obtain the same light curve. In addition we cannot find the direction of the orbital motion from the light curve alone. Moreover the shape of the light curve is unchanged if we keep the binary period constant but change the geometry of the whole system (the sizes of the stars and the binary separation) by, for example, a factor two. Consequently we cannot use the light curve to determine the semimajor axis of the orbit, but we can get some idea of the relative sizes of the two stars. In general the light curves are difficult to interpret and so we shall start with a few simple examples before mentioning some of the difficulties and complications that can arise, together with the means of tackling them.

Algol-type light curve

The simplest case to consider is that of two stars that are both spherical, that both appear uniformly bright over their surface (no limb darkening), and that have circular orbits. In this case we can easily distinguish between the two different types of eclipse, partial and total. When i is close enough to 90° for eclipses to occur, but not close enough for total eclipses to occur, each star does not quite manage to obscure the other, even at the minimum of the light curve, and the eclipses are only partial.

To see this, imagine the disc of one star, let us call it star A, passing across the face of the other, star B. The eclipse begins when the disc of A first appears to touch the disc of B and the light curve begins to dip. The light curve continues to decrease until at the minimum, when the maximum fraction of disc B is covered by disc A. Thereafter the light curve increases symmetrically until the two discs again appear to touch. Hence when the eclipse is partial, the shape of the dip in the light curve is that of a decrease, followed by a rounded minimum and a symmetrical increase. We should also note that the eclipse immediately following, when star B eclipses star A, will be exactly similar in shape and that the maximum amount of star B that is eclipsed at one minimum is equal to the maximum amount of star A that is eclipsed at the next (figure 5.12).

When i is nearly 90°, the two eclipses are a total eclipse and a transit. Suppose star A is smaller than star B and imagine the minimum caused by the eclipse of B by star A. The eclipse again begins when the two discs appear to touch externally – this is called FIRST

CONTACT and the light curve begins to dip at this point. A short time later the two discs appear to touch internally – second contact. After second contact star A proceeds to transit across the face of star B until the discs again appear to touch internally at third contact. Because star B is uniformly bright, the amount of light cut out by A as it transits across B is constant and thus the light curve stays constant between second and third contact. The light curve increases between third contact and fourth contact (when the discs appear to touch externally) in a symmetric manner to the transition from first to second contacts. The next eclipse, when star B obscures star A, will clearly be a total eclipse. First, second, third and fourth contacts can be defined similarly and since the orbit is circular each takes place exactly half a period later than their counterpoints in the previous eclipse. Between second and third contacts, star A is totally hidden by star B (total eclipse) and the light curve therefore again remains constant (figure 5.13). As before for partial eclipses, the amount of star B that is obscured by star A is exactly equal to the amount of star A obscured by star B half a period later. The depth of the eclipse in an ALGOL-TYPE SYSTEM is a measure of the surface brightness of the eclipsed star – that is of the temperature of the eclipsed star. The hotter star is obscured at primary minimum. We also note that outside eclipses the light curve should stay constant.

We have seen that for a simple eclipsing system such as that considered here we can expect to obtain information about i from the shape of the eclipses. We can find out, for example, whether they are partial or total eclipses, and can determine information on radii from the length of duration and actual shape of the eclipses.

Ellipsoidal variables

We noted above that when the two binary stars are spherical, the light curve remains constant outside of eclipses. However, when two stars are close enough together, the force of gravity is so high that each component raises huge tides on the other, so that both are pulled out to form elongated egg shapes. When the distortion is slight, each star is the shape of a prolate ellipsoid (stretched out along one axis). As the stars orbit one another, the long axis of each egg-shape turns around to face the other and so the surface area presented by each star to a fixed observer varies through the orbit. In addition, those parts of the star that are furthest from its centre (i.e. the parts at the ends of the egg) do not shine as brightly as the rest. Even when the stars do not eclipse each other, their apparent brightness depends on the direction from which they are viewed and so varies with the orbital period P. Non-eclipsing systems that just fail to be eclipsing but show periodic light variations because of their distortion are called ELLIPSOIDAL VARIABLES.

Beta-Lyrae-type light curve

When ellipsoidal variables eclipse, they produce a light curve that is typified by the star system β Lyrae. Because the stars are distorted, the light curve away from an eclipse is not flat, but rather shows a smooth variation. Moreover, in general, the surface of a star is not uniformly bright, because of limb darkening, so that during an eclipse the amount of light from the eclipsed star that is blocked out varies through the eclipse and the eclipse is therefore not flat-bottomed. The distortion of the stars and gravity darkening exacerbates this effect. The light curve of the eclipsing system is never flat but shows a smooth variation throughout the cycle (figure 5.15). If the distortion and limb darkening are not too large, it is possible to make allowance for them. When allowance has been made, by a process that is called rectification of the light curve, the light curve should look much more like an Algol type; the analysis of the light curve can then proceed as before. In the star β Lyrae itself, the stars are so close and one of the stars is so distorted by the companion, that the outer layers are more attracted to the companion than to itself, and it spills matter down on to the companion's surface. Such a star is called a SEMI-DETACHED BINARY SYSTEM.

W-Ursae-Majoris-type light curve

This group of stars, of which the prototype is W Ursae Majoris, are binary stars that are so close together that they are in contact. The binary system consists of two stellar cores, orbiting around one another, surrounded by a common envelope. Again, the light curve varies smoothly around the cycle often varying from cycle to cycle. The two minima are almost exactly equal, even though the two stellar cores may have different masses and luminosities.

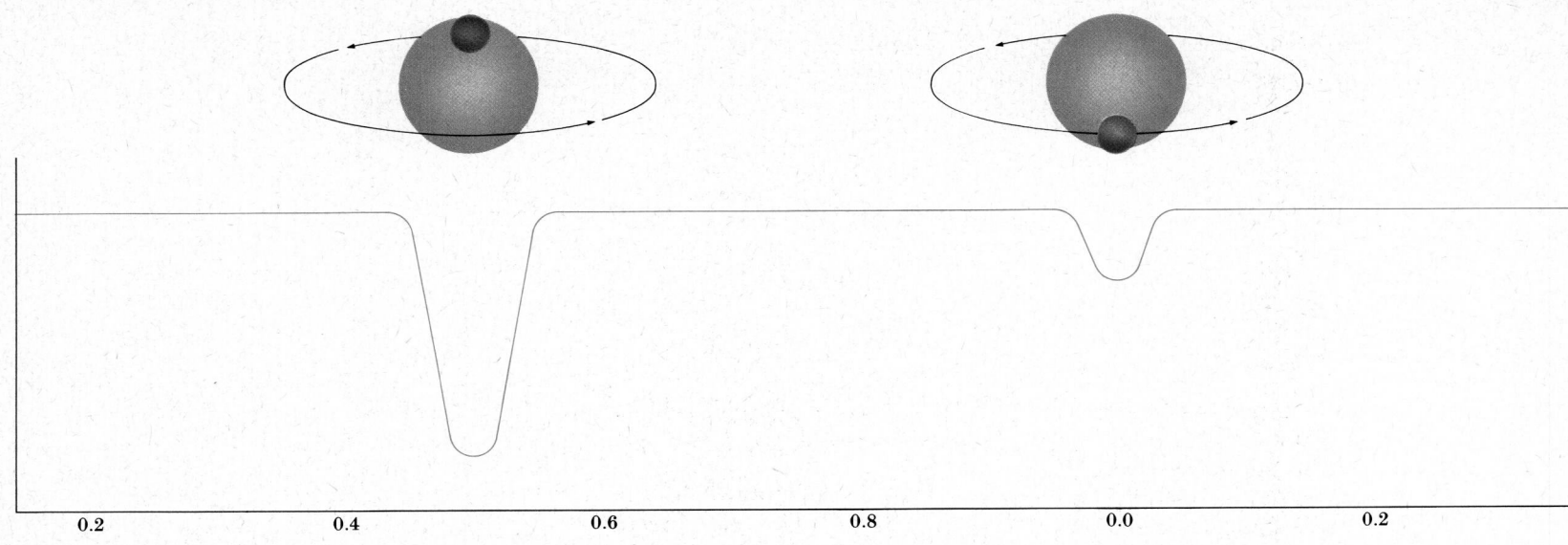

0.2   0.4   0.6   0.8   0.0   0.2

5.12: *Algol-type light curve : partial eclipses.
The apparent brightness of the binary system
is measured as a function of time measured in
orbital periods.*

5.13: *Algol-type light curve : total eclipse and
transit. The times of first (t_1), second (t_2),
third (t_3) and fourth (t_4) contact are shown.*

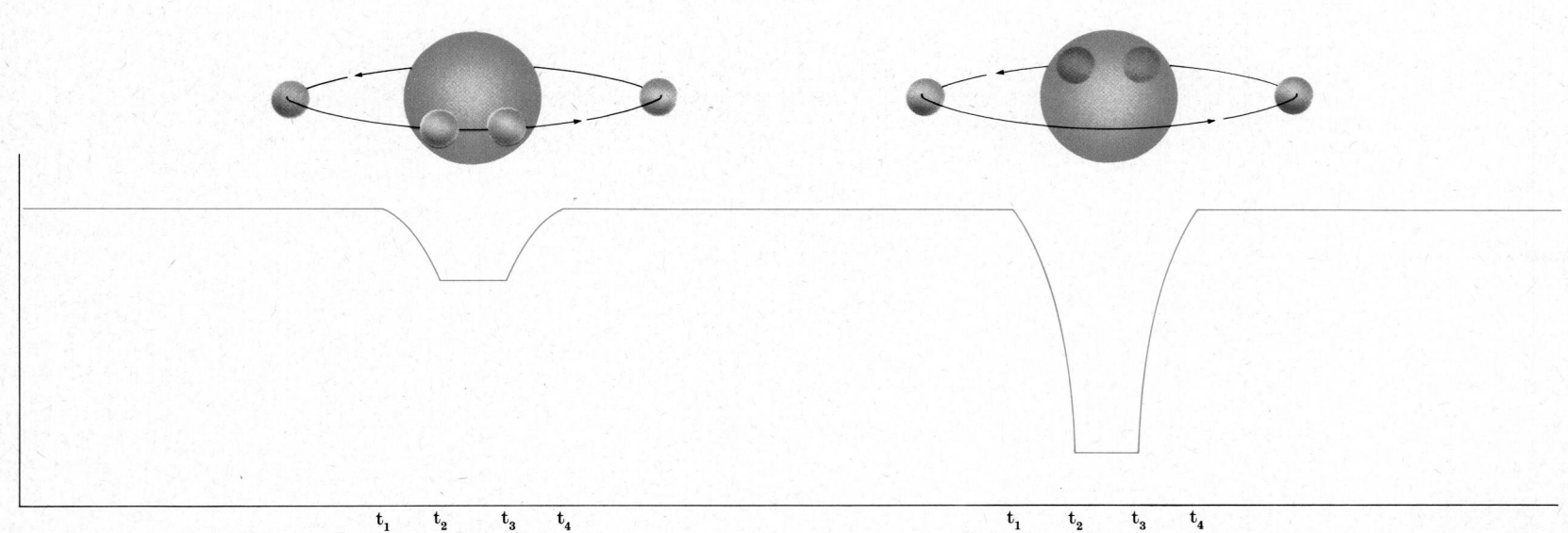

t_1 t_2 t_3 t_4 t_1 t_2 t_3 t_4

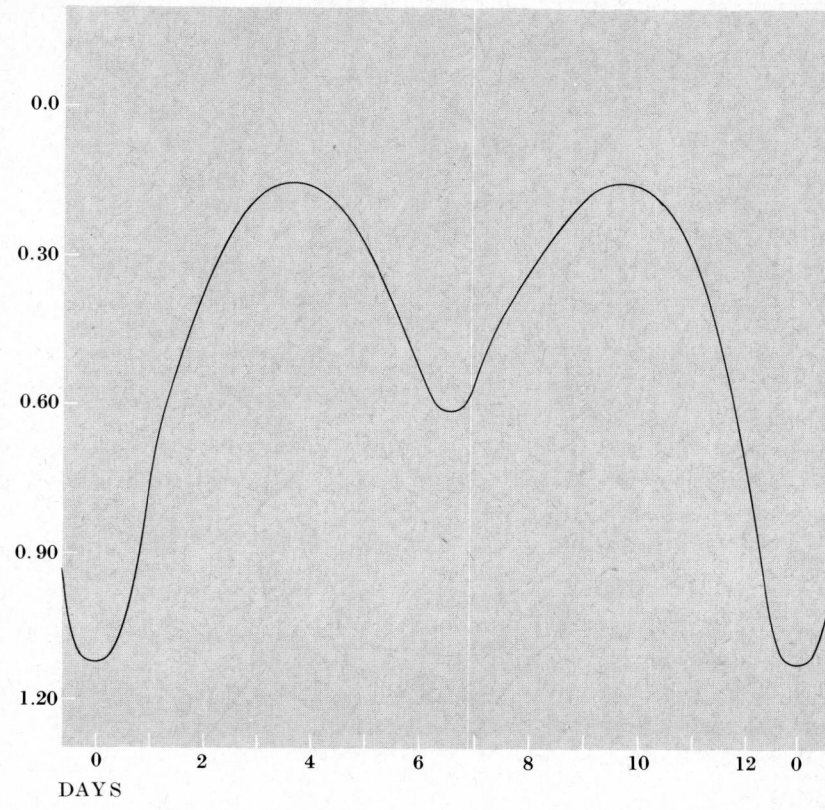

5.14: *Light curve of an ellipsoidal variable. The star appears brighter when more of its surface is visible.*

5.15: *Light curve of β-Lyrae.*

Light curve synthesis

We have seen that the light curve of an eclipsing (or of a nearly eclipsing) binary system can be complex and difficult to interpret. The most important effects that must be taken into account are the following:

DISTORTION. A single star, like the Sun, is essentially spherical. When two stars are close together, however, mutual gravitational forces distort each star. The problem of what shape such stars are has not been solved, but it is possible to get a good idea of the answer by approximate methods. If both stars are rotating at the same speed as the system as a whole, and if each star may be approximated by taking all its mass to be concentrated at its centre while the rest of it consists of a massless fluid, the stars take up the shape defined by *Roche potentials*.

LIMB DARKENING. A stellar atmosphere appears to be of varying brightness when viewed from different angles. At the edge of a star we are viewing the atmosphere obliquely, while at the centre we look straight down into it. The edges of a star appear less bright than its centre.

GRAVITY DARKENING. When a star is distorted, those parts of the atmosphere that are furthest from the centre of the star are in general cooler. The effective temperature varies over the surface of a distorted star and allowance must be made not only for the relative brightness of various parts of the star, but also for the filter through which observations are being made.

REFLECTION EFFECT. When two stars are close enough, each of them can subtend an appreciable angle to the other. Each can intercept a significant fraction of the light emitted by the other. The result is that those parts of the stars in close proximity to each other are hotter than might be expected.

A computer can be used to take all these effects into account, to calculate what each star looks like from various phases of the orbit, and to determine how much of one star is obscured by the other at each moment in time. In effect, if the computer is given the size (relative to the orbital separation) and luminosity of each star, it can compute a synthetic light curve for an eclipsing system. The synthetic curve can then be compared to the real one. If there are differences between the two, some of the initial parameters must be changed. By trial and error and a judicious choice of the parameters of the synthetic system at each stage, it is possible to produce a good imitation of the real light curve and hence a good estimate of the actual orbital elements.

5.16: *The radius of a single star like the sun plotted as a function of time. For about the first 10^{10} years hydrogen burning occurs in the centre and the radius slowly increases. Thereafter the star grows to become a red giant and helium burning occurs. Eventually the outer envelope of the star is dispersed (probably as a planetary nebula) leaving a white dwarf as remnant. If a close binary companion is present, interaction between the two stars becomes more likely as each single star evolves.*

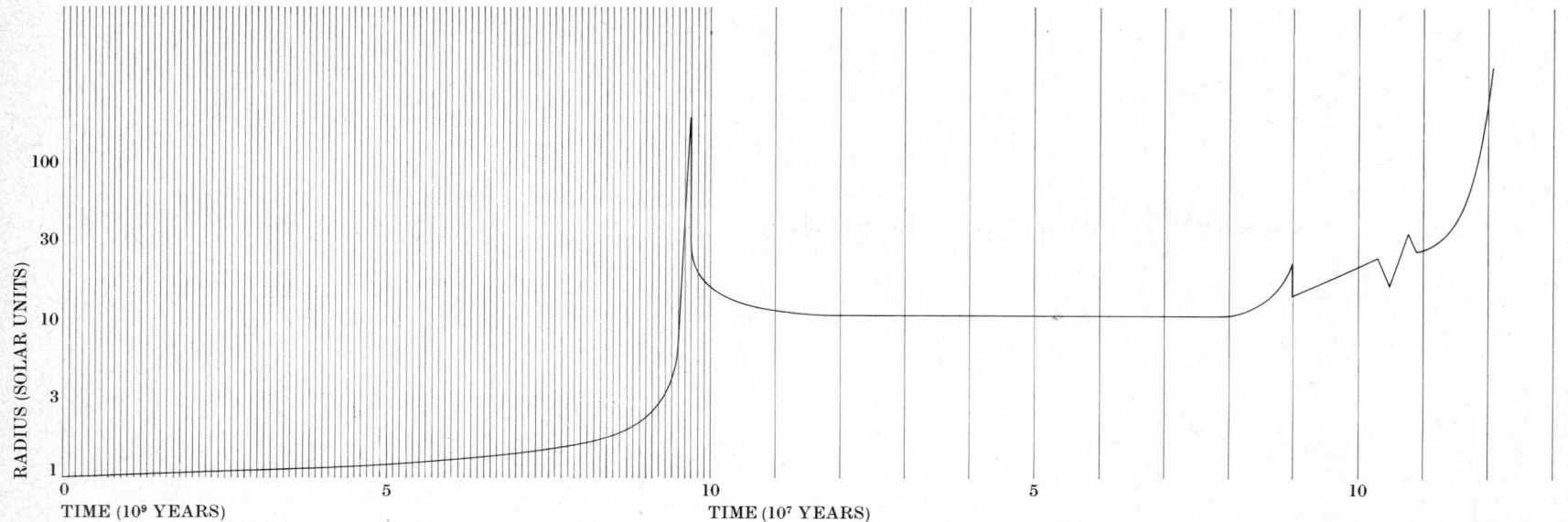

Close binary systems

As a star evolves and burns its nuclear fuel its radius slowly increases (figure 5.16). If, therefore, the star is in a binary system it is possible for it, during the course of evolution, to swell up and interact with and possibly even to engulf a companion star. If the two stars are near enough together for this possibility to occur we call them a CLOSE BINARY SYSTEM. When we consider the evolution of a single star we can assume, for the most part, that the mass of the star is a constant. We see immediately that the evolution of stars in close binary systems is fraught with additional complications, since it is possible for matter to be transferred from one star to another. Before proceeding further we consider more precisely the manner in which the two stars interact.

A single star is spherical; in other words, the equipotential surfaces (that is, surfaces over which the gravitational field is constant) around a point mass are spheres. To see this more clearly, imagine that space can be represented by a stretched rubber sheet (we suppress the third dimension for the moment). A point mass stretches the sheet as shown in figure 5.17 to form a POTENTIAL WELL. We may imagine a star as being a point mass surrounded by a massless fluid. Then however much fluid is put into the potential well, the surface of the fluid is always a circle. If we could imagine the same process in three dimensions with the 'sheet' being stretched in the fourth dimension, the surface would be a sphere. Figure 5.17 shows the contours of the well, known as the EQUIPOTENTIAL SURFACES.

5.17: *The potential well of an isolated gravitating mass point (a single star) in which the third space dimension has been suppressed. The star is spherically symmetric and the contour lines (equipotentials) are circles in two dimensions (or spheres in three dimensions).*

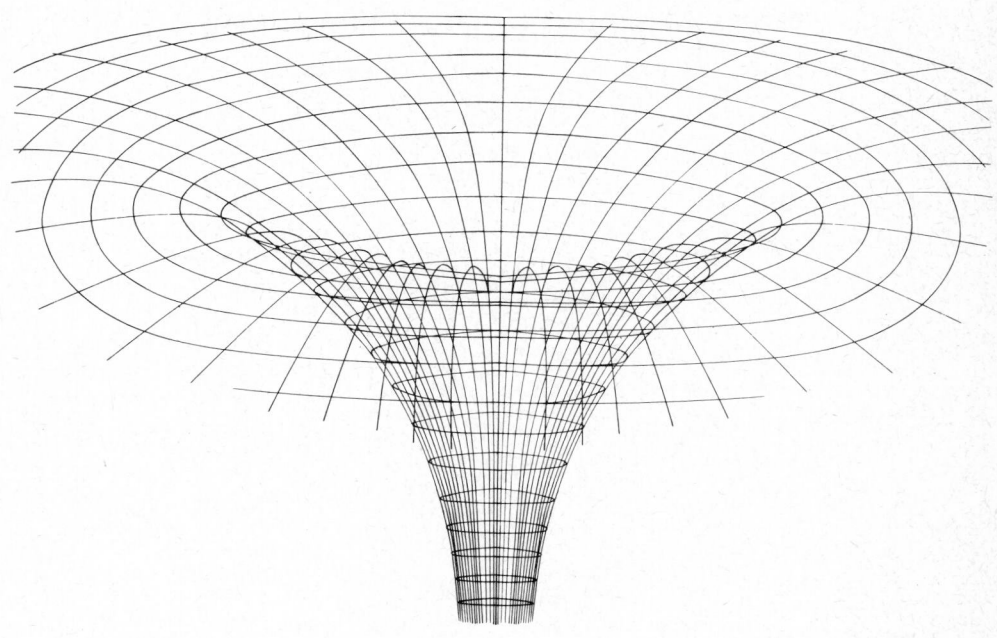

When two stars are close to each other it is clear that the equipotential surfaces cannot be spheres. The gravitational potential well of each star interferes with that of the other. The shapes of the equipotential surfaces in this case were first calculated by Roche and they are therefore known as the ROCHE POTENTIALS. An example is shown in figure 5.18. We see that close to each mass point the surfaces are almost spherical, and that as we start to fill the wells with our massless fluid the stars are initially almost spheres. Such a system is called a DETACHED BINARY SYSTEM. If the stars eclipse they give rise to the Algol-type light curve described above.

If we continue to fill one of the wells we find that the surfaces become less spherical and the star more distorted. Eventually the star cannot get any larger; it starts spilling matter on to its companion at the INNER LAGRANGIAN POINT, marked L_1 in figure 5.18. If such a distorted star is eclipsed it gives rise to the β-Lyrae-type light curve. We call this type a semi-detached binary system; the star which is losing mass is said to fill its ROCHE LOBE. The material tipped off the surface of the star starts to fall towards the companion, but, because the system is rotating, it is deflected by Coriolis force. The path it follows is shown in figure 5.19. This gas stream from the larger star may either strike the companion star directly, or orbit the star until it strikes itself. In the latter case it interacts with itself to form a ring or a disc around the companion star. These circumstellar rings are observed in many systems. In the *dwarf novae* it is possible to see a luminous patch called the hot spot, where the incoming gas stream crashes into the disc (figure 5.19). In certain binary systems the disc can emit intense X-ray radiation.

If we continue to fill both of the potential wells, we find eventually that the stars are immersed in a common envelope of gas. We term this type of binary a CONTACT BINARY, of which the prototype is W Ursae Majoris. If the filling process continues we see that the system must spill matter eventually, through the outer Lagrangian point L_2 (figure 5.18).

5.18: *The equipotential contours of two interacting mass points (a binary star). The inner Lagrangian point L_1 lies at the base of a valley connecting the two stars. The closed contour line through this point defines two Roche lobes. A similar valley at L_2 implies that a contact binary star in which all the material corotates with the binary system cannot exceed the closed contour through L_2.*

5.19: *Mass flow in a semi-detached binary system in which the accreting is so small that the stream of transferred material forms a ring or disc around it. The Roche lobe of the accreting star is also shown.*

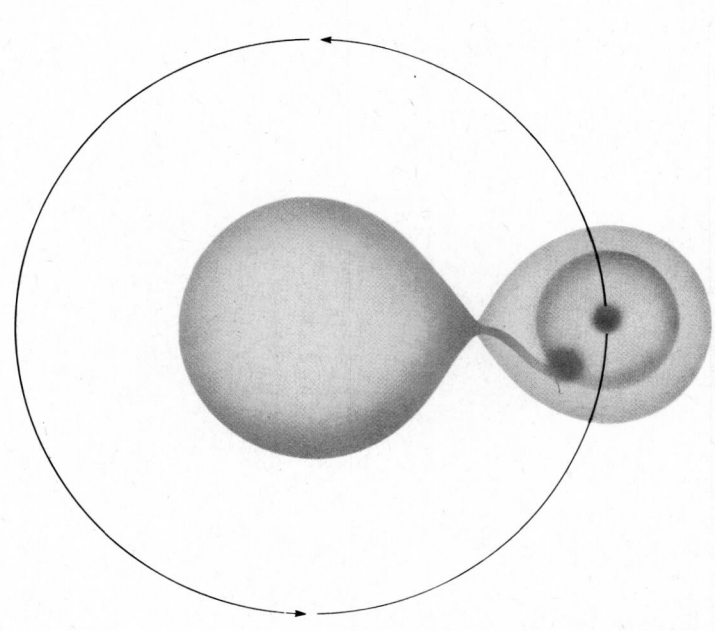

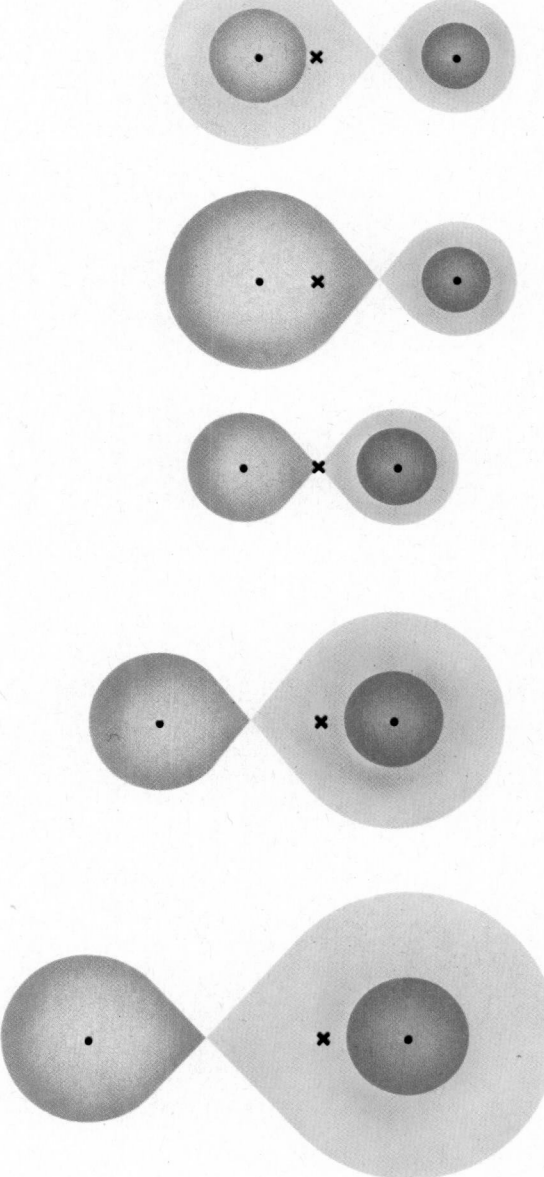

Observations of interacting binary systems

When mass transfer is taking place from one star to the other in a binary system, there is a considerable amount of gas flowing in the Roche lobe of the star that is receiving the mass. The splash as the gas stream strikes the star is probably sufficient to produce a flow of gas around the whole system as well. The gas streams can have unfortunate effects when we attempt to derive the orbital elements of the system. The gas stream can, for example, produce confusing spectral lines, whose Doppler shifts are unrelated to the orbital motion. Worse still, these lines may just blend in with the stellar spectral lines and shift them systematically. The main effect of this is to make the orbit look eccentric, whereas it may in fact be perfectly circular! In addition stellar light reflected from the gas or light generated by friction in the gas flow itself can interfere with the eclipse light curve of the binary star and induce spurious results. Even greater confusion will arise if the gas streams also give rise to additional eclipses.

We now have a confession to make: Algol is a semi-detached binary system. We should perhaps further confess that it is in fact a triple system with the two eclipsing stars, of orbital period 2.8 days, orbiting around a third body in a period of 1.8 years. The more massive star in the system, which is also the brighter star and the one eclipsed at primary minimum, lies well inside its Roche lobe, and is, therefore, almost spherical. Since this star contributes most of the light in the system, the light curve outside eclipse is almost flat even though the fainter companion is highly distorted. Therefore, strictly, to produce an Algol-type light curve it is only necessary for the brighter star to be undistorted. The fainter companion is less massive and fills its Roche lobe. The effect of the resulting gas flow is not very marked.

On the other hand, in the binary system β Lyrae, the brighter star is the less massive of the two and also overfills its Roche lobe. This star contributes most of the light in the system, and because it is so

5.20: *Evolution of a close binary system in the initial stages. The initial system is detached with the more massive star on the left. The Roche lobes are also shown. As this star evolves it expands to fill its Roche lobe and transfers mass to its companion which eventually becomes the more massive star. The centre of each star is shown as well as the centre of mass of the binary system. As mass is transferred, the more massive star is the one which is closer to the centre of mass of the system. The last configuration shown resembles the semi-detached star Algol.*

distorted gives rise to the characteristic β-Lyrae-type light curve. The effects of the gas streams in β Lyrae are quite considerable and caused much confusion for many years. It now seems clear that there is a disc of gas flowing around the fainter star, which is inside its Roche lobe, as well as streams from the brighter star to the disc through the inner Lagrangian point and from the disc back to the brighter star.

Perhaps the most spectacular example of gas flow in a binary system is seen in the dwarf novae. These are very close binary systems with orbital periods of a few hours; the prototype of them is U Geminorum. This star system consists of a main-sequence star filling its Roche lobe and transferring mass to a heavier, but more compact, white dwarf companion. The gas flow does not strike the white dwarf directly but, rather, forms a disc around it. The inner parts of the disc orbit the white dwarf more rapidly than the outer parts. (This is similar to orbits in the Solar System, where just the inner planets have shorter years than the outer ones). The disc in a dwarf nova is therefore rotating differentially. Friction in the disc between the layers rotating at different speeds causes the whole disc to light up. Often the disc itself is brighter than the central white dwarf. In addition a lot of energy is released where the mass stream crashes into the outer part of the disc, producing a highly luminous hot spot. To an optical astronomer, this hot spot can be the brightest object in the system. That is, in some dwarf novae, more light comes from the hot spot than from either of the two stars! As you may imagine, an attempt to analyse the eclipse light curve of such a system by the classical methods described above can be somewhat frustrating.

An exception

Of course, not all eclipsing binaries can be analysed in the way we have described above; often a certain amount of guess-work has to be employed. A case of particular interest is the star ζ Aurigae. This is an eclipsing binary system consisting of a small, blue, bright B star with radius 5 solar radii and a large, red, K giant with radius 245 solar radii. Eclipses occur every 972 days and last for about 35 days. The B star is much smaller than its companion and is the brighter star in the system. Therefore we can analyse the eclipses as being due to a point source of light (the B star) disappearing behind a large opaque disc (the K giant). If the disc had a sharp edge we would expect the onset of the eclipse to be almost instantaneous.

The most likely explanation for these phenomena is that the outer layers of the giant star's atmosphere are so diffuse that even after the onset of the eclipse we see the bright star gradually disappearing behind denser and denser layers of the giant's atmosphere. The eclipse starts earlier (and ends later) when viewed in ultraviolet, rather than optical, light because ultraviolet photons are more easily absorbed in the atmosphere of the giant star than optical ones. In fact it is possible to use the blue star as a probe to shine through the various outer layers of the giant star and to give us information on its atmospheric structure.

The evolution of binary stars

It is reasonable to assume that the two stars in a binary system were formed at the same time. The chance of a collision between two single stars in the Galaxy is very small; the chance of the capture of one by another of a different age to form a binary system smaller still. It is, therefore, usual to assume that the two stars formed simultaneously as a binary system and that they began burning their nuclear fuel at the same instant. A more massive star burns its nuclear fuel at a much faster rate than a less massive one and its radius therefore expands at a faster rate as well (figure 5.20). We therefore expect the more massive star to be the first one to fill its Roche lobe and to start transferring mass on to its less massive companion. This initial stage of mass transfer is separated into three types which depend on how far the more massive star has evolved before it has expanded to fill its Roche lobe and mass transfer begins.

If mass transfer begins while the star is still burning hydrogen in its core, the expanding star transfers most of its mass to its companion in a relatively short-lived but possibly spectacular burst of mass flow. By short-lived, we here mean about ten thousand years, that is, short compared to the total lifetime of the binary system. The star that was originally less massive is now the more massive one and it becomes a bright main-sequence star with luminosity corresponding to its new mass. The star filling its Roche lobe is now the less massive and continues to burn nuclear fuel and expand slowly, trickling matter on to its companion. What happens next depends on the parameters of the binary system. There are essentially two possibilities:

Either the (now) less-massive star runs out of hydrogen in its core and begins a phase described below.

Or the rejuvenated, and now more-massive, star burns its nuclear fuel rapidly and expands to fill its Roche lobe as well. If this latter possibility takes place the star becomes a contact binary system and its future evolution is not well understood.

With this outline of mass transfer we now consider further the Algol system. Algol itself, and a number of similar binary systems, consists of a small bright blue star well inside its Roche lobe and a less massive, but larger, red star that fills its Roche lobe and is losing mass from its surface. Before the process of mass transfer had been studied, astronomers were puzzled by this behaviour, since it seemed that the less massive star had evolved and expanded to fill its Roche lobe more rapidly than its more massive companion. This seemed flatly to contradict the theories of stellar evolution. The reader may have noticed that the resolution of the paradox is already at hand. The initial burst of mass transfer takes place very rapidly and therefore the probability of our seeing it is correspondingly small. It may be, however, that β-Lyrae-type systems are examples of this. After this transfer, the now less massive but evolved star continues to trickle matter on to its now more massive, but unevolved, companion for a considerable length of time. It is this process we are witnessing in Algol-type systems. It is these binaries that give us some confidence that our ideas on mass transfer are at least qualitatively correct.

Now we consider what happens when the hydrogen fuel is exhausted in the core of an evolving star. The core collapses until it has reached a temperature and density at which helium can be burnt. As the core contracts, the outer envelope of the star expands. If the star fills its Roche lobe during this phase of expansion, another kind of mass transfer begins. This case is relatively easier to understand because once the star has formed a dense helium-burning core (and therefore becomes a red giant), this core is fairly oblivious of how much material is in the diffuse envelope surrounding it. Therefore as much of this envelope is lost as is necessary to bring the star completely within the Roche lobe (figure 5.20). If the helium core is less than about four solar masses it is able, eventually, to become a white dwarf once nuclear burning has ceased. The binary system then consists of a massive bright main-sequence star (which was originally the less massive but is now rejuvenated by acquiring matter from its companion) and a less massive white dwarf. We note that Sirius is just such a system – Sirius A is a 2.25 solar mass main-sequence star and Sirius B is a white dwarf of about one solar mass. If the helium core is more than about four solar masses it probably cannot shed enough mass to become a white dwarf and may well eventually collapse to form a neutron star or a black hole.

When a star, now a red giant, has exhausted its helium fuel, its core collapses until carbon burning can start. If mass transfer begins during the corresponding expansion of the stellar envelope, when the outer layers are now diffuse, very little energy is required to drive the mass transfer and the flow takes place very rapidly. The subsequent history of such systems is uncertain. It is probably similar in many respects to that described in the previous paragraph.

Wolf-Rayet stars and X-ray binaries

Many Wolf-Rayet stars are found in close binary systems that consist of a massive, luminous, main-sequence O star and a less massive, smaller, yet even more luminous companion. Because it is so luminous, the small star expels the outer parts of its atmosphere in the form of a dense stellar wind, which produces a complicated but characteristic spectrum. It seems probable that such stars are the result of mass exchange. For example V444 Cygni has an orbital period of 4.2 days. The bright star has a mass of about ten solar masses and is probably a helium star which has transferred most of its original mass to its companion. The O star has a mass of about 25 solar masses and is presumably now brighter than it was originally because of its increase in mass. A number of X-ray stars are found to be binary stars consisting of an O-type supergiant and a compact object – either a neutron star or a black hole. Astronomers speculate that when the helium star in V444 Cygni runs out of nuclear fuel and collapses, and when the O-type main-sequence star evolves and expands to become a supergiant, V444 Cygni could become an X-ray star.

6. Dense states of cosmic matter

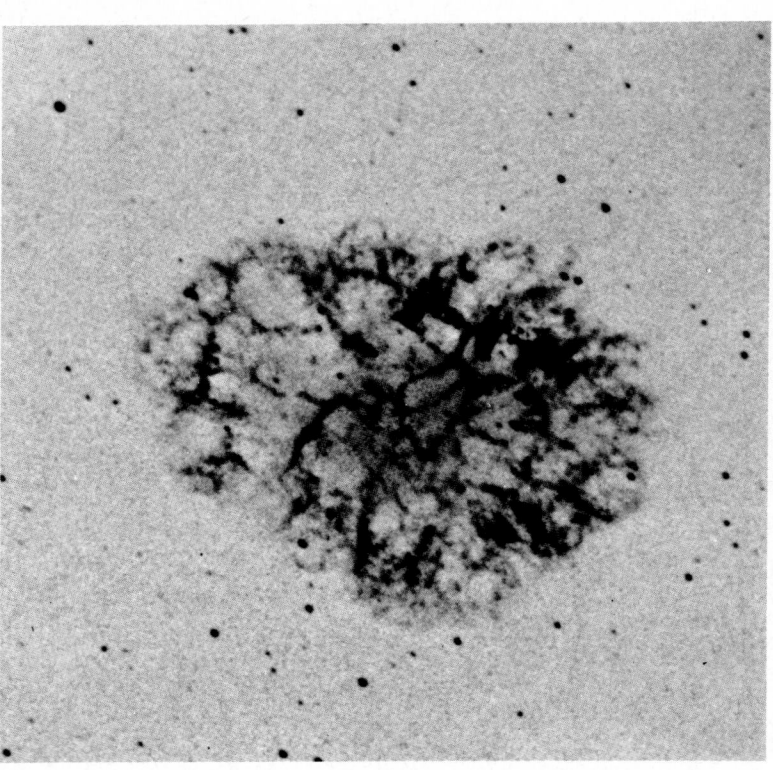

6.1: *The Crab Nebula is kept shining by energy supplied by the pulsar in its centre. The pulsar is a rapidly-spinning neutron star, the very compact remnant of the supernova explosion which produced the gas in the nebula. (Kitt Peak National Observatory, USA)*

Introduction

As a star evolves and burns its ever-diminishing supply of nuclear fuel, it becomes less and less able to support itself against the inexorable force of gravitation. The material in the centre of our Sun is only about 100 times as dense as water, but the centres of some collapsed stars in which the supplies of nuclear fuel have been exhausted contain matter so dense that a pinhead made of it would weigh over a million tonnes. Some of the most energetic phenomena in the Universe involve such collapsed stars. In this chapter we consider the properties of matter at high densities and of the objects in the Universe that are made of it.

The volume of an atom comprises mainly empty space. The bulk of the atomic mass resides in the central *nucleus*, which is composed of *protons* and *neutrons*, each of which is about 1840 times more massive than one of the surrounding *electrons*. An atom is about 10^{-10} m in diameter, but the atomic nucleus, which contains most of the mass of the atom, measures a mere 10^{-15} m across. This is the distance at which the nuclear forces, as opposed to the *electromagnetic force*, have dominant influence. The size of the atom is determined by the electron cloud – with comparatively negligible mass – which is about 10^{-10} m in diameter. It is the electrons that decide the physical and chemical properties of ordinary matter as we experience it in our everyday lives; the nuclear force has no effect for most practical purposes on the behaviour of ordinary matter. For everyday purposes we may consider the protons in the nucleus to be present merely to keep the matter electrically neutral and the neutrons to act as stabilizers for the nucleus.

The factor of 10^5 in linear size between the atom and the nucleus means that there is approximately a factor of 10^{15} in density between the two. Since the density of ordinary solid matter, which consists of closely-packed atoms, is a few tonnes per cubic metre, we can conclude that the density of nuclear matter is of the order of 10^{15} tonnes m^{-3} (or 10^{18} kg m^{-3}). To emphasize this point, it may be noted that 99.95 per cent of the mass of the Earth resides in nuclei which, if they were packed tightly together, would fill a sphere with a diameter of about 200 metres! It is difficult to visualize that this is so, because the obvious rigidity and opacity of the Earth give the impression that ordinary matter is completely solid. However, as we explain below, all of the obvious properties of ordinary matter are due to the electrons, not the very dense nucleus.

What would happen to the structure of matter on Earth if the Earth's mass increased? Imagine a situation in which rocks are piled on the Earth from outside. Initially hills and valleys arise, but as they become too extreme these structures would crumble under their own weight and the material supporting them would flow like a liquid because of the enormous pressure of over-lying rocks. Mountains formed out of ordinary rock cannot be much higher than about 20 kilometres on Earth. This is why the Earth has no 'corners'. In fact because of its own gravity a lump of rock in space cannot appreciably deform from a sphere unless its diameter is less than about 400 km.

If the combined mass of the Earth and the added material were to become much greater than that of the giant planet Jupiter, the atomic electrons would no longer be able to maintain any pretence of structure. Immense internal pressures would crush the normal atomic structure, and the electrons would become a free-electron gas! The radius of the Earth would now decrease if more material were to be added. Eventually, with the addition of more matter, it would have a radius similar to that of the original Earth again, but would have some of the properties associated with the *white-dwarf stars*. Application of extreme pressure might cause it to become a *neutron star*, by which time it would be only about 15 km in radius. The density would then be similar to that of nuclear matter and the object would resemble one enormous nucleus. Finally as more matter is added, exotic effects associated with gravitation would build up: it would disappear from view and become a *black hole!*

We have, of course, passed over many important points in this imaginary experiment, not least of which is the release of gravitational energy. If you drop a stone on the ground it releases energy, mostly in the form of heat. The addition of all the hypothetical material to the Earth would release an enormous amount of energy that might well prevent the experiment from continuing at certain stages. Nevertheless, it should be stressed that many of the superficial appearances of matter at the densities to which we are normally accustomed are determined by the atomic electrons. If enough cold matter is contained in a sphere held together by its own gravity, the effect of the electrons may be completely washed out and nuclear densities prevail throughout. Some fraction of a dying star will eventually pass into at least one of the three terminal states of evolution (white dwarf, neutron star or black hole) unless it is completely dispersed. Many observed objects are identified as white dwarfs and neutron stars, and there are even some good candidates for black holes. Studies of these extreme objects, reveal properties of matter unattainable on Earth. Many of the violent and highly active phenomena in space involve compact objects. As we have mentioned, a small stone dropped onto the surface of the Earth makes a noise. Drop a small stone onto a neutron star and it will release as much energy as a hydrogen bomb! Discoveries made by astronomers in the late-1960s and continuing in the 1970s inspired a great upsurge in the study of very dense matter, for which the relevant experimental results come mainly from astronomical observation (figure 6.1).

Matter at high densities

The properties of very dense matter are so peculiar that you may not be familiar with the underlying physical principles. In order to appreciate the implications for astrophysics of these principles we give here a brief outline of the behaviour of matter at high densities. Naturally the presentation involves some elementary algebra. All of the elements can solidify at extremely low temperatures; that is to say, if their atoms are made to move slowly enough, they lock into a solid structure (they freeze). There must, therefore, be some attractive force between the atoms which can bind them together in the form of a crystal if the atoms are not too energetic. Just as

important, there must also be a second, repulsive, force which prevents the crystal, once formed, from collapsing altogether under the influence of that attraction. What are these forces?

Gravitation is far too weak and nuclear forces have too short a range. Although each atom is, as a whole, electrically neutral, the attractive force is in fact electrostatic. The motions of the outer electrons of each atom are related in such a way that the nucleus of each atom sees another nucleus as attractive. Counteracting this is the dominant repulsive force which, especially in dense matter, is caused by the *degeneracy pressure* of the electrons.

Heisenberg's UNCERTAINTY PRINCIPLE states that the uncertainty in a measurement of the momentum, of (for example) an electron and the uncertainty in the measurement of its position, are related thus:

(momentum uncertainty) × (position uncertainty)
is greater than 6.6×10^{-34} J s

where 6.6×10^{-34} J s is PLANCK'S CONSTANT and will be denoted by h. The meaning of this famous uncertainty principle is that if we devise an experiment to measure at some instant the speed of an electron to a high degree of accuracy (that is to say the momentum error is small), then we shall not be able to predict the position of the electron at that instant very accurately (because the positional error is then large). Conversely, if we fix an electron in space with sufficient precision, its momentum is unpredictably large. This principle is fundamental to microphysics, and the uncertainties mentioned occur even in an ideal experiment. Since Planck's constant is so small, we are unaware of the uncertainty principle in everyday life. For example, the average inaccuracy due to the uncertainty principle incurred in dropping a pebble onto a given spot from a height of 10 metres is 10^{-16} m – about a tenth of the radius of a nucleus! But, as we shall now see, there are circumstances in physics when the uncertainty principle is critically important.

The position of an electron that is under the influence of an atomic nucleus is well specified, and consequently its momentum is ill-defined. The probability of our observing the electron at rest under such circumstances is vanishingly small. This ceaseless motion of the electron exerts a pressure, termed DEGENERACY PRESSURE, on its surroundings, just as ordinary gas pressure is caused by the continual motion of the gas molecules. (As a simple but valid analogy we may consider the trapping of an unwilling creature in a box with movable walls. The more it is confined, the more wildly it rushes around, the more frequently it collides with the walls, and the more pressure it exerts on the walls of the box.) We should stress that although the bound electron is in motion and has energy, this energy cannot be removed, since doing so would decrease its momentum, and thus degenerate matter may be thought of as cold.

The pressure, P, of a collection of particles may be written approximately as $P = nmv^2$ where n is the number of particles per unit volume, m is the mass of a particle and v the average velocity.

Consider the degeneracy pressure of the electrons in a lump of solid hydrogen of volume V which contains N atoms. Clearly the number, n, of particles per unit volume is N/V. Because of PAULI's EXCLUSION PRINCIPLE, which states that no two electrons (or protons or neutrons) can occupy the same state, the effective volume available to any one electron is not the total volume, but is rather V/N, the volume occupied by an atom. Thus each electron is effectively confined to a volume V/N, or to a small distance $(V/N)^{\frac{1}{3}}$. The momentum is m v which, by the uncertainty principle, is equal to h/(distance uncertainty). If we now gather these relations together, we have $v = \dfrac{h}{m}\left(\dfrac{N}{V}\right)^{\frac{1}{3}}$.

Our pressure equation for a degenerate electron gas is therefore given by:

$$P \approx \frac{h^2}{m_e}\left(\frac{N}{V}\right)^{\frac{5}{3}}$$

where m_e is the mass of an electron. We can make a further modification by noting that the density of the matter, which we shall denote by ρ is given by (number of particles) × (particle mass)/(volume), that is $\rho = Nm_e/V$, and consequently:

$$P = h^2\, m_e^{-\frac{8}{3}}\, \rho^{\frac{5}{3}}$$

This is known as the EQUATION OF STATE of such a gas. We note that, unlike ordinary pressure, degeneracy pressure is independent of temperature, and depends just on the density and the mass of the degenerate particle.

But how important is degeneracy pressure? In the Earth's atmosphere the air pressure is almost all due to ordinary heat pressure, with degeneracy pressure contributing less than one part in 10^5. In the central core of a *red-giant star*, however, the density exceeds $10^8\,\mathrm{kg\,m^{-3}}$ and degeneracy pressure can dominate despite the high temperature (10^8 K). In an ordinary gas at a fixed temperature the pressure is proportional to the density. Since degeneracy pressure depends on the five-thirds power of the density, it will become more important than the gas pressure at sufficiently high densities, whatever the temperature. We have somewhat laboured this point because the extraordinary properties of dense matter are due to unfamiliar laws of physics. We have one final complication to discuss before returning to the astronomical aspects of dense matter. If the density is sufficiently high, the momentum of an electron becomes so large that its velocity approaches the speed of light. The motion is governed by Einstein's *theory of special relativity*, and the electrons are said to become relativistic. Then the pressure of a relativistic degenerate electron gas is given by:

$$P \approx hc\left(\frac{N}{V}\right)^{\frac{4}{3}} = hc\, m_e^{-\frac{4}{3}}\, \rho^{\frac{4}{3}}$$

The important point here is that once again the pressure is independent of temperature, but in this case it is proportional to the four-thirds power of the density.

White dwarf stars

We have seen how *main-sequence stars* are supported against gravitational collapse by the enormous gas pressures sustained by the fusion energy. Since fuel for the nuclear reactions runs out eventually, gravity must dominate ultimately unless other forces become important. Low-mass stars that have run out of energy are eventually stabilized against collapse by the electron degeneracy pressure discussed above and they are known as WHITE DWARFS.

The structure of a white dwarf is a result of balance between the outward pressure of degeneracy forces and the inward-acting gravitational force. This latter force is proportional to the product of the density of the white dwarf and its mass, divided by the square of its radius; (this is a particular form of *Newton's law of gravitation*). The density clearly also depends upon the mass of the star and the cube of its radius. Therefore we can say that the gravitational force increases as the square of the mass divided by the fifth power of the radius. We know from our discussion of the equation of state for degenerate matter that the pressure varies as the five-thirds power of the density. The outward radial force is just the pressure gradient, so we divide pressure by the star's radius. The result is a force that is proportional to the five-thirds power of the mass divided by sixth power of radius. Hence at sufficiently small radii, the degeneracy pressure force exceeds the gravitation. If we now balance these two forces we obtain a radius which depends upon the inverse cube root of the mass. A curious feature of white dwarfs is that increasing the mass decreases the radius. The white dwarf has to become smaller because confining its electrons more is its only way of increasing its outward pressure forces and supporting the extra mass.

The mass of a white dwarf cannot exceed a certain critical value. If we consider higher-mass stars, the electrons move faster and faster with increasing mass until their speeds approach that of light. The equation of state now changes (as we have discussed immediately above) and the degeneracy pressure force is now proportional to the inverse sixth power of the radius. We can no longer bring the two opposing forces into equilibrium by suitable adjustment of the stellar radius and no stable solution for the star is possible using electron pressure. The critical mass at which this catastrophe occurs is known as the CHANDRASEKHAR MASS for a white dwarf. It is about 1.4 solar masses for white dwarfs composed of the proportions of material likely to result when a star approaches the end of its life. Note that a pure hydrogen white dwarf cannot exist, since at nuclear densities the hydrogen would immediately burn explosively to form helium.

In summary, a degenerate object decreases its size when increasing its mass. This is a consequence of the uncertainty principle, since a decrease of size means an increase in momentum and hence degeneracy pressure. The speed of light proves to be the limitation, for when the electron velocities approach this value the gravitational force increases at the same rate as the degeneracy pressure force, and equilibrium is unattainable (figure 6.2).

The fate of a white dwarf that captures so much matter that its mass exceeds the Chandrasekhar limit is uncertain. Initially it would collapse, releasing a large quantity of gravitational energy. Some material is probably then blasted off and any remnant star would consist of exceedingly dense matter. We outline the properties of this dense matter below.

Observed properties of white dwarfs

In 1844, F.W.Bessel deduced from the motion of Sirius that it must have an unseen companion. This companion, Sirius B, was discovered in 1862 by A.Clark; it is a tenth-magnitude object, eleven magnitudes fainter than Sirius A, and yet both components have the same surface temperature. The large difference in brightness must therefore be due to a difference in size. This means that Sirius B must be smaller in radius than Sirius A by a factor of about 100. Since Sirius A has a radius of about 10^6 km, the radius of Sirius B is about 10^4 km, which is less than the diameter of the Earth. On the other hand, a study of the orbital motion of the two stars indicates that Sirius B has a mass of about $1\,M_\odot$. We conclude therefore that Sirius B must be a white dwarf (figure 5.3).

Many more white dwarfs have since been discovered, both as single stars and as members of *binary systems*. No correlation is found between the radii of white dwarfs and their temperatures, in agreement with our finding that degeneracy pressure is independent of temperature. The radius of a white dwarf is fixed by its mass and by the proportions of the various chemical elements it contains. Once an isolated white dwarf has been formed, it has no alternative but to cool – eventually to very low temperatures – since no nuclear reactions are taking place to replenish its lost heat. Unlike an ordinary star, it does not need energy to provide the pressure required to support it against gravity. Indeed the only white dwarfs we can see are the hotter, more luminous ones. In the Galaxy, there are undoubtedly huge numbers of cool white dwarfs, which we should perhaps call black dwarfs, that are too faint to be visible. Our Sun will eventually become such an object, though, of course, not for another 10^{10} years or so.

The optical spectra of white dwarfs are varied. Some show absorption lines of hydrogen and others very few, if any, features. The atmospheres of some white dwarfs appear to contain no hydrogen at all. The spectral lines are always broad, due to pressure broadening. A few white dwarfs rotate fast enough for rotational broadening to become important as well. Centrifugal forces become important at high rotation rates and may provide sufficient additional support against gravity to enable some white dwarfs to exceed the Chandrasekhar limit by up to a factor of about two. If the rotation period is much less than 10 seconds, however, these centrifugal forces will rip the star apart. From some white dwarfs, polarized light has been detected, indicating surface magnetic fields of up to 10^4 tesla (10^8 gauss), about a billion times more than Earth's field.

Since the mass of a white dwarf cannot exceed about $1.4\,M_\odot$, single stars less massive than this probably evolve to form white

6.2: *All the objects in the Universe can be plotted on this diagram: position on the diagram is determined just by the mass and the radius of an object. For an object of a given mass, gravity tries to diminish its radius and in so doing the object traverses a horizontal path in the diagram from right to left. Various physical effects can prevent this from happening. In the region labelled 'stars', nuclear fusion can produce sufficient thermal pressure to counteract gravity. Along the line marked 'degenerate dwarfs', electron degeneracy pressure balances the gravitational force. Neutron degeneracy pressure acts in a similar manner along the line marked 'neutron stars'. When an object becomes sufficiently compact, gravity overcomes all other forces and the object collapses to become a black hole.*

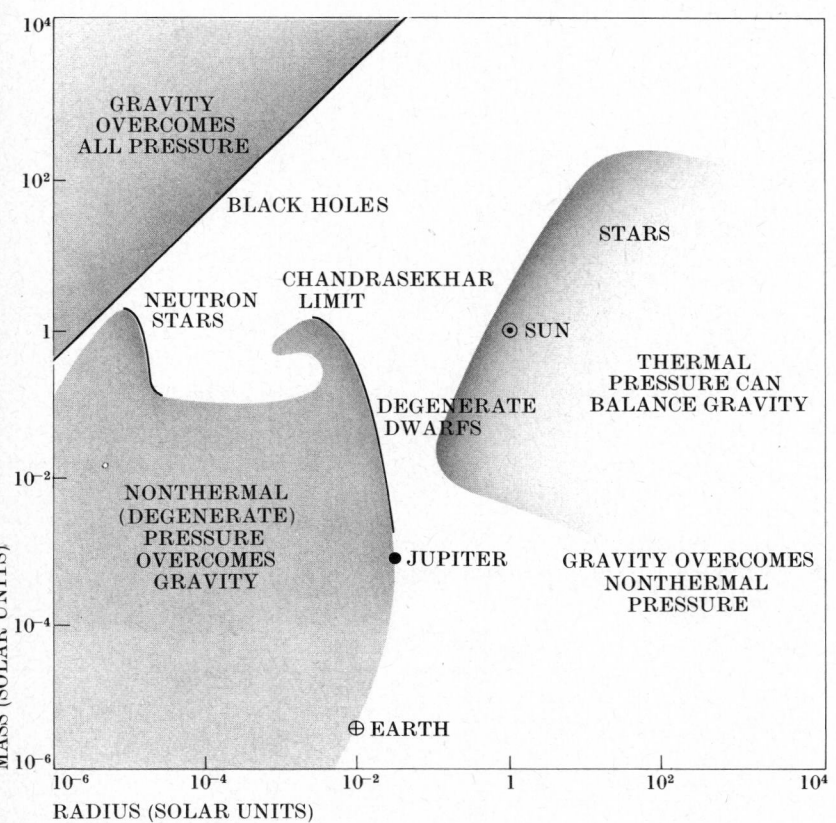

dwarfs. The time they take to do so is 10^{10} years or longer. From this we can see that unless stars lose mass during their lifetimes, white dwarfs should only be seen in old stellar systems where such ancient stars have had time to evolve. The fact that white dwarfs are seen in young clusters, such as the Hyades (perhaps 20 million years old), and in binary systems containing young stars (for example Sirius) is proof that mass loss must occur during the evolution of some stars. In a binary system the mass can be shed by dumping it onto the companion, but if the star is single the mass must be expelled in the form of a wind. *Planetary nebulae* appear to be new-born white dwarfs which have just expelled a large quantity of material.

Although an isolated white dwarf continues to cool indefinitely, a white dwarf with a close binary companion can remain luminous for much longer. Such an attendant can spill over some of its material to the white dwarf and the energy released when the material crashes onto the surface of the white dwarf corresponds to about $10^{13}\,\mathrm{J\,kg^{-1}}$. (One kilogram of material therefore releases as much energy as a 100 megawatt power station generates in a day.) This gravitational energy is then radiated by the white dwarf. For example Mira B, the white-dwarf companion to the variable star Mira (o Ceti) appears luminous because it is gathering material from the dense stellar wind emitted by Mira itself.

6.3: *The internal structure of a white dwarf. The existence of a solid crystalline core depends on the constituents and temperatures of the white dwarf. The white dwarf shown has about the same mass as the Sun and the radius is slightly greater than that of the Earth.*

6.4: *The composition of degenerate material at high densities relevant to neutron star matter. Neutron drip occurs when the density exceeds $4 \times 10^{14}\,kg\,m^{-3}$. Neutrons are then the most abundant constituent. At densities above a few times $10^{17}\,kg\,m^{-3}$ the nuclei dissolve into their component protons and neutrons. At even higher densities other elementary particles appear.*

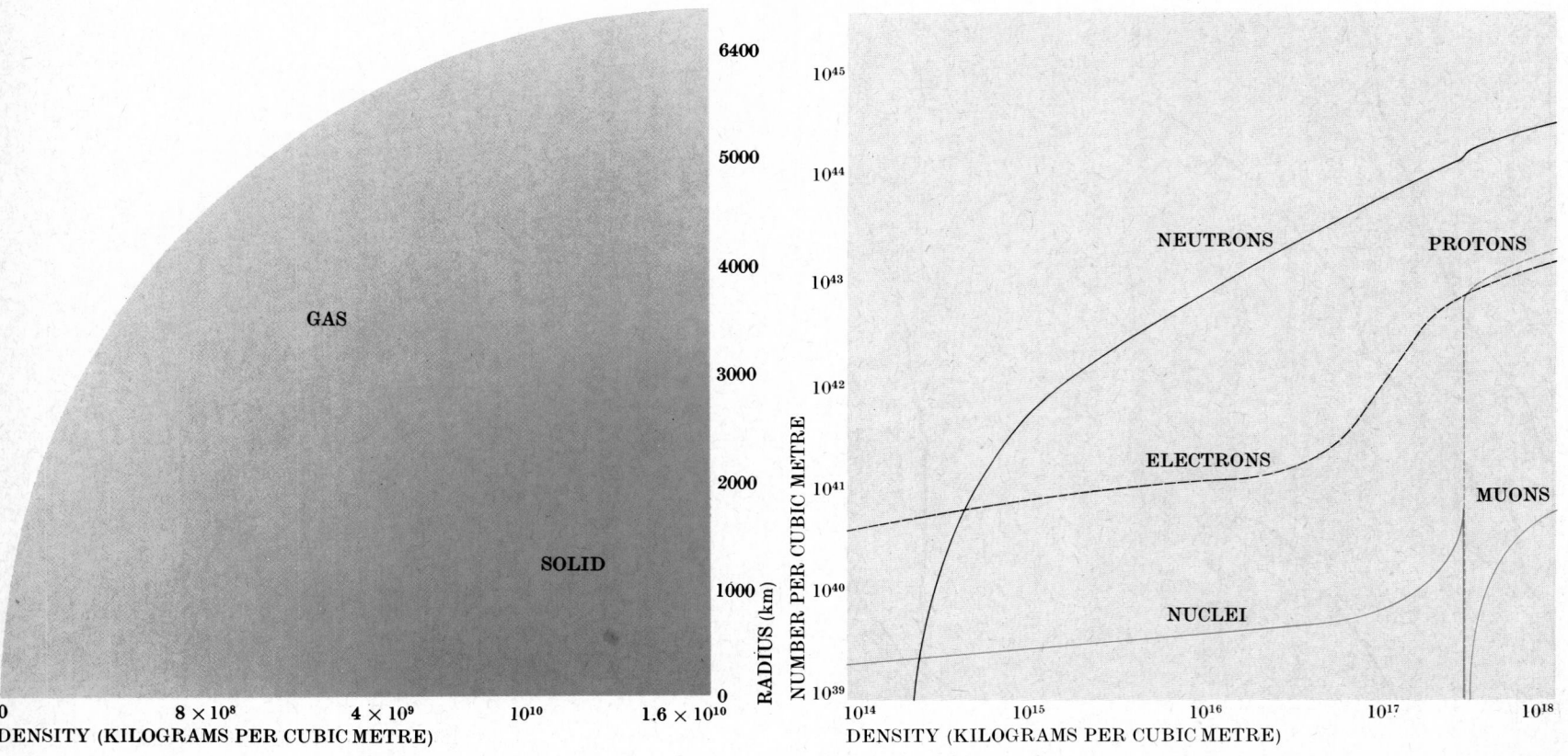

NOVAE are binary systems in which material is being transferred slowly from one star (a low-mass, main-sequence star) to its companion white dwarf. In dwarf novae the accretion takes place onto the white dwarf in sporadic bursts, producing flares at irregular intervals. In novae, the matter appears to accumulate on the white dwarf at a steady rate. The density of the accreted material, once it has settled on the surface, it quite high (more than about $10^7 \, \mathrm{kg \, m^{-3}}$). As more matter accumulates the density rises, and nuclear burning of hydrogen can occur spontaneously. Thus if the transferred material is mostly hydrogen, when a sufficient amount (about $10^{-4} \, \mathrm{M_\odot}$) has accumulated on the surface the hydrogen starts to burn. However, since the burning matter is degenerate, the temperature increase due to the burning does not affect the pressure and so the density initially stays the same. Since a slight increase in temperature yields a large increase in burning, the nuclear reactions run out of control and an explosion results. Such an explosion is thought to be the cause of a nova outburst.

6.5: *Phase diagram which shows the physical state of dense matter at various temperatures. The relevant values are indicated for matter at the centre of the Sun, white dwarfs and neutron stars. The region in the bottom left-hand corner represents conditions accessible in the laboratory.*

6.6: *The internal structure of a neutron star. The star has the same mass as the Sun but is only 15 km in radius. The radius of a black hole of the same mass would be only 3 km.*

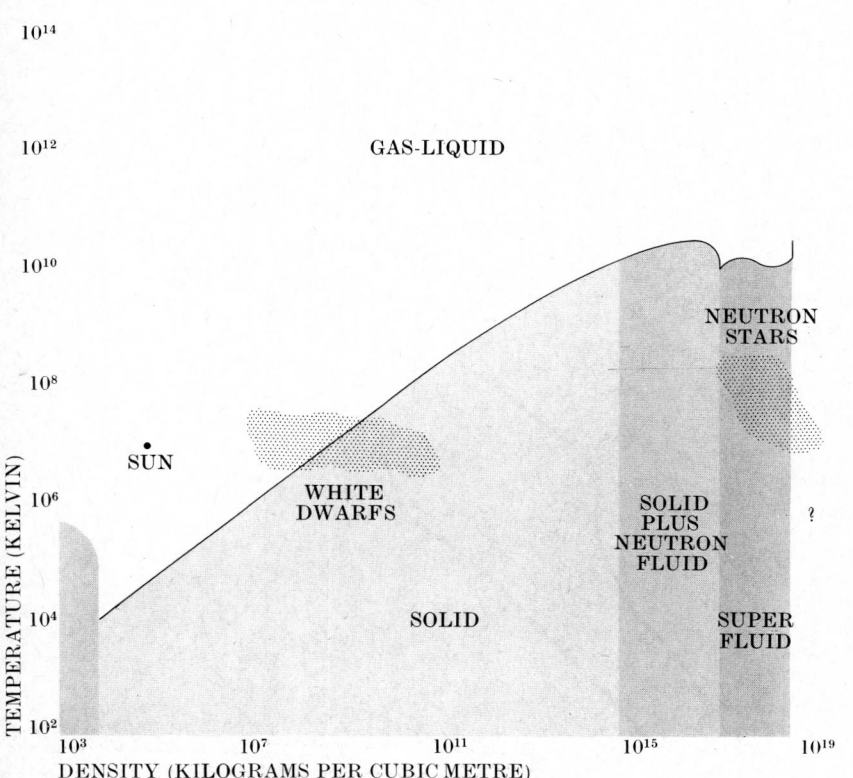

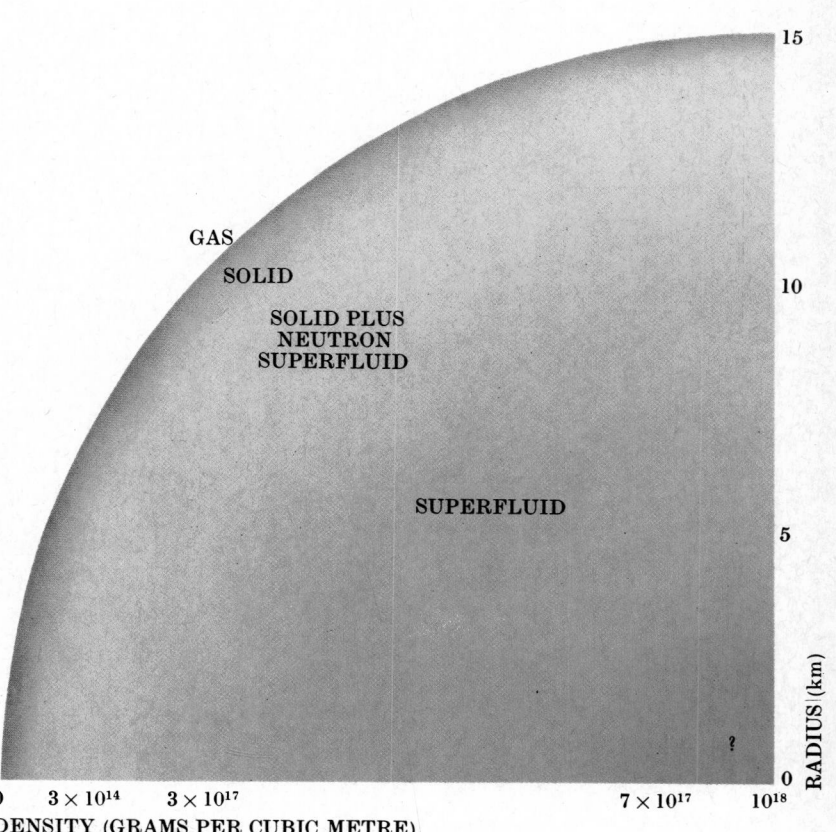

Matter at nuclear densities

A single isolated *neutron* decays into a *proton*, an *electron* and an *anti-neutrino* with a half-life of 12 minutes. This is an example of β-decay. However, in matter in which the electrons are moving at nearly the velocity of light, the reverse process can take place: an energetic electron collides with a proton to form a neutron, emitting a neutrino in the process. The density at which this starts to take place depends on the constitution of the matter: it is about 10^{10} kg m^{-3} for hydrogen and about 10^{12} kg m^{-3} for iron. Normally, the neutron-rich nuclei so formed would undergo radioactive fission, expelling the electron again, but at sufficiently high densities the presence of other free electrons prevents this. There is simply nowhere for the expelled electron to go; once again we are seeing *Pauli's Exclusion Principle* at work inside a star.

As the density of the matter increases, the formation of more neutrons proceeds and consequently nuclei with more and more bizarre neutron-to-proton ratios are formed. However, because there are now so many neutrons compared to protons in each nucleus, the binding forces of each nucleus become weaker. Eventually, when the density is as high as about 4×10^{14} kg m^{-3}, the neutrons start to 'drip' out of the nucleus, in a process called NEUTRON-DRIP. At higher densities, after neutron-drip has occurred, the matter consists of essentially three components: the nuclei are able to arrange themselves in the form of a crystal lattice of electrons, nuclei and free neutrons. At densities of about 10^{17} kg m^{-3} the nuclei have completely dissolved (figure 6.4).

The matter consists almost entirely of free neutrons together with 0.5 per cent protons and electrons. Such a neutron fluid may well be a SUPERFLUID, having the property of zero viscosity (absolutely no resistance to flow) similar to liquid helium. The few protons present may also be superfluid, and, in addition, make the fluid SUPERCONDUCTING (no resistance to electric current). There are so few electrons present that the main pressure in material at nuclear densities is due to NEUTRON DEGENERACY PRESSURE. This is exactly analogous to electron degeneracy pressure except that the particles exerting the pressure are the free neutrons. The equation of state is similar to the case of electron degeneracy, with the neutron mass replacing the electron mass.

Neutron stars

A self-gravitating object which is supported by neutron-degeneracy pressure is known as a NEUTRON STAR; they were investigated theoretically long before they were discovered in space. Their properties are analogous to those of white dwarfs except that their radii are smaller by a factor of about 1840 (the ratio of neutron mass to electron mass). Thus a one solar-mass neutron star has the tiny radius of only 10 km. Similarly, we expect an upper limit to the mass of a neutron star, analogous to the Chandrasekhar limit for a white dwarf. However, when the density increases to such an extent (about 10^{18} kg m^{-3}) that the neutrons are moving at relativistic velocities, collisions between the particles lead to the formation of other *elementary particles*. In addition, although neutron degeneracy pressure is important, the density is so high that nuclear interactions cannot be neglected, and the equation of state is more complicated than we have postulated. Therefore, although an upper limit to the mass of a neutron star is expected, it is not easy to calculate, but is estimated to be in the region of 1.5–3 $M_{\odot}$.

The structure of a neutron star more closely resembles a planet than a star, but on a smaller and denser scale (figure 6.6). The atmosphere, if any, is unlikely to be more than a few centimetres thick. The outer layer of the star, known as the crust, is solid and crystalline and is probably a kilometre or so thick. The gravitational field at the surface is so large that the highest mountains are only about half a centimetre high. However, a would-be mountaineer requires 10^{11} joules of energy to climb such a mountain – more energy than a human being generates in his whole lifetime! Inside the crust is a region of neutron fluid containing a few protons and electrons to stabilize it. As we mentioned before, this fluid may have the properties of a superfluid. This fluid region may extend to the centre of the star. It may be, however, that in the more massive neutron stars a solid crystalline core forms at the centre (figure 6.6).

6.7: *Successive pulses from the first pulsar discovered, CP 1919, are here superimposed vertically. The pulses occur every 1.337 seconds. They are caused by a rapidly-spinning neutron star.*

Pulsars

Discovery

The possibility that the degeneracy pressure of neutrons might stabilize a self-gravitating object was first noted in the 1930s by L.D.Landau and F.Zwicky. W.Baade and F.Zwicky emphasized that they might exist as the stellar remnant of a supernova explosion. Interest in neutron stars was aroused by the discovery of X-ray stars in 1962. Because a neutron star is so small (radius of 10 km), in order to radiate energy at a rate comparable to the Sun it needs to have a much higher surface temperature, namely several million degrees. Radiation emitted by material at such a high temperature is X-radiation. It was thought at the time that some of the X-ray stars might be hot, cooling neutron stars. However the variable luminosity of these stars made this hypothesis inconclusive.

The situation changed dramatically with the discovery of PULSARS (pulsing radio sources) in late-1967 by astronomers at the Cavendish Laboratory, Cambridge. The first pulsar to be discovered, CP 1919 (an abbreviation for Cambridge pulsar at 19 hr 19 min right ascension), is a radio source which flashes regularly every 1.33730 seconds with each flash lasting only 50 milliseconds. In fact, the flashes are so regular that the pulsar could be used as a clock that is accurate to one part in a hundred million. Since then many more pulsars (about 200) have been discovered, with periods ranging from four seconds down to the pulsar in the Crab Nebula which has a period of 33 milliseconds. This last-mentioned pulsar is of special importance, since it proved beyond all reasonable doubt that pulsars are magnetized neutron stars; the regularity of the pulsed radio signal is provided by the rapid rotation of such stars and only a neutron star can rotate that rapidly (figure 6.7).

The Crab pulsar

The supernova that created the *Crab Nebula* was observed and recorded by oriental astronomers in 1054 AD. The radio, optical and X-ray emission from the nebula itself is highly polarized, indicating that the radiation is emitted by the *synchrotron process*. In a given magnetic field, the more energetic an electron, the higher the frequency of the synchrotron radiation it emits and the faster it loses its energy. The high-energy electrons that give rise to the X-radiation from the nebula, lose their energy within 10 years. This means that there must be in the nebula a source of high-energy electrons that is still operative some 900 years after the supernova explosion. It is this source of energy which provides the necessary 10^{31} watts to keep the nebula alight.

One star in the remnant, known as Baade's star and long thought to be of some significance on account of its odd spectrum, was identified as the pulsar in 1969. The star is also seen to pulse at optical frequencies and X-ray energies at the same period of 33 milliseconds. The period is slowly getting longer at a rate such that the interval between successive pulses is about one part in 10^{12} greater than the preceding one.

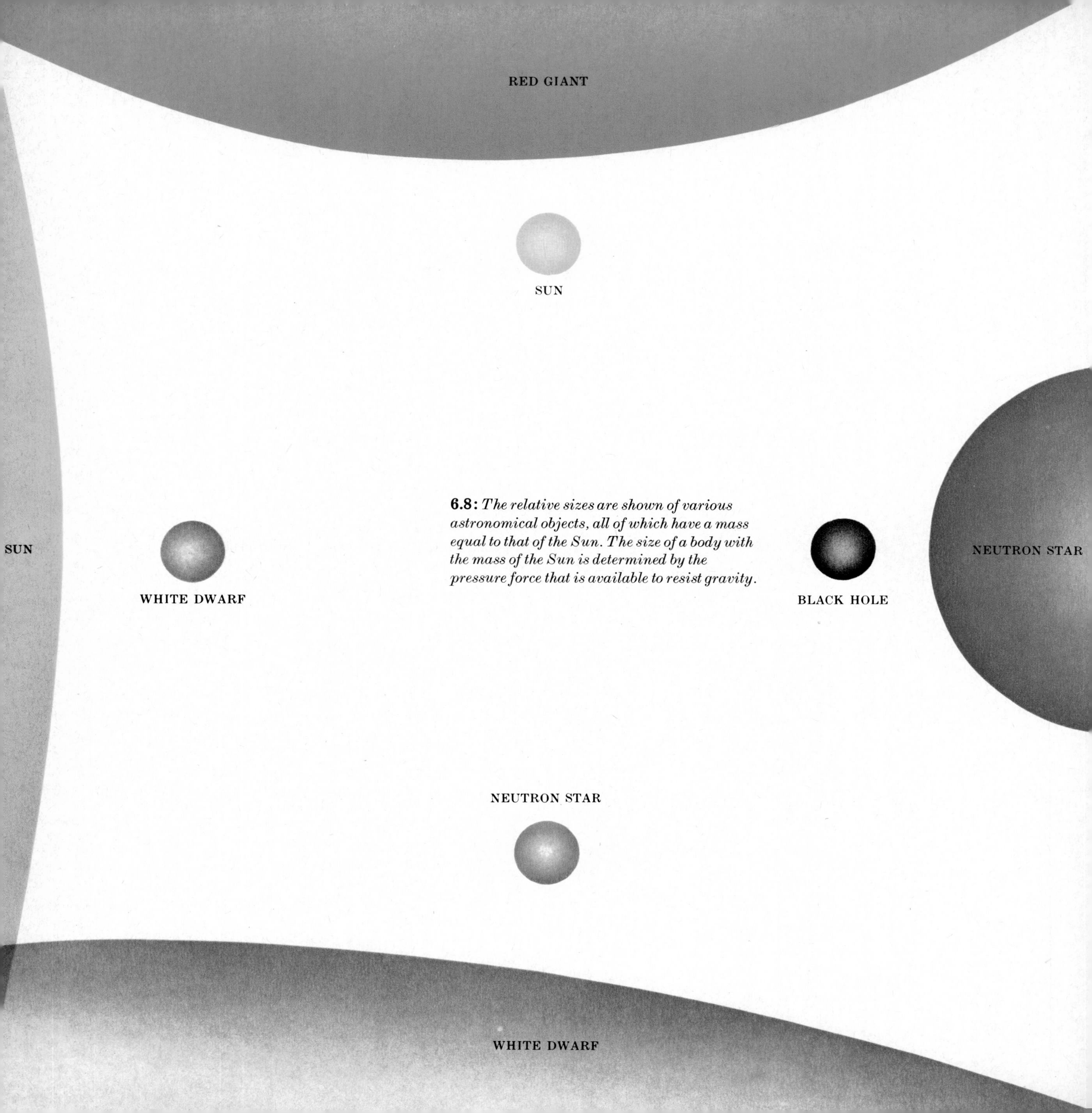

RED GIANT

SUN

SUN

WHITE DWARF

6.8: *The relative sizes are shown of various astronomical objects, all of which have a mass equal to that of the Sun. The size of a body with the mass of the Sun is determined by the pressure force that is available to resist gravity.*

BLACK HOLE

NEUTRON STAR

NEUTRON STAR

WHITE DWARF

The minimum rotational period of a star is of a similar magnitude as its fundamental pulsational period. Both vary inversely as the square root of the star's average density. Therefore, to get a short period (rapid rotation) we need a dense star. If a white dwarf rotates faster than about once a second, it will tear itself to pieces by centrifugal forces. We see therefore that the Crab pulsar must be a solid body which is over a thousand times denser than a white dwarf; in short it must be a neutron star. In fact, the energy lost by a neutron star that is rotating 30 times a second and that is slowing down with the observed timescale of a few thousand years is precisely the same as that which is required to keep the Crab Nebula glowing. Somehow the rotational energy of the Crab pulsar is being fed into the surrounding nebula, much of it in the form of fast particles which, together with the ambient magnetic field, produce synchrotron radiation.

Pulsar emission

The Sun has a present average surface magnetic field of about 10^{-4} tesla, a rotation period of 26 days, and radius of 700 000 km. Consider its properties if it were forced to collapse to form a neutron star of radius 10 km. Just as a pirouetting ice skater spins up as he brings in his arms, so the Sun would spin up until its rotation period was only 0.4 ms. The magnetic field would be compressed to a value of 5×10^5 tesla. The neutron stars that give rise to pulsars are thought to have magnetic fields as high as 10^8 tesla. As they emit radiation, they lose energy and slow down.

Such a strongly magnetized and rapidly rotating neutron star acts like a rotating bar magnet and radiates electromagnetic waves at its rotation frequency. The rotating magnetic field also generates such strong electric fields that electrons and protons can be dragged off the surface of the star, creating currents and setting up a *magnetosphere*. The particles in the magnetosphere rotate with the neutron star out to the distance at which their velocities approach the velocity of light (figure 6.9). There are many unsolved problems related to the studies of pulsars and it is safe to say that this is a branch of astronomy in which observations far outstrip the theory. Somehow and somewhere in the rotating magnetosphere, coherent (laser-like) radio emission is produced. This emission is concentrated into a narrow beam, and, like the flashing of a lighthouse, produces a radio pulse every time the sweeping beam crosses the earth. In addition, very fast (relativistic) particles are emitted.

The Crab pulsar, which has the shortest period known, is the only one from which pulses have been unambiguously detected right through the electromagnetic spectrum, from radio waves to gamma rays. This may be related to its comparative youth. Pulsed emission diminishes rapidly, particularly at optical and higher frequencies, as a pulsar ages and slows down. Because of this ageing process, most observed pulsars are intrinsically faint and have been discovered only because they are relatively close to us. There are probably many tens of millions of undetected pulsars in the Galaxy, some of them active, yet with beams that never

6.9: *Magnetic field of a rotating neutron star. Field lines trail the rotation. Far from the pulsar the lines move at the speed of light.*

sweep the Earth and many that are now defunct, or so feeble as to be undetectable by present radio telescopes. Moreover, distant pulsars are difficult to recognize because their characteristic pulsations become increasingly smeared out by the free electrons in interstellar space.

Neutron starquakes

Because the emission from pulsars is poorly understood theoretically, they tell us little about the nature of neutron stars. Only those pulsars that show occasional abrupt changes in pulse period – termed GLITCHES – as observed in the Crab and Vela pulsars provide such information. These glitches are due to starquakes, or a sudden release of elastic strain in the crust or core of the neutron star. The glitches can be useful tools in revealing the structure of neutron stars, just as seismology tells us about the interior of the Earth.

The glitches in pulse arrival times as seen in several pulsars may be interpreted to reveal the inner structure of the underlying neutron star. The Crab pulsar, for example, probably consists of a thin crust encasing a superfluid interior. Initially this crust is deformed from a truly spherical shape because of the centrifugal forces associated with its rapid rotation. An equatorial bulge forms, just as in the case of the planets Earth and Jupiter. The subsequent spin-down due to the radiation of rotational energy then reduces the centrifugal forces. Being a solid lattice, the crust cannot follow these changes and cracks at some stage. Such starquakes then cause a readjustment of material in the neutron star and a change in the spin rate. The observer detects this as a change in pulse arrival times.

It is only the crust that initially readjusts, because it takes time for the change in spin rate to be spread throughout the star. We can visualize this if we recall that if a cup of coffee is suddenly rotated there is some delay before the coffee begins to rotate. Therefore the sudden glitch is followed by a slower change in pulse rate as the effects of the starquake spread themselves throughout the neutron star. A close study of this can reveal details of the nature of the superfluid region.

The binary pulsar

An important parameter to measure is the mass of a neutron star. This can best be determined in the same manner as for ordinary stars, by the observation of a *binary system* that contains a neutron star.

To get the masses unambiguously we really need an eclipsing, double-lined binary, in which both components give us radial velocity measurements. Neutron stars have not as yet revealed any spectroscopic lines, but the pulses due to their rotation are just as useful! In fact no spectroscopic measurements would be necessary at all if we could find two pulsars orbiting each other. Unfortunately such a system has not yet been found, although a binary system with one pulsar has been discovered. The binary pulsar PSR 1913 + 16 consists of a pulsar with a 59.03 ms period in orbit round an invisible companion. This unseen companion cannot be much larger than a white dwarf, and could indeed be another neutron star or even a *black hole*.

The high eccentricity of the orbit (0.615), the short period (0.323 days), and high accuracy to which pulse times can be obtained may still allow us to determine the masses of the two components. The last two of those factors mean that Doppler effects, predicted by the *theory of special relativity* are measurable. These lead to a determination of the inclination of the orbit relative to the plane of the sky. APSIDAL MOTION, a gradual shift in the position of *periastron*, is 4° per year. There are three possible causes for this: first, tidal distortion of the unseen companion, second, rotation of this star and third, general relativistic *precession* similar to the precession of 43 seconds of arc per century of the perihelion of the planet Mercury. The first two may be ignored if the unseen companion is as compact as a neutron star or black hole. The rate of apsidal motion then yields the sum of the masses of the stars. This, together with the inclination angle and the data determined from the radial velocities, gives the individual masses of the components. Preliminary analyses suggest that they are each about 1.4 solar masses, but this does depend upon the assumption that the apsidal motion is solely due to effects of relativity.

A precise clock (the pulsar) in a close simple orbit around a companion provides us with a beautiful laboratory for performing experiments. In such a star system, gravitational theories can be put to the test. Most theories predict a similar rate for apsidal advance, but those predicting the emission of *gravitational waves*, such as Einstein's theory of general relativity undergo at least one further test. The emission of gravitational waves results in a reduction in the separation of the two stars. The associated change in binary period should be detectable by about 1986.

Black holes

In 1798 Laplace, in his book the 'Exposition of the system of the world', stated the following theorem: a luminous body in the Universe of the same density as the Earth, whose diameter is 250 times larger than the Sun, can, by its attractive power, prevent its light rays from reaching us. Consequently, he continued, the largest bodies in the Universe could remain completely invisible. An object that is invisible to us because its light is imprisoned by a mighty gravitational field is termed a BLACK HOLE. The proof of Laplace's theorem is very simple and we shall now give it. For a projectile to be able to leave a gravitating body like the Earth, its kinetic energy must be sufficient that it can climb out of the gravitational field, or potential well, of Earth. In other words, its velocity must exceed the escape velocity from the surface of that body. The escape velocity from the surface of the Earth is about $11 \, \text{km sec}^{-1}$. The escape velocity from a body of a given density is proportional to its radius. Therefore if a body had the same density as the Earth, but a radius 250 times that of the Sun, the velocity of escape would exceed the speed of light. The mass of such a hypothetical body would be about a hundred million times greater than that of the Sun.

Similarly we find that for a body of mass M, it has to have a radius greater than a critical radius $R_s = 2GM/c^2$, known as the SCHWARZSCHILD RADIUS, in order that light leaving its surface might reach an external observer. We note that the Schwarzschild radius of an object is proportional to its mass. As we have seen, the Schwarzschild radius of a body with a mass of 10^8 solar masses is some 250 times larger than the Sun. Proportionally, the Schwarzschild radius of the Sun is only 3 km. Therefore if we took a neutron star of one solar mass, and radius about 10 km, and squeezed it down to 3 km radius, we would find that it would turn into a black hole. For this reason it is speculated that if matter were to be added to a neutron star until the mass of the star exceeded the maximum mass for neutron stars, the star would collapse to form a black hole.

Because, according to the *theory of special relativity*, nothing can travel faster than light, once an object has collapsed to form a black hole it cannot re-emerge from it. Similarly if anything falls into a black hole it cannot escape from it again. In particular, if you want to know what is inside a black hole, it is no good asking a friend, or anyone else, to go and look for you. You will have to go and look for yourself, and you could never come back! Suppose we want to carry a black hole around in a box, for use as a rather effective rubbish disposal unit. Could it be done? Suppose we can carry a kilogram or so. A simple calculation tells us that the size of a black hole weighing a kilogram is about 10^{-27} metres. Since the size of an atom is only 10^{-15} m or so, such a black hole would fall out between the atoms of our box! It would be too small to swallow anything. Perhaps we would really prefer a decent-sized black hole, say a centimetre across. Such a black hole would have a mass of 10^{25} kg – the mass of the Earth! We see then that black holes are very compact objects indeed.

Black holes in astronomy

Two questions arise when discussing the astronomical consequences of the possibility of the existence of black holes. Where would we expect to find them, and how would we detect them?

To form a black hole we need to find places in the Universe which are much denser than their surroundings. The matter in the Universe was at its most dense at the origin of the Universe – the *big bang*. The earliest time at which we can hope to apply known gravitational theory is the so-called PLANCK TIME which is 10^{-43} seconds after the big bang. A black hole formed at this time has a mass of 10^{-8} kg and a radius of 10^{-35} m. Anything with a smaller radius would not form a black hole, and anything with a much larger radius would not just form a black hole, but would cut itself off from our Universe and form a tiny Universe of its own! There could be a large number of such mini black holes around without us noticing them. One possibility for finding them is that they could be mistaken for heavy particles in detectors of cosmic radiation.

When a star like the Sun has evolved so far that it has run out of nuclear fuel, it becomes a white dwarf which gradually cools and fades away. When a star more massive than about four solar masses has run out of nuclear energy, however, its core is too massive to form a white dwarf. According to present theories, the core collapses to form a neutron star – possibly a pulsar – and the energy released in the collapse blows off the outer layers of the star in the form of a *supernova explosion*. However, if a star exceeding about eight solar masses runs out of nuclear fuel, the compact remnant it would wish to leave behind is too massive to become even a neutron star. There are then two possibilities. Either the core of the star is blown apart in the supernova explosion or the core collapses to form a black hole. We would expect the masses of such black holes to be three solar masses and greater. If all the stars that have existed in the Galaxy with masses greater than eight solar masses left black holes as their remnants there could be as many as 10^8 black holes in the Galaxy at present. That is, about one in one thousand of all starry objects could be a black hole!

Another region of space where the density of material is higher than in the surroundings is in the core of a *globular cluster*. This has a much higher density of stars than its surroundings. It is quite possible that at the same time as the cluster formed, a large amount of gas collected in the centre of the cluster and collapsed to form a black hole. The mass of such a black hole could be as much as a thousand solar masses. Similarly, it is entirely possible that at the same time as a galaxy forms, a large quantity of gas collects in the nucleus and creates a black hole. Such a black hole could contain as much as 10^9 solar masses. It has also been suggested that some gas clouds, collapsing to form galaxies, may have overshot and formed black holes themselves – containing as much as 10^{12} solar masses. Perhaps a nascent *cluster of galaxies* could have overshot the mark, to form a black hole of some 10^{14} solar masses. It has even been suggested that the Universe itself is a giant black hole – after all nothing can escape from it, by definition! This is not, however, a useful concept and we shall not pursue it further.

The detection of black holes

If black holes are really objects from which no light, nor anything else, can escape, how can we detect their presence? There are three main possibilities which we take in turn.

First, there is the discovery by the Cambridge astrophysicist Stephen Hawking that black holes are not completely black. Matter-antimatter pairs of particles are continually being produced throughout space, even in a perfect 'vacuum'. This may be considered a consequence of a variant of the *Uncertainty Principle*; large amounts of energy are available for proportionally brief periods of time. This energy may be sufficient to create an electron-positron pair, say, which then annihilates almost instantaneously. The net effect is nothing produced from nothing. In the extreme gravitational environment close to the *Schwarzschild radius* of a black hole, one of the newly-created particles may be dragged within the black hole. This time the net effect is a free particle outside the hole. We cannot get something for nothing however, and the black hole decreases in mass by an amount proportional to the mass and energy of the free particle. In this way a black hole evaporates away its rest mass energy. The rate of evaporation is proportional to the inverse square power of the mass of the hole. For this reason, this effect is only important for the less massive, smaller black holes; for example, a black hole of one solar mass would last 10^{67} years! On the other hand, black holes with masses of less than about 10^{11} kg, which were formed at the origin of the Universe some 10^{10} years ago, would all have evaporated by now. In fact those with masses of around 10^{11} kg would be completing their evaporation at this moment. It is possible that astronomers might detect the final stages of the evaporation as the former black hole disappears with a flash of gamma rays.

The second property of the gravitational field of a black hole that we can make use of to help us to detect such objects is its ability to bend light rays. Light passing close to any gravitating body is deflected, the amount of deflection being proportional to the strength of gravitational field encountered. The Sun bends light rays which pass close to it by a small amount and the verification of this is one of the key experiments in support of the theory of relativity. Light passing close to a black hole can be bent through a substantial angle. In this way a black hole can act as a GRAVITA-TIONAL LENS, magnifying objects which lie behind it and distorting them in a characteristic manner. Unfortunately the chance of a black hole and a distant object lining up in this manner is small, but if astronomers could find an unusually magnified object they could conclude that the object responsible for the magnification was a black hole.

Third, because the effective escape velocity from a black hole is the speed of light, an object which falls towards a black hole reaches velocities approaching the speed of light before it disappears from view. In other words, the kinetic energy of the object before it disappears is comparable to its rest mass energy. When it disappears, however, it takes almost all of its energy with it. If we could find some means of tapping this energy, we would have at our disposal the most efficient means of transforming matter into energy that is theoretically possible. For example, if we were to lower a particle of mass one kilogram into a black hole on a string over a pulley, we could use the other end of the string to generate power. The amount of energy we could obtain theoretically is 42 per cent of the rest mass energy of the kilogram, that is 4×10^{16} joules. If the string were made of even the strongest materials we know, however, it would break under its own weight and we could only obtain a minute fraction of the rest mass energy. Fortunately astronomers do have quite a strong 'string' available. It is the same 'string' which prevents the Earth from crashing into the Sun, that is, centrifugal force.

Suppose we have a quantity of gas which is circling in orbits around a black hole. Then, for the same reason that the inner planets circle the Sun at a faster rate than the outer ones, the gas closer to the black hole orbits it at a faster rate than the gas which is further away. The gas therefore forms a disc of gas that rotates more slowly further from its centre. Friction between the parts of the disc attempts to speed the outer parts up, and to slow the inner parts down, allowing them to fall inwards. In the disc, friction transfers angular momentum to the outer parts and allows the material in the disc to spiral slowly inwards. The heat produced by the friction, which stems originally from the gravitational energy that is being released by the matter falling inwards, is radiated away. Because the inner parts of the disc are so close to the black hole, a large amount of energy can be released for every kilogram that is accreted by the hole in this way. Such an ACCRETION DISC can radiate away up to about 40 per cent of the rest mass energy of the accreted material. Because an accretion disc is such an efficient converter of matter into radiation, we might expect some of the most luminous objects in the Universe to be powered by accretion discs. Among the possibilities are *quasars*, *galactic nuclei* and *X-ray stars*.

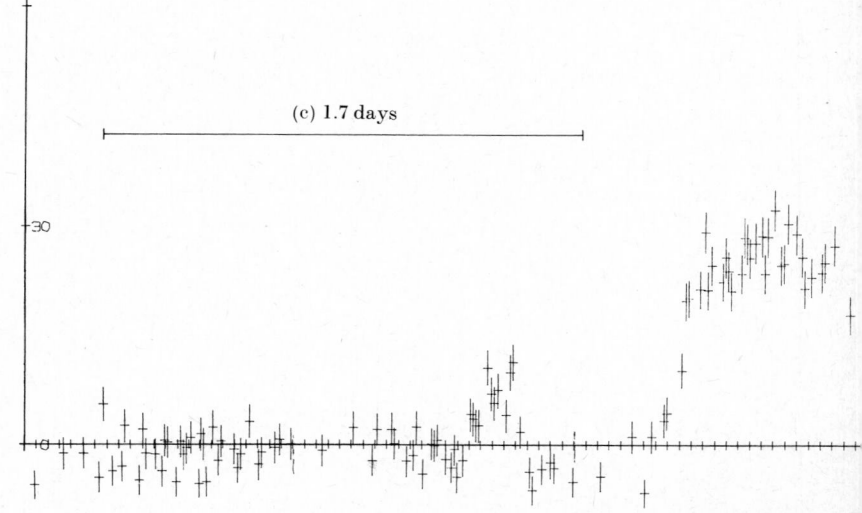

(c) 1.7 days

6.10: *X-ray light curves from compact objects. Cygnus X–1 (a and d) displays variability on all time scales measured, from years to milliseconds. No periodic variations have been detected from this source, which orbits its stellar companion every 5.6 days. The so-called Rapid Burster (b) emits thousands of intense bursts of X-rays every day. As can be seen, these bursts are not periodic, although the interval between bursts depends upon the size and duration of the previous burst. The source occasionally appears to switch off for intervals of many months. Hercules X–1 (c) is rich in periodicities. The 1.7 day eclipsing behaviour is modulated on a 35 day cycle giving rise to the overall envelope of the light curve. Not discernible here are the 1.24 sec pulsations. Note that the eclipses appear to widen as the 35 day cycle proceeds. This is due to a varying amount of obscuration before the X-ray source is eclipsed by its stellar companion.*

X-ray stars

X-rays are associated with high-energy phenomena. The Sun emits most of its radiation at frequencies corresponding to visible light and has an effective surface temperature of about 5800 K. X-ray photons are roughly a thousand times more energetic than the photons of ordinary light, and so to produce X-rays we need either temperatures of several million degrees, or particles with energies more than several thousand electron volts. Although ordinary stars emit most of their radiation in optical light, there are also bodies in the Universe which emit most of their radiation as X-rays. Early studies with rocket-borne detectors of these cosmic sources of X-rays showed a class of objects within our own Galaxy radiating up to a million times more powerfully than the Sun. With the launch of the X-ray satellite Uhuru in 1970, over a hundred such objects were rapidly discovered within the Galaxy and a few more in the Small and Large Magellanic Clouds (figure 6.10).

These X-ray stars in the Milky Way are characterized by their high luminosity and by the strength and rapidity of their variability. For example, the star Cygnus X–1 (the first X-ray source to be discovered in the constellation of Cygnus) varies on a timescale of milliseconds as well as by factors of five over a few minutes. Even more spectacular are the transient X-ray sources, sometimes called X-RAY NOVAE which appear from nowhere within a day or so and then die away over a period of months. There are also the soft gamma-ray or hard X-ray bursts; several bright ones are seen per

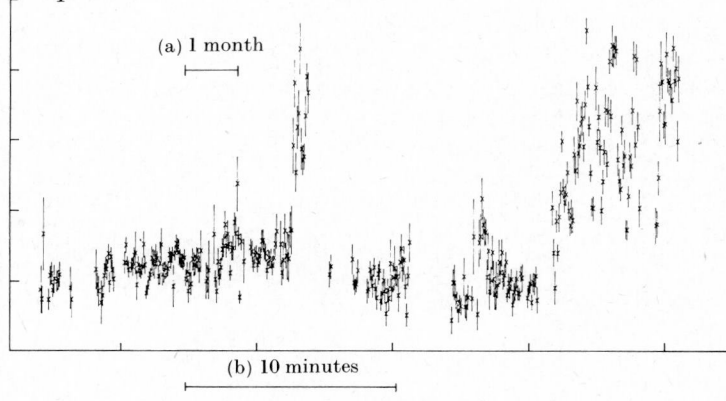

(a) 1 month

(b) 10 minutes

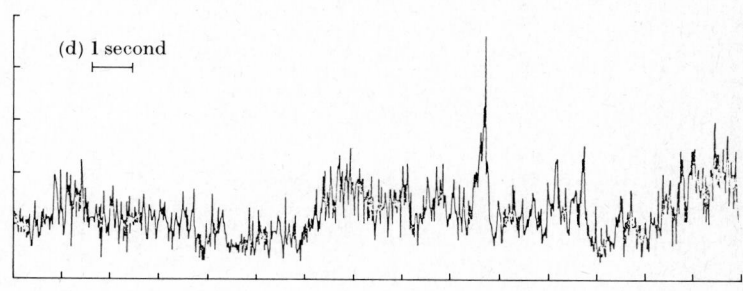

(d) 1 second

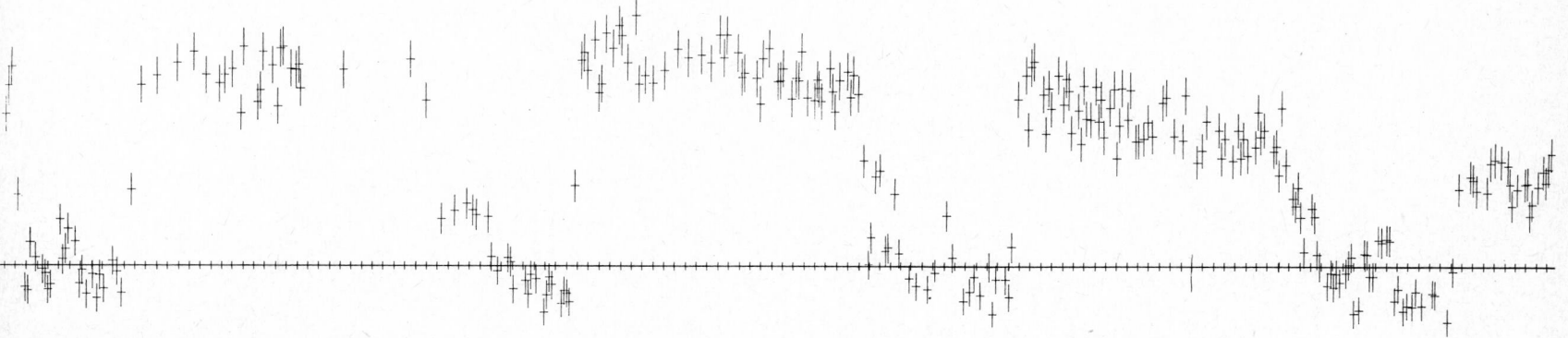

year and although they are as luminous as the other X-ray sources they last only a matter of seconds or less. Much of the variability associated with X-ray stars is highly irregular, but some do vary in a periodic manner. The X-radiation from the sources Hercules X–1 and Centaurus X–3 is regularly pulsed with periods of 1.24 and 4.84 seconds, respectively. In addition, these two sources and a number of others display regular eclipses with periods of a few days, indicating that these sources at least are members of *binary star systems*.

Because of the short timescales involved, the X-ray emission must originate from relatively small, compact objects. Three classes of object fit this description: white dwarfs, neutron stars and black holes. The escape velocity from a neutron star, which is the same as the velocity achieved by a particle falling radially onto its surface, is about a third of the velocity of light. A white dwarf has about the same mass as a neutron star but is about a thousand times larger, and so the escape velocity is about thirty times smaller. The velocity achieved by a particle falling onto a black hole approaches the speed of light.

What energy source powers the luminous sources of X-rays? The pulsar in the Crab Nebula emits pulsed X-radiation with the same pulse period of 33 milliseconds as that observed at radio frequencies. Rotation is the most credible source of such regular pulses and the only known object that can rotate once every 33 milliseconds without being torn apart by centrifugal force is a neutron star. In the case of the Crab pulsar the observed slow-down of the rotation period and consequent decrease of the rotational kinetic energy of the star indicate that the source of energy is indeed the rotational kinetic energy. However the Crab pulsar is unique among X-ray stars in this respect. Centaurus X–3 has a much larger pulse period of 4.84 seconds and has therefore correspondingly less stored rotational energy. If rotation powered this X-ray source it would slow down in less than ten years. This is observed not to be happening; in fact the star is actually spinning up. Thus the bulk of the X-ray stars, unlike radio pulsars, are not powered by their stored rotational energy.

As we mentioned above, when a blob of matter falls onto a neutron star it reaches a velocity of about a third of the speed of light. This means that about a tenth of the blob's original rest mass energy is converted into kinetic energy during infall and is dissipated as heat when the blob strikes the stellar surface. Similarly up to about 40 per cent of the rest mass energy of matter trickling into a black hole from an accretion disc is released as radiation. A hundred millionth of a solar mass falling onto a neutron star per year is sufficient to heat the star to X-ray temperatures and to provide the observed amount of radiation as well. A comparable trickle of matter through an accretion disc, heats the disc to X-ray temperatures.

A lone neutron star in interstellar space captures material from its surroundings. The density of material in space is so low that the amount of matter that can be acquired heats the star up to only about 100 000 K giving rise to a faint source of ultraviolet radiation.

X-ray binary stars

In a close binary system, the stars are near enough to transfer matter from one to the other. Mass-flux rates of up to about a millionth of a solar mass per year have been observed by optical astronomers. A compact object in a close binary system can, therefore, receive enough matter to power it as an X-ray source.

Let us now take a closer look at how the mass transfer takes place and how the X-ray emission arises in a binary system. There are two ways in which the mass transfer can take place. In a sense these are two extremes and in practice the transfer is probably due to a combination of the two. Firstly, imagine the compact object to be in orbit around an ordinary, fluffy star. As the ordinary star burns its nuclear fuel its central regions contract, and its outer regions correspondingly expand. Eventually, as the star gets bigger, some parts of its surface layers will be attracted more to the circling compact object than itself. This surface material peels off, and falls onto the compact object and mass transfer begins. Secondly, there is mass transfer by means of a stellar wind. The bright O and B stars, with which some X-ray sources are known to be associated, are much more massive and much more luminous than the Sun and are believed to have dense stellar winds. These winds are so dense that a neutron star or black hole circling such a star would be able to accrete enough material from the wind to power itself as an X-ray source. In whatever way the mass transfer takes place, because the binary system is rotating, the infalling material has, in general, too much angular momentum to be able to fall straight onto the compact object, just as the Earth (luckily!) has too much angular momentum to be able to fall straight into the Sun. Instead the material forms a 'disc' around the compact object.

If the compact object is a white dwarf, a black hole or a neutron star with a magnetic field less than about 10^4 tesla, the accretion disc extends right down to the surface of the star, or, in the case of a black hole, down to the innermost stable circular orbit. The same friction that gives rise to the angular momentum transfer in the disc also produces a large amount of dissipation of kinetic energy and generation of heat. Thus, as we mentioned above, although material falling radially onto a black hole generates very little radiation, material spiralling into a black hole through an accretion disc can in fact radiate away up to about 40 per cent of its rest mass energy. This is the most efficient means known of transforming matter into energy and it is not surprising that this is one possibility for the explanation of such luminous objects as X-ray sources. The material at the inner edge of a disc around a black hole just falls down the black hole without radiating further. However, if the disc has a star at the centre, about half of the radiation observed is emitted by the disc, and the other half is emitted when the accreted material at the inner edge of the disc crashes into the stellar surface, dissipating the rest of its kinetic energy as heat.

If, however, the compact object is a neutron star with a strong magnetic field the story is quite different. For the neutron stars associated with the pulsating radio sources, magnetic fields as high as 10^8 tesla (10^{12} gauss) have been suggested, and there seems no reason why such strong fields should not exist on X-ray-source neutron stars as well. Such a strong field controls the flow of material out to a distance of several hundred times the radius of the neutron star. The accreting material is highly conducting and so can flow only along the lines of magnetic force and not across them. The shape of the magnetic field of a neutron star is basically similar to that of the Earth in that it is a dipole – that is, there are two magnetic poles, one north and one south. As for the Earth, there is no reason to expect the magnetic poles and the axis of rotation of the star to be coincident. The accretion disc is, in this case, disrupted a large distance from the neutron star, and the infalling material is funnelled by the magnetic field onto the magnetic poles. At each pole the energy dissipated by the infalling matter produces a hot spot, about a kilometre across, which is a very luminous X-ray emitter. If these hot spots lie well away from the rotation axis, then as the star rotates we see first one spot and then the other – in order words the X-ray emission from the source is pulsed with a period between the pulses equal to, or half, that of the rotation period of the neutron star. This is indeed thought to be the case for the two pulsing X-ray sources Cen X–3 and Her X–1.

Hercules X–1 pulses every 1.24 sec and undergoes eclipses lasting 5.8 hours every 1.7 days. The 1.24 sec pulse period actually varies smoothly with a 1.7-day period just as if it were orbiting an unseen companion, and this gives conclusive evidence of the association of X-ray sources with binary systems. The star HZ Herculis varies regularly in brightness by a factor 4 with a period of 1.7 days. If HZ Her were a solitary star, it would be a rather uninteresting star with a surface temperature of some 7000 K. However the close proximity of its energetic and luminous companion causes the side of it nearest the X-ray source to be heated to over 20 000 K and the rotation of the system as a whole causes the observed regular variation in brightness. This is, however, by no means the end of the story. As well as the two periodicities, Her X–1 has a third 35-day period associated with it. For 10 of the 35 days the X-ray source is on, whereas in general, for the remaining 25 days, few X-rays are seen at all. Another odd thing is that whereas the X-ray source Her X–1 appears to turn on and off, the heating of its companion HZ Her remains more or less constant throughout. This means that for most of the time the X-ray source manages to shine X-rays at the companion star but not at us. How it achieves this still remains something of a mystery.

The X-ray source Cygnus X–1 was unidentified for some time, but in March 1971 a radio source appeared close to the expected X-ray position (a number of binary systems, e.g. Algol, are known to have weak, but variable, radio sources associated with them, though the cause of this radio emission is still unknown). The radio source, whose position could be determined much more accurately than that of the X-ray source, coincided with a very young luminous supergiant star HDE 226868. The spectral lines of the star are observed to vary sinusoidally in wavelength over a regular period,

indicating that it does indeed have an unseen companion. Because the supergiant star is so massive (about 20 times more massive than the Sun), its companion must also be massive (at least six times and probably ten times more massive than the Sun), in order to be able to swing it around at such a speed. Thus the mass of the unseen companion is well above the theoretical upper limits to the masses of neutron stars and white dwarfs, and it is widely speculated that this object must be a black hole (figure 6.11).

6.11: *The star field in the neighbourhood of the X-ray star Cygnus X-1, which may consist of a black hole orbiting the visible star. (Palomar Sky Survey, USA)*

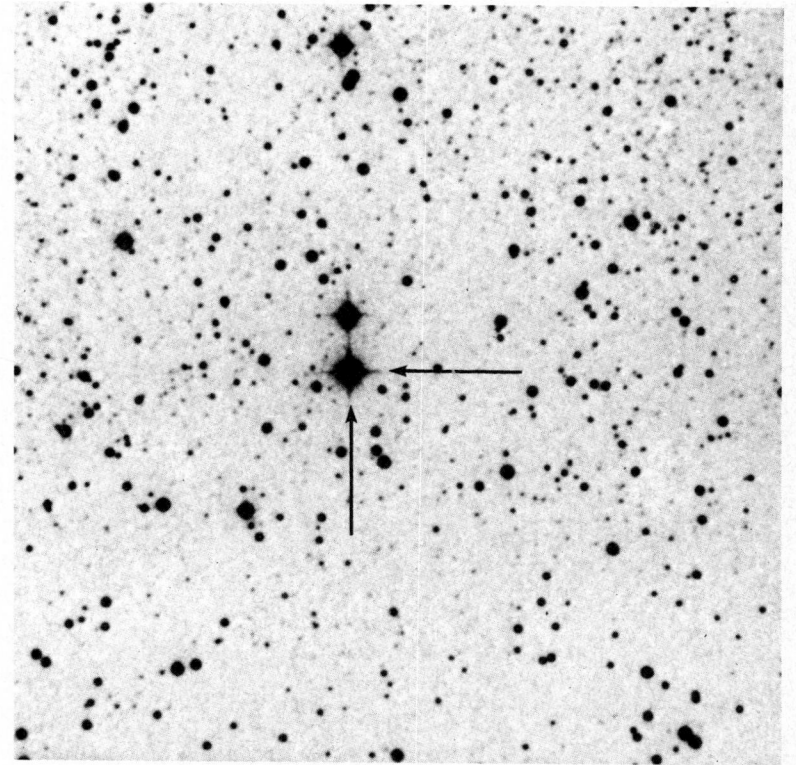

7. The distribution and origin of the chemical elements

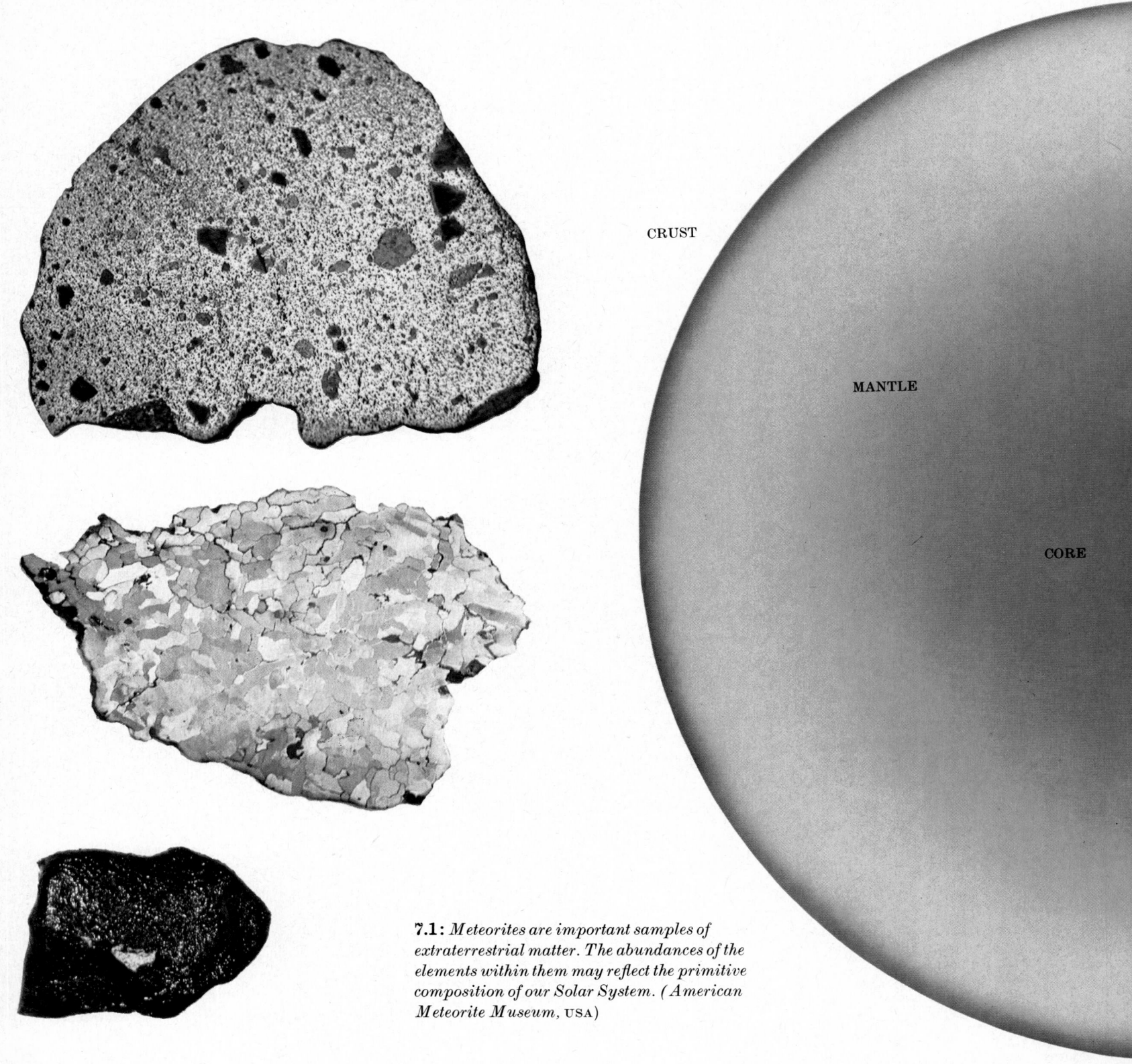

CRUST

MANTLE

CORE

7.1: *Meteorites are important samples of extraterrestrial matter. The abundances of the elements within them may reflect the primitive composition of our Solar System. (American Meteorite Museum, USA)*

The composition of the Universe

The discovery of the chemical composition of every type of astronomical body, from our planet Earth, through planets, stars and interstellar gas, to distant galaxies is a major occupation of astrophysicists in our own time. Since nuclear science realized the dream of the alchemist, to transmute the elements from one to another, we have come to understand how the everyday materials that we take for granted have not always existed as such. The chemical elements are largely the by-products of nuclear reactions in stars, galaxies, and the early Universe. Nuclear astrophysicists apply the knowledge of the physics of *nuclear reactions* to fit together the data on the distribution of the elements to form a unified picture of the origin and evolution of the constituents of the Universe. Attempts are made to answer the questions: what was the composition of the Universe when it was first created? What chain of events has resulted in the variety of chemical elements (92 natural ones) that can combine into almost an infinity of compound materials, and the complexity of life that can speculate on its own earliest beginnings? It is not, perhaps, widely appreciated that scientists can now be reasonably sure that all the atoms on Earth, for example, had to be created inside a generation of stars that evolved before the birth of the Sun and planets. The elucidation of the processes by which elements were and are created in the cosmic environment will stand in history as one of the great advances of the physical sciences in the twentieth century.

The methods and results of abundance analysis

There are only two basic ways in which abundances, or the relative quantities of each element in the Universe, may be determined: the direct chemical analysis of samples, and deduction from analysis of *absorption* and *emission-line spectra*. We include here the parts of the spectrum outside the visible range, because some of the most exciting discoveries about the interstellar medium have resulted from microwave and *radio astronomy*.

Direct chemical analysis has so far been possible only for the surfaces of the Earth and Moon, and for *meteorites* (figure 7.1). Its great advantage is the accuracy with which the composition of any individual sample can be assessed under laboratory conditions; even the relative amounts of different *isotopes* can be determined. However, finding the compositions of the Earth and Moon as whole objects is more difficult because of the chemical separation that has taken place since they formed. The Earth's interior must have a composition different from its crust as the average density of the Earth ($5500\,kg\,m^{-3}$) is considerably greater than that of typical rocks in the crust ($2400\,kg\,m^{-3}$). The existence of several layers in the Earth's interior is confirmed by studies of the way earthquake waves travel through the Earth. The interior structure of the Earth is shown schematically in figure 7.2. The core must be predominantly iron and nickel to account for the average density of the planet, and the presence of a metallic core is confirmed by the existence of the Earth's magnetic field. The layer between the crust and the core, the mantle, is probably made of olivine rock, a

7.2: *A schematic representation of the interior structure of the Earth. The core must be made of heavy elements, such as iron and nickel, in order to account for the average density.*

mineral of iron and magnesium silicate. 98 per cent of the crust is composed of only eight elements: oxygen, silicon, aluminium, iron, calcium, magnesium, sodium and potassium.

Apollo astronauts left *seismometers* on the Moon. Studies of the weak naturally-occurring moonquakes, and artificially-created ones show that the Moon too has several layers, but no metallic core. The surface rocks that have been analysed are similar in nature to terrestrial rocks, but they have a significantly different composition. In particular, more titanium, uranium and rare earth elements are present. This is one example of abundance data teaching us about astronomical history. In the face of the composition difference, it seems unlikely that the Moon was part of the Earth, except perhaps in the very earliest phase of the Solar System.

The Earth, Moon, and inner planets have very little of the lightest and volatile elements, presumably because these elements (e.g. hydrogen and helium) rapidly escape into space from a small body under the influence of solar heat. The giant planets, on the other hand, are further from the Sun so the heating is weaker and they are largely composed of the light elements. Because of the different evolutionary history of each planet, it is not possible to use planetary abundances to gain a completely precise picture of the abundance of the elements in the material from which the Solar System formed. For this we have to turn to the Sun. The composition of the Sun itself is probably the best clue to the nature of the material from which the Solar System formed. The composition of the outer layer that is responsible for the Sun's absorption-line spectrum remains unchanged despite the nuclear processes going on in the interior. From the lines in the spectrum of the Sun it is possible to deduce the relative composition of the solar atmosphere. The solar abundances are confirmed by results from a surprising source, namely the relative proportions of the elements found in certain meteorites: one type of meteorite, the CARBONACEOUS CHONDRITES, contains 20 per cent water and compounds of volatile elements, the presence of which suggests that these meteorites have never undergone heating, so that they presumably have their original composition. Their name arises from the small spherical bodies, or chondrules, that they contain, and only a handful have ever been discovered.

When the effects of heating and consequent chemical separation have been taken into account, the results from the Sun, meteorites, Earth, Moon and planets are not remarkably different, and the abundances of all the elements in the Solar System have been drawn up on the basis of this data. Figure 7.3 shows the abundances of the elements plotted on a graph against *atomic mass*, A. The general features of this curve tell us a great deal about how the elements could have been created. Note that there is a general decrease in abundance towards heavier elements. On top of this general trend, there are two particularly notable features. One is the great dip corresponding to the light elements lithium, beryllium and boron. The other is the spike around $A = 56$; this is the so-called IRON PEAK.

Perhaps it is surprising that most stars whose spectra have been examined have compositions similar to the Sun's. Some of those

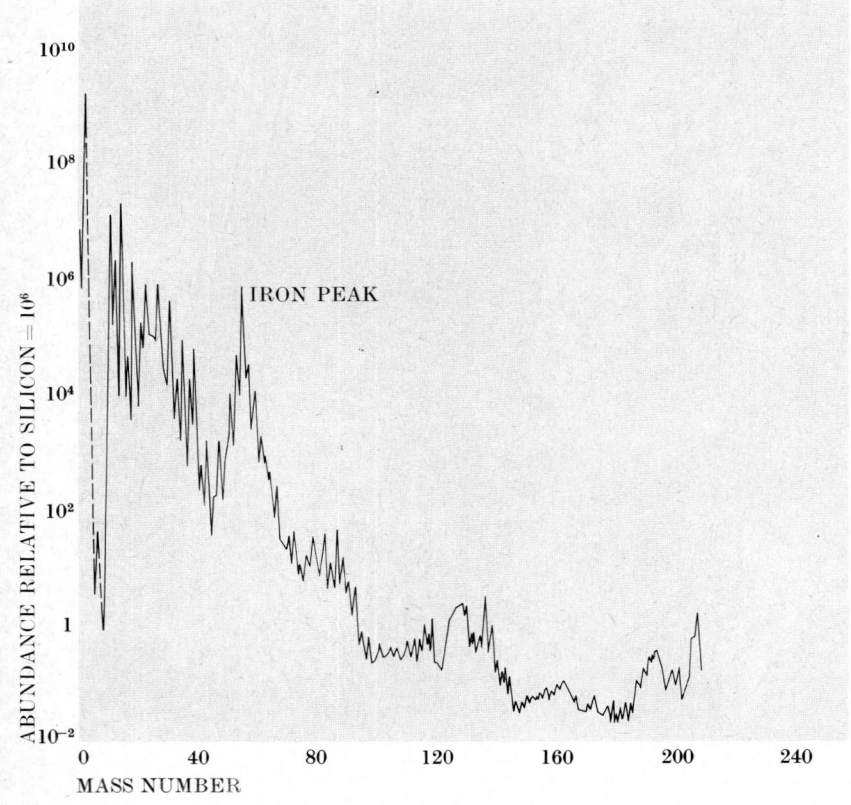

7.3: *The relative abundances of the elements in the Solar System plotted against atomic mass. Astrophysicists have shown how the main features of this curve arise. All elements other than hydrogen and helium have been manufactured in cosmic nuclear furnaces and explosions.*

that do not can be explained by circumstances peculiar to the particular stars. However, the metal-deficient stars form an interesting group. These are stars that have significantly less of the elements heavier than helium (metals) than the Sun and they have been found to belong exclusively to *Population II*. These are all old stars in globular clusters, or in high-velocity orbits perpendicular to the plane of the Galaxy. There is a clear indication that younger stars have richer compositions, though even old stars near the galactic centre are not metal deficient. The composition of a star depends on both its age and its location in the Galaxy, a reflection of the changing composition of the Galaxy as a whole as time progresses.

It is not possible to gain a detailed picture of the chemical composition of other galaxies, but we can infer from their spectra that they cannot be grossly different from our Galaxy. The ratios of the abundances of some elements can be determined, especially for galaxies with emission lines in their spectra, and these do not show spectacular deviations from the Solar System abundances.

The processes of nucleosynthesis

The term NUCLEOSYNTHESIS means the creation of new elements in nuclear reactions. Before we can consider how the present-day mix of elements may have come into being, we need to look at the various processes that could have contributed. It used to be supposed that the Universe has always had the composition we observe today, but since we now know that nuclear reactions are occurring inside stars, we must consider the possibility of a composition that has changed significantly, because stars are modifying the elemental mix.

Stars on the *main sequence* derive their energy from converting hydrogen to helium: hydrogen nuclei essentially fuse together in a series of reactions. The consumption of a nuclear fuel in this way is called burning, though it is not combustion in the normal sense. The two main processes are called the *proton-proton (p-p) chain* and the *carbon-nitrogen (CN) cycle*. Energy is released in these reactions, which only occur in the first place because the temperature (about 10^7 K) becomes sufficiently hot in the core of a star to give the particles the necessary speeds. The p-p chain can occur in material that is initially pure hydrogen. If there is already some carbon or nitrogen present, then the CN cycle can operate. When all the hydrogen that is hot enough has been converted into helium, no further reactions occur in the stellar core until the temperature exceeds 10^8 K, at which stage helium burning can commence. Helium nuclei combine to form the isotopes of carbon and oxygen, ^{12}C and ^{16}O. These reactions and successive changes in the internal processes of a star cause structural changes that move the star away from the main sequence.

Another increase in temperature to about 10^9 K takes place when all the helium has been consumed, and this allows carbon and oxygen burning reactions to occur with the production of heavier elements such as neon, sodium, magnesium and silicon. Up until this point, only elements with a mass number that is an exact multiple of four have been created (i.e. ^{12}C, ^{16}O, ^{20}Ne, ^{24}Mg, ^{28}Si, ^{32}S, etc., up to ^{56}Fe) in the more massive stars that are able to reach the requisite central pressures. At a temperature of 3.5×10^9 K silicon burning will take place in the later evolution of $20 M_\odot$ stars for example. Two silicon nuclei (^{28}Si) combine to form nickel-56 (^{56}Ni), which emits two positrons to make cobalt (^{56}Co) and ultimately iron (^{56}Fe). In this way all the iron we find in our everyday surroundings is thought to have been cooked up in a stellar furnace at a temperature of 3.5×10^9 K.

Now we must examine the origin of elements with mass numbers that are not multiples of four. Any further temperature rise is sufficient to cause protons and α-*particles* (helium nuclei) to be removed again from some of the nuclei that have been built up and thus trigger a whole host of new reactions. They can then recombine until, gradually, all the elements with mass numbers up to the iron peak (^{56}Ni, ^{56}Co, ^{56}Fe etc.) are created with the consequential release of energy. By the time the temperature has soared to 4×10^9 K, nearly all the nuclei will have become iron-peak elements. However, there the build-up ends because any further fusion demands the input of energy, and it is therefore necessary to look for other means to create the elements heavier than iron.

A popular explanation for the origin of many of the heavy elements is that they have built up gradually by the NEUTRON CAPTURE PROCESS. Relatively plentiful iron-peak nuclei act as 'seeds' that pick up neutrons one at a time. After the capture of a neutron, a nucleus may be unstable and, if so, the emission of an electron (β-*decay*) follows. When this happens, the number of protons in the nucleus increases by one, and thus a new element is created. If there is a large number of neutrons about, several may be captured by one seed nucleus before it has time to decay via emission of an electron. This rapid capture of several neutrons has been termed the R-PROCESS. If the flux of neutrons is small, so that any unstable nucleus has time to decay before the next neutron comes along, the situation is described as the slow, or S-PROCESS. Some examples will make this clear. If we add neutrons one at a time to ^{56}Fe we make ^{57}Fe, ^{58}Fe, and ^{59}Fe. Now ^{57}Fe and ^{58}Fe are stable, but ^{59}Fe is not. In the r-process (many neutrons around) ^{60}Fe, and ^{61}Fe, form successively, but ^{61}Fe decays to ^{61}Co in around 6 minutes. In s-process synthesis (not many neutrons) the ^{59}Fe decays to ^{59}Co before it can pick up an unattached neutron. A continuation of our agument would show that the two mixtures of elements that result from r-process and s-process syntheses are not identical. The r-process forms nuclei that are neutron-rich relative to the s-process. This leads us to the interesting possibility of determining which route led to the formation of the heavy elements in the Solar System.

There is remarkable evidence that the material of the Solar System has been subjected to the s-process. Nuclei that easily capture neutrons are quickly destroyed when there are neutrons about, so it would be expected that the greater an element's ability to capture neutrons, the less there will be of that element. The quantity that is a measure of a nucleus' ability to catch neutrons is called its capture cross-section (σ). The s-process predicts that the product of the abundance, N, and σ is roughly constant over certain ranges of atomic mass. The Solar System abundances fit the s-process prediction rather well, as shown in figure 7.4 where the solid line is the theoretical prediction that fits the observations best. Unfortunately, the r-process cannot be tested in the same way. The prediction is a rather random distribution of (σN) with atomic mass that cannot be reliably connected with the observed abundances.

Some heavy isotopes cannot be manufactured by either of the two neutron-capture processes, notably those isotopes that are relatively rich in protons. It is thought that they may be produced by proton capture (P-PROCESS). The source of neutrons and protons to allow these processes to occur is uncertain, but it is thought that they may be produced in large numbers in the later stages of stellar evolution, or it may be that these events all happened under special circumstances early in the life of the Galaxy.

Nucleosynthesis in the Galaxy

Nucleosynthesis is closely linked with cosmology. The present composition of the Galaxy has arisen because the history of the Universe took the course it did. Some early theories investigated single processes in the early Universe that might have resulted in the present abundances. One of these was the ALPHA-BETA-GAMMA THEORY, so-called because it was proposed by the three physicists Alpher, Bethe and Gamow. This theory is based on the idea of a very hot, dense, early stage to the Universe (the *primaeval fireball*) where protons and neutrons might combine rapidly, but of itself it fails to account for the amounts of heavier elements we have now. Another idea was the EQUILIBRIUM THEORY. If a high enough temperature can be reached ($>5 \times 10^9$ K) under suitable conditions, then the nuclear reactions that are occurring are just as frequently reversed, so that the composition remains fixed, depending only on the actual temperature. Again, this one process, which, it was supposed, might have taken place in the early Universe, cannot account for the abundances of all the elements at once, though such a process might have occurred at some point.

The observational and theoretical evidence all suggests that a sequence of events has changed the composition of the Universe, including our Galaxy, and that the heavier elements have been built up from light ones. As the outer layers of some of the oldest stars in the Galaxy are metal-poor, they are thought to represent the original composition of the Galaxy. These stars are still in existence because their masses are low and their consequent rates of evolution are slow. Massive stars that were born at the same time have long since evolved. Many of these will have exploded as *supernovae*, scattering some of the contents of their evolved interiors into the *interstellar medium*, though exactly how much mass is lost by stars in this way is uncertain. Recent research has shown that during the explosion itself, conditions are right for nucleosynthesis to occur. This may turn out to be a major source of heavier elements.

If the rate at which supernova explosions occur has always been

7.4: *The s-process curve for the Solar System abundances. The filled circles represent isotopes produced by the s-process only with known values of* σ. *The crosses represent isotopes with estimated values of* σ. *Open circles represent isotopes produced partly by the r-process for which a contribution has been subtracted. The solid line is a theoretical result.*

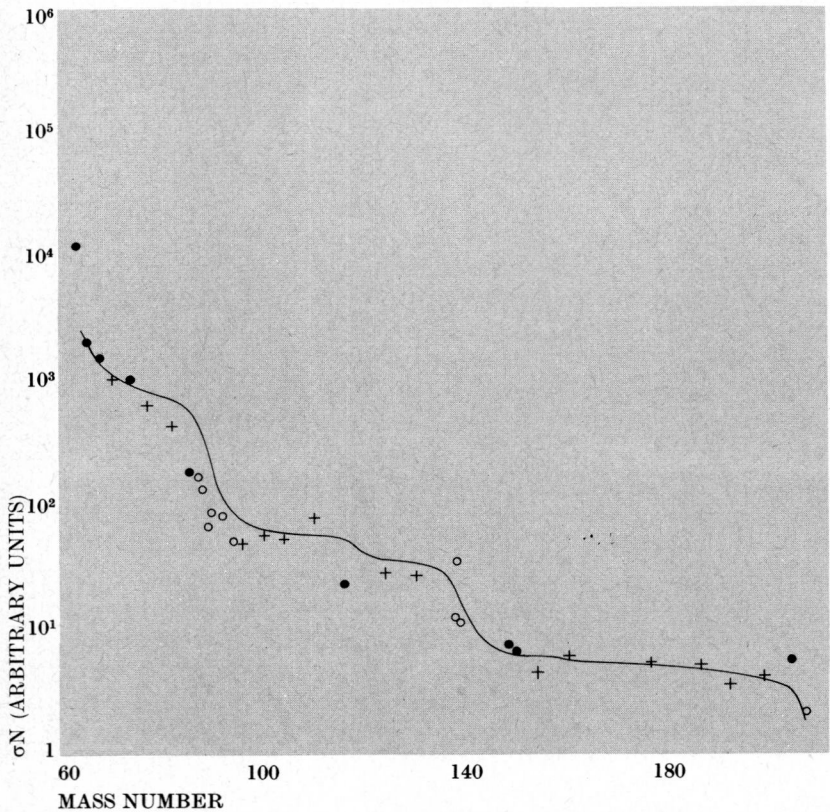

the same as it is now, it could not explain the observed enrichment of stellar material. As only the oldest stars have the metal-poor composition, it looks as though a burst of element production took place in the Galaxy, after the first stars were formed. Perhaps early in the history of the Galaxy, there were many more massive stars than we observe today; these would rapidly have become supernovae. Of course, much of the material that is converted into heavier elements remains locked up in the remnants (*white dwarfs* or *neutron stars*) of highly-evolved stars and is not available for new stars. The tendency for the stars poorest in metals to be found away from the galactic centre suggests that this may have been the site of the earliest and most intense element production. However, there remain many problems in piecing together a unified theory, and this is still very much an area of active research.

We have been much concerned with the production of heavy elements, but one of the worst headaches is the so-called HELIUM PROBLEM. The question is, essentially: was all or some of the helium present today part of the original composition of the Universe? One of the troubles is that helium is notoriously illusive to detect. Its spectral lines are measurable only in the hottest stars (O- and B-types), so we cannot be sure of the exact abundance of helium in the Galaxy, though it seems to be around 25 per cent by mass in younger stars. Only about 2 per cent of the matter is in the form of heavier elements, the remainder being hydrogen.

Astrophysicists are reasonably agreed that the hydrogen is primaeval (i.e. it dates from the earliest phase of the Universe, or shortly after); but although helium is a major product of hydrogen burning in stars, it in turn is consumed in successive processes. If only 10 per cent of the mass of the Galaxy has been changed into the helium that is observable now, (i.e. not counting that which has subsequently been turned into heavier elements, or will be used up in time in low-mass stars), the amount of energy released would have been so great that the total luminosity of the Galaxy would sometime have had to be at least 50 times greater than it is now. Furthermore, if all the helium was produced in stars, it is difficult to account for the proportions of helium and heavier elements. One theory that tries to explain this suggests that hypothetical super-massive stars ($>100\,M_\odot$) might have exploded after they had converted a substantial proportion of their hydrogen to helium, but before the helium had been changed into other elements.

The idea favoured by most astronomers is that most of the helium found in our Galaxy has not been assembled inside stars, since the problems of explaining its ubiquity in the observed high proportion (one-quarter of all cosmic matter) seem insurmountable. It is thought that helium could have been made in the primaeval Universe by the following process. In the laboratory, the free neutron decays in about 10 minutes to produce a proton and an electron. It has been shown theoretically that all the helium could have been formed in the first ten minutes of the Universe's existence, before half the neutrons would have naturally decayed. In the primordial neutron-proton soup, neutron-proton collisions produce deuterons. Deuteron-pair collisions result in the production

of helium-3 and helium-4 (^{3}He and ^{4}He). The exact details depend on the model of the Universe that one adopts, but it does seem entirely plausible that the observed helium was made in the primordial *big bang*.

The light elements, lithium, beryllium and boron have also presented some special difficulties. These are rapidly destroyed in stellar interiors. Although their abundances are low compared with elements of neighbouring mass, the fact that they exist at all needs explanation. A plausible theory is that they are produced when *cosmic rays* collide with heavy nuclei and break them up.

Out of the tangled web of data from nuclear physics (information on energy levels in nuclei and nuclear reaction rates) and spectroscopy (abundance and distribution of the chemical elements), astronomers have drawn a coherent picture of the history of matter. Elements are assembled inside the stars and then broadcast through space by supernova explosions. From the enriched interstellar medium, new stars and possibly planets form, incorporating the ashes of a previous generation. All common materials of our world were made in stellar furnaces before our Sun and planets formed; every atom of our bodies was fused together in past aeons of an almost fantastic galactic history. In truth we are the children of the Universe.

Table 7.1: Summary of fusion reactions in stellar interiors

Hydrogen burning (10^7 K) *p-p chain (simplest form)*
1) $p + p \rightarrow {}^2H + e^+ + \nu$
2) $^2H + p \rightarrow {}^3He + \gamma$
3) $^3He + {}^3He \rightarrow {}^4He + p + p$

CN cycle
1) $^{12}C + p \rightarrow {}^{13}N + \gamma$
2) $^{13}N \rightarrow {}^{13}C + e^+ + \nu$
3) $^{13}C + p \rightarrow {}^{14}N + \gamma$
4) $^{14}N + p \rightarrow {}^{15}O + \gamma$
5) $^{15}O \rightarrow {}^{15}N + e^+ + \nu$
6) $^{15}N + p \rightarrow {}^{12}C + {}^4He$

Helium burning (10^8 K)
$3\,{}^4He \rightarrow {}^{12}C + \gamma$
$^{12}C + {}^4He \rightarrow {}^{16}O + \gamma$

Carbon burning (5×10^8 K) *examples*
$^{12}C + {}^{12}C \rightarrow {}^{24}Mg + \gamma$
$^{12}C + {}^{12}C \rightarrow {}^{23}Na + p$
$^{12}C + {}^{12}C \rightarrow {}^{20}Ne + \alpha$

Oxygen burning (10^9 K) *examples*
$^{16}O + {}^{16}O \rightarrow {}^{32}S + \gamma$
$^{16}O + {}^{16}O \rightarrow {}^{31}P + p$
$^{16}O + {}^{16}O \rightarrow {}^{31}S + n$
$^{16}O + {}^{16}O \rightarrow {}^{28}Si + \alpha$

Silicon burning (2×10^9 K) *typical process*
1) $^{28}Si + \gamma \rightarrow 7\,{}^4He$
2) $^{28}Si + 7\,{}^4He \rightarrow {}^{56}Ni$
or $^{28}Si + {}^{28}Si \rightarrow {}^{56}Ni$
$^{56}Ni \rightarrow {}^{56}Co + e^+ + \nu$
$^{56}Co \rightarrow {}^{56}Fe + e^+ + \nu$

8. Our Sun

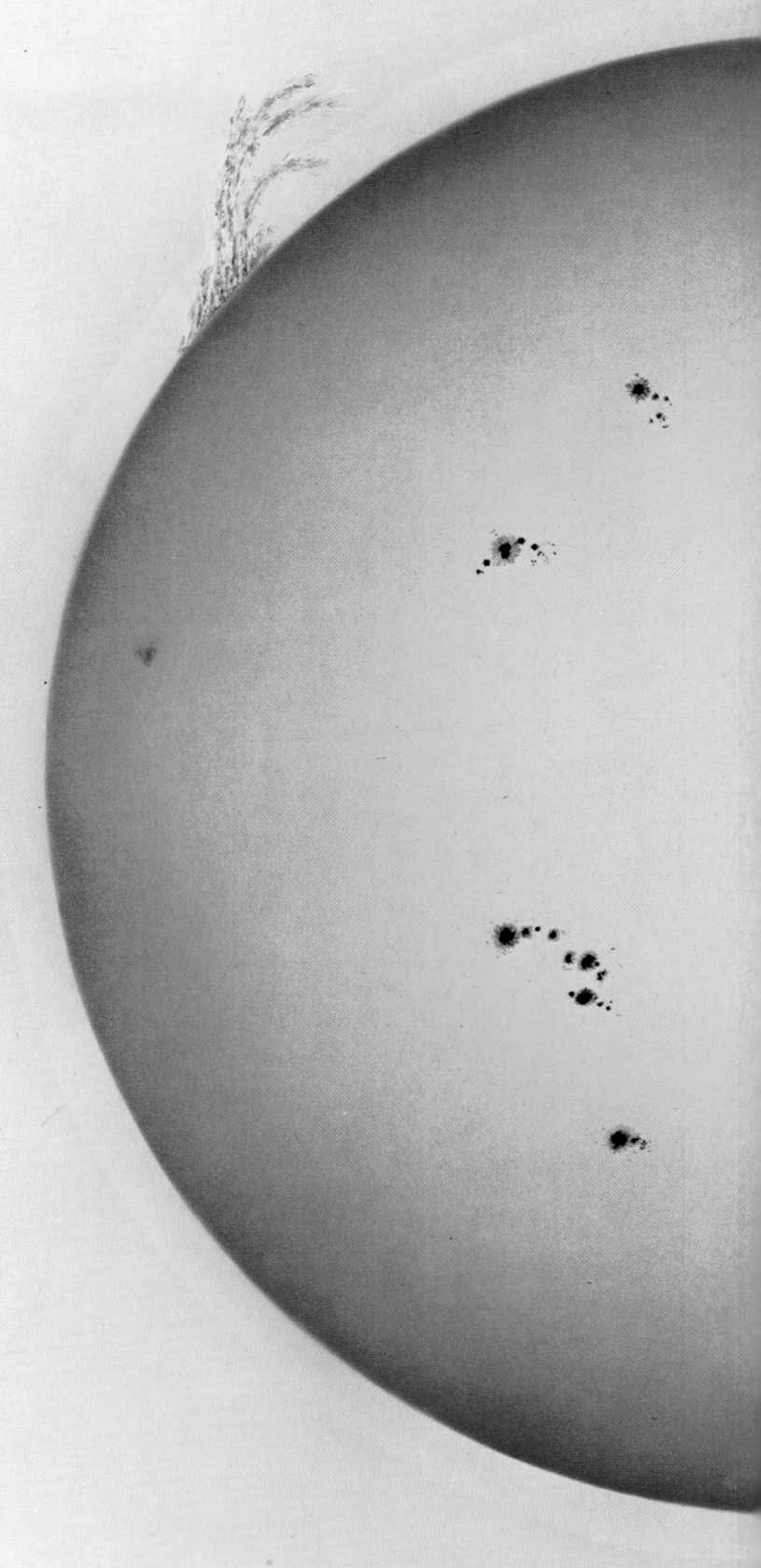

Table 8.1 : Properties of the Sun

Property	*Value*
Average Sun–Earth distance	149,598,000 km
Angular diameter	32 minutes of arc
Radius	696,000 km (108 Earth radii)
Mass	1.99×10^{30} kg (3.28×10^5 Earth–Moon mass)
Average density	1.41×10^3 kg m^{-3} (0.26 Earth density)
Luminosity	3.90×10^{26} watts
Surface temperature	5,800 K
Spectral type	G2
Apparent magnitude	-26.8 mag
Absolute magnitude	4.79 mag
Composition	75 per cent : hydrogen
	25 per cent : helium
	0.8 per cent : oxygen
	0.3 per cent : carbon
	0.5 per cent : other elements

Introduction

The Sun is a typical star, but is unique as far as we are concerned because of its proximity to Earth; it is about 150 million km away. A summary of basic solar properties is given in table 8.1. Solar energy provides virtually all the heat and light which our planet receives, and it therefore sustains every living entity. The character of our own environment is strongly influenced by solar radiation which has been a major factor in determining the course of natural evolution on Earth. The Sun is important to astronomers and physicists because it enables them to investigate physical conditions, which are typical of most stars, in detail. Historically, the study of the Sun led to significant advances in atomic physics, nuclear physics, magnetohydrodynamics, and plasma physics. An understanding of solar processes is therefore of biological and physical interest, and several fundamental areas of scientific research are furthered by observing this local astrophysical laboratory. Satellites have enabled space scientists to probe more closely the interaction between the Sun and the Earth, especially the influence of the Sun on the magnetic field of the Earth.

Before describing the Sun in detail we must issue an important warning about observing the Sun: intense solar radiation permanently damages the tissue of the human eye. The Sun must never be viewed directly with a telescope or binoculars, which would have the effect of concentrating a massive dose of radiation on to the delicate tissue. The solar filters sold with many cheap telescopes are not an adequate safeguard because they may admit a dangerous dose of invisible ultraviolet light or may shatter unexpectedly. They should be destroyed in order to remove the temptation to use them. With a little experimentation, good images of the Sun can be produced by projecting through an eyepiece on to a piece of stiff card. This arrangement is adequate for viewing sunspots or the progress of an eclipse. An *eclipse* may also be observed by the unaided eye by looking at the Sun through a really dark filter or looking at the reflection in a dark container of still water, but even these methods require caution. We repeat: **to look directly at the Sun through binoculars or a telescope is a dangerous act that can cause permanent blindness.**

Solar structure

Inside the Sun

The Sun condensed about 5 000 million years ago from a pocket of *interstellar gas* that contracted under the attractive forces of its own gravity. An important property of the Sun is its mass (330 000 times the Earth's mass), which results in a pressure and temperature at the centre of the Sun sufficiently high to cause the nuclear reactions that sustain the prodigious output of energy. A rather small proportion of the total volume of the Sun, known as the core, contains most of the mass and is responsible for the entire luminosity: within the central sphere of one-quarter the solar radius (1.5 per cent of the volume) is concentrated half the mass, and it is here that 99 per cent of the energy is generated. Originally the core consisted of about 75 per cent hydrogen, almost 25 per cent helium and around 1 per cent of heavier elements. Although the outer part of the Sun still has this original composition, nuclear burning has altered the make-up of the core.

The source of solar energy is the *proton-proton cycle*, in which hydrogen nuclei are converted to helium nuclei. Today, after more than 4 500 million years of fusion in the core, the concentration by mass of hydrogen has been reduced from 75 per cent to about 35 per cent; consequently the helium abundance has risen to around 65 per cent. Fusion is accompanied by a mass loss, which appears as energy. To generate the observed solar luminosity of 4×10^{26} watts demands the destruction of mass at the rate of $5 \times 10^{9} \, \mathrm{kg \, s^{-1}}$. Even at this rate the change in the Sun's mass due to fusion while it is a *main-sequence star* will be below 0.1 per cent. The Sun can maintain essentially its present output for about 5 000 million years. After this the exhaustion of hydrogen at the centre will induce structural changes that turn the Sun into a *red-giant* star. Ultimately the Sun will become a *white dwarf*.

Figures 8.1 and 8.2 illustrate the variations of the solar temperature and density with increasing distance from the centre. The central temperature is about $1.5 \times 10^{7} \, \mathrm{K}$, and it decreases steadily, reaching a surface value of 5800 K. At the centre, the density is nearly $1.6 \times 10^{5} \, \mathrm{kg \, m^{-3}}$, or 12 times the density of lead. The density falls rapidly with increasing distance; for example, it reaches the value for water half-way from the centre. These extreme physical conditions in the core cause the complete *ionization* of matter.

8.1: *It is impossible to measure the temperature inside the Sun by direct methods, but theoretical studies have indicated that the temperature at the centre of the Sun is about $1.5 \times 10^{7} \, K$. It drops to 5 800 K at the surface, following the steady decrease illustrated here.*

8.2: *Calculations have shown that the density of matter in the Sun varies from $1.5 \times 10^{5} \, kg \, m^{-3}$ at the centre to $10^{-4} \, kg \, m^{-3}$ at the surface. The average density is 1.4 times that of ordinary water. A consequence of the rapid fall in density with increasing distance from the centre is that 90 per cent of the mass is enclosed by the inner half of the solar radius.*

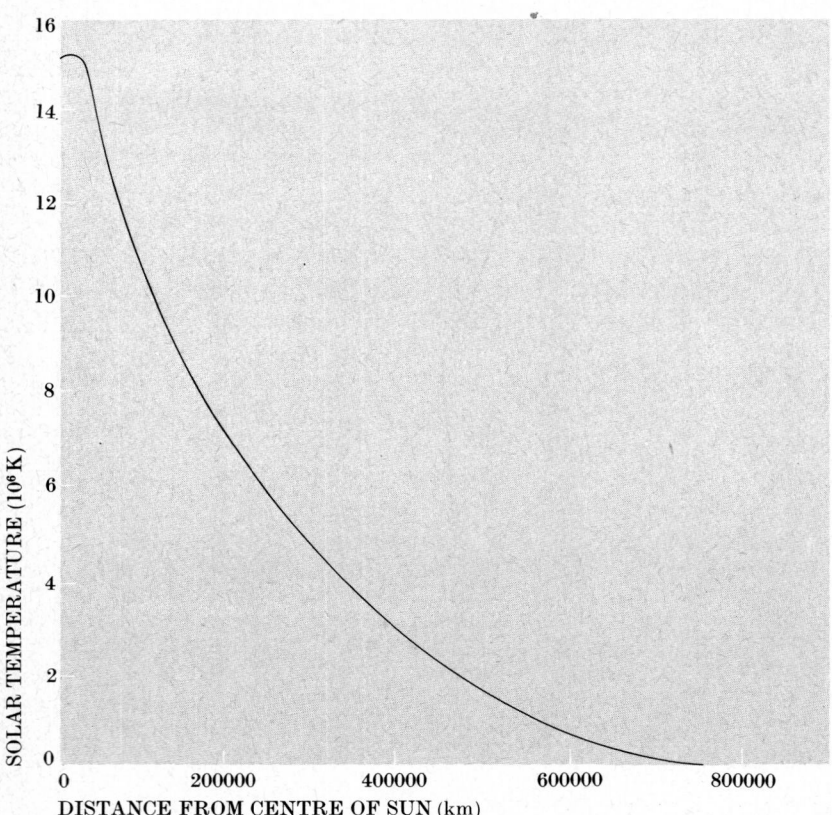

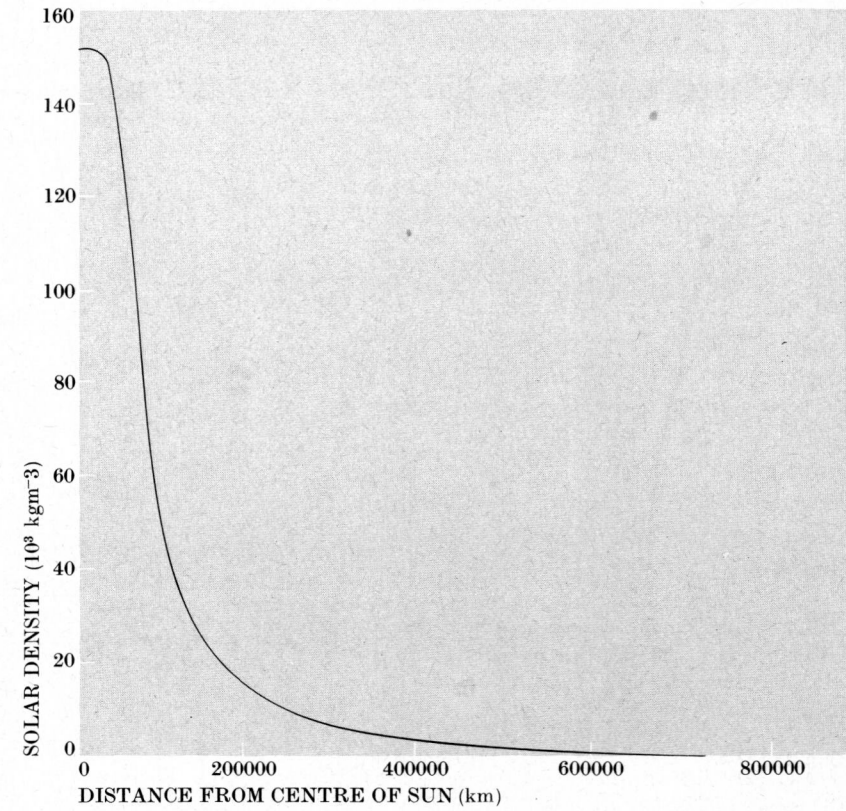

Even nuclei of the heavy elements are unable to retain orbital electrons. Therefore the solar core consists primarily of hydrogen nuclei (*protons*), helium nuclei (*alpha particles*), and free electrons. Most of the energy released from the nuclear fusion reactions is in the form of gamma-ray photons, X-ray photons, and weird particles called *neutrinos*. The neutrinos have such a small probability of interacting with matter that they stream straight out of the Sun. For the photons a different situation prevails because the free electrons readily scatter photons, and the nuclei can participate in non-elastic collision with photons. These properties of the electrons and nuclei make the core essentially *opaque* to electromagnetic radiation. Consequently it takes about 10^6 years for electromagnetic energy to diffuse from the core to the surface of the Sun. This long diffusion time is a major contributor to the stability of the Sun.

Out to a distance of around 0.85 solar radii, energy is transported primarily by radiation. The absence of convection in this part of the Sun prevents the helium made in the nuclear reactions being carried out of the core. At the distance 0.85 solar radii and beyond, the temperature has fallen sufficiently to enable the heavier nuclei to recapture outer orbital electrons and so form partially ionized atoms. These outer electrons of the atoms can easily absorb photons, and this leads to a sharp increase in the opacity of the solar material to radiation. Convective instability is then triggered because the radiation streaming out of the core is suddenly blocked; the transport of energy is primarily by turbulent circulating currents of gas and each element of rising gas takes energy directly to the surface. This zone of convection extends from a depth of 150 000 km or so up to the visible surface itself. At the surface, radiation again predominates as the means of energy transport.

Currents in the convection zone are thought to arrange themselves in three major tiers, as shown in figure 8.3. Deepest are the GIANT CELLS, each encompassing possibly 200 000 km. At an intermediate layer, SUPER-GRANULAR CELLS about 30 000 km in diameter are located. Finally, a layer of small currents roughly 1 000 km across and up to 2 000 km deep reaches to the surface. The tops of this upper layer make up the Sun's visible surface.

An important check on our knowledge of the solar interior has come from attempts to detect the abundant flux of neutrinos, which is released in the core to escape into space easily on account of the almost negligible interaction of neutrinos with matter. An experiment started in the late-1960s utilized a neutrino detector that contained 600 tonnes of liquid tetrachlorethylene (C_2Cl_4). This substance is relatively effective in recording certain of the neutrinos thought to be emerging from the Sun because they have the appropriate energy to interact with the chlorine atoms. The *neutrino telescope* was positioned deep in a gold mine to reduce spurious responses caused by *cosmic rays*. After the experiment had run for several years it consistently recorded the number of solar neutrinos to be less than the theoretical predictions. Subsequently, experimental and theoretical refinements reduced the

discrepancy somewhat, but the reasons for the lack of agreement are not clear. The experiment has demonstrated that our understanding of solar physics is perhaps not as complete as the simplified outline given here would suggest. One possibility, among several, is that the Sun's luminosity may vary slightly over a time scale of 2×10^8 years; this might also account for some of the major ice epochs experienced on Earth.

8.3: *Close to the solar surface, the material is broken up into three zones of convection, shown here. The highest tier of convection gives rise to the solar granulation.*

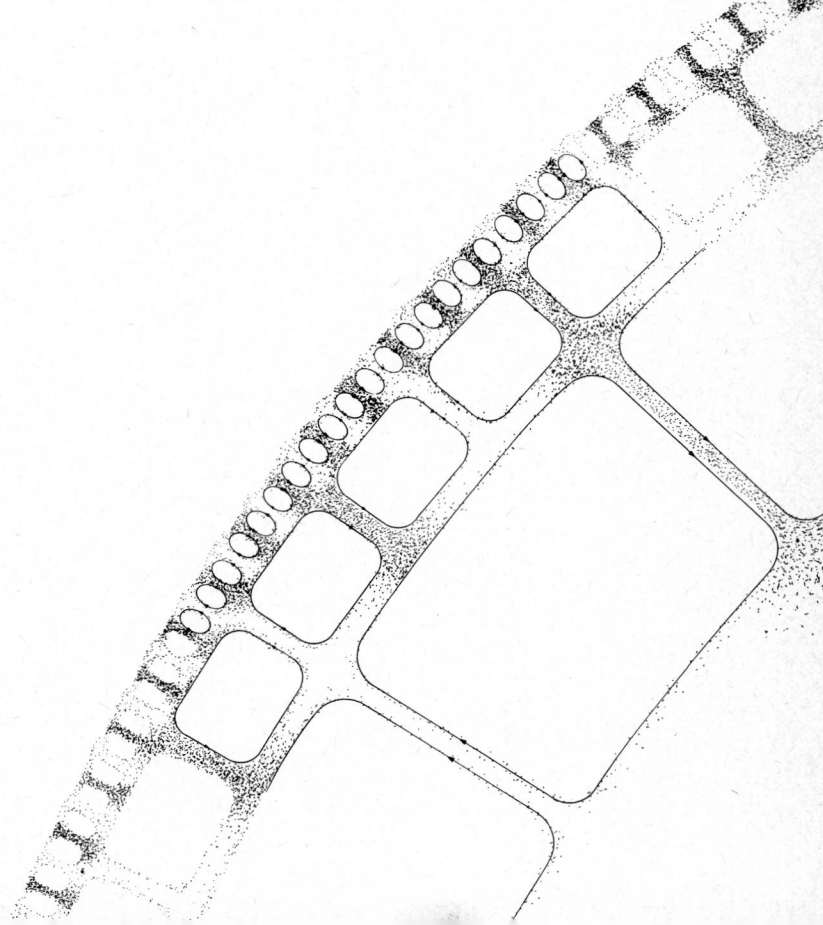

The visible surface

The highly luminous surface of the Sun is called the PHOTOSPHERE. The photosphere is the sharp disc as observed with the eye or a small telescope. Larger telescopes used under excellent observing conditions show that the photosphere is not uniformly bright, but has a mottled texture termed GRANULATION (figure 8.4). Graduations in this structure exist, but the smallest granules consist of bright patches of light, about 1 000 km across, with a dark border. The pattern is changing continuously as granules dissolve away and are replaced by new ones, so that the appearance changes completely in only a few minutes. Measurements of the *Doppler shifts* present in light from the photosphere have shown that the bright centre of a granule is moving upwards, whereas the boundary is cooler, descending gas. Almost certainly the solar granulation is associated with the highest convective tier in the Sun. Doppler-shift measuring techniques have also revealed large-scale motion of the photosphere. Within supergranular cells 30 000 km in diameter the gas moves predominantly horizontally from the centre to the edge of the cell. Disturbances deep in the convection zone may also be the cause of the rhythmic rising and falling of the photosphere on a cycle time of five minutes.

A remarkable property of the photosphere is that its edge, or LIMB, appears sharp to the naked eye, rather than merging gradually into the blackness of space, which is how we might expect an incandescent ball of gas to appear. This indicates that the layer from which most of the light is coming is shallow in comparison to the solar radius. The reason for this is as follows: as photons move through the convection zone, the temperature, pressure and density fall steadily. At visible wavelengths the negative hydrogen ion, which is a hydrogen atom that has temporarily captured a second electron, is a major contributor to the emission and absorption of radiation. Above the convection zone the density of this ion decreases much more rapidly than the total density of the solar atmosphere because it is extremely sensitive to changes in the temperature. One consequence of this is that most of the radiation that we can see is emitted in a layer only 500 km thick. Below this the Sun is opaque and above it is completely transparent.

The photospheric disc appears slightly less bright at the edge when observed visually or photographically (figure 8.5); this phenomenon is termed LIMB-DARKENING. It arises because a line of sight to the centre of the visible disc penetrates the solar atmosphere vertically and enables us to view slightly deeper, and therefore hotter, more luminous layers, as illustrated in figure 8.7a. Towards the edge of the disc, the line of sight passes obliquely through a greater thickness of cooler and partially opaque atmosphere. Consequently we see only to a slightly higher level; where the temperature is lower the material is less luminous, and therefore the limb appears darker. The magnitude of the effect is dependent on wavelength: it is most noticeable in blue light.

There are several ways of deriving a temperature for the Sun's

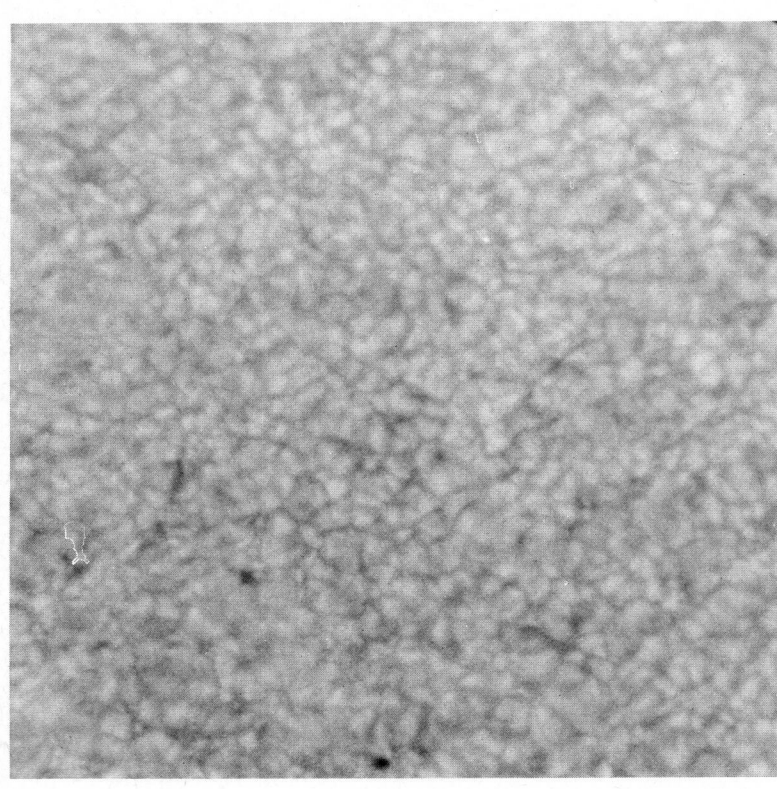

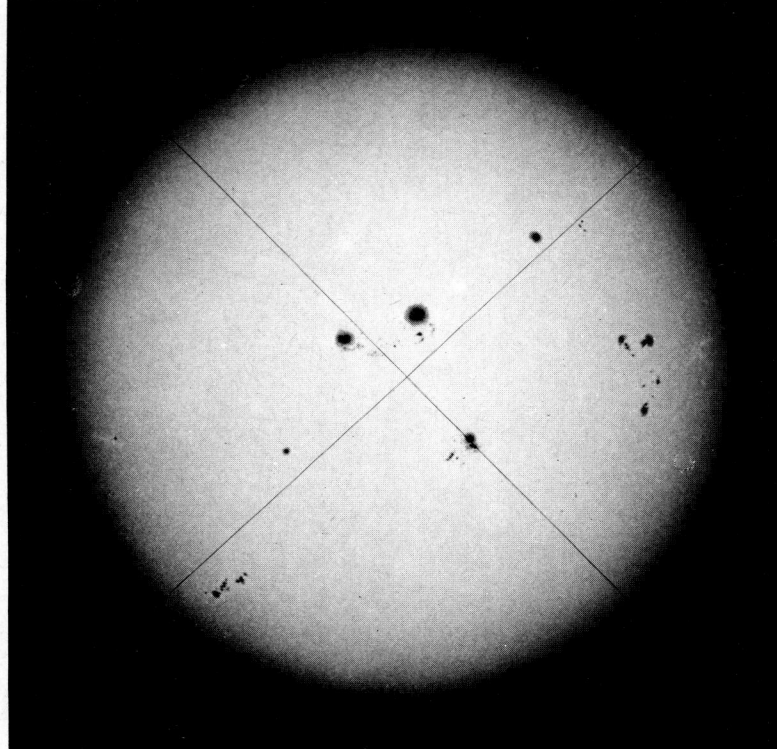

8.4: *Under excellent conditions it is possible for telescopes to photograph the fine mottling of the solar surface, known as the granulation. The gas within 150 000 km of the surface forms convection zones, and the top layer of convective material gives rise to the seething granules. (Sacramento Peak Observatory,* USA*)*

8.5: *In this photograph of the Sun's disc, darkening can be seen towards the edge, or limb. This arises because less light is received from the edge of the Sun, compared to the centre of the disc. Several magnificent sunspots can also be seen. (Royal Greenwich Observatory)*

8.6: *The visible light spectrum of the Sun. Some of the principal absorption lines, the elements producing them, and the wavelengths are given in the table. (Sacramento Peak Observatory, Air Force Cambridge Research Laboratories,* USA*)*

Table 8.2: Principal lines in the solar spectrum

Identifying symbol		Wavelength (nm)	Element
Fraunhofer	Other		
C	Hα	656	hydrogen
D		589	sodium
	b	516, 517, 518	magnesium
F	Hβ	486	hydrogen
	Hγ	434	hydrogen
	Hδ	410	hydrogen
	Fe	404	iron
H		396	calcium
K		393	calcium

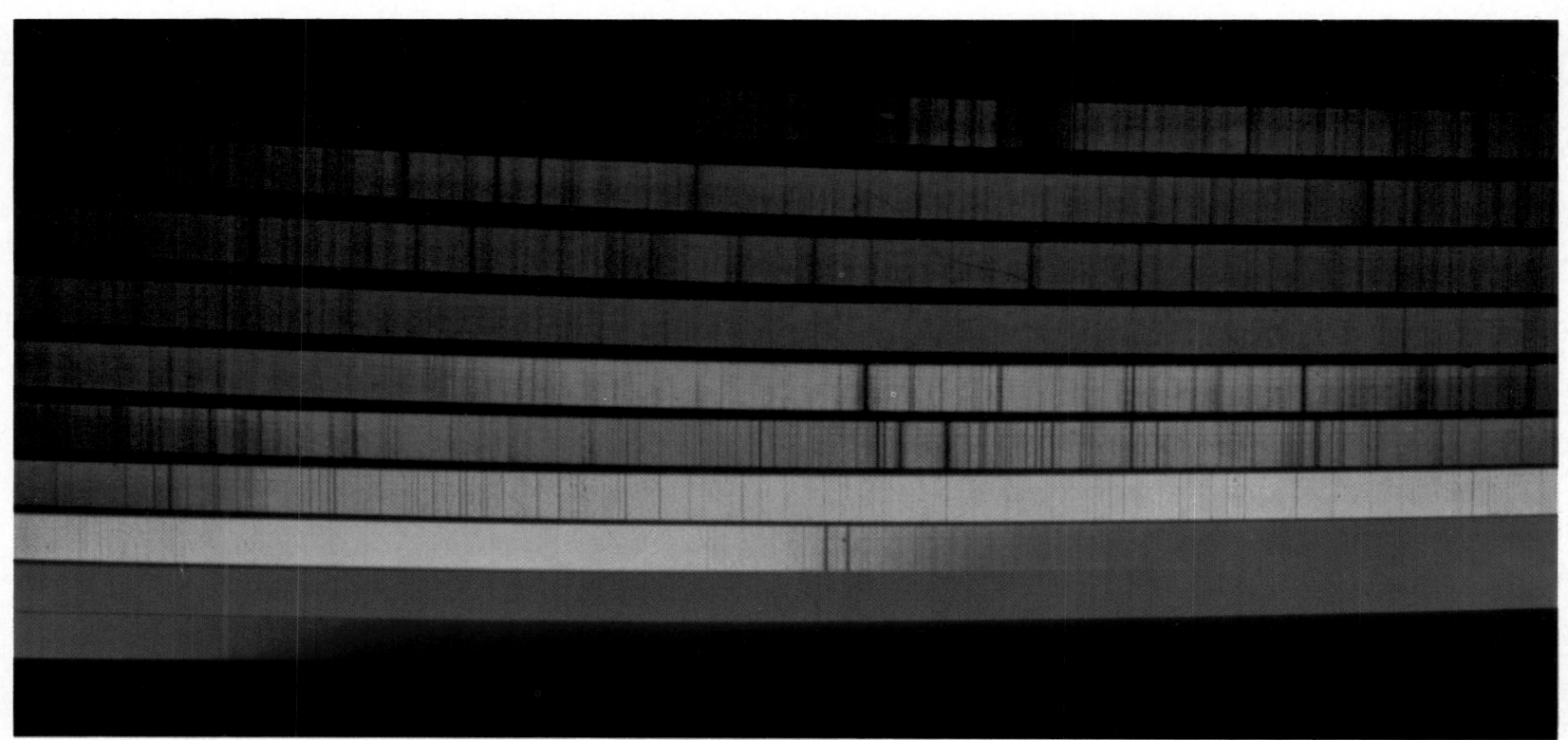

visible surface. The BLACK-BODY TEMPERATURE is 6 000 K. This is obtained by matching the spectrum of the continuum radiation from the Sun to theoretical curves derived from radiation laws.

The EFFECTIVE TEMPERATURE is related to the Sun's surface luminosity, which is 6.44×10^7 watts m^{-2}. According to the *Stefan–Boltzmann law*, an object radiating at 5 800 K would match this value. We see that the temperature obtained from the shape of the spectrum is greater than the temperature derived from the luminosity. This is because the radiation we receive is coming from a 500-km layer in the solar atmosphere, and the temperature varies in this layer. At the centre of the disc most of the energy is coming from a zone with a temperature of 6 500 K, whereas at the limb lower values prevail. For this reason it is not possible to define a unique temperature for the Sun's surface.

At the temperature of 6 200 K all substances are entirely gaseous; tungsten is the most refractory of all known elements, melting at 3 643 K and boiling at 6 200 K.

The solar atmosphere

Radiation from the photosphere produces a continuous spectrum without emission or absorption lines. Above the photosphere is a layer of gas about 500 km thick, within which the effective temperature declines steadily from about 6 000 to 4 000 K. Consequently, solar radiation has to traverse a layer of relatively cooler gas, and this absorbs radiation at wavelengths characteristic of the atoms and ions in the solar atmosphere. Within this cooler zone the *absorption-line spectrum* of the Sun, first described in some detail by *Fraunhofer* in 1814, originates. The absorption lines indicate that the mean temperature just above the photosphere is about 4 500 K. In older textbooks the cool zone is sometimes termed the REVERSING LAYER, and it is described as if there were a sharp transition between the hot radiating region and the overlying absorbing layer. In practice the layers merge, with continuum radiation and absorption taking place simultaneously; radiation dominates at the lower levels and absorption dominates higher up.

From the absorption-line spectrum, solar physicists have deduced the composition of the Sun's atmosphere, and, by implication, the composition of the whole region outside the core. The elements that produce the strongest lines, such as iron, which is responsible for several hundred, are identified simply by matching features in the solar spectrum against laboratory measurements for known atoms and ions. For the fainter lines, or the less abundant elements, or the regions of the spectrum which

8.7a: *Limb darkening arises because the light received from different parts of the solar photosphere arises from different depths in the outer layers of the Sun. A light beam from the solar limb directed towards Earth has to traverse a much greater thickness of the solar atmosphere, and consequently only light from the higher layers of the atmosphere, where the temperature and light intensity are lower, reaches us. When we look at the centre of the disc we receive light that has ascended the solar atmosphere vertically, and it is therefore possible to see to greater, hotter, depths. Consequently the centre appears brighter than the edge.*

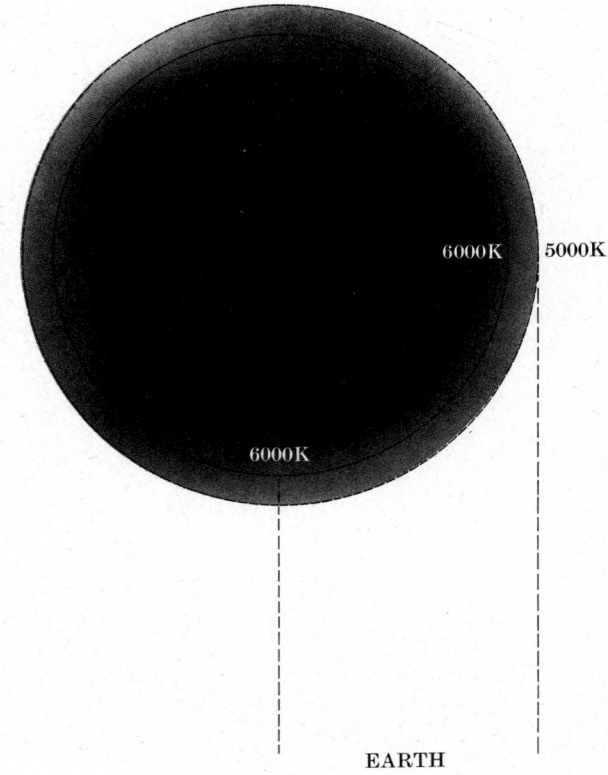

EARTH

are crowded with lines impressed by the Earth's atmosphere (telluric absorption lines), a partly theoretical approach is necessary in order to identify the lines. Table 8.2 lists the elements which have been tracked down in the Sun by means of spectroscopy. Strong lines are produced by iron, sodium, magnesium, aluminium, calcium, titanium, chromium, and nickel.

The relative abundances of the elements in the Sun's atmosphere are deduced from the strength of the lines which they produce, with due account being taken of the effect on the spectrum of the solar temperature and pressure. These latter exert a powerful influence: ionized calcium produces intense absorption in the visible region, whereas hydrogen gives weak lines even though it is nearly a million times more abundant. This phenomenon misled the early astrophysicists into believing that the Sun mainly consisted of heavy elements. More than two-thirds of the natural chemical elements are definitely present in the Sun. During the 1868 solar eclipse, spectroscopists observed a brilliant yellow emission line in the spectrum of the Sun's chromosphere. Because the line could not be matched to any element known at that time, scientists attributed it to a substance called helium (from the Greek noun 'helios' which means Sun). In 1895 helium was isolated in the laboratory for the first time.

Scattering of light in our atmosphere makes it impossible for us to observe the Sun's outer atmosphere easily. Light scattered from the main solar disc is blinding in comparison to the faint glow of the solar atmosphere. During a total *eclipse* of the Sun, however, the Moon blocks the direct light from the disc and the Sun's outer atmosphere is visible as a luminous halo extending several solar diameters into space. For a few seconds before and after totality of the eclipse a very thin crescent of pinkish light flashes into view. This light comes from the solar CHROMOSPHERE, a region extending from the photosphere to a height of about 2 000 km; this includes the 500 km of the reversing layer.

When the solar spectrum is observed during an eclipse, the absorption lines remain so long as part of the photosphere is visible. Once the photosphere is completely blocked, however, the absorption-line spectrum is replaced by a bright emission-line spectrum. This is the chromospheric or FLASH SPECTRUM, which is shown in figure 8.7b. It has over 3 500 identifiable lines, and many of the bright ones are identical to lines in the Fraunhofer spectrum.

The temperature at the bottom of the chromosphere is about 4 500 K. At an altitude of 1 500 km or so it starts to rise to perhaps 20 000 K and finally reaches 10^6 K where it merges with the outermost region, known as the *corona*. The height of the chromosphere actually varies and it can reach 30 000 km. In reality the interface between the chromosphere and the corona is not sharply definable, and therefore authorities differ as to its precise extent and temperature. The pinkish colour is mainly due to emission in the red *Balmer line* of hydrogen at 656.3 nm. The flash spectrum also has lines of neutral and ionized helium, as well as some ionized metals that are not present in the photospheric spectrum. This shows that parts of the chromosphere are hotter than the photosphere.

The intense emission from the first Balmer line offers a method of observing the chromosphere. The 656.3-nm line is one of the strongest absorption features in the photospheric spectrum. Therefore photographs of the Sun taken through filters which only admit light from about 656.25 to 656.35 nm record next to nothing from the photosphere (where the hydrogen is absorbing light), but a great deal of light from the chromosphere (where there is intense emission). Before the manufacture of highly-selective filters a special instrument known as a SPECTROHELIOGRAPH, invented in 1890, was used to secure photographs of the Sun in a narrow wavelength range. Astronomers now generally use filtergrams taken in Hα (656.3-nm wavelength) and the line of calcium (393.4-nm) to explore the structure of the chromosphere and its activity.

8.7b: *The flash spectrum of the chromosphere taken during an eclipse. The usual spectrograph slit, which is used to ensure narrow images of spectral lines, is not used to obtain this spectrum since the chromosphere is itself a narrow source of light. Each emission line produces an image in the shape of a narrow crescent. Many of these lines correspond to features in the photospheric spectrum, which is displayed in table 8.2. (Hale Observatories, USA)*

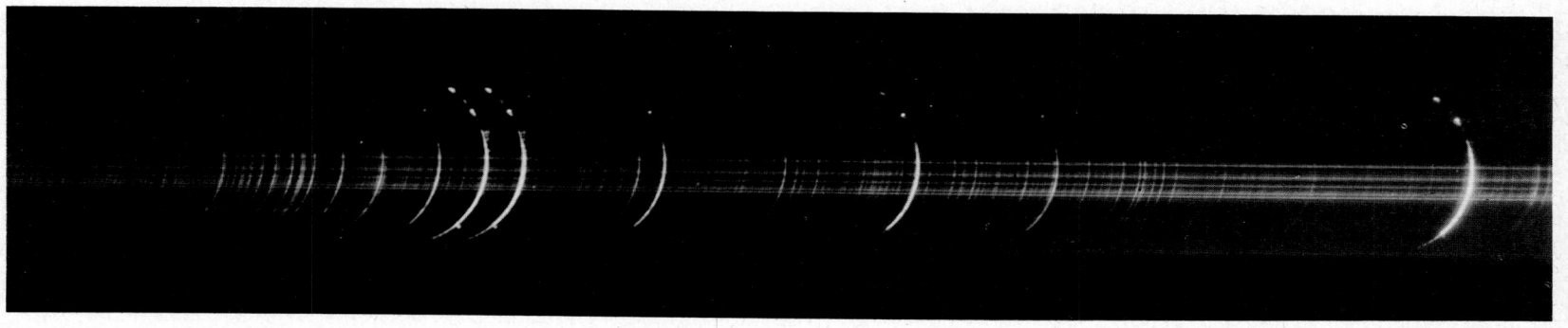

When the solar disc is photographed in either of the above lines, a network of cells, approximately the size of the supergranules, is generally visible. There may also be patches of brightness, due to high-temperature regions in the chromosphere which are produced by strong magnetic fields. High-resolution photographs also reveal many fine, dark, short lines, resembling scattered blades of grass; these are called FIBRILS (figure 8.8). Although the fibrils are absorption features when viewed against the bright disc, they appear as luminous gas in photographs of the limb of the Sun. As figure 8.9 illustrates, the fibrils look like jets or flames, and they are then termed SPICULES. They arise in the lower part of the chromosphere and may reach altitudes of 10 000 km. Each spicule lasts 2–10 minutes.

The chromosphere is not a uniform atmospheric layer. Essentially it is a turbulent froth churned up by the photosphere. Pressure waves generated in the convection zone are thought to be the main cause of heating in the chromosphere, which gets hotter with increasing distance from the Sun (figure 8.11). The density of matter decreases with altitude, and this causes the pressure waves to accelerate. In so doing they bring about more energetic collisions of particles which are driven along by the waves. The directed motion of the waves is thus converted to the kinetic energy of random motion of the particles, that is, to heat energy. Consequently the chromospheric temperature rises from 4 300 K at its base to near-coronal values of 10^6 K in only 3 000 km or so.

8.8: *To see fine detail on the surface of the Sun, astronomers often restrict their photography to a very narrow range of wavelength. By this technique it is possible to record features that are emitting or absorbing at the wavelength concerned, and cut out the flood of light from the photosphere at all other wavelengths. This high-resolution photograph obtained in the red light of hydrogen (Hα at 656.3-nm wavelength) shows the coarse mottling, outlined by the dark lines termed fibrils, in the solar chromosphere. (Sacramento Peak Observatory, USA)*

8.9: *This Hα photograph illustrates the dense packing of spicules, which are identical to the fibrils illustrated in figure 8.8. They outline the boundaries of supergranule cells. (Sacramento Peak Observatory, USA)*

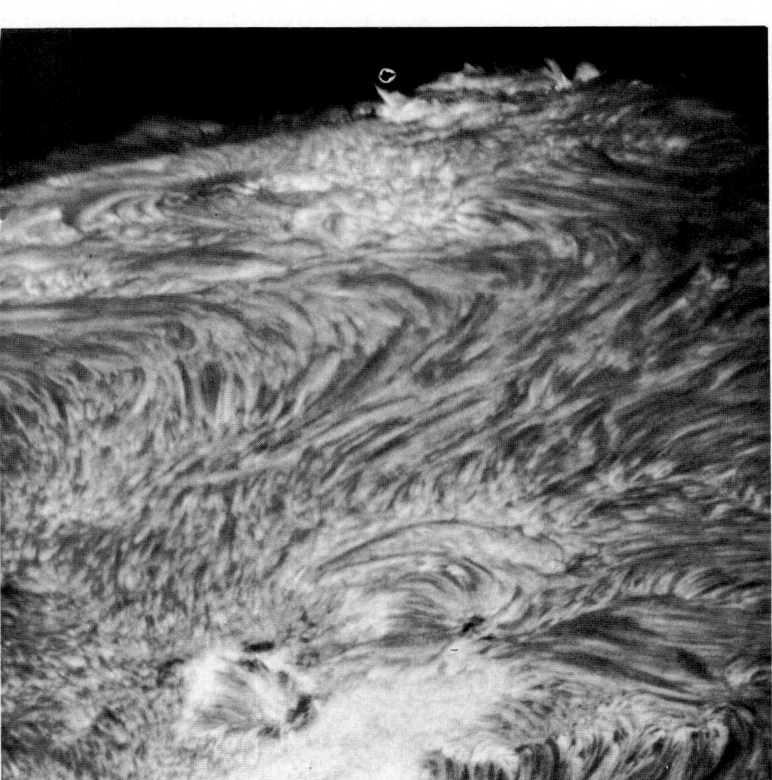

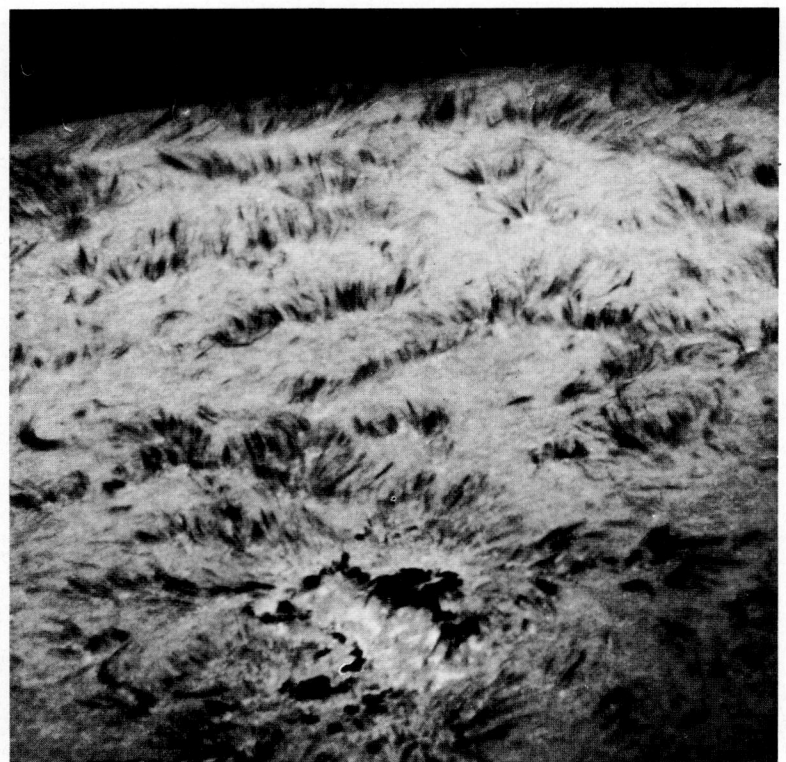

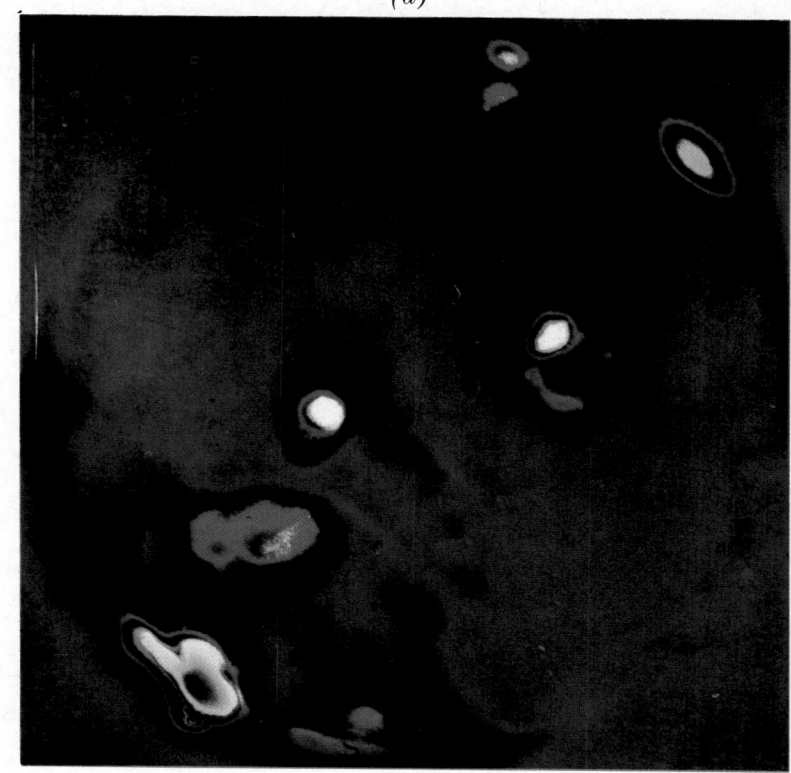

(a)

8.10: *A triumph of space astronomy has been the study of celestial objects in wavelength regions that are not accessible on the surface of the Earth. This series of X-ray images, shown here in false colour, illustrates several important features of the X-ray Sun. (a) The Sun in soft X-rays is shown here ; the red regions are the faintest and the white the brightest. (b) In this composite picture an X-ray flare has emerged from the tiny emitting region shown in the central inset. (c) In this full disc image most of the typical inner coronal features that can be seen in soft X-rays are shown. The active regions appear as two large and over-exposed bands near to the equator. Many bright points of X-ray emission are also present. (American Science and Engineering,* usa*/Marshall Space Flight Center,* usa*/NASA,* usa*)*

(b)

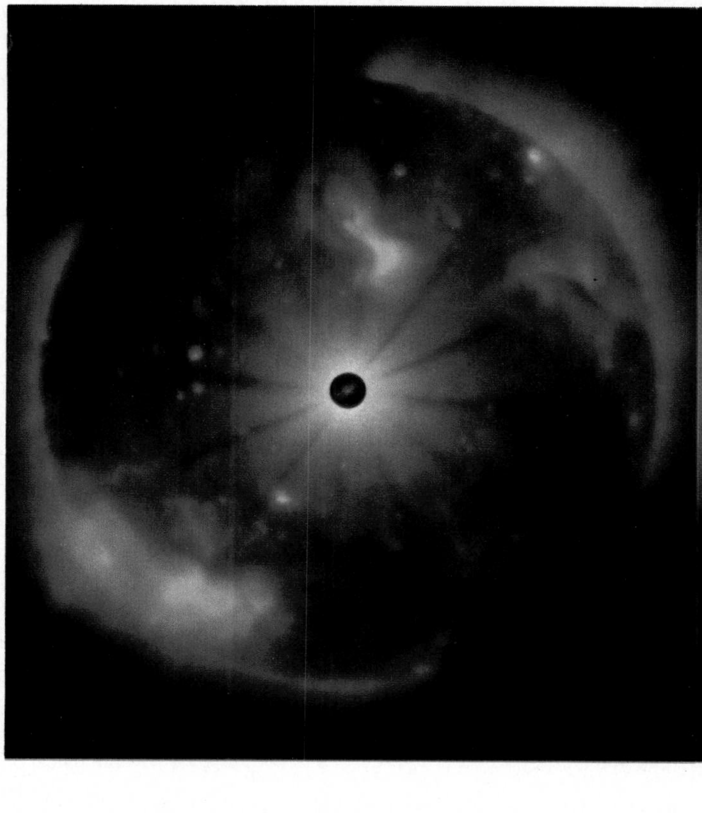

(c)

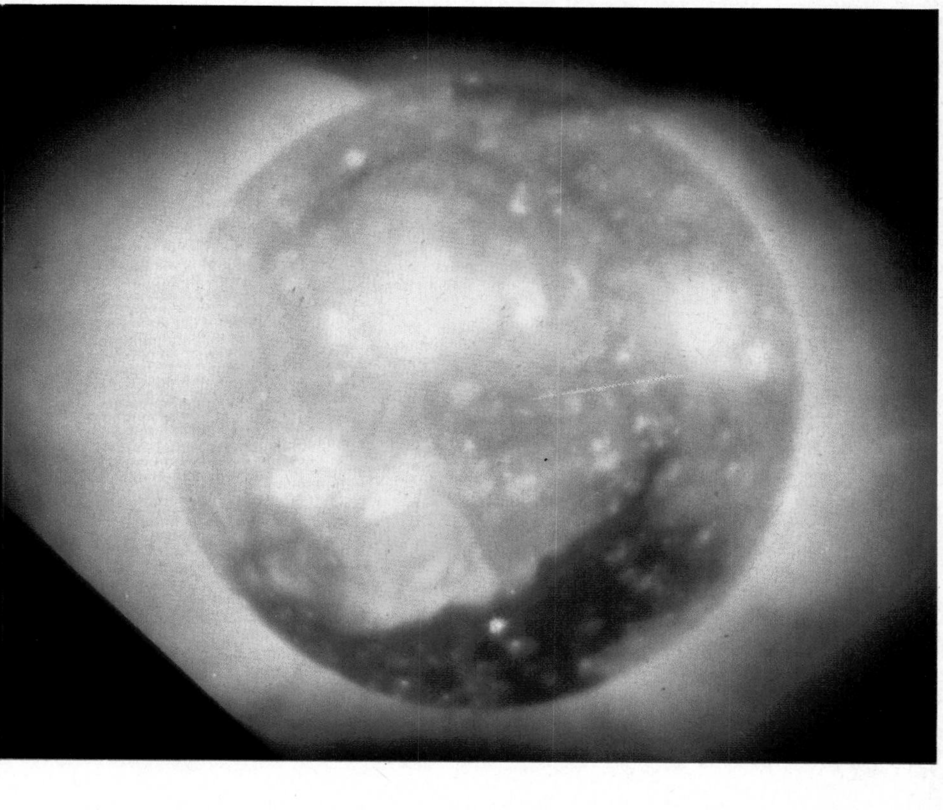

Above the chromosphere we come to the solar CORONA, a region of low density and high temperature that merges imperceptibly with interplanetary space. It is difficult to observe, since its intensity in the visible region of the spectrum is only equivalent to that of the full Moon. The brilliance of the photosphere and the scattering of sunlight in our own atmosphere render it undetectable, unless the photospheric light is blocked, as happens at a total solar eclipse or in an instrument known as a CORONOGRAPH. Although Kepler observed the corona, serious interest in it did not develop until the nineteenth century. Observations of the corona during eclipses are not easy. On average, suitable eclipses occur less than annually; they are frequently over oceans or remote parts of the land; the weather cannot always be relied upon; and only a few minutes are available for obtaining data. Despite these difficulties, great efforts are made to send expeditions to eclipse sites since certain observations can only be carried out at totality.

In the coronograph, the light from the disc is blocked off artificially by positioning an opaque disc, with diameter exactly equal to that of the Sun's image, at the focus of the objective lens. To minimize the effects of scattered light it is essential to eliminate dust and blemishes on the objective lens and to place the coronograph at a high altitude, or even to use it above the atmosphere in a rocket or satellite. Mirrors are not normally used in coronographs, because minute surface blemishes in the aluminium coating scatter too much light.

8.11: *The chromosphere has a vague transition zone where it merges with the hot corona. Within the intermediate region the temperature rises rapidly to about 10^6 K. Pressure waves propagating outwards from the convection zone carry energy which is turned into heat in the chromosphere.*

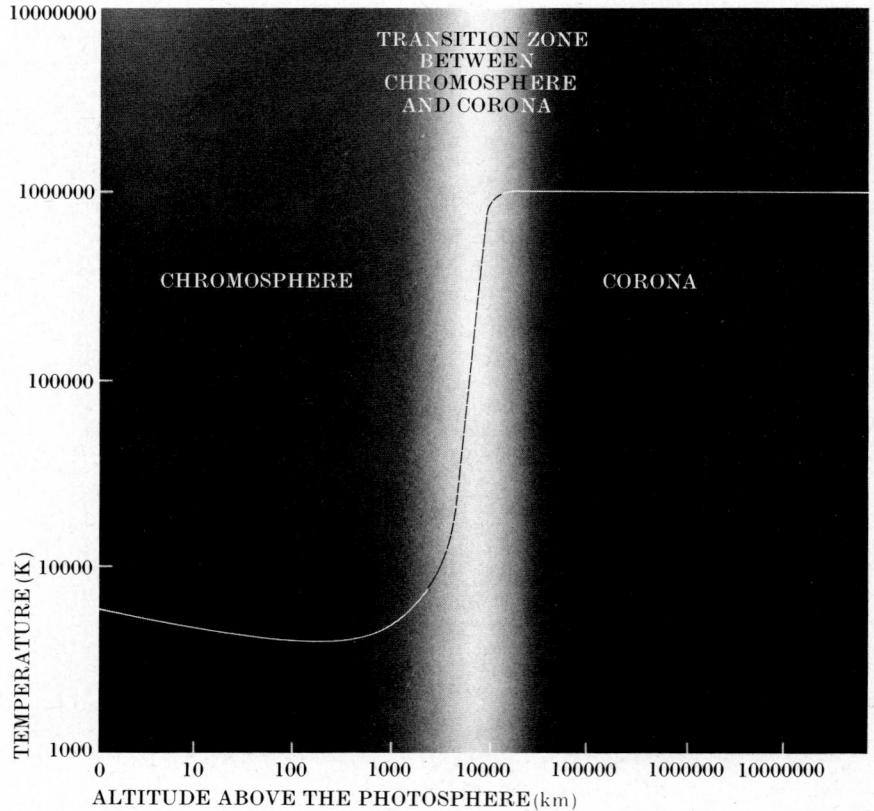

Spectroscopically, the inner corona (or K-CORONA) shows a continuum crossed by emission lines; these are fainter and less numerous than in the chromosphere. The continuum is primarily visible light from the photosphere which has been scattered towards Earth by free electrons in the corona. The Fraunhofer spectrum cannot be distinguished in the spectrum of the inner corona because the large random motions of the scattering electrons introduce large random Doppler shifts that smear out the absorption features. Beyond a few solar radii scattering of the photospheric light by dust particles takes place. These have smaller motions, and the Fraunhofer lines are not completely washed out. This region is termed the F-CORONA.

A handful of intense emission lines in the coronal spectrum intrigued the early astrophysicists. Among these lines are a strong red line at 637.4-nm wavelength and a brilliant green line at 530.3-nm wavelength; the latter was first noted by Young in 1869. These and other lines could not be matched to the characteristics of any familiar element, and so scientists speculated that an unknown element, coronium, was responsible, just as helium had accounted for once unrecognizable photospheric lines. Later work, however, filled in the remaining gaps in the periodic table of the elements, and it became apparent that no element's atoms could account for the coronal lines. The resolution of the paradox came in 1941 when it was realized that familiar elements, but in a highly-ionized state, were emitting the mysterious lines. The prominent green line (530.3 nm) is from atoms of iron that have been stripped of 13 outer electrons, designated Fe^{13+}, while the red one (637.4 nm) is from iron that has lost nine electrons, Fe^{9+}. Other lines can be attributed to Fe^{4+}, Fe^{6+}, Fe^{8+}, and Fe^{12+} (which has two intense infrared lines), and to nickel and chromium ions. There are still a few unidentified or doubtfully-identified coronal emission features. Several of the OSO (Orbiting Solar Observatory) satellites carried spectrometers. With these, the ultraviolet spectrum of the corona was observed and many new emission lines, due to highly ionized atoms, were discovered.

The high state of ionization in the corona indicates that it is at a much higher kinetic temperature than either the photosphere or chromosphere (figure 8.11). An enormous amount of energy is needed to dislodge 13 orbital electrons from a neutral iron atom and so form Fe^{13+} ions. Collisions between atoms and ions only become powerful enough to strip these electrons at temperatures of about 10^6 K; occasionally a temperature of 2×10^6 K is reached in the outer corona, and individual hotspots may temporarily reach 4×10^6 K. Because the coronal gas is rarefied (the density is 10^{11} particles m^{-3}, compared to 10^{25} particles m^{-3} in Earth's atmosphere) the total amount of energy stored in it is not great. Even so the intense heating of this tenuous gas has long puzzled solar physicists. The continual dumping of energy into the corona by shock waves and turbulence arising at the photosphere could be the most significant source of coronal heating. Solar flares, and other forms of activity discussed below, may be contributory agents.

Much of the radiation from the corona falls beyond the visible region in the extreme ultraviolet and X-ray domains of the spectrum. This is because the corona is very hot and highly ionized. X-ray images of the Sun show areas of locally higher particle density and higher temperature in the inner corona. These hotspots are generally located high above active regions on the surface of the Sun. The detailed structure evident in such photographs (figure 8.10) proves that the corona is non-homogeneous.

The corona is in dynamic rather than static equilibrium, as it expands under its own pressure gradient, against the Sun's gravitational field, into the near-vacuum of interplanetary space. The flow of material out of the corona, called the *solar wind*, takes about five days to reach Earth. It has a considerable effect on the magnetic fields of the planets since the ionized matter of which it is composed cannot cross magnetic field lines. In the neighbourhood of planetary magnetic fields, the wind flows round a protective magnetic shell.

Solar activity

Solar weather and magnetic field

So far in this chapter the Sun has been considered as a static ball of hot gas: energy is created in the core, and streams out to space through the convection zone, photosphere, and solar atmosphere. We might expect that the release of energy from the surface regions should be uniform over the solar disc. Although standard evolutionary models account for the Sun in terms of normal stellar processes, no account is taken of the weather, or activity, in the Sun's outer layers, which we can see because of our proximity. Even violent solar storms only involve 10^{-6} of the solar luminosity, so that the weather has no significant effect on the standard models of evolution. Nonetheless the displays in the solar atmosphere are scientifically interesting, frequently of dramatic beauty, and often affect the Earth. The study of solar activity includes a description of solar magnetism, sunspots, prominences, and flares. The variety of phenomena is considerable, and it would be confusing to discuss all of them in detail here.

It is widely believed that solar activity is stirred up by the interplay between the solar MAGNETIC FIELD and the Sun's DIFFERENTIAL ROTATION. At its surface the Sun has a general magnetic field that is approximately like a dipole and of strength 10^{-4} tesla (1 gauss). The Earth has a similar dipole field with a strength of 6×10^{-5} tesla (0.6 gauss). Symmetry and a precisely-defined axis are lacking. The weak surface field does not arise from a dipole inside the Sun; it results from many localized surface fields.

The Sun does not rotate rigidly like Earth; this is not surprising since we know that the Sun is gaseous throughout. The polar regions of the photosphere take 37 days to rotate once with respect to the distant stars, whereas the equator takes 26 days. As observed from Earth, which is moving around the Sun, the corresponding synodic periods are 41–27 days. Several authorities quote rotation

8.12: *The rotation of the photosphere takes between 26 days (equator) and 37 days (poles), so that an imaginary line drawn across the Sun from pole to pole will orbit the Sun more rapidly at the equator than at the pole.*

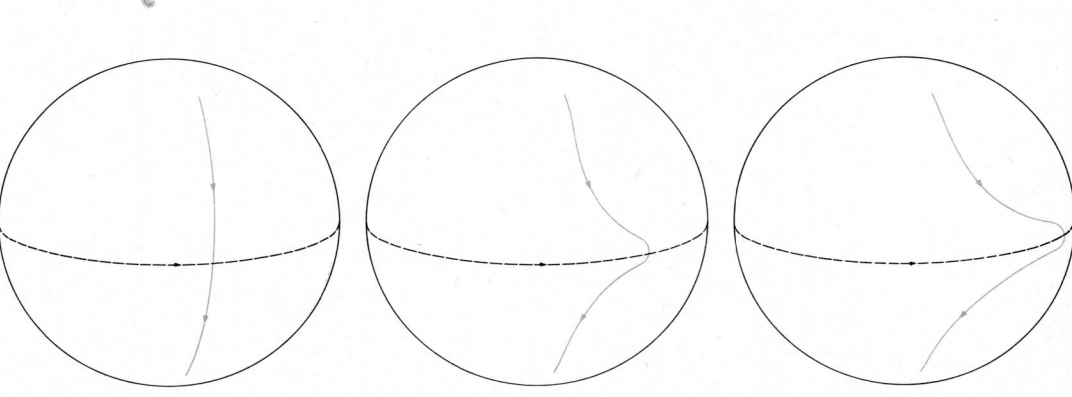

periods which are slightly shorter than these. The periods given here are based on the observed Doppler shifts of photospheric lines and not, as is more common, on the observed rotation rate of sunspots, which rate is probably influenced by the Sun's internal magnetic field. The faster rotation indicated by the magnetic field may be caused by a rapidly rotating core. The Sun is said to rotate differentially because the material at progressively lower latitudes takes progressively less time to make one circuit (figure 8.12).

It is possible that the non-rigid rotation of our Sun is caused by rapid rotation of the solar interior, which would lead to a shear stress, and swifter rotation, at the equator of the visible surface. Extremely delicate measurements made in 1970 showed that the Sun is not precisely spherical; rather it is oblate, the deviation being of order 0.005 per cent, or about five times as large as one would predict for a core rotating in about 30 days. This observation may also be accounted for in terms of the centrifugal force present in a rapidly rotating solar core. However, this controversial measurement has not been confirmed independently so caution must be exercised in drawing any conclusion.

We now consider the relationship between the Sun's magnetism and its differential rotation. First it is essential to emphasize that matter in the Sun is a good conductor of electricity: most of the particles, being free electrons or ions, are electrically charged. When the electrical conductivity is large, as it is below the photosphere, it is not easy for matter to move relative to a magnetic field. If it attempts so to do, secondary magnetism results from induced currents; the resulting magnetic force opposes the motion (this is *Lenz's law of magnetism*). Consequently the field in a plasma, which is a good conductor, becomes 'frozen-in', and is largely constrained to move with the plasma. This situation is pertinent to the solar interior. Because the Sun rotates differentially, the frozen-in field lines get progressively stretched out by the shear in the rotation, as figure 8.13 illustrates. The shearing action winds up the internal magnetic field, steadily increasing its strength.

If we imagine starting this process with a simple dipole field, we can visualize that it evidently gets twisted and amplified into an intense toroidal field, tightly encircling the Sun at lower latitudes. We can anticipate that eventually the density of field lines becomes sufficiently great for magnetism occasionally to burst out of the interior, on account of the repulsion between adjacent lines of the same polarity. Once the strength of the field exceeds about 1 tesla (10^4 gauss) it exerts a force on the surrounding plasma that exceeds the Sun's gravitational attraction. Gas in the vicinity that contains charged particles becomes buoyant and therefore aids the process. Another effect is of adjacent magnetic field lines 'reconnecting', or short-circuiting the magnetism.

Observations show that solar activity is cyclic, with a characteristic time of 22 years. Over this period the internal magnetism rises to a crescendo and then collapses; this takes about 11 years. After the decrease the solar field reverses its polarity, and during the second 11-year period differential rotation winds the strength up once more, until the new field also short-circuits and a further reversal follows. It therefore takes 22 years for the Sun to return to its original magnetic state, although most of the observable effects of the process repeat at roughly 11-year intervals.

During each 11-year cycle, magnetic energy builds up as the rotation amplifies the field. This energy is released through *sunspots*, solar active regions, and *solar flares*; the latter provide the most violent release. After the peak the field dies away and reverses, and the memory of the magnetic field during earlier cycles is soon erased. Superposition of weak fossil fields from old disturbed regions probably accounts for the weak general field of the solar surface.

8.13: *Magnetic lines of force inside the Sun become trapped by moving plasma because it has a high electrical conductivity. The differential rotation (figure 8.12) of the Sun causes the frozen-in lines to become distorted, and slowly wound up in the equatorial region. After a few years the internal magnetic field of the Sun is shaped rather like a doughnut.*

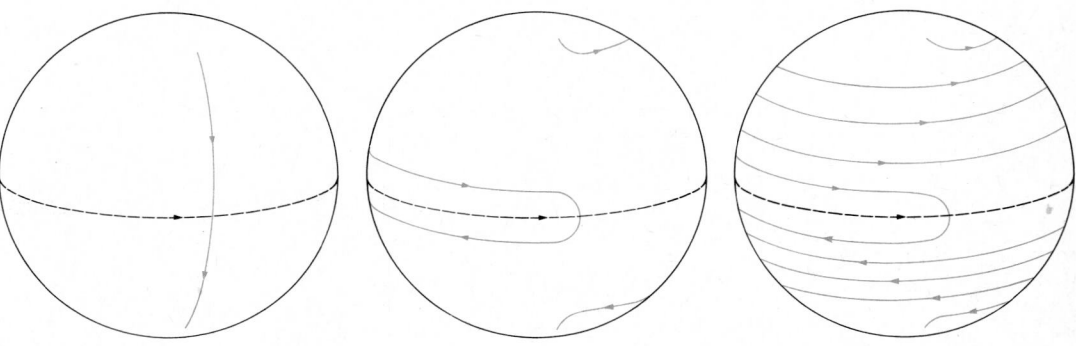

Sunspots

SUNSPOTS are the sole sign of solar activity that is occasionally detectable to the eye. Known since antiquity, according to Greek sources, they were rediscovered by Europeans in 1611, after Galileo's epochal application of the telescope to astronomical investigations. Despite this fact, the European school of natural philosophy steadfastly held the Sun to be a perfect, unblemished sphere for more than a millennium during the Dark Ages! Do not look for sunspots yourself by positioning an instrument between your eyes and the Sun; it may cause you to go blind permanently – see the beginning of this chapter. It is not dangerous to look at the red disc of the Sun as it is about to set on a hazy horizon at sea level. On such occasions you may sometimes see large spots with the naked eye. (Do not use any instrument.)

Sunspots look like irregular holes in the Sun's surface (figure 8.14). Although they appear to be dark areas, this is entirely a contrast effect. A large spot radiates as much light as the full Moon, but appears black against the brilliant photosphere. The black inner region is termed the UMBRA and the more luminous surrounding fringe the PENUMBRA. An average size for a spot would be 10 000 km, but ones as big as 150 000 km have been recorded.

It is usual for spots to occur in pairs or in more complex groups. The larger spots are often associated with the smallest type of spot which is known as a PORE; these range in size from about 3 000 km down to the instrumental limit. Generally a pore only lasts a few hours, whereas true sunspots remain for a week or more. Large sunspots persist for several weeks, during which time solar rotation will take them out of view for a couple of weeks. Spectroscopy has shown that the temperature in the black region of a spot is 4 000 K, some 2 000 K less than the surrounding photosphere. Observations of sunspots approaching the limb of the Sun prove that they are depressions, not elevations, in the photosphere, since when a spot approaches the limb the near side becomes practically invisible whereas the far side is enlarged; this is the WILSON EFFECT.

Early explanations of sunspots seem bizarre today: some astronomers thought they might be planets inside the orbit of Mercury, and others that they were mountains poking through the photosphere. Galileo opined that they were clouds, whereas Sir William Herschel speculated that they were holes in the fiery clouds through which one could see the dark, and presumably habitable, surface. Modern science provides a model that is simpler than any of these: sunspots are regions of unusually high magnetic field in which the photospheric temperature is 2 000 K cooler than average.

For nearly 250 years astronomers have kept worthwhile records of the number of spots visible on the Sun. They are the most readily observable tracer of the solar magnetic cycle. The number varies from day to day and year to year. About every 11 years the activity reaches a maximum; this is the period of the SUNSPOT CYCLE, first described in 1843. Conventionally, the sunspot cycle is recorded by means of an arbitrarily-defined quantity, the ZURICH SUNSPOT NUMBER, Z:

$$Z = C(S + 10G)$$

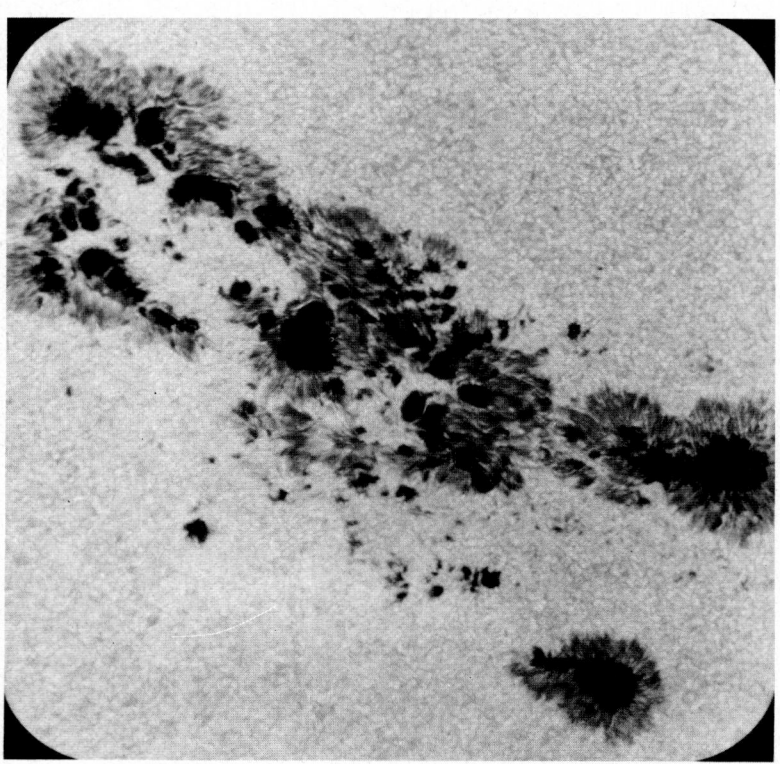

8.14: *This complex group shows several large sunspots, some pores, and the solar granulation. The black region, known as the umbra, has a temperature of 4 000 K. Highly-structured sunspot groups such as this usually occur at the maximum of the solar cycle. (Sacramento Peak Observatory, USA)*

where S is the number of individual spots, G is the number of groups, and C is a correction factor designed to correct for variations in observer enthusiasm, equipment, and weather. Figure 8.15 shows the variation in sunspot numbers since 1700, and figure 8.16 displays recent cycles in more detail. Over the last 50 years the cycle time has averaged 10.4 years. It can be as short as 7 years or as long as 17 years. Besides the variations in the number of visible spots, another feature of the cycle is that at the start of the cycle, spots appear in the vicinity of latitudes $+40°$ and $-40°$. As the cycle progresses, these two zones in which most spots are located migrate to within about $5°$ of the equator. At this stage the first spots of the next cycle erupt at high latitudes. A diagram which depicts the change in latitude during the cycle is in figure 8.17.

Spots are only one manifestation of the solar cycle. Many other features, such as the extent of the chromosphere and corona, or the frequency of solar flares, become more exaggerated or intense as the maximum of sunspot activity is approached. The sunspots are merely the most observable manifestation of solar activity, not the root cause of it.

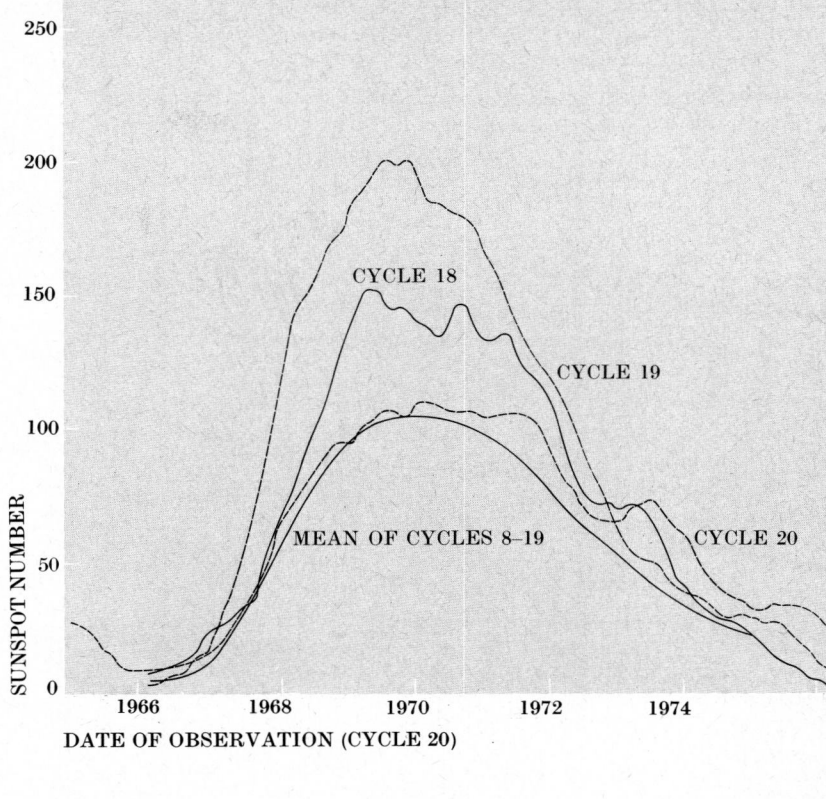

8.15: *The variation in mean sunspot number from 1700 to 1977 clearly shows the 11-year cycle of solar activity, as well as suggesting that there may be a longer-term cycle of around 80 years. The quantity plotted on the vertical axis is the Zurich sunspot number.*

8.16: *This detailed graph of recent solar cycles shows the random fluctuations that are superimposed on the 11-year cycle. Cycle 19, which spanned April 1954–October 1964, resulted in the highest sunspot activity ever recorded.*

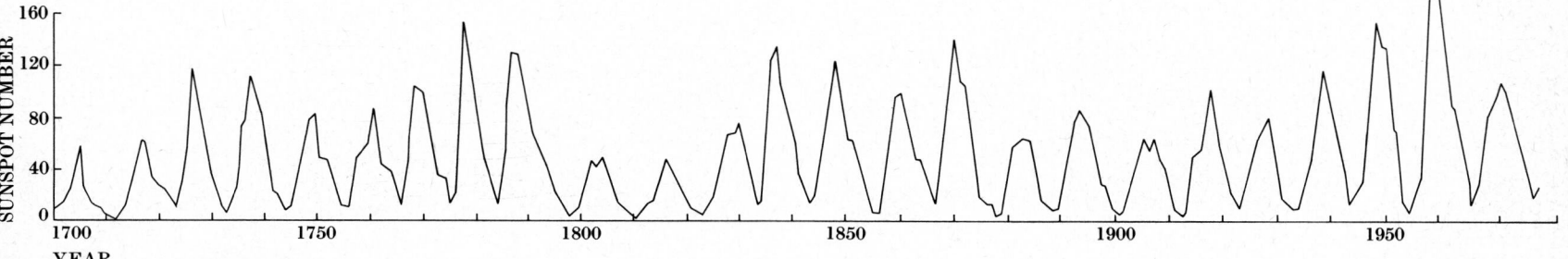

8.17: *The sunspot butterfly diagram (also called the Maunder diagram after the scientist who plotted it) plots date on the vertical axis and latitude on the Sun horizontally. The migration of the spots towards the equator as time advances is clearly evident.*

8.18: *It is possible to analyse the light from the Sun in such a way as to obtain an image of the distribution of magnetic field. The phenomenon exploited is that of the Zeeman effect, which causes a narrow spectral line to split into several components when a strong magnetic field is present. (Hale Observatories, USA)*

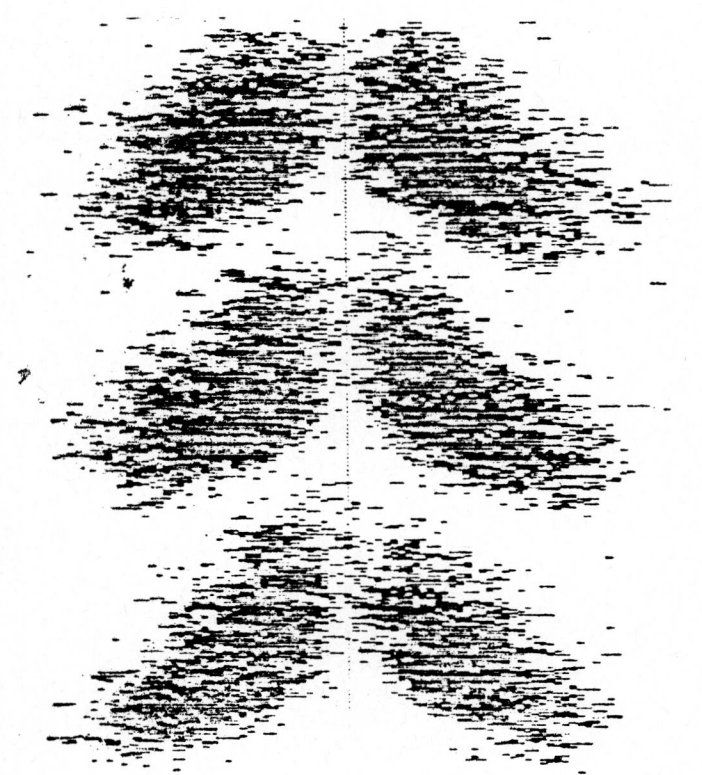

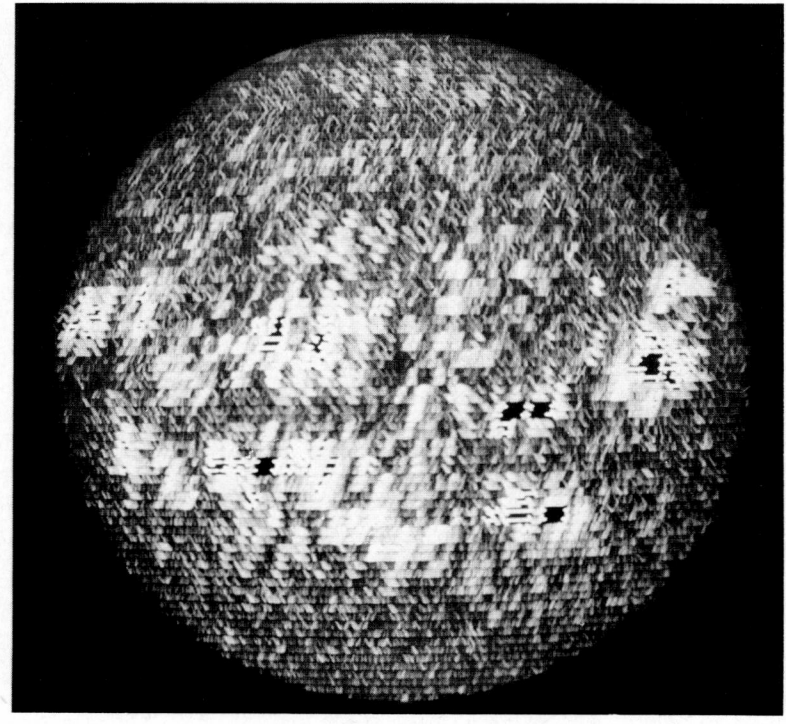

Investigations of the magnetic fields of sunspots probably started in 1908. In that year George Hale noted that the spectral lines from the spots could be resolved into several components, each of which was polarized (figure 8.18). The splitting of lines is caused in this case by the ZEEMAN EFFECT, which occurs when atoms emit or absorb light in an intense magnetic field. Strong magnetic fields modify the energy levels in atoms and thus introduce extra structure into the spectral lines. The presence of Zeeman splitting provides a powerful means of probing the magnetism of sunspots because the separation of components of a given line depends on the field strength. This can be as high as 0.4 tesla (4 000 gauss): this is thousands of times stronger than the geomagnetic field and may extend over an area exceeding the surface area of Earth. Such powerful fields cannot possibly be due to permanent magnets embedded in the Sun, but must be caused by circulating electric currents in the interior. Within the spot umbra, the field lines emerge more or less vertically.

Frequently sunspots appear as close pairs aligned parallel to the solar equator; these are called BIPOLAR SPOTS. Magnetic field measurements demonstrate that the two spots in a pair have opposite polarities: the field lines emerge from the surface at one spot and re-enter at the other, as shown in figure 8.19. During a particular sunspot cycle, and in a given solar hemisphere, the polarity of the western spot (the one leading in the direction of solar rotation) is always the same. In the other hemisphere the

8.19a: *The formation mechanism of a loop prominence.*

8.19b: *In a pair of sunspots, the magnetic field leaves the surface at one spot and re-enters at the other. This can lead to the formation of loop prominences, such as that shown here as dark-coloured material. (Sacramento Peak Observatory,* USA*)*

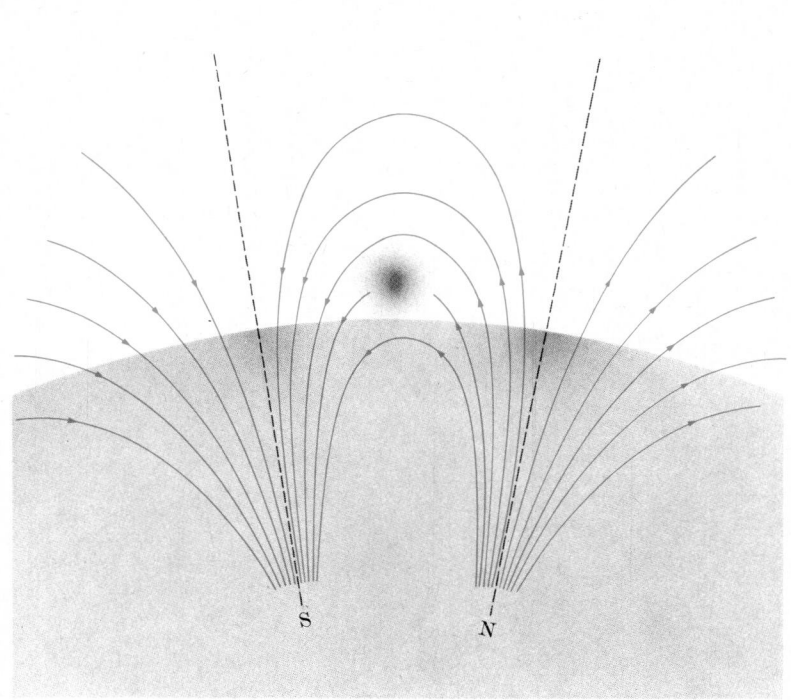

bipolar groups follow an analogous relation but the sense of the polarities is opposite (figure 8.20). This behaviour persists throughout the solar cycle; then, at the commencement of the next cycle, the polarities reverse in both hemispheres. We see that the magnetic behaviour of the bipolar groups follows the full solar cycle of 22 years. In the case of large spots that are apparently magnetically isolated, because no spot of opposite polarity can be found nearby, it usually turns out that the magnetic field is much stronger in an adjacent area of the photosphere where, often, sunspots have formed and disappeared.

Sunspots are not vortices or tornadoes in the photosphere as some books suggest. The distinctive feature of a sunspot is the strong vertical magnetic field, and we shall use this property to make a model of sunspot behaviour. The fact that differential rotation builds up a shell of strong magnetic field under the photosphere has already been mentioned. Convection, in all probability, further twists and jumbles the field, as rising bubbles of conducting gas drag the field lines with them (figure 8.21). Kinks in the ropes of magnetic field lead to even stronger fields. Eventually the magnetic pressure is great enough to make the field buoyant: it wells up, bursts through the photosphere (figure 8.22), and forms sunspots. Solar physicists have shown that this will first occur in latitudes $\pm 40°$, because that is where the shearing forces are greatest; the eruptions lessen the field at higher latitudes and strengthen it nearer the equator. Therefore the spots gradually migrate to the equator, in accordance with the observations. The lower temperature inside sunspots arises partly because the intense magnetic field suppresses the ingress of new energy supplies from the convection zone and partly because the gas density is lowered as plasma flows out along the field lines.

8.20: *A representation of the magnetic polarities in sunspots. During a given cycle, all the spots in one hemisphere are polarized in one sense and all in the other hemisphere in the opposite sense. As the cycle progresses, the spots migrate towards the solar equator. When a new cycle begins the polarities are opposite to those of the cycle immediately preceding.*

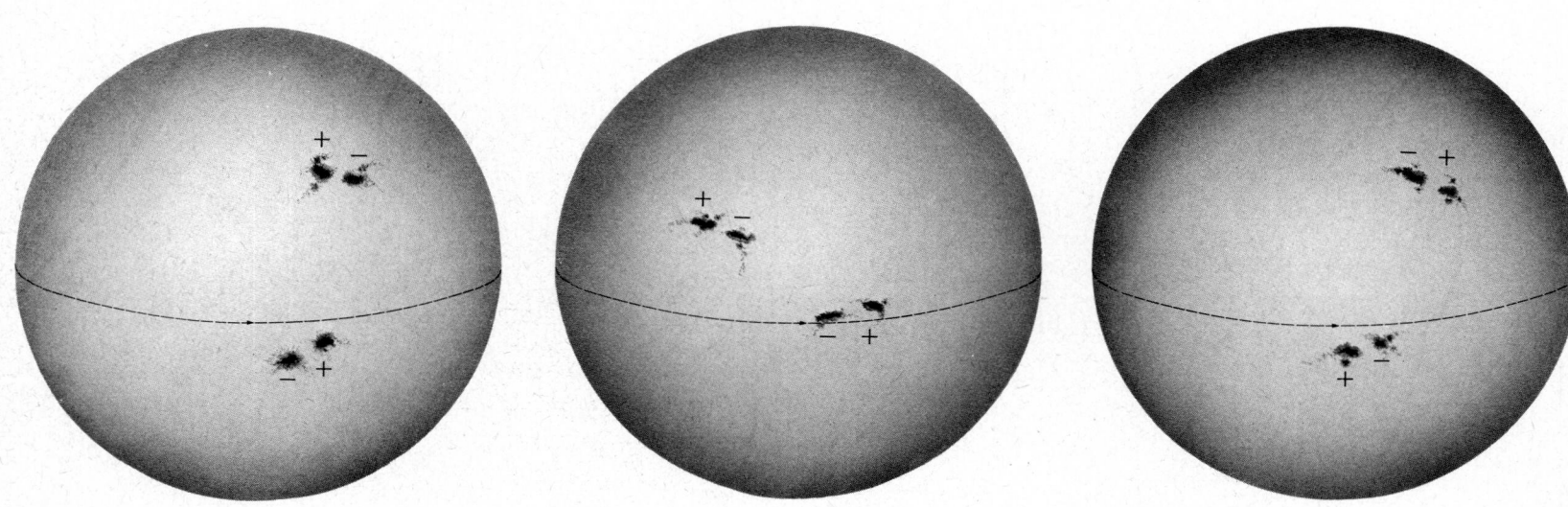

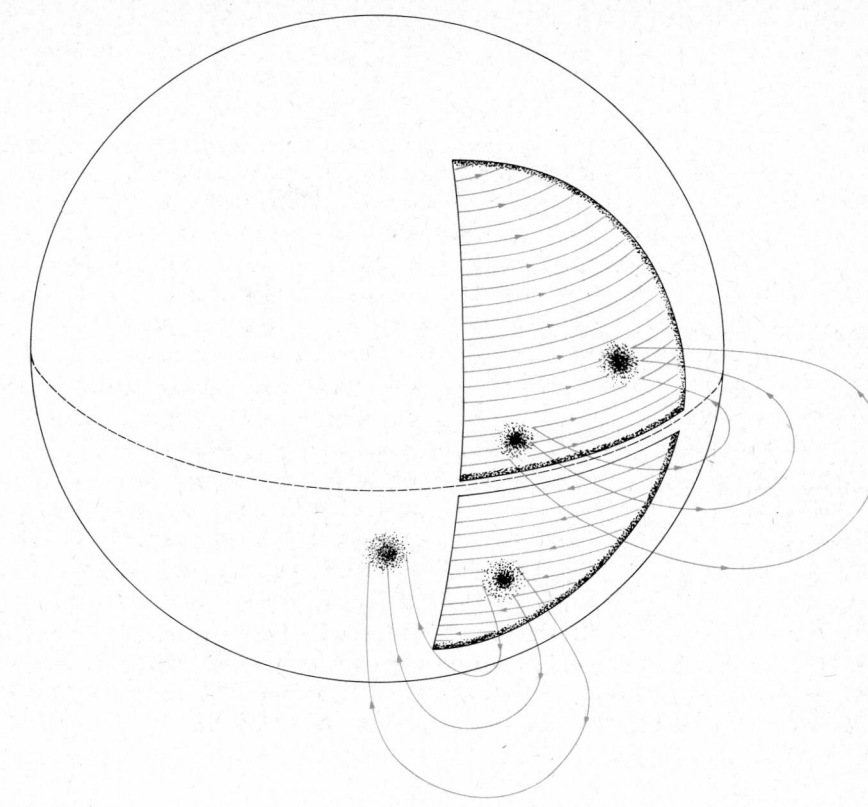

8.22: *Sunspots appear to be regions of the solar surface that have been pierced by magnetic loops from the interior.*

8.21: *Uniform magnetic field below the solar surface gets tangled by the turbulent gas in the convection zone, so that the field can burst through the photosphere and form a sunspot pair.*

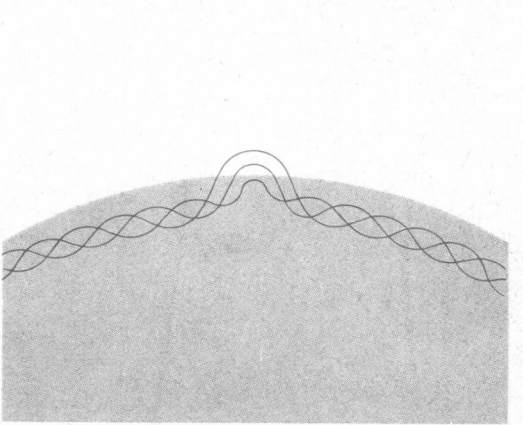

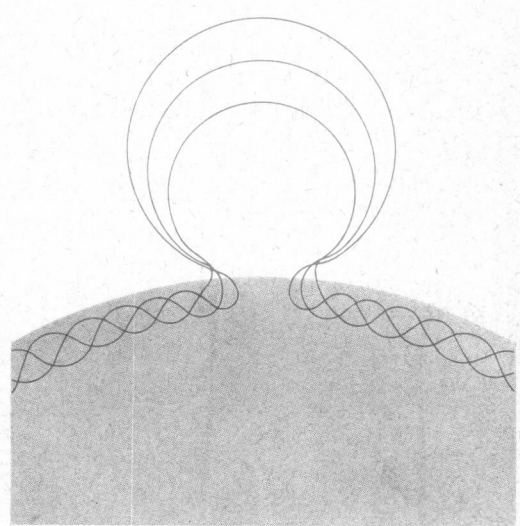

Solar active regions

An active region on the Sun (one is shown in figure 8.23) includes not only sunspots but related phenomena: plages, prominences, faculae, and flares, to name but a few. One feature common to all these natural phenomena is the strong magnetic field.

PLAGES are highly disturbed zones in the chromosphere. They usually appear before the spots and outlive them. Plages show as regions of intensified emission in photographs taken in Hα or the K-line of calcium. Local concentrations of magnetic field in the chromosphere apparently heat the gas to incandescence.

Brightening around an active region can also be seen in the white light from the photosphere. Such areas are called FACULAE, and they are located in the photosphere. They were first described in the seventeenth century by Hevelius.

FILAMENTS show on chromospheric photographs as dark streaks above a region of high magnetic field. They are actually prominences seen in absorption against the bright disc.

PROMINENCES are among the most beautiful astronomical phenomena. Best seen when they extend beyond the Sun's limb in an eclipse (or coronograph picture), they are luminous clouds of gas that appear in the corona. Spectra indicate a temperature of 10 000–20 000 K for prominence material. QUIESCENT PROMINENCES last for several solar rotations; they are regions of locally enhanced density that are falling out of the corona back to the photosphere (figure 8.24). LOOP PROMINENCES are those in which the condensing material returns to the photosphere along a loop of magnetic flux similar to those in figure 8.22. Early solar physicists thought that prominences were pyrotechnic displays in which matter is violently spewed out of the photosphere, but time-lapse photography shows that the material is usually descending from the corona to the photosphere. Rarely, energetic ERUPTIVE PROMINENCES, which are spectacular surges in the vicinity of sunspots, do throw material in a burst that may extend 3×10^5 km above the photosphere (figure 8.25).

The appearance and extent of the corona are modulated by the solar cycle. The density increases twofold and the temperature by 20 per cent between solar minimum and maximum. Structural asymmetries are pronounced in the inner corona, where the details of plasma flow are under the control of the magnetic field. At sunspot maximum the corona attains its greatest extent and is generally at its most symmetrical. Condensations, loops, and local enhancements hover over the active regions. Figure 8.26, taken at solar maximum, shows the coronal streamers extending to several solar radii. POLAR PLUMES have sprouted at the magnetic north and south poles. Large streamers, known as HELMET STREAMERS, overlie prominences in the lower corona. The corona of the active Sun evidently incorporates much structure which is controlled by complex magnetic fields.

8.23: *This high-resolution photograph shows a solar active region near the limb of the Sun. (Kitt Peak National Observatory, USA)*

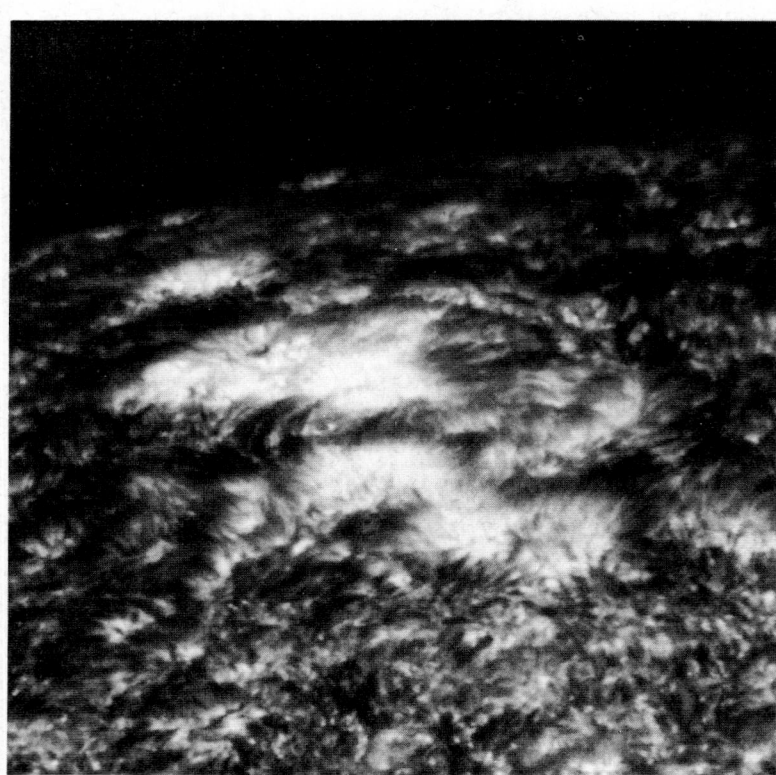

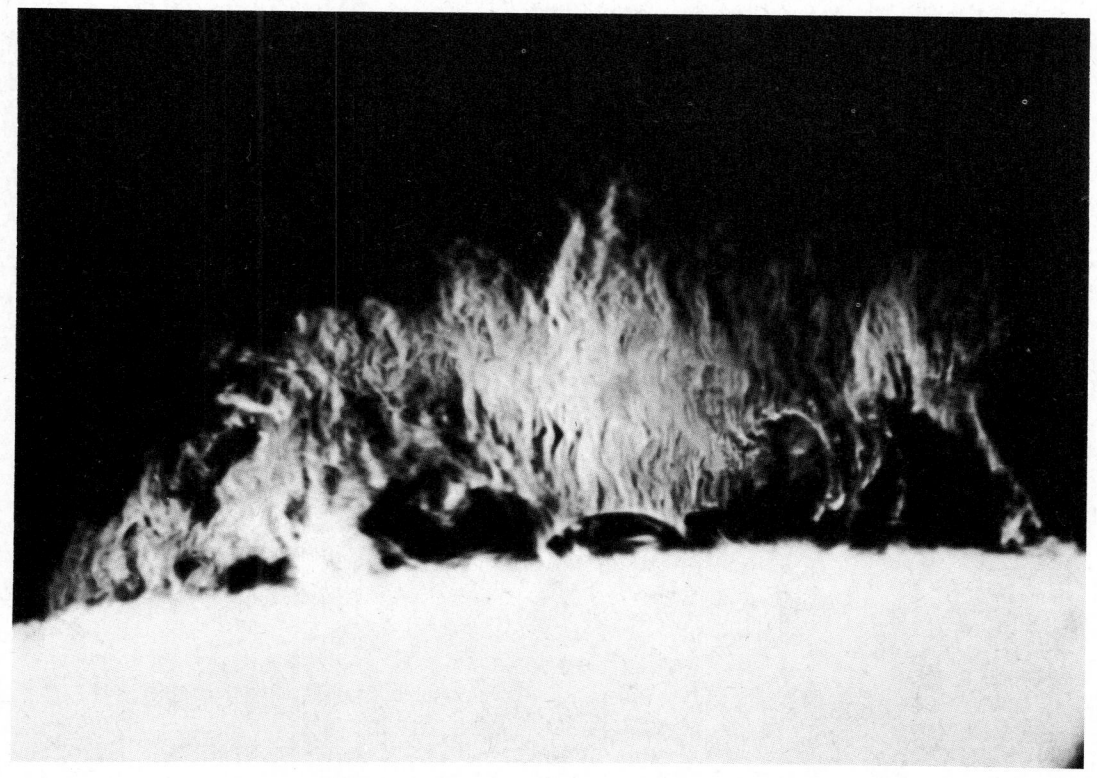

8.24: *A small quiescent prominence on the solar limb, about 50 000 km high, shows the characteristic vertical structure, which remains static even while the material flows back to the surface. The descending gas is channelled along lines of magnetic force that give the delicate tracery shown here. (Sacramento Peak Observatory, USA)*

8.25: *This dramatic view of an eruptive prominence conveys clearly the violent expulsion of material from the solar surface. (Sacramento Peak Observatory, USA)*

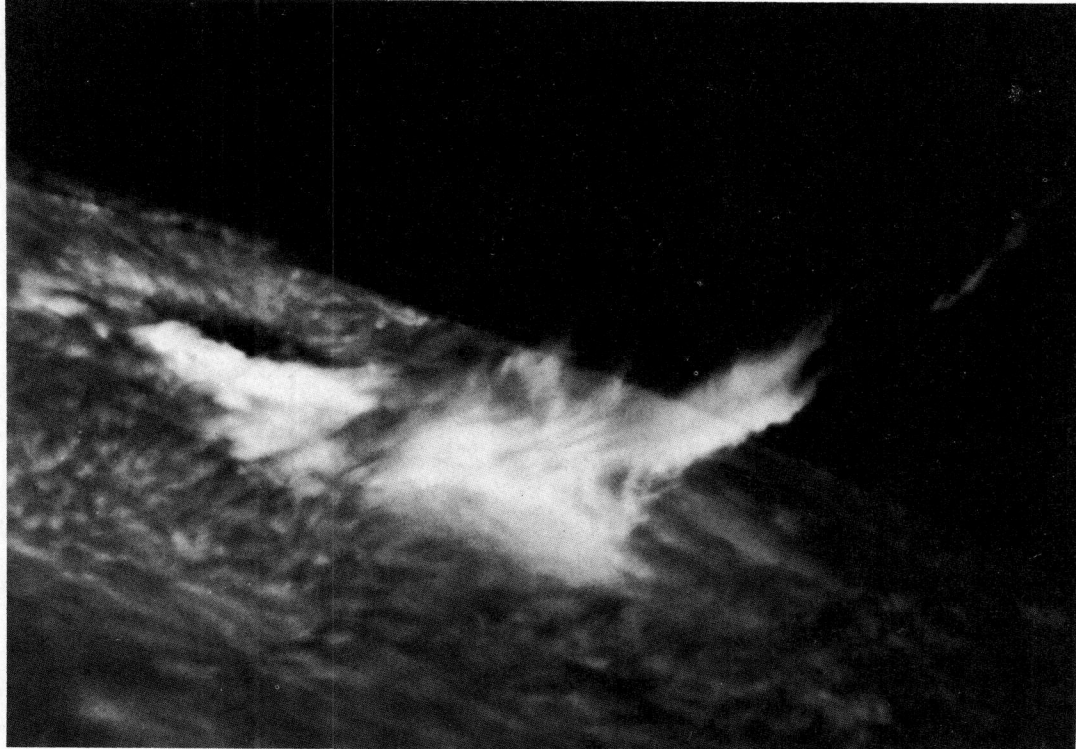

Solar flares

Brilliant flashes of light in the solar atmosphere, lasting less than an hour, or even perhaps only a few seconds, are named SOLAR FLARES. The brightest are visible in white light, but they are easier to see in the light of hydrogen or calcium lines. A flare is a highly concentrated, explosive release of energy, usually in the vicinity of an active region. Hα photographs typically show a starlike brightening in the lower atmosphere, within a plage region, which spreads rapidly to cover areas the size of the Earth (figure 8.27). Most of the energy in a flare is released in about five minutes across the entire electromagnetic spectrum from radio waves to X-rays.

Flares spring up in active regions where the magnetic field has been stressed into a strong, unstable, configuration. A major puzzle in solar physics is the reason for the sudden release of energy through the flare mechanism. Once they have started to release energy at a particular place they may flash on and off several times. Violent shock waves tear through the photosphere and chromosphere at velocities of $2\,000\,\mathrm{km\,s^{-1}}$. Simultaneously X-ray and ultraviolet detectors register intense blasts. In the hard X-ray region, the total emission from the Sun may rise by 100 times during a flare. For this reason it is considered hazardous to send astronauts into space at times when strong flares are likely to erupt on the Sun. Flares also eject copious bursts of energetic charged particles, such as protons and electrons, from the Sun. After a major outburst it is not uncommon to see material crashing back to the Sun in the form of a loop prominence.

Flare studies expanded considerably once engineers had developed instruments that could be launched in rockets and satellites. The copious X-ray emission can only be monitored outside Earth's atmosphere. When a flare occurs, a sharp burst of hard X-rays (wavelengths shorter than $0.1\,\mathrm{nm}$) is detected, followed by a gradual rise and fall of soft X-rays (wavelengths between 0.1 and $2\,\mathrm{nm}$). In the soft spectrum are emission lines from highly ionized species, such as Fe^{24+} and Fe^{25+}. The continuum is thermal radiation with a characteristic temperature $2-3\times10^7\,\mathrm{K}$. On the other hand the hard X-rays have a non-thermal spectrum. This may be produced when intense streams of relativistic electrons collide with other particles. The same electron beams may also create the *synchrotron radiation* from flares which is detected by microwave radio telescopes.

Flares have observable consequences for Earth. The energetic particles streaming into our atmosphere about two days after a flare excite atoms and electrons, causing them to emit light when they de-excite (i.e. return to their normal state); the result is the auroral displays, which are strongest at high latitudes where the magnetic field emerges vertically from the Earth's surface, and at solar maximum. The X-ray bursts indirectly cause the fadeout of shortwave radio communications on the sunlit side of Earth and cause geomagnetic disturbances. Powerful surges in the Sun's radio emission also occur.

8.26: *The solar corona. Structural features such as polar plumes and helmet streamers can be seen in the corona, which here extends to a solar radius. (Royal Astronomical Society, UK)*

8.27: *The development of a solar flare on 7 August 1972 is shown in this sequence. Flares are explosive releases of energy in the vicinity of active regions on the Sun. (Big Bear Solar Observatory, USA)*

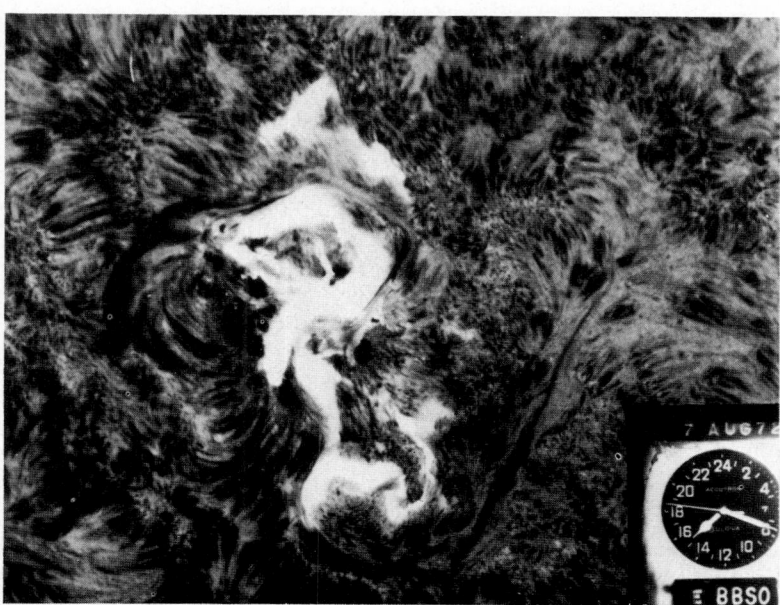
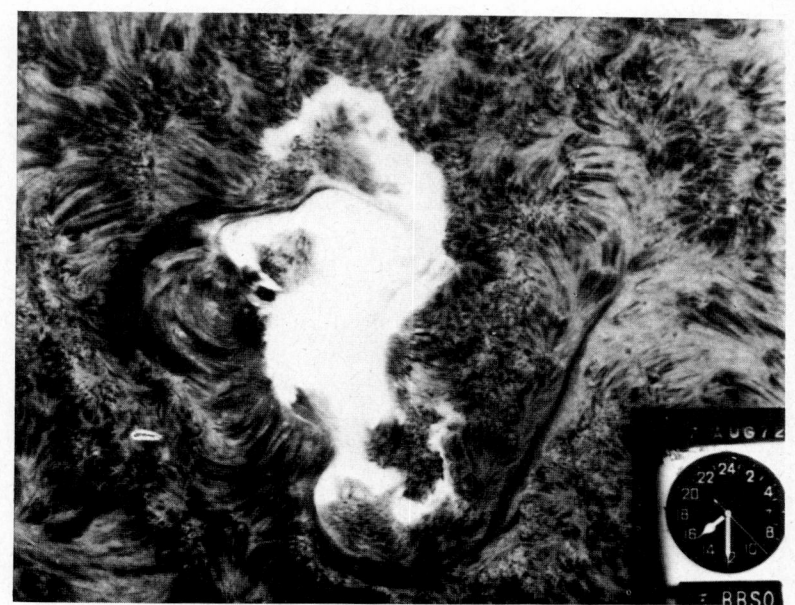

Radio waves from the Sun

As early as 1900, a British physicist, Sir Oliver Lodge, attempted to detect radio waves from the Sun. His failure to do so can be attributed mainly to the primitive equipment then available. Marconi, in 1916, and various radio enthusiasts thereafter, surmised that the static disturbances might be of solar or cosmic origin. Military investigations at radar stations in Britain during 1942 left no doubt that the Sun is a radio source, which occasionally radiates bursts of amazing intensity. The behaviour of the Sun at radio frequencies is quite different to its features in the optical domain: the radio disc is larger, and the fluctuations in intensity are more marked since the total solar radio flux can increase by one to 100 000 times during active storms.

Radio emission from the quiet Sun is best mapped at periods of sunspot minimum, since solar activity is then least likely to modify the radio picture. As we saw when discussing the sharpness of the optical disc, most radiation at a given frequency comes from regions where the atmosphere is just becoming transparent at that frequency. The properties of the radio Sun are mainly governed by the electron density in the chromosphere and corona, since free electrons are the major source of opacity at radio wavelengths. The electron density decreases with distance above the photosphere, but in the lower parts of the atmosphere it is sufficiently great to absorb long wavelengths. Consequently only radio waves shorter than a few millimetres propagate in, and are detectable from, the lower chromosphere. Wavelengths below 10 cm travel in the upper chromosphere unimpeded and metre-wavelength radiation is only encountered in the corona.

By mapping the solar radio emission at a series of wavelengths it is possible to investigate the physical conditions at different heights in the solar atmosphere. At longer radio wavelengths the Sun subtends a larger angular size and the emission comes from regions with an electron temperature of 10^6 K, since the corona is the major source. Radio observations show limb brightening in the corona at wavelengths longer than 10 cm, giving added confirmation that temperature is higher in the corona. The variation of brightness temperature, as a function of distance from the centre of the Sun's disc, is shown in figure 8.28.

Radio observations of the solar corona are also made indirectly by observing the transmission through the corona of signals from very remote radio sources, such as *quasars*, as they are occulted by the outer solar atmosphere. In this way scattering and refraction by the corona and solar wind have been detected out to 1.5×10^8 km.

The Sun is studied daily at many radio observatories in order to keep track of the various manifestations of solar activity. At Culgoora in Australia, there is a 96-element radio heliograph. This interferometer is able to map solar radio waves from the entire disc every few minutes. At centimetre wavelengths the total radio power varies gradually on a day-to-day basis. This S-COMPONENT of the solar emission correlates almost exactly with the surface

8.28: *The radio picture of the Sun gives a larger disc that shows limb brightening.*

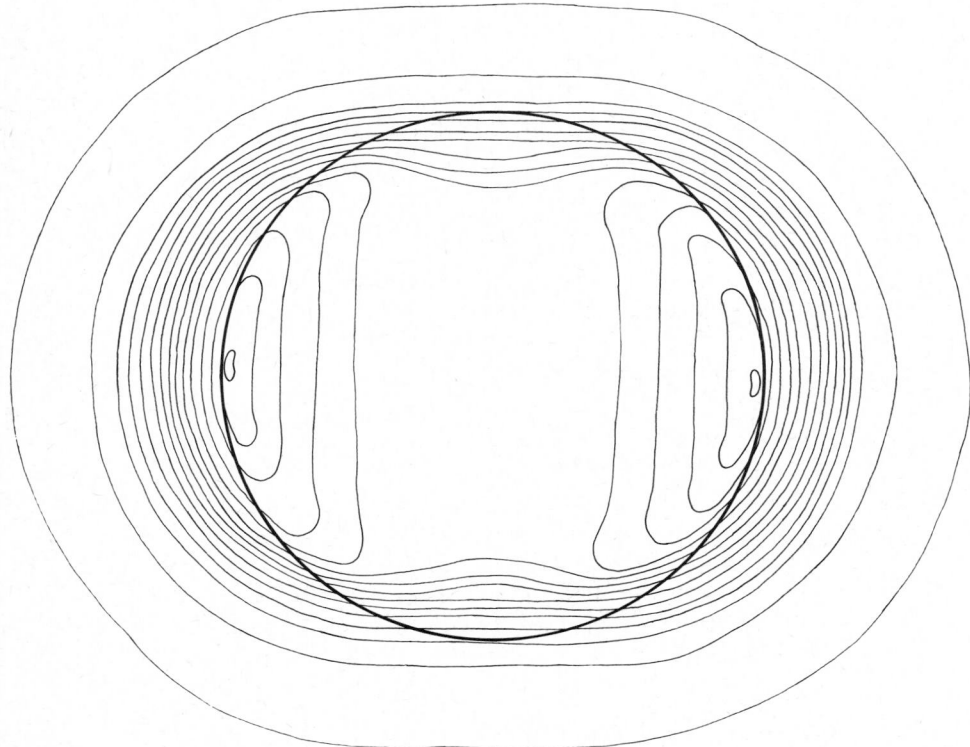

area of the disc that is covered by sunspots; so the S-component is presumably associated with active regions. High-resolution observations have shown that the radio waves are emitted from regions in the corona which are larger in size than the sunspots (figure 8.29). Because the regions correspond to the plages mentioned earlier they are called RADIO PLAGES. They have a brightness temperature of 10^6 K, and are due to higher-density regions in the corona overlying the sunspots; thermal emission from dense regions in the corona probably accounts for the radio plages.

It was an intense NOISE STORM on the Sun which led to the discovery of solar radio emission in 1942. The subject of radio bursts from the active Sun is a complex and fascinating part of solar studies, which has made important contributions to plasma physics. Several types of radio burst have been differentiated; those identified at metre wavelengths are designated as types I–V.

TYPE I BURSTS are a prominent feature of solar activity at metre wavelengths. They are the only type of burst which is not specifically associated with solar flares. When their intensity is plotted against time they appear as myriads of spikes of radio emission, lasting 0.1–10 seconds, imposed on a greatly increased background. They are associated with sunspots, and the high brightness temperature of 10^{11} K signifies that the radiation is not thermal in origin. Noise storms have durations of a few hours to several days.

The larger solar flares are frequently accompanied by outbursts at metre wavelengths lasting up to 30 minutes as well as strong X-ray bursts. These are termed TYPE II BURSTS. One of their interesting properties is that the burst is detectable at a later time at lower frequencies: the emission drifts from higher to lower frequencies at about 1 MHz/sec during the burst. Consequently special radio receivers had to be developed for studying the type II bursts. Research conducted by J. Paul Wild and his colleagues in Australia suggests that the frequency drift is a consequence of the stream of radiating particles' motion from the Sun which excites lower frequency waves as it gets higher up in the atmosphere. High-resolution radio maps, made during the course of solar bursts, have essentially confirmed this model.

After a flare begins, TYPE III BURSTS may be detectable as short duration spikes which drift down in frequency by about 20 MHz/sec. These also appear to be caused by clouds of electrons being expelled from the Sun, possibly at velocities 0.25 that of light.

Sometimes a type II burst is followed by emission covering all wavelengths, from microwaves to tens of metres, and lasting an hour or so. These are TYPE IV BURSTS. They are caused by synchrotron radiation from electrons that they have been trapped and accelerated to relativistic velocities by the magnetic fields in active regions. Solar cosmic rays are frequently ejected during type II bursts.

TYPE V is a broadband emission lasting a few minutes which displays some frequency drift.

The interaction of the Sun with the planets

The Sun and Earth

The radiations from the Sun influence the Earth and planets in many ways apart from the obvious effects of heating and illuminating their surfaces. The study of the interactions between the Sun and Earth is a branch of astronomy termed solar-terrestrial relations. The short-wavelength photons from the Sun have sufficient energy to ionize any constituents in the outer atmospheres of planets. The resulting IONOSPHERES, as the ionized outer layers are termed, affect the propagation of radio waves; in particular they make long-distance radio communication possible on Earth because the ionosphere forms a reflecting screen. Since the extreme ultraviolet and X-ray emissions from the Sun are highly variable, the height of the ionosphere and concentration of the ions are also variable.

Charged particles may be trapped in planetary magnetic fields, and so give rise to *radiation belts* encircling the planet. The total extent of the planetary magnetic field is restricted to a region termed the *magnetosphere* by the pressure of the solar wind streaming past the planet. When a solar storm occurs, shock waves and clouds of plasma propagate out and can interact with a magnetosphere to give rise to magnetic storms and aurorae.

Many of these phenomena were unknown, or their existence only indirectly inferred, before the era of space vehicles. The direct probing of the interplanetary space in the vicinity of Earth has now allowed detailed pictures to be constructed of conditions and processes, largely unattainable on Earth itself, which take place as the emissions from the Sun interact with the planets.

The solar wind

The continuous expansive motion of the coronal gas gives rise to the SOLAR WIND. At the distance of the Earth its velocity is normally about $400\,\mathrm{km\,s^{-1}}$, the particle density about $10^7\,\mathrm{m^{-3}}$, and the temperature approximately 10^5 K. Even though the total outflow of material from the Sun is about one million tonnes per second the mass-loss has a negligible influence on the Sun's evolution. The high coronal temperatures ensure that the constituents of the solar wind (mainly electrons, protons and alpha particles) are ionized; the low density of particles prevents the recombinations of ions and electrons even at large distances, where the temperature may have dropped considerably. This ensures that the solar wind is electrically high conducting. Consequently it can be influenced by magnetic fields, and indeed it drags some of the magnetic field of the Sun with it into interplanetary space. The wind itself blows approximately radially outwards from the corona, but the interplanetary magnetic field, firmly rooted to the Sun, is drawn out into spirals on account of the rotation of the Sun; this is frequently referred to as the garden-hose effect. The large-scale regions of different magnetic polarity on the Sun, mentioned above, are reflected in the sectorial structure of the solar wind (figure 8.30). Magnetic fields in the wind scatter low-energy cosmic rays, thus preventing us from measuring directly the interstellar cosmic-ray flux.

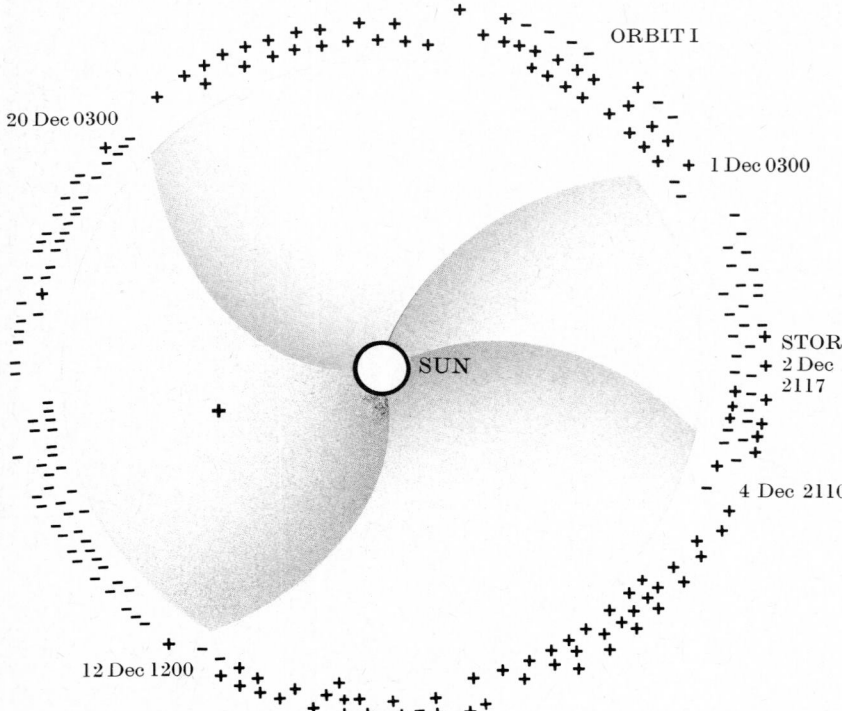

8.29: *An aerial view of the solar observatory at Culgoora in Australia, showing the 96-element radio telescope that scans the Sun continuously to map waves from the disc. (CSIRO Division of Radiophysics, Australia)*

ORBIT I

20 Dec 0300

1 Dec 0300

SUN

STORM
2 Dec
2117

4 Dec 2110

12 Dec 1200

8.30: *The sectored structure of the solar wind as determined by interplanetary spacecraft.*

Back in the last century, the aurorae were related to streams of charged particles emitted from the Sun. Later, a similar hypothesis was used to explain magnetic storms and changes in cosmic-ray counting rates after solar flares. In the 1950s, a model invoking more uniform emission of particles was proposed by L. Biermann to explain why comets' tails point away from the Sun; ordinary electromagnetic radiation pressure is insufficient for this. The first direct evidence for the solar wind (a phrase coined by E.N. Parker, a pioneer in this field) came in 1959 and 1962 from charged-particle detectors carried in early space probes to the Moon and Venus. These results have since been amply confirmed, and now the solar wind had been detected out beyond Jupiter. Somewhere beyond the orbit of Pluto the solar wind probably merges with the interstellar medium.

At times of solar activity, such as a solar flare, much plasma is ejected from the Sun both in the form of relativistic (energies exceeding 1 GeV) and non-relativistic particles. The less energetic plasma is preceded by a shock wave, which greatly distorts the interplanetary magnetic fields as it passes them. The interaction of first the shock front and then the compressed, hot plasma with a planetary magnetosphere leads to a *magnetic storm* being recorded down on the surface of the planet.

Inhomogeneities and fluctuations in the coronal and solar wind density near the Sun can cause the SCINTILLATION OF RADIO SOURCES. This phenomenon occurs in much the same manner as the optical twinkling of stars observed on Earth, which is attributable to turbulence in our atmosphere. A point source of light, such as Sirius, twinkles violently to the eye, but the twinkling of individual parts of the apparent disc of Jupiter tends to even out and render it relatively steady. Similarly only the smallest radio sources show scintillation at radio wavelengths, caused by natural variations in the density of the corona and solar wind. Studies of scintillation have improved our knowledge of the outer corona especially in directions as yet inaccessible to spacecraft, and have also permitted estimates of the angular sizes of small radio sources.

The environment of the Earth

The absorption of solar *Lyman-α* (121.6 nm) and X-radiation by the upper atmosphere of the Earth results in the ionized regions known as the *ionosphere*. The ions and electrons are here present to such an extent that radio-wave propagation is seriously affected, and indeed reflection occurs at long wavelengths. The D-REGION lying between about 60 and 90 km can be explored from the ground by means of radio propagation techniques, but the effective study of the upper layers ($E-$, F_1-, and F_2- regions) require rocket and satellite instrumentation. Above about 500 km the density is low enough for the particles to be in orbit about the Earth and here the magnetic field is a dominant influence. This region is the MAGNETO-SPHERE (figure 8.31).

In its simplest form, the magnetic field of the Earth may be pictured as a dipole (or straight permanent magnet) displaced about 400 km from the centre of the planet. The positive, or north-

8.31: *As the solar wind sweeps past a planet with a magnetic field, it distorts the planetary magnetism to form a protective shield, known as a magnetosphere. These magnetic cages surrounding some of the planets have been explored by means of interplanetary and terrestrial probes.*

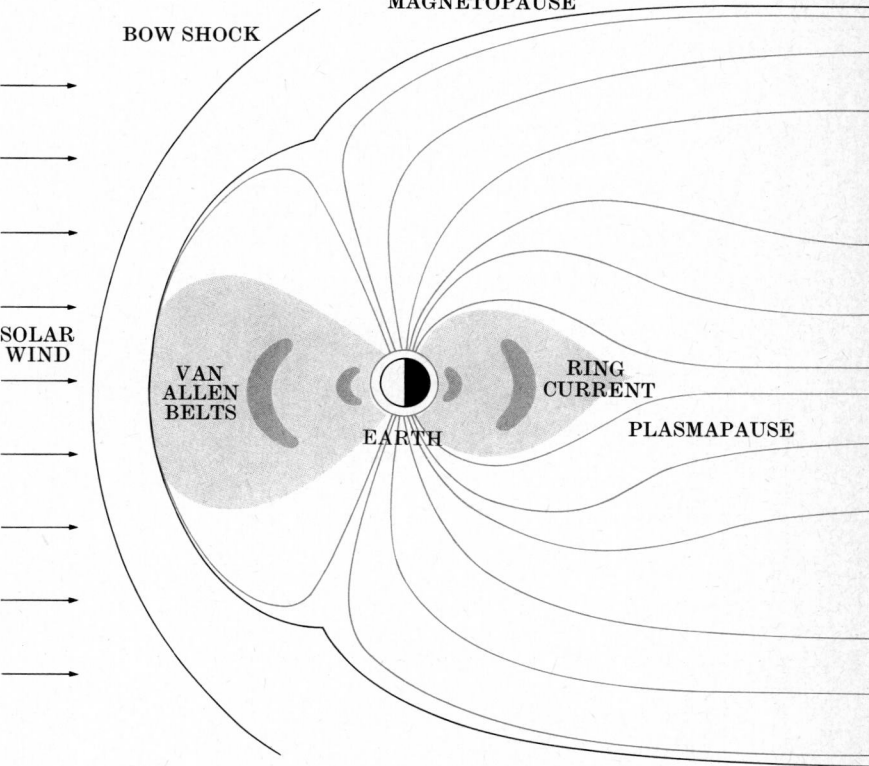

seeking pole, is actually the one on the southern hemisphere and vice versa. The magnetic field lines, which indicate the directions to which a freely-suspended magnetic compass would point, emerge vertically at the Earth's surface at about 75.6°N, 107°W and 66.3°S, 141°E (1965 positions). These positions change slowly with time, as does the intensity of the field. The intensity is presently decreasing at a rate such that, if it continued unchanged, it would be zero at about AD 4 000; such an extrapolation is not particularly justified however. Studies of partially magnetized rocks have shown that the magnetic field of the Earth has reversed at irregular intervals frequently in the past.

The magnetic field of the Earth strongly influences the charged particles, such as cosmic rays, that are incident on the Earth. Cosmic rays of energies less than a few giga-electron-volts (GeV) cannot approach the atmosphere at mid-latitudes and those that do get down at higher latitudes follow extremely tortuous paths. There are certain regions around the Earth where charged particles can orbit the Earth in relatively stable configurations. These zones have crescent-shaped cross-sections and are regions in which particles become trapped. As they contain a relatively high density of charged particles, they are called the RADIATION BELTS, or VAN ALLEN BELTS after their discoverer (figure 8.32).

8.32: *Within Earth's magnetic neighbourhood there are two zones known as the Van Allen belts that have imprisoned charged particles from the Sun.*

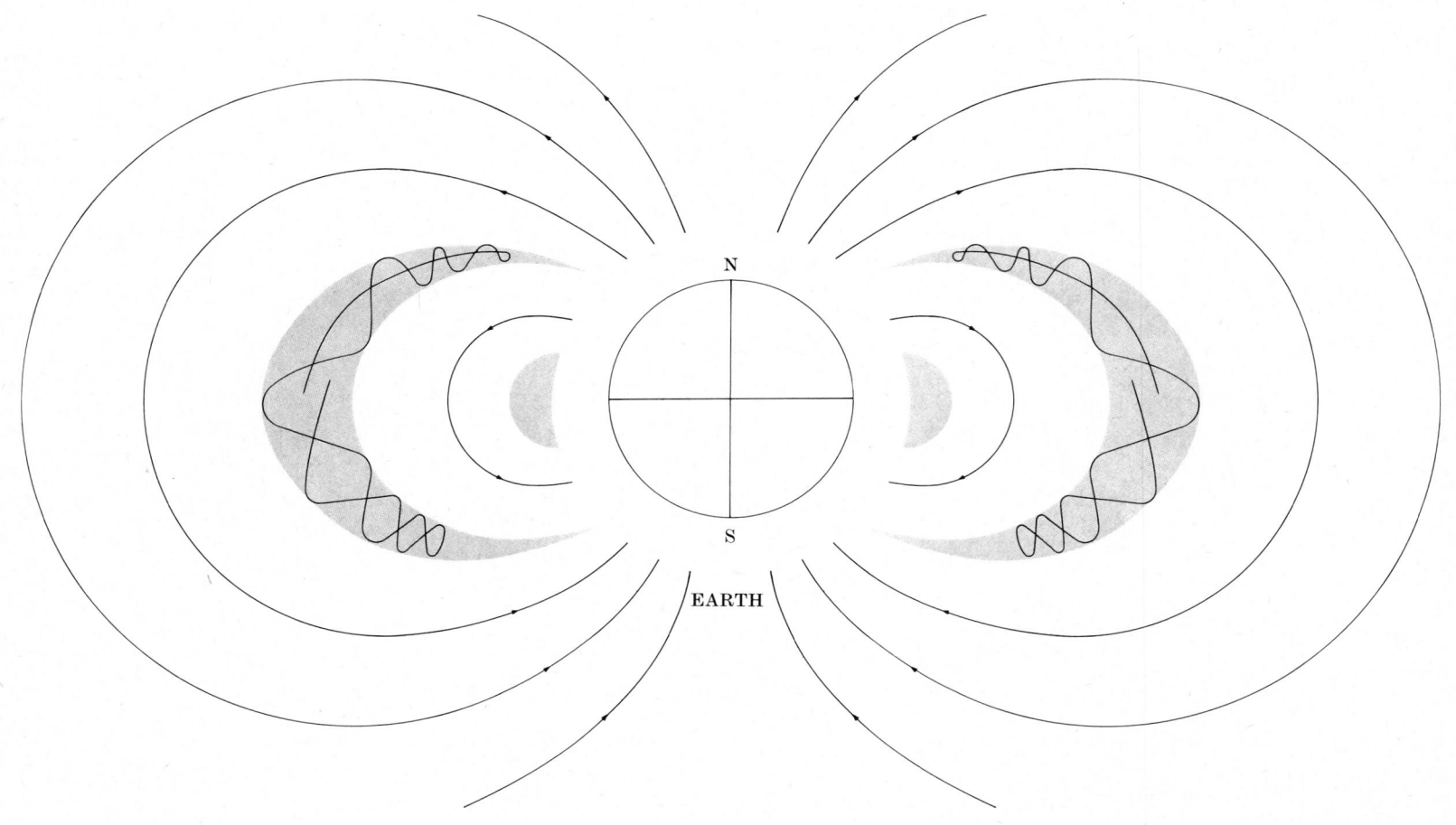

The particles spiral about the field lines, mirroring back on themselves near the magnetic poles, with periods of 0.1–3 sec. for the journey from pole to pole. Superimposed on this rapid motion is a general westward drift of protons, and eastern motion of electrons. Evidence for these radiation belts came from the earliest Russian and American satellites. The work of J.A. Van Allen of the USA and his colleagues in 1958 provided the first picture of their shape and distribution. Their simple Geiger counters on Explorer 1 registered no charged-particle radiation when they were carried above about 1 000 km. Laboratory tests and later satellite experiments showed that the null reading was in fact caused by complete saturation of the Geiger counters. Initially the researchers identified two radiation belts, but such a clear distinction is perhaps misleading. Generally the protons with energies exceeding about 30 MeV form a relatively compact belt (the inner belt) centred at about 1.5 Earth radii. The lower-energy electrons and protons occupy a much more extensive zone out to about five Earth radii.

Some of the protons in the inner belt may be indirectly accounted for by higher energy cosmic-ray protons smashing into the Earth's upper atmosphere. Any neutrons thus released are not influenced by the magnetic field and may stray out to the inner belt region. The half-life of a free neutron is about 12 min; the proton and electron resulting from its decay can be trapped in the radiation belt. The remainder of the particles may be due to the diffusion of cosmic rays and solar wind plasma from interplanetary space.

Several artificial radiation belts were produced in 1958 and 1962 by the detonation of nuclear bombs in space before international agreement to ban such experiments was obtained. The Starfish explosion of 9 July 1962 produced an inner belt that persisted for several years and caused several satellites to become inoperational because their solar cells were damaged. These are probably the most abrupt large-scale environmental changes that Man has made.

If the magnetic field of the Earth faithfully followed that of a dipole even at large distances, then the solar wind would be influenced beyond 100 Earth radii. The pressure exerted by the solar wind is sufficient to compress the Earth's magnetic field and restrict its influence to about 10 Earth radii to the sunward side of the Earth. In the opposite direction, the solar wind drags the field lines back to distances beyond that of the Moon's orbit.

Some of the outer field lines in the tail of the magnetosphere (the MAGNETOTAIL) that are closed (that is, run continuously from one hemisphere to another) are so distorted that regions of opposite polarity run parallel to one another and in close proximity. Strong currents can flow in this NEUTRAL SHEET and charged particles can be accelerated when the region is disturbed, as the field lines annihilate and distribute their energy into particle motion. The boundary of the magnetosphere, which as we have seen is far from spherical, is known as the MAGNETOPAUSE (figure 8.31). In the same way that a bow wave forms in front of a stick held in a fast-flowing stream, so a shock front stands off the front of the magnetopause. The intermediate zone between the shock wave and the magnetopause is called the MAGNETOSHEATH.

Solar storms and magnetic storms

SOLAR STORMS, described above, are spectacular outbursts due to the sudden transformation of a considerable amount of energy (about 10^{26} joules) into electromagnetic and charged-particle radiation within an hour or so. A typical event is a solar flare, which, apart from the burst of radio, optical and X-radiation, releases electrons and protons with energies that can range up to 100 GeV. The highest energy, relativistic particles, arrive at the Earth almost simultaneously with the visible activity and they can be recorded by neutron monitors located below ground. These neutrons do not come directly from the Sun; they are produced when the solar cosmic-ray protons smash into the terrestrial atmosphere at height of about 20 km. Twentyfold increases in counting rate have been recorded in intervals of a quarter of an hour or so.

The sudden local injection of energy into the solar wind above a flare creates a shock wave that propagates out to the distance of the Earth in about two days. The resultant sudden compression of the magnetosphere is recorded on the ground by a sudden change in the magnetic field at the surface. This is the sudden commencement of a magnetic storm. This change reverses itself later as the plasma sweeps over the *magnetosphere*, and partially replenishes the *radiation belts* and changes the currents flowing in them. The MAGNETIC STORM, as this sequence of events is termed, takes several days to run its course, after which Earth's magnetism returns to normality.

Cosmic rays are reflected by the distortion of the interplanetary magnetic field associated with the shock wave spreading out in the interplanetary space and this gives rise to a decrease in detection rate. Changes occur in the ionosphere as well as radio fadeouts over the sunlit hemisphere. Polar blackouts, in which cosmic radio noise is strongly attenuated at latitudes above the arctic circles, are frequently observed.

Disturbances of the geomagnetic field are extremely complicated and have been recorded for centuries. A measure of worldwide activity is given by the KP INDEX; this is a three-hourly mean of fluctuation in the magnetic field observed at twelve stations between latitudes 40° and 63°. Many of these disturbances are caused by currents flowing in the magnetosphere and ionosphere, among which is that due to the opposing drifts of positively and negatively charged particles in the radiation belts.

A large variety of everyday phenomena have been correlated with solar activity, and the 11-year solar cycle. These include the prices of shares and certain commodities, political upheavals, geophysical effects such as earthquakes, and the weather. Many of the claimed relationships are undoubtedly spurious, but there is an increasing body of evidence to suggest that some aspects of the weather are linked to activity on the Sun. The precise mechanism is unknown, but the cycle is evident in counts of tree rings. More recently it has been found that the large-scale movements of air masses over the Earth are regulated by the sectorial structure. Changes are noted a few days after a sector boundary has swept across the Earth's magnetosphere.

There is a notable similarity between solar and magnetic storms in that magnetic field energy is converted into particle energy. This occurs in a solar flare, which later triggers a similar conversion in the Earth's magnetotail. Satellite measurements in this latter region can provide direct observations of a universally occurring phenomenon, the conversion of magnetic energy to kinetic energy, that is currently little understood.

The Aurorae

The AURORAE BOREALIS and AUSTRALIS have been associated with magnetic activity since the eighteenth century. Most of the light in these displays is produced by excitation and ionization of the upper atmosphere at high latitudes by an influx of electrons with energies about 10 keV. Disturbances of the magnetic field configuration within the magnetotail energize these electrons; in their propagation towards the Earth they become deflected towards high latitudes. In each hemisphere they arrive in thin sheets mostly within an area called the AURORAL OVAL. The extent and position of this depends upon magnetic activity, but generally it has a width of about 5° and comes within about 12° of the geomagnetic poles on the sunward side and about 22° on the dark side. The rotation of the Earth underneath the oval, causes aurorae to be visible over a large zone in the course of a single day. Aerial and satellite studies have confirmed the shape of the oval inferred from ground-based observations.

The aurorae in the oval visible to the naked eye often have curtain-like structures. The lower border is at a height of about 100 km and may extend several thousands of kilometres. Vertical striations appear in rayed arcs and more complicated forms occur in so-called draperies showing folds and curls. Spectral lines are observed, and in particular a green oxygen line at 557.7 nm is present. Rocket and balloon measurements indicate X-ray emission produced by *bremsstrahlung* from the particles impacting on the atmosphere. The auroral zones march equatorward in times of increased solar and magnetic activity and indeed aurorae have been observed from Singapore.

Interplanetary space and planetary magnetospheres

Centrifugal forces due to the rotation of the Sun may cause the solar wind and the interplanetary magnetic field to vary away from the solar equatorial plane. Consequently, space probes that journey out of the ecliptic are important for filling in the details that cannot be provided by the usual interplanetary missions. The motion of the Sun through interstellar space probably creates a similar, although much larger-scale, magnetospheric-shock wavetail structure as occurs near the Earth.

The ZODIACAL LIGHT appears as a conical glow extending upwards along the *ecliptic*. It is visible on clear, moonless evenings and at dawn just at the end of twilight. Zodiacal light visible before morning twilight is popularly called the false dawn. It is easiest to

8.33: *Beautiful aurora displays photographed in Alaska. The light in these displays is produced by electrons from the Sun disturbing atoms at high altitudes. The white spots are stars. (University of Alaska,* USA*)*

see when the ecliptic is perpendicular to the horizon. For this reason it is most conspicuous in the tropics, and on spring evenings or autumn mornings in temperate zones. Polarization and other studies suggest that the zodiacal light is caused by sunlight reflected from interplanetary dust particles several microns in size. Interactions with the solar wind and radiations will charge these particles to several volts positive. Enhancements of the zodiacal light have been reported after intense solar flares. Related to the zodiacal light is the more feeble GEGENSCHEIN or COUNTER-GLOW. It is visible on exceedingly dark and clear nights as a luminous elliptical area exactly opposite the Sun's position in the sky. This also is caused by the reflection of sunlight by interstellar dust.

The solar wind blows on all the planets and their satellites, and its effect on these depends upon their magnetic fields, atmospheres and electrical conductivities. A planet such as Jupiter, which has a relatively strong magnetic field, has a well-developed magnetosphere. The rapid rotation of the body of the planet and its magnetic field leads to a large centrifugal force on the particles in the radiation belts, which thus acquire a flattened shape.

The nearby satellite, Io, strongly interacts with this magnetosphere and trapped particles, producing decametric radio bursts.

Planetary magnetic fields are usually considered to be due to rotation of some fluid mass exciting a dynamo action. We therefore only expect magnetic fields for planets satisfying these condi-

tions. Saturn provides an interesting possibility in which the planet's rings may be of some influence.

A slowly-rotating planet such as Venus offers no magnetic field sufficient to develop radiation belts and a magnetosphere, although its ionosphere makes it appear conductive to the solar wind and a bowshock is observed. In the anti-Sun direction a plasma shadow with subsequent turbulent motions occurs. Mars has little magnetic field and so its interactions are similar to that of Venus. The lack of a lunar atmosphere allows the solar wind to impinge directly on to the Moon's surface. The magnetic field of Mercury is capable of producing a magnetosphere, although the weakness of this field and the proximity to the Sun mean that the magnetopause is only about 2 000 km from its sunward surface. The source or cause of Mercury's magnetic field is not yet understood.

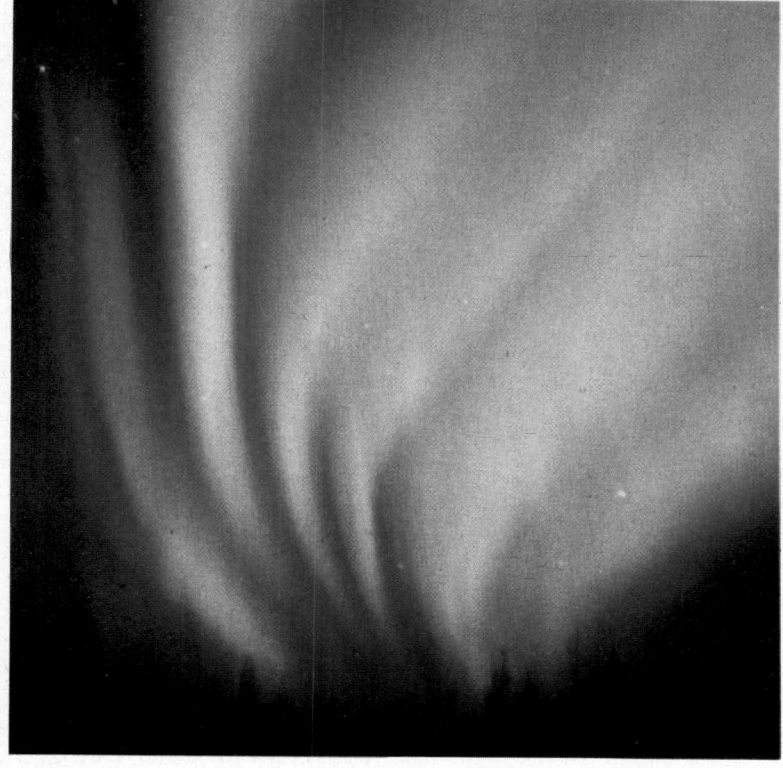

9. The Solar System

Orbits of the planets

The main bodies of the Solar System are the Sun and, in orbit round it, the nine major planets. In order of increasing distance from the Sun these are Mercury, Venus, Earth, Mars, Jupiter, Saturn (all known since antiquity), Uranus, Neptune and Pluto. Sir William Herschel discovered Uranus in 1781 during a review of the entire sky which was so systematic as to be virtually certain to reveal any such object. A planet more distant from the Sun than Uranus was predicted independently by John Adams in 1843 and by Urbain Le Verrier in 1846. These predictions enabled Johann Galle and Heinrich d'Arrest to find and identify the planet which is now known as Neptune. In 1915 Percival Lowell published calculations predicting another planet beyond Neptune; this ninth planet was found in 1930 by Clyde Tombaugh and named Pluto.

Several of the planets have systems of satellites, or moons, in orbits round them which in several ways mimic the system of Sun and planets. There is also a whole host of lesser objects: minor planets or *asteroids*, *comets*, *meteoroids*, and dust, as well as the *solar wind*.

The word planet is derived from the Greek noun πλανητης (planetes) which means wanderer. This name arose because of the way in which the planets wander against the backcloth of distant stars. According to Ptolemy, the Earth lay at rest at the centre of the Universe, while the Moon, Sun and planets moved in orbits around it. This view was generally accepted until the middle of the

9.1: *The elliptical orbit of a planet around the Sun. The Sun is at one focus and there is nothing at the other. The eccentricity, e, has been exaggerated here; real planetary orbits are almost circular and the Sun is quite near the centre.*

9.2: *Each shaded area in the planet's orbit is equal and, by Kepler's second law, the planet takes the same time to cover the arcs of the orbit determined by these areas. Its speed is therefore greater when it is nearer the Sun than when it is further away.*

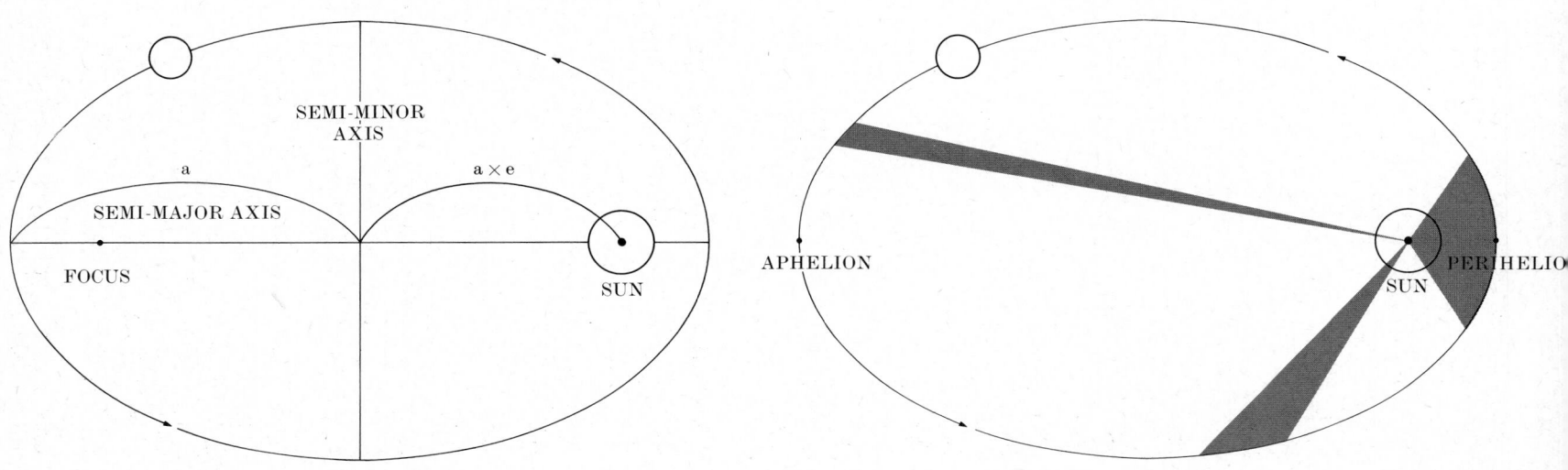

sixteenth century when Nikolaus Copernicus argued that it was the Sun which should be at the centre. This view was bitterly opposed at the time but gradually became accepted. Copernicus followed Ptolemy's views in one respect: he built planetary orbits up from circles. The theories of both Copernicus and Ptolemy suffered from a great defect: they did not predict the positions of the planets with sufficient accuracy. The true nature of planetary orbits was eventually elucidated by Johannes Kepler in the early seventeenth century when he published three relationships describing planetary motion. These are usually referred to as KEPLER'S LAWS. The first of these laws is K1: Each planetary orbit is an ellipse with the Sun at one focus. An elliptical orbit is shown in figure 9.1. The SEMI-MAJOR AXIS, a, determines its size and the ECCENTRICITY, e, its shape. The eccentricity is less than one for elliptical orbits; if it is zero we have a circle with both foci at the centre. As e increases towards one, the ellipse becomes more elongated and the foci move further from the centre.

Kepler's second law is K2: The line joining any one planet to the Sun sweeps out equal areas in equal times. This constant rate of sweeping out area is different for each planet.

It follows from this law that the speed of a planet varies along its orbit (see figure 9.2). It is greatest at PERIHELION, the point at which the planet is nearest to the Sun, and least at APHELION, at which it is furthest away. Our Earth is at its perihelion about 2 January each year; the near coincidence with the start of the calendar year is fortuitous.

Kepler's third law, K3, can be expressed thus: For any pair of planets, the squares of the periods are proportional to the cubes of the semi-major axes of their orbits. As a result the further a planet is from the Sun, the longer it takes to go once round its orbit.

The Earth's orbit lies in a plane which passes through the Sun and which is called the ECLIPTIC. The orbit of each one of the other planets also lies in such a plane which is inclined at a small angle to the ecliptic. Because this angle is small, but not zero, a planet passes above and below the ecliptic as it moves around its orbit, but by only a relatively small amount. Each planet goes around its orbit in the same direction as the Earth does.

The Earth's rotation axis is not perpendicular to the ecliptic but is tilted by an angle of 23° 27′; this angle is called the OBLIQUITY OF THE ECLIPTIC. The axis points in a direction which is almost fixed in space as the Earth moves round its orbit. We can see that during the year this causes the Sun to appear to move northwards and southwards relative to Earth (see figure 9.3). The SUMMER SOLSTICE is the time of the year (22 June) when the Sun appears at its most northerly position. It is then overhead at a latitude of 23° 27′ N; the line joining all points with this latitude is called the TROPIC OF CANCER. Six months later, at the WINTER SOLSTICE (22 December) the Sun is at its most southerly and is overhead at a latitude of 23° 27′ S (TROPIC OF CAPRICORN). Twice a year the Sun appears overhead at the equator; these occasions are the VERNAL EQUINOX on 21 March and the AUTUMNAL EQUINOX of 23 September. It is customary to use each of the terms Summer

9.3: *The direction of the Earth's rotation axis is almost fixed in space. The axis is tilted by 23° 27′ so that it is not perpendicular to the plane of the orbit. As the Earth goes round its orbit the north and south poles are alternately tilted towards the Sun.*

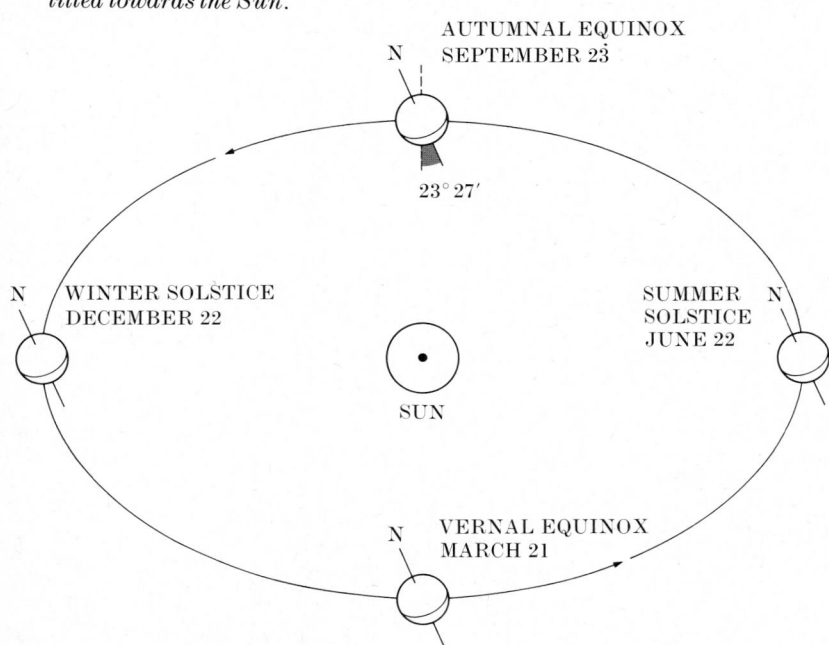

Solstice etc. to describe both a particular time, as above, and the position of the Earth in its orbit at that time. In particular the vernal equinox, or more precisely, the direction from the Earth to the Sun at the vernal equinox, is used as a standard direction in many astronomical *coordinate systems*. This direction is also called the direction of the FIRST POINT OF ARIES.

Over a period of 25 800 years the Earth's axis sweeps out a cone; this motion is called PRECESSION. The obliquity remains very nearly constant while the direction of the axis varies. This has the interesting consequence that the pole star Polaris will only be over the Earth's north pole for a few hundred years more. Relative to the stars, the equinoxes and the direction of the first point of Aries moves once round the Earth's orbit in this time. As a result the TROPICAL YEAR of 365.24219 days, which is the time from one vernal equinox to the next is slightly shorter than the SIDEREAL YEAR of 365.25636 days, which is the orbital period of the Earth relative to a fixed direction in space.

To describe completely the orbit of a planet or other object round the Sun it is necessary to specify six parameters known as ORBITAL ELEMENTS. The choice of elements is not unique, but the set most commonly used for planetary orbits is shown in figure 9.4. The elements i and Ω determine the position of the orbital plane, ω the orientation of the orbit in the plane, a and e its size and shape and P and T the position of the planet in its orbit. Values of orbital elements are given in table 9.1. The ASTRONOMICAL UNIT is defined to be equal to the semi-major axis of the Earth's orbit.

The same elements can be used to describe the orbit of a comet when this is an ellipse. Some comets, however, move in orbits that cannot be distinguished from parabolas. In this case the eccentricity, e, is equal to one. The period, P, and the length of the semi-major axis, a, are both infinite and are not used. The size of the orbit can be specified by using q, the distance of the comet from the Sun at perihelion. This element, q, can also be used for elliptical orbits; in this case it is equal to $a(1-e)$.

Kepler's Laws are not laws in the sense of modern science. Rather they are a model, or set of rules, that give us a satisfactory account of how the planets move. But why do they move in this way? The answer was given in the middle of the seventeenth century by Sir Isaac Newton who discovered laws of motion and of gravitation that explained why the planets have their observed motions. He was then able to predict theoretically that the planets would move very nearly in accordance with Kepler's empirically-derived laws. The agreement is not exact because the planets have non-zero masses; this has two effects. First, the motion of the Sun, which is being tugged at by nine planets, must be taken into account. Second, the planets attract one another and these perturbations cause deviations from exact elliptical orbits. With modern computers it is possible to calculate the motions over long periods of time and to issue accurate predictions of the positions of planets and satellites. Comparison of such predictions with observations shows that Newtonian mechanics and gravitation give a very accurate description of motions in the Solar System,

9.4: *The orbital elements of a planet completely specify the shape, size and orientation of the orbit and the position of the planet at any time can be calculated from them. Not shown are P, the period and T, the time the planet reaches perihelion.*

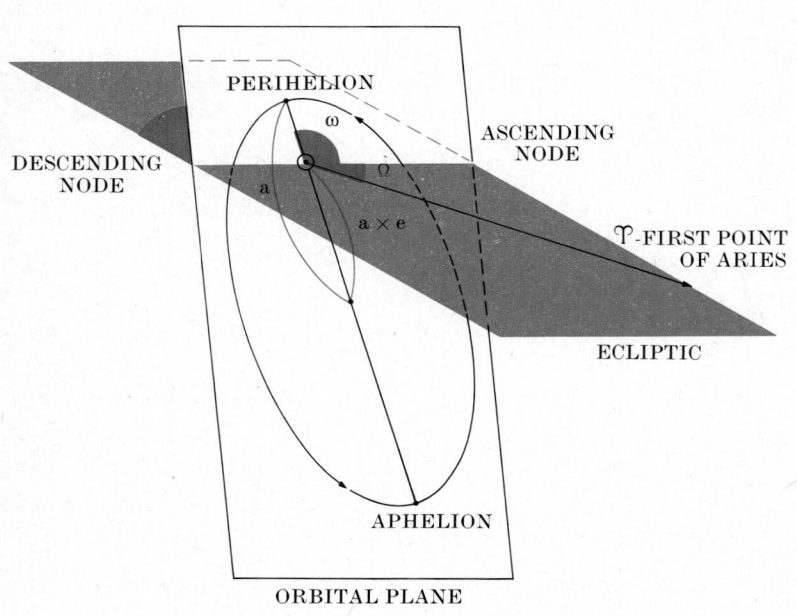

although the *general theory of relativity* has to be used in the case of Mercury's orbit.

After the discovery of Uranus, astronomers found that irregularities in its motion could not be explained by perturbations caused by the planets then known. It was the analysis of these discrepancies which led Adams and Le Verrier to predict another planet in a triumph for the gravitation theory. Later, more irregularities in the motion of Uranus were found which led Lowell to predict yet another planet beyond Neptune. This turned up in 1930 and was named Pluto. Although it was acclaimed at the time as yet another victory for theoretical astronomy, it is now considered that the discovery was mainly the result of good fortune.

Are there any more planets beyond Pluto? If there were a TENTH PLANET beyond Neptune and Pluto it would cause perturbations in the motions of the outer planets. These deviations would be very small. All observations of planetary positions have a small error and no discrepancy larger than these errors has been seen with any degree of certainty. It is also possible to use observations of certain comets, such as Halley's comet, to make predictions of planets not yet seen but none of these calculations has resulted in the finding of a planet. Astronomers now consider that no further planets, comparable to those known, remain to be discovered.

One of the effects of the mutual perturbations of planets is to cause their orbits to rotate in their own plane so that there is a steady change in the direction of perihelion. For Mercury the observed PRECESSION OF PERIHELION per century is 574 arc sec. According to the Newtonian theory of gravitation, this shift should be only 532 arc sec, which leaves an unexplained discrepancy of about 42 arc sec. Einstein's general theory of relativity agrees very closely with Newton's theory of gravitation, when applied to the Solar System, but it does also predict this extra shift. Within the accuracy of the measurements (about one second of arc per century) there is full agreement between observation and the predictions of the general theory of relativity. This result and the corresponding results for the smaller shifts of the perihelia of Venus and the Earth form one of the main experimental verifications of the general theory of relativity. For the Earth the total shift of the perihelion is 1165 arc sec per century, so that in 111 270 years, perihelion moves once round the orbit. Of this shift only 3.8 arc sec per century is due to relativistic effects.

We are now in a position to discuss how astronomers have worked out the size of the Solar System. From Kepler's third law and measurements of the orbital periods of the planets it is possible to calculate the relative sizes of planetary orbits; for example the semi-major axis of each orbit can be expressed in astronomical units. We can then use the theory of gravitation to predict the distance, in astronomical units, between any two planets at any time. Now if we can find just one such distance in kilometres, the length of the astronomical unit in kilometres can be obtained, and all distances in the Solar System are then known in kilometres. The

Table 9.1 : Mean orbital elements of the planets

Planet	Mean distance a		Sidereal period P		Synodic period	Mean orbital velocity	Eccentricity e	Inclination to the ecliptic i	Mean longitude of: ascending node Ω	perihelion ω
	astronomical units	millions of kilometres	tropical years	days	days	km/s		degrees	degrees	degrees
Mercury	0.387099	57.9	0.24085	87.969	115.88	47.89	0.2056	7.00	48	77
Venus	0.723332	108.2	0.61521	224.701	583.92	35.03	0.0068	3.39	76	131
Earth	1.000000	149.6	1.00004	365.256	—	29.79	0.0167	—	—	103
Mars	1.523691	227.9	1.88089	686.980	779.94	24.13	0.0934	1.85	49	336
Jupiter	5.202803	778.3	11.86223	4332.589	398.88	13.06	0.0485	1.30	100	14
Saturn	9.53884	1427.0	29.4577	10759.22	378.09	9.64	0.0556	2.49	113	93
Uranus	19.1819	2869.6	84.0139	30685.4	369.66	6.81	0.0472	0.77	74	170
Neptune	30.0578	4496.6	164.793	60189.0	367.49	5.43	0.0086	1.77	132	44
Pluto	39.44	5900.0	247.7	90465.0	366.73	4.74	0.250	17.2	110	223

modern method of making such a measurement is to use radar. A large radio telescope is pointed towards another planet (which in practice is Venus) and a pulse of radio waves is transmitted. Some of the radio waves are reflected by Venus back to the Earth where they are received several minutes after transmission. The time for the journey is measured and since the velocity of radio waves is known to be $299\,792.458\,\text{km}\,\text{s}^{-1}$ the distance between the radio telescope and the surface of Venus can be calculated with great precision. A series of such observations is made over a period of several months. This produces a more accurate value of the astronomical unit than would a single measurement and enables other quantities, such as the radius of Venus, to be measured. The *astronomical unit* is now known to be $149\,597\,870\,\text{km}$.

Radar can also be used to measure the time that a planet takes to revolve on its axis. Because a planet is moving relative to the Earth, the reflected radio waves in a radar experiment suffer a *Doppler shift*. The revolution of a planet about its axis causes this shift to be different for different parts of the planet's surface, and the smearing of the returned radar pulse is used to calculate the period of revolution.

It is generally possible to determine the elements of the orbit of a planet or comet from its positions at three different and known times. The uncertainties in the positions inevitably result in uncertainties in the elements, but these can be reduced by using more than three positions spread over as long a time as possible. This has been done for all the planets and their orbits are known with great accuracy. As mentioned above, each planet, as it moves around the Sun, suffers only small perturbations from the other planets which are relatively easy to allow for when making predictions of future planetary positions. The Moon presents a much more difficult problem, as its orbit around the Earth is affected so much by the Sun that the Sun cannot be considered a small perturbation. All three bodies, Moon, Earth and Sun, must be considered together; astronomers call this the THREE-BODY PROBLEM. The problem has no exact solution like the elliptical orbit of the two-body problem. Over the centuries, the theory of the lunar motion has improved but it has still not yet reached a completely satisfactory state from which the position of the Moon can be predicted as accurately as it can be measured.

In 1772 Johann Bode drew attention to a curious numerical relationship which had been discovered some years earlier by Titius. For many years this intriguing relationship was unfairly called Bode's Law although recently the name TITIUS-BODE LAW has come into use. The law starts by taking the numbers, 0, 3, 6, 12, 24, 48, 96, 192 and 384. After 3 each of these is twice its predecessor. The value 4 is now added to each number. If the distance of the Earth from the Sun is taken as 10, this series of numbers gives the distances from the Sun of all the planets, except Neptune, remarkably accurately as table 9.2 shows. In 1772 Uranus, Neptune and Pluto were unknown, but when Uranus was discovered in 1781 it fitted the law very well. Neptune does not fit but Pluto does if it is taken to follow Uranus. The law predicts a planet at a distance of 28 on the scale being used here. Such a planet was discovered by G. Piazzi on 1 January 1801, the first day of the nineteenth century. This was Ceres, and on the scale of the Titius-Bode law its distance from the Sun was 27.7, in satisfactory agreement with the predicted value of 28. Later, many other objects at a similar distance from the Sun were found; they are now known as MINOR PLANETS because of their small size compared to the other, MAJOR PLANETS. Nobody has yet devised a satisfactory explanation for the Titius-Bode law. It is most probably a mere coincidence. Although this may sound implausible we must bear in mind the fact that the 'law' has several degrees of freedom! The starting points 0 and 3 are chosen arbitrarily, then we choose the doubling law, then we decide to add 4 to each number. None of these choices is based on physical arguments. Even after playing about to find numbers that fit the inner planets we have trouble with Neptune which does not harmonize.

Table 9.2: Distances of the planets from the Sun as predicted by the Titius-Bode law compared to actual distances

Planet	Distance by Titius-Bode law	Actual distance
Mercury	4	3.9
Venus	7	7.2
Earth	10	10.0
Mars	16	15.2
—	28	—
Jupiter	52	52.0
Saturn	100	95.4
Uranus	196	191.8
Neptune	—	300.6
Pluto	388	394.4

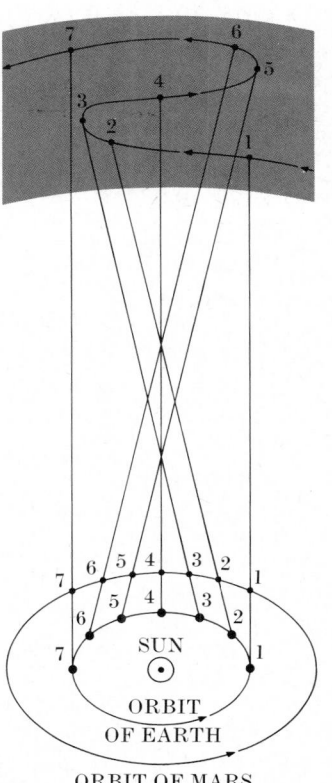

9.5: *The motion of Mars when viewed from the Earth is the combined effect of the orbital motion of each. Mars and the Earth are shown at monthly intervals and the lines joining the positions indicate where Mars is seen against the background of stars. Most of the time Mars appears to move from west to east; this is called direct motion. Mars is at opposition at point 4 and for a time around then (between points 3 and 5) it appears to move from east to west (retrograde motion). Because the orbit of Mars is inclined to that of the Earth, the apparent motion is not along a straight line but along either a Z-shaped curve as here or a loop.*

SUN

ORBIT
OF EARTH

ORBIT OF MARS

The planets as seen from the Earth

The path of a planet in the sky as seen from the Earth results from a combination of the effects of the orbital motion of both the Earth and the planet. The form of the observed motion depends primarily on whether the planet is nearer the Sun than the Earth (an INFERIOR PLANET), or further away (a SUPERIOR PLANET). Mars is a typical superior planet and its motions are illustrated in figure 9.5. When the Earth and Mars are in line with the Sun and on the same side, Mars is said to be at OPPOSITION. At this time Mars is nearest to the Earth and best placed for observation. Figure 9.6 illustrates the terms opposition, CONJUNCTION, QUADRATURE and PHASE ANGLE for Mars. These terms are also used for the other superior planets: Jupiter, Saturn, Uranus, Neptune and Pluto. Technically, opposition is defined to occur when the celestial longitude of the planet differs from that of the Sun by 180°. Conjunction occurs when the difference is zero, and quadrature when it is 90°.

For Mars the greatest phase angle is 47°, for Jupiter it is 12° and for the other superior planets it is smaller still. As Mars and the Earth move round the Sun the varying distance between them causes the angular diameter of Mars to vary from 25 arc sec at opposition to 3.5 arc sec at conjunction.

Figure 9.7 shows the orbit of Venus, one of the two inferior planets; the other is Mercury. As Venus moves along its orbit it appears successively at INFERIOR CONJUNCTION, GREATEST WESTERN ELONGATION, SUPERIOR CONJUNCTION, GREATEST EASTERN ELONGATION before returning to inferior conjunction. At its positions of greatest elongation Venus appears 48° away from the Sun in the sky. The planet is best placed for visual observations from the Earth when it is near these positions. During its orbital motion Venus turns varying parts of its illuminated hemisphere towards the Earth so that it shows phases similar to the Moon. At inferior conjunction the dark side is towards Earth, but, as Venus moves, the illuminated hemisphere is gradually turned towards Earth: at greatest western elongation half the visible hemisphere is illuminated and at superior conjunction all of it is. In the other half of the orbit the phases occur in the reverse order. Meanwhile the apparent diameter of Venus is varying between 64.5 arc sec at inferior conjunction, when it is nearest to Earth, and 9.9 arc sec at superior conjunction when it is furthest away. Because of its varying phase and distance Venus does not attain its brightest apparent magnitude at either conjunction, but near to its positions of great elongation. The changing phases make it an interesting subject for binoculars or a small telescope.

Mercury shows the same phases as Venus but because of its smaller orbit its greatest elongations are 28° from the Sun. At inferior conjunction, Venus and Mercury may pass in front of the Sun's disc. Such a TRANSIT does not occur every time because of the inclination of the planets' orbits to that of the Earth. A list of some transits is given in table 9.3; it can be seen that transits of Mercury are much more common than those of Venus. Transits can only occur when the planet is near one of the nodes of its orbit, since otherwise it passes above or below the Sun. Mercury passes through its nodes on 9 May and 10 November, Venus on 7 June and 9 December and so transits can only occur close to these dates.

Because the orbits of all the planets are inclined to that of the Earth, each planet is seen to move along a different path against the background of stars. None of the inclinations is very great and as a result the apparent paths of all the planets are confined to a narrow band in the sky called the ZODIAC.

The name SIDEREAL PERIOD is given to the true time of revolution of a planet round the Sun relative to the distant stars. The SYNODIC PERIOD is the average time of revolution relative to the line joining the Earth to the Sun, that is the average time between two successive oppositions or corresponding conjunctions.

Table 9.3: Some transits of Mercury and Venus

Mercury		Venus	
1960	November 7	1639	December 4
1970	May 9	1761	June 5
1973	November 10	1769	June 3
1986	November 13	1874	December 8
1993	November 6	1882	December 6
1999	November 15	2004	June 7
		2012	June 5

9.6: *The orbit of Mars, a typical superior planet. At opposition and conjunction Mars is in line with the Sun and the Earth. If the phase angle is divided by 180 it gives the fraction of the Martian hemisphere seen from the Earth that is in darkness. This is greatest when Mars is at quadrature, i.e. when the angle Sun-Earth-Mars is a right angle.*

9.7: *The orbit of Venus, a typical inferior planet. Conjunction occurs when Venus is in line with the Earth and the Sun and is called superior when Venus is beyond the Sun or inferior otherwise. At greatest elongation, Venus appears furthest from the Sun in the sky and is best placed for observation after sunset at easterly elongation and before sunrise at westerly.*

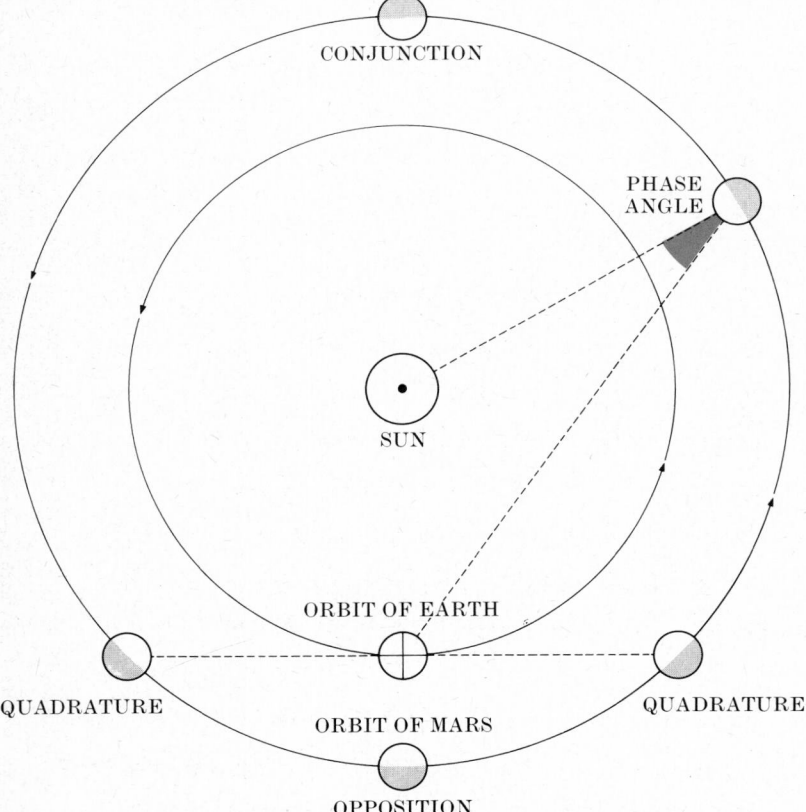

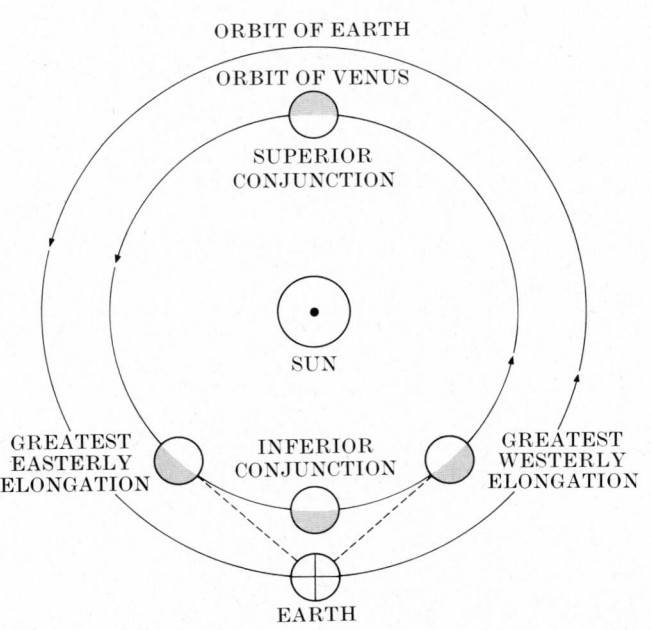

The Sun and stars seen from the Earth

As the Earth rotates on its axis, the stars appear to move round the sky in the opposite direction. Since the Earth is travelling around the Sun, the Sun as viewed from Earth appears to move against the background of stars. Because of this it is possible to measure (or to define) the length of a day in two different ways. A SIDEREAL DAY is the time for the stars to move once round the sky and return to the same positions in the sky relative to the Earth. A SOLAR DAY is the corresponding time measured using the Sun rather than the stars. The Earth rotates on its axis in the same direction as it revolves around the Sun, so the solar day is longer than the sidereal day (figure 9.8). In a year the number of sidereal days is exactly one more than that of solar days, because the Earth, in orbiting the Sun, has effectively made one less rotation relative to the Sun. The difference in the length of the two days is 1/365.24 sidereal days which is about four minutes. If we measure time by the Sun the stars will therefore be in the same positions in the sky four minutes earlier each day (or two hours earlier each month). The length of the solar day varies throughout the year because of the ellipticity of the Earth's orbit and the tilt of its axis to the ecliptic. The position of the real Sun determines what is called APPARENT SOLAR TIME. For practical purposes it is much more convenient to use MEAN SOLAR TIME which is obtained by making all days equal in length to the average length of a solar day. The difference between apparent and mean solar time is called the equation of time and it can be as large as a quarter of an hour (figure 9.9). A basic sundial gives apparent solar time although it is possible to mark the dial so that mean time can be used.

9.8: *The difference between the sidereal and solar day. The Earth's orbit is viewed from above the north pole. The heavy line is fixed in the Earth and at A it points towards the Sun. When the Earth has moved to B it has rotated once on its axis so that the heavy line again points in the same direction as at A. Because of the Earth's orbital motion this is no longer the direction to the Sun; the Earth must move on to C for the heavy line to point towards the Sun again. The sidereal day is the time to move from A to B, the solar day from A to C.*

9.9: *The variation through the year of the equation of time (= apparent solar time – mean solar time).*

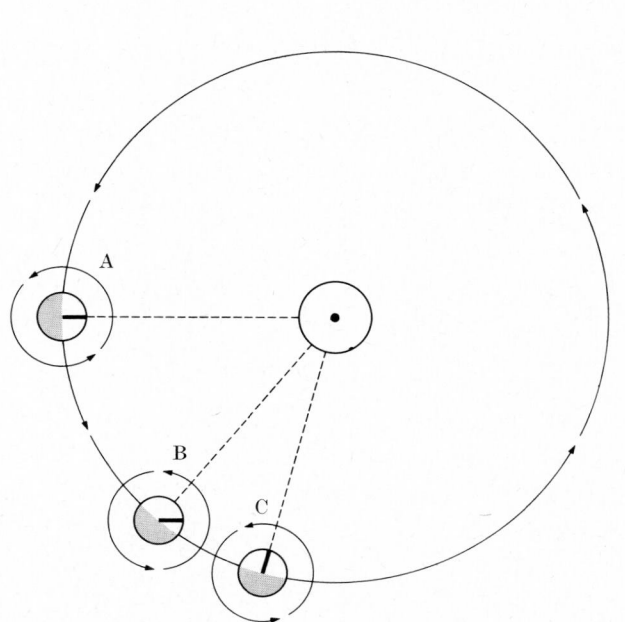

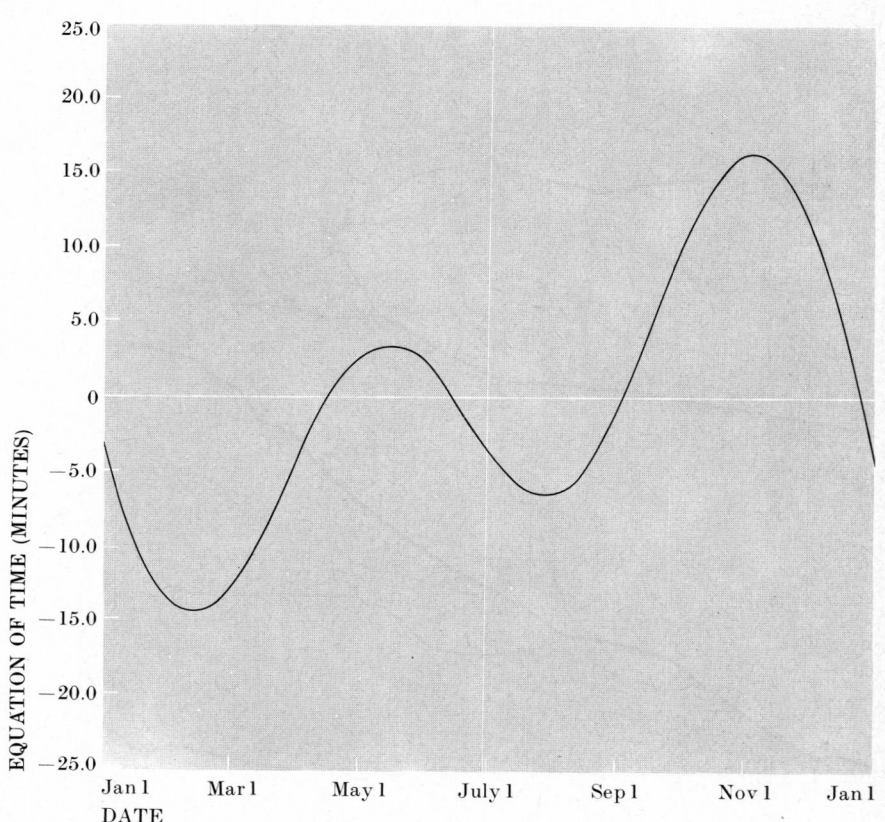

The motion and phases of the Moon

The Moon is in orbit around the Earth, and, like a planet orbiting the Sun, its motion is along an ellipse with semi-major axis 384 390 km and eccentricity 0.0549. Because of the ellipticity of the orbit the distance between the Earth and the Moon varies between a minimum of 356 400 km and a maximum of 406 700 km. The point of the orbit closest to the Earth is called PERIGEE and the point furthest away APOGEE. These terms are also used for artificial satellites in orbit around the Earth and correspond to the perihelion and aphelion of an orbit around the Sun. The Moon goes round its orbit in the same direction as all the planets go round the Sun, in a SIDEREAL MONTH of 27.3217 days, after which time it returns to the same place among the stars. Because of the Earth's motion round the Sun, the Moon takes 29.5306 days to return to the same position relative to the Sun; this interval is called a SYNODIC MONTH (figure 9.10). As the Moon orbits the Earth it turns a varying proportion of its illuminated face to the Earth; this gives rise to the PHASES of the Moon, which are illustrated in figure 9.11.

The Moon's orbit is inclined at 5° 9′ to the plane of the Earth's orbit (the ecliptic). The orbit has an ASCENDING NODE, where the Moon crosses the ecliptic from south to north and a DESCENDING NODE where it crosses from north to south. The gravitational pulls of the Sun and the planets perturb the Moon's orbit and this has two important effects. First, the perigee moves round the Earth

9.10: *The synodic month (A to C) is longer than the sidereal month (A to B). At A the Moon is between the Sun and the Earth. B is one sidereal month later than A. At B the Moon appears in the same direction against the background of stars but because of the Earth's orbital motion it is not between the Sun and the Earth. This does not happen until C, which is one synodic month later than A.*

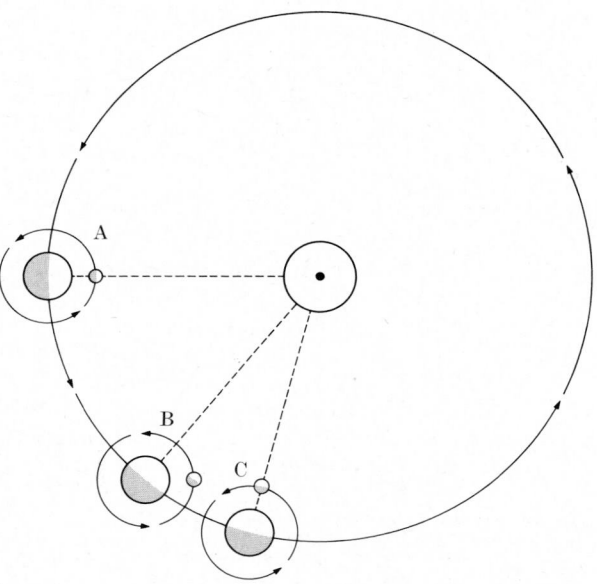

with direct motion, i.e. in the same direction as the Earth rotates, with a period of 8.85 years. (This is also the direction in which each of the planets orbits the Sun and the Moon orbits the Earth.) Second, the line joining the nodes, which is the line along which the orbits of the Earth and the Moon intersect, has RETROGRADE motion in the ecliptic, i.e. the opposite of direct motion, with a period of 18.61 years, the so-called NUTATION PERIOD. This motion has a counterpart in the nutation of the Earth's axis, a slight nodding of 9.210 arc sec with the same period. The time between successive passages of the Moon through the same node is consequently less than a sidereal month and is equal to 27.2122 days, the DRACONITIC, or NODAL MONTH.

As the Moon goes round its orbit, it broadly presents the same face to the Earth; this is due to the equality of its rotation period and its period of revolution, the sidereal month. The part of the Moon seen from the Earth is not exactly the same because of several wobbles, or LIBRATIONS. The Moon's equator is inclined at an angle of 6° 41′ to its orbit which causes a libration in latitude of 6° 41′. The Moon rotates on its axis at a uniform rate, but, in accordance with Kepler's second law, the Moon's motion in its elliptical orbit is not at a uniform speed and consequently there is a libration in longitude of 7° 36′. As the Earth rotates on its axis, a terrestrial observer sees the Moon from different positions; he can thus see round the edges a little and this is called a daily libration. The combined effect of these librations, and a number of much smaller ones, is to make 59 per cent of the Moon's surface visible from the Earth at least some of the time; of this 41 per cent is always visible and 18 per cent occasionally comes into view.

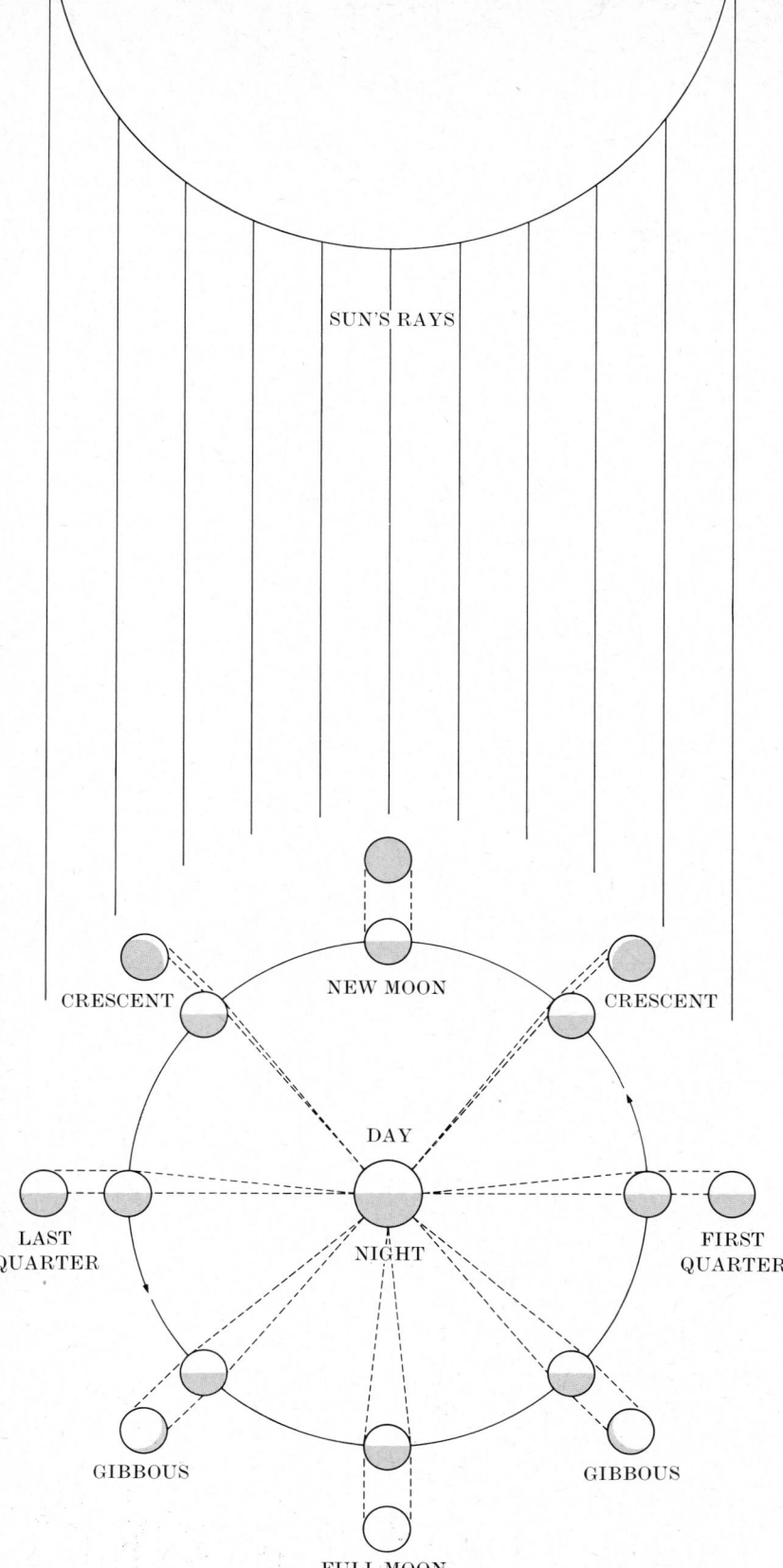

9.11: *The phases of the Moon. The Moon, with one hemisphere illuminated by the Sun, is shown at eight points in its orbit around the Earth. From the Earth parts of each of the illuminated and unilluminated hemispheres can be seen, giving the various phases as shown outside the orbit. The terms new Moon, first quarter, full Moon and last quarter refer to the particular points in the orbit shown whereas there is a crescent Moon whenever less than half the hemisphere seen from the Earth is sunlit and a gibbous Moon when more than half is sunlit.*

Eclipses of the Moon and Sun

The Earth and the Moon throw long conical shadows into space and when one of these bodies moves into the shadow cast by the other there is an ECLIPSE. The shadow has two parts: the total shadow, called the UMBRA, and the partial shadow, termed the PENUMBRA. The Sun is totally obscured to an observer in the umbra but in the penumbra it is partially visible.

The umbra of the Earth's shadow extends into space for 1 382 000 km on average, but because of the ellipticity of the Earth's orbit this distance varies by 22 500 km between its greatest and least values. Since the length of the umbra is more than three times the distance of the Moon from the Earth it must strike the Moon if it is pointing in the proper direction: i.e. if the Moon, Earth and Sun are in line as shown in figure 9.13; there is then a total eclipse of the Moon. Such an eclipse starts when the Moon enters the penumbra. The darkening that results is not very conspicuous and may not be noticed by someone who is not fore-warned. The more conspicuous partial phase starts when the Moon enters the umbra and the eclipse is total when all of the Moon is in the umbra. When the total phase ends, there are second partial and penumbral phases before the eclipse is finally over. Although those parts of the Moon in the umbra are not illuminated directly by the Sun they are not completely dark. The Sun's rays which pass through the Earth's atmosphere without striking the Earth's surface are refracted and scattered slightly so that some light enters the umbra and illuminates the Moon during the eclipse. Since red light is refracted less than blue, the Moon is given a coppery-red hue (figure 9.12). The exact colour and intensity of this light depends on the conditions in those parts of the atmosphere where the light is refracted and astronomers speak of dark and bright eclipses. Dust in the atmosphere can also have an effect. The phenomenal volcanic eruption at Krakatoa in August 1883 sent a great amount of dust into the atmosphere and caused some subsequent eclipses of the Moon to be very dark indeed.

There can also be partial eclipses when the Moon enters the umbra but is not completely immersed, and penumbral eclipses when the Moon only enters the penumbra. As is the case with the penumbral phases of partial and total eclipses, a penumbral eclipse is often not noticed by people who do not know that it is taking place.

An eclipse of the Moon can only occur at Full Moon. However, there is not an eclipse every month for the following reason: because the Moon's orbit is inclined to the ecliptic, the Moon often passes to the north or south of the Earth's shadow. Whether there is an eclipse depends on how far the Sun and Moon are from a node of the Moon's orbit. If the difference is greater than 12° 15′ a total eclipse of the Moon cannot occur; if it is less than 9° 30′ an eclipse must occur. For positions between these limits, eclipses may or may not occur according to other circumstances. When an eclipse does occur, its duration depends upon the exact circumstances, but the partial and total phases can last at most 3 hr 40 min of which

9.12: *A total eclipse of the Moon (with north to the top). The Moon is totally immersed in the Earth's shadow so that no light can reach it directly from the Sun. The coppery-red hue is caused by sunlight refracted into the shadow by the Earth's atmosphere. The amount of this light and its colour vary across the Moon depending on the distance from the edge of the shadow. (Norton Scientific, Arizona, USA).*

totality is at most 1 hr 40 min. The eclipse will be visible (weather conditions permitting) from the hemisphere of the Earth for which the Moon is above the horizon.

Since the Moon is smaller than the Earth, the umbra of its shadow extends into space for only 375 000 km on average. This distance is less than 384 390 km, its average distance from the Earth. Under these average conditions, the Moon's umbra cannot reach the surface of the Earth when the Moon is between the Earth and Sun. However, the umbra is longer than average when the Earth and Moon are further than average from the Sun; the longest possible shadow occurs when the Earth is at aphelion. Similarly the Moon can be nearer to the Earth than average. Under the most favourable circumstances the Moon's umbra can

extend 29 300 km beyond the Earth's surface. A TOTAL ECLIPSE occurs in this case and the Sun is totally obscured (figure 9.14). The greatest possible diameter of the umbra at the Earth's surface is 269 km but if the shadow falls obliquely onto the Earth the projected shadow is approximately an ellipse with a minor axis of 269 km and a larger major axis. As the Moon moves round its orbit its shadow moves across the Earth to give a zone of totality.

More common than total eclipses are ANNULAR ECLIPSES which occur when the umbra fails to reach the Earth's surface. At a total eclipse the Moon appears slightly larger than the Sun and is able to cover it completely; at an annular eclipse the Moon appears slightly smaller than the Sun and the rim of the Sun is visible all round the Moon. The fact that the Sun and the Moon have almost

9.13: *During a total eclipse of the Moon, the Moon must pass through the penumbra before and after the total phase when it is totally immersed in the umbra. As the Moon moves between the umbra and penumbra, there is a partial phase to the eclipse. Sometimes the Moon never fully enters the umbra (partial eclipse) or only enters the penumbra (penumbral eclipse).*

9.14: *At an eclipse of the Sun, the umbra of the Moon's shadow (darker tone) may or may not reach the surface of the Earth. When it does not (a) the Moon appears smaller than the Sun and at some places the rim of the Sun is seen to encircle the Moon; this is an annular eclipse. At a total eclipse (b) the Sun is completely obscured at those points on the Earth that are inside the umbra of the Moon's shadow.*

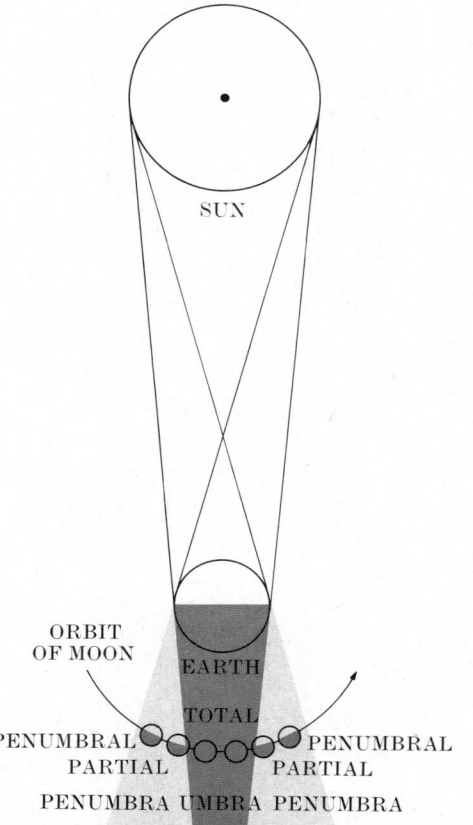

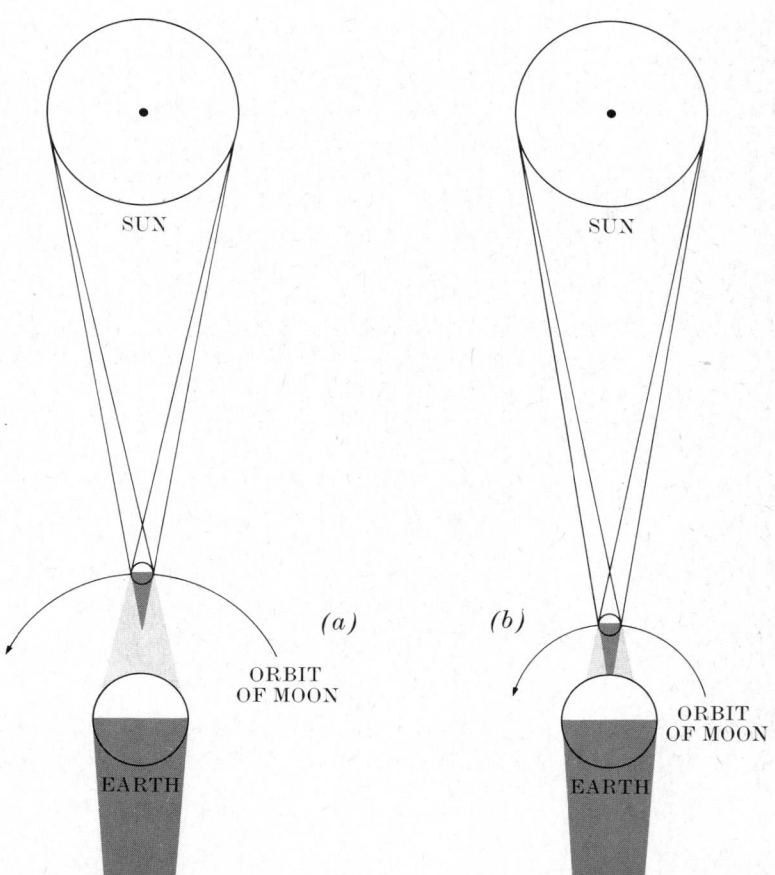

9.15: *The Earth viewed from space during the eclipse of the Sun of 30 June 1973. The shadow at exactly 12 noon UT is shown with the dark central part where there was a total eclipse and the lighter surrounding area where the eclipse was partial. As the Moon moved around its orbit, the shadow moved across the Earth in about five hours so that at various times during the day points in a long narrow strip (shown by a dashed line) had a total eclipse. Surrounding this strip is a much larger area (also shown with a dashed line) in which a partial eclipse occurred at some time. At other eclipses these areas are placed on other parts of the Earth.*

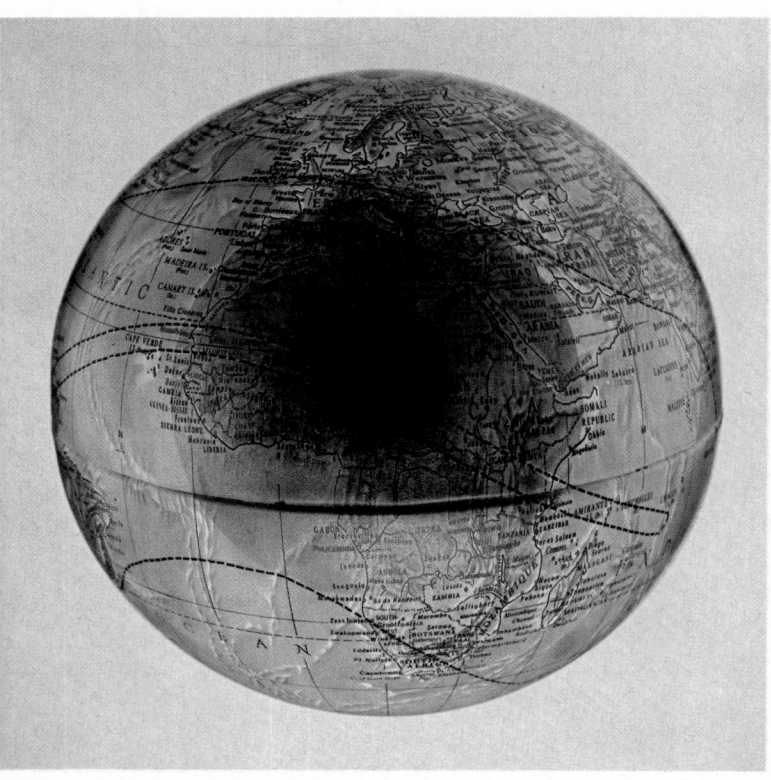

the same angular diameter is a pure coincidence. Sometimes an eclipse can be total at some places on the Earth and annular in other places. At both annular and total eclipses the penumbra of the Moon's shadow falls on part of the Earth's surface. In these regions the Sun is only partially obscured and a partial eclipse is visible about 3000 km on each side of the eclipse path.

The Moon's shadow moves rapidly across the surface of the Earth (figure 9.15). The slowest possible speed is 1680 km/hr and this can only occur at the equator, where a total solar eclipse can last at most 7 min 40 sec. Elsewhere the maximum duration is shorter; for example at latitude 45° it is 6 min 30 sec. Annular eclipses can be longer; at the equator the maximum is 12 min 24 sec.

A total eclipse of the Sun starts with the partial phase when the Moon covers part of the Sun. As totality approaches, the visible part of the Sun becomes a narrow crescent. Immediately before totality this crescent is broken up by the irregularities of the mountains at the edge of the Moon's visible disc to form what are known as BAILY'S BEADS. The last visible part of the Sun can give the appearance of a DIAMOND RING. During totality the Sun's atmosphere, the *corona* becomes visible (figure 8.26). Since the corona is much less bright than the Sun's disc, it is not normally visible against the glare of the Sun, but at totality this glare is removed and the corona emerges in splendour. The resultant spectacular view of the corona is only possible because of the coincidence that the apparent diameters of the Sun and Moon are very nearly equal. After totality the partial phases are repeated in reverse order.

If you want to view an eclipse please take great care. The Sun is a very bright object and the dangers of looking at it directly cannot be overstressed. For naked-eye observations, a very dark filter is required to prevent eye damage. To view the Sun directly through a telescope can result in blindness. The only satisfactorily safe method for the amateur to view the Sun with a telescope is to project the image onto a screen.

Eclipses of the Sun can only occur at New Moon but, as with eclipses of the Moon, there is not an eclipse every month. The Moon's shadow may miss the Earth completely and whether there is an eclipse or not depends on how far the Sun and Moon are from a node of the Moon's orbit. If the difference is more than 18° 31′, a solar eclipse cannot occur and if it is less than 15° 31′, an eclipse must occur.

Because of the restrictions on the Moon's position in its orbit at an eclipse there can be at most seven eclipses during a year, of which either four or five are eclipses of the Sun. There must always be at least two eclipses (both of the Sun). Solar eclipses are more common than lunar eclipses but, at a given location, lunar eclipses are more frequent because such an eclipse can be seen from a much larger part of the Earth's surface. On the average there is a total eclipse of the Sun visible somewhere on the Earth once every 18 months but because of the narrowness of the band on the Earth's surface inside which an eclipse is total, a total eclipse occurs at any one place only once every 360 years on average.

It has been known for several thousand years that eclipses recur at an interval of 18 years 11 days 8 hours – the so-called Saros cycle. This period is almost equal to 223 synodic months, or 242 nodal months or 19 eclipse years. An ECLIPSE YEAR is the interval at which the Sun passes the ascending node of the Moon's orbit; it is 346.6200 days long. At an eclipse the Moon is near one of the nodes of its orbit and is at either the full or new phase; consequently the Sun must also be in the direction of one of the nodes. After the passage of a Saros cycle this situation is repeated and there is another eclipse of the same type. Because the periods are not exactly equal, a sequence of eclipses ends after a long period. Similarly, new sequences start from time to time. Since the Saros cycle is not an exact number of days in length, the eclipses in a sequence are not all at the same place on the Earth's surface. The odd eight hours in the length of the cycle causes each eclipse to be 120° to the west of the previous eclipse. Three such displacements add up to 360° so that the eclipse position repeats itself almost exactly after three Saros cycles, that is after 54 years and 34 days.

Lists of lunar and solar eclipses from AD 1977 to 1985 are given in tables 9.4 and 9.5.

Table 9.4: Eclipses of the Moon from AD 1977 to 1985

Date of mid-eclipse	Type of eclipse	Duration of totality (min)	Sub-lunar longitude	latitude at mid-eclipse
1977 Apr 4	partial	—	64 W	6 S
1978 Mar 24	total	90	115 E	2 S
1978 Sep 16	total	82	73 E	3 S
1979 Mar 13	partial	—	45 E	3 N
1979 Sep 6	total	52	164 W	7 S
1981 July 17	partial	—	71 W	21 S
1982 Jan 9	total	84	63 E	22 N
1982 July 6	total	102	112 W	23 S
1982 Dec 30	total	66	171 W	23 N
1983 June 25	partial	—	126 W	23 S
1985 May 4	total	70	60 E	16 S
1985 Oct 28	total	42	90 E	13 N

Note: Penumbral eclipses are not included. It is easy to determine whether a given eclipse is visible from a particular point on the Earth's surface by means of a globe. Turn the globe so that the position of the sub-lunar point at mid-eclipse is uppermost and the eclipse can be seen from any point in the upper-half of the globe.

Table 9.5: Eclipses of the Sun from AD 1977 to 1985

Date	Type of eclipse	Maximum duration of total phase min	sec	Track
1977 Apr 18	annular	—	—	Atlantic Ocean, SW Africa, Tanzania Indian Ocean
1977 Oct 12	total	2	37	Pacific Ocean, Peru, Brazil
1978 Apr 7	partial	—	—	Antarctic
1978 Oct 2	partial	—	—	Arctic
1979 Feb 26	total	2	48	Pacific Ocean, USA, Canada, Greenland
1979 Aug 22	annular	—	—	Pacific Ocean, Antarctica
1980 Feb 16	total	4	8	Atlantic Ocean, Congo, Kenya Indian Ocean, India, China
1980 Aug 10	annular	—	—	South Pacific Ocean, Bolivia, Brazil
1981 Feb 4	annular	—	—	South of Australia and New Zealand, Pacific Ocean
1981 July 31	total	2	3	USSR, North Pacific Ocean
1982 Jan 25	partial	—	—	Antarctic
1982 June 21	partial	—	—	Antarctic
1982 July 20	partial	—	—	Arctic
1982 Dec 15	partial	—	—	Arctic
1983 June 11	total	5	11	Indian Ocean, East Indies, Pacific Ocean
1983 Dec 4	annular	—	—	Atlantic Ocean, Equatorial Africa, Somalia
1984 May 30	annular	—	—	Pacific Ocean, Mexico, USA, Atlantic Ocean, Algeria
1984 Nov 22–23	total	1	59	East Indies, South Pacific Ocean
1985 May 19	partial	—	—	Arctic
1985 Nov 12	total	1	55	South Pacific Ocean, Antarctica

10. The inner Solar System

Introduction

The best known part of the Solar System is, naturally enough, that part of it nearest to the Earth. Mercury, Venus, the Earth and Mars are known as the TERRESTRIAL PLANETS, but only because of their position in the inner Solar System, not because they are just like the Earth. The Moon, by comparison with its primary, the Earth, is a very massive satellite which is often, with justification, considered to be a planet in its own right. Mars has two tiny satellites to make a total of seven known bodies in the inner Solar System. Other bodies – *asteroids, meteorites* and *comets* – also enter this region of space; they are considered in chapter 12. Occasionally, claims have been made that there is a planet (Vulcan) inside the orbit of Mercury. Each time, the observations have been shown to be spurious and we can be sure that there are no unknown planets of any significant size in the inner Solar System.

The advent of spacecraft observations has increased our knowledge of the inner planets so much that planetary astronomy is effectively only 10 to 15 years old. Before 1965, no features smaller than several hundred kilometres across could be seen on Mars whereas several per cent of the surface has now been observed with a resolution of 100 m. Much the same is true for the other inner planets. The resultant new interest has also had an effect on studies of the Earth, which can now benefit from comparison with the other planets.

10.1: *The variation of density with depth in the Earth, showing the division into a mantle, outer core and inner core with sudden changes in the density at the boundaries. The surface crust is between 10 and 40 km thick and so is too thin to show on this figure. The centre of the Earth, at a depth of 6378 km, is marked by the right-hand end of the curve.*

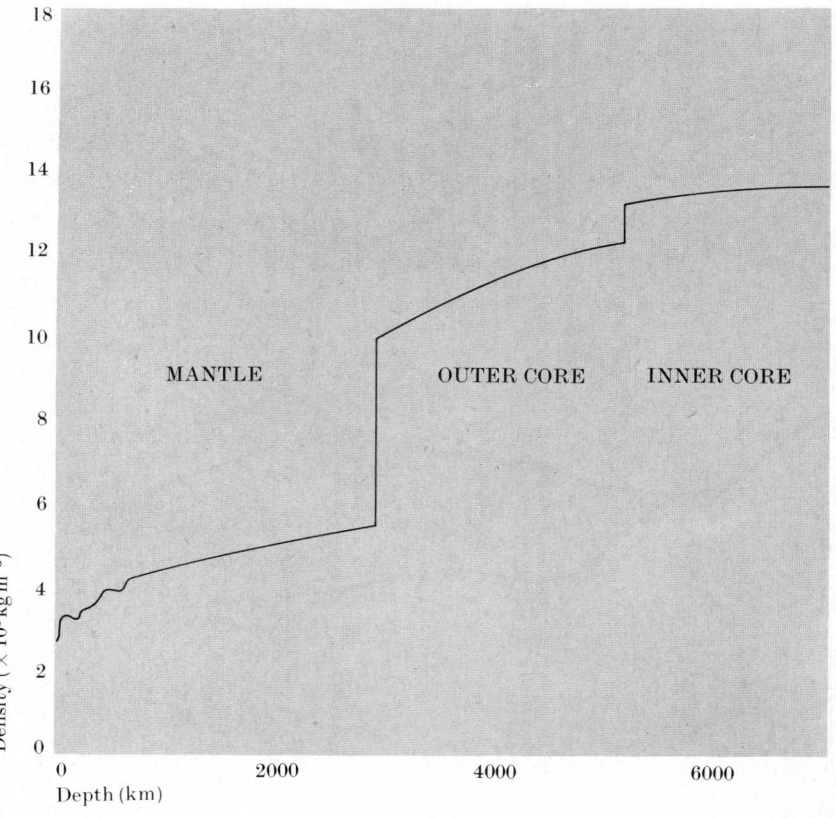

Interiors

The interiors of the planets are totally inaccessible to direct observations. The deepest hole drilled into the Earth goes to a depth of about 10 km, just a small fraction of the 6378 km distance to the centre. Information about the interior must therefore come from indirect methods and in practice the most important method by far is the study of SEISMIC WAVES. These waves are generated by earthquakes or artificial explosions, travel through the body of the Earth, and can be picked up by sensitive recording instruments called seismometers. There are four types of waves, of which two, LOVE WAVES and RAYLEIGH WAVES, only travel near the surface of the Earth and so tell us nothing about the interior. P-WAVES and S-WAVES travel through the body of the Earth and are distinguished by the direction of the small displacements which make up the waves. A P-wave is like a sound wave in air and the vibrations are along the direction of travel of the wave, whereas they are at right angles for S-waves. An important consequence of this difference is that S-waves can travel only in solids whereas P-waves can travel in any medium. S- and P-waves typically have velocities around 10 km s^{-1} but this varies with depth. By observing the times at which the waves from a particular event arrive at various places around the Earth, geophysicists have been able to deduce much about the variation of density with depth in the Earth (figure 10.1). There is an outer superficial layer called the CRUST whose thickness varies between 30 to 40 km beneath the continents and about 10 km under the oceans. The composition of the continental crust is given in table 10.2. Below the crust there is an abrupt increase in density in the region called the MANTLE.

The boundary between the crust and the mantle is called the MOHOROVIČIĆ DISCONTINUITY (or MOHO for short). The mantle transmits both S- and P-waves and so it must be a solid layer. Its density varies from 3300 kg m^{-3} at the Moho to 5500 kg m^{-3} at its base, which is at a depth of 2900 km. Here we meet the WIECHERT DISCONTINUITY where the density increases suddenly to 10 000 kg m^{-3}. Below this discontinuity we are in the CORE. S-waves do not propagate into the core so its outer layers at least must be liquid. P-waves can enter the core and in 1936 it was shown that they suffer an abrupt change in velocity at a depth now measured to be 4980 km (i.e. 1390 km from the centre) so that the core is divided into distinct inner and outer parts. The inner core has been shown to be solid with a probable density of 13 000 kg m^{-3}. On average, the core is about twice as dense as the mantle, so that although it occupies only 16 per cent of the Earth's volume it has about 32 per cent of the mass. Overall the mean density of the Earth is 5518 kg m^{-3}, calculated directly from the mass and radius.

Further subdivisions of the Earth's interior can be made on the basis of sudden changes in the velocities of seismic waves at various depths. The main such division is at a depth of about 700 km to give an upper and lower mantle.

At four places on the Earth's surface there are outcrops of rock

Table 10.1: Physical elements of the inner planets

	Mercury ☿	Venus ♀	Earth ⊕	Moon ☾	Mars ♂
Reciprocal mass[1]	5 972 000	408 520	328 900	27 069 000	3 098 710
Mass[2] (Earth = 1)	0.0558	0.8150	1.0000	0.01230	0.1074
Mass[2] (kg)	3.332×10^{23}	4.870×10^{24}	5.976×10^{24}	7.350×10^{22}	6.421×10^{23}
Equatorial radius (km)	2425	6070	6378	1738	3395
Equatorial radius (Earth = 1)	0.380	0.950	1.000	0.2725	0.532
Angular diameter[3] at	10″.90 *inferior conjunction*	61″.0 *inferior conjunction*	—	31′ 06″ *mean distance*	17″.88 *opposition*
Ellipticity[4]	0.0	0.0	0.0034	0.002	0.009
Mean density (kg m^{-3})	5600	5200	5518	3340	3950
Equatorial surface gravity[5] (m s^{-2})	3.78	8.60	9.78	1.62	3.72
Equatorial escape velocity (km s^{-1})	4.3	10.3	11.2	2.38	5.0
V magnitude[3] at	−0.2 *greatest elongation*	−4.22 *greatest elongation*	−3.84 *seen from the Sun*	−12.73 *full Moon*	−2.02 *opposition*
Sidereal rotation period	58.65 days	243 days *(retrograde)*	23 hr 56 min 04.1 sec	27.322 days	24 hr 37 min 22.6 sec
Inclination of equator to orbit	7°	3°.4	23° 27′	6° 41′	23° 59′

Notes:
1. *The reciprocal mass is the mass of the Sun divided by the mass of the planet (including the atmosphere and any satellites).*
2. *These masses exclude the satellites.*
3. *Because of the ellipticity of planetary orbits, these quantities are not constant and the mean value is given. For example the angular diameter of Mars at opposition varies from 14 to 25 arc sec.*
4. *The ellipticity is defined as $(R_e - R_p)/R_p$, where R_e and R_p are the equatorial and polar radii. For the Moon the equatorial radius towards the Earth is used.*
5. *This includes the centrifugal term.*

Table 10.2: The relative abundances (percentages) of major elements in the Earth's crust

		by mass	by number of atoms
Oxygen	O	46.5	62.1
Silicon	Si	28.9	22.0
Aluminium	Al	8.3	6.5
Iron	Fe	4.8	1.8
Calcium	Ca	4.1	2.2
Potassium	K	2.4	1.3
Sodium	Na	2.3	2.1
Magnesium	Mg	1.9	1.6
Titanium	Ti	0.5	0.2
Everything else		0.3	0.2

which are thought to have come from the mantle during mountain building. Even if this is mantle material, it is quite possible that it has been changed in some unknown way by the very process that put it into its present place. Apart from these outcrops, none of the material of the Earth's interior is accessible for chemical study. Geophysicists can make estimates of the composition at various depths by using the seismic data discussed above. Although the increase of density towards the centre can be accounted for as being due to the enormous pressure inside the Earth, there must be an abrupt change of composition at the core-mantle boundary. It is generally assumed that the core is mainly iron with some nickel and that the mantle is mainly composed of silicates such as olivine $(Mg,Fe)_2SiO_4$. The core may be similar to iron *meteorites* and the mantle to stony meteorites, but because meteorites vary widely in composition and probably come from parent bodies much smaller than the Earth, it is difficult to make reliable deductions about the Earth's interior from them. By analogy with iron meteorites, the proportion of nickel in the core is often assumed to be about six per cent. Whatever the composition of the core it must have a high density and be an electrical conductor, to account for the magnetic field. Alternatives to a mixture of iron and nickel have been suggested but none has been found satisfactory. The solid inner core has a higher density than the liquid outer core, but the difference appears to be too great to be just that between a solid and a liquid of the same chemical composition and there must be some variation in composition.

The temperature at the centre of the Earth is about 4000 K and decreases steadily towards the surface. Since heat flows from high to low temperatures there is an outward flow; at the surface it is about 0.06 watt m^{-2} on average, and although this is much less than the heat received from the Sun, it is the heat from the interior that supplies most of the energy for volcanoes, earthquakes and mountain building. It is now generally believed that the Earth formed from solid particles with a temperature of 500 K or less, so we must ask where the Earth's heat has come from. The answer is from the radioactive decay of elements such as uranium and thorium. There is also an appreciable contribution from elements such as potassium, which are only weakly radioactive but are sufficiently common to be almost as important as uranium. Although there is some uncertainty about the exact amounts of radioactive elements inside the Earth, there is no question that they can provide the necessary energy to explain the present temperatures.

Radioactive decay is not the only source of heat. As the Earth grew, its gravitational attraction increased and with it the energy released by an infalling body; the gravity is sufficient in certain circumstances, such as *meteors*, to cause complete vaporization. The total energy released during the formation of the Earth was sufficient to heat it to a temperature of at least 20 000 K. This energy was released at or near the surface and it is likely that most of it was quickly radiated away, leaving radioactive decay as the main internal energy source.

Roughly speaking, the *radioactive elements* important to the

Earth's heating can be divided into two types: short-lived with half-lives of one to ten million years and long-lived with half-lives of a billion years or so. If there were sufficient quantities of the short-lived elements, then the Earth would have heated up quickly after it was formed, whereas the long-lived elements would have taken much of the Earth's lifetime to heat it up. Since all the short-lived elements have long since decayed, it is not known how important their contribution was. At some stage the central regions of the Earth must have melted and it was probably at this time that the separation into a core and a mantle took place. A similar process occurs when iron is melted in a steelworks and the non-metallic parts separate out from the iron to form a lower density slag on the surface.

Although the mantle is solid, it is not completely rigid. The outermost layer, the LITHOSPHERE, is between 70 and 100 km thick and has considerable strength, but below this is a weaker layer called the ASTHENOSPHERE, which extends to a depth of a few hundred kilometres. Geophysicists believe that the material of this layer can flow and that there are convection currents which carry some of the outward flow of the Earth's heat. Since the material is solid, its motion can be only very slow, but over a long period of time there can be significant movement. It is thought that these convection currents are responsible for movements of the Earth's crust giving rise to continental drift (see *plate tectonics* below). The mantle below the asthenosphere, the MESOSPHERE, is thought to have appreciable strength, like the lithosphere; neither of these layers exhibits convection.

Among the many instruments carried to the Moon have been several seismometers which have returned much important information. Their observations of lunar seismic waves, including some induced artificially by deliberately crashing spacecraft onto the surface, have shown that the Moon has a crust, mantle and dense core. The core has a radius of about 500 km and the mantle is 1200 km thick. The core therefore occupies only two per cent of the Moon's volume compared to 16 per cent for the Earth and therefore the mantle is relatively more important on the Moon than on the Earth and the mean density is lower. Similarly the crust is relatively much thicker on the Moon. The seismic observations allow a rigid lithosphere to be distinguished from an asthenosphere and show that it extends to a depth of 1000 km. The thin lithosphere on the Earth is fractured into plates which can move about and is thin enough to allow lava to be transported from the asthenosphere to the surface. The enormous armoured layer of the Moon's lithosphere just cannot be fractured in this way and so, apart from the small core, the Moon is a dead body. The Moon could have been heated up by radioactive decay as was the Earth and acquired a dense core in the process, but because of its smaller size it would have cooled down more quickly to give the thicker lithosphere and mantle that we observe today.

Although the results are by no means certain, both theory and observation indicate that Mercury, Venus and Mars are also differentiated into a mantle and a dense core. Because of their dif-ferent distances from the Sun, the inner planets are likely to have formed with different proportions of the elements. According to theoretical studies, Mercury and Venus should have massive iron-nickel cores whereas the core of Mars should also contain sulphur so that all, or nearly all the iron is present as ferrous sulphide (FeS) and there is little free iron. Ferrous sulphide has a lower density than iron, and a core of this material would explain why the mean density of Mars is lower than that of Mercury, Venus or the Earth. Mercury's iron core appears to contain about 80 per cent of the planet's mass and to have a radius of 1800 km. The core of Venus has a radius of 3100 km, so that as far as we can tell the interior of Venus is very much like the Earth. Figure 10.2 shows the relative sizes of the planetary cores.

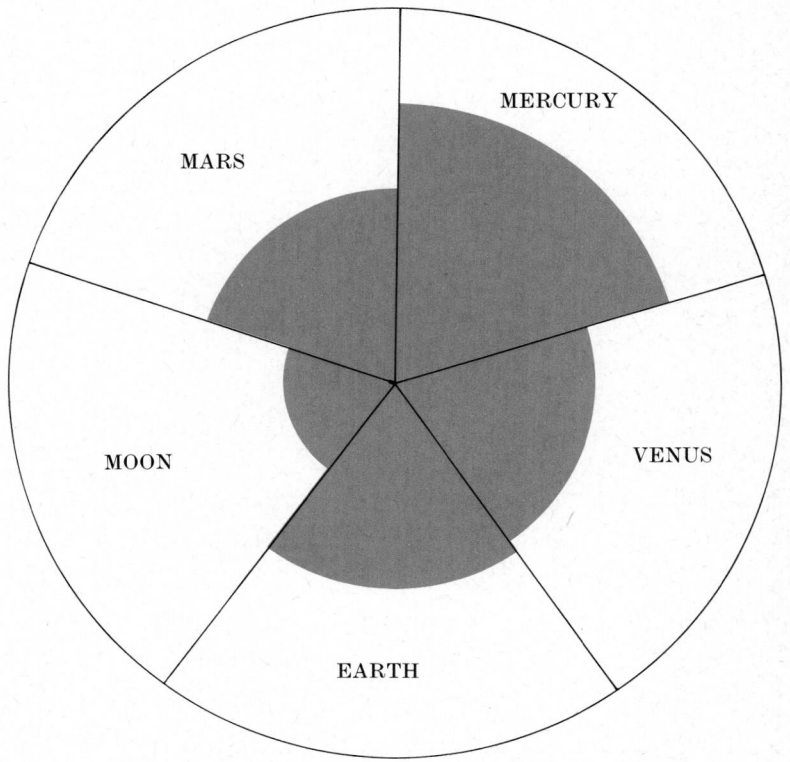

10.2: *Cutaway views of the inner planets scaled to have the same diameter to show the relative sizes of the core (shaded inner region) and the mantle (outer region). The crusts are too thin to be shown.*

Magnetic fields

On the Earth, a pivoted magnet will swing round to point roughly north-south and, if it is free to tilt, will take up an inclined position with the northern end pointing downwards in the northern hemisphere and upwards in the southern. Such a magnet can be used to plot the direction of the Earth's magnetic field which is causing it to move. Similarly it is not difficult to measure the strength of the field. The strength is measured in units called TESLAS; the field varies over the surface of the Earth from 7×10^{-5} to 2.5×10^{-5} tesla. GEOMAGNETISM, the study of the Earth's magnetic field, is a complicated subject because the field varies not only from place to place but also with time. Part of the place-to-place variation is due to permanently magnetized rocks. When molten rock forces its way to the surface and appears as lava from a volcano, it cools and is magnetized by the Earth's general magnetic field. The direction of the magnetization is the same as that of the Earth's field at the time when the rock cools. By studying such rocks, scientists are able to compare the Earth's field in the past with what it is today. Laboratory measurements during the last 400 years have shown that the Earth's MAGNETIC FIELD varies substantially over periods of a hundred years or so. The study of magnetized rocks has revealed the effects of these changes but has also shown that the field completely reverses in direction every few hundred thousand years. Each FIELD REVERSAL seems to take only one or two thousand years.

The field outside the Earth is roughly the same as that outside a uniformly magnetized sphere or, which is the same thing, that of a dipole at its centre. (A magnetic dipole is a simple magnet whose two poles are very close together.) Such a field has two magnetic poles where a magnetized needle stands vertically and a magnetic equator where it lies horizontally. The dipole that best fits the Earth's field has an axis inclined at $11\frac{1}{2}°$ from the rotation axis so that the magnetic poles are at latitude $78\frac{1}{2}°$N and S: the northern pole is in the northwest of Greenland. The differences between the best-fit dipole field and the actual field are quite substantial and reach 20 per cent in places. There are regions a few thousand kilometres across, over each of which there is a systematic difference. These regions are not correlated with any surface features such as oceans, continents or great mountain chains, so the cause of the non-dipole field is certainly not to be found in the surface layers of the Earth.

The variations of the field with time point to the same conclusion. 300 years ago the non-dipole field was quite different and, if present trends continue, it will be quite different again in another 300 years. The dipole part of the field, however, has hardly changed in this time. Typical of the changes are a $35°$ swing in the direction of the compass between 1580 and 1820 at London and a 30 per cent decrease of the horizontal component of the field in 100 years at Cape Town. The timescale for these changes is so short that it is inconceivable that they are due to changes in the solid part of the Earth, which would have other cataclysmic consequences. From measurements of the field over the whole surface of the

Earth it is possible to deduce that apart from some minor effects, the cause of the changes in the field must lie within the Earth. We have already excluded the solid part of the Earth; this leaves the fluid outer core where we can hope for motions that are sufficiently rapid to explain the variations in the field.

One explanation of the magnetic field can be immediately excluded: that the Earth is a permanent magnet. There is no known fluid that can be permanently magnetized, and even if there were, the motions in the core would soon mix up the various parts so that there would be no general magnetism. Another common way in which a magnetic field can be produced is by electric currents, and it is now generally accepted that these are indeed responsible for the Earth's field. The outer core is thought to be composed largely of molten iron and is therefore a good conductor. If a current were started in the core and just left, it would die away on a timescale of ten or twenty thousand years so there must be some mechanism to maintain the currents. The only satisfactory explanation is that there is some kind of dynamo generating the currents and hence the magnetic field. Figure 10.3 shows a simple type of dynamo, the disc dynamo, and shows how the external circuit can be arranged to generate the magnetic field and produce a SELF-EXCITING DYNAMO. If a constant torque is applied to the axle, the dynamo will settle down to a steady state with a constant field. If both the current and magnetic field in figure 10.3(b) are reversed, the dynamo will work as before. This is what we want: a dynamo which will give a field in either direction. The simple system in figure 10.3(b) will not, however, reverse of its own accord, although more complicated systems will.

Obviously the dynamos discussed here are not what we expect to find in the Earth's core. They have a very simple motion but a rather complex structure. In the Earth we will have a simple structure and so to produce a self-exciting dynamo, the motion must be complicated. It is a very difficult problem to decide whether there are any possible motions that are suitable, but physicists have now demonstrated that there are. This is, of course, not the same as determining what the motions going on inside the Earth are and this is one of the major research problems of geomagnetism. We know already that for any dynamo to work the flow speed in the Earth's core must be at least $0.3\,\mathrm{mm\,s^{-1}}$, which appears to be quite reasonable.

We do not know what the forces are that drive the dynamo. The outward flow of heat through the Earth is likely to cause convective motions in the Earth's core and the combined effect of these and the Earth's motion is generally believed to be responsible. An alternative view ascribes the motions to the *precession* of the Earth. The fluid core may not be able to follow the precession exactly and an eddying motion may be produced. Quite possibly both these mechanisms play a part. It is generally true of fluid motion that the motion is more complicated than its cause. We can see this in meteorology: the Sun shines on and warms up one hemisphere and out of this simplicity grows all the complexity of weather and climate. Similarly we can expect that the motions in the Earth's core are sufficiently turbulent to cause the observed irregularities and changes in the field. Finally we can note that at the speed of 0.3 mm s⁻¹ the time to move 1000 km, a distance comparable to the core size, is 100 years, the timescale for variations of the field.

Measurements from spacecraft have shown that none of the other inner planets has a magnetic field as large as the Earth's. Typically, the surface fields of Venus, the Moon and Mars are no more than a few times 10^{-8} tesla, i.e. less than 0.001 of the Earth's field. In each case it seems that a dynamo mechanism cannot work; Mars and the Moon are probably too small to have a sufficiently large conducting fluid core and Venus is rotating too slowly. If the driving force for the Earth's dynamo is precession, which is caused by the Moon, rather than convection currents, then similar dynamos on Venus and Mars would still be quite impossible. The magnetic field of the Moon appears to be due to permanent magnetism; the same is presumably true for Venus and Mars. On the Moon this magnetism is widespread and it is definitely established that there are magnetized lava flows (due to domains of iron in the rocks) there. If a material is heated above its CURIE TEMPERATURE, it loses its magnetism and can only be remagnetized if it cools in a magnetic field. The Curie temperature of iron is 780°C so the rocks must have lost their magnetism when they were melted to form lava. The Moon must therefore have had a field of internal origin to magnetize the lava flows when they cooled. The most likely explanation is that the Moon once had a field generated by a dynamo. When the Moon was young it is likely that the radioactive energy sources driving the convection were stronger than they are now so that a dynamo was possible. As the convection became weaker, a time would come when the dynamo could no longer function. Another possibility is that the fluid core of the Moon is probably smaller than it used to be because of cooling and subsequent solidification of its outer regions. A combination of both these effects is also a possibility.

Because of its small size and slow rotation, astronomers predicted that Mercury would have no intrinsic magnetic field, except possibly for a small field due to permanent magnetism induced by the solar wind and the Sun's field. However the Mariner 10 spacecraft in 1974 and 1975 measured a field with a strength about one per cent of the Earth's and showed that it was due to an intrinsic dipole (figure 10.4). This result was a great surprise even though Mercury probably has a large iron core. It may not be sufficient to say that dynamos can work in less favourable circumstances than astronomers previously thought, for if Mercury has one then why does not Venus? Now that information about the fields of all five inner planets, with their ranges of radius and rotation rate, is available it should be easier to sort out the valid theories from the invalid ones. Perhaps Mercury's field is not due to a dynamo at all but to permanent magnetism (which is unlikely), an interaction with the solar wind, or to some cause not yet imagined.

The effect of the *solar wind* on the Earth's magnetic field and the way in which it is confined within the *magnetosphere* has been dis-

10.3: *The disc dynamo. At (a) a disc is rotating in a magnetic field perpendicular to itself. If an external circuit is connected to the axle and the rim of the disc by brushes a current is generated and flows in the direction indicated. This current can itself be used to generate the field by an arrangement such as that shown at (b).*

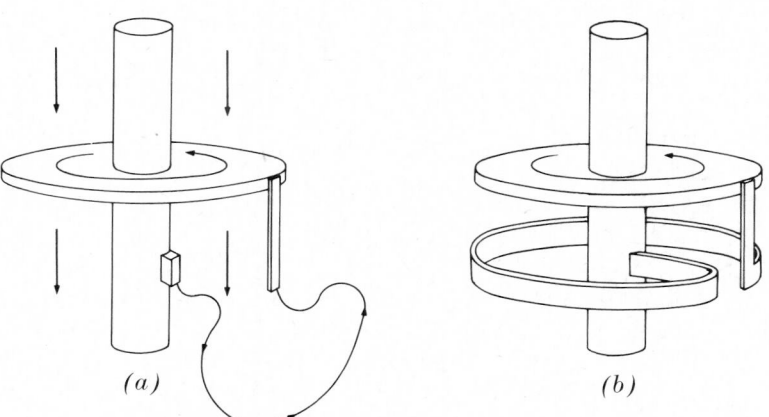

(a)   *(b)*

cussed in chapter 8. As figure 10.4 shows, Mercury has a similar magnetosphere although it is much smaller because the field is weaker and, being nearer to the Sun, the solar wind is stronger. For both Mercury and the Earth, the particles of the solar wind cannot enter the magnetosphere and so they do not reach the planetary surface. This effect cannot operate on Venus or Mars because of their minute fields, but both are surrounded by an *iono-sphere*. A sufficiently high electron density here can permit electric currents to flow and to induce magnetic fields which are strong enough to divert the flow of the solar wind and prevent it imping-ing directly on the surface. There is then a dividing surface, the IONOPAUSE, analogous to the *magnetopause*. Spacecraft measure-ments show that the electron densities for both Venus and Mars are greater than the theoretically-calculated minimum values required to form an ionopause. The Moon has no atmosphere and hence no ionosphere and it seems that the solar wind impinges directly onto its surface.

10.4: *The magnetic field of Mercury. The field is basically that of a dipole but it is disturbed by the solar wind and confined to the region inside the magnetopause.*

10.5: *The tides. At (a) we see the Moon in orbit around the Earth. Both bodies in fact move around their common centre of gravity and their total mutual gravitational attraction has just the right strength to keep them in their orbits. Locally at A, however, the Moon's gravity is stronger than at C, the centre of the Earth and the force is greater than that required to maintain the orbital motion. Similarly, at B the force is not sufficient. Material at A and B is therefore forced away from the centre of the Earth to form a bulge. For the oceans this bulge is quite substantial. It also occurs in the solid body of the Earth but because of the rigidity the bulge is very small. This simple theory predicts that bulges on the Earth would be at the point directly below the Moon and the antipodal point. The Earth is rotating and there is sufficient friction to drag the tidal bulge around in the direction of rotation (b). High tide occurs when a particular point on the Earth is carried past the bulge by the rotation. The varying depths of the Earth's seas and oceans and the arrangements of the land masses also affect the times of high and low tide; this is particularly true in shallow seas and along coastlines. The Sun also raises tides on the Earth, about one-third the size of those due to the Moon. At new and full Moon these act together to give spring tides (c) which are greater than the neap tides produced at first and last quarters (d).*

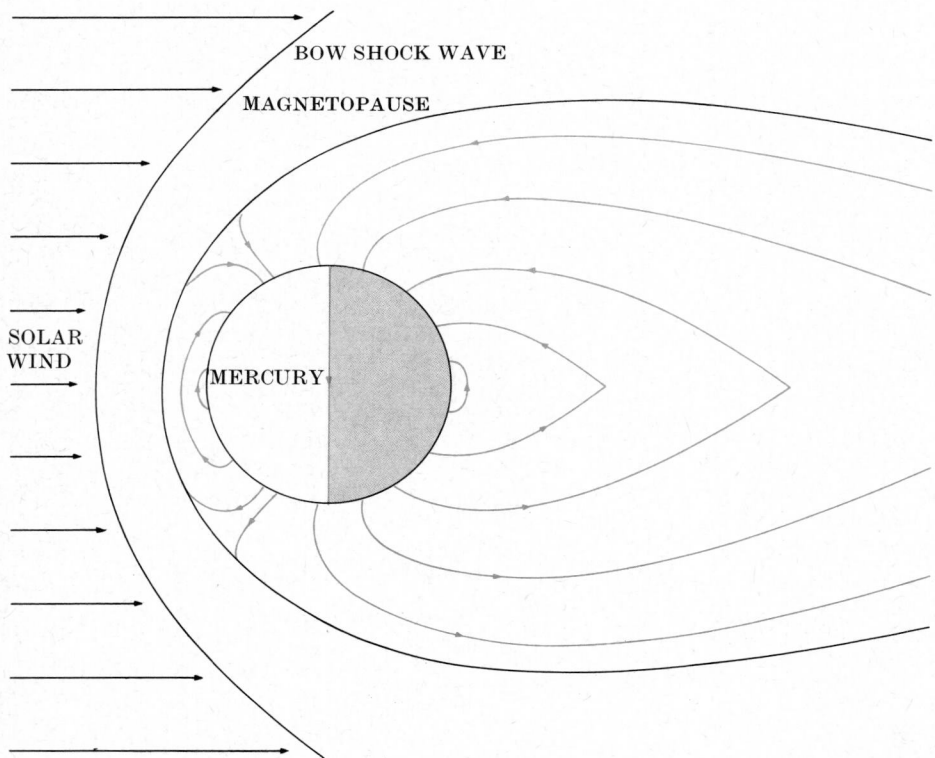

BOW SHOCK WAVE

MAGNETOPAUSE

SOLAR
WIND

MERCURY

Rotation

In 1889, G.V.Schiaparelli announced that his extensive observations of Mercury had shown that the planet rotated on its axis in the same time, 88 days, that it took to revolve around the Sun and that as a result it always kept the same face turned towards the Sun. This result was confirmed by several other astronomers between 1889 and 1965. It therefore came as a great surprise when radar observations in 1965 by G.H.Pettergill and R.B.Dyce showed conclusively that the rotation period was in fact 59 days, with an uncertainty of about five days. More recent and accurate measurements have shown that the period is 58.65 days, precisely two-thirds of the orbital period. This has been confirmed by observations from the spacecraft Mariner 10 in 1974 and 1975. The earlier, erroneous value, based on visual observations, arose from two effects. Firstly, Mercury is always close to the Sun in the sky and is a small planet, so that it is difficult to see surface features with certainty. Secondly, because of the eccentricity of Mercury's orbit only some elongations are favourable for visual observations. In general, several successive favourable elongations occur at such an interval that Mercury turns more or less the same face to the Earth at each to give the impression of synchronous rotation.

Because of the extensive cloud cover, the surface of Venus cannot be seen and it was only the use of radar that enabled the rotation period, of 243 days, to be measured. The rotation is retrograde (opposite to the orbital motion), unlike that of all the other planets except Uranus. If the period is 243.16 days, then the same face of Venus will be turned towards the Earth at each *inferior conjunction*.

The rotation periods of the other inner planets can be easily measured by direct observation. The Moon is in synchronous rotation so that it turns the same face towards the Earth, and Mars rotates in just 41 minutes more than does the Earth.

Mercury, Venus and the Moon therefore have their rotation locked into an orbital motion to give what is known as RESONANCE. Astronomers believe that all the inner planets were formed with periods of several hours or a day and that in some cases tidal friction was sufficient to slow down the rotation until it became locked into the resonance observed today. The most obvious tidal effect is the regular rise and fall of the Earth's seas and oceans twice a day (figure 10.5). Tides are also raised in the solid bodies of the planets. Because of the rigidity of solid matter, these tides are much smaller than those in the oceans. The actual sizes of these tides are not known and it is likely that there are substantial variations between the planets. Tidal friction causes the rotation of the Earth to slow down. To conserve angular momentum the orbit of the Moon must be simultaneously increasing in size. The Moon's gravity acts on the elongated shape produced by the tidal bulges and causes a torque which tries to pull the bulges back in line with the Moon and this has the effect of slowing down the Earth's rotation. The same effects apply on the Moon although,

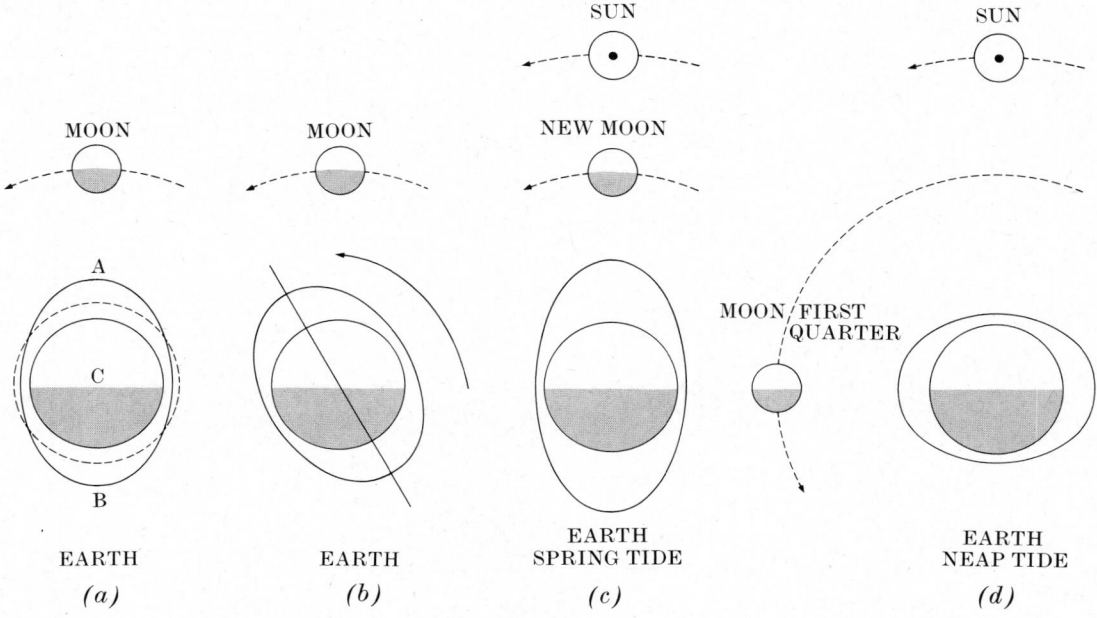

EARTH	EARTH	EARTH SPRING TIDE	EARTH NEAP TIDE
(a)	*(b)*	*(c)*	*(d)*

because there are no oceans, there are only tides in the solid body. The radius of the Moon towards the Earth is about four kilometres greater than it is in directions at right angles. This is in fact much greater than any tidal effect and the Moon's elongated shape must have been formed when the Moon was younger and hotter and been frozen in as it cooled and formed its extensive lithosphere. The effects of tides in the solid body of the Moon slowed down its rotation until it locked into synchronism with its orbital motion. Today there is no net torque on the Moon but were it to spin up or spin down, the torque on its elongated shape would in each case act to return the rotation to synchronism; the situation is stable.

The resonance of Mercury's rotation with its orbital motion depends on the planet's elongated shape but the two to three ratio of periods is only possible because of the high orbital eccentricity. The long axis points towards the Sun at *perihelion* but is at right angles at *aphelion*. The orientation at perihelion tends to give stability and outweighs the destabilising effect of the orientation at aphelion because of the 52 per cent greater distance at aphelion (figure 10.6).

The rotation of Venus appears to be controlled by the Earth. For this to be possible, Venus must be elongated with its long axis towards the Earth at each inferior conjunction. Because of the great distance to Venus, this asymmetry must be rather large and it is not certain that Venus is strong enough to maintain the required shape. From the Earth, measurements of the actual shape cannot be made sufficiently accurately to detect the expected departures from a spherical shape and the question of their existence is unlikely to be resolved until suitable measurements are made from a spacecraft in orbit around Venus.

Plate tectonics

A glance at any atlas shows that the Atlantic coastlines of Africa and South America have very similar shapes. The coastline does not truly represent the shape of a continent, as it depends on the level of the oceans. A much more significant feature is the edge of the continental shelf where the sea bottom falls comparatively rapidly to a depth of around four kilometres. The fit between the two continents at this edge is quite striking. Other coastlines fit together nearly as well and it is possible to assemble all the continents into just two pieces which themselves fit together, although not was well. This led to the suggestion that at some time in the past there was a single continent called Pangaea, which split into two parts, Laurasia and Gondwanaland. These drifted apart and subsequently broke themselves up to give the present-day northern and southern continents respectively. This whole process was called CONTINENTAL DRIFT. More direct evidence for such movements of the continents across the face of the Earth comes from the direction of the permanent magnetism of the rocks, which shows that in many places there has been a substantial change in latitude since the rocks were laid down. There is also the existence of coal deposits, which form in tropical areas, in the now frozen wastes of Antarctica.

10.6: *The apparent path of the Sun as seen from Mercury. The elongation of the planet in the directions of longitudes 0° and 180° is exaggerated to make it visible. The distances and positions are drawn to scale and marked at eleven-day intervals. The diagram covers 176 days, i.e. two orbital periods or three rotation periods but, for Mercury, only one solar day.*

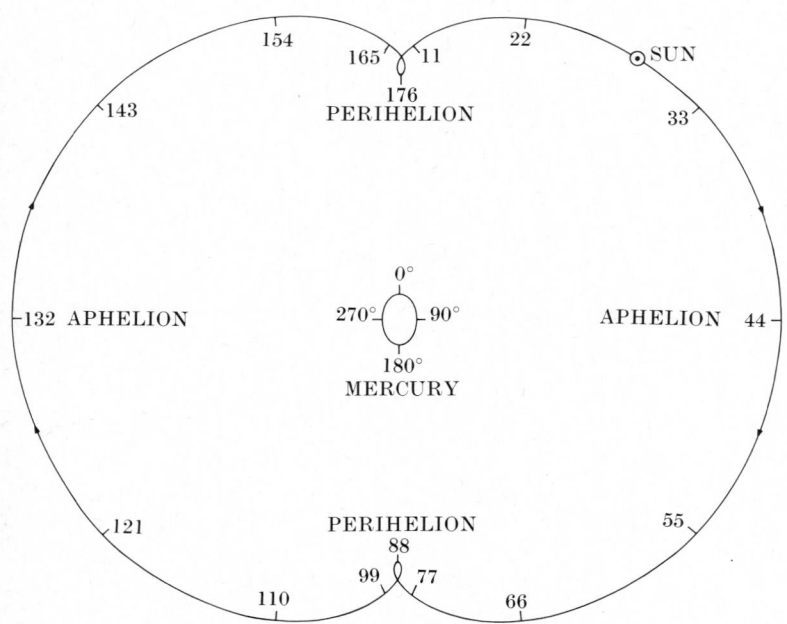

This simple theory of continental drift has now been superseded by PLATE TECTONICS since it is now realized that the crust under the oceans is involved just as much as the continents. The present theory says that the entire surface of the Earth is divided into a series of internally rigid, but relatively thin (about 100 km) PLATES which together form the lithosphere. There are at least fifteen plates of various sizes but most of the Earth's surface is accounted for by seven large plates. A plate may include both oceanic and continental areas. The plates are in continuous motion and this causes virtually all the earthquake, seismic, volcanic and mountain-building activity. This activity marks the active zones of the Earth's crust and closely follows the boundaries of the plates. There are four principal types of boundary between plates. At spreading ridges the plates are separating and material rises from the mantle to fill the gap and form a ridge of new plate material. These ridges mainly occur in the centres of oceans and in places reach the ocean surface to form volcanic islands. At subduction zones two plates are moving towards one another and one is consumed. They often occur at the edge of a continent and the plate carrying oceanic crust is forced under the continental plate and down into the mantle where it is destroyed. The crustal material is less dense than the mantle and so it rises back towards the surface. Some breaks through to the surface to form a string of volcanoes, such as those in the Andes towards the western coast of South America. In other places the subduction zone is under the ocean and a string of volcanic islands is formed such as the Aleutian, Kurile, Japanese and Marianas islands in the northwest Pacific. Ultimately an ocean can be completely destroyed by a subduction zone so that two continents come into collision and a collision zone is formed. Some material is still forced into the mantle but some is pushed upwards to form a chain of mountains, such as the Himalayas. Finally there are transform faults where two plates are simply gliding past one another with no formation or destruction of plate material. These occur at intervals along spreading ridges to form a series of offsets along the plate boundary.

The molten material ejected by volcanoes is called MAGMA. Although the mantle below the lithosphere is semi-molten so that the slow convection currents responsible for driving the plate motions are possible, it is not magma. The heat-flow in the mantle forms magma preferentially at the disturbed areas along plate boundaries. Only some of this is released to the surface by volcanoes; the rest cools and solidifies underground to form rocks such as granite.

Venus has almost the same size and density as the Earth so it is quite possible that tectonic processes similar to those on the Earth are taking place. Radar mapping is the only technique used so far to study large-scale surface features and the best maps have a resolution of about ten kilometres. This makes it difficult to distinguish impact craters from the results of tectonic activity but it is most probable that both are present. The best evidence of tectonic activity is a linear trough, 1500 km long, that runs northeast-southwest across the equator. This can be compared to the East

African rift valley on the Earth which is known to have been caused by crustal movement. Other features found on Venus are a large volcano and mountain areas. The volcano is about 300 km across and one kilometre high with a central crater 80 km across.

Mars, too, shows similar evidence of tectonic activity. It has the largest volcano in the Solar System, Olympus Mons, which is about 600 km across and whose summit rises 25 km above the surrounding terrain! Near the summit are a number of *calderas*, which were once the vents for the molten lava that built up the volcano. The volcano forms a shield whose edge is marked by an escarpment two kilometres high; presumably this cliff face was formed by erosion of the softer surrounding rocks to leave the harder volcanic rock. Close to Olympus Mons are four more large shield volcanoes (one of them greatly eroded) located along the Tharsis ridge. It seems that tectonic activity lifted the edge of a plate by about ten kilometres to form this ridge and that the shield volcanoes formed at places of particularly high stress. On the Earth, plate movements are mainly horizontal but on Mars there is no sign of such movements and the plates can only move vertically. This difference may account for the gigantic size of the shield volcanoes on Mars. There is also a giant canyon, the Valles Marineris (also known as Coprates Canyon) which is 4000 km long, 150 km or more wide and 2–3 km deep. This looks like a rift valley and is therefore further evidence of tectonic activity.

The driving force for tectonic activity is the convection in the asthenosphere, the semi-molten layer of the mantle below the rigid lithosphere. If a planet has a sufficiently thin lithosphere then the convection currents can break it into plates and move them around. The Moon has a vast lithosphere and tectonic activity there is quite impossible. Although Mercury has an Earth-like interior, its surface is very like the Moon and it too does not appear to have present-day tectonic activity.

Craters

The most obvious features on the surface of the Moon are the circular walled areas called craters. These have been known since telescopic observations began. The Earth has very few easily recognizable craters of any great size, although in recent years careful observations have revealed many more which are somewhat obscured by water, vegetation, erosion and so forth. Astronomers expected that Mercury, Venus and Mars would be like the Earth, rather than the Moon, and it was a great surprise when the Mariner 4 spacecraft flew past Mars in 1965 and revealed a crater-strewn surface similar to the Moon. These observations covered only a small part of the surface and it was not until the planet-wide photographic coverage by Mariner 9 in 1972 that large areas relatively free of craters were discovered. Mariner 10 photography in 1974 covered nearly half the surface of Mercury and showed this planet to have a surface very similar to that of the Moon. Radar mapping of Venus in the 1970s has shown that it too is covered with craters although the number of small craters is less than on Mars, Mercury or the Moon.

For many years the origin of the lunar craters was a matter of great controversy between supporters of volcanic origin and those of meteoritic impact origin. It was only settled to most people's satisfaction when spacecraft data became available. Most astronomers now believe that the majority of lunar craters were formed by meteoritic impact, although some are of volcanic origin.

If a large meteorite, or small asteroid, collides with the surface of the Moon the relative velocity is some tens of kilometres per second, which is greater than the speed of sound in the lunar material. This material cannot move out of the way of the meteorite faster than sound and so it is therefore compressed. This slows down the meteorite and the energy of its motion is converted into heat which can be sufficient to vaporize a large mass of material. Eventually the meteorite is stopped some kilometres below the surface having formed a pocket of hot, highly compressed and vaporized rock. This then explodes and it is the explosion that forms the crater. If a graph is drawn of crater diameters against depths for lunar craters, terrestrial meteorite craters, and craters caused by man-made explosions, all the points lie on the same smooth curve, thereby confirming the explosive origin of the lunar craters. An objection sometimes raised to this impact theory is that meteorites generally strike the Moon obliquely and that the craters should be elliptical and not circular. This would be true if the meteorite simply gouged out a hole, but in fact the explosion after the meteorite has stopped is not affected by the direction of impact and so a circular crater is formed which completely obliterates any elliptical feature produced when the meteorite initially penetrated the surface. The theory of impact origin is now well understood and is supported by laboratory experiments. As a result most workers in this subject agree that impact-produced craters have the following features (figure 10.7 (c)):

A nearly circular rim crest with the slope of the rim steeper on the inside than on the outside.

Interior walls that are terraced in large craters and steep in smaller ones.

A surrounding hummocky and undulating blanket of material ejected in the explosion that caused the crater. It has radial and dune-like features, is usually brighter than its surroundings and extends at least one crater diameter outward from the rim crest.

A system of radial rays extending beyond the ejecta blanket due to projectiles from the impact site that form secondary craters.

A depression inside the rim that is generally deep. When it is large, there is a central peak that was probably formed by the elastic rebound of rock from beneath the surface during the impact event.

Although the crater itself is not appreciably affected by the angle of impact, the ejecta blanket and the rays form preferentially on the side opposite the direction of impact. In contrast to these features, volcanically-produced craters display the following characteristics:

A usually polygonal form.

A rim with the interior and exterior slopes nearly the same and with few, if any, wall terraces.

A relatively smooth ejecta blanket which is often darker than the surroundings.

No extensive ray systems.

Craters that are usually shallow with collapsed depressions on the rim and in the floor.

10.7a, b, c: *Three striking lunar panoramas taken from satellites orbiting the Moon. (a) Earthrise viewed from lunar orbit. The visible land area is the western portion of Africa, and, above this, heavy cloud conceals much of the Atlantic Ocean. (b) The large crater, Goclenius (foreground), is nearly 65 km from rim to rim. An unusual feature is the prominent rille that crosses the crater rim at the right. Figure (c) shows part of the near side of the Moon dominated by the impact crater Copernicus (90 km diameter) almost exactly at the centre. Many other craters in the photograph are also of impact origin but some can be identified as volcanic. The large smooth circular area to the north of (above) Copernicus is Mare Imbrium. The crater Plato on the northern border of Mare Imbrium (top centre of photograph) has been flooded with mare material to give it a smooth flat bottom. Many other craters have been flooded in this way. At the bottom is Mare Nubium, an example of a mare with an irregular outline. (NASA, Apollo 8 and Orbiter IV, USA)*

(a)

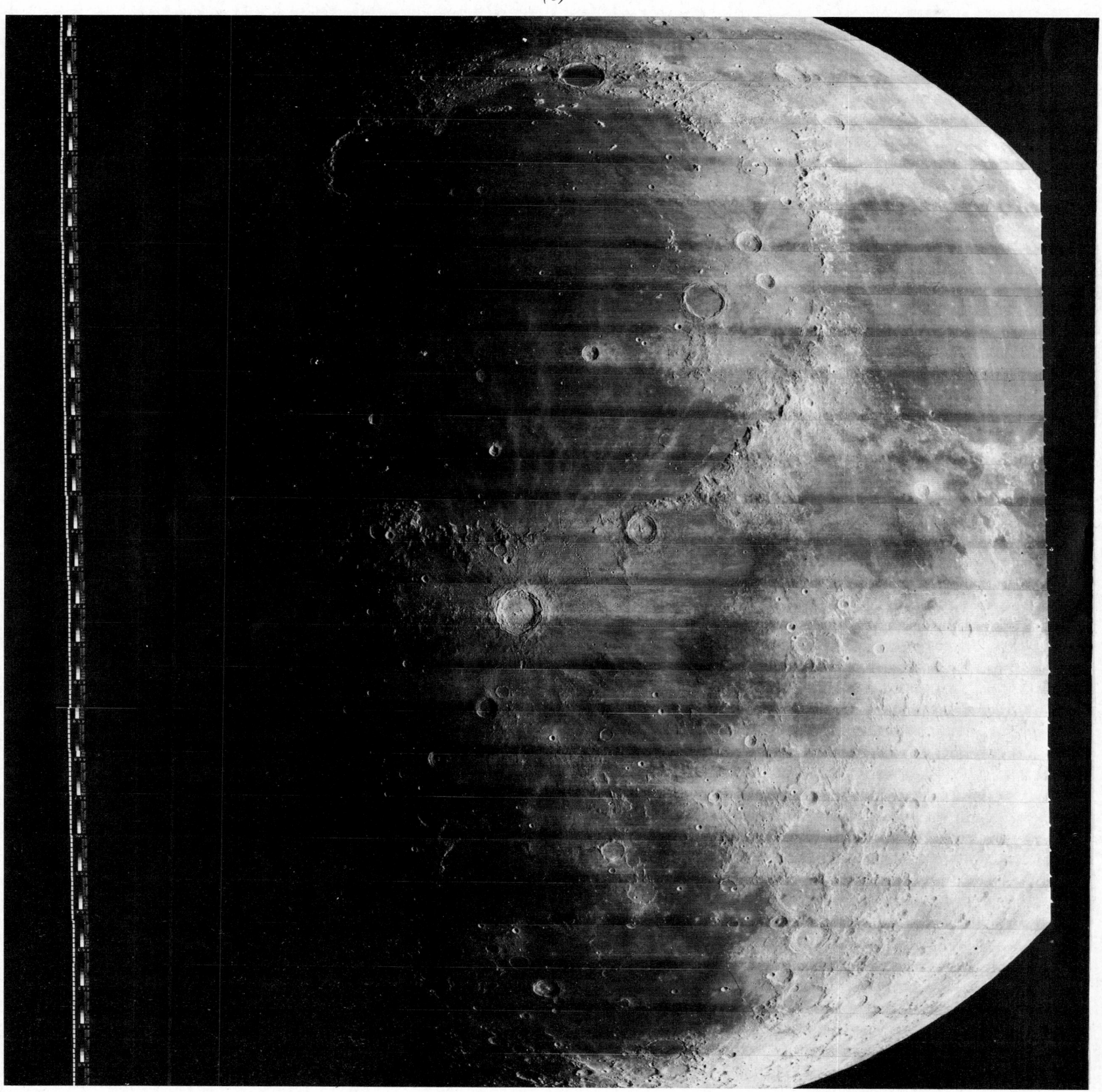

The distinction between the two types of crater is most easily made for the fresh, young features such as Maunder and Kopff shown in figure 10.8. Older craters, however, have generally had their features subdued by later events and it is not always easy to make a distinction. Being depressions, craters are the hosts of varying amounts of fill. The very large craters, such as the basins of Serenitatis, Nectaris, Crisium, Imbrium, Moscoviense, Ingenii and Orientale are partly or nearly filled with dark mare material. For example, in the case of Orientale (figure 10.8) the dark *mare* material appears to overlie the lighter material in the interior of the basin. Some small craters occur in CRATER CHAINS which can be as much as 300 km long; they occur over most parts of the lunar surface. The individual craters are usually less than 15 km in diameter. It would be too much of a coincidence for them to have been formed by the random process of impact and so they must be of volcanic origin. They presumably mark out lines of crustal weakness.

The Earth is the only planet known to have volcanoes active today. We have referred above to the way in which they are almost always found along plate boundaries. Of particular interest to the study of the large craters on other planets are those volcanic craters on the Earth which are larger than two kilometres across and are known as CALDERAS. It is popularly supposed that these volcanoes have blown their tops off but this is incorrect; the material now present is newly cooled magma. The largest calderas develop late in the history of a volcano during a violent eruption. It seems that the underground reservoirs of magma are emptied by the eruption and that the summit of the volcano, having lost its support, collapses to leave a crater. The Earth's largest caldera, at Aso-san in Japan, is 23 km by 16 km – much less than the 65 km diameter of the caldera of Olympus Mons on Mars.

The Moon's surface

The surface of the Moon can, roughly speaking, be divided into two contrasting types – dark, comparatively smooth areas called MARIA (singular: mare) and brighter, more rugged regions called TERRAE. The maria cover about one-third of the Moon's near side but are almost completely absent from the far side. Maria is the Latin word for seas and was used because of their sea-like appearance in small telescopes, although it is now known that these low-lying regions are completely waterless. They are of two types:

Nearly circular regions generally surrounded by circular mountain areas or fault scarps. Examples are Mare Imbrium, Mare Crisium and Mare Moscoviense (figure 10.7 (c)).

Regions of irregular outline without bordering mountain walls or fault scarps. Examples are Mare Tranquilitatis, Mare Nubium and Oceanus Procellarum.

The whole lunar surface is dominated by the craters described above although these occur more frequently on the terrae than on the maria; this is particularly true of the large craters. The maria show numerous other irregularities in their apparently smooth surfaces. Lunar DOMES are almost circular surface bulges, and their diameters range up to several kilometres, but they are never more

10.8: *The magnificent three-ring Orientale basin. The rings have diameters of 480, 620 and 930 km. These concentric structures were probably formed by the impact of a large body at the centre of the basin. The outermost ring is surrounded by an enormous ejecta blanket also produced by the impact. Inside the inner ring is the dark material of Mare Orientale on which can be seen a number of craters. The largest two are Maunder on the northern (upper) edge and Kopff to the east (right). Maunder, 55 km in diameter, is believed to be a meteorite impact crater, whereas Kopff, 45 km in diameter, appears to be volcanic in origin. Orientale cannot be seen properly from the Earth as it is on the edge of the visible hemisphere and it was not until spacecraft photographs became available that astronomers had any inkling of its true nature. The horizontal lines on figures 10.7 (c) and 10.8 are due to the way in which the pictures were scanned in the Orbiter spacecraft a narrow strip at a time. After radio transmission to the Earth these strips were reconstructed individually and rejoined. (NASA, Orbiter IV, USA)*

than 100 m or so in height. At least three quarters have a small crater at the top. Only a few have been detected with certainty in the mountainous terrae. Also on the maria are several types of linear features, collectively known as LINEAMENTS. RILLES, or RIMAE are long trench-like features between a half and five kilometres wide, rarely more than 400 m deep but extending across the lunar surface for hundreds of kilometres. They usually cross craters, hills and other features with little change in direction or width, showing that they must have formed later than most other lunar features. WRINKLE RIDGES are sinuous, irregular and apparently smooth elevations up to 30 km wide, but rarely more than 100 m high. FAULTS are dislocations of the surface with either vertical (dip-slip) or essentially horizontal (strike-slip) movement which manifest themselves as discontinuities in various other features or as linear scarps. The best known lunar fault is Rupes Recta (the Straight Wall) in Mare Nubium, a linear scarp about 120 km long. It is the surface expression of a normal dip-slip fault with a vertical displacement of more than 300 m.

The terrae are mountainous, heavily-cratered regions often known as the lunar HIGHLANDS and, in contrast with the maria, were given the Latin name for continents. The craters are of all sizes up to 250 km in diameter and are scattered over the highlands in great profusion; frequently they overlap one another. Some craters have walls rising to over 3000 m above the surrounding terrain. Most of the principal mountain ranges in the lunar highlands form borders to the maria and should, perhaps, be considered to be part of the maria.

The lunar rocks that have been brought back from the Moon by Apollo astronauts were only taken from the topmost few centimetres. However we can be confident that a proportion of these rocks were originally tens of kilometres deep until they were scattered by the impacts that produced most of the craters. Most of the rocks are composed of what is called ANORTHOSITIC material and so the lunar crust is most probably composed predominantly of this type of material. Anorthositic rocks are mainly made up of one mineral – plagioclase feldspar ($CaAl_2Si_2O_8$) – and are formed in pools of lava. To have produced a crust 60 km thick, the lava must have been about 200 km deep over the whole surface of the Moon. All the planets are believed to have formed by accretion of cold particles, but the kinetic energy of this material was sufficient to melt the whole planet. Although most of the heat would have been quickly radiated away, it seems that enough must have been retained by the Moon to melt the outermost 200 km. Although the theory behind this idea is not at all certain, there does not appear to be any way to melt the surface after the Moon was formed. Being exposed to space, the molten surface would quite quickly cool down but not before a low density crust of anorthositic rocks had formed.

Another constituent of the lunar rocks is KREEP NORITE. This type of rock is named after potassium (K), rare earth elements (REE) and phosphorous (P). Although these elements are only minor constituents of lunar (and terrestrial rocks) they, and others such as barium, uranium and thorium are fifty to a hundred times more abundant in KREEP norite than in other rocks. KREEP norite has a relatively low melting point and will separate out from the lunar crust if there is partial melting of the anorthositic rocks. The rock can be detected from orbiting spacecraft by the *gamma rays* emitted by the high concentration of the radioactive elements, uranium and thorium, as well as by direct analysis of rock samples. Such observations have shown that it is concentrated mainly in the broad area of Mare Imbrium and Oceanus Procellarum. The source of the heat required to form the KREEP material is a mystery.

The next stage of lunar history was the formation of the main surface features during a period of major impacts about four billion years ago. As the radioactive elements in rocks decay, the proportions of the various decay products change and hence they can be used as a clock to determine the age of the rocks. If rocks are heated sufficiently, the decay products can be released and the clock is reset to zero. The rocks of the lunar highlands are four billion years old, although it is thought the rocks were formed shortly after the Moon – about four and a half billion years ago. They must have been heated four billion years ago, almost certainly by the violent impacts that excavated the basins of the huge circular maria and threw debris out to blanket much of the near side of the Moon. Because these impacts obliterated any older features, we do not know whether they were the only ones of this magnitude or whether they just marked the end of a period of major impacts that started when the Moon was formed. One unexplained aspect of the maria is the way in which they almost all lie on the near side of the Moon. The Earth was presumably responsible, but in what way remains to be discovered.

When these impacts had come to an end, or possibly while they were diminishing, vast quantities of lava erupted onto the lunar surface. This lava flowed into the circular maria basins where it solidified to give them their present relatively smooth appearance. Other low-lying areas were also flooded to produce the irregular, non-circular maria. The solidified lava forms the rock type known as BASALT. Comparison of lunar and terrestrial basalts show that those on the Moon have been systematically depleted of the more volatile elements such as lead, sodium and potassium. This suggests that the Moon was formed from particles in the solar nebula at a somewhat higher temperature than those that went to make up the Earth. Successive lava flows are clearly visible in the maria, and the lava continued to issue from the interior for almost a billion years. The composition of the lava changed with time; for example the oldest samples collected contain more titanium than the younger ones. This appears to be due to a change in the depth at which the lava was generated from 150 km initially to 240 km or more later on. Although the lunar interior was being heated by radioactive decay at this time, the outer layers were more affected by loss of heat to space and cooled down so that the layers hot enough to generate lava moved inwards. This process has continued during the last three billion years until today we have the situation described above, with a rigid lithosphere about 1000 km thick. These three billion years have been a period of quiescence for the Moon. There have been very few major impacts since the maria were formed, and they have kept their smooth appearance to the present day. They are not completely smooth, for close-up views have shown them to be pockmarked with small craters formed by minor impacts. One way of determining the relative ages of different parts of the lunar surface is to count the number of craters; the more craters per unit area, the older the surface. Since we do not know how the rate of impacts has changed with time, this method only allows us to put different areas in order of age.

Tracking of spacecraft in orbit around the Moon showed, in 1968, that the pull of gravity above the circular maria was about one per cent stronger than above adjoining regions. It is not possible conclusively to determine the origin of these gravity anomalies but it is highly significant that thin plates one or two kilometres deep that just covered the circular maria would do the job nicely. The pressure at the base of the lithosphere is the same over the whole Moon and can support the same mass per unit area at all points. The situation in which this is the case is called ISOSTASY. Astronomers generally believe that isostasy does not hold below the circular maria and that there is extra mass in their basins. This extra mass is called a MASCON (abbreviated from mass concentration) and it must be supported by the rigidity of the crust. The origin of mascons is uncertain but one theory, due to S.K. Runcorn, is shown in figure 10.9. The irregular maria do not contain mascons. Runcorn's theory will only work if the initial mare basin formed by meteorite impact is deep, about 20 km or so. It is reasonable to suppose that the lava in the irregular maria is only a couple of kilometres thick, covering a depression in the original terrain.

10.9: *A possible mechanism for the formation of a mascon. At (a) a meteorite impact has formed a mare basin, about 20 km deep. Because matter has been removed from the crust, gravity is weaker over the mare than elsewhere. This lack of mass causes stresses in the crust and lithosphere just as large as would be caused by a corresponding amount of extra mass. These stresses produce cracks which allow fluid lava (magma) to be forced into the basin from the asthenosphere until pressure balance is restored. This occurs when the mass above the asthenosphere per unit area is the same everywhere and gravity above the mare is then the same as elsewhere. Since the lava is denser than the crustal material, pressure balance is restored when the basin is only partly full. When the lava solidifies, it contracts and the surface drops by about ten per cent of the depth of the basin, i.e. by about two kilometres. If the cracks remain open, more fluid lava could rise to the same height as before giving the extra mass to form the mascon and produce the observed gravity anomaly.*

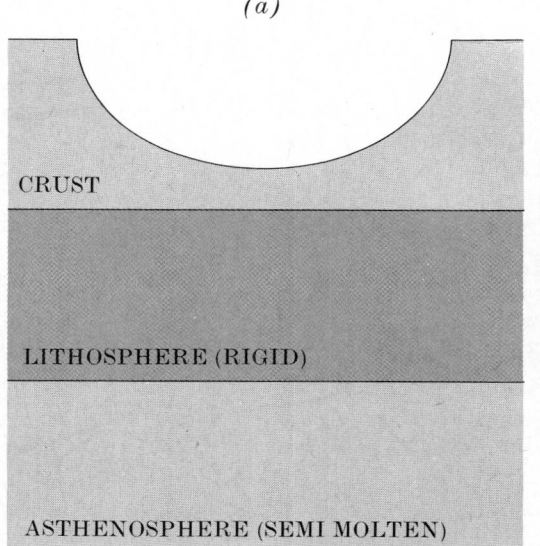

(a)

CRUST

LITHOSPHERE (RIGID)

ASTHENOSPHERE (SEMI MOLTEN)

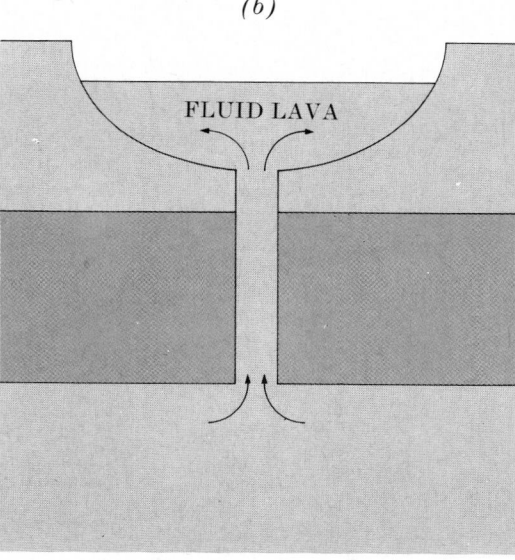

(b)

FLUID LAVA

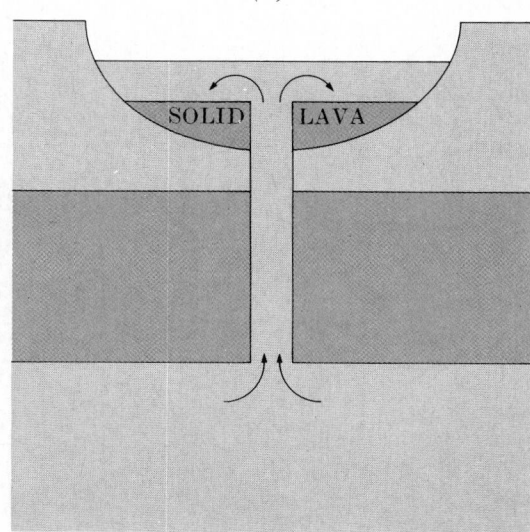

(c)

SOLID LAVA

The surface of Mars

Perhaps the most remarkable aspect of the Martian surface is the distribution of craters larger than 10 km in diameter, which are much commoner in the southern hemisphere than in the northern. Much of the northern hemisphere has been flooded with lava and this has evidently obliterated the craters that must have existed at one time. Using estimates of the present rate of crater formation on Mars, we can deduce that most of the large craters in the southern hemisphere were formed early in the planet's history, probably during the first billion years. The lava plains that have covered the northern hemisphere are very similar to the lunar maria. There is plenty of variation in the density of craters on these plains with the most heavily marked regions having ten times as many craters as the least marked. This variation shows that the lava flooding must have extended over a considerable period from more than a billion years ago until almost the present. Why the flooding should have occurred preferentially in the northern hemisphere is not known, but the reason is probably connected with the fact that much of this hemisphere lies several kilometres below the average level of the southern hemisphere. The lava plains are not the only volcanic features on Mars; there are also the volcanic craters already described in the section on *plate tectonics*.

Martian craters show a wide variation in the extent to which they have been degraded. On the volcanic plains of the northern hemisphere nearly all the craters have a fresh appearance, showing that since the plains were formed there has been little significant erosion. Earlier in the history of Mars, the erosion must have been much more rapid and detailed studies of the forms of craters have shown that the time of most rapid erosion occurred near the end of the initial cratering episode that produced the major southern features.

Long before the advent of spacecraft observations, it was recognized that there could be no liquid water on the surface of Mars. It came as a surprise when sinuous channels up to 1500 km long and 200 km wide were discovered. They look just as if they were formed by erosion due to a running liquid; they have tributary systems and almost without exception the direction of flow is downhill. The channels are quite unlike the lava channels (*rilles*) found on the Earth and the Moon and it is clear that a liquid much less viscous than lava was responsible. The most likely candidate is water, and if this is correct then Mars, or at least the equatorial regions where the channels mainly occur, must once have been warmer and wetter than it is today. The source of the water is not clear for most of the channels, but in some cases it appears to have been a region of what is called CHAOTIC TERRAIN. Such terrain is a depressed region characterized by a disorderly array of broken slabs of rock. It is thought to be due to the withdrawal of subsurface material and the subsequent melting of surface ice. FRETTED TERRAIN is another landform that may have resulted from the melting of ice below the surface causing landslides. This terrain is a flat lowland, bordered by steep cliffs with an intricate geometry. Close to the cliffs there are numerous small elevated plateaus.

It must be pointed out that these sinuous channels have no con-

10.10: *The seasons on the Earth. The diagram shows beams of sunlight with equal cross-sections falling on the Earth at the summer and winter solstices. The light and heat is spread over a smaller area in the summer than in the winter so that summer is warmer than winter. Clouds permitting, the rate of solar heating is greatest at the summer solstice but the Earth takes some time to respond so that on average the warmest weather occurs some weeks later. The same effect also operates on Mars.*

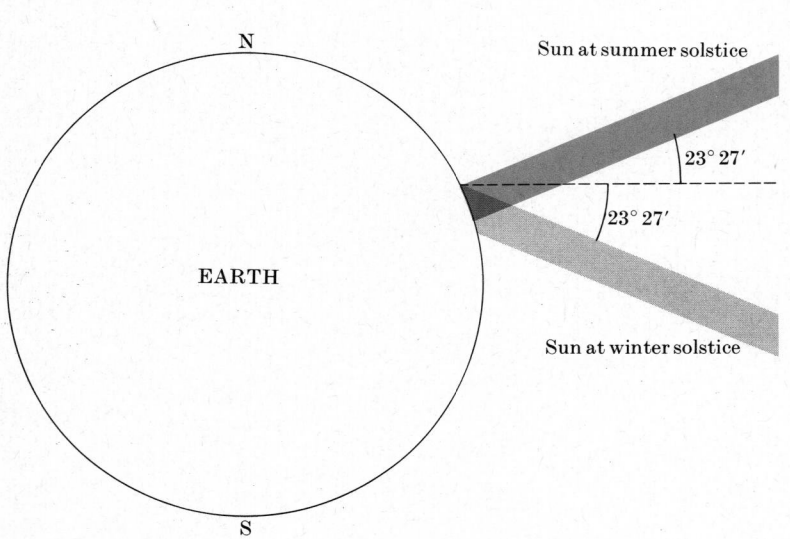

nection with the canals reported by observers in the late nineteenth and early twentieth centuries. These canals were supposed to be long, accurately straight features on the limits of telescopic observations and some people fancifully took them to be a network of irrigation canals constructed by inhabitants of Mars to carry water from the polar caps to the rest of the planet. Spacecraft photographs have shown conclusively that the canals do not exist and that most of them are totally spurious features. In a few cases it appears that the observer's eye mentally joined together several smaller features that happened to lie in a more or less straight line.

The tilt of the Martian rotation axis is very nearly the same as the Earth's and as a result there are seasons on Mars (figure 10.10). The orbit of Mars around the Sun is appreciably elliptical and the planet is at perihelion during the southern summer. As a result the southern summers are hotter and shorter than those in the north. Mars has polar ice caps which contract each summer and grow again during the following winter. At maximum extent they can reach down to a latitude of 60°. The southern cap disappears almost completely during some summers, but because of the cooler summers in the northern hemisphere the polar cap there is never reduced to such a small size. The caps are made partly of carbon dioxide ice which vaporizes directly and condenses again without passing through the liquid state. A large fraction, possibly as much as 20 per cent, of the atmospheric carbon dioxide is held in the polar caps. There is also probably some water ice in the caps. This never melts and may form the permanent cap left each summer. At latitudes above 45° the ground below the martian surface is always below the freezing point of water and a layer of permafrost may have formed there similar to that in the Earth's polar regions. There may also be more water trapped in the REGOLITH, the granular material that lies above the bedrock. Altogether about one per cent of the surface material could be water, enough to form a layer a few tens of metres deep if it were all melted and spread evenly over the surface.

The surface of Mercury

Because Mercury is so much nearer to the Sun, it receives ten times as much solar energy per unit surface area when it is at perihelion than does the Moon. Because of the coupling between Mercury's orbital motion and rotation (figure 10.6) the meridians at 0° and 180° longitude receive two and a half times more radiation overall than do longitudes 90° and 270° Mercury's rotation axis is almost perpendicular to its orbit and there are no seasons as on the Earth or Mars, but there is instead a seasonal variation with longitude.

Photographs of Mercury have only been obtained for longitudes between 10° and 190° (all longitudes are measured westwards), yet this hemisphere is clearly divided into two by the varying nature of the surface. Between longitudes 10° and about 100° the surface could easily be mistaken for the Moon. One significant difference, though, is the presence of conspicuous smooth areas, or plains, in the highlands, something not seen in the generally heavily-cratered lunar highlands. There are also many fewer craters between 20 and 50 km in diameter on Mercury than on the Moon. One reason for these differences is the higher gravity on Mercury which confines the material ejected in an impact to an area only one sixth of the size covered by a similar impact on the Moon. It is therefore likely that recent impacts on Mercury have not obliterated earlier features to the same extent as on the Moon.

Another important difference is the large number of shallowly scalloped cliffs, called LOBATE SCARPS that run for hundreds of kilometres across Mercury. They are not present on the Moon or Mars and suggest that the interior of Mercury has shrunk so that the surface became wrinkled like an old apple. This shrinking may have occurred as the large iron core slowly cooled and contracted. The very large craters on Mercury are well preserved and are probably three or four billion years old, indicating that there has been no migration of plates on the planet since that time.

The other half of the observed surface, between longitudes 100° and 190° shows large areas of smooth plains. These must be younger than the heavily-cratered areas or they too would be covered with impact craters. Like the lunar maria, they appear to be lava flows. A particularly notable feature of this part of Mercury is Caloris Basin, 1400 km in diameter, which is entirely filled with smooth plains material and must have been formed by an impact comparable to the one that produced Mare Imbrium on the Moon.

The surface history of Mercury was probably very similar to that of the Moon, despite the quite different interiors. After formation of the planet, there must have been a planet-wide obliteration of surface features to give a smooth surface which we can still see today in the smooth plains between the craters. This was followed by a heavy bombardment that produced the craters. Towards the end of this phase there was the impact that gouged out the Caloris Basin and, possibly, other giant basins were similarly formed in the so-far unphotographed hemisphere. After Caloris Basin was formed widespread outflows of lava filled this basin and other low ground to give the large smooth maria-like plains. This was the last active phase of the surface history and it has been followed by a quiescent period lasting to the present. The smooth ground is marked only by a light peppering of impact craters, many of which show conspicuous rays. Remarkably, the distribution of these on Mercury, the Moon and Mars shows that over the last three billion years or so all three of these planets have been subjected to the same total amount of bombardment.

The surface of Venus

Owing to the thick clouds we know little of the surface of Venus. Reference has already been made to the craters observed by radar. There is a scarcity of small craters; this is to be expected because the dense atmosphere would burn up the smaller meteoroids which would otherwise produce these craters. Venus is a very flat planet with few features more than a kilometre in height but again the hot, dense corrosive atmosphere may have been responsible by causing more rapid erosion than on Mars. This is not certain, for the winds at the surface may not be strong enough to pick up the dust which, by sandblasting, is thought to be the major cause of erosion on Mars.

Spacecraft have softlanded on Venus and sent television pictures of the nearby surface back to Earth. These showed a mixture of smooth rounded stones and angular rock fragments typically 30 to 40 cm across which appear to form a geologically young landscape. By contrast, the other spacecraft landed in a smoother area with large flat boulders that is apparently geologically older. This shows that erosion does occur on Venus even though there is no liquid water and possibly insignificant windborne dust.

The face of the Earth

From measurements of radioactive decay products, it is possible to measure the age pattern of the Earth's continents. They are found to have an ancient nucleus, at least 2.5 billion years old, onto which successively younger extensions have been welded, a process still continuing today. The growth has not been regular and in particular there were world-wide interruptions marked by intense deformation and igneous activity around 2.7, 1.8 and 1.0 billion years ago. Although a surprisingly large proportion of the continental crust was already in existence 2.5 billion years ago, most of it is younger – in marked contrast to the surfaces of the other planets. The Earth must have been subjected to the same intense bombardment four billion years ago that was responsible for the large craters still seen on the other planets but tectonic activity since then has destroyed these early surface features.

The surface of the Earth is also being changed by weathering and erosion. Chemical reactions and frost shattering can weather rocks to produce debris which is worn away and transported elsewhere by erosion. Together, weathering and erosion result in the sculpturing and eventual lowering of the landscape. The main agents of erosion are rivers, glaciers, waves, currents and wind. Loose material can also fall, slide or creep downhill just under the force of gravity. Erosion is rapid in steep areas with high rainfall and in semi-arid regions only poorly protected by patchy vegetation, but slow in deserts and cold lowlands. It has been estimated that the average rate of erosion of the land is 8.6 cm per 1000 years. Since this is rapid enough to wear Mount Everest down to sea level in only 100 million years we can see that erosion alone would have long ago destroyed craters formed four billion years ago. Today we see the net effect of tectonic mountain building activity and the levelling due to erosion.

The rock materials removed and carried away by weathering and erosion are generally deposited at the bottom of a river or ocean to form sediments. If the pressure is sufficiently high the sediments are compressed into a more compact and hardened state and are then known as SEDIMENTARY ROCKS. Such rocks cover more than two-thirds of the Earth's surface. IGNEOUS ROCKS are produced by the solidification of *magma*. The third main type of rocks are the METAMORPHIC ROCKS, which are produced from other rocks by the action of heat (but not sufficient to melt the rocks) and pressure.

Atmospheres

Compared to the Earth, Mars has a thin atmosphere and Venus a thick one whereas Mercury and the Moon do not have one at all. Table 10.3 lists some of the gases which we might expect to find in planetary atmospheres because they are volatile compounds of the cosmically common elements. If a planet ever gets an atmosphere from anywhere it will gradually lose it because some of the molecules are moving sufficiently fast to escape from the planet's gravity. Molecules move faster at higher temperatures and at any particular temperature light molecules move faster than heavier molecules. It seems likely that Mercury and the Moon have lost any atmospheres they may once have had because of their low surface gravities and low escape velocities. In the case of Mercury there is also the high surface temperature which reaches a maximum of 700 K on the equator at noon. Mars has an escape velocity only a little greater than Mercury's but on account of its greater distance from the Sun and consequent lower temperature it has been able to retain an atmosphere. Hydrogen and helium are cosmically the most abundant elements but, because they also have the lightest molecules, none of the inner planets has been able to retain these elements in their atmospheres.

Accurate studies of how planets lose their atmospheres are made difficult because the atmospheric temperature, and hence the rate of loss, depends on the composition. For example, if the Moon once had an atmosphere we do not know what its temperature was and hence cannot predict how rapidly it would have been lost. We can however say that the present planetary atmospheres are being lost at rates that are so slow that they are generally negligible, even over a period as long as the age of the Solar System.

Table 10.4 gives some data for the planetary atmospheres. The presence of the various constituents has been established spectroscopically. The only detected major constituent for both Mars and Venus is carbon dioxide (CO_2). In the case of Venus, Venera spacecraft have entered the atmosphere and shown that it contains 97 per cent carbon dioxide. This proportion is similar on Mars; nitrogen and argon, which have been detected by the Viking spacecraft, constitute about two per cent of the atmosphere each. A number of minor constituents have also been detected in the two atmospheres. One notable molecule not detected on Venus is oxygen, which must be at least 50 times less abundant than carbon monoxide. On Mars there are twice as many carbon monoxide molecules as oxygen molecules. Carbon monoxide is thought to be formed from carbon dioxide in upper atmospheres by the action of ultraviolet light from the Sun. The two gases are formed in the relative amounts seen on Mars. Oxygen is presumably formed in the same way on Venus but quickly carried lower in the atmosphere where it combines with some other substance, possibly sulphur which may be found in the clouds.

The clouds on Venus are so thick that they always keep the planet's surface hidden from view. In visible light, the cloud tops are a featureless pale yellow but in ultraviolet light a complex pattern of bright and dark swirls is visible. Ultraviolet photo-

Table 10.3: Some possible constituents of planetary atmospheres

The molecular weights give the relative masses of the molecules in the various compounds or elements.

		molecular weight
Hydrogen	H_2	2
Helium	He	4
Water	H_2O	16
Carbon monoxide	CO	28
Nitrogen	N_2	28
Oxygen	O_2	32
Argon	Ar	40
Carbon dioxide	CO_2	44

Table 10.4: Planetary atmospheres

Planet	*Venus*	*Earth*	*Mars*
Surface pressure (atmospheres)	90	1	0.006
Mean surface temperature (K)	750	300	230
Known atmospheric constituents:			
major	CO_2, N_2, Ar	N_2, O_2, Ar	CO_2
minor	HCl, HF, CO, H_2O	CO_2, H_2O, etc	O_2, H_2O, CO, Kr, Xe
Amounts (kg m^{-2})			
CO_2 atmosphere	700 000	10	700
crust	(small?)	700 000	?
H_2O atmosphere	<1000	10	0.1
crust (including oceans)	(small?)	3 000 000	?
Cloud amount (per cent)	100	50	5

graphs of Venus are customarily processed by computer to enhance the contrast since the light areas are only a few per cent brighter than the dark ones. Observations of the *Doppler shift* of the light from the clouds and of the motion of cloud features across the disc show that the clouds and upper atmosphere of Venus rotates in the same retrograde direction as the planet itself, but with the much shorter period of only four days. This period corresponds to wind speeds of about $100\,\text{m s}^{-1}$ (i.e. 360 km per hour) at the equator. Measurements by softlanding craft have shown wind speeds at the surface of only one or two metres per second. Astronomers have not yet succeeded in satisfactorily explaining the high speeds observed in the upper atmosphere and indeed some have suggested that the observations have been misinterpreted and that the winds are much slower.

Figure 10.11 shows the variation of temperature and pressure with height in the atmosphere of Venus. The visible cloud features are at an altitude of about 60 km but the cloud layer extends from about 80 km down to 35 km. This layer reflects or absorbs much of the incident solar radiation. Only about one per cent of the radiation reaches the surface and here it is mainly absorbed and re-emitted as long-wavelength infrared radiation. This is absorbed by the atmosphere and the clouds; it cannot directly escape back into space. Consequently the atmosphere has been heated up to give a surface temperature of about 750 K; this whole process is called the GREENHOUSE EFFECT. In the atmosphere below the visible clouds,

heat is transported mainly by convection; this limits the temperature gradient to about 10 degrees per kilometre.

Spectroscopically, liquids and solids are more difficult to identify than gases and as a result the composition of the clouds is not known with certainty. The commonly held view is that the clouds are mainly droplets of concentrated sulphuric acid containing about one quarter water. Such droplets are white, not yellow, so it is likely that there are impurities as well. The ultra-violet markings can be explained by differences of a few per cent in the diameters of the droplets between the darker and lighter parts of the clouds. In the lower clouds the droplets may coagulate to form a rain which would be the most corrosive fluid in the Solar System!

Unlike the dense atmosphere of Venus, with its surface pressure of 90 atmospheres, that of Mars is very thin – only 0.006 atmospheres at the surface. Figure 10.12 shows the variation of temperature with height in the Martian atmosphere for three locations. Unlike Venus, Mars shows horizontal, as well as vertical variations in temperature. There is no greenhouse effect in the thin atmosphere so the average surface temperature is 230 K, below the freezing point of water. In general there is only a small amount of cloud, about five per cent of the surface being covered at any one time. At middle latitudes clouds of water-ice are seen; nearer the poles they are of solid carbon dioxide. The clouds are often associated with surface features. As the winds blow over a large

10.11: *The variation of temperature and pressure with altitude in the atmosphere of Venus, showing the cloud layer between altitudes 35 and 80 km. The pressure at an altitude of 50 km is the same as at sea-level on the Earth. At the surface the pressure is 90 atmospheres, the same as at a depth of 900 m in the Earth's oceans. The surface temperature is high enough to melt lead.*

10.12: *The variation of temperature and pressure with altitude in the atmosphere of Mars. The unit of pressure (millibar) is almost exactly 0.001 atmosphere. Because of the variation of temperature over the surface of Mars, curves are given for three locations: (A) 15°S, 64°W, (B) 38°S, 282°W and (C) 87°S, 342°W. The dashed parts of the curves represent uncertain findings. Because the atmosphere of Mars is so thin, the Sun can heat it almost equally at every height and there is much less variation of temperature with altitude than on Venus. The altitude is measured from the mean surface of Mars, where the pressure is 6 millibars.*

crater, a pattern of LEE WAVES is set up. Where the air is rising it expands and cools and ice-clouds can form by condensation. Such clouds are also found downwind from terrestrial mountains. Nearer the equator localized condensation clouds are sometimes found. They form when air rises and cools as it passes over highly elevated surface features.

Mars also has dust storms. Small storms are common but once every Martian year there is a great storm and a large part of the surface is obscured by dust in the atmosphere. The storm starts when Mars is close to perihelion. It normally begins at about the same place in the southern hemisphere and within a month almost all this hemisphere is obscured. Sometimes the storm spreads into the northern hemisphere as well and the entire planet can be shrouded by dust. The dust generally settles over a period of a few months. During a storm, the atmospheric temperature can rise by as much as 50 K because of absorption of solar radiation by the dust. The storms appear to be produced by something similar to a terrestrial hurricane which pumps dust from the dry surface to an altitude of 20 km whence it spreads out in a layer between 20 and 30 km high.

The main external drive for the large-scale behaviour of the atmospheres of the inner planets is the larger amount of radiation received per unit surface area at the equator than at the poles. This causes a temperature contrast between the equator and poles although it is quite different for each planet. In terms of the mean

atmospheric temperature the contrast is less than 2 per cent for Venus, 16 per cent for the Earth and 40 per cent for Mars. Because of its large mass, the atmosphere of Venus responds very slowly to the influx of solar radiation and since the atmospheric motions can carry heat from the equator to the poles more rapidly than this there is very little horizontal temperature variation. The atmosphere of Mars has little mass so that it rapidly responds to the solar radiation and a larger temperature contrast is possible. For similar reasons there is little difference between day and night-time temperatures on Venus but a large difference on Mars. This large diurnal variation on Mars causes strong winds.

Volcanic activity on Venus, Mars and the Earth is likely to have released an atmosphere predominantly of carbon dioxide, water vapour and nitrogen. On the Earth the most abundant constituent, water, has condensed to form the oceans whereas carbon dioxide has reacted chemically with the oceans and surface rocks to leave nitrogen as the most abundant atmospheric species. The appearance of photosynthesising plants on the Earth about two billion years ago was responsible for the release of oxygen which now makes up about 20 per cent of the atmosphere. There is no evidence of similar life on any other planet, which explains the absence of major amounts of oxygen in the atmospheres of Venus and Mars. Judging by the amounts of carbon dioxide in their atmospheres (table 10.4) we can see that Venus has had a release of gases by volcanic activity similar to the Earth, but that Mars has been much less active. There can have been little loss of carbon dioxide from either the Earth or Mars or loss of water from the Earth, whereas, although Mars has little water now, it has been estimated that $5000 \, \mathrm{kg \, m^{-2}}$ have been lost to space. If this is correct, then the relative amounts of water and carbon dioxide emitted to the atmospheres were similar for Mars and the Earth. In contrast there is very little water on Venus compared to the amount of carbon dioxide. Why this is so is not certain but it seems quite likely that at the distance of Venus from the Sun the temperature was too high for water to condense from the primitive solar nebula so that Venus never had any crustal water to emit to the atmosphere. By contrast, carbon dioxide could condense chemically combined into carbonates which would release the gas when heated.

10.13: *The Moon photographed from various distances.*
(a) A view from Apollo 11 showing part of the hemisphere visible from the Earth to the left. This photograph shows clearly how the maria (the dark, relatively smooth areas) are predominantly found on the side of the Moon turned towards the Earth. Several systems of bright rays, centred on craters, are visible.
(b) Part of Sinus Medii, a small mare at the centre of the lunar disc as viewed from the Earth. North is upwards. The low elevation of the Sun (nearly 6° in the east but less than 1° in the west) emphasizes the undulations which occur in this apparently smooth mare area. The largest crater, Bruce, is about 6 km across.
(c) The forked Diamondback Rille in Mare Tranquillitatis. A footprint-shaped crater is an interesting feature at top left.
(d) The almost perfect outline of the traction cleats on the astronaut's boot implies that the lunar soil has a very fine texture. A much coarser material would not have allowed the appearance of such fine detail.
(e) A view across the rim of a 40 m diameter crater. The interior slopes are strewn with rocks and boulders. The crater rim casts shadows in the foreground which show how intensely black are shadows on the lunar surface.
(f) The lunar farside crater Tsiolkovsky, 150 km in diameter, which was discovered by Lunik 3 in 1959. The crater is remarkable for its very dark floor of mare-like material.
(NASA, Apollo 8, 10 and 11, USA)

(a)

(d)

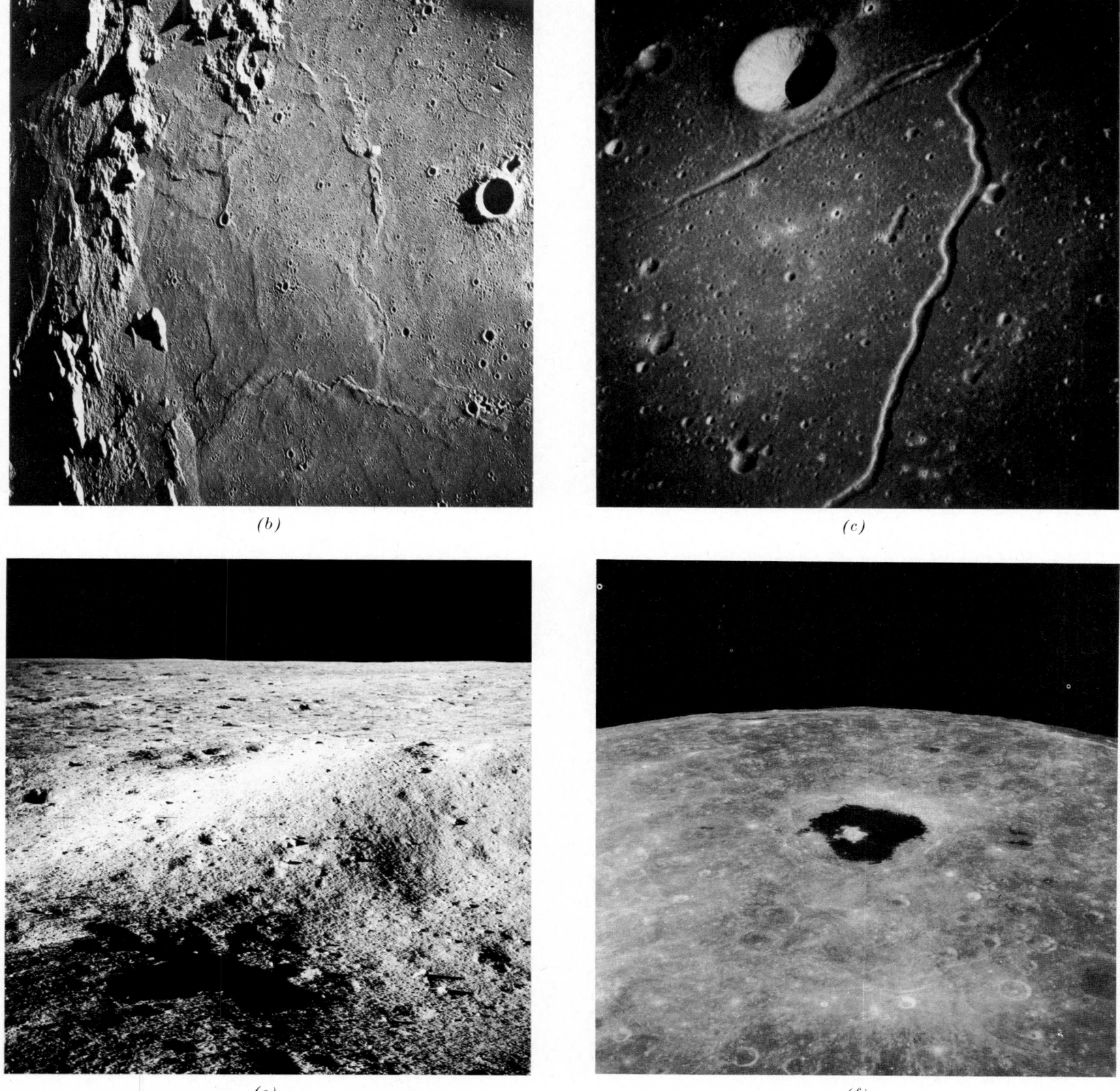

(b)

(c)

(e)

(f)

Table 10.5 : The satellites of Mars

	Phobos	Deimos
Discoverer	A. Hall	A. Hall
Year of discovery	1877	1877
Mean distance from Mars (km)	9380	23,500
Sidereal period (days)	0.318910	1.262441
Inclination of orbit to equator of Mars	1°.0	2°.0
Eccentricity of orbit	0.018	0.002
V magnitude at mean opposition	11.5	12.6
Size (km)	20 by 23 by 28	10 by 12 by 16

Satellites of Mars

Mars has two small satellites, PHOBOS and DEIMOS, details of which are given in table 10.5. They are irregularly shaped, very dark objects liberally covered with craters (figure 10.14). This gives them the appearance of modestly-sized *asteriods* but their almost circular orbits make it unlikely that they are simply captured asteroids. Several astronomers have suggested that they are the shattered remains of an earlier large single satellite of Mars. Each satellite moves in an orbit remarkably close to the planet and Phobos has the unique distinction of having an orbital period less than the rotation period of its primary. Because of this, Phobos appears to rise in the west and set in the east and, furthermore, does this twice every martian day. Both satellites are in synchronous rotation, always keeping the same face turned towards Mars.

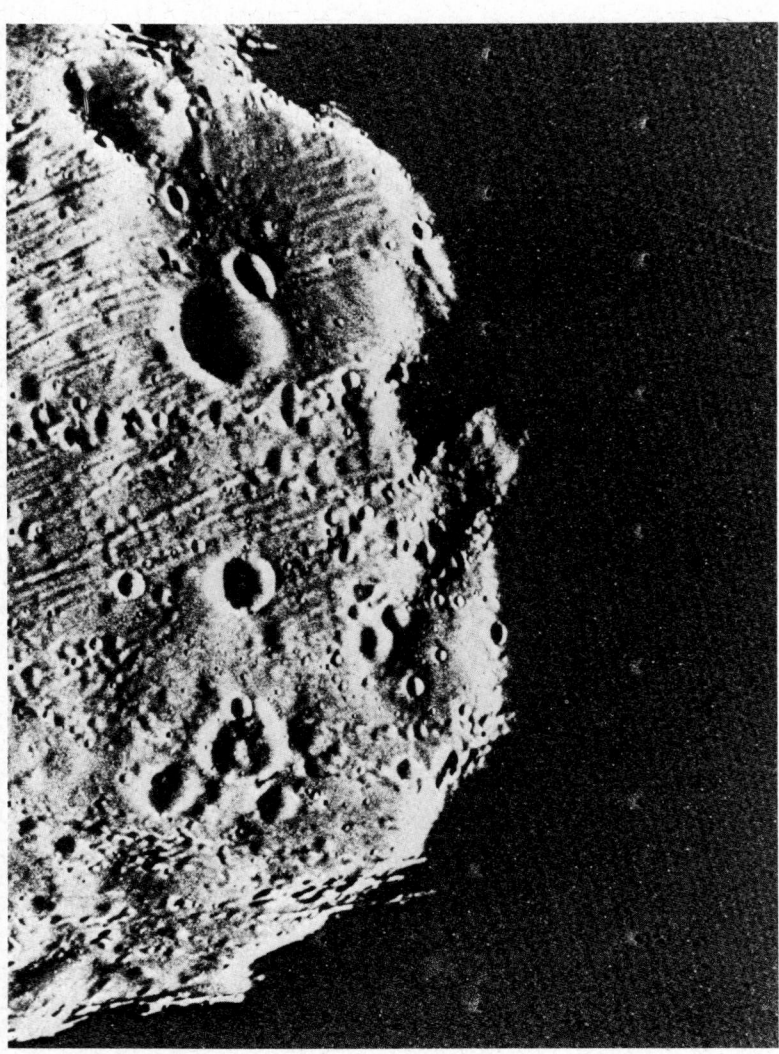

10.14: *Phobos, the inner and larger of the satellites of Mars, photographed from a distance of 880 km on 18 September 1976. The smallest object visible on the original photograph is about 40 m across. Phobos is heavily cratered, as astronomers expected, but surprisingly it also shows striations and chains of small craters. On Mars and other planets these are formed by secondary cratering from the debris ejected by a larger impact. The photograph shows an area about 18 km by 9 km – about a quarter of the surface. (NASA, Viking Orbiter 2, USA)*

10.15: *Mercury, showing its strong resemblance to the Moon.*
(a) A small bright-rayed crater 30 km in diameter, surrounded by dark areas.
(b) A cratered area also showing hummocky terrain and faults. The crater with a central peak just below centre is 60 km in diameter.
(c) Terraced craters probably of impact origin. The largest, with a double central peak, is 100 km across.
(d) Cratered and smooth plains. The crater at the centre of the left-hand edge is 85 km across and has a 12 km diameter crater on its floor close to the central peak.
(NASA, Mariner X, USA)

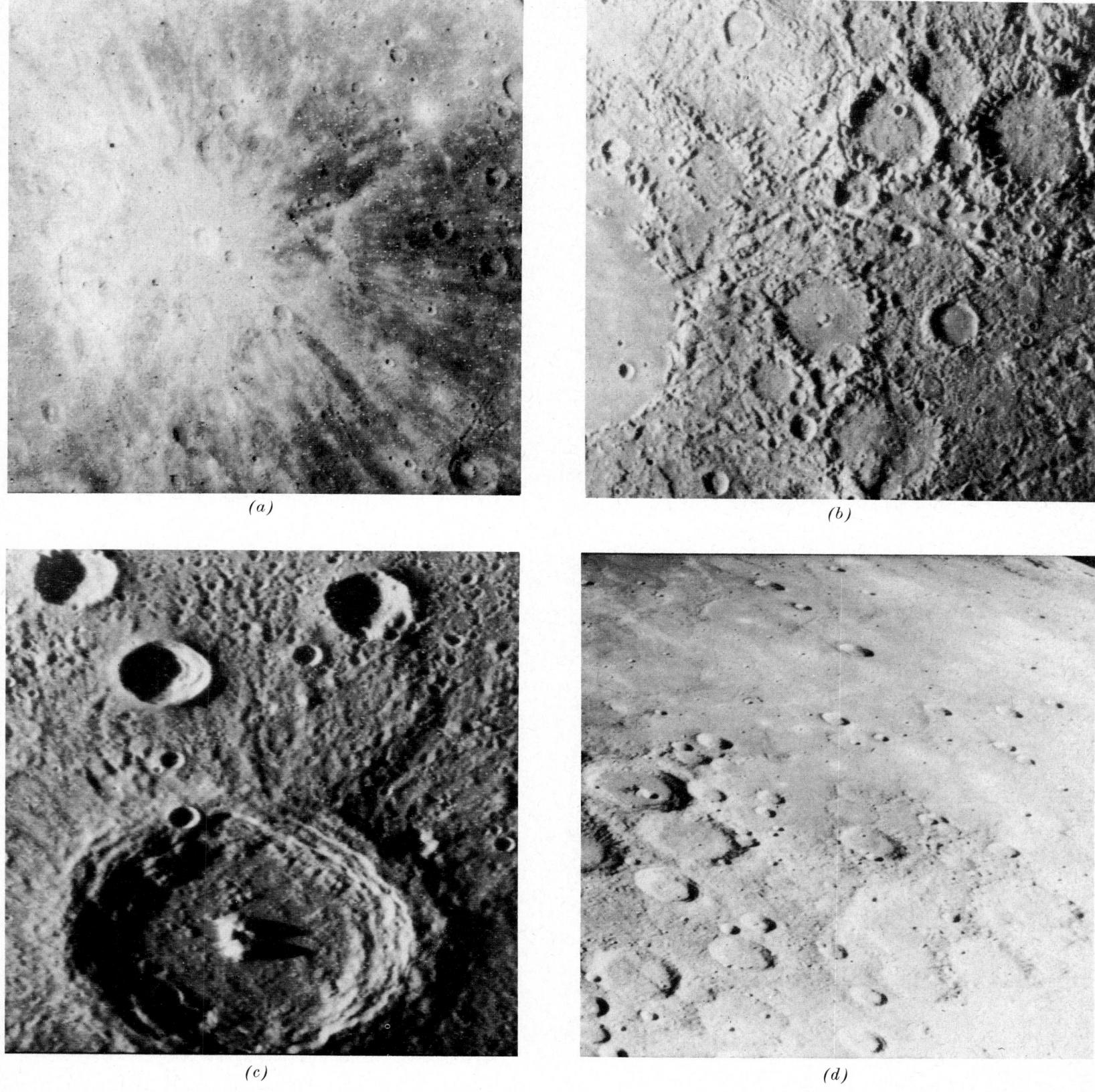

(a)

(b)

(c)

(d)

(a)

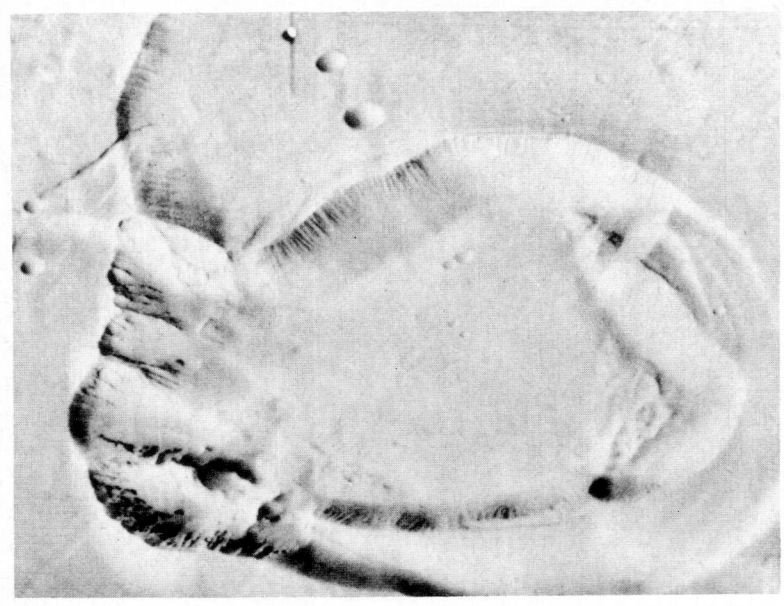

(b)

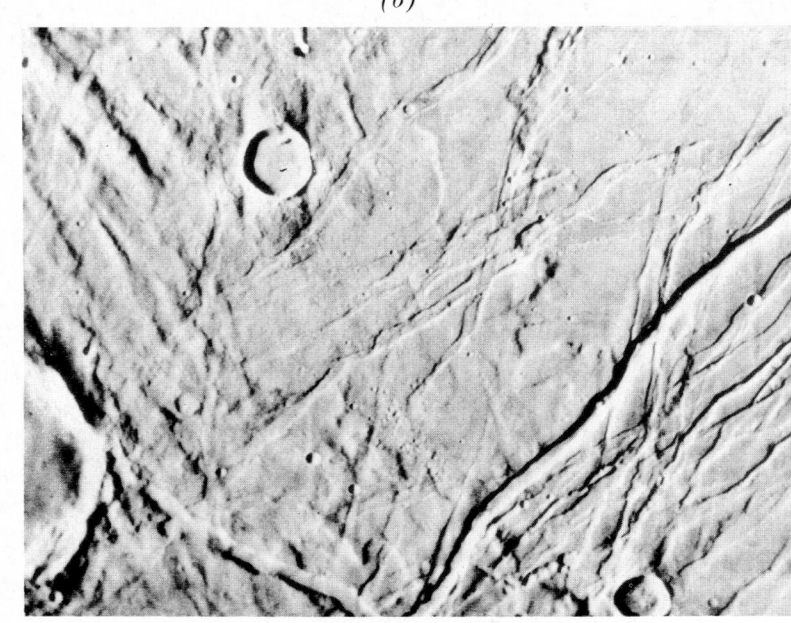

(a)

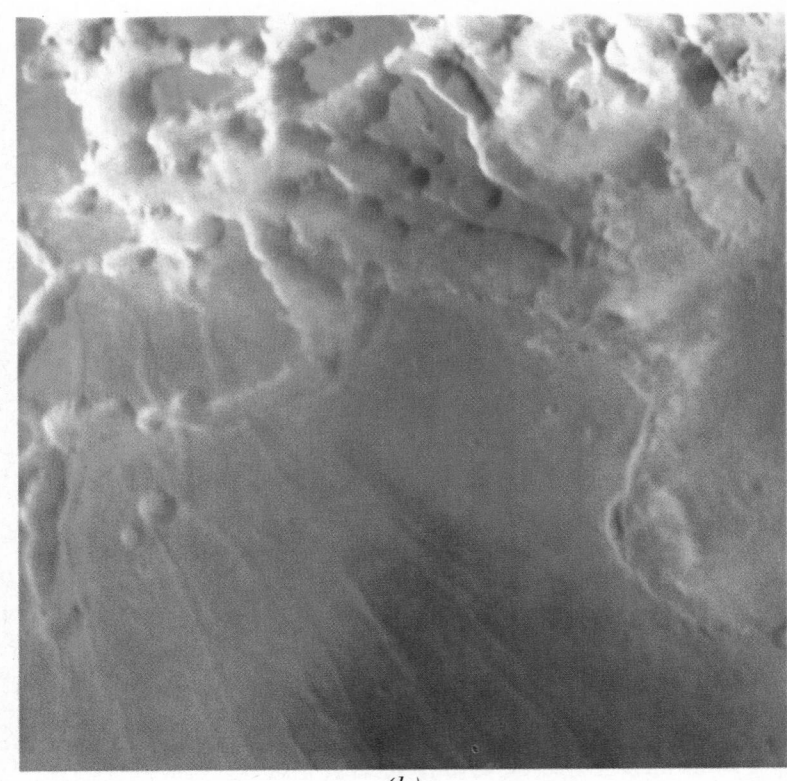

(b)

10.16: *Mars. (a) The 60 km diameter caldera (crater) of one of the volcanoes on Tharsis Ridge. The rim shows upper fluted cliffs and lower slopes of debris as well as evidence of multiple collapse. (b) A fine example of fractured and faulted terrain. (NASA, Mariner IX, USA)*

10.18: *Part of the Valles Marineris on Mars showing the branching pattern of tributary canyons that look as if they may have been formed by running water. Today the atmospheric pressure on Mars is so low that any extensive body of free liquid water on the surface would quickly evaporate. The Viking spacecraft have found evidence that early in Martian history there was a sufficiently dense atmosphere to make the rivers flow. (NASA, Mariner IX, USA)*

10.17: *Mars. (a) A view from the Viking 1 lander about 15 minutes before sunset. The low Sun (only a few degrees above the horizon) emphasizes the surface features, such as the shallow depression at the centre. Instruments on the Viking landers shows that Mars is seismically very quiet.*
(b) A Viking orbiter view of sunrise over Noctis Labyrinthus at the west end of Valles Marineris. The clouds in the canyons of this high plateau region may be due to water that condenses onto the canyon's east facing slopes in the late afternoon; it then vaporizes when warmed by early morning sunlight. (NASA, Viking 1, USA)

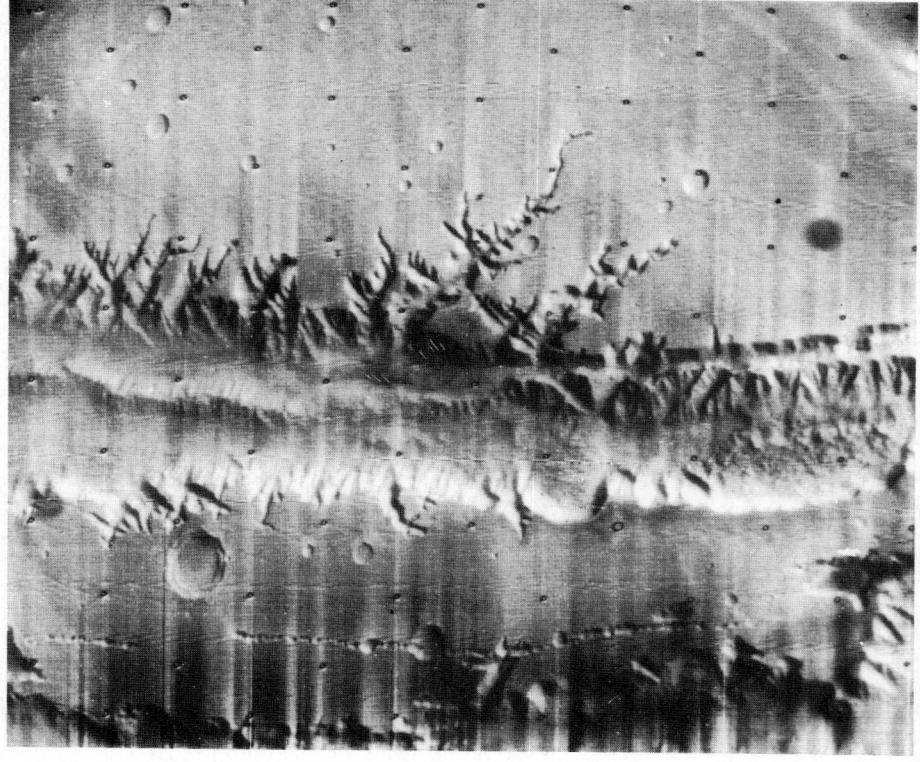

(a)

10.19: *Panoramas of the surface of Venus returned by Venera 9 (a) and 10 (b). Venera 9 landed on a slope so that the horizon appears only 100 m away whereas the Venera 10 horizon is quite distant. The two sites are 2200 km apart. At (a) both angular and rounded rocks can be seen, suggesting a geologically young setting, compared to the smoother and probably older landscape at (b).*

The fish-eye effect is introduced by the camera system and is not due to atmospheric refraction. The photographs have not been touched up and still show vertical stripes due to periodic interruptions in the picture transmission containing scientific and engineering data. (Novosti Press Agency, UK)

10.20: *Views of a photomosaic globe of Mars constructed from Mariner 9 photographs. (a) A view centred on the equator at longitude 120°W with north upwards. Olympus Mons, 600 km across, is the large circular area to the upper left with the central volcanic crater. To the lower right, Valles Marineris, the grand canyon of Mars, runs parallel to the equator. (b) The north and (c) south polar caps. The*

(a)

(b)

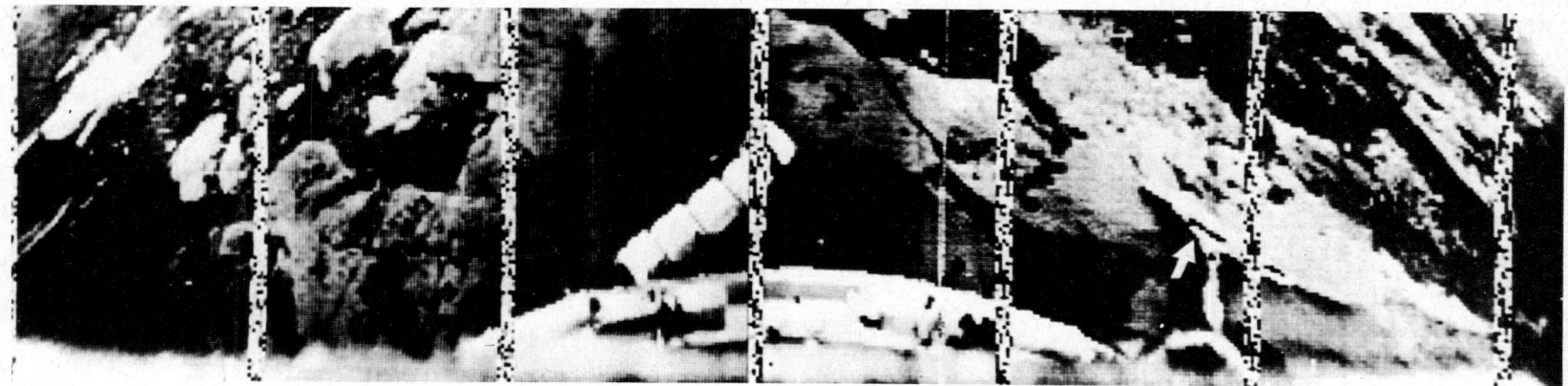

(b)

north polar cap shows a series of almost
concentric ridges which are thought to be the
edges of frozen layers around the pole.
Similar, though smaller, features are seen in
the southern cap. Measurements by the Viking
spacecraft in late 1976 suggest that the caps
have a permanent layer of water ice on which
lies a seasonal carbon dioxide layer which
grows during winter and contracts in summer.
(Jet Propulsion Laboratory, California, USA)

10.21: A radar map of Venus showing surface
features otherwise hidden by the thick clouds.
The mapping technique uses a combination of
Doppler shift and journey time to pinpoint
positions on the surface. Near the equator this
is not sufficiently accurate and a black band is
shown instead. (Jet Propulsion Laboratory,
California, USA)

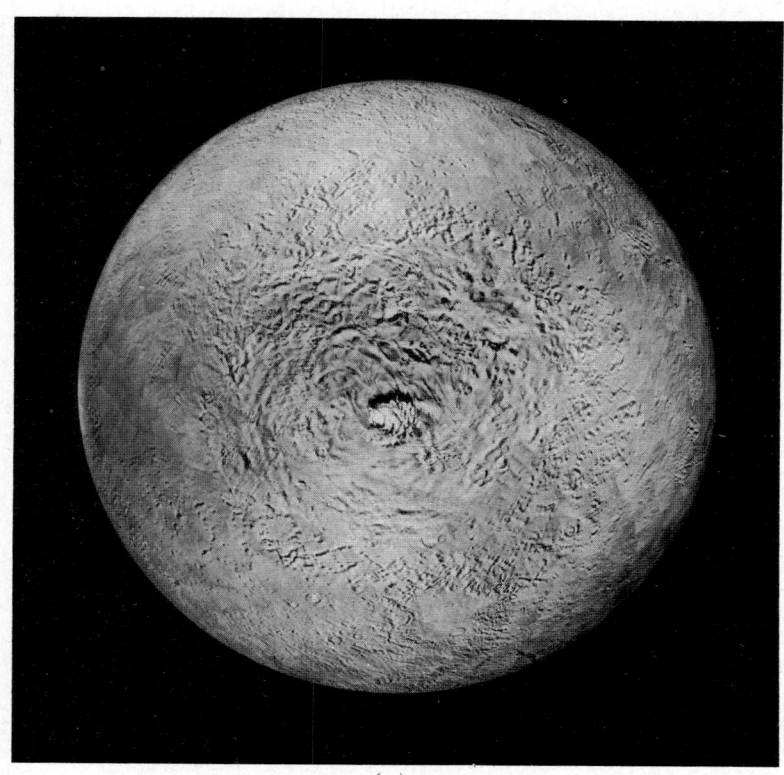

(c)

11. Giants of the Solar System

11.1: *Jupiter photographed from Earth under the best possible conditions. Comparison with Pioneer photographs on the following pages shows how spacecraft have revolutionized studies of Jupiter by the wealth of detail that they reveal. (International Planetary Patrol, USA)*

11.2: *The belts and zones in Jupiter's atmosphere. The photographs show that the boundaries between the belts and zones are not as regular as in this schematic diagram. The SEB frequently appears double, being divided in two by a narrow light zone, and at times a thin belt, the Equatorial Band, appears along the centre of the EqZ. A disc representing the Earth to the same scale is shown for comparison.*

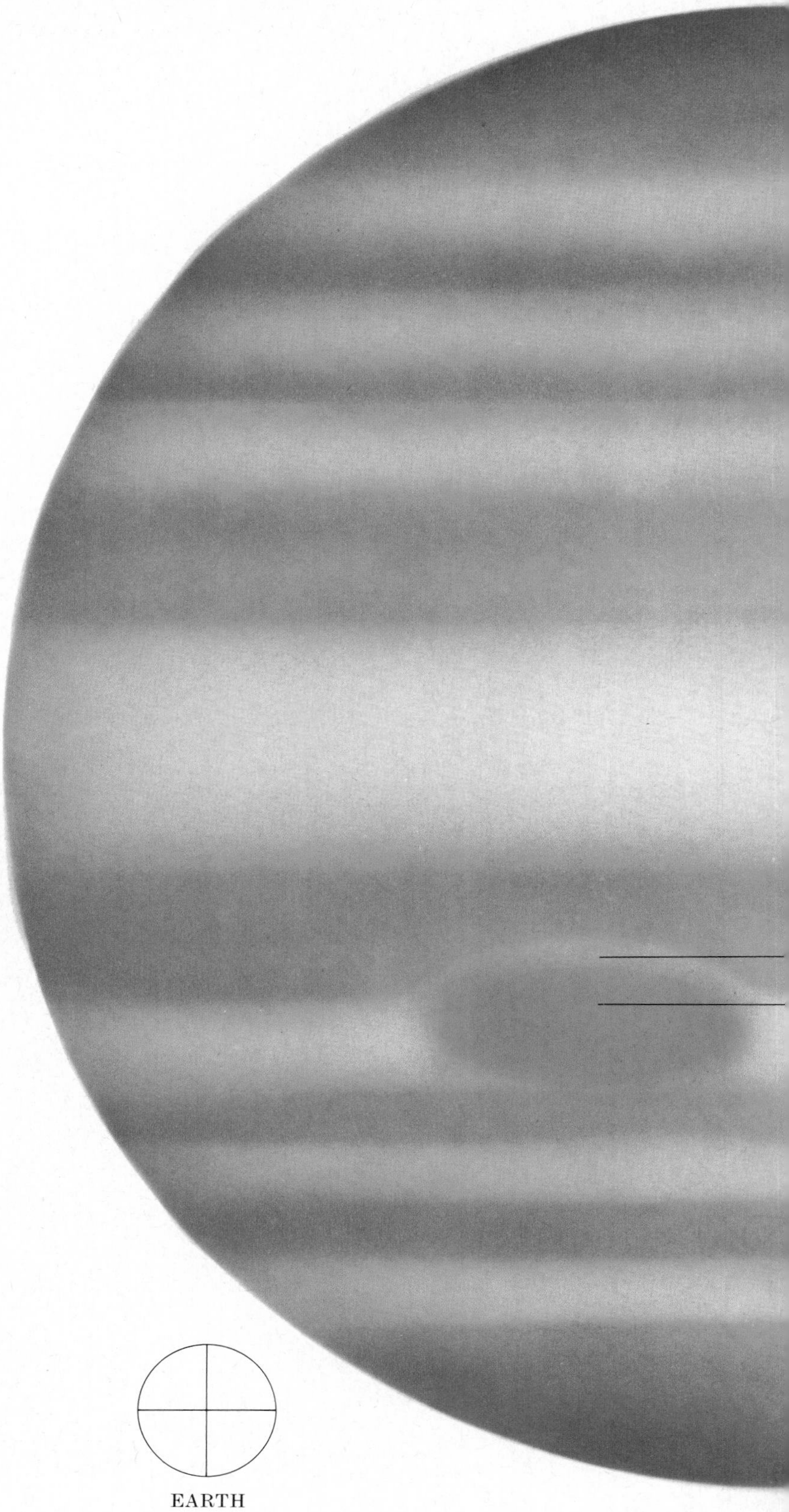

EARTH

N

NORTH POLAR REGION (NPR)

NORTH NORTH TEMPERATE ZONE (NNTZ)

NORTH NORTH TEMPERATE BELT (NNTB)

NORTH TEMPERATE ZONE (NTZ)

NORTH TEMPERATE BELT (NTB)

NORTH TROPICAL ZONE (NTrZ)

NORTH EQUATORIAL BELT (NEB)

EQUATORIAL ZONE (EqZ)

SOUTH EQUATORIAL BELT (SEB)
—— RED SPOT HOLLOW
—— GREAT RED SPOT
SOUTH TROPICAL ZONE (STrZ)

SOUTH TEMPERATE BELT (STB)

SOUTH TEMPERATE ZONE (STZ)

SOUTH SOUTH TEMPERATE BELT (SSTB)

SOUTH SOUTH TEMPERATE ZONE (SSTZ)

SOUTH POLAR REGION (SPR)

S

The outer Solar System

The inner planets and their satellites, described in the previous chapter, comprise less than half of one per cent of the planetary mass in the Solar System: more than 99.5 per cent of the planetary matter is found beyond the orbit of Mars. This region includes most of the *asteroids* and *comets*, the giant planets Jupiter, Saturn, Uranus and Neptune and their 30 or so satellites, plus the planet Pluto, a body more like a detached satellite than a companion planet to the giants. The giant planets differ markedly from the bodies of the inner Solar System. They have mean densities between 704 and 1600 kg m^{-3}, much less than the Earth's value of 5518 kg m^{-3}. They are comparatively large, with radii between 3.7 and 11.2 times that of the Earth, which is itself the largest terrestrial planet. All four rotate rapidly, with periods ranging from just under 10 up to 15 hours. This fast rotation produces a pronounced flattening, particularly of Jupiter and Saturn. Orbital elements for the outer planets have already been given in table 9.1, and physical elements are listed in table 11.1.

Jupiter

Jupiter, the nearest of the giant planets, is also the largest and most massive. It appears brighter than any other planet apart from Venus; at times it may even cast a shadow. Some of its surface features, and the four brightest satellites, can easily be seen in a small telescope, or even in binoculars. Jupiter's mass is more than twice that of all the other planets put together, and it is determined by observing the periods of Jupiter's satellites and the sizes of their orbits and applying Newton's *law of gravitation* to the data. It is not essential to use observations of a natural satellite; similar calculations can be performed for any body that passes near the planet. For example, the spacecraft Pioneers 10 and 11 flew past on 4 December 1973 and 3 December 1974 respectively. The radio transmitters on these craft broadcast on accurately known frequencies, so that by observing the *Doppler shift* in the received signal the velocity of the craft along the line of sight could be calculated. This velocity changed as each spacecraft was attracted by Jupiter's gravitational field and the Doppler shift measurements were then used to calculate the mass. These observations show that Jupiter has a mass 317.89 times that of the Earth. However, although Jupiter is such a massive planet we should note that it is still much smaller than the Sun, whose mass is 1047 times greater.

Jupiter is noticeably flattened. Its equatorial radius is 71 600 km, which is 11.23 times that of the Earth, whereas the polar radius is 67 300 km, about six per cent smaller. The volume of Jupiter is therefore 1330 times that of the Earth. Since its mass is only 318 times that of the Earth its mean density is lower: 1314 kg m^{-3} compared to 5518 kg m^{-3}. Because the density of Jupiter is so much lower than that of the Earth and the other terrestrial planets it cannot possibly have a similar composition. If Jupiter did have a terrestrial composition the higher internal pressure caused by its greater mass would result in a greater density than that of the Earth and not a lower one.

Jupiter observed

When we look at Jupiter we see only the uppermost cloud layers in its atmosphere. The composition of the atmosphere at this level can be determined spectroscopically (figure 11.1). The first reported observations of dark absorption bands in Jupiter's spectrum were made by Angelo Secchi in 1863. It was not until the early 1930s that the bands were shown, by Rupert·Wildt and T.Dunham, to be due to the presence of methane (CH_4) and ammonia (NH_3). Although these bands are the dominant feature of Jupiter's optical spectrum it is wrong to deduce that methane and ammonia are the main constituents of the atmosphere. Some spectral features are intrinsically much weaker than others. An important molecule with such intrinsically weak lines is molecular hydrogen (H_2). It was not until 1960 that these lines were identified, by C.C.Keiss, C.H.Corliss and H.K.Keiss, in Jupiter's spectrum. Although the lines are very weak, molecular hydrogen is undoubtedly the major constituent of Jupiter's atmosphere. This finding agrees with the low mean density, which requires the predominant constituents of Jupiter to be hydrogen and helium, the lightest elements.

Because of Jupiter's low atmospheric temperature, no lines of helium can be present in the optical spectrum and the element cannot be detected, if present, by means of Earth-based observations. Detection from an Earth-orbiting satellite is very difficult. It has been traditional to assume that helium is present in Jupiter's atmosphere in much the same proportion as in the Sun. Since almost all the hydrogen must be in molecular form this gives a number ratio $He/(He + H_2)$ of about 0.12. The first direct evidence of the presence of helium on Jupiter was the observation by Pioneer 10 of a spectral line in the ultraviolet at 58.4 nm, but it has not been possible to determine the abundance of helium from this observation.

Small amounts of four other molecules have also been detected; these are water (H_2O), ethane (C_2H_6), acetylene (C_2H_2) and phosphine (PH_3). There is also a trace of two isotopes of elements: deuterium (heavy hydrogen) and ^{13}C (carbon-13) have been detected in methane as CH_3D and $^{13}CH_4$ respectively. Further molecules are undoubtedly present but have not yet been detected because their lines in the accessible part of the spectrum are too weak. In particular it is expected that sulphur is present as the molecule hydrogen sulphide (H_2S).

Although Jupiter is completely cloud covered like Venus, the

Table 11.1: Physical elements of the outer planets

Some of the elements for Pluto are extremely uncertain and are enclosed in brackets.

	Jupiter	*Saturn*	*Uranus*	*Neptune*	*Pluto*
Symbol	♃	♄	♅	♆	♇
Reciprocal mass[1]	1047.357	3498.1	22 759	19 332	(3 000 000)
Mass[2] (Earth = 1)	317.893	95.147	14.54	17.23	(0.11)
Mass[2] (kg)	1.899×10^{27}	5.686×10^{26}	8.69×10^{25}	1.030×10^{26}	(6.6×10^{23})
Equatorial radius (km)	71 600	60 000	25 900	24 750	(3000)
Equatorial radius (Earth = 1)	11.23	9.41	4.06	3.88	(0.5)
Angular diameter at mean opposition	46″.86	19″.52	3″.60	2″.12	(0.22)
Ellipticity[1]	0.0637	0.102	0.01	0.0266	?
Mean density (kg/m³)	1314	704	1210	1670	?
Equatorial surface gravity[3] (m/s²)	22.88	9.05	7.77	11.00	(4.3)
Equatorial escape velocity (km/s)	59.5	35.6	21.22	23.6	(5.3)
Mean V magnitude at opposition	−2.55	0.75	5.52	7.84	14.90
Sidereal rotation period at equator[4]	9 hr 50 min	10 hr 14 min	10 hr 49 min	15 hr 48 min	6.3874 day
Inclination of equator to orbit	3° 05′	26° 44′	97° 55′	28° 48′	($\gtrsim 50°$)

Notes:
1. *These terms are defined at table 10.1. The reciprocal mass includes the atmosphere and satellites.*
2. *These masses exclude the satellites.*
3. *This includes the centrifugal term.*
4. *Jupiter and Saturn rotate somewhat more slowly away from the equator; see the text for details.*

visual appearance is quite unlike that of the almost featureless venusian clouds. Even in a small telescope much detail is visible and this detail is always changing. The most prominent features are a series of dark belts and light zones which run parallel to the planet's equator (figure 11.1). Since the Earth is never far from the plane of Jupiter's equator these appear straight when viewed from the Earth. They seem to be permanent features and have been given the names shown in figure 11.2. As this figure indicates, the belts and zones are found at equatorial and intermediate latitudes but not in the polar regions. Their colours vary somewhat but in general the zones are whitish or yellowish whereas the belts are more often brownish or reddish.

The belts and zones are not the only features visible on Jupiter. The better photographs taken from the Earth (figure 11.1) and those taken from spacecraft (figures 11.4–11.7, 11.9 and 11.10) show a wealth of intricate detail due to spots, festoons, plumes and waves. Colours such as grey, blue and black can be seen; although most features are pastel-coloured some show quite intense colours. Apart from the belts and zones, most of Jupiter's visible features have a limited lifetime and are seen to form and later disappear, typically after a few weeks or months.

The visible clouds, or at least their upper layer, are composed of small particles of frozen ammonia similar to the water-ice cirrus clouds of the Earth. These must be rather tenuous so that, at least near the centre of the planetary disc, it is possible to see through them to a second, more substantial cloud layer. The composition of this lower layer is not certain, but particles of ammonium hydrosulphide (NH_4SH) seem most likely. Various suggestions have been made for the source of the coloration. One is that the dominant yellowish colour is due to ammonium sulphide ((NH_4)$_2$S) in the ammonium hydrosulphide cloud layer. Other possibilities are the ammonium sulphide polymers and the element sulphur itself.

Spacecraft measurements have shown that the tops of the zones are about 9 K cooler than the tops of the belts and that the zones reach about 20 km higher in the atmosphere than the belts.

Although the observed features of Jupiter's disc have a limited lifetime they do, in general, last long enough for measurement of their rotation periods. Such measurements show that there are two distinct rotation systems. The equatorial zone, which extends to about latitudes 10° north and south, forms what is known as SYSTEM I and rotates about 360 km hr^{-1} more rapidly than the rest of the planet, which forms rotation SYSTEM II. Neither system rotates uniformly, but standard rotation periods have been assigned as follows:

System I : 9 hr 50 min 30.003 sec = 9.8416675 hr
System II : 9 hr 55 min 40.062 sec = 9.9277950 hr

These rotation periods define two systems for measuring longitude. On the Earth, which has a solid surface, longitude is measured

11.3: *Part of the optical spectrum of Jupiter with a comparison laboratory spectrum at each side. Jupiter reflects light from the Sun so its spectrum contains all the lines in the solar spectrum plus others, mainly due to methane and ammonia, caused by absorption in its own atmosphere. The lines are tilted because of Jupiter's rotation and the consequent variation of the Doppler shift between one limb of the planet (top of spectrum) and the other (bottom). (Lowell Observatory, Arizona,* USA*)*

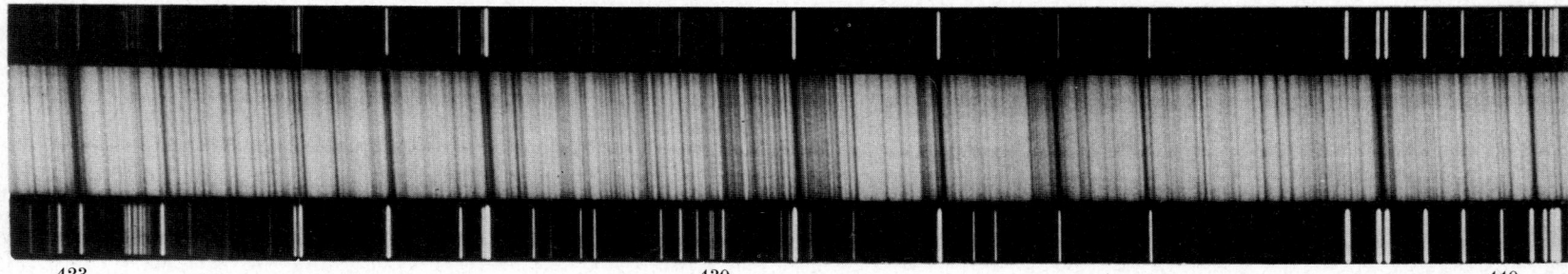

423   430   440
Wavelength (nm)

11.4: *Pioneer 10 took this photograph of Jupiter as it approached the planet, the first spacecraft to do so. The Great Red Spot at lower left has just been carried into daylight by the planet's rotation. Just to the right of centre is the dark shadow of the satellite Io, itself outside the picture to the right. (NASA, Pioneer 10, USA)*

11.5: *Jupiter viewed from below the equator so that detail around the south pole can be seen in a way that is not possible from the Earth. A plume trails leftwards from a bright nucleus in the equatorial zone (above centre). Material appears to rise in the nucleus, which is in the equatorial jet, and move to a higher level in the atmosphere where it trails behind the nucleus because of the slower rotation there. (NASA, Pioneer 11, USA)*

relative to a meridian fixed on the surface; the particular meridian is the one through Greenwich. Since Jupiter does not have a solid surface this procedure cannot be used. Instead a decision was made that at a certain time the central meridian of Jupiter was to be defined as having longitude zero. Using System I the longitude of the central meridian must then increase by $360°/9.8416675 = 36°.579$ per hour, or by $0°.60965$ per minute. After one complete rotation period the longitude of the central meridian has increased by $360°$ so that the meridian of zero longitude is again the central meridian. In System II the increase in longitude is $36°.262$ per hour, or $0°.60436$ per minute. Tables are published that show the longitude of the central meridian in both Systems I and II at regular intervals; the longitude at any other time can then be readily calculated. The longitude of an actual feature on Jupiter can be determined by noting the time at which it transits (i.e. crosses the central meridian) and then looking up the longitude in the tables. In the equatorial zone, System I is used; elsewhere on the planet it is System II. A feature that rotates with exactly the standard period for its appropriate system has the same longitude at every transit. If it rotates more slowly, the longitude increases from one transit to the next; rotation faster than the standard period results in a decreasing longitude. In general, features on Jupiter do show a changing longitude because they do not rotate at exactly the standard rate. The actual rotation period can be easily calculated from the change in longitude from one transit to the next;

for most features the rotation periods are not constant but change during their lifetime.

The existence of these different rotation periods, and particularly that of the EQUATORIAL JET which constitutes System I, shows conclusively that the visible surface of Jupiter does not form a solid surface. As discussed below it is not even certain that Jupiter has a solid surface at all, but if it does its rotation period is most likely equal to that of the magnetosphere; this is determined from radio measurements described below. In 1962 a SYSTEM III rotation period of 9 hr 55 min 29.37 sec was adopted for the standard radio period. Unfortunately more recent measurements have shown this value to be incorrect; the best measurement is now 9 hr 55 min 29.75 sec. This means that a feature which rotates with this latter period will, in System III, drift to greater longitudes at a rate of 3°.6 per year. Since the magnetic field of Jupiter is generated in the central regions of the planet, the rotation period of these regions is likely to be equal to the radio period.

11.6: *Jupiter viewed from above latitude 49° N showing detail smaller than 300 km in size. The sharp edges are the boundaries of the picture as transmitted to the Earth. Going from the South Tropical Zone (at lower right) to within 7° of the north pole the cloud bands have an increasingly complex structure at higher latitudes. Around the poles the alternating bands and zones of the tropical and temperate zones give way to disorganized mottlings. Light circular spots may be hurricane-like storms. (NASA, Pioneer 11, USA)*

11.7: *Part of Jupiter's northern hemisphere photographed less than eight hours after the closest approach by the Pioneer 11 spacecraft. Along the bottom is the Pacific standard time and date at which the picture was taken. (NASA, Pioneer 11, USA)*

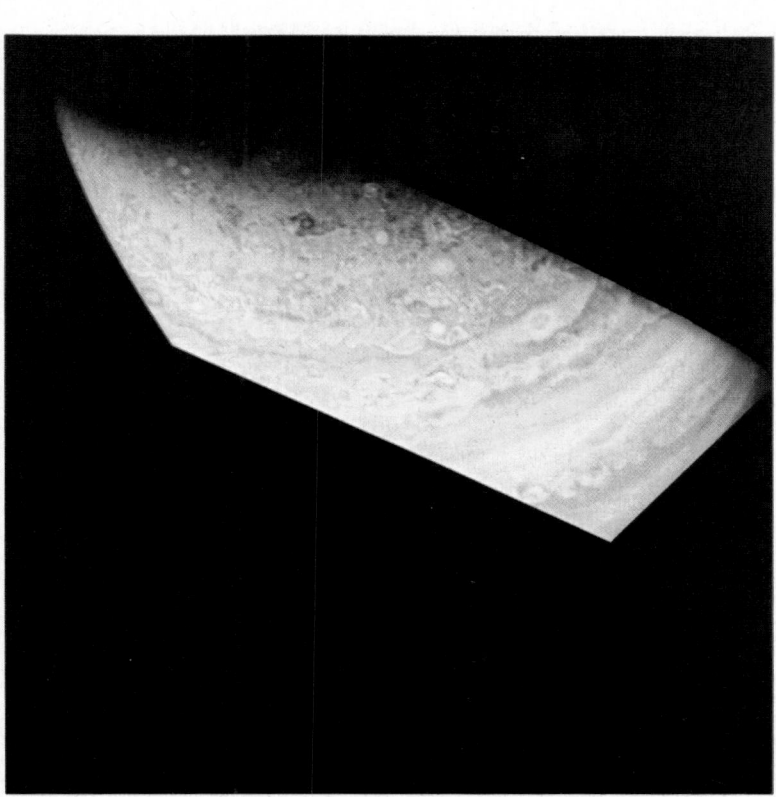

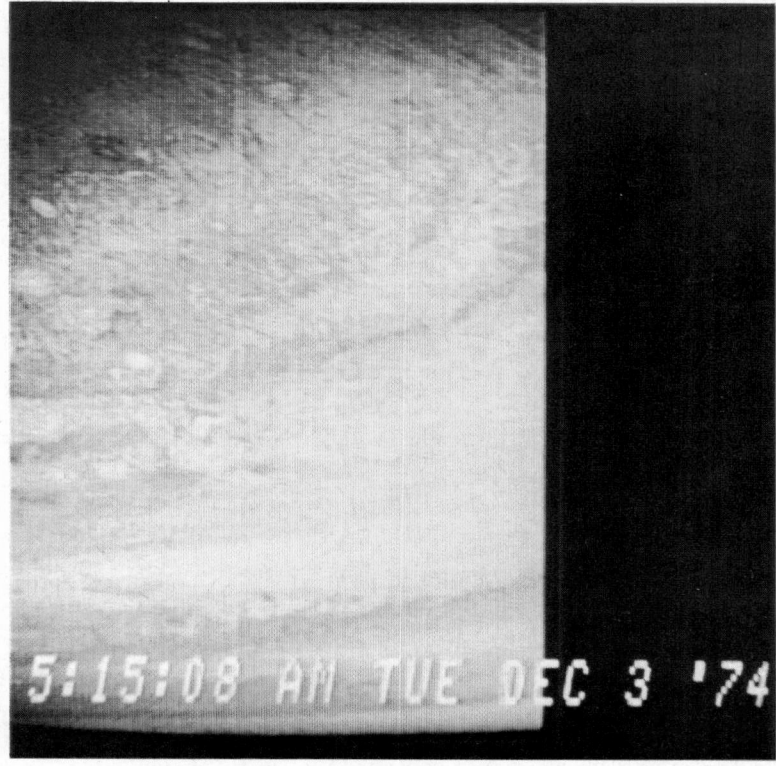

5:15:08 AM TUE DEC 3 '74

Great Red Spot

The most prominent and permanent feature of the visible surface of Jupiter is the GREAT RED SPOT (figure 11.9). It is an elongated area of variable size; at its largest, in the 1880s, it was about 38 500 km long by 13 800 km wide and had a surface area about equal to that of the Earth. The spot lies in the south tropical zone but protrudes somewhat into the latitudes occupied by the south equatorial belt, to form what is called the RED SPOT HOLLOW in this belt. In 1878 it first became really prominent when it developed from a pink oval object into a brick red area. This startling red colour only lasted until 1882 when the spot began to fade. Since then the spot itself has from time to time been invisible but has always been recognizable by its characteristic hollow, which has persisted at all times. This hollow has been found on a drawing by Schwabe made in 1831. It is probably on another drawing made by Robert Hooke in 1664 and was recorded intermittently between then and 1713. The spot revives from time to time, as, for example, it did in 1939. Typical of the changes in the spot are those observed during the years 1962–9. It was very prominent in 1962 and 1963 and remained prominent until 1965. In 1966 it started to fade and by February 1968 it was very weak. It then suddenly began to strengthen and quickly resumed its prominence of four years earlier.

The most remarkable feature of the spot is the fact that it does not appear to be fixed to a solid surface. Measurements of its longitude reveal that its rotation period is not constant so that relative to its mean position it has wandered over a wide range of longitude, amounting to about 1200° (more than three revolutions) during the last century. The latitude of the spot has always remained nearly fixed at about 22° south; it deviates by up to 1° in latitude. Various associated features have been seen in addition to the hollow in the south equatorial belt. For example, in January 1966 a small dark spot was seen moving along the edge of the south temperate belt. It approached the red spot along its southern side and then circulated round it, with a period of about nine days, about one and a half times before disappearing. During 1967 four similar spots appeared although at least two of these came from the south equatorial belt. These spots had periods of about 12 days. They were only seen to move part way round the red spot.

The spot has a lower temperature than its surroundings and there is less gas above it. These differences show that it extends about 8 km above the surrounding cloud tops. Material is observed to rise in the centre of the spot, move outwards and then descend at the edge. During its outward motion the material also moves round the spot somewhat in an anti-clockwise direction.

The nature of the spot is not known with certainty. At one time, many astronomers thought that it was some kind of solid island floating in a dense atmosphere. It is now thought that no solid substance can have a sufficiently low density to float in the upper atmosphere of Jupiter. If an island were to have a larger vertical extent so that it reached down to a region of much higher density it would be disrupted and would also move towards the equator. As a

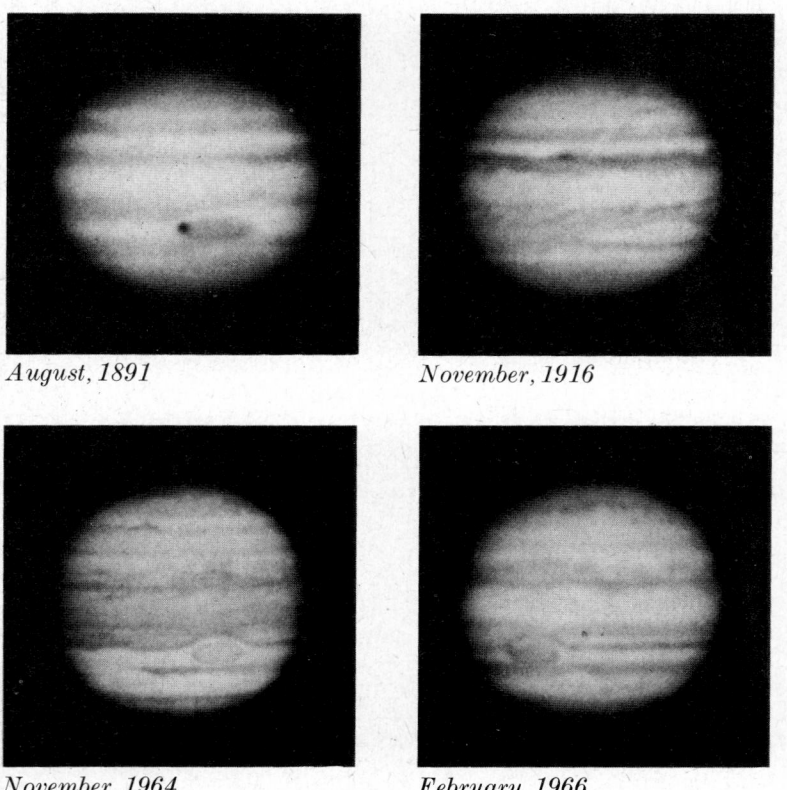

August, 1891   *November, 1916*

November, 1964   *February, 1966*

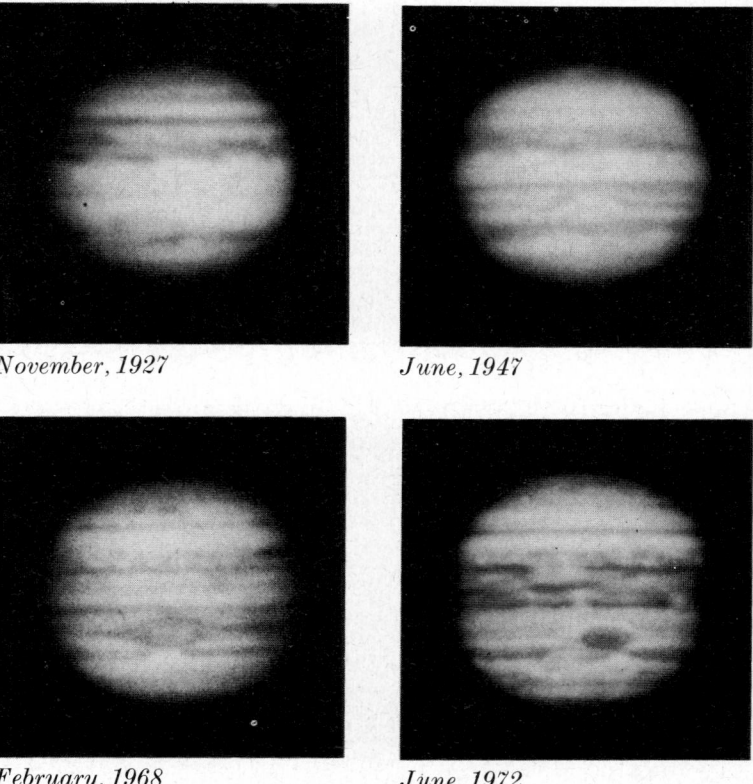

November, 1927   *June, 1947*

February, 1968   *June, 1972*

result the theory of a floating island is no longer accepted.

A more recent suggestion is that the spot is the top of a TAYLOR COLUMN. This is a stagnant column of fluid that can result when an atmospheric flow is unable to surmount some topographic feature. Because of the spot's motion in longitude this feature cannot be attached to a rigid solid surface. In any case it is believed that Jupiter has at most only a small solid core. A further suggestion is that the cause of the column is some local feature of the magnetic field or of the internal convective motions. There are many objections to this theory and it is not even certain that such a column would form in Jupiter's atmosphere, even if there were a suitable topographic feature to disturb the atmospheric flow.

The most widely accepted explanation of the spot is that it is the vortex of a long-lived cyclonic storm – a suggestion first made by Gerard Kuiper. For this theory to be acceptable it is necessary that the lifetime of such a cyclone or eddy be longer than the 300 or so years for which the spot is known to have existed. Recent calculations suggest that major changes in the circulation of Jupiter's atmosphere take at least 300 000 years. If the great red spot is a long-lived eddy as suggested, then it would last about this long, which is indeed longer than the observed minimum age of 300 years. This theory also explains other spots in the same way. These smaller spots would have shorter lifetimes in accordance with observations.

11.8: *Jupiter photographed from the Earth showing how the belts and the Great Red Spot change over the years. (Lowell Observatory, Arizona,* USA*)*

Energy balance of Jupiter

The apparent magnitude of Jupiter varies to some extent because of its varying distance from the Earth, but this is not sufficient to explain all the observed changes. Since 1862, the mean opposition magnitude has ranged over 0.45 magnitudes so that, at the brightest opposition, Jupiter was reflecting 50 per cent more light than at the faintest. This means that, as the patterns of the clouds of Jupiter vary, the ALBEDO, which is the fraction of the incident sunlight which they reflect, also varies. The albedo also depends on the wavelength of the light or other radiation being measured, but in the visual range it is typically between 30 and 50 per cent.

The solar energy that is not reflected by Jupiter's clouds is absorbed by the atmosphere. If just this amount of absorbed energy were re-emitted then Jupiter would have an effective temperature of 105 K, i.e. it would radiate the same amount of energy as a *black body* of this temperature and of the same size. Most of the energy is radiated at infrared wavelengths. Measurements show that the effective temperature is actually 125 K, so that Jupiter is radiating twice as much energy as it absorbs from the Sun. There is therefore an internal energy source of equal power to the absorption of solar energy. This energy source has important effects on theories both of the internal structure of Jupiter and on the structure of its atmosphere. Spacecraft measurements show that the day and night sides of Jupiter have the same temperature. This implies that the absorbed solar energy is carried to the night side of Jupiter by the planet's rotation much more quickly than energy is lost from the atmosphere, in agreement with theoretical calculations.

The belts, zones and other features of Jupiter's atmosphere show that its structure varies from point to point and from time to time. We can however first consider the average structure of the atmosphere and ignore the local variations (weather) and the details of the dynamical processes. Calculations of a standard model atmosphere can then be made.

About 45 per cent of the incident energy is reflected and more than 10 per cent is absorbed fairly high in the atmosphere so that slightly more than 40 per cent must be absorbed by the clouds in the main body of the atmosphere, which is known as the TROPOSPHERE. A similar amount of energy comes from the internal source and enters the troposphere at its base. In the upper troposphere the energy is transported by radiation, whereas in the deep atmosphere the main transport mechanism is convection.

The theoretical models of the atmospheric structure are subject to many uncertainties because the physical processes involved are not fully understood and the chemical composition is not completely known. Figure 11.12 shows the way in which temperature, pressure and density vary with depth according to one set of calculations. Despite the uncertainties involved, these results probably give a good idea of the overall atmospheric structure.

As mentioned above, the visible surface of Jupiter consists of two cloud layers. The upper layer of ammonia cirrus has its base where the temperature is about 150 K and extends upwards to a

11.9: *The Great Red Spot contained in the broad whitish South Tropical Zone. The spiral structure within the spot suggests an anticlockwise flow of material. The white spot near the bottom right is over half the size of the Earth. (NASA, Pioneer 11, USA)*

11.10: *Striking views like this are unobtainable from the Earth. The north pole is at the top, roughly on the terminator (the boundary between the day and night sides). The Great Red Spot is at lower right and there is a plume at lower left. (NASA, Pioneer 11, USA)*

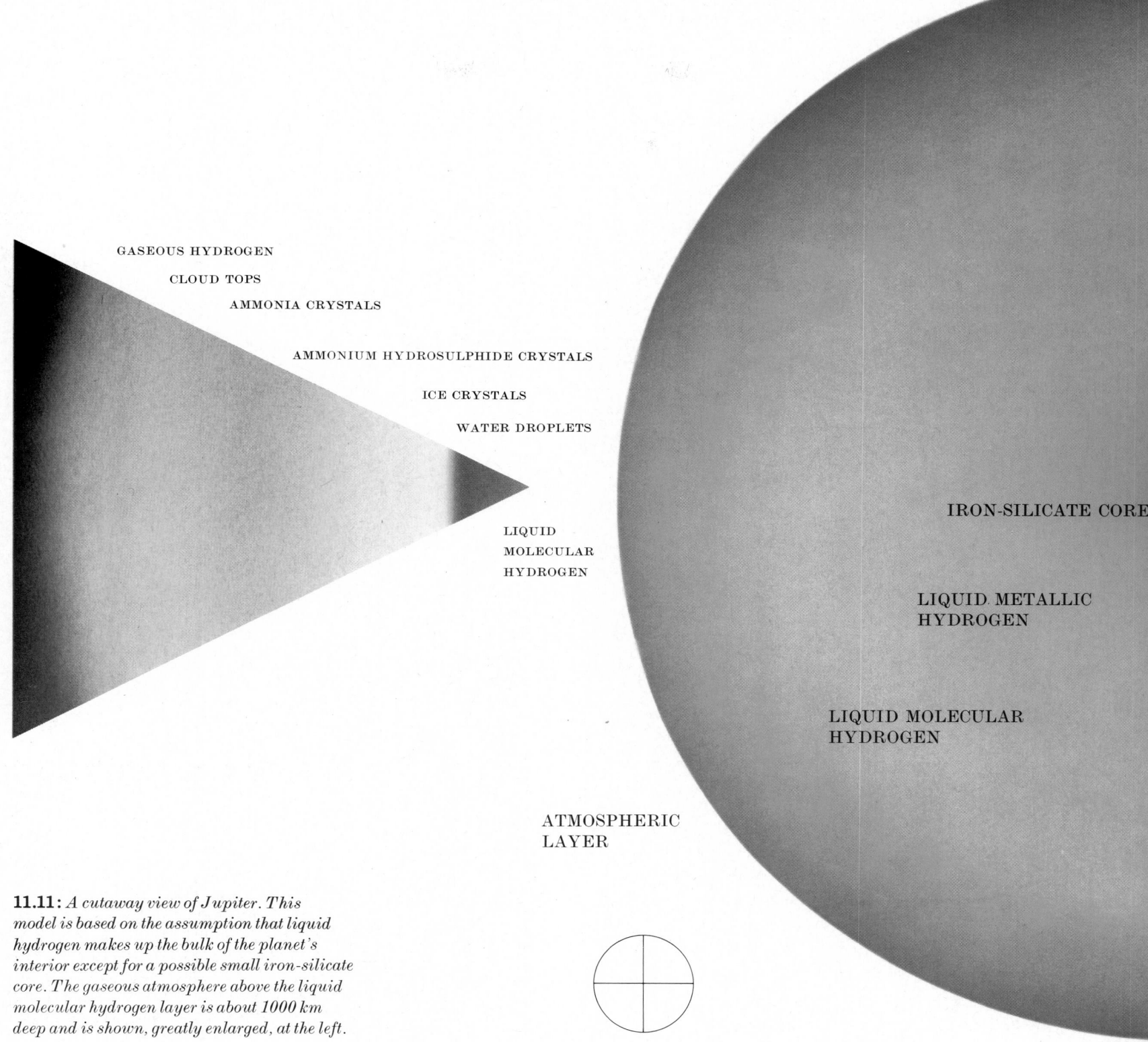

GASEOUS HYDROGEN

CLOUD TOPS

AMMONIA CRYSTALS

AMMONIUM HYDROSULPHIDE CRYSTALS

ICE CRYSTALS

WATER DROPLETS

LIQUID
MOLECULAR
HYDROGEN

IRON-SILICATE CORE

LIQUID METALLIC
HYDROGEN

LIQUID MOLECULAR
HYDROGEN

ATMOSPHERIC
LAYER

11.11: *A cutaway view of Jupiter. This model is based on the assumption that liquid hydrogen makes up the bulk of the planet's interior except for a possible small iron-silicate core. The gaseous atmosphere above the liquid molecular hydrogen layer is about 1000 km deep and is shown, greatly enlarged, at the left.*

EARTH

temperature of 106 K – the point of zero depth in figure 11.12. The position of the base of the lower cloud layer is less certain; somewhere in the layers where the temperature lies between 200 and 225 K seems likely.

The two-dimensional structure of belts and zones strongly suggests that the thickness of the upper cloud layer varies considerably over the disc. The zones are known to reach about 20 km higher in the atmosphere than the belts. Jupiter's atmosphere is driven by the internal energy source rather than by the incident solar energy. This heat enters the atmosphere from below and sets up convection currents in the atmospheric material. As a result of the Pioneer missions, astronomers believe that the rising, heated material reaches the visible surface in the bright zones, where it cools, and then descends in one of the adjacent dark belts. Because of the planet's rapid rotation the regions of ascending and descending material form into regular belts and zones of constant latitude rather than into an irregular pattern of small cells, as happens on the Sun for example. An internally driven, rapidly rotating atmosphere such as Jupiter's is inherently more stable than a more slowly rotating atmosphere that is driven by the incident sunlight such as is the case for the Earth's atmosphere. There is also no variation in temperature during the day and night to disturb the atmosphere. As a result, large-scale changes in structure will take much longer on Jupiter than on the Earth.

11.12: *The structure of the upper parts of Jupiter's atmosphere showing the probable positions of the cloud layers. This is probably the best currently available theoretical model. The depth is measured from the tropopause, the level at which the temperature is a minimum.*

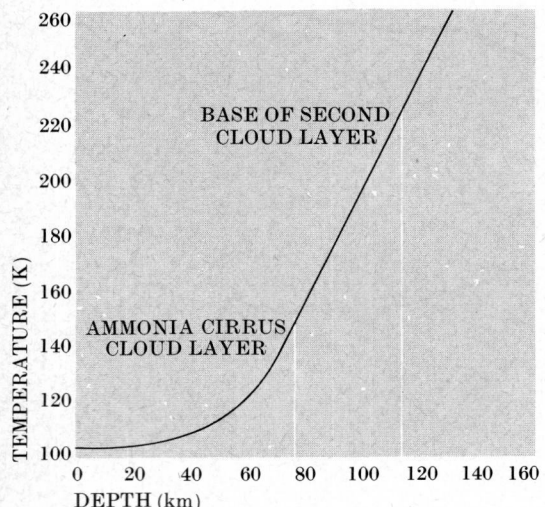

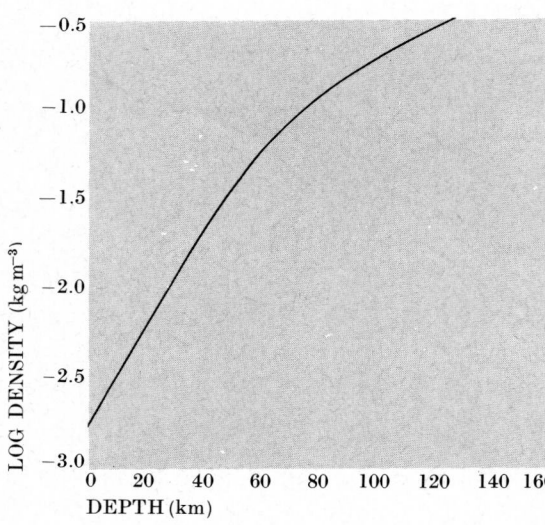

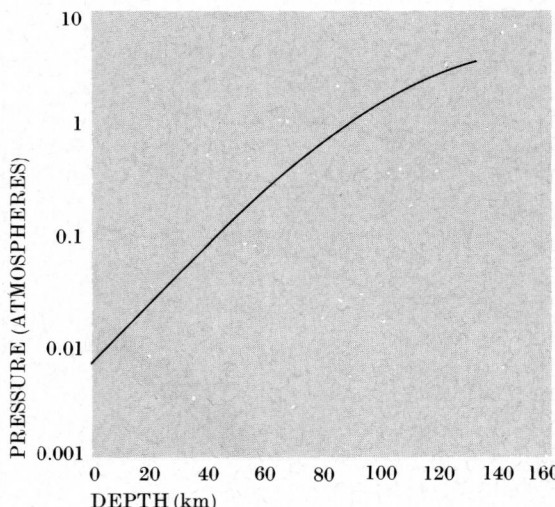

Inside Jupiter

Direct measurements of the conditions deep inside Jupiter are of course impossible. Calculations of these conditions are, however, constrained in a number of ways. The low mean density, only 1.3 times that of water, implies that the composition must be very different from the *terrestrial planets*, with their typical mean density of five times that of water. Jupiter must be composed almost entirely of hydrogen and helium, since only these two elements can have such a low density at planetary temperatures and pressures. By laboratory standards, although not by astronomical standards, the temperatures and pressures inside Jupiter are very high and it is necessary to predict the properties of the materials making up the planet. It is less difficult to do this for hydrogen and helium than for other elements. Any theoretical model of the interior of Jupiter must explain the origin of the large internal heat source and the way in which the energy is transported to the surface. Because of the relative simplicity of the properties of the material in Jupiter, and this need to include the internal heat source, it is likely that the understanding of Jupiter's internal structure will soon improve to such an extent that it will be quite accurately known. The interior of Jupiter may then be better understood than any other planet – except possibly the Earth!

One theory for the origin of Jupiter is that it formed in a similar manner to a star. In the nebula from which the Sun condensed, there was a second region where the density was sufficiently greater than average for the material to collapse under its own gravitation. Because of the very low mass, the internal temperature never became hot enough to start nuclear fusion. For a condensation of the mass of Jupiter, the temperature would soon reach a maximum of about $40\,000\,K$ after which the body would cool rapidly. It seems that it would reach a state with the present radius and energy production of Jupiter after about 4×10^9 years, which is just the age of the Solar System.

An alternative theory assumes that there is a high density core with a composition similar to that of the terrestrial planets. This core must have formed first and then built up a body the size of Jupiter by gravitational capture of interplanetary gas. This gas would be part of the nebula from which the Sun formed and as such would presumably have the same composition as the Sun, i.e. almost entirely hydrogen and helium.

In the liquid and solid states, hydrogen and helium can only mix together in certain proportions. Because of this there may be separate layers of hydrogen-rich material and helium-rich material inside Jupiter; the details depend on the central temperature. One theoretical model, which has only hydrogen-rich layers, except for a possible dense core, is shown in figure 11.11. Another possibility is a helium-rich core surrounded by a layer rich in metallic hydrogen above which is a molecular-hydrogen-rich atmosphere. Again there may be a dense heavy-element core. In each layer, energy is carried outwards by convection, whereas across the boundaries the energy flow is by conduction.

The most probable source of the internal energy is gravitation.

If Jupiter contracted by just one millimetre per year, then, with a central temperature of $10\,000\,K$, the observed excess luminosity would result. Alternatively there may be gravitational separation of the hydrogen and helium; this can give the present luminosity with a lower temperature. It is very unlikely that simple cooling, by radiating the heat acquired during formation, is a major contributor to the energy production. Table 11.2 shows the results of one calculation of the pressure and density in the interior of Jupiter. Like all the theories described here, these results are uncertain and should be treated with some caution, but they do give the probable general trend of the conditions inside Jupiter.

Table 11.2: A typical model of Jupiter's interior

The values in this table give the probable general trend of the conditions inside Jupiter.

Radius (km)	Fractional mass	Pressure[1] (Mbars)	Density (kg m⁻³)
69 000	0.99	0.004	30
65 000	0.97	0.24	400
60 000	0.90	1.1	700
55 000[2]	0.80	2.5	1100
50 000	0.70	4.5	1600
45 000	0.60	7.6	1900
40 000	0.40	11	2300
35 000	0.30	15	2600
30 000	0.20	20	3000
25 000	0.10	24	3400
20 000	0.06	28	3700
15 000	0.03	32	3900
10 000	0.01	35	4100
5 000	0.001	36	4200
0	0	37	4200[3]

Notes:
1. 1 Mbar = 10^6 bar $\simeq 10^6$ atmospheres.
2. *The transition between molecular hydrogen and metallic hydrogen probably occurs at about this radius.*
3. *This value for the central density does not include a possible dense core.*

Jupiter's magnetic field

In 1955, when radio astronomy was still a comparatively new science, astronomers near Washington DC were looking for previously undiscovered radio sources of small apparent size. Their telescope picked up strong waves at a frequency of 22.2 MHz, corresponding to a wavelength of 13.5 metres. At first they attributed these radio waves to terrestrial sources such as faulty car-ignition systems. The interference persisted and continued observations showed that the source moved relative to the stars and that it was in fact Jupiter. Planets were not then considered likely radio sources and so it was several months before this identification was made – although Jupiter was shining brightly overhead for all to see. The nature of the observed radio waves indicated the existence of a magnetic field and energetic particles around Jupiter. Both of these were first directly observed by the Pioneer 10 spacecraft in late 1973.

11.13: *The effect of the satellite Io on the decametre radiation from Jupiter. The diagram shows Jupiter and the orbit of Io to scale. The majority of the stronger source B emission events and most of the source A events occur when Io is within a few degrees of the positions indicated.*

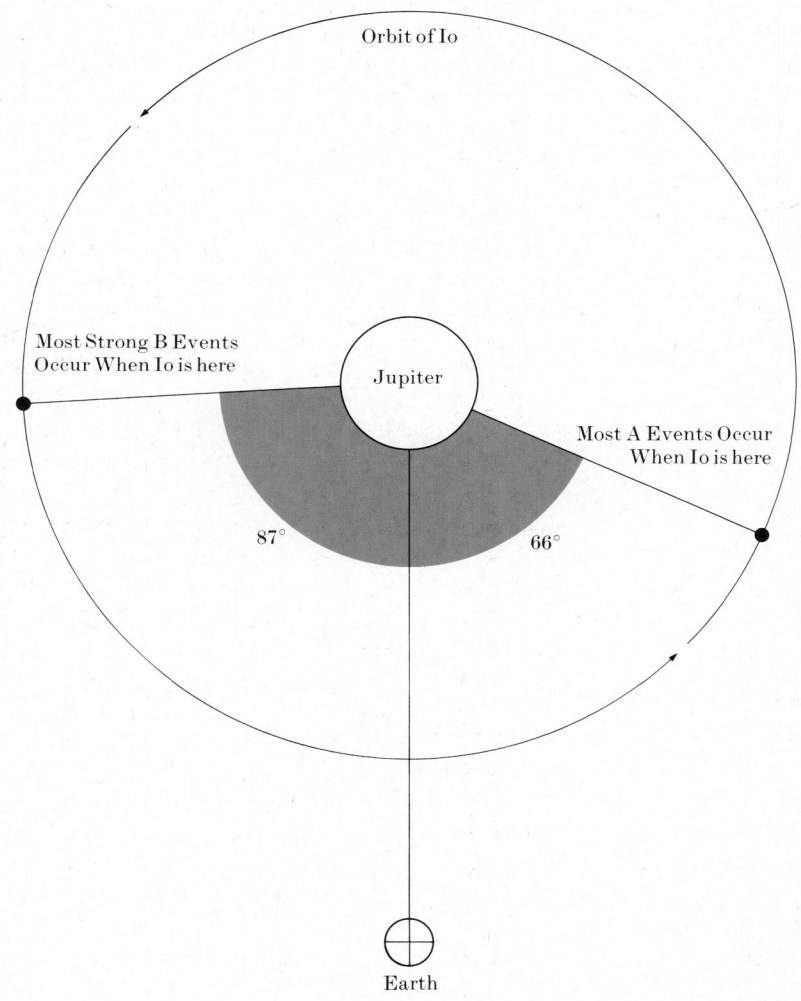

A description of the RADIO EMISSION FROM JUPITER can be divided conveniently into three parts. At wavelengths shorter than 7 cm the emission is mainly thermal in origin and comes from the body of the planet. At longer wavelengths, the emission is primarily non-thermal and has two clearly distinguishable components. One is a centimetre and decimetre component, with wavelengths below about one metre, and the other is a decametre component, which is important at wavelengths longer than 7.5 metres.

The DECAMETRE RADIATION component has been detected at frequencies between 450 kHz and 39.5 MHz, i.e. wavelengths between 670 and 7.5 metres. At the longer end of this wavelength range the radio waves cannot penetrate the Earth's own ionosphere and the observations have been made from Earth-orbiting satellites. Unlike the steady emission below one metre, the decametre radiation is emitted sporadically in short intense bursts of radio noise. The emission is strongest around 10 MHz (30 m). Many bursts occur during a period, usually between several minutes and several hours long, to form a JOVIAN NOISE STORM. Between the storms are quiescent periods which may last for hours, days or weeks. Most of the individual bursts last between 0.5 and 5 seconds and are known as L BURSTS. Shorter (S BURSTS) and longer bursts also occur. Each burst contains just a narrow band of frequencies somewhere within the total observed range for all bursts. The decametre emissions are highly polarized; it is likely that they are polarized at the point of origin but that the magnetic field of Jupiter substantially modifies the polarization of the radiation on its way to the Earth.

A characteristic feature of these bursts is that they occur preferentially when the longitude (*System II*) of the central meridian has certain values, which implies that the emission is coming from certain preferred longitude zones. These are not identical at all frequencies but at 18 MHz three zones A, B and C have been identified. The constancy of longitude in System II is not exact and a radio rotation period of 9 hr 55 min 29.37 sec was adopted in 1962 as a best fit to the observations. This is the *System III* referred to above. As mentioned there, a better value of 9 hr 55 min 29.75 sec has been obtained from more recent observations.

The decametre emissions are also affected by the satellites Io and, to a lesser extent, Europa. Bursts from zones A and B are most likely to occur when Io is in certain positions in its orbit (figure 11.13). Not all bursts, however, occur when Io is near these positions. The explanation for this effect is unknown but it seems likely to be connected in some way with the ionosphere of Io which was detected by Pioneer 10. Also unexplained is the origin of the decametre radiation itself. Although it is known that individual bursts probably come from regions less than 400 km across, the exact positions are not known. This lack of important information is a main reason for the origin remaining unexplained.

The shorter CENTIMETRE and DECIMETRE wavelength RADIO RADIATION from Jupiter is quite different from the decametre emission. Between about 5 and 300 cm, the radiated power is constant and comes from an area much larger than the planetary disc (figure 11.14). The emitting region sways as the planet rotates. The radiation is linearly polarized and the direction of polarization rocks back and forth 10° each side of its mean direction. From observations such as these a rotation period can be obtained; it is the same as that obtained from the longer, decametre emission. These Earth-based observations strongly suggest that, like the Earth, Jupiter has a magnetic field and belts of energetic particles and that the centimetre and decimetre radio emission is *synchrotron radiation*. The existence of the magnetic field and the energetic particles have now been confirmed by spacecraft measurements.

Jupiter has an intrinsic MAGNETIC FIELD which is described reasonably accurately by a magnetic dipole. The dipole is tilted 10°.77 to the rotation axis towards (in December 1974) System III longitude 230°.9. The dipole is offset from the centre of Jupiter by a distance of 0.101 times the planet's radius in the direction of latitude 5°.12 north and System III longitude 185°.7. The dipole currently points in the opposite direction to that of the Earth so that a terrestrial compass would point towards Jupiter's south pole. The maximum field at Jupiter's visible surface is about 20 times greater than the corresponding value for the Earth. Because of the tilt of the magnetic field relative to the spin axis, any phenomena connected with the field will show a wobble as Jupiter rotates. This applies particularly to the radio emission and so the rotation period measured from radio observations is in fact the rotation period of the magnetic field. Since the central parts of Jupiter are liquid, the magnetic field is most probably generated by the same dynamo effect that is thought to be responsible for the Earth's field.

Jupiter's MAGNETOSPHERE, as the region where Jupiter's magnetic field dominates over that of the Sun is called, has several basic parts (figure 8.31). In the inner magnetosphere, which extends about 20 Jupiter radii from the planet, the field of the dipole predominates. The rotation of the field closely follows that of the dipole. The observed field is generally relatively smooth except that significant perturbations caused by the satellites Europa and Ganymede, whose orbits are in this part of the magnetosphere, have been observed. In the inner region the magnetosphere behaves in a similar way to that of the Earth.

Further out from Jupiter, the field is much more complicated. In the middle magnetosphere, between 20 and 50 Jupiter radii from the planet, there is a thin, disc-like region in which the magnetic field is nearly constant at 10^{-8} tesla. The field traps a low-energy plasma. Electric currents flow in this, forming what is called a current sheet, and are responsible for the field. Because of the tilt of Jupiter's magnetic axis, this sheet is warped so that it is above the equator on one side of the planet and below it on the other. Like the inner magnetic field this warped sheet rotates with the planet. Away from this disc-like region, the field in the middle magnetosphere is weaker and more like that of a dipole. In the outer magnetosphere the field is very irregular and, as with the Earth, it extends away from the Sun in a comet-like tail. The distance of the magnetosphere boundary from Jupiter towards the

Sun varies considerably in short times between extreme values around 50 and 100 Jupiter radii.

Jupiter's magnetic field traps energetic particles, mainly electrons and protons, in the same way as the Earth's does although Jupiter's radiation belts appear to be 10 000 times more intense than the Earth's *Van Allen belts*. In the middle magnetosphere the particles are concentrated into the same disc-like region as the magnetic field. The particles in this outer radiation belt are probably not completely trapped so therefore they continually leak away. At the same time other particles are captured from the interplanetary medium. There is also an inner radiation belt of particles trapped in the inner magnetosphere, but unlike those in the outer belt the particles here are firmly trapped. As well as the energetic particles, Jupiter's magnetosphere contains a plasma of low-energy particles which is not confined to the current sheet of the middle magnetosphere.

As mentioned above, astronomers deduced that the centimetre and decimetre radio emission from Jupiter was due to synchrotron radiation produced by energetic charged particles moving in a magnetic field. These particles can now be identified with those detected in the inner magnetosphere by the Pioneer spacecraft. The strength of the synchrotron radiation depends on both the energy of the charged particles and the strength of the magnetic field. The Pioneer observations confirmed that the particle energies and magnetic field strength have the correct values to produce the observed radio emission.

11.14: *The radio emission from Jupiter at 10-cm wavelength. The colour sequence blue, yellow, orange, red corresponds to increasing intensity of emission. The peak emission does not come from the body of the planet (shown as a circle). The source of the radio waves is a doughnut-shaped region around Jupiter.*

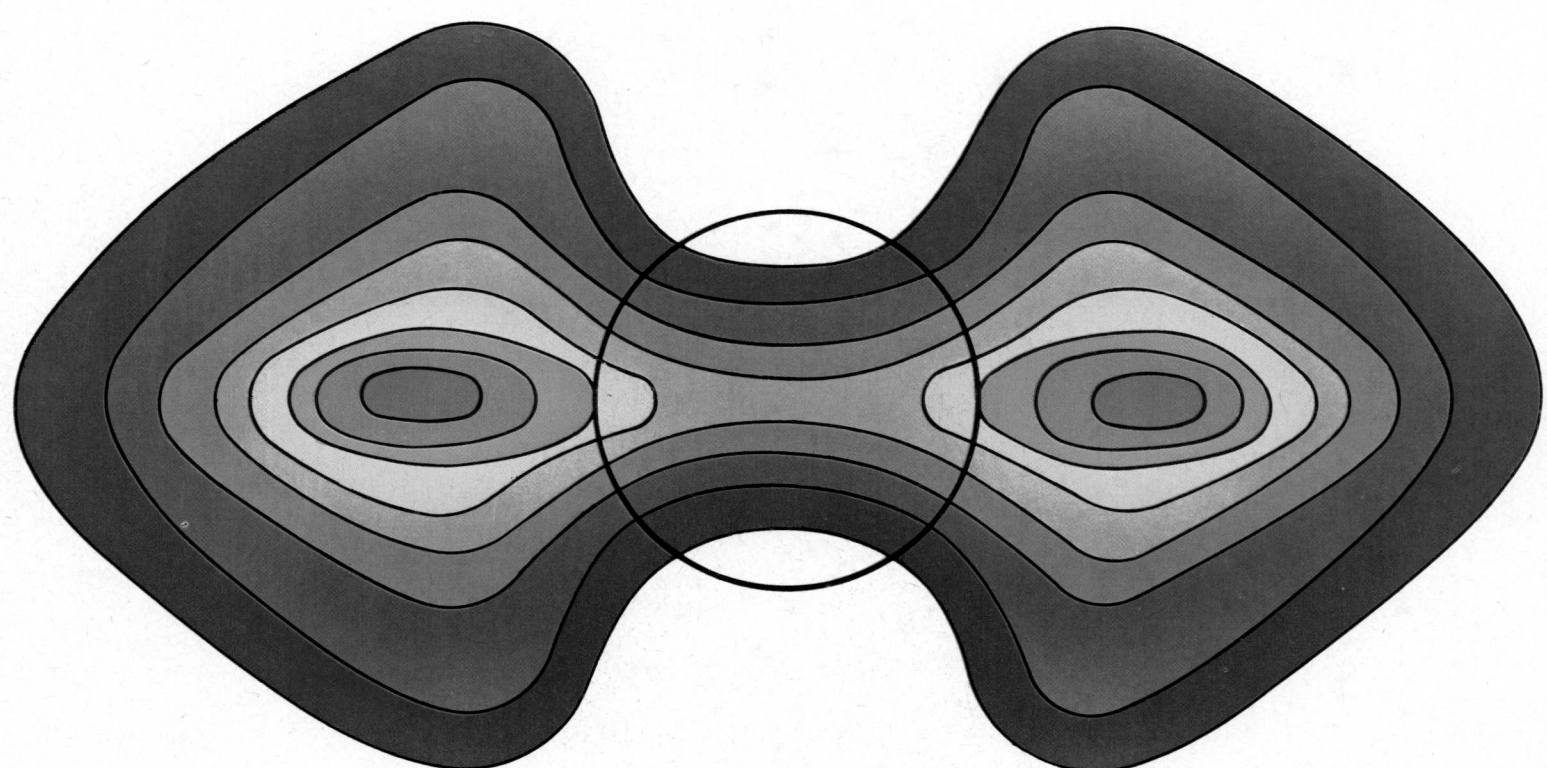

Saturn

Beyond Jupiter is Saturn, the most distant planet that was known to the ancients. With the obvious exception of the rings, it appears to be similar to Jupiter in many ways. *Saturn's rings* effectively consist of an enormous number of minute satellites and are considered, together with the ten known satellites in the next chapter.

Saturn is the least dense of all the planets. Its density of $704\,\text{kg}\,\text{m}^{-3}$ is less than that of water so that one might imagine Saturn being placed in a tank of water and floating! Like Jupiter, Saturn must be composed predominantly of hydrogen and helium. We know much less about Saturn than Jupiter, since no spacecraft have yet passed in its vicinity. Our knowledge is confined to that which can be obtained by conventional Earth-based observations. We receive about 16 times less light from Saturn than from Jupiter and the geometric resolution of the surface as seen from Earth is only half as good. Consequently most studies of Saturn draw heavily on analogy with Jupiter.

Saturn's mass is 95.147 times that of the Earth. The equatorial radius is $60\,000\,\text{km}$. The polar radius is 11 per cent smaller, making Saturn by far the most flattened planet. The average density of $704\,\text{kg}\,\text{m}^{-3}$ follows from these figures; this is about half the average density of Jupiter and one-eighth that of the Earth.

Molecular hydrogen was first positively identified on Saturn in 1962, two years after the corresponding discovery on Jupiter; methane had been discovered earlier during the 1930s (figure 12.2).

11.15: *Saturn and its magnificent ring system. The dark Cassini division divides the bright inner ring B from the outer ring A. The body of the planet shows belts and zones similar to those of Jupiter and at upper rights its shadow partly obscures the rings. (International Planetary Patrol,* USA*)*

Ammonia, the other major contribution to the spectrum of Jupiter, has not been definitely identified on Saturn. The observational evidence is conflicting; some observers have claimed to have seen spectral lines of ammonia while others have said that they cannot detect any. Ammonia may well be on the limit of what can presently be detected. It is also possible that the amount of gaseous ammonia in the atmosphere (which is what is detected spectroscopically) is variable since small changes in the atmospheric temperature would cause large changes in the amount of ammonia which is condensed into clouds. There can be little doubt, though, that ammonia is present. The same is true for helium, although as is the case of Jupiter, it cannot be detected from the Earth. Apart from phosphine (PH_3), discovered in 1975, no other atoms or molecules have yet been definitely detected in Saturn's atmosphere.

As with Jupiter, the visible surface of Saturn is the cloud layers of the upper atmosphere. There is a system of cloud belts with light zones between them which are sufficiently permanent to have received names (figure 11.17). The intricate details of cloud structure seen on Jupiter are largely absent on Saturn. This makes the determination of the rotation period more difficult; the most satisfactory technique is to use the variation of the *Doppler shift* across the disc to measure the rotation speed and hence the period. The period at various latitudes is as follows:

Latitude	Rotation Period
0° (equator)	10 hr 2 min
27°	10 hr 38 min
42°	10 hr 50 min
57°	11 hr 8 min

Each of these values has an uncertainty of several minutes.

WHITE SPOTS occur on Saturn on rare occasions and persist for a few days or weeks. They never achieve the prominence or lifetime of the spots seen on Jupiter and nothing remotely like the *great red spot* has ever been seen. The longest lasting spot that has been observed was seen during a 490-day period between October 1969 and February 1971. Its average rotation period was 10 hr 36 min 27.9 sec but the actual period varied somewhat. The spot itself measured 8000 km from north to south and 6000 km from east to west. As well as being the longest lasting, this spot set a record for the greatest southern latitude: 57.3° S. Another prominent spot was one discovered in August 1933 by Will Hay the famous comedian, who was also an amateur astronomer. The spot appeared in the equatorial zone and rapidly became very conspicuous. It gradually lengthened and the portion of the disc behind it darkened. The spot faded quickly and disappeared completely after a few months.

The rotation periods of the spots seem to be shorter nearer to the equator than further away. They do not appear to agree with the rotation periods measured by Doppler spectroscopy, but the measurements are not sufficiently precise for this result to be certain. In any case, it is well established that spots on Jupiter do not, in general, have the same rotation period as the surrounding

Table 11.3: The internal structure of Saturn

This table gives the probable general trend of conditions inside Saturn. It does not include a possible dense core. There is a transition between an inner region of metallic hydrogen and an outer region of molecular hydrogen at a radius of about 30 000 km. (1 Mbar = 10^6 bar $\simeq 10^6$ atmospheres.)

Radius (km)	Fractional mass	Pressure (Mbars)	Density (kg m^{-3})
57 000	0.98	0.001	10
55 000	0.95	0.01	60
50 000	0.84	0.1	300
45 000	0.8	0.4	600
40 000	0.7	0.9	900
35 000	0.6	1.9	1100
30 000	0.5	2.5	1400
25 000	0.4	4	1700
20 000	0.3	5	1900
15 000	0.25	6	2000
10 000	0.2	7	3000
5 000	0.05	10	3000
0	0	10	3000

11.16: *The structure of Saturn's atmosphere according to what is probably the best currently available theoretical model. It goes to a greater depth than the corresponding model for Jupiter in figure 11.12 but does not include a lower layer of ammonium hydrosulphide clouds. The altitude has been arbitrarily measured from the level at which the pressure is one atmosphere.*

clouds, so a similar result for Saturn is no surprise. Jupiter has a distinct equatorial jet with a sharp change in rotation period near latitudes 10° north and south. It is not yet known whether Saturn has a similar jet, but analogy strongly suggests that it does.

The colour of Saturn's clouds varies over the disc from white through pale yellow to brownish yellow (figure 11.15). Experienced observers have reported seeing colours such as orange and blue in places, but any such shades are extremely subtle. These colours presumably originate in the same way as those on Jupiter. The visible clouds are probably ammonia cirrus but somewhat more dense than those on Jupiter.

It is difficult to measure the *albedo* of Saturn because of the rings that generally obscure part of the disc and also contribute unwanted light of their own to the measurements. Measurements have been made though, and show that Saturn as a whole reflects less of the incident light than does Jupiter. In blue light the albedo of Saturn is about 60 per cent of Jupiter's; in red light it is about 90 per cent. In the infrared the situation is the reverse and Saturn reflects more of the incident solar radiation than does Jupiter.

Measurements of the energy radiated by Saturn are seriously hampered by radiation from the rings and the results are less certain than they are for Jupiter. If Saturn radiated just the energy absorbed from the incident sunlight then its effective temperature would be 71 K; in fact it is 97 K. It follows that Saturn is radiating three and a half times as much energy as it absorbs

from the Sun. Although this figure is rather uncertain there can be very little doubt that Saturn, like Jupiter, has an important internal energy source.

The problems of understanding the structure of Saturn's atmosphere are similar to, but greater than those for Jupiter. Several important quantities are less well known; these include the details of the composition and the magnitude of the internal energy source. Saturn has a much lower surface gravity than does Jupiter: $9.05\,\mathrm{m\,s^{-2}}$ compared to $22.88\,\mathrm{m\,s^{-2}}$ at the equator. This causes a major difference in the structure of the two atmospheres; the SCALE HEIGHT of the atmosphere is much greater on Saturn than on Jupiter. The scale height is a measure of the change in altitude over which the pressure or density changes by a factor of $e = 2.71828\ldots$ Figure 11.16 shows the results of one computation of the structure of Saturn's atmosphere. Saturn's clouds are expected to be denser than those of Jupiter. This is confirmed by optical observations which show that there is no penetration of radiation through the top cloud layer from below as does occur on Jupiter.

Studies of the INTERNAL STRUCTURE of Saturn proceed along the same lines as those for Jupiter. Some calculations suggest that to produce a model of the correct mass and volume and with an internal energy source of the observed strength, a high fraction of helium, about three quarters by mass, is necessary. This is generally considered unlikely as a composition roughly like the

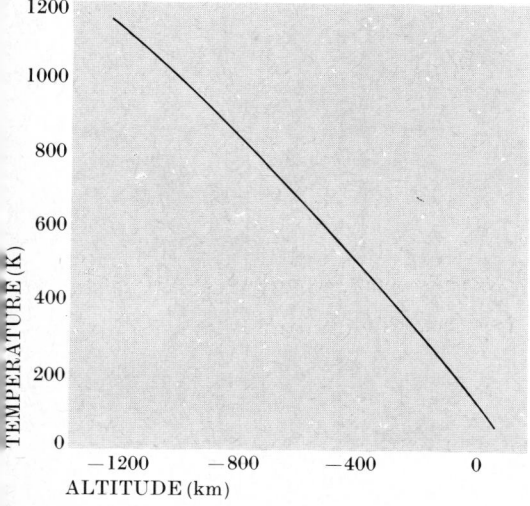

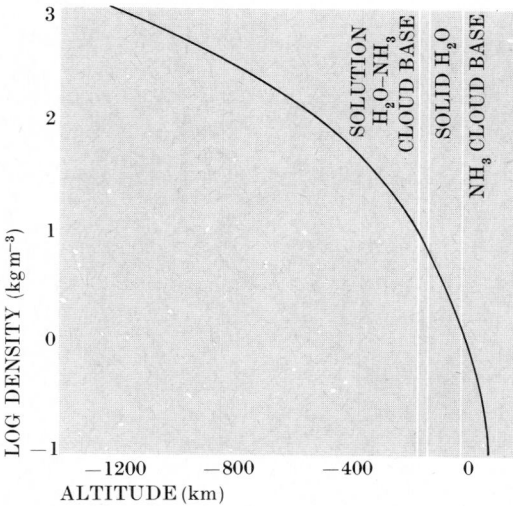

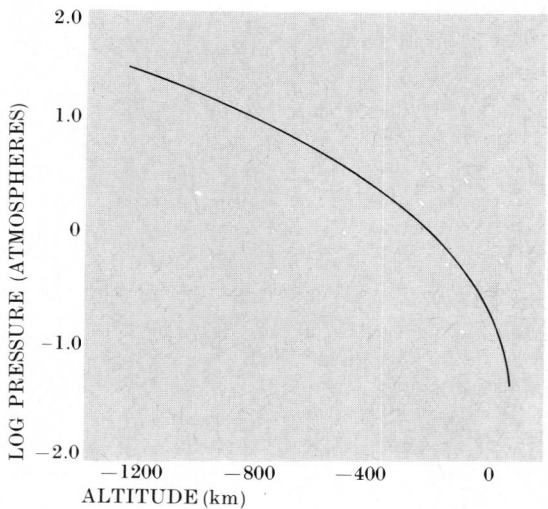

Sun with one quarter helium by mass is more plausible. As discussed above, the size of the internal energy source may be smaller than present measurements indicate because of confusion with radiation from the rings. If this is true then a smaller fraction of helium is necessary. A small high-density core would also reduce the proportion of helium required to explain the observations. Such a core might consist of a rocky centre with a layer of ice (figure 11.18). Table 11.3 shows the results of one model and probably gives the correct general trend of conditions inside Saturn.

RADIO EMISSION from Saturn has been detected over the wavelength range from about 1 mm to 94 cm. All this radiation appears to be due to thermal emission from the atmosphere. There is no evidence that there is any non-thermal radiation as there is from Jupiter. From the Earth a magnetic field on Saturn would only be detectable indirectly by observations of such non-thermal radio emission. Consequently there is at present no evidence that Saturn has a magnetic field.

11.17: *The belts and zones of Saturn's visible surface, with the rings omitted for clarity. This diagram is drawn to the same scale as figures 11.2, 11.11, 11.18 and 11.20.*

EARTH

N

NORTH POLAR REGION (NPR)

NORTH NORTH TEMPERATE BELT (NNTB)

NORTH TROPICAL ZONE (NTrZ)

NORTH TEMPERATE BELT (NTB)

NORTH EQUATORIAL BELT (NEB)

EQUATORIAL ZONE (EqZ)

SOUTH EQUATORIAL BELT (SEB)

SOUTH TEMPERATE BELT (STB)

SOUTH TROPICAL ZONE (STrZ)

SOUTH SOUTH TEMPERATURE BELT (SSTB)

SOUTH POLAR REGION (SPR)

S

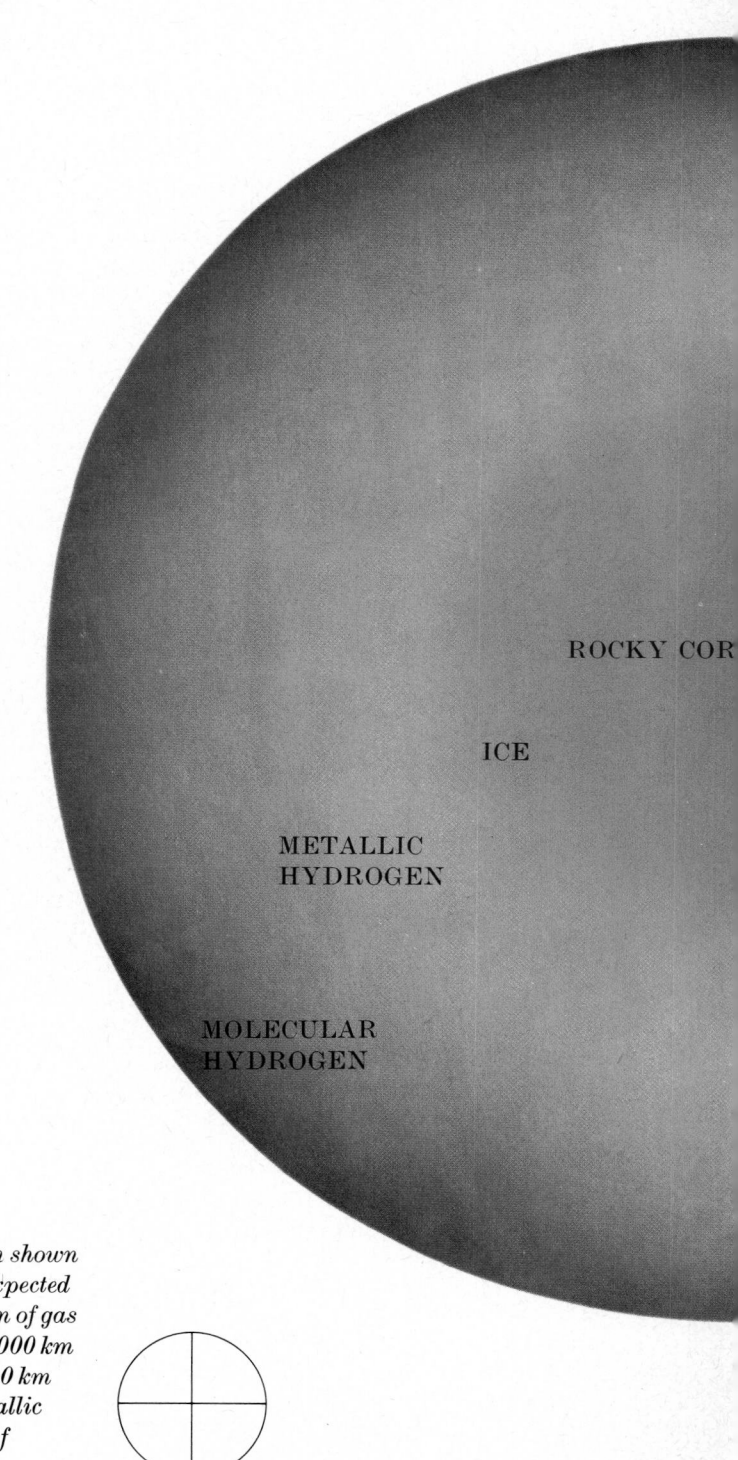

ROCKY CORE

ICE

METALLIC HYDROGEN

MOLECULAR HYDROGEN

11.18 : *The internal structure of Saturn shown in cross-section. This is the structure expected if the planet formed by the accumulation of gas onto a rocky core. This core is about 20 000 km in diameter and is surrounded by a 5000 km layer of ice and an 8000 km shell of metallic hydrogen. There is also an outer layer of molecular hydrogen.*

EARTH

11.19: *The rotation axis of Uranus has an inclination of 98° so that it lies almost in the plane of the orbit. As Uranus revolves around the Sun, the rotation axis points always in the same direction in space. At A the Sun is overhead at the north pole and at C at the south pole. In the intermediate positions B and D the Sun is overhead at the equator. Because the inclination is not exactly 90° the subsolar point at A and C is not exactly the pole but at latitude 82°.*

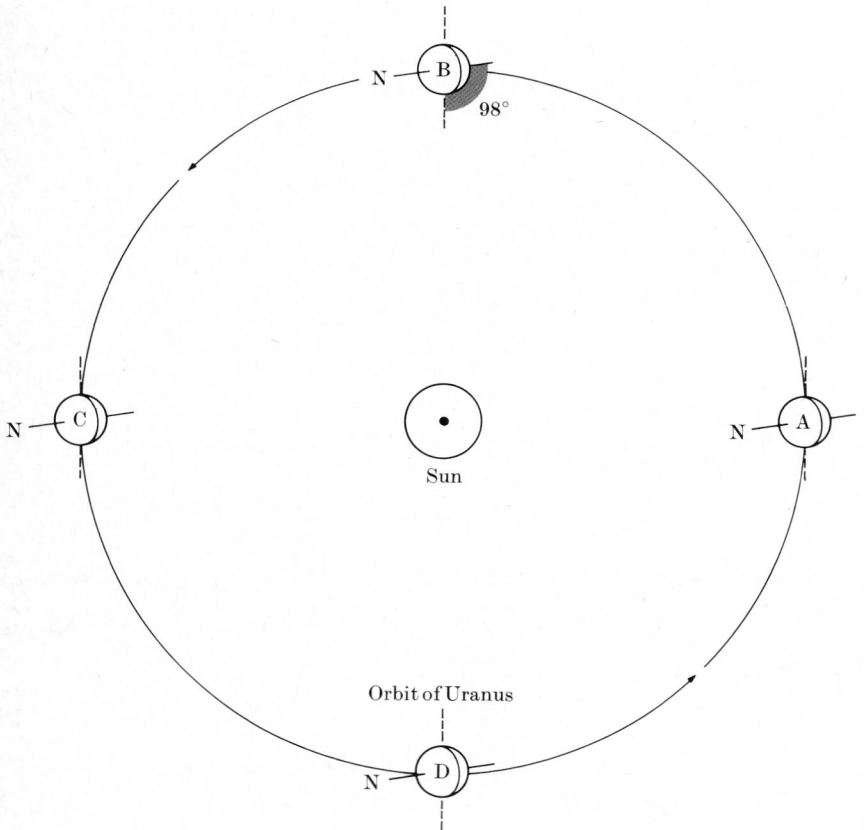

Uranus and Neptune

Uranus and Neptune are difficult bodies to study. The radiation received at the Earth from Uranus is less than one-thousandth of that received from Jupiter and from Neptune it is even less. The greater distances of the two planets make surface details more difficult to detect than on either Jupiter or Saturn. No planets are exactly the same but Uranus and Neptune are more nearly alike than any other pair. Neptune was once thought to be the larger of the two but modern measurements show that the equatorial radius of Uranus is just five per cent greater than that of Neptune although Uranus has 15 per cent less mass. Because of their similarities it is convenient to consider the two planets together.

Molecular hydrogen has been detected on both Uranus and Neptune. A feature seen by G.P.Kuiper in the spectra of both planets was shown by G.Herzberg in 1952 to be a molecular hydrogen line at a wavelength of 827 nm. Other lines have subsequently been detected in the spectrum of each planet.

The detection of methane in the atmosphere of Uranus followed the same pattern as for Jupiter and Saturn. In 1869 Angelo Secchi was the first person to observe the absorption lines in the spectrum of Uranus. Rupert Wildt suggested in 1932 that these might be caused by methane and in 1934 Adel and V.M.Slipher confirmed that this was indeed the case. In the first decade of the twentieth century V.M.Slipher had shown that the spectrum of Neptune was very like that of Uranus, except that the absorption was even stronger. It therefore followed that methane was also present on Neptune. No other atoms or molecules have been identified on either planet. However it is expected that ammonia and helium are both present. Unlike Jupiter and Saturn, any ammonia is only expected deep in their atmospheres.

The effective temperatures of Uranus and Neptune are calculated to be 57 and 45 K respectively if the only energy source is the absorbed sunlight. Temperature measurements agree with these values, which suggest that these planets do not have appreciable internal energy sources (which would raise the effective temperatures). In the case of Neptune, however, it is possible that there is such a source, which may be caused by tidal friction produced by Triton, Neptune's very large and close satellite.

All but one of the planets have rotation axes roughly perpendicular to the planes of their orbits. The exception is Uranus, which has an axial inclination of 98° so that the axis is more or less in the plane of the orbit (figure 11.19). Twice in each orbit of the Sun, the axis is at right angles to the direction to the Sun; this last occurred in 1966. In between these times, one or other of the poles points more or less directly at the Sun. If north and south are defined by the direction of the rotation the north pole will face the Sun continuously in 1985. It is believed that there is very little effective heat exchange between the two hemispheres. The poles will therefore heat up when they face the Sun, possibly by as much as 20 per cent. The poles actually receive more heat per orbit of the Sun than does the equator and hence are the hottest parts of Uranus.

Telescopically, Uranus appears as a small bluish-green disc

about four seconds of arc in diameter. The best modern observations, even with large telescopes or from balloons, show no surface features. Yet, at times of superior seeing, the best classic visual observers have usually reported two faint equatorial belts on either side of a bright zone and darker poles. Certainly these belts, if they exist, must be right on the limit of what can be detected. Neptune shows a disc of the same bluish-green colour but just 2.5 seconds of arc in diameter. There are a few reports of some very weak spots of irregular shape, but none of any band structure.

Certainly neither planet has any surface features that can be used to determine the rotation period. The currently-used rotation periods of 10.8 hours for Uranus and 15.8 hours for Neptune were derived from the variation across the disc of the Doppler shifts of the spectral lines. The measurements are somewhat uncertain and could be in error by as much as half an hour or an hour respectively. An alternative way to obtain the period is to observe any changes in the light from the planet caused by regions of different brightness passing across the visible disc as the planet rotates. Observations of Uranus are in disagreement as to whether such fluctuations do take place and it is not known whether any of those reported are real. The situation for Neptune is similar.

The greenish-blue colour of the two planets is caused by the tremendous absorption of red light, for which the methane in the atmospheres is largely responsible. Uranus reflects about 50 per cent of the incident short wavelength (blue) light but only 10 to 20 per cent of the long wavelength (red) light. The albedo of Neptune is much the same as that of Uranus.

Much less is known about the atmospheric structures of Uranus and Neptune than for Jupiter and Saturn. The visible layers in the atmospheres must have temperatures roughly equal to the effective temperatures quoted above. Deeper in the atmosphere the temperatures will be higher. Radio emission from both Uranus and Neptune has been detected over a wide wavelength range. This is thermal emission coming from below the visible layers of the atmospheres where the temperature is between 130 and 200 K. If, as expected, ammonia is present on Uranus then a cloud layer of solid ammonia particles must form where the temperature is about 170 K and the pressure about eight atmospheres. This layer is much deeper in the atmosphere than are the corresponding layers on Jupiter and Saturn and it is well below the visible part of the atmosphere. There should also be a thin methane haze with its base at 60 K and 0.4 atmospheres. On Neptune the ammonia cloud layer must be deeper in the atmosphere where the pressure is higher than it is on Uranus. There may also be thin argon clouds high in Neptune's atmosphere.

Like Jupiter and Saturn, Uranus and Neptune are believed to contain large amounts of lighter elements, but are not thought to be as rich in hydrogen. In recent years the radii of both Uranus and Neptune have been remeasured and found to differ by around ten per cent from previous measurements. This means that the calculated mean densities have altered by 30 per cent. A consequence of this is that theoretical models of the internal structure of Uranus and Neptune calculated during the 1960s using the old, erroneous values are now obsolete. It is not known whether the two planets have hot or cold interiors or whether they have a solid surface. One possibility, shown in figure 11.20, is that each has a rocky core 16 000 km in diameter surrounded by an 8000 km layer of ice. The rest of the planet consists of molecular hydrogen.

Pluto

Pluto has the largest, most eccentric and most highly-inclined orbit of any of the known planets. Because of this large eccentricity, Pluto, when near perihelion, is actually closer to the Sun than Neptune can ever be; this will next occur in 1989. The highly-inclined orbit takes Pluto as much as a billion and a quarter kilometres above the plane of the ecliptic – a distance almost as great as Saturn's average distance from the Sun. Because of this there is no chance of a catastrophic collision with Neptune. Calculations of the motions of Neptune and Pluto in their orbits have been made taking account of the perturbations which result from their mutual gravitational attraction. These calculations show that Neptune and Pluto never come closer together than 16.7 astronomical units even though the closest points in the two orbits are much nearer to each other than this. It is interesting to note that this minimum distance between Pluto and Neptune is more than that between Pluto and Uranus, which is 10.6 astronomical units.

R.A.Lyttleton has suggested that Pluto may be an escaped satellite of Neptune. The orbit of Neptune's satellite, Triton, is unusual for such a large satellite as it is highly inclined and Triton's orbital motion is retrograde. Lyttleton and G.P.Kuiper have suggested that Pluto and Triton were both in orbit around Neptune until an interaction took place that sent Pluto into orbit around the Sun and Triton into its present orbit. This theory is not wholly satisfactory since it is difficult to see how Pluto could end up in an orbit which does not closely approach that of Neptune.

The angular diameter of Pluto is only about a quarter of a second of arc (figure 11.21), which corresponds to a diameter of 5860 km, but this could be in error by as much as 50 per cent. A more accurate value could be obtained if Pluto occulted a star. Such an occultation would be a rare event and none has been observed; a near miss occurred in 1965 and this showed that Pluto's diameter is at most 6800 km.

The mass is obtained by measuring Pluto's perturbations of Neptune. These are very small because of Pluto's low mass and hence are difficult to measure. Although Pluto was only discovered in 1930, earlier observations of what were thought to be stars have now been shown to have been pre-discovery records of Pluto. These date back to 1846 but since then Pluto has made only half a revolution of the Sun, and satisfactory mass determinations cannot be made from less than a complete orbit. Account must also be taken of the perturbations of other planets, particularly Saturn and Uranus, and a small error in the mass of either of these would cause a large error in the derived mass of Pluto. The best value for the mass of Pluto is 0.11 times that of the Earth but this is subject to a very large uncertainty. This mass, together with a diameter of 5860 km gives a density of 6200 kg m^{-3}, but this value is also highly uncertain.

The rotation period of Pluto was first measured in 1955 by observing the regular changes in its brightness. The latest value for the period is 6.3874 days. This period is quite constant but the mean magnitude and the range both vary. Over a 20-year period the mean V magnitude, after allowing for the varying distances from the Earth and the Sun, has decreased by 0.20 and the amplitude of the variations has increased from 0.11 to 0.22 magnitudes. If Pluto has bright polar caps, a patchy equatorial region and a highly-inclined rotation axis, then such a change would result as Pluto's motion around its orbit caused it to present a varying aspect to the Earth.

No atmosphere has been detected on Pluto and it may not have one. The surface temperature must be around 40 or 50 K and at such a low temperature molecules such as carbon dioxide, water and ammonia would lie frozen on the surface. The surface gravity is probably sufficiently low for the light gases hydrogen and helium to escape from the planet altogether. Minute amounts of gaseous methane or nitrogen could be present but these would be almost entirely frozen on the surface. The heavier inert gases such as neon and argon could form a permanent atmosphere but they are difficult to detect spectroscopically.

Because the radius of Pluto is so poorly known, it is pointless to convert its brightness at various wavelengths into *albedo* values. The measurements do show that Pluto reflects more of the incident red and blue light than of the green light. Similarly the lack of accurate knowledge of the density means that no meaningful studies of the internal structure are possible. A large magnetic field is unlikely, since Pluto is small and rotates slowly. The slow rotation will also result in considerable differences between day-side and night-side temperatures with a maximum of perhaps 50 K.

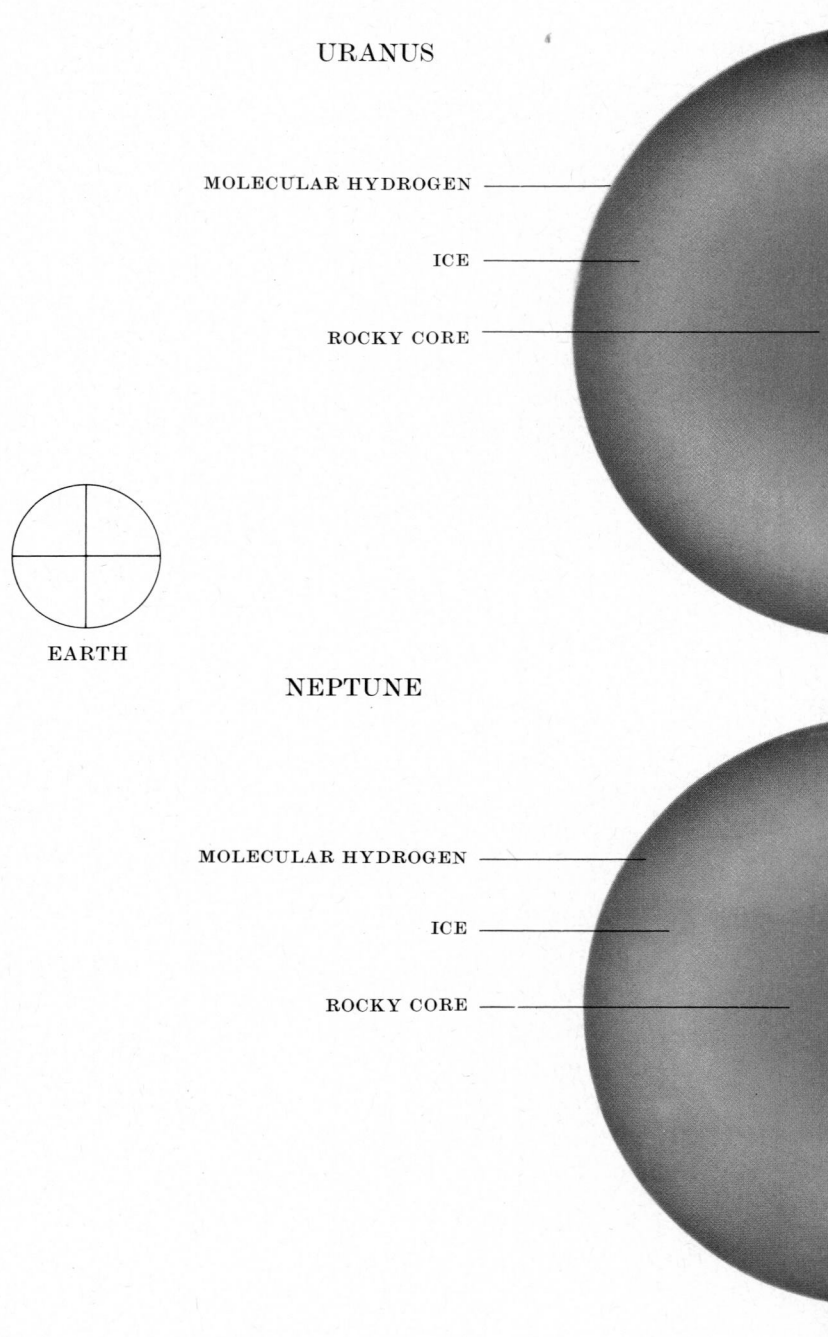

URANUS

MOLECULAR HYDROGEN

ICE

ROCKY CORE

EARTH

NEPTUNE

MOLECULAR HYDROGEN

ICE

ROCKY CORE

11.20: *Cutaway views of the interiors of Uranus and Neptune to be compared with those of Jupiter and Saturn (figures 11.11 and 11.18) at the same scale. These planets of almost identical size probably have rocky cores about 16 000 km in diameter surrounded by an 8000 km layer of ice inside an outer layer of molecular hydrogen.*

11.21: *The same starfield photographed on successive days in January 1950 showing the motion of Pluto. The planet is so small that it looks like a star and it is only its motion across the sky that allows it to be distinguished as a planet. (McDonald Observatory,* USA *)*

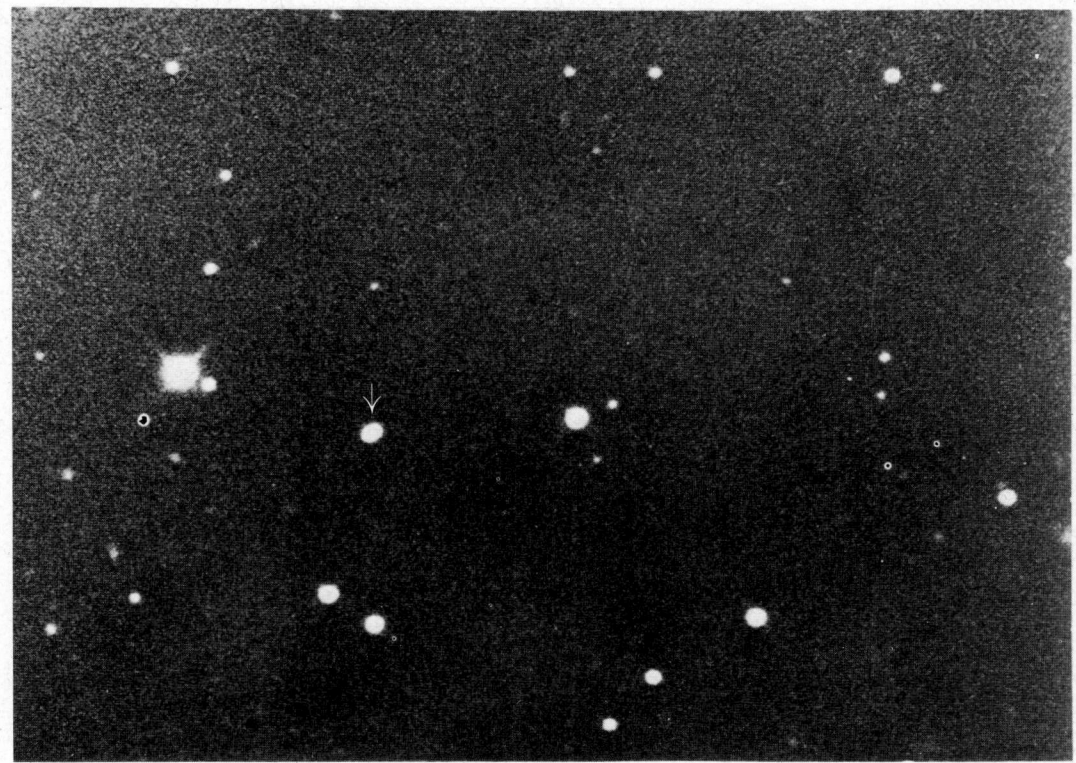

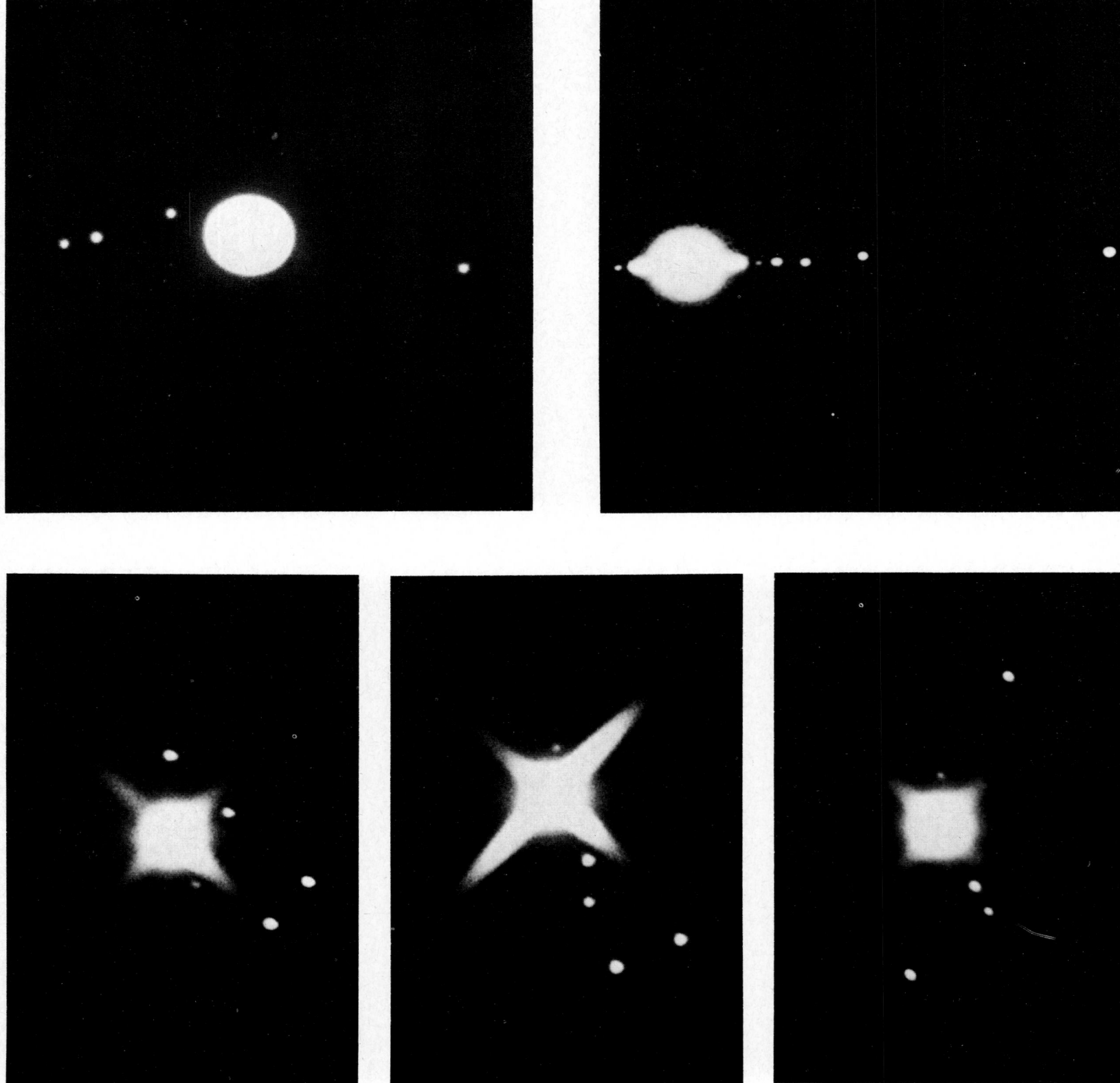

12. Minor members of the Solar System

The planets form the bulk of the Solar System, but many other bodies are known which, though much smaller or less massive than planets, are full of interest. These minor bodies include the glorious set of rings around Saturn, tens of planetary satellites, hundreds of comets, thousands of asteroids, countless meteors, and other small particles which are seen as the *zodiacal light* and the *gegenschein*.

Satellites of Jupiter

In addition to our Moon and the two tiny satellites of Mars, a further 31 natural satellites are known in the outer Solar System. They are in orbit around the four giant planets: Mercury, Venus and Pluto have no known satellites whereas Jupiter has fourteen, Saturn has ten, Uranus five and Neptune two. Five satellites – Io, Ganymede, Callisto, Titan and Triton – are bigger than the Moon, and of these Ganymede and Titan (certainly), and Callisto and Triton (possibly), are larger than Mercury. A number of other satellites are larger than Ceres, the largest asteroid. At the other extreme are bodies about ten kilometres across, at the limit of what can be detected by present-day techniques. In addition the rings of Saturn consist of what are effectively myriads of tiny satellites.

Jupiter has fourteen known satellites (table 12.1) which have been numbered in order of discovery. Some of these are shown in figure 12.1. The innermost five, Amalthea, Io, Europa, Ganymede and Callisto, move in circular orbits in Jupiter's equatorial plane. They appear to rotate on their axes in the same period as they revolve around Jupiter, so that they keep the same face always turned towards the planet. The remaining nine satellites can be divided into two groups on the basis of their orbital elements: (a) XIV, XIII, VI, X, VII, (b) XII, XI, VIII, IX. Table 12.1 shows clearly that the members of each group have similar mean distances from Jupiter, periods, and orbital inclinations. All nine are at great distances from Jupiter so that their orbits are significantly perturbed by the Sun. The members of the outer group move in retrograde orbits. Almost nothing is known about these nine bodies because of their small sizes, and the radii in table 12.1 are very rough estimates based on their observed brightness. The small satellites are probably captured asteroids, rather than true satellites formed at the same time as, and close to Jupiter. The innermost satellite, Amalthea, moves in an orbit only 1.54 Jupiter radii from the planetary surface, where observations are severely hampered by glare from Jupiter.

The remaining four satellites are all comparable in size to the Moon. They are commonly referred to as the GALILEAN SATELLITES after Galileo, who discovered three of them on 7 January 1610; six days later he noticed all four at the same time. Galileo was probably the first person to realize what it was that he had seen but he was not the first to see the satellites as is commonly stated elsewhere. This honour belongs to Simon Marius (or Meyer), who saw them ten days before Galileo, and who proposed the names by which these satellites are known today: IO, EUROPA, GANYMEDE and CALLISTO.

12.1: *Jupiter (top left), Saturn (top right) showing their brighter satellites, and Uranus (bottom) showing all its five known satellites on three different nights. The photographs have been correctly exposed for the satellites and this has resulted in overexposed images of the planets and of Saturn's rings. From left to right the satellites of Saturn are Enceladus, Mimas, Tethys, Dione, Rhea and Titan. On 10 March 1977 Uranus occulted the star SAO 158687. The observations showed a series of secondary occultations which must have been caused by a ring of small, otherwise unobserved satellites. These satellites have orbits about 20 000 km above the surface of the planet and some may be as much as 100 km across. (Jupiter and Saturn: Lowell Observatory, Arizona; Uranus: McDonald Observatory, Texas, USA)*

All four Galilean satellites are relatively bright objects and, were it not for the glare of Jupiter, they would be visible to the naked eye. A very few people claim that they can see the satellites clearly and distinguish them individually from the general glare. Most of us are not sufficiently keen-sighted to do this but can possibly see them as an extension of the light of the planet whenever two or more are situated on the same side of the planet.

The biggest Galilean satellite, Ganymede, is larger than Mercury, and Callisto is almost the same size. Io is larger than the Moon and the smallest of the four, Europa, is not much smaller. In 1971 Io occulted the star β Sco C and in 1972 Ganymede occulted SAO 186800. Observations of these events gave the diameter of Io accurate to within about 5 km and of Ganymede to within 100 or 200 km. Every six years, the Earth passes through the plane of the satellites' orbits and mutual occultations are then visible. From observations of these in 1973 the diameters of Europa and Ganymede have now been obtained to within 50 to 100 km and of Callisto to within 200 km. Actual values of the radii are given in table 12.2 together with other physical data. These data include masses of the satellites obtained from the flights of the Pioneer spacecraft in 1973 and 1974.

Table 12.1 : Satellites of Jupiter

Satellite		Discoverer	Year of discovery	Mean distance from Jupiter (km)	Sidereal period (days)	Orbital inclination[1,2] (degrees)	Orbital eccentricity[1]	Radius[3] (km)	V magnitude at mean opposition
JV	Amalthea	E. Barnard	1892	181 000	0.418 178	0.455	0.003	80	13
JI	Io	S. Marius, Galileo	1610	422 000	1.769 138	0.027	0.000	1818	4.9
JII	Europa	S. Marius, Galileo	1610	671 000	3.551 181	0.468	0.000	1530	5.3
JIII	Ganymede	S. Marius, Galileo	1610	1 070 000	7.154 553	0.183	0.001	2610	4.6
JIV	Callisto	S. Marius, Galileo	1610	1 883 000	16.689 018	0.253	0.007	2445	5.6
JXIII	Leda	C. Kowal	1974	11 110 000	239	27	0.147	3	21
JVI	Himalia	C. D. Perrine	1904	11 476 000	250.566	28	0.158	50	14.2
JX	Lysithea	S. B. Nicholson	1938	11 700 000	259.22	29	0.12	8	18.8
JVII	Elara	C. D. Perrine	1905	11 737 000	259.65	26	0.207	12	17
JXII	Ananke	S. B. Nicholson	1951	21 200 000	630	147	0.169	8	18.7
JXI	Carme	S. B. Nicholson	1938	22 600 000	692	163	0.207	9	18.6
JVIII	Pasiphae	P. Mellote	1908	23 500 000	739	147	0.40	10	18
JIX	Sinope	S. B. Nicholson	1914	23 600 000	758	156	0.275	9	18.6

Notes:
1. The eccentricities and inclinations of the inner five satellites are slightly variable. Those for the outer eight satellites are extremely variable.
2. To the equatorial plane of Jupiter.
3. Apart from the four Galilean Satellites, these values are extremely uncertain.
4. Satellite XIV was discovered in 1976 but details have not been confirmed.

The occultation of SAO 186800 by Ganymede also provided the first direct evidence of an atmosphere on a Galilean satellite. The density is uncertain but it is definitely very much less than at the surface of the Earth. Another occultation, this time of a radio transmitter on board Pioneer 10, showed the existence of free electrons in Io's atmosphere and also of an atmosphere of neutral particles having a surface pressure between about 10^{-8} and 10^{-10} atmospheres.

Io is eclipsed by Jupiter's shadow in every orbit. As it emerges from the shadow into the sunlight it is sometimes seen to be about 0.1 magnitude brighter than usual. This excess brightness was first noticed in 1964. It does not occur after every eclipse and when it does it disappears after about 15 minutes. It was suggested that the cause was the condensation of part of an atmosphere as Io cooled in the darkness of an eclipse. The condensed material could form a bright layer on the surface which would only gradually evaporate when the satellite re-emerged into the sunlight. However the Pioneer 10 results show that Io does not have a sufficiently dense atmosphere for such an explanation to be possible. In any case the observations of the excess brightness are difficult to make because of the proximity of Jupiter and it is possible that the brightening does not really occur.

Another oddity of Io is the yellow glow surrounding it which was discovered in 1974. This glow extends outwards from Io for several times its diameter and is due to the characteristic light of sodium (emission in the D line). Io's orbit is within Jupiter's *magnetosphere* and the surface of the satellite is continuously bombarded by the energetic particles in Jupiter's radiation belts. If the surface of Io is covered at least partly with compounds of sodium, such as common salt (sodium chloride), the bombarding particles could knock sodium atoms off the surface to form a cloud around the satellite where they could then emit their characteristic yellow light. Observations also show a corresponding cloud of hydrogen, although this fills the whole of Io's orbit, forming a torus, instead of being confined to the immediate vicinity of the satellite.

Observations of the visible and infrared sunlight reflected by the Galilean satellites and an examination of the fraction reflected at different wavelengths show that the surface properties vary considerably from satellite to satellite. Europa and Ganymede are coated largely with water frost at a temperature of about 150 K and with grains about 0.1 mm across. The proportion of water frost in the surface layer is around 75 per cent and 60 per cent respectively for these two satellites whereas it is at most a minor constituent for Io and Callisto. Io has a very high *albedo* at near infrared wavelengths; between 1 and 3 μm it is over 90 per cent. This can be explained by a surface layer of minerals containing a large amount of water of crystallization. This is consistent with the requirement for a proportion of sodium compounds to explain the D-line glow.

Little is known about surface features on the satellites. Faint markings can be seen from the Earth through large telescopes; these show that each of the four satellites keeps one face turned towards Jupiter as it revolves around it. Pioneer 10 took photographs of Ganymede which seem to show a bright region near its south pole. This might be an ice cap, possibly composed of methane rather than water. One Pioneer 11 photograph showed an ice cap on Callisto quite clearly.

Ganymede and Callisto have mean densities of 2000 and 1740 kg m⁻³ respectively. If they were balls of rock their densities would be at least 3000 kg m⁻³. These two satellites must therefore contain sizeable quantities of low-density frozen solid or liquid material such as water, ammonia, and possibly, methane. This material probably forms a thick mantle around a rocky core of hydrated silicates. These mantles will be liquid if there is even a small amount of radioactive decay in their interiors. Io and Europa both have a higher mean density, around 3500 kg m⁻³ in each case, and could contain a high proportion of rock so that they have a large core and a relatively thin mantle. All four should have at least a thin solid crust. Except on Io, this may be ice, although on Callisto there must be additional dark material on the surface itself in order to explain the low albedo.

Table 12.2: Physical data for the Galilean satellites of Jupiter

	Io (JI)	*Europa* (JII)	*Ganymede* (JIII)	*Callisto* (JIV)
Mass (Jupiter = 1)	4.696×10^{-5}	2.565×10^{-5}	7.845×10^{-5}	5.603×10^{-5}
Mass (Moon = 1)	1.213	0.663	2.027	1.448
Mean radius (km)	1818	1530	2610	2445
Mean density (kg m⁻³)	3540	3230	2000	1740
Mean surface gravity (m s⁻²)	1.80	1.46	1.43	1.14
Escape velocity (km s⁻¹)	2.56	2.09	2.75	2.38
Rotational change in V magnitude	0.16	0.31	0.15	0.15

Saturn's rings

With this review of Jupiter's satellites complete we now consider SATURN'S RINGS. When Galileo turned his telescope towards Saturn in 1610 he saw the planet in three parts. Later, in 1612, it looked quite regular and he feared that his earlier observations may have been in error. In 1614 C.Scheiner drew Saturn as a planet with two handle-like extensions. G.B.Riccioli drew it as a triple body in 1640 but between 1647 and 1650 he too showed two handles.

The true explanation of this mysterious appearance was eventually discovered by Christiaan Huygens. In 1655 he saw a narrow arm on each side of the planetary disc. Early in 1656 these appeared to have completely disappeared and he saw the planet simply as a round disc, and by October of that year the narrow arms had reappeared. Huygens soon realized what was happening, and in 1656 he published a paper about his discovery in the previous year of the first-known satellite of Saturn. At the end he included an anagram of the Latin text: 'Annulo cingitur tenui, plano, nusquam cohaerente, ad eclipticam inclinato'. Translated this is, 'It is surrounded by a thin, flat ring not connected with the planet in any place and inclined at an angle to the ecliptic'. Huygens published a full account of this discovery in 1659.

Because of the inclination of the rings to the ecliptic, their aspect presented to the Earth varies during Saturn's orbit around the Sun. Twice during the orbit, we on the Earth are able to see the rings open to the fullest extent; on one occasion the view is from the north and on the other from the south. At these times we are directly above latitude 28° on Saturn. Halfway between two successive fully-open positions the rings are viewed edge-on and, except in powerful telescopes, they seem to disappear completely. Viewing from the Sun, one would, of course, always see the sunlit side of the rings. Because of the Earth's own orbital motion it is sometimes possible for the other, unlit, side of the rings to be visible; they then appear as a dark narrow band across the planet's disc. This can only happen when the Earth is passing through the plane of the rings. Again because of the Earth's motion around the Sun, this passage through the plane of the rings may occur three times at fairly short intervals instead of just once. In 1966, for example, the Sun passed through the plane of the rings on June 15 but the Earth passed through on 2 April, 29 October and 18 December.

In 1675 G.D.Cassini realized that the ring around Saturn was double, with a dark gap between the inner and outer rings. This gap is now known as the CASSINI DIVISION, (figure 12.3). W.Struve named the outer ring RING A and the inner one RING B. Ring B is noticeably brighter than Ring A. A gap in Ring A was first noticed on 25 April 1837 by J. Encke and is now named ENCKE'S DIVISION after him. A third ring, inside Ring B, was seen by J.G.Galle in 1838. This is now called the CRÊPE RING, or simply RING C. It is tenuous and the planet can be plainly seen through it. Galle's discovery was ignored and the ring was rediscovered in 1850 by G.P.Bond and, independently, by W.R.Dawes. There has been

Table 12.3: Dimensions of Saturn's rings

	Kilometres	*Saturn radii*
Equatorial radius of Saturn	60 000	1.00
Outer edge of ring D	72 600	1.21
Inner edge of ring C	76 800	1.28
Inner edge of ring B	92 000	1.54
Outer edge of ring B	117 800	1.97
Inner edge of ring A	120 400	2.01
Outer edge of ring A	136 450	2.28
Mean distance of Janus from Saturn	168 700	2.81
Division between rings C and D	4200	—
Division between rings A and B (Cassini division)	2600	—

considerable controversy for many years about the presence of a fourth, extremely tenuous ring outside Ring A. This ring has been called RING D but its existence is by no means certain. Rather more certain is a ring inside Ring C. It is separated from Ring C by a dark division and reaches virtually down to the atmosphere of the planet. This ring has also been named Ring D, a logical choice, but one which can obviously lead to confusion. The radial dimensions of the rings are given in table 12.3.

The rings are undoubtedly very thin; this makes an actual measurement of their thickness very difficult. Certainly the thickness cannot be less than 500 m, is unlikely to be more than 4 km, and a value of 2 to 3 km seems most likely. The rings cannot be solid or liquid. James Clerk Maxwell showed this theoretically in 1857 and in 1895 J.E.Keeler found that the rings were in differential rotation (the inner parts take a shorter time to revolve around Saturn than do the outer parts) (figure 12.2). The rings consist of particles that move in individual orbits around Saturn according to *Kepler's laws*. The particulate structure is confirmed by at least six observations of stars seen right through Ring A, even though they were of magnitude 7.2 or fainter. Two stars of eighth magnitude have also been seen through the brighter, more dense Ring B. Observations such as these show that for light falling perpendicularly onto the rings about 35 to 50 per cent passes straight through Ring B and about 60 to 70 per cent through Ring A. The visual surface brightness of Ring B and parts of Ring A are somewhat higher than the mean surface brightness of Saturn itself. This indicates that the particles in the rings have a very high albedo. Spectroscopic studies of the light reflected from the rings have shown that the particles are largely ice or at least ice-covered, although the ice cannot be pure. Measurements of the infrared radiation from the rings have shown that the ring particles have a surprisingly high temperature, which implies that the particles must be fairly large and be warmer on the side facing the Sun and the Earth than on the other side.

Saturn's rings are the most distant objects to have been observed by radar; the radio waves take about 2 hours 40 minutes to make the round trip to Saturn and back. In the early 1970s R.M.Goldstein and G.A.Morris showed that the rings were efficient radar reflectors by transmitting and receiving strong echoes from them at a wavelength of 12.6 cm. The Doppler spread of the echoes matched that expected from the known range of orbital velocities of the particles in the bright inner Ring B. The radar reflectivity of the rings is five to ten times higher than for any of the other objects observed by radar: the Moon, Mercury, Venus, Mars and the asteroids Icarus, Toro and Eros. The radar observations require the reflecting objects to be centimetre-size or larger.

This minimum size of a few centimetres for the size of the ring particles is supported by several lines of evidence. Solar ultraviolet radiation and protons in the solar wind knock water molecules off the icy surface of the particles; this is technically known as SPUTTERING. During the lifetime of the Solar System several centimetres of ice would be eroded so that particles smaller than this would have completely disappeared by now unless they were of recent origin, which is thought to be unlikely. The POYNTING-ROBERTSON EFFECT would also clear the ring system of particles smaller than about 3 cm. This effect arises because forces other than gravity – especially radiation pressure – cause the orbits of particles to become gradually smaller so that they spiral in towards Saturn. The effect is greater for smaller particles than for large ones so that only those below a certain size could have spiralled all the way to Saturn's atmosphere since the Solar System was formed.

The evidence as a whole suggests that the ring particles have sizes measured in centimetres but this is by no means certain. Other poorly-understood aspects of the rings are their dynamics and origin. Some astronomers believe that the particles rarely collide with one another whereas others believe that collisions are very frequent. The gaps in the rings are thought to be caused by dynamical interactions with the satellites of Saturn, similar to the *Kirkwood gaps* in the asteroid belt. The ring particles may have condensed where they are at the same time as Saturn and its other satellites were formed. Alternatively the rings may be the result of the break-up of a larger object (or objects) by tidal disruption or as the result of a collision.

12.2: *Part of the spectrum of Saturn and its rings flanked on each side by a comparison laboratory spectrum. From the tilt of the lines, caused by the Doppler shift, can be calculated the rotation velocity at various points in the rings. This shows that the rings rotate not as a rigid body, but according to Kepler's laws, they must consist of separate particles. (Lowell Observatory, Arizona,* USA*)*

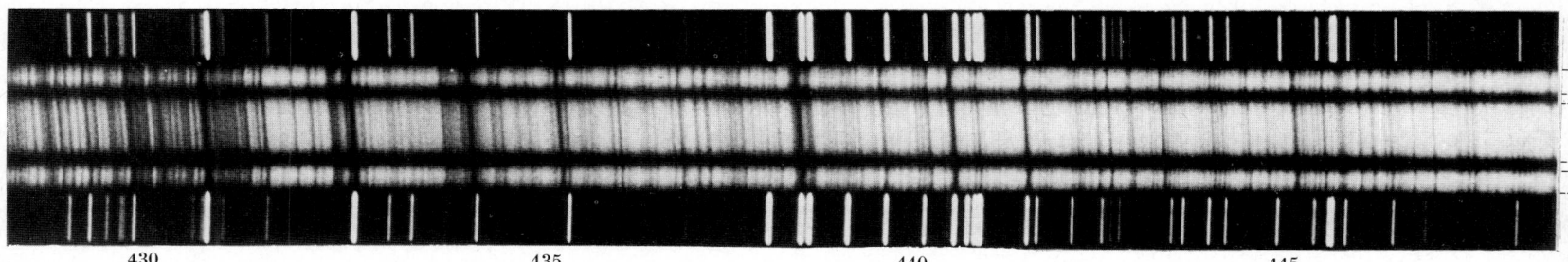

Wavelength (nm)
430   435   440   445

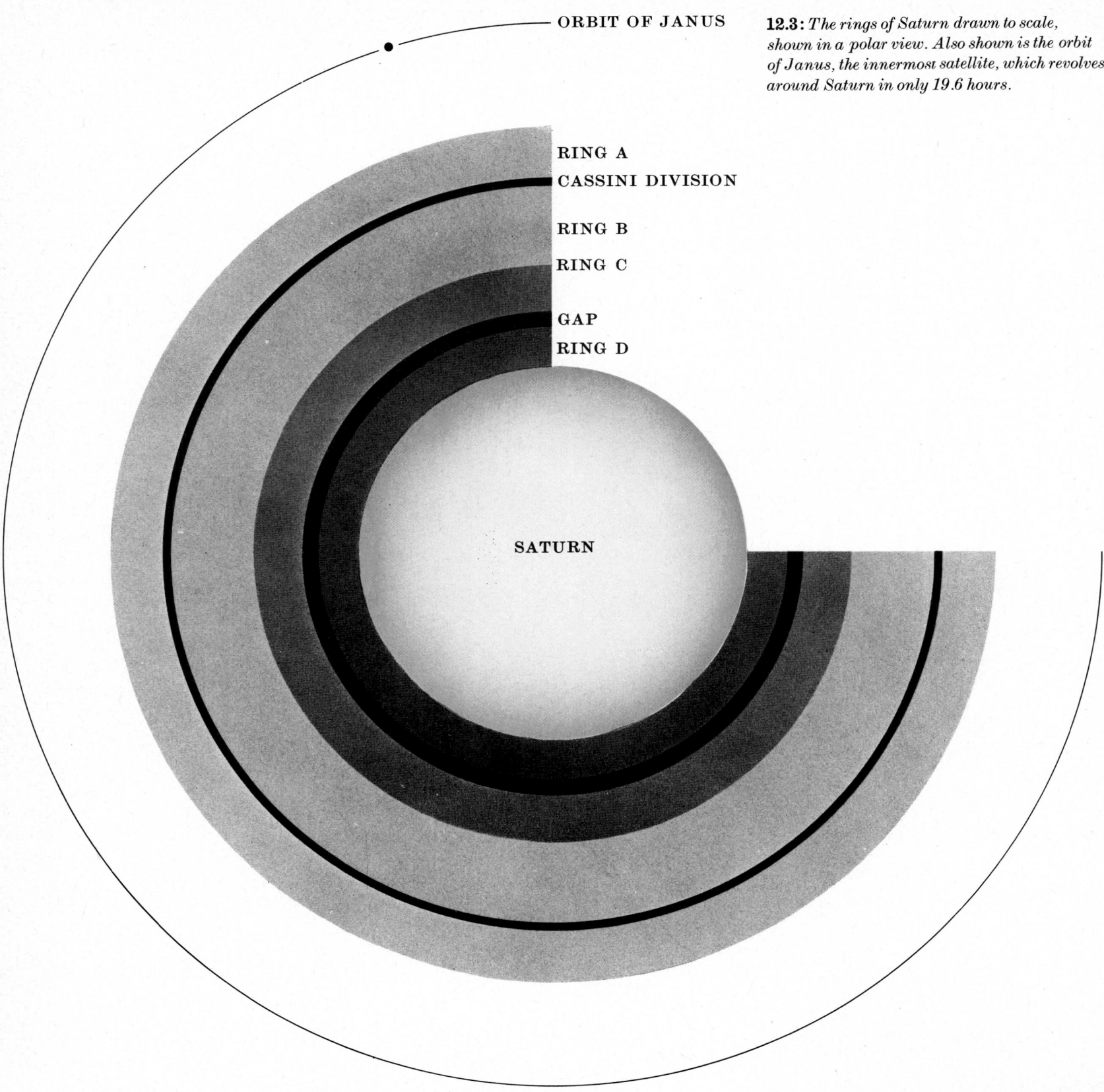

ORBIT OF JANUS

RING A
CASSINI DIVISION

RING B

RING C

GAP
RING D

SATURN

12.3: *The rings of Saturn drawn to scale, shown in a polar view. Also shown is the orbit of Janus, the innermost satellite, which revolves around Saturn in only 19.6 hours.*

Satellites of Saturn

In addition to the ring particles, there are ten SATELLITES of SATURN (table 12.4). The diameters of the satellites are difficult to measure from the Earth. Turbulence in the Earth's atmosphere blurs the image by at least 0.1 to 0.2 arc sec. This causes an appreciable error for an object whose apparent size may be only 0.3 second of arc, as is the case for Rhea. An opportunity to obtain more accurate values occurred on 29 March 1974 when the dark limb of the Moon occulted Saturn and its satellites. This was the first time that such an occultation of Saturn was observed by *photoelectric devices*, which enabled the time for each satellite to pass behind the lunar limb to be measured accurately. Observations were made of Iapetus, Rhea, Tethys, Dione and Titan and the derived values of the radii are given in table 12.4. In the case of Titan the strong signal showed that this satellite is definitely highly *limb-darkened* and has a radius of 2900 km. This value is substantially larger than the previously adopted value of 2500 km. Titan is now known to be the largest satellite in the Solar System although its mass is less than that of Ganymede.

Masses of most of the satellites have been obtained by observing their mutual perturbations. Most of these are uncertain and consequently even moderately reliable densities are only available for three satellites: Tethys, Dione and Titan. The ten satellites are rather substantial bodies for the most part. All of them are larger than the outer irregular satellites of Jupiter and at least five are bigger than the largest asteroid. Titan can be seen in a 5-cm telescope and Rhea, Dione and Tethys are visible in an 8-cm instrument.

TITAN is certainly the most interesting of Saturn's satellites as it is the largest and has an extensive atmosphere. Methane (CH_4) was detected there by Gerard Kuiper in 1944 and is the only constituent of the atmosphere to have been definitely identified. In 1972 L. Trafton claimed to have detected molecular hydrogen, and there are unidentified features in the spectrum which suggest the existence of at least one other gas on Titan. Ethane (C_2H_6) seems to be the most likely but ethylene (C_2H_4) or an isotope of methane have also been suggested. The interpretation of the spectrum is further complicated by the probable existence of an opaque cloud deck in the satellite's atmosphere. Titan's albedo decreases rapidly through the blue, violet and near ultraviolet, behaviour that is entirely opposite to what happens with a gas, and virtually the only explanation is the presence of an aerosol.

Before 1974 the mean density of Titan was believed to be 2100 kg m^{-3}. When the radius was remeasured and found to be larger than previously thought, the density dropped to 1400 kg m^{-3}. The radius obtained from the occultation data refers strictly to the cloud tops and not to the real surface. The height of the clouds is not known but D. Hunten has estimated about 150 km. This value decreases the radius to 2750 km and increases the density to 1600 kg m^{-3}. Whichever value is correct, Titan has a very low den-

Table 12.4: Satellites of Saturn

	Satellite	Discoverer	Year of discovery	Mean distance from Saturn (km)	Sidereal period (days)	Orbital inclination[1] (degrees)	Orbital eccentricity	Radius[3] (km)	V magnitude at mean opposition	Mass[4] (Saturn=1)	Mass[4] (Moon=1)	Mean density (kg m^{-3})	Rotational change in V magnitude[4]
X	Janus	A. Dollfus	1966	159 000	0.7490	0	0.0	150	14	?	?	?	?
I	Mimas	W. Herschel	1789	186 000	0.942422	1.517	0.020	200	12.2	6.6×10^{-8}	0.00051	?	?
II	Enceladus	W. Herschel	1789	238 000	1.370218	0.023	0.004	300	11.8	1.5×10^{-7}	0.001	?	(0.4)
III	Tethys	G. D. Cassini	1684	295 000	1.887802	1.093	0.000	500	10.5	1.10×10^{-6}	0.0085	1200	0.16
IV	Dione	G. D. Cassini	1684	377 000	2.736916	0.023	0.002	400	10.6	2.04×10^{-6}	0.0158	4300	0.20
V	Rhea	G. D. Cassini	1672	527 000	4.417503	0.35	0.001	800	9.9	(3×10^{-6})	(0.025)	?	0.19
VI	Titan	C. Huyghens	1655	1 222 000	15.945449	0.33	0.029	2900	8.3	2.462×10^{-4}	1.905	1400	0.00
VII	Hyperion	W. Bond	1848	1 483 000	21.276657	(0.28–0.93)[2]	0.104	220	14	(2×10^{-7})	(0.0015)	?	?
VIII	Iapetus	G. D. Cassini	1671	3 560 000	79.33084	15	0.028	800	10.7	(4×10^{-6})	(0.02)	?	1.92
IX	Phoebe	W. Pickering	1898	12 950 000	550.33	150	0.163	120	15	?	?	?	0.25

Notes: 1. To plane of rings. 2. Varies between 0.28 and 0.93 degrees. 3. The uncertainty in these values is at least 100 km. 4. In these columns values in brackets are highly uncertain.

sity and, like Ganymede and Callisto must be composed largely of low-density material such as solid ammonia, water and methane.

Another interesting satellite is IAPETUS, which is much brighter when to the west of Saturn than when it is to the east. This variation in brightness, of nearly two magnitudes, was immediately noticed by J.D.Cassini when he discovered Iapetus, and suggested, 'but it seems, that one part of his surface is not so capable of reflecting to us the light of the Sun which maketh it visible, as the other part is.' This has indeed proved to be the case, because Iapetus keeps one face turned towards Saturn as it revolves. It has a bright hemisphere, which reflects about 50 per cent of the incident sunlight and a dark hemisphere which reflects only 10 per cent. The best explanation of the cause is that Iapetus had a thin ice crust which has been eroded from only one hemisphere by bombarding *meteoroids*.

The inner eight satellites move in regular orbits almost exactly in the plane of Saturn's equator. They would seem to be true satellites formed together with Saturn, although the orbits of Titan and Hyperion are somewhat eccentric. Further out is Iapetus with an orbit inclined by 15° to Saturn's equator. Astronomers are uncertain whether Iapetus is a true satellite or a captured *asteroid*. The most distant satellite, Phoebe, is almost four times further from Saturn than is Iapetus. It moves in a noticeably elliptical and inclined orbit in a retrograde sense and is most probably a captured asteroid.

Satellites of Uranus and Neptune

Details of the SATELLITES OF URANUS and NEPTUNE are given in table 12.5. The radii of all five satellites of Uranus are too small to be measured directly, but values can be calculated from their observed brightness and an assumed albedo. If they are ice-covered, the radii could be as small as 100 km (Miranda) to 350 km (Titania) whereas extremely dark surfaces give radii as large as 650 to 2000 km. The tabulated values are a compromise between these two extremes.

W.Lassell detected Neptune's larger satellite, Triton, on 10 October 1846, less than a month after the identification of Neptune itself by J.G.Galle. The only other known satellite of Neptune is Nereid, discovered by G.P.Kuiper on 1 May 1949. The two satellites are quite unlike each other. Triton is in retrograde motion in an orbit close to Neptune with no detected eccentricity whereas Nereid is in direct motion in a highly eccentric orbit far from Neptune. This orbit takes Nereid as close as 140 000 km to Neptune and as far away as 9 500 000 km. From the observed brightnesses, Triton is apparently large and massive and Nereid is the opposite.

Triton's retrograde motion suggests that it is a captured asteroid whereas its circular orbit suggests that it is a true satellite. This apparent conflict has led to the suggestion that the planet Pluto is an escaped satellite of Neptune, which sent Triton into its peculiar orbit when it escaped. Pluto is not known to have any satellites.

Table 12.5 : Satellites of Uranus and Neptune

Satellite		Discoverer	Year of discovery	Mean distance from planet (km)	Sidereal period (days)	Orbital inclination[1] (degrees)	Orbital eccentricity	Radius[2] (km)	V magnitude at mean opposition	Mass[2] (planet = 1)	Mass[2] (Moon = 1)
Uranus :	Miranda	G. Kuiper	1948	130 000	1.414	0	0.00	120	16.8	1×10^{-6}	0.001
	Ariel	W. Lassell	1851	192 000	2.52038	0	0.003	350	14.3	15×10^{-6}	0.018
	Umbriel	W. Lassell	1851	267 000	4.14418	0	0.004	250	15.1	6×10^{-6}	0.007
	Titania	W. Herschel	1787	438 000	8.70588	0	0.002	500	13.9	50×10^{-6}	0.059
	Oberon	W. Herschel	1787	586 000	13.46326	0	0.001	450	14.1	29×10^{-6}	0.034
Neptune:	Triton	W. Lassell	1846	355 000	5.87654	160	0.00	1900	13.6	0.0013	1.8
	Nereid	G. Kuiper	1949	5 562 000	359.88	28	0.75	120	19.1	?	?

Notes : 1. To equator of planet. 2. These values are extremely uncertain.

The minor planets

The *Titius-Bode law* predicted that there should be a planet between Mars and Jupiter about 2.8 astronomical units from the Sun. In 1800 six astronomers, with Johann Schröter as president and Baron von Zach as secretary, worked out a scheme jointly to search for this missing planet. However, before their plans could be put fully into effect, another astronomer, G.Piazzi, discovered a planet on 1 January 1801 while he was compiling a star catalogue. The starlike object moved from night to night and Piazzi took it for a tail-less comet; however, he made enough observations for an orbit to be worked out. This showed that the object was not a comet, but a planet 2.77 astronomical units from the Sun, which is very close to the predicted 2.8. Piazzi named the planet CERES, after the patron goddess of Sicily where he was director of the Palermo observatory.

Ceres was found to be a very small body, about 400 km in radius and hardly seemed worthy of the name planet. The search for a missing planet continued and in March 1802 H.Olbers discovered another object, now called PALLAS, with a size and orbit very similar to those of Ceres. Olbers suggested that the two bodies may have formed when a larger object met with some disaster. This idea suggested the existence of other similar objects and Karl Harding discovered JUNO in 1804 and Olbers found VESTA in 1807. These two resembled Ceres and Pallas and the four became generally known as MINOR PLANETS or ASTEROIDS. The next asteroids to be found were Astraea in 1845 and Hebe in 1847, both discovered by K.L.Hencke. J.R.Hind found another two in 1847 and not a year has passed since then without at least one discovery. Vesta is the brightest asteroid, as seen from the Earth, and can sometimes be seen with the naked eye. Several others are within the range of binoculars and small telescopes.

When an asteroid has been sufficiently observed for a satisfactory orbit to be worked out it is given a number; these numbers therefore roughly give the order of discovery. There is also a temporary nomenclature which is used until a permanent number can be assigned. Since 1 January 1925 this has comprised the year of discovery followed by a pair of letters. The discoveries of January 1 – 15 are AA, AB, etc., of January 16 – 31 BA, BB, etc., up to December 16 – 31 when YA, YB, etc. are used (the letter J is not used). At the time of writing almost 2000 asteroids have been given permanent numbers and about another thousand still have only temporary nomenclature. In general these have been seen for a short period only, much less than an orbital period, and then never seen again. Asteroids are only named officially (generally by the discoverer) when they receive a permanent number.

The early asteroids were given dignified names from mythology but in time the supply of these names became exhausted and discoverers have resorted to other sources. Some are quite odd, such as 724 Hapag, the initials of a German navigation line, the Hamburg Amerika Paketfahrt Aktien Gesellschaft, and 694 Ekard. Ekard is Drake spelt backwards and was named by two members of Drake University in the USA.

Some representative asteroids are listed in table 12.6.

Systematic searches have been made for asteroids on two occasions: the McDonald survey from 1950 to 1952 and the Palomar-Leiden survey in 1960. From these surveys the number of asteroids brighter than photographic magnitude 21.2 at mean opposition has been found to be near 500 000. It has been estimated that the total mass of all these asteroids is only 2.4×10^{21} kg, which is 0.0004 of the Earth's mass. The largest asteroid, 1 Ceres, accounts for nearly half of this mass.

Nearly all asteroids have orbits with a mean distance from the Sun between 2.17 and 3.3 astronomical units which places them between the orbits of Mars and Jupiter. The lower limit appears to be due to the influence of Mars. Asteroids in smaller orbits would pass sufficiently close to Mars for their orbits to be significantly perturbed and the region closer to the Sun than 2.17 astronomical units has been almost entirely swept clean.

Figure 12.4b gives the distribution of asteroids with distance from the Sun, and this shows clearly that there are very few asteroids at certain distances: these are the so-called KIRKWOOD GAPS, named

after their discoverer (1866). At these gaps the orbital periods of the asteroids and Jupiter are in a simple ratio (i.e. they are in RESONANCE or are COMMENSURABLE). For example, at the 5:2 resonance five circuits of an asteroid's orbit take the same time as two of Jupiter. The gaps at the 2:1, 3:1 and 5:2 resonances are particularly prominent but there are several others. The 2:1 resonance in fact marks the outer limit of the main asteroid belt at 3.3 astronomical units from the Sun. An asteroid that was in one of the Kirkwood gaps would repeatedly pass Jupiter at the same small number of points in their orbits and the perturbations that it received would normally move it quickly into a different orbit. This does not always happen, however, and it is possible for an asteroid to become locked into an orbit at one of these distances under rather special circumstances. The most important of these asteroids are the TROJAN ASTEROIDS which have the same mean distance from the Sun and the same orbital period as Jupiter (the 1:1 resonance). There are two groups of Trojans, the ACHILLES GROUP whose members move an average of 60° ahead of Jupiter, and the PATROCLUS GROUP 60° behind (figure 12.5). 588 Achilles was the first such asteroid found

Table 12.6: Some representative asteroids

Number and name		Radius (km)	Mass (kg)	Rotation period (hr)	Orbital period (yr)	Mean distance from Sun (astronomical units)	Orbital eccentricity	Orbital inclination (degrees)
1	Ceres	380	1.17×10^{21}	9.08	4.60	2.766	0.079	10.6
2	Pallas	240	2.6×10^{20}	10.0	4.61	2.768	0.235	34.8
3	Juno	100	2.0×10^{19}	7.22	4.36	2.668	0.256	13.0
4	Vesta	240	2.4×10^{20}	10.68	3.63	2.362	0.088	7.1
6	Hebe	110	2.0×10^{19}	7.28	3.78	2.426	0.203	14.8
7	Iris	100	1.5×10^{19}	7.12	3.68	2.386	0.230	5.5
10	Hygiea	160	6.0×10^{19}	18.0	5.59	3.151	0.099	3.8
15	Eunomia	140	4.0×10^{19}	6.08	4.30	2.643	0.185	11.7
16	Psyche	140	4.0×10^{19}	4.30	5.00	2.923	0.135	3.1
51	Nemausa	40	9.0×10^{17}	7.78	3.64	2.366	0.065	9.9
433	Eros	7	5.0×10^{15}	5.27	1.76	1.458	0.223	10.8
511	Davida	130	3.0×10^{19}	5.17	5.67	3.190	0.177	15.7
1566	Icarus	0.7	5.0×10^{12}	2.27	1.12	1.078	0.827	23.0
1620	Geographos	1.5	5.0×10^{13}	5.23	1.39	1.244	0.335	13.3
	Apollo	0.5	2.0×10^{12}	—	1.81	1.486	0.566	6.4
	Adonis	0.15	5.0×10^{10}	—	2.76	1.969	0.779	1.5
	Hermes	0.3	4.0×10^{11}	—	1.46	1.290	0.475	4.7

12.4a: *Asteroid 1976 AA, the first to be discovered in 1976, photographed on 14 January that year. During this 10 minute exposure the asteroid moved 71 seconds of arc to the north west (top right). 1976 AA and 1976 UA are the only asteroids known with orbital periods of less than a year. (Table Mountain Observatory, California, USA)*

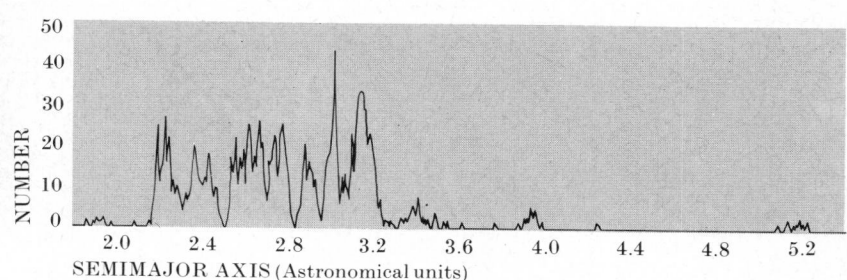

12.4b: *The distribution of 1563 asteroids with semimajor axis (the mean distance from the Sun). The diagram shows the number of asteroids in each interval of 0.01 astronomical unit. At some distances there are very few asteroids. These Kirkwood gaps are caused by the gravitational influence of Jupiter. The gap at 2.5 astronomical units, for example, marks the distance at which an asteroid would have an orbital period exactly one-third that of Jupiter.*

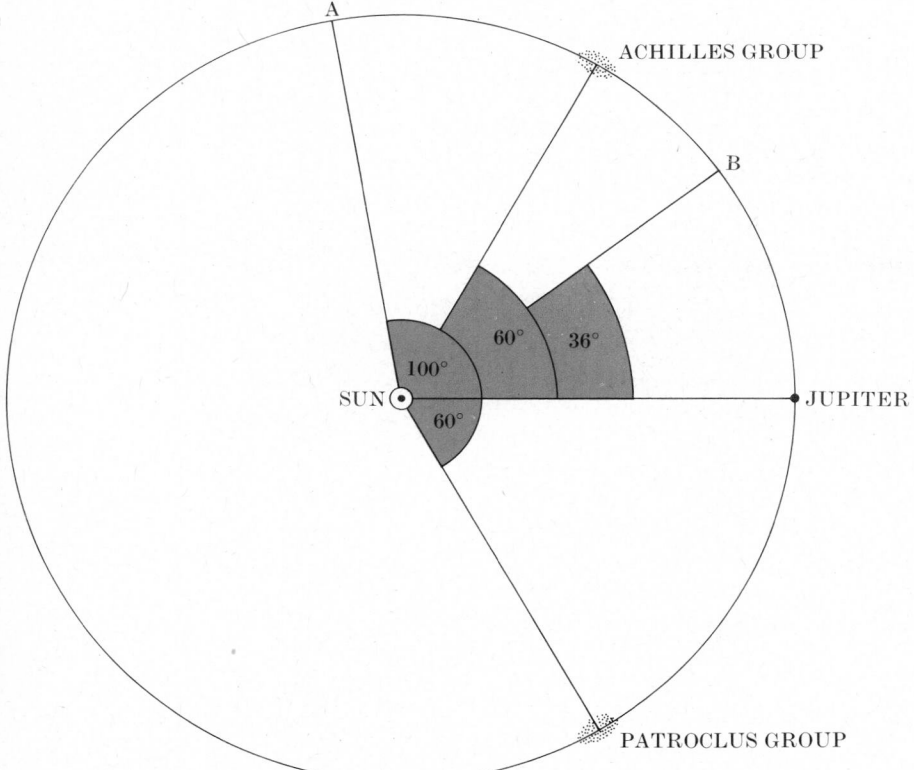

12.5: *The two groups of Trojan asteroids have the same orbital periods as Jupiter. The members of each group remain 60° ahead of, or behind, Jupiter on average, but can move appreciable distances away from their mean positions. An example is given by 1437 Diomedes which varies its position between the points marked A and B. These asteroids also vary their distances from the Sun.*

(1906) and subsequent discoveries were given names of other combatants in the war between Greece and Troy and the whole group came to be known as the Trojans. Special surveys have shown that there are about 700 asteroids brighter than mean opposition magnitude 20.9 in the preceding Achilles group but only about half that number in the following Patroclus group. The outer satellites of Jupiter are probably captured Trojan asteroids.

Apart from the main belt, there are a number of asteroids that come much closer to the Sun. Those that cross the Earth's orbit are called Apollo asteroids after the first to be discovered to do so. Apollo was first seen on 24 April 1932 by Karl Reinmuth and was followed only until 15 May of that year when it became too close to the Sun in the sky to be seen, although on that day it was only 11 000 000 km from the Earth. The orbit was determined from the observations and showed that at *perihelion* Apollo was just 0.65 astronomical units from the Sun and inside the orbit of Venus. From its brightness Apollo is estimated to be only about one kilometre across. Nineteen asteroids are known in the APOLLO GROUP and some details are given in table 12.7. Their diameters are between about one kilometre for Adonis, Hermes and 1976AA and 6 km for 1972XA, except for minute P–L 6344 and 1976UA which may be only 200 m across. The Apollo asteriod 1566 Icarus, 1976UA and 1976AA are particularly notable as they have the smallest known orbits. Asteroid orbits are shown in figures 12.6 and 12.7.

The closest observed approach of an asteroid was made by Hermes in 1937 when it passed only 780 000 km from the Earth, barely double the distance of the Moon. Hermes could come even closer and pass between the Moon and the Earth!

One very special object is 944 HIDALGO, the asteroid with the largest known orbit. Its mean distance from the Sun is 5.8 astronomical units but because of the high eccentricity (0.66) it moves as far out as 9.7 astronomical units from the Sun and as close as 2.0 astronomical units. It is also the only asteroid ever known to approach within one astronomical unit of Jupiter, having passed within 0.38 astronomical units in 1673.

The bulk of the asteroids, those in the main belt between Mars and Jupiter, have orbital eccentricities smaller than the Apollo group but larger than the major planets. The mean eccentricity of the objects in the Palomar-Leiden survey is 0.147 with a range from 0 to 0.385. The average inclination of asteroid orbits is about 4° near the inner edge of the main belt rising to 11° near the outer edge. The larger asteroids have, on average, larger inclinations so that they are less well confined to the ecliptic than the smaller ones.

The study of the structure of asteroids requires a knowledge of their masses and radii. Only three masses are known and one of these is very uncertain. These three were obtained by observing the gravitational perturbations of one asteroid on the orbit of another. These perturbations are normally too small to measure but they have been large enough for useful measurements to be made in two cases: a series of close encounters of 4 Vesta with 197 Arete and for the mutual interaction of 1 Ceres and 2 Pallas. From the observations astronomers have been able to calculate the following masses:

Table 12.7: The known Apollo asteroids

Name	q	Q	i
1566 Icarus	0.19	2.0	23
1936 CA (Adonis)	0.44	3.3	1
1976 UA	0.46	1.2	6
1971 FA	0.56	2.4	22
1971 UA	0.58	1.6	16
1937 UB (Hermes)	0.62	2.7	6
1973 EA	0.62	2.9	40
1932 HA (Apollo)	0.65	2.3	6
1685 Toro	0.77	2.0	9
1976 AA	0.80	1.1	19
P-L 6743	0.82	2.4	7
1620 Geographos	0.83	1.7	13
1947 XC	0.83	3.7	1
1959 LM	0.83	1.9	3
1950 DA	0.84	2.5	12
1972 XA	0.87	2.9	41
1973 NA	0.88	3.7	67
1948 EA	0.89	3.6	18
P-L 6344	0.94	4.2	5

Q and q are the distances from the Sun at aphelion and perihelion respectively (in astronomical units) and i is the orbital inclination (in degrees). The P-L in two of the names refers to objects found in the Palomar-Leiden survey. The data for these two asteroids and 1947 XC are uncertain.

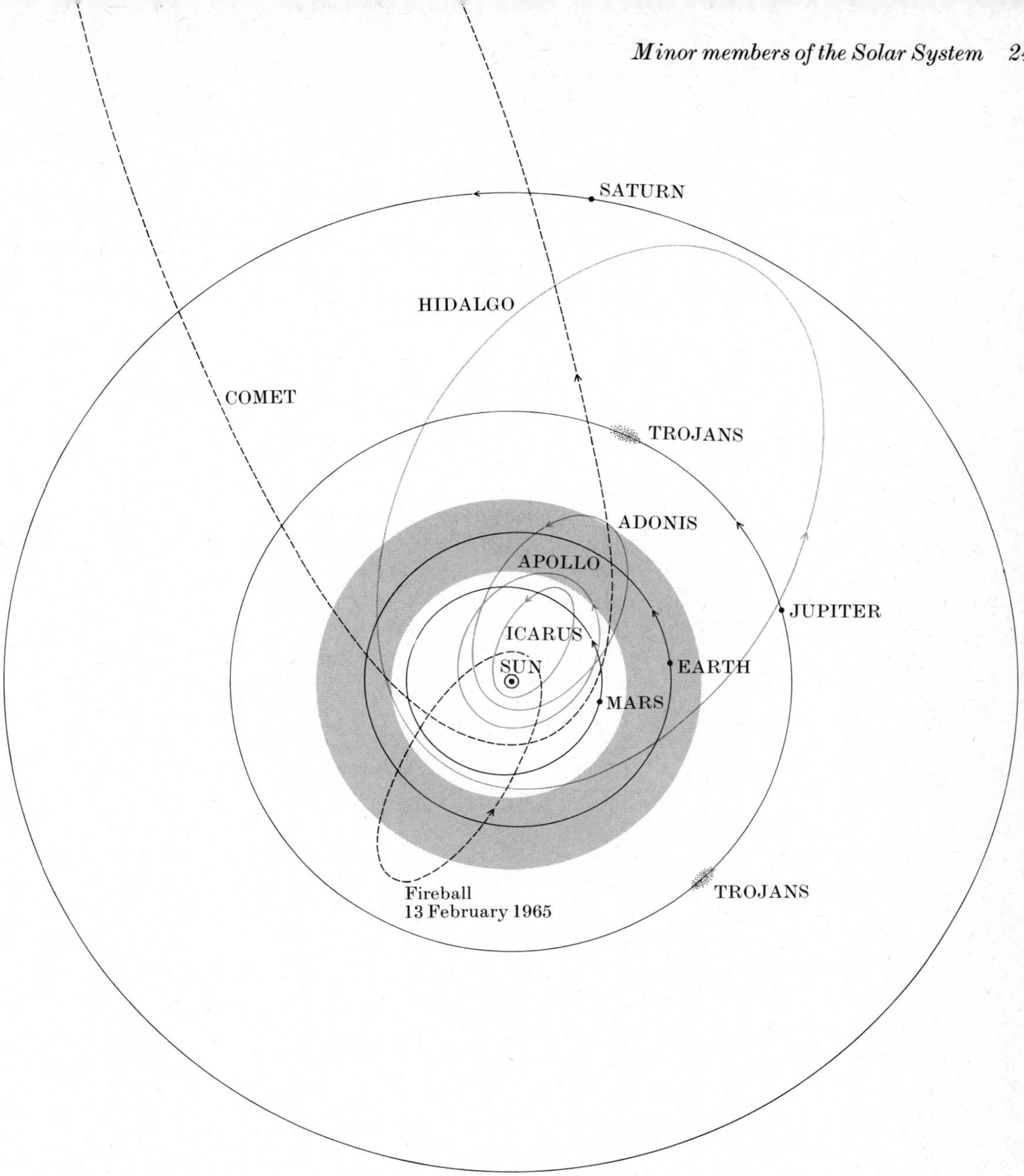

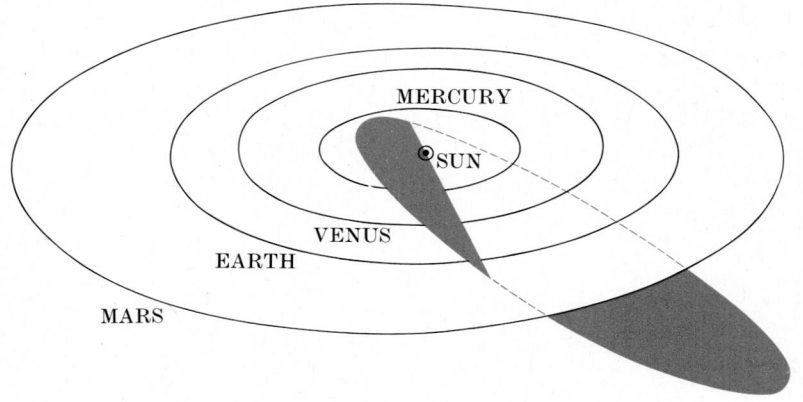

12.6: *The orbit of Icarus which is one of the smallest asteroid orbits known; the mean distance from the Sun is only 1.078 astronomical units. Because of its high orbital eccentricity of 0.827, Icarus is only 0.186 astronomical units from the Sun at perihelion and is inside the orbit of Mercury. At aphelion it is 1.97 astronomical units from the Sun. Although this is beyond the orbit of Mars it is still inside the main asteroid belt. Icarus was only discovered because it crosses the ecliptic close to the Earth's orbit so that a close approach to the Earth is possible.*

12.7: *Some representative asteroid orbits as seen from above the Solar System. Most asteroids move in a belt between Mars and Jupiter (here shown tinted). Apollo, Adonis and Icarus are members of the Apollo group with orbits that pass inside that of the Earth. Hidalgo has the largest asteroid orbit known which takes it out as far as Saturn. Also shown are orbits of a typical comet and of a meteor which grazed the Earth's atmosphere and caused a fireball in 1965.*

1 Ceres	$(11.7 \pm 0.6) \times 10^{20}\,\mathrm{kg}$
2 Pallas	$(2.6 \pm 0.8) \times 10^{20}\,\mathrm{kg}$
4 Vesta	$(2.4 \pm 0.2) \times 10^{20}\,\mathrm{kg}$

The uncertainty in the mass is particularly large for 2 Pallas. Some other masses, based on the radius and an assumed value of the density, are given in table 12.6

Only the first four asteroids have diameters sufficiently large to have been measured directly, but two other, indirect, methods are available for obtaining diameters. An asteroid of a particular visual magnitude may be small, but highly reflective, or large and very dark. However the asteroid heats up more in the second case than in the first, both because it is larger and because it absorbs more of the incident light, and it therefore emits more infrared radiation. By comparing the amount of this radiation with the reflected visual radiation, an astronomer can determine the asteroid's albedo and then, from its visual magnitude, its diameter. This technique was first applied to asteroids in 1970 by David Allen and Dennis Matson and several astronomers have now used it to obtain the diameters of some tens of asteroids.

The second indirect method uses measurements of the amount of polarization in the sunlight reflected from an asteroid and the way in which this varies with direction. This approach has been used by Joseph Veverka, Ben Zellner and Edward Bowell to obtain the diameters of a couple of dozen asteroids. They make measurements of the polarization and then use the results of laboratory experiments to deduce the albedo. A measurement of the apparent visual magnitude and a simple calculation then give the diameter. Some of the results from all three methods are compared in table 12.8, which shows that the values obtained by the photometric and polarimetric methods agree quite well with each other but are obviously systematically larger than the direct measures. It must be remembered, however, that the direct measurements are of angular diameters of, at most, only a few tenths of a second of arc and are therefore subject to large errors.

Most asteroids have an irregular shape or some variability in reflectivity over their surfaces (or both) so that as they rotate the amount of light that they reflect to the Earth varies. It is therefore generally possible to measure the rotation period by observing the light curve and this has been done for about 50 asteroids. The accurately measured periods range from 2.273 hours for 1566 Icarus to 18.813 hours for 532 Herculis, but there appear to be a few objects with much longer periods. An example of the difficulties of interpreting the light curves of asteroids is furnished by 4 Vesta. Astronomers have known for many years that Vesta varies its light by about 0.15 magnitude with a maximum every 5 hours 20 minutes. Two interpretations of this variation are possible. Vesta could be a nearly spherical, spotty body with a rotation period of 5.33 hours, or an elongated body with twice this period. Tom Gehrels made a detailed analysis of photoelectric observations in 1967 which appeared to show conclusively that the shorter period was correct. However in 1971 R.C.Taylor made a new series of observations which clearly showed that successive maxima of Vesta's

12.8: *The light curve of the asteroid 433 Eros, measured photoelectrically by R.L.Millis on 24 December 1974, when the amplitude was close to the maximum possible. The curve covers nearly one complete rotation of Eros, during which there are two maxima and two minima. The two curves at the bottom of the B − V (blue minus yellow) and U − V (ultraviolet minus blue) colour indices show virtually no change indicating that the light variations are predominantly due to the elongated shape of Eros.*

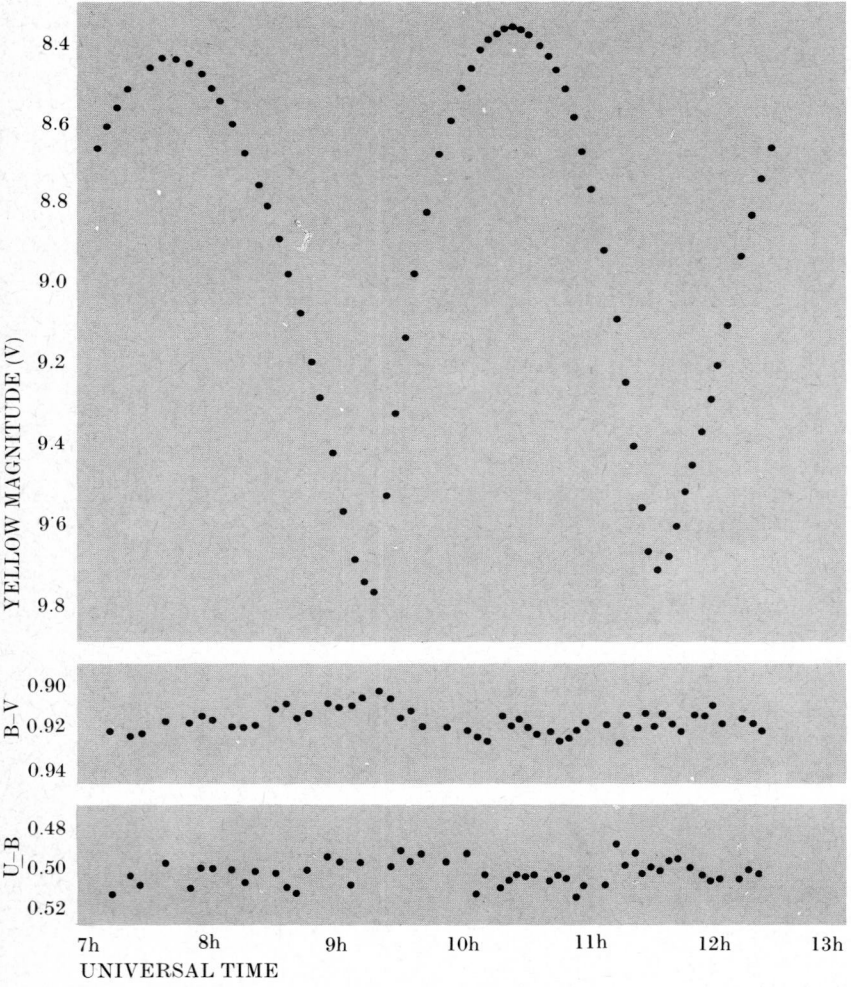

light curve alternated in height so that the true period was 10 hours 41 minutes during which two maxima and two minima occur. These observations were made at a time when Vesta's southern hemisphere was turned towards the Earth. When we view the northern hemisphere the two maxima during each rotation period become indistinguishable because of the different albedo variations in the two hemispheres. The observations can be explained if Vesta is a spheroid with one diameter 15 per cent longer than the other two. There is a flattened region near the south pole which may be a large impact crater like those on *Phobos* and *Deimos*.

Now that astronomers are able to measure the radii of asteroids accurately, they can convert measurements of the light reflected at various wavelengths into albedos and deduce something about the composition. Roughly speaking, there are two classes of asteroid. Some are moderately bright reddish objects which reflect 10 to 20 per cent of the incident blue light and 14 to 23 per cent of the red light. The others are dark grey and reflect nearly the same amount of the incident sunlight at all wavelengths; this amount varies between about three and nine per cent. This means that most asteroids are at least as dark as the Moon and some, such as 324 Bamberga (the blackest asteroid known), are much blacker still. In very general terms we can say that the red asteroids are composed largely of silicate-type material and the dark grey asteroids of carbonaceous chondritic type.

Many astronomers have suggested that there is a connection between asteroids and *meteorites*. Clark Chapman and John Salisbury have made detailed comparisons of the albedos of asteroids and meteorites. They have found only three asteroids which resemble ordinary *chondritic meteorites*: the Apollo asteroid 1685 Toro and, from the inner edge of the main belt, 8 Flora and 43 Ariadne. A further five, 2 Pallas, 4 Vesta, 16 Psyche, 29 Amphitrite and 192 Nausikaa, match other, less common, types of meteorite. More important than these matches is the fact that there are many asteroids that resemble no known meteorite and meteorites that resemble no studied asteroid. This is consistent with the idea that most stony meteorites are derived from a few atypical asteroids.

Three asteroids, 433 Eros, 1566 Icarus and 1685 Toro have been detected by radar when close to the Earth. Icarus and Toro have been only marginally detected but improved techniques and the favourable circumstances of its close approach to the Earth in 1975 resulted in data of much higher quality for Eros. The observations were made at a wavelength of 3.8 cm and show that the surface of Eros must be rough on a scale of centimeters. Since the results from the optical polarimetry used to measure the diameter also tell us that Eros is dusty, the radar results suggest that the dust is too thin to smooth out rock outcrops, edges and depressions on a scale of centimetres.

The width of the radar spectrum, together with the rotation period, gave a measurement of the diameter of Eros independent of the results from the polarimetric and photometric methods. All agree that the longest and shortest diameters are about 36 and 15 kilometres.

Table 12.8: Asteroid diameters (in kilometres)

Asteroid		Direct measurement	Radiometric measurement	Polarimetric measurement
1	Ceres	770	1000	1050
2	Pallas	490	530	560
3	Juno	195	240	225
4	Vesta	390	530	515
8	Flora	—	170	155
15	Eunomia	—	260	260
17	Thetis	—	100	90
21	Lutetia	—	120	100
23	Thalia	—	120	90
40	Harmonia	—	120	95
63	Ausonia	—	110	110
511	Davida	—	300	270
532	Herculina	—	170	120

12.9: *The Leonid meteor shower photographed in a 3½ minute exposure on 17 November 1966, showing the apparent divergence from the radiant. Two meteors that directly approached the camera appear as dots instead of trails. (D.Milon, USA)*

Meteors, meteoroids and meteorites

If you view the sky on a clear moonless night you may see streaks of light several times per hour. These luminous streaks are called shooting stars or METEORS (figure 12.9). The Solar System contains a large number of small particles moving in orbits around the Sun. In the vicinity of the Earth these particles typically have a speed of $65\,\mathrm{km\,s^{-1}}$. The orbital speed of the Earth is $30\,\mathrm{km\,s^{-1}}$, so that a relative speed anywhere between 35 and $95\,\mathrm{km\,s^{-1}}$ is possible. If one of these particles intercepts the Earth and enters the atmosphere, the air resistance quickly heats up the particle to incandescence and it is visible as a streak of light. At the same time the air along the meteor trail is ionized. The light of a meteor can, with only very rare exceptions, be seen only at night but the trail of ionized gas reflects radio waves and can therefore be detected by radar both by day and by night. Typically, a meteor is completely vaporized in less than a second. The larger and brighter meteors may last longer and give a trail hundreds of kilometres long. The brightest meteors emit so much light that they are able to cast shadows. They are called FIREBALLS and may even be seen during daylight (figure 12.10). They are occasionally accompanied by a sound like thunder which is presumably a sonic boom like that associated with supersonic aircraft. Fireballs sometimes explode in flight and are then called BOLIDES. Although most meteors are completely destroyed during their flight through the Earth's atmosphere a few penetrate to the surface. They are then known as METEORITES. The word meteor is used somewhat loosely to describe either the visible trail, the associated ionized gas or the actual solid particle responsible for these. It is now customary to use the word METEOROID for the particle before it reaches the surface of the Earth, and METEOR for the observable trail which it produces in the atmosphere.

If a meteor trail is photographed from two places its path can be obtained by surveying techniques. The two observing stations need to be about 30 km apart: this is far enough to provide a good baseline but not so far that the meteors are not visible from both stations! Meteors typically become visible about 100 km up since the Earth's atmosphere is too tenuous at greater heights to raise the particle to incandescence. The brighter meteors remain visible down to a height of 55 km or less while fainter (and smaller) ones fade at about 80 km. The speed of a meteoroid may be obtained by the use of a shutter which periodically cuts off the light to the camera and breaks the photographed meteor trail up into segments. The orbit of the meteoroid around the Sun, before it entered the Earth's atmosphere, can then be determined. Radar observations of meteor trails can also be used in a similar manner. All the orbits so far determined are elliptical, indicating that the meteoroids come from within the Solar System; no hyperbolic orbits, indicative of an interstellar origin, have been found. The spectra of the brightest meteors can be obtained by placing a prism over the objective of a meteor camera. The results indicate that meteoroids have a composition similar to meteorites.

Although a single, naked-eye, observer will see about six to eight meteors per hour he is only seeing the brightest meteors over a small part of the Earth's surface. The total number of particles entering the atmosphere every day is enormous, but when allowance is made for the very small mass of each particle, a total mass of about 1000 tonnes falls on the Earth each day, although this figure is extremely uncertain. Most of this mass is in the form of MICROMETEORITES. These are particles that are so small that the air resistance is very large compared to their masses. They are slowed down so much that they do not glow and vaporize, but instead drift undamaged to the ground. They are smaller than a few micrometres across and can be found in large quantities on the ground and in deep-sea sediments. Naturally it is difficult to distinguish them from ordinary terrestrial dust. A better way to collect micrometeorites is with rockets and spacecraft.

The rate at which meteors appear is not constant and varies both during the night and over a year. It is always greater after midnight than before, and in northern latitudes it is greater in the autumn and winter months. On some nights a much greater number of meteors than usual appears to give what is known as a METEOR SHOWER. Meteors not in a shower, that occur at all seasons, are called SPORADIC METEORS. The meteors in a shower seem to radiate from one point in the sky, called the RADIANT; in a few cases there are two radiants within one shower. The apparently divergent trails are an effect of perspective on the actual trails which are parallel. These meteor showers recur each year regularly at the same date, although the actual number of meteors may vary. A list of the main

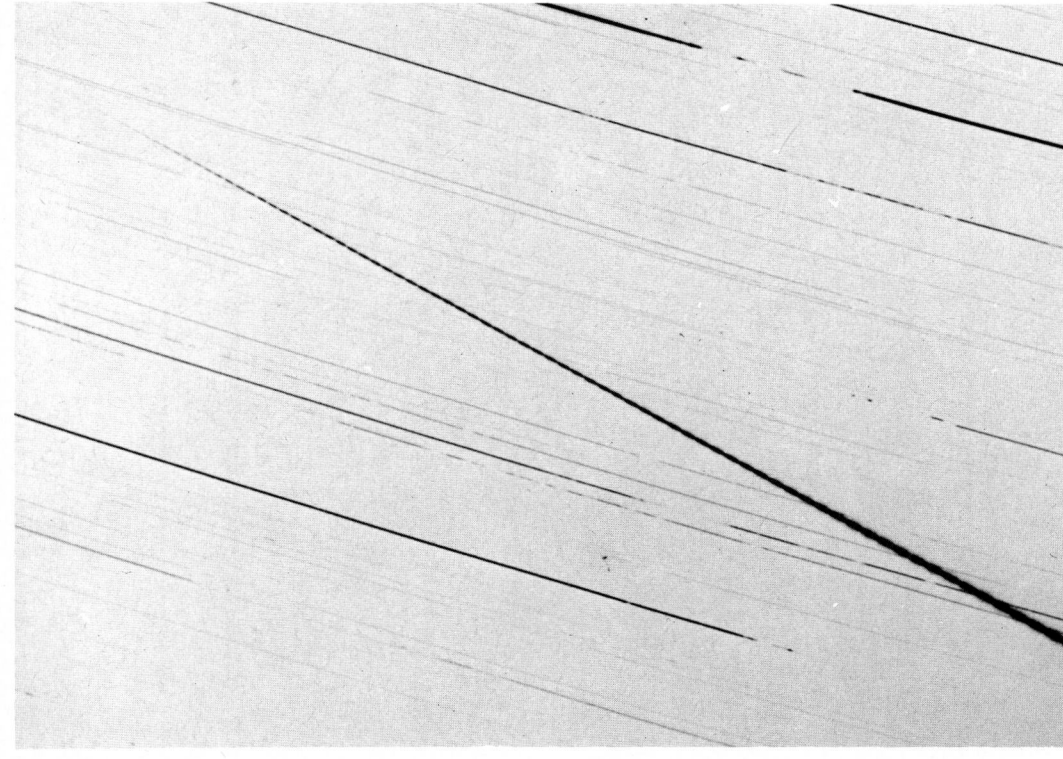

12.10: *The Primbram fireball in a negative photograph taken on 7 April 1959. A rotating shutter cut off the light ten times every second. The number of breaks in the trail shows that the meteor took seven seconds to cross the photograph. (Ondrejov Observatory, Czechoslovakia)*

Table 12.9: Meteor showers.

The list of night-time showers includes all the major and minor showers

Name	Duration	Maximum	Radiant R. A. h m	Dec °	Zenith hourly rate at maximum
Night-time showers					
Quadrantids	*Jan 1–6*	*Jan 4*	15 28	+50	110
Corona Australids	*Mar 14–18*	*Mar 16*	16 20	−48	5
April Lyrids	*Apr 19–24*	*Apr 22*	18 08	+32	12
η Aquarids	*May 1–8*	*May 5*	22 24	00	20
June Lyrids	*June 10–21*	*June 16*	18 32	+35	8
Ophiuchids	*June 17–26*	*June 20*	17 20	−20	6
Capricornids	*July 10–Aug 15*	*July 25–26*	21 00	−15	6
δ Aquarids	*July 15–Aug 15*	*July 27–28*	22 36 / 22 36	00 / −17	35
Pisces Australids	*July 15–Aug 20*	*July 31*	22 40	−30	8
α Capricornids	*July 15–Aug 25*	*Aug 2*	20 36	−10	8
ι Aquarids	*July 15–Aug 25*	*Aug 6*	22 32 / 22 04	−15 / −06	6
Perseids	*July 25–Aug 18*	*Aug 12*	03 04	+58	68
κ Cygnids	*Aug 19–22*	*Aug 20–21*	19 20	+55	4
Orionids	*Oct 16–26*	*Oct 21*	06 24	+15	30
Taurids	*Oct 20–Nov 30*	*Nov 8*	03 44 / 03 44	+14 / +22	12
Cepheids	*Nov 7–11*	*Nov 9*	23 30	+63	8
Leonids	*Nov 15–19*	*Nov 17*	10 08	+22	10 ?
Phoenicids	*Dec 4–5*	*Dec 4–5*	01 00	−55	5 ?
Geminids	*Dec 7–15*	*Dec 14*	07 28	+32	58
Ursids	*Dec 17–24*	*Dec 22*	14 28	+78	5
Day-time showers					
o Cetids	*May 13–23*	*May 15*	02 00	−03	15
ζ Perseids	*June 1–16*	*June 8*	03 56	+22	40
Arietids	*May 30–June 18*	*June 8*	02 56	+23	60
β Taurids	*June 25–July 7*	*June 29*	05 40	+17	24

showers is given in table 12.9. Most of them are named after a star close to the radiant or the constellation containing the radiant. In general a shower lasts just a few days each year, although some, such as the best known, the PERSEIDS, are visible for a month or more. The number of meteors in a shower is often measured by the ZENITH HOURLY RATE (Z.H.R.) at maximum. The observed rate at which a naked-eye observer sees meteors depends strongly on the altitude of the radiant and is greatest when the radiant is at the zenith (i.e. directly overhead). At a radiant altitude of 27° the observed rate is reduced to a half of this and at 2.6° to only 10 per cent. The ZHR is the hourly rate for an observer watching under very good conditions with the radiant at the zenith. The figures in table 12.9 are for an experienced observer who can see meteors as faint as magnitude 6.5. The actual rates vary somewhat from year to year; for some showers the variations are substantial. The most extreme example of these variations is shown by the Leonid shower. This shower gave spectacular displays in 1799, 1833 and 1866, suggesting a period of 33 or 34 years. Few meteors were seen in 1899 or 1933 and the general expectation was that this would continue in 1966. In fact the most spectacular display in meteor history occurred. After a steady climb over several hours, the rate suddenly peaked sharply over a few minutes at 150 000 meteors an hour.

Many meteor showers have been associated with *comets*, particularly in the cases where there is little difference between the orbits of the comet and the meteoroid particles. For example the Leonids are associated with comet 1866 I (P/Temple-Tuttle), the η Aquarids and Orionids with P/Halley and the Taurids with P/Encke. Matter from comets is spread around the comet's orbit, and when the orbit passes close to the Earth's, the Earth will intercept the cometary material once (or occasionally twice) a year and produce a meteor shower. In some cases the matter is unevenly spread around the cometary orbit so that the shower strength varies from year to year; this is particularly so for the Leonids.

On 7 April 1959 a Czech fireball of magnitude − 19, which led to the Pribram meteorite fall, was successfully photographed by accident. This showed the possibility of predicting impact points of meteorites by the photography of fireballs. Three networks of automatic cameras were set up to cover large areas of the American and Canadian prairies and most of Czechoslovakia and West Germany, a total of three million square kilometres of the Earth's surface. The results of the photography showed that fireballs are about ten times more frequent than was previously thought but that only about one per cent of them actually lead to a meteorite fall. Most of the meteorites that cause fireballs must be made of fragile material, possibly of cometary origin, which is destroyed in the Earth's atmosphere. The few objects that survive to become meteorites are probably of a different nature and, quite possibly, are effectively very small asteroids. This is confirmed by the photographs of the Pribram fall and of a fall on 8 January 1970 at Lost City, Oklahoma, which showed that the orbits of the meteorites around the Sun were elliptical with *aphelia* in the asteroid belt.

Detailed calculations have shown, however, that the supply of material from the asteroid belt is insufficient to provide the parent bodies of more than a small fraction of the bright meteors.

About 500 meteorites fall on the Earth each year. Since only 30 per cent of the Earth's surface is land the number that is accessible for recovery should be about 150, but of these only about ten are actually recovered. A meteorite is generally named after the town or village nearest to which it was found or some readily identifiable topographical feature.

Meteorites are classified according to composition and structure. The basic classification is into IRONS, STONY-IRONS and STONES. Most of the stones contain small spheroidal aggregates known as CHONDRULES which are typically one millimetre across. The stones are therefore divided into CHONDRITES (those with chondrules) and ACHONDRITES (those without). About 60 minerals are known in meteorites but many of these are only minor constituents; the common minerals are listed in table 12.10. These differ in several ways from terrestrial minerals: for example nickel-iron is practically absent from terrestrial rocks. The common meteorite minerals are largely magnesium-iron silicates whereas quartz (silicon dioxide) and aluminosilicates are abundant on Earth. Meteorites are largely anhydrous (i.e. free from water of crystallization) whereas hydrated minerals are common and abundant on Earth. From the types of minerals found we can deduce much about the conditions under which meteorites formed; for example iron and nickel must have been present largely as the free metal. Meteorites do not contain minerals formed under high pressure, which would indicate formation as part of a large parent body. The only exception to this is the diamond found in iron fragments of the Canyon Diablo meteorite which formed the Arizona Meteor Crater (figure 12.11) and the small group of meteorites known as ureilites. This diamond appears to have been produced by the shock of impact in the first case and by extraterrestrial shock effects in the second.

Figure 7.1 shows photographs of some typical meteorites. Most meteorite finds are irons, which are resistant to weathering and are easily recognized as peculiar objects. An iron is therefore more likely to be found than a stone. This bias in the relative proportions of irons and stones can be largely overcome by considering only those meteorites which are seen to fall. About 84 per cent of falls are chondrites with nine per cent achondrites, six per cent irons and one per cent stony-irons.

Table 12.11 shows the chemical composition of meteoritic matter. The average compositions of iron meteorites and the metal in chondrites are almost identical, indicating a common origin. The differences between the other types, both in the proportions of the various elements and of the minerals that they make up, show that however the meteorites may have formed, they do not come from a single parent body.

There is another small class of meteorites which we have not yet mentioned, the CARBONACEOUS CHONDRITES, which differ fundamentally from the other classes and consist mainly of the mineral serpentine $(Mg,Fe)_6Si_4O_{10}(OH)_8$. They are remarkable for the

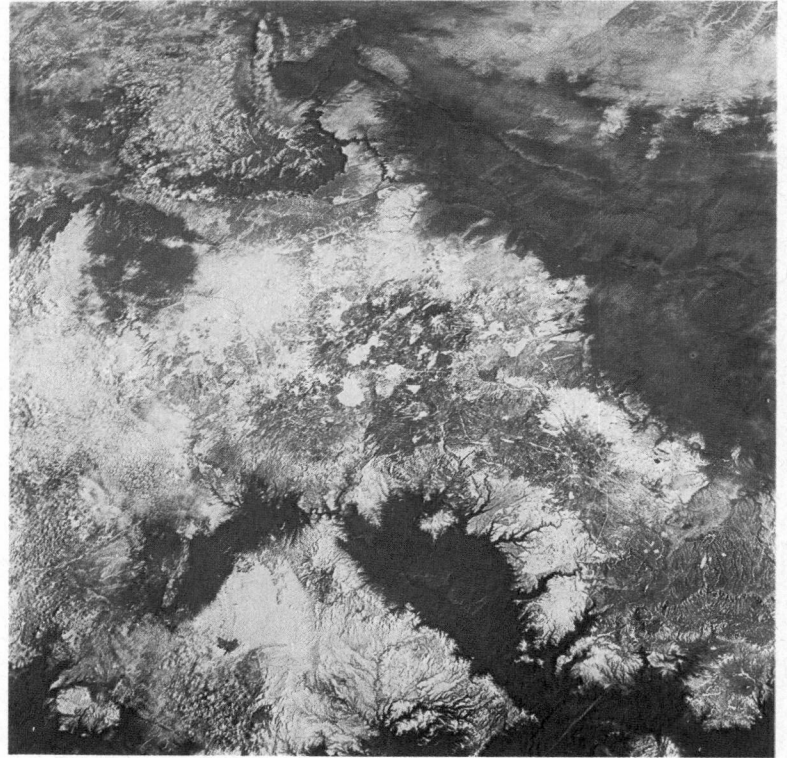

12.11: *An oblique view of northeast Arizona. The very small bright circle is the best known terrestrial meteor crater, a kilometre and a half across and 170 m deep, the result of the impact of an iron meteorite probably weighing a million tonnes. (NASA, Apollo 9, USA)*

Table 12.10: The common minerals in meteorites

Kamacite	α — (Fe, Ni)	(4–7 per cent nickel)
Taenite	γ — (Fe, Ni)	(30–60 per cent nickel)
Troilite	FeS	
Olivine	$(Mg, Fe)_2SiO_4$	
Orthopyroxene[1]	$(Mg, Fe) SiO_3$	
Pigeonite	$(Ca, Mg, Fe) SiO_3$	
Diopside	$Ca (Mg, Fe) Si_2O_6$	
Plagioclase	$(Na, Ca) (Al, Si)_4O_8$	

Note:
1. Orthopyroxine is divided into enstatite, bronzite and hypersthene according to the ratio of iron to magnesium.

considerable amounts of organic compounds of extraterrestrial origin that they contain and for the close correspondence between their chemical composition and that of the Sun. Chondrites, and especially carbonaceous chondrites, are now recognized to be relatively well-preserved samples of the non-volatile material of the nebula from which the Sun and planets formed. Most chondrites show signs of having been heated within their parent bodies to around 800°C or higher. If a fairly small proportion of these parent bodies reached 1400–1500°C they would have melted and separation of the various constituent elements could have occurred (as in the Earth) to give the achondrites, irons and stony-irons.

The cooling rate, and hence the size of the parent body, can be deduced from examination of a meteorite. Such studies have indicated that 90 per cent of iron meteorites have come from at least six and possibly as many as eleven parent bodies and that all but one of them were larger than 200 km in diameter. Similarly, there were at least five, or as many as ten, parent bodies for the chondrites with diameters in the range 180 to 300 km.

Table 12.11: The chemical composition of meteorites (weight per cent)

	Metal (from irons)	Metal (from chondrites)	Silicate (from chondrites)	Average chondrite
Oxygen	—	—	43.7	33.2
Iron	90.8	90.7	9.88	27.2
Silicon	—	—	22.5	17.1
Magnesium	—	—	18.8	14.3
Sulphur	—	—	—	1.93
Nickel	8.59	8.80	—	1.64
Calcium	—	—	1.67	1.27
Aluminium	—	—	1.60	1.22
Sodium	—	—	0.84	0.64
Chromium	—	—	0.51	0.39
Manganese	—	—	0.33	0.25
Phosphorus	—	—	0.14	0.11
Cobalt	0.63	0.48	—	0.09
Potassium	—	—	0.11	0.08
Titanium	—	—	0.08	0.06

Interplanetary light

The dust which reaches the Earth, or is collected by spacecraft as micrometeorites makes its presence known in another way. The particles that make up this dust travel in elliptical orbits around the Sun and are concentrated in the plane of the ecliptic. They reflect the light of the Sun to give a luminous band around the sky. As seen from the Earth, the brightness of the light falls away rapidly with increasing angular distance from the Sun and the ecliptic to give what is known as the ZODIACAL LIGHT (figure 12.12). This phenomenon has been known since antiquity and was described as the false dawn in the Rubaiyat of Omar Khayyam, the Persian astronomer-poet, around AD 1100. Because of the tilt of the Earth's axis, the zodiacal light is most easily seen after sunset in spring and before sunrise in autumn in the northern hemisphere, and vice versa in the southern. It is best seen on a clear moonless night somewhere well away from the glare of city lights. A casual observer is often convinced that it is twilight that he is seeing because of the brightness and large extent of the light. The term zodiacal light is generally used just for the light seen within about 90° of the Sun. In 1854 T.J.Brorsen discovered a patch of light in the night sky exactly opposite the Sun; he named it the GEGEN-SCHEIN, which in English means reflection or counterglow. Later Brorsen also discovered a light bridge or ZODIACAL BAND joining the gegenschein to the true zodiacal light and thereby completing a band of INTERPLANETARY LIGHT along the whole ecliptic. Figure

12.12: *The zodiacal light photographed at Chacaltaya in Bolivia. (D.E.Blackwell, Oxford, UK)*

12.13: *The interplanetary light visible to the naked eye. The contour lines join points of equal brightness and are labelled with numbers proportional to this brightness. Visible observations are only possible within about 10 to 15° of the ecliptic where the contrast and brightness are sufficiently high. This diagram is based on observations made by Cuno Hoffmeister in Namibia in the 1930s.*

12.13 shows the relative brightness of the various parts of the interplanetary light that are visible to the naked eye. P.J.van Rhijn and others have shown that substantial amounts of interplanetary light are visible in all parts of the sky. Away from the ecliptic, the contrast is very low and as a result the light is not noticed by visual observers.

Studies of the interplanetary light are somewhat hindered by the other sources of light in the night sky. As well as scattered moonlight and more local effects such as city lights and *aurorae* there are two other contributions to the undisturbed light of the night sky, the nightglow and integrated starlight. Together with the zodiacal light these three sources provide roughly equal amounts of light. The NIGHTGLOW is emitted by atoms and molecules in the Earth's atmosphere at an altitude of about 80 km. Because this is relatively low, an observer on the ground sees minimum brightness directly overhead and an increase towards the horizon. INTEGRATED STARLIGHT is the combined effect of faint stars that cannot be seen individually by the naked eye. Because of the very flattened shape of the Galaxy this light is largely confined to the region of the galactic equator. To study the interplanetary light, nightglow and integrated starlight, astronomers must first separate their relative contributions. The nightglow is the easiest to remove because it is well known how it varies with altitude and it does not move around the sky as the Earth rotates. The zodiacal light moves relative to the stars as the Earth orbits the Sun and this motion allows its separation from the integrated starlight. The uncertainties inherent in these methods mean that it is not unusual for studies to differ by a factor of two or more. Satellite observations can be made above the Earth's atmosphere in order to eliminate the nightglow. Spacecraft are being sent further and further from the Earth, and when observations from beyond Saturn become available in the 1980s it is expected that these will show only a small contribution from the interplanetary light and will allow more accurate studies of the integrated starlight. Astronomers hope that in due course these new techniques will allow them to distinguish more accurately the three phenomena and learn more about each.

ELONGATION WEST OF SUN

Comets

Comets have excited interest in men's minds from time immemorial. There are two classes of comets. First, but less important, are the SHORT-PERIOD COMETS moving in eccentric orbits at planetary distances from the Sun, and of these about a hundred are known. Second, are the far more numerous LONG-PERIOD COMETS, of which almost 500 have been observed through the ages, the periods of which are so long, anything from a thousand years to several million, that there must be many million of them gravitationally bound to the Sun and destined to arrive eventually in the inner reaches of the Solar System to become observable from the Earth. Although comets move under the gravitational influence of the Sun and planets, none has ever been found to produce any disturbance itself, though some have even passed within the satellite system of Jupiter.

Comets are usually discovered by systematic searches, using a low-power 'comet-seeker' with a large field-of-view, but discovery occurs from time to time on photographic plates, often taken with some other purpose in mind, and this is becoming more frequent with wider and wider sky surveys for different objects. In a few cases, comets have suddenly come into view close to the Sun during total eclipses, suggesting that many comets are present only ever in the daylight sky and escape observation altogether. Perhaps the most remarkable cometary discovery of all happened in 1896 when Perrine, at the Lick Observatory, received information stating the latest position of a comet he himself had discovered shortly before, but the telegram was garbled and gave the wrong position more than 2° away from the true one. Naturally quite unaware of this, Perrine made observation in the stated place and by an amazing coincidence found an entirely new comet right there in the middle of the eye-piece!

The practice for newly-discovered comets is to assign them the names of their discoverer or discoverers, sometimes with an added parenthetical number if the observer already has other comets to his credit, though in a few cases the names given are those of astronomers that have made special theoretical study of a comet, as for instance Halley and Encke. But it has been found more useful to supplement this nomenclature by labelling comets as successively detected in any year by the letters a, b, c, etc. in turn, with the letter P often added for the return of a periodic comet. Thus 1976e P/d'Arrest was the fifth comet discovered in 1976 and a return of comet d'Arrest first found in 1851. Often considerably later, when the precise times of perihelion have been established, all comets coming to perihelion in a given year are re-labelled with a Roman numeral affixed to the year concerned: thus 1971b P/Holmes became 1972I, while 1971c became 1972XI. This notation has obvious advantages, and its uniqueness of designation can fail only for the rare exceptions of comets that undergo large perturbations into entirely different orbits.

The short-period comets are no more than the minor remnants of

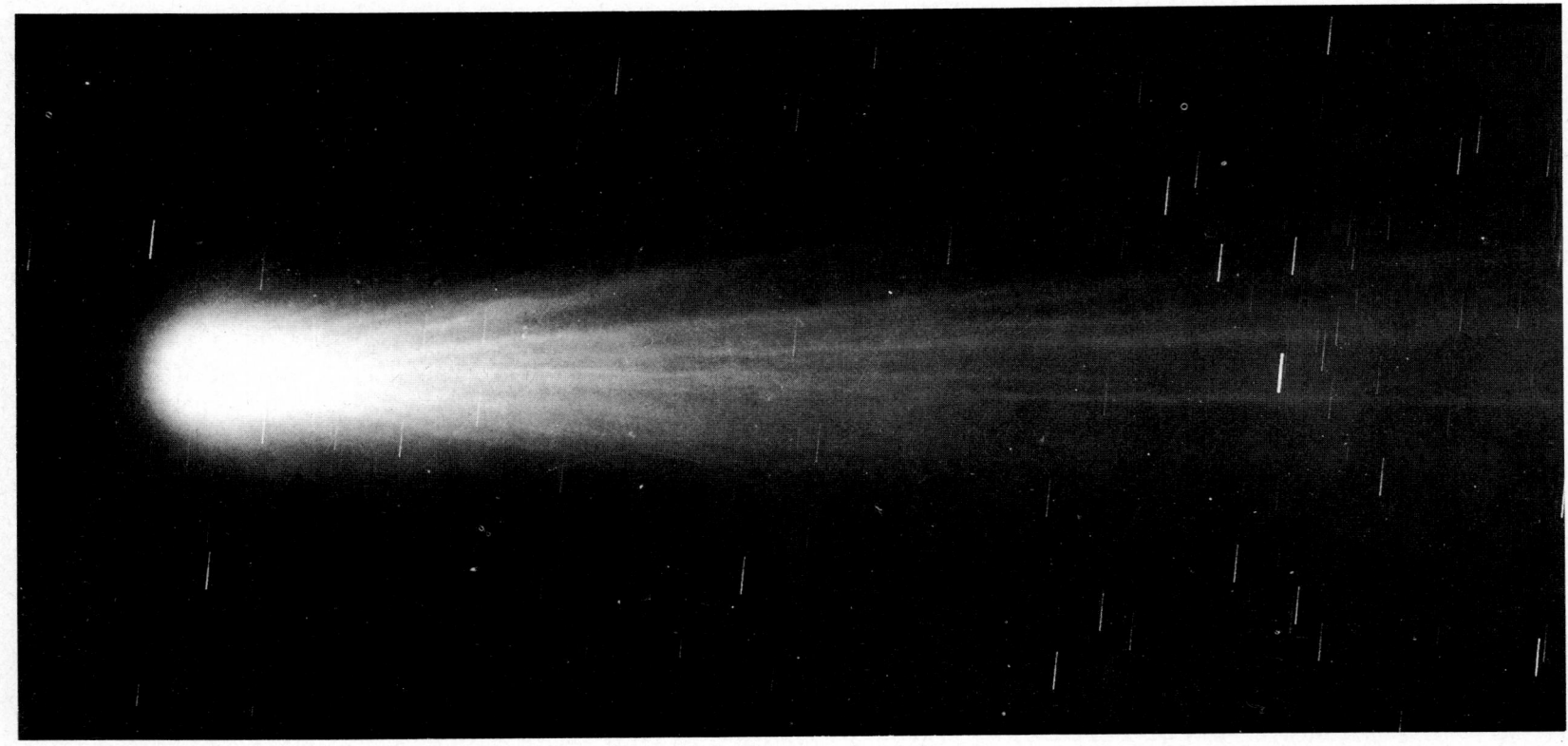

former long-period comets that have chanced to pass close to Jupiter and be deflected into their present orbits. The Earth itself passes quite close to the paths of some of these comets, and, as we have mentioned, at the appropriate time of year there is an accompanying *meteor shower* in which tens to even hundreds of thousands of meteors can be seen from any station on Earth. The comet itself may be far away at another part of the orbit. These meteors associated with comets are tiny solid particles – none has ever been known to reach ground level – that have gradually moved away from the main mass of the comet, and they establish that comets when quiescent are nothing more than a vast swarm of widely-separated dust particles. Stars are seen undimmed right through the heads of comets.

At the distances from the Sun at which they move, short-period comets cannot hold themselves together by their own gravitation, and it is through collisions and solar radiation acting on their particles that they become spaced out into meteor streams in a few thousand years. By radio techniques, some meteor streams have been found spread all round an orbit, but with no associated comet remaining. Halley's comet, of which records exist going back over 2,000 years, has orbital period ten times the average short-period comet, and so may be that much longer lived than most. It is due to return close to the Sun early in 1986, but detailed studies already made suggest that it is unlikely to be at all a brilliant object as seen from the Earth.

12.14: *Comet Bennett, the great naked-eye comet of 1970. As with all comets, the tail streams away from the direction of the Sun. The equal density tracing of this photograph shows the structure in the tail and head. (Tautenberg Observatory, DDR)*

On the other hand, the long-period comets can hold themselves together gravitationally when at great distance from the Sun, even though their masses may be only about a millionth that of the Moon and spread through a volume several times that of the Sun. It is at such distances, thousands of times the Sun-Earth distance, that in accordance with the laws of motion they must spend practically all their time, and this may be hundreds of thousands or even millions of years, before coming back in to the immediate neighbourhood of the Sun.

It is this huge irregularly shaped dust-swarm structure of comets that gives them seemingly most curious properties when they arrive at planetary distances and come under the dominating influences of solar gravitation and also solar radiation which can repel small particles of the order of the wavelength of sunlight in size as well as certain gaseous molecules. Leonardo da Vinci was fascinated by comets, and was moved to write: 'Why, this comet seems variable in shape, so that at one time it is round, at another long, at another divided into two or three parts, at another united, and sometimes invisible and sometimes become visible again.' All these phenomena are understandable as a result of the development of a vast irregular swarm of tiny particles (some comets are larger than the Sun even in their observable overall bulk and may in fact have far greater extent still) as it pursues its orbit, and the chance relationship of the position of the Earth to the comet at its most active stages when it is nearest the Sun.

Through inevitable dynamical causes, a comet must turn itself inside out, as it were, on the part of its orbit nearest the Sun, those particles at first moving on one side of the median plane crossing through it in one direction and those to the other side crossing through to meet them as two opposing streams. The relative speeds are sufficiently high that a great deal of gas and much finer dust particles are released as a result of collisions, and then solar radiation can come into operation to repel certain of the gases and minute dust particles and bring about the impressive tail-effects so well known. When a comet first appears on the way in, it is usually no more than a large hazy patch of light so dim as to be scarcely distinguishable from the background sky, but as it approaches the Sun it contracts in some of its dimensions, as seen from the Earth, and may even extend in others, and it may increase in brightness far more rapidly than could be accounted for by mere approach towards the Sun. The quality of the light may also change, at first being mainly scattered and reflected sunlight but then beginning also to emit light of its own apparent making. The greatest depths in the line of sight through the comet may often give the appearance of higher condensation of light within the general COMA (the overall visible head of the comet), and occasionally within this condensation there may seem to develop a starlike point of light, which is termed the NUCLEUS. Only a small proportion of comets come to exhibit a nucleus, and then not at all times, while on the other hand a few comets have shown more than

12.15: *Comet Kohoutek provided a spectacular display in 1973–74. This is a very long-period comet which will not again come into our part of the Solar System for many thousands of years. Other comets, such as Comet Halley, have been captured by the planetary system, and they swing in past the Earth more frequently. The next appearance of Halley will be in 1986.*
(Hale Observatories, California, USA)

12.16: *Comet West blazed through the sky in 1975, accompanied by a glorious fan-shaped tail.*
(Table Mountain Observatory, California)

one nucleus at times. But it has to be remembered that this is merely the impression that the human eye reports to the brain, and there can be no question of any sizeable object being present within a comet capable of emitting an unresolvable point-source of light.

As to where these comets come from in their millionfold numbers, (there must be these huge numbers to keep up the observed average annual supply), study of their orbits reveals remarkable properties that throw considerable light on the question. They are found to be by no means randomly distributed. For instance, ten so-called SUN-GRAZING COMETS are known that all come in from almost exactly the same direction in space, and in almost identical orbits, apart from their different timing. There are over fifty such COMET GROUPS, as they are termed, though with fewer members. There is found to be a very strong association of these directions from which the long-period comets approach the Sun and the direction of motion of the Sun itself relative to the surrounding stars in the Galaxy. Indeed, it has been known for almost a century that more than 60 per cent of comets have their perihelion-points within no more than 45° of the solar apex, which means only 15 per cent of the whole area of the sky. This is exactly the opposite of what would be expected if comets simply came in, as they are, from interstellar space. (It may be added that careful dynamical calculations inescapably show that comets all come in from finite, though in some cases, very large distances.) Moreover, the directions on the celestial sphere from which they come are found to be strongly concentrated to the galactic plane in a kind of belt-like distribution. These correlations reinforce the theory that comets represent dense aggregations of interstellar dust formed by the gravitational focusing action of the Sun as it pursues its orbit in the Galaxy and from time to time finds itself passing through one of the vast gas-and-dust clouds that abound in the Galaxy and lie near the galactic plane. Examination of this mechanism explains exactly why comets move in the highly elongated orbits they do, near-parabolas which bring them in almost directly towards the Sun and then back out again on a nearly parallel path.

12.17: *Long-period comet Humason came round in 1962. This one had a perihelion distance of 2.13 AU so that it never ventured inside the orbit of Mars. The elongated head is several thousand kilometres in diameter, and the tail shines largely by reflected sunlight.*

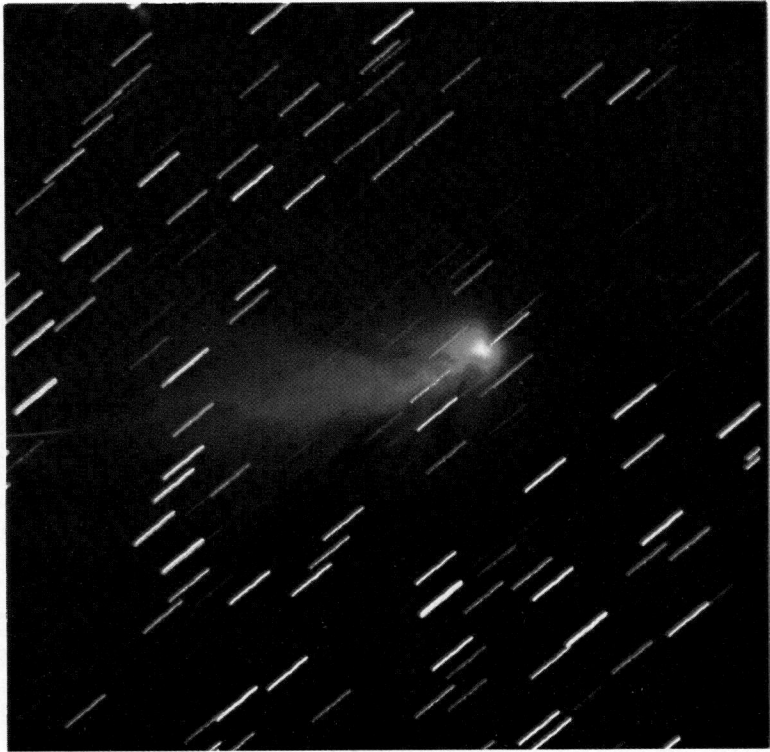

Unlike the planetary orbits, which are stable for tens of millions of years at the least, these elongated cometary orbits are highly sensitive to the action of the great planets, Jupiter especially because of its great mass. At each return to the Sun, so weakly bound are the long-period comets, there is a high probability, something like an even chance for a comet selected at random, of its being ejected altogether from the Solar System in a hyperbolic orbit, never to return. This makes it almost certain that comets, by astronomical standards, are recent additions to the Solar System, and not all formed at the same time. Much the same conclusion is also indicated by the fact that at each return to the Sun, a comet loses a small but finite proportion of its mass. Halley's comet, for example, loses material in tail production, which goes on for a matter of months, and decay to meteors (there is a meteor stream associated with the comet), and if at each approach it lost only a

millionth of its mass (almost certainly it loses a good deal more), then going backwards in time to the beginning of the Solar System its initial mass would need to be far greater than that of the Sun!

As a consequence of the highly elongated orbits, even a bright comet (most remain faint telescopic objects) may arrive unexpectedly and leave to become undetectable after a few months. This unpredictability, except for the faint short-period comets, leads to their not receiving the degree of attention by means of large telescopes and professional astronomers as do less erratically moving objects. Discovery of comets is made mainly by amateurs using powerful binoculars or small telescopes with large fields of view. But despite this, comets may well be objects of the highest astronomical interest, for they may represent samples of interstellar material accessibly deposited in the Solar System instead of remaining for ever beyond the reach of man.

The material of different comets may well have quite different ages, and differ from the age of the Solar System; this would be a question of the greatest interest to be able to answer. The material of short-period comets is eventually swept into the Sun as a result of the dissipative action of solar radiation on small particles.

There is a great deal still to be learnt about comets, much of it possibly only by means of space missions to the few that are both predictable and accessible. Finally, since every star in the Universe may have a retinue of comets in number of the same order as does the Sun, comets may have special importance if only as the most numerous class of celestial objects in the Universe.

12.18: *With increasing exposure time, the apparent size of the head of a comet increases, the actual dimensions in this case being 3500, 6000, 13 000, and 22 000 km. These observations of Comet Kohoutek were made with an image-intensifier camera. (Lowell Observatory, Arizona, USA)*

The origin of the Solar System

The origin of the planets constitutes one of the central problems of astronomy, perhaps the more so as it includes the origin of the Earth itself. The problem has remained a permanent challenge down the years, and has stimulated many attempts which even if not yet entirely successful have led to important new lines of study. Thus the most famous equation in physics, $\nabla^2 \varphi = 0$, was first come upon in 1787 by Laplace in a study of the *rings of Saturn*, while the theory of rotating gravitating liquids, which has application to the planets, has led to important advances in both dynamics and pure mathematics.

Many lines of evidence show inescapably that not only the Earth but the Sun itself cannot be infinitely old, but we do not yet know if the same holds for the Universe. Radioactivity sets a limit to the age of the Earth of not more than 5000 million years. The question has always been of wide interest whether other solar systems exist moving round other stars, but even if such systems existed in abundance there is but the slenderest possibility of detecting other planets, even if as large as Jupiter at stellar ranges. Only if the mechanism of formation of planets were fully understood might it become possible to know if other stars possessed planetary systems. Yet another reason for study of the problem is to make sure that the Solar System can happen within the laws of science, without invoking any supernatural cause.

We cannot yet be certain that existing laws of nature and knowledge of the contents of space itself are adequate for the problem to be solved. For generations, it was widely believed that the whole history of the world could be encompassed in a time-span that went back only to the year 4004 BC, and the possibility raised by Newton's work of tracing the planets backwards in time to that date must have given many the thrilling prospect of determining the circumstances of Creation itself! But it soon became clear how doomed to failure this was, and increasingly so amid the deeper and deeper knowledge of the astronomical world since attained.

The celebrated NEBULAR HYPOTHESIS of Laplace (1749–1827) in some of its features has proved the most enduring perhaps of all, for, after almost a century of excursions into hypotheses of other kinds, most recent theories bear considerable resemblance in broad appearance to the Laplacian scheme. In this hypothesis, it is assumed that the planets condensed from a nebula that itself finally contracted into the primitive Sun. Unbeknown to Laplace, it seems, similar ideas to this had been proposed verbally in less precise form by Swedenborg as early as 1734, and also by the great Kant in 1755 who assumed that such a nebula would heat up as a result of contraction. But he incorrectly supposed that it would develop rotation of its own accord, and do so increasingly rapidly for the nebula to shed a succession of rings at its outer rim that would collect lengthwise into the several planets. Laplace understood the need for endowing the nebula with rotatory momentum from the outset, and he also assumed that it would take on the form of a lens-shaped distribution distended by the high initial temperature, with subsequent cooling bringing about the necessary contraction and increasing rotational speed. Although these developments were not established with much rigour, the theory obviously held out the possibility of explaining at least the closely circular and co-planar character of the planetary orbits.

The seeming successes of the hypothesis must for a time have shielded it from much criticism, and first serious misgivings seem to have arisen from a study by Maxwell (1831–1879) of the rings of Saturn, a study that showed that a fluid or gaseous ring could not aggregate into a single mass, as had been supposed it could. A wider question, impossible to meet at the time of Laplace or indeed of Maxwell, was that of the origin of the postulated nebula itself, and it is to the answering of this that most modern theories have in the first place been addressed. Another serious difficulty is that if any such nebula extended out to the distance of Neptune and were rotating sufficiently quickly at that stage to have become unstable at its outer edge, the angular momentum of the whole mass would have been so great that the central end-product, the Sun, would have been left rotating very much more rapidly than it does, an unsatisfactory implication that any hypothesis must avoid if it is to be acceptable, as the Sun contains well over 99 per cent of the mass of the whole system.

Following these criticisms, attention began to return to so-called CATASTROPHIC HYPOTHESES. The earliest known attempt on such lines had already been made far earlier by Buffon (1770), who suggested that some great body, inappropriately termed a comet, had collided with the Sun to generate the planets in an unspecified way. In 1880 Bickerton revived the idea, but perceived that only an object of stellar mass could be expected to be capable of removing material from the powerful gravitational field of the Sun. From the appearance of *spiral nebulae* (whose nature was then unknown), Bickerton conjectured that the Sun underwent grazing impact with another star for each to acquire a tongue of gaseous material so heated by the collision as to extend out into the requisite nebula. The orbits of the planets were to be associated with the plane of motion of the two stars in their encounter. A fatal defect attends any such process, however, for although material might be removed from the two stars, such an encounter cannot endow it with more than a minute fraction of the rotatory momentum associated with the great extent of the actual system compared with the size of the Sun: Jupiter moves at 1000 solar radii, and Neptune at about 6000.

Some appreciation of this defect may have moved Chamberlain (1843–1928) and Moulton (1872–1952) to develop their famous PLANETESIMAL THEORY in which the star passes much further out from the Sun, but disturbs it by strong tidal action causing it to erupt a succession of so-called bolts of material to distances comparable with those of the great planets on the side nearer the star, and less violent ejections on the remoter side carrying the bolts to the distances of the terrestrial planets. The inner remains of these bolts went to form the initial cores of the planets, while the outer parts would expand and cool into a vast swarm of infinitesimal solid particles spread out into a disc-like distribution rotating round the Sun in a plane and direction determined by the motion of the passing star. The cores, by gradually gathering in the planetesimals, would round up their initially highly eccentric orbits. The main objection is of the same nature as before in that for serious tidal action to take place the star would need to pass far too close to the Sun to supply the angular momentum requisite for the vast scale of the Solar System.

Not long before this, Jeans (1877–1947) investigated purely tidal action as a means of removing material from the Sun, examining the mechanism mathematically rather than merely asserting verbal conclusions. It was shown that, if a similar star passed within a few diameters of the Sun, so gigantic would be the tidal wave on the solar surface that it would more or less constitute a gaseous arm reaching out towards the other star. From the outermost tip of this arm would become detached successive blobs of gas, mere droplets compared with the Sun, and these primitive planets would be drawn sideways into orbits about the Sun by the pull of the receding star. Such planets would inevitably be at high temperature and gaseous to start with, and so only large planets could be formed: planets with as little mass as Mercury and Mars, and even more so the Moon, could not survive in gaseous form but would dissipate into space.

A more general objection was raised by Jeffreys who pointed out that bodies drawn off the Sun by gravitational forces could not rotate much more rapidly than the Sun itself, whereas the majority of planets still do so, some even 50 or 60 times as fast. To overcome this difficulty, a grazing collision was reintroduced, which would lead to a ribbon-like stream stretching out between the stars. In producing this from the outer layers, sliding past each other at hundreds of kilometres a second, turbulent viscosity would generate strong vorticity in the mingling material, and when the stream segmented into embryo planets through internal gravitation, this vorticity would lead to the necessary rapid rotations.

Much invalid criticism was levelled at both the tidal and collision theories on the quite erroneous grounds that the prior probability of so close an encounter was too small to permit such a postulate. But the first person to perceive clearly an insuperable difficulty common to all mechanisms of encounter with the Sun was H.N.Russell (1877–1957). His objection, so simple that it is amazing that it had so long been overlooked, is in essence the following. On any theory, the planetary material must acquire angular momentum far greater than would correspond to any object circling the Sun just outside its surface. But if a particle were so moving, and its velocity doubled by some means, that would certainly double its angular momentum, but it would endow it with such energy that it would escape altogether from the Sun, and not remain bound to it in a planetary orbit. In fact Jupiter possesses over thirty times the angular momentum it would have if in a circular orbit skimming the Sun, and Neptune nearly eighty times as much. Even Mercury could not be put into its present orbit by any single mechanism that removed mass from the Sun.

A simple means of escape from this difficulty was not long in coming with the proposal that, before the existence of the planets, the Sun may have been a *binary star*, examples of which abound in the Galaxy. If the scene of encounter with a third passing star is transferred to the companion star already moving at the distance of the great planets, any material removed from it and from the colliding star will automatically have the necessary angular momentum from the outset. It can be shown too that the encounter can cause the companion star to escape from the Sun for ever. Whether material so removed by a grazing collision of two stars could immediately aggregate into planets is a question that has never been settled, though the extreme violence of the process would seem to render it doubtful. But it would be sufficient if an amount of order somewhat greater than the total planetary mass were captured in gaseous form, for this on cooling down would surround the Sun with a Laplacian disc of dust and gas. It is to be noticed also that the intrinsic angular momentum would prevent the material falling into the Sun to any appreciable extent, and thus the solar rotation would not be speeded up.

Variants on this theory were later proposed. First, that the companion star to the Sun was itself a very close binary which, as a result of addition of interstellar material, merged into a single star that would automatically be rotationally unstable and undergo such violent break-up as to throw the resulting components apart at speeds far above those needed for escape from the Sun. At the same time, between the two separating components there would be left a mere wisp of material captured by the Sun – less than one per cent would be quite enough – that again would give a nebula from which planets could develop. Another suggestion was that a companion much more massive than the Sun developed to the *supernova* stage to throw off vast amounts of material at high temperature and containing the heavy elements needed for most of the planets.

Almost all recent discussions adopt the view that the first requirement of any theory is to endow the Sun with a primitive nebula by some orderly rather than catastrophic process. If this happens as part of the mechanism of formation of the Sun itself, then a rapidly rotating primitive Sun as end-product seems inescapable, though the suggestion has been made that this can be dealt with by postulating subsequent enormously strong magnetic coupling to condensations within the nebula. On the other hand, material for such a nebula could simply be captured by the Sun as it moves through interstellar space. Since the Galaxy contains a great many vast clouds of gas and dust, occupying something like 15 per cent of its volume, planetary systems if initiated in this way may be very numerous, even if only a small proportion of stars have successfully undergone such an event.

There is no possibility of planets condensing under gravitational forces within the gaseous component of such a nebula for the simple reason that the volume-density would be far too low. About one per cent of a nebula so derived would consist of dust particles, or come to contain this proportion if originally entirely gaseous, and this solid material would quickly settle into a thin disc as a result of collisions between the particles. The rings of Saturn are an example of this: if any particle were not moving strictly in the plane of the ring, its motion perpendicular to that plane would be rapidly damped out by collisions. If the whole of the mass of the four inner planets were spread out into a circular disc extending out just beyond the orbit of Mars, it would be a few centimetres thick. The vital point is that because of the high density of the material of the disc, aggregations can form within it and continue to grow despite the shearing motion of circulation round the Sun. Clumps of material would form almost everywhere in the disc and so great would be the congestion that only when bodies of order 100 km in radius had grown could they be spaced out in separate circular orbits. But through perturbations, strictly circular orbits would not be possible, so collisions would continue to occur at low relative speeds and give rise to larger bodies still. The process would end, though never quite completely, with a few large bodies each dominating the original zone of the disc from which its mass had been collected.

Up to the final stage, there would necessarily remain some of the original dust and debris of collisions, always in the form of a disc. This material would provide a kind of dissipative medium tending to round up any non-circular orbits of the large aggregations, and it would provide precisely the conditions in which a body such as the Moon, at first moving as an independent small planet near the orbit of the Earth, could come to be permanently captured. Purely as a result of the combined action of the Sun and Earth, the latter could temporarily capture the Moon in an orbit much larger than the present orbit, but the slightest addition of mass to the Earth or Moon or both at this stage, which would occur from the material of the residual disc, would draw them together and render them permanently bound gravitationally, getting closer as more material showered down on their surfaces. Evidently the material of the disc was effectively exhausted before the Moon was drawn into the Earth completely.

As for the great outer planets, they too could only start to form by growth within a dust-disc. But once a primitive planet had accumulated, at or beyond the distance of Jupiter, and attained a mass about equal to that of the Earth, it would then have a sufficiently strong field to collect in hydrogen and helium and any other gaseous components of the nebula. The temperature of the material at these distances would be much lower than at those where the terrestrial planets formed, and so the thermal speeds would be sufficiently small for such bodies to collect in even the lightest gases and continue to do so until the whole nebula had become exhausted.

The rotations of the planets are readily explicable on any such theory by the vorticity inherent in the material of the disc, and the surrounding gaseous nebula, resulting from the orbital motion about the Sun. This vorticity or spin is in the same sense as the orbital motions, and would mean that the rotation of any aggregation would be about an axis perpendicular to the plane of the disc.

Belated collisions and coalescence of large planets could of course act to disturb to some extent the precise directions of the rotation axes. The curious direction of the axis of Uranus, which lies almost in the orbital plane of the planet, suggests that the final stage of formation of this particular planet was by the collision and elision of two bodies, their relative orbital angular momentum of encounter, which might be in almost any direction, necessarily becoming part of the rotatory momentum of the combined single mass, and probably the greater part.

An important feature of the process of growth is that, because of the extreme thinness of the disc, material will fall to the surface of a growing planet only in a very narrow great-circle band, and not at all parts of its surface. Only when the mass had reached a value about that of the Moon at present would the energy of infall be enough to liquefy the particles and the surface material stopping them. Up to this point, a growing planet would remain sufficiently cool always to be solid. Even when it reached more than lunar mass, and infalling material caused melting, such material would flow polarwards away from the plane defined by the disc, and spread thinly over the surface. Any theory of the present kind for the origin of planets would imply that the terrestrial planets, and in particular the Earth, began their existence in entirely solid form, the very opposite of what was for so long believed.

13. Between the stars

The interstellar medium
The emptiness of space

The briefest glance at the night sky reveals one of the most remarkable features about the Universe: its inhomogeneity. Most of the matter in the Universe is clumped together rather than spread out uniformly. This is true of our Solar System, which consists of planets with 'space' between them, of our Galaxy, which consists of stars with 'space' between them, and of the Universe which consists of galaxies and clusters of galaxies with 'space' between them. These three types of space are usually described as interplanetary, interstellar and intergalactic, and the matter, if any, which fills them is referred to as a medium. The properties of the interplanetary, interstellar and intergalactic media are quite different. This chapter is purely concerned with the interstellar medium; the others are described in chapters 8 and 18.

The main constituents of the INTERSTELLAR MEDIUM are gases, mainly hydrogen and helium, and minute solid dust particles. As far as we know there are no liquids in interstellar space. Although interstellar space is nowhere truly empty, it is in most places far more sparsely filled than even the best laboratory-produced vacuum. For example, one cubic metre of air at sea level contains about 5×10^{25} atoms. At the height at which artificial satellites orbit the earth, say $300\,km$, the density has fallen to $10^{15}\,m^{-3}$. In interstellar space the density is often a billion times less than this, with only one atom in each cubic centimetre. A ray of light leaving the surface of the Earth and travelling in a straight line across our Galaxy would intercept more gas in the first ten kilometres of its path through the Earth's atmosphere than on the whole of the rest of its journey. This would also be true of a ray of light passing through the intergalactic medium to distant quasars in the Universe. Nevertheless, the volume of interstellar space is so great that the total quantity of interstellar material is very considerable. Our own Galaxy contains about $10^{10}\,M_\odot$ of it, comprising some 10 per cent of its total mass. Most of this interstellar matter lies in the spiral arms and the disc of our Galaxy, in a layer a few hundred parsecs thick.

The interstellar medium affects and often hinders many of our studies of distant objects. Although there is, on average, only about one dust grain in every $100\,000$ cubic metres of space, there are enough of them along the line of sight to many stars to render these stars almost invisible. Radio waves are attenuated and delayed by free electrons; ultraviolet and X-rays are absorbed by hydrogen and oxygen atoms. The night sky is confused by scattered light and by glowing gas clouds; interstellar magnetic fields deflect and jumble fast-moving cosmic-ray particles in their paths across the Galaxy.

On the other hand, the interstellar medium presents us with a cosmic laboratory on a scale which could never be achieved on Earth. In it we can study the physics and chemistry of matter at very low densities. For example, whereas most gaseous elements on the Earth exist as molecules, such as H_2, O_2, or NH_3, in the low density of interstellar space single atoms are more usual. Collisions

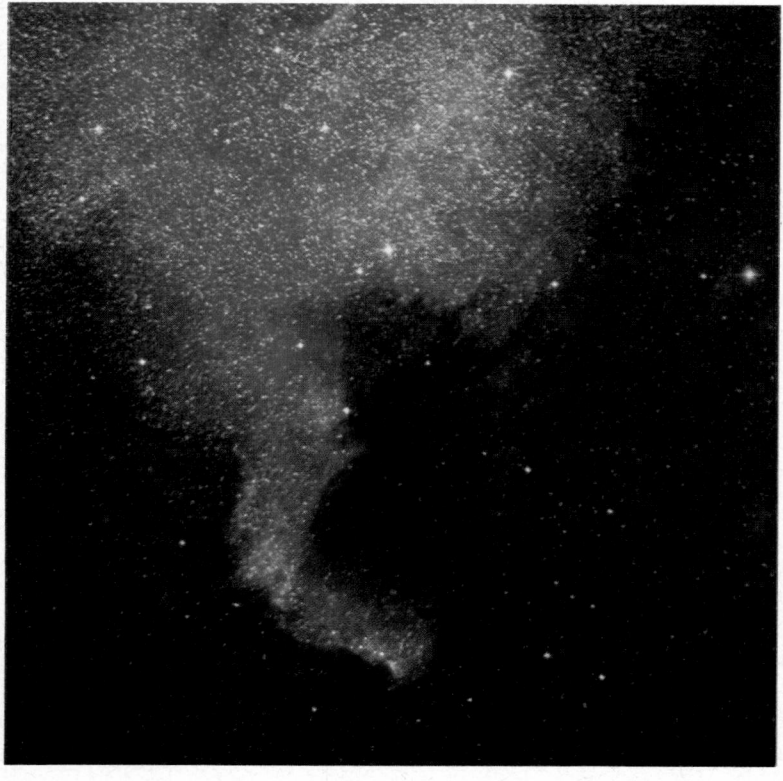

13.1: *The North American Nebula, so named because of its resemblance to a map of the USA and Mexico. The pink glow comes from a cloud of hydrogen gas between the stars.* (*Hale Observatories,* USA)

between atoms are rare in space so spectral lines retain their sharpness and are in some cases enhanced to a degree unobtainable in a terrestrial laboratory. Chemicals that are too reactive to exist on earth for more than a few moments are sometimes abundant in space. A gas cloud may be so massive that its motions are governed by its own gravity rather than that of a nearby object; another may be ionized and supported by a magnetic field. The study of the interstellar medium is thus the study of matter in a completely different environment.

The nebulae

The most noticeable manifestations of the interstellar medium are NEBULAE. The term 'nebula' is used fairly loosely in astronomy; the word is derived from the Latin for cloud, and can refer to almost any object that appears fuzzy or extended through a telescope. One of the early catalogues of nebulae was that of Messier, who in 1781 published a list of about 100 nebulous objects. His designations, for example M 42 for the *Orion Nebula*, are still in use for some of the brightest objects. Messier's list includes many different kinds of astronomical phenomena, many of which have nothing to do with the interstellar medium; about a third of his objects are galaxies, and over half are clusters of stars. The term 'nebula' is nowadays not much used for either of these classes of object. Thirteen of the Messier objects are bright clouds of interstellar matter; one is a *reflection nebula*, four are *planetary nebulae*, seven are *ionized hydrogen (H⁺) regions*, and one is a *supernova remnant*. The last three types are sometimes referred to as GASEOUS NEBULAE.

The difference between these four types of nebula lies mainly in the way they are illuminated and on whether their dust or their gas makes them more prominent. A reflection nebula contains dust grains which reflect and scatter light from nearby stars. The light from planetary nebulae and ionized hydrogen regions, on the other hand, is generated by a fluorescent process, in which ultraviolet photons from a very hot star excite interstellar atoms to an ionized state, whence they recombine and emit visible light. Supernova remnants, of which the *Crab Nebula* is a famous example, are the result of gigantic stellar explosions.

There is another important class of nebula not represented in Messier's catalogue; these are the *dark nebulae*. These are clouds of gas and dust that are so opaque that they prevent light from stars or bright nebulae passing through them. They can only be detected if they are large enough and thick enough to obscure so many stars that a prominent 'hole' appears in the sky. Some of these dark nebula have names, such as the 'Horsehead' (figure 13.2) and the 'Southern Coalsack'. They contain approximately the same sort of mixture of gas and dust as the bright nebulae, but have no suitable stars to illuminate them.

There are, of course, many more nebulae than are listed in Messier's catalogue. Some are simply very small or very faint.

13.2: *The Horsehead Nebula in Orion. Both bright and dark nebulae are prominent in this picture. The 'horsehead' itself is an extension of the dark cloud which covers the lower half of the picture. Notice that there are fewer stars in the lower half of the picture than in the upper half, indicating that distant stars are being obscured by the dust. The pink glow is from ionized hydrogen gas, while the bright white cloud in the lower left corner is a reflection nebula. (Hale Observatories, USA)*

Others, hidden from us, can be detected by their emission or absorption of radio, microwave or infrared radiation rather than visible light. Such objects are commonly called *interstellar clouds*; the term refers to a concentration of gas or dust whether or not it is visible to us on Earth as an optical nebula.

The variety in types of interstellar cloud is an indication of the variety of conditions found in the interstellar medium. For example, temperature and density variations of a factor of a million are found between different regions, with the faintest and most extended objects losing their identity as individual nebulae and blending into the general background of the interstellar medium. Other important variables include the ratio of gas to dust, and the state of ionization of the hydrogen in a cloud; different regions of space may be either predominantly molecular (H_2), neutral (H^0) or ionized (H^+), depending on their density, temperature, and proximity to bright stars. The various different sorts of interstellar cloud are discussed in chapter 14; their importance is that these are the regions of the Galaxy where there is the strongest interplay between the stellar and interstellar components of the Galaxy.

Recycling the interstellar medium

The relationship between the interstellar medium and the stars is a dynamic one; matter is exchanged between them all the time. Our Sun, for example, emits particles in the form of a *solar wind*, and absorbs others in the form of *cosmic rays*. In this case the amount of mass exchanged is small compared with the total mass of the Sun. Under certain conditions, however, much more drastic exchanges of matter between the stars and the interstellar medium take place; these events involve the births and deaths of stars.

New stars may be formed when the density of an interstellar cloud exceeds a critical value. Its internal gravitational forces then compress the cloud until it is hot enough to become a star in its own right. This process was very common when the Galaxy was young, and is still happening now in certain regions. Old stars, on the other hand, tend to expel matter into space by one of several processes; *red-giant* stars blow it off gradually, whereas *planetary nebulae* and *supernovae* eject it in an explosive event (figure 13.3). Matter therefore alternates between being part of a star (or its associated planets) and being part of the interstellar medium. By doing so it becomes steadily enriched in the heavy elements, as these are synthesized in the stars. These heavy elements in interstellar space may exist in a gaseous state, like the hydrogen and helium, or may condense to make dust grains.

As yet, we do not know to what extent the depletion of the interstellar medium by star births, and its regeneration from old stars balance each other. It is possible, for example, that the older our Galaxy becomes the less interstellar matter it will contain.

13.3: *The planetary nebula NGC 6781 in the constellation of Aquila. The glowing red shell of gas has been recently ejected into space from the star in the centre of the ring.*
(Hale Observatories, USA)

Dust grains in space

Extinction and reddening

The interstellar medium is nowhere completely transparent and nowhere completely opaque; a dusty region of space dims rather than blocks the light passing through it. This dimming process is called INTERSTELLAR EXTINCTION. Interstellar extinction in front of a star can be expressed quantitatively, and is usually given the symbol A_v where A_v is the number of magnitudes by which the star's light is dimmed by the dust at visual wavelengths. For example, a star behind a dust cloud with $A_v = 2$ would appear two magnitudes fainter than if the dust cloud had not intervened. The extinction due to the interstellar dust varies enormously from place to place. In the plane of the Galaxy, A_v is typically two magnitudes for every kiloparsec the light travels through it, but there are some clouds that are so dusty that A_v reaches values of several hundred magnitudes per parsec.

The amount by which light is dimmed by the interstellar medium depends on its wavelength. Red light suffers less extinction than blue light with the result that the apparent colour of a star is altered if it is observed through a patch of dust. This phenomenon is called INTERSTELLAR REDDENING, and it is a consequence of the fact that the particles causing the extinction are smaller than the wavelength of light. A similar kind of reddening occurs in the Earth's atmosphere, and is the cause of the Sun's apparent daily colour changes as it rises and sets. The reddening effect of the Earth's atmosphere is small when the Sun is high in the sky; in the evening, however, when sunlight has to travel a long distance through the atmosphere at a shallow angle, the effect becomes more pronounced and the setting Sun appears orange rather than white.

Interstellar extinction and reddening are important in the infrared and ultraviolet parts of the spectrum as well as the visible. In this context the term 'reddening' is used, with some chromatic licence, to indicate the relative enhancement of long-wavelength over short-wavelength radiation. Figure 13.4 shows how the extinction (A_λ) varies with wavelength from 0.1 to 10μm. The curve shows that at short ultraviolet wavelengths the extinction is several times larger than for visible light, while longward of 2μm it is reduced by a factor of at least ten. This dramatic improvement in the transparency of the interstellar medium at long wavelengths is of great importance as it allows astronomers to see through layers of dust with $A_v = 50$ magnitudes or more, which would be impenetrable at shorter wavelengths. Several 'bumps' have been found in the interstellar extinction curve, and others will probably be discovered as techniques improve. The three features shown in figure 13.4 are at wavelengths where graphite, ice and silicate particles preferentially absorb radiation, but these chemical identifications are not yet certain.

Reflection nebulae

Two things can happen to light rays when they meet a dust particle; they can be either absorbed into the grain or scattered back

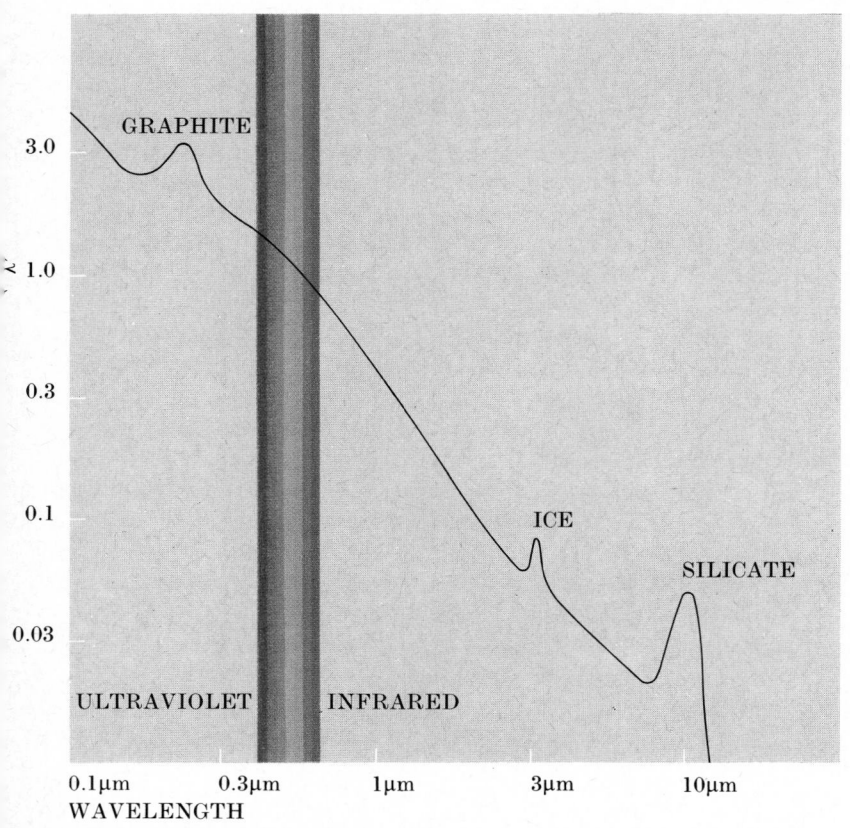

13.4: *Average extinction curve for interstellar dust particles showing how radiation of different wavelengths suffers different amounts of extinction. The curve is compiled from measurements on a variety of stars, and is normalized so as to have $A_V = 1$ magnitude. The identifications of the 0.2 μm, 3 μm and 10 μm features as being due to graphite, ice and silicate grains are tentative.*

into space. The relative importance of these two processes depends on the *albedo* of the grain, which is defined thus:

$$albedo = \frac{light\ scattered}{light\ scattered + light\ absorbed}$$

The albedo of a grain depends on its size, its shape and its composition, and also on the wavelength of the radiation being scattered. For interstellar dust grains at visible wavelengths the albedo is about 0.5, so that approximately equal amounts of light are absorbed and scattered. Starlight that has been scattered no longer travels in a straight line from its parent star. When observed from the Earth, therefore, such light appears to shine from the patch of interstellar dust where it was last scattered rather than from the star itself. The dust therefore appears to be shining.

Scattered starlight makes up about a quarter of the light of the Milky Way. Usually the scattered light is too diffuse for either the star or the dust cloud to be identified, but if a bright star lies close enough to a dense patch of dust a REFLECTION NEBULA may be seen. A good example of reflection nebulae is shown in figure 13.5. The Pleiades cluster consists of a group of over 3000 young stars situated at a distance of some 120 pc from the Sun in the constellation of Taurus. The brightest stars in this group, though not the nebulosity surrounding them, are visible to the naked eye. Spectroscopic analysis confirms that the light from the nebulae has the same characteristic absorption lines as the B-type stars illuminating them. However, since blue light is scattered more

13.5: *Reflection nebulae surrounding stars of the Pleiades cluster M45. The blue colour is the result of light being scattered by dust particles near the stars. The streaky patterns show the irregular distribution of dust grains within the nebulae. The regular circles around the stars, however, like the crosses through them, are artifacts of the telescope used to take this photograph.* (*Hale Observatories,* USA)

13.6: *Reflection nebula CRL 2688. At the position of the cross is a hidden F supergiant star and a powerful infrared source. Light from this nebula is 40 per cent polarized.* (*Steward Observatory,* USA)

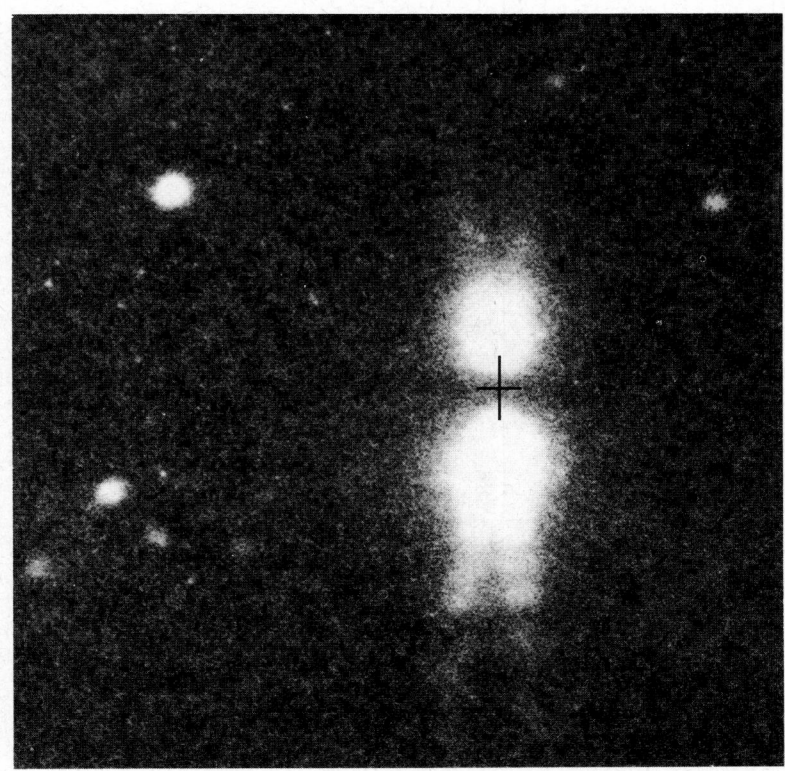

than red light the nebulae appear bluer than their illuminating stars.

The blue colour of reflection nebulae is a useful method of distinguishing them from *ionized hydrogen (H+ regions)* which they sometimes resemble. A more clear-cut distinction, however, can be made on the basis of the spectrum of the light from the nebula. A reflection nebula has a continuous spectrum with stellar-type absorption lines, whereas the light from an H+ region is predominantly in the form of emission lines. Two further differences between the two types of nebula are that the light from reflection nebulae is often *polarized* whereas that from H+ regions is not and that reflection nebulae are usually associated with B-type stars, H+ regions with O-type stars.

A reflection nebula can sometimes reveal the presence of a hidden star. The object shown in figure 13.6 was discovered in 1974 as a result of an infrared survey of the sky. The spectrum of the light from the two bright blobs indicates that they are being illuminated by an F-type supergiant star lying in the dark lane between the blobs and hidden from earth by a very thick layer of dust.

Polarization

Most celestial bodies emit light which is unpolarized. The few exceptions include certain *white dwarf* and *peculiar A stars*, sources of *synchrotron radiation* such as the *Crab Nebula*, and *reflection nebulae*. Nevertheless the light from many ordinary stars contains a measurable degree of *linear polarization*. The amount of polarization is greatest for stars which are the most reddened, so it is a natural conclusion that the polarization arises during the passage of the starlight through the interstellar medium. The measured polarization is very approximately one per cent for every magnitude of visual extinction (A_v). Consequently very few bright stars have polarizations of more than a few per cent. The amount of polarization varies with wavelength and has a maximum value near $\lambda = 0.55\,\mu m$.

Several thousand stars have had their polarizations measured. These stars are shown in figure 13.7, plotted in *galactic coordinates*. It may be seen that there is a tendency for stars close to each other to be polarized in the same direction, and for stars at low galactic latitudes to be polarized parallel to the galactic plane. The reason for these patterns is probably the *interstellar magnetic field*. The field acts on those grains which have an elongated rather than a spherical shape, and tends to make them all line up in the same direction. It is this alignment of dust grains that is the cause of interstellar polarization.

Circular polarization has also been measured in a few stars. This is a much smaller effect than linear polarization, and is therefore much more difficult to measure. The largest known value of interstellar circular polarization is 0.06 per cent in the star VI Cygni 12.

13.7: *The polarization of starlight in and around the galactic plane. Each line represents one star. The length of the line is proportional to the amount of polarization, while the angle of the line shows its direction. The stars are shown superimposed on a map of hydrogen clouds in the vicinity of the Sun (see figure 14.2).*

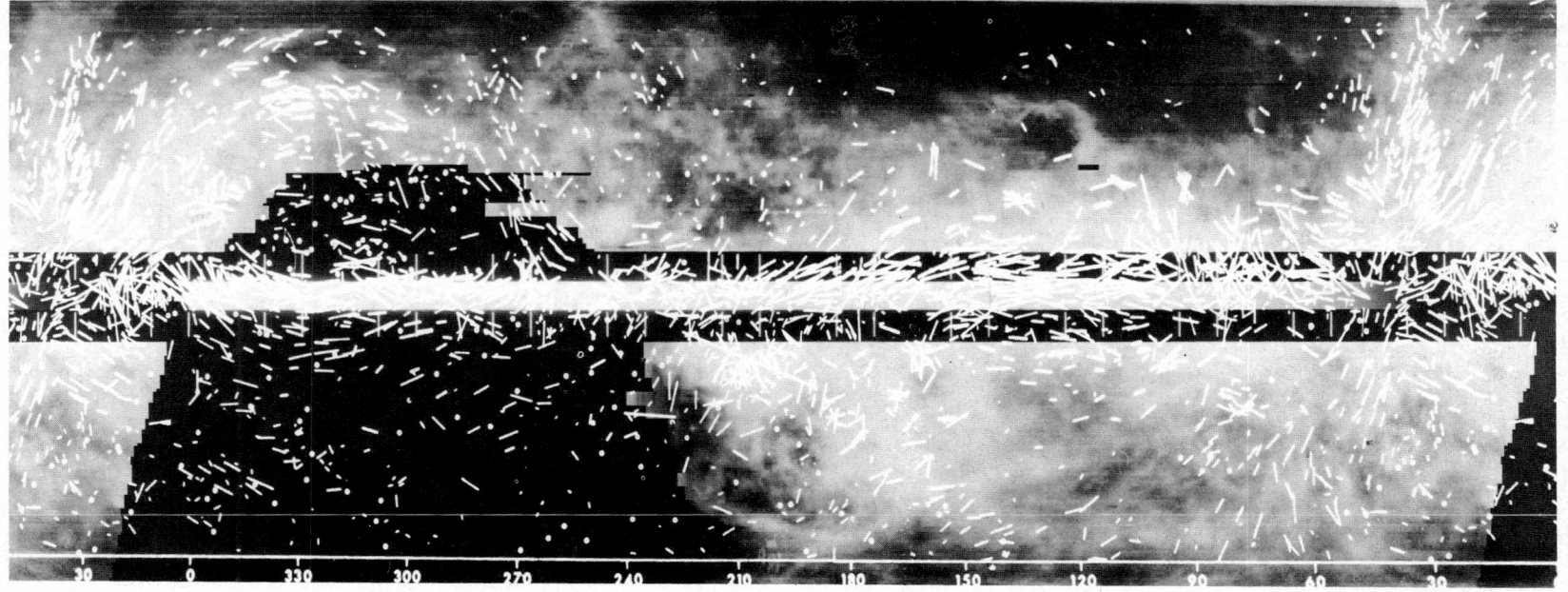

GALACTIC LONGITUDE

Infrared sources

Since starlight carries energy, any light that is absorbed (as opposed to scattered) by a dust grain tends to increase the temperature of the dust grain. This absorption of energy is balanced by the energy that the grain reradiates into space. The wavelength of the radiation from the grain depends on its temperature. Normal interstellar dust, at a temperature of a few tens of degrees kelvin, radiates at very long infrared wavelengths of 100 μm or more. This radiation is faint and difficult to observe. Grains close to stars become hotter and therefore radiate at shorter wavelengths. They rarely emit visible light, however, since most grains are destroyed by being heated above a few hundred degrees kelvin.

Infrared emission from heated grains is most easily observed when there are thick layers of dust in the immediate vicinity of luminous stars. Such a situation commonly occurs in dense clouds associated with the birth of stars in the nuclei of some galaxies. Many late-type stars also show strong infrared emission from dust grains. The fourth-magnitude star μ Cephei, an M 2 Ia supergiant, is an example. Shortward of 7 μm its energy distribution resembles that of a 4000 K black-body, as would be expected for a star of this spectral class (figure 13.8). Instead of continuing to decrease longward of 7 μm, however, the flux density increases sharply at 10 μm and again at 20 μm. These are wavelengths at which heated dust particles radiate most efficiently; the presence of these infrared 'bumps' indicate that there is a shell of warm dust surrounding the star. The dust particles absorb about ten per cent of the light from the star and reradiate this energy as infrared waves. The dust shell is too small to be seen directly, and its presence can only be inferred from its infrared radiation.

A more extreme example of a star surrounded by a dust shell is provided by the object IRC + 10216. In this case essentially all of the light from the star, a carbon star at a temperature of 2000 K, is absorbed in the dust shell and reradiated at infrared wavelengths (figure 13.8). As a consequence, this object is hardly visible even on red-sensitive plates taken with large telescopes (figure 13.9). At infrared wavelengths, however, it is very luminous and at 20 μm is one of the ten brightest objects in the sky. Most of the infrared flux comes from a shell of dust 0.4 arc sec in diameter at a temperature of 600 K. The distance to IRC + 10216 may be about 200 pc. If so, then the dust cloud has a diameter of 80 AU (the same as Pluto's orbit around the Sun) and a luminosity of 25 000 L$_\odot$.

The nature and origin of dust grains

We cannot examine interstellar dust in a laboratory. Small interplanetary particles that reach the Earth or that are intercepted by spacecraft are characteristic only of our Solar System and are probably quite different from those found in interstellar space. What knowledge we have about the size, shape and composition of interstellar grains is based on our observations of how grains absorb, scatter, polarize and radiate electromagnetic waves, and on our ideas about what kinds of materials are plentiful enough and stable enough to exist in space.

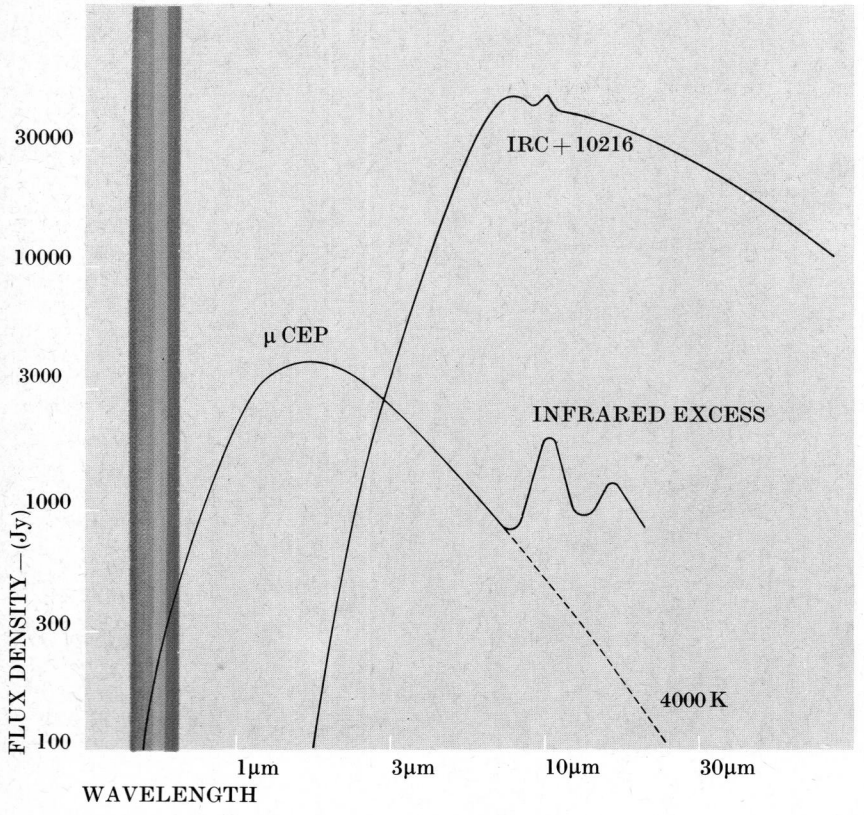

13.8: *Infrared emission from circumstellar dust shells. The bright star μ Cephei emits about ten per cent of its energy in an infrared excess at 10–20 μm. The more extreme infrared source IRC + 10216 emits essentially all of its energy at wavelengths longer than 3 μm.*

The extinction curve (figure 13.4) gives us the most information. From it astronomers have deduced that most of the dust grains which cause extinction at visible wavelengths have diameters of about 0.1 μm. Such grains weigh only 10^{-18} kg each. Even smaller particles are necessary to provide the extinction at ultraviolet wavelengths, but we do not yet have much idea about the total range of grain sizes in interstellar space. We also know almost nothing about the shapes of grains.

The three bumps on the extinction curve indicate that graphite particles, ice crystals and some silicate material, such as magnesium silicate, are probably present. Other substances which have been suggested as constituents of dust grains include magnesium carbonate, silicon carbide, iron, diamond, and various organic molecules including complicated polymers. Different materials may be present in the same grain, and a favoured model consists of a small silicate particle surrounded by a thicker layer of ice.

Grains can be formed by condensation from the gas in the outer atmospheres of late-type stars; the dust in the infrared shells of μ Cephei and IRC + 10216 was made in this way. Different sorts of stars make different sorts of grain. An oxygen-rich star, for example, tends to produce silicate grains, a carbon-rich star graphite or silicon carbide grains. The grains are eventually blown away from the star into interstellar space. New grains are then formed from new material leaving the star's surface. Not all dust is made this way. Some grains may condense out of gas as it contracts to form new stars, and others grow by steadily accreting extra atoms and molecules from the interstellar medium. Grains are destroyed either by being incorporated into new stars or by being subjected to high temperatures or harsh radiation fields. Whatever the material the grains are made of, and however they form, we do not expect that on average more than one per cent of the mass of the interstellar medium is in the form of dust at any time. The reason for this is that only those atoms in the interstellar medium which are not hydrogen or helium are of much use in making grains. Such elements altogether comprise less than one per cent of the mass of the Galaxy.

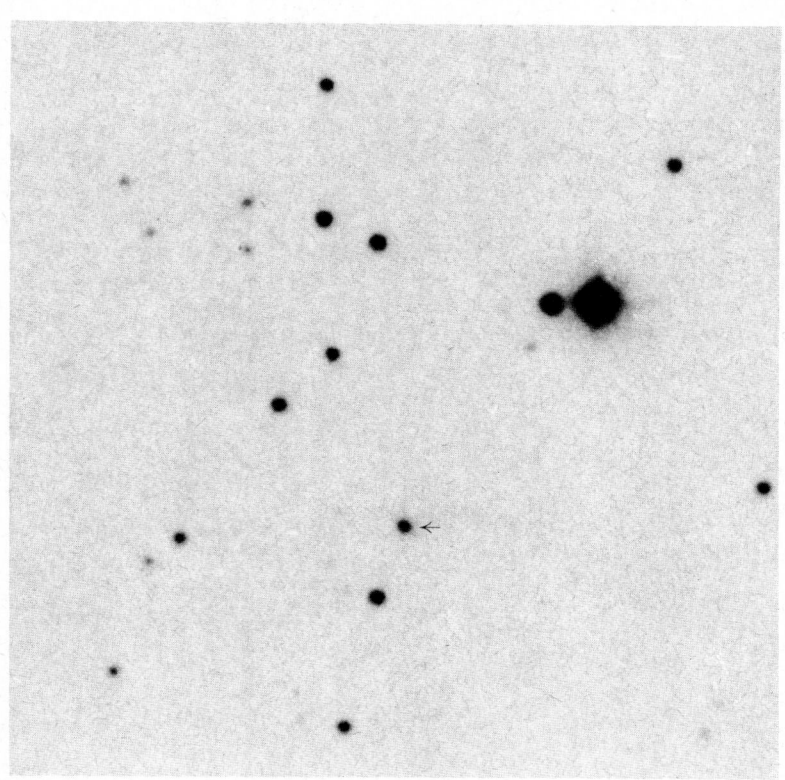

13.9: *The infrared source IRC + 10216 photographed in red light. It appears fainter than 18 mag at visible wavelengths, but at 20 μm is one of the brightest objects in the sky. (Palomar Sky Survey,* USA*)*

Interstellar gas

The hydrogen 21-cm line

Interstellar gas is more difficult to see than interstellar dust, despite the fact that there is much more of it. The reason for this is that while solid particles absorb and emit radiation over a wide range of wavelengths, gases emit and absorb only at certain discrete wavelengths. In studying the gas, one is therefore constrained to observing a limited number of spectral lines. Most of what we know about interstellar gas has come from the study of a single spectral line: the 21-CM RADIO WAVELENGTH transition of atomic hydrogen. This transition arises as follows. Hydrogen, in its lowest energy state, can exist in two forms. In one case the spins of the proton and electron are parallel, in the other they are opposed. There is a very slight energy difference between these states; the difference corresponds to a photon of 1420.4 MHz frequency or about 21-cm wavelength. In interstellar space very nearly three-quarters of the hydrogen atoms are in the higher energy state (spins parallel) and one-quarter in the lower. Transitions between the states are rare and usually occur only as a result of a collision with another particle. This may happen to a particular atom only about once every 400 years. Nevertheless the number of interstellar hydrogen atoms is so large that the 21-cm line can be detected in nearly every direction of the sky with a moderate-sized radio telescope.

The 21-cm line can be seen in both emission and absorption. The left diagram in figure 13.10 shows a stationary cloud emitting radiation only at frequencies very close to 1420.4 MHz. In general, the more hydrogen there is in a cloud the stronger will be the emission line. If the cloud is moving either towards or away from the observer, the frequency of the line will be altered by the *Doppler effect* (middle diagram). These frequency shifts are extremely useful as they allow us to distinguish between clouds at different velocities along the same line of sight, and hence to study the motions of distant parts of the Galaxy. Absorption at 21 cm can occur when radio emission from a bright, distant object such as a quasar, a radio galaxy or a supernova remnant passes through a cloud of hydrogen. The amount of absorption depends on the temperature of the cloud; cold gas absorbs more than hot gas. By comparing the amount of emission and absorption produced by the same cloud of gas one can measure its temperature. Figure 13.11 shows this technique in use. The lower profile shows the 21-cm absorption spectrum of the distant radio galaxy Cygnus A due to hydrogen in our Galaxy. The spectrum contains several strong, narrow lines. The upper profile is the emission from the same clouds of hydrogen, as measured along a direction a fraction of a degree of arc away from Cygnus A. The emission profile shows that there is much hydrogen moving at velocities between $+20$ and -20 km s^{-1} and smaller amounts moving at all velocities between $+30$ and -130 km s^{-1}. Much of the hydrogen is hot, more than 1000 K, and

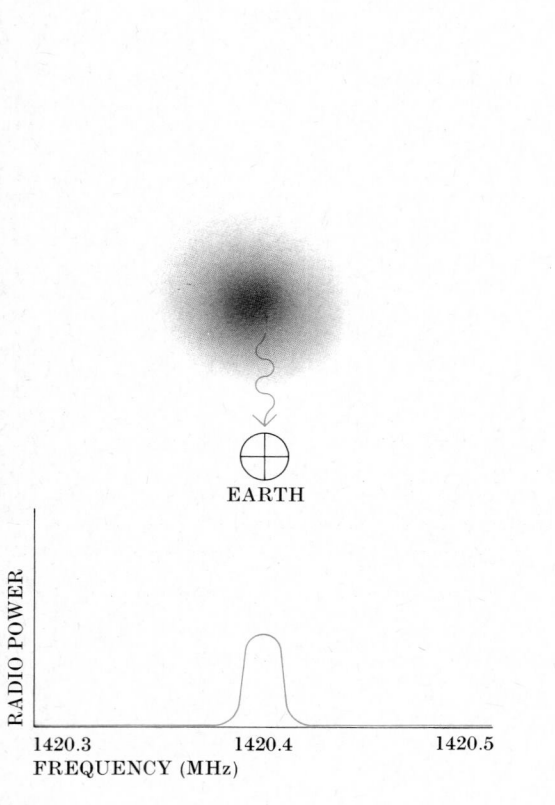
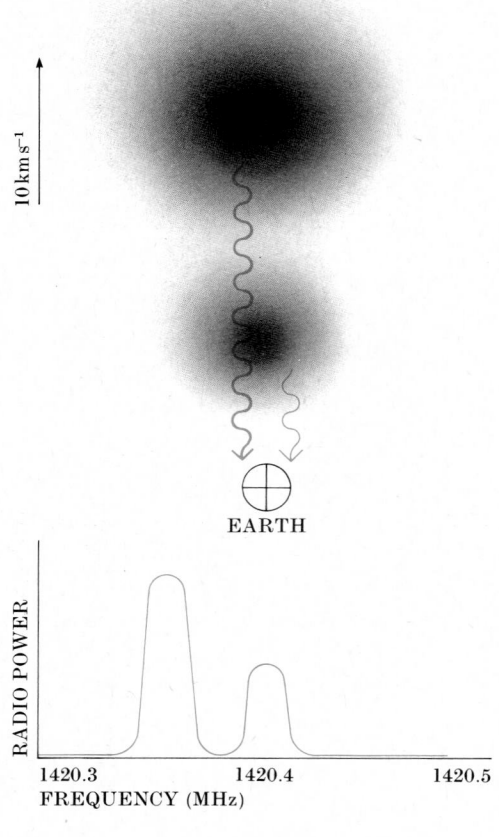
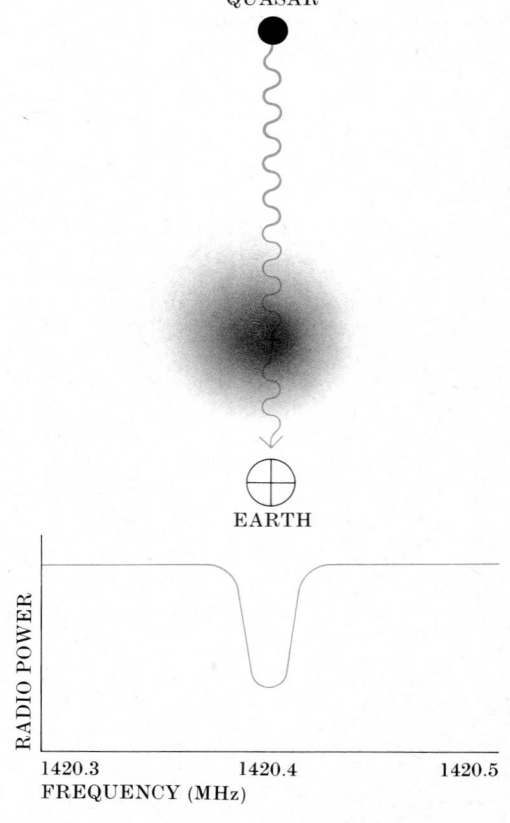

so does not absorb strongly, but there are some patches which are much colder, about 100 K, and give rise to the deep absorption lines. The most prominent cold clouds are moving at velocities of $+11, +4, 0, -10, -18$ and $-85 \, \mathrm{km \, s^{-1}}$ away from us.

The 21-cm line is seen only in hydrogen when it exists in the form of free, neutral atoms. Hydrogen which is ionized and hydrogen in the form of H_2 molecules must be studied by other methods.

Visible and ultraviolet absorption lines

The original discovery of interstellar gas preceded the development of radio astronomy by several decades. In 1904 it was discovered that certain of the absorption lines in the spectrum of the binary star δ Orionis did not change in wavelength as the star moved around its orbit. It soon became clear that this particular absorption was taking place not in the atmosphere of the star, but in a region of interstellar space uninfluenced by the motion of the star. Since that time interstellar absorption lines have been observed in the spectra of several hundred stars. The lines are usually much narrower than those formed in stellar atmospheres and sometimes have multiple Doppler-shifted components, corresponding to absorption in clouds with different radial velocities.

Only four atoms, sodium, potassium, calcium and iron, and only two ions, those of singly-ionized calcium and titanium can be seen by their visible absorption lines. Of these, the neutral sodium and ionized calcium are by far the strongest. A large number of atoms and ions, however, have absorption lines at ultraviolet wavelengths and can be studied by the use of satellite or rocket-borne telescopes. Of all the ultraviolet lines, the Lyman-α transition of neutral hydrogen at 121.6 nm is by far the strongest.

Despite the fact that most of the hydrogen is neutral, some interstellar elements, including both calcium and sodium, exist primarily in an ionized state. Along the line of sight to the star ζ Ophiuchi, for example, it is estimated that 90 per cent of the gaseous calcium is in the singly ionized form Ca^+, 9 per cent in the doubly ionized form Ca^{++} and one per cent in the form $Ca°$. The ionization of calcium and other elements is produced by the general background of starlight and, to some extent, by collisions with cosmic-ray particles. An atom which has been ionized will remain so until it collides and recombines with a free electron. The low density of the interstellar medium ensures that such collisions are rare; the probability that an atom is in an ionized state at any particular time can therefore be quite large.

A few simple interstellar molecules have been detected by their absorption lines. CH, CH^+ and CN are seen at visible wavelengths; CO and H_2 at ultraviolet wavelengths.

The composition of the interstellar gas

More than twenty different elements have now been detected by their visible or, more commonly, by their ultraviolet interstellar absorption lines. Most of these elements exist both in their neutral and their ionized state; sulphur, for example, has been identified as $S°$, S^+, S^{++}, and S^{+++}. Since the number of each kind of atom can be

13.10: *Emission and absorption in the 21-cm hydrogen line. A single cloud of hydrogen emits radio radiation only at a frequency of 1420.4 MHz (left). The denser cloud in the middle of the diagram is moving away from the Earth; its emission is therefore Doppler-shifted to a lower frequency. Radio emission from a distant bright source, such as a quasar, is absorbed by a cold hydrogen cloud (right).*

13.11: *Emission (top) and absorption (bottom) profiles for the 21-cm line in the direction of the radio galaxy Cygnus A.*

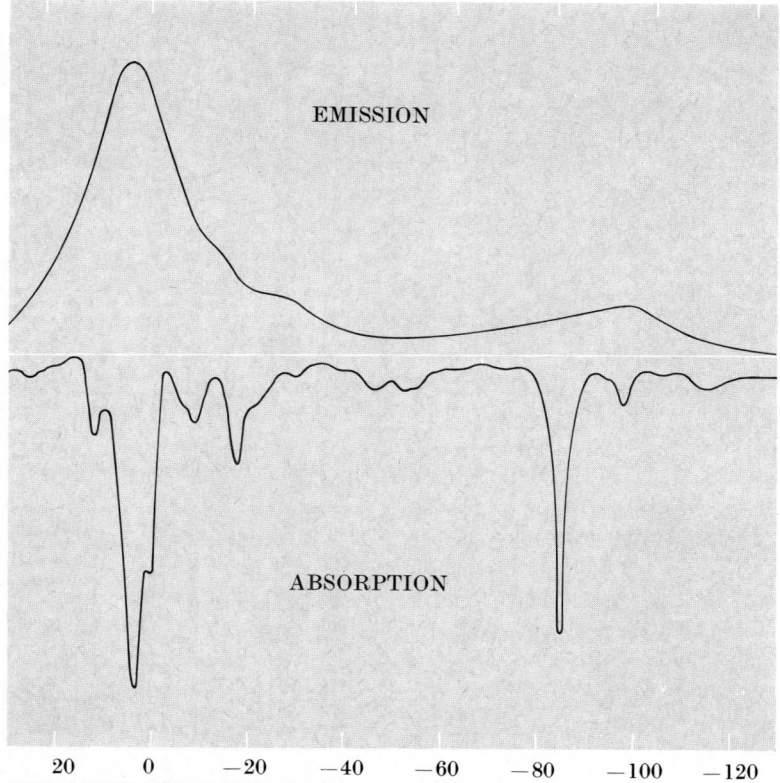

FREQUENCY (MHz)

1420.4   1420.7   1421.0

EMISSION

ABSORPTION

20   0   −20   −40   −60   −80   −100   −120
VELOCITY RELATIVE TO EARTH (km s⁻¹)

calculated from the depth of its absorption lines, we can compare the constitution of the interstellar medium with that of the stars.

The two most abundant elements are, of course, hydrogen and helium. Together these elements make up over 99 per cent by mass of the interstellar medium, as they do in most stars. It is in the abundances of the rarer, heavier, elements that differences between the interstellar medium and stars are found. The most carefully studied section of the interstellar gas is that in the line of sight between the Earth and the star ζ Ophiuchi. Here it is found that almost all the elements are much rarer as compared with hydrogen than is the case in stars. The interstellar gas contains only a tenth of the sodium, a hundredth of the iron and less than a thousandth of the calcium that stars do.

What is the reason for this difference? The answer is that most of these 'missing elements' are in the interstellar grains, which we take no account of in studies of absorption lines. ζ Ophiuchi has a visual extinction of about one magnitude. Calculations show that if all the missing elements from the gas are combined chemically to produce a mixture of suitable grains, the dust that would result would provide almost exactly the observed amount of extinction. The actual ratio of gas to dust in the interstellar medium is about 200:1 by mass. This ratio is fairly uniform over a large scale, but anomalously high or low ratios are sometimes found where grain destruction or grain formation processes are particularly lively.

The diffuse interstellar lines

The spectrum of a reddened star generally contains a number of interstellar absorption lines which cannot be attributed to any simple atom, ion, or molecule. These so-called DIFFUSE INTERSTELLAR LINES, or BANDS, are quite different in appearance from the atomic absorption lines in that they are much broader. Whereas an atomic line is typically less than 0.02 nm wide, the interstellar bands are usually 10 to 100 times more diffuse. The great breadth of the lines is too large to be explained by Doppler shifts and is believed to be intrinsic to the type of material giving rise to the lines.

Nearly 40 diffuse lines have been detected, the strongest being at 443.0, 628.4 and 617.7 nm. In the visible wavelength range, the diffuse lines absorb about six times more light than do the atomic and ionic lines. The absorption is, however, still less than a thousandth of that produced by the dust grains. The strength of the diffuse lines correlates well with the amount of extinction in the same line of sight. It is therefore probable that the material causing the absorption exists either in or on the grains. So far, there has been almost no success in identifying this material or group of materials. The width of the lines indicates that the material is solid rather than gaseous, but as yet we do not know if it is primarily organic or inorganic. The successful identification of these mysterious lines might give us an enormous insight into the nature and evolution of the interstellar medium.

Extreme ultraviolet and X-ray absorption

At wavelengths shorter than 91 nm it is not only the dust grains in the interstellar medium which absorb starlight. At these extreme ultraviolet (EUV) wavelengths the hydrogen atoms themselves are very strong absorbers of radiation by virtue of their ability to become ionized by such energetic photons. It is in the wavelength range just short of 91 nm that the interstellar medium is most opaque. A sensitive experiment aboard the USA–USSR Apollo–Soyuz spacecraft in 1975 was able to see only a handful of celestial objects at these wavelengths, and all of these are comparatively close to the Sun.

At wavelengths around 90 nm the absorption is about 20 magnitudes per parsec, or 10 000 times greater than that at visible wavelengths. Shortward of this wavelength the absorption decreases again fairly quickly, but at about 4 nm (corresponding to a photon energy of about 0.3 keV) absorption by other atoms, such as carbon, nitrogen and, especially, oxygen, become important. Although these atoms together number less than 1 per cent of the number of hydrogen atoms, they absorb so much more energy per ionization that it is they, not hydrogen, that are the main cause of opacity in the X-ray region. They greatly hinder observation of X-ray sources, at energies less than about 2 keV.

The X-ray absorption efficiency of atoms like carbon, nitrogen and oxygen is essentially unaffected by whether or not they are incorporated into molecules or dust grains. By measuring the X-ray absorption in any given direction and comparing it with the amount of hydrogen as estimated using the 21-cm line it is possible to check on the abundances of the heavy elements without having to consider the extent to which they are condensed onto dust grains. Early experiments of this kind have tended to confirm previous ideas about the expected heavy element abundances, but more sensitive techniques which will become available soon are expected to indicate some anomalies.

Table 13.1: Interstellar molecules discovered up to early 1977

H_2	hydrogen
OH	hydroxyl
SiO	silicon monoxide
SiS	silicon sulphide
NS	nitrogen sulphide
SO	sulphur monoxide
CH	methylidyne
CH^+	methylidyne ion
CN	cyanogen
CO	carbon monoxide
CS	carbon monosulphide
H_2O	water
N_2H^+	dinitrogen monohydride ion
H_2S	hydrogen sulphide
SO_2	sulphur dioxide
CCH	ethynal
HCN	hydrogen cyanide
HNC	hydrogen isocyanide
HCO^+	formyl ion
HCO	formyl
OCS	carbonyl sulphide
NH_3	ammonia
C_2H_2	acetylene
C_3N	cyanoethynyl
H_2CO	formaldehyde
HNCO	isocyanic acid
H_2CS	thioformaldehyde
H_2CNH	methanimine
H_2NCN	cyanamide
HCOOH	formic acid
HC_3N	cyanoacetylene
CH_3OH	methanol
CH_3CN	methyl cyanide
$HCONH_2$	formamide
CH_3NH_2	methylamine
CH_3C_2H	methylacetylene
$HCOCH_3$	acetaldehyde
H_2CCHCN	vinyl cyanide
HC_5N	cyanodiacetylene
$HCOOCH_3$	methyl formate
$(CH_3)_2O$	dimethyl ether
C_2H_5OH	ethanol (ethyl alcohol)

Astrochemistry

Molecules in space

Like atoms, molecules absorb and emit radiation only at specific wavelengths, as they make transitions from one energy state to another. A molecule is a much more complicated object than an atom, however, and consequently has many more transitions available to it, especially at infrared and microwave wavelengths. This richness not only results in molecular spectroscopy being much more complex than atomic spectroscopy, but it potentially makes an enormous amount of astrophysical information available to astronomers. Molecular spectroscopy is of rapidly increasing importance in astronomy, not only because of the light it sheds on interstellar chemistry, but also because it is allowing us to study dark regions of space from which little or no light emerges.

The transitions of a simple molecule such as carbon monoxide (CO) can be divided into three main types: electronic, vibrational and rotational, as depicted in figure 13.12. ELECTRONIC TRANSITIONS involve changes in the shape of the cloud of electrons surrounding the constituent atoms. They are very analogous to the transitions seen in single atoms, and occur at similar wavelengths, namely visible and ultraviolet. Electronic transitions in interstellar molecules can be studied only by looking at the absorption in front of a bright star. Only rather few, relatively transparent regions of space can be studied in this way, so although ultraviolet and visible observations of molecules can be useful in forming a general picture of the diffuse interstellar medium, they provide no clue to what happens in the denser, more opaque regions.

VIBRATIONAL TRANSITIONS occur as a result of elasticity within the molecule allowing its atoms to oscillate to and fro with respect to each other. Changes in the amplitude of these vibrations generally lead to transitions at infrared wavelengths. Although infrared spectroscopy is potentially one of the most promising methods for studying molecular clouds in our Galaxy, the technique is currently not very sensitive, and is confined to observations of cool stars or infrared sources such as IRC + 10216.

ROTATIONAL TRANSITIONS, resulting from changes in the rate a molecule is spinning, give spectral lines which are usually at microwave or millimetre wavelengths. Large numbers of molecules have been observed by their rotational transitions, although the commonest molecule, hydrogen, like other symmetric molecules including oxygen, nitrogen and carbon dioxide, is unfortunately unobservable by this technique. Nevertheless, as described in the next section, the study of molecules by their microwave transitions has led to a spectacular increase in our understanding of molecular clouds in the past five or ten years. Most of our knowledge about interstellar chemistry is based on these very recent observations, many of which are of regions whose existence was unsuspected a decade ago.

Radio spectroscopy

The first molecule to be discovered in space at radio wavelengths was the hydroxyl radical (OH) in 1963. Starting in 1968, there then came a rush of new molecule discoveries. Most of these were made at wavelengths of less than one centimetre by groups of astronomers using the 11-metre radio telescope of the US National Radio Astronomy Observatory at Kitt Peak, Arizona. In some cases molecules were identified on the basis of a pattern of spectral lines, but sometimes only a single transition has been seen. In most cases the lines are observed in emission rather than absorption.

Table 13.1 lists the interstellar molecules seen by radio telescopes up to early 1977. Although a few inorganic molecules have been found (e.g. NH_3, SiO, H_2S), most of the molecules are organic. They range in complexity from diatomic molecules such as CH, CO, CN and CS to molecules with as many as nine atoms (e.g. $(CH_3)_2O$, C_2H_5OH). The number and complexity of the molecules discovered in the early seventies was a great surprise to astronomers and chemists alike, who up to that time had believed that none but the simplest molecules could form and survive in space.

Interstellar radio spectroscopy has now become so sophisticated that it is in some cases easier to study the spectrum of a molecule in space than in a laboratory. Such a case is illustrated in figure 13.13; on Earth the N_2H^+ ion is so reactive that at the time of its discovery in space it had never been possible to isolate enough of it for spectroscopic study. In the low-density regions of space, however, the molecule can survive in large enough quantities that spectral lines can be seen that are sufficiently clear for scientists to measure the detailed structure of the molecule for the first time.

Interstellar molecules are very unevenly distributed in space. Most of the molecules listed in table 13.1 have been seen in less

13.12: *The three most important types of transition which a molecule such as carbon monoxide can make. In an electronic transition, the molecule changes the shape of its electron cloud; in a vibrational transition it alters the amplitude of the to-and-fro motion of its atoms, and in a rotational transition the speed of its end-over-end spinning is changed. The different types of transition tend to produce ultraviolet, infrared, and millimetre wave photons respectively.*

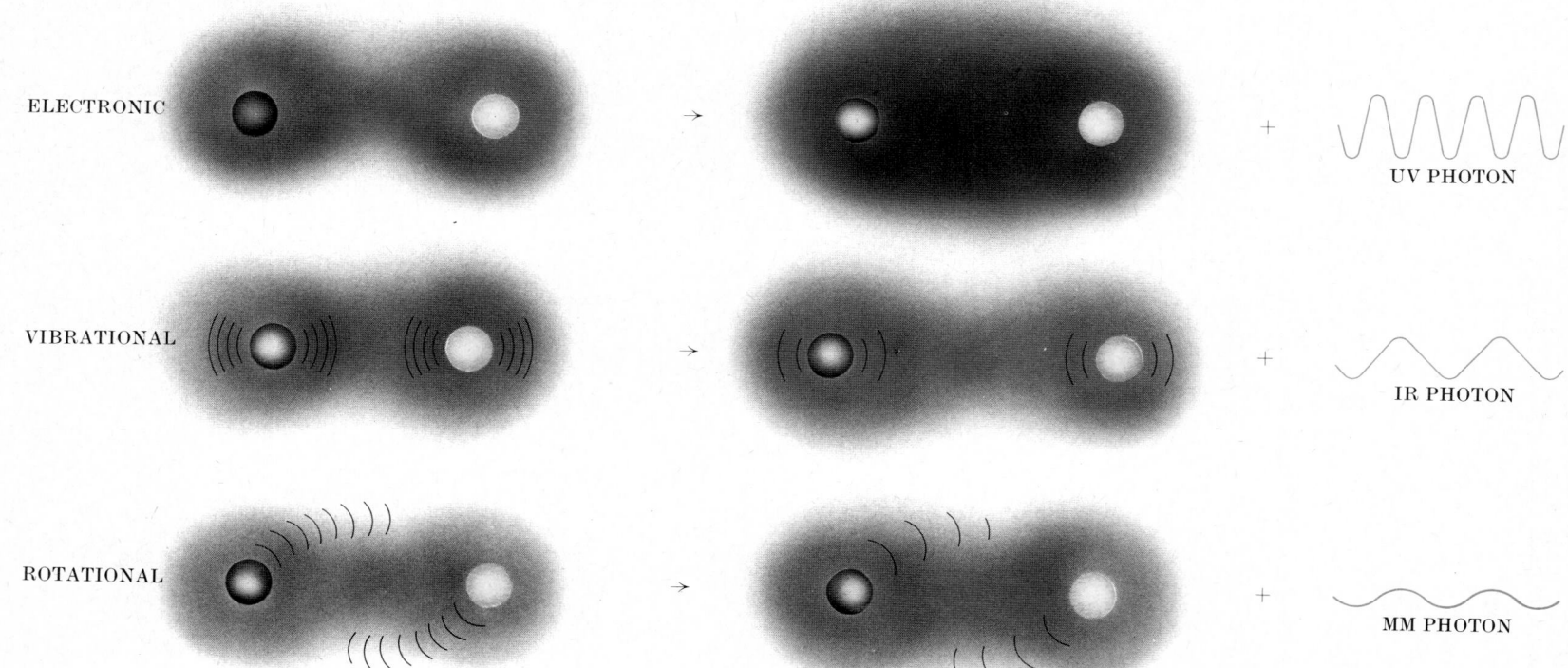

ELECTRONIC → + UV PHOTON

VIBRATIONAL → + IR PHOTON

ROTATIONAL → + MM PHOTON

than a dozen locations in the sky and many in only one place — the giant interstellar cloud Sagittarius B2, very close to the centre of our Galaxy. Molecules are plentiful only under certain interstellar conditions, chief of which are a high gas density (typically 10^{10} molecules m^{-3}), and sufficient dust to provide a shield from the destructive effects of ultraviolet starlight. A few molecular clouds are associated with old stars, but most of them are regions where new stars are condensing out of the interstellar medium. These clouds include the most massive objects in the Galaxy; although the clouds themselves are usually invisible at optical wavelengths, they are often found associated with known H^+ regions.

Most of the radio lines are caused by rotational transitions. A simple molecule, such as carbon monosulphide, spends most of its time with no angular momentum; sometimes, however, as a result of a collision with another molecule (most probably an H_2 hydrogen), it can be made to spin in an end-over-end fashion. If undisturbed, it will (on average) then remain in this rotational state for just a few hours before emitting one or more millimetre-wavelength photons and reverting to its ground state. Because carbon monosulphide molecules drop out of their excited states so rapidly they are seen only in regions where molecular collisions are very frequent, namely where the molecular hydrogen density is $10^{12}\,m^{-3}$ or more. The molecule carbon monoxide behaves in many ways much like carbon sulphide, but does not have to be excited by molecular collisions nearly as frequently as does carbon sulphide. It can therefore be seen in regions of comparatively low density, typically 10^8 molecules m^{-3}. For this reason, carbon monoxide is used for mapping out the moderate-density clouds in our Galaxy, whereas carbon sulphide and certain other molecules show us the location of the densest parts of these clouds.

In the places where several different molecules have been seen, estimates can be made of their relative abundances by comparing the strengths of their spectral lines. Although molecular hydrogen is very difficult to observe directly, there is little doubt that it is by far the dominant species in these clouds. Of those molecules observed at radio wavelengths, carbon monoxide is much the most widespread, with something like one molecule for every 10 000 of hydrogen. Carbon monoxide is so common, and is seen in so many directions in space, that it can be used to study the structure of our Galaxy in a way that complements the observations of atomic hydrogen. The next most abundant molecules are hydroxyl and ammonia, although they are only one per cent as common as carbon monoxide. All other known molecules are rarer still, though the as-yet unobserved nitrogen molecule (N_2) is probably widespread. As described in the next section, the relative abundances of different molecules give us clues to the processes of interstellar chemistry. A more speculative calculation was performed by the discoverers of interstellar ethyl alcohol in 1974; they estimated that the 'proof' (a measure of the ratio of alcohol to water) in the molecular cloud Sagittarius B2 was somewhat less than 1°. Despite this dilution, the cloud contains enough alcohol for 10^{28} bottles of whisky.

13.13: *Microwave spectrum lines from the N_2H^+ ion in the interstellar cloud OMC2. This molecule was first discovered in space and only subsequently isolated in a laboratory.*

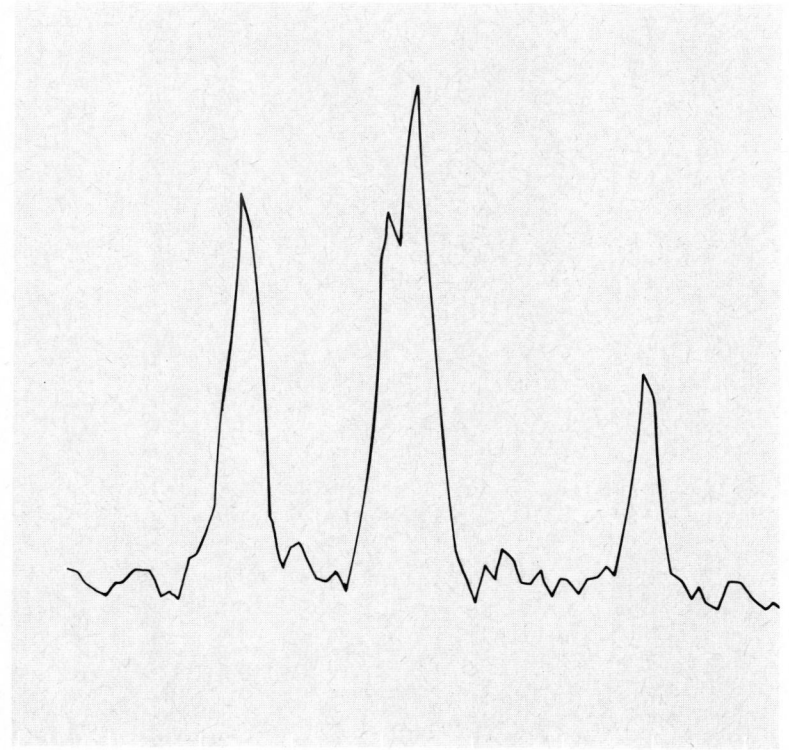

RADIO POWER

93.170   93.175

FREQUENCY (GHz)

Chemistry in space

Molecules are fragile objects; they cannot survive long in normal interstellar space because they are usually rapidly destroyed in bombardment by ultraviolet starlight. It follows, therefore, that the molecules we detect were formed only recently and that the dense clouds where we see them are the chemical 'factories' where they are produced. For a chemical reaction to take place, the participating atoms or molecules must collide or, at least, approach each other very closely. The clouds where molecules are found must therefore be relatively dense, and collisions in them frequent occurrences. Also, in order to prevent the destruction of molecules by starlight, a cloud rich in molecules must contain a high enough concentration of dust grains that light is excluded from its interior. This dust may serve an additional role in aiding the actual production of molecules, in that gas atoms landing on the surface of a dust grain may combine with other atoms already there, using the dust surface as a catalyst.

Some clues as to how interstellar molecules are formed may be obtained by examining the classes of molecules that are known to exist and, just as important, which molecules up to now have not been detected. As we would expect if large molecules are made by synthesis from small ones, we find that complicated molecules are in general rarer than simple ones. A more unexpected phenomenon is that in almost every case where two carbon atoms are joined together, it is by a single bond (C—C) or a triple bond (C≡C)

13.14: *Spectrum of the OH maser associated with the H⁺ region W3, measured at 18-cm wavelength. The thick and thin lines represent the signals of different circular polarizations.*

13.15: *The distribution of sources of OH maser emission in W3. The crosses represent the errors in the position of each 'spot', the diameter of each is much too small to be shown in this picture. This map was made using the Very-Long-Baseline-Interferometer technique; it covers a region of sky only 3 arc sec square.*

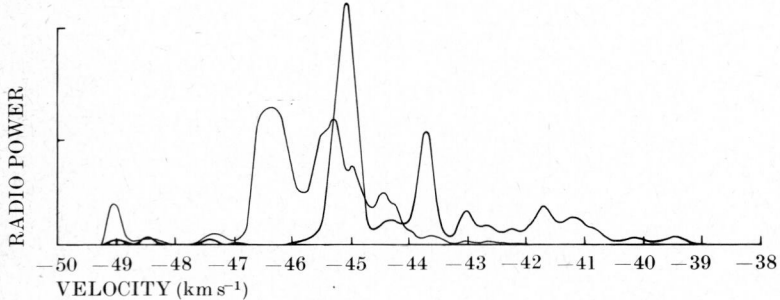

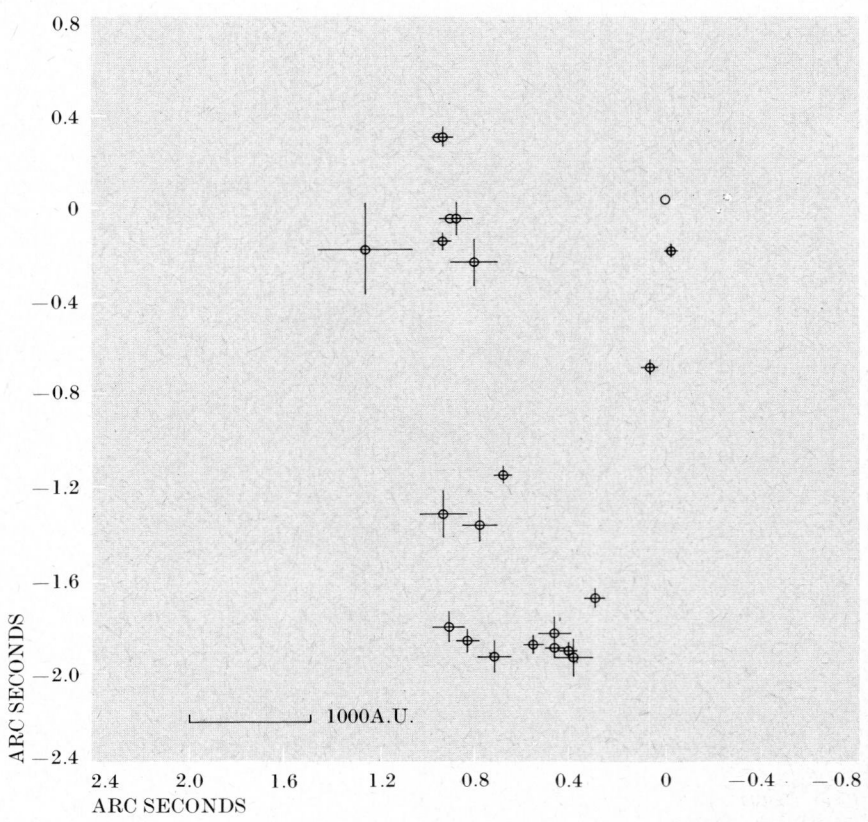

rather than by a double bond (C=C). Another strange feature is that no oxide of nitrogen, nor any molecule containing a nitrogen-oxygen bond has yet been seen. Similarly ring molecules, such as pyridine (C_5H_5N), although common in terrestrial chemistry, are rare in interstellar space. From clues such as these, astronomers are trying to work out the chemical reactions by which molecules are synthesized. One possibility under discussion is that while the simplest molecules are formed catalytically on the surface of grains, the more complicated molecules are built up by direct collisions among the gaseous molecules and ionized radicals. One of the difficulties in solving the problem of INTERSTELLAR SYNTHESIS is that many of the chemical reactions considered important in interstellar space are insignificant at terrestrial densities, and hence have been ignored until now. Consequently there is nearly as much activity by chemists in their laboratories discovering and measuring new reactions as there is among astronomers in their observatories looking for their products in space.

Although the chemistry of interstellar molecules has turned out to be much richer than anticipated, the complexity of the compounds discovered to date is still many orders of magnitude less than that of even the simplest living organism. Biological cells are made up of vast chains of amino acids, the simplest of which is glycine ($NH_2.CH_2.COOH$). Even if, as it not unlikely, some individual amino acids are discovered in interstellar clouds, the implications for the origin of life on planets such as ours are few; any molecules present in the cloud out of which the Solar System formed would probably not have survived the heat given out as the Earth condensed. Thus, although there are some interesting analogies between biology and interstellar chemistry, there is probably no causal relationship between them.

OH and other interstellar masers

The first interstellar molecule to be discovered at radio wavelengths, the OH RADICAL, is still the most difficult to understand. Although in some dark clouds the OH molecule behaves in a simple fashion, there are many locations in the Galaxy where the OH emission shows characteristics quite unlike those of a normal interstellar molecule. The OH EMISSION LINES in these sources consist of a group of very narrow spectral lines instead of a single broad line (figure 13.14); these narrow lines are usually polarized and vary over a period of months. The emission appears to come from very small volumes; a typical OH source displays emission from a dozen or more 'hot spots', each 5–10 AU across and about 1000 AU apart, whereas a normal molecular cloud is something like a million AU across (figure 13.15). Finally, the strengths of these lines are millions of times stronger than would be expected if the OH molecules in an interstellar cloud behaved normally. The implication of these observations is that the OH lines are being amplified by some means. The process must be akin to that in a MASER (an acronym for Microwave Amplification by Stimulated Emission of Radiation). By a process that is not yet fully understood, the OH molecules absorb energy, probably from collisions, or from infrared or ultraviolet radiation fields, and convert some of it into radiation at a wavelength of 18 cm. Theoretical calculations show that this masering process can take place only under special conditions of density, temperature, motion and magnetic field, though astronomers differ in their opinions as to just what these conditions are.

The original OH MASERS were found at a wavelength of 18 cm. Subsequently maser emission from OH molecules has been found at other, shorter, wavelengths. Several other molecules are now known to exhibit maser action as well as OH; the most notable of these are water vapour, H_2O, and silicon monoxide, SiO. Water-vapour masers are even more powerful than OH masers; the source called W49, for example, emits as much power in the single spectral transition at 1.35 cm wavelength as does the Sun at all wavelengths. Hydroxyl, water-vapour and silicon-monoxide masers are usually found close to each other in the sky, but are not actually coincident.

There appear to be two main types of OH maser source, namely those associated with late-type stars and those associated with H^+ regions. Only certain late-type stars are OH sources, namely some M supergiants such as NML Cygnus and VY CMa, and some Mira variables such as R Cas. These OH stars are all cool, red objects with oxygen-rich atmospheres. Almost all have infrared emission which comes from a shell of hot dust around the star. Two common characteristics of this type of maser are that they regularly vary in strength with a period of about a year, and that the OH lines are double, with the two components separated by a frequency which corresponds to a Doppler shift of 20–40 km s^{-1}. The reason for this splitting is still very much a mystery, though it must be somehow related to the expansion or rotation of the cloud of OH molecules surrounding the star.

The OH and H_2O masers that are found in H^+ regions appear to be connected with an early stage of star formation. They are almost always coincident with either a very compact H^+ region, a strong infrared source, or both. The infrared sources are probably the hot central regions of *protostars*, which are clouds in the process of collapsing to form new stars. Eventually, the study of these masers may give us a great deal of information about the velocities, temperatures and densities in a protostar, but at the moment our lack of understanding of the maser process itself greatly hinders such an interpretation of the data.

Interstellar cosmic rays

Almost all our knowledge of the Universe comes from the study of photons, whether they be of X-ray, visible, infrared or radio wavelength. There is, however, an increasingly important branch of astronomy that is concerned with quite different particles, COSMIC RAYS. The term cosmic ray is applied to elementary particles, usually protons, electrons or the nuclei of atoms, which travel through space with a velocity close to that of light. Since most of these particles are absorbed by the Earth's atmosphere they must be studied from the tops of high mountains, or from rockets, balloons, or satellites.

Most photons can travel across the Galaxy from their point of origin to the Earth with almost no deflection from a straight line. This is not true for cosmic rays. Protons, electrons and nuclei all possess electric charge and are therefore continuously deflected in different directions as they encounter the constantly-changing magnetic fields of interstellar and interplanetary space. Except possibly for the very highest energy particles, we cannot tell where a cosmic ray came from by looking at the direction it was travelling when it reached the Earth. The observational problems faced by cosmic ray astronomers are somewhat analogous to those of optical astronomers if the latter were forced always to observe the skies through a frosted glass window which randomly scattered all starlight as it entered the telescope!

The main properties of cosmic rays that can be measured are their energies and the numbers of the different types of particles reaching the Earth. It is found that some 90 per cent of the particles are protons, the nuclei of hydrogen atoms, with most of the rest being α-particles, the nuclei of helium atoms. The bulk of the particles detected have energies around 10^8–10^9 eV, but many particles with much greater energies are also seen. Figure 13.16 shows how the number of particles of a given energy depends on the energy. Above 10^9 eV the particle flux drops steadily with increasing energy all the way to 10^{20} eV. We know very little about cosmic rays with energy greater than 10^{19} eV because so few of them arrive on the Earth each day. There is, nevertheless, very great interest in such particles, as they have energies many orders of magnitude greater than can be generated by particle accelerators in terrestrial laboratories. The energy contained in a single 10^{20} eV cosmic-ray proton is about 16 Joules – enough to lift this book several centimetres off the table.

High-energy cosmic rays possess so much momentum that they are essentially undeflected as they pass through the Solar System. Cosmic rays with energies less than 10^9 eV, however, are much more susceptible to the influence of the Sun, in particular of the *solar wind*. As a result, comparatively few cosmic rays with energies below 10^8 eV reach the Earth, as shown in figure 13.17. This effect, known as SOLAR MODULATION, prevents us from measuring the true flux of low-energy cosmic rays in interstellar space.

The only place in the Galaxy where we can measure cosmic rays directly is the vicinity of our Sun. Several lines of indirect evidence, however, indicate that the flux of cosmic rays we detect on Earth is

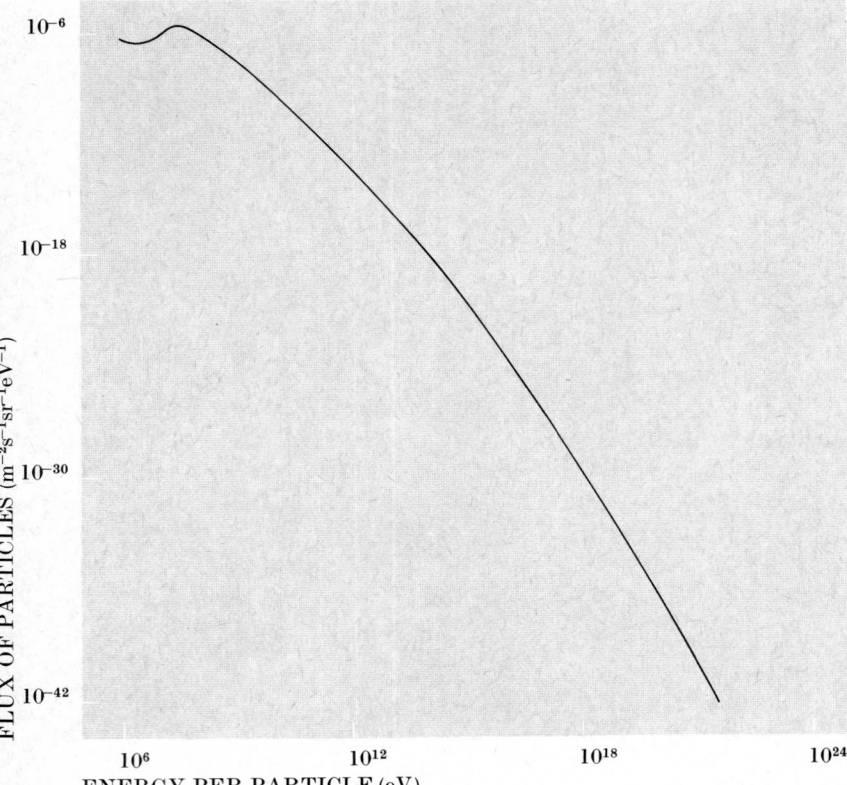

13.16: *The flux of interstellar cosmic rays near the Earth as a function of their energy. At low energy the cosmic rays, which are mainly protons, are detected by a satellite or balloon-borne experiments. At energies above 10^{14} eV information comes from air-shower experiments on the ground.*

typical of many regions of the Galaxy and that cosmic rays are a universal constituent of the interstellar medium. In the rest of this section we will describe some of the secondary effects of cosmic rays such as radio and gamma-ray emission, and also discuss what is known about their origin and propagation.

Galactic radio emission

The interstellar medium is a very strong source of radio waves. Besides individual bright objects such as the supernova remnant Cassiopeia A and the H^+ region Orion A, there is diffuse emission visible from all directions in the sky. This radio emission is the result of the interaction between cosmic-ray electrons and the Galactic magnetic field.

A map of this diffuse radio emission is shown in figure 13.17. There is a strong concentration towards the plane of the Galaxy, but there are other prominent features as well. The largest of these, the North Polar Spur, rises from the plane near galactic longitude 30°, and may possibly be the result of a supernova explosion near the Earth some 10^5 years ago. The diffuse radio emission is seen at frequencies from about 1 MHz to 1 GHz, and, in common with many other celestial objects such as radio galaxies and supernova remnants, is strongest at long wavelengths, declining towards higher frequencies. Such a spectrum is characteristic of SYNCHROTRON RADIATION, which arises when high-speed electrons spiral around magnetic field lines. The realization around 1950 that the diffuse

13.17: *Map in galactic coordinates of the 150 MHz radio emission from cosmic-ray electrons in the interstellar medium. The bright (orange and yellow) regions correspond in general to the plane of the Milky Way.*

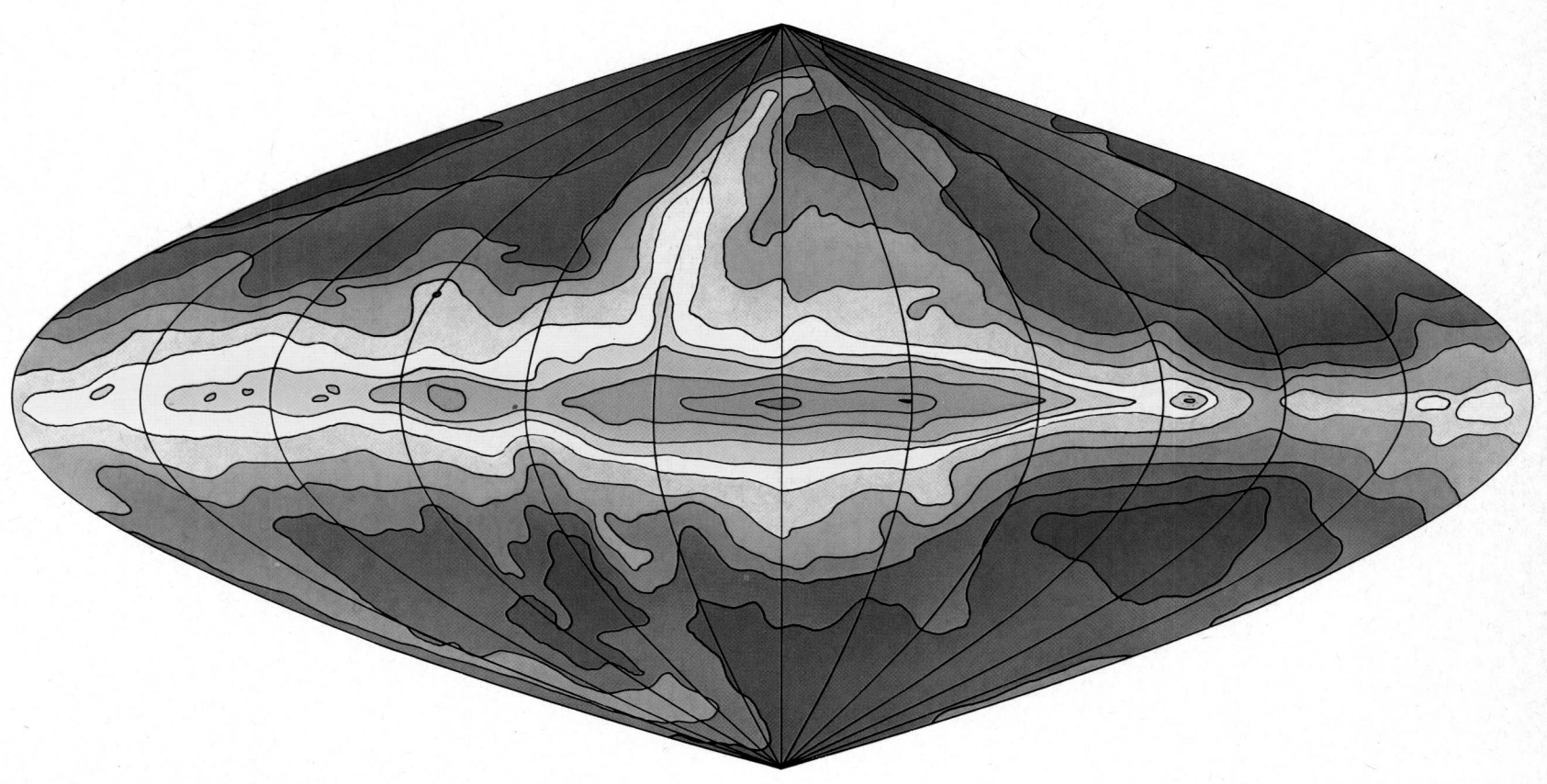

galactic radio emission was due to the synchrotron process was the first evidence for the existence of cosmic-ray electrons, as opposed to protons, in the interstellar medium. At most energies, cosmic-ray electrons are outnumbered 100 to 1 by protons and it was only in the 1960s that cosmic-ray detection techniques became sensitive enough to detect cosmic-ray electrons at the top of the Earth's atmosphere directly.

The radio frequency at which a synchrotron electron radiates depends on its energy and on the strength of the magnetic field about which it is spiralling. For example, a 3-GeV electron in a magnetic field of 3×10^{-10} T (3μG) radiates predominantly at about 300 MHz, a typical radio-astronomy frequency. In the same way that gamma rays can tell us about distant cosmic-ray protons, therefore, radio astronomy gives us a picture of the cosmic-ray electrons throughout the Galaxy. Neither case is straightforward, however, since the gamma rays are dependent also on the hydrogen density distribution, and the radio flux depends on the galactic magnetic field.

We do not know very much about the interstellar magnetic field. We cannot measure it directly because it is so much weaker inside the Solar System than that of the Sun or the Earth. We must therefore use indirect means. One method is to measure the *Faraday rotation* of the plane of polarization of cosmic radio waves, as they pass through the interstellar medium. Another is to look for the *Zeeman splitting* of the 21-cm hydrogen line as it is absorbed in an interstellar cloud containing a magnetic field. Rough estimates of the interstellar field strength can also be made on the basis of the optical polarization of starlight and from a comparison of the

13.18: *The distribution of high-energy gamma rays around the galactic plane. The large peak is towards the central regions of the Galaxy, while the smaller, narrower peaks are probably due to the Crab and Vela supernova remnants.*

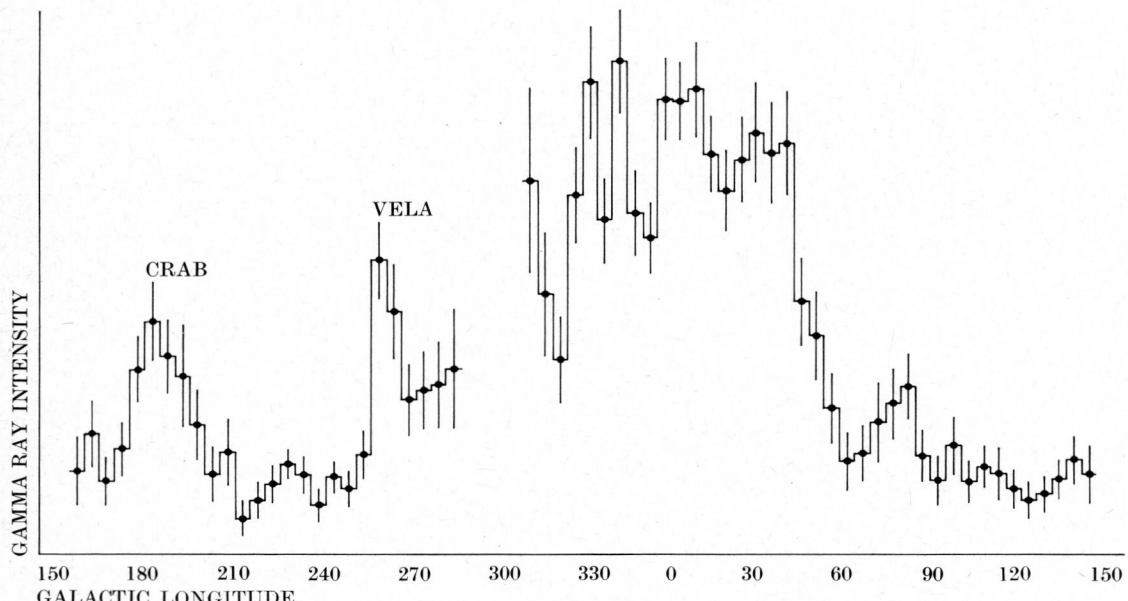

measured spectrum of the diffuse galactic radio emission with that predicted from the cosmic-ray electrons as observed near the earth. All these methods suggest that magnetic fields in the range 10^{-10} to 10^{-9} T are fairly typical in our Galaxy, although stronger fields must exist in the denser regions of the interstellar medium. The direction of the magnetic field appears to be in the plane of the Galaxy in most places and, near the Sun, probably runs along the local spiral arm.

Galactic gamma rays

One of the few methods of detecting cosmic rays in distant parts of the Galaxy is provided by the very new science of gamma-ray astronomy. When high-speed cosmic-ray protons collide with hydrogen atoms in the interstellar medium, nuclear reactions take place between them and a number of π°-mesons are created. These π°-mesons, or pions, are unstable and themselves decay almost immediately to produce a pair of gamma rays. These gamma rays have an average energy of about 100 MeV each, corresponding to a wavelength of 10^{-14} m, and can pass right across the Galaxy with almost no hindrance by the interstellar medium.

Figure 13.18 shows the distribution of these gamma rays as a function of galactic longitude around the Milky Way, as measured by the SAS-2 satellite in 1973. Apart from a couple of subsidiary peaks which are due to gamma-ray emission from the Crab and Vela supernova remnants, the distribution of gamma rays is very similar to that of the interstellar hydrogen in the Galaxy. The measured intensity of the gamma rays in any direction is close to what is expected from the pion decay process if the intensity of cosmic-ray protons is about the same throughout the Galaxy as it is at the Earth. This is very encouraging support for the assumption that the cosmic rays we detect on Earth are typical of the Galaxy as a whole. As gamma-ray telescopes become more sophisticated in the next few years we may be able to locate sources of cosmic rays by this technique.

The origin of cosmic rays

There is little doubt that most of the disc of the Galaxy is filled with cosmic rays. What is not certain is whether or not they are also found in large numbers in the deeper reaches of extragalactic space, apart from such special places as quasars and radio galaxies. At present this question is controversial, but the more conservative view is that all except the most energetic cosmic rays are confined to and produced within the Galaxy. The main motive behind this attitude is the very large number of cosmic rays; at a typical point in the Galaxy there is as much energy in cosmic rays as in starlight, with the result that cosmic rays play a significant role in the heating, ionization and pressure balance of the interstellar medium. It is difficult enough to think of ways to produce the cosmic rays which fill the galactic disc; to make sufficient additional particles to fill the whole of the space between the galaxies is a daunting problem for all but the most courageous theoretical astrophysicists.

There may be several different kinds of celestial objects capable of producing cosmic rays, but it is generally agreed that supernovae are probably the most important. The reason for this conclusion is the fact that supernova remnants are very strong sources of synchrotron radio emission and that they must therefore have the ability to generate their own high-velocity electrons. Some of these electrons, and presumably other particles such as protons, are ejected from the supernova remnant into the interstellar medium and contribute to the background of cosmic rays. The problem of how the particles become accelerated to such high velocities is unsolved, but it is conjectured that either the electromagnetic fields of a rotating pulsar, or the shock waves in an expanding supernova shell may be powerful enough.

How long do the cosmic rays spend on their tortuous paths from their points of origin to the Earth? An important clue is obtained from looking at the concentrations of the elements lithium, boron and beryllium in cosmic rays. We find that these elements are a million of times more common in cosmic rays than in the stars. This effect is the result of SPALLATION; when a fast-moving cosmic-ray nucleus collides with a stationary atom of interstellar matter, nuclear reactions can take place. Most frequently, these reactions lead to the production of new atoms of the light elements. From the amounts of Li, Be and B found in cosmic rays it is deduced that an average cosmic-ray proton passes through $50 \, \text{kg} \, \text{m}^{-2}$ of interstellar matter on its path to the Earth. The length of time it takes the proton to negotiate this much of the interstellar medium depends on the region of space it is confined to move within. If the interstellar magnetic field restricts it to the disc of the Galaxy, a proton would have to live for 3×10^6 yr and travel 10^6 pc in order to pass through this much matter. If, as some astronomers believe, the cosmic rays travel in addition within the halo of our Galaxy occupied by the globular clusters then they must be more than 10^7 years old. In either case, the time is vastly greater than the few thousand years it would have taken a relativistic proton to travel in a straight line from a typical supernova to the Earth. This time difference of a thousand or more is an indication of the twistiness of the path that a cosmic ray takes as it transverses the Galaxy.

14. Clouds, nebulae, star births and deaths

14.1: *The H⁺ region M8, also known as the Lagoon Nebula.*
(Hale Observatories, USA*)*

Interstellar clouds

The unevenness of the interstellar medium

The previous chapter described the ways in which the interstellar medium can be observed, and summarized the major properties of the dust, the gas, and the cosmic rays which comprise it. This chapter is concerned with the way in which the interstellar medium is generally concentrated into clouds, particularly clouds associated with the births and deaths of stars.

There are many mechanisms which have the effect of stirring up the interstellar medium and generating clouds, nebulae, and other structural features. These include:

(a) *Density waves* associated with rotating galactic spiral arms.

(b) *Thermal instabilities* which tend to separate interstellar gas into regions which are either cool and dense or hot and rare.

(c) Gravitational collapse of clouds to form new stars.

(d) Ionization of certain parts of space (H^+ *regions*) by the ultraviolet radiation from O- and B-type stars.

(e) Expulsion of matter from old stars in the form of *planetary nebulae* or *supernovae*.

(f) Magnetic fields.

The various types of cloud produced by these processes are transient objects that are generally in a state of either expansion or contraction. Most evolve with timescales of thousands or millions of years which, though long by human standards, are short compared with the lifetime of the Galaxy. The study of clouds is therefore primarily the study of the evolution of the interstellar medium and of its interaction with the stars.

Atomic clouds

The most crucial factor on which the properties of an interstellar cloud depend is the state of its most prevalent constituent, namely hydrogen; the state of the helium and of the heavier elements is of secondary importance. Although the various different forms of hydrogen can coexist to some extent, it is a reasonable simplification to divide space into three basic types of region: those in which the hydrogen is in predominantly molecular form (H_2), those in which it is predominantly atomic (HI or H^0) and those in which it is predominantly ionized (HII or H^+). Molecular hydrogen and ionized hydrogen appear to exist mainly in discrete clouds, leaving most of interstellar space filled with atomic hydrogen.

The unevenness of the atomic hydrogen can be seen in figure 14.2. This diagram shows the strength of the 21-cm hydrogen emission line around the whole sky, with the exception of the galactic plane and some southern regions. Most of the gas seen in figure 14.2 is within 100 pc of the Sun; it exists largely in the form of loops, filaments, and clouds rather than as a uniform galactic atmosphere. In the case of this local hydrogen the interstellar magnetic field is one of the most important influences; for example, comparison of figure 14.2 with figure 13.7 shows that many of the hydrogen filaments are elongated along magnetic field lines.

Close to the galactic plane, 21-cm spectra generally indicate the existence of atomic hydrogen at a variety of distances along the line of sight. Part of the variation is due to the presence of *spiral arms* and part is due to the presence of clouds. As described on page 266, spectra such as those in figure 13.11 indicate that different parts of the gas are at different temperatures. In particular, there are patches of hydrogen which are much colder than the average, and so absorb strongly. These patches are cool atomic clouds, which lie within a hotter 'intercloud medium'. Clouds vary greatly, but typical ones may have densities of between 5×10^6 and 10^8 atoms m^{-3}, and sizes of up to a few parsecs across. The temperature of the gas inside a cloud is about 100 K, whereas that of the intercloud medium is much greater. In the region of the galactic plane a few per cent of the volume is occupied by clouds, whereas the rest is filled by the intercloud medium.

This separation of the interstellar atomic hydrogen into 'cloud' and 'intercloud' regions is partly the result of THERMAL INSTABILITIES in the interstellar medium. Interstellar gas is heated by a mixture of ultraviolet starlight, X-rays and *cosmic rays*. It is cooled by photons which are emitted as a result of collisions between the interstellar particles. At typical interstellar temperatures and densities an increase of density at some point leads to an increase in the rate of collisions and therefore in the rate of cooling. The resultant drop in temperature is under certain circumstances enough actually to decrease the pressure at that point, leading to an instability as neighbouring gas rushes in and increases the density even more. A gas which is initially at uniform density will therefore, if it is disturbed slightly, separate itself spontaneously into cold, dense regions and hot, rare regions. The theory behind this process is known as the TWO-PHASE MODEL of the interstellar medium.

14.2: *The distribution of high galactic latitude neutral hydrogen in the vicinity of the Sun. Blue areas show hydrogen moving towards the Sun, red away from the Sun. The blank strip in the middle of the diagram shows the location of the galactic plane; the blank area to the lower left is the region of sky invisible from the northern Californian location of the radio telescope where these data were obtained.*

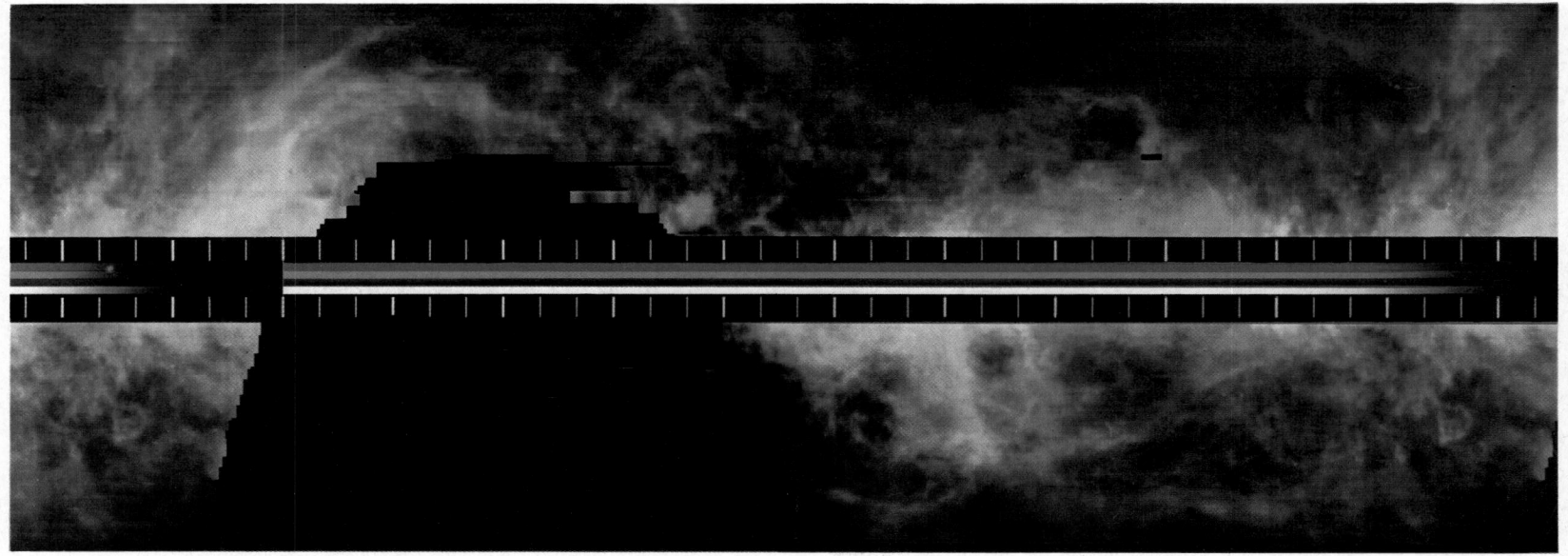

Dark clouds and molecular clouds

The thickest and densest interstellar clouds consist mainly of molecular hydrogen. The reason for this is that the formation and preservation of molecules is facilitated by a high concentration of gas (and consequently a greater frequency of atomic collisions) and also a high concentration of dust grains which assist the formation of hydrogen and shield it from the destructive effects of ultraviolet starlight. Ultraviolet observations with the Copernicus satellite have shown that clouds which have an extinction (A_v) of less than 0.3 mag are predominantly atomic, whereas those with an extinction greater than this contain an appreciable amount of molecular hydrogen.

Clouds that produce visual extinction of a few magnitudes or more may become detectable because of the obscuration they cause. They are often referred to as DARK NEBULAE or DARK CLOUDS. The Horsehead Nebula (figure 13.2) and the Coalsack are the classic examples of these objects. Sometimes the dark nebulae manifest themselves simply as apparently blank areas of sky, devoid of stars (figure 14.3). Alternatively, they may appear as very dark patches in front of bright nebulae (figure 14.9). It is very common for dark clouds to be found closely associated with H^+ regions and with reflection nebulae. Dark clouds occur in a wide variety of sizes. Small clouds, such as those in figure 14.9 are called GLOBULES, and may have diameters no larger than the Solar System; large clouds may be several parsecs in diameter.

The dust content of dark clouds may in some cases be estimated by comparing the number of stars visible through it with the number estimated to be behind it. The gas content is more difficult to obtain. The 21-cm line is no use since the hydrogen in dark clouds is predominantly molecular, not atomic. The ultraviolet spectral lines of molecular hydrogen cannot be studied since the cloud is opaque at these wavelengths. It is therefore necessary to observe other molecules such as formaldehyde, hydroxyl or carbon monoxide. Figure 14.4 shows contours of the strength of the formaldehyde absorption at 6-cm wavelength from different parts of the ρ-Ophiuchi dark cloud. The regions of strongest absorption correspond well with thick parts of the obscuring cloud, confirming that the dust and the molecules are co-extensive in this cloud. The hydrogen molecule density in dark clouds is typically 10^9–10^{10} atoms m^{-3}. Because of the increased rate of cooling at high densities and the fact that ultraviolet and X-radiation cannot penetrate to heat the middle of the cloud, the temperature of dark clouds is lower (around 10 K) than in atomic clouds.

The MOLECULAR CLOUDS which are the main focus of attention of the radio spectroscopists are generally hotter (30–100 K) and denser (10^{10}–10^{12} atoms m^{-3}) than visible dark clouds, though they are much less common in the Galaxy. These warm molecular clouds are also strong sources of infrared radiation by virtue of the heated dust grains they contain. They are frequently found in the vicinity of giant H^+ regions, and are thought to be places where new stars are forming. The nearest such clouds to the Sun are associated with the *Orion Nebula*, (figures 14.13, 14.14).

14.3: *The dark nebulae Barnard 68 and Barnard 72 known as the 'Snake'. Although the black patches appear to be holes in the sky they are, in fact, dense interstellar clouds through which light from distant stars cannot pass. This photograph gives some idea of the vast number of stars which are visible in certain directions of the Milky Way. (Palomar Sky Survey, USA)*

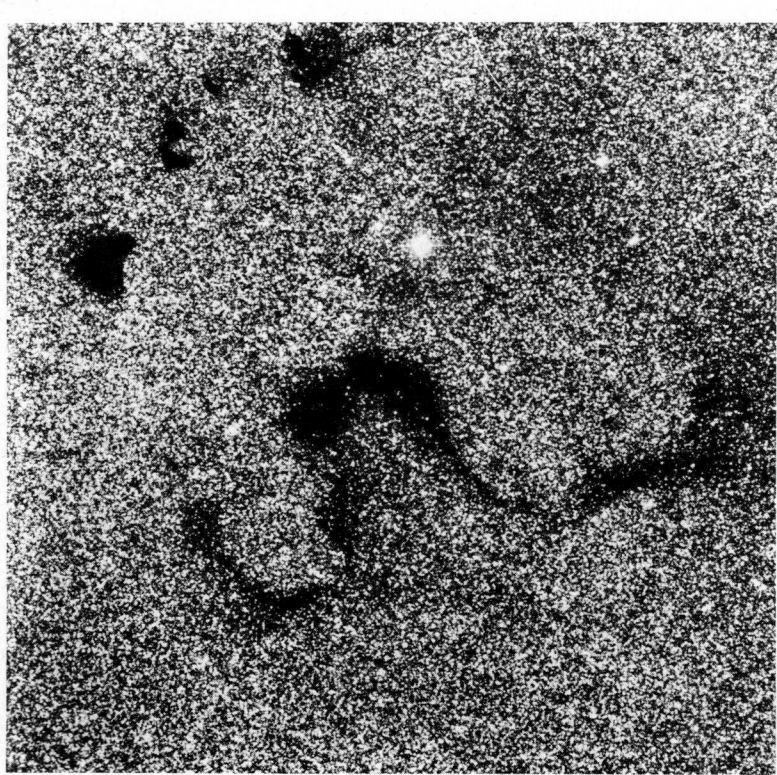

The intercloud medium

Less is known about the intercloud medium than about the clouds. The intercloud medium appears to contain both atomic and ionized hydrogen, and there are several lines of evidence to suggest that the average concentration of free electrons in the intercloud medium is about 3×10^4 atoms m^{-3}. Observations at 21-cm wavelength suggest that the intercloud medium is a warm, partially-ionized gas with a density of about 2×10^5 atoms m^{-3}, a temperature of perhaps 8000 K, and with about one hydrogen atom in seven ionized by some means. Ultraviolet observations, however, do not completely support this picture and suggest that the free electrons exist in low density H$^+$ regions, separate from the atomic hydrogen. These H$^+$ regions are ionized by distant O and B stars or, alternatively, by the X-rays from the occasional *supernovae* that explode in the Galaxy.

Ultraviolet studies have also demonstrated the existence of yet another form of interstellar gas, namely an ionized component with an extremely low density, but a temperature in excess of 100 000 K. These regions are thought to represent 'holes' in the interstellar medium caused by *supernova explosions*. These holes can reach a diameter of 50 pc and, it is conjectured, may join up with each other and produce a network of tunnels through the interstellar medium, rather like a Swiss cheese.

One of the most prominent effects of the free electrons in the interstellar medium is to delay radio waves as they pass through the Galaxy. The delay is most noticeable in the case of signals from *pulsars*, and the phenomenon is therefore often called PULSAR DISPERSION. The delay is greater for low-frequency radio signals than for high-frequency ones; a 300-MHz signal from a 300-pc distant pulsar would be delayed by about 0.5 sec by the interstellar medium, whereas a 150-MHz signal would be delayed by 2 sec. This 1.5 sec time difference in the arrival of the different frequency pulses is easily measured, and can sometimes be used to make an estimate of the distance to the pulsar.

Another effect attributable to free electrons is INTERSTELLAR SCATTERING. Irregularities, such as clouds, in the density of the free electrons can lead to scattering of radio waves as they pass through the Galaxy. The effect is small and significant only at low frequencies; at 80 MHz the scattering is typically a few tenths of a second of arc. The effect can nevertheless impede the measurement of the true sizes of compact radio sources such as *quasars* and *OH masers*.

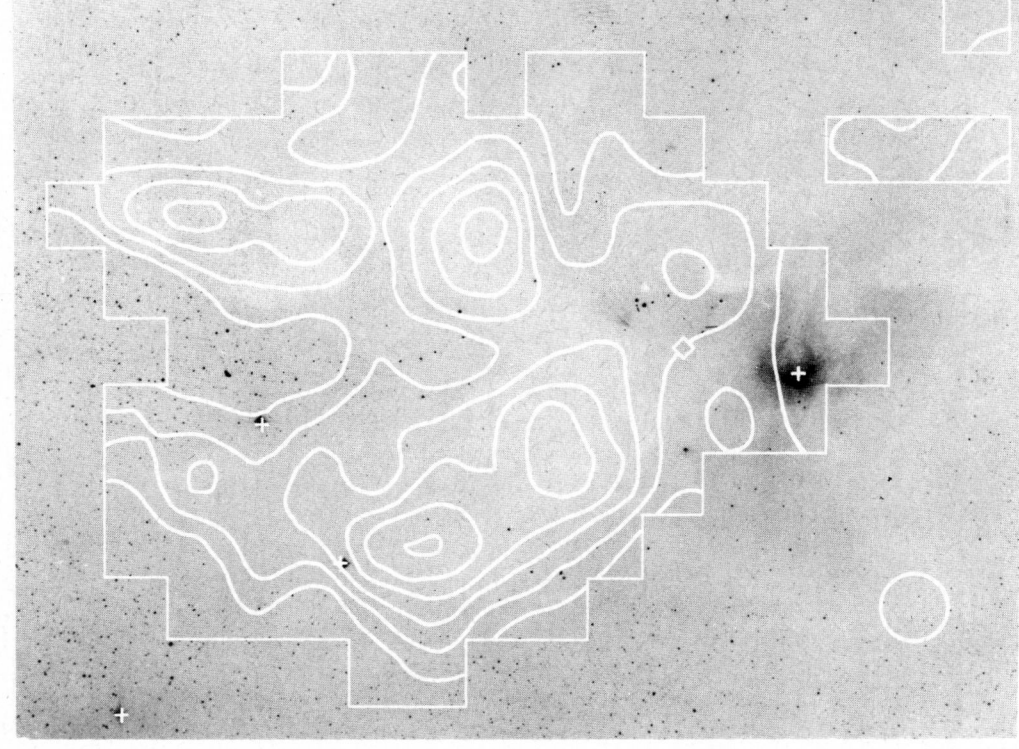

14.4: *Negative photograph of part of the ρ Ophiuchi dark cloud. The empty white areas represent the regions where the absorption of light is the greatest. The contours show the variation of the strength of the 6-cm wavelength formaldehyde absorption. The black patch to the right of the picture is a reflection nebula. (Photograph: Hale Observatories, USA)*

14.5: *The young cluster M 16. The bright stars to the top and left of centre are O stars formed about two million years ago. The red glow and the dark streaks are parts of the gas and dust cloud out of which the stars condensed. Another association of young stars with interstellar matter is seen in the Pleiades cluster (figure 13.5); in that case the brightest stars are type B, not type O. (Hale Observatories, USA)*

The birth of stars

Star formation at the present epoch

The birth of a star is a rare, slow event; all but a very few of the stars visible to the naked eye have existed longer than mankind. It is therefore first necessary to consider the evidence that new stars are being formed in the Galaxy at the present time.

As explained in chapter 3, the energy which a *main-sequence star* radiates into space is generated by the conversion of hydrogen to helium at its centre. By comparing the rate at which energy is being emitted to the mass of hydrogen fuel in such a star we can estimate its potential lifetime. It is found that the main-sequence lifetime of a star depends strongly on its mass; low-mass stars (such as type M) are small, cool, and long-lived; however high-mass stars (such as type O) are large, hot and short-lived. Our Sun is now half-way through its total main-sequence lifetime of 10^{10} years, but an *O star* with a mass 30 times greater than the Sun would live for only a few million years. The fact that such bright stars are seen to exist today implies that star formation must have taken place within the last few million years; since our Galaxy is about twelve thousand million years old, it is reasonable to assume that somewhere in the Galaxy the same process is taking place even now. Recent estimates are that the equivalent of several stars the size of the Sun are born somewhere in the Galaxy each year. At the time when the Galaxy first formed, however, the rate of star formation was many times higher than this.

Stars cannot in general move very far across the Galaxy in a few million years. Any O stars we find must therefore still be fairly close to the places where they were formed. Searches for O stars have shown that they are almost always found in the close vicinity of gas and dust clouds (figure 14.5); we may therefore conclude that it is out of such clouds new stars condense. These surveys have also shown that O and B stars almost always exist in either *associations* or *open clusters* and that most of these clusters and associations are in the spiral arms of our Galaxy. The same appears to be true of new stars of low mass, such as the *T Tauri stars*, and it is now generally accepted that essentially all stars are formed by the gravitational collapse of interstellar clouds in the spiral arms of our Galaxy, and that all types of stars form in groups rather than singly.

Collapse and fragmentation of interstellar clouds

The evolution of a cloud of interstellar gas depends on a balance between internal gravitational forces tending to make it contract and thermal pressure tending to make it expand. James Jeans, in 1926, first showed that a cloud of given temperature and density can collapse only if its mass is above a certain minimum value. Large, dense, cool clouds contract, while small, low density, warm ones expand. The Jeans mass (M_J) can be calculated in solar units from a simple formula:

$$M_J \geq 3 \times 10^4 \sqrt{T^3/n} \text{ solar masses}$$

The density of the cloud (n) is expressed as the number of hydrogen atoms per cubic metre, while the temperature (T) is measured in Kelvins. Table 14.1 shows the Jeans mass as calculated for various components of the interstellar medium.

The fact that the Jeans mass for these different types of cloud is much more than the mass of a typical star (1 $M_\odot$) explains why stars generally form in groups; only large accumulations of gas have sufficient gravitational pressure to contract. Since the Jeans mass in the first line of the table is larger than any collection of stars in the Galaxy, it is clear that stars do not form out of the intercloud medium. On the other hand the Jeans mass for atomic clouds, 3000 $M_\odot$, corresponds to the typical mass of an open cluster or association, suggesting that it is out of such regions of interstellar space that new stars begin to form. Smaller groups of stars can subsequently be formed in dark clouds.

The metamorphosis of an interstellar cloud into a cluster of stars must involve the breaking up of the cloud into smaller pieces as it collapses. This process is called FRAGMENTATION and can also be explained by the simple theory of collapse under gravity. As a cloud collapses, its density must increase as its radius decreases. A 3000 $M_\odot$ cloud such as the one in table 14.1 would start with a diameter of 13 pc. Over a period of some 10 million years it would collapse to about 3 pc, increasing its density from 10^8 m^{-3} to 10^{10} atoms m^{-3}. The Jeans mass for a cloud with density 10^{10} atoms m^{-3} and the same temperature is only 300 $M_\odot$, so it would be possible for small fragments of the cloud to collapse themselves, and for the cloud to separate into up to ten pieces. The fragmentation process would then continue (figure 14.6), with each fragment having the possibility of subsequently breaking into yet smaller fragments as its density increases and its Jeans mass gets less.

The process of fragmentation can only take place if the temperature of the cloud stays cool. In a low-density cloud, heat can easily escape, but as the fragments become denser and denser the heat is trapped by the dust in the fragments, and their temperatures start to rise. A fragment then no longer breaks up into smaller fragments but becomes instead a PROTOSTAR. One of the current unsolved problems in astrophysics is to predict into how many pieces a cloud will fragment at each stage in its collapse. The importance of this calculation is that it is the fragmentation process which primarily determines the ratio of the numbers of each different type of star in the Galaxy.

Table 14.1

	Particle density n (m^{-3})	*Temperature* T (K)	*Jeans mass* M_J (solar masses)
Intercloud medium	2×10^5	8000	5×10^7
Atomic clouds	10^8	100	3000
Dark clouds	10^9	10	30

14.6: *The fragmentation of an interstellar cloud. As the density of the collapsing cloud increases, smaller parts of it become unstable and are therefore able to collapse on their own. The cloud therefore fragments into progressively smaller and smaller pieces which become protostars and ultimately stars.*

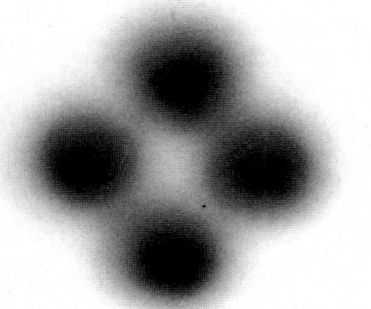 → 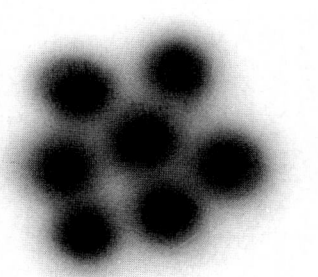 →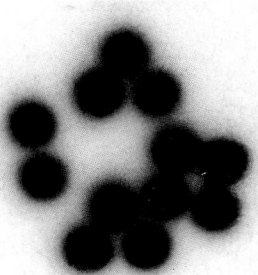

The evolution of a protostar

The evolution of a protostar from being an isolated fragment of an interstellar cloud to becoming a main-sequence star takes hundreds of thousands or even millions of years; astronomers attempting to follow this process must therefore resort to computer calculations rather than direct observations. These calculations are very complicated since they involve estimating simultaneously the density, temperature, velocity, and heat flow in every part of a continually-changing cloud. For this reason, only the simplest protostar models have been considered – namely spherical ones with no rotation or magnetic field. Another difficulty is that the evolution of a protostar depends somewhat on its shape, temperature, and density immediately after its last fragmentation, and since we do not yet have a proper theory of fragmentation, we are forced to start the calculations from conditions which are little more than intelligent guesswork.

The simplest case that has been calculated is that of a $1\,M_\odot$ protostar collapsing from a uniform cloud with an initial density of 6×10^{10} atoms m^{-3}, a temperature of $10\,K$, and a radius of $0.05\,pc$. As the gravitational forces in the cloud start the collapse, the density at the centre begins to increase. At first the increase is fairly gentle, but after 400 000 years the density and temperature at the centre both rise dramatically and a hot core region is formed within the protostar. This core soon itself collapses, forming the nucleus of the future star, and, for another 100 000 years the

mass of this nucleus steadily increases as the remainder of the protostar falls onto it. The overall appearance of the protostar on an *HR diagram* is indicated in figure 14.7; when, after 400 000 years, the nucleus of the protostar forms, the object appears at point A, with a luminosity about equal to the Sun, but a very low temperature – less than a hundred Kelvins. As the nucleus grows, the protostar becomes hotter and more luminous, moving across the HR diagram approximately from A to B. The evolution from B to the main sequence (point C) is very much slower, and takes about 5×10^7 years. During this stage of evolution, (sometimes called the pre-main-sequence or PMS stage), the star as a whole contracts while its centre becomes steadily hotter. When its central temperature reaches about $10^7\,K$, thermonuclear conversion of hydrogen to helium can begin, and the star can take its place on the *main sequence*.

Stars more massive than the Sun evolve more rapidly and in a different way. Figure 14.7 shows the evolution of a protostar which starts off with $60\,M_\odot$. A nucleus forms in much the same way as for a single solar mass star (point D), but it now grows so quickly that after only 20 000 years (point E) it is hot enough for thermonuclear reactions to start. The nucleus now somewhat resembles a main-sequence star except that it is surrounded by the thick gas and dust outer layer of the protostar. The mass and luminosity of the nucleus increase as matter continues to fall on it, until after another 2500 years (point F) the nucleus is so bright that

14.7: *The evolution of protostars on a Hertzsprung-Russell diagram. The thick line is the Zero Age Main Sequence. The track ABC is that followed by a 1 $M_\odot$ protostar, while DEFGH is that of an object initially of 60 $M_\odot$. The infrared protostars W3-IRS5 and Orion BN are also marked. The shaded area shows where T Tauri stars are usually found.*

14.8: *The very young cluster NGC 2264. Many of the stars seen in this photograph are T Tauri stars, and have not yet reached the main sequence. (Lick Observatory, USA)*

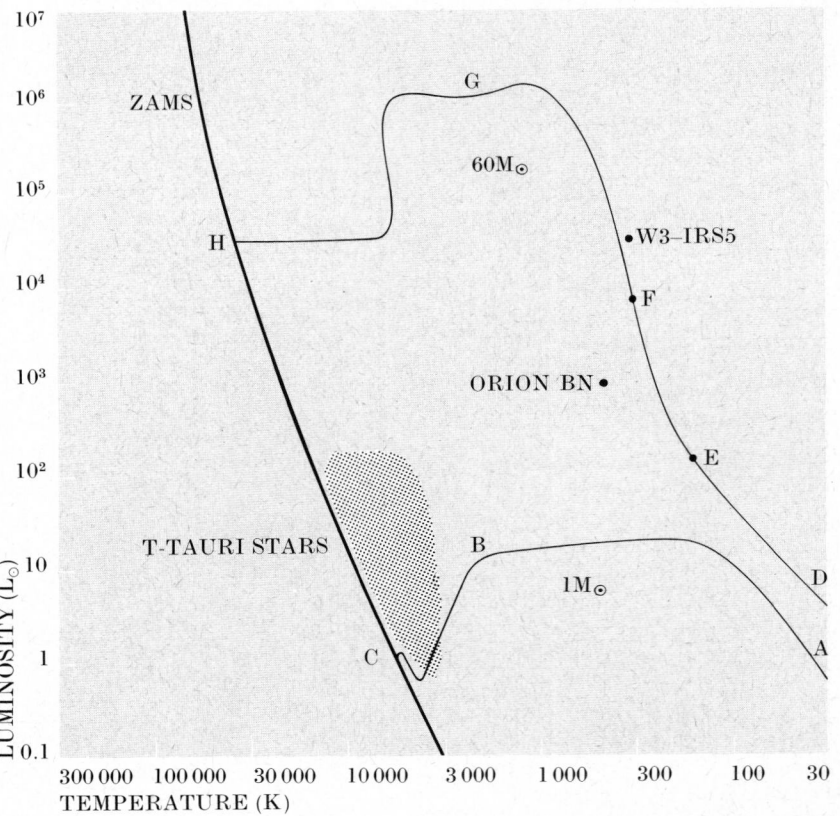

radiation pressure acts to stop any more matter falling inwards. Consequently some $43\,M_\odot$ of the original $60\,M_\odot$ cloud is expelled back into space, and a $17\,M_\odot$ remnant is left behind which, after a very brief luminous period (region G), becomes a normal main-sequence O star (H).

If a cloud is rotating as it collapses to form a star, the law of conservation of angular momentum requires that the speed of this rotation increases as the cloud becomes smaller. This effect can be very large and is an obstacle to star formation, since a rotational speed increase of a million could be expected during the collapse of a protostar from a 0.1-pc diameter cloud to a star like the Sun. This rotation leads to centrifugal forces which tend to oppose the contraction of the protostar. As a result of turbulence and of galactic rotation, all interstellar clouds probably possess enough rotation to prevent collapse to stars unless there is some way of reducing their angular momentum. One way in which a protostar can lose angular momentum is to divide itself into two or more pieces which revolve around each other – in other words it can form a binary or a multiple system. The fact that binary systems are very common emphasizes the importance of this process, but as yet the problem of the evolution of a proto-binary star is nowhere near solved.

Observing star formation

Because star formation takes a long time by human standards, the astronomer interested in this subject must take on the role of a cosmic archaeologist. He finds varied examples of collapsing clouds and young stars and attempts to put them in the correct evolutionary sequence. From measurements of the size, density, and temperature of an interstellar cloud one may calculate whether or not the cloud is likely to be expanding or contracting. From data such as these, we know that some of the cold, dark clouds are almost certainly in a state of gravitational collapse, and it has been conjectured that some of the small globules such as those in figure 14.9 are in fact protostars of around one solar mass. Some of the warm molecular clouds, such as those in the Orion Nebula region also appear to be collapsing.

The stages of star formation involving the creation and accretion of the hot nucleus are more difficult to observe. There is a star called FU Orionis which in 1936 flared up in a few months in what some astronomers believe is an example of this phenomenon. A similar behaviour was seen in the star V1057 Cygni in 1969, though other interpretations of these events, not involving the formation of new stars, are possible. The most likely candidates for protostars are certain infrared sources, such as the Becklin-Neugebauer object in the Orion Nebula and W3–IRS5 (figure 14.12) in the constellation of Cassiopeia. As shown in the HR diagram (figure 14.7), these sources have temperatures of a few hundred degrees and luminosity at least a thousand times that of the Sun. They both lie at the centres of molecular clouds, show H_2O *maser* emission, and are very close to compact ionized hydrogen regions. Neither is visible optically, and both were unknown until the advent of infrared astonomy. As a protostar evolves further and the light from its nucleus begins to shine through and reflect off the outer layers of dust, a small nebula may be seen. This process is thought to be the origin of the so called *Herbig-Haro objects* which are sometimes found associated with young stars.

The pre-main-sequence stage of star formation (B to C in figure 14.7) is, for low-mass stars, a comparative slow process. A lot of stars are therefore visible in the region of the HR diagram just above the main sequence. Some of these stars belong to the *T Tauri* class of irregular variables, with emission lines and strong ultra-violet and infrared excesses. Such stars often occur in very young clusters which also contain signs of gas and dust (figure 14.8). The Be and Ae *emission-line stars* are probably similar to the T Tauris except that they have a larger mass. The most massive stars evolve so quickly that the outer layers of the cloud out of which the star formed remain as an opaque cocoon for some of the main-sequence lifetime. Since O stars give out mainly ultraviolet radiation, a compact ionized hydrogen region is formed in the cocoon, and the star becomes visible (indirectly) through its radio and infrared radiation rather than by the light it emits. Finally, forces such as *radiation pressure* and supernova shocks will blow away the remaining gas and dust and will leave only the cluster of new stars.

14.9: *The Rosette Nebula. This large region of ionized hydrogen in the constellation Monoceros contains 11 000 M$_\odot$ of ionized hydrogen in a cloud 16pc in diameter, 1.4kpc distant from Earth. The gas is heated and ionized by the cluster of O stars in the central hole of the nebula. The black streaks visible in the lower part of the nebula are dust-filled globules of molecular hydrogen that lie in front of the emission nebulosity.*
(Hale Observatories, USA*)*

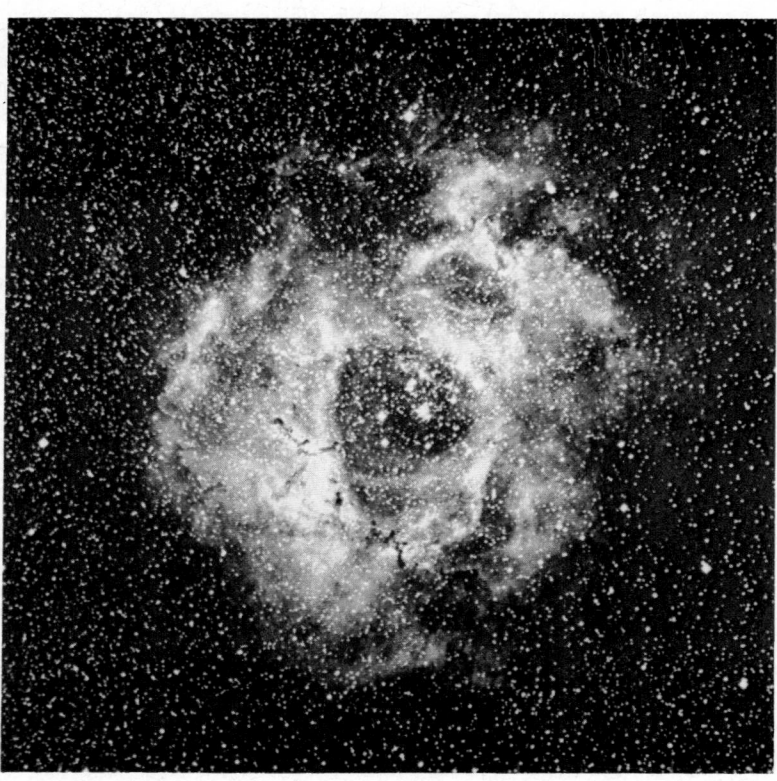

Ionized interstellar clouds

H$^+$ regions

As its name implies an H$^+$ REGION (or HII REGION as it is often written) is a part of space where the hydrogen in the interstellar medium is in an ionized rather than in a neutral state. The most common situation where this occurs is in the immediate vicinity of O-type stars, since these stars have a large ultraviolet flux; an 05 main-sequence star emits 6×10^{49} photons per second which have an energy great enough to ionize hydrogen atoms. If there is enough gas close to an O star, then a prominent nebula may be formed (figure 14.9). Within this region, almost all the gas is ionized, and there is a close balance between the rate at which electrons and ions recombine and the rate at which the resultant neutral atoms are re-ionized. There is often a comparatively sharp boundary, known as an IONIZATION FRONT between the H$^+$ region and the surrounding neutral gas.

H$^+$ regions sometimes look approximately circular (figure 14.9) but more often appear quite irregular, either because of the odd shape of the gas cloud itself, or because of patchy obscuring matter in front of it (figures 13.1 and 14.5). The ionization may be from a single star or from a cluster of them. The temperature of the ionized gas in an H$^+$ region is always close to 10 000 K, but the density can vary from about 10^7 to 10^{12} ions per cubic metre. Sizes can range up to several parsecs across, depending on the density of the gas and the ultraviolet luminosity of the ionizing stars.

Of all interstellar clouds, the H$^+$ regions are the easiest and most rewarding to study; they emit many different kinds of radiation and can be detected in large numbers all over the Galaxy. In H$^+$ regions, the interaction between the stars and the interstellar medium is seen at its strongest; an H$^+$ region usually comes into being as the by-product of star formation, and is made visible only as a result of the radiation from the stars it contains.

The line spectrum of H$^+$ regions

The light from an H$^+$ region is of a quite different character from that of a star. Whereas a normal star emits a continuous spectrum with dark absorption lines, an H$^+$ region emits almost all its light in a few comparatively narrow emission lines (figure 14.10). The most important of these emission lines are those of hydrogen, helium and oxygen. The visible hydrogen lines form the so-called 'Balmer Series', and arise as electrons in the upper states of a hydrogen atom drop to the second lowest state. Helium lines are only seen from 'high-excitation' nebulae – in other words those with very hot exciting stars; the ionization potential for helium is much larger than that for hydrogen (24.6 electron volts instead of 13.6), so that only stars which have a large flux shortward of 50.4 nm can ionize helium in the nebula.

The hydrogen and helium lines are sometimes called RE-COMBINATION LINES, since they occur as an indirect result of the recombination of an electron with a hydrogen or helium ion. When the recombination takes place the resultant neutral atom is probably in an excited rather than in the ground state; it then cascades down to lower and lower energy states, emitting a photon at each transition, until it reaches the ground state, where it will remain until it is ionized again by an ultraviolet photon from the exciting star. In a nebula with density 10^9 ions m^{-3} and radius 1 pc a hydrogen atom would typically remain ionized for some 100 years before recombining. It would then cascade to the ground state in a fraction of a second, and then remain there for something like two months before being ionized again.

In most nebulae the strongest spectral lines are not those of hydrogen or helium, but those of the oxygen ions O^{++} at 495.9 and 500.7 nm, and O^+ at 372.6 and 372.9 nm. The prominence of these lines is remarkable not only because oxygen ions are a thousand times rarer than hydrogen ions, but also because these particular spectral lines are extremely difficult to produce in a terrestrial laboratory. The atomic transitions that give rise to these lines are called FORBIDDEN TRANSITIONS and are normally too weak to be seen. Under the extreme low-density conditions found in interstellar clouds, however, these lines come to dominate the spectrum. The oxygen ions, in fact, act as a thermostat that keeps all H^+ regions at much the same temperature (about 10 000 K) by absorbing kinetic energy from the fast-moving electrons in the nebula and radiating the energy away as emission lines. The physics of why these forbidden lines are so strong is complicated, and for many years after the discovery of these lines in nebular spectra, their origin was a mystery. For a while there was speculation that the lines were due to a hypothetical chemical element NEBULIUM, and it was only in 1927 that the lines were correctly identified. Since then, forbidden lines have been seen from other elements such as nitrogen, neon and sulphur and are much used to measure the temperature and density of H^+ regions and of some other astronomical objects including *planetary nebulae* and *quasars*.

Emission lines are also seen at infrared and radio wavelengths, superimposed on the strong continuum. Spectra at these wavelengths are particularly useful for the study of distant and of obscured H^+ regions because of the fact that infrared and radio radiation is much less absorbed by dust than is light. At infrared wavelengths, the brightest lines are certain forbidden lines, such as the 12.8 µm line of Ne^+. At radio wavelengths, it is the hydrogen and helium recombination lines that are the most important; for example, the transition from the 110th to the 109th energy level of hydrogen occurs at a radio frequency of 5.009 GHz and has been much studied. These radio recombination lines are particularly useful in that they allow the radial velocities of H^+ regions to be measured, even if they are invisible from the Earth. For many obscured H^+ regions the radial velocity is the only clue we have to its distance, through a model of the rotation of the Galaxy.

14.10: *Optical spectrum of the Orion Nebula in the green-blue-violet region showing emission lines of hydrogen and helium atoms and of oxygen, sulphur, neon, and iron ions. The wavelengths are indicated in nanometres. (Royal Astronomical Society, UK)*

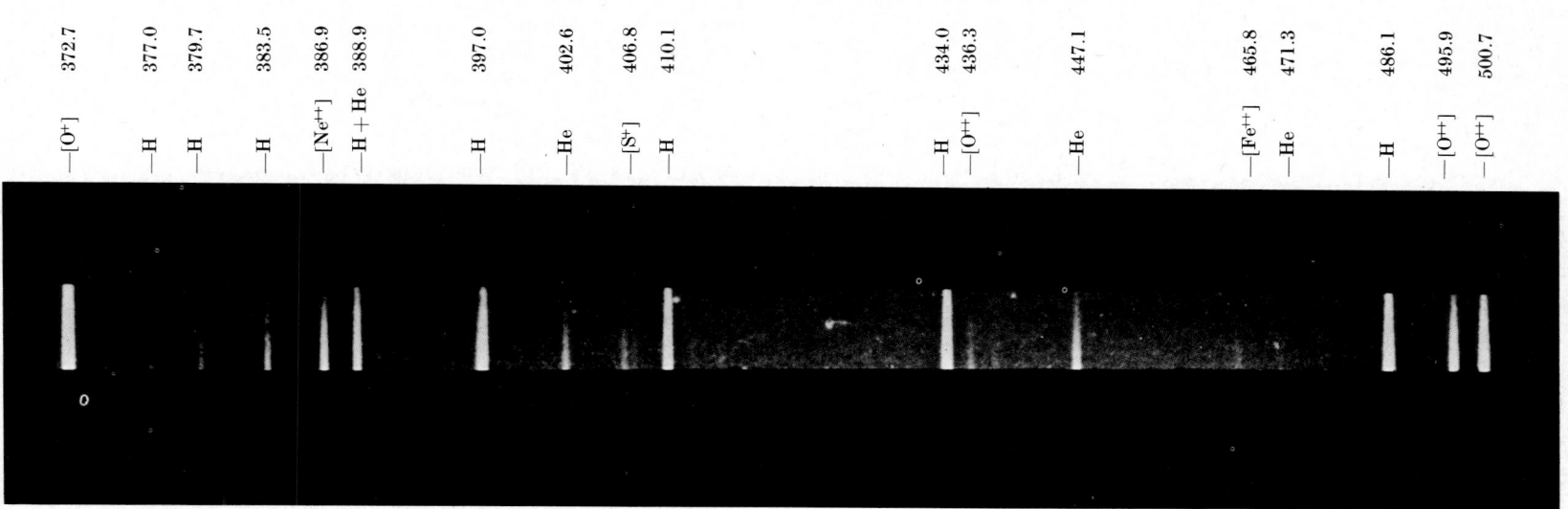

Continuous emission from H+ regions

Although most of the visible light from H+ regions is in the form of emission lines, the same is not true at longer wavelengths, where most of the energy is radiated in a continuum. There are, in fact, two continua: *bremsstrahlung* or *free-free emission* from the ionized plasma, which causes the radio flux, and thermal radiation from dust grains, which dominates the infrared region shortward of about 3-mm wavelength (figure 14.11).

Free-free emission occurs as a result of random encounters between electrons and ions. As an electron moves through the plasma, it experiences ever-changing accelerations due to electrical forces between it and the charged ions. Every burst of acceleration generates electromagnetic radiation over a wide range of frequencies. The term free-free refers to the fact that, as opposed to the situation in an ionization or recombination, the electron is not attached to an atom either before or after the encounter. The net result of all these collisions is a continuous band of almost uniform emission at radio and infrared wavelengths. At low frequencies (below perhaps 1 GHz, depending on the H+ region), the emission decreases due to reabsorption of the free-free radiation by the gas, so radio astronomers prefer to study H+ regions at high radio frequencies if possible. Modern *aperture synthesis radio telescopes* can produce pictures of the radio emission from an H+ region which have almost as much detail as an optical photograph (figure 14.12), but which are completely free from interstellar extinction. In many cases the radio emission is the only information we have about H+ regions, since a large fraction of these objects, especially those on the far side of the Galaxy, are obscured at visible wavelengths. For optically visible H+ regions, a comparison of the radio and infrared continua with the visible hydrogen recombination lines can provide a reliable guide to the amount of dust in front of the object.

Almost all H+ regions show a large infrared continuum at wavelengths in the range 3–3000 μm. The emission arises from small dust grains at temperatures between 30 and 300 K. Some of the dust grains exist within the ionized regions and become heated by absorbing radiation from the ionizing stars and from the ultraviolet recombination lines in the nebula. Other, cooler dust grains exist in the neutral gas that surrounds many H+ regions, and are heated by the light that emerges through the ionization front. Many H+ regions have so much dust associated with them that essentially all the visible and ultraviolet light from the ionizing stars is converted to infrared radiation. H+ regions are therefore among the most powerful sources of infrared radiation in our Galaxy, and have luminosities of up to $10^7 L_\odot$. In some cases, however, including the Orion Nebula, some of the infrared emission may come from *molecular clouds* very close to the H+ region rather than from the immediate vicinity of the ionized gas. Weak continuum emission is also seen in the visible spectrum of H+ regions. The emission is due partly to starlight scattered off the dust grains in the nebula and partly to atomic processes in the plasma.

14.11: *The radio and infrared continuum emission from H+ regions, in this case the group of objects known as W3. The radio emission comes from 'free-free' collisions in the ionized gas, while the much stronger infrared emission is from dust grains associated with the gas. The temperature of the dust is about 70 K.*

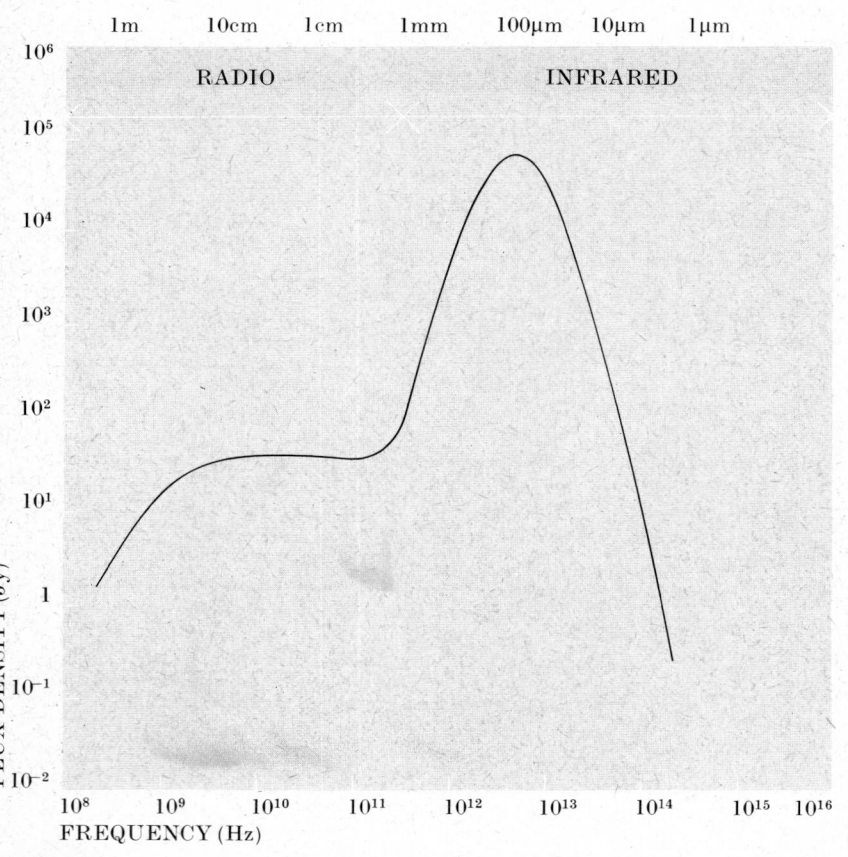

The evolution of an H+ region

Since an H+ region is at a much higher temperature than the neutral gas which surrounds it, it exerts an outward pressure at the ionization front. The main characteristic of the evolution of an H+ region is therefore one of expansion. The birth of an H+ region is generally a by-product of the birth of an O star. The gas which becomes ionized is part of the cloud out of which the star formed. At first, the H+ region is very dense and compact, and is invisible optically because of the dust in the outer, neutral layers of the cloud. A group of five compact H+ regions is shown in figure 14.12; each of these contains at least one newly-formed O star. The differences in size and brightness between these five objects is a result of differences in their ages and in the O stars at their centres. These very young H+ regions are embedded in a warm cloud of molecular hydrogen and are expanding into it at a rate of the order of one parsec every 100 000 years. As they expand they will ionize more and more of the surrounding neutral hydrogen and disperse the obscuring material that is currently concealing them from the view of optical astronomers.

Optical nebulae such as the Rosette Nebula (figure 14.9) and the North American nebula (figure 13.1) are much older than the compact H+ regions in figure 14.12, but are probably evolved from objects not unlike them. As these H+ regions continue to expand they will become less and less dense and will eventually blend into the background of the interstellar medium.

14.12: *Contour map of the radio emission from the group of compact H+ regions known as W3. These objects are not visible at optical wavelengths, and must be studied by either radio or infrared techniques. Each compact H+ region contains at least one newly-formed O- or B-type star. The crosses show the positions of infrared sources and interstellar masers, including the protostar W3-IRS5. (Mullard Radio Astronomy Observatory, Cambridge, UK)*

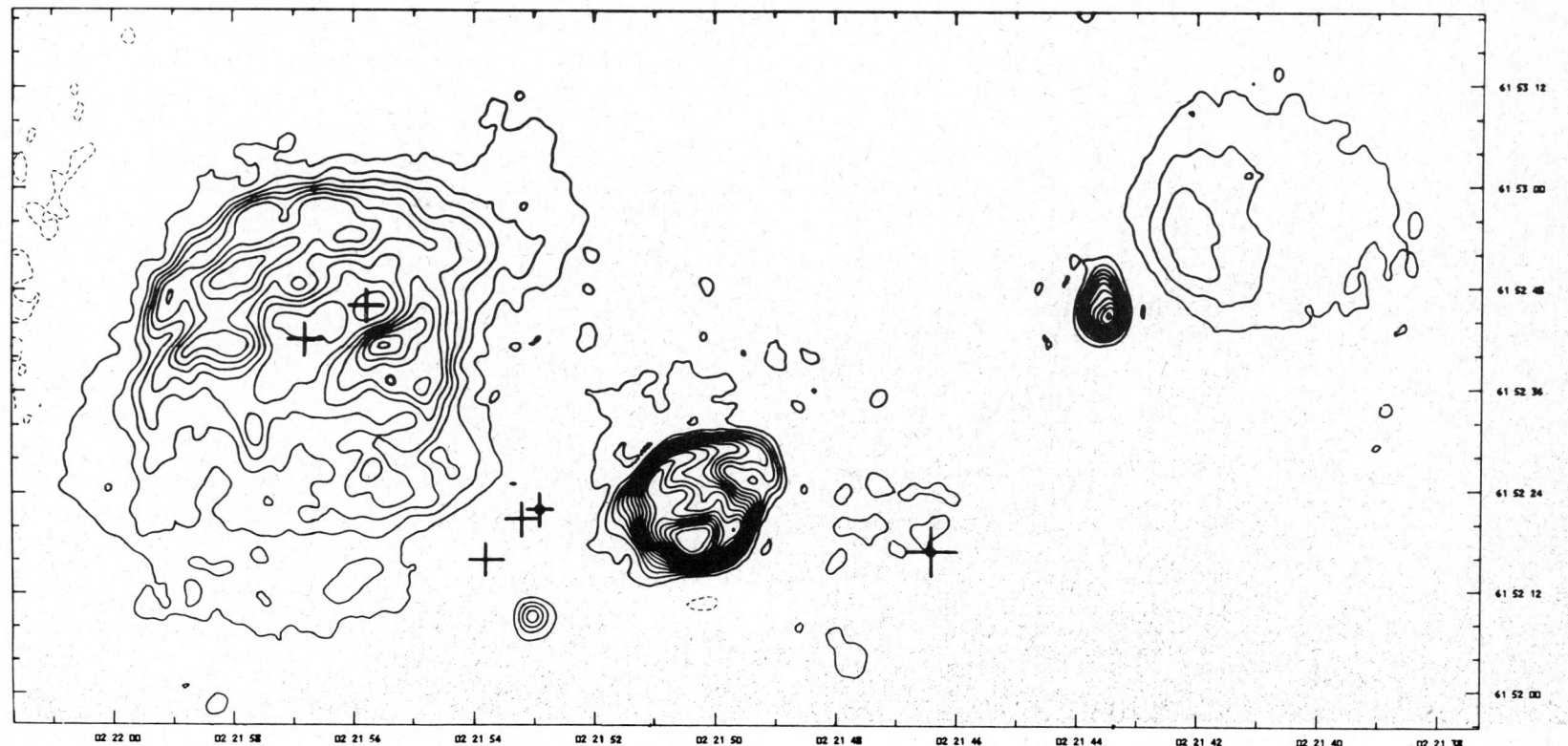

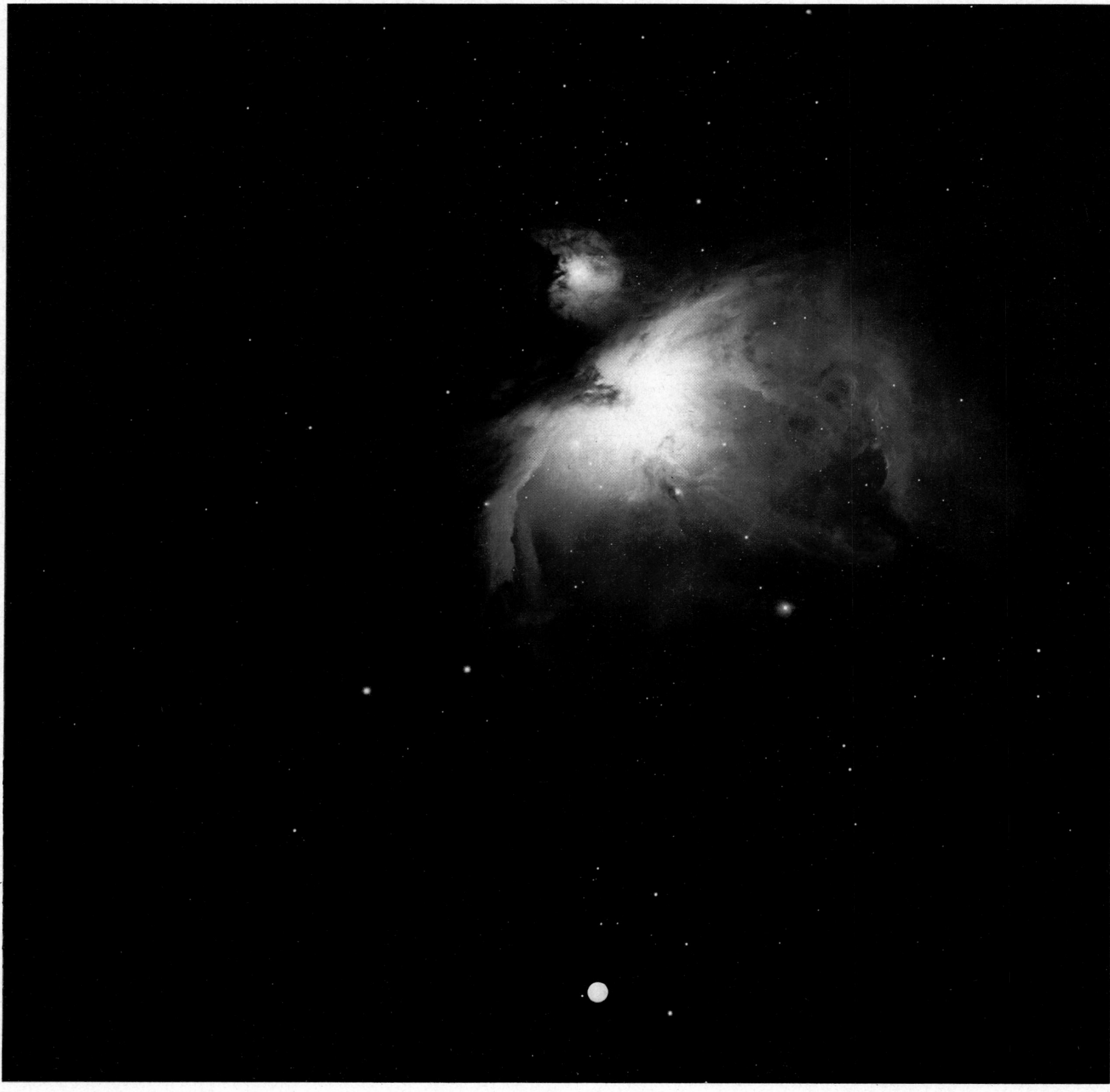

The Orion Nebula

The Orion Nebula is the nearest H+ region to the Earth and the one that has received the greatest attention from astronomers. It is visible as a 4th magnitude fuzzy patch of light in the Sword region of the Orion constellation. On long exposures (figure 14.13) the nebula appears to be about half a degree across and to consist of a beautiful series of loops and filaments which emit the characteristic red light of hydrogen gas. Most of the light, however, comes from a more compact region a few minutes of arc across which appears white and over-exposed in figure 14.13.

The Orion Nebula is ionized by a small group of O and B stars known as the Trapezium Cluster. The brightest of these stars is of spectral type O6. The cluster lies very close to the brightest part of the nebula and is surrounded by a rather uneven distribution of ionized gas. To the immediate east of the Trapezium stars is a thick cloud of neutral gas, known as the Dark Bay, which has not yet been ionized by the stars. To the west and south the density of the gas appears to decrease more gradually.

Behind the nebula, but invisible to optical astronomers is a cloud of molecular hydrogen. The contours in figure 14.14 show the approximate extent of this cloud, and they are based on radio measurements of the strength of carbon monoxide and formaldehyde emission. The cloud has two prominent peaks, the southern of which, OMC1, lies fairly close to the Trapezium Cluster and contains some 500 $M_\odot$ of hydrogen. Each cloud contains at its centre a cluster of infrared sources, at least one of which, the Becklin-Neugebauer object (figure 14.7) is almost certainly a protostar. The temperature and density of the molecular clouds is highest close to the infrared sources, and it therefore seems very likely that these are the parts of the clouds where gravitational collapse and star formation have been happening most recently. The presence of a group of OH and H_2O masers close to the infrared sources in OMC1 provides additional evidence for this conclusion.

The relationship between the H+ region and the molecular cloud behind it is not completely clear, but it seems likely that the two regions are in physical contact and that the H+ region is eating its way into the molecular cloud. At the present time, the southern infrared cluster generates about the same total amount of power (at infrared wavelengths) as does the Trapezium cluster at optical wavelengths. The stars being born there are therefore potentially O stars. We may thus anticipate that some tens of thousands of years in the future, as the H+ region fades away, a new H+ region will be formed inside what is now the molecular cloud, ionized by the stars that we currently see in the process of formation.

14.13: *The beautiful Orion Nebula, about 500 pc from the Earth, is the most prominent H+ region in the sky. The glowing red gas is hydrogen. The central part of the nebula is so bright that the four bright stars which ionize it are hidden in this picture. Their location is indicated by the red dots in figure 14.14.*

14.14: *Behind the Orion Nebula is a large cloud of molecular hydrogen. It gives out no light but can be seen by radio telescopes. The southern and northern peaks of this cloud are known as OMC1 and OMC2 respectively. At their centres are clusters of infrared protostars and OH and H_2O masers, all of which are probably the result of the collapse of the molecular clouds. North is up, east to the left.*

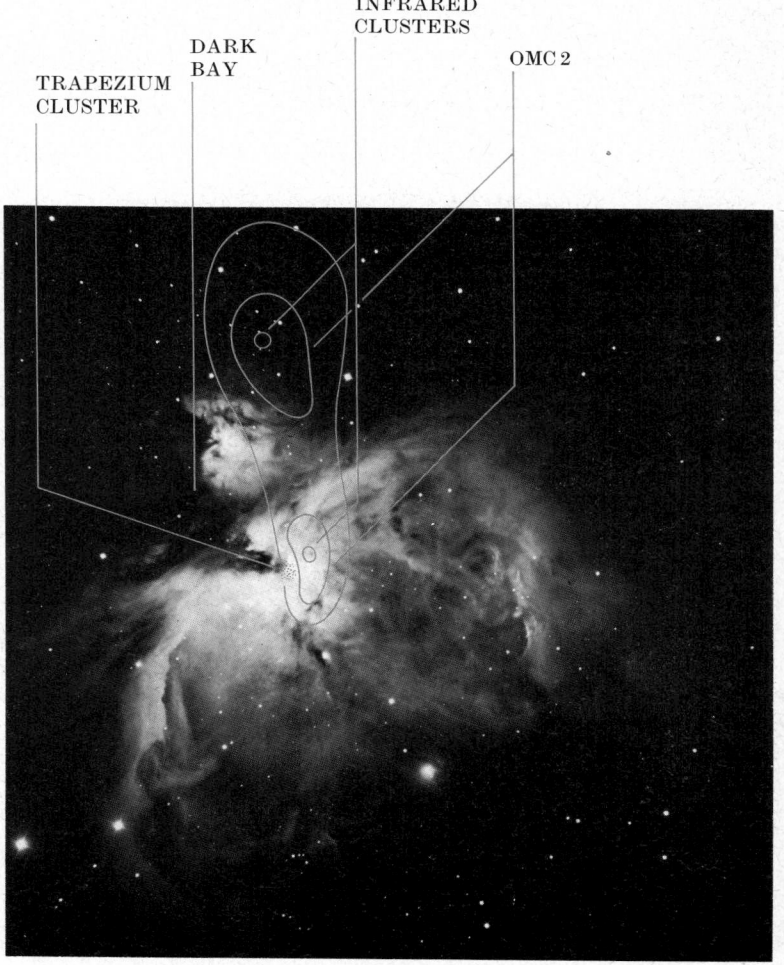

TRAPEZIUM CLUSTER · DARK BAY · INFRARED CLUSTERS · OMC 2

Planetary nebulae

Similarities to H⁺ regions

Like an *H⁺ region*, a PLANETARY NEBULA is a cloud of interstellar gas, mainly hydrogen, ionized by a hot star. The important difference between the two types of nebula is generic; while H⁺ regions are usually a by-product of the birth of highly luminous O stars, planetary nebulae are old objects, formed by the expulsion of gaseous material from the outer layers of a dying star. The name planetary nebula is misleading, and arose historically because of the visual resemblance between certain small circular nebulae and terrestrial planets such as Uranus.

Although in a few particular cases there is some uncertainty about whether a particular object is a planetary nebula or an H⁺ region there are a number of general observational differences:

(a) Planetary nebulae are usually much more symmetric in appearance than H⁺ regions.

(b) They occur isolated from each other and from other interstellar clouds and star clusters.

(c) They have a much smaller mass of gas (about $0.2\,M_\odot$) than most H⁺ regions.

The optical spectrum of a planetary nebula is similar to that of an H⁺ region in that it consists mainly of bright emission lines such as the *Balmer series* of hydrogen and the *forbidden lines* of ionized oxygen, nitrogen, and other such elements. The central star of a planetary is generally hotter than that of an H⁺ region, with a temperature in the range $50\,000$–$100\,000\,\mathrm{K}$ rather than $25\,000$–$50\,000\,\mathrm{K}$; the higher stellar temperatures mean that many more highly excited ions, such as Ne^{4+} and, in particular, He^+ are seen in the ionized shell.

The radio and infrared properties of planetary nebulae are rather like those of H⁺ regions. Free-free emission produces a radio-wavelength continuum, while dust grains absorb ultraviolet photons from the star and from the nebula, and re-emit the energy as infrared radiation. These dust grains appear to have a different chemical composition to normal interstellar grains, but their concentration and method of formation is uncertain. Emission from carbon monoxide molecules has been detected from some planetary nebulae; this result indicates that there must be molecular hydrogen associated with at least some planetary nebulae, but we do not yet know whether this neutral gas exists outside the ionized region or in small, dense globules within it.

Expansion of the shell

Almost all planetary nebulae have a remarkably symmetric structure, often in the shape of a ring (figures 13.3, 14.15, 14.16) but sometimes more like an hourglass (figure 14.17). The differences in shape are presumably mainly due to variations in the way the gas shell was initially expelled from the star. The speed of rotation of the star, its radiation pressure and its magnetic field are probably also very important, though as yet no adequate theory exists for the dynamics of planetary nebula shells.

There are two pieces of evidence to show that planetary nebulae are expanding away from their central stars. Firstly, photographs of the RING NEBULA (figure 14.15) taken 40 years apart show that it is slowly increasing its diameter. Secondly, the *Doppler shifts* of the light emitted from different parts of the shell can be measured. In a symmetrical nebula, light comes partly from the side of the shell nearer the Earth, and partly from the side beyond the central star; if the shell is expanding there will be a difference in wavelength in the light from the front and back. This difference can be measured, and it shows that in many cases the gas is expanding away from the star at a speed of about $20\,\mathrm{km\,s^{-1}}$. Since a typical planetary nebula is about $0.5\,\mathrm{pc}$ in diameter the shell must have been produced by the star some 10^4 years ago.

The variations of colour seen across the faces of some nebulae are due to changes in the degree of ionization in different regions. For example, the green colour of the inner parts of the Ring Nebula is an indication that in these regions, oxygen is doubly ionized. In the outer regions, oxygen is only singly ionized and the dominant green spectral lines of O^{++} are absent. The red colour here (and in many other nebulae) is due to a mixture of the Hα line of hydrogen and of a forbidden line of ionized nitrogen.

Planetary nebulae and stellar evolution

About 1000 planetary nebulae are known. The best-studied ones have angular diameters between about 10 arc sec and several arc minutes, but planetaries can range in size from giant objects such

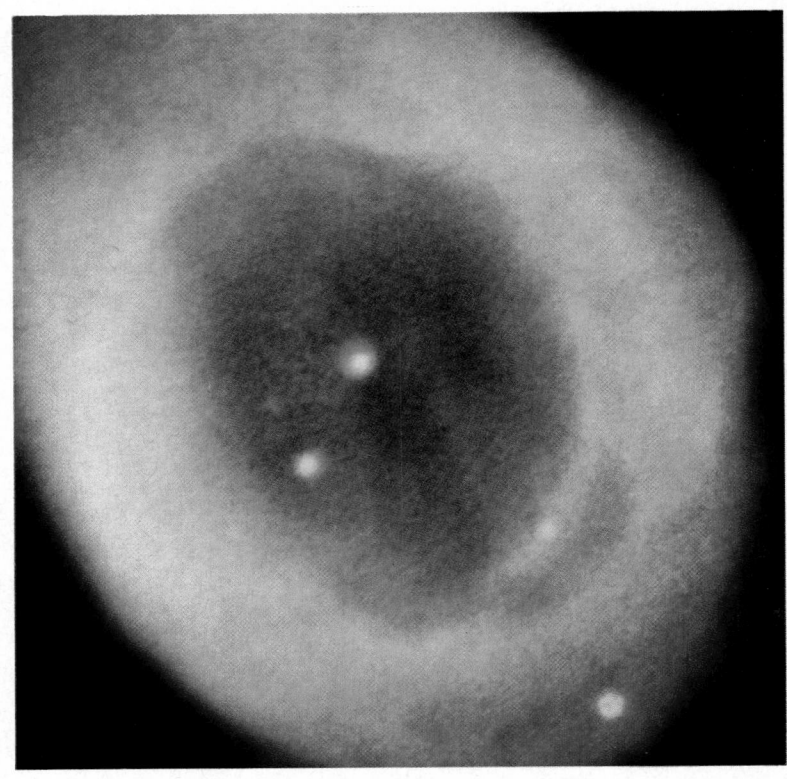

as NGC 7293, the Helix Nebula (figure 14.16), which is about one degree in diameter, to objects so small that they appear starlike even on the best optical photographs. These so-called stellar planetaries were discovered by searching the sky with a very low dispersion spectrograph and looking for objects which, though otherwise resembling stars, give out most of their light in narrow emission lines.

Most planetary nebulae lie within a few degrees of the galactic plane, with the greatest concentration of objects lying towards the Galactic Centre. Planetary nebulae have a typical *disc distribution* rather than that of *Population I or II*; they show concentrations towards neither spiral arms, interstellar clouds nor young stars, but occupy instead the region of the Galaxy populated by evolved stars such as *novae* and *RR Lyrae* variables. The implication of this distribution is that planetary nebulae are associated with the later rather than the earlier stages of stellar evolution.

It is now generally believed that planetary nebulae are a normal stage in the late evolution of single stars with masses of between 1 and $4 M_\odot$. Pulsations of such a star during its helium-burning, *red-giant* stage can lead to the swift expulsion of essentially the whole of its hydrogen-rich envelope to form the shell of the nebula. This gas expands outwards at 20–$30 \, \text{km s}^{-1}$, leaving behind the extremely hot burnt-out core as a very compact blue-hot star. This star is the source of the ultraviolet ionizing radiation for the nebula, but cools over a period of 10^5 years, becoming an ever-fainter *white dwarf* and,

finally, a *black-dwarf* star. Long before the star has cooled this far, however, the ionized gas shell will have become so diffuse that it has blended with the general interstellar medium, eventually to become embroiled in a subsequent round of star-formation. The total amount of matter returned to the interstellar medium by all the planetary nebulae in the Galaxy is about $5 M_\odot$ per year, which amounts to perhaps 15 per cent of all the matter expelled by all sorts of stars. Planetary nebulae therefore play a significant role in the evolution of the whole Galaxy.

14.15: *The Ring Nebula in Lyra. This planetary nebula is formed by the expulsion of a shell of gas from the central blue star, which then keeps the gas ionized.* (*Kitt Peak National Observatory,* USA)

14.16: *The Helix Nebula. This southern-hemisphere planetary appears as the largest as seen from the Earth, about one degree in diameter, but it is too faint to be seen with the naked eye.* (*Hale Observatories,* USA)

14.17: *The Dumbbell Nebula. The hour-glass shape of this planetary is a contrast to the more usual ring appearance.* (*Hale Observatories,* USA)

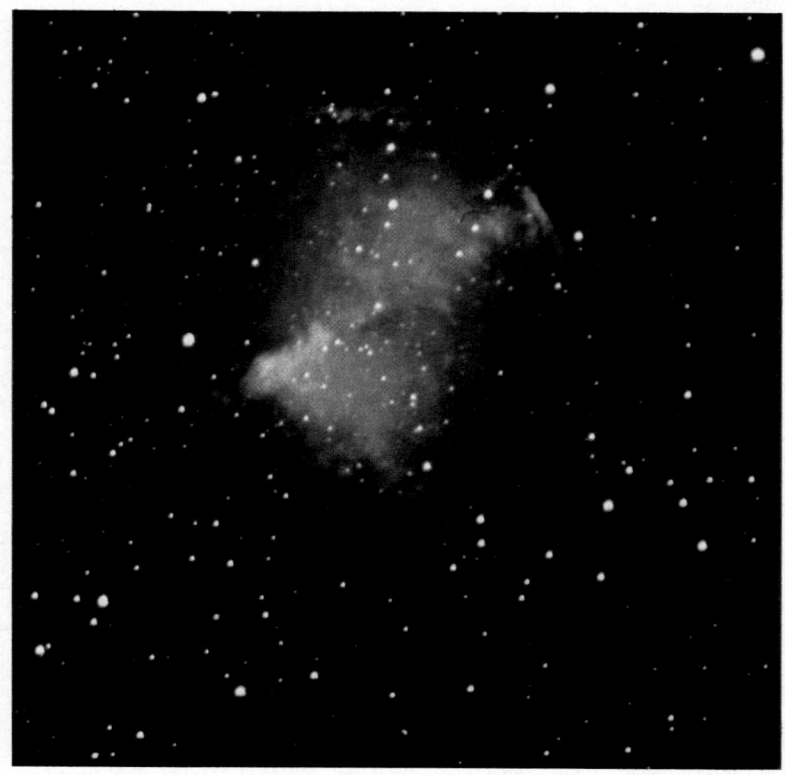

Supernova remnants

The explosion of a supernova

SUPERNOVA EXPLOSIONS are the most spectacular events that occur in our Galaxy. During the first week of its supernova phase, a star can reach an absolute magnitude of −20.5, which is 10 billion times more luminous than the Sun, and as bright as many complete galaxies. Supernova explosions are rare events – only five are known to have taken place in our Galaxy in the past thousand years – but the debris from explosions such as these remain visible to astronomers for hundreds of thousands of years. These supernova remnants (sometimes abbreviated to SNRs) are among the brightest X-ray, gamma ray and radio sources in the sky, and are therefore a very important constituent of the interstellar medium. SNRs are particularly important in a galactic context since they are a major (and possibly the only) source of *cosmic rays* and of many of the heavy elements.

Most of what we know about supernova explosions is derived from the study of galaxies exterior to the Milky Way system. These studies have shown that supernova explosions can be divided into two classes, Type I and Type II, depending on their optical spectrum. Type I supernovae are all very similar to each other, and are probably all derived from the same type of star. We do not know just what sort of star this is, but a plausible guess is that it is a comparatively small object, of around $1.4 M_\odot$ or maybe some sort of binary. Type II supernovae are more of a mixture; they are found only in galaxies containing *Population I* objects, so are generally believed to have been produced by the collapse of massive stars, larger than perhaps $4 M_\odot$. The details of what happens during supernova explosions are very uncertain, but we know that they occur when the inner part of a star suffers severe gravitational collapse to something like a *black hole* or a *neutron star*. The large amounts of energy liberated by this collapse are imparted to the outer layers of the star, which are thereby ejected into space with a velocity of $10-20\,000\,\mathrm{km\,s^{-1}}$. It is the radiation from this hot, fast-moving gas and its subsequent interaction with the nearby interstellar medium that make the supernova remnants visible. The collapsed object at the centre is much more difficult to detect, but in some cases it may manifest itself as a *pulsar*.

Radio emission from supernova remnants

There are about a hundred known supernova remnants in our Galaxy. Although visible, X-ray and gamma radiation have been detected from a few of these, most are seen only at radio wavelengths. The radio emission is caused by high-speed electrons, produced within the supernova, spiralling around magnetic field lines. This process, called *synchrotron radiation*, is also the origin of the radio emission from *quasars*, *radio galaxies* and the general *galactic radio background*, but is quite different from that which causes the emission from H$^+$ regions. It is therefore easy to distinguish between H$^+$ regions and supernova remnants purely on the basis of their radio emission, despite the fact that they are often found in fairly close proximity to each other. In particular the

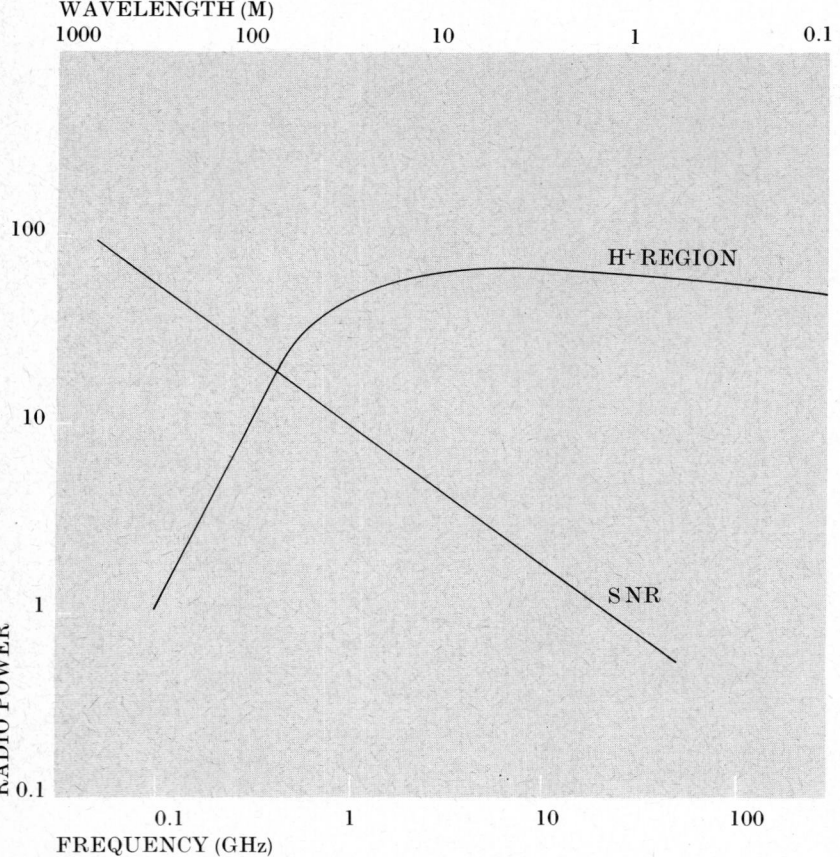

14.18: *Typical radio spectra from H$^+$ regions and from supernova remnants (SNR). The mechanism for the former is the thermal free-free emission from an ionized plasma at 10 000 K; the emission from the latter is synchrotron radiation.*

WAVELENGTH (M)

H$^+$ REGION

SNR

RADIO POWER

FREQUENCY (GHz)

observable differences are:

(a) The emission from an SNR declines with increasing radio frequency (figure 14.18) while that from an H⁺ region increases or stays constant.

(b) Emission from SNR's is often polarized; that from an H⁺ region never is.

(c) H⁺ regions show hydrogen radio recombination lines while SNR's do not.

Supernova remnants may also be distinguished from H⁺ regions by their shape. H⁺ regions are usually comprised of a group of compact sources; supernova remnants, on the other hand, often have a very distinctive roughly circular shell shape several arc minutes in diameter. A classic example of a young shell-shaped supernova remnant is provided by CASSIOPEIA A – the object which, after the Sun, is the strongest source of radio emission in the sky as seen from the Earth (figure 14.19). There is no historical record of the supernova explosion that gave rise to Cas A, but from the measured rate at which the supernova is expanding we know that the event must have taken place in the late seventeenth century. At some positions around the shell, nebulous filaments can now be seen on sensitive red photographs. These filaments have an emission-line spectrum, which has allowed their velocities to be measured via the *Doppler effect*; they are found to be moving at speeds of up to $9000 \, \mathrm{km \, s^{-1}}$ from the Earth, and to have proper motions of up to 0.5 arc sec per year. These velocities are consistent with the idea that they were produced in the original explosion, 3000 pc away, 300 years ago.

The evolution of Cas A is rapid enough for changes to be seen in both its radio and optical appearance in a few years. Some of the radio knots seen in figure 14.19 altered their positions and strengths between 1969 and 1974, while brightness variations in the optical knots have typical timescales of 20 years. The total emission of Cas A at radio wavelengths decreases steadily with time at the rate of about 1 per cent per year. This decrease is equivalent to a cooling down of the relativistic gas as the SNR expands. In 1975, however, it was reported that the flux density of Cas A at 38 MHz (one of the lowest frequencies used in radio astronomy) had started to increase again. As yet we do not know whether or not the increase will continue or whether it comes from a part or from the whole of the SNR. The reason for the increase is also a mystery.

There are two other supernova remnants that are known to date from explosions seen at about the same time as Cas A originated. The Danish astronomer Tycho Brahe witnessed a supernova in 1572, and Kepler saw one in 1604. Both of these objects now appear as radio shells looking very much like figure 14.19. Their diameters are about 10 pc – larger than Cas A – but they are considerably fainter than it. The most famous supernova remnant, the Crab Nebula, does not have a shell structure and is, in many ways, different from almost all the other SNRs in the Galaxy. Since it is the best studied of all the SNRs, it is worth devoting the whole of the next section to a description of it.

14.19: *Radio photograph of the 300-year-old supernova remnant, Cassiopeia A. This is the brightest radio source in the sky outside of the Solar System. The ring of emission shows where the gas in the supernova remnant is colliding with the interstellar medium. (Mullard Radio Astronomy Observatory, Cambridge, UK)*

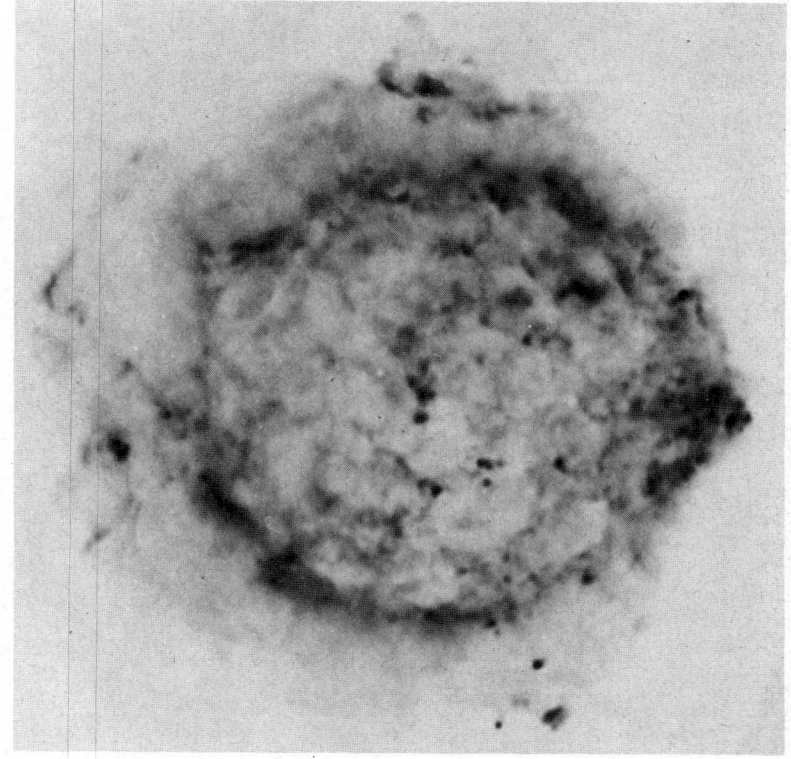

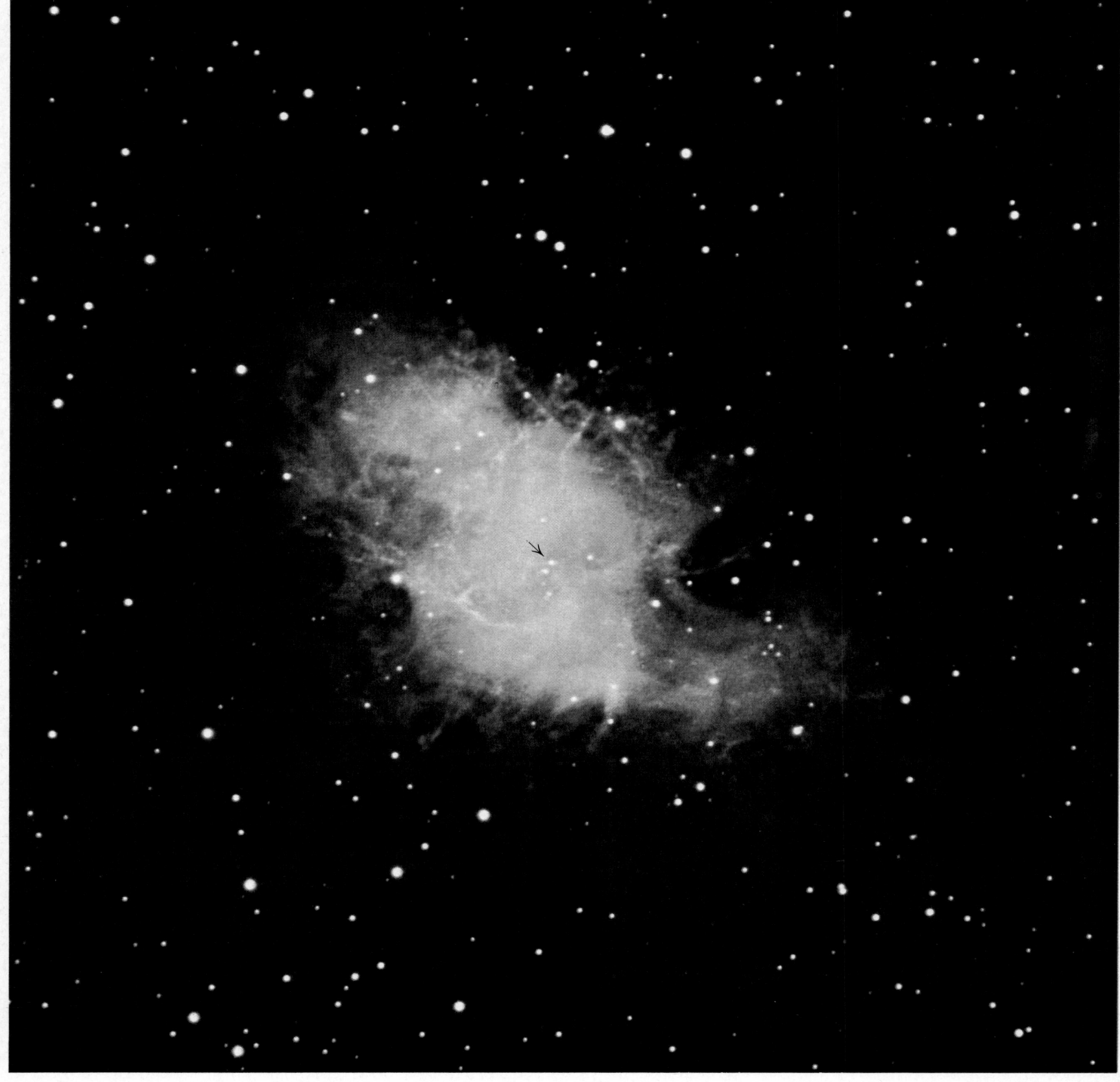

The Crab Nebula

The CRAB NEBULA is almost certainly the result of a supernova explosion (figure 14.20) which was observed by Chinese astronomers on 4 July 1054. This supernova was so bright that it was visible in full daylight for three weeks. Strangely, however, there is no record of its having been seen in any of the European or Arabian observatories known to have been in existence at that time. Possibly the apparition was regarded as too ominous to contemplate, or perhaps Europe had an abnormally cloudy summer that year!

The Crab Nebula is about 2000 pc away and is now about 4 pc in diameter. Its mass is about $1\,M_\odot$. *Synchrotron radiation* is emitted at all wavelengths from radio to X- and possibly gamma rays; the whitish diffuse glow seen in figure 14.20 is from this process, and shows a high degree of *polarization*. The pink-coloured filaments that give the nebula its characteristic crab-like shape and comprise most of its mass, are ionized gas. The pink colour is due to the dominance of the Hα line in the emission-line spectrum of these particular regions. The ionization in the filaments is maintained not by a star, but by the ultraviolet continuum of synchrotron radiation.

In the case of the Crab Nebula, we can actually identify the star which exploded to form the supernova. It is arrowed in figure 14.20 and was originally identified because ripples of synchrotron light appear to move outwards from it about every three months, presumably carrying new relativistic electrons into the nebula. The extraordinary nature of this object was not fully appreciated until 1967 when it was found to be flashing off and on 30 times a second. This star was the first, and remains the only, optical *pulsar* known, but its pulsations can also be seen at radio, infrared, X-ray and gamma-ray wavelengths. The pulsar is crucial to the nebula since it is the reservoir for the power the nebula radiates into space. A *neutron star* spinning 30 times a second contains a vast reserve of *kinetic energy*. From the rate at which the pulsar is slowing down we can calculate the rate at which the energy is being lost by the pulsar. We find that this power is equal to the total power radiated by the nebula (mainly at X-ray wavelengths). By some process which we do not understand the rotating neutron star is able to accelerate streams of electrons to almost the speed of light. These electrons then carry energy away from the pulsar and radiate it as synchrotron radiation in the outer regions of the nebula. The presence of this internal energy source, in the form of a pulsar, is probably the main reason that the Crab Nebula appears so different from the shell-shaped remnants such as Cassiopeia A.

14.20: *The Crab Nebula. This object resulted from the explosion of the arrowed star in the year 1054. The white emission is synchrotron radiation from electrons produced from the vicinity of the exploded star which is now seen as a pulsar. The pinkish regions are filaments of ionized gas.*
(Kitt Peak National Observatory, USA)

X-rays and gamma rays from supernova remnants

X-rays have been detected from several supernova remnants by the use of satellite-borne telescopes. The case of the Crab Nebula has already been mentioned; here the X-rays are almost certainly due to synchrotron radiation. Most SNRs, however, do not contain a pulsar that can maintain the supply of the ultra-relativistic electrons which are necessary for X-ray synchrotron emission.

In these other cases, the X-radiation is probably thermal emission from very hot gas that has been heated to temperatures of the order of ten million Kelvins. The heating results from the collision between the expanding supernova shell and the static interstellar medium which surrounds it. X-rays are seen from young supernova remnants such as Cas A (figure 14.19) and also from much older ones such as the CYGNUS LOOP (figure 14.21). This latter object is probably the result of a supernova explosion some 50 000 years ago. The remnant now has a diameter of about 30 pc and is composed mainly of interstellar matter that has been swept up by the blast. The X-rays from the Cygnus Loop are of lower photon

14.21: *The Cygnus Loop in red light (right) and in X-rays. In the X-ray picture the white and red areas are the brightest, and the blue areas the faintest. (Palomar Sky Survey, USA and Mullard Space Science Laboratory, UK)*

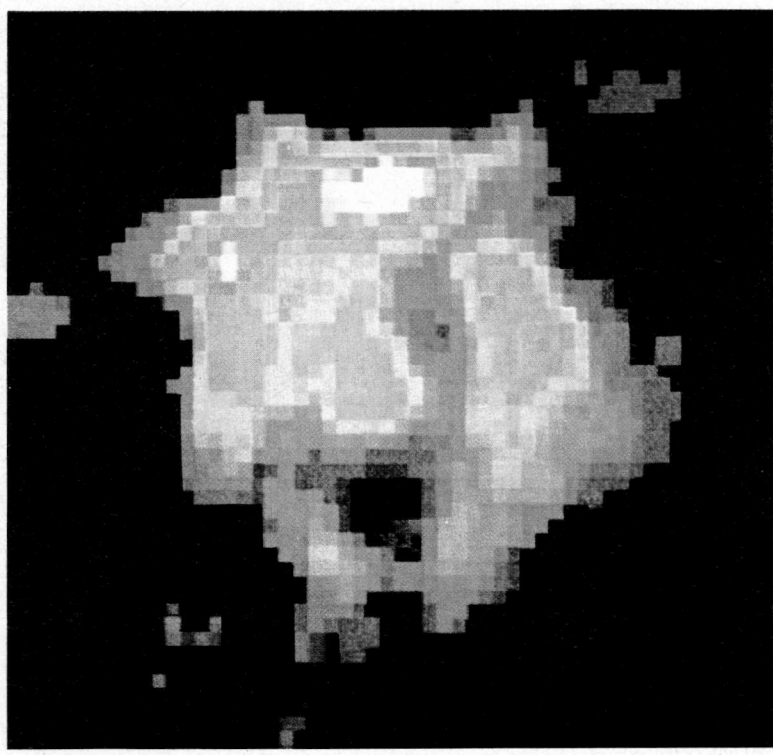

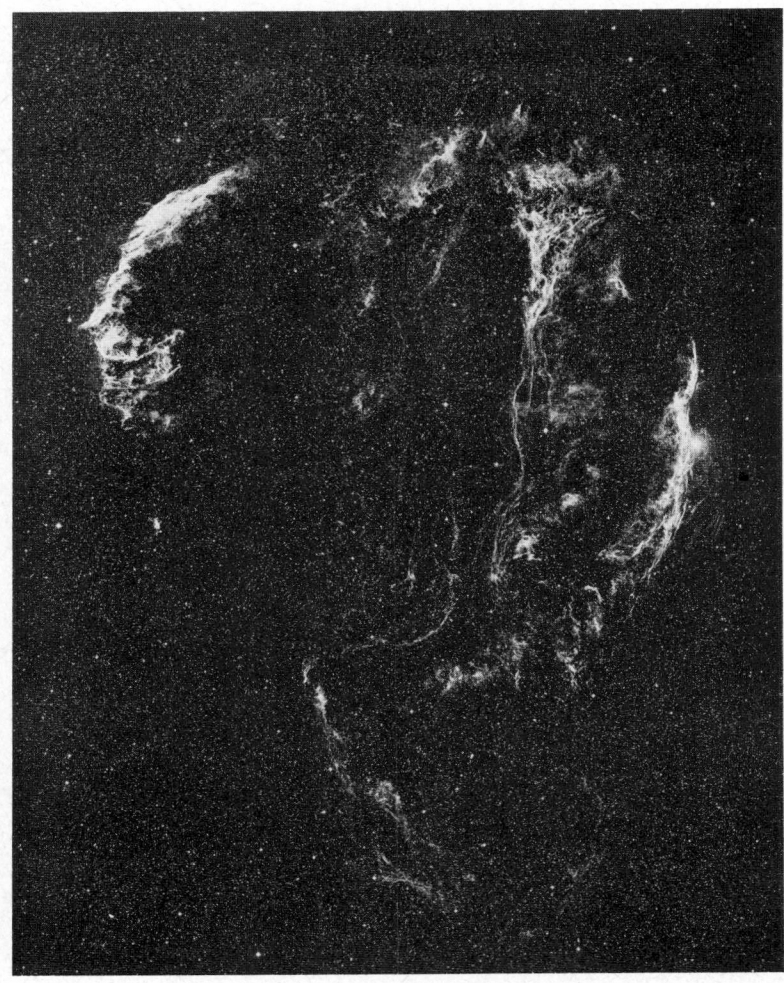

energy than those from Cas A. The reason for this may be that the expansion rate of the Cygnus Loop has been slowed down over the years by its interaction with the interstellar medium; as a result the heating produced currently by the collision is weaker than in Cas A, and the resulting temperature is insufficient to lead to the emission of any photons with energy greater than 1 keV.

Two supernova remnants appear to be sources of gamma-ray emission in the energy range around 100 MeV; these are the Crab Nebula and the Vela supernova remnant, a comparatively old SNR. As it happens, these are the only two SNRs which are definitely associated with pulsars, but this may be only a coincidence. We do not yet know what causes the gamma-ray emission; a possible mechanism involves the production and decay of pions as a result of the interaction of the cosmic ray protons produced in the SNR with the nearby interstellar medium. Current gamma-ray telescopes, however, have insufficient resolution to allow measurement of the angular diameters of these gamma-ray sources, and the possibility remains that the gamma rays are produced very close to the pulsar rather than in the shell. A synchrotron origin for the gamma rays is also possible.

The ages of supernova remnants

Apart from the handful of remnants in our Galaxy which can be identified with particular explosive events, the ages of supernova remnants must be determined by indirect means. In some cases, such as Cas A, this may be done by comparing the diameter of the remnant with its expansion velocity; in general, however, one must calculate models of interstellar explosions in order to find a theoretical explanation for the variations that are seen among SNRs. We now believe that the evolution of a supernova remnant takes place in several fairly distinct phases. The initial stage comprises the unimpeded expansion of the hot gas away from the central collapsed object. After about 100 years the original expansion velocity of 10–20 000 km s^{-1} will start to decrease as a result of the ram pressure of the surrounding interstellar medium, with the result that the interstellar gas swept up by the SNR is compressed into a shell. Hydrodynamic calculations show that it is instabilities in this shell that lead to the uneven ring of strong synchrotron radiation that is characteristic of remnants in the second stage of expansion, such as Cas A (figure 14.19). The shell expands steadily over the next 20 000 years, cooling and slowing down as it does so. The third phase begins when the shell becomes cool enough (about 10^6 K) that radiation by line emission becomes important, cooling the gas even more. The Cygnus Loop (figure 14.21) is near the beginning of this stage, and is currently expanding at 100–200 km s^{-1}. Finally, after several hundred thousand years the shell slows down to a velocity of a few kilometres a second, and loses its identity in the general interstellar medium.

The lifetimes of supernova remnants are therefore less than the lifetimes of even the shortest-lived main-sequence stars. There are, however, longer-term effects from supernovae. *Pulsars* are probably visible for about 10^7 years – long after the remnant has disappeared. The galactic spurs and the general galactic-background radio emission have their origins in supernova remnants, as do some, or perhaps all, of the galactic *cosmic rays*. Although the total rate of mass return to the interstellar medium is smaller for supernovae than for certain other types of evolved stars, the material in the supernova shells is unique in that it is enriched in the elements heavier than iron. As important as the mass is the energy that the SNRs put into the interstellar medium; the turbulence produced by the passage of shock waves may provide at least 10 per cent of the total kinetic energy of the interstellar gas. The very hot (10^5 K) regions of interstellar gas discovered by ultraviolet satellites may also have their origins in supernova remnants.

With the estimates we now have of the ages of SNRs in our Galaxy we can calculate the rate at which supernova explosions must have been taking place in order to produce the number of remnants that are now seen. This calculation is very uncertain, but indicates that there is something like one supernova explosion somewhere in our Galaxy every 50–150 years. This number is broadly consistent with both the observations of supernovae in other galaxies and with the expected rate of star deaths in our own. The fact that only four of the five explosions in the last millennium have actually been seen from the Earth can be explained by the presence of interstellar extinction. The frequency of Galactic supernova explosions is just high enough to give every astronomer the hope that he will witness one during his own lifetime – preferably on a night when he himself is at a telescope!

15. Our Local Group of galaxies

The stars of our Galaxy

A faint luminous band can be observed in the clear night sky, spanning a great circle on the celestial hemisphere. This band varies in width around an average of some 20°. Dark patches are seen in it, but it is clearly brighter than the sky background and hence it was long ago named the MILKY WAY on account of its appearance to the naked eye (figure 15.1). Inspection with a moderately powerful telescope reveals that the light comes from a vast number of faint stars. This observation of the stellar nature of the Milky Way gives a first indication of the structure of the world beyond our Solar System: an enormous mass of stars, distributed over a flattened region of space. The Sun is one among these stars. In this section we survey the space around us to summarize its principal contents and their distribution.

When a radio signal is sent forth from Earth, as was done in 1975 with the Arecibo radio telescope to indicate our presence to possible alien civilizations, the wave carrying the message expands into space with the velocity of light, almost 300 000 km s^{-1}. This is the highest velocity known to experimental physics, and no material particle or radiation can travel any faster. On its journey outward, the signal passes the outermost planet of the Solar System after about 5.5 hours. Thereafter it will traverse space for 4.3 years before the next sizeable object is reached. This is the star α Centauri C, the third member of the triple-star system α Centauri, one of the brightest stars in southern skies. Because it is

15.1: *Full view of the night sky. All of the celestial sphere is shown projected in galactic coordinates. The north galactic pole is at the top, the south pole at the bottom. The Milky Way with its dust patches, H$^+$ regions and stars is prominently visible, as are the Magellanic Clouds (in the southern sky). (Lund Observatory, Sweden)*

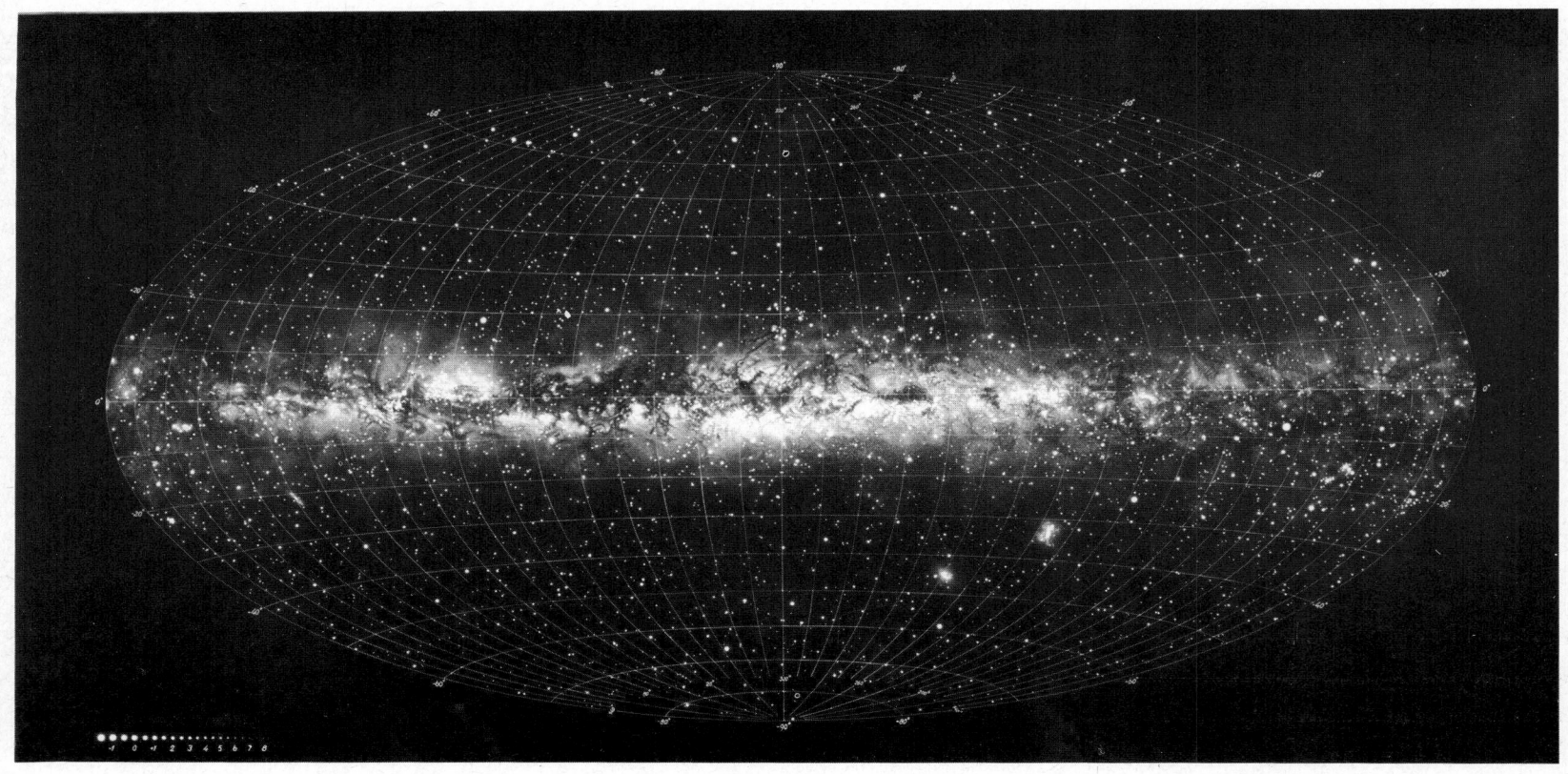

the star nearest to us, α Centauri C is also called Proxima Centauri. Its distance of 4.3 light years corresponds to 30 million times the diameter of the Sun, or 7000 times the diameter of the Solar System. To visualize this immensity, imagine what would happen if people were separated by 30 million human diameters; one's nearest neighbour would then be as far away as one tenth of the distance to the Moon! Evidently stars are very sparsely distributed in space: the average distance between stars is about five light years. Within 17 ly (5 pc) from the Sun, only 45 stars have been found (figure 15.2).

The nearest stars appear to be distributed at random in space. At larger distances, however, there exist many loosely-bound groups of some 100 stars each. They are called *associations* and *open clusters*. The nearest of these is reached by our signal after 68 years. This is the Ursa Major star cluster, which is so close that its 100 or so members spread over a region on the sky of 20° diameter; several of the visible stars in the constellation Ursa Major, though not all of them, are members of this association. Further well-known groups are the Hyades (at 140 light years or 43 pc) and the Pleiades (125 pc). When the positions in space of these open clusters are plotted, it becomes clear that their distribution is not random at all. They lie in the Milky Way: of the nearest 30 open clusters, half lie within 5° from the middle of that luminous band. This distribution defines a plane in space, analogous to the plane of the *ecliptic* which is approximately defined by the positions of the planets. This GALACTIC PLANE, in projection on the sky, forms the central line of the Milky Way. The mean distance of the open clusters from the plane is only 70 pc. Because such clusters are, on average, seen to distances of about 3 kpc, the thickness/diameter ratio of the galactic plane is smaller than 0.002 (i.e. 70/3000). The corresponding ratio of our Solar System is 0.034; therefore the open clusters are at least 15 times more narrowly confined to their plane than are the planets.

The open clusters and associations which define the galactic plane are very young. Their ages are found by two independent methods. Firstly, most of them contain stars of certain types, especially *T Tauri variables* and *O-type stars*, which are known from studies of *stellar evolution* to be no older than between 10^5 and 10^6 years. (For comparison, the age of the Sun exceeds five billion years). Secondly, the clusters have a low star density: some thousands of stars at most, within a diameter of about 5 pc. This means that they are loosely bound, that is to say the mutual gravitational attraction of the stars in the cluster, which holds the group together, is so small that a star manages to escape about once in every 100 000 years. This evaporation effect limits the age of open clusters to around 100 million years.

There exists another distinctive type of local condensation in the stellar field: the groups called *globular clusters* because of their spherical appearance. Among the nearest of these to be passed by our signal, after 9000 years, is the object Messier 4 (M4), which contains about a million stars within a diameter of 10 pc. The distance of M4 indicates that globular clusters are much sparser than open clusters. In fact, whereas the mean distance between globulars is some 3 kpc, the open clusters are on the average only 100 pc apart. Another important distinction is that globulars are not concentrated towards the galactic plane. Precise determinations of their distances show that they are distributed in a roughly spherical volume of some 20 kpc radius. They are concentrated towards the sphere's centre, which is a point at a distance of 10 kpc from the Sun in the direction of the constellation Sagittarius. This point lies exactly in the galactic plane. The globular clusters are old systems that contain stars which are known to have existed for billions of years.

15.2: *Stereogram of the 45 stars nearest the Sun (circled dot). This diagram can be viewed in a stereoscope, or at 50 cm distance with the eyes crossed until the left and right images merge. Notice several binary stars. The farthest star is 5 parsec (17 light years) from the Sun.*

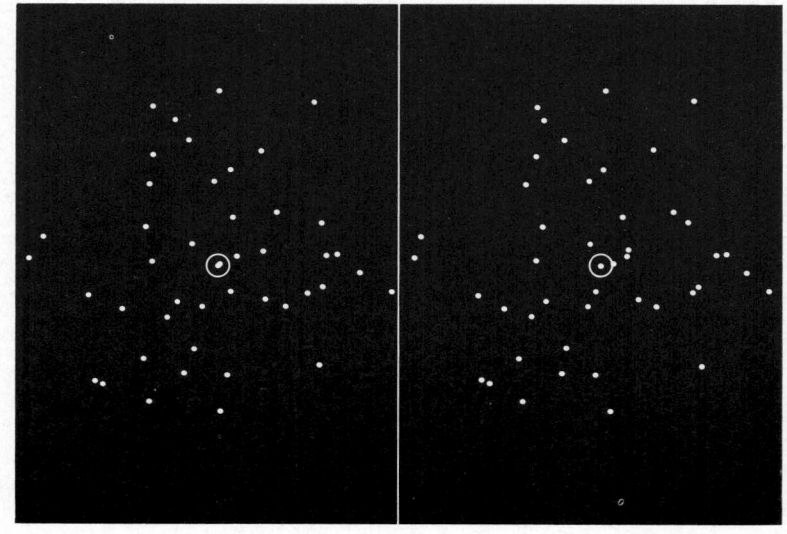

So, we now see the following rough picture of our starry surroundings emerge. The Sun lies in a vast stellar system, our Galaxy. The Galaxy may be divided into two sub-systems. One sub-system consists of stars confined to a narrow plane in space. This galactic plane coincides with the central line of the Milky Way and is outlined by young stars in associations and open clusters. The planar component has been named POPULATION I. The other system fills a spherical volume of space centred upon a point in the galactic plane. This spherical component contains old objects, such as globular clusters, and it has been named POPULATION II. It should be noted that there is no sharp distinction between the two populations. Rather, this classification is a simplified form of a scheme in which the stars are arranged continuously according to properties such as age, content of heavy elements, and mean height above the galactic plane. For practical purposes, this continuum is subdivided into the five population classes listed in table 15.1. The total matter density of the entire assembly shows a strong concentration towards the galactic plane.

We now have to sketch into the above schematic picture some important details of the stellar distribution. As has been said, observation of the stellar component with the naked eye readily indicates the disc-like shape of the Galaxy. A similar, but more refined approach to the determination of galactic structure is to count the number, per square degree on the sky, of stars in a given interval of apparent brightness. One may try an attempt to find the spatial distribution of the stars by such a statistical method as is graphically explained in figure 15.3. The reconstruction of the third dimension (depth) can never be achieved satisfactorily, because some information is always lacking. One source of ambiguity is the fact that not all stars have the same intrinsic luminosity, so the apparent brightness is not an honest measure of distance. Worse still, starlight is dimmed by interstellar matter.

Whereas the Population II objects show a smooth distribution in the plane, the extreme Population I exhibits a clear inhomogeneity. The distances to O and B stars can be determined by spectroscopic means, and the distances to the *Cepheids* are found using the relationship between their period and luminosity. When their positions in the galactic plane are plotted, these stars appear to be concentrated in clumpy bands (figure 15.4). These are thought to be parts of spiral structure extending throughout the plane and so O and B stars and Cepheids are called SPIRAL TRACERS. In the solar neighbourhood, a section at right angles across a spiral arm as delineated by these stars appears like a very flat ellipse with axes of about 1000 and 150 pc.

Throughout the Galaxy, many objects are found which are not ordinary stars (like the Sun or Sirius, say), but which have nonetheless a stellar ancestry. Among these are the *planetary nebulae, novae, supernova remnants, pulsars, X-ray binaries,* and possibly *black holes.* There is no evidence that they are of great importance in the overall structure of the Galaxy.

Table 15.1: Classification of stellar populations

Halo Population II	*Intermediate Population II*	*Disc Population*	*Older Population I*	*Extreme Population I*
Subdwarfs	High-velocity stars with velocities greater than 30 km s^{-1} normal to the galactic plane	Stars of galactic nucleus	A-type stars	Open clusters and associations
Globular clusters with large velocities normal to the galactic plane	Long-period variables with periods less than 250 days and spectral types earlier than M5	Planetary nebulae Novae RR Lyrae stars with periods below 0.4 days	Strong-line stars	Supergiants Classical Cepheids T Tauri stars
RR Lyrae stars with periods longer than 0.4 days		Weak-line stars		Supernova remnants Pulsars

15.3: *Determining the distribution of stars in space (right column) from star counts (middle) on the sky (left). In this computer-generated example, the size of the 'stars' indicates their apparent magnitude. (a) The sky as it would appear if space around the Sun were uniformly filled with stars. The star counts are expected to fall on a straight line (grey band). (b) The appearance of a lack of stars at some distance from the Sun. The star count clearly shows excesses at high and low brightness (points above grey band). (c) Excess of stars at some distance from the Sun. Notice again the deviation from the uniform distribution.*

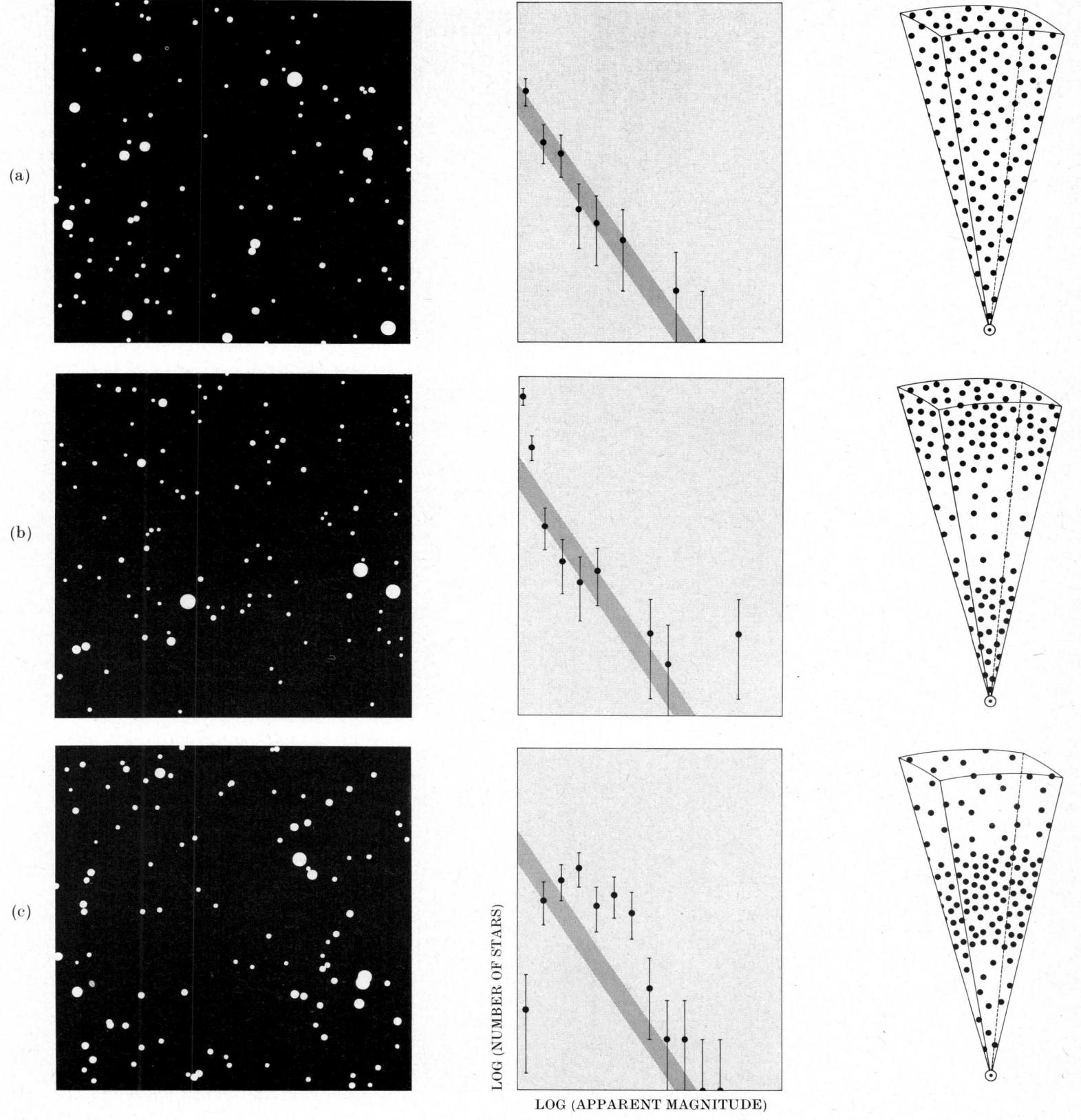

(a)

(b)

(c)

LOG (NUMBER OF STARS)

LOG (APPARENT MAGNITUDE)

Between the stars

Two simple observations with the naked eye show that the Milky Way contains gas. Firstly, certain nebulae such as the Orion Nebula have a fuzzy appearance (figure 14.13). Secondly, the presence of obscuring matter may be inferred from the existence of the dark patches in the Milky Way that were mentioned in chapter 14. This matter is much less conspicuous than the stars, because it does not itself generate energy. If all the matter in stars near the Sun were distributed evenly through the same volume of space, its density would be $7 \times 10^{-21}\,\mathrm{kg\,m^{-3}}$, hence at most 12 per cent of the total mass in the solar neighbourhood consists of gas and dust. Although it is very tenuous, this dispersed matter is an important constituent of the Galaxy.

The dimming of light as it travels through interstellar matter presents a formidable obstacle to the determination of the structure of the Galaxy. Light passing through a typical part of the galactic plane is dimmed by two magnitudes for every kiloparsec it travels. Consequently, optical observations in the plane are limited to the nearest 3 kpc (figure 15.4), so that only local information can be obtained by optical telescopes. Worse still, the degree of obscuration depends strongly on the direction in which the observations are made (figure 15.1). All of the structure determinations done in the early years by the technique of star counts have been proven invalid because of the then unsuspected irregularity of interstellar extinction. The dimming of the light depends also on

15.4: *Spiral tracers in the neighbourhood of the Sun, looking down onto the galactic plane from the galactic north pole. The visibility of tracers becomes worse with distance, due to extinction. Also, their position along the line of sight becomes more uncertain. Although the distribution is clearly not uniform, the bands are not very crisp. Blue dots are Cepheid variables, red dots are star clusters.*

0   5 kpc

the angle which the line of sight makes with the galactic plane. From measurements of the change of absorption with galactic latitude, it has been deduced that the mean thickness of the layer of interstellar matter is 150 pc. This is only 100 times the average distance between stars, so apparently the gas layer is extremely thin with respect to its extent in the plane.

The layer of gas forms a curious galactic atmosphere, pervaded by a magnetic field; but the flux density is only 50 nT (nanotesla), which is 100 000 times weaker than the field of Earth. It appears that this field is too weak to influence galactic structure on scales larger than about one hundred parsec. Likewise, other aspects of the 'galactic weather', such as the propagation of blast waves from exploding *novae* and *supernovae*, the local ionization by hot stars, and the diffusion of *cosmic rays*, do not influence large-scale structure, but merely generate clouds with sizes up to hundreds of parsecs.

These phenomena leave long-lived traces in the galactic atmosphere. For example, the blast waves from exploding stars disperse matter into interstellar space. Since the stars that generate these shells of debris have changed part of their hydrogen by nuclear fusion into heavier elements (especially carbon, nitrogen, oxygen and iron), the chemical composition of the interstellar medium is modified by the addition of these heavy elements. In supernovae, elements much heavier than iron are made in the blast wave itself. Composition changes in the interstellar medium are also caused by highly energetic cosmic rays which collide with interstellar atomic nuclei and smash them up. The splinters left over from the collision are nuclei of light elements, especially those lying in the range between helium and carbon. It is now known that processes like these are important for galactic structure: new stars form from some of this modified matter, and then change it further by their own nuclear processes. Thus a record of the galactic weather is kept by the composition of stars and the interstellar matter; the evolution of the Galaxy may be traced by analysing spectral lines in order to deduce this composition. It is fairly certain that our Galaxy formed about 12–14 billion years ago, from a collapsing cloud of hydrogen (about three quarters of the total mass) and helium (one quarter). (For comparison, note that the age of the Universe is probably 13–20 billion years.) Between 80 and 90 per cent of this gas condensed into a first generation of stars within a few hundred million years. After, or perhaps due to, this initial burst of star formation, the Galaxy settled down into the form it still presents to us today. We will now look at that form as it appears in radio astronomy.

Radio observations and the galactic centre

At optical wavelengths, interstellar matter has proved to be more a hindrance than a help for the determination of galactic structure. Happily, in the radio domain (this is the region of the electromagnetic spectrum where the wavelengths are longer than one millimetre), the converse is the case: firstly because the galactic atmosphere is almost everywhere transparent to waves of nearly all radio frequencies, and secondly because the matter itself is a source of weak radio radiation. And just as in the optical case, this radiation shows a continuous spectrum (*continuum*) with spectral lines in absorption and emission superimposed on it. The radio continuum intensity is highest in a band coinciding with the Milky Way (figure 15.1). Within this diffuse band, numerous compact radio sources can be seen. The majority of these are thermal sources: clouds of ionized hydrogen (H^+ *regions*) with temperatures up to 10 000 K. Because of their strong concentration towards the galactic plane, these regions belong to the extreme Population I, the most youthful component of the Galaxy. Their distribution indicates the presence of spiral arms, which is not surprising since they receive their energy from O and B stars, which are tracers of the spiral structure. The majority of the remaining compact radio sources are supernova remnants.

Apart from the individual thermal sources in the Galaxy there is also the continuum associated with the diffuse background. This shows a *non-thermal spectrum*, which indicates that this radiation is not caused by hot gas, but instead is *synchrotron radiation*, emitted by cosmic-ray electrons as they diffuse through the galactic magnetic field. Because the kinetic energy of the electrons is very large, they ascend to heights exceeding 2 kpc above the galactic plane and thereby form a GALACTIC HALO. Just how far this galactic halo of faint radio emission extends is still a matter of controversy. Possibly it is so extended as to coincide with the enormous volume through which the globular clusters are distributed. The halo is extremely tenuous: at heights beyond 2 kpc, its density is less than 10^{-25} kg m^{-3}, which is a ten-thousandth of the density of interstellar matter in the plane.

The non-thermal radio emission from the Galaxy is by no means featureless, even on a large scale. Outside the galactic plane, numerous ridges of enhanced radio emission can be seen to extend into the halo. These SPURS are probably remnants of the shells of nearby supernovae which exploded more than 100 000 years ago. Such ancient shells have diameters up to 150 pc which means that at close range, radio astronomers observe them as circles with very large angular radius projected on the sky. For example, the NORTH POLAR SPUR traces a gigantic loop with a radius of 50°. Its radio waves are strongly polarized, which indicates that the object must be near by. We can deduce this interesting fact because if it were far away, the blurring caused by the galactic atmosphere (*Faraday rotation*) would largely have destroyed the polarization, which is imposed on the radiation by the magnetic field of the blast wave. Objects like these are too small to be of direct importance for galactic structure as a whole. They look spectacular to us merely because they are not very far away. Indirectly, however, they help to maintain the galactic atmosphere by the injection of fast particles, probably even cosmic rays, which replenish and heat the interstellar medium.

In the galactic plane, regions of enhanced radiation occur in places where the line of sight happens to run along a local spiral arm (e.g. in the direction of Cygnus). But the most conspicuous extended source in the galactic plane lies in Sagittarius (figure 15.5). In this region, most of the stars are obscured by interstellar dimming, but some can be seen through low-absorption WINDOWS. Because these windows occur at somewhat higher galactic latitudes, the stars seen through them must lie a kiloparsec or so from the plane. These distant stars form the CENTRAL BULGE of our Galaxy, which contains the Sagittarius radio source complex (figure 15.5). This is about 10 kpc from the Sun, at the very centre of the Galaxy. The central region consists of an oblate spheroidal cloud of stars, with a radius of 1 kpc, a thickness of 400 pc.

In the equatorial plane of this spheroid lies a rotating disc of gas with radius 750 pc, and a varying thickness that decreases from 250 pc on the periphery to 100 pc at the centre. The edge of the disc spins at 230 km s^{-1}. The density is about 10^{-21} kg m^{-3}; this amounts to 8 million solar masses, half of which is in the form of neutral hydrogen, half is molecular hydrogen, and a small admixture (about one per cent) dust.

Inside the central region of the Galaxy, a number of small radio sources are observed. The brightest of these are called Sagittarius A and B (figure 15.5). The source Sgr A is only a few parsecs in extent. This object is the galactic centre, situated at right ascension 17 hr 42 min 37 sec and declination $-28°$ 57' (for the equinox and epoch of 1950.0). It forms a reference point for the HELIO-CENTRIC GALACTIC COORDINATES. Heliocentric galactic coordinates are defined as a right-handed spherical coordinate system centred on the Sun. Its longitude l is measured in the plane of the Galaxy from 0 (on the galactic centre at ra 17 hr 42 min 37 sec, dec $-28°$ 57') to 360°. Its latitude b ranges from $-90°$ to $+90°$, the latter value being reached at the GALACTIC NORTH POLE, which is situated at ra 12 hr 49 min 0 sec, dec 27°4' (1950.0). In projections, it is customary to look upon the galactic plane from the north pole.

The central region of the galaxy has many unique features. It contains the galactic dynamical centre, coinciding with Sgr A. The region centred on this point is the most rapidly rotating section of the Galaxy: it turns around its axis once every 50 000 years. From this high speed we can deduce that it has the highest average density: within one parsec of the centre are contained four million solar masses. The central density is therefore a million times higher than the density near the Sun. If all of this is stars, the average distance between the stars is only 20 light days! A resident of a hypothetical planet orbiting a star in the galactic centre would be able to see its neighbouring stars resolved in an optical telescope: the apparent angular diameters would be upwards of 2 seconds of arc. Planets around these stars could easily be seen, from our hypothetical planet, since a planet like Jupiter would have an

apparent visual brightness of 6 mag. Another unique object is the source Sgr B2, which is part of the Sgr B complex. It is probably the most massive cloud in the Galaxy: three million solar masses concentrated within a radius of 3 pc. More species of *interstellar molecules* have been detected in Sgr B2 than in any other galactic cloud. Infrared observations reveal a number of similar, though less massive, molecular clouds. From information about their velocities it has been deduced that they form an expanding ring (or at least a large sector of a ring) around the centre of the Galaxy.

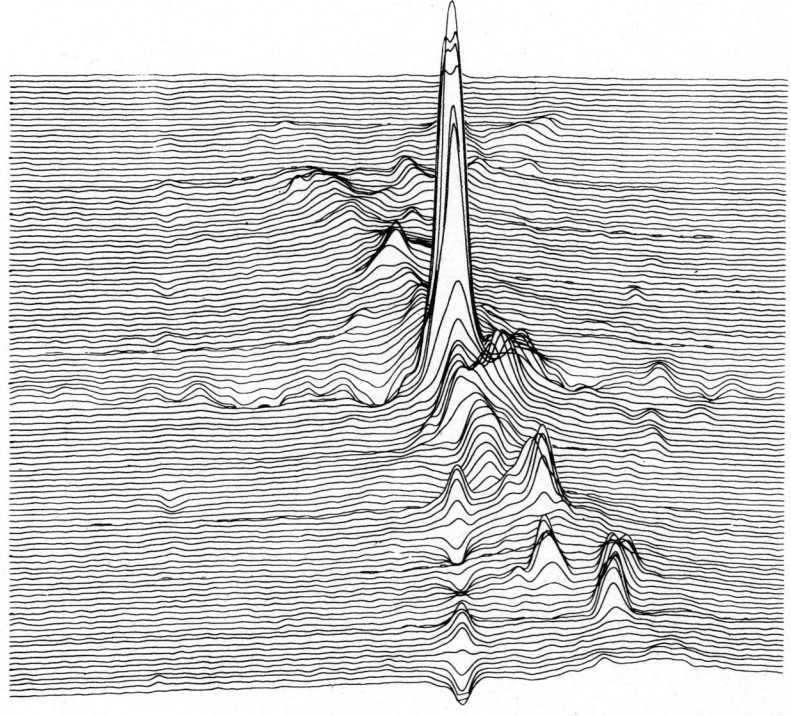

15.5: *Early observation of the galactic centre at the radio frequency 158 MHz. The height of the hills corresponds to the intensity of the radio radiation. Valleys are artefacts. The galactic plane is seen slanting across the picture, through the entire Sagittarius complex.*

The restless Galaxy: the motion of the stars

The order and regularity of the planetary motions provided the key to the structure of the Solar System and the discovery of the law of gravitational attraction. Likewise, the study of galactic dynamics has been, and is, essential to a determination of the structure of the Galaxy. Careful observations of stellar *radial velocities* (motion of the star along our line of sight) and *proper motions* (motion across the celestial sphere), revealed a certain amount of orderliness. These velocities are due to the simultaneous effect of two causes. Firstly, since no star is attached to the others, every one has a certain RANDOM VELOCITY with respect to the LOCAL STANDARD OF REST (that is the centre of mass of the Sun and its nearest neighbours). Secondly, all stars move in their orbits around the galactic centre. The random velocity of the Sun causes the proper motion vectors of the other stars to point systematically away from a certain point in the sky (the *apex*) towards a point diametrically opposite (the *antapex*): the apparent trajectories seem to be radiating from a point in the direction of motion of the observer (the same effect that causes the 'radiant' of a meteor swarm). The orbital motions of the neighbours are best understood by making the simplification that all the mass within the solar orbit is concentrated in the galactic centre and that all stars have the same orbital energy. Then, classical mechanics tells us that all orbits have the same length of semi-major axis, and the magnitudes of all orbital velocities near the Sun are the same.

The solar apex lies at right ascension 18^h and declination $30°$, towards which point the Sun moves with a velocity of $20\,km\,s^{-1}$ with respect to the local standard of rest. The two streams, caused by the presence of non-circular orbits, appear in the motion of the HIGH-VELOCITY STARS, that is, those stars which have velocities in excess of $63\,km\,s^{-1}$ (figure 15.6). These stars all belong to the galactic halo; it follows, then, from these dynamical data, that the younger Population I stars move in the plane in approximately circular orbits around the galactic centre, whereas the older Population II stars follow non-circular orbits in the halo.

Once these large-scale motions have been determined, astronomers can study the more subtle dynamical effects. The object of this effort is to determine the distribution of the mass in the Galaxy, and to find the total mass of the Galaxy. Clearly, such knowledge is of enormous importance for the understanding of the structure, and ultimately the history, of our Milky Way system.

The most obvious difference between galactic and planetary motion is that the latter is almost entirely governed by the central gravitational attraction of the Sun, whereas the Galaxy is held together by the gravitational attraction of its widely-distributed stars, gas and other constituents. This difference is reflected in the way in which the systems rotate. In the Solar System, rotation is described by *Kepler's third law*. In the Galaxy, as we shall see, the situation is vastly more complicated. Consider firstly the motion of the Sun in its galactic orbit: it is in equilibrium between its centrifugal acceleration and the attraction of all the mass in the Galaxy enclosed by the solar orbit (figure 15.7). A star with a galactic

15.6: *Proper motions of the high-velocity stars. All velocity vectors point away from the same spot in the sky, due to the orbital motion of the Sun in the plane of the Galaxy. The asymmetric distribution of the velocities is due to the orbital motion of the stars in rosette orbits out of the galactic plane. As seen from the Sun the velocity distribution gives the appearance of two streams of stars sweeping past the Sun.*

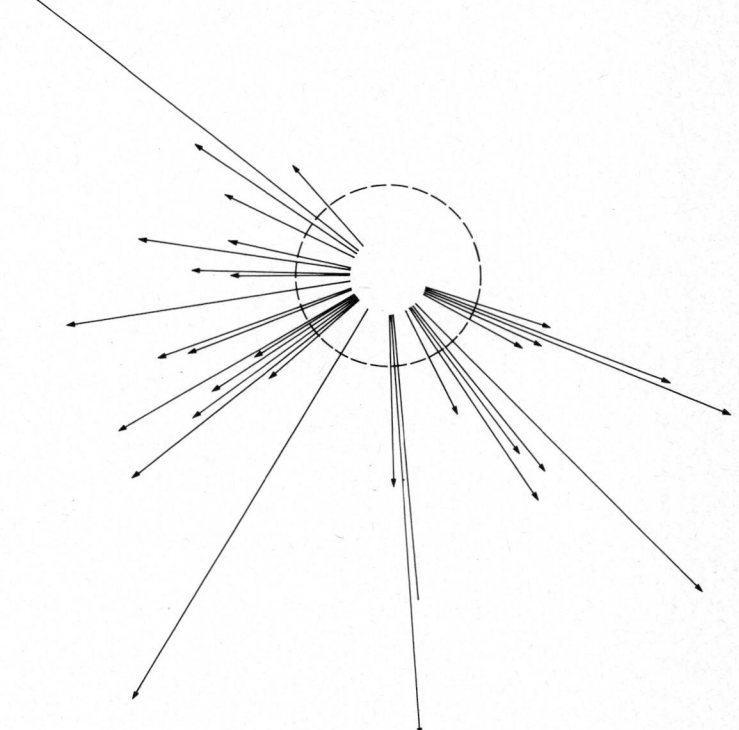

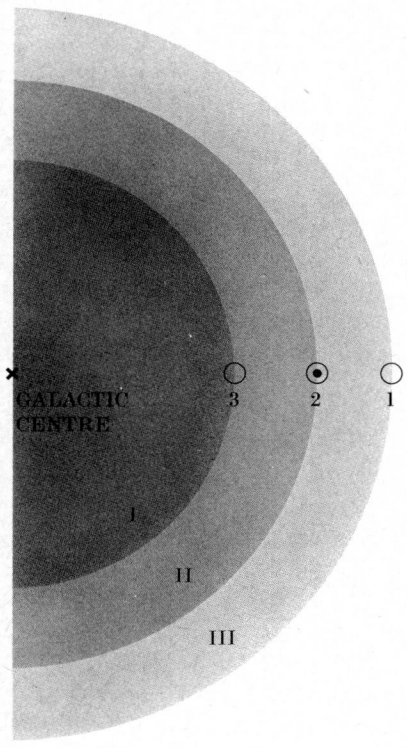

15.7: *The origin of the rotation curve of our Galaxy. Stars far away from the centre (circle 1) are kept in orbit by almost the entire mass of the Galaxy. Stars further in (2,3) see progressively less mass within their orbits (regions II + I and I), so that their orbital speeds fall more and more below the Keplerian curve.*

GALACTIC CENTRE

3 2 1

I

II

III

15.8: *Computer-generated rosette orbit of a star in the lower halo of our Galaxy. (a) plan view from the galactic north pole (b) side view in the galactic plane. Dashed line: orbit of the Sun.*

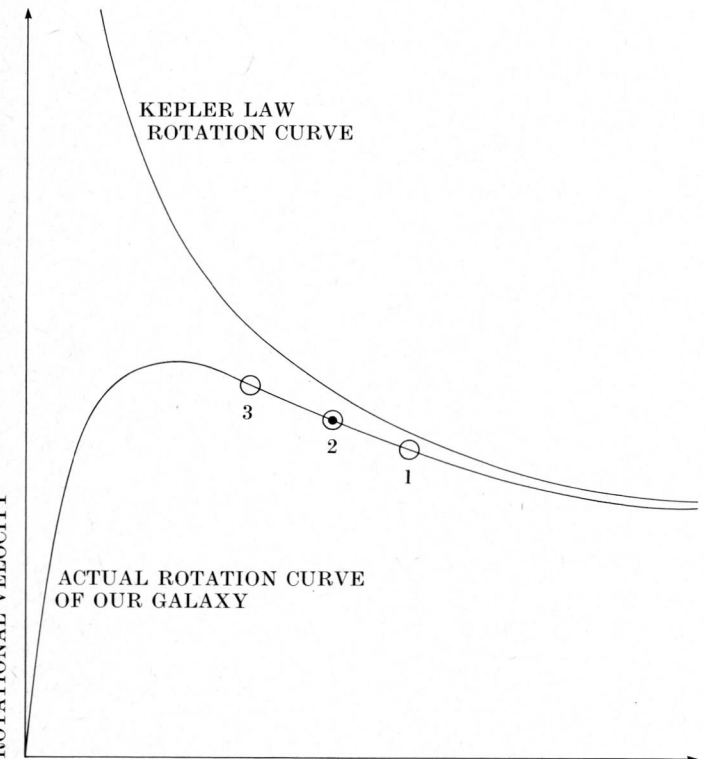

KEPLER LAW
ROTATION CURVE

3

2

1

ACTUAL ROTATION CURVE
OF OUR GALAXY

ROTATIONAL VELOCITY

RADIUS

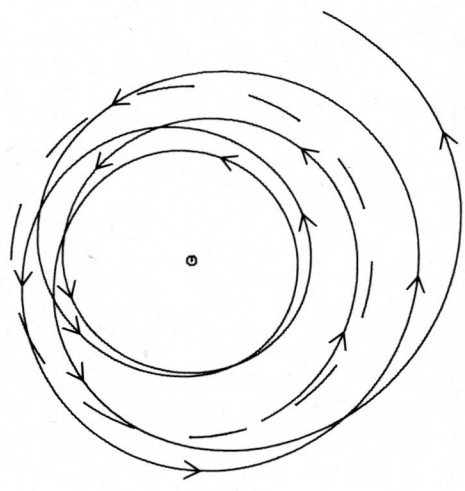

orbit greater than that of the Sun will experience the attraction of a greater mass, because the larger orbit encompasses more matter (figure 15.7a). Conversely, a star within the solar orbit is effectively attracted by a smaller mass. This effect of the variation of attractive force with position in the Galaxy causes the galactic law of rotation to differ markedly from Kepler's third law (figure 15.7b). This difference shows up in the motion of the stars.

Stellar orbits are not restricted to a plane: the path which a typical halo star traces is rather reminiscent of a three-dimensional figure known as a LISSAJOUS PATTERN (figure 15.8). Even if a star moves exactly in the galactic plane its path is not an ellipse, but is a ROSETTE ORBIT as in figure 15.8a. It has been already mentioned that the distance between stars is very large, and that interstellar matter is extremely tenuous. Therefore, a star can move on an orbit as in figure 15.8 without noticeable hindrance from stellar collision or slowing down by friction with the gas or dust. Hence the mass distribution as it is observed today is essentially the same as it was when the Galaxy formed. The presence of a halo therefore indicates that the *protogalaxy* (the gaseous cloud from which the Galaxy formed by gravitational contraction in the early phases of the Universe) was originally roughly spherical. The presence of a disc shows that somehow the matter which did not turn into stars early on, has collapsed to a very flattened sub-system. Subsequently, later generations of stars have formed, and are still doing so, from the gas in the disc. This course of events is also indicated by the fact that halo stars are poor in heavy elements compared with disc stars. Nuclear fusion processes associated with stars constantly increase the amount of heavy elements in the interstellar medium, because some stars disintegrate at the end of their evolution. Hence the halo stars were apparently the first to form, before this nuclear enrichment had really got under way.

Gas dynamics

In the optical spectrum of some bright nearby stars, spectral lines are observed which have not formed by absorption in the stellar atmosphere, but which arose by the interception of the starlight by interstellar matter. These *interstellar absorption lines* appear to occur at wavelengths which differ from those at which the corresponding atoms in the laboratory absorb radiation. This is due to the *Doppler effect*: we must conclude from these absorption lines that there exist interstellar clouds that move through the Galaxy. Comparison of the interstellar lines of stars close together in the sky shows that different clouds often have approximately the same velocities: apparently there is a systematic (that is, well-organized) motion in the interstellar gas. As we have seen, optical observations in the galactic plane are limited by observation to distances of a few kiloparsecs, but fortunately spectral lines also occur at radio wavelengths. The strongest of these lines are emission lines of atomic neutral hydrogen. The most extensively used to date is the line at *21-cm wavelength*, due to a hyperfine transition in the hydrogen atom at 1421 MHz, theoretically predicted in 1946 and first observed in 1951. The radio spectral lines also show the Doppler effect, and since they can be seen right across and throughout the Galaxy it is possible to study the state of motion of the galactic gas on a very large scale (tens of kiloparsecs).

The mass distribution and the total mass of the Galaxy are closely connected with the shape of the GALACTIC ROTATION CURVE. Therefore, in order to determine these extremely important properties of our island in the Universe, it is crucial firstly to obtain the rotation curve. Radio astronomers have succeeded in doing this by observing the neutral hydrogen in a hypothetical circle drawn about a point half-way between the Sun and the galactic centre, and passing through the Sun (figure 15.9). Let us assume that the gas moves in circular orbits about the galactic centre. Simple geometry then shows that at every point of the hypothetical circle the line of sight from the Sun makes a tangent to one particular circular orbit in the galactic plane. Therefore, all orbital velocities of matter which happen to pass across this SUBCENTRAL CIRCLE point directly towards the observer. This fact makes the subcentral circle very special, for on this circle the observed radial velocities are the highest attained along any chosen line of sight! In principle, it is possible to dream up odd-looking rotation curves for which this is not true, but the Galaxy could not stay very long in such a peculiar state of motion. Thus all of the above gives us the following recipe to determine the galactic rotation curve.

Firstly, observe the neutral hydrogen in a number of directions between longitudes 0° and 90°. Secondly, from the observed 21-cm line profile and the Doppler formula, find the velocity of the fastest-moving cloud along every line of sight. Thirdly, find out where these lines of sight intersect the subcentral circle. Fourthly, because the maximum velocities must lie on these intersections, we know what the velocity of rotation is on every circular orbit between the Sun and the galactic centre! However, as this recipe shows (and figure 15.9 confirms), the rotation curve can only be found between the Sun and the galactic centre (figure 15.10).

When these difficulties have been overcome, there still lies some hard work ahead to derive from the rotation curve the distribution of mass in the Galaxy. In order to see how such a MASS MODEL is arrived at, consider again figure 15.7. It was mentioned there that any object moving in a circular orbit about the galactic centre feels a net attraction only from the material within its orbit. Outside this orbit, the attractive forces on the moving body all cancel each other exactly, because of the symmetrical distribution of the matter. Therefore, we reach the important conclusion that the difference of the velocities on two orbits (say orbits 2 and 3 in figure 15.7) depends exclusively on the difference in the amounts of mass encompassed by these orbits (this difference is equal to the mass in region II of figure 15.7). Building a mass model, then, means constructing a series of nested shells of galactic matter, adjusted in such a way that the rotation curve of the model equals the rotation curve of the Galaxy. The adjustment is achieved by varying the shape and the density of the layers of this galactic onion. The number of mass shells taken is very large, so that the model appears smooth, for in reality the Galaxy is continuous instead of layered. Unfortunately, the adjustment in shape and in density leaves us too much freedom: many mass models are possible for one and the same rotation curve, because we have no information about the velocities everywhere in the Galaxy, especially at large distances from the plane and outside the solar orbit. The adjustment in shape must occur between two extreme models, namely the one in which the Galaxy is supposed to be entirely flat, and the one in which it is supposedly spherical. For both extreme cases, and for these only, it can be proven that there is a simple recipe to calculate the mass distribution. If the Galaxy is supposed to be perfectly flat, the mass within a certain radius is proportional to the square of the orbital velocity at that radius. If it is fully spherical, the mass is proportional to the radius times the square of the velocity. In between these extremes, everything is possible (figure 15.11). Our Galaxy lies probably closer to the first extreme.

Once the rotation curve is determined, we have at our disposal a relationship between velocity and distance. If all interstellar gas moved accordingly, it would be possible to obtain the distance to every cloud by a simple measurement of its velocity. As an analogy, consider the Solar System, where the velocity-distance correlation is expressed in Kepler's third law. Imagine that the planets are replaced by thin rings of neutral hydrogen gas. At a given geocentric longitude (the longitude measured from Earth) in the plane of the ecliptic, each imaginary ring of hydrogen which is cut by the line of sight gives an emission line at a certain velocity. When the observations at all longitudes are completed, the height of each hydrogen emission line is plotted against its longitude and its velocity. Each imaginary ring-shaped mock planet shows up as a ridge in this diagram. In observed longitude-velocity diagrams for interstellar gas (figure 15.12), ridges are clearly seen, so there appear to be structures in the disc which are

15.9: *Motion of hydrogen clouds in the plane of the Galaxy. The orbital velocities (black arrows) are seen in projection (open arrows) along the line of sight. On the subcentral circle (dashed) this projected velocity is exactly equal to the real velocity, as shown for a cloud in the innermost orbit. As long as the Sun and the clouds follow circular paths about the galactic centre, all projected velocities in the direction of the centre are zero (see second cloud in the innermost orbit).*

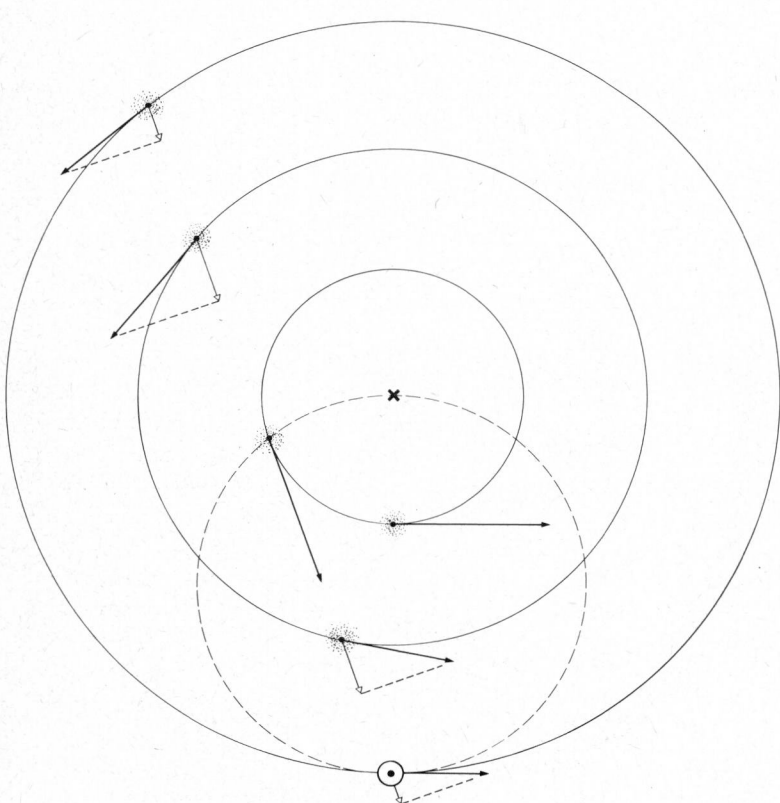

roughly ring-shaped. Closer inspection reveals that these features are probably sections of *spiral arms* (figure 15.12). However, there are many possible reconstructions of the lost third dimension, unless one assumes strictly that the gas clouds in the Galaxy all move in circular orbits. This appears unlikely, especially in the central regions. Therefore there is severe ambiguity in the interpretation of the 21-cm observations of the Galaxy: a line profile observed in a certain direction can be due to masses with radically different velocities and distributions in space.

Uncertainties of this kind have led to controversy over the distribution and dynamics of gas in the Galaxy. Especially near the centre of the system (within 5 kpc from the nucleus, say) problems are severe, because the longitude-velocity diagram of that region is very complicated. The most remarkable aspect of these observations is the presence of gas with non-zero velocities at zero longitude. As figure 15.9 shows, this should not happen if galactic rotation were purely circular. Apparently radial motions in the central region occur systematically over distances of many kiloparsecs. Analysis shows that cloud collisions would destroy these motions well within the lifetime of the Galaxy. Therefore, there must be some agent which has thrown vast amounts of galactic gas out of its regular circular orbit in the plane. Probably, an explosion occurred in the galactic nucleus some 12 million years ago, hurling gaseous clouds of a million solar masses in two

15.10: *Observed rotation curve of our Galaxy (red line), and the basic mean rotation curve derived from it by smoothing (black).*

15.11: *Density and mass distributions in the galactic plane, as derived from the rotation curve, the inferred distributions depend on assumptions about the shape of the Galaxy. Possible extremes: entirely flat (lower bounds of coloured areas) or entirely spherical (upper bounds).*

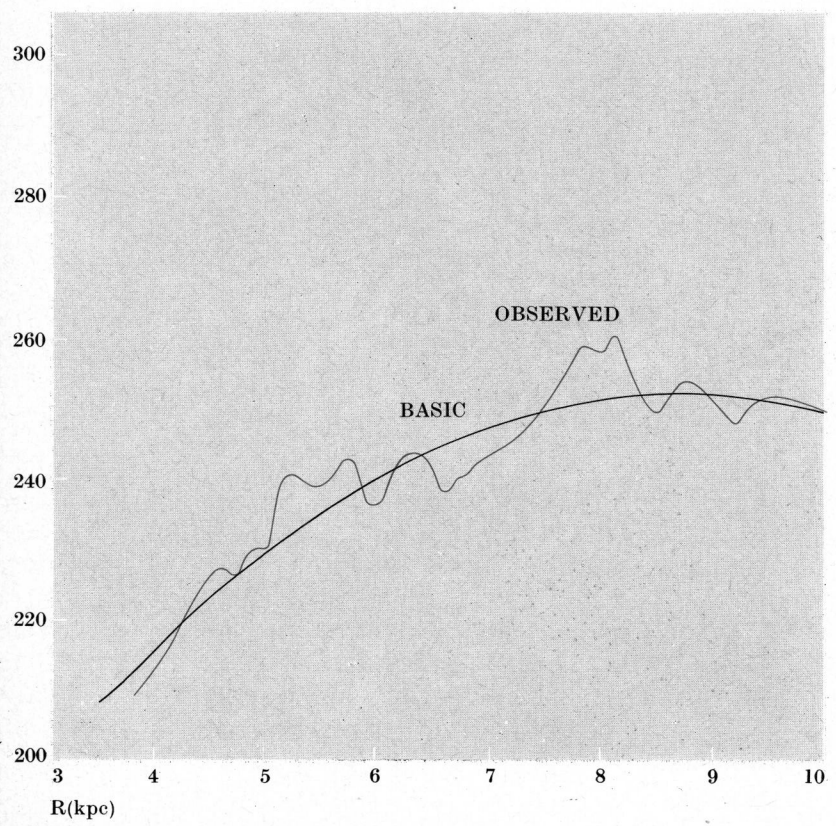

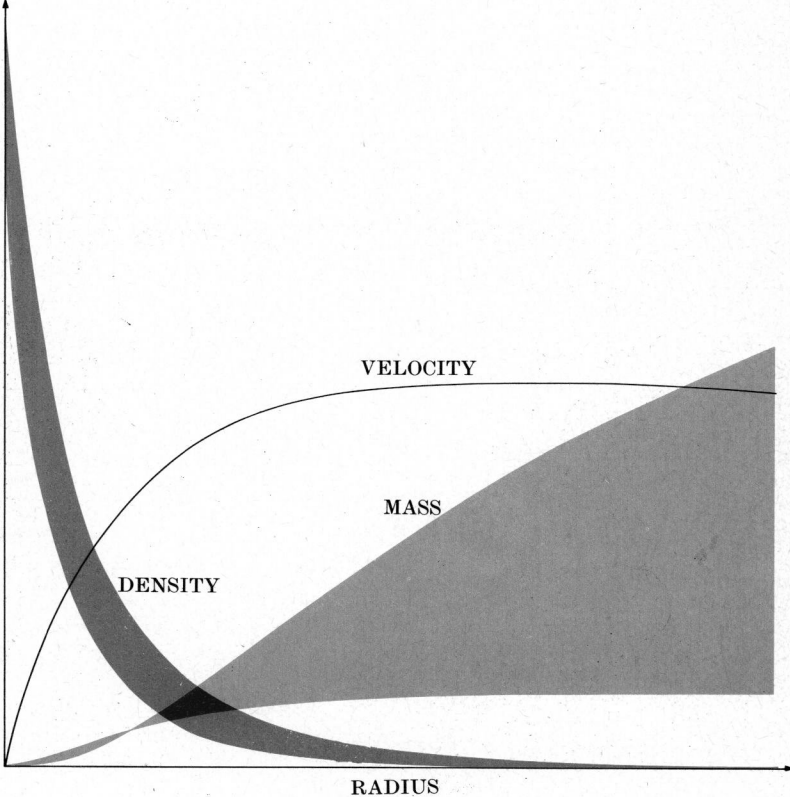

opposite directions inclined about 30° out of the plane. This matter traversed the relatively empty regions of the lower halo and fell back into the plane at about 3.5 kpc from the centre, where it caused the radial motions which we observe today. If not all of the gas has yet fallen down, we expect to see gas with radial velocities outside the plane. Such motions are observed, in support of the notion that the nucleus was recently the scene of violent activity.

The overall strength of the 21-cm signal in the central part of the Galaxy is smaller than elsewhere in the disc. This does not necessarily mean that the centre is empty of gas, because the 21-cm line is only emitted under favourable circumstances. If the temperature is too high (1000 K and higher), not enough atoms are in the correct state to emit the line. If the temperature is too low (below 100 K), most atoms form H_2 molecules and thereby lose the ability to emit the 21-cm line. In hot regions, such as the ionized regions near the galactic nucleus, it becomes feasible to use the radio *recombination lines* instead of the 21-cm line, with the same type of analysis as described above. In cold regions, the H_2 molecule is of no avail, for it is a reluctant emitter. The carbon monoxide molecule, CO, is relatively abundant in cold regions and readily emits a radio spectral line (at 2.6 mm wavelength); these properties make it well suited as a probe for cold clouds, and the spectral lines can be analysed as above.

15.12: *Observed longitude-velocity diagram of our Galaxy (left), and a theoretical interpretation of it (middle) as derived from a spiral-arm model (right). Colours indicate observed intensity of the hydrogen 21-cm line (red = high, violet = low). The red ridges are due to spiral arms (shaded).*

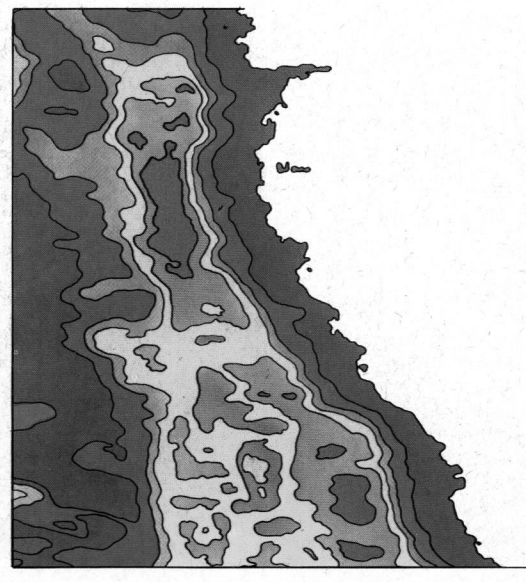

GALACTIC LONGITUDE

RADIAL VELOCITY OF HYDROGEN

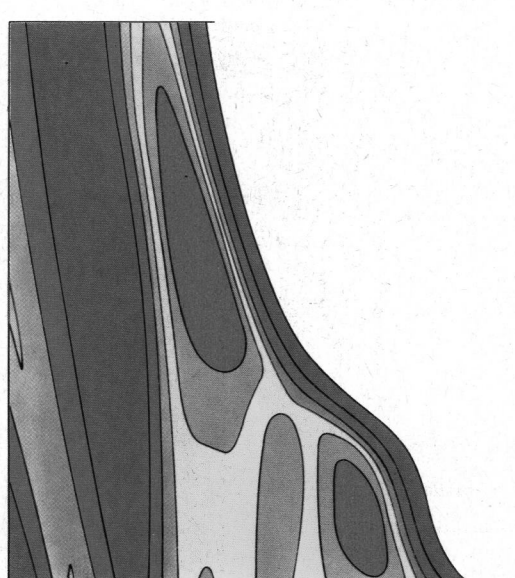

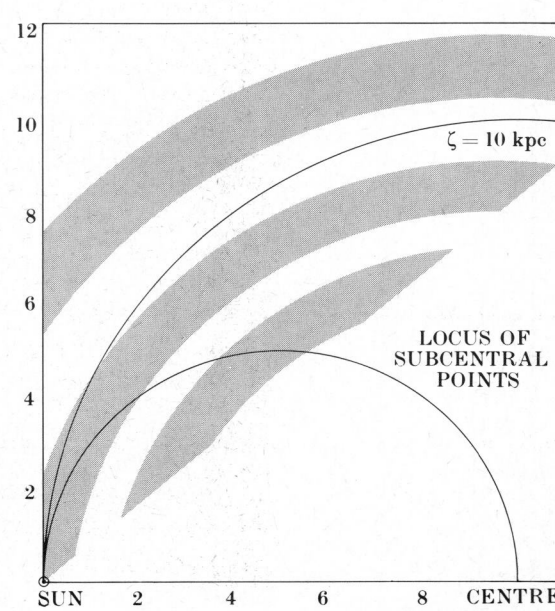

$\zeta = 10$ kpc

LOCUS OF SUBCENTRAL POINTS

SUN   2   4   6   8   CENTRE

A model of the Galaxy

Our Galaxy is a vast system of 100 billion stars, occupying a volume of space with a diameter of 60 kpc. The youngest stars form a disc some 500 pc thick. Half the stars are contained within 1 kpc from the disc, and the oldest stars pervade a roughly spherical halo with 30 kpc radius around the centre of the disc. Between the stars, a tenuous galactic atmosphere of mainly hydrogen and helium extends throughout the plane, to a thickness of about 200 pc. In the disc, spiral arms with a cross section of 400 by 2000 pc are observed to contain very young stars (100 000 yrs or less in age) and H^+ regions. The galactic centre consists of a stellar bulge which is strongly concentrated towards the nuclear region (figure 15.5), containing an active radio source in a flat, rapidly rotating, gaseous nuclear disc. The entire system rotates about an axis through the nucleus at right angles with the plane, and the angular velocity decreases steadily outward. The tangential velocity in the plane first increases and then, after having reached a maximum at 8 kpc, slowly decreases outward. The Sun lies in the galactic plane, 10 kpc from the centre (table 15.2; figure 15.13).

15.13: *Cutaway sketch of our Galaxy. The various components (see also table 15.2) are shown roughly to scale.*

Table 15.2: Gross inventory of our Galaxy

Total numbers

Stars	10^{11}, of which	70% is double or multiple
		15% white dwarfs
		11% O-B type
		41% A-F type
		48% G-M type
Gas	10^5 atoms per cubic metre	
	of which	73% hydrogen
		25% helium
		1% carbon, oxygen, nitrogen, neon
		1% heavier elements
		15% is hot (8000 K)
		85% is cold (100 K)
Assorted objects	planetary nebulae 700 known	
	globular clusters (10^6 stars average)	500
	open clusters (100 stars average)	18 000
	novae 2.2 average per year	
	supernovae 1 per 50 years	
	supernova remnants 1000	
	pulsars 160 detected	
Mass	$1.4 \times 10^{11} M_\odot$	
Colour	like a G2 star (yellowish)	
Absolute magnitude	−20.5 mag	
Radius	25 000 pc (Sun is at 10 000 pc from centre)	
Rotational speed	200 km s^{-1} at the Sun	
Thickness	1000 pc (stellar disc)	
	100 pc (gaseous disc)	
Distance between stars	1 pc average	

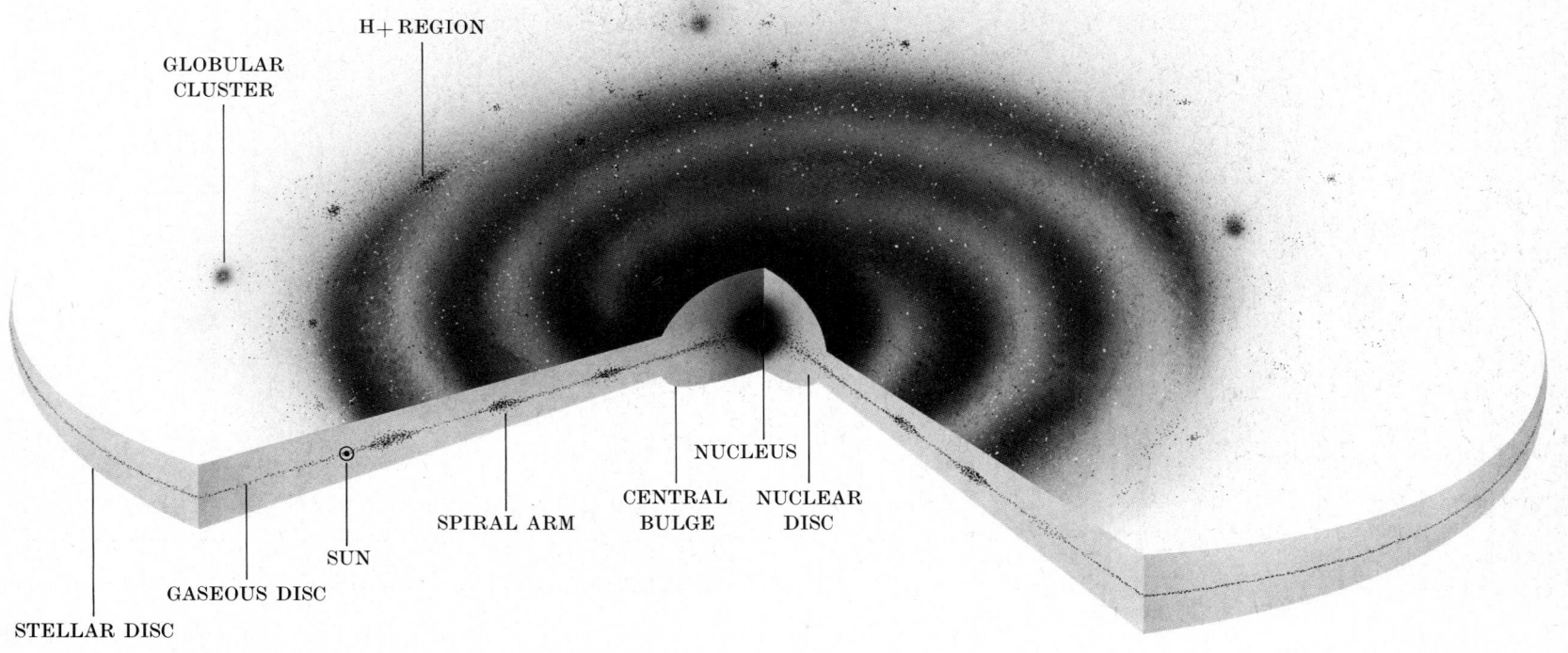

GLOBULAR CLUSTER   H+ REGION

STELLAR DISC

GASEOUS DISC

SUN

SPIRAL ARM

CENTRAL BULGE

NUCLEUS

NUCLEAR DISC

The Local Group of galaxies

To an observer in the southern hemisphere, the existence of galaxies beyond our own should be as evident as the existence of stars beyond the Sun: the two nearest external galaxies, the LARGE and the SMALL MAGELLANIC CLOUD, (LMC and SMC) are readily visible to the naked eye (figures 15.14, 15.15). At their distances of 50 and 60 kpc respectively, they lie certainly (but only just) outside our Galaxy, of which they are satellites. From places on Earth above latitudes 30°N the Magellanic Clouds are always below the horizon. But another external galaxy can be seen, without any telescope, as a fuzzy patch of light about a third of a degree across, in the constellation Andromeda. This object is not a satellite of the Galaxy and it is 690 kpc away. These distances, of course, cannot be determined with the unaided eye; it is only with hindsight that we know the Clouds and the Andromeda Nebula (also known as Messier 31 or M 31) to be extragalactic.

In fact, it was not until the late 1930s that most astronomers admitted the existence of galaxies, similar to our own, elsewhere in space. The distance to the Magellanic Clouds had been known since the investigation, early in this century, of Cepheids in the Clouds. Because M 31 is a dozen times more distant, Cepheids and novae in it were not discovered until the construction of sufficiently large telescopes in the late 1920s. The last doubts as to the extragalactic nature of M 31 were finally dispelled in 1943, when

15.14: *The Large Magellanic Cloud in the light of the hydrogen-alpha line. The diffuse band of the 'bar' runs across the picture. Note the giant H⁺ region 30 Doradus at the upper left end of the bar. (UK Schmidt Telescope Unit, Australia and UK)*

15.15: *The Small Magellanic Cloud in visible light. Note the resolution into individual stars, and the globular cluster at the left. (UK Schmidt Telescope Unit, Australia and UK)*

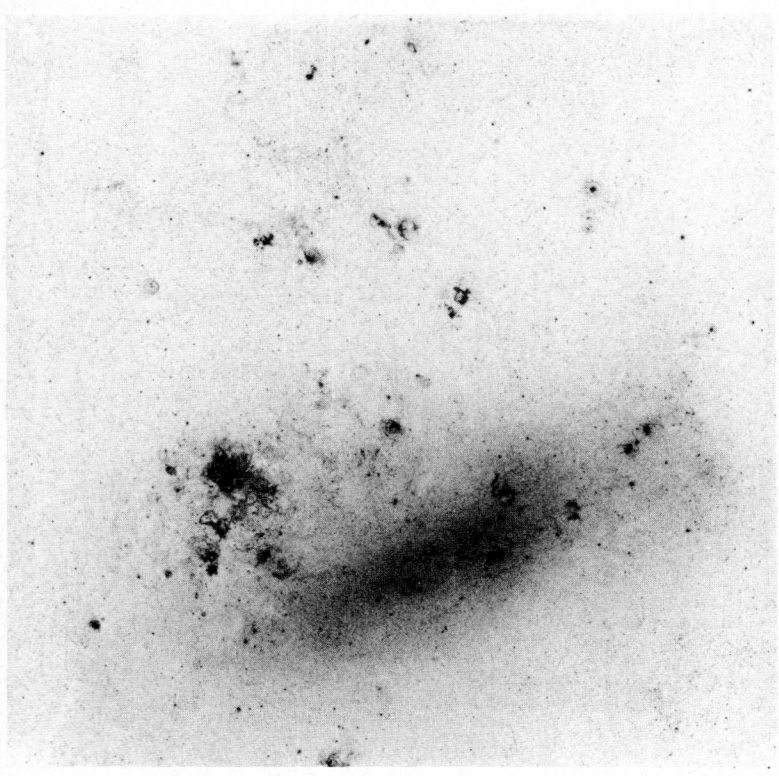

the advent of fast red-sensitive photographic plates allowed the central region of this galaxy to be resolved into individual stars for the first time; their apparent brightnesses left no doubt as to their comparatively great distance. But more than two decades before that time, some observers already believed M31 to be a galaxy like ours; long-exposure photographs (figure 15.16) showed it to be quite unlike any galactic object and also different from the Magellanic Clouds.

A search for nearby galaxies reveals that they occur in small clumps. For example, the Galaxy, the LMC and the SMC are evidently bound together by gravitational attraction. Likewise, the Andromeda Nebula has a number of satellites, some of which even have a nucleus, as is the case with elliptical M32. These clumps, in their turn, form a small swarm of galaxies with 500 kpc radius. No galaxies are found within the immediate vicinity (a thousand kiloparsecs, say) of this swarm, which therefore is considered to be a separate entity, the LOCAL GROUP OF GALAXIES. By the end of 1977, 28 members were known. Some are listed in table 15.3. It is interesting to compare their distribution in space (figure 15.17) to that of the nearest stars (figure 15.2). Note firstly, that the distribu-

tion of the galaxies is evidently less random than is that of the stars. Secondly, we see that the average distance between the dominant galaxies (M 31, the Galaxy and M 33) is only about a dozen galactic diameters, whereas the corresponding distance between stars is some 30 million stellar diameters! Clearly, galaxies are very close neighbours in relation to their size. Also, the Local Group is very diffuse as compared with a galaxy: the average density of matter in the galactic plane, smearing out the stars evenly in space, is about 10 million particles per cubic metre, but the average density in the Local Group, smearing out its galaxies is only about 15 particles m^{-3}.

Because we live in the plane of the Galaxy, galactic structure can be determined only in a roundabout and ambiguous way. Therefore, it is of advantage to study external galaxies, and obviously the nearest ones – the Local Group – are of prime importance for a comparison with the Galaxy. But immediately a problem arises because merely looking at the member galaxies reveals a baffling variety of appearances: tight spirals (M 31 and the Galaxy), an open spiral (M 33), irregulars (LMC and IC 1613), ellipticals with nucleus (M 32), spheroidals without nucleus.

Table 15.3: Local Group of galaxies

Galaxy	Type	Linear diameter (kpc)	Distance (kpc)	Absolute mag.	Rotation velocity (km/s)	Recession velocity (km/s)	Log (mass) ($M_\odot$)
LMC	Ir I	7	52	−18.7	95	+270	10.0
SMC	Ir I	3	63	−16.7		+168	9.3
And neb. M31	Sb	16	670	−21.1	280	−275	11.5
NGC 221	E2	1	660	−16.3		−210	9.5
NGC 205	E5	2	640	−16.3		−240	9.9
Tri neb. M33	Sc	6	730	−18.8	104	−190	10.1
NGC 147	Ep	1	660	−14.8		−250	9
NGC 185	Ep	1	660	−15.2		−300	9
IC 1613	Ir I	1	740	−14.8	60	−240	8.4
NGC 6822	Ir	2	470	−15.6	110	− 40	8.5
Sculptor system	E	1	85	−12			6.5
Fornax system	E	2	170	−13		+ 40	7.3
Leo I system	E4	1	230	−11			6.6
Leo II system	E1	1	230	− 9.5			6.0
Draco system	E		67	− 8.5			5
UMi system	E		67	− 9			5
Maffei I	SO		1000	−20			11.3

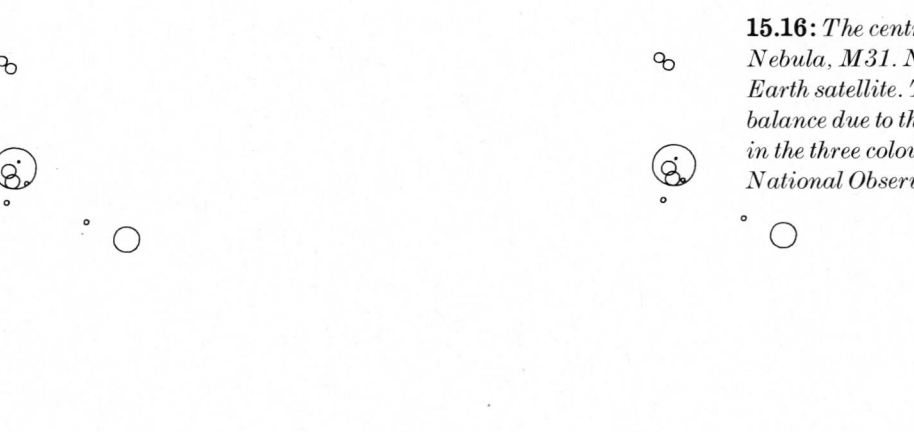

15.16: *The central parts of the Andromeda Nebula, M31. Notice the trail of an artificial Earth satellite. The colours are somewhat off balance due to the unequal reciprocity failures in the three colour emulsions. (Kitt Peak National Observatory,* USA*)*

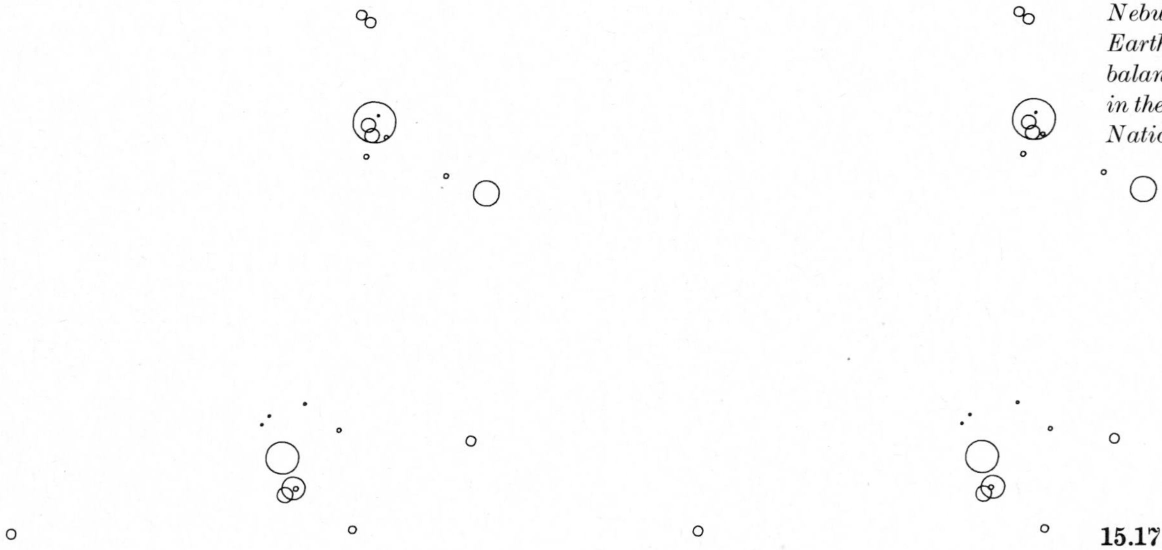

15.17: *Stereogram of the Local Group of Galaxies (to be viewed in the same way as figure 5.2). The surface of the circles is proportional to the magnitude of the objects. Top right is the M31 group and M33. Bottom middle is our Galaxy and the Magellanic Clouds. Bottom left is IC1613.*

The Andromeda Nebula

The ANDROMEDA NEBULA, M31, is a GIANT SPIRAL galaxy. With a mass of 300 billion solar masses ($M_\odot$) it is the most massive member of the Local Group; it is twice the mass of the Galaxy. Its total absolute magnitude $M_v = -21.1$ makes it also the brightest member. In the sky, the optical image measures 75×245 minutes of arc, which at its distance of 690 kpc corresponds to a disc with radius 25 kpc, seen at an inclination of 77°. This rather high inclination makes it difficult to decide whether the numerous ionized hydrogen (H^+) regions, of which about a thousand have been found, form continuous rings or spiral arms. Other spiral tracers show the same difficulty: the *OB associations*, of which there are about 200, mostly in the plane of the galaxy between nine and 18 kpc from the centre, and the Cepheids occur in bands which are so foreshortened that they might be spiral arms or closed circles. By analogy with other spiral galaxies it is generally assumed that M 31 is a spiral galaxy with tightly wound arms. Nearly 200 globular clusters accompany M 31; the furthest are at a distance of 30 kpc from the centre. These findings show that M 31 has stellar populations similar to those of our Galaxy. A remarkable fact is that the properties of the populations of the disc and the lower halo are dependent on the distance to the centre: what we are seeing in these stars is that the amount of elements heavier than helium (mostly carbon, nitrogen and oxygen), increases towards the galactic centre. This indicates that the processing of material through stars, via rapid mass loss and enrichment of the interstellar medium, is larger in the central parts of M 31 than it is in its outskirts. Information of this type is important because it enables astronomers to work out what happened to the galaxy in the past.

The Andromeda Nebula has a nucleus which at optical wavelengths looks like an ellipse with axes of five and eight parsecs, and a very large surface brightness compared with the rest of the galaxy. Its power output in the infrared is about equal to that of the nucleus of our Galaxy, and since most of this radiation is scattered starlight it follows that the structure of the star clouds in both nuclei are very much alike. But in the radio continuum, the galaxy's nucleus is more than 20 times fainter than is Sagittarius A.

Our Galaxy ranks second in the Local Group, and the third most massive member is the TRIANGULUM NEBULA, Messier 33 (M 33; figure 15.18). It is clearly a spiral galaxy with an open-armed pattern, covering 68×40 minutes of arc in the sky, corresponding to a disc with a radius of seven kiloparsecs with an inclination of 50°. It contains a Population II component, with perhaps an increase of heavy elements towards the centre similar to that observed in M 31. But the most striking feature of this galaxy is its very strong Population I component. Even in the nucleus, a bright region of five parsecs diameter, young blue stars and accompanying regions of ionized hydrogen are observed. Along the spiral arms many more

15.18: *The central parts of the Triangulum Nebula, M33. Note the nucleus in the picture centre and the dust lanes along the spiral arms. Several H^+ regions are visible as reddish clumps, especially the giant H^+ region at the top right, which measures about 250 pc across.*

of these are found, sometimes clumped together as in the giant H⁺ region in the northeast (figure 15.18), which measures 270 pc across.

The remaining members of the Local Group are relatively unimportant, for together they comprise only a tenth of the total mass of the group. The galaxies NGC 6822 and IC 1613 resemble the Magellanic Clouds. They all measure a few kiloparsecs across and have masses between 400 million and 6 billion $M_\odot$. Roughly speaking, they contain the selection of objects to be found in the giant spirals, although they do not show the regular plane-halo arrangement of the three dominant galaxies. They look rather irregular, with perhaps a tendency to have an elongated concentration of stars and gas in their central regions. Both populations are present, and there are indications that the amount of heavy elements they contain is rather less than in our Galaxy.

This difference in chemical composition shows that the Clouds have a history rather different from that of our Galaxy. Probably they collapsed more slowly, and their initial star formation was some five times less efficient than was this process in the Galaxy. Therefore the Clouds contain much more gas relative to their total mass. Also, later star formation was less efficient, so that overall the fraction of heavy elements added to the interstellar gas in the Clouds was less than in the Galaxy. This also explains why the SMC is practically free from dust particles, since these form from heavy elements.

Magellanic Clouds

Only the Magellanic Clouds are observed to contain a few *globular clusters*, presumably because the Clouds are more massive than NGC 6822 and IC 1613. *Open clusters* and *associations* are very patchily distributed through all these galaxies, tracing no discernible structure. Some associations are rather large, and the LMC contains a vast clumping of H⁺ regions, called the 30 DORADUS COMPLEX, spanning 3×1 kpc in the sky (figure 15.14). The largest single region of this complex has a diameter of 230 pc, which is only slightly less than the giant cloud of ionized hydrogen in M 33. Imagine what would happen if 30 Doradus were at the distance of the Orion Nebula: it would be visible throughout the day and cast shadows at night! In the LMC, a dozen probable supernova remnants are observed, and both clouds together have about 50 planetary nebulae. As everything in the clouds is at roughly the same distance from the Sun, they are a good collection of objects for internal comparison purposes. This feature, combined with their closeness, makes the Magellanic Clouds very important, notwithstanding their modest mass: a 50-cm telescope can easily do as much work on the Clouds as can a 5-metre telescope on the Andromeda Nebula. A dramatic example of this importance was the discovery, after the turn of the century, of a correlation between the brightness and the period of LMC Cepheid variables; because these all are about equally far (50 kpc) from the Sun, this directly yielded the celebrated *period-luminosity law*. A drawback is that the Magellanic Clouds are not readily comparable with the large spiral galaxies. As has been said, they look very different, and it is found that some of their properties are different too. For example, the gas content of the SMC is about a third of its total mass, and although the gas content is smaller in the LMC, the latter may well have a quarter of its mass in gaseous form. This is about six times as much as the Galaxy or M 31. Also, the dust content of the SMC gas is ten times lower than is that of the Galaxy. These differences have to be taken into account when, for example, we try to obtain information on the rate of star formation.

From our vantage point, we have a convenient overall view of the Clouds, which immediately shows that young stars of the O and B types, ionized hydrogen clouds, dense neutral hydrogen clouds, and late-type supergiants all occur near each other, in small dense clumps. There is about 200 times more gas in them than there is in the form of stars. Most young clumps measure some tens of parsecs across, so the 30 Doradus nebula is an outsized example of such an aggregate. Only weak magnetic fields are observed. There is a possibility that supernova remnants are present in a few associations. Far away from the young clumps old red stars come to the fore, with practically no associated gas. The life history of a star, of which we see here a snapshot, apparently goes as follows. Firstly, tenuous and cold hydrogen clouds with masses of a few thousand solar mass contract by gravitation, slowly at first, but gradually more and more rapidly. Somehow such a cloud breaks up into fragments, and a smaller number of these (half a per cent or so) manage to contract so far that their temperature and density become high enough for nuclear hydrogen fusion to begin. The most massive of these young stars give off so much ultraviolet radiation that the gas around them is ionized and blown away through the newly-formed association. In a few hundred thousand years, these stars may explode as supernovae. Their less massive, and hence more sedate, brethren slowly evolve and move away to mingle with their distant surroundings. Although almost all stages of stellar evolution are presented to us in a picture of the Clouds, we cannot apply any derived results directly to our Galaxy.

The remaining members of the Local Group are rather featureless clumps of stars. They are very numerous (14 out of the 21 members) but have a very small mass, whence they are called DWARF ELLIPTICAL GALAXIES. Typical absolute magnitudes range around $M_v = -10$, and their surface brightness is so low (about 24 mag. per square second of arc), that almost all were discovered in the last 30 years, when photographic plates improved. Even with today's *electronographic detectors*, they are practically undetectable beyond 500 kpc. It is unlikely that this situation will improve until devices are used that automatically remove the unwanted radiation due to the brightness of the night sky, which has a surface brightness about equal to that of a dwarf elliptical galaxy.

Still, there is a striking resemblance in the star content of globulars and dwarf elliptical galaxies: both contain exclusively old Population II stars, with the exception of a very small Population I within a few hundred parsecs of the centres of NGC 185 and NGC 205. No interstellar gas has been observed in any dwarf elliptical, but dust appears to be present in a few patches in the centre of NGC 105 and in two sizeable dust lanes across NGC 205. The masses of dust involved are at most a few hundred solar masses. Although the dust indicates the presence of at least silicon and carbon, the spectra of stars in these galaxies show that they contain less heavy elements than do the dominant spirals.

It should be clear from the above, that the members of the Local Group have much in common. They appear to be built out of the same materials, which is something worth considering; for it is not at all obvious that a cloud of stars that has formed 700 kpc away from us should contain essentially the same kind of stars as are to be found in the solar neighbourhood. The building blocks differ in detail, though, and notably the different abundances of the heavy elements show that not all members of the Local Group have gone through the same past evolution, while all do seem to have approximately the same age.

Dynamics of Local Group galaxies

The distance to external galaxies makes it difficult to resolve them into stars, and hence the motions of their stars have been but poorly studied. In the nearby Magellanic Clouds, such studies are quite possible in principle; in fact, however, in important regions the stars are so close together in the sky that it becomes very difficult to obtain separated spectra from which to determine individual radial velocities. As *planetary nebulae* are relatively rare and obvious objects, they are not subject to this crowding. By a survey of their radial velocities it has been determined that the inner 2 kpc of the LMC rotate like a solid body, revolving once in a few hundred million years. Towards the outer parts, the rotation curve flattens, and at 4 kpc distance from the centre the tangential velocity is about 30 km s^{-1}. The latter value is not the true value because the rotation axis of the LMC is inclined to the line of sight at an angle somewhere between 25° and 45°. This lack of precision leads to an uncertainty in the mass, which probably is about six billion solar masses. In the SMC, no reliable observations of this kind have been made.

The stellar motions in the dwarf elliptical galaxy M 32 have been studied in some detail. Since it is at present out of the question to measure the velocities of individual stars in such a densely-packed faint object, a spectrum had to be taken of the light of all stars together, thus measuring the average Doppler effect. From this it appears that M 32 has a nucleus with a diameter of eight parsecs, which rotates as a solid body with a tangential velocity of about 100 km s^{-1}, thus revolving once in half a million years. Outside this nuclear region, the rotation curve drops rapidly to zero velocity at a radius of 30 pc. This indicates that the outer regions of the centre of M 32 rotate at best very slowly. The mass within 30 pc is 18 million solar masses, equivalent to a mean distance between stars of 1.9 pc.

In a similar way, the nuclear region of the Andromeda Nebula was analysed. It is of interest to present this in detail, because the nuclei of some galaxies are the site of puzzling and highly energetic phenomena. As we have seen in the case of our Galaxy, the central clouds of gas and stars may well be considered as a giant galactic thundercloud, and we should like to know the behaviour and especially the origin of its outbreaks.

Spectra taken through the nucleus with the slit parallel to the major axis of the galaxy yield a strange rotation curve. It rises from zero velocity straight to 200 km s^{-1} at a radius of 200 pc, which implies that this part of the stellar cloud rotates as a solid body with a period of six million years. Between 200 and 400 pc from the nucleus, the curve shows a sharp dip with a minimum of 100 km s^{-1}. Thereafter, it decreases from 200 km s^{-1} at 400 pc to 100 km s^{-1} (perhaps even to 50 km s^{-1}) at 1600 pc.

These two features are very surprising, although the latter effect is not unlike the rapid decrease in the rotation curve of M 32. An explanation for this behaviour might be that the stellar orbits are not on the average circular, but instead show systematic motions away from the galactic nucleus. Indeed, spectra taken with the spectroscope slit parallel to the minor axis show radial motions up to $100\,km\,s^{-1}$. It is an unsolved puzzle how these systematic motions are created and maintained in the central region. The problem is that a star moves once around the nucleus in 10 million years or so, whereas the age of most of these stars is about four billion years: in their lifetime they have orbited the nucleus 400 times, so that all systematic motions present at their formation should have been smeared out long ago.

The motion of the galaxies in the Local Group

As figure 15.17 shows, the least massive members of the Local Group cluster around the dominant galaxies. At a distance of 50 kpc from the centre of a $10^{11}M_\odot$ galaxy, the escape velocity is about $140\,km\,s^{-1}$. Because the dwarf elliptical galaxies in the Local Group move more slowly than this, it appears fairly certain that they are satellite galaxies orbiting in the gravitational field of giant galaxies. Their orbital periods are about 500 million years, so they must have orbited their central galaxies a score of times during the history of the Universe, rather like globular clusters in galactic haloes. Because we observe only a snapshot of the satellites, evidence of orbital motion must be obtained indirectly.

One effect to be considered is that the central galaxy tends to pull stars away from a satellite. The outer stars, which are weakly bound, run the risk of being peeled off, thereby stripping the satellite down to its *tidal radius*. The existence of this tidal limiting has been confirmed by the study of the distribution of light in the ellipticals. Likewise, we may expect gas from the satellite to be torn away by the gravitational pull of the central galaxy. Strong evidence for such an occurrence is the MAGELLANIC STREAM, a huge lane of neutral hydrogen streaming off the Magellanic Clouds across the south galactic pole, presumably to end near our Galaxy (figure 15.19). Along this stream, the gas velocity equals the velocity of the Clouds at that end, and approaches the velocity of our Galaxy at the other. This is additional evidence that the Magellanic Stream is a tidal bridge of gas, caused by the gravitational interaction between the Galaxy and the Magellanic Clouds in their orbit. Theoretical calculations confirm that long narrow bridges can be formed between a satellite and its central galaxy (figure 16.24). Observations of the neutral hydrogen in the outer parts of our Galaxy show that the galactic plane is warped, possibly as much as 1 kpc at a radius of 15 kpc. This might be due to the disturbing effect of the Magellanic Clouds. A similar effect can explain the warp in the plane of M 33, although this galaxy has no obvious satellites which can be held responsible for the distortion.

Another phenomenon which is possibly connected with the interaction between the Galaxy and its satellites is the existence of HIGH-VELOCITY CLOUDS of neutral hydrogen. These are found in many different places in the sky, measure a few degrees across, and move very rapidly: some towards the Sun with maximum velocity of about $200\,km\,s^{-1}$, some away with half that speed. As we have seen, typical velocities far away from the Galaxy do not nearly span a range of $300\,km\,s^{-1}$! It appears likely, therefore, that the high-velocity clouds are not very distant from the Sun, and that they arise from an interaction between intergalactic gas and the upper reaches of the galactic atmosphere. The origin of the infalling gas could be a tidal interaction between the Galaxy and the Magellanic Clouds, which are very rich in gas.

The observation of satellite motions makes it possible to estimate the masses of the central galaxies, just as the mass of the Sun can be derived from planetary motions. Likewise, the average positions and velocities of globular clusters can be used to measure galactic masses. In general, the masses thus obtained agree well with those found from the analysis of the rotation curves.

The satellite galaxies have almost no influence on the large-scale motions in the Local Group because of their small masses. The only really important galaxies are M 31, the Galaxy and M 33. Our Galaxy moves with respect to the centre of mass of the Local Group with a velocity of about $170\,km\,s^{-1}$ along a line through $l=10°$, $b=0°$. The radial velocities of M 31 and M 33, after correction for this motion, are -68 and $-11\,km\,s^{-1}$, respectively. The absolute average velocity of the dominant members of the Local Group is therefore $83\,km\,s^{-1}$ or more, because motions at right angles to the line of sight cannot as yet be measured. The escape velocity at 350 kpc from the Galaxy is only $60\,km\,s^{-1}$, so that one might conclude that the three most massive galaxies move too rapidly to be bound to each other by gravitation. Then the existence of the Local Group would be merely due to chance. However, there is evidence that the Group is a bound unit. Firstly, there are no comparable massive galaxies nearby for at least 1000 kpc around. Secondly, small groups of galaxies like ours are very common in the Universe; it appears unlikely that these are together by chance only, rather than being bound by mutual gravitational attraction.

This is a real poser: if the Local Group is gravitationally bound, how can it be that its members move so rapidly? The galaxies we see around us do not contribute enough mass to prevent the dissolution of the Local Group that these velocities would imply. The only solution appears to be, that there must be more matter in the Group than we can readily observe. By itself, this is not very difficult to accept, because only the matter which is concentrated in stars, or in highly energetic gas streams like supernova remnants, emits a substantial amount of radiation for a given amount of mass. In other words, the mass-to-luminosity ratio of stars and the like is probably very much smaller than is that ratio for matter in general. As we have seen in the discussion of rotation curves, the attraction which a particle in an orbit experiences is proportional to the mass encompassed by that orbit. Classical mechanics tells us that the escape velocity is proportional to the square root of the mass within the orbit. Therefore, in order to make the escape velocity exceed $120\,km\,s^{-1}$, which is about what is needed to bind the Local Group together, the total mass of the Group must be at least four times the mass observed in the galaxies.

If this is the solution of the problem, in what form could the material be? The number of possibilities is practically infinite. Almost any dense object which is not of itself luminous would escape detection. For example, the HIDDEN MASS (also called MISS-ING MASS) might be in the form of football-size rocks, but given the enormous amount of equally possible alternatives (e.g. golfball-size rocks) it is not very fruitful to pursue the point. It is of more interest to determine the distribution in space of the hidden matter. There are two alternatives. Either the mass is present somewhere in the galaxies, more specifically in an extended halo, or it pervades the whole of the Local Group as an INTERGALACTIC MEDIUM. The second possibility appears slightly more probable than does the first, because it is somewhat difficult to reconcile the presence of a massive halo with the observations of the motions of globular clusters and satellite galaxies. But it is not at present known with certainty which solution is correct.

The galaxies of the Local Group individually, or, if the Group is gravitationally bound, as a unit, move under the influence of more distant galaxies and groups of galaxies. The nearest of these are a few million parsecs away from our Galaxy. On a cosmic scale, this is not very far: only a hundred galactic diameters. Some of the problems we have encountered here, do also occur on this larger scale of organization.

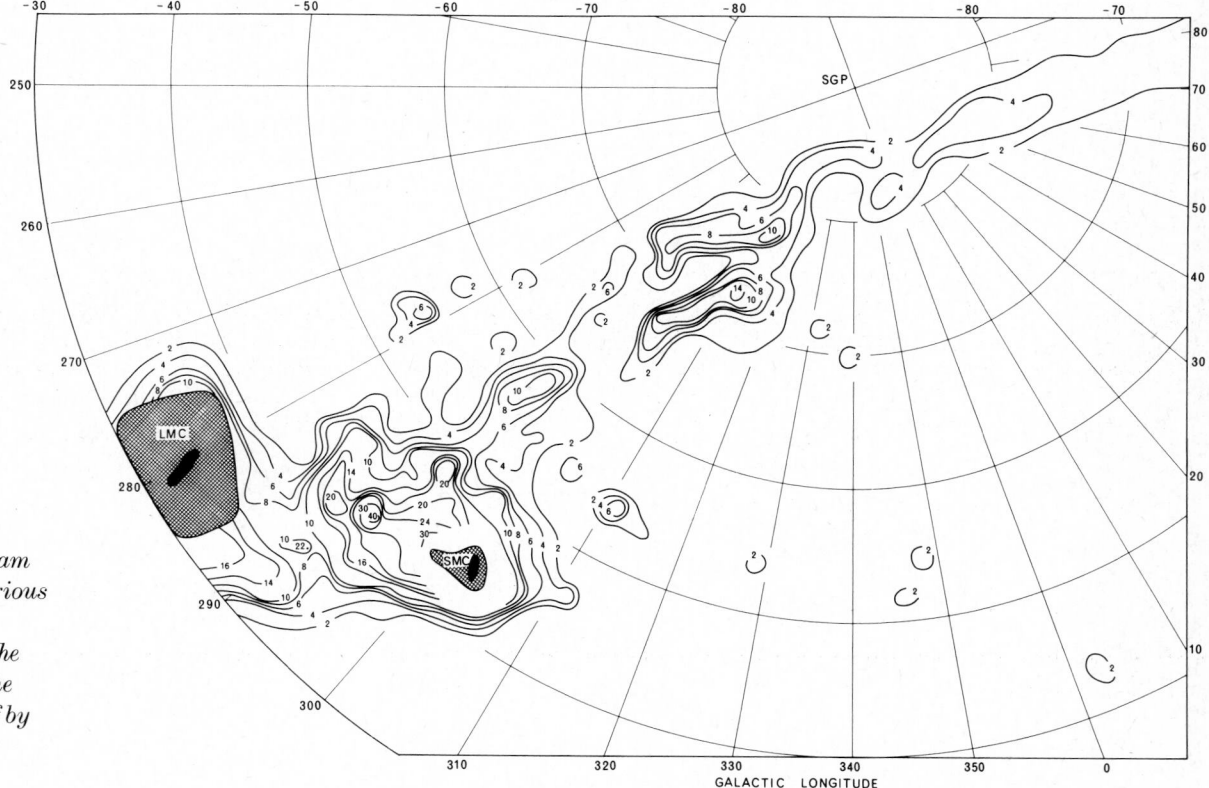

15.19: *Radio maps of the Magellanic Stream in the 21-cm line. Top: positions of the various clouds in the Stream, projected in galactic coordinates. Right: more detailed view of the Stream around the Magellanic Clouds. The hydrogen stream was probably stripped off by the tidal action of our Galaxy.*

16. The nature of normal galaxies

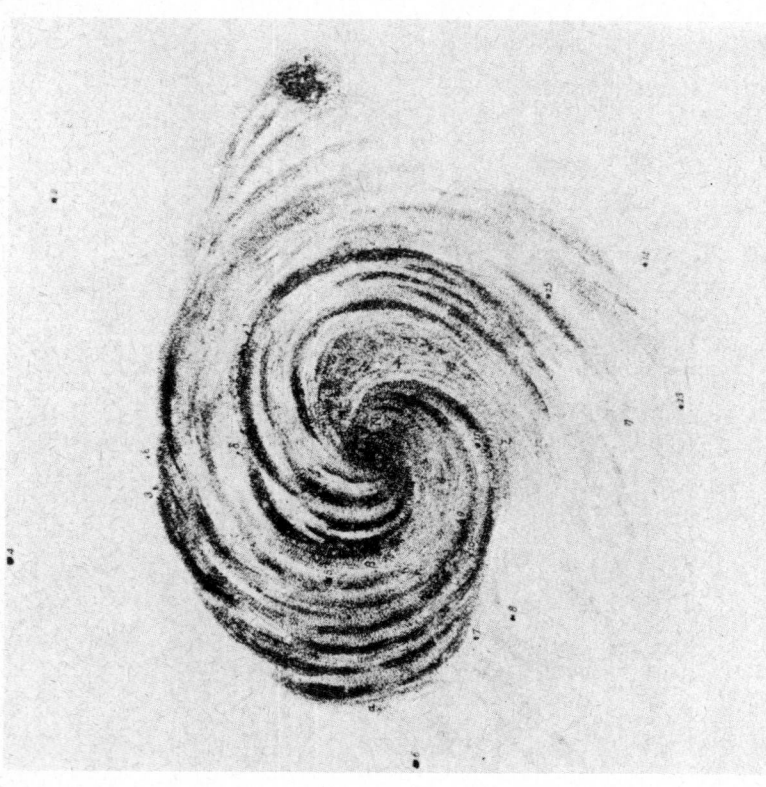

16.1: *Earliest sketch of the spiral galaxy M51 in Canes Venatici. The object at the top is now known to be an elliptical galaxy passing by, distorting the outer parts of the spiral galaxy by gravitational tidal action (see figures 16.13 and 16.25).*

Beyond our Galaxy

Just as Earth is not the only planet in the Solar System, and just as our Sun is not the only star in the Galaxy, so our Galaxy is not the only one in the Universe. But it was only 50 years ago that this important fact was established, even although SPIRAL NEBULAE – distant galaxies like our own – had been known since the end of the eighteenth century (figure 16.1). Throughout the nineteenth century, theoretical astronomers worked on the possible extent of the material Universe; however, the establishment of some nebulae as extragalactic systems was wholly a feat of modern observational astronomy. The realization that there are other galaxies far beyond the Milky Way proceeded apace with the technology of optical observation, and it provides a fascinating success story of recent astronomy.

By the beginning of the twentieth century, work with the existing refracting telescopes had led to the listing of some 8000 nebulae, most of which were known to belong to our immediate neighbourhood since they were *emission* or *reflection nebulae* associated with bright stars; the Orion Nebula (figure 14.13) is an example of an emission nebula. But the observers found that some were rather different because of their colour and shape: they were whiter, emitting a smaller fraction of their light in the red Hα line than do the galactic nebulae, and many possessed the distinctive spiral shape shown in figure 16.1.

In 1917 the discovery of an exploding star (now known to have been a *supernova*) in the nebula NGC 6946 prompted a search for stellar outbursts in other nebulae. Within a few years, astronomers found 22 in the Andromeda Nebula, M 31. Comparison of the stars' peak apparent magnitudes with the peak absolute magnitude of galactic *novae* (at that time thought to be −4 mag) put M 31 at a distance of 200 kiloparsecs, a good 10 times the estimated diameter of our Galaxy. But this method of distance measurement did not prove the extragalactic nature of the Andromeda Nebula beyond all doubt, for one of the 22 exploding stars was fully 12 magnitudes brighter at its peak than were any of the others: we now know that a supernova caused the most brilliant outburst, whereas the others were due to ordinary novae. Therefore observers sought further evidence to strengthen the extragalactic hypothesis, and this was found when they used large telescopes and new photographic emulsions to resolve M 31 and M 33 (Triangulum Nebula) into individual stars. Comparison of these with galactic stars showed M 33 to be 300 kpc away from the Sun, and therefore extragalactic. But the evidence was denied by some observers who maintained that the images of the individual stars were partially resolved and were therefore clouds, which should not be compared to galactic stars.

The interpretation of many astronomical observations hinges on distance determination, and the final resolution of the problem of the nebulae yielded to this method. The spiral nebulae were once and for all proven to be extragalactic in 1924 when the analysis of *Cepheid variables* in M 31, M 33 and NGC 6822 showed that their distances far exceed the diameter of our Galaxy. Even so, these three external galaxies are relatively near by: they are in fact members of the *Local Group*.

In addition to the above methods, there are other ways to determine the distances of galaxies. One possibility is to use the fact that ionized hydrogen (H⁺) regions are normally smaller than 200 pc diameter; thus, by determining the apparent diameters of the H⁺ regions in a galaxy, its distance can be estimated. For example, if such a diameter were 5 arc sec, then the galaxy would be 8 Mpc away. Another method is to measure the apparent brightness of an entire galaxy and to compare it with that of a similar galaxy with known distance. On the assumption that similar-looking galaxies have similar absolute magnitudes, this comparison gives a *distance modulus*. Both methods are imprecise because of the enormous differences in the size and composition of galaxies.

Nearby galaxies

Soon after the establishment of spiral nebulae as galaxies beyond our own, practical astronomers put a major effort into the determination of their optical apparent luminosities, colours, angular sizes, radial velocities, distances and shapes. From these data, galaxies appear to be the most massive single concentrations of stars known in the Universe. This deduction should not be taken to mean that they are in fact the most massive, or in any sense, the most important, for there are many ways in which matter can escape detection. Matter that is not of itself sufficiently luminous can be found only with difficulty, for example by the scattering or absorption it causes to radiation from elsewhere. Furthermore, luminous matter can be virtually undetectable when it is spread out over such a large area as to yield a low surface brightness. In the latter case the light from the object may be drowned by the night sky, by the *zodiacal light* or by the *galactic background*. Only gravitation reveals the presence of all matter in the Universe, but this very indirect method of detection gives as yet highly uncertain results. Consequently all one may say is that galaxies are very conspicuous components of the Universe, but equally impressive amounts of matter could be completely invisible to our telescopes.

In order to get some feeling for the appearance of these components, let us inspect a part of a typical photograph of the night sky (figure 16.2). With a little practice, images that are starlike can be distinguished from fuzzy ones. The latter are almost exclusively galaxies. Most of them look rather small and faint because of the great distances separating them from us: very faint galaxies have been recognized out to ten billion parsecs. Nearby ones, however, usually appear as spectacular disc-like systems of stars, gas and dust (figure 15.16) or large spheroidal concentrations of stars.

16.2: *Galaxies and stars. Centre: photograph in blue light of a few square arc seconds of the sky. Left: same picture with the galaxies removed. Right: same picture with the stars removed.*

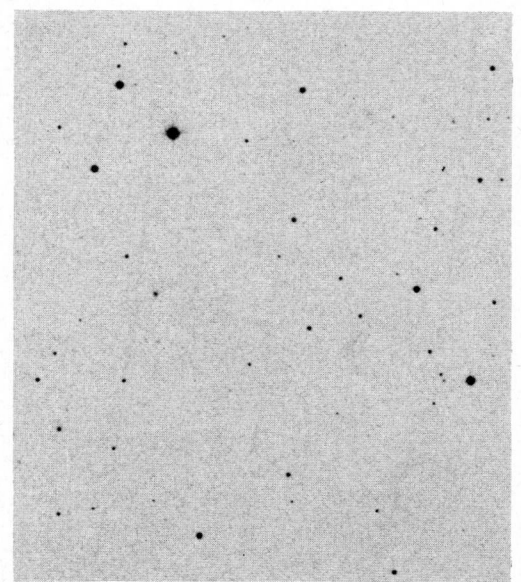
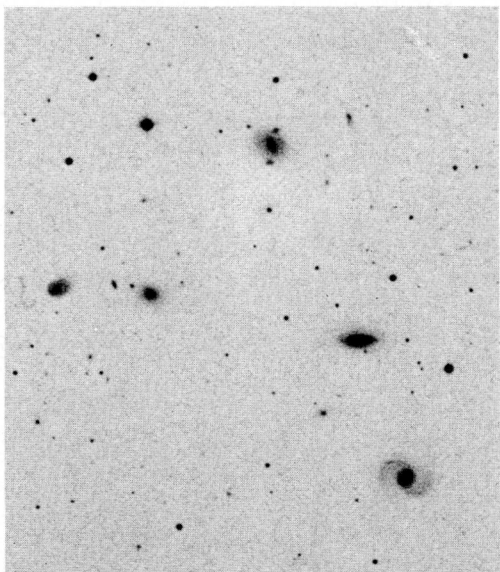
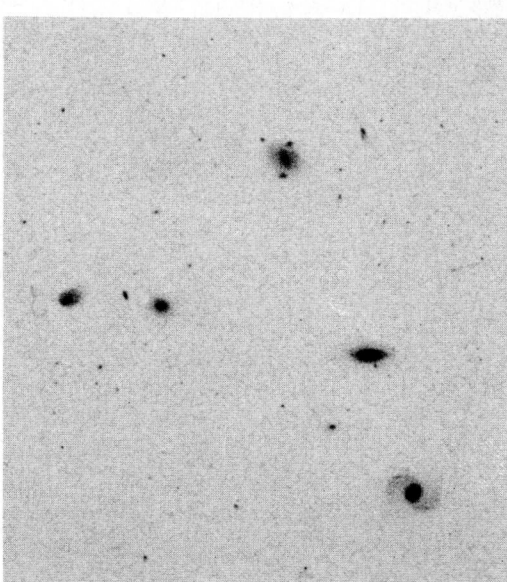

Apart from occasional patches radiating the blue continuum and red hydrogen-alpha line emission, characteristic of massive young stars and their attendant regions of ionized hydrogen, the predominant colour of galaxies is yellowish. The *colour index* B–V lies usually between 0.6 and 1.0, and most probably near 0.8 corresponding to stars of late G type. (These stars are slightly yellower than the Sun.)

The sizes of galaxies have a much larger range than do their colours: diameters lie between approximately two and 50 kpc. The smallest galaxies are probably the most numerous, although our knowledge of these midget systems is severely limited by the selection effects (difficulty of detection) mentioned above. But the total amount of mass contained in these DWARF GALAXIES is quite negligible, since their individual mass is only a few hundred million solar masses. At the other end of the mass range, the GIANT GALAXIES with masses up to $10^{13} M_\odot$ are extremely rare (less than one per million cubic megaparsec). Galaxies of intermediate size, having a diameter of about 20 kpc and a mass of about 50 billion solar masses, are sufficiently numerous (one per 50 cubic megaparsec) to make up most of the luminous matter in the Universe. Although individual galaxies are very massive, the mean density of visible matter in the Universe is almost incredibly tiny. If all the matter in galaxies were smeared out uniformly in space, the resulting mass density would be $2 \times 10^{-28}\,\mathrm{kg\,m^{-3}}$; that is equivalent to one atom per ten cubic metres. This is ten million times less than

16.3: *The Sa galaxy M 104, known as the Sombrero Nebula. Notice the prominent dust band in the plane of the galaxy, and the large central bulge. On close inspection, some globular clusters are visible in the halo. (David Dunlap Observatory, Canada)*

16.4: *The giant elliptical galaxy M 87 in Virgo. This galaxy lies in the middle of the Virgo cluster of galaxies: notice the neighbours. Small fuzzy patches in the outskirts of M 87 are globular clusters. Compare this long-exposure photograph with figure 18.7. (David Dunlap Observatory, Canada)*

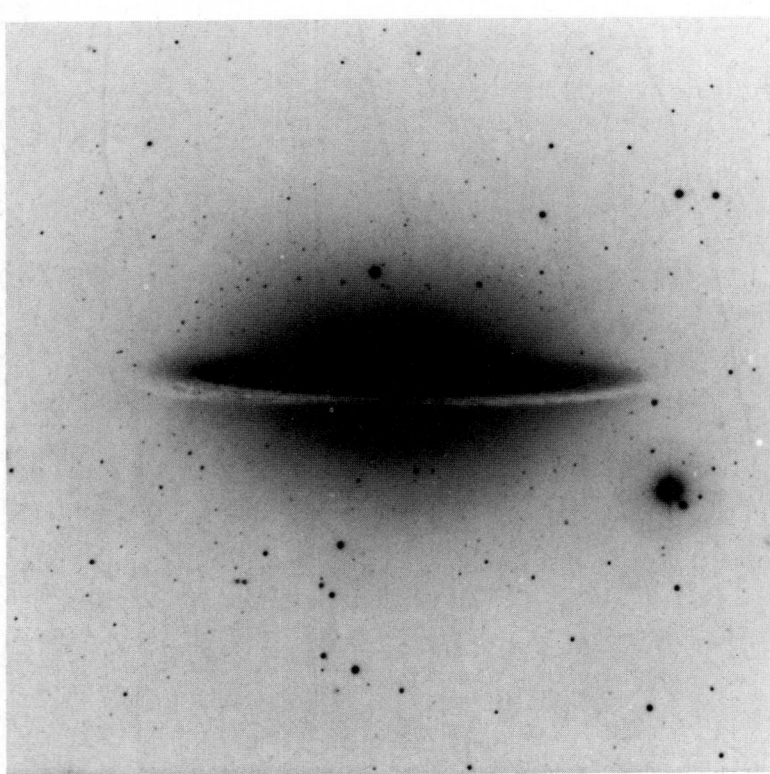
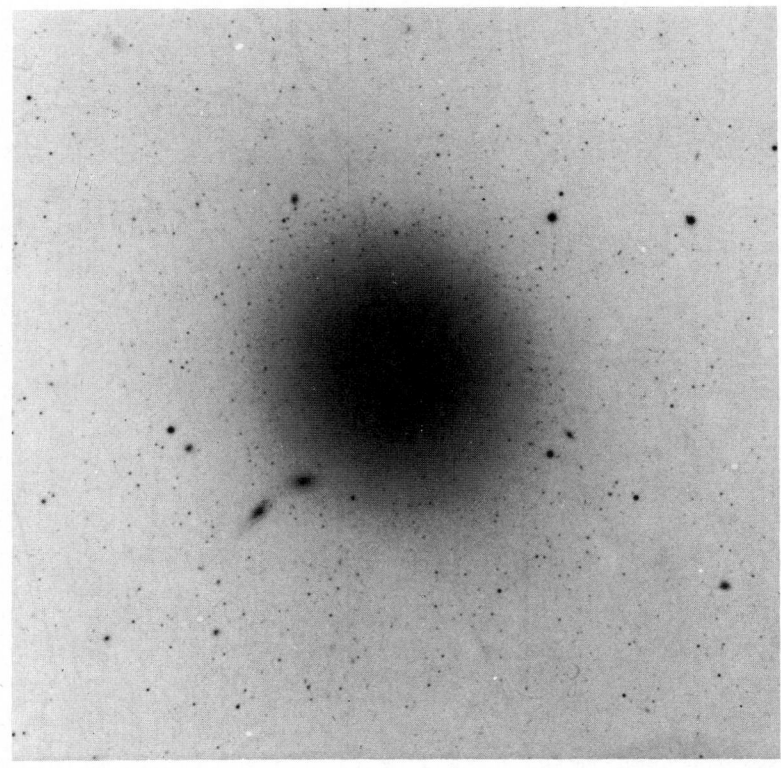

the density of the *interstellar medium*. If the Moon were expanded to the average cosmic density, it would fill a sphere around the Sun encompassing the nearest 10 stars!

The mean distance between two intermediate-sized galaxies is about three megaparsecs, or 150 galaxy diameters. Therefore, galaxies are rather near neighbours: in everyday terms we can picture them, on the average, as being about as far apart as are the inhabitants of a country village. For comparison, the mean distance between stars in the plane of our Galaxy is 30 million stellar diameters. Because of their relatively small mutual distances, we may expect to find a sizeable number of galaxies near ours.

Let us, therefore, look at a sample of neighbouring galaxies. As it turns out, the nearest ones, the Magellanic Clouds, have less than average masses and are so close (about 60 kpc) as to be satellites of our Galaxy. The nearest truly external large galaxy is the Andromeda Nebula (figure 15.16): its distance is only 690 kpc. Our Galaxy is part of a local concentration of galaxies, the *Local Group*.

Another nearby galaxy is M 87, near the northernmost boundary of Virgo. This one (figure 16.4) looks entirely different from M 81. The angular diameter is four minutes of arc, apparent magnitude 10.7, colour index 0.97 (early K-type), distance 13 Mpc, linear diameter 15 kpc. Outside this average diameter, it has an extensive halo, which contains so many stars that M 87 is the most massive galaxy known: about $10^{13} M_\odot$. Its shape might lead one to believe that it is an outsized *globular cluster*, but in reality the galaxy itself contains a very large number of true globular clusters (figure 16.4).

The galaxy M 104, near the southern edge of Virgo, is different again (figure 16.3). The central part looks like a spheroidal cloud of stars with a colour index 0.98; but the galaxy also contains a disc terminating in a prominent dust ring with a diameter of seven minutes, which at its distance of 12 Mpc corresponds to 24 kpc. The central bulge contains numerous resolved patches, which are globular clusters caught in snapshot on their 100 million-year orbit in the galaxy's halo. The mass of M 104 is probably $5 \times 10^{11} M_\odot$, slightly more than M 31.

The galaxy known as NGC 3992, near the star γ Ursae Majoris, represents yet another structural variety. Spiral arms are seen out to a diameter of seven minutes, winding inwards until, at about 1.5 arc minutes from the centre, they abruptly stop. Within that region a bar-like structure extends on opposite sides of the galaxy's nucleus. This central region has a linear diameter of 15 kpc, for the distance of the galaxy is probably about 17 Mpc. NGC 3992 is slightly whiter than any of the preceding galaxies (B–V = 0.85, like a late G-type star), whereas its mass is roughly equal to that of our Galaxy. The last galaxy in this series of examples is NGC 4449 (figure 16.5), near the eastern border of the constellation Canes Venatici. Although its size is quite ordinary (apparent magnitude 10.3, mass $5 \times 10^{10} M_\odot$, diameter 12 kpc for a distance of 8 Mpc), its shape is nowhere near as regular as any of the other examples. Also, its colour is very much bluer; the B–V index is 0.38, like an early F-type star. This is due to the blue light contributed by the relatively large number of regions of ionized hydrogen.

16.5: *The irregular galaxy NGC4449. Notice the unorganized structure and the large, knotty regions of ionized hydrogen (this galaxy is too far away for individual stars to be seen: bright dots are H⁺ regions).*
(Yerkes Observatory, USA)

The stellar contents of galaxies

Apparently, there is great variation among galaxies. In order to understand their properties, and ultimately their history, it is of prime importance to search carefully for common features to distinguish the typical from the incidental. The first such feature is indicated by the colour of galaxies: yellowish, approximately corresponding to *black-body radiation* with a temperature of 5000 K. At first glance, this suggests that all galaxies are stellar systems consisting mainly of ordinary stars more or less like the Sun. Especially luminous individual stars are observable in nearby galaxies. For example, the apparent magnitude of a star in M31 with absolute magnitude $M_v = 0$ would be about 24, so that only *main-sequence stars* with a spectral type hotter than B5, or *giants* more luminous than K0 type can be seen individually.

So a typical galaxy is primarily a vast cloud of stars, and this raises the question: of what kind of stars are galaxies made? The observation of giant stars emphasizes a complication which makes this question a difficult one to answer: it is quite possible that the light received from a galaxy is mainly emitted by only a few, but nevertheless very luminous, giants or supergiants, whereas the bulk of the mass consists of dwarf stars whose contribution to the galaxy's luminosity is small. At second glance, therefore, the colour alone of a galaxy gives rather poor information about the stellar make-up of the galaxy. Evidently, the whole spectrum of the system must be considered, not merely the colour indicators. There are two ways in which attempts are made to find the stellar constitution of a galaxy; theorists speak of making a POPULATION MODEL or an EVOLUTIONARY MODEL, and we shall look at these in turn.

A population model is a recipe for making a concoction of stars which looks as much like a galaxy as possible. The prescription is to observe the galaxy's spectrum in as many narrow wavelength bands as observational constraints allow (say 30). The next step is to take a *Hertzsprung-Russell diagram* and divide it into the same number of boxes (also 30, in this example) as there are spectral points available. The final step is to put such a number of stars into each box that they together reproduce the galaxy's spectrum (figure 16.6). Although the contribution of faint dwarf stars remains highly uncertain, this method gives a reasonable amount of insight into the composition of bright galaxies (table 16.1). An important result obtained is that galaxies have a composition in their outskirts which differs from that in the centre. This information indicates that the abundances of heavy elements (all those heavier than helium) steadily increases towards the inner parts of the galaxy. These particular elements are formed by nuclear reactions in the cores of stars and in stellar explosions; they are subsequently thrown into the interstellar medium if a star containing them explodes. Therefore, the observed COMPOSITION GRADIENT indicates three possibilities: either (i) the original population of stars near the centre contained a larger proportion of massive stars, thus giving rise to more stellar explosions; or (ii) material rich in heavy elements has accumulated in the galaxy's centre, there forming new stars; or (iii) the rate of star formation (and consequently also of

star explosions) increases towards the centre.

The more ambitious evolutionary model tries to produce a galaxy by starting with a collection of stars all on the *zero-age main sequence*, that is stars newly formed, and then letting every star run along its *evolutionary track*. Within a few hundred million years, the most massive stars will have ended their life by explosion, those of intermediate mass ($2 M_\odot$, say) have evolved into giants, and the low-mass stars are still close to the main sequence (figure 16.7). By suitable adjustment of the initial stellar population, model galaxies like those observed can be obtained. This adjustment is somewhat arbitrary, of course, but evolutionary models have the advantage that they can be tested against observations of galaxies at large distances, which are presumably in an earlier stage of their evolution. Also, evolutionary models are useful for studying abundance gradients, because the birth of new stars may be included as an additional feature, so that the chemical evolution of a galaxy can be modelled.

From a determination of the stellar content of the brighter part of a galaxy by the above methods, it appears that most of the stars are dwarfs about 10^{10} years old. Most of the light of a galaxy is due to giant stars, whereas dwarfs make up most of the mass. A small number of massive stars with ages less than 100 000 years are usually present too; these young blue stars are so luminous as to be highly conspicuous. Other spiral galaxies contain basically the same *stellar populations* as does our Galaxy: young (Population I)

16.1: Population model for M31

Spectral type	Percentage of mass	Percentage of V light
G0V–G4V	0.77	11.56
G5V–K0V	0.76	5.10
K1V–K2V	0.40	2.29
K3V–K4V	0.78	3.07
K5V–K7V	1.12	1.24
M0V–M2V	0.73	0.27
M3V–M4V	10.3	1.09
M5V–M6V	4.6	0.15
M7V	69.4	1.74
M8V	10.2	0.03
G0IV–G4IV	0.35	11.88
G5IV–G9IV	0.26	8.79
SMR K0–K1IV	0.13	6.74
SMR K2 III–IV	0.12	26.57
SMR K3 III	0.03	12.23
SMR K4–5 III	0.01	5.98
M5III–M6III	0.003	1.22

Note: SMR = super-metal-rich stars.

and old (Population II). The proportions in which these populations occur vary from one galaxy to another. Their distribution is discussed below (see also table 15.1). Among the stars in other galaxies, many types of special stars known in the Milky Way are also found, such as *novae*, *supernovae* and *Cepheid variables*. The latter are especially important as distance indicators, but differences in composition between galaxies make a careful calibration necessary.

Not all stars are evenly distributed over a galaxy; there exist clusters and associations in addition to the general distribution. *Open clusters* and *OB associations* are Population I objects, and are usually quite prominent because of the high luminosity of their massive young members (figure 16.7). *Globular clusters* are Population II objects, and can be seen as fuzzy patches far into the haloes of nearby galaxies. Globular clusters are useful distance indicators because they can be readily identified and their apparent magnitudes can be compared with globular clusters of known distance close to the Milky Way. Also, they are important as probes of a galaxy's gravitational field: their velocities are proportional to the square root of the mass within their orbit, so that velocity measurements yield an estimate of the mass distribution in a galaxy. This method is especially instructive because it can serve to detect indirectly the presence of matter with low luminosity in a galaxy's outskirts. Since most of the light of a galaxy comes from giant stars, enormous numbers of faint dwarfs could exist in the halo without being detected optically. However, mass determinations from the velocities of globular clusters agree with those obtained by other means, and speak against but do not quite exclude the existence of a large amount of hidden mass in galactic haloes.

As we have seen, all galaxies contain stars, and most contain gas and dust, but the total mass of the latter is small compared with the stellar mass. Also, the gas content differs enormously from one galaxy to another. Some, like M 87 (figure 16.4), are observed to contain gas in their innermost regions only, and even that is only a tiny percentage of the central mass. Others, like NGC 4449 (figure 16.5) have gas distributed throughout the system, sometimes amounting to 25 per cent of the total mass. Dust is observable directly only in those galaxies of which about one per cent or more of the mass is in the form of gas (figures 15.16 and 16.5). Indirectly, its presence can be inferred from the infrared radiation that some galaxies emit.

Gas in a galaxy is detected by means of *emission lines* in its spectrum. In the optical part of the spectrum, these lines are primarily due to atoms of hydrogen, helium, nitrogen, oxygen and neon. These, and carbon which is difficult to observe spectroscopically, are precisely the elements that are most abundantly generated by the nuclear reactions in stellar cores. Therefore a measurement of the relative amounts of these elements can give valuable information about the history of a galaxy. The *abundances* of the elements are determined from a comparison of their line strengths, just as in galactic nebulae. To radiate the emission lines, the gas must be *excited* by atomic collisions or by radiation. Because the gas is very tenuous (typically a few million atoms per cubic metre, and often considerably less), the collision frequency is low, and excitation usually occurs near bright young stars. Therefore, abundance determinations are possible in regions of ionized hydrogen only. Because these *ionized hydrogen regions* occur only in a small number of places in certain special kinds of galaxy, our knowledge of the composition of galactic interstellar matter is rather incomplete. It turns out that the deduced abundances are similar to those in the neighbourhood of the Sun. For example, the ratio of the number of helium atoms to the number of hydrogen atoms in NGC 4449 (figure 16.5) is 0.088, and 0.101 in the Orion nebula. The abundance ratios for the heavier elements, carbon, oxygen, nitrogen and neon with respect to hydrogen, show larger differences: the mean value is about a thousandth, but deviations with a factor of two or three do occur. The abundance of deuterium cannot yet be determined with any confidence, because its spectral lines are too close to those of ordinary hydrogen. This is unfortunate, for the deuterium content of galaxies is a significant quantity in cosmology.

Observations of abundances in various parts of galaxies indicate that the gas, like the stars, shows an abundance gradient: in the ionized hydrogen regions nearest the centre of a galaxy, elements heavier than helium are on the average twice as abundant as they are in the outermost ionized hydrogen regions. Because the motions of the stars generally differ radically from those in the gas, it is not obvious that the abundance gradient in the one component should resemble the other. The fact that they do is a notable constraint on the possible history of galaxies.

The properties of the dust in galaxies other than ours are almost entirely unknown. Photographs of spirals that appear edge-on from our vantage point do, however, show that dust is a prominent component of some spiral galaxies. The knowledge of the size and composition of dust grains in our Galaxy is based on observations of the scattering of starlight by clouds of these grains, but the amount of light reaching Earth from stars in external galaxies is so small that these observations are impracticable. Observations of the central regions of galaxies in the infrared suggest that grains with sizes around one micron are common in these parts.

Molecules are difficult to detect in external galaxies. Individual stars appear so faint that high-dispersion spectroscopy, necessary for the detection of optical interstellar absorption lines, is not feasible. But hydroxyl (OH), carbon monoxide (CO) and formaldehyde (HCOH) have been detected by their *microwave lines* at 18, 0.26 and 6.2 cm wavelength, respectively. The CO emission lines are most suitable for detection. Radio astronomers have detected absorption lines of carbon monoxide and formaldehyde against the continuum radio sources in the central parts of NGC 253.

Many galaxies emit *non-thermal radio waves* by the *synchrotron radiation* mechanism. This radiation is generated by very fast electrons diffusing through a magnetic field. From this observation theorists conclude that galaxies often contain *cosmic rays* and magnetic fields.

The nuclei of galaxies

Short-exposure photographs of the central regions of galaxies usually show a bright spot which is star-like in appearance, or just resolved (one second of arc diameter or less). This is the NUCLEUS which, although frequently absent in some small galaxies, is a characteristic feature of the larger ones. The angular diameter of one second corresponds to a linear size of 3.3 pc at M 31, 16 pc at M 81 and 63 pc at M 87. Because the size of the nuclear image is usually determined by atmospheric seeing, these values are upper limits to the true sizes of the nuclei. Hence one can safely say that a galaxy's nucleus is small compared with its overall size.

Like a galaxy itself, the nucleus usually emits a black-body continuum with an effective temperature around 5000 K. This suggests that it consists of stars very much like those that the rest of a galaxy contains. However, the greater brightness of the nucleus leads to the conclusion that its star density must be about a million times the average density in a galaxy. Population models of nuclei are made in the same way as they are of galaxies. A complication arises because the nucleus has such a faint appearance, even though it is one of the brightest spots in the galaxy, that the region to be observed must have a diameter above 10 seconds of arc in order to collect enough light for photometry. This means that the sample thus obtained contains a considerable amount of light from stars well outside the nucleus. The populations deduced from these measurements resemble those of the underlying galaxy, so that galaxies which have many ionized hydrogen regions tend to have blue nuclei due to the presence of young massive stars, whereas galaxies without such a strong young component tend to have redder nuclei in which the bulk of the light comes from G-, K- or M-type giants. There is a clear tendency for the nuclei to be somewhat redder than their galaxies, and it seems fairly certain that this is so because the nuclei contain a larger amount of elements heavier than helium.

Notwithstanding these general properties of a galaxy's central parts (in the range 10–60 arc seconds apparent diameter), the innermost, and usually unresolved, part of the nucleus is often less predictable. Such a semi-stellar nucleus may be rather different in colour from its surroundings, either redder or bluer. It is often a fairly strong radio source, as in our Galaxy (the Sagittarius A radio source), sometimes it is weaker, as in M 31, or even absent, as in M 33. Some nuclei emit infrared radiation in the region near 300 micron wavelength. This radiation cannot be ascribed to fluorescence of dust grains near giant stars, for most of this emission occurs at about 2 or 3 microns. It appears therefore to be certain that many galaxies contain in their nuclei one or more sources of radiation that are not stars. In *active galaxies*, nuclear sources are usually very prominent. What these sources are is one of the most important unsolved astronomical problems.

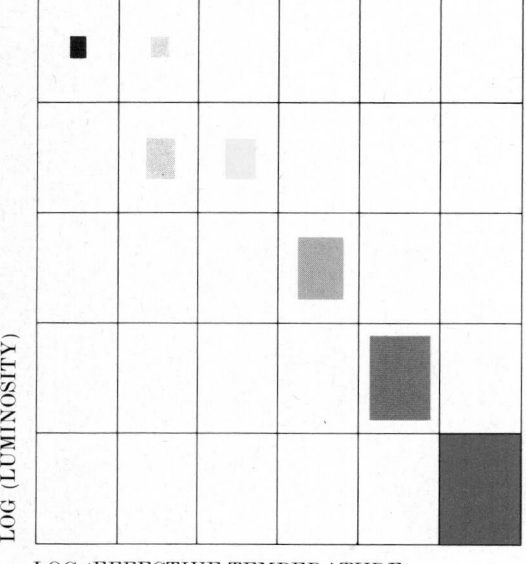

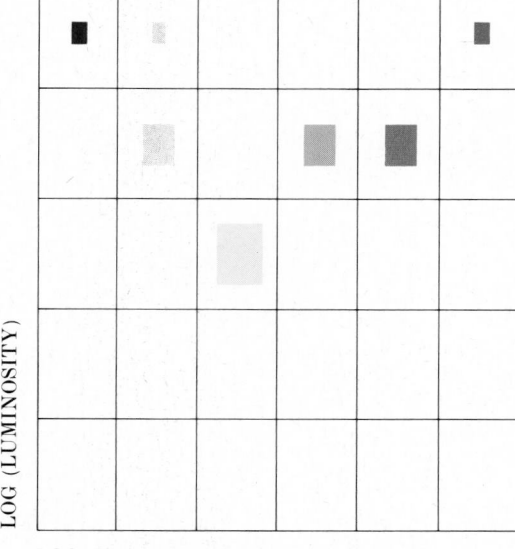

LOG (LUMINOSITY)

LOG (EFFECTIVE TEMPERATURE)

LOG (LUMINOSITY)

LOG (EFFECTIVE TEMPERATURE)

GALAXY SPECTRUM

GALAXY SPECTRUM

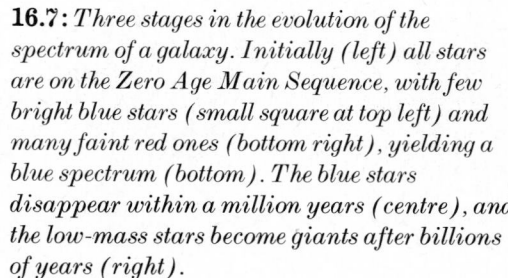

16.6: *Synthesis of a galaxy spectrum with a population model. Cells in the temperature-luminosity diagram are filled with a number of stars (coloured squares), and the spectra of these are added to give the galaxy's composite spectrum (bottom). Two different ways of filling the cells (left, right) may give identical spectra!*

16.7: *Three stages in the evolution of the spectrum of a galaxy. Initially (left) all stars are on the Zero Age Main Sequence, with few bright blue stars (small square at top left) and many faint red ones (bottom right), yielding a blue spectrum (bottom). The blue stars disappear within a million years (centre), and the low-mass stars become giants after billions of years (right).*

The nucleus of a galaxy is often seen to emit a spectral line at 372.7 nm, due to a *forbidden transition* in singly ionized oxygen. The apparent presence of ionized oxygen serves to indicate the existence of gas in the nucleus, and also the presence of some ionizing agent. The amounts of ionized gas are relatively small, of the order of 100 000 solar masses (i.e. less than one per cent of the total nuclear mass). Spectroscopic studies of some nearby nuclei show that the gas is probably ionized by a few very hot stars (50 stars with an effective temperature of 40 000 K are sufficient) or perhaps by a weak non-thermal ultraviolet source. Also, it is not excluded that some of the ionization is due to collisions with fast electrons.

16.8: *A spiral galaxy, which is seen almost exactly edge-on. From comparisons with less inclined galaxies it can be concluded that this galaxy is an S-type. The smallness of the central bulge (bright area in centre) would indicate that this is an Sc or Sd galaxy. (US Naval Observatory,* USA)

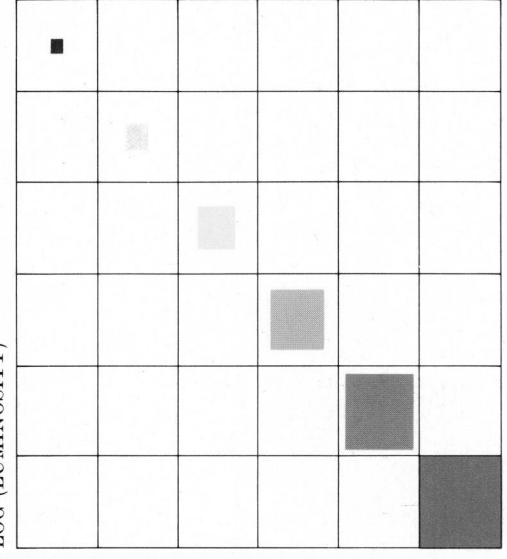

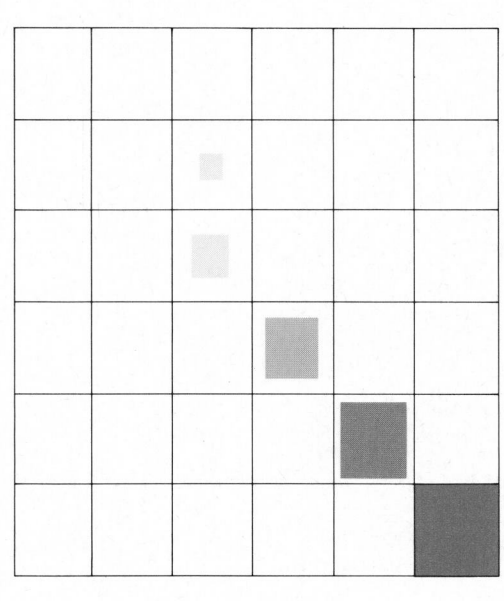

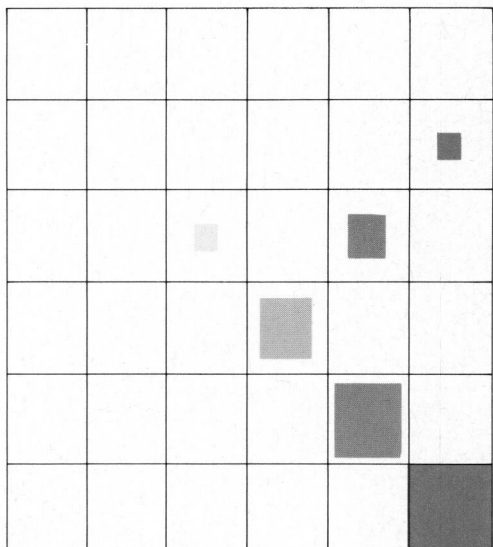

LOG (LUMINOSITY)

LOG (EFFECTIVE TEMPERATURE)

GALAXY SPECTRUM INITIALLY

AFTER 10 MILLION YEARS

AFTER 10 BILLION YEARS (NOW)

16.9: *The spiral galaxy M81, photographically deprojected to show what it would have looked like when viewed face-on. Note the striking difference in appearance with the original of M81 as seen in the sky (figure 16.10, fourth photograph). (University of Cambridge,* UK*)*

The emission of infrared radiation with a wavelength of a few microns indicates the presence of dust grains which intercept the light of stars in the nucleus and re-emit this at a wavelength approximately equal to the grain size. Where dust is present, one expects to find other cool components of the interstellar matter as well. Possibly the observed radio emission line of carbon monoxide is also emitted near the nucleus. In addition, the 21-cm emission line of neutral hydrogen has sometimes been observed. The problem is, however, that many nuclei are continuum radio sources, and it is very difficult to separate this continuum from the emission lines. Radio absorption lines due to hydroxyl and to formaldehyde have been observed against nuclear sources. It is inferred that nuclei contain at least as much neutral as ionized gas, and possibly up to 10 times more.

We have seen that the contents of other galaxies are very much like those of our Galaxy. Yet it is not obvious that matter in the Universe should appear to be the same everywhere; the observation that it is apparently the same, is extremely important. The fact that galaxies throughout the Universe are made of about the same kind of stars and interstellar matter indicates that the formation of these objects was a natural consequence of the properties of matter and of the way these arose in the early Universe.

The large-scale structure of galaxies

Galaxies display a great variety of appearances and in studying this diversity, it is difficult to distinguish the typical from the incidental. The contents of a galaxy do not readily change, because of the slowness of evolution of the low-mass dwarf stars that make up most of a galaxy's mass. But what about the evolution of a galaxy's shape? This could conceivably change as rapidly as it takes a star to cross from one end of the galaxy to another. Since this crossing time is at most a few hundred million years, it is possible in principle that a galaxy's shape is ephemeral in its lifetime of 10 billion years.

Many galaxies are remarkable for not showing any special features. These look like symmetrical clouds of stars, usually denser in the middle and containing a nucleus, but sometimes without such a condensation. These are called ELLIPTICAL GALAXIES. They closely resemble one another, the main variation being the degree of flattening and the rate at which the surface brightness decreases outward. The colours are virtually the same in all ellipticals; the spectrum typically resembles that of a K0-K5 star. Population models show that the bulk of the light from ellipticals comes from K and M giant stars, whereas most of the mass is in dwarfs smaller than the Sun (table 16.1). Towards the centre, the colour becomes redder; this may be in part due to slight changes in population. However, spectroscopic indications, notably the strength of the absorption bands of titanium monoxide in the stellar spectra, show that the colour changes mainly because the amount of elements heavier than helium decreases from the centre outwards.

For dynamical reasons, the stars in elliptical galaxies are thought to occupy a volume in space known as an oblate spheroid, which is the figure obtained by spinning an ellipse about its minor axis. The flattening of the spheroid is expressed by the ELLIPTICITY n, which equals 10 times the difference between the apparent lengths of the major and minor axes, divided by the apparent length of the major axis. The type of an elliptical galaxy is then indicated as En. In this system, a spherical galaxy such as M 87 has type E0, whereas M 32 is an E2 galaxy. Most ellipticals have type E0, a few have type E7 and none are flatter than this. A complicating factor is that the ellipticity of a galaxy image depends on the distance from the centre of the galaxy. In consequence of this, a short-exposure photograph of an elliptical galaxy shows a different ellipticity to that displayed in a long exposure of the same object, usually in the sense that the central parts look more nearly circular than the outskirts. The measured distribution of ellipticities is only apparent, because we see galaxies as projected in the sky. For example, many E0 and E1 types are really flatter (E4, say), but are seen almost pole-on instead of edge-on. If one makes the obvious assumption that galaxies are oriented at random in space, the true distribution of ellipticities can be deduced from the apparent one.

The mass of a galaxy is determined by several dynamical methods: (i) by analysis of the *rotation curve*; (ii) by using the motion of its globular clusters; (iii) by means of the *velocity dispersion* of the stars in the galaxy; or (iv) by measuring the orbital parameters of interacting galaxies (see page 346). The range of masses of elliptical galaxies is tremendous: from *dwarf ellipticals* like the Draco system with a mass of only 100 000 $M_{\odot}$ to SUPERGIANT ELLIPTICALS like M 87, with almost 10^{13} $M_{\odot}$; this latter colossus is the most massive galaxy known. In terms of the entire Universe, the dwarf ellipticals are probably the most numerous, whereas the giants and supergiants are extremely rare. Most of the mass locked in the elliptical galaxies actually resides in the intermediate population, which is characterized by a mass of 10^{11} $M_{\odot}$. These determinations show that ellipticals are much more massive than would be expected on the basis of their total luminosity. For if these galaxies did consist of stars of about 0.6 $M_{\odot}$, as the galaxies' effective temperatures would suggest, the ratio of the mass of the galaxy to its luminosity would be 4 (taking the solar *mass/luminosity ratio* to be unity). But most mass determinations show that M/L is about 50 in an elliptical galaxy, which is fully 12 times the expected value. These elliptical galaxies contain much matter in a form which is not especially luminous.

Stars shed mass quietly in the form of stellar wind, or sometimes more violently by generating *planetary nebulae*, or nova or supernova explosions. In cool stellar winds, certain kinds of dust particles are formed in the outer layers of stars. In a galaxy consisting of 10^{11} stars, a few solar masses per year are returned to the interstellar medium by these processes. Considering that the age of a galaxy is about 10^{10} years, we might reasonably expect that any galaxy should contain a large amount of gas and dust, but ellipticals typically do not. Furthermore those that do are always peculiar for other reasons (for example, NGC 5128 corresponds to the intense radio source Centaurus A and it is swathed in dust). Only in the nuclei of some elliptical galaxies do we find traces of gas, and even then it is less than a few tenths of a per cent of the nuclear mass. Clearly, the gas we expect to find in ellipticals is somehow removed, a point that we return to below.

The elliptical galaxies are rather faceless, but there are galaxies with salient features (or personalities!). Those like M 81 and M 104 (figures 16.9 and 16.3) are called SPIRAL GALAXIES, NGC 1300 is called a *barred spiral* (figure 16.17), and asymmetric, more or less chaotic ones like NGC 4449 are called *irregular* (figure 16.5).

Spiral galaxies are recognizable by either luminous or absorbing lanes, or both, winding outwards from their central parts. These lanes are called SPIRAL ARMS, and many photographs of spiral galaxies (e.g. figure 16.10) give the distinct impression that these arms lie in a rather thin plane. An attempt to reconstruct M 81 as it would be seen when looking directly onto this plane is shown in figure 16.9. The fact that spiral galaxies are rather flat is emphasized by the existence of many of these systems seen apparently edge-on (figures 16.8, 16.16). The spiral arms are clearly inclined with respect to a circle about the centre of the galaxy. This inclination, usually called the pitch angle, varies from one spiral galaxy to another. When the pitch angle is small, the spiral arms are said to be tightly wound, whereas loosely-wound spirals have a large pitch angle.

Classification of spirals

The tightness of winding is the feature that is most commonly used to characterize the overall shape of a spiral galaxy. Because the pitch angle is not always the same at every distance from the nucleus, spiral types are not simply distinguished by a number giving that angle. Instead they are indicated by S followed by a, b, c or d, in order of decreasing tightness, where 'a' corresponds to a pitch angle of about 10° (tightly wound), 'b' to about 15°, 'c' to 20° and 'd' to 25° (loose structure). Galaxies with more open patterns than Sd are sometimes called Sm. The borderlines between these classes are necessarily somewhat vague, but the sequence is still quite recognizable (figure 16.10).

Formerly, it was thought that this sequence of shapes was due to a real evolution in the course of time. A galaxy was then expected to start as an Sm type with very open arms, much gas and young stars, to evolve through a winding up of the arms and the dying of the massive stars, towards an Sa type, eventually leaving an elliptical galaxy behind. This notion is now known to be completely wrong. Still, many classification schemes for the appearance of spiral galaxies have been proposed in the hope that they might lead to an understanding of the causes of these shapes. Only the above classification by pitch angle corresponds reasonably well with other physical properties, which will be mentioned below.

Spiral galaxies are made of the same basic ingredients as ellipticals, but in rather different proportions. The greatest similarity is found between ellipticals and the NUCLEAR BULGE of a spiral – the somewhat extended, elliptical-looking cloud of stars centred on the nucleus of a spiral galaxy, which can be most clearly seen in edge-on systems.

The great difference between spirals and ellipticals is to be found in the *Population I* component (young stars, gas and dust). In elliptical galaxies it is absent outside the nucleus itself, but it shows up as a disc with some gas and dust in Sa galaxies, increasing its prominence through the Sb and Sc types, until its light completely dominates the Sd galaxies. The fraction of the mass of a galaxy in the form of neutral hydrogen accordingly increases from about two per cent in Sa types to 15 per cent in the open-armed Sd galaxies (figure 16.19). Another difference is that spiral galaxies are much bluer than are ellipticals: whereas the latter typically have a B–V colour index around 0.9, this parameter for Sc types lies between 0.5 and 0.6. This difference in colour is caused by the presence of young massive stars in spiral galaxies. The average number of such stars and their attendant regions of ionized hydrogen increases with increasing pitch angle, so that Sa galaxies contain a few ionized hydrogen regions whereas Sc and Sd types are completely dominated by them. This has two important implications. Firstly, it shows once more that where there is much gas, there are many new stars being formed. Secondly, it shows that in spiral galaxies the relative importance of the Population I component is correlated with the spiral type (figures 16.10 and 16.11). This is an extremely significant conclusion, because it shows that spiral patterns are not random, but have some fundamental connection with the other properties of spiral galaxies. In general the ionized hydrogen lies along the spiral arms (figure 16.12). These intriguing clues to the origin of spiral structure are expounded below. It is dangerous to jump to conclusions from such correlations but they are certainly relevant.

The Population I component in spiral galaxies also shows its presence at radio wavelengths. The ionized hydrogen in the vicinity of bright young stars emits a thermal continuum which is

16.10: *Spiral galaxies arranged according to decreasing winding tightness. Notice that the thickness of the central bulge also decreases from left to right. Galaxies shown are NGC 1201 (SO) NGC 2811 (Sa) NGC 488 (Sab) M81 (Sb) and M74 (Sc). (Hale Observatories,* USA*)*

16.11: *Correlation between the gas content of galaxies and their spiral type. The more open its spiral pattern, the more gas a galaxy usually contains. Such a correlation shows that the mechanism which generates spiral arms is probably directly or indirectly linked with the gas content of a galaxy.*

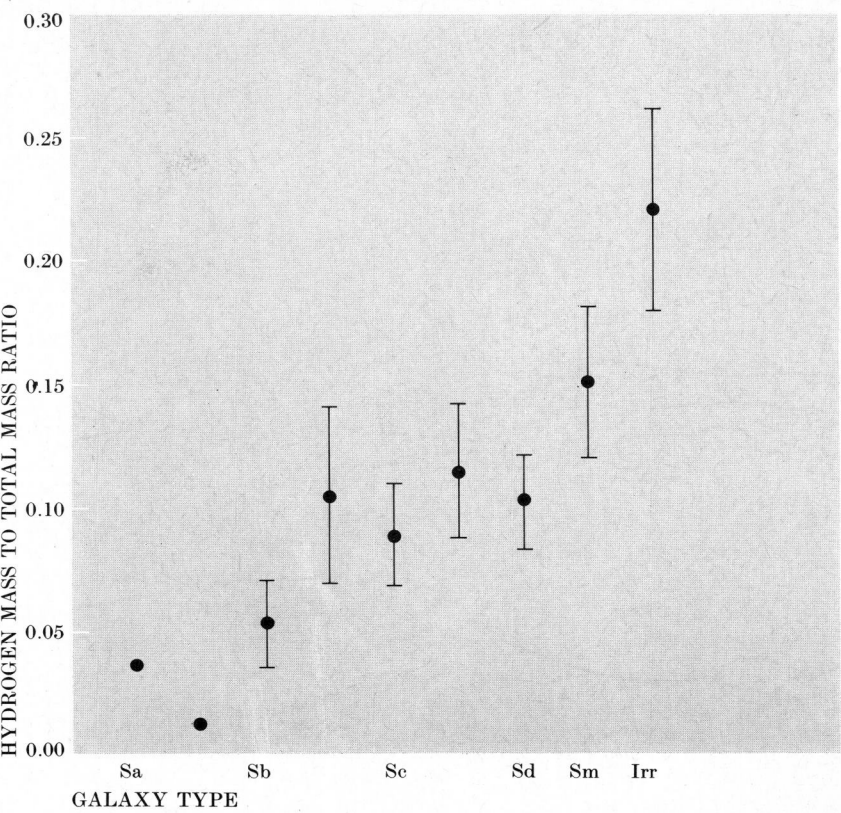

detectable at centimetre wavelengths, if the source is bright and relatively nearby. For example, the giant cloud 30 Doradus, in the Large Magellanic Cloud would still be detected at a distance of 5 Mpc, that is 170 galaxy diameters from the Sun. The most distant H+ region known lies in the galaxy NGC 3310, at 20 Mpc from our Galaxy. But at decimetre wavelengths these sources are rather small and weak compared to the non-thermal continuum from a galaxy. If such radiation is detected, it comes either from the galactic nucleus or from the disc, or both. Apparently the cosmic rays and the magnetic fields, which together generate this radiation, are confined to the disc, anchored somehow to the gas in the plane of the galaxy. In some cases, the continuum shows ridges that follow the spiral arms (figure 16.12), which is evidence that the density of fast electrons and magnetic fields is larger inside than it is outside the spiral arms. Also, the maximum intensity of the radio emission coincides with the dust lanes in the optical spiral arms.

Apart from the continuum, the radio spectrum of spiral galaxies often contains spectral lines. Molecular lines like those of *hydroxyl* and *formaldehyde* have been found in absorption against the continuum of some nuclei, and *carbon monoxide* has been seen in emission in a score of galaxies. Most information to date has come from the *21-cm line* of neutral atomic hydrogen. This radiation is emitted from the plane of spiral galaxies, and in many cases shows ridges that beautifully follow the optical spiral arms figure (16.12).

Radio astronomers have discovered that the total extent of the neutral hydrogen plane is often considerably larger than the optical image of the galaxy. Its radius may be 1.5–2 times the optical radius. These outermost regions of the disc are often warped or otherwise distorted, as is true for both our Galaxy and M33.

The total mass detected from the 21-cm line is thus far the only practical indicator of the gas content of a spiral galaxy (figure 16.11). Regions that are too cold to emit the 21-cm line could be analysed from the 2.6-mm carbon monoxide line, whereas those regions that are too hot could be observed by means of hydrogen radio *recombination lines*. But these emissions are too faint to be of practical value as yet.

16.12: *The spiral galaxy M51 with the 1415 MHz radio continuum contour map superimposed. Notice the exact coincidence between the dust lanes and the radio ridges. (Westerbork Synthesis Radio Telescope, Netherlands)*

16.13: *Photograph in visible light of the spiral galaxy M51. Compare with the drawing in figure 16.1. (Hale Observatories, USA)*

16.14: *Lenticular galaxy NGC2855. Notice the almost circular absorption lanes in the disc of the galaxy. (Hale Observatories, USA)*

Lenticular, irregular and barred spiral galaxies

Since there is a correlation between the gas content of a galaxy and its spiral type, it is natural to ask whether there are any spiral galaxies with either no gas at all, or at any rate less than the few per cent contained in Sa types, or else with more gas than the Sd galaxies. Such systems do indeed exist; they are the LENTICULAR and IRREGULAR GALAXIES respectively.

Lenticular galaxies strongly resemble the Sa types, but they lack the extreme Population I component (i.e. gas and dust). Usually they have a large nuclear bulge, and where seen edge-on they show a characteristic outward cusp due to the stars in the plane of the galaxy. Many appear to contain no interstellar matter, although a small proportion shows absorption lanes when seen edge-on. These inconspicuous dust lanes appear to be practically circular when a lenticular galaxy is seen face-on (figure 16.14). Because of their similarity to Sa types, the lenticular galaxies are held to belong to the spiral sequence, and therefore are often called S0 galaxies. It is less certain whether the lenticulars form a true intermediate state between spiral and elliptical galaxies. On the one hand, the large nuclear bulge of many lenticulars is reminiscent of an E7 type, but on the other hand the difference between a spheroidal star cloud and a system with a fundamental plane is very profound, in shape as well as dynamically (see page 344). Also, the idea of an E–S transition is in conflict with the finding that among the flattest stellar systems known there are many lenticular galaxies (figure 16.14). Lastly, there is the curious fact that the masses of spiral galaxies are much more sharply defined than are those of ellipticals. Whereas E types range from 10^6 to almost 10^{13} solar masses, the S types are typically found between 10^{10} and a few times 10^{11} $M_\odot$. Perhaps this effect is connected with the possible existence of large haloes around galaxies or perhaps it is a selection effect, but its cause is not yet known. If it is real, this phenomenon speaks against lenticulars forming an E–S transition.

Irregular galaxies are more or less chaotic stellar systems. There exist two kinds of irregulars, which are usually easily distinguishable by their colour. The so-called TYPE I IRREGULARS are very blue, with a B–V index around 0.35; the TYPE II IRREGULARS have the ordinary yellowish colour of about 0.8. The Irr I are held to be intrinsically irregular, whereas the Irr II are made irregular by some disturbance, for example an explosion in the nucleus, as in M82 or a galaxy collision. Only the intrinsically irregular galaxies are considered here. They have the largest gas content of all galaxies (figure 16.11). New stars formed from this gas give the systems their blue colour, while generating regions of ionized hydrogen that completely dominate the optical picture of the galaxy (figure 16.5). Although some irregulars look vaguely like Sd galaxies with a very open spiral-like pattern, it is not certain whether the irregulars belong to the spiral sequence. The mass of an irregular galaxy is typically lower (10^{10} $M_\odot$) than that of an average spiral. Also, irregulars less frequently have nuclei; the composition of their interstellar matter is sometimes highly atypical, as in the case of the Small Magellanic Cloud (figure 15.15) which has one third of its mass as gas, but practically no dust.

Many spiral galaxies have a pattern that winds inwards until, at a radius of five to 10 kpc, it breaks off, being replaced by what looks like a bar-like structure centred on the galaxy's nucleus. Such systems are called BARRED SPIRAL GALAXIES. Apart from their inner shape, they resemble ordinary spirals in every respect. They show a steady progression in the tightness of winding of their spiral parts (figure 16.17). Accordingly, their shapes are indicated as SBa through SBd. Much less is known about their gross properties than is known about ordinary spirals, partly because there are no nearby ones visible from the northern hemisphere, where most large observatories are located. Bars also exist in other types of galaxy. For example, the equivalent of the lenticulars are the THETA GALAXIES, named after their similarity to the Greek letter Θ. Barred irregular galaxies also appear to exist; for example the Large Magellanic Cloud (figure 15.14) contains a distinct elongated cloud of stars.

16.15: *Distribution of the neutral atomic hydrogen in the spiral galaxy M81 (see also figures 16.9 and 16.10d). Blue is high intensity, red is low: see inset strip. The rectangle on the lower right indicates lengths of 2 kpc in the plane of the galaxy. Dot shows the radio telescope resolution. (Westerbork Synthesis Radio Telescope, Netherlands)*

16.16: *Edge-on spiral NGC 821 with its 2.7 GHz radio contours (National Radio Astronomy Observatory, West Virginia, USA)*

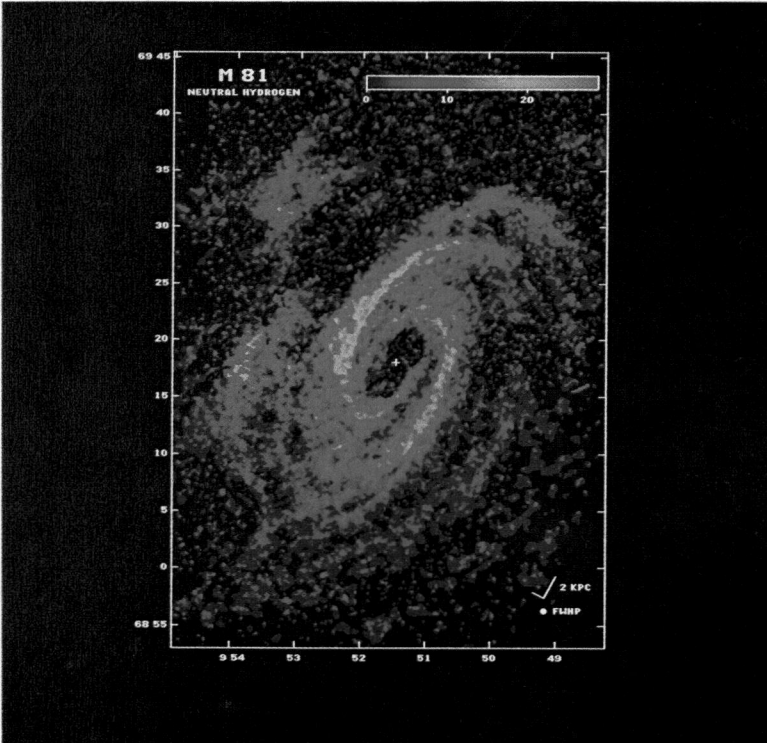

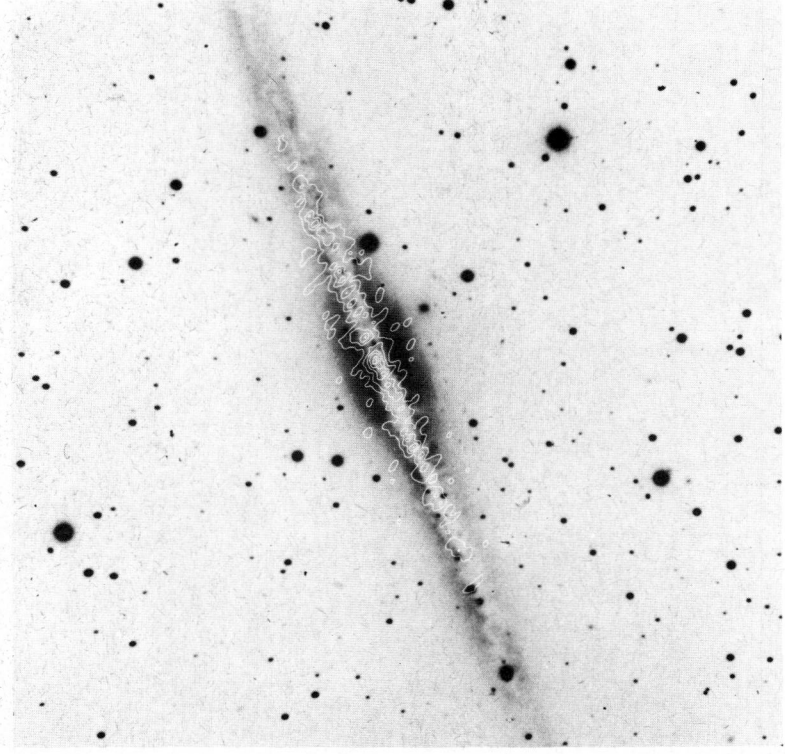

16.17: *Barred spiral galaxies arranged according to decreasing tightness of spiral arm winding (left column top to bottom, then right column likewise). The sequence is analogous to the one shown in figure 16.10. The top left galaxy is a theta galaxy. Barred spirals have not yet been sufficiently studied to say if correlations like the one in figure 16.11 exist. (Hale Observatories, USA)*

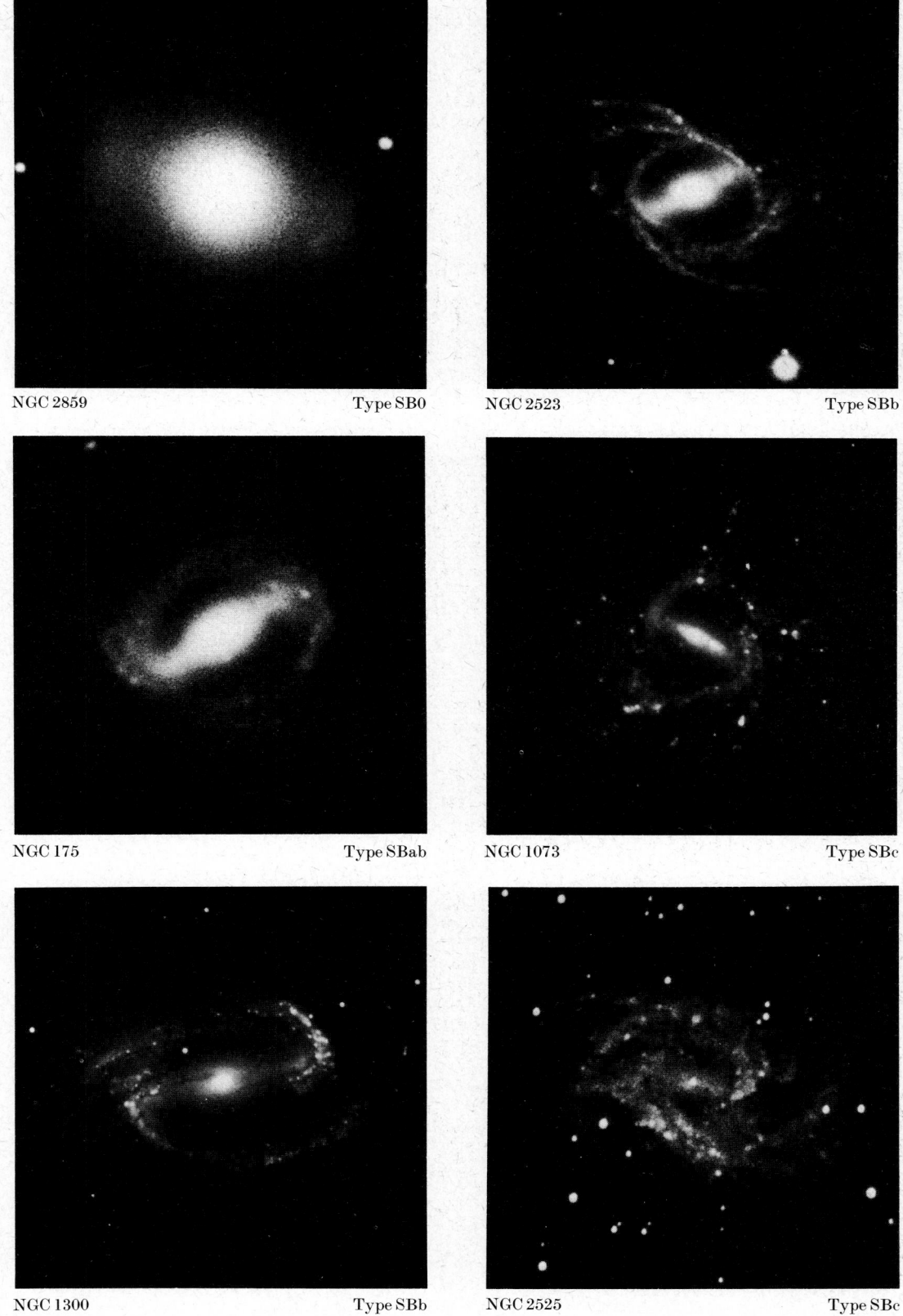

NGC 2859   Type SB0

NGC 2523   Type SBb

NGC 175   Type SBab

NGC 1073   Type SBc

NGC 1300   Type SBb

NGC 2525   Type SBc

The large-scale dynamics of galaxies

So far, we have limited ourselves to a consideration of the outward appearance of galaxies, somewhat like a taxonomist classifying the shapes of plants and animals. A taxonomist knows that his subjects are part of a large chain of evolution, allowing the recognition of order in the living diversity; also, he probably recognizes the function of many of his subjects' features. But anyone studying galaxies knows that although they evolve, they have no parents or offspring, and their shapes are certainly not due to adaptation to their environment. Thus it is difficult to find the causes underlying the diversity of galaxies.

Little progress can be made in this respect unless, like the biologist, we also consider behaviour: the motions of the various components of the galaxies, or their dynamics. Before turning to the more complicated systems, let us consider elliptical galaxies. Motion is observed by means of the *Doppler shift* of a spectrum. As its bulk consists of stars only, the study of an elliptical's dynamics requires the observation of the stellar velocities. Unfortunately only a few nearby ellipticals can be resolved into individual stars, and even in these cases the stars are too faint to allow detailed spectra to be made; these are necessary to determine the Doppler shift of spectral lines. One is therefore reduced to trying to obtain velocity information from an entire section of the galaxy, so that the spectrum observed is a composite of the spectra of all stars along the line of sight (figure 16.18). This has four major disadvan-

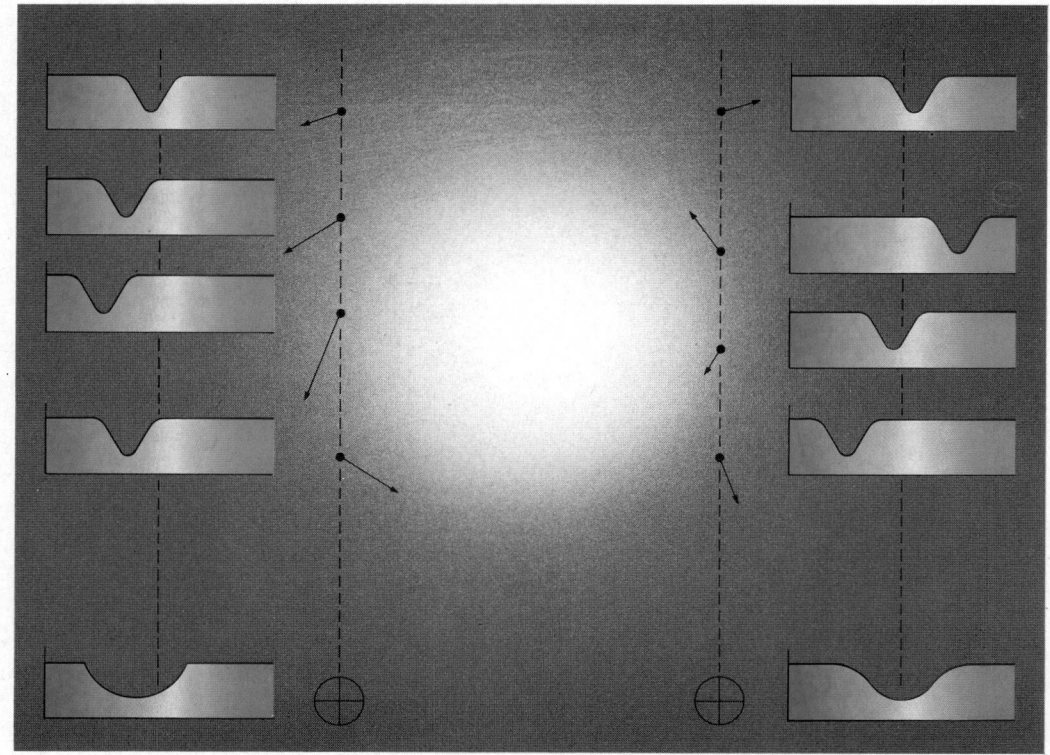

16.18: *The formation of galaxy absorption lines. In the left column, four absorption-line spectra of typical stars in the galaxy are shown as they would appear if the galaxy rotated smoothly. Added together, along the line of sight to Earth, all such spectra would merge and yield the semicircular absorption dip shown at the bottom. This line is off-centre due to the net Doppler shift of the galaxy's rotation. In the right column, spectra of randomly moving stars are added to give the centred bell-shaped absorption line at the bottom. In reality, the line shape is something in between the left and right extremes.*

tages. Firstly, not all stars in the galaxy are of the same spectral type, so that a wide variety of stellar line shapes are blended together. Secondly, one looks right through the galaxy, which means that it is impossible to determine the velocity of a small region. Thirdly, not all stars are in perfectly circular orbits; most of them have a certain random velocity which usually is of the same order of magnitude as the systematic velocity due to galactic rotation. Finally, not every volume along the line of sight contains the same amount of stars, and consequently the central parts of the galaxy contribute much more to the light than do the outskirts. These four disadvantages show that we are effectively looking at something which is a mixed, if not muddled, bag of material. It is therefore not surprising that there is practically no information about the rotation curves of ellipticals; only a couple are known with some confidence (figure 16.19). We see therefore that the masses of elliptical galaxies cannot be found by the method of integrating the rotation curve.

Fortunately, the systematic motions are not the sole source of information about a galaxy's dynamics: the random motions can be used too. These are measured by observing the width of the absorption lines in a section of a galaxy (figure 16.18). The random velocities of the stars in such a section cause a broadening of the absorption profile, because of the random superposition of Doppler shifts. The random velocities are of the order of 100 or $200\,\mathrm{km\,s^{-1}}$. Such a measurement can be translated into a mass by using the fact that virtually the only influence on the motion of a star is gravity, and that in a not-too-flattened system a star is on the average influenced only by the mass encompassed by its orbit. Thus one expects the stars in the outskirts of an elliptical galaxy to have a velocity corresponding to that of a Keplerian orbit about a central mass equal to the mass of the galaxy. By the laws of classical mechanics, this implies that the square of the velocity dispersion (i.e. spread in random velocities) is proportional to the galaxy's mass divided by a typical orbital radius. Since the average orbit is about as large as the galaxy itself, it follows that the square of the velocity dispersion is proportional to the mass of the galaxy divided by its radius. Therefore, measurement of the radius (five kiloparsecs, say) and the velocity dispersion ($100\,\mathrm{km\,s^{-1}}$ or so) yields an estimate of the mass (10^{10} solar masses in this example). By use of masses so determined, astronomers have found that the mass-to-luminosity ratio of an elliptical galaxy is typically 50. Since the M/L ratio of a spiral galaxy is about 5, an elliptical that is as luminous as a spiral contains 10 times as much mass. For example the companion of M 51 (figure 16.13) is almost as massive as the spiral galaxy itself!

16.19: *Rotation curve of the elliptical galaxy NGC 4697. Velocities are in $km\,s^{-1}$, distances in seconds of arc. The curve should be antisymmetric about the centre, that is, the nucleus of the galaxy.*

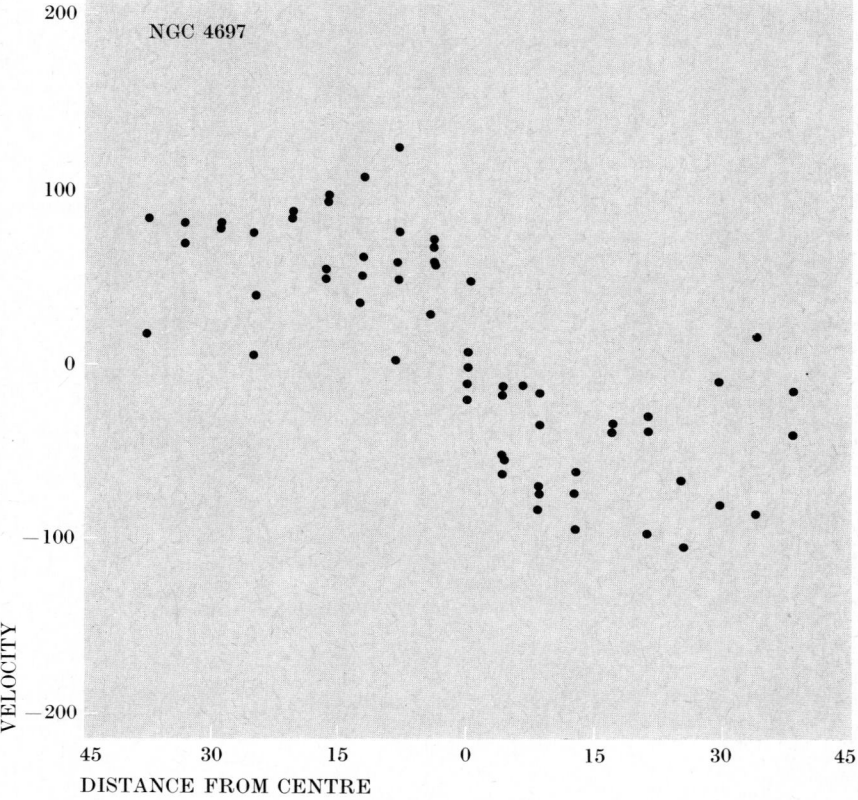

Interpretation of elliptical galaxies

We have outlined the contents and dynamics of elliptical galaxies, and we now interpret these observations by a sequence of theoretical models. We have to explain how a cloud of stars can be made and maintained so that:

(i)   it has a density which is highest in the centre and which smoothly decreases outwards;

(ii) it looks like an oblate spheroid with radius about five kiloparsecs, and is never flatter than E7;

(iii) it is 10^{10} years old and contains some 10^{11} solar-type stars, but next to no gas or dust.

The average star-star distance in a galaxy with 10^{11} stars and a radius of five kiloparsecs is about 20 million stellar diameters. Any star moving with a speed of $100\,\mathrm{km\,s^{-1}}$ through such a sparsely-populated space has a probability of colliding with another star once in 10^{19} years, that is 10^{8} stellar lifetimes. Imagine encountering only one neighbour in a hundred million human lifetimes! Accordingly, the cloud of stars that form a galaxy is said to be collisionless. Since the electric and magnetic fields carried by some stars are imperceptibly weak over distances of millions of stellar diameters, there is only one natural force to govern stellar motion, namely the force of gravity. The problem of describing an elliptical galaxy is thereby reduced to that of describing the behaviour of a large number of point-like masses, moving under gravity.

The laws of classical mechanics tell us that, on average, two stars must move past each other within about 100 stellar diameters before their gravitational interaction deflects them by more than 90° from their former paths. Such an interaction is strong enough to be considered as a collision, even if the stars do not actually touch. To a star in an elliptical galaxy, this kind of gravitational collision is expected to happen once in 10^{14} years, that is once in a thousand times the galaxy's lifetime. Accordingly, ellipticals are collisionless with respect to gravitational interaction too. Therefore the stars interact primarily with the average gravitational field of the galaxy, caused by the mean attraction of all distant stars. The attractions due to neighbours form but a small perturbation on the motion in the average gravitational field. This estimate also shows that once the shape of an elliptical is established, it will change only on a timescale of 10^{14} years. We therefore conclude that the elliptical galaxies assumed their shape right at the time when they were formed, shortly after the beginning of the Universe.

Once an elliptical has settled to its final state, a very quiet period starts. Stars orbit in the galaxy, very few being able to escape: in order to attain the escape velocity, they must be accelerated by a close encounter, which for a given star has an average chance of occurrence of once in a thousand galaxy lifetimes. The absence of collisions also ensures that the galaxy does not collapse, because this can only happen when the stars suffer close encounters so frequently that many of them are knocked into orbits passing through the inner parts of the galaxy. The orbits traced out by the stars in their courses about an elliptical galaxy can be likened to a ball of string that is so loose that it never ties itself into a knot.

Dynamics of spiral galaxies

Spiral and irregular galaxies look so much more complicated than do ellipticals, that it is reasonable to expect their dynamics to be vastly more complex too. Consider firstly the motions of the stars. Since spirals are so highly flattened, the method of velocity dispersion can fruitfully be used only in the nuclei and central bulges, which are sufficiently nearly spherical for the velocity dispersion to reflect the total mass. Typical velocity spreads are of the order of a hundred kilometres per second. Using the estimate outlined above (page 339) it follows for example that the inner 20 pc (5 arc sec as seen from Earth) of M 31 contains $2 \times 10^{8}\,\mathrm{M_{\odot}}$, and the inner 2 kpc of the central bulge about $10^{10}\,\mathrm{M_{\odot}}$. As in the case of elliptical galaxies, the systematic motions in the stellar component are very difficult to observe. Measurements of the central parts of M 31 have been made, with some puzzling results, but their reliability is doubtful.

Observations of the systematic motions of stars are essential for the study of the dynamics of galaxies like lenticulars that contain practically no gas. Because observations of the stellar velocities are extremely difficult, most of our knowledge of dynamics is restricted to spiral types, where the spectral lines emitted by the gas can be used to determine the velocity fields. In the optical part of the spectrum, the emission lines most frequently used are the *Balmer series lines* due to atomic hydrogen and a nearby line of singly-ionized atomic nitrogen. In the few cases where comparison is possible, the velocity of the gas corresponds moderately well to the velocities of the stars. Within about one kiloparsec of the centre of an ordinary spiral, the orbital velocity in the plane of the galaxy typically increases in direct proportion to the distance from the centre. This implies that the swirling matter in this region rotates as if it were a solid body. Beyond this radius, the velocity increases less rapidly, and after reaching a maximum at a radius usually between three and eight kiloparsecs, slowly decreases outwards.

Such ROTATION CURVES can also be observed by using the *21-cm hydrogen line*. The radio line spectrum of a whole galaxy can be obtained at once. At optical wavelengths only the surfaces of the interstellar clouds are observed, whereas the radio waves can be seen from practically all the hydrogen gas in the disc.

16.20: *Spiral density waves. (a) A collection of stellar orbits with random orientations. No pattern is discernible. The orbits are presumed to be elliptical for simplicity. (b) Stellar orbits with a strict phase correlation between adjacent orbits. A two-armed spiral pattern is evident, forming the crest of a density wave. In reality, a spiral galaxy is somewhere between these extremes of order and disorder.*

Interpretation of spiral galaxies

Since most of the mass of a spiral galaxy is in the form of old (Population II) stars, let us consider the stellar component first. As in the case of ellipticals, the stars form a collisionless system, so that we expect the mass distribution to change extremely slowly. The evolution time turns out to be a thousand galaxy lifetimes, a fact which is hardly changed at all by the presence of gas. This can be seen by imagining a typical star like the Sun, tunnelling its way at a typical velocity of $200 \, \text{km sec}^{-1}$ through an interstellar gas with a typical density of one hydrogen atom per cubic centimetre. Such a star would at most intercept $500 \, \text{kg}$ matter per second, or in other words, it would intercept a mass equal to its own after a billion galaxy lifetimes! Therefore, the way in which the stars are on the average distributed through a spiral galaxy must date from the galaxy's birth, just as in the case of ellipticals.

The gas behaves in a very different fashion, because it is dominated by collisions. Since stars occupy only a minute fraction of the volume of a galaxy, the gas does not interact directly with them. The fate of interstellar gas on a large scale (kiloparsecs) is determined roughly by four processes: heating by starlight and cosmic rays, cooling by radiation, stirring and heating by blast waves from active stars (e.g. *novae* and *supernovae*), and gravitational interaction. The first three effects never quite balance, but roughly speaking they lead to the establishment of a galactic atmosphere with a mean density of a million atoms per cubic metre and temperatures between 100–$5000 \, \text{K}$. This atmosphere is rather turbulent and tries to settle in the average gravitational field formed by the stars in the galaxy. The settling is governed by the inertia of the gas and its tendency towards equilibrium between the forces of gas pressure and gravity. Thus the gas seeks the points of lowest gravitational energy, thereby forming a very thin layer in the plane of the galaxy, that is, at right angles to the axis of the galaxy's rotation. This is the origin of the disc of gas in spiral galaxies. The thickness of the gaseous disc is maintained at a few hundred parsecs by gas pressure and turbulence. The radial extent of the disc is determined by the balance between the inward pull of gravity and the centrifugal acceleration due to rotation. The rapid rotation of spiral galaxies causes the radius of the gaseous disc to be at least as large as that of the stellar disc, and often up to twice as large.

The typical disc structure of a rapidly rotating galaxy containing gas and stars has now been explained, but this is only the first part of the problem. The second part is to account for the origin and maintenance of SPIRAL STRUCTURE. The observations summarized in the previous section indicate that *spiral arms* survive for up to a hundred galactic years. This means that they cannot be permanent condensations, because these can only survive as a pattern if the whole galaxy rotates as a solid body. The rotational velocity of spiral galaxies never increases in direct proportion to the radius, except sometimes in their innermost parts, so that DIFFERENTIAL ROTATION rather than solid-body rotation prevails. Consequently any material structure in a galactic disc is wound up and entirely obliterated in only a few galactic years, and the spiral arms must therefore be a wave phenomenon: what we perceive as spiral patterns are not permanent ridges of matter, but instead comprise the locus of wave crests of a DENSITY WAVE. Therefore,

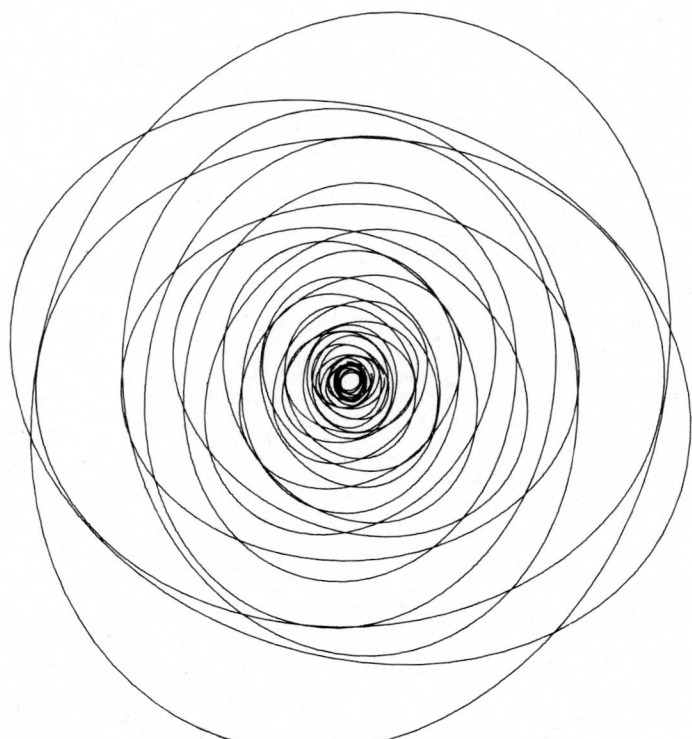

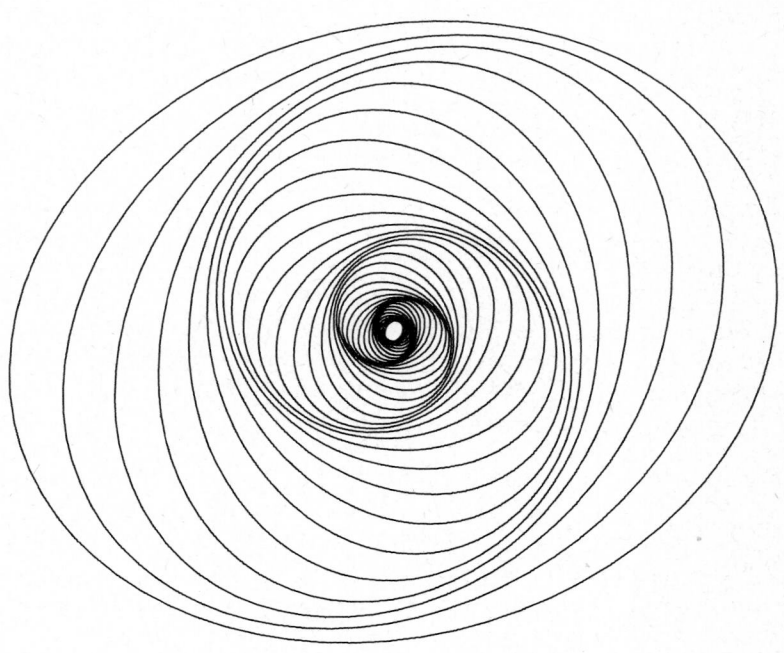

the crucial problem is to show that the material in the plane of a spiral galaxy can oscillate in such a way that density waves are formed with a wave-crest pattern that looks like a trailing spiral and rotates as if it were a solid body.

Waves occur as small perturbations of an equilibrium. In the case of waves on a pond, the ripples are the perturbations and the equilibrium state is the level surface of the water. The ripples move out from a disturbance, but the water in the pond oscillates in small ellipses, without outward motion. Spiral arms are density perturbations, and the equilibrium state is the simple rotating disc structure described above. The surface of a pond is in equilibrium between the pull of gravity and hydrostatic pressure. The disc of a galaxy is in equilibrium between the inward pull of gravity and the centrifugal effect of inertia. A water wave is formed when water particles oscillate around their equilibrium state in unison with neighbouring particles; similarly, a spiral density wave can only occur if there is a certain unison between the motions of the matter at neighbouring radii in the plane. The stars are expected to make up the bulk of the wave, because most of a galaxy's matter is in the form of stars. Stellar orbits in a galaxy are *rosette orbits* (figure 15.8), so it is not easy to visualize stars moving in some semblance of order; for greater clarity, let us pretend that the orbits are ellipses around the galaxy's centre. When there is no unison between their oscillations, the orbits form a random collection, but when every orbit is related in a methodical manner to its neighbours, a pattern emerges (figure 16.20).

In water waves, the ordering of neighbouring water particles is brought about by molecular forces. In spiral waves, the force of gravity between stars acts as the maestro for orchestrating the stellar motions. The resulting pattern is not fixed with respect to the stars but is rather a fleeting density enhancement, moving around the galaxy as a wave. As the figure shows, the shape of the spiral depends on the shape of the individual stellar orbits. Since we know that these orbits do not change appreciably during the galaxy's lifetime, it is to be expected that the pattern is permanent as well.

This explanation would suffice to solve the problem of spiral structure, if it weren't for the fact that waves are subject to decay. As we know from everyday experience, waves eventually die out; this is known as DAMPING. To the dismay of density wave theorists, it has been shown that these waves, if left to themselves, would decay within half a dozen galactic years. Consequently, the problem now to be considered is the way in which the waves are maintained; this is a fascinating but as yet unsolved problem.

Because the gas is such a small fraction of a galaxy's total mass its gravitational influence on a density wave is practically negligible. Instead of acting itself, the gas is acted upon by the gravitational potential associated with the density wave. The response of the gas to the spiral potential well can be calculated with the methods of *hydrodynamics*. Here again, the fact that the gas is *collision dominated* has remarkable consequences. The wave moves with respect to the matter in the galaxy's disc with a velocity of

some 30 km sec⁻¹ on the average (except certain special regions in the galaxy which are not considered here). For a star, which is a collisionless particle, this means that it feels a gravitational bump which merely deflects its orbit a little. A gas particle, however, is collision dominated, so that it follows not only the imposed gravitational field but also the pressure forces from the neighbouring gas. These forces propagate with the velocity of sound, about 10 km sec⁻¹ at most. Because the speed of the density wave is three times larger than the sound speed, the gas is forced to go faster than sound during part of its motion around the galaxy. The theory of hydrodynamics predicts that this must cause the formation of SHOCK WAVES near the spiral arms. Since these shocks are accompanied by a strong compression of the gas (figure 16.21), and since interstellar dust is swept along with the gas, the *dust lanes* seen in the spiral arms of many galaxies are thought to be the place where these cosmic sonic booms occur. Thus the presence of sharp dust lanes indirectly confirms the existence of a density wave.

Stars are formed from gas, and it is reasonable to expect that compression will make interstellar matter more liable to star formation. Hence theorists speculate that young, massive stars occur preferentially in spiral arms because they form more readily when the gas is compressed by a density wave. Too little is known about star formation to allow this guess to become a theory. Moreover, the occurrence of shock waves is a serious complication.

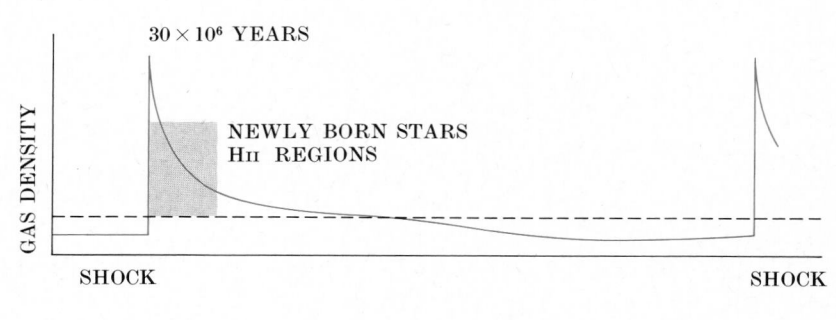

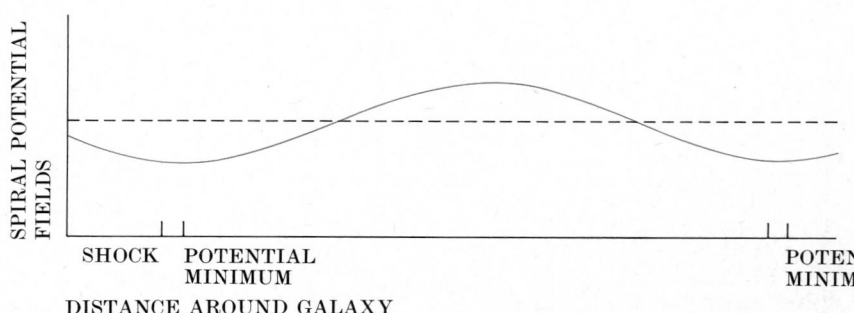

DISTANCE AROUND GALAXY

Young galaxies

Possibly the most fascinating aspect of astronomy is its intimate connection with origins. As we have seen, the mass distribution due to the stars in a galaxy has remained virtually unchanged since the time the galaxy formed. Hence, the structure of galaxies should give us some clues about their origin.

The formation of our Galaxy must have taken place some ten billion years ago. This estimate follows from three independent age determinations. Firstly, the chemical composition of the Galaxy, and especially the relative abundances of certain radioactive elements, has been used as an atomic clock. Secondly, the theory of *stellar evolution* enables us to determine the ages of the stars. Thirdly, observers have found that the Universe expands; calculating backwards in time by using the theory of *cosmology* (chapter 19), we can demonstrate that there was a time when the Universe was so hot and dense that no galaxies, nor even stars, could exist. These three clocks give roughly the same readings. How, then, did galaxies form?

The answer to this intriguing question is not known, but certain aspects of galaxy formation have become clearer in recent years. Cosmology tells us that no objects as dense as stars could have existed in the Universe until it had cooled by expansion to a temperature below 10 000 K. From this we conclude that a galaxy formed from a more or less uniform gas cloud. At the time the critical temperature (10 000 K) was reached, the cosmic gas consisted almost entirely of hydrogen (75 per cent of the total mass) and of helium (25 per cent). The hydrogen, which until then had been ionized, cooled during further expansion and finally recombined at 3000 K to form neutral hydrogen. The Universe had already expanded so far, that only gravity remained important to govern the motions of the gas on the large scales involved in galaxy formation. Consequently, a galaxy must have formed from a gas cloud collapsing under its own gravitational attraction.

16.21: *Shock waves in the interstellar gas. The gravitational attraction of the stars in a density wave causes a potential well as shown at the bottom. Gas moving through such a well is forced to be supersonic during part of its orbit in the plane of the galaxy. This creates shocks immediately before a potential minimum, that is, the place where a spiral arm occurs. The high compression in a shock probably shows up as dust lanes. Also, the compression may give rise to enhanced star formation, creating H+ regions along spiral arms.*

Protogalaxies

It is not known how the Universe came to develop regions of above average density, or perturbations, which eventually formed these PROTOGALAXIES, but the end product of the initial million years of cosmic evolution seems reasonably certain: a hydrogen-helium cloud with a temperature of a few thousand kelvin, and a density around $10^{-19} \mathrm{kg\,m^{-3}}$. The range of masses and sizes of protogalaxies is very uncertain; guided by hindsight, we shall start with a $10^{11} \mathrm{M_\odot}$ cloud with a radius of a few kiloparsecs. At the epoch we are now considering, the protogalaxies were still expanding, but theorists presume that some of them did so slightly more slowly than did the rest of the Universe. These 'lagging' clouds eventually stopped expanding and contracted by their own gravity. On top of this large-scale motion, it seems probable that the protogalaxies had some chaotic internal motions on smaller scales, but the properties of this turbulence are a major uncertainty.

At this stage, protogalaxies were extremely near neighbours: their average separation was little more than their average size. Consequently, the clouds must have interacted fairly strongly. The gravitational torques between protogalaxies passing close to each other may have set them rotating, over and above the spin they probably had as a consequence of their inner turbulence. Some clouds were so close together that they could not escape each other's gravitational pull: they remained to form BINARY GALAXIES.

The protogalaxy expands more and more slowly, until after some 20 million years its expansion stops and reverses to gravitational collapse. At this stage, our sample cloud measures about 80 kpc across. Possibly some stars have already formed in the turbulent interior of the cloud, but since the average density has been going down to about $10^{-22} \mathrm{kg\,m^{-3}}$ during this stage, there probably were not many. As soon as the protogalaxy starts to collapse, however, the increasing density makes it easier for stars to form (figure 16.23). During the initial stages of collapse, the cloud is so tenuous that radiation can escape freely from it. Thus it is possible for smaller condensations to form and radiate away their excess energy into the space between the protogalaxies. These subcondensations are supposed to have formed the first generation of stars in the galaxy. Some of them were probably very massive (more than a hundred solar masses) and rapidly evolved to explode as *supernovae*. Others somehow divided the available mass among many small stars, thereby forming *globular clusters*.

Galaxy formation

The collapse now proceeds faster and faster. The central parts of the protogalaxy contract more rapidly than do the outskirts; the formation of a *nuclear region* is thus started. In many cases the nuclear region may have started to contract even before the outer parts of the cloud have expanded to their maximal extent. More stars form, some of which pick up matter that has already been processed by the first supernovae and mixed into the rest of the gas by the ubiquitous turbulence. As soon as a star has been formed, it becomes separated from the rough and tumble. Virtually unhampered by the gas, extremely unlikely to collide with another star, it follows a path dictated by the average gravitational field of the protogalaxy. Since this field changes rapidly in the course of time because the collapse is still proceeding, the star experiences a rapidly changing gravitational pull. This affects the star as if it were undergoing a huge collision: roughly speaking, one could say that the star collides with the whole protogalaxy! Consequently, this 'collision' flings the star into an orbit which mimics the average state of motion of the cloud. This process of VIOLENT RELAXATION smoothes the distribution of the stars over the system and causes the symmetrical shape of elliptical galaxies and the nuclear bulges of spiral galaxies.

Not all the gas in a protogalaxy forms stars: a certain amount is left behind, partly because some gas moves too chaotically to contract smoothly, partly because the radiation from the stars that happen to form at an early stage heats up the gas surrounding them. This heating, which increases the gas pressure and hampers contraction, occurs especially in the later stages of collapse, when the protogalaxy has become so dense that some radiation is intercepted on its way out. Let us consider two extreme cases.

If the star formation is very efficient and almost complete before the protogalaxy enters its later stages of collapse, violent relaxation serves to give the galaxy a smooth shape: an elliptical galaxy is formed. If the galaxy happens to rotate, contraction is first stopped in the equatorial plane by the centrifugal acceleration. The contraction at right angles to the plane comes to a halt as soon as the random motions of the stars reach equilibrium with the average gravitational pull of the galaxy. The laws of mechanics show that such equilibrium is almost always reached before the thickness of the galaxy is less than a third its diameter, thereby explaining that no ellipticals are flatter than E7.

If, on the other hand, the stars do not form very efficiently, some gas will be left. This, as we have seen, behaves rather differently from the stars. Being *collision dominated*, it settles as a thin disc in the equatorial plane of the galaxy. There, it is slowly used up in the formation of subsequent generations of stars, which form fitfully in irregular galaxies and more or less regularly along the arms of spirals. It is not known what causes the differences in efficiency of the formation of the first generations of stars. Possibly the rotation of a galaxy plays a decisive role: it is to be expected that a rapidly rotating protogalaxy has a more violent internal turbulence than does a slow rotator. This interferes with star formation because centrifugal acceleration counteracts gravitation.

These two extreme cases illustrate the way in which the populations of a galaxy are established. The first generations of stars and the globular clusters form very early, so that they do not usually contain many elements heavier than helium, which are added to the interstellar gas by exploding stars. Also, violent relaxation freezes their orbits to mimic the shape the galaxy had when they were formed. Therefore, the extreme Population II objects are old, poor in heavy elements, and occupy the halo. At the other extreme, the population of the galactic plane is young and rich in heavy elements. Depending on their collapse history, galaxies contain various proportions of these populations and their intermediates.

A few hundred million years after the beginning of its contraction, a protogalaxy has been shaped by the forces of the collapse into a young galaxy. Probably faint wisps of infalling gas, the straggling remains of the outermost layers of the initial cloud, still continue to drizzle into the galaxy. Otherwise, a very quiet period begins: ten billion years without any action even remotely resembling the dramatic events during the first one per cent of that time.

A galaxy's first hundred million years

The initial stages of the collapse of protogalaxies were taking place when the Universe was a few hundred million years old. The *cosmological redshift* corresponding to this epoch is about 10. Considering that the largest redshift observed to date is about four, it seems doubtful that galaxy formation will be amenable to direct observation in the near future. However, it is useful to anticipate and try to determine what we should expect to see.

Most of the action occurs in the first hundred million years, when the first generation of stars formed. Evidence about the chemical composition of the objects in our Galaxy strongly indicates that many of these early stars, which created most of the heavier chemical elements, must have been very massive. The theory of stellar evolution predicts that such stars rapidly evolve to explode as *supernovae*. It is often speculated that the formation of *galactic nuclei* was accompanied by even more violent events. Let us be optimistic and estimate that a young galaxy can just be observed when it has an apparent luminosity of 24 mag. At the distance corresponding to a redshift of 10, the absolute magnitude must then be -23, or about 25 supernovae radiating at any one time. Considering that the decay time of a supernova flash is about a month, we may expect the young galaxy to be just barely visible if it generates one supernova per day, that is 20 000 times as many as our Galaxy produces now. Assuming that all the mass passes once through a supernova phase, and assuming that each supernova involves $50 M_\odot$, a $10^{11} M_\odot$ protogalaxy could keep up this explosion rate for five million years. Since the collapse time is of the order of a hundred million years, this flash is very brief, so that at first sight the chances of observing a galaxy's birth seem slim. However, the above estimate tacitly assumes that the light is emitted as continuum radiation. This need not be the case, for it may be emitted in emission lines. Let us assume the extreme case that all the supernova radiation is in the hydrogen alpha line, and that the line width corresponds to a random Doppler velocity of $10\,000\,\mathrm{km\,sec^{-1}}$. Then the peak intensity of the line is about 200 times that which the continuum would have had, so that the supernova rate needed to make the young galaxy visible is 200 times less than the previous estimate: only one per 200 days. A protogalaxy with a mass of $10^{11}\,\mathrm{M_\odot}$ could well sustain this rate for a hundred million years, that is during the entire collapse time.

Although these estimates are rather too optimistic for present-day observational techniques, they show that under favourable circumstances the birth of galaxies is observable with optical telescopes. It is also possible that young galaxies are powerful radio sources, but the formation mechanism is far too uncertain to allow predictions of their strengths and spectra.

When the collapse proper has ended, the rate of star formation is negligible as compared to its previous pace. The more massive stars (above $5\,\mathrm{M_\odot}$ or so) reach the end of their evolution within a few hundred million years (figure 16.7) and the galaxy looks almost as exactly as it would today.

Interactions between galaxies

If we were to be really pedantic we could assert that a normal galaxy is an abstraction: all galaxies, when inspected sufficiently closely, deviate from the norm. Most of the peculiarities are minor, but there are quite a few puzzling ones (see also chapter 18). An important class of PECULIAR GALAXIES are those which were originally normal but have been disturbed by a collision with a neighbour (figure 16.22). The probability of a GALAXY COLLISION can be estimated just as it was for stars. A representative $10^{11}\,\mathrm{M_\odot}$ galaxy with a diameter of 50 kpc moves typically with a random velocity of a few hundred kilometres per second. The mean distance between these galaxies is about 3000 kpc, so that it follows that a galaxy can be expected to collide with a similar one once in 10^{13} years, that is once in a hundred galaxy lifetimes. On the average, therefore, the collision probability is quite low. But in regions where the galaxies have clumped together (such as *clusters of galaxies*), average distances can be as small as 500 kpc, while random velocities of $1000\,\mathrm{km\,s^{-1}}$ and above occur. The mean time

16.22: *Spectacular results of close encounters between galaxies. These are tidally disrupted systems. (Hale Observatories, USA)*

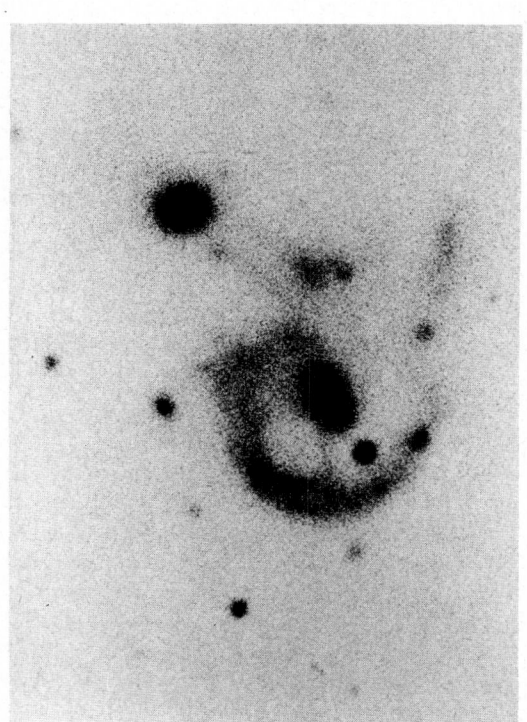
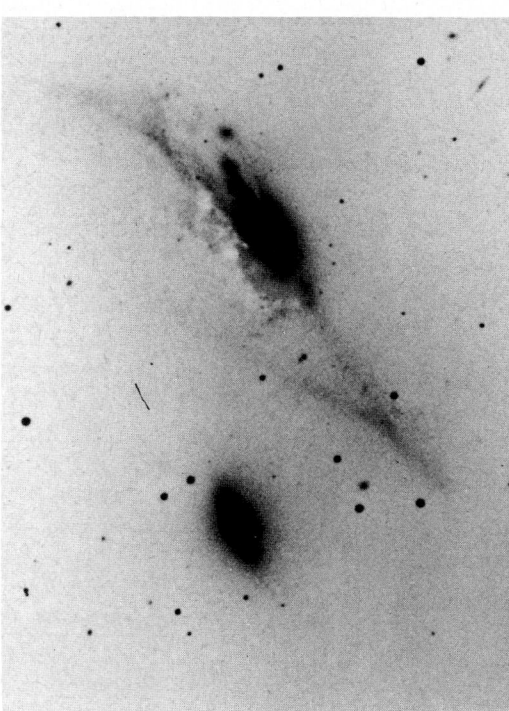
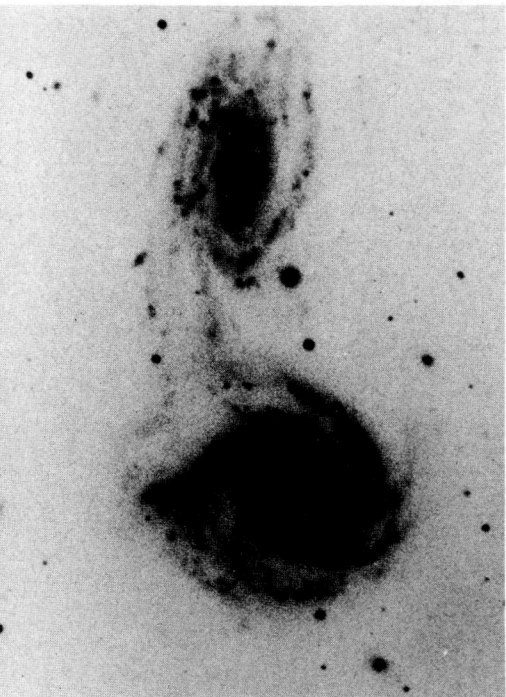

between collisions accordingly reduces to 15 billion years, so that a galaxy has a better than even chance to collide with a neighbour once in its lifetime.

Not many of these encounters are expected to have spectacular consequences. Usually the galaxies stay far enough apart for their internal structure to remain undisturbed. Even so, close encounters are astronomically useful because they make it possible to measure the masses of the galaxies. By observing the relative velocities and distances, and by application of the laws of mechanics, it is found that the masses so determined agree rather well with those derived from rotation curves. The interacting-galaxy method is especially important for elliptical galaxies, whose rotation curves are virtually unobservable. These mass determinations show that the mass/luminosity ratio is about five for spiral galaxies and some ten times larger for ellipticals. The pair encounters indicate that spiral galaxies probably have no massive low-luminosity haloes. If they did, either the observed masses should be at least a factor 10 higher, or we must assume that the haloes of the interacting pair interpenetrate. In the latter case, the inner motions of the galaxies should be much more disturbed than is actually observed.

The derivation of masses from encounters illustrates how an interaction can serve to probe the colliding objects. In a few cases, the observed collision leads to spectacular disturbances which

16.24: *Two models of known interacting galaxies. (a) The 'Antennae', bottom as seen in projection in the sky, top as in plan view of the orbital plane. Particles in the same colour originally belonged to the same galaxy. (b) The 'Mice', bottom as in the sky, top in plan view. (Adapted from work by Toomre and Toomre).*

16.23: *Artist's conception, in cutaway view, of the later stages of the formation of a spiral galaxy. A protogalaxy (left), having reached its maximum size, begins to collapse under its own gravity. Early globular clusters form in the galaxy's halo (next diagram) and the central parts become much denser. A thick gaseous disc begins to form, contracting to a thinner one as the collapse proceeds (next diagram) and the galaxy increases its rotation speed. Hot, supermassive blue stars form in the centre; globular clusters are left orbiting in the halo. Finally (right) the galaxy settles into a disc-halo form.*

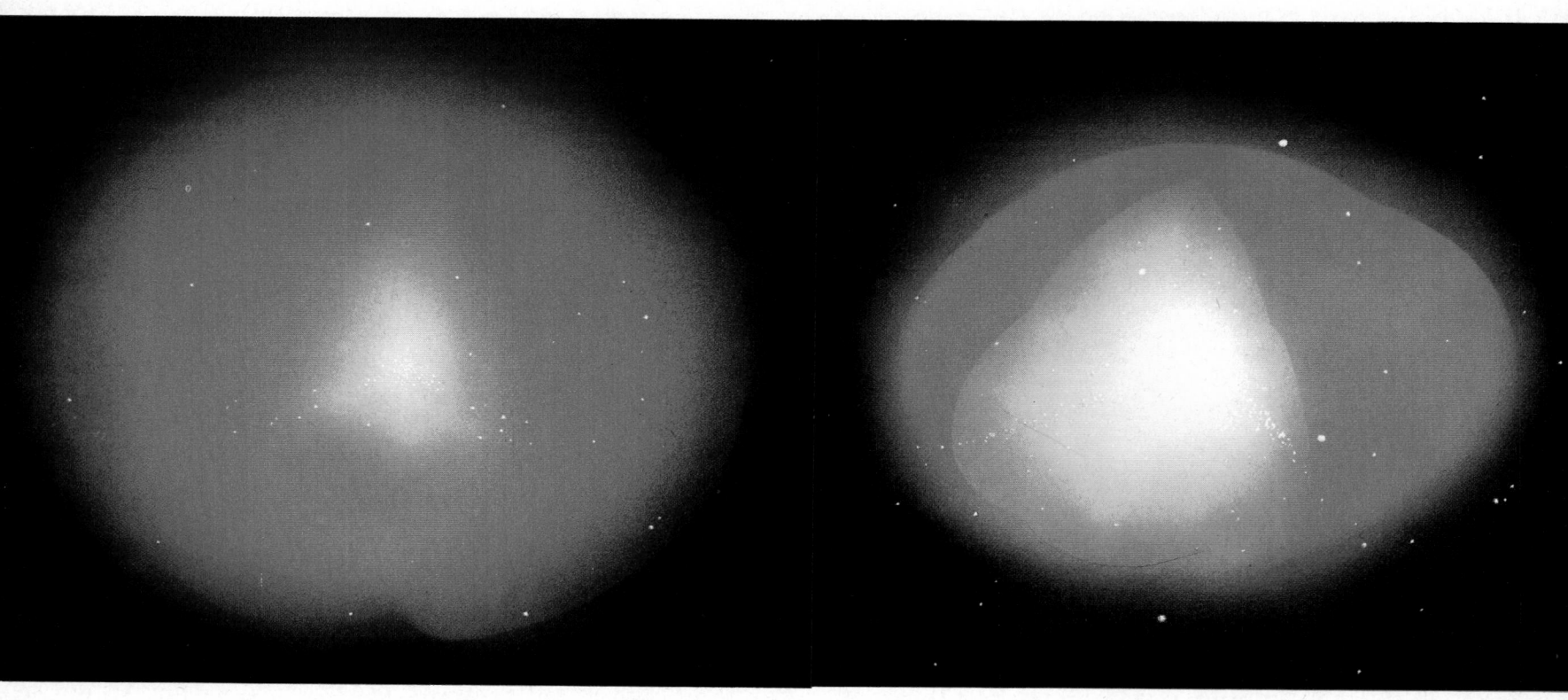

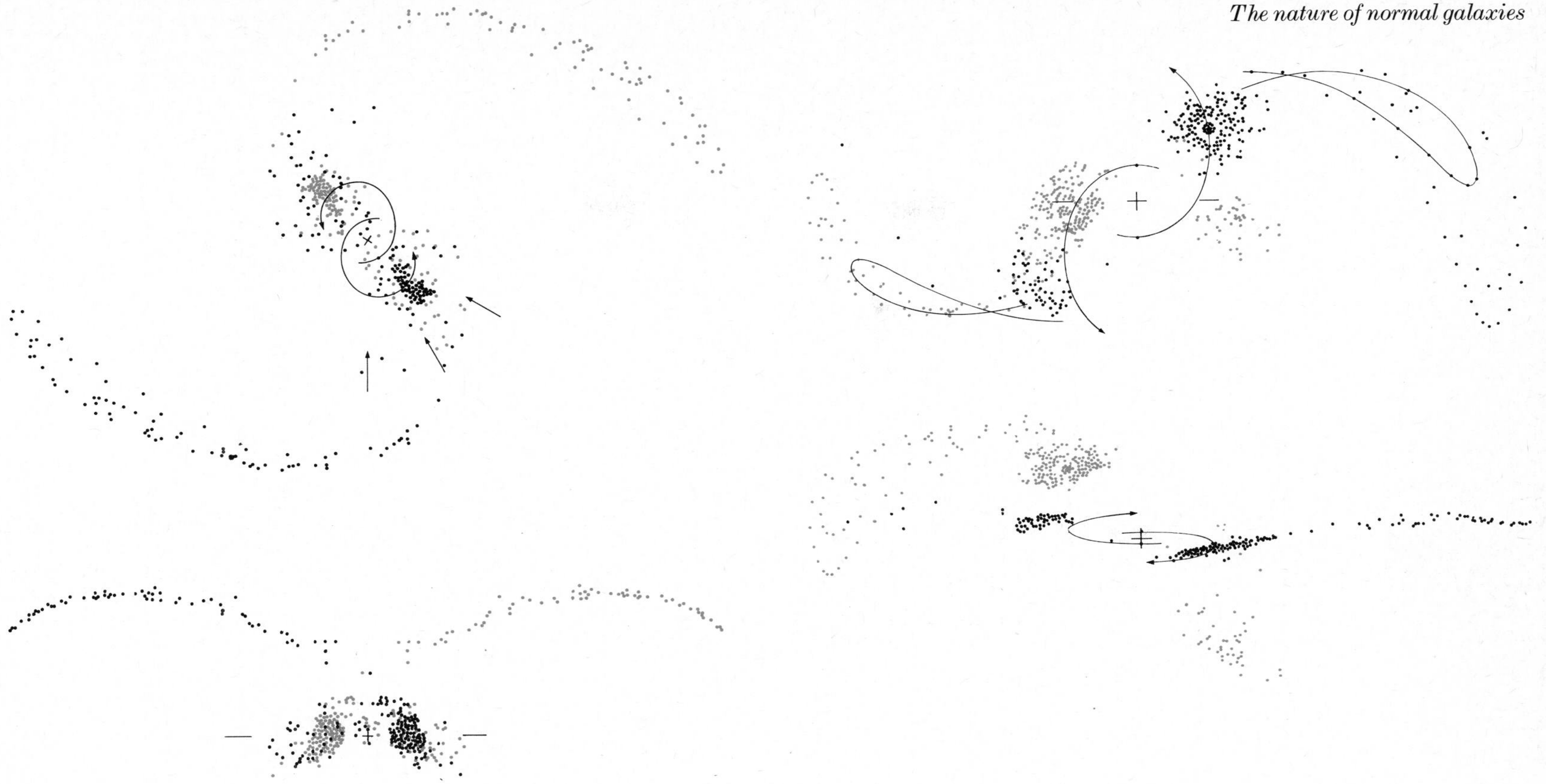

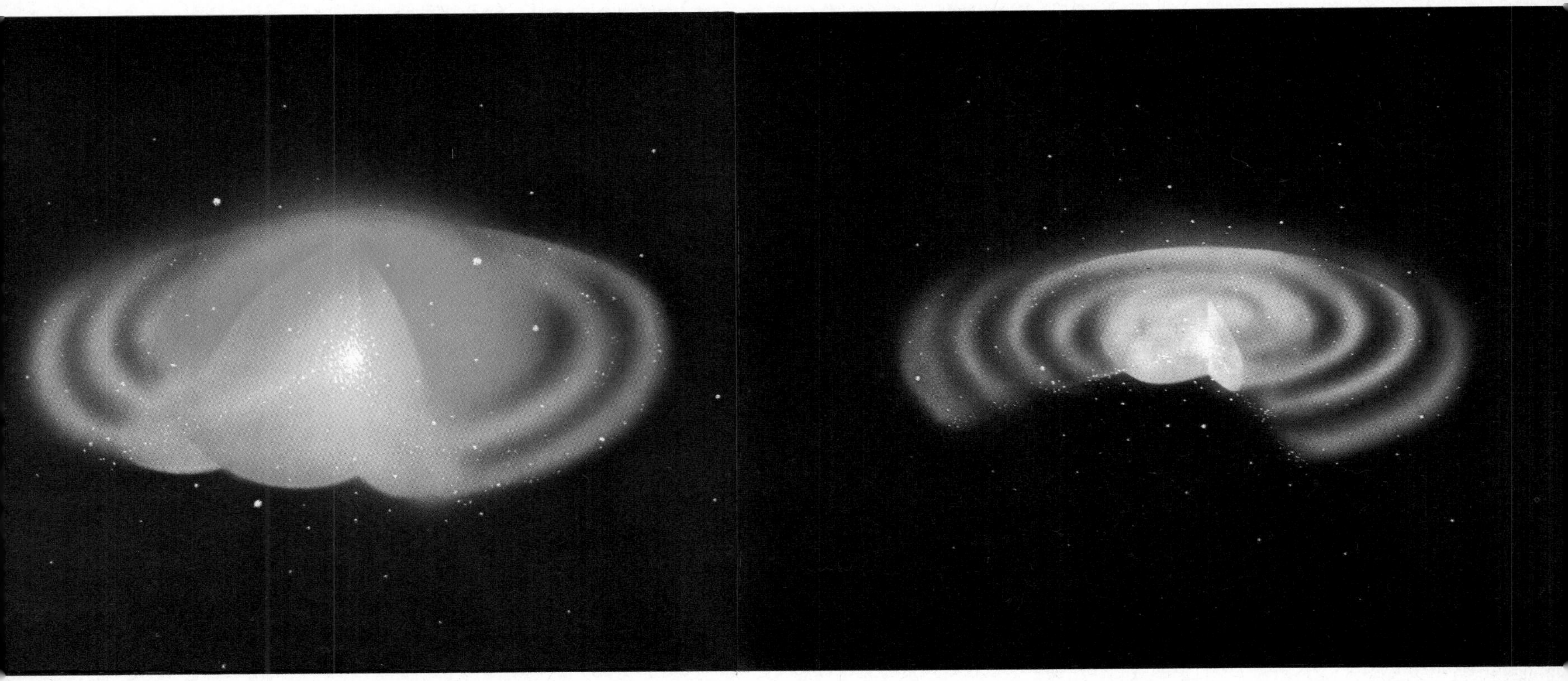

enable astronomers to probe even deeper into the internal constitution of the galaxies. A method which has been used with considerable success in recent years is a form of model building: with the aid of computers, a number of collisions is simulated until the end result looks like an interaction which is actually observed. Because the interaction picture is only a snapshot, the model building is necessarily ambiguous for lack of data; even so, relatively simple models have yielded striking results. In this approximation, two massive point-like bodies are sent on a close-encounter course. Each of these has an attendant cloud of test particles which initially move on bound circular orbits. These particles are allowed to move in the gravitational field of the two massive bodies; the mutual attractions between the test particles are neglected. During an encounter, every particle has its orbit distorted (figure 16.24), and together the particle clouds often form the BRIDGES and TAILS characteristic of many observed galaxy collisions (figure 16.25). In some cases, it is suspected that the tidal distortions induced by the encounter strongly influence the formation of *spiral structure* (figure 16.25), but here further studies are necessary in which the test particles are allowed to interact with each other.

The tidal forces that occur during a collision have the largest influence on the most weakly-bound particles, that is the ones in the outskirts of a galaxy. Usually these particles are torn away, and the majority is captured by the more massive of the two galaxies. Thus small galaxies orbiting near larger ones are stripped of their outer layers. Such TIDAL LIMITING is observable by measurement of the way in which the surface brightness of a galaxy decreases outwards; for example the outer brightness profile of M 32 is due to interaction with the Andromeda Nebula, M 31.

The most spectacular results of all are to be expected in the rare case where two galaxies collide head-on. Then all stars, including the innermost ones, experience such a rapidly changing gravitational field that a situation arises that is comparable to the collapse stage of galaxy formation. Unless the colliding galaxies go so fast that their interaction time is too short, the encounter leads to an actual merging of the galaxies. This is expected to occur most effectively when the collision velocity is of the order of the random velocity of the stars, say a few hundred kilometres per second. For in that case, stars from one galaxy find it relatively easy to follow the gravitational field of the other: they are, as it were, at a loss to determine to which galaxy they belong! The violent relaxation due to the changing gravitational field smoothes the stellar distribution, so that the merged product comes to look like a single galaxy.

The fate of the interstellar gas during a galaxy collision is almost entirely unknown. The approximations which hold for the stars are not applicable to the gas, which is collision dominated. For example, an orbital cross-over like that illustrated in figure 16.25 could never happen in gas flow. Thus, full hydrodynamic computa-

16.25: *Computer-generated film of the collision of two galaxies, modelling the M 51 system.*

tions are necessary, which present such formidable obstacles that this aspect of the encounters between galaxies is only just beginning to be studied.

Two-galaxy collisions are rare, and encounters between three galaxies are correspondingly rarer. But SMALL GROUPS OF GALAXIES are observed, in which the distances between the members are only a few tens of galaxy diameters (figure 16.26). Our *Local Group* is one of these. The relatively large number of such groups can only be explained if the galaxies in them are held together by their mutual gravitational attraction. It could be argued that the groups arise when galaxies happen to stand close together in the sky but have a large separation along the line of sight. Calculations show, however, that such projection effects do occur, but too infrequently to explain all groups.

Small groups of galaxies are rather loose structures. Their members are typically half a megaparsec apart, moving with a few hundred kilometres per second relative to the centre of mass of the group. Under these circumstances, collisions are rare: one collision per galaxy per hundred billion years.

The small groups are interesting because the motion can be studied exactly with computers. It is found that the small groups usually contain up to twice as much mass as can be accounted for by adding the masses of the individual galaxies, assuming normal mass-to-light ratios. To explain this finding, we must assume either that the groups are not bound together, which conflicts with the fact that there are so many of them; or that the galaxies have massive haloes, which conflicts with other mass determinations; or that the extra matter is in between galaxies, which is problematic because it must be in such a form that it could hitherto have escaped direct detection.

The HIDDEN or MISSING MASS PROBLEM has not been solved yet, but the study of the dynamics of small groups has yielded some interesting results about their appearance. It had been known for a long time that there exist chains of galaxies (figure 16.26). At first sight, these alignments seemed rather enigmatic. But numerical calculations showed that a gravitationally bound group of five galaxies assumes an apparent chain configuration about five per cent of the time. Consequently, unless it can be shown that they are held together by other forces, the existence of chains indirectly proves that small groups of galaxies must be gravitationally bound; for the chances that a random encounter would yield such a configuration are entirely negligible.

We have now concluded our rather lengthy review of the properties of normal galaxies. We have devoted a relatively large amount of space to these topics because we believe that the main thrust of astrophysical research between now and the end of the century will be among the realms of the wheeling galaxies.

16.26: *Small groups of galaxies in chain-like configurations. These are only temporarily aligned; in a few hundred million years, the orbital motions of the galaxies will have displaced them so that the chain is broken up. (Hale Observatories, USA)*

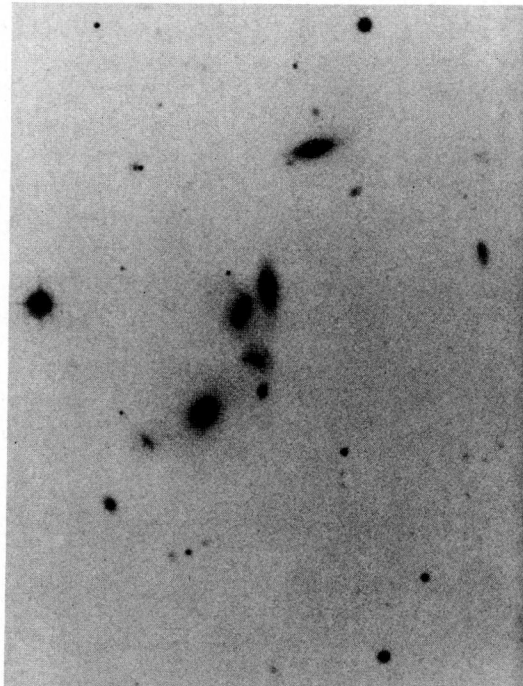
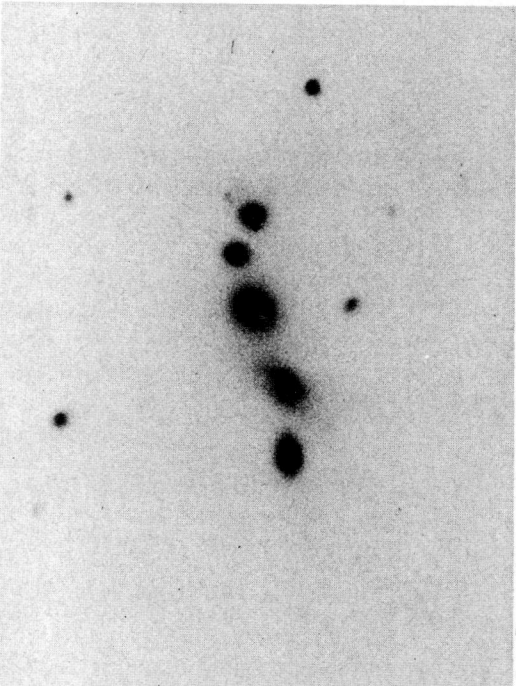

17. Clusters of galaxies

17.1: *(a) Nearby galaxies plotted on an equal-area equatorial projection from the 1932 catalogue of Shapley and Ames. The prominent band containing few galaxies is the zone of avoidance, and is due to obscuration in our own Galaxy. The concentration of galaxies above and to the right of centre is the Virgo cluster of galaxies. (b) An equal number of galaxies to those shown above as they might appear, from our viewpoint in the Galaxy, if all galaxies were distributed at random.*

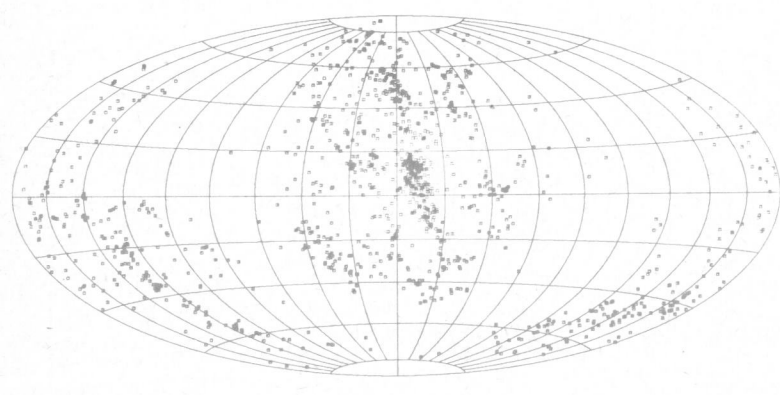

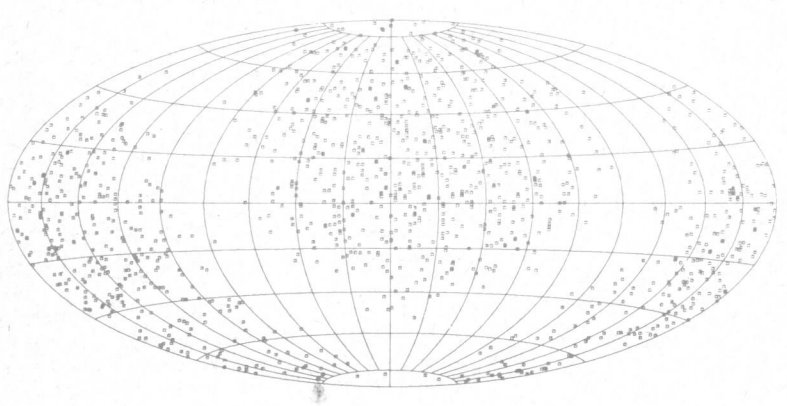

Introduction

The distribution of galaxies in the sky is far from uniform. The Herschels remarked on the unevenness of the distribution of nebulae on the celestial sphere in the nineteenth century. Part of the variation is due to the uneven distribution of obscuring matter in our Galaxy, and there is a ZONE OF AVOIDANCE at low galactic latitudes within which few galaxies are found. Even in the two windows that are available however, one centred over the north galactic pole and one over the south, the galaxies follow a patchy distribution (figure 17.1).

Statistical studies of the distribution of galaxies show that they tend to clump and cluster together. Few galaxies are really single or isolated: most are members of binary, triplet or multiplet systems of galaxies. Our own Galaxy is a member of the *Local Group*, which extends over a few megaparsecs and contains several tens of galaxies. There are much richer groupings of galaxies, called CLUSTERS OF GALAXIES, which occupy a similar volume to the Local Group, but which are composed of as many as several thousand galaxies. There appears to be a complete, and continuous, range for clumping of galaxies from binaries, through clusters, up to the largest entities known as SUPERCLUSTERS.

This introduces us to the concept of a HIERARCHICAL UNIVERSE, in which galaxies are grouped together to form clusters, and clusters constitute superclusters, and so on. There is at present no evidence for clustering of superclusters, but such a statement is really a measure of our ignorance. It is usually assumed in cosmology that the Universe is quite uniform (homogeneous), a view that may appear contrary to the clustering discussed here. The discrepancy is overcome when it is realized that cosmologists are generally unconcerned with the detailed structure of the Universe on length scales of much less than 100 Mpc. At least this is the case when models for the complete Universe are being studied, although of course it is hoped that cosmological theory will eventually explain clusters, galaxies and smaller-scale phenomena.

Counts of galaxies down to various limiting magnitudes in given regions of sky have been used to support the concept of homogeneity on a large scale. This technique is widely used throughout astronomy and appears under different guises depending upon the wavelength range and nature of the objects counted. For the present we shall assume that the objects are of the same intrinsic luminosity. Counting objects down to some limiting brightness is then the same process as counting all the objects within a sphere surrounding the observer. The radius of this sphere is proportional to the square root of the limiting brightness (since brightness varies as distance squared). If the density of objects is uniform, then the number in the sphere varies as the radius cubed, or limiting brightness to the three halves power. Deviations from this proportionality then tell us about the homogeneity of the objects. Galaxies do have differing luminosities, but the principle still applies, and the same proportionality results, although it then becomes more difficult to interpret discrepancies. The beauty of this test for homogeneity lies in its simple observable requirements: number and magnitude.

E. Hubble, and later other astronomers, have used this method to show the approximate uniformity (to within a factor of 2), of the visible Universe out to redshifts of approximately 0.5, or distances of about 2000 Mpc. Radio and X-ray astronomers find similar evidence for homogeneity.

On scales much less than 100 Mpc inhomogeneities are quite evident, and the more extreme examples of these are the subject of much of this chapter. Before discussing them in more detail, however, it is worth stressing that it is not yet clear which clumps of galaxies are dynamically associated and which are not. By a dynamical association we mean a clump within which the interactions (mostly gravitational) are large and long-lived enough to affect significantly the evolution of that clump. It is possible that galaxies appear clustered on some scale, but do not really influence each other. Some clumps may result from purely random motions; others perhaps from an oddity related to the formation of the galaxies. This situation is perhaps most serious in the case of superclusters. It is generally assumed that galaxies are dynamically associated within clusters. The rich clusters are indeed considered to be gravitationally bound, meaning that the individual members do not have sufficient velocities to escape from the cluster by overcoming the combined gravitational pull of all the other members. As we shall see, there are problems in establishing the validity of this assumption. One simple way of testing the physical influences between galaxies on large scales is provided by the velocity-distance relation (*Hubble's law*). Deviations from this may reflect the overall gravitational interaction existing within, say the local supercluster.

Clusters of galaxies consist of hundreds or thousands of galaxies within a volume of diameter a few megaparsecs. They can be roughly classified into two types: regular and irregular. The REGULAR CLUSTERS have a high central concentration and appear spherically symmetrical: they resemble globular clusters of stars. Elliptical galaxies predominate, especially in the core of the cluster, and giant spirals are rare. A typical example of a regular cluster is that in the constellation of Coma. IRREGULAR CLUSTERS are similar to open star clusters, and show no marked central concentration or symmetry. They may contain galaxies of all types and range from being very richly populated down to much sparser groupings such as the Local Group. The Virgo cluster is an irregular cluster.

Various catalogues of galaxies have been used to compile lists of clusters of galaxies. Early catalogues of bright galaxies such as that of Shapley and Ames clearly show the Virgo cluster, some 20 Mpc distant. G. Abell has studied the National Geographic Society Palomar Observatory Sky Survey plates and catalogued 2712 rich clusters of galaxies. Part of these data are sufficiently homogeneous that they can be used for statistical purposes. F. Zwicky and his colleagues have made lists of thousands of clusters and galaxies.

Radio observations have detected emission from clusters of galaxies. Very extended radio sources have been mapped over several of the nearer clusters. Many of the rich clusters also appear to be sources of X-ray emission. The cores of these clusters are thought to contain gas at temperatures of 10^7–10^8 K.

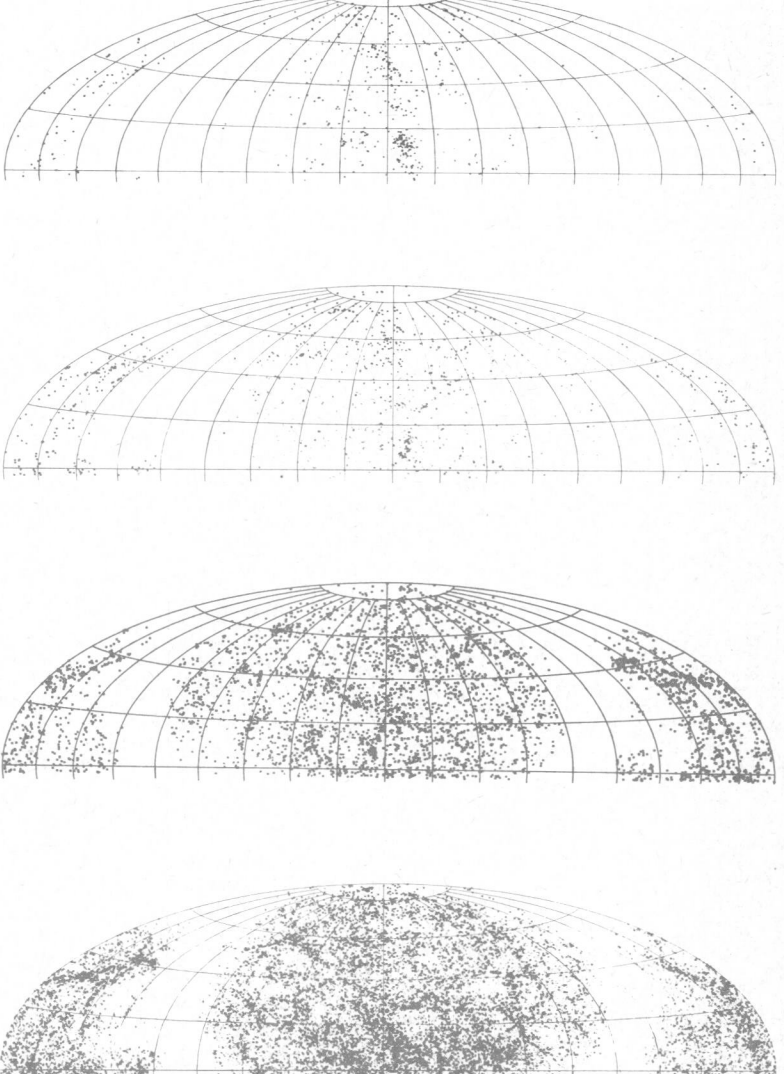

17.2: *Equal-area equatorial projections of the galaxies in the catalogues of Zwicky and his co-workers published in the 1960s, illustrate the clumping of galaxies (a) galaxies brighter than 13 mag; (b) galaxies between 13 and 14 mag; (c) galaxies between 14 and 15 mag; (d) galaxies between 15 and 15.7 mag.*

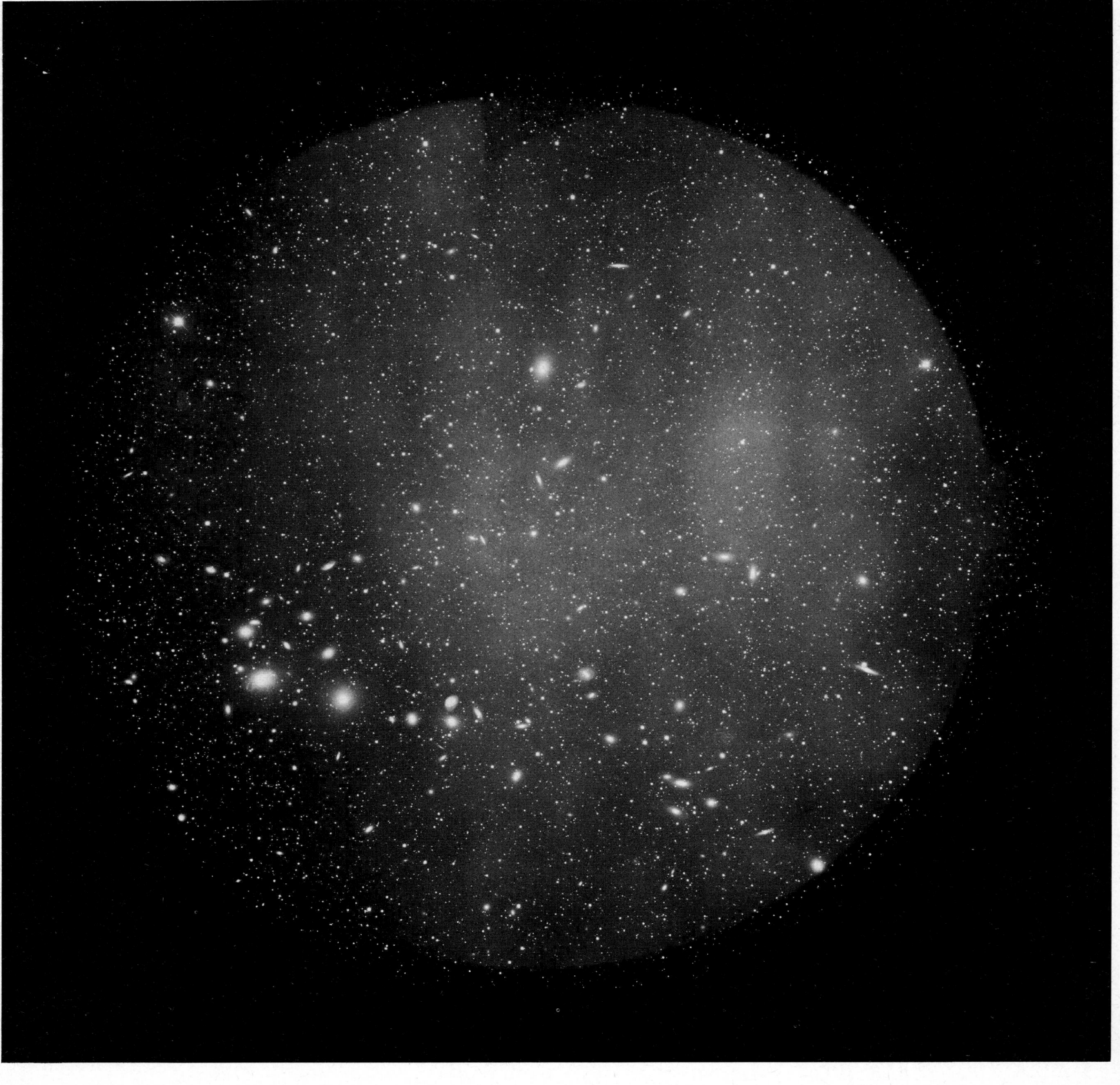

Clusters of galaxies are clear landmarks that can be traced out to large distances. It is generally hoped that they will be of great use in surveying the Universe and testing cosmological models. The brightest galaxies in clusters seem to fall within a narrow enough range in brightness for them to be used in determining the cosmic constants for universal expansion. Clusters of galaxies should also be instructive in teaching us about the formation of galaxies and revealing what large-scale density enhancements survived the early phases of the Universe. Most of the observational sides of these issues are clouded with uncertainties and a lack of sufficient data. Future studies will hopefully resolve these problems and throw up new questions. For the present, however, we define what we mean by a cluster of galaxies and attempt to outline some of its properties.

The distribution of galaxies on the sky

Galaxies are not distributed randomly on the sky (figure 17.2). There are clear gaps where the plane of the Galaxy obscures our line of sight. It can be shown without doubt that the probability of obtaining by chance the observed distribution of galaxies on the sky is negligible. Studies of the clumping for galaxies of different brightnesses and distances show that the clustering cannot be due solely to galactic obscuration. Such an effect would presumably cause clumps of near and far galaxies to occur in the same direction, which is contrary to observation.

17.3: *Optical photograph of the Perseus cluster of galaxies. The brightest galaxy, NGC 1275, shows evidence of surrounding filamentary structure. A prominent chain of galaxies stretches westward from NGC 1275. The bright galaxy in the upper half of the photograph, half a degree from NGC 1275 is NGC 1265, associated with a head-tail radio source (figure 17.8).*
(Asiago Observatory, Italy)

A detailed investigation requires the application of statistical methods. The Universe presumably consists of galaxies scattered throughout three-dimensional space. These galaxies are inter-related and clumped in some manner reflecting their origin, formation and interactions. We have to discover the nature and underlying form of these groupings in order that we can unwind the past and understand the evolution of galaxies. Unfortunately, however, we see these galaxies from only one vantage point through a relatively dirty window. More important, we see only a two-dimensional projection of these galaxies. Exact distances are not available for a sufficiently large number of galaxies for this projection to be reconstructed as a true image of space. Workers minimize distance spread by restricting their attention at any one time to narrow bands of galactic magnitudes. The results of such work rely upon the dispersion in galaxy luminosities: the LUMINOSITY FUNCTION of galaxies (figure 17.4).

We are presented with a classical observational problem: plenty of data (in the form of catalogues), but a lack of knowledge of what to look for. Aggregations such as the Coma cluster are not too difficult to pick out, but how do we define weaker clusters? We have already stressed in the introduction that there is a difference between groups of galaxies that are gravitationally bound together, and groups which appear by chance, or birth. There are two fairly well-defined approaches that we can make to this problem. One is to think up some models for the clustering and fit them to the data. The other is to apply many unbiased tests and interpretations to the data before drawing any conclusion. In practice a combination of the two is used. Certain properties may be plotted against each other in a search for correlations. For example, a comparison of the absolute brightness of stars with their spectral types reveals a striking correlation (the *Hertzsprung-Russell diagram*). There is no such definitive case for galaxies, or their distributions, although an interesting limit was published by E.F. Carpenter in 1938. Carpenter plotted the number density of galaxies in well-defined clusters and groups against the diameter of that group or cluster. A distinct upper limit emerged (figure 17.5). This was interpreted to mean that a cluster of given extent may have no more than a certain limited density which is larger for smaller clusters. Smaller clusters must therefore be more densely populated than larger ones, although in total the larger ones contain far more galaxies. A similar limit does not show up if the same parameters are plotted for galactic star clusters. This is clearly an important result, and the population densities in all clusters and groups strongly suggest that they are all members of a more universal distribution. The distinction between groups and clusters becomes arbitrary and only based upon convenience!

This has not taken us far in finding out the distribution of all galaxies however. We must avoid splitting off the richest groups and clusters and discussing them only for they may merely be extreme cases: what models shall we try? Hubble and his contemporaries favoured a relatively random distribution of field galaxies dotted here and there with clusters. More recent studies suggest that the percentage of real field galaxies is in fact small. A powerful statistical approach to our problem can be found by studying the frequency with which various angular separations occur between randomly selected galaxies. We are, of course, interested in how such a frequency distribution differs from one compiled from a chance arrangement of galaxies. The initial results for pairs and triplets of galaxies indicate that excess small separations are more likely than large ones. Significant excesses are found even out to separations of 10° or more, depending upon the magnitude limit of the sample. This indicates that most galaxies are correlated on linear scales up to about 30 Mpc. The frequency distribution is fairly smooth and is similar in form to Carpenter's limit, which involved the richer clumps only.

There may be some weakly preferred scales for clustering, the evidence for which is lost in the partial smearing inherent in reconstructing the three-dimensional image from the observed flat projection. The results do appear inconsistent with Hubble's picture of clusters embedded in a relatively smooth distribution of field galaxies. The behaviour observed is common on all scales up to about 30 Mpc and it strongly suggests that the same mechanism that has produced the clumpiness, or caused it to evolve, applies both to the distribution of galaxies on the scale of a small group and to superclusters extending tens of megaparsecs.

We now describe some specific examples of well-studied clusters; those in the constellations of Coma, Perseus, Virgo and Centaurus. Remember that these are clear enhancements in the observed surface densities of galaxies and can be isolated and discussed as such. Surrounding them is a complete spectrum of matter clumping from pairs of galaxies, through sparsely populated groups to the rich clusters. Clusters of galaxies have best been studied at present by optical means. X-ray observations are making it clear that not all matter is optically visible and the detection of extended X-ray emission from clusters suggests that observations will be more varied in the future. The advent of fast computerized plate scanners that can recognize galaxies will also considerably speed up our knowledge of their distribution.

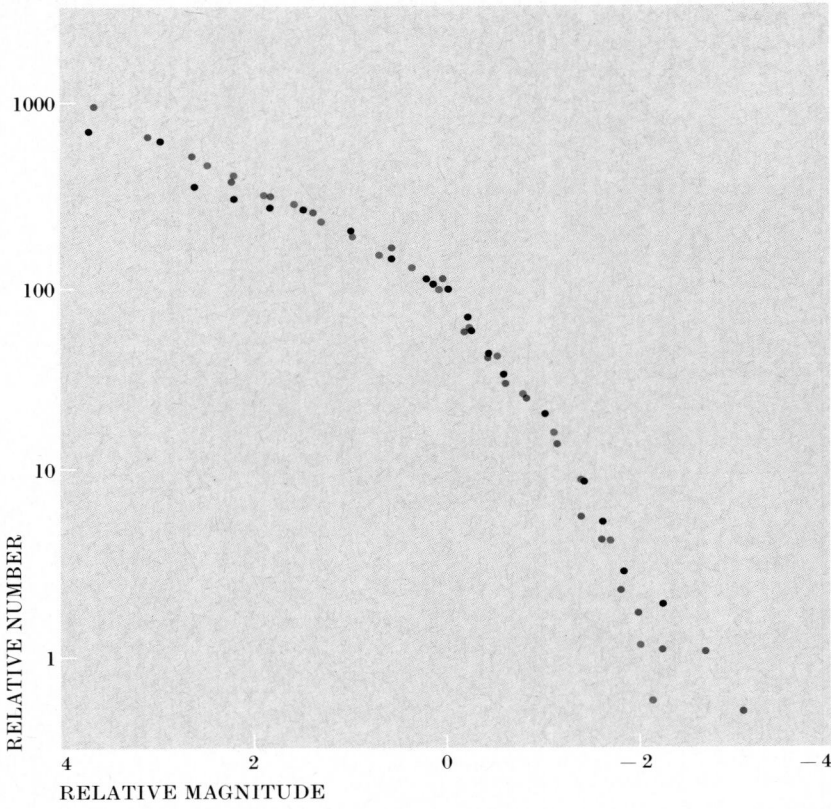

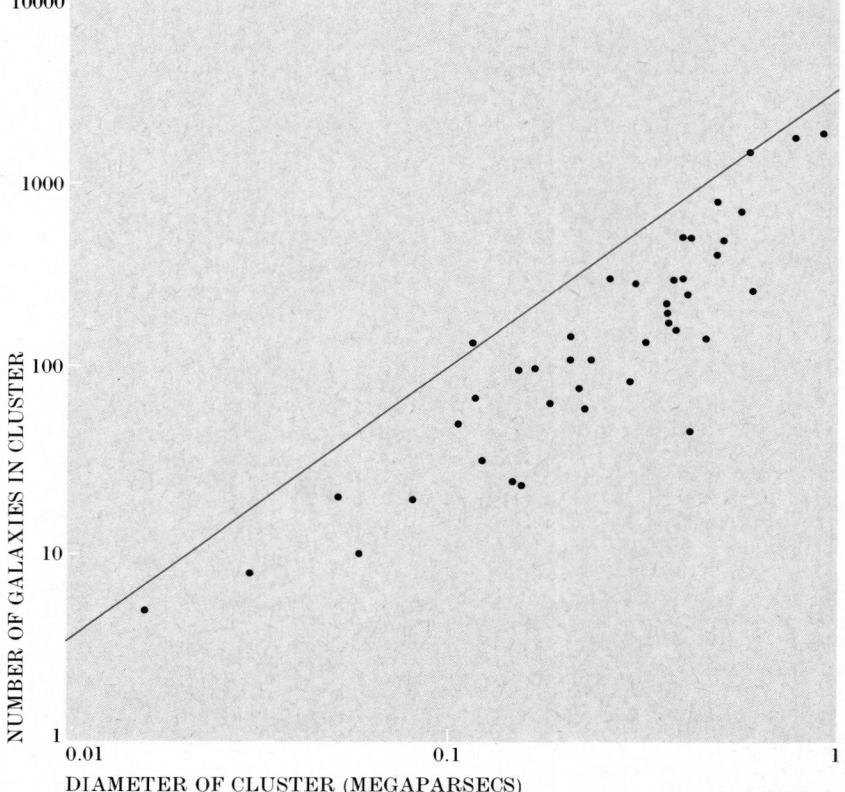

17.4: *Counts of galaxies brighter than certain magnitudes within a cluster comprise its luminosity function. Assuming that all the galaxies lie at the same distance, then the shape of this function depends upon the spread in intrinsic luminosity of galaxies within that cluster. Note the knee used to give the origin for this logarithmic plot, and the steepness of the brighter end. The results for four Abell clusters – red, A1656; blue, A2065; green, A151 and black, A2199 – give similar curves.*

17.5: *Carpenter's plot of the number of galaxies in a cluster against cluster diameter. The three points at upper right are very rich clusters. A distinct, continuous upper bound appears. Clusters to the lower right would be difficult to identify as such owing to their low density.*

Classification of clusters

Most of the clusters we describe are termed RICH CLUSTERS of galaxies. This implies a fairly high degree of central concentration of galaxies. Abell's catalogue tabulates 2712 rich clusters, which are numbered in order of increasing right ascension preceded by the letter A: examples are the Coma and Perseus clusters, A1656 and A426 respectively (figures 17.7 and 17.3). Abell clusters are mostly in the northern celestial hemisphere. Apart from the rich clusters, F. Zwicky and his colleagues have produced diagrams of the distribution of galaxies that reveal many more clusters that are not necessarily rich. The advent of survey material from observatories in the southern hemisphere means that similar, and even more detailed, catalogues of the southern regions are now available.

Abell classified his clusters according to richness and distance. In this scheme, the larger the richness and distance class the more centrally concentrated and distant is the cluster. He also differentiates in form between regular and irregular clusters. Distance classes range from near to extra-distant; distance estimates are based upon estimates of galaxy absolute magnitudes. Other classification schemes have been devised which inquire more into the brightness contrast between the galaxies, or the form of the cluster.

Clusters can also be classified by their radio or X-ray properties. For example some, and perhaps most, rich clusters contain extended radio sources as well as more complex radio sources associated with member galaxies. Many clusters are observed to emit X-rays. At present, however, these properties are ill-defined and no clear-cut classes are apparent.

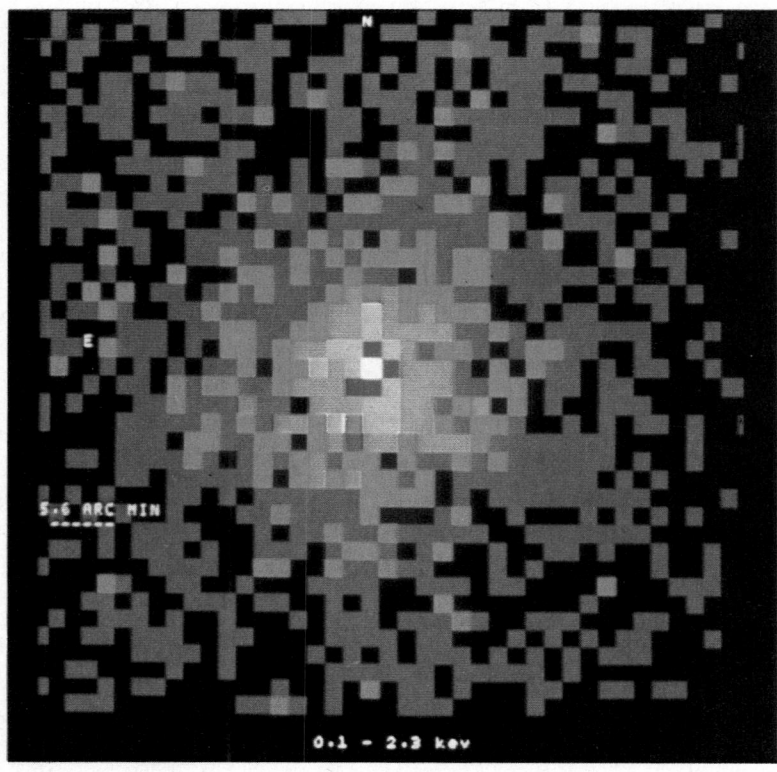

17.6: *X-ray intensity representation of the Virgo cluster of galaxies, obtained with an imaging X-ray telescope carried on board a sounding rocket. The white box in the centre is M87. The total size of the picture is about one degree. Note the extended nature of the X-ray emission surrounding M87; the telescope is capable of resolving features separated by more than about three of the image elements. (Harvard College Observatory, USA)*

The Coma cluster

One of the nearest rich regular clusters is situated two degrees from the north galactic pole in Coma Berenices (figure 17.7). It is ideally situated for observation, and the effects of galactic obscuration may be ignored. The cluster extends over several degrees, its total radius being difficult to define. Galaxies are usually assigned to a cluster if their *redshift* is similar to that of the core, or central region of the cluster. Over 800 redshifts are available for the Coma cluster, the mean implying a recession velocity of $6888\,km\,s^{-1}$ and the spread, or velocity dispersion – assumed due to the intrinsic velocities of member galaxies with respect to each other – being characterized by a value of $861\,km\,s^{-1}$. For a Hubble constant, H_0, of $75\,km\,s^{-1}\,Mpc^{-1}$, this implies a distance of about 90 Mpc, and one minute of arc is about 25 kpc at that distance.

The distribution of galaxies within the Coma cluster mimics that of stars in an elliptical galaxy, or stars in a globular cluster. This is what might be expected from a system of self-gravitating objects which has had sufficient time to interact and share its kinetic energy amongst its members. Such a distribution is characterized by a core, which is of about 240 kpc radius for the Coma cluster. Counts of galaxies have shown galaxies with similar redshifts to that of the Coma cluster out to 12° from the centre. It is not clear just how these apply to the cluster, if at all, for they may belong to less rich neighbouring clusters. The Coma cluster contains over 1000 bright members in the central regions, and this estimate may

increase to 10 000 if galaxies similar to the lesser members of our Local Group are included. The luminosity function of galaxies in Coma and other clusters has been determined, and shows that low-brightness members do not dominate the total mass or brightness. The average separation between brighter members is about 200 kpc in the central regions, and decreases within the core. Two super-giant galaxies, an elliptical NGC 4889 and an S0 galaxy, NGC 4874 dominate this core. It is devoid of spiral galaxies, and spirals are found only in the more outer regions. The main core population consists of elliptical and S0 galaxies. The lack of gas in these core galaxies has in the past been attributed to galaxy collisions. These are somewhat unlikely, however, and perhaps more probable is the following mechanism, known as RAM-PRESSURE STRIPPING. The presence of a hot intracluster gas is indicated by the observed X-ray emission, and galaxies ploughing through this will be stripped of gas. Several of the more massive elliptical galaxies are *active galaxies*, and explosive events within them may act to clear them of much of their gas. Studies of the redshifts of member galaxies at differing distances from the core show that rotation of the whole cluster is small.

The Coma cluster contains an extended radio source, which is presumably due to *synchrotron radiation*. The source of the relativistic electrons responsible is not known, although it is possible that some originate in the massive central galaxies. NGC 4874 itself exhibits a complex radio source, and NGC 4869, another galaxy in

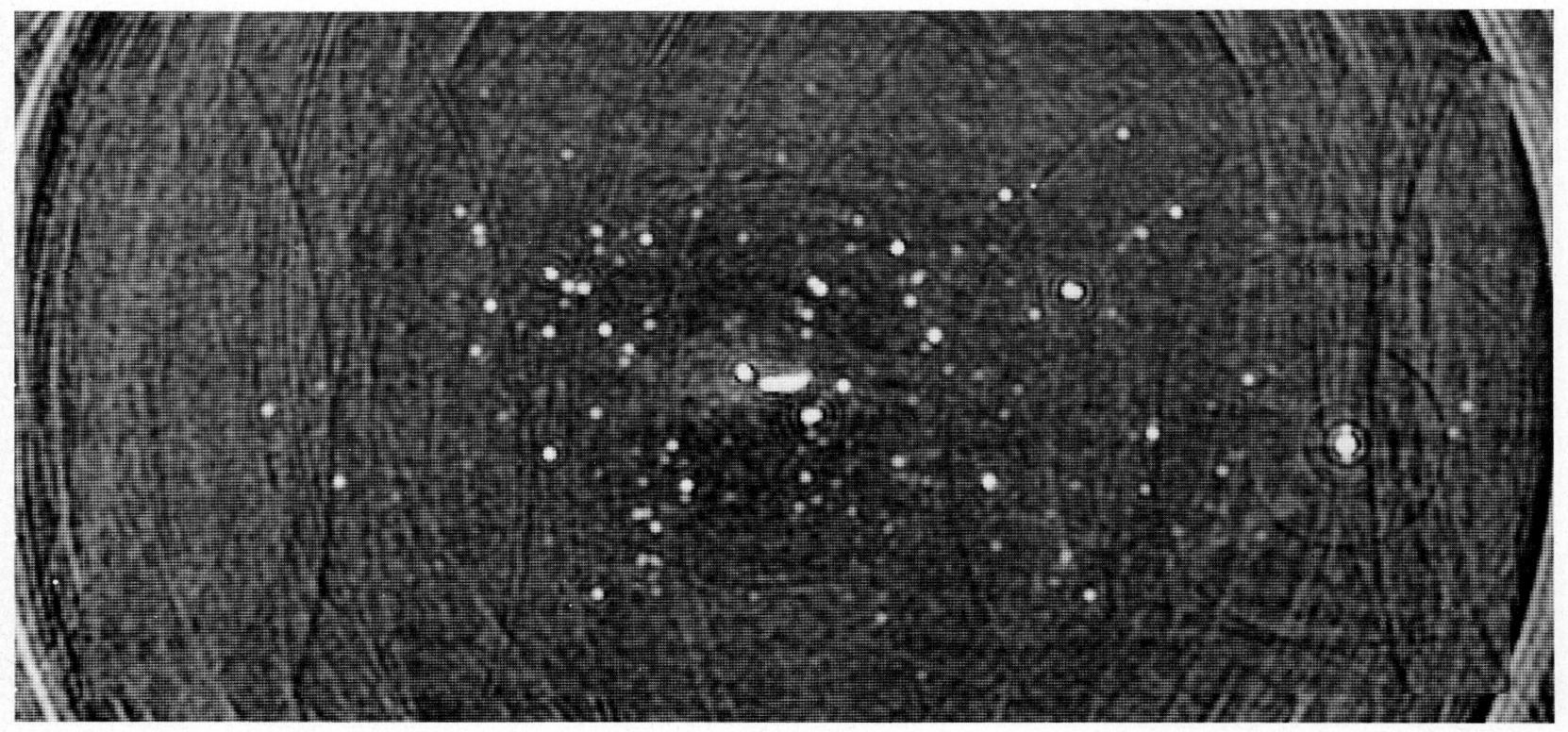

17.7: *Radio photograph of the field containing the Coma cluster of galaxies. The field is 3 degrees square, having been compressed by a factor of two in the N-S direction. This makes the telescope response circular, as can be seen from the diffraction rings. The lack of sources at the edge is due to instrumental effects. About 20 of the sources in the centre are associated with the Coma cluster. Note the tailed radio galaxy, NGC 4869, and diffuse radio source at centre. Coma A (not associated with the Coma cluster) is at right. (Leiden Observatory, Netherlands)*

17.8: *Radio contour map of NGC 1265 superimposed upon an optical photograph (Compare with figure 17.3). Note the blobs in the radio tail. (Leiden Observatory, Netherlands)*

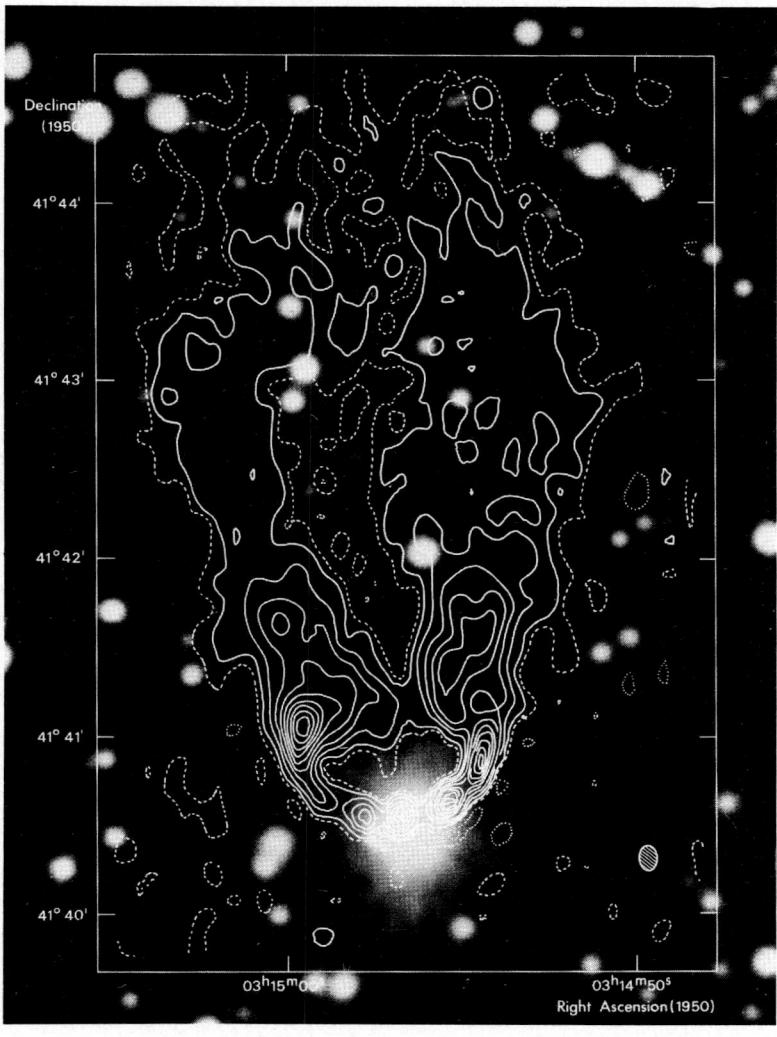

the core is an example of a 'head-tail' radio source. An extended X-ray source (0.5° extent), centred on the core of the cluster has been detected by Earth-orbiting satellites. X-ray emission is expected from electrons scattering the microwave background, and more probably from *thermal bremsstrahlung radiation* from hot intracluster gas (temperatures of about 10^8 K). X-ray spectral studies, although not well advanced, support this hypothesis. We do not expect anyway that the formation of galaxies is completely efficient, and some residual gas which did not participate in the creation of galaxies seems quite reasonable.

The Perseus cluster

The rich cluster in Perseus lies much nearer to the galactic plane than the Coma cluster, so has not been so well studied. Moreover it is not as symmetrical, the brightest galaxy members lying in an east-west line. It is possible that this projected line, which stretches for about 1°, is a transient effect observed in a cluster which is on the average much more symmetrical. A disc-shaped system seen nearly edge on is another possibility, although no rotation has been detected. The mean redshift of the Perseus cluster indicates a recession velocity of 5490 km s^{-1} and hence a distance of 72 Mpc. Over 50 redshifts give a velocity dispersion of about 1400 km s^{-1}, increasing in the core regions, the highest velocity dispersion yet recorded (figure 17.3).

Counts of galaxies in the Perseus cluster indicate a core radius of about 240 kpc, similar to that found in Coma, and indeed this seems to be a common value for rich clusters.

The core of the Perseus cluster is dominated by the *Seyfert galaxy* NGC 1275. An extended radio source exists over much of the cluster and there are several interesting radio sources including the one (Perseus A) located at NGC 1275. The Perseus cluster is one of the brightest extragalactic X-ray sources, and this is again most probably due to radiation from hot gas at a temperature of about 10^8 K. The extended X-ray emission is sharply peaked in the vicinity of NGC 1275 (figure 17.9).

The Perseus cluster contains several HEAD-TAIL RADIO SOURCES, the best studied example of which is NGC 1265. This lies about 0.5° ($\sim$1 Mpc) from NGC 1275. As the radio map shows (figure 17.8), extended emission can be traced for about 8 arc min north of the galaxy itself. This radio trail is itself double (figure 17.8) and there appear to be discrete blobs strung out in a semicircle which eventually merge into the tail. Radio polarization studies show that the magnetic field is aligned along the tail, and the degree of polarization itself increases with distance from the galaxy. The length of the tail (a few hundred kiloparsecs) seems to be similar to that expected from a source emitting synchrotron radiation and moving with a velocity of 1000 km s^{-1} or so. It is possible that we are viewing a radio trail, in which perhaps outbursts of activity from the galactic nucleus every few million years eject blobs of plasma that fall back from the galaxy, losing energy as they move through the cluster. Such an interpretation provides indirect evidence for the presence of an intracluster gas.

The Virgo cluster

Sixteen of the 34 galaxies listed in the Messier catalogue are members of the Virgo cluster, which lies near the north galactic pole and is a good example of an irregular cluster (see figure 17.10). Its mean redshift translates to about 1140 km s^{-1} implying a distance of only 16 Mpc, and the spread in velocities is about 670 km s^{-1}. It should be noted that the Virgo cluster of galaxies is part of the chain of systems used to determine distances independent of redshift.

There is little in the way of a central concentration of galaxies, although the ellipticals are somewhat more spherically symmetric than the rest. The whole cluster seems to be highly structured. No marked separation of galaxy types is observed. The galaxy M87 (NGC 4486) is a prominent member of the Virgo cluster. Short photographic exposures reveal a jet, and deep surveys show an extensive halo of globular clusters.

The X-ray luminosity of the Virgo cluster is about 2 per cent of the Perseus cluster. It is centred upon M87, which lies about 1° from the cluster centre. The emission extends for about 50 arc min and again it is probably due to hot gas, although emission from compact sources in the galaxy and globular cluster halo may contribute also. The X-ray luminosity of clusters of galaxies seems to be correlated with velocity dispersion: the clusters with the higher velocities are the more luminous. These clusters are likely to be more massive and contain more gas, thus more X-ray emission is expected.

Many groups and chains of galaxies lie between the Virgo cluster and the Local Group. The apparent flattening and concentration of these systems has encouraged G. de Vaucouleurs to name them the Local, or Virgo, Supercluster. The physical and dynamical reality of this supercluster is in doubt, and it is not clear how chance groupings of objects interfere with the interpretation.

The Centaurus cluster

Several rich clusters are known in the southern hemisphere, and one of the most prominent lies in the constellation of Centaurus. Some tens of its member galaxies have had redshifts measured and the mean of 3740 km s^{-1} implies a distance of about 50 Mpc. The velocity dispersion is about 950 km s^{-1}.

The distribution of galaxies in the Centaurus cluster is irregular and exhibits two major concentrations, so it is possible that it consists of two separate clusters close to each other by chance. Near one of the peaks lies NGC 4696, an elliptical galaxy with an associated radio source. The X-ray emission from the Centaurus cluster is rather weak when compared with the Perseus cluster, and there appears to be a concentration in the vicinity of NGC 4696.

17.9: *X-ray intensity representation of the Perseus cluster of galaxies, produced by the same telescope system as figure 17.7. The central white spot is associated with NGC 1275.*
(Harvard College Observatory, USA)

17.10: *Part of the Virgo cluster of galaxies. M87 is the prominent elliptical galaxy in the lower left-hand corner. M82 is the apparently flat galaxy (displaying a marked dust band) near the right-hand edge, about one and a half degrees from M87.*
(Tautenberg Observatory, DDR)

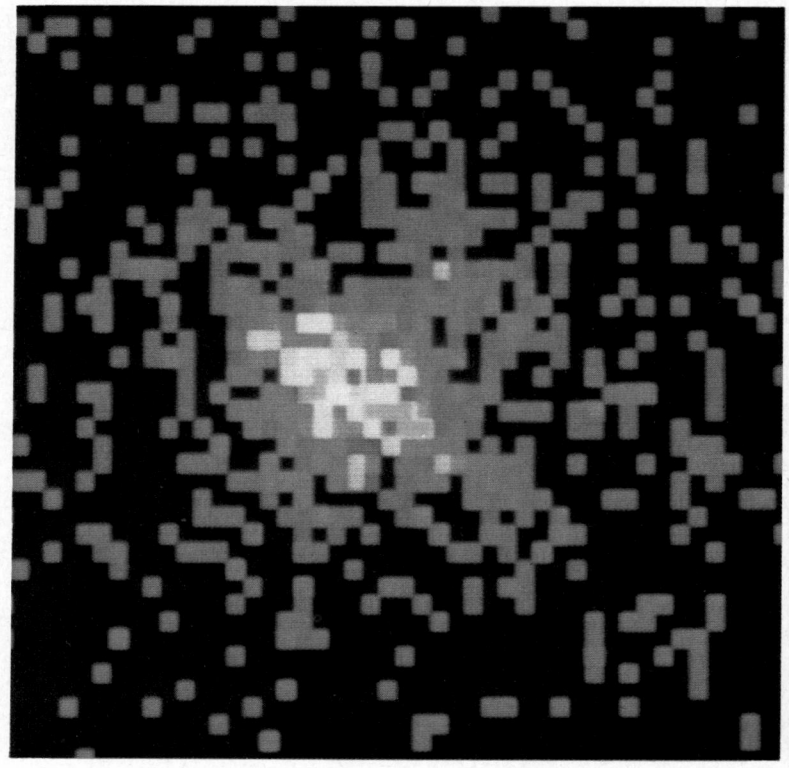

17.11: *Observational constraints on the missing mass in the form of gas in the Coma cluster. The clumpiness is defined as the ratio of the total cluster volume to the total volume occupied by gas, and must exceed unity. The gas (taken as 90 per cent hydrogen + 10 per cent helium) will be ionized if hotter than 10^4 K. Regions to the right of line 1 are excluded because more soft X-rays would be emitted than are observed. Similarly other constraints are placed by the observed lack of: Lyman alpha emission due to the hot gas recombining, 2; radio emission from thermal bremsstrahlung 3; neutral hydrogen emission at 21 cm, 4 and neutral hydrogen absorption, 5. (The last two do not apply to ionized gas.) The gas must exceed the 2.7 K temperature of the microwave background giving limit 6. The unshaded region is all that remains acceptable. The gas must be ionized and occupy less than 0.01 per cent of the cluster volume. Theoretical considerations further reduce this region.*

The dynamics and masses of clusters of galaxies

Rich clusters of galaxies are certainly not due to chance associations or random encounters between galaxies. They are systems in which galaxies are dynamically interacting with each other and with any intracluster gas. In terms of the spatial distribution of member galaxies the richest clusters especially appear stable and gravitationally bound. Unlike the Solar System for example, which matches all the requirements for a stable, gravitationally-bound system, mass estimates made for galaxy clusters do not agree with their being bound. We now examine the dynamics and motions of galaxies within a cluster, which are somewhat more complicated than those of the planets.

A typical cluster galaxy does not describe a simple orbit about the centre of mass of the cluster. It is continually being deviated from its path by the gravitational pulls of all the other galaxies. Close encounters and collisions must be rare, especially in the less dense regions of the cluster, but the cumulative effect of all the distant galaxies is significant. In a region uniformly populated with galaxies, the gravitational attraction from any individual galaxy falls off as its distance squared, but the number of such galaxies increases as the distance squared. Consequently equal shells around any specified galaxy contribute the same total pull independent of distance. Of course if everything is completely symmetrical the pulls cancel, but the distribution of galaxies and gas in a real cluster gives rise to important effects. The overall tendency

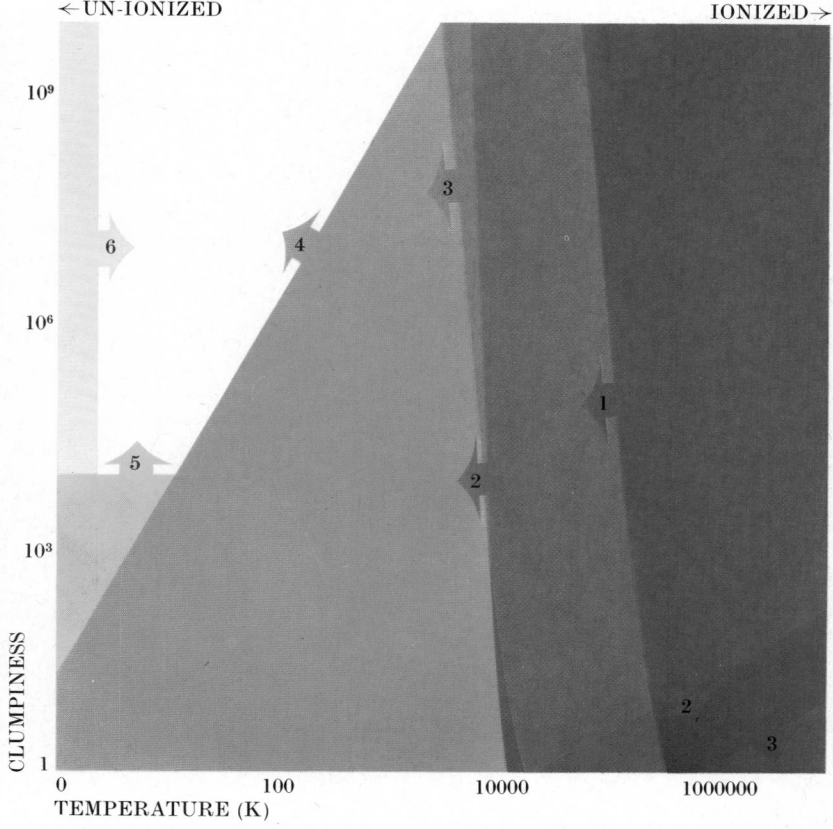

is for kinetic energy to be shared among the individual galaxies. The time taken after a disturbance for the system to restore equilibrium, in which all galaxies have on average the same energy as any other, is known as the RELAXATION TIME.

The relaxation times for the dense cores of the richest clusters are of the order of the age of the Universe and so these regions may be considered relaxed and therefore stable. It is possible that conditions in the initial collapse of these cores were such that somewhat shorter relaxation times occurred in the past. If clusters were unbound, then they would tend to evaporate away in a timescale similar to that which a galaxy would take to cross the whole cluster, if its present velocity were unchecked. In the case of the Coma cluster core, for example, this time (usually referred to as the CROSSING TIME) is approximately 3×10^8 yr, which is much shorter than the age of the Universe. The dispersal of cluster cores would moreover introduce large numbers of elliptical galaxies into the regions between clusters of galaxies. Only subsequent rapid changes in the form of elliptical galaxies could produce the observed lack of ellipticals in these regions. There is no known mechanism for such changes nor observational basis for its occurrence. These arguments strongly suggest that rich clusters are stable and gravitationally bound.

The mass of a cluster of galaxies can be measured basically in two ways. The first method is to study the spread in motion of the cluster galaxies. In the same way that stellar masses and galaxy masses can be estimated from binary pairs, masses of large collections of objects can be deduced from their average motion. The greater the mass of the cluster, the greater will be the gravitational pull that the galaxies exert on each other. These forces hold the cluster together, but it is prevented from collapsing completely by orbital motions, as with a binary pair. A relaxed self-gravitating system left to itself and examined at various later stages should on average be found to be in a state such that twice the sum of the kinetic energy of the components should equal the total gravitational potential energy. This is known as the VIRIAL THEOREM and the masses derived from it VIRIAL MASSES. Simply the mass $M = V^2 R/G$ where V is a weighted mean of the galaxy velocities (obtained from the velocity dispersion of the cluster), R is a characteristic radius (the harmonic average of the separations of galaxies) and G the gravitational constant.

The VELOCITY DISPERSION is a measure of the spread of galaxy velocities (determined from redshift measurements), and, as observed, relates to motions along the line of sight (a geometrical factor ($\sqrt{3}$) must be included to change this into the true velocity dispersion). For the Coma cluster the characteristic radius is about 3 Mpc. The virial mass of the Coma cluster is then approximately 5×10^{15} $M_\odot$.

Another method for determining the mass of a cluster of galaxies is to add up the individual masses of the member galaxies. Analyses of galaxy *rotation curves*, luminosity distributions, and studies of binary galaxies have been used to obtain the masses of galaxies themselves. These give mass-to-luminosity ratios (M/L ratios) of 30–70 $M_\odot/L_\odot$ for ellipticals and between 1 and 10 $M_\odot/L_\odot$ for spirals. The estimated total luminosity for the Coma cluster, found by summing the individual galaxies; is about 3×10^{13} $L_\odot$. A mass-to-luminosity ratio of nearly 200 $M_\odot/L_\odot$ is therefore required to explain the virial mass. The discrepancy between the mass-to-luminosity ratios for the cluster as a whole and its individual members is at least a factor of 5 and perhaps more.

Similar procedures have been followed for many other clusters and the mass discrepancy always seems to occur, with factors of 10 or more being common, and seeming to increase with the size of the system. This suggests that it cannot all be a statistical fluctuation or a chance projection of galaxies occurring in the Coma cluster. The mass discrepancy is independent of the value of the *Hubble constant*. Drastic approaches such as new laws of physics, involving, for example, a slight change in the inverse square law of gravitation, have been suggested.

We shall take the view here that there is a mass discrepancy and look at the various explanations in terms of MISSING MASS. The optical luminosity of the cluster is an estimate of the luminosity of detected objects. There may be much more hidden or invisible mass, and if so it must be distributed in space roughly in the same way as the galaxies. If it were much more extended it could not hope to bind the core, and if it were much more compact it would tidally distort the central regions more than is observed. We discuss in detail the Coma cluster since this is well studied, but most of the arguments apply to other clusters.

One obvious candidate for the missing mass is INTRACLUSTER GAS. This has probably been detected by its X-ray emission, and it has an implied density, if distributed fairly smoothly, of about 10^3 ions per cubic metre. The radio trail galaxies also point to its presence. One further test would be the detection of a dip in the intensity of the microwave background as seen through a cluster. This would result because the thermal electrons collide with the microwave background photons, changing their direction and energy. Preliminary results of searches for this effect suggest that it does occur. Unfortunately the total mass of hot gas is only about 10 per cent of the virial mass. Thus it cannot overcome the mass discrepancy by itself. It is possible that denser clouds of cooler gas are embedded in this hot gas. Under certain circumstances fairly dense clouds of, say, molecular hydrogen might be virtually undetectable. Searches for cluster gas have been carried out at many wavelengths. These include looking for redshifted *Lyman-α* emission in *quasar* spectra, Hβ emission, *bremsstrahlung* emission at radio and optical frequencies and 21-cm emission and absorption. The results for the Coma cluster are summarized in figure 17.11. It appears that the cluster cannot be bound by ionized gas.

Other possibilities centre on more condensed matter. Studies of obscuration and colour changes in the centre of the cluster indicate that dust similar to that in our Galaxy is not responsible. However, larger dust particles ranging in size up to football-sized lumps could easily bind the cluster and remain undetectable, but there is no obvious means for producing such objects. Intergalactic *black holes* might work, as might a population of 'brown' dwarfs – stars with masses less than about one-tenth that of the Sun. Presumably most of such objects (if the black holes are of stellar mass) would lie in the haloes of galaxies, and in fact there are tentative indications that massive galaxies are surrounded by extensive haloes.

Increasing the mass-to-luminosity ratio for galaxies to about 170 is possible but it is not generally considered likely. Such massive galaxies would tend to distort each other tidally far more than is observed to be the case. They might also tend to interact with each other in such a way as to gobble each other up. This might well result in more mass segregation of galaxies than is observed.

The missing mass problem may be resolved by pushing to their limits many of the suggestions listed above. The virial theorem ought to apply in a fairly precise way to a rich and apparently stable cluster such as the Coma cluster. This intriguing problem has sparked off many interesting investigations and taught us that not everything in the Universe is visible – at least not to present-day instruments. Perhaps some new physics, such as the spontaneous creation of galaxies, or non-velocity redshifts, lies behind the frustrating results so far. Few astronomers believe this, but extragalactic astronomy is bedevilled by problems related to the interpretation of redshifts and the measurement of extended objects. Several groups of galaxies, such as Stephan's Quintet, appear to have mass discrepancies large enough to make the Coma problem pale into insignificance. Such groups could, and probably do, contain chance associations, making it difficult to be at all rigorous.

Clusters of galaxies as cosmological probes

Clusters of galaxies are the largest entities known and studied in the Universe. They are also very luminous, with integrated brightnesses rivalling those of quasars. This property, along with their radio and X-ray emission, enables them to be discovered and investigated at large distances. It is generally hoped that this will lead to the use of clusters of galaxies in testing models of the Universe. No outstanding results have as yet been obtained, nor are they likely to be gained until far more is known about the forms, populations, luminosity functions, and other properties of a large sample of clusters. Computer analyses of large-field photographs should gradually change this situation, as this is the only reasonable way of processing the quantity of data involved.

One obvious cosmological use for clusters is in defining the cosmic constants for expansion of the Universe. Here the useful distance criterion is the apparent magnitude of the first, or third, or tenth brightest member. The behaviour of the brighter end of the galaxy luminosity function means that there is only a small spread in the absolute magnitudes of such galaxies. Selection effects cloud the usefulness of this: for example, very distant clusters may be selected because they are richer than average or contain some exceptionally bright or unusual galaxy or emission property. Obviously if a cluster of galaxies contains an unusually luminous galaxy or galaxies, then any distance assigned on the basis of the mean magnitude of other brighter cluster galaxies will be under-estimated. Such effects are really important when deciding whether the universal expansion is slowing down or speeding up. If the rate of expansion was greater in the past than it is now, then a distant galaxy or cluster will have a greater redshift than if no change in expansion rate occurred. Consequently underestimating the distance to a cluster mimics overestimating the amount of deceleration.

The evolution of the overall brightnesses and spectra of galaxies is largely unknown. Consequently it is not safe to assume that the luminosity function for galaxies has always been the same as it is now. It is not even known which way to correct the magnitudes of the brighter and more massive galaxies. Although earlier they contained bright young stars which have since dimmed, the individual massive galaxies within the cores of clusters may have grown in mass. This they can do at the expense of their neighbours, by tidal disruption. Intracluster gas may also be accreted into such galaxies, whilst interstellar gas can be expelled by violent events. The redshift of distant galaxies means that radiation emitted in the ultraviolet now becomes visible.

Another way in which clusters may be instrumental in determining the deceleration of the Universe is the so-called angular diameter-redshift test. An extended object of fixed size should appear smaller when viewed from increasing distances. The curvature of space may cause it to pass through a minimum angular size and then get bigger again. Clusters of galaxies are extended and they should show this effect although clusters at redshift of unity or more may be needed in order to observe a minimum. Difficulties arise in assigning some characteristic length to a cluster, especially for those of high redshift, and hence distance. Clusters probably also evolve in diameter thereby introducing further uncertainties.

Clusters of galaxies must have formed at large redshifts and studies of them now may give clues to the formation and evolution of galaxies. It is not clear whether the clusters formed first and then the galaxies, or whether it happened the other way round. Computer models reproduce details of the Coma cluster if it is assumed that the galaxies formed and then clustered. This is consistent with a picture in which gravitational instabilities gave rise to the large-scale features in the Universe in the periods after recombination of the helium and hydrogen atoms.

The discovery of intracluster gas is important in showing us another constituent of the Universe, hitherto undetectable. Such gas may be the remnant of infall into clusters from some all pervading intergalactic medium, leftovers from the process of galaxy formation, or gas expelled from individual galaxies. The diffuse X-ray background at kilovolt energies may partly originate in a hot intergalactic medium. The spatial structure of this radiation may thus be instructive in mapping further details of the large-scale matter distribution in the Universe.

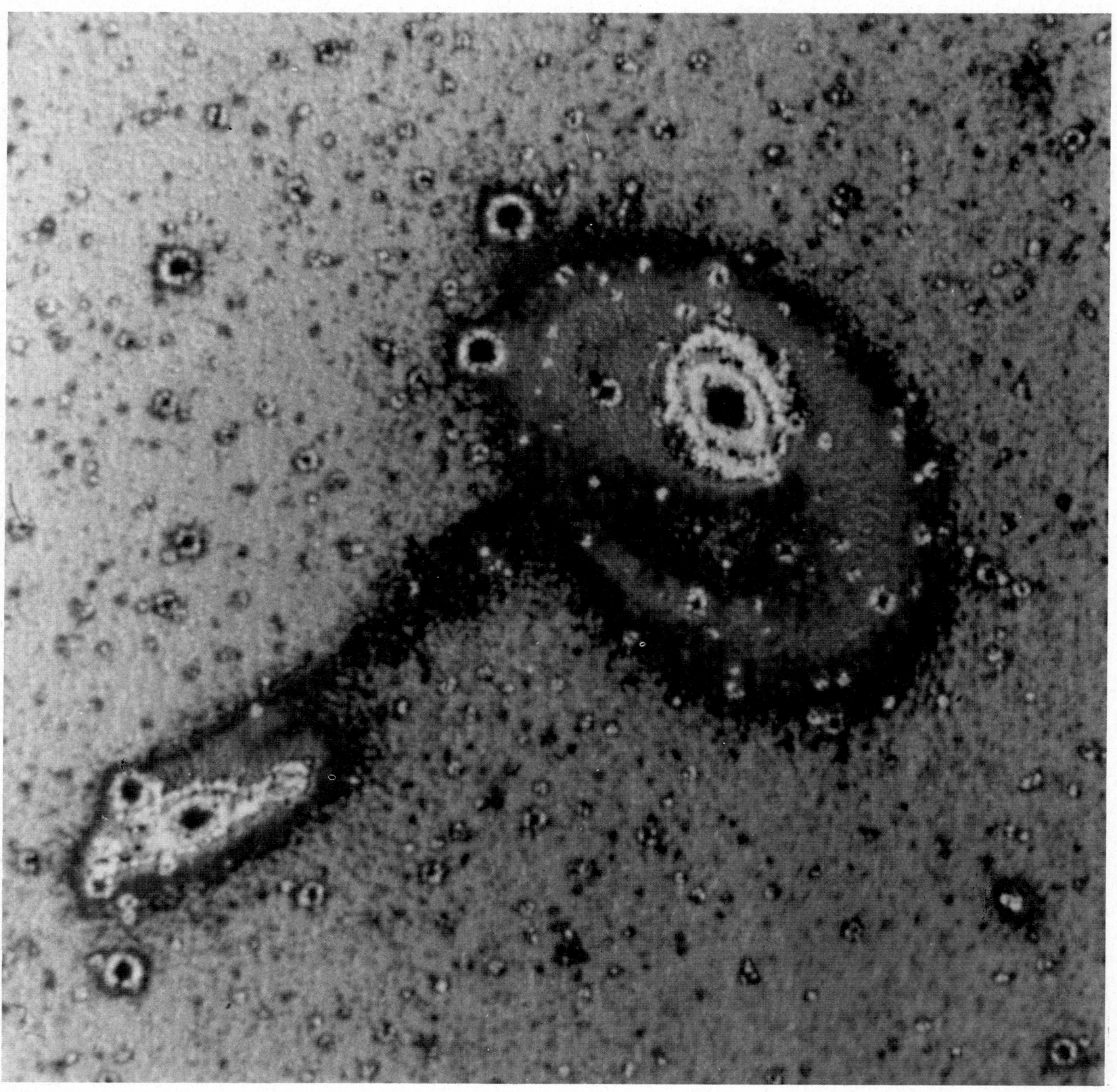

18. Active galaxies and radio galaxies

Introduction

The previous chapters described the general properties of normal galaxies in detail. The vast majority of galaxies are normal in the sense that they have general properties in common. In particular, their present rate of evolution, as measured for example by their rate of star formation, is consistent with their age as indicated by their stellar *populations*.

A relatively small number of galaxies, however, show levels of energetic activity that could not be sustained for more than a small fraction of the total expected lifetime of a galaxy. Despite the considerable variety of activity exhibited, these objects are usually grouped under the general heading of active galaxies. Active galaxies are of considerable interest to astronomers since they are objects which represent the extremes of galactic structure. The activity in these galaxies is accessible and therefore more easily measured than in normal galaxies. Such observations can give valuable clues to phenomena that are present to a much lesser extent in many galaxies but that are nevertheless of great importance to our understanding of them all. It is important to appreciate that most classes of active galaxies have been discovered largely by accident, as a by-product of work on relatively normal objects. Only in the case of the radio galaxies have the properties of active galaxies been surveyed systematically and comprehensively. It may well be that it is the haphazard way in which they were discovered that is responsible for their apparently great diversity. Because of this, we shall concentrate on the various forms that this activity can take and then look at a few of the better-studied objects in some detail. As the strong *extragalactic radio sources* and *quasars* have been studied fairly systematically, they will be described separately.

The signs of activity in galaxies

The common feature of all the forms of energetic galactic activity is that all are relatively short-lived. We have a fairly good idea of the ages of stars and galaxies as well as of the way in which they evolve. ACTIVE GALAXIES are those that appear to be evolving in a manner that they could not sustain for more than a small part of their total lifetime without the presence of some source of energy much more powerful than that needed to account for the properties of *normal galaxies*. It is in the nuclei of these galaxies that we often see the many and varied signs of activity.

Galaxies with abnormally luminous nuclei

We know from studies of normal galaxies that regions of recent star formation are particularly luminous. It is possible to account for the high nuclear luminosity of certain galaxies by supposing the galaxy to be very young. This would mean that we were seeing its initial burst of star formation. Such an explanation undoubtedly accounts for some of the COMPACT GALAXIES and is confirmed by their spectra which show them to be similar to giant *ionized hydrogen regions*. They also are found to contain large amounts of neutral hydrogen; this implies that they are, indeed, fairly young

18.1: *Much of modern research has centred on understanding the unusual galaxies that seem to have been overwhelmed by cosmic catastrophe. Computer processing techniques such as that shown here enable scientists to extract more information on the nature of galaxy interactions. A tidal interaction is pictured here.*
(Kitt Peak National Observatory, USA)

so that only a small fraction of the total gas content of these galaxies has yet been able to collapse to form stars. Apart from the young galaxies, there are also objects which have abnormally luminous nuclei but which are believed to have a considerable age. These include the normal or supergiant elliptical galaxies, found in rich regular clusters of galaxies. Giant elliptical galaxies with active nuclei are often associated with strong radio emission and their origins may well be related.

Galaxies with unusually broad lines in their spectra

The width of the lines in a spectrum of an object can indicate either the temperature of the emitting region or it can give the range of velocities found within the emitting region. A number of galaxies have particularly wide lines in their spectra. If the broad lines are attributed to high temperatures, these are much greater than found in normal galaxies and resemble the temperatures found in *supernova remnants*. Alternatively, the line widths could indicate the velocity dispersion within the nuclei of these galaxies. This might imply that clouds of gas are moving about rapidly (up to 5000 km s^{-1}) within the nuclei of these galaxies. However, with such high speeds the clouds could only be bound gravitationally to the nucleus if it was extremely massive. Otherwise the clouds must be moving rapidly away from the nuclear region and we may have to consider the possibility that they have been ejected from the nucleus of the galaxy.

Galaxies with non-thermal continua

Most active galaxies have an optical spectrum rich in *emission lines*. These are superposed on a continuum spectrum which normally has essentially a *black-body* (thermal) form determined by the temperature of an object. In some active galaxies, however, the continuum spectrum appears to be of a non-thermal origin, in that it cannot be due to an object with a single temperature or, indeed to the superposition of a large number of objects of different temperature. It is likely that in these cases the continuum is produced by *synchrotron radiation*, generated when energetic electrons move through a region containing a weak magnetic field.

Galaxies which emit strongly at radio wavelengths

The radio radiation emitted by normal galaxies is very weak indeed. However some of the most distant galaxies ever found have been discovered by radio astronomers because of the great intensity of their radio emission. These are the strong extragalactic radio sources described below. Many active galaxies radiate at radio wavelengths with intermediate strength. High-resolution radio telescopes enable astronomers to estimate the amount of energy needed to account for the radio emission. These amounts are not enough to sustain the phenomenon for more than a fraction of a galactic lifetime. This suggests that radio emission is either a transient phenomenon or that there may be hidden energy sources within radio-bright galaxies.

Galaxies with rapid variability

Normal galaxies probably reach the peak of their luminosity soon after they are formed, and subsequently fade away relatively slowly. The most violently active galaxies show variations in their optical and radio brightness, sometimes in only a few days. Although the radiating regions are extremely compact, measurements suggest that the disturbances responsible for the variability must move through the emitting region with a velocity close to that of light.

Galaxies with unstable jets or tails

Normal galaxies are dynamically stable: they will change their large-scale structure only very gradually. Certain active galaxies exhibit structures that must be short-lived. The jets or tails seen attached to some galaxies can only last until the gravitational attraction of the parent galaxy pulls them back towards the galaxy. Indeed their very presence suggests that they must have been ejected from their parent galaxies in the fairly recent past.

It is clear from the above survey that there is tremendous variety in the forms and violence of the activity in galaxies. In the next section we look at the variety found in active galaxies and search for features common to a number of different classes.

The classification of active galaxies

The many classes of active galaxies are primarily a consequence of the haphazard way in which they were discovered. Very few active galaxies fit neatly into one class; consequently there is considerable overlap between the various classification schemes used. With this proviso we now review the main properties of several classes of active galaxies.

Markarian galaxies

These are objects discovered in the early 1970s by the Russian astronomer B.E.Markarian of the Byurakan Observatory in Armenia. He used a *Schmidt telescope* with an objective prism to search for galaxies with a strong ultraviolet continuum. The objects found fall mainly into two types: galaxies (often spirals) with a bright nucleus that is the source of the ultraviolet continuum, and diffuse galaxies with the ultraviolet sources spread throughout the object. Many of the first group are *Seyfert galaxies* whose spectra show broad emission lines. Others in this group have narrow emission lines in their spectra. The fainter members of the second group have spectra very similar to those of ionized hydrogen regions, and are occasionally referred to as intergalactic H$^+$ regions. They are faint irregular galaxies generally with a very low metal content. It is probable that these galaxies have been formed within the past 100 million years. The brighter MARKARIAN GALAXIES are fairly diverse in their general properties. HARO GALAXIES were first found in 1956 by Haro of the Tonantzintla Observatory in South America using a survey technique similar to that of Markarian. They are essentially the same as the diffuse Markarian galaxies.

Compact galaxies

While the Californian astronomer Fritz Zwicky was compiling a catalogue of clusters of galaxies, he found a number of COMPACT GALAXIES of high surface brightness that are barely distinguishable from stars. The red compact galaxies found by Zwicky are probably normal galaxies with an unusually high surface brightness, while the blue galaxies in Zwicky's list are probably small intergalactic ionized hydrogen regions.

N-type galaxies

These are objects with most of their luminosity in a bright, starlike nucleus and surrounded by a faint, relatively compact nebulous envelope (figure 18.2). The nuclei of N-TYPE GALAXIES have colours like *quasars*, whereas the envelopes have colours similar to those of giant elliptical galaxies. In many respects N-type galaxies are similar to relatively luminous, distant Seyfert galaxies, described next.

Seyfert galaxies

These are galaxies first classified as a group by Carl Seyfert in 1943 as part of a survey of spiral galaxies. They have starlike nuclei that emit a rich emission-line spectrum with very broad lines. SEYFERT GALAXIES are relatively common. Approximately 10 per cent of the brightest galaxies are Seyfert-type galaxies although they are much less common among fainter galaxies. Seyfert galaxies differ from the other Markarian galaxies in that they show substantial non-thermal emission which is seen most easily at the ultraviolet end of their spectra. Indeed it is generally found that objects with broad emission lines in their spectra also show non-thermal nuclear continuum. The colours of Seyfert nuclei are rather similar to those of *quasars*.

The emission lines found in Seyfert spectra are both the permitted hydrogen *Balmer lines* and the lines of ionized oxygen, nitrogen and neon. Seyfert galaxies may be divided into two sub-types on the basis of their spectra. These are Type 1 (such as shown in figure 18.3) where the Balmer lines are broader than the lines of ionized metals and Type 2 (such as shown in figure 18.4) where the Balmer lines and the metal lines are of similar width. The Balmer lines of Type 1 Seyferts are often several thousand km s^{-1} wide whereas the metal lines of Type 1 and all the lines of Type 2 Seyferts are usually 500–1000 km s^{-1} wide.

The complexity of Seyfert galaxy spectra has made it difficult to reach any firm conclusions about the origin of Seyfert-type activity. In certain respects, Seyfert galaxies are like quasars. Spectroscopically, quasars are similar to Type 1 Seyfert galaxies and the faintest quasars have a brightness in the range of the brightest Seyfert galaxies. A particularly interesting nearby Seyfert galaxy is IC4329A which has an exceptional Hβ flux which is only one-third of that of the well-known quasar 3C 48.

Seyfert galaxies are often optically variable sometimes over a few months. It is almost always the continuum which varies while the emission lines remain constant. This implies that the region

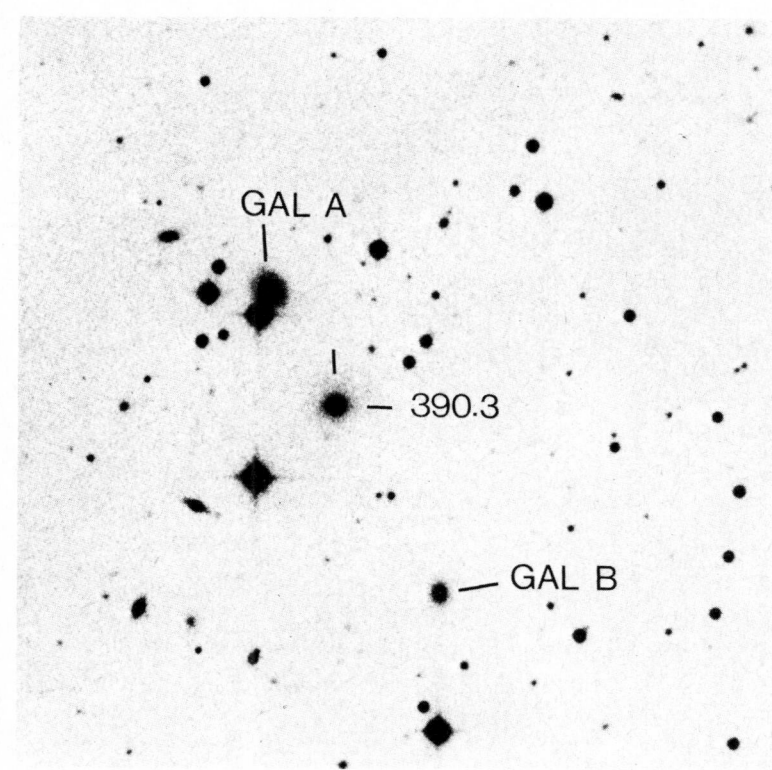

18.2: *Radio source 3C 390.3 matches the N-type galaxy which is a member of a galaxy cluster. Galaxy B is another member. Galaxy A is probably a foreground galaxy. (Royal Greenwich Observatory, UK)*

that generates the non-thermal continuum is much more compact than the region that produces the emission line radiation. Detailed spectroscopic studies suggest that the considerable line width in Seyfert galaxy spectra is a result of the emission lines coming from a number of distinct clouds of gas close to the centre of the galaxy. The velocities of these clouds can be as high as $700 \, km \, s^{-1}$ relative to the centre of the galaxy. The extended widths of the Balmer lines of Type 1 Seyferts imply much higher velocities, typically $3000 \, km \, s^{-1}$ relative to the centre of the galaxy. These probably originate in turbulent regions closer to the centre of the galaxy where the gas density is high enough to stop any *forbidden lines* being produced. A correlation is observed between the width of the Balmer lines and the intensity of the non-thermal continuum. This might arise if the ultraviolet continuum radiation is responsible for ionizing the gas that then produces the Balmer lines.

Most Seyfert galaxies have small radio sources in their nuclei; these are between 10 and 1000 times brighter than those found in the nuclei of normal spiral galaxies. None, however, has the characteristic double structure commonly found amongst the stronger extragalactic radio sources. Some Seyfert galaxies emit a considerable quantity of X-rays.

18.3: *NGC 4151, a classical Seyfert galaxy. Its rich emission-line spectrum reveals a wealth of astrophysical information on conditions within its nucleus. This object has a Type I spectrum.*
(Hale Observatories, USA)

18.4: *Peculiar galaxy ESO 116–IG15 is 150 Mpc away. It has a Type II Seyfert spectrum. Gas motions of 800 km s⁻¹ are present in its active centre.*
(European Southern Observatory, Chile)

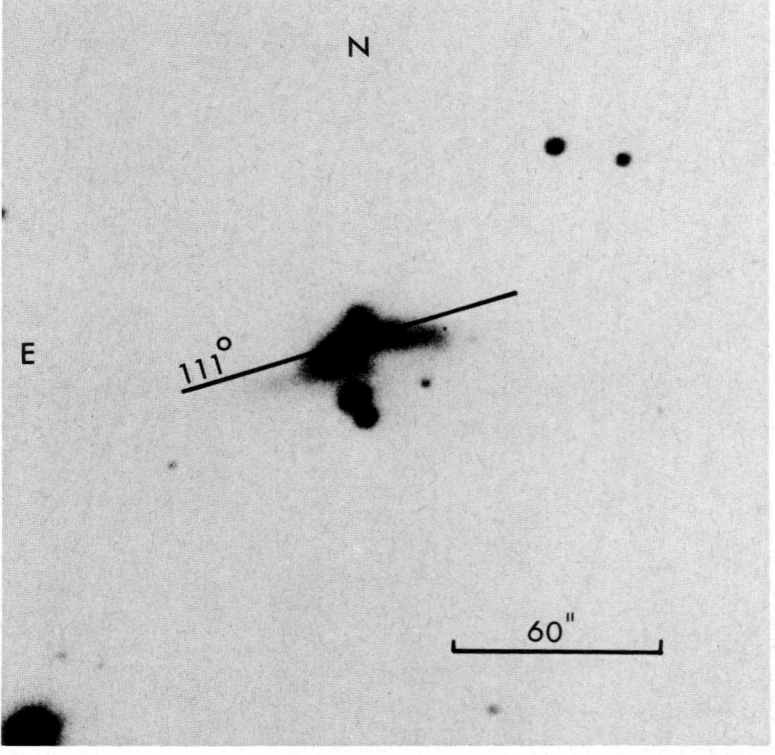

The exploding galaxy M82

This is the nearest galaxy in which we see evidence of violent activity. The first sign of activity came with the discovery of a small, weak, radio source in its nucleus. Optical studies showed that a large amount of gas had been ejected above and below the plane of M82 and the velocity of the gas suggested the ejection had started about 1–10 million years ago. It has also been found that the radiation from the filaments of ejected gas is strongly polarized. This was first thought to show that the outburst had given rise to optical *synchrotron radiation*, but more recent work has shown that both the optical continuum and the emission lines are strongly and similarly polarized. As synchrotron radiation cannot generate emission lines, polarized or not, another explanation had to be sought. Figure 18.6 shows evidence of substantial quantities of dust – so much so that the nucleus of M82 can only be penetrated by infrared wavelengths longer than about 700 nm. It is now believed that the dust grains above and below the plane of M82 are aligned by the radiation from the nucleus and that the way in which they scatter light towards us is responsible for the polarization. As there is no evidence for a bright stellar nucleus, even after the obscuration produced by the dust has been accounted for, it is evident that M82 is not a Seyfert galaxy. There is, however, a very strong infrared source in the nucleus. There are also considerable non-circular motions of the ionized gas throughout the galaxy and it is probable that these motions were also caused by disturbances in the nucleus of M82.

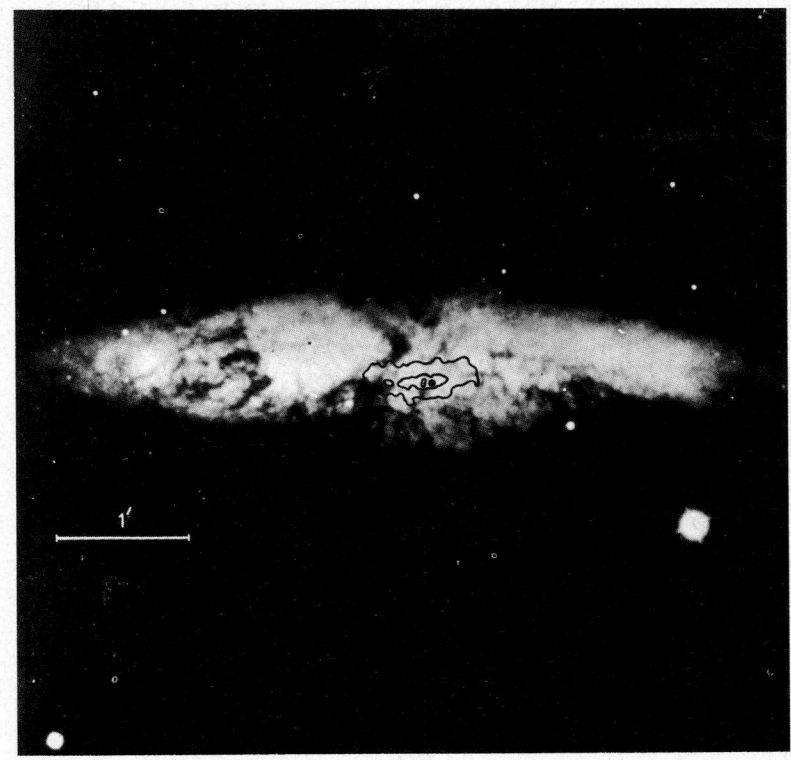

18.6: *Active galaxy M82 consists mainly of billowing clouds of gas and dust. The contours indicate the extent of the radio source shown in figure 18.5.*
(Hale Observatories, USA)

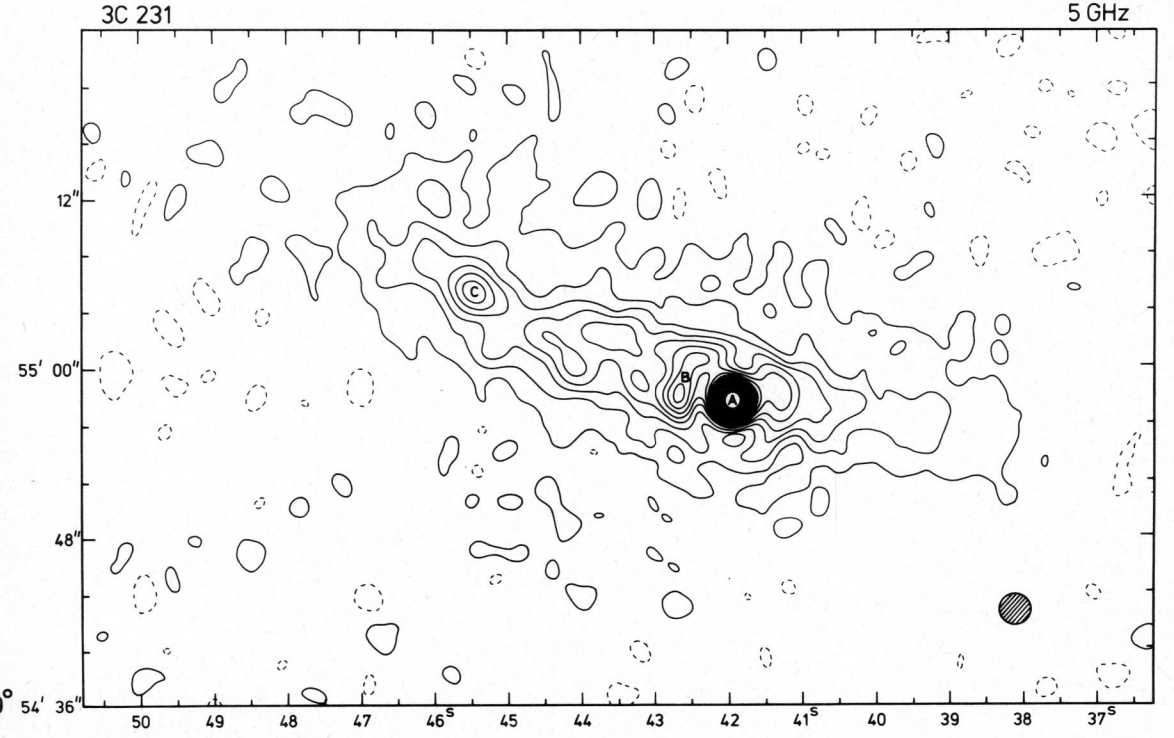

18.5: *Radio source 3C 231 has several compact emission regions marked A, B and C, associated with the active centre of galaxy M82. (Mullard Radio Astronomy Observatory, Cambridge, UK)*

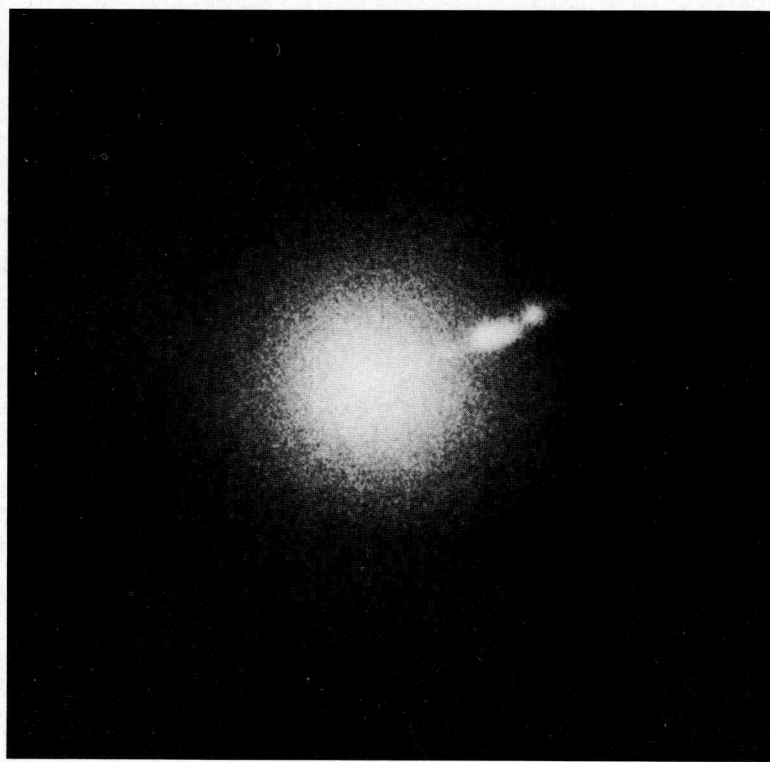

18.7: *Galaxy M87 is famous for the jet of intense blue light that emerges from the nucleus. This object emits by the synchrotron process, and contains as much material as a million suns. Radio maps show that M87 has two jet-like radio sources as well. This is a prime example of an extremely active galaxy. The entire galaxy is illustrated in the long-exposure photograph figure 16.4.*
(Hale Observatories, USA and University of Cambridge, UK)

The giant elliptical galaxy M87

M87 is the biggest and brightest galaxy in the Virgo cluster. It is the nearest giant elliptical (at a distance of 15 Mpc) in which there is clear evidence of activity, both within the nucleus and well outside it. The first direct evidence came with the discovery by H.D.Curtis in 1918 of a remarkable optical jet in the galaxy (figure 18.7). It was found much later that M87 is also a powerful radio source and that a considerable fraction of the total radio emission comes from the jet. It is frequently referred to as Virgo A and 3C 274, the names given to it by radio astronomers. The radio emission is clearly *synchrotron radiation*, and this emission is now known to be partially polarized. Optical studies have shown that the light from the jet is also probably synchrotron radiation.

Synchrotron radiation is caused when electrons move across magnetic field lines. If the electrons are extremely energetic (10^{11} or 10^{12} eV) they radiate at optical wavelengths. However at these wavelengths the electrons lose their energy relatively quickly (within a few hundred years in the jet of M87). This jet is probably about 2000 pc long, so particles travelling with the speed of light will take around 6500 years to travel the whole length of the jet. If all the energy that gives rise to the jet was generated in the nucleus of M87, no particles could have enough energy left to radiate optically near the end of the jet. This shows us that the electrons in the jet must actually be given the energy which they eventually radiate while they are moving along the jet. How this might happen is difficult to guess, and astronomers are a long way from understanding how the jet of M87 is energized.

The nucleus of M87 is itself remarkable. It contains a very compact non-thermal high-frequency radio source which is less than three light-months across. Within 300 pc of the centre of M87 are found clouds with velocities which may be as high as 900 km s^{-1}. In addition to the radio structures associated with the jet (and those on the opposite side of the nucleus of M87 where a fainter jet has been reported), there is a low-brightness halo of radio emission.

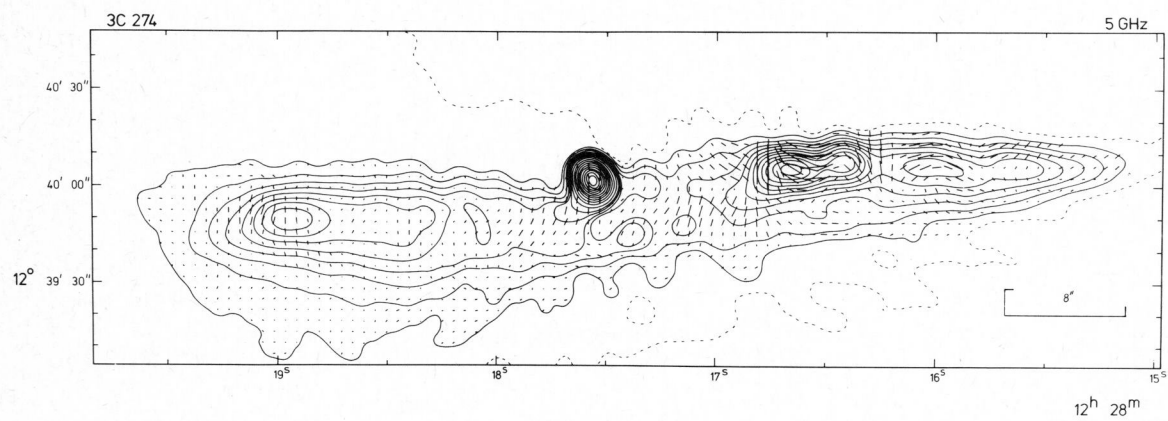

NGC 1275 or Perseus A

NGC 1275 (figure 18.8) is the brightest galaxy in the Perseus cluster and it is a strong radio source. It was by far the most distant of the twelve galaxies originally listed as Seyfert galaxies. Since the Perseus cluster is rich in elliptical galaxies it has been suggested that NGC 1275 might be an active elliptical galaxy and not a spiral galaxy like all the other Seyferts, but this is not the case. However NGC 1275 is clearly not a normal spiral galaxy. It has a bright central part several kiloparsecs in diameter, outside which are found broad, extended structures as well as absorbing clouds. There are also numerous filamentary structures (figure 18.8) due to ejected gas.

Spectroscopic studies of the nuclear gas in NGC 1275 show lines with widths corresponding to velocities of several thousand kilometres per second. Immediately outside the nucleus, gas is present moving with a velocity of approximately $3000\,\mathrm{km\,s^{-1}}$ relative to the centre of the galaxy. Direct photographs taken in the light of the Hα line centred on each velocity system have been taken by American astronomers (figure 18.8). They clearly show the remarkable extent of the filamentary structure which was presumably generated by an enormous explosion in the centre of the galaxy. In some respects the filamentary structure is reminiscent of that of the *Crab Nebula*. The optical continuum from the nucleus of NGC 1275 has a considerable non-thermal component which is polarized in the ultraviolet.

The radio structure of NGC 1275 is complex; it has a number of discrete components with sizes ranging from nearly 100 kpc down to 0.1 pc. The compact core is variable at radio wavelengths.

The activity in the Perseus cluster is not restricted to NGC 1275: there is evidence that the influence of this dominant Seyfert galaxy emanates throughout the cluster. For example, a large, low-brightness halo of radio emission extends through the cluster. The other bright galaxy in the cluster, NGC 1265, has a most unusual radio structure (figure 18.9), with the appearance of a galaxy moving through space trailing radio-emitting clouds out behind it. Astronomers are not agreed as to the reason for this structure but it is known that NGC 1265 has a considerable velocity ($2500\,\mathrm{km\,s^{-1}}$) relative to the cluster as a whole. Probably the radio blobs are indeed being shed by NGC 1265 as it travels through the extremely tenuous intergalactic medium in the cluster. It is not clear whether NGC 1275 is itself a radio galaxy or whether the radio emission is generated by the motion of the galaxy through the intergalactic medium in the cluster. The Perseus cluster is also a strong X-ray source and there are another two much weaker radio-trail sources in the cluster.

18.8: *NGC 1275 shows a tangled structure when imaged in the red light of hydrogen. Its nucleus may be exploding.*
(Kitt Peak National Observatory, USA)

18.9: *The radio image of galaxy NGC 1265, in the Perseus cluster, shows a long tail. The white bars indicate the predominant polarization.*
(Leiden Observatory, Netherlands)
Many other trail galaxies have been found by radio astronomers. The radio contour maps are expanded details of small portions of the optical fields indicated by the black bars.
(National Radio Astronomy Observatory, USA)

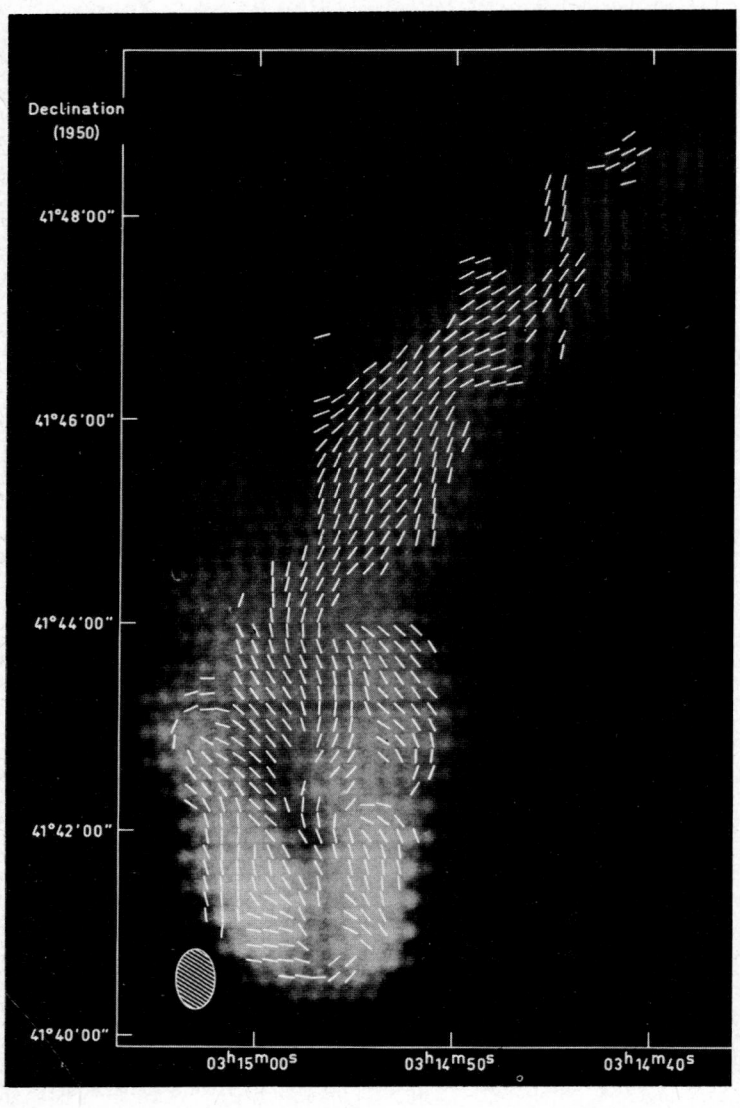

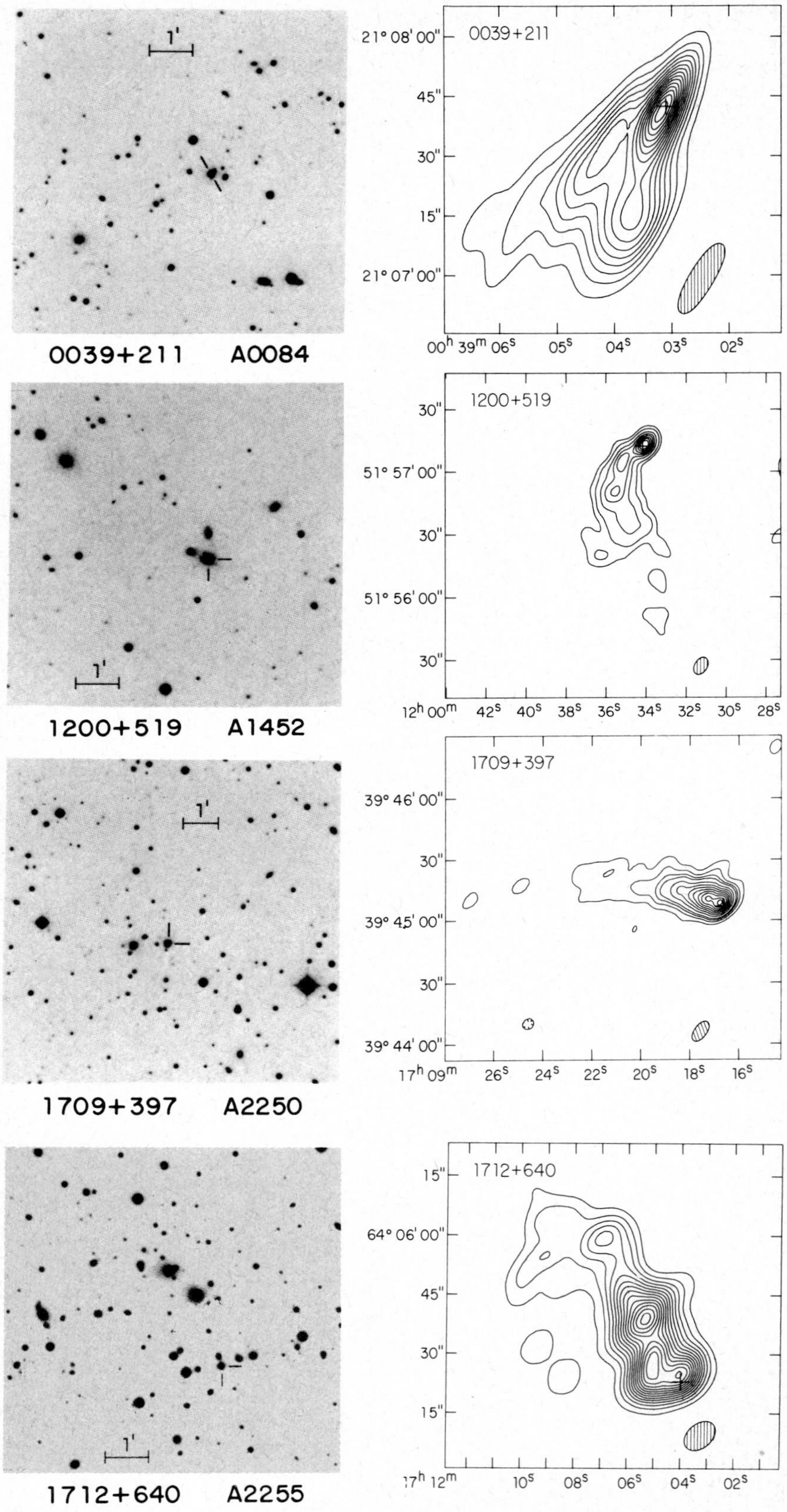

0039+211   A0084

1200+519   A1452

1709+397   A2250

1712+640   A2255

Radio galaxies

Until the discovery of radio galaxies in the early 1950s, radio astronomy was hardly more than an interesting sideline to the primary study of stars and galaxies by optical telescopes. However, in only a few years rich new vistas of research were opened up. A momentous breakthrough came in about 1954, when British and Australian astronomers managed to construct *interferometer* telescopes which enabled them to pinpoint a few dozen radio sources with enough precision for optical astronomers to link the radio emitters with visible objects. The then recently-completed 5-m reflector at Palomar turned its penetrating gaze to the strongest radio source, in Cygnus. There Walter Baade and Rudolph Minkowski found a disturbed 16-mag galaxy coincident with strong radio emission. On obtaining a spectrum, their initial suspicions became amply confirmed because the object showed many intense emission lines – a sure sign of unusual activity. Furthermore the lines were displaced to the red end of the spectrum with a *redshift* of $z = 0.057$, at the time one of the largest known. It indicates a recession speed of $17\,000\,\mathrm{km\,s^{-1}}$ and a distance of around $170\,\mathrm{Mpc}$.

The amazing nature of this discovery lies in the fact that CYGNUS A, as the object is called, is one of the brightest objects in the radio sky, but it is at an immense distance from our Galaxy. The radio luminosity is a fantastic 10^{38} watts, which is millions of times more energetic than the background of radio emission from our own Galaxy. With the discovery of such titans, extragalactic astronomy was launched on a golden age of expansion.

There are many thousands of radio sources beyond our Galaxy that appear in catalogues drawn up by radio astronomers. Roughly one-third to one-half of these EXTRAGALACTIC RADIO SOURCES coincide in position with galaxies that are visible on deep photographs of the sky. A galaxy that is a strong source of radio emission is known as a RADIO GALAXY; naturally, with the growth of the subject the variety of galaxies that show radio emission has increased considerably, but we concentrate here on a presentation of the major observed features of radio galaxies.

The radio emission itself has a very characteristic spectrum. For most objects, the FLUX DENSITY at a particular frequency (which is the radio astronomer's term for the energy received per unit bandwidth) is proportional to the frequency raised to some power, called the spectral index. In mathematical language, this can be expressed as:

$$S(\upsilon) = \kappa \upsilon^{-\alpha}.$$

where $S(\upsilon)$ denotes flux density at frequency υ, κ is a constant of proportionality, and α is the spectral index. The unit of measurement of the flux density is the jansky (Jy), in honour of the pioneering American radio scientist Karl Jansky; it is measured in $\mathrm{watt\,m^{-2}\,Hz^{-1}}$, and $1\,\mathrm{Jy}$ is $10^{-26}\,\mathrm{watt\,m^{-2}\,Hz^{-1}}$. Observed flux densities from galaxies in the frequency range $10\,\mathrm{MHz}$ to $10\,\mathrm{GHz}$ span a range of 10^{-2} to $10^{5}\,\mathrm{Jy}$. Note that in radio astronomy very low energies are in fact being received, despite the great intrinsic luminosity of the radio sources. For example, a flux density of $1\,\mathrm{Jy}$

18.10: *Centaurus A, the giant radio galaxy in the southern hemisphere, is only 4 Mpc away. It is crossed by a dense lane of dust. Radio emission spreads for many degrees on each side. (Cerro Tololo Inter-American Observatory, Chile and USA)*

falling on a telescope with a collecting area of 100 m² only gives a signal strength of 10⁻¹⁸ watts with a bandwidth of 1 MHz. In figure 18.11 are plotted the spectra of a representative sample of radio galaxies, including cases where the spectral index α is not constant over all the spectrum.

From the radio spectra of galaxies we glean some useful information. Firstly, all the strong radio galaxies have spectra of the type described above, and this indicates that they are probably all energized by the same basic mechanism. Secondly, this power-law spectrum is exactly what we expect when electromagnetic radiation is released by synchrotron emission. In this process the fastest electrons radiate at the highest frequencies, and they are the first to run out of energy (i.e. slow down). This explains why the spectra of some radio galaxies, such as Cygnus A, bend over at high frequencies, where the electrons have become somewhat depleted.

The architecture of radio galaxies is explored with interferometers, because only these can attain the requisite resolving power of a few arc seconds or less. Most radio galaxies are less than one minute of arc in diameter, mainly because they are at a great distance and so subtend a small angular size. The normal methods of displaying data on the structure of a particular radio source are either by means of a contour map, or by processing the data so that it is displayed on a television screen as if it were a photograph. Most strong radio galaxies consist of two large clouds of radio emission symmetrically disposed on either side of the galaxy (figure 18.12). Therefore the radio waves are in fact coming from regions of space which are usually well beyond the visible confines of the associated galaxy. The radio clouds may be 10 kpc–1 Mpc from the galaxy, and may measure 1–50 kpc in diameter. We can see from these values that the radio clouds are often larger than their parent galaxies. Indeed, the very largest radio sources, such as 3C 236 and DA 240, are as big as an entire *cluster of galaxies!*

At first sight one might think that the predominant double structure of radio galaxies implies that they are surrounded by a ring (or doughnut) of radio emission. That this is not the case is clear from the fact that we never see such doughnuts face on. Therefore we conclude that the radio waves are coming from a pair of cloud-like regions. High-resolution maps show that these clouds often contain compact emission regions, particularly at the periphery of the clouds, and the latter may indicate a reaction between the clouds and invisible matter in extragalactic space. By studying the polarization of the radio emission it is possible to map out the structure of the magnetic fields inside extragalactic radio sources, and this work has tended to show that such structure is rather complex.

The picture of radio clouds emerging from these data is of a vast region of space populated by exceedingly energetic electrons and threaded by a tangled magnetic field. The double structure suggests that these rather exotic materials are somehow cast out of the optical galaxies, perhaps by immense explosions in the centres. Certainly the activity observed in the nuclei of other galaxy types encourages us to proceed along these lines.

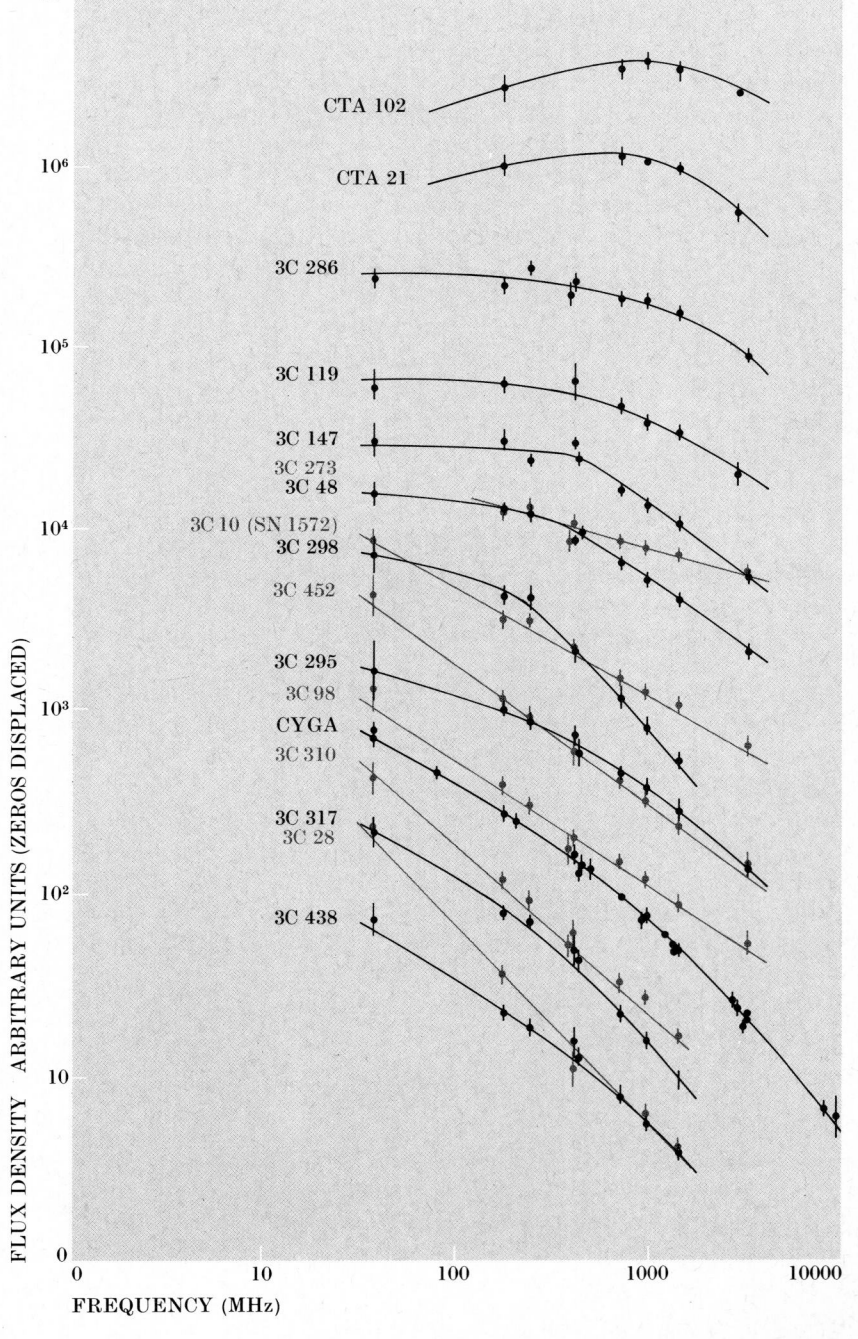

18.11: *Spectra of several radio sources on a logarithmic plot of intensity against frequency. The characteristic shape of these spectra is due to emission by electrons in a synchrotron process.*

When the synchrotron radiation idea is linked to the structural information we can get a notion of the energy requirements of a radio galaxy. This is because the total amount of energy stored up in the magnetic field and the fast electrons is related to the volume of the source and the spectrum of the radiation. We have no way of knowing the detailed distribution of energy in the radio cloud, but the sum total is lowest if we assume (conservatively) that it is equally split between fields and particles. In that case we find stores of energy ranging upwards from 10^{49} joules to 10^{52} joules. Recall that the total rest mass energy of the Sun is 2×10^{47} joules, and the total energy that it will release while on the main sequence is roughly 10^{45} joules, and you can appreciate how powerful a radio galaxy is.

Among the radio galaxies deserving a brief mention we may include Cygnus A, Centaurus A, and 3C 236. Cygnus A is often taken as the prototype since it is among the most powerful known. Its optical counterpart has a rich spectrum of emission lines, like an over-excited Seyfert galaxy, displaying a redshift of 0.057; this places it at a distance of around 170 Mpc. The two radio clouds are around 50 kpc from the optical nucleus, and they both contain a brilliant, condensed, region of radio emission. Radio astronomers in the southern hemisphere have an object of immense angular size, Centaurus A, available for study. It is a puny 4 Mpc from us, but has radio emission spanning 600 kpc of space. Despite this generous expansiveness, it has only one-thousandth the energy of Cygnus A. An interesting feature of Centaurus A (figure 18.10) is that it contains a further double radio source which has not yet broken free of the galaxy. Finally we briefly mention 3C 236 because it appears to be one of the biggest radio galaxies found in the Universe. This object has the usual double structure, centred on a faint galaxy. From the redshift (i.e. distance) of the galaxy and the measured angular size of the radio lobes, astronomers have concluded that 3C 236 stretches for almost 6 Mpc! This is nearly ten times the distance from ourselves to the Andromeda nebula.

The principal problems that radio galaxies pose for theorists are: the origin of the immense energy; the translation of this energy into magnetic fields and energetic electrons; and the origin of the double structure. It is widely considered that unknown processes in the central regions of certain elliptical galaxies are at the root of these problems.

18.12: *Giant radio source DA 240 is one of the largest objects in the Universe. The two puffs of radio emission are as large as a galaxy cluster. They lie symmetrically about an active galaxy. (Leiden Observatory, Netherlands)*

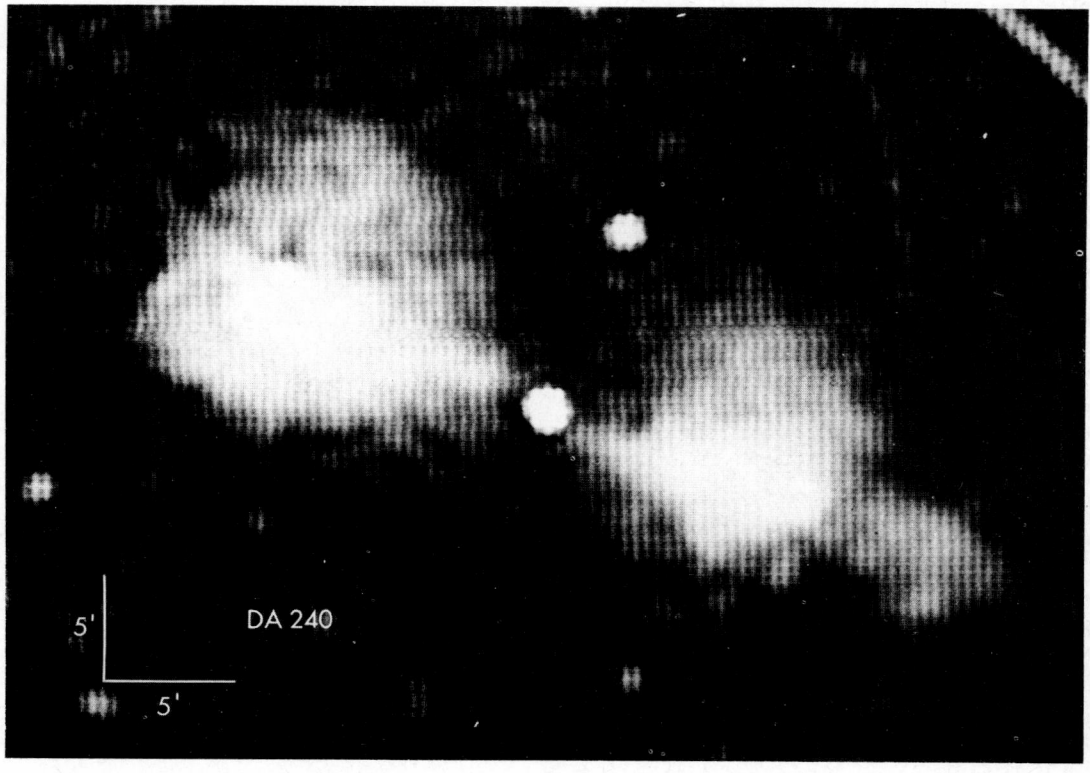

Quasi-stellar objects

The remarkable properties of *radio galaxies* spurred astronomers on in their efforts to find the optical counterparts to radio sources. This stimulus was partially responsible for the discovery, in the early 1960s of quasi-stellar objects or QUASARS. These are extra-galactic radio sources that match up optically with objects that cannot be resolved, i.e. they are star-like or quasi-stellar (figure 18.13). But how do we know that these are not galactic stars that emit radio waves? The answer is contained in the optical spectrum, which invariably has a large *redshift*, the principal hallmark of a quasar. The first two quasars that were investigated, 3C273 and 3C48, have redshifts of 0.158 and 0.367 respectively, which, in the mid-1960s, were considered large. They imply distances of approximately 480 and 1100 Mpc if we assume that the redshift is due to the systematic recession of distant objects in the expanding Universe.

Gradually, optical and radio astronomers have found quasars of larger and larger redshifts. This has required considerable effort because the higher redshifts results in ultraviolet emission lines being shifted into the visible region, so in the early days at least astrophysicists were on unfamiliar ground. By the end of 1976 several redshifts of nearly 4 had been encountered, with some dozens of objects displaying redshifts exceeding 2.

At higher redshifts we have to take into account the *theory of special relativity* in order to convert the redshift, z, to a velocity of

18.13: *Quasar (Q) has an image like a star but the spectrum indicates that it is far beyond our Galaxy. (Hale Observatories, USA) The horizontal pair of round images in the centre of the right-hand photograph are two quasars with different redshifts. The brighter one is a member of the cluster of fuzzy galaxies to the right. The hexagonal pattern is due to the image-tube used to intensify the image. (University of Hawaii, USA)*

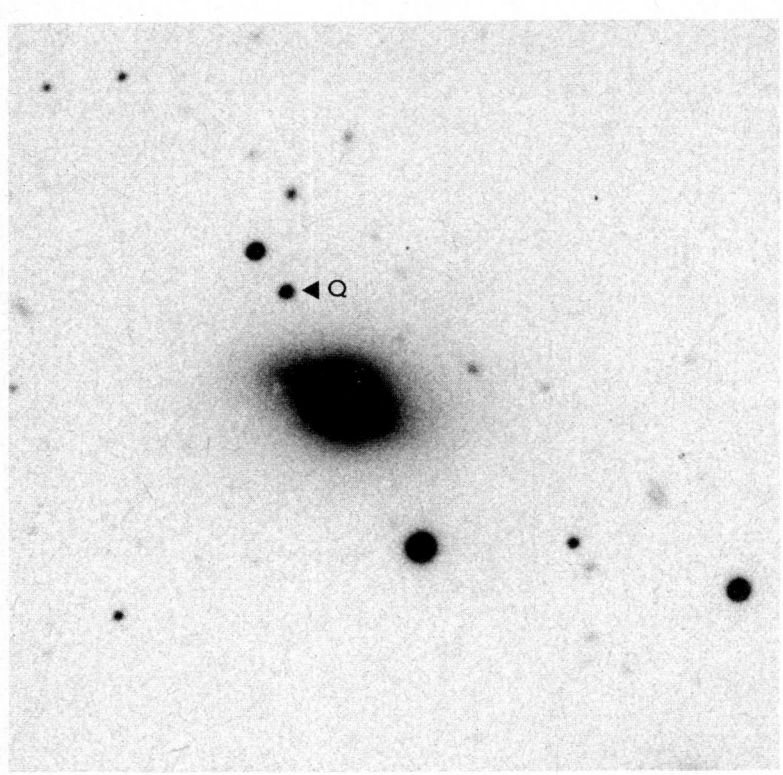
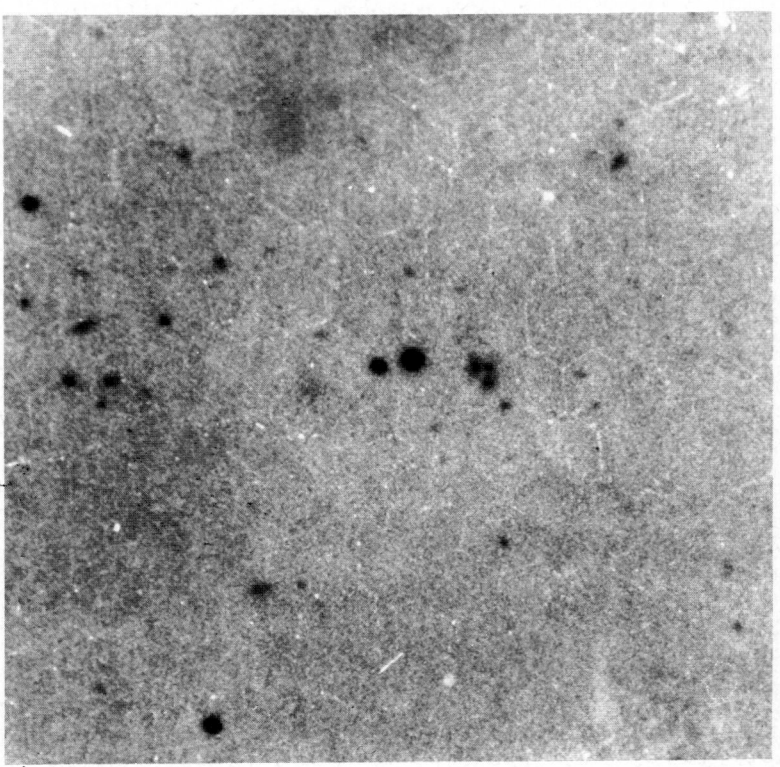

recession, v. The light is shifted from its rest wavelength λ to an observed wavelength (1 + z)λ at velocity v in accordance with

$$1 + z = \sqrt{\frac{c+v}{c-v}}$$

a relation which is graphed in figure 18.14. Here c denotes the speed of light. For velocities below about 0.4c an approximate formula z = v/c is sufficiently precise. For a quasar with a redshift of 2 the recession speed is 0.8 c, i.e. 80 per cent the speed of light.

Quasars quite frequently have a rich spectrum of emission lines and absorption lines. The emission lines can generally be arranged neatly into a sequence of spectral lines that display one redshift. For the absorption lines astronomers have noted that a different arrangement is not uncommon. In a given quasar the absorption lines may belong to several different systems, each with a different redshift that is less than the emission-line redshift. An example, PHL 957, will clarify this finding: its emission-line redshift is 2.69, but the array of absorption lines seems to slot into five spectral sequences with redshifts of 2.67, 2.55, 2.54, 2.31, and 2.23. An obvious, and likely, explanation is that the emission-line redshift is the intrinsic redshift, but the quasar has shed several clouds of matter at speeds approaching that of light. Radiation from the quasar that passes through such an expanding shell will have a lower-redshift absorption spectrum impressed upon it.

A further optical property of quasars, and one that they share with the nuclei of active galaxies such as Seyferts, is variability. The brightest quasars are present on patrol photographs dating from the nineteenth century. Archival material and modern photometric data show that quasars vary on timescales from a few days and upwards to decades, and with amplitudes from 0.1 to 3 mag. Variations on a timescale of weeks would indicate that the region generating the bulk of the luminosity is less than 0.1 pc in size. Now, these tiny volumes are pouring out to the Universe up to 100 times as much energy as a galaxy, so we see once more the scale of the energy problem faced by theorists.

Quasars are remarkably similar to radio galaxies when their radio properties are compared. Many quasars show the double structure and have the spectrum that is characteristic of synchrotron radiation. Faced with a spectrum and radio map of a newly-found double radio source, it would not be possible without optical observations to tell whether it was a radio galaxy or quasar. However, some quasars are highly-compact radio sources, unlike the radio galaxies. *Interferometers* with an intercontinental baseline have demonstrated that the radio components in some quasars are less than 0.001 arc sec in size. Furthermore, there is ample evidence that these structures are short-lived because they alter significantly in only a few months; this is additional evidence that the major part of the energy is generated in remarkably small regions embedded inside the quasars.

Skilled optical astronomers have gone to extraordinary lengths, using the world's finest telescopes, to detect structure around quasars. Generally this has been a disappointing endeavour, although a few wisps of gas seem to be present round 3C48. It appears to be fairly certain that some quasars at least are in clusters of galaxies (figure 18.13). This is because a few quasars have the same redshift as very faint galaxies that are only a small angular distance away.

18.14: *The relation between velocity and redshift.*

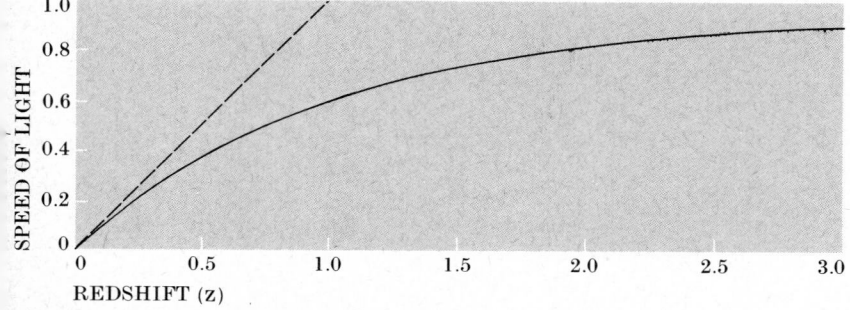

The redshift controversy

Observations made with great care and skill by Allan Sandage and collaborators at the Hale Observatories showed, in the mid-1970s, that in the case of the brightest galaxies in rich clusters, the *Hubble law*, linking redshift with cosmic distance, probably holds good to a redshift of at least 0.46. Beyond the distance corresponding to that redshift there is no direct empirical evidence relating redshift and distance for any object. Recall that the radio galaxies and quasars present a formidable energy problem: if we use their redshifts to give distance via the Hubble law, then very large energy stores are required, and in the case of quasars they are packed into very tiny volumes. The magnitude of the problems involved has led some researchers to propose that the Hubble law breaks down in certain cases: at large redshifts and for quasars.

The arguments that have been advanced against the interpretation of quasar redshifts as distance indicators are several. Firstly there is the energy problem, which is a good deal less acute if quasars are nearer than their redshifts indicate. Secondly there is the formidable evidence brought forward by the distinguished observer Halton Arp. He has found several examples of apparently related objects with different redshifts, such as faint bridges between objects having different redshifts. He has also found that some quasars are remarkably close to bright galaxies (figure 18.13). Through Arp's careful research there runs a consistent theme: not all the redshifts that we measure for extragalactic objects are in agreement with Hubble's law; how, therefore, can we be sure that unusual objects, such as quasars, obey it? Arp has certainly made interesting points and challenged the establishment view commendably, but it is hard to assess the significance *a posteriori* of the alleged relations between quasars and bright galaxies. Thirdly we may consider statistical evidence. Some researchers have tried to show that quasars are, on the average, in configurations relative to galaxies that are most unlikely to arise by chance. Therefore, the argument runs, the quasars must be somehow related to a set of nearby objects, galaxies, and cannot be at the cosmological distance derived from the redshift.

Several models have been advanced to explain how quasar light might be redshifted by a means other than the recession phenomenon associated with the expanding Universe. One idea, popular after the realization that *black holes* might really exist, is that quasars contain a very massive object which causes the emitted radiation to have a high *gravitational redshift*. This theory does not account for the very high redshifts. Another notion is that light from quasars might somehow get 'tired' on its long journey to us, and, in using energy on its travels, become redshifted. However, nobody has got this light-fatigue model to work convincingly. Yet another concept that has been tried is to alter the laws and constants of physics for large times and at large distances. Most physicists prefer to play the game by keeping the 'constants' constant under all conditions; once they are changed there are repercussions for all of physical theory, and it seems preferable to keep the present structure for the foreseeable future.

An important discovery in connection with the redshift controversy was the discovery of BL Lacertae objects, or LACERTIDS, named after the prototype. These are variable radio emitters that resemble quasars photographically but that have no emission or absorption lines in their optical spectra. The finding of quasar-like objects with featureless spectra showed that there might be a whole range of related extragalactic radio sources – active galaxies, lacertids, and quasars – differing mainly in the degree of activity in the nucleus.

Further important clues came with the realization that the nuclei of *Seyfert galaxies* and *N-type galaxies* are just as variable as quasars. Until variability in quasars was established, no careful observations had been made of changes in galactic nuclei. Once the variability had been found in other extragalactic objects, quasars seemed a little less unusual. Another factor was the detective work that led to the discovery of quasars in clusters of galaxies with a common redshift. This showed that some quasars at least behave as galaxies do rather than being a class apart.

In retrospect it seems that the redshift controversy grew up as an accident caused by the order in which key discoveries were made. If quasars had been found after Seyfert galaxies had been studied more closely, after the work on compact objects as energy sources had been started, after the discovery of lacertids, and after the exploration of a whole variety of galactic nuclei, they would have been accepted more or less immediately as a natural extension of phenomena already satisfactorily explained. We prefer to take the view that quasars do follow the Hubble law, and therefore that they are remote objects in the furthest reaches of our expanding Universe. This conclusion allows us to treat quasars as cosmological probes, that is, as observable test objects in the far-off Universe, a universe that has properties rather different from those prevailing at our time and in our locality.

The unity of active galaxies

Our survey of active galaxies and quasars looks rather like a zoo of various cosmic beasts. In each compartment we have a type of galaxy, frequently named for its discoverer (e.g. *Markarian galaxy*), or location (e.g. *lacertid*), or the technique of discovery (e.g. *radio galaxy*). What systematic trends emerge when we study these species collectively? One recurrent theme is that of active nuclei. Since the early 1960s it has been emphasized more and more that the central regions of galaxies are the seat of violent activity. What became clear over a period of two decades or so was the astonishing variety of this central activity.

Beginning with our own Milky Way, there is a powerful radio source, Sagittarius A at the galactic centre, and ample evidence that the central regions are expanding fast. Some astronomers interpret this as evidence for an explosion in recent times at the centre of the Galaxy. Not far away is another exploding galaxy, M82 (figure 18.6) and the galaxy with the optical jet, M87 (figure 18.7). In the Seyfert galaxies the nuclei are certainly active and are responsible for the rich emission-line spectrum. The same applies to the optical properties of radio galaxies; opinion is firmly in favour of the idea that the clouds of plasma responsible for the radio structure must have emerged from galactic nuclei. Quasars are certainly small, as we expect for a galactic nucleus. Could it be that in quasars the nuclear emission is so intense that the light from any underlying galaxy is totally swamped? That this could be the case is strengthened by the facts that wisps are found round 3C48 and that a few quasars are members of clusters of galaxies. Even lacertids can be neatly accommodated into this unified picture: they may be galaxies with strong continuum emission from the nuclei but with no gas that can be excited to give the emissions that characterize quasars.

A unified model of all delinquent galaxies has great attractions for the theorist since it is one of the tasks of science to organize apparently unrelated facts into a rational sequence, and then to extract new facts from this ordering. It appears very possible that the ultimate source of energy in the excited nuclei is some form of highly-condensed object. If a great deal of matter (millions of solar masses) is concentrated into a small volume or volumes of space (kilometres or planetary size), prodigious quantities of energy may be extracted – tens of times the energy available via *nuclear reactions*. The compact objects could be *neutron stars* or *black holes*, for the theoretical study of these has certainly demonstrated the possibilities of their producing vast supplies of energy, much of it in the exotic form (electrons moving at the velocity of light, for example) that is required. There is every hope that the variety of galaxies will one day be ordered and explained, just as the astrophysicists of the early twentieth century ultimately made sense of the apparently bewildering selection of stellar spectra and star types.

18.15: *This rare and spectacular ring galaxy, the Cartwheel, may be the relic of a collision between galaxies.*
(UK *Schmidt Telescope Unit, Australia and* UK)

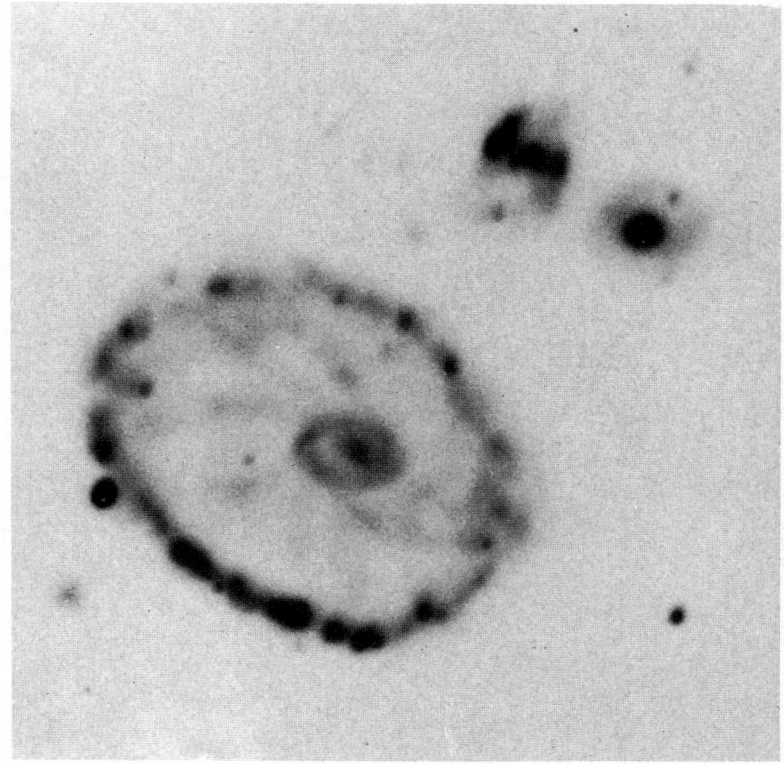

19. Cosmology, the nature of the Universe

19.1: *The expansion of the Universe. The velocity with which a galaxy appears to be receding is plotted against its distance as inferred from its apparent brightness. The recession velocity is observed to be directly proportional to the distance. The slope of the line indicates the rate at which the Universe is expanding, this is about 75 kilometers per second for every megaparsec of distance. The simplest interpretation of this diagram is that the Universe 'exploded' many billions of years ago. The galaxies used in compiling this diagram are of several different kinds, and different symbols have been used to emphasise this. The scattering of the points reflects the difficulty of determining the large distances to the furthest galaxies.*

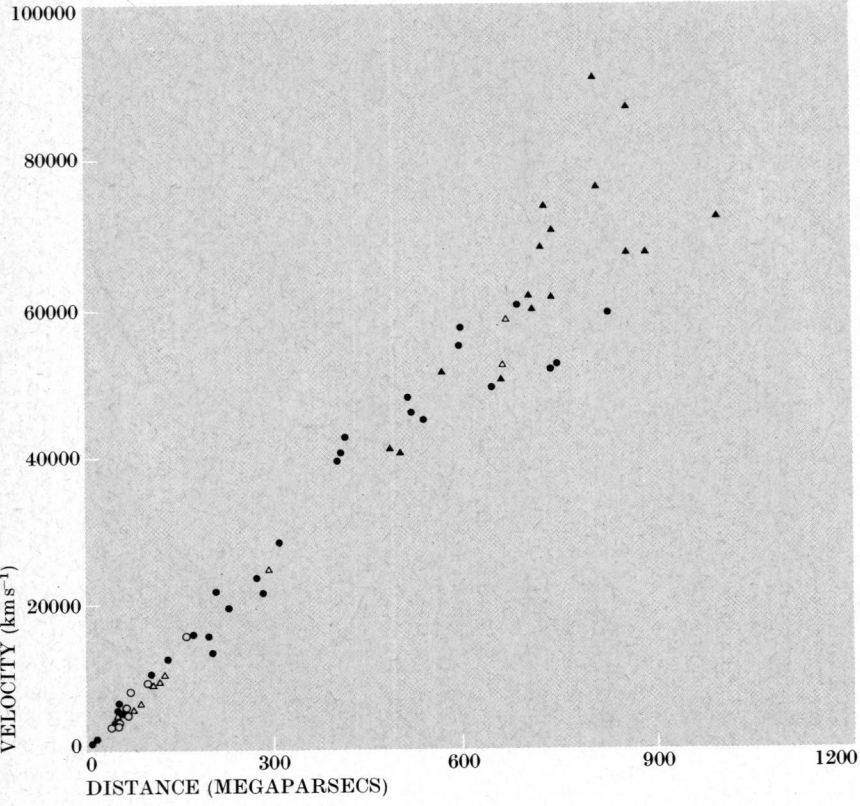

The birth of extragalactic astronomy

With the passing of time, Man has been able to look increasingly further into the depths of space. Each step has produced new insight into the nature of the Universe and our position within it. To the Greeks and Romans, the Earth was the centre of all things. The furthest they could see was the Milky Way, although its true nature was not realized until well over a thousand years later when Galileo resolved it into stars with the first telescopes. At the beginning of the nineteenth century, William Herschel studied the Milky Way in greater detail and estimated distances to the stars. At that time, it was not realized that the so-called 'nebulae', the cloud-like objects catalogued by Messier and the Herschels, were in fact other galaxies so distant that their individual stars could not be resolved. Using his giant 72-inch reflecting telescope, Lord Rosse later discovered that some of these objects possessed spiral structure. But it was the advent of astronomical photography during the last years of that century that heralded the birth of extragalactic astronomy. The first photographs of 'nebulae' revealed complex and beautiful structures that Lord Rosse's telescope could only hint at. Until that time, little was known about the relationship between these systems and the Milky Way, but the new photographs inspired a number of eminent scientists to speculate about the nature of the nebulae.

The major point of contention during the early part of this century was: how far away are the nebulae? At that time, Harlow Shapley was able to map out the scale of the Milky Way by using Bailey's discovery of *RR Lyrae stars* in globular clusters and Leavitt's discovery of *Cepheid variables* in the Magellanic clouds. He put the Sun at some 10 kpc from the galactic centre, that is, about two-thirds the way to the edge of the Galaxy. The distances to the nebulae, however, did not come for another decade. After much heated debate, Edwin Hubble presented convincing evidence that the three nebulae M31, M33 and NGC 6822 were systems considerably more distant than the most remote parts of our Milky Way. Notwithstanding a few inconsistencies between various distance estimates, there was no longer any doubt that these were indeed 'island universes' not unlike the Milky Way.

Hubble then turned his attention to the systematic study of these extragalactic systems and OBSERVATIONAL COSMOLOGY was born. No longer was cosmology the domain only of the philosopher and theologian, it had entered the arena of the scientist.

The expanding Universe

Hubble's most remarkable and important discovery came soon after his establishing that many of the nebulae were extragalactic systems. He found a systematic increase in the *redshift* of their spectral lines with increasing distance. Adopting the most straightforward interpretation of the redshift as being a *Doppler shift* due to the recession of the source, we can see an immediate interpretation of Hubble's result: the Universe is expanding, and the most distant galaxies are rushing away the fastest. Taken at face value, we are led by this discovery to the conclusion that the Universe was denser in the past than now, and we may even speculate that there may have been a time in our past when all the matter in the Universe was highly compressed. Such are the possible ramifications of Hubble's discovery, a discovery that surely ranks as one of the outstanding achievements of modern physics. Of course, we should proceed with care. It is possible that the simple interpretation of the redshift is not correct, and that the expansion is illusory. Even if we accept the fact of expansion, it does not necessarily follow that the Universe was denser in the past than now, for implicit in that conclusion is the assumption that matter in the Universe is neither created nor destroyed. It is the task of the astrophysicist to put these ideas to the test, to distinguish clearly what is well-established, and perhaps that some ideas are, a priori, more plausible than others. So, with regard to the redshift, the hypothesis that it is a Doppler shift due to the RECESSION OF THE GALAXIES is scientifically acceptable: it is consistent with the laws of physics as we know them. No other scientifically acceptable hypothesis has yet been proposed. On the other hand, we have no proof that this is the explanation. We take the simplest course and assume that the cosmic expansion is real. We can do a lot better as regards supporting the contention that the Universe was denser in the past, and we can moreover provide strong evidence that it was also much hotter.

Before presenting this further evidence for the HOT BIG BANG THEORY, it should be remarked that in the time since Hubble's discovery of the expansion, much more data has become available which provides striking confirmation of Hubble's linear relationship between recession velocity and distance. The HUBBLE LAW, as it is now called, is known to extend a distance a hundred times that investigated by Hubble, and there is no obvious deviation from a simple-straight line relationship:

Velocity = Hubble's parameter × distance in Mpc

From the modern data, the Hubble parameter is found to be 75 kilometres per second per megaparsec with a possible uncertainty of 25 km/sec/Mpc. That is, for every extra megaparsec away in distance from us, the galaxies recede faster by 75 kilometres per second. This is the present RATE OF EXPANSION OF THE UNIVERSE. It should also be noted that because light travels at a finite speed, the more distant galaxies are being observed as they were a considerable time in our past. There is therefore the possibility of inferring the nature of the cosmic expansion at much earlier times.

There is an interesting side-issue relating to the cosmic expansion and the redshifting of the light from distant galaxies: this is the so-called OLBERS' PARADOX, which may be set forth as follows. If the Universe were infinite, yet not expanding, every line of sight from Earth would eventually intersect the surface of a star. In that case, the sky would be everywhere as bright as the surface of a typical star, in other words, as bright as the Sun's surface! Olbers recognized the darkness of the night sky as an important paradox. Now we can understand the resolution of the paradox in terms of known facts about the Universe. Stars which lie in galaxies at great distances from us have their light redshifted out of the optical wave-

band and into the infrared or beyond. Thus they do not contribute to the optically visible light of the night sky and that is why the sky is dark at night.

Homogeneity, isotropy and evolution

Hubble also embarked on some deep surveys of the distribution of galaxies in the Universe, as far out as his telescopes and the then-available photographic plates would allow. Two things struck him about these surveys. Firstly, notwithstanding the manifest clustering of galaxies on scales of a few megaparsecs, the Universe when viewed on very large scales looks HOMOGENEOUS. There is no sign of the number of galaxies significantly thinning out as we approach the limits of the Universe accessible to our most powerful optical telescopes. Secondly, the Universe looks very much the same in all directions, and moreover, the cosmic expansion is proceeding at the same rate in all directions. Astronomers describe this by saying the Universe is ISOTROPIC. An important consequence of the apparent homogeneity and isotropy of the Universe is that there is no meaningful centre. Our Galaxy, the Milky Way, does not occupy a privileged position. It has taken less than five hundred years to displace mankind from the very centre of all things to a small planet orbiting a rather average star of a galaxy that is typical of millions of others.

Recently, radio astronomers have been able to put stringent limits on the isotropy of the Universe. By observing at centimetre wavelengths, they have discovered a component of radiation that is not due to either known radio sources or noise within their receiving systems. Moreover, this residual radiation is seen to be isotropic to better than 0.1 per cent, that is, any deviation from the radiation being the same in all directions is likely to be less than this amount. The high degree of isotropy excludes the possibilities of the radiation originating in the Solar System or in the Galaxy. It is therefore concluded that this radiation must be of cosmic origin, and it is referred to as the COSMIC BACKGROUND RADIATION. We shall have more to say about this radiation field later: it is of central importance in understanding our Universe. Here we are only concerned with its isotropy, for if the radiation is indeed of cosmic origin, then this is the most stringent constraint on the isotropy of the Universe. (Indeed, this isotropy measurement is probably the most accurately known parameter that characterizes the Universe). Unless we believe that we are in a privileged position at the centre of the Universe, this radiation also tells us that, in the large, the Universe is homogeneous.

Hubble's deep surveys probably included large numbers of galaxies receding from us at about one-third the speed of light, and whose distance from us is to be measured in thousands of megaparsecs. However, the galaxies which are so typical of the ones observed by Hubble emit very little light and radio-frequency radiation as compared with the *quasars* and *radio galaxies*. Hence these latter objects allow us to probe the Universe to greater depths and at the same time look a long way into the past. Indeed, the most distant quasar yet observed has a redshift factor of about

3.5, some four times the redshift of the furthest galaxy for which a redshift has been measured. The significant fact that has emerged is that the actual number of quasars and radio galaxies was much greater in the past than now. It was this fact that first established that the Universe was different in the past than now. Not only is this conclusion gratifying in providing support for the most straightforward interpretation of the cosmic expansion, but it also poses a serious problem for cosmological theories such as the *Steady State* theory which proposes that the Universe looks the same at all times. Of course, it might be argued that we do not properly understand the nature of either quasars or radio galaxies, but notwithstanding such arguments, it would take a fairly serious step, such as abandoning the conventional interpretation of the redshift, to fault the conclusion that we live in a Universe that changes with time.

A hot Big Bang

By 1950, there were two rival interpretations of Hubble's observations: the BIG BANG and the STEADY STATE theories. Although we shall have more to say about theories of the Universe later on, it is appropriate to mention this famous controversy at this point since it was instrumental in motivating many important observations bearing on cosmology. Both theories accepted the simple view that the Universe, in the large, is homogeneous and isotropic, and expanding against the pull of gravity. Where they differed was that whereas the Big Bang theory took the conservative view that matter is neither created nor destroyed spontaneously, the Steady State theory did not. A direct consequence of the Big Bang hypothesis is that, at a finite time in our past (roughly 20 billion years ago as calculated on the basis of current data), all the matter in the Universe was piled up in a state of infinite density – the COSMIC SINGULARITY. On largely philosophical grounds, this singularity was regarded by some as a serious defect of the theory, and an ingenious way out was suggested by Herman Bondi, Tommy Gold and Fred Hoyle. It was proposed that matter might be spontaneously created at just the rate required to make up for the decrease of density resulting from the cosmic expansion. The density of the Universe thus remains constant and there is no singular event of the kind encountered in the Big Bang theory; such a Universe has an infinite past and infinite future.

One of the strongest protagonists of the Big Bang theory was George Gamow. Gamow saw the early Universe not only as a dense place, but also a hot one where nuclear reactions might take place. At that time, Gamow's hope had been to synthesize all the elements in their cosmically-observed amounts. Although this hope was not to be fulfilled, Gamow's theory nevertheless resulted in two important predictions. It was possible to predict firstly that there should be a universal cosmic abundance of helium of about 25 per cent by mass. Secondly, that we should now observe the left-over radiation from this early hot phase as an isotropic radiation field having a *black-body spectrum* corresponding to a temperature of a few degrees absolute. The first of these has since been well verified;

nowhere has an abundance of helium which is low compared with the cosmic value been observed. Moreover, astrophysicists find it difficult to understand under what circumstances this helium might have been produced if not in a hot Big Bang. The second prediction has led to the most important discovery in cosmology since Hubble's discovery of the expansion of the Universe. In 1965, Arno Penzias and Robert Wilson discovered an isotropic radiation field whose intensity corresponded closely to Gamow's prediction. Ten years of subsequent observations have strongly confirmed the isotropy of the radiation and have shown, in addition, that the spectrum of the radiation is thermal with a temperature of 2.7 K. The remarkable isotropy of the radiation convinces astrophysicists of its cosmic origin. The shape of the spectrum tells us that the radiation was once in *thermodynamic equilibrium* with matter, from which we conclude that the Universe must have been considerably denser and hotter in the past than now.

19.2: *The cosmic background radiation spectrum. The brightness of the sky is plotted at a variety of frequencies where measurements have been made. The solid line fitted to the data is a 2.7 K Planck curve. The observation that the radiation is highly isotropic, taken together with the impressive fit to a Planck curve, provides the strongest evidence for the 'hot big bang' theory of the Universe. The observations from 3 mm to 1 m has been obtained with ground-based radio telescopes. At shorter wavelengths the best data comes from balloon-borne bolometers. Future technology will provide the crucial data shortward of 1 mm. The dashed lines represent the contributions from the galaxy (longward of 1 m) and from combined infrared sources (shortward of 0.1 mm).*

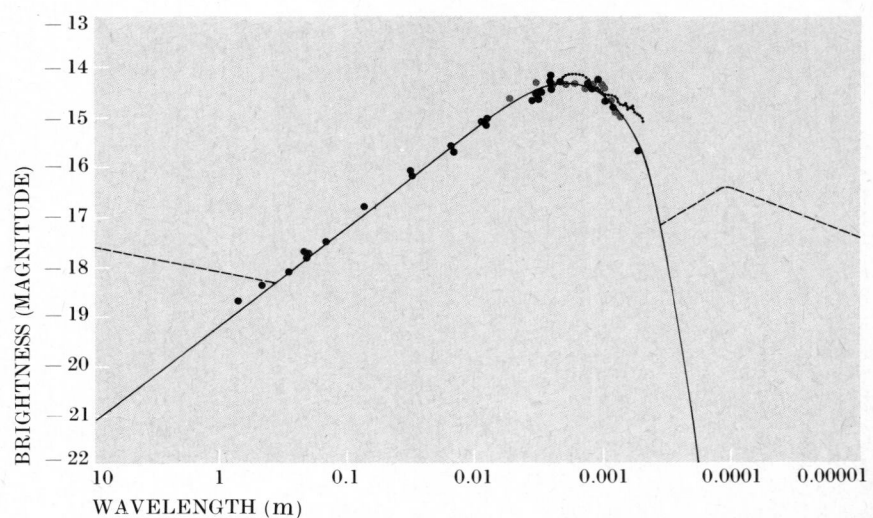

19.3: *The past density of the Universe. The diagram shows how dense the Universe was at a given time in our past, for a given present density. This latter quantity is only poorly determined and so two curves are shown covering the probable range of values. The denser model is dense enough that the present expansion will eventually be halted by gravity. Such a universe is said to be 'closed'. The other model will expand forever and is said to be 'open'. The present age of the closed model is about 7.4 billion years, while the age of the open model is 13 billion years. The age of the Sun, a typical star in our own Galaxy, is about 5 billion years. The numbers on each curve refer to the observed redshift corresponding to light emitted at a given time in our past. Thus the light from a quasar observed at a redshift of 3 was emitted some 6.6 billion years ago in the denser model, or 9.8 billion years ago in the open model. This quasar turned on 0.8 billion years after the big bang in a closed Universe, or 3.2 billion years after the big bang in the open Universe.*

The role of gravity and the fate of the Universe

Can we reconcile this overall view of the Universe with the known laws of physics? It is here that we leave the domain of observed fact and enter the realm of speculation. If the observed Universe can indeed be understood in terms of the laws of physics, then our confidence in our Earth-based laws is increased. However, and this is perhaps the exciting prospect, if the Universe cannot be understood in this way we may be led to seek out new laws of physics! First of all, we must decide which force controls the Universe. Of all the known forces, the force of gravity is the only one that has a long enough range of influence to affect the most distant parts of the Universe. As far as we know, gravity is always an attractive force. Gravity dominates the motions of the planets and satellites of the Solar System, it most probably dominates the motions of stars in galaxies, and it is reasonable to speculate that it governs the motions of the galaxies and the dynamics of the Universe.

The Universe is expanding, whereas the effect of the force of gravity is to try to hold it together. A basic question the cosmologist would like to answer is: is the force strong enough eventually to halt the expansion and to reverse it? There is a useful analogy here in thinking of a rocket launched from the Earth. If the rocket has a great enough velocity it will leave the Earth's environment. On the other hand, if the velocity is below the escape velocity the gravitational force exerted by the Earth will stop the rocket and bring it back down. Correspondingly, there are two possible fates for the Universe. It may expand forever so that there will come a time when even the largest telescopes would fail to see more than a few galaxies. Alternatively, the force of gravity will dominate, the expansion will be reversed and the Universe will be crushed into the same kind of singularity from which we believe it emerged. It is, in principle, a simple matter to decide which fate awaits us.

Consider a typical volume of space which is expanding at a known rate (inferred from observing the motions of the galaxies). The force exerted by gravity on that volume depends on the density of material in the volume: a high density is associated with a strong gravitational pull, and conversely a low density is associated with a weaker pull. Hence the FATE OF THE UNIVERSE can be decided simply by comparing the relative values of the expansion rate and the averaged density of matter in the Universe. Astronomers believe that the rate of expansion is about 75 kilometres per second for every megaparsec of distance from us. There is less certainty as regards the density of the Universe. The sum total of the observed luminous matter (mostly galaxies) gives a density equivalent to one hydrogen atom for every 10 000 litres. However, there could be significant quantities of non-luminous material (black holes, snowballs or bricks, for example) whose existence could only be deduced indirectly, if at all. Thus the quoted density of observed matter is in fact a lower limit. However, a simple calculation tells us that it would require a density in excess of one hydrogen atom per 100 litres to provide a strong enough gravitational pull eventually to reverse the present observed expansion. If there is not much more matter in the

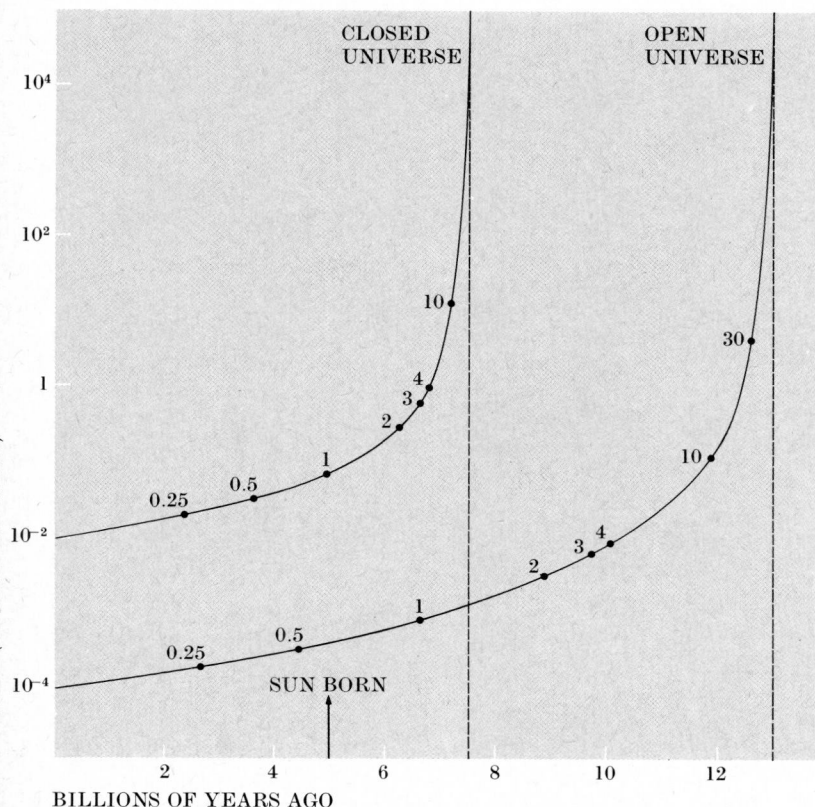

Universe than is seen through the largest telescopes, and if the force of gravity behaves the way our Earth-based experiments would have us believe, it seems that the ultimate fate of the Universe is to expand into nothingness. The Universe observed by our descendants long in the future will be a very sparsely populated place. To avoid this conclusion would require that the observed matter is only one per cent or so of all that constitutes the Universe.

The cosmologist's kaleidoscope

How can this elementary yet profound deduction be checked? It is at this point that the theoretical cosmologist enters the picture. His task is to exploit the assumption that the force of gravity dominates the evolution of the Universe. He uses *Einstein's theory of general relativity* to map out the history of the competition between expansion and gravitation. In doing so, he constructs what are known as COSMOLOGICAL MODELS. It turns out that there is a large number of evolutionary histories for the Universe which are consistent with both the known laws of physics, and the observed expansion and density of the Universe. They have one feature in common: they all possess a singularity, a finite time in our past. The existence of such a singularity – a Big Bang – is an inescapable consequence of Einstein's theory. There is no way of avoiding the Big Bang which is suggested so strongly by a naive extrapolation of the observed cosmic expansion into our past, without changing Einstein's theory of general relativity, or abandoning some fundamental tenet of modern physics. We have already mentioned the example of the Steady State theory which avoided the problem by invoking some new physics.

The cosmologist must decide which of these cosmological models best describes the Universe. In spite of the great number of candidates, some are obviously more suitable than others. The cosmologist favours those which have a hot beginning because in these there is a ready explanation of the origin of the radiation field observed at centimetre wavelengths to pervade the Universe. This radiation becomes the relic of the earlier hot phase, cooled down by the cosmic expansion. Cosmologists favour those models which at the present time look the same in all directions. The observed cosmic background radiation is isotropic to better than one part in a thousand, so this eliminates all but a relatively small number of the models. The question still remains however: which model best describes our Universe?

Among the cosmological models remaining at this stage of the argument, some have magnetic fields, some have matter and anti-matter initially, and others have turbulence. To progress with the question of which cosmology, the cosmologist now has to change his tactics. He considers the very simplest among these models and sees how far he can get with these towards accounting for the properties of the observed Universe. If he reaches an impasse, he is prepared to modify the simple assumptions underlying the model and try again. It is perhaps remarkable that the very simplest models are, with only minor modifications, capable of

providing a satisfactory picture of the Universe. The modifications referred to arise from a wish to understand the complex question of the origin of galaxies.

The simplest models are those that are homogeneous and isotropic at all times, and which have the desirable feature of being hot at the beginning. As such a model universe expands, its density and temperature decrease in a way that can be calculated from the laws of gravity and thermodynamics. The density histories of two such models are depicted in figure 19.3. The models differ only in that one has a present density of one hydrogen atom per 10000 litres, whereas the other has a density of one hydrogen atom per 100 litres. The latter model will, at sometime in the future, stop expanding and recollapse: the cosmologist refers to this as a CLOSED UNIVERSE. The other model expands forever, and is called an OPEN UNIVERSE.

Before following the life histories of these universes, we should ask: how far into the past of the Universe can we confidently apply the terrestrially-established laws of physics? We should certainly start to lose confidence when the densities of matter greatly exceed nuclear densities, and the temperatures exceed hundreds of billions of degrees. We have no direct experience of such conditions and our knowledge of the structure of matter is hardly adequate to allow any more than an informed guess. Nonetheless, this ignorance relegates only the first fraction of a second of the Universe to the realm of scientific speculation.

Nucleosynthesis and neutralization

The simple model universes were selected for discussion because they provide a straightforward explanation for the origin of both the element helium and the cosmic background radiation, and because of their lack of complicating features. Nevertheless, it is by no means a simple task to discover all of their properties and construct cosmic histories which may possibly be confronted with observation. So, in order to set the scene, let us begin by tracing the history of such a model universe, and looking at its principal features. First of all, consider what it is like at the age of about 25 seconds. According to the simple model, its temperature is about four billion degrees, and its density roughly 2 tonnes per litre! At this time the principal constituents are radiation (*photons*) and *neutrinos*, with a very small admixture of matter in the form of protons, neutrons and electrons. The density of the matter component is less than 0.01 kg per litre, some ten times the density of air at sea-level. Since radiation vastly outweighs the matter, the Universe is said to be radiation-dominated. The protons cannot combine with either the electrons (to form hydrogen atoms) or the neutrons (to form deuterium): such products would be broken apart by the intense radiation almost as soon as they were formed at this time. It is not until the Universe is some 200 seconds old that the radiation temperature has fallen enough to allow deuterium to form, and it is another million years before the electrons can combine with the protons to form neutral hydrogen gas (the EPOCH OF NEUTRALIZATION).

These two events, the synthesis of deuterium and the combination of electrons and protons, mark two very important events in the history of the Universe. With the onset of deuterium formation, *nucleosynthesis* begins abruptly and a chain of *nuclear reactions* takes place that converts almost all of the deuterium that is formed into helium. Within a matter of minutes, one quarter of the matter in the Universe is turned into helium. The other event, the formation of neutral hydrogen, marks the end of a radiation era and, as we shall see, the beginning of the era of galaxy formation. Once all the electrons have combined with the protons, the cosmic radiation field can no longer interact with anything, and propagates virtually unhindered to us now where it is observed as the cosmic radiation field.

Let us consider in a little more depth the significance of the nucleosynthesis period in terms of the simple cosmological models, and of the Universe in which we live. The simple models indicate that between 25 and 27 per cent of the mass in the Universe was converted into helium. Not only is helium very difficult to destroy, it is also very difficult to make in stars in significant quantities. If our simple models of the universe were reasonable representations of the real Universe, astronomers should see an almost uniform abundance of the element helium, there being nowhere less than 25 per cent or so by mass. This is indeed what is seen. Not only is this regarded as strong evidence in favour of the simple models we have considered, but also as an indication that our extrapolation of the laws of physics so far into our past may not be unreasonable. Moreover, it is possible to compute the yield of helium expected from different cosmological models. Some of these contain magnetic fields, some have antimatter, and others rotate; but most do not produce the required quantity of helium.

It is now thought that most of the isotope deuterium must have been made in the early Universe. This is because astrophysicists have not yet been able to find a way of making the required quantity of deuterium in stars without at the same time making much more beryllium and boron than is observed. In cosmological nucleosynthesis, the deuterium that is left over is just a small amount that was not consumed in the making of helium and other elements. If we make the assumption that the observed deuterium is of cosmological origin, the logical question to ask is: do our simple models produce the required amount? Now we come to a very sensitive test of the simple model universes. The fraction of the Universe that is turned into helium is about 25 per cent in all simple models whose present mass density lies in the range one atom per 10 000 litres to one atom per 100 litres. The helium observation does not allow us to distinguish observationally the open and closed models. However, whereas one atom in every 10^5 or so left over from the nucleosynthesis era in the open model is a deuterium atom, only one in every 10^{10} is a deuterium atom in the closed model. The observed deuterium abundance is nearer to one part in 10^5, and so the open simple model is strongly favoured if we believe the deuterium we observe is of cosmological origin.

The origin of galaxies and stars

It is fair to say that our Universe is on the whole well represented by one or other of these simple homogeneous and isotropic cosmological models. They certainly provide a basis for understanding the gross features of the Universe. But what about the galaxies and stars that are the basic building blocks of the Universe, what does our simple model have to say about these? In the preceding discussion, we tacitly assumed that the early Universe was a gas or plasma, and based many of our arguments on this premise. Can we support this assumption in view of the fact that what we see through our telescopes are mainly stars and galaxies? Two arguments can be given which suggest that the gaseous models are a reasonable assumption at early times. According to the simple models, the density of matter at the epoch of neutralization (a redshift of about 1000) is of the order of 10^7 atoms per litre. This is at least a thousand times the density of a typical galaxy, so we can argue with confidence that whatever the Universe was made of at such early times, it was not galaxies as we know them now. The argument against stars at this time is less direct: if the Universe had been made up entirely of stars, it would be difficult to understand the origin of the cosmic background radiation. Of course, it is yet more difficult to rule out a mixture of stars and gas except by saying that we do not know how stars could have formed in the early Universe! In the face of such problems, we sidestep the issue by asking a slightly different question: how can we account for the existence of galaxies and stars within the framework of the simple model universes?

The question of the origin of galaxies is a crucial one for any cosmological hypothesis. We would like not only to explain the fragmentation of the Universe into sub-units, but also to explain why galaxies have the mass and rotation we observe. These parameters should arise in a natural way in any cosmological theory. Let us concentrate on the question of the origin of galaxies in a general sense, without worrying for the moment about explaining their properties. There are two views one can take about this: firstly, the Universe was, at all times in our past, at least as lumpy as it is now; or secondly, the Universe was, in the past, fairly smooth, and by some physical process became lumpy. The first view, represents a significant departure from the simple Big Bang theory, but no doubt a theory of this kind can be constructed and may be quite difficult to refute observationally. Perhaps the strongest argument is that such a lumpy Universe would not look like the simple model at the time of nucleosynthesis, and so is likely to give the wrong amounts of deuterium and helium. This is not a problem if we take the second view, but of course there we have the problem of finding a mechanism by which galaxies can condense out of the Universe. Two such mechanisms have been proposed. There is the GRAVITATIONAL INSTABILITY picture, where the force of gravity acts so as to enhance any slight irregularities, and there is the COSMIC TURBULENCE picture where lumps are created by hypothetical eddies crashing into one another.

The gravitational instability picture

Consider a small region of the Universe where the density of matter is slightly higher than elsewhere. The gravitational force holding this region together will be slightly greater than for comparable volumes elsewhere. Therefore, if gravity is the only force acting, the expansion of the overdense region will lag behind the expansion of the Universe as a whole. The contrast in density between this region and the rest of the Universe will be enhanced as time goes on. If the contrast becomes sufficiently great, the force of gravity may halt the expansion of the lump and cause it to collapse. The hope is that a lump of suitable mass would collapse to form a star, a galaxy or a cluster of galaxies. This is fine if no force other than gravity is acting, but if the Universe is hot enough, pressure forces may resist the compressing effect of gravity. This is a particularly important point before the electrons and protons have combined to form neutral hydrogen, for then the radiation exerts a tremendous pressure by colliding with the free electrons. This pressure is so great that at that time, the force of gravity cannot dominate except for enormous lumps having masses in excess of 10^{18} solar masses. Consequently inhomogeneities on scales of clusters of galaxies or smaller cannot be gravitationally enhanced during the fireball phase of the Universe. Once the electrons and protons combine, however, there are no longer any free electrons and the matter no longer feels the pressure of the radiation. Gravity then enhances all structure on scales exceeding 10^5 solar masses. On smaller scales, the pressure arising from the mutual collisions between atoms can resist gravitational amplification. Thus although gravity cannot form stars, it can certainly cause objects of galactic size to condense out of the Universe.

The neutralization of the cosmic plasma takes place according to simple models when the Universe is some hundred thousand years old. This event, according to the gravitational instability theory, marks the beginning of the process of galaxy formation. It may take another hundred million years for gravity to halt the expansion of the lump, but once that happens, the lump (referred to as a PROTOGALAXY at this stage) goes into rapid collapse. It is not difficult to envisage the possible sequence of events during the collapse of the protogalaxy, though to establish the chain of events rigorously is another matter: this is a most complex problem in theoretical astrophysics. As the protogalaxy starts to collapse it may fragment, and the first generation of stars will form within the fragments. Some of these stars may evolve and explode before the protogalaxy has stopped collapsing. These will enrich the protogalactic material with elements such as carbon, oxygen and nitrogen. Strong gravitational interactions organize the stars into a stellar system of the kind we observe. Any gas not converted into stars may form a flattened disc by the time the collapse is halted by the build-up of pressure forces. Speculative? Certainly, but this scenario is not totally without theoretical foundation. In this theory the galaxies form as a result of a succession of competitions between gravity and opposing pressure forces. First the pressures prevent gravitational enhancement, but at neutralization it is gravity that wins, only to be forestalled later by the build-up of pressure forces within the collapsing protogalaxy.

Cosmic turbulence

The picture described above provides one explanation of why the Universe may have become lumpy. We are, however, a long way from being able to verify such a theory by observation: galaxies bear few birthmarks that might provide rather indirect clues to their origins. It is not surprising, therefore, that cosmologists have been able to dream up a variety of theories for the origin of galaxies. The cosmic turbulence theory provides an important viable alternative to the gravitational instability picture. Ever since the discovery of spiral galaxies, it has been remarked that they resemble cosmic whirlpools. This is just what the cosmic turbulence theory proposes: that galaxies are fossilized eddies left over from a previous era when the Universe was turbulent. Prior to the time when the Universe became neutral, the intense radiation pressure would have caused the hypothetical turbulent whirls and eddies to bounce off one another, creating smaller eddies. Immediately after neutralization, the radiation can no longer affect the motion of matter, and when the eddies collide and mix there is nothing to prevent them from generating enormous shock waves and lumps which are later to be identified with galaxies. Unfortunately, turbulence is poorly understood and consequently it is rather difficult to calculate precisely what should be expected on the basis of the cosmic turbulence theory. Nevertheless, the theory has intuitive appeal in producing the cosmic whirlpools directly. An objection to the theory is that at the very early times when nucleosynthesis takes place, such a turbulent Universe represents a radical departure from the simple models. It seems unlikely that a turbulent Universe would provide the required quantities of deuterium and helium.

We see in the galaxy formation theory an important application of the Big Bang hypothesis. The hypothesis tells us that in the past there was a time before which the matter was ionized and after which the matter was neutral. This EPOCH OF NEUTRALIZATION marks the onset of the galaxy formation process in both theories we described. The hot Big Bang hypothesis tells us also that at very early times the synthesis of deuterium and helium took place. The requirement that all the observed deuterium and helium be synthesized cosmically allows us to impose constraints on the various theories of galaxy formation without even looking at galaxies!

Cosmic meditations

During these past fifty or so years, we have discovered our Universe and set it within the framework of the laws of physics. A concrete and coherent picture has emerged. This picture is indeed compelling: there are few (if any) viable alternatives, and the theory has satisfied every test demanded of it. But is our confidence any more justified than, say, that of the Greeks in their cosmologies, which were after all consistent with their view of the Universe? On the basis of historical precedent we might surmise that the theory will be continually altered to incorporate new data. This will happen either until the theory departs so far from the original concept that it can hardly be regarded as the same idea, or until so much additional structure is required to support the theory that it is no longer a simple theory. At that time a new view can easily displace the old theory. In this context we might think of the modifications to Newton's theory of gravity that were introduced to account for the slight anomaly in the motion of the planet Mercury. There were several ad hoc attempts to set matters right, including the suggestion that the anomalies might be due to a planet whose orbit lay within that of Mercury. But it was not until the formulation of the *General Theory of Relativity* that a truly satisfactory answer to the problem was found. However, notwithstanding the radical change in viewpoint engendered by the theory of relativity, Newton's law remains a very good description of what is going on. Similarly the Big Bang theory may be a good approximation to the state of affairs, even if some drastic conceptual innovations should ultimately prove necessary.

In an attempt to stretch our theory of the Universe to its limits, we might well begin by trying to isolate those points at which our theory may encounter difficulty, or to ask questions which our theory may not be able to answer. In this way we build up a list of fundamental cosmological problems which are so often the subject of debate, and which lie on the ill-defined boundary between physics and metaphysics. Because these questions arise frequently, we shall say something about a few of those which are questions of physics rather than philosophy.

Perhaps one of the central issues concerning the Big Bang cosmology is the issue of the cosmic singularity. If our ideas about the nature of matter are correct, and if in addition Einstein's theory is the appropriate framework within which to discuss cosmology, the existence of a singularity in our past is inevitable. A breakdown of the presently-accepted laws of physics is required in order to avoid the conclusion that our Universe evolved from a singular state. One such modification led to the Steady State theory, which is indeed singularity-free; however, we have seen that this theory is not consistent with the observational data. Indeed, if we invoke the nucleosynthesis arguments, we have good reason to suppose that any such changes in the laws of physics would only have been of importance during the first few seconds of the life of the Universe. Let us pursue this point a little further and ask: when might the laws of physics have been sufficiently different from the presently observed laws? We might well believe

that matter exhibits peculiar properties when its densities exceed nuclear densities. There is no experimental information on this point, though it is not clear that any anomalous behaviour would necessarily have the required effect of removing the singularity. (The kind of anomalous behaviour we are looking for is, for example, the pressure of the cosmic medium becoming negative.) We have no reason to doubt the validity of general relativity in the kind of physical regimes observed so far, but as yet we have never studied a situation where the space-time curvature is very high. Ultimately, there comes a point when space-time can no longer be viewed classically and we should have a merger between general relativity and quantum theory. In the Universe, this would happen when the density is some 10^{90} kilograms per litre! Even if it were shown that the assumptions leading to a singularity break down at this point, it seems to be somewhat a matter of semantics as to whether we should say a singularity has been avoided!

If the Universe is closed, the force of gravity will eventually halt the expansion and cause the Universe to collapse towards another state of infinite density and temperature. This future singularity is as inevitable in a closed Universe as is the past singularity we have just been contemplating. A breakdown in the laws of physics in the vicinity of such a singularity might cause the Universe to bounce back and start another phase of expansion. In this way we arrive at the notion of an OSCILLATING UNIVERSE which has an infinite past and an infinite future. Classical thinking leads us to suspect that such a Universe might run down in much the same way as a bouncing ball eventually comes to a stop. However, such deductions can hardly take proper account of the all-important mechanism for the hypothetical bounce. The strongest argument against the oscillating Universe concept is that we do not appear to live in a closed Universe. If that is correct, then the cosmic singularity is a unique event.

We turn our attention now to a rather different problem which is rarely discussed in the popular literature on cosmology. It is one of the most important, as yet unanswered, questions: why is the Universe homogeneous and isotropic? A possible answer is 'because it started off that way', but as we shall see, this answer is inadequate and only sidesteps the central issue. Before going on to discuss this rather deep question, the reader may like to consider the following analogous phenomenon. A race is to be run with each of the competitors running in different neighbouring stadia. One starting-pistol is fired, and all the runners are seen to start simultaneously before any of them could have heard the report of the gun! If we observed such a scene, we would indeed be puzzled and wonder how the runners knew when to start. What we observe in the Universe is directly analogous. The homogeneity of the Universe implies that all parts must have commenced expanding in unison, and yet there is apparently no physical agency through which different regions could have communicated so as to synchronize their histories.

We can best illustrate the cosmological situation by reference to a space-time diagram (figure 19.4). Consider two cosmic observatories A and B, and suppose that the Universe as observed from A and B is homogeneous and isotropic. Because the Universe expands, each of A and B will see more of it as time goes on. At sufficiently early times A and B will not be able to see each other, since the light rays emitted from A will not have had enough time to reach B, and vice versa. A and B are then said to lie beyond each other's HORIZON. They are causally disconnected, by which we mean that at that time, nothing that has happened in the vicinity of A can affect B, and vice versa. At some later time, A receives the first signals from B. B is then said to have come within A's horizon, and this is the first A knows of B's existence. Subsequent to that time A and B can compare their respective environments, and eventually there comes a time when they realize that they have experienced almost identical cosmic histories. Although A and B

could not communicate at very early times (and were even unaware of each other's existence), the Universe somehow went bang simultaneously in both places. Thus our observation of the homogeneity and isotropy of the Universe on immense scales seems to imply some breakdown of the basic notion of CAUSALITY that the cause precedes the effect by at least as much time as it takes a light ray to travel from the point of cause to its point of effect. The feeling among some cosmologists is that this breakdown of causality must have occurred at or before the time when the picture of space-time as continuous breaks down. Needless to say, we are not yet sophisticated enough to cope with this problem theoretically: there has to date been relatively little success in merging the theory of relativity with quantum theory.

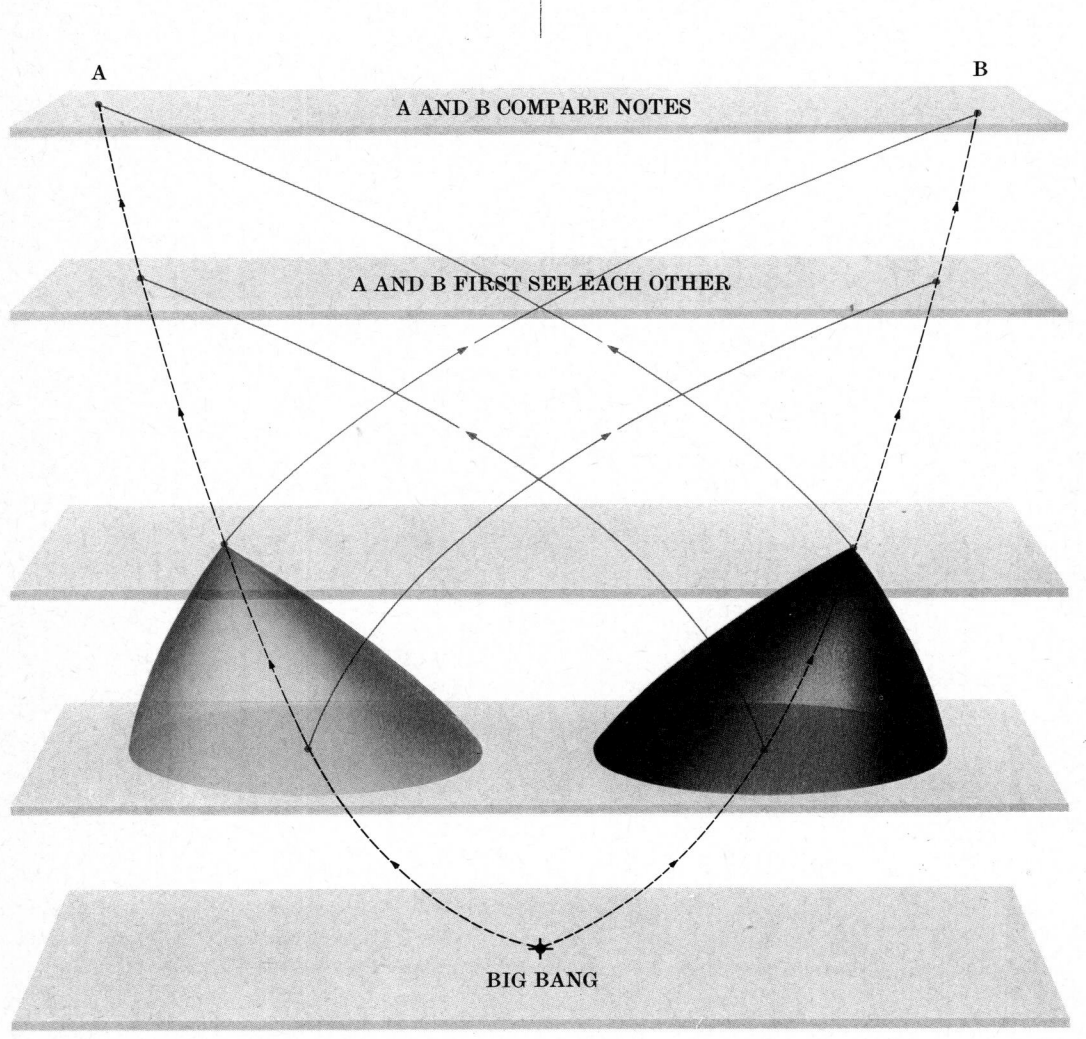

19.4: *Why is the Universe isotropic? This space-time diagram shows how two observers A and B emerge from the big bang. Time is plotted vertically and the three dimensional world is shown compressed into two dimensional slabs. The diagram displays the cosmic expansion, A and B get further apart on successive slabs. It also shows the part of the Universe which can be seen at any instant by an observer: his 'past light cone'. The further away an observer looks, the further he sees into his past. The surface of the past light cone is the only part of space-time that is accessible to observation at any instant. Thus A can only communicate with B when B lies on A's past light cone. During the earliest phases of the expansion, A and B can know nothing of each other since not enough time has elapsed to allow them to communicate. It is a mystery, then, why the parts of the Universe in the vicinity of observers A and B should apparently have identical past histories.*

A AND B COMPARE NOTES

A AND B FIRST SEE EACH OTHER

A   B

BIG BANG

Mach's Principle

In the past, MACH'S PRINCIPLE has been considered a central cosmological issue. Mach's principle is an ill-defined concept, but broadly speaking asserts that our local physical laws are influenced by the large-scale distribution of matter. An often-quoted example that illustrates this is that of the Foucault Pendulum. If a pendulum is set up by suspending a ball on a string from the ceiling, and then sets swinging back and forth, the ball traces a straight line on the floor. The plane in which the pendulum swings rotates once every twenty-three hours, fifty-six minutes and four seconds. This is just shorter than the length of the day, so it is not the Sun that drags the pendulum around. In fact the plane of the swing of the pendulum is fixed relative to the distant stars and galaxies. Accordingly, we attribute the rotation of the plane of the pendulum directly to the influence (presumably gravitational) of the most distant matter in the Universe. At least, that is what Mach did. One of Einstein's hopes when thinking about the general theory of relativity had been to rediscover Mach's principle as a consequence of a proper theory of gravitation. However, it is not clear to what extent Einstein's theory achieves this. For example, there are solutions to Einstein's equations in which the Universe rotates. What is meant by the rotation of the Universe here is that an observer sitting in a terrestrial *inertial frame* sees the Universe rotating relative to this particular frame. Thus, such a Universe is not Machian in the sense that the coordinate system in which the distant stars are fixed is not an inertial frame.

It is possible to turn this doubt concerning Mach's principle and Einstein's general relativity into a strong cosmological principle by asserting that the only physical cosmological solutions to the Einstein equations are those which are Machian. Enunciated in this form, Mach's principle immediately excludes rotating cosmological models as physically acceptable models for the Universe. The principle also excludes the curious vacuum universes which have no matter at all, and yet display the cosmological redshift phenomenon. Most importantly, it seems that the simple homogeneous and isotropic cosmological models are Machian. Thus if we add Mach's Principle to the general theory of relativity, we may go part of the way to explaining the isotropy of the Universe.

Attempts have been made to modify General Relativity so as to incorporate Mach's principle explicitly. It is possible to construct cosmological models from these modified theories of gravitation and so test the theories indirectly by seeing if these models are observationally validated. Since these Machian cosmologies behave somewhat differently near the cosmic singularity from the Einstein-theory models, the nucleosynthesis arguments may be used to eliminate some of them as being inconsistent with cosmology. More direct tests of non-Einstein gravitation theories will be possible using satellite-borne gyroscopes.

Where do we go from here?

Cosmology has changed from a subject of philosophical and theological introspection into a branch of the physical sciences. There is now an established framework which delineates the arena of cosmic physics. It is not thought that future developments will change the basic picture, but will rather define the picture more precisely. Thus we expect to be able to describe the Universe in greater detail in future, as a result of further observations and advances in theoretical physics.

On the observational side, there are prospects for mapping out the expansion law of the Universe in greater detail, and for studying the spectrum and distribution of the cosmic background radiation. The number of galaxies with measured redshifts and magnitudes is only in the thousands, but we do not understand galaxies well enough to utilize even that much data. It is to be expected that this quantity of data will increase significantly owing to the development of automatic photographic-plate measuring machines and the building of large telescopes and specialized peripheral equipment for them. With an increased knowledge of the properties of galaxies, the prospects indeed look bright for achieving such goals as characterizing the clustering of galaxies and determining the *Hubble law*. Just as the discovery of the cosmic background radiation field engendered a renaissance in cosmology, the detailed study of all aspects of the radiation will provide us with direct information about the Universe at the early times when the radiation spectrum was established.

On the theoretical level, there is little doubt that the success of the nucleosynthesis arguments in constraining the number of possible cosmological models will be thoroughly exploited. Much of that work will be based on models for stellar and galactic evolution. Theoretical work, combined with observational data will tell us about the origin of galaxies, and this will in turn, via our models for galaxy formation, tell us about the Universe. The development of high-speed, super-computers will enable cosmologists to simulate various aspects of cosmology, such as the growth of clustering of galaxies and the evolution of galaxies. At a deeper level there is now a realistic and exciting prospect of forging a link between the microscopic world of elementary particle physics and the theory of gravitation.

20. Life in the Universe

20.1: *The DNA molecule. The DNA/RNA molecule is common to all terrestrial life-forms. It contains the blue-prints for the manufacture of proteins, the basic constituents of cellular material. The plan for the construction of a given protein is given by a particular sequence of 'bases' lying along the DNA molecule. The interpretation of a given base sequence is called the Genetic Code. (MRC Laboratory, Cambridge, UK)*

Are we alone?

A typical galaxy contains some hundred billion stars, most of which are not unlike our own Sun. The largest telescopes can photograph some billions of galaxies. The observable Universe therefore contains some 10^{20} stars! How likely is it that the Sun is the only one among these which is orbited by a life-bearing planet? This fundamental question is not one that can easily be answered. The only life-forms we know of are here on Earth, and we are only just now beginning to understand terrestrial life; the *genetic code* was cracked only twenty-five years ago. Given only a shallow understanding of life on Earth, one might well wonder whether discussion of hypothetical extraterrestrial life-forms is any more than a speculative exercise. Even more so, one might well ask whether life on Earth has any relevance to possible extraterrestrial life-forms. It is clear that if we are to make any progress towards answering the question 'are we alone?' scientifically, we must, at the outset, base our discussion on facts deduced by observing the terrestrial environment. We are, of course, immediately guilty of terrestrial chauvinism, but anything else would belong firmly in the domain of science fiction. The fundamental question should therefore be asked in a different, more scientific way: what does modern science have to say about the possibility of life similar to our own existing elsewhere than on Earth?

There are several facets to the problem. There is the astronomical problem of deciding what kind of stars are likely to be accompanied by a retinue of planets. There is the biological problem of finding a suitable definition of life and evaluating the circumstances under which life may evolve. Then there are the problems of interstellar communication: if there is intelligent life somewhere else, should we try and let it know of our existence? Such life-forms may be trying to communicate their existence to others: should we search for their signals and if so, how? To answer each of these questions scientifically we must inevitably fall foul of terrestrial prejudices simply because life on Earth is the only kind we know. The way we are going to approach the problem is as follows. We shall examine the evolution of a star and discuss whether or not we should expect a planetary system to form. We shall then look at the formation of the planets and ask ourselves how likely it is that planets similar to the Earth are to be found orbiting stars like the Sun. Strong arguments can be presented suggesting that terrestrial planets are not uncommon. So encouraged we shall follow the various stages of the development of life on Earth, as we understand it, and try to gauge how likely it is that a similar sequence of events has occurred on another Earth-like planet. Then we may make the final extrapolation, and speculate about the emergence of intelligent life. To do that requires some understanding of what has happened on Earth: what distinguishes Man from other terrestrial life-forms? This is a highly Earth-orientated picture, but at least it minimizes the speculative aspect of the subject. Speculation is, however, one of the most exciting, and occasionally fruitful aspects of scientific research. We should not ignore the possibility that totally dissimilar life-forms exist elsewhere in the Universe.

Since we are going to adopt such an Earth-biased basis for discussion, it is important to lay bare the prejudices that underly the whole approach. There are two basic sources of bias. First, we live on a planet in an almost circular orbit around a rather typical G-star. The almost constant distance to the Sun has ensured a temperature range in which the water that is essential to terrestrial life is a liquid. Second, all organic compounds are based on the element carbon. We could certainly imagine life developing on a planet orbiting a smaller star than our Sun, an M-dwarf, for example. The temperature range would be right for liquid water if the planet were nearer the star than the Earth is to the Sun. On the other hand, it is often argued that because stars more massive than the Sun have shorter lifetimes, life is less likely to develop on any planets they may have. This argument rests on the assumption that life takes billions of years to evolve. But what about the liquid water requirement? There is clearly a very strong terrestrial bias on this point. Crystalline or gaseous life-forms are by no means inconceivable, and indeed the pages of science fiction abound with such ideas. What is perhaps more relevant, and less terrestrially biased, is the need for a particular range of temperatures. Life must depend on complicated chemical reactions, otherwise such a sophisticated level of organization could not be achieved. At too high temperatures, complex molecules cannot survive, whilst at very low temperatures, chemical reactions proceed relatively more slowly. Of course, the carbon-based organic chemistry underlies all such arguments, yet it is not inconceivable that somewhere life may be based on a nitrogen or silicon organic chemistry. Our present knowledge of chemistry is inadequate to provide a firm basis for ruling out such a scheme, so we must simply admit that it is yet another possibility.

What is life?

Life is the most complex state of organization of matter known in the Universe. Living systems achieve this state of organization by using energy that they extract from their environment. Many physical systems do this, but a living system is distinguished in that it uses the energy to convert the material taken from its surroundings into a form characteristic of itself. This process is known as METABOLISM. It may be argued that metabolism is a sufficient condition for life for any individual organism. But in order to have a LIFE-FORM, that is a collection of similar living organisms, the individuals must also possess the ability to grow and reproduce. According to this definition of life, a virus is not alive (it is not a metabolic system), nor can a collection of crystals be considered alive. A more precise definition of life is not really possible. According to the most widely-held view, life did not appear spontaneously but there was a transition from the non-living to the living. Just where in this metamorphosis life began can only be a matter of semantics.

Although speculation on the nature and origin of life has a long history in theology and philosophy, the basic scientific viewpoint which has set the tone for subsequent debates was put forward in the 1920s by A.I.Oparin in the Soviet Union, and J.B.S.Haldane in Britain. Haldane enumerated the broad categories into which theories for the origin of life would have to fall. Firstly, one might assert that life had no origin, but is an integral part of the Universe that has been propagated from star to star by some means. Such a point of view is quite definitely ruled out by current ideas in cosmology, where all the evidence points to the Universe having originated some tens of billions of years in our past. Secondly, there are theories which assert that life is the consequence of some supernatural event. The very nature of such hypotheses puts them beyond scientific investigation. Finally, we may suppose that life evolved as a result of chemical processes. There are two theories that fall into this third category. There is the theory that although life on Earth is a spontaneous result of achieving a certain level of chemical complexity, the chain of events is so long, that the origin of life is very improbable. On this view, the Earth may be the only abode of life in the entire Universe since elsewhere the conditions were never all just right. The other theory simply asserts that life will appear automatically once a certain level of chemical complexity is reached. This is the view towards which a majority of scientists today would lean. It is a good scientific hypothesis since it is possible to perform laboratory experiments which may shed light on the origin of life. A consequence of this hypothesis is that life will appear wherever terrestrial conditions are present. Accordingly, a clear understanding of the development of life on Earth is of direct relevance to the question of life elsewhere, and the strategy adopted from here on will be to find the answer to what happened on Earth. We draw on astronomical, geological, biological and chemical evidence. We argue that the first astronomical, geological and chemical conditions that existed on the primitive Earth were also likely to have been realized elsewhere. The question of the origin of life elsewhere in the Universe will then be reduced to a speculation concerning the probability of making a transition from the non-living world of complex organic systems to the living.

Suitable planetary systems

How likely is it that systems similar to the Solar System exist elsewhere in the Galaxy? This, like many of the questions raised when discussing extraterrestrial life, is a highly controversial issue. It should be remembered that we have no direct evidence for the existence of any planetary system other than the Solar System. The issue thus rests on indirect arguments that are essentially theoretical.

The first point to note is that the Solar System is a dynamically stable system. The orbits of the planets have probably been much as they are now for most of the past life of the Solar System, and it is expected that this situation will persist for as long as the Sun is a stable main-sequence star. Such stability is not a characteristic of planetary systems in binary or multiple star systems in general, and so we should look at single stars in search of planetary systems. A large fraction of solar-type stars appear to be members of multiple stellar systems. However, the number of candidate-stars in our Galaxy for having solar systems probably exceeds 10^9 and may be as high as 10^{10}.

A second point concerns the rate at which the Sun is spinning about its rotation axis. If a typical interstellar cloud of one or two solar masses were to collapse to form a star, the resulting star would be spinning at least ten times faster than our Sun. It would therefore seem that the Sun's rotation has been braked by some means during the formation process. One theory for the braking of the Sun's rotation is that the rapidly spinning proto-Sun interacted with its surroundings in such a way as to cause the surrounding regions to rotate at the expense of the Sun's own rotational energy. The interaction could be via magnetic fields such as are observed to pervade the Galaxy, or by generation of turbulence in the surroundings. Thus 'slow' rotation of a star might be construed as evidence in favour of a pre-planetary system that absorbed the star's rotational impetus. The observations on the rotation velocities of various kinds of stars indicate that G, K, and M stars have much lower rotational velocities than O, B, A, or F stars. The main-sequence G, K and M stars have rotation velocities around ten kilometres per second, while the main-sequence O, B, A and F stars have rotation velocities of the order 100 kilometres per second or more. Thus, not only are the G, K, M stars intrinsically slow rotators, they are slow compared with other stars. This could be symptomatic of the existence of planetary systems about these stars, though it has been suggested as an alternative view that the G, K, M stars are slow rotators because they are old and their stellar winds have had a long time to carry away a large fraction of the star's rotational energy.

There are almost a hundred stars within twenty light years of the Sun. Most of these have masses in the range of 0.1 to 1 solar mass, but only a few have luminosities similar to the Sun's. Stars of spectral type G0 to G5 have temperatures in the range 4000 K–6000 K, and luminosities in the range 0.05 to 1.5 solar luminosities; they therefore make obvious candidates for a first search for evidence of planetary systems. There are 17 such stars within 20 l.y. of the Sun, all but five of which are components of multiple star systems. The stars which belong to multiple systems can be excluded on the grounds that they are less likely to possess stable planetary systems. This leaves ε Eri, ε Ind, τ Cet, σ Dra, δ Pav as the candidate stars for a first investigation. As remarked earlier, this list is constructed on the prejudice that solar-type stars are the ones most likely to possess planets with suitable environments. If we go to smaller and fainter stars, the size of the list increases significantly.

It is known that a number of stars have very small companions whose existence can only be inferred by observing the motion of the stars relative to more distant stars. The small companion exerts a force on the main star which causes the star to describe a small orbit about a point called the MASS-CENTRE of the system. Thus the Sun describes a complicated orbit about the mass-centre of the Solar System. This mass-centre lies close to the surface of the Sun,

and, as seen from afar, the Sun would appear to wobble about its path through space through a distance of about a solar radius. The planets Jupiter and Saturn are mainly responsible for this effect. Distant astronomers might detect Jupiter and Saturn by noticing that the Sun's wobble has components with periods of about twelve and thirty years, though it should be remarked that the wobble is so slight that it would be almost undetectable by present terrestrial techniques from the nearest stars. There are seven stars for which there is evidence of a wobble in the motion across the sky. It is clear from the preceding comments that the wobble is caused by bodies considerably larger than Jupiter and Saturn combined, otherwise no peculiarities in the motion could have been detected.

The case where there is least doubt is that of Barnard's star. BARNARD'S STAR, a 9.5 mag M5V star, is the nearest star in the northern equatorial hemisphere. The star has a large proper motion and photographic plates exist showing the star's track across the sky during the past 60 years. The deviations from a smooth track amount to only a few hundredths of an arc second and show a roughly periodic structure. Analysis of these deviations show that the motion of Barnard's star can be explained in terms of two planets orbiting the star in circular orbits with periods of 11.5 and 20–25 years. The innermost of the planets has a mass very close to that of Jupiter, while the outermost has a mass nearly half that of Jupiter. These are indeed planets! There is considerable confidence in the orbital characteristics of the inner planet, and the somewhat uncertain state of affairs regarding the outer planet should improve with continuing observations. One of the exciting aspects of this discovery is that evidence of a planetary system has been found in a very small sample of nearby stars where an effect could be detected. The planetary system of Barnard's star might have been detected had Barnard's star been three times further away, but of course there would be less certainty in the result. There are fewer than fifty stars in such volume.

The origin of the Solar System

Given that other stars have planetary systems, what is the likelihood that the planetary system resembles our Solar System? If we can answer that, we may be able to decide whether the evolution of life on Earth has any relevance to life elsewhere in the Universe. The only planetary system we have any knowledge of is the Solar System, so we must discover how this system originated, and see whether any exceptional circumstances went into its formation.

According to the best available solar models, our Sun is at least 4.65 billion years old. The oldest dated rocks on Earth are between 3.3 and 3.6 billion years old, and some Moon rocks have been dated at 4.1 billion years. The first life-form that we have any evidence of was present 2.7 to 3.2 billion years ago although this does not preclude the existence of life at even earlier dates. These numbers indicate that it took the Earth 0.5 to 1 billion years to form and solidify, and that rudimentary life-forms existed within the following 500 million years. This period is one about which we have little knowledge, but it is nevertheless possible to advance a number of plausible hypotheses based on our ideas of how the Earth formed, and on our understandings of simple biological processes. It is this period that is crucial to the origin of life on Earth, and we must understand it as well as possible if we are to attempt an assessment of the chances of finding life in other terrestrial environments.

The currently held view of the *origin of the Solar System* goes back to the Solar Nebula theory of Laplace. According to the modern view, the Sun condensed inside an extensive dust cloud. If the interstellar clouds we see now are anything to go by, the primitive solar nebula out of which the planets formed would be cold and already contain organic molecules like methyl alcohol (CH_3OH), acetaldehyde ($HCOCH_3$), methyl cyanide (CH_3CN) and methylacetylene (CH_3C_2H) to name but a few, besides the familiar carbon monoxide (CO), water (H_2O), and ammonia (NH_3) inorganic molecules. The cloud collapses and becomes hotter and denser in the centre, until a point is reached where nuclear reactions start up there. A star is then born. By this time the process of slowing down the rotation of the star will be well under way, and the outer regions will have settled into a spinning, flattened, disc. The energy radiated by the newly-formed star will be enough to boil away the lighter molecules in the central regions of the disc. At the same time, the refractory materials (iron and silicates) condense out nearer the star, while the less refractory materials (ices of carbon, nitrogen and oxygen) condense at greater distances. Thus the basic compositional difference between the inner and outer planets of the Solar System can be understood at a very simple level, and this leads us to suspect that such a division may not be uncommon in other planetary systems. The planets are thought to have been built gradually through the collision and coalescence of the condensed solid particles into planetesimals, and then into planets. The force of gravity would help this process along and at the same time sort out the orbits of the protoplanets into a fairly regular and well-spaced configuration. Although all the details of this scenario have not yet been completely worked out, there are a number of very impressive (and almost equally convincing!) theoretical discussions of various stages of the process. In this regard, the computations have shown the build-up of planets and the organization of their orbits in a way that leads one to believe that other planetary systems may bear considerable resemblance to the Solar System.

Let us now turn to consider the evolution of one of these protoplanets. As the protoplanet contracts under its own gravitation, the centre heats up and melts. A crust is formed through which the lighter gases like methane (CH_4), carbon dioxide (CO_2), carbon monoxide (CO), water vapour (H_2O) and ammonia (NH_3) can escape to form an atmosphere. It is generally believed that there was no free oxygen at this stage. The primitive atmosphere will certainly contain some of the simple organic molecules that existed in the pre-stellar cloud, together with some of the more complex molecules formed during the period when the solid material first condensed out of the solar nebula. The lack of oxygen is an important factor in the origin of terrestrial life for a number of reasons. There would have been no ozone (O_3) to protect the surface from the Sun's powerful ultraviolet radiation. The solar ultraviolet radiation could therefore have played an important role in the synthesis of organic molecules at the earliest times. Moreover, the presence of significant quantities of free oxygen would have seriously inhibited the formation of the organic molecules that are necessary to life. We have direct evidence for the absence of oxygen two billion years ago in rocks of that age which were weathered without being oxidized. Indirect evidence for there being no significant amount of oxygen around before that time comes from the observation that the Earth has had liquid water since 3.3 to 3.6 billion years ago. (The oldest rocks show evidence of having solidified under water.) The Sun was colder in the past, and the water would have been frozen if the Earth's atmosphere had contained as much oxygen as it does now. On the other hand, a reducing atmosphere, containing a small amount of ammonia, could act as a greenhouse and keep the Earth's surface at a higher temperature. (A similar phenomenon is observed on Venus now.) One of the uncertainties in this latter argument arises because we do not know how much heat the Earth could have produced internally.

The possible existence of complex organic compounds at times before the Earth even formed is an important point as regards the very first steps towards the building of the highly complex organic structures that are characteristic of terrestrial life. The evidence of this comes from the observation that certain kinds of meteorite, the CARBONACEOUS CHONDRITES, contain natural carbon compounds of very high molecular weight. The bulk of these compounds resemble crude oils and tarry substances found on Earth, but there is also a small component of amino acids, purines and pyrimidines present. These latter compounds contain the essential ingredients of terrestrial life: the amino acids are the building bricks of proteins, and purines and pyrimidines are the code-units of DNA, the genetic molecule. It appears that some of these meteorites may have ages in excess of four billion years. Thus we have direct evidence that extensive synthesis of extremely complex organic compounds may have taken place even before the planets formed. Just how much organic material could have been made in this way is impossible to estimate. It is possible that the continual rain of meteorites on the Earth might have been a major source of organic material. The most important point, however, is that we have direct evidence that it is easy to synthesize complex organic molecules during the early history of the Solar System.

The synthesis of organic materials

We have seen that the primitive atmosphere of the Earth would have contained, at a very early stage, organic compounds of varying degrees of complexity. Indeed, the picture described so far is likely to be a fairly common one wherever planetary systems have formed; no extraordinary events have been postulated. The next step must be the construction of the proteins and nucleic acids that are the basic building blocks of terrestrial life. PROTEINS are long chains of organic compounds called AMINO ACIDS and the NUCLEIC ACIDS are long strings of compounds referred to as bases. We must first understand how the amino acids and bases themselves formed, and then ascertain the conditions under which they may form these long chain-like structures (POLYMERS). Two processes are needed to achieve this; there must be an enrichment of the appropriate organic material, and then it must be concentrated to the point where polymers can be formed. The enrichment process is facilitated by the absence of free oxygen and the fact that the atmosphere is exposed to a number of sources of energy that can promote the formation of molecules. Examples of such energy sources are: solar ultraviolet radiation, volcanic activity, meteoritic bombardment of the atmosphere, cosmic rays, and lightning from atmospheric thunderstorms. Some twenty-five years ago, Stanley Miller performed some fundamental experiments demonstrating that the action of electrical discharges on a mixture of water vapour, methane and ammonia could produce reasonable yields of simple amino acids (glycine, $HCHNH_2 COOH$ and alanine, $CH_3 CHNH_2 COOH$). Subsequent experiments along the same lines by Leslie Orgel have confirmed Miller's findings, and shown that most of the smaller building blocks of biochemistry are also produced in this way. As an aside, it is of interest to note that the Miller-Orgel experiments simulated an environment rather similar to the lower atmospheric regions of Jupiter, where it is known that there are violent thunderstorms. Accordingly we would expect to find basic biochemical substances there: Jupiter may well be the best candidate in the Solar System for rudimentary extraterrestrial life!

Heavy molecules formed in the Earth's atmosphere drift downwards to the Earth's surface. These add to the stock of molecules put there by volcanic activity, or deposited by meteoritic and cometary impact. There are then a number of processes whereby these amino acids and bases may be concentrated and turned into biologically important polymers, the proteins and *polypeptides*. The evaporation of molecule-containing lakes, or even the freezing

of such lakes, could increase the concentration to the point where polymerization can take place. Absorption of organic molecules onto clay or mineral surfaces could have the same effect. The basic problem, however, is more complicated than merely obtaining polymers of amino acids and bases: we need the right polymers, the proteins and nucleic acids. A considerable amount of research effort has gone into the synthesis of organic molecules from primitive conditions. We have just mentioned Miller-Orgel experiments that produced amino acids, sugars and fatty acids under conditions that one might readily accept as being primitive. On the other hand, although the nucleotides and pyrimidines which are basic elements of DNA and RNA have been produced in some experiments, it is not generally agreed that the conditions imposed were really primitive. Moreover, no experiment has yet produced proteins or nucleic acids spontaneously.

This is a crucial point in the story. It has often been argued that once the proteins and nucleic acids assembled, then we have made the transition from chemical evolution to organic evolution. This is the origin of life since, before this point, everything that happens does so merely by chance. So let us look more closely at the question: what is so special about the proteins and nucleic acids? At this stage, let us take it for granted that amino acids and bases can be synthesized in the primordial soup. We have seen how amino acids may join up with one another to form polymers of amino acids. The simple chains of amino acids are called POLYPEPTIDES. The proteins, the fundamental constituents of living cells, are very special polypeptides. Not only does each protein have a very specific construction, but it is folded into a special three-dimensional configuration which it maintains as long as it is biologically active. The properties of the protein molecule cannot be deduced from its chemical constitution alone; the properties depend crucially on what parts of the molecule lie close to one another in virtue of the three-dimensional structure. Many proteins can act in such a way as to speed up certain chemical reactions, without themselves being affected by the reaction. Such proteins are called ENZYMES: they catalyze organic reactions. During that period of the Earth's history when polypeptides were being made, some were perhaps easier to synthesize than others, and a few of these may in turn have acted as catalysts for other chemical reactions. We might therefore envisage a kind of natural selection operating at a pre-biological stage, favouring the formation of a small class of important proteins.

Nucleic acids, cells and intelligent life

We have a basis for understanding the synthesis of elementary proteins. This is but the first rung on the ladder towards the evolution of life as we know it. As we climb this ladder, the system adapts itself more strongly to the terrestrial environment and so it is from here on that the divergences between life-forms on various planets will increase. There is a long way to go from the simple protein to homo sapiens, but if we are to get some feeling for the likelihood of there being an intelligent life-form elsewhere in the Universe, it is of interest to follow through the chain of events as we believe they happened on Earth.

Here then is the crux of the story of the emergence of intelligent life. The first stages of the argument are the most speculative, but as we move closer to the present the picture is clarified by the observations of fossils and other biological evidence on the evolution of life. The piecing together of diverse facts that go into the picture is one of the most fascinating examples of detective work in modern science. For example, there is good reason to suppose that all life on Earth is descended from a common ancestor. Furthermore, Man has spent such a short time on this planet that any intelligent life on other planets is likely to be so far out of step with us on the evolutionary track that we could never communicate with it.

The most important thing to begin with is an appreciation of what features are essential to an entity's being classed as alive. We have already discussed this point at the beginning of this chapter, where we saw that the two essential features are the ability to metabolize and the ability to reproduce. Both features imply a complexity of organization that must derive from a sufficiently complex organic basis. On Earth, this basis is provided by proteins and nucleic acids. Nevertheless, the mere presence of proteins and nucleic acids is not in itself sufficient to ensure metabolism and reproduction. They must be organized into higher structures, and act in a coherent way.

Proteins are the basic constituents of the cell; they perform the numerous tasks by virtue of which we say the cells are alive. They are responsible for the structure and activity of the cell. The function of the nucleic acids (like DNA and RNA) is to manufacture proteins according to a specified pattern, and a typical cell may turn out thousands of protein molecules every minute. The nucleic acids are enormous structures resembling twisted ladders whose rungs are pairs of substances called NUCLEOTIDES. The twisted sides of the ladder make the famous DOUBLE HELIX. Only four nucleotides are used in the construction of a DNA MOLECULE, and the sequence of nucleotide pairs that form the ladder-rungs constitutes the GENETIC CODE. The genetic code is indeed a code in the usual sense; the plans for a protein molecule are expressed as linear sequences of organic molecules. Since proteins occurring in nature are made from only 20 amino acids, four nucleotides grouped in pairs are more than enough of an alphabet to describe the construction of a given protein molecule. Interestingly, the first definite coding scheme was put forward by George Gamow in 1954.

Although the details of Gamow's theory were subsequently proved wrong, the importance of his contribution is generally acknowledged by molecular biologists today.

The way in which protein molecules are made raises a fundamental question: which came first, the protein or the nucleic acid that contains the protein plan? This is analagous to the famous chicken and egg dilemma, and may of course be resolved similarly by saying that the present system is highly evolved. But what did it evolve from, and how?

As to the how, it is generally felt that some sort of natural selection operated in favour of the development of our particular genetic code, though it is not yet possible to describe the selection in detail. As remarked earlier, this is a crucial point; the onset of natural selection in some primitive form is often considered to be the point at which life began. An interesting and possibly very important fact about the genetic code is its ubiquity on Earth. The DNA molecule contains the plans of proteins in a coded form where each amino acid of the protein is described by three successive rungs of the DNA ladder. What is striking is that the coding is identical in all terrestrial life. A possible implication of this is that all life descended from a single ancestral system. If more than one ancestor were involved, we might reasonably expect to see considerable variations in the coding. The single ancestor theory is not the only possible explanation of the universality of the genetic code, but there are other peculiarities of the code which are also consistent with this particular theory. It should be remarked that this does not exclude the possibility of there having been other kinds of primitive life-form on Earth in the remote past. But it does imply that one of these (our ancestor) was more successful than the others and succeeded in taking over the Earth by eliminating them.

There is an independent piece of evidence also favouring the single ancestor theory. This concerns the optical activity of amino acids. In a laboratory, any complex amino acid can exist in one of two forms which differ only in that they are mirror images of one another. The forms are referred to as right-handed (dextro) and left-handed (laevo) in analogy with the gloves of a pair that are identical in all respects except that they are mirror images. In biological systems, all amino acids are left-handed. (This is not just a matter of semantics, a left-handed molecule rotates the plane of vibration of an electromagnetic wave one way, while a right-handed molecule rotates it the other way. Thus handedness can be measured using polarized light.) There is no obvious reason why both forms of amino acid should not coexist; if amino acids are made in a laboratory, both forms are produced in equal amounts. This is true of the Miller-Orgel type of experiment. One way of explaining the left-handedness phenomena is in terms of life being descended from a single event and place!

The final stages, from proteins and nucleic acids to cells and then to plant and animal life, represents a long and complicated story. Let us tackle the formation of cells first. This requires a combination of two processes: a high concentration of protein material and a subsequent organization of the protein molecules to form large molecular structures. An interesting idea has been put forward to explain the high concentrations that are needed. As a solution of protein molecules gets more and more concentrated, (through evaporation, for example), the polymers form and grow until they reach a certain critical size. At that point, very concentrated droplets separate out of the solution. These droplets are called COACERVATES. They can selectively absorb substances from the external medium and can grow bigger and more complex. A kind of natural selection will operate to favour the continued existence of those droplets whose structure is such that they can benefit from their environment. Such droplets could be the sites for the origin of a genetic code.

What about the formation of organized macromolecular structures ? It is believed that once protein molecules come into contact they will arrange themselves automatically into a special macromolecule. Quite how this works we do not know, but it is certainly a well-observed phenomenon. In some experiments, tissue made of protein is dissolved and the solution stirred up. This destroys the elaborate macromolecular structure of the original tissue (such structure can be seen with an electron-microscope). If the dissolved molecules are then precipitated out of the solution, it is observed that the structure of the original tissue reappears spontaneously. The order present in large aggregates of protein molecules is apparently inherent in the structure of the protein itself.

From here the story is one of continual building and natural selection. It may, for example, be favourable for survival for an agglomerate of protein molecules to be surrounded by a membrane. In this way, primitive cellular structures may develop. Later on, the cells may develop a nucleus and could resemble living cells more closely. It is interesting that we have some fossil evidence on the development of cells. The oldest known fossils are bacteria and calcareous sedimentary structures called STROMATOLITES associated with blue-green algae. These are dated at 3.2 billion years of age. What is of inportance about these life-forms is that their cells are especially primitive in comparison with the cells of animals and plants. The bacteria and blue-green algal cells have no organized nucleus. Such life-forms are grouped under the heading of PRO-CARYOTES and they form the expected precursor to the present-day cellular structures (EUCARYOTES) which have a cellular nucleus.

If life on Earth evolved by a process of growth, modification and selection, and if it is descended from a single ancestor, we should be able to identify the times at which the various innovations to the structure of life appeared. This is the grandest of all family trees ! The tree can be constructed by modern investigation of the protein structures of various life-forms. In this way we learn for example that plants and animals separated 1.1 billion years ago, and we can trace the evolution of the great biological families (phyla). The tree is shown in figure 20.2.

It has clearly been a long and difficult route to the evolution of man. So many things could have happened on the way that it is probably safe to say that extraterrestrial intelligence will differ

20.2: *A schematic reconstruction of the pathways followed by life-forms on Earth. The relationships between the main groups of living things is indicated. Well established dates are included, but there is a great deal of uncertainty about the older parts of the history.*

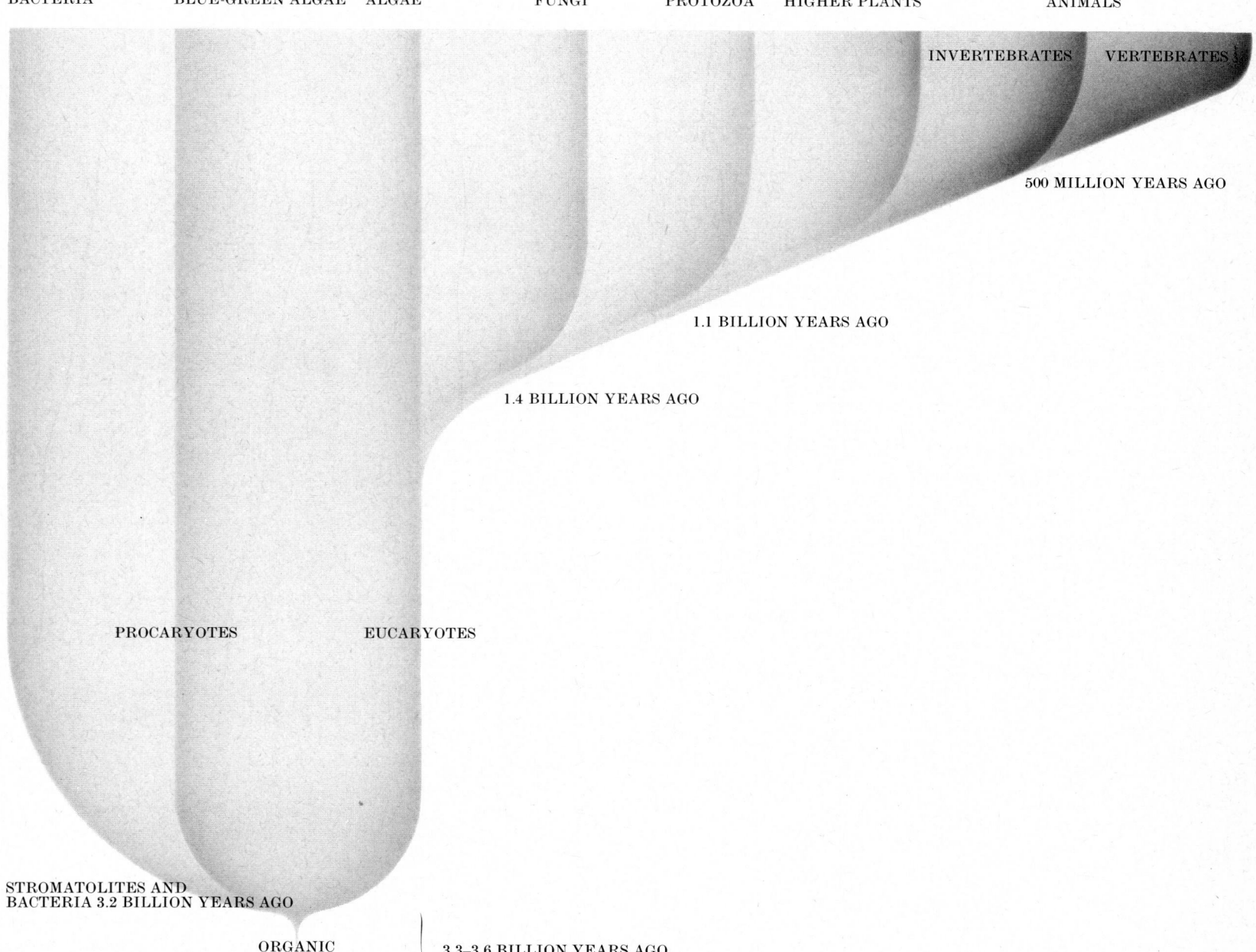

BACTERIA　　　BLUE-GREEN ALGAE　ALGAE　　　　FUNGI　　　PROTOZOA　HIGHER PLANTS　　ANIMALS

INVERTEBRATES　　VERTEBRATES

500 MILLION YEARS AGO

1.1 BILLION YEARS AGO

1.4 BILLION YEARS AGO

PROCARYOTES　　　　　　EUCARYOTES

STROMATOLITES AND
BACTERIA 3.2 BILLION YEARS AGO

ORGANIC　　　　3.3–3.6 BILLION YEARS AGO
INORGANIC　　　　LIQUID WATER

considerably from us, if, indeed, it exists. In that context, it is important to understand what distinguishes homo sapiens from other animals; it is certainly more than mere intelligence.

'Man' has created a world of culture by documenting his intellectual efforts. Animals, however intelligent, do not have this, though many undoubtedly have emotions, senses, memories and even perhaps creative imagination. Man can acquire knowledge about the world from his fellows, whereas an animal's knowledge of the world is gained only from personal experience. The world of culture was created by man and the development of language must have been of paramount importance in this process. Man achieved self-conciousness through communication with his fellows.

There is a danger of putting 'Man' on too high an intellectual plane. What we believe to be objective knowledge arises as a result of the processing of our sense data by our brains. It is entirely conceivable that we are being fooled, and that another superior intelligence might come to differing conclusions about the same sense data. The human brain has evolved considerably even though it has only doubled or tripled in size in the two million years since our ape-like ancestors walked the Earth. What might a further ten million years do? It should be noted that there are stringent physiological constraints on the future development of Man. One reason for this is in the way humans are born: the infant's head must pass through the pelvic girdle at birth, and this puts an upper limit on the size of the human brain at birth. The fate of our species may therefore be a rather stagnant one like the spider, in which any further growth of the brain would constrict the ingestion of food. There may also be social constraints on further development such as found in ants which seem to have used their intelligence to create a homogeneous and almost static society.

It has been remarked that language and our understanding of the world have developed together. The link between our understanding of the world and the language we use may be such a powerful one that our knowledge is actually constrained by our language structure. So even in mathematics, which one might have thought of as existing quite independently of the real world, we can identify only a few basic structures like topological structures and algebraic structures. Is this because that is all there is to mathematics, or is our mathematical knowledge constrained by the way it was acquired via language? Our mathematical knowledge may even be constrained by the simple structure of our brains that formulate both the language and the mathematics. Life-forms evolving completely different means of communication, and having different brain structures might have different mathematics, and so their technologies could be inconceivably different from ours! We must be humble about our present position and beware of intellectual chauvinism.

The communication problem

Suppose that we are not the sole intelligent life-form in the Universe. Discovery of another life-form and subsequent communication with it would be one of the most important events in the history of the human race. But how should we go about searching for such a life-form, let alone communicate with it? The question of search can be answered to a limited extent, but only within the framework of our present technology. The problem of communication is far more severe in view of our total ignorance regarding the possible nature of such life-forms. Nor is it a simple matter of science; there are economic problems too. It is certain that an efficient search for extraterrestrial intelligences would cost a great deal of money; a sum comparable with the Apollo Moon programme could be involved. Moreover such a search may take decades before extraterrestrial intelligence is discovered or before it can be fairly well established that civilizations like our own are very rare. It is clearly difficult to justify such a vast expenditure of money when the success of such a venture can in no way be guaranteed. So at present the search for extraterrestrial life must be a by-product of more general astronomical exploration.

There have been a few searches using present telescopes for evidence of extraterrestrial civilizations which may be trying to communicate their existence to others. The first such search was project Ozma conducted at the National Radio Astronomy Observatory in Virginia in 1960. The stars observed were τ Ceti and ε Eridani. Since then there have been more observations, generally of nearby G, K or M stars. The searches have not yielded anything that could be construed as a signal, but they do lead us to discuss a number of very interesting problems. We might ask ourselves how many stars we might expect to observe using a given technique before obtaining a result. What is the optimal wavelength to search at? What constitutes a 'signal' and how shall we recognize it as such? Then there are questions like: suppose we discover evidence of an extraterrestrial civilization, how will we understand its communication? What would be the result of such contact between civilizations? Our terrestrial experience of contact between different civilizations is a history of the decimation of the less advanced societies. Extraterrestrial communication does not involve physical contact, so the effect may be more akin to the influence of ancient Greek philosophers and Biblical prophets on present European society, and that is certainly not insignificant!

Such problems have been considered and debated at considerable length. International conferences have been organized to bring together the thoughts of scientists in many disciplines from many countries. In the face of our total ignorance about extraterrestrials, and of our own rapidly growing but evidently primitive technology, such discussions must be regarded as remarkably ingenious. However, one is sobered somewhat by (and one may derive amusement from) the thought of how similar debates might have proceeded only a hundred years ago! Bearing this in mind, let us make a few comments on these questions.

Consider first the question of the likelihood of discovering an extraterrestrial civilization. That depends on many things. It depends on the probability of the existence of life on a planet orbiting a given star, on the extent to which the civilization has developed, on the nature of the instrument used in the search and on whether or not the civilization is trying to signal its existence to others. We have already discussed the evolution of rudimentary life on Earth, and the development of technological civilization, so the reader can judge the likelihood of the same process occurring elsewhere. An important factor here is how long such civilizations can survive, once established. If, for example, the lifetime is a mere hundred years following the development of nuclear technology, we would have to observe that civilization during that short period between the birth of its technology and the annihilation of its society. Unless technologically-advanced societies are stable over periods of perhaps millions of years, we may never discover any. Of course, if the civilization continues to advance it will become more readily detectable simply by virtue of the energy it radiates in the maintenance of its civilization.

The problem of what kind of instruments should be built to optimize the search for extraterrestrial civilizations is a difficult one. Even if we assume that some civilization has established a beacon to let others know of its existence, we have no way of guessing in advance what frequency to look at. The 1420 MHz line of neutral hydrogen has been suggested on the grounds that it is an 'obvious' choice in the absence of any information, but really there is no reason to exclude the possibility of signalling with some other radio line (which may be less noisy), or at optical or even X-ray frequencies. In fact, since searches for extraterrestrials will in the foreseeable future be based on existing equipment, the search frequency may be dictated more by terrestrial conditions than anything else. The most ambitious project proposed to date is PROJECT CYCLOPS, an array of more than a thousand 100-metre dishes. The waveband to be searched by this instrument would be from 1420 MHz to the OH-transition at 1662 MHz, a band known picturesquely as the 'waterhole'. The main advantage of such an array would be that it can be added to as money for the project becomes available, and will be capable of doing important radio astronomy at the same time.

If extraterrestrial civilizations do not set up beacons, they could be detected by virtue of the energy they emit in the maintenance of their society. The problem is then even more difficult, for not only are we ignorant of the best frequency to use, but we would have to eavesdrop and the power emitted may be rather low in comparison with what a specially constructed beacon might achieve. Moreover, in the absence of any special signal, it will be more difficult to establish that an extraterrestrial civilization has in fact been observed. If, for example, a civilization radiates most energy away at infrared wavelengths, we have the problem of distinguishing this infrared source from hundreds of others that are due to circumstellar dust shells.

Another way to look for evidence of extraterrestrial civilizations is to look here on Earth! It is conceivable that a highly-developed super-civilization may have had time to visit most stars in the Galaxy, and in particular may have visited the Earth. If the Earth provided a suitable environment for the visitors, they may have colonized the Earth. The absence of any obvious extraterrestrials on Earth indicates either that the Earth was a hostile environment and not colonized, or that there are no civilizations in the Galaxy with the capability of such extensive exploration. Visiting extraterrestrials, finding the environment hostile, may nevertheless have left evidence of their visit, either accidentally or intentionally. It is not clear what form such evidence might take. To be found now it would have to survive many thousands or even millions of years, and not get lost as a result of geological activity. One possibility that comes to mind is an artificial satellite orbiting the moon while emitting occasional strong bursts of radiation. What does seem clear, however, is that such a technologically advanced civilization would not need to construct landing sites or astro-navigation aids of a kind resembling the archaeological relics found all over the world today. Whatever the correct interpretation of such sites or of petroglyphs, it makes no sense whatever to ascribe such things to an extraterrestrial civilization with the technological capability of interstellar space travel. Of course, there may be evidence around that we are not yet capable of recognizing. The previous example of a moon-orbiting satellite could not have been recognized until this century, and it is certainly conceivable that a highly-advanced civilization has left a sign that only comparable intelligence could appreciate. There is yet another possibility that we were visited and our visitors were, in their wisdom, careful not to leave any sign for fear of disturbing the development of a primitive life-form. Such visitors might even observe us rather as we might observe animals in a zoo, and this ingenious idea has been called the zoo hypothesis. The hypothesis is, of course, irrefutable and so is not therefore a properly scientific one.

The possibilities are enormous, and speculation is part of the intrigue of science. The search for extraterrestrials must begin somewhere if we are to ascertain our true position in the Universe. We now have the technology to begin a search, and to signal our awakening to other civilizations. Accordingly, we should award some of our scientific effort to this problem now, even if it is only as a part of scientific research. It has taken several centuries for us to benefit from the dawn of the age of science and technology. It may take a long time to reap the benefit of interstellar communication, but if we are to succeed, it may herald the birth of a new era in human civilization.

21. Major trends in the history of astronomy

Introduction

Astronomy, being the oldest of the exact sciences, has a very long historical tradition going back many thousands of years. For the greater part of this time, the study of the skies has been inseparable from astrological and religious traditions. Indeed, in the past, astronomy was more intricately woven into the fabric of civilization than is the case today. Not until the time of Galileo and Newton do we find the scientific aspects of astronomy to be distinguishable from its mystical overtones. To review the long evolution from the many primitive views of the cosmos to our own complex picture would be a vast task, and one which would be out of place in an encyclopaedia of modern astronomy. Our purpose, therefore, is to take four of the significant themes and show how these were slowly developed by individual scientists to give us our present understanding.

The selection of topics for a limited discussion must be somewhat arbitrary. We have chosen to describe the following major trends:

The development of theories of the planetary system, with particular reference to the impact of these theories on man's understanding of the Universe and to the thrust given to the branch of mathematics known as celestial mechanics.

Methods by which cosmic distances are evaluated and their relationship to the model of the Universe adopted in working out the distances.

The rise of astrophysics as a separate discipline, and the attempts of physicists to deduce the nature of stars and the Sun through analyses of the known laws of physics.

The discovery of the vast Universe beyond our Galaxy and the calibration of the extragalactic distance scale.

The adoption of this scheme brings out more clearly the main steps involved in the calibration of the distance scale, for example, at the expense of a strictly chronological story. Since our aim is to show how parts of astronomy developed in practice, rather than to give a detailed account of every small advance and major setback, we feel justified in abandoning the traditional order of presentation.

Our story does not begin in deepest prehistory. We could have started with a survey of primitive astronomy and proto-astronomy throughout the world, drawing in the contributions of Babylonia, Central America and neolithic Europe, together with description of alleged observatories such as those at Stonehenge and Carnac. Although this is in itself a fascinating tale, it cannot be linked in an unbroken chain to the present day. Hence we shall begin in the classical world of the Mediterranean, where the earliest planetary models that we can still describe with certainty were invented.

I. Theories of the planetary system:
Early planetary schemes

Behind all the complex hypothetical machinery to move planets through the sky lay a simple aim: to predict the positions of planets and the Sun and Moon in the foreseeable future in order to cast horoscopes, make forecasts and construct a calendar. In achieving these aims, it did not matter that the solution appeared to be contrived. So long as it saved the phenomenon (hardly any of them did!), that was enough.

Although the early astronomers of Egypt and Babylonia had been keen observers of the apparent motions of the Sun, Moon and planets, they did not use geometrical models of their paths through the sky. With the Greeks, the emphasis changed from a strictly observational role to one that required rational explanations for observed changes in the sky. They began to make geometrical models of planetary motions with some attempt being made to fit the appearances. The earlier attempts were not too successful from the observer's point of view; that is, the observed positions of planets and the positions calculated theoretically did not agree very closely. However, a model was developed by the second century AD which satisfied the observations with a fair degree of accuracy and which was accepted, with minor changes in the constants from time to time, until the sixteenth century. This model was developed by Claudius Ptolemaeus, or Ptolemy as he is usually called, an astronomer from the school of Alexandria.

Hipparchus, (active c. 160–126 BC), was the author of the first systematic star catalogue. His researches were to culminate in the 'Great Synthesis' of Ptolemy, or 'Almagest', as it is commonly called from its Arab translation. Ptolemy's work is a masterpiece of complicated geometrical computation, and its success relied heavily on previous planetary observations, many of which came from Hipparchus. Ptolemy attempted only to explain the appearances, not the actual orbit in space; his model was a geometrical device to permit correct predictions of celestial positions against the background of fixed stars from an observed fixed position on a stationary Earth.

The 'Almagest' treated each planet separately, and, although the mathematical scheme for each had the same general pattern, there was no connection between them to produce an integrated system. It was concerned only with apparent position; the actual size of the planetary orbit was of no consequence – Ptolemy assumed the accepted order of the celestial bodies adopted by the ancients. The general structure of the celestial sphere is described with the Earth at the centre, and the path of the Sun, the ecliptic, defining the reference plane. The motion of the Sun is taken as the reference body for describing the positions of the other planets, which can then be demonstrated fairly simply. Since the motion of the Sun is not uniform, the centre of the circle is displaced very slightly from the Earth and the resultant true position of the Sun calculated with respect to the Earth. The motion of the planets required two extra features, the equant and the epicycle.

In the period following Ptolemy's death, (c. 151 AD), astrono-mers accomplished little: compilations and commentaries replaced observations, so the Ptolemaic theory remained unchanged. Only in the eighth and ninth centuries with the birth of Arab schools in Baghdad, Cairo and the Arab West (Spain and Morocco) did astronomical observations once more become important. New astronomical tables based on the principles laid down in the 'Almagest' were drawn up and minor improvements made to the theory, which basically remained the same. Ptolemy became known to the West about the middle of the twelfth century through the books of Al-Battani and Al-Farghani. The 'Almagest' was first translated into Latin by Gerhard of Cremona in about 1175. Around the same time, translations of Aristotle's works on scientific subjects became available and, as with his well-known works on logic, they exerted considerable influence over mediaeval thought. A new set of astronomical tables, the 'Alfonsine Tables' published in 1252, was to last for the next two centuries. By this later date, discrepancies between the tabulated and observed positions, particularly for the planet Mars, became unacceptably large. In Europe, and in particular in Vienna and Prague, there was a concern on the part of the Catholic Church to rationalize the dates of the Easter festival. The reliability of current tables had to be tested and more positions obtained. A closer study of the 'Almagest' was necessary and two astronomers, George von Puerbach (1423–61) and his pupil Johann Müller (or Regiomontanus) (1436–76) were invited to investigate the problem. This resulted in the Nuremberg 'Ephemerides', the most detailed and accurate astronomical information then available. The next change was to be fundamental.

In a book published in 1543, 'De Revolutionibus Orbium Coelestium', Nikolaus Copernicus (1473–1543), a Polish canon, for the first time offered an alternative to the 'Almagest' for the serious astronomer. Analysing a vast amount of data, as had Ptolemy, he reconsidered the whole problem of planetary motions with the Sun rather than the Earth at the centre of the system. From the modern standpoint, it makes little difference which reference point one uses, but the relocation of the centre played a significant role in the history of astronomy. In his scheme for inner and outer planets Copernicus, like Ptolemy, believed in the necessity for uniform, circular motion; the mathematical techniques in both the 'Almagest' and 'De Revolutionibus' are essentially the same. Copernicus got rid of the five planetary epicycles but he had to add a large number of small epicycles to remove eccentrics. What he did provide was a uniform planetary system in which all the planetary distances were linked to the Sun-Earth system. From a historical point of view, he also re-opened the whole question of the Earth's mobility and demonstrated that accurate planetary predictions could be made from a heliocentric system. The Copernican revolution in fact lay in the after-effects of 'De Revolutionibus' rather than in the contents of the text itself. The removal of the Earth from the centre, within a thorough mathematical treatment of planetary orbits, had consequences which Copernicus, steeped in mediaeval traditions, could not anticipate, and the introduction of a rotating Earth was another major conceptual advance.

The motion of Mars

The Copernican theory fitted the planet orbits of small eccentricity (Venus, Earth, Jupiter and Saturn), but, as with the Ptolemaic theory, Mars remained a problem. Discrepancies of more than a degree, unacceptable by any observational standards, still persisted. To Johannes Kepler (1571–1630), enthralled with the beauty and symmetry of the heavens, the Copernican fit was not sufficient. He considered there must be a simple, geometric relation describing the motions of the celestial bodies.

His first thoughts on the geometric configuration of the heavens were published in 1596 in the 'Mysterium Cosmographicum'. This account of the relations between the numerical quantities occurring in the Solar System represents the beginning of his search for a harmonic relationship between the sizes of orbits of the various planets and their periods of revolution about the Sun, a search which was to last about 25 years. But first he had to find out why Mars would not obey the Copernican heliocentric theory. He began this project under the supervision of Tycho Brahe, (1546–1601), around the year 1600. Tycho had made an incomparable series of observations including regular observations of Mars over a long period. After Tycho's death in 1601, Kepler fortunately succeeded in getting control of the greater part of them. Many years of arduous computation and guess-work began.

Initially, Kepler proceeded along Copernican lines. Eventually he abandoned this approach in favour of an entirely new one. He decided to try and determine the actual shape of the orbit so a whole new series of calculations began. He first tried combination after combination of eccentric, epicycle and equant until he reached a scheme which could represent the observations to an accuracy of eight minutes of arc. This was not close enough, so he forsook circles in favour of various ovals. Finally he achieved the long-sought and far-reaching synthesis with an ellipse and found that, if the Sun were at one focus, it satisfied the problem beautifully. He had solved the problem of the shape of the orbit, and proceeded to find out how the planet moved in this known orbit. Again many attempts were necessary before he made his second elegant discovery, that the straight line joining the planet to the Sun sweeps out equal areas in equal times. Both these results, now known as *Kepler's laws* were published in the 'Astronomia Nova' in 1609. His full investigation of Mars, 'Commentaries on the Motions of Mars' was also published in that year. In the following years he satisfied himself that these rules applied to the whole Solar System and investigated other astronomical problems.

By 1619 he had proposed a further empirical rule – the square of the period of revolution of any planet is proportional to the cube of its mean distance from the Sun. This was published in his 'Harmony of the World' and is now known as *Kepler's third law*. Kepler's three rules suddenly made the problem of describing planetary motions look simple. They were, however, empirical rules with no dynamical basis. The link between these rules and the laws of physics was found by Newton.

The Law of Universal Gravitation

Isaac Newton's 'Mathematical Principles of Natural Philosophy' (or 'Principia') was published in 1687. This work dealt with observed properties of bodies and their motions from which could be derived certain general laws relating to the forces of nature, general laws that could be used to predict other natural phenomena. The 'Principia' was divided into three parts, the first two dealing with the general principles of motions and forces, the third, his System of the World. In the third, Newton propounded the mutual forces of gravity between the planets and the Sun, and from these forces, deduced their motions. All the planetary motions, described empirically by Kepler's three laws, could be deduced from one fundamental law, the LAW OF UNIVERSAL GRAVITATION: the force between two bodies is directed along a line connecting them, is directly proportional to the product of their masses, and is inversely proportional to the square of their separation. Astronomy, the most ancient of sciences, and dynamics, were united by this law.

The concept of a mutual attraction between objects, along with ideas on the nature of motion of terrestrial bodies, had been developing throughout the seventeenth century. Kepler and other physicists mentioned the possibility of an inverse square attraction between objects, although none of them provided any test for it. Galileo, one of the pioneers in dynamics, had built up a theory of falling objects in which the notion of uniform acceleration occurred for the first time and he formulated an example of the law of inertia (a more general form of which became Newton's first law). In his 'scientific method', his emphasis on the necessity for repeated careful experiment, Galileo could be called one of the first moderns. Important work was also done by Christiaan Huygens (1629–95) on the theory of the pendulum and allied problems describing the motion of a body in a circle or other curve. One of the principles which he introduced and examined was that of centripetal force, the force which holds a body moving in a circle in that motion, a very useful concept for celestial as well as terrestrial mechanics. Newton's greatness lay partly in his ability to synthesize all the important results of his predecessors, but also in his insight into the real nature of the problem; none of his predecessors saw as clearly as he the universality of gravity.

Although the 'Principia' was not published until 1687, Newton had tested the validity of the law of gravitation as early as 1666. Using the known distance to the Moon and calculating its rate of 'fall', he determined that the force maintaining it in its orbit was the same as the force of gravity observed in terrestrial bodies. The delay in publication can be partly explained by a natural reticence on Newton's part, but also by certain inherent difficulties in the theory. The exact relationship governing the attraction of a sphere on an external point, and the search for a general solution to the three-body problem (i.e. Moon-Earth-Sun) occupied Newton and many mathematicians after him.

European developments after Newton

Towards the middle of the eighteenth century, European rather than British mathematicians began to investigate the remaining problems in the lunar and planetary theories. Although Newton had provided a solid foundation for the theory of the motions of the Moon and planets, he was not able to account for all the inequalities in their orbits. Newton's calculated motion of the Moon's *apogee* was only half the observed result. Similarly, perturbations in the planetary orbits, particularly for Jupiter and Saturn, could not be explained. It appeared that the Solar System might not be stable and therefore must from time to time require some divine intervention to balance out the inequalities.

The LUNAR THEORY was the least satisfactory. Newton himself was concerned by its disagreement with Flamsteed's observations, and at the time of publication of the 'Principia' had only given a qualitative account of lunar inequalities. The Swiss mathematician Euler (1707–83) and the French mathematicians, Clairaut (1717–65) and D'Alembert (1717–83), all provided distinct solutions to the problem of three bodies in a form suitable for the lunar theory. Clairaut first attempted an alteration in the inverse square law, i.e. in the form $\frac{a}{r^2}+\frac{b}{r^3}$, which gave a satisfactory result. Later, however, he discovered terms in the lunar equations that he had previously omitted which could account for the discrepancies in the Moon's orbit, and Newton's theory was saved. Euler and D'Alembert also reached satisfactory solutions without assuming any alteration in the inverse square law. The lunar tables of Tobias Mayer (1755), capable of giving longitude at sea to within half a degree, were based on Euler's methods. Euler, Clairaut and D'Alembert had one distinct advantage over Newton in their treatment of lunar inequalities; they used analytical rather than geometrical methods. However, they still were not able to explain all aspects of the motion of the Moon satisfactorily. The secular acceleration was later accounted for by Laplace as being due to an indirect planetary effect, causing a slow increase in the Moon's motion and thus a resultant decrease in the length of the month; his result agreed almost exactly with observations.

There are two types of inequality in an orbit – periodic and secular. By the middle of the eighteenth century, it was believed that the latter was cumulative and therefore that the Solar System was unstable. Such secular changes were known for the inclination of an orbit, the eccentricity and the length of the orbit axis. During the last quarter of the eighteenth century, a remarkable series of investigations on secular inequalities were undertaken by two French mathematicians, Lagrange in Berlin and Laplace in Paris. Laplace explained the slow change in the rates of motion of Jupiter and Saturn as being due to a periodic disturbance; since their times of revolution are nearly proportional to two whole numbers, a disturbing force is produced. He found this inequality to have a period of about 900 years. Lagrange obtained general expressions for the secular changes in the inclination of an orbit and the length of axis, and found these changes to be necessarily periodic. Laplace showed that allegedly secular variations of the eccentricity were also of a periodic nature. Their combined results indicated that any changes in axis, eccentricity and inclination of a planetary orbit are restricted within definite limits.

These results were summarized in Laplace's masterpiece, the 'Mécanique Céleste', published from 1799–1825. The Solar System was shown to be a stable system in which all the motions could be accounted for fairly accurately by means of the law of gravitation.

Thus it was that the eventual production of the theory of universal gravitation enabled scientists to give a harmonized view of motion within the heavens. One simple theory swept aside the spheres within spheres and wheels within wheels of the ancients, and this theory holds good even today, unless the velocities of the moving bodies are a significant fraction of the speed of light. Paralleling the long road to Newton's theory was an even longer road to the distance scale. Newton needed to know some distances in order to test his theory, but as we shall see in the next section, scientists in Newton's lifetime were a very long way from knowing the structure of the Universe on large scales.

II. Measuring cosmic distances:
Early measurements of the Universe

A spherical Earth was accepted very early, although the first conclusive physical argument in favour came from Aristotle. He pointed out that during a lunar eclipse the shadow cast by the Earth on the Moon was circular, which would not be the case unless the Earth were spherical. Aristotle alluded to certain measurements of the size of the Earth in his writings, but the first fully-recorded account, although second-hand, is that of Eratosthenes, (276–195 BC). Using only a gnomon (shadow-stick) he measured the length of the shadow cast by the noon-day Sun on the summer solstice at Alexandria, while the Sun was directly overhead (in the zenith) at Syene, a city some 5000 'stades' (850 km) due south of Alexandria. He found the angle of the Sun at Alexandria to be 7° 12′ away from the zenith. From this observation he arrived at an Earth circumference of 250 000 stades (equivalent to a diameter of about 42 500 km), only 5 per cent lower than the modern value. For some reason this value was later ignored by Ptolemy and the less accurate result (180 000 stades) of Posidonius adopted.

Speculative estimates of the scale of the Solar System had also been made by the third century BC. The first-known estimate is that of Anaximander (611–546 BC), a philosopher of the Ionian school, who put the Sun's distance at 27 times the radius of the Earth and that of the Moon at 18 times the radius of the Earth. The Pythagorean school of philosophers also made estimates of the sizes of planetary orbits in the early fifth century, based on their analogy of the orbits with musical scales. They sought a harmony of the Universe in the distances of the planets, and from musical proportions arrived at the relative distances of the orbits. There are other references to distances in the classical sources, but very little remains of the methods adopted. During the third century BC, however, a series of measurements were made by Aristarchus of Samos, in an account entitled 'On the sizes and distances of the Sun and Moon', which is still extant. Aristarchus is now famous for his anticipation of the heliocentric system, which we know of only through second-hand sources.

To obtain the relative distances of the Moon and Sun, Aristarchus observed the Moon at *quadrature*, when the Earth, Moon and Sun form a right-angled triangle. His measurements gave the angle Moon-Earth-Sun as 87°, which corresponded to a triangle in which the Earth-Sun distance was 19 times the Earth-Moon distance. He also reported that since the Sun and Moon subtend the same angle at the Earth, the Sun must then be 19 times larger than the Moon. Modern measurements give the ratio of distances as 400:1 rather than 19:1. This discrepancy would have arisen from the difficulty of the measurement. In practice it is extremely tricky to determine the exact moment of quadrature (when the Moon is at precisely half phase), and even a slight miscalculation produces a large error in the final result.

The observation mentioned above gives only the relative measures of the Sun-Moon distances. Aristarchus was also able to arrive at an absolute distance by using his observations of the Earth's shadow during a lunar eclipse. By measuring the time elapsed for the Moon first to appear totally eclipsed, and the total time of obscuration, he concluded that the Earth's shadow at the Moon's distance was twice the size of the Moon. Since he knew the actual diameter of the Earth, by use of simple geometrical arguments he was able to arrive at the absolute distances of the Sun and Moon. His value of the Sun's distance, of the order of six million kilometres, was grossly underestimated primarily because of the difficulties in the initial measure of the relative distances, but the method which he used was ingenious.

A more tenuous method of obtaining the scale of the Solar System was through a synthesis of the Aristotelian mechanistic scheme of the Universe with the Ptolemaic mathematical model of the planets. Many attempts were made in the post-Ptolemaic period, particularly among the Arabs, to fit the epicyclic theory more satisfactorily into the concept of thick spherical shells. This combination allowed the relative dimensions of the Ptolemaic scheme to be transformed into absolute distance by utilizing the known distance of the innermost sphere, the sphere of the Moon. Each shell was thick enough to allow both for each planet's nearest and farthest approaches to the Earth. From a knowledge of the relative sizes of the epicycle and deferent, they calculated the ratio of the inside and outside diameters of each sphere. Since the spheres were all nested together, the outer diameter of one determined the inner diameter of the next so that knowledge of the distance of one sphere sufficed to determine the distances of all the others. Implicit in this whole scheme was the belief that no empty spaces existed between the spheres. A void was not permissible.

After the fifth century AD, estimates based on the concept of space-filling spheres became quite common. Al-Farghani, the ninth-century Arabic astronomer, provided a well-known set of cosmological dimensions using this method.

The downfall of a compact Universe

Mediaeval astronomical measurements assumed the model of a two-sphere Universe. This model postulated the segregation of Earth and sky: the laws of motion and the constitution of the heavens were considered quite separately from the physical relationships governing the behaviour of matter on the Earth. Philosophers considered the heavens to be perfect and unchangeable: all celestial bodies moved with the most perfect motion, uniform circular motion, about the Earth. During the sixteenth century, however, Aristotelean physics and the concept of a geocentric Universe came under increasing attack. By the end of the seventeenth century, the postulated duality of Earth and Sky had been overthrown by the concept of a unified Universe in which Earth and Sky alike were governed by the *law of universal gravitation*.

The change in cosmological outlook was characterized by a new interest in the stellar sphere itself. Events such as *comets*, which in earlier times would have been attributed to atmospheric effects, were now watched enthusiastically in an attempt to explain the new evolving cosmos. This new interest in the heavens was accentuated by the demands of navigation. With trade and expansion dependent on accurate means of navigation, countries sought to solve the problem of determining longitude at sea. Many felt that the clue lay in more precise knowledge of celestial positions, which could then be observed by navigators in order to deduce their own positions. So, around the middle of the seventeenth century, State observatories were set up in France, England, and later other countries, to prepare extensive catalogues of stellar and lunar positions. At the other end of the scale further attention was paid to the shape and size of the Earth to see if it satisfied the predictions of Newtonian gravitation.

The overall revolution in astronomical thinking began with the work of Nikolaus Copernicus. Although Copernicus began the so-called revolution, very few of the changes mentioned above were anticipated by him. Observed planetary positions at this time were found to differ by as much as several degrees of arc from their predicted positions. Copernicus re-analysed planetary motions and concluded that a new model of the Solar System would fit the observations more closely. 'De Revolutionibus Orbium Coelestium' adhered to the mediaeval concept of a compact Universe bounded by the sphere of the stars, but it positioned the Sun, rather than the Earth, at the centre. Unlike the 'Almagest', it provided a uniform planetary system, the mathematical application of which would reveal the relative sizes of the planetary orbits in space. In other words, from the Copernican system one could obtain the actual scale of the Solar System. The displacement of the Earth from the centre had another dramatic effect – it meant that the diameter of the hypothesized celestial sphere would have to be at least 2000 times greater. With the stars any closer than this, one would expect to be able to detect stellar parallax (cyclic changes in the observed positions of the stars due to the motion of the Earth round the Sun), which had not at the time been observed. Despite this massive increase in stellar distances, the Copernican world picture was much like the mediaeval one.

One of the early converts, Thomas Digges, added a new outlook to the Copernican picture. In a popular account of the Copernican theory published in 1573, he depicted the stars stretching outwards beyond the orbit of Saturn and he maintained that they extended to infinity. It was Giordano Bruno, however, who became the leading proponent of the idea that the Universe extended infinitely and had no particular centre and his doctrines spread throughout Europe like wildfire. Bruno's theory implied a plurality of inhabited worlds and a rejection of traditional religious doctrine; this led to his execution in 1600, and also provoked suspicion of the Copernican theory among theologians.

The overthrow of classical concepts

In the midst of these cosmological expansions, several events culminated in the abolition of the concept of solid, classical spheres required by mechanistic models of the Universe. Copernicus' Universe deprived the stellar sphere of its earlier function as the driving force behind celestial motions. A succession of uncommon celestial events showed that the spheres were a redundant feature of the models. These rarities included the sighting of a supernova in 1572 and the appearance of the great comet, visible in daylight, in 1577. Tycho Brahe observed both of these and was ingenious enough to take a few measurements of them; from the lack of visible parallax of the nova and the very small parallax of the comet he deduced that they must both be far beyond the atmosphere of Earth, and therefore celestial phenomena. Such observations of transient events cast serious doubt on the existence of immutable planetary spheres and re-opened the question of the whole mechanism of the Solar System.

At this point, although the concept of space and the size of the Universe was changing, actual distance measures had not advanced. Copernicus' value for solar parallax was remarkably similar to Ptolemy's, and only the estimated distances to the stars had increased. The most meticulous observer of the day, Tycho Brahe, had attempted to determine the trigonometrical parallax of the star Polaris with his great quadrant but met with no success. Consequently he rejected the notion of a moving Earth and instituted instead an alternative planetary scheme. Another objection to a moving Earth was the immense stellar diameters (of the order of 2000 times that of the Sun) obtained from the new distances if the apparent angular sizes were converted to linear measurements. This objection was eliminated by Galileo's observations of stars through a telescope, the first-known telescope to be used for astronomical purposes. To Galileo's surprise, the stars continued to appear as mere points of light, despite magnification; this demonstrated that apparent sizes were, after all, misleading. The telescope also revealed an infinitude of stars, hitherto unseen, particularly in the Milky Way where Galileo's telescope could resolve star images. Gradually a picture of layers of stars at varying distances replaced the old model of a sphere of fixed stars. To determine their distances, Galileo suggested a new method of parallax determination based upon differential measurements of distances between the components of optical pairs of double stars. His idea was that of two stars close together in the sky, the brighter could be assumed to be the nearer; if this were true, the apparent separation of two close stars should vary as the Earth orbits the Sun, on account of parallax.

Contemporary with Galileo's telescopic observations, Johannes Kepler was providing the final blow to the classical picture of the Universe. After several unsuccessful attempts over many years Kepler finally discovered that the orbit of Mars could be accurately represented by an ellipse. He extended the model to the rest of the planets, and also revealed the first accurate period-distance relation now known as *Kepler's third law*. Kepler attempted to find the absolute scale of the Solar System by obtaining the parallax of Mars, but he was unable to detect any such parallax. He concluded that the distances of Mars and the Sun must be greater than had been supposed: in his estimate, the distance to the Sun would have to be three times greater than the currently-accepted value (that is, a solar parallax of about 1 arc minute) and the distances to stars at least 400 000 million kilometres.

Estimates of solar parallax were to become more exact in the seventeenth century. In 1671, Jean Richer undertook an expedition to Cayenne, in co-operation with Picard and Cassini. Together with other observers back in France they determined the parallax of Mars and thus, solar parallax. 1671 was a particularly good time to observe Mars as it was then in opposition, the point at which the Earth and Mars come nearest to each other in their orbits. Their combined efforts produced a solar parallax of around 9.5 arc seconds, or approximately 140 000 000 km.

Extensive star catalogues, particularly that of John Flamsteed, the first Astronomer Royal, were also being published. Despite the much greater accuracy of the instruments, parallax still escaped detection. A new method, developed by Christiaan Huygens around 1650, initiated what could be called the photometric method of parallax determination. In this method, Huygens compared the observed brightness of the Sun and Sirius. On the assumption that both stars had the same intrinsic brightness, he estimated the distance of Sirius to be about 29 000 times that of the Sun (that is, a parallax of about 3 arc seconds). This method was used by Newton, Gregory, and others after them, to arrive at possible stellar distances. The historical importance of this development lay in the assumption that the Sun and the distant stars are physically the same, since their apparent brightnesses could only give reliable distance estimates if this were the case.

Throughout the seventeenth century, estimates of solar and stellar distances increased as more precise data became available. The development of the micrometer, first used by William Gascoigne and later, independently, by Christiaan Huygens, contributed to this greater accuracy. Jean Picard was the first to introduce the systematic use of micrometer sights on the telescope in about 1667, after which they became a common tool of the observational astronomer. At first, however, there was the occasional objector; Johann Hevelius, for example, insisted on the superiority of naked-eye observations throughout his life. With the establishment of the Greenwich and Paris observatories during the second half of the seventeenth century, astronomers, assured of limited State support, began thorough investigations of planetary and stellar positions. In about 1720 Edmond Halley undertook at the age of 63 the task of obtaining precise lunar positions over a complete synodic period (18.6 years).

Universal gravitation

Meanwhile, investigations into the physical mechanism of the planets culminated in 1687 with the publication of Isaac Newton's 'Principia'. Although others had made important contributions to the question of the mutual attraction of bodies, Newton was the first to assimilate it all and to derive the exact equations for the fall of a body on Earth and the equivalent fall of a satellite, such as the Moon, in its orbit. After this masterly synthesis of cosmic and terrestrial physics Newton proceeded to calculate the motions of the various members of the Solar System. He included in his calculations the mutual perturbations of the planets on each other, to see if the observed and predicted positions were in close agreement. As with all his endeavours, Newton expected experimental or observational confirmation of his theories, and rejected hypotheses which he believed to be unverifiable.

Newton's work presented a whole new consistent world view, just as Aristotle's had done many centuries before. Although this new structure did not materially affect the state of observations, it did mean that a variety of observations which would perfect the constants of Newtonian physics were made. Different philosophical frameworks require different observations. With the concept of a Solar System as a mechanism in which each member influences the motion of every other member in accordance with the law of universal gravitation, the various irregularities in the motions of planets took on new importance.

Transits of Venus

The desire to detect both solar and stellar parallaxes provided great incentive for observational astronomers during the eighteenth century. Lunar distances also were important because observations of the Moon were felt to be a viable approach to the problem of determining longitude at sea.

One of the most elaborate scientific expeditions of the eighteenth century was concerned with the accurate measure of solar parallax through observations of the transits of Venus in 1761 and 1769. Attention had been drawn to these important events by Edmond Halley in 1716 in an attempt to unite and stimulate young astronomers by the accuracy the method offered. Halley's idea (mentioned earlier by Kepler and others) was based on his observation of the transit of Mercury in 1677. Essentially it uses the circumstance that the apparent path of Venus across the Sun is not the same for observations conducted at different points on Earth's surface. Hence, two different observers at different latitudes will see two different paths, the difference depending on the size of the Earth, position of the observers and the scale of the Solar System. Since the first two of these factors were known, the third, the distance to the Sun, could be deduced from the differences between the observed paths.

Governments, scientific societies and individuals went to incredible trouble and expense to prepare for these transits since their occurrence, due to the inclined paths of Venus and the Earth, is rare. Expeditions were despatched throughout the world to ensure the best possible results. Unfortunately a combination of effects – optical, instrumental and atmospheric – led to results that did not live up to expectations.

For the first transit (1761), values for the solar parallax ranged from 7.5 to 10.5 seconds of arc; for the second, values were much better, ranging mostly from 8.5 to 8.8 seconds of arc. Some astronomers deduced values close to the presently accepted one but the data were uncertain, so that such results held no more weight than others. The whole set of observations was re-analysed by Encke in 1835, who deduced a value of 8.571 seconds of arc.

The first distance to the stars

Vital steps were taken towards the detection of stellar parallax during the eighteenth century through the collection of extensive and precise stellar catalogues. In addition, more precise instruments, impossible for the crude technologies of earlier times, were being constructed. Both these factors contributed to many false alarms until the actual minuteness of stellar parallaxes was ascertained.

Flamsteed's catalogue, the 'Historia Coelestis Britannica', led the way in the new science of exact astronomy. Published posthumously in its revised form in 1725 (after a pirated edition in 1712) it included positions of about 3000 stars down to an accuracy close to 10 seconds of arc. The previous extensive catalogue, that of Tycho Brahe, could only claim accuracies down to about 1 minute of arc. The second Astronomer Royal, Edmond Halley (1656–

1742), did not improve on this observational limit but he did contribute to the problem in his discovery of the first actual motion of stars, known as their *proper motion* (or motion across the line of sight). Using proper motions astronomers could determine the relative distances of those stars which had detectable proper motions and thus select the best candidates for a measurable parallax.

Halley's successor, James Bradley, (1693–1762), added many refinements to both instrumental construction and observing techniques. With respect to the latter, he produced an excellent table of the refraction of light through the atmosphere, thus allowing the effects of temperature and barometric pressure on all measurements to be removed. Bradley attempted to measure the parallax of the star γ Draconis but instead discovered a phenomenon called *aberration*, an equally strong proof of the Copernican theory and a confirmation of Roemer's discovery of the finite velocity of light. Upon further reduction of his results, he noticed another small perturbation that he later concluded to be *nutation*, a wobbling of the Earth's axis due to the gravitational attraction of the Moon. From these results Bradley showed that any parallactic displacement must be less than 2 seconds of arc and probably less than 0.5. In addition to these discoveries, he compiled a catalogue of about 3000 stars of unrivalled accuracy which was published in 1798 and 1805, long after his death.

Other countries were also producing extensive catalogues. Nicolas de Lacaille, a French astronomer, published a catalogue of about 10 000 southern stars while at the Cape, South Africa. Lalande, as director of the Paris Observatory, published his 'Histoire Céleste Française', which included recorded observations of nearly 50 000 stars down to 10th magnitude. At the same time the list of stars of known proper motion was expanding. Halley had measured four (Sirius, Aldebaran, Betelgeuse, Arcturus) in 1718.

One of the great astronomers of this period, Sir William Herschel (1738–1822), often called the father of sidereal astronomy, also examined the problem of parallax. He hoped to measure it by observing double stars and then using the method of differential parallax suggested by Galileo. With such a pair, the remote one could be used as a fixed reference point with which to compare any displacement of the nearer one. Herschel was very successful after an examination of many double stars, not in the determination of parallax, but in the discovery that double stars existed as actual physical pairs (binary stars). Previous to this, such pairs had been considered to be optical, or coincidental, doubles. This discovery meant that such pairs could not be used since they were equidistant from the Sun.

The final discovery of parallax came from three very different quarters in fairly close succession: Bessel in Germany, Henderson at the Cape and Wilhelm von Struve in Russia. Bessel and Struve had both equipped themselves with the best optics then available, developed by a young Bavarian optician, Joseph Fraunhofer, famous for his work on the solar spectrum. The final detection in 1838 ended several debates over previous illusory discoveries, since the small quantities actually involved could not have been ascertained by earlier instruments.

Bessel's discovery came after many years of assiduous labour. In 1818 he published Bradley's catalogue of 3000 positions reduced to the equinox of 1760; for the first time a catalogue contained not raw data, but positions corrected for the effects of *precession*, *nutation* and *aberration*. He then proceeded to extend the catalogue and was able to compile a catalogue with positions for over 63 000 stars. With the completion of his catalogue, Bessel acquired a HELIOMETER, developed by Fraunhofer at Königsberg (the principle of this instrument is the separation of two distinct images of the same object by a measurable amount). With the exquisite defining powers of this instrument, he attacked the problem of stellar distances; for this he used observations of the star 61 Cygni, which has an unusually large proper motion. A year later, at the end of 1838, he published a result of 0.3136 second of arc for 61 Cygni.

This result was followed closely by two others. In January, 1839, Thomas Henderson announced a parallax of about 1 second of arc for α Centauri, the result of observations made earlier while he was director at the Cape. Struve's measurements extended over roughly the same period as Bessel's. His telescope, mounted with an equatorial drive, used an object glass developed by Fraunhofer and contained the finest micrometer then available. His result, 0.2613 second of arc for α Lyrae, was announced in 1840.

The results signified a new age of instrumental precision and exploration beyond the Solar System. The original purpose behind the search – the proof of a moving Earth – had long been a moot point. As can be expected of any search which spans such a long period, the ultimate results may lie in an area completely alien to the originators of the search. Proof of a moving Earth was no longer necessary, since it had become an accepted part of theory. The results were more interesting in their own right – as distance determiners – and were important to the nineteenth century as a method of ascertaining the intrinsic brightness of stars. Both these interests, one lying in exact astronomy the other in astrophysics, represented an entirely new outlook on astronomy, an outlook completely different from that of the original pioneers of a moving Earth.

III. The rise of astrophysics

The discovery at the turn of the nineteenth century that the light from the Sun dispersed through a spectroscope produced not only a continuous spectrum, as Newton had shown in 1666, but one crossed by dark lines – the *Fraunhofer lines* as they came to be known – provoked much concern among astronomers, physicists and chemists as to their nature. Both continuous and bright-line spectra had been observed previously, but the interruption of a continuous spectrum by numerous dark lines was a new phenomenon.

To add to the mystery of these lines, some were found to coincide in position with the bright lines obtained from normal laboratory spectra of the elements. In 1840–60, a number of experiments were undertaken, primarily by scientists in England, France and Germany, that came very close to the final interpretation. However, they did not arrive at the general explanation of spectra; this was provided by Gustav Kirchhoff.

Kirchhoff had conducted experiments on the spectra of flames and metallic vapours, with particular emphasis on a certain line in the solar spectrum known, according to Fraunhofer's classification, as the sodium D-line. He noted that by superimposing a sodium flame on a solar spectrum, the dark solar D-line changed into a bright line. Similar experiments were conducted with other elements, and in 1859 Kirchhoff was able to announce the two basic laws of spectroscopy which are named after him: firstly, that incandescent solids or liquids produce a continuous spectrum, while gaseous substances produce either bright lines or bands with each chemical element producing a characteristic spectrum; and secondly that each element is capable of absorbing the same radiation that it emits. These rules formed the basis of early spectroscopy, and immediately opened the doors to a new field of investigation – the science of astrophysics.

Early solar observations

Nineteenth-century ideas on the nature of the Sun can be divided into two distinct periods; the first characterized by the simple visual observations of *sunspots*, the second, by the application of photography and spectroscopy to the Sun.

In the early nineteenth century, sunspots were the major clue to the nature of the Sun. The common interpretation of sunspots as mountains or volcanoes emerging through an incandescent ocean, was an intuitive one. In 1774, a British astronomer, Wilson, showed that this interpretation was wrong. From purely geometrical reasoning, he argued that the spots must be depressions rather than elevations. The idea was expanded upon by William Herschel in 1795 to produce a general picture of the Sun, one which was accepted until around the middle of the nineteenth century. According to it, the spots were interruptions in the cloud layers, exposing the solid body of the true Sun. There were two cloud layers, an upper luminous one (called the *photosphere* by Schroter), and an inner one protecting the surface from much of the hot, outer layer. Beneath this was a cold and solid globe like a gigantic planet. At the time very little was known about the nature of heat, so this theory was acceptable.

Later, closer studies of sunspot activity began. From observations carried out at the Cape of Good Hope, John Herschel concluded that spots could be compared to tornadoes, an idea which has survived to the present day. At about the same time, a German amateur, H.S.Schwabe, showed that the number of sunspots varied over a 10-year period. A similar period was found by the astronomer J.Lamont in 1851 for the variation of the Earth's magnetic field. In the same year, Sir Edward Sabine found that the number of magnetic storms varied over a 10-year period and that the variations were parallel to those of solar activity. This exciting correlation, the cause of which was a mystery at the time, stimulated interest in the study of solar activity. R.Wolf, a Swiss astronomer, undertook a statistical study of the maxima and minima of solar activity back to 1750 (observations before this were too irregular), and provided the framework for such statistical studies to be used as an index of solar activity. Another systematic study was undertaken by the English astronomer R.C.Carrington, who was able to announce a new result in 1859 – the Sun rotated differentially. He also noted that the mean latitude of spots varied systematically through a complete cycle; the result was obtained independently by a German amateur, G.Sporer, whose name is usually associated with it.

Attempts to determine the overall brightness and temperature of the Sun and the amount of solar radiation received on Earth, were made by John Herschel and by Pouillet in France. The main problem lay in the allowance for atmospheric absorption. Pouillet found that the Sun's rays falling on a square centimetre of the Earth's surface could raise the temperature of 1.7633 grams of water 1°C per minute. He called this number the solar constant. Taking a mean between this result and his own, Herschel calculated that the ordinary expenditure of the Sun per minute would have enough power to melt a cylinder of ice 50 m in diameter reaching from the Sun to α Centauri. A much more difficult problem was the calculation of the solar temperature. Pouillet estimated a temperature somewhere between 1461 and 1761°C, whereas Waterston obtained a potential temperature of 12 880 000°F.

Throughout the century, estimates of temperature ranged from several thousand to several million degrees. The exact relationship between the temperature of the surface and the amount of radiation emitted was not solved until 1879, when the Austrian physicist J.Stefan announced what we now call *Stefan's law of radiation*. Stefan showed that the total radiation increases as the fourth power of the temperature, a relationship subsequently derived theoretically by Ludwig Boltzmann. Application of this rule gave temperatures close to the present value, 6000°C; at the time, however, the relationship was mistrusted, partly because of its simplicity. More accurate temperatures were dependent on more precise values of the solar constant. In 1875, the French physicist Violle was the first to obtain an accurate result by observations of the Sun from Mont Blanc; this resulted in a solar constant of 2.5 cal cm^{-2} min^{-1}. Studies of solar radiation were aided by the invention in 1880 of a type of *bolometer* by the American physicist Langley. The instrument was used to study the variation of atmospheric absorption with wavelength, so as to produce a more accurate solar constant.

The source of energy remained a mystery until the first half of the twentieth century. In the 1840s the belief that energy must be conserved began to establish itself. Geological evidence required the Solar System to be much older than the biblical age of 6000 years; this meant that chemical burning (coal, oil, wood) was inadequate, so some other mechanism had to be introduced to account for the Sun's heat. Mayer, in 1848, suggested that the heat was produced by the impact of meteorites on the solar surface. However, the density of meteorites required would cause the Sun's mass to increase at an appreciable rate, resulting in an observable alteration in the Earth's orbit. A theory which did become accepted was that expounded by Hermann von Helmholtz in a popular lecture in 1854, and it was to remain the accepted model for nearly 50 years. According to this new theory, the Sun's heat was a direct result of shrinkage through cooling. By a decrease in diameter of 120 m per year, Helmholtz calculated that the radiation could last 22 million years. Towards the end of the century even this lifetime became unacceptably small by comparison to geological estimates of the age of the Earth, but a better explanation had to await the discoveries of nuclear physics.

The study of the solar spectrum

The dark lines in the solar spectrum, noted by Wollaston in 1802, were first mapped systematically by the physicist Joseph Fraunhofer. By 1817 Fraunhofer had described hundreds of lines and bands, the principal ones to which he assigned letters A, B, C and so on, which are used even today. Furthermore, he believed that the lines were caused by the nature of sunlight and not a result of diffraction or some other external factor. Brewster, in 1833, using better equipment, showed that at least some of the lines were due to absorption by the Earth's atmosphere. Fraunhofer proceeded to turn his spectroscope on to the Moon, Venus, Mars and certain bright stars and was impressed by the appearance in most of these of a strong line in the orange region, the D line, a line which also appeared in the spectrum of a sodium flame.

Kirchoff attributed the solar FRAUNHOFER LINES to the absorption of the continuous spectrum produced by the photosphere by vapours in the extensive solar atmosphere, which he associated at the time with the corona. He suggested that the photosphere was a hot, incandescent liquid. The region in the solar atmosphere where the reversal of the lines was supposed to occur was called the *reversing layer*. Kirchhoff's theory implied that the solar atmosphere must be at a very high temperature, since the metals had vaporized, with the photosphere being at a higher temperature still since the lines appear in absorption, which meant that the temperature of the Sun must increase inwards. The French astronomer H.Faye proposed a new solar theory in 1865 on the basis of these ideas. Faye considered the entire mass of the Sun to be gaseous, with the heat reaching the outside by means of ascending and descending convection currents.

The study of the solar spectrum underwent rapid development. Kirchhoff identified many lines with terrestrial elements such as sodium, iron, and calcium. S.P.Langley developed an easy method of distinguishing the intrinsic solar lines from the terrestrial ones by comparing spectra from opposite limbs of the Sun. The solar lines are displaced due to solar rotation, a phenomenon not affecting the terrestrial lines. This effect, an example of the *Doppler shift*, had been described in a general way by Christian Doppler in 1842; in 1848 Fizeau had pointed out that spectral lines could be used to measure velocities. A systematic study of spectra from different parts of the Sun by Sir Norman Lockyer revealed that sunspots contained more numerous and stronger lines than the photosphere; this indicated that spots were regions of lower temperature. Apart from these specific discoveries, more extensive studies of the lines were undertaken. A.J.Ångström published the wavelengths of 1000 lines; an important identification by him and Thalin was that of hydrogen. This type of work culminated with the publication between 1886 and 1895 of the tables of the American physicist, H.A.Rowland, which provided the wavelengths of 14 000 solar lines from the ultraviolet to the red.

During the late nineteenth century, the application of spectroscopy and photography at a group of total eclipses led to rapid advances in solar physics and particularly on the nature of the outer solar atmosphere. In the 1868 eclipse, bright-line spectra of prominences were obtained which definitively showed that they belonged to the Sun. Janssen and Lockyer independently developed methods for studying prominences out of eclipse. Lockyer noted that prominences emanated from a gaseous envelope, which he called the *chromosphere*, close to the solar surface. At the 1869 eclipse, the first good photographs of the outer layers of the Sun were taken. W.Harkness discovered the corona's continuous spectrum, together with a single bright line in the green region of the spectrum. In 1868 Lockyer found that the yellow-orange line emitted by prominences could not be identified with any known element and called the unknown element responsible for it helium. He maintained that it was a new element, but general opinion held it to be the line of a familiar element under exceptional conditions of excitation. In 1895, the British chemist, Sir William Ramsey, isolated helium for the first time. Another important result of the 1869 expedition was the observation by the American astronomer C.A.Young of the flash spectrum. The eclipses that followed continued to reveal many details of the structure and chemical composition of the chromosphere, prominences and corona.

Modern research into solar physics can be said to date from the invention in 1891 of the 'spectroheliograph' by the American astronomer G.E.Hale and the independent invention of a very similar instrument, the spectral velocity recorder by the French astronomer, H.Deslandres. Both instruments relied on constructing a monochromatic image of the chromosphere. They differed in that Hale's did a continuous scan of a very narrow wavelength band, whereas Deslandres' isolated a much wider band and moved discontinuously. The two astronomers later became involved in a dispute over the priority of the instrument! In 1905 Hale, supported by the Carnegie Institution of Washington, set up a large solar observatory on Mount Wilson. His subsequent work revealed, among other things, the existence of the magnetic fields of sunspots and later a general magnetic field about the Sun. The study of solar magnetism begun by Hale provided much of the currently accepted information on the Sun.

Stellar studies from 1850 to 1900

In the mid-nineteenth century, very little was known about stars other than positions, apparent magnitudes, and, in a few cases, distances. The method of determining distance, by trigonometrical parallax, was limited to those stars within a hundred parsecs of the Sun; thus, even by 1890 fewer than 100 stars had known distances. Spectral analysis did not suffer from this limitation. As long as sufficient light from a star could be collected, much information could be gathered about that star and in the early 1860s these studies were begun by William Huggins and Angelo Secchi. Their different interests characterize the two different aspects of the field which were to develop. Huggins, working with W.A.Miller, was interested in the detailed spectra of stars so as to analyse their chemical composition. In 1864 they published a paper on the spectra of some 50 bright stars, from which they concluded that stars have a similar chemical composition to the Sun and that most of these elements – hydrogen, sodium, magnesium, calcium, iron and so on – play an important role in terrestrial physics and organic life. This link with organic life and consequently its evolution, a major controversial issue at the time, played an influential role in the discussions on the evolutionary order of the stars. The argument ran that as a species evolves, so must a star, and thus a picture of the linear evolutionary development of stars soon followed. The actual sequence was established by the classification of stellar spectra begun by Secchi. In 1868, Secchi published a catalogue of 4000 stars which he divided into four classes according to the appearance of their spectra. The idea that each sequence indicated successive stages in the life of a star was soon taken for granted. Secchi's classification was achieved by a visual examination of the spectra; the wet collodion process used by photographers at the time was too crude. In the 1870s the development of dry gelatine plates meant that a closer study of the spectra could be made, including a broader band of the spectrum as photographs revealed the ultraviolet region of the star's radiation. Both aspects of the work that followed – the detailed examination of structure and the large-scale classification and consequent evolution – involved a close interaction with developments in the chemical laboratory, where experiments were being made on the varying effects of different conditions on the spectra of gases.

An important by-product of Huggins' work was the determination of the first line-of-sight velocity of a star. The French physicist, Fizeau had pointed out in 1848 that spectral lines provided very good markers for measurements of the Doppler effect. In 1868, Huggins announced a very small shift in the lines of Sirius, indicating a velocity of recession of $47 \, \mathrm{km \, s^{-1}}$.

Stellar data were accumulating rapidly and, as a result, a more definite picture of stellar evolution. Secchi had classified the stars into four types – white stars like Sirius, yellow stars such as the Sun, orange and reddish stars like Betelgeuse and faint red stars – according to the appearance of their spectra. He thought that his classification represented a temperature sequence, but he was more interested in actual spectral differences.

By the end of the century, there was little doubt of the order of evolution of the four major classes – helium stars into Sirean, Sirean into solar-type and these into red stars with banded spectra – although certain newly-found groups of stars, such as the *Wolf-Rayet stars*, did not automatically fit into it. The observation that the helium stars and gaseous nebulae have the same distribution about the galactic plane added support to the view that the white stars represented the youngest stage in the sequence. Also the inclusion in this class of the *Algol-type variables*, the prototype of which had been found by Vogel in 1888 to be a binary system, supported the general belief. Vogel had concluded that Algol was a binary system from a study of its radial velocity, obtained from measures of the shift in spectral lines throughout its cycle. The eclipsing nature of Algol was used by Pickering in 1880 to calculate its diameter, another important parameter in calibrating the evolutionary series. Most of the observations strengthened the belief in the general view of evolution. Disagreement was aimed rather at the causes of the changes in the spectral lines: was temperature the main factor involved, or density? The answer was not forthcoming until the great advances in atomic theory in the early twentieth century. The Danish physicist Niels Bohr published his model for the structure of the atom in 1913. M.N.Saha used this model in 1920–1 to explain the appearance of the spectrum in terms of the excitation and ionization in stellar atmospheres, which could be calculated from the pressure and temperature of the atmosphere.

The extensive catalogues published during the second half of the nineteenth century provided virtually unlimited amounts of stellar data for the astronomers of the early twentieth century. The spectral classification developed at Harvard by E.C.Pickering and Antonia C.Maury was so detailed and extensive that all other classification schemes were soon swept into oblivion. In the first 'Draper catalogue', published in 1890, they proposed a classification scheme of stellar spectra including sixteen classes denoted according to the letters A–Q. The massive project was made possible by the introduction of the objective prism by Pickering in 1885 and

funded as a memorial to Henry Draper, an early pioneer in astronomical photography. The actual classification scheme was somewhat modified with the publication of the second volume, including southern stars, in 1897 with certain groups being omitted or combined with other groups. At this time Maury added a second parameter ('a', 'b' or 'c') to classify the spectra, a parameter related to the sharpness of the line, since she noted that definite differences in sharpness did occur; this important factor was used by E.Hertzsprung in 1905. The extensive work was continued by Annie J. Cannon with the resultant classification of over 225 000 stars in the catalogues published between 1918 and 1924 into the sequence of decreasing temperature accepted now O, B, A, F, G, K, M, R, N, S. At the beginning of the twentieth century, the physical reasons behind such a temperature sequence still evaded astrophysicists. The catalogue has been hailed by leading astrophysicists as the greatest single work in the field of stellar spectroscopy.

Stellar astrophysics after 1900

The Draper catalogues provided astrophysicists with the massive numbers of spectra needed for statistical studies of the distribution of stellar types, which in turn might provide clues on stellar evolution. Two independent studies of particular interest, one by E.Hertzsprung, a Danish astronomer, the other by the American astronomer H.N.Russell, resulted in one of the corner-stones of modern astrophysics – a diagram now named after both of them (the *Hertzsprung-Russell diagram*) which describes the distribution of stars as a function of their luminosities and temperatures.

In 1905 Hertzsprung used a statistical method for obtaining distances to examine some of the stars on A.Maury's list. He found that stars at the beginning of the classification scheme, now called O, were extremely luminous, and also that the red stars of classes K and M contained two types – one of faint absolute luminosity, the other, very high luminosity. In addition these distinctions in luminosity were correlated with the sharpness of the spectral lines noted by Maury. Hertzsprung proposed the names dwarf and giants for the two types of stars. At about this time Russell, engaged with obtaining distances by photographic methods, found that there was a definite correlation between luminosity and spectral type. These results suggested to him an evolutionary sequence similar to Lockyer's with the luminous red stars at the young end of the scale, the faint red stars at the other extreme. On hearing of Hertzsprung's discovery of two luminosity classes, Russell believed his theory to be confirmed. Hertzsprung, on the other hand, considered that the results indicated two parallel series of evolution.

In 1911 Hertzsprung found that a plot of the apparent magnitude against colours for stars in the Pleiades and Hyades clusters yielded a narrow band distribution with stars becoming redder with decreasing brightness. Russell produced a similar plot (rotated by 90°) for all stars, which he discussed in 1913 at the Royal Astronomical Society and later that year at the American Astronomical Society. The distribution of the majority of the stars in a narrow band across the diagonal of the plot (now called the *main sequence*), demonstrating the distribution of spectral classes, was agreed by most astronomers to be the result of varying surface temperatures. However, there was no general agreement over the causes of the luminosity difference between the horizontal line (giant branch) and the diagonal band, that is, between the dwarfs and giants, as named by Hertzsprung. Russell's view was that density was the main cause of the difference; the order of evolution was one of increasing density from the giant branch through the O stars along the main sequence to the faint red stars with the temperature first rising, and then, along the main sequence, falling. This picture was finally overthrown in the 1920s with the large-scale use of photo-electric *photometry* (introduced by Stebbins about 1910) to examine the colour-magnitude diagrams of stars in open and globular clusters. These studies revealed that the straightforward linear picture of evolution had to be significantly modified.

An important by-product of the work on luminosity differences was the method of *spectroscopic parallax*. Hertzsprung, by 1911, had suggested that if the luminosity of a star could be obtained from its spectrum its distance could be deduced. However, he did not pursue the idea. In 1914, the American astronomer Adams and the German astronomer A. Kohlschütter announced results which led to the introduction of the method in 1916. They found that giants and dwarfs of the same spectral class produced lines of different intensity. Using stars with known distances, they were able to calibrate intensity ratios of certain lines so that the observation of these same lines in another star provided its absolute luminosity, which, on knowing the star's apparent magnitude, provided its distance. This method, much more powerful than the method of trigonometrical parallax, led to a rapid increase in the number of known stellar distances.

Somewhat earlier, the determination of the actual sizes of stars had been calculated by combining the laws of thermal radiation with estimates of stellar temperatures. These results showed that the names giant and dwarf could be interpreted literally to refer to the relative sizes of the two classes. An interferometer mounted on the 2.5-m telescope at Mount Wilson was used by A.A.Michelson and F.G.Pease in 1920 actually to measure directly the sizes of certain supergiant stars; their measurements confirmed earlier calculations. Another method for obtaining the dimensions of stars was developed by H.N.Russell and H.Shapley at Princeton from a detailed study of the light variations in eclipsing binaries; their study meant that the sizes of stars of all classes could be obtained.

In addition to the *spectroscopic* and *eclipsing binaries*, *variable stars*, particularly *Cepheids*, provided new insight into the nature of stars. Shapley had shown in 1914 that the Cepheid phenomenon could not be explained by a binary system, as had been supposed up to this time. He suggested that the light variations were due to actual pulsations. A pulsation theory was soon developed by the British astrophysicist A.S.Eddington, from which it was possible to derive the sizes of Cepheids. His theory also provided an explanation for the correlation between the period and magnitude of Cepheids just discovered by Henrietta Leavitt. Later, Eddington

developed a theory of stellar interiors which still forms the basis for such studies. In a series of investigations between 1918 and 1924 he presented the theory of *radiative equilibrium* of stars, a theory which requires the centre of stars to be at extremely high temperatures. At the time, no energy mechanism was known which could retain such high temperatures for long periods of time. A solution was only reached in 1938 when H.Bethe in the United States and C. von Weizsäcker in Germany discovered a nuclear reaction in which hydrogen is transformed into helium. The discovery of this reaction meant that for the first time estimates of the energy source of the Sun were sufficient to satisfy modern estimates of the age of the Earth.

This concludes our brief survey of the development of stellar astrophysics. In many ways this subject must be seen as one of the great triumphs for theoretical researchers. Even though only one star can be examined in great detail, and despite the fact that we cannot see inside any stars, physicists have learned much about the basic physical processes through the application of the laws of thermodynamics and nuclear physics as deduced on Earth. We are next going to look at the sequence of events that led to an understanding of the nature of the non-stellar objects – the nebulae. Here we see less direct application of physics. Our interest mainly lies in the fact that the extragalactic nebulae – galaxies as we now term them – hold the key to determining the large-scale structure of our Universe. We begin our story with William Herschel, one of the finest observers, who made the first detailed listing of the nebulae. He was not able to discriminate the gaseous nebulae of the Milky Way from the external galaxies; that step was not in fact made until the present century, and it is at that point that our description ends.

IV. The Universe beyond our Galaxy:
The nature of nebulae

Certain nebulous patches, such as the Magellanic Clouds in the south and the Andromeda Nebula in the north, are clearly visible to the naked eye and have undoubtedly been observed from early times. Comments on the Andromeda Nebula date back to the Arabs in the middle of the tenth century. Similarly, the nebulous band of light stretching across the sky, called the Milky Way, is also a conspicuous feature of the night sky. (The name 'Galaxy', which we now use to refer to our stellar system comes from the Greek 'galaxias' which translates as Milky Way.) In the seventeenth century, Galileo applied his telescope to this hazy band and found much to his surprise that it could be resolved into myriads of faint stars. On examining some of the nebulous patches, he found that they also were dense regions of stars. From this he concluded that most nebulosities could be resolved into stars.

Those that could not be resolved were simply called nebulae and by 1700 about 10 of these were known. The first extensive list of these objects, comprising 42 southern nebulae, was the work of Nicolas de Lacaille in 1755. Often, in fact, the discovery of nebulae was the by-product of another goal – the search for comets. The next extensive list of nebulae, consisting of 103 nebulous objects and clusters, was compounded by Charles Messier and Pierre Méchain in 1784 in order to keep track of nebulae during their regular comet searches. In general, eighteenth-century astronomers were too concerned with the problems of the Solar System to be bothered about the curiosities in Messier's list. Certain eighteenth-century philosophers, on the other hand, considered these objects and the Milky Way to be quite worthy of speculation.

Emanuel Swedenborg, the Swedish philosopher, described the Milky Way as a rotating mass of stars in the shape of a sphere. According to him, the Universe was filled with such spheres. Thomas Wright, the English instrument-maker and mathematician, also considered that the Milky Way was one among many, but he presented an entirely different view of its structure. In his 'Original Theory', or 'New Hypothesis of the Universe' he considered the Milky Way as a vast disc containing concentric rings of stars. In the same work he proposed another model closer to Swedenborg's; however later writers preferred the former model, which became known as the 'grindstone theory' of the Milky Way. Later works of Wright, discovered by a London book dealer in 1966, presented views very reminiscent of the mediaeval philosophers and inclined to a theological view of the Universe.

Wright's ideas were drawn to the attention of Immanuel Kant who became interested in a correct interpretation of the Milky Way, and he furthered the disc theory by replacing Wright's poetic ideas with Newtonian physics. In the 'General History of Nature and Theory of the Heavens', published in 1755, Kant compared the Milky Way to Saturn, a system with swarms of particles rotating about it. The shape of the Milky Way and the nebulous stars could be explained by their rotation. Kant considered the nebulae to be other universes or Milky Ways and the term ISLAND UNIVERSES is usually attributed to him. He argued that a flattened, circular array of stars would look smooth and elliptical if seen from a distance, thus accounting for patches such as the Andromeda Nebula.

William Herschel was the first astronomer who carefully examined the heavens to study the stars for their own sake. Largely self-taught, he constructed his own reflecting telescope (1773) and began observations. In this, and most of his later endeavours, he was aided by his sister Caroline who became an astronomer in her own right. As his enthusiasm increased, he spent much time grinding and polishing mirrors for bigger and better telescopes. Together he and Caroline swept the skies systematically, and during one of these surveys in 1781 he discovered Uranus, an achievement for which he was amply rewarded.

Herschel had obtained a copy of Messier's catalogue of nebulae and star clusters and he proceeded to examine each of the objects on the list with his 6-m focal-length telescope of 40-cm aperture. He was able to resolve many of them into stars and by 1785 had concluded that all nebulae must consist of stars. Over a period of seven years spent in the regular sweeps of the sky, he and Caroline were able to add 2000 nebulae to the list. From their distribution, in general away from the plane of the Milky Way, he concluded that they must be separate systems.

In addition to his interest in the nebulae, Herschel was intent on determining the structure and scale of the Milky Way. He had developed his own model by 1784 and was determined by the method of 'star-gauging' to obtain some scale to this model. His method involved counting the number of stars in the field-of-view of the telescope over a large number of regions. Assuming the stars to be uniformly distributed and their faintness to be an indication of their distance, the number of stars in a particular region was then proportional to the extent of that region. Since no stellar distance had yet been obtained, Herschel used the distance of Sirius as his measuring stick. The relationship between distance and faintness was a poor one and Herschel realized from his discovery of binary systems that it was crude. However, there was no other method available for estimating distance. His results indicated a diameter for the Milky Way of 800 times the distance of Sirius, or 2 kpc. Later, Herschel became more sceptical of this method because of the limitations of his 6-m telescope, which he felt had led him to underestimate considerably the size of the Milky Way. He revised his diameter to 2300 times the distance of a first magnitude star, or about 6 kpc.

In later years, Herschel turned from a spatial description of the Milky Way and the nebulae to an evolutionary one. He began classifying his objects into an evolutionary sequence, with the start of the sequence represented by a uniform, static Universe of scattered stars. However, the planetary nebulae, which he discovered and named such because of their appearance, would not fit into his stellar scheme. As he studied these objects more closely, it became more and more obvious that they were stars in actual association with nebulosity. Therefore, true nebulosity did exist and all nebulae were not necessarily unresolved stellar systems at remote distances. The existence of island universes could no longer be assumed, and, because of Herschel's great authority, it suffered a decline in popularity in the first quarter of the nineteenth century.

Nineteenth-century research on nebulae

Herschel's discovery of stars embedded in nebulosity, the so-called planetary nebulae, reinforced a possible interpretation of the nebulae as planetary systems in the making. Such an interpretation correlated very well with the accepted theory of the origin of the Solar System developed by Pierre Simon de Laplace towards the end of the eighteenth century. According to Laplace's theory the Sun contracted from an immense rotating cloud; during the contraction several rings of matter detached themselves to become planets. Planetary nebulae must then be one of the final stages in the evolution of an immense cloud or nebula into a solar-type system.

Towards the middle of the nineteenth century the island universe theory was revived after observations with the large telescope of Lord Rosse, William Parsons, of Parsonstown. In February, 1845, Rosse successfully completed a 2-m mirror mounted in a 16-m tube. Together he and Robinson examined one of the nebulae in John Herschel's list (an extension of Sir William's) and found that it could be resolved into stars. They also verified the suggestion by John Herschel that M51 could be considered an analogue to the Milky Way system. M51 was observed later by Nichol and found to have a definite spiral pattern, a pattern also observed in several other nebulae. By 1848, fifty nebulae had been resolved by Rosse's telescope and this brought into question once more the existence of true nebulosity. In the enthusiasm to resolve nebulae even Orion and the Crab Nebula were added to the list and the former, according to G.P.Bond, displayed a certain amount of spiral structure! In 1852 Stephen Alexander of New Jersey suggested that the irregular appearance of the Milky Way could be explained by the existence of *spiral arms* and unsuccessful attempts followed to determine its exact structure and scale.

Sir William Huggins was the first to examine nebulae with a spectroscope. In 1864, he studied Orion and found it to display several bright lines, similar to the spectrum of a hot gas. This compelling evidence seemed to contradict reports that Orion could be resolved into stars, so Huggins concluded that the objects they observed must not have been stars but rather masses of tenuous gas. Similarly, photographs of Orion and the Crab revealed no stars. Huggins found that of sixty nebulae and clusters examined, one-third displayed a bright-line spectrum. Within the spiral nebulae he consistently found a stellar-type spectrum, and in the planetary nebulae, a bright-line spectrum. The existence of true nebulosity was for the first time definitively shown.

During the latter part of the nineteenth century, data on the nebulae accumulated. John Herschel's observations of nebulae from the Cape of Good Hope, published in 1847 as the General Catalogue, extended his father's list of 1802 by 2500. His results

revived his father's ideas on the coexistence of stars and nebulosity. They also emphasized the distribution of nebulae away from the galactic plane and towards the poles, and drew attention to the peculiar *zone of avoidance* noted earlier by William Herschel. The strange distribution was used by some to argue for the physical association of the nebulae with the Milky Way, and occasionally by others for the opposite.

The spectroscopic results, combined with increasing interest in Laplace's nebular results furthered the decline in popularity of the island universes. More and more evidence seemed to indicate that they were all part of our own system. Isaac Roberts, an energetic amateur astronomer specializing in astronomical photography, took photographs of M31 in 1888 which revealed not only its spiral structure but two satellite objects, M32 and NGC205. Roberts speculated that these two satellites were protoplanets in an early stage of condensation so that the system represented a perfect example of Laplace's nebular theory at work.

The question of the nebulae was intricately linked up with the structure of the Milky Way. Three models of the Milky Way were considered during the nineteenth century – the disc model of Kant and Herschel, an unlimited slab of stars, and a central cloud surrounded by a distant ring of stars. Its spiral nature was suggested by its noted similarity to M51, which Robinson had observed to be spiral. C.Easton published the first diagram displaying the Milky Way as a spiral in 1900, in which he placed the centre in the constellation Cygnus and the Sun about a third of the way from the centre to the edge. The scale was still very dubious as there were no reliable distance indicators. At the end of the nineteenth century, its exact nature was as mysterious as that of the nebulae. The question of the uniqueness of our stellar system could not be separated from the question of the true nature of the nebulae. At this time astronomers felt the evidence weighed heavily in favour of the nebulae being part of the Milky Way.

Shapley and star clusters

Progress on the nebulae in the early twentieth century was stimulated by the construction of large telescopes in good climates and the regular use of permanent records such as photographic plates and spectrograms. The Harvard telescope in Peru, the Crossley 1-m reflector at the Lick Observatory and the Mount Wilson 1.5-m played an important role in the closer examination of the nebulae. The photographic plates revealed hitherto unsuspected numbers of fainter nebulae, a large portion of which appeared to be spiral. The nature of the spiral became one of the searching questions in astronomy.

Spectrograms of M31 by Scheiner and, independently, by Huggins, showed a continuum due to stars. Similarly, a 12-hour exposure of M31 by Wilson revealed bright patches which looked very much like star clusters; Wilson considered them excellent confirmation of Laplace's nebular hypothesis. This observation was taken by Sir James Jeans as evidence for the spirals being early stages in the formation of *globular clusters*. Moulton used the spiral shape to add weight to his and Chamberlain's theory of the origin of the Solar System, which explained the formation of the planets as due to material pulled off the Sun by a passing star. He argued that the tidal material pulled off by the star would form a double-branched logarithmic spiral, so that spiral nebulae were interpreted as planetary systems in the making. Coincident with these ideas, though somewhat subdued, was the idea that the spirals were stellar systems like the Milky Way. We can see that although there was no shortage of ideas on the nebulae at the turn of the century, no accurate means of estimating the scale of the Universe existed which would enable models to be tested.

At about this time, however, a 'standard candle' became available for obtaining distances. In 1885 a dramatic flare-up of a *nova* in M31 indicated that, unless this nova, S Andromedae, was very unlike galactic novae, the Andromeda Nebula must be fairly close. In 1895, a second extremely bright nova was found in the spiral NGC5253. In 1911, Very estimated the size of the Milky Way from the expansion parallax of nova Persei to be about 35 pc; assuming S Andromedae to be similar to this he calculated a distance of 500 pc for M31. In the following year, Wolf applied a different method. He compared the size of dark holes in M31 with some in the Galaxy to get a distance for M31 of 8 kpc. At this point, another distance indicator became available. Henrietta Leavitt at Harvard, while examining the Small Magellanic Cloud for variables, discovered the *period-luminosity law* for Cepheid variables, which enabled distances to be found from apparent magnitudes. E. Hertzsprung obtained a distance of 8 kpc for the Small Magellanic Cloud after he had calibrated the period-luminosity law.

In 1914, V. Slipher of Lowell Observatory found that M31 was approaching us at a velocity of 300 km s^{-1}, the largest radial velocity then known. Slipher continued his study of radial velocities and found that of 15 nebulae, 11 showed velocities of recession; the average velocity was 800 km s^{-1}. The high velocities made it clear that the spirals were very different from ordinary stars. Slipher also noted that the spectral lines of certain spirals were tilted, which indicated rotation. The high velocities and rotation rates suggested the intriguing possibility that spirals might have measurable proper motions and angular rates of rotation. H. D. Curtis of the Lick Observatory obtained an average proper motion of 0.033 arc seconds per year from 66 spirals, and this result combined with the average radial velocity, indicated an average distance of 3 kpc. Angular rates of rotation, became the long-term project of A. van Maanen of Mount Wilson. For the first spiral he examined, van Maanen found a period of rotation of 85,000 years. Similar results followed over a period of 10 years and van Maanen's high rotation measures became the main evidence against the spirals being external galaxies.

Harlow Shapley revolutionized the scale of the Galaxy by using the globular clusters as boundary markers to plot its extent. On the assumption that the Cepheids in globular clusters were the same as those defining the period-luminosity relationship, he arrived at the incredible diameter of 80 kpc for the Milky Way with the Sun

20 kpc from the centre. The average distance of spirals of 3–6 kpc put them well inside this Galaxy.

Meanwhile, there was more evidence for the spirals being very remote. In July 1917 Ritchey at the Mount Wilson Observatory discovered a nova in the spiral NGC6946, which, on comparison with galactic novae, implied a vast distance. This discovery encouraged a closer study of stars associated with the spiral nebulae by Curtis. He became convinced that spiral systems were like our own Galaxy, and that the spectacular novae of 1885 and 1895 were unusual; Curtis later (1921) suggested that the novae could be divided into two magnitude classes. In March 1917 he had discovered a nova in NGC4527 and two more in NGC4321, all of about 14 magnitude. Curtis, always a very cautious astronomer, awaited more evidence before publishing his results; an examination of plates files soon revealed many more novae, all of which indicated the existence of island universes.

In 1920 a meeting was arranged by the National Academy of Sciences to discuss the question of the nebulae openly: were the spirals island universes or part of our own Galaxy? The two sides were represented by H. D. Curtis and H. Shapley respectively. Essentially the two men defended different aspects of the problem – Shapley arguing for the large size of the Galaxy, Curtis, for spirals being external galaxies. Shapley felt, partly on the basis of van Maanen's large rotations, the spirals had to be nearby. Curtis considered Shapley's distance measures to be unreliable and preferred to trust the old accepted size of the Milky Way, which meant that the nebulae could be well outside its boundaries. The meeting did not answer the question because insufficient data were available.

However the required information soon followed. In 1922 J. C. Duncan found variables in M31, and, from photographs of NGC 6822 showed it to contain both stars and nebulae. Edwin Hubble became interested in the latter and took a series of photographs with the 2.5-metre telescope which resulted in the discovery of 15 variables, 11 of which were Cepheids. In 1923, Hubble identified one of the variables in M31 as a Cepheid and several more in M31 and M33 soon afterward. Using the period-luminosity relationship he calculated a distance of 230 kpc for NGC6822. With the continuation of his search for Cepheids with the 2.5-m telescope, he soon discovered 35 in M33 from which he calculated a distance of 250 kpc. The spirals were definitely island universes far beyond our Galaxy.

One question had been answered but many remained. The nature of our own system was still uncertain. The nebulae had been separated into two separate categories, the galactic objects – planetary and diffuse nebulae – and the extragalactic systems, but little was understood of their structure or evolution.

The expansion of the Universe

Hubble had shown definitively that spiral nebulae were external galaxies. In the 1930s he continued work on these objects with the Mount Wilson 2.5-m reflector, which was then the world's largest telescope. Studies over the next decade revealed that the extragalactic nebulae could be divided into four main classes: *irregular, elliptical, normal spiral* and *barred spiral*. On the basis of their shape alone he arranged them into a sequence known as Hubble's 'Tuning Fork' diagram. Hubble warned that the sequence was not necessarily an evolutionary one. He estimated the distances to two dozen galaxies by 1929 and found that their velocities were in direct proportion to their distances; for example galaxies at twice the distance of other galaxies receded twice as quickly. This result caused a great stir among cosmologists since one of the deductions of *general relativity* is the unstable state of the Universe; that is, according to Einstein's theory, the Universe should be either expanding or contracting. Hubble's relationship was immediately used as evidence for a Big-Bang-type Universe. For observers it had another use: for galaxies too remote for the resolution of Cepheids or novae, the standard distance indicators, the Hubble relationship could be reversed to infer distances from velocities, easily measured from the *redshift* in the spectrum of the galaxy.

The new distances to the nearby spirals gave rise to several problems. First of all, the spirals in general seemed much smaller than the Milky Way, the size of which had been determined by Shapley. Secondly, the novae and globular clusters seemed much fainter than those in the Galaxy; in addition Hubble had only been able to resolve stars in the outer regions of M31, and none in the nucleus. The results conflicted with the normal assumption of astronomers – namely the uniformity of nature. Only through the assumption of the similarity of objects (i.e. Cepheids, novae) in remote galaxies with those of known distance in our own could distances be obtained.

Meanwhile, studies of the motions of stars in the solar neighbourhood provided new insight into the structure of our own Galaxy. In the early part of this century, two opposing streams of stars had been detected, one moving away from the direction of Sagittarius, the other towards it. At right angles to these two streams was a small number of stars moving at extremely high velocities. In 1921 the Swedish astronomer Lindblad explained the phenomenon by supposing the rotation of our Galaxy about some point in Sagittarius. Later he proposed the existence of two separate sub-systems of stars in the Galaxy – a spherical system to which the globular clusters and high-velocity stars belonged, and the flat disc system to which the other stars belonged. Lindblad's ideas were hypothetical, but in 1927 the Dutch astronomer, Jan Oort, provided evidence. Examining stars lying directly between us and the centre of the Galaxy, Oort found that they displayed a zero radial velocity. Stars in intermediate directions appeared to recede or approach depending on the direction. The pattern indicated rotation about a point lying in the direction of Sagittarius, the centre of Shapley's globular cluster distribution. From his stellar velocities, Oort cal-

culated the distance of this point from the Sun as 6 kpc, a value only one-third that obtained by Shapley. Oort also confirmed the distinction pointed out by Lindblad between stars of the spherical system and those of the highly flattened system.

The discrepancy between Oort's and Shapley's distances for the centre of the Galaxy was explained several years later by Robert J. Trumpler of the Lick Observatory. Trumpler had been collecting data on a large number of galactic clusters, and determined distances for about one hundred of them. From the angular dimensions of these clusters he was able to calculate their actual sizes. His result indicated that remote clusters were about twice the size of nearby ones. Trumpler was not willing to accept this anomaly and explained it instead by the existence of interstellar absorption, that is, dust. This dust absorbed light, so causing more distant clusters to appear fainter and therefore more remote than they actually were. This exaggerated distance, together with the measured angular size, led to the estimated larger size of the more remote clusters. The correction due to this absorption was small for nearby objects but quite considerable for more remote ones. Shapley's distance to the centre of our Galaxy had therefore been exaggerated by about a factor of two. Similarly, the apparently small size of M31 was explained, although there still remained some discrepancy – the Galaxy still appeared to be considerably larger.

The distance scale was further revised in the 1940s when Walter Baade announced the existence of at least two distinct stellar populations in spiral galaxies. Baade reached this conclusion after long exposures of the nucleus of M31, when he succeeded in resolving the nucleus into great numbers of red stars, and found similar results for the two elliptical companions of M31. On plotting the colour-magnitude diagram of these stars he saw that they were quite different from the red stars found by Trumpler in *galactic clusters,* but very similar to the bright red stars in *globular clusters*. A new type of system discovered by Shapley, exemplified by the Sculptor and Fornax systems (bigger than globular clusters but dwarfish compared to ellipticals) also exhibited the same kind of properties. Baade called the stars found in ellipticals, globular clusters, nuclei of galaxies *Population II* stars and those in the disc of spiral galaxies *Population I* stars. One of the results which followed was that not all Cepheid variables followed the same period-luminosity relationship; Cepheids in globular clusters were four times fainter than those in the disc of the galaxy. This meant that distances based on Cepheids in globular clusters had to be increased by a factor of two. Thus the problem which had baffled astronomers – the small size of M31 and faintness of globular clusters and novae within it – was solved, as M31 was doubled in size. Another discrepancy, the great brightness of S Andromedae which had exploded in the nucleus of M31 in 1885 was clarified by the division of such objects into two classes, novae and supernovae, an idea suggested earlier by Curtis. A study by F. Zwicky in 1936 at Palomar revealed that the latter were very rare. Once more the compelling assumption – the uniformity of nature – could be relied on to extrapolate to more remote regions of the Universe.

While the revisions to the distance scale were being made, investigations were under way to find some indication of spiral structure in our own Galaxy by comparison of the content of the Galaxy with the spirals. Baade had shown that the luminous stars in M31 lie along the spiral arms; further examination revealed that regions of ionized gas (i.e. emission nebulosities) also lie exclusively along the spiral arms. A survey of these H^+ *regions* in the Galaxy by Morgan, Sharpless and Osterbrock produced in 1952 a map which indicated the existence of several sections of nearby spiral arms.

The long struggle to determine the structure of the Milky Way and the nature of the nebulae, begun in earnest by William Herschel, had come to a fitting conclusion. The island universes of Kant did exist and the Milky Way had unfolded itself as a very typical representative.

The growth of radio astronomy

In the midst of the early turmoil over the distance scale and the internal structure of stars, a few vague attempts were made to examine a whole new aspect of astronomy. Until this time, astronomers had been observing only in the optical part of the spectrum, that part ranging from about 300 to 1000 nm. Then, suddenly in 1931–2, an accidental discovery was made: Karl G.Jansky of the Bell Telephone Laboratories, while in the process of studying high-frequency radio disturbances found a strange source of interference. At first he linked it with the Sun, but on further examination he found that it came from a fixed direction in space, somewhere near the constellation Sagittarius.

Although Jansky discovered cosmic radio waves he did not follow up the findings. The first radio telescope was built during the middle 1930s by Grote Reber, an American radio engineer and amateur astronomer. Reber was impressed by Jansky's work and built a parabolic radio antenna to examine more closely the peculiar cosmic radio noise. Interaction with astronomers began when he took his results to the Yerkes Observatory to discuss the implications of this noise from the Milky Way. His research paper in the 'Astrophysical Journal' in 1940 stirred more interest. With his measures of intensity he produced the first radio map which indicated strong sources in Sagittarius, Cassiopeia and Cygnus.

Development of radar techniques resulted in great advances in receiver technology. With the possibility of more precise radio-astronomical instruments the stage of data collection began. In addition to wartime technical developments, the discovery of a radio source, the Sun, occurred on the British early-warning radar system in February, 1942, although it was only publicly announced after the war. J.S.Hey, an English radio astronomer, concluded that an unusually intense outburst coincided with the appearance of a large solar flare, and he thus found a connection between radio emission and solar activity. Soon, systematic observations began in Britain and Australia, and later other countries, to examine more closely the radio Sun and the cosmic noise. The construction of bigger, better and more expensive instruments began, partly stimulated by the discovery of the first discrete source, Cygnus A,

by the English astronomers J.S.Hey, S.J.Parsons and J.W.Phillips. More accurate telescopes were needed to pinpoint the location of such radio objects to enable them to be linked with optically-visible objects.

Practical astronomers in England and the Netherlands turned eagerly to radio astronomy since, unlike optical astronomy, it is not interfered with by clouds and fog. In 1947, L.S.McCready, J.L.Pawsey and R.Payne-Scott designed a radio *interferometer* for achieving moderate resolving power. A variety of designs were completed in the next few years: two separate arrays at Cambridge, two 27-m paraboloid dishes in the Owens Valley built by the California Institute of Technology, and the Mills Cross near Sydney, Australia. Most of the designs favoured interferometers since they were easier to build and less expensive than the single great dishes, while providing the necessary resolution. However, a large steerable paraboloid reflector has the advantage of great versatility and a number of these were also constructed. The largest was the 75-m dish at Jodrell Bank, England, completed in 1957 under the direction of Sir Bernard Lovell. The results obtained by these great instruments quickly influenced astronomical research. Using interferometric techniques F.G.Smith, then working at Cambridge, and B.Y.Mills, in Australia, were able to establish the positions of the strongest radio sources accurately enough for W.Baade and R.Minkowski to use the Hale Observatory 5-m telescope to make optical identifications in 1952–4. About the same time, H.I.Ewen and E.M.Purcell of Harvard detected the first radio line, the *21-centimetre line* of neutral hydrogen. Independent discoveries in the Netherlands and Australia were announced simultaneously. The line had been predicted by the Dutchman H.C. van de Hulst in 1944. It provided a new and impressive way of mapping the structure of the Galaxy, a technique unencumbered by the dust and gas that interfere so much with optical studies. In 1953–4, the Dutch radio scientists succeeded in mapping the outer spiral structure of the Galaxy.

In the decade spanning the late 1950s and early 1960s, the great catalogues of radio sources, among them the famous Third Cambridge (3C) catalogue, were produced. By the mid-1960s, electronic developments and increased funding for big science placed radio astronomers in the position where they could compete on equal terms with optical astronomers. With the opening of this new window on the heavens, previously invisible objects could be studied. The discoveries of *radio galaxies*, *quasars*, *pulsars*, the *solar wind*, and *interstellar molecules* influenced profoundly the future direction of astronomical research. Theoretical developments in the nature and origin of the radio emission, and clues to the origin of the Universe from the extensive counts of radio sources developed alongside. Objects requiring a whole new look at the physics of the energy mechanism revealed themselves for the first time.

Astronomy entered the age of big science from about 1955 onwards. The most searching questions became dependent upon an observatory equipped with the latest developments technology could offer and with a budget to match.

22. Ground-based astronomy

22.1: *Much of the radiation entering the atmosphere from space is absorbed before it reaches the ground. Only at radio, optical and certain infrared wavelengths does the radiation penetrate to the ground. In some cases the radiation is mainly absorbed near to sea level; it is possible to observe at these wavelengths from high-flying aircraft (as in the far infrared). Otherwise rockets or satellites are needed to reach above the atmosphere: X-ray and gamma-ray astronomy rely almost entirely on satellite-borne detectors.*

ULTRAVIOLET

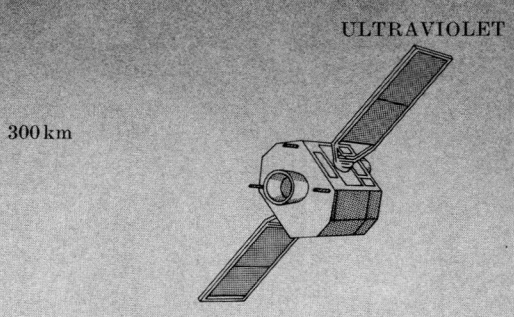

300 km

100 km

X-RAYS

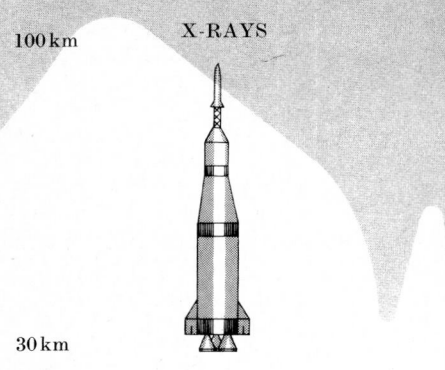
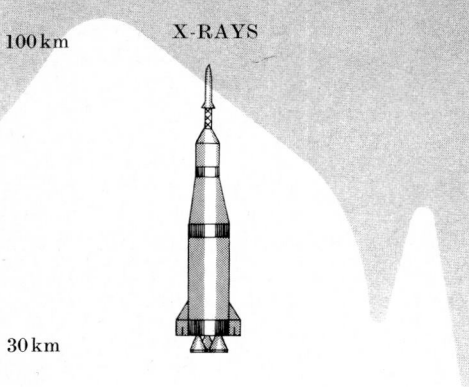

INFRARED

30 km

10 km

INFRARED

RADIO WAVES

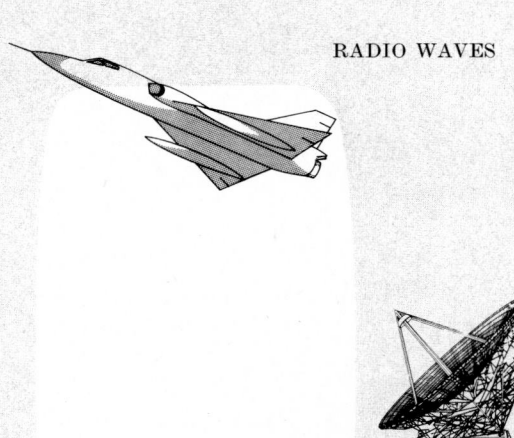

VISIBLE

3 km

The absorption of radiation in the Earth's astmosphere

The surface of the Earth is covered in a thin layer of gas called the ATMOSPHERE of our planet. It is made up of a large number of constituent gases of which nitrogen, oxygen, argon, carbon dioxide and water vapour are the most abundant, with ozone being important at high altitudes. Much of the radiation entering the top of the atmosphere is completely absorbed or reflected before it reaches the ground. Life on the surface of Earth is only possible because the atmosphere protects us so efficiently from the intense ultraviolet radiation produced by the Sun. Unfortunately for astronomers, this means that much of the radiation from distant stars and galaxies gets no nearer the surface of the Earth than the top of the atmosphere, and thus it restricts substantially our view of the Universe.

In figure 22.1 we see what happens to the various forms of electromagnetic radiation as they pass into the Earth's atmosphere. The outermost layer of the atmosphere that affects the passage of electromagnetic radiation is called the IONOSPHERE. It consists of a layer of hot, ionized gas (called a PLASMA) which reflects long-wavelength radio waves back into space. Long, medium and short waveband radio stations on Earth make use of this ability of the ionosphere to reflect radio waves. Radio waves are reflected from the underside of the ionosphere, so that signals may be received clearly from broadcast stations far beyond the horizon of the transmitter. However, radio waves with wavelengths from about 1 mm to 10 m pass through the atmosphere almost without absorption. From 1 nm to about 1 mm (from the near infrared to the millimetre wavebands), electromagnetic waves are strongly absorbed by molecules in the upper atmosphere, notably water and carbon dioxide. In the visible part of the spectrum (350 nm–700 nm), the atmosphere is transparent and most of this radiation reaches the surface of the Earth. Waves of shorter wavelength are strongly absorbed: the ultraviolet waves by molecules, X-rays by individual atoms and gamma rays by atomic nuclei. This means that the ground-based astronomer can only work satisfactorily in two spectral regions: from 1 mm to 30 m (the RADIO WINDOW) and from 350 nm to 700 nm (the OPTICAL WINDOW). With care it is also possible to work in parts of the infrared region of the spectrum, provided the astronomer chooses a site which is as high and dry as possible. An example of such a site is Mauna Kea on Hawaii at an altitude of 4500 m. Such a site minimizes the amount of water vapour between the telescope and the top of the atmosphere.

One might suppose that it should be possible to observe relatively bright objects in other parts of the spectrum, even if only a few per cent of the radiation from the object penetrates to the Earth's surface. Unfortunately this is not usually possible. The temperature of the Earth's atmosphere varies by only a fairly small amount, in the range 240 K–310 K. Although it absorbs vast amounts of energy from the Sun it maintains its temperature in this narrow range by re-radiating nearly all of the energy it absorbs.

We cannot see the stars in the daytime because the sky is so bright, due to the scattering of sunlight. As soon as the Sun sets, the sky darkens quickly. Note, however, that in the infrared part of the spectrum the atmosphere is radiating because it is hot; it cools only slowly so that the infrared sky remains bright all night long. It is often easier, therefore, to observe in wavebands where the absorption and hence re-radiation of the atmosphere is small.

Emission of radiation by the night sky

Outside the radio and optical windows, the main source of night-sky emission is the re-radiation which accompanies absorption. In the radio window the sky is very dark, by day and by night, since it radiates very little indeed. Radio observations at wavelengths longer than a few centimetres are therefore just as easy by day as by night and are unaffected by clouds or rain, though they are affected by man-made and natural terrestrial interference. Radio radiation from the Sun can interfere with observations of faint objects in directions close to that of the Sun. Our Galaxy produces a faint band of radio radiation, concentrated along the Milky Way, which can hamper observations of the faintest sources at wavelengths of 0.5 m or longer. However, both these effects are fairly small and much less serious than the NIGHT-SKY RADIATION.

There are a number of mechanisms that produce diffuse optical background radiation, which brightens the night sky and makes it more difficult to observe the faintest objects. Our planet is continually sheathed in a faint nocturnal glow (NIGHTGLOW or AIRGLOW) that is seldom noticed. It is caused by chemical reactions in the upper atmosphere that result in the emission of light.

Another source of unwanted radiation is the stream of energetic charged particles repeatedly shot out from the Sun. Many of these particles become tangled with the Earth's magnetic field. They then radiate their energy as the beautiful polar aurorae, mostly in the zones 20° to 25° from the geomagnetic poles.

A minor component of the Solar System is a diffuse distribution of dust grains in its plane. These dust grains scatter sunlight to produce the ZODIACAL LIGHT. Apart from moonlight and the aurora, the zodiacal light is the brightest component of the night-sky radiation. It can be an impressive spectacle, especially in the tropics where the plane of the Solar System (the ECLIPTIC) is almost vertical to the horizon.

Sunlight and moonlight are the main contributors to the brightness of the night sky. Therefore observations of the faintest optical objects must wait until the Sun is well down below the horizon and until the Moon has either set or waned so that it produces only a little light. The contributions of sunlight and moonlight are much less important in the infrared than in the visible region of the spectrum. Because of this, it is often possible for infrared astronomers to work during twilight and on moonlit nights when many optical astronomers find the sky too bright for useful observations of faint objects. Some far-infrared observations can even be made throughout the day.

Refraction in the atmosphere and the ionosphere

On a hot day we can look along a surfaced road at a distant object and see that it seems to shake and shiver as we look at it. This happens because 'bubbles' of hot air rise from the surface of the road. The fluctuations in air density caused by these bubbles of hot air deflect the light beams passing through the air from the distant object, making the air appear to shiver before our eyes. The bending of light rays is called refraction. Similar but much smaller density variations are found everywhere in the atmosphere. They cause the light from a star, for example, to be slightly deflected from its original path in a random manner. On the timescale of a few seconds, this causes the light from the most compact point object, such as a star, to be smeared over a disc of typically a few arc seconds diameter. When this disc is large, we refer to the observing conditions as BAD SEEING. Images better than one arc second diameter are observed only under conditions of GOOD SEEING. The quality of the seeing changes from hour to hour and from day to day. In addition, atmospheric irregularities cause fluctuations in the brightness of the stars known as SCINTILLATION. On a dark night we observe the random atmospheric refraction as the twinkling of stars. Twinkling tends to be most severe under conditions of poor seeing. The more they twinkle the poorer is the seeing. (Note that planets do not twinkle, because they are extended objects; the twinkling of each part of a planet's disc averages out to give a steady image.) There is not very much that the astronomer can do to reduce the effects of seeing. For very bright objects it may be possible to build devices which sense the seeing deflections very quickly and move the images slightly to correct for the deflection. However the light from all but the brightest objects is too faint to allow this to be done. Further, as large apertures average out the seeing deflections, such a technique is only of use with relatively small telescopes. The only other way to reduce the effects of seeing is to choose the best possible observing site where the air is very dry and stable, or else to take the telescope above the Earth's atmosphere in a balloon or on an Earth satellite.

In addition to the random refractions that produce seeing, visible and infrared waves are also refracted by the layer of atmosphere which surrounds the Earth. We may see the same effect if we look at an object through a slab of glass. As the glass is tilted, the object appears to move by an amount which is greatest when the light from the object to the observer is passing through the glass at a glancing angle. Similarly ATMOSPHERIC REFRACTION causes the apparent positions of stars to be changed as they move closer to the horizon. However, this effect is on a large scale and is highly predictable so it does not degrade the quality of the image near the horizon though it does alter the apparent angular separation of two objects. Nevertheless, astronomers prefer not to observe objects near the horizon if possible: the seeing is often poorer there, since the light must travel through many more atmospheric density fluctuations, and there is usually more absorption of the light by dust and pollutants near the horizon.

Radio waves longer than 10 cm are refracted by the ionosphere as well as by the atmosphere in much the same way that visible and infrared waves are refracted by the atmosphere. As these are large-scale effects and are fairly predictable and repeatable they do not seriously disturb the work of the radio astronomer.

Choice of observing sites for telescopes

No terrestrial observing site is perfect and any one site can only be a compromise between the many, often conflicting requirements of a so-called site. What makes a good site for an optical or infrared observatory? Firstly, it must have many good, clear nights. Then it must be as dark as possible. This means that the site should not be too near the polar regions if the aurorae are to be avoided. A major component of the light of the night sky is man-made street lighting. There are always enough dust or water droplets in the atmosphere to ensure that street and advertisement lighting cause a bright glow over a city which can have a substantial effect on the sky brightness many tens of kilometres from the city. There are many parts of the world where towns and cities are so close together that there are few truly dark sites over large areas (figure 22.2). For example, urban development has been so rapid over the last thirty years in California that the great observatories on Mount Wilson, Mount Palomar and at Lick are substantially affected. However, Kitt Peak in Arizona is less affected because the Tucson city authorities have installed baffles on street lighting to minimize the effects to the telescopes 80 km away. In recent years the substantial growth of city lighting (10 per cent per annum) has forced astronomers to choose observing sites on small mountainous islands with a limited potential for growth.

The next requirement of a good site is that the atmosphere above it should be stable, to ensure that the seeing is as good as possible. Seeing generally improves with altitude and the best sites are those which are above the INVERSION LAYER in the atmosphere. This is the height above which hot air from the surface of the Earth does not normally rise. Above the inversion layer the atmosphere is particularly steady, clear and free from dust or water vapour. This last aspect – freedom from water vapour – is of particular importance to infrared astronomers and for this the most important single factor is altitude. Mauna Kea on Hawaii (4500 m) is, therefore, an excellent infrared site. It is also a good optical site along with the Chilean sites (Las Campanas, Cerro Tololo, La Silla) and the Canary Island sites (Tenerife and La Palma).

Radio observatories may be sited in poor northern climates since radio observations are largely unaffected by cloud or rain, except at wavelengths below 10 cm. The largest, most sensitive telescopes have to be built away from sources of man-made interference such as that produced by electrical machinery. In addition, there are a number of radio wavebands which are protected from use throughout the world and which are used for radio astronomy.

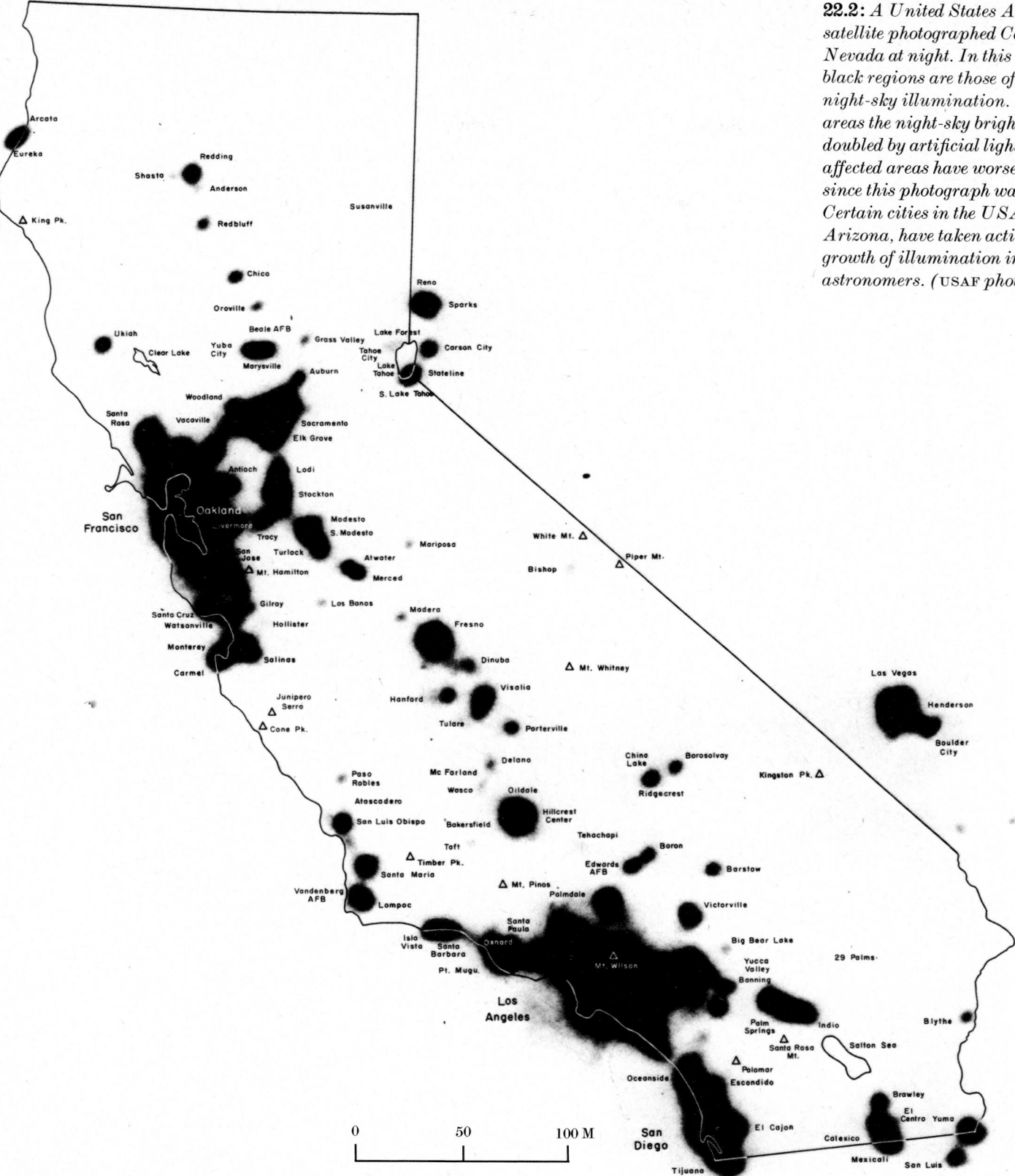

22.2: *A United States Air Force weather satellite photographed California and part of Nevada at night. In this negative print the black regions are those of intense artificial night-sky illumination. At the edges of these areas the night-sky brightness at the zenith is doubled by artificial lighting. Already the affected areas have worsened considerably since this photograph was taken in 1972. Certain cities in the USA, such as Tucson, Arizona, have taken action to reduce the rate of growth of illumination in order to help astronomers.* (USAF *photograph*)

Radiation collectors

Once the radiation from an astronomical object has passed through Earth's atmosphere, it must be gathered into a form that enables us to detect it fairly easily. Only after this detection has taken place and the signal from the object recorded can any analysis of the data take place.

Astronomical objects are so far away that they have a low apparent luminosity. Radiation which reaches Earth from any one point in the cosmos is travelling in a parallel beam for all practical purposes. It is clear, therefore, that a collector of electromagnetic radiation, or TELESCOPE as it is usually called, has two main functions: firstly, it must collect radiation from as much of the parallel beam as it can and, secondly, it must concentrate or FOCUS this radiation onto the detector so as to give a sharp image of the object.

It is important to remember in the following discussions that although radio, infrared, optical, ultraviolet, X-ray and gamma-ray telescopes often look very different, the principles of optics which govern their design are the same. No particular wavelength is implied in this discussion based on general principles unless it is explicitly stated.

Image-forming devices

One of the simplest image-forming devices is a concave mirror (figure 22.3). If the mirror is parabolic, on-axis rays which make up a parallel beam are deflected and converge at a single point. The radiation from different parts of an extended object, such as a galaxy, reach the mirror from slightly different directions (greatly exaggerated in figure 22.3). They are then deflected and brought to a focus at slightly different points in the FOCAL PLANE of the telescope to form other elements of the image.

The formation of an image is more complicated than this in practice. Electromagnetic waves consist of rapidly-varying electric and magnetic fields. If these waves are to add together to produce a sharp, luminous image it is important that they all reach the focal plane of the telescope with approximately the same PHASE. Otherwise the radiation in the out-of-phase waves will subtract from the total, reducing the net luminosity of the image. This gives the most important constraint on the precise shape of the mirror of the telescope, namely that all the rays in a parallel beam incident on the telescope should reach the focal plane with approximately the same phase. In practical terms, it is usual to require the shape of a telescope to be accurate to within about one-twentieth of the wavelength of the radiation the telescope is designed to collect. This means that an optical telescope working at a wavelength of 500 nm has to be polished to within $\approx$ 25 nm, whereas a radio telescope working at a wavelength of 21 cm may be built much more crudely with a surface accuracy of only 1 cm.

Another important parameter of a telescope is the area of the radiation collector. The larger the telescope, the more radiation can be gathered (in proportion to the square of the diameter of the telescope). A larger telescope means that observations may be

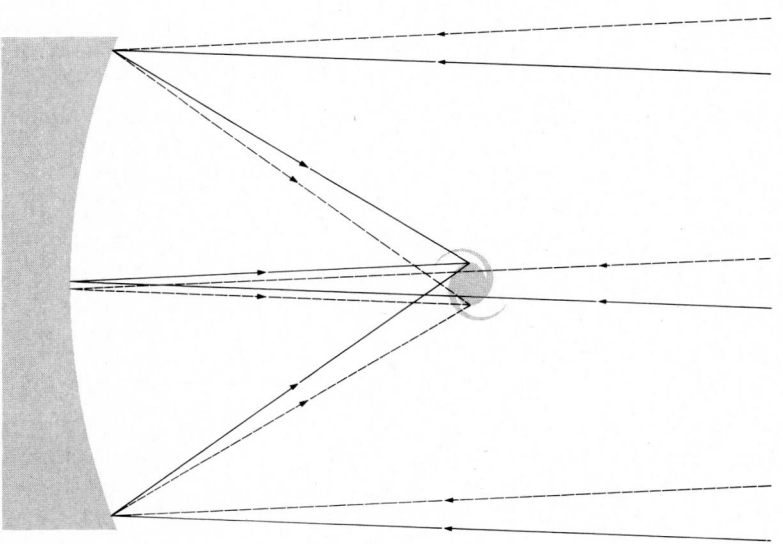

22.3: *A specially curved mirror deflects the parallel rays from one distant source of radiation so that all are brought together at one point which is the focus of the mirror. Other sources of light produce images at different points in the focal plane so that extended sources produce extended images.*

made more rapidly and of much fainter objects. It also improves the amount of detail visible in the image. This is set by the resolution of the telescope in the following way. Suppose that there are two objects, such as stars, close together on the sky. If we are to resolve them, that is to form images of the two objects which do not overlap, then we require that the radiation forming the image of one of the objects must not add together to give an appreciable signal at the position of the image of the other object. In figure 22.4, the first object is on the axis of a telescope of diameter D which works at wavelength λ. The rays from the second object travel in a direction which makes a very small angle with the rays from the first object (this angle is the ANGULAR SEPARATION of the two objects in the sky). Some of the radiation from the second object is reflected to the position of the image of the first object, but we see from figure 22.4 that the rays from the second object to the edges of the telescope have a path-length difference of l between them. This path-length difference produces a phase difference in the received rays which reduces their net intensity. When $l \simeq \lambda/2$ the extreme rays are of opposite phase and we see that $\beta = \lambda/2D$ (since β is small so $\sin \beta = \beta$). It is usual to define the RESOLVING POWER of a telescope as the smallest angle between two point objects that produces distinct recognizable images. It is usually given as $\beta = 210\,000\lambda/D$ arc sec.

The larger the telescope, or the shorter the wavelengths used, then the better the resolving power. However it is not always possible to improve the resolution of a telescope indefinitely. An optical telescope of 10 cm diameter has a resolution of about 1 arc sec. If the diameter was increased to 1 m, the telescope itself would have a theoretical resolving power of 0.1 arc sec, but we have seen that the radiation which has passed through the Earth's atmosphere is spread over an angle seldom less than 0.5 arc sec by fluctuations in the atmosphere. For this reason the largest optical telescopes in the world have resolving powers no better than that of 20-cm telescopes – but they are able to gather much more radiation than small ones. Because of the longer wavelengths they use, infrared astronomers are much more affected by diffraction limits than optical astronomers. At a wavelength of 10 μm, a 2-m telescope has a diffraction-limited resolving power of about 1 arc sec – again the limit of seeing at these wavelengths.

We will find it convenient to talk about the FOCAL RATIO (or F-RATIO) of a particular telescope focus. This is the ratio of the effective focal length of the telescope to the diameter of its primary reflector. The focal length of a telescope is the distance of the focal plane from the mirror. The MAGNIFICATION of the image is proportional to the focal length of the telescope. Note, however, that large magnifications can be undesirable for faint objects if their light is spread over too great an area.

Radio waves are much less affected by the Earth's atmosphere and the size limits of radio telescopes are set largely by difficulties of construction. These problems may be avoided by the use of *interferometers* (described later). At a wavelength of 2 cm, an interferometer of 5-km baseline has a resolving power of about 1 arc sec.

22.4: *An image of a point source of radiation is formed at the point at which the rays striking opposite edges of the mirror have travelled equal distances from the source. Two sources an angular distance β apart on the sky are imaged at different positions in the focal plane (A and B).*

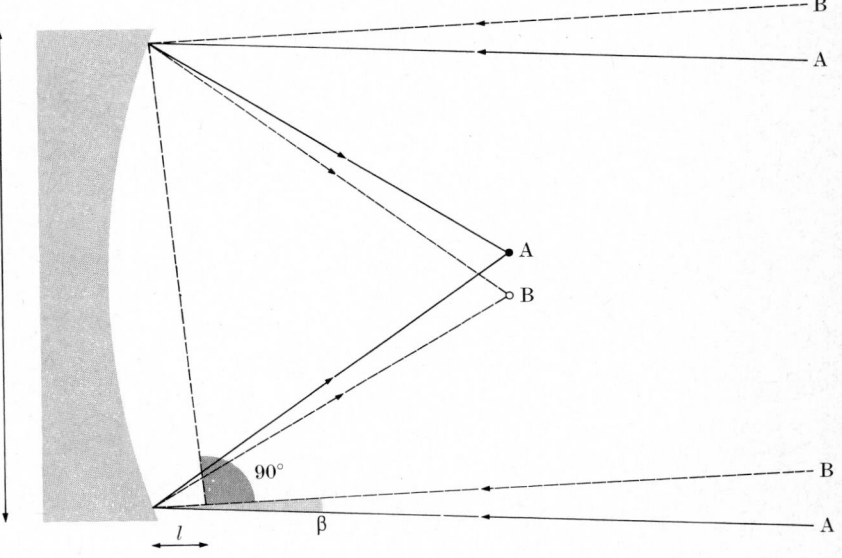

22.5: *The three most common foci of optical telescopes are these : (a) Prime focus, in which the light is reflected once only. (b) Cassegrain focus, where a curved secondary mirror intercepts the converging beam before prime focus to give a focal plane behind the primary mirror. (c) Coudé focus, where three additional mirrors provide a focal plane on the main telescope floor which does not move with the telescope.*

The parabolic reflector

The commonest shape for the primary mirror of a reflecting telescope is a simple paraboloid. It gives excellent images at the centre of the flat focal plane although the area over which acceptable images are produced can be small. Much of the variety seen in telescope design is a consequence of getting an observer or a detector to the focused image. The most straightforward focal position is the PRIME FOCUS (figure 22.5a). At this focus, the rays from the object being observed have only been reflected once so that the reflection losses are minimized. Many radio telescopes are of this construction (figure 22.6a). In the largest optical telescopes there is sometimes provided a small observing cage at prime focus in which the observer and his equipment remain during an observation. In smaller telescopes such an obstruction of the mirror would be unacceptable and an additional mirror is provided to give the NEWTONIAN FOCUS. This is a traditional configuration often used by amateur astronomers. Another arrangement is the CASSEGRAIN SYSTEM, where a small convex secondary mirror intercepts the ray path before prime focus. The rays are then reflected through a hole at the centre of the primary mirror to a focus just behind the mirror. This focus is often more easily acces-

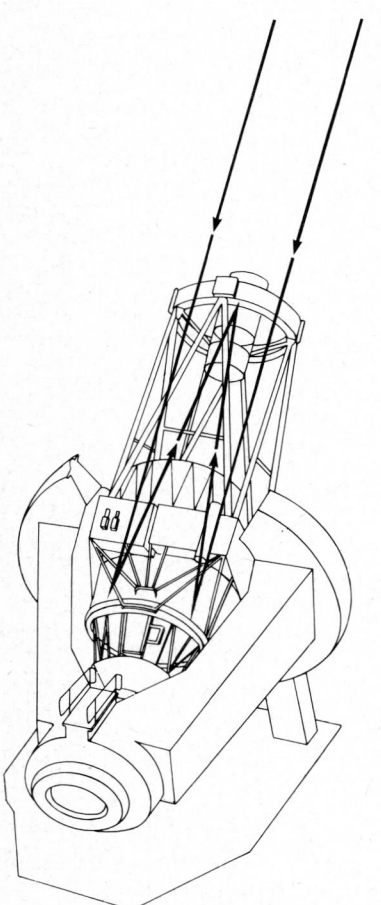

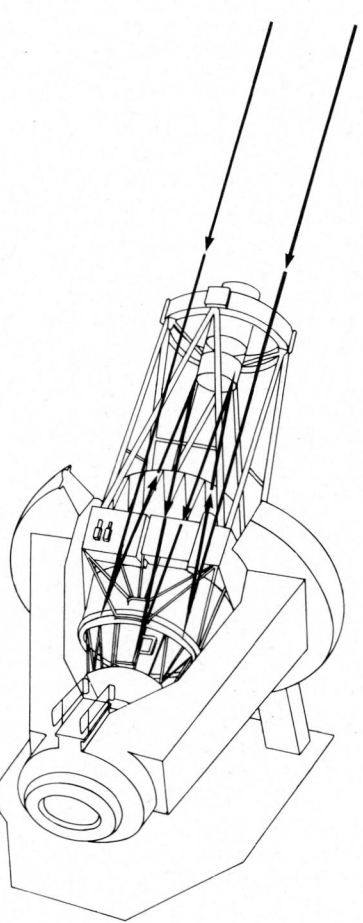

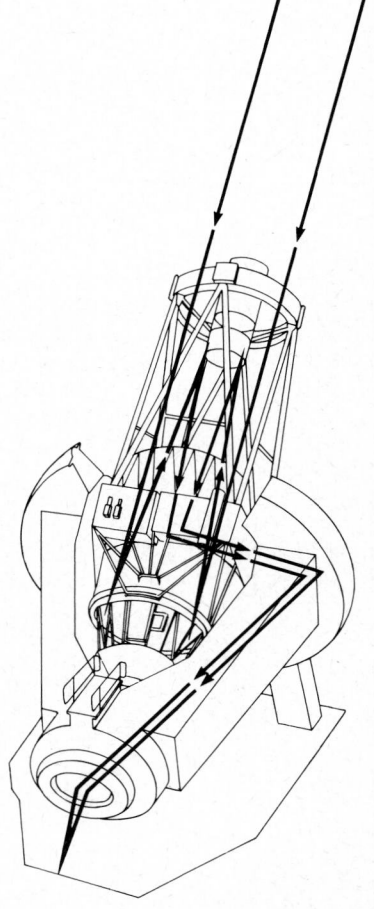

(a)   (b)   (c)

sible than the prime focus and is capable of having much heavier equipment attached (figure 22.6b). For certain kinds of optical observations, such as high-resolution spectroscopy, special equipment is needed which is much too heavy to be attached directly to the telescope or its mounting. For such observations a COUDÉ FOCUS is provided some way from the telescope tube (figure 22.5c). The presence of a prime-focus cage or of secondary mirrors in the primary beam of the telescope does not produce images with holes in their centres. Each part of the beam of radiation from the object contains essentially the same information about the object. If one part of the beam is obstructed by a secondary mirror, for example, the main effect is to reduce the intensity of the final image. A hole in the image could only be produced by an obstruction in the converging beam after the radiation had been reflected by the primary mirror, and even then only if the obstruction was fairly close to the focal plane of the telescope. The supports of the prime-focus assembly or the secondary mirror are responsible for the cruciform appearance of stellar images. The supports cause some of the starlight to be diffracted out of its original path. These produce the DIFFRACTION SPIKES seen around bright stars on most astronomical photographs.

22.6: *Radio telescopes are constructed using the same principles as optical telescopes to give: (a) Prime focus. (b) Cassegrain focus. The coudé focus is not used with radio telescopes.*

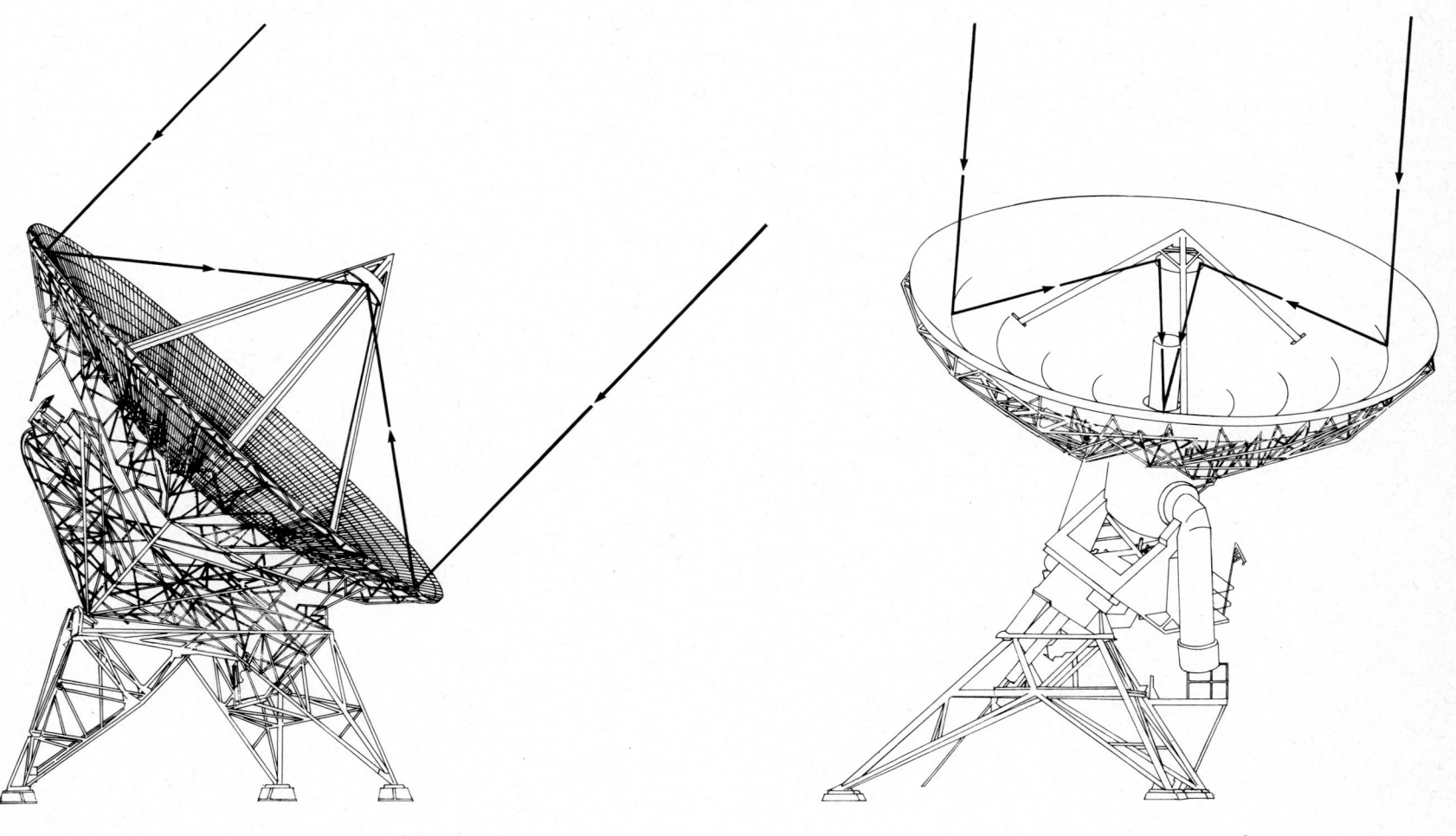

(a) (b)

The first optical telescopes built did not use reflecting mirrors. Instead, a lens was used to focus the light to give an image. The largest existing refractor now in use is the 1-m telescope of the Yerkes Observatory, University of Chicago. Difficulties of mounting and supporting the objective lens so that the image stays fixed and in focus as the telescope moves to follow the sky impose a limit on the size of refracting telescopes which may be built.

One of the biggest disadvantages of most reflectors is that while the images are excellent on the axis of the instrument, they rapidly deteriorate with angular distance from the axis. We say that there is a fairly small FIELD OF VIEW over which the images are of acceptable quality (where the word 'acceptable' depends on the type of observations being made). Spherical reflectors suffer from SPHERICAL ABERRATION which causes the rays from the edge of the mirror to come to focus at a different position from the inner rays. Bernard Schmidt of the Hamburg Observatory realized that it was possible to correct for this by placing a thin corrector lens in the path of the rays before they struck the mirror. Such an arrangement produces excellent images over a very wide field, often several degrees across. Telescopes based on this principle are called SCHMIDT TELESCOPES (figure 22.7).

22.7: *The 1.2-metre Schmidt telescope constructed by the UK Science Research Council at Siding Spring mountain in Australia. Modelled on the Schmidt telescope at Mount Palomar USA, its main work has been to survey the southern sky to very faint levels, which it has achieved with outstanding success. (UK Science Research Council)*

22.8: *The 3.9-metre Anglo-Australian telescope at Siding Spring mountain in Australia. For prime focus observations (such as direct photography), the astronomer travels with the telescope in the prime focus cage attached to the top end of the telescope (a). The telescope is moved until it is nearly horizontal for the observer to climb into the cage (b). The astronomer sits on the seat (c) and may rotate the whole cage for comfort as the telescope is driven across the sky. The photographic plateholder fits into the square hole in the middle of the cage. Beside it are eyepieces which help with the positioning of the telescope. A view of the Cassegrain focus is shown in (d). Equipment here is operated remotely, often under computer control (Anglo-Australian Observatory, Australia)*

(a)

(b)

(c)

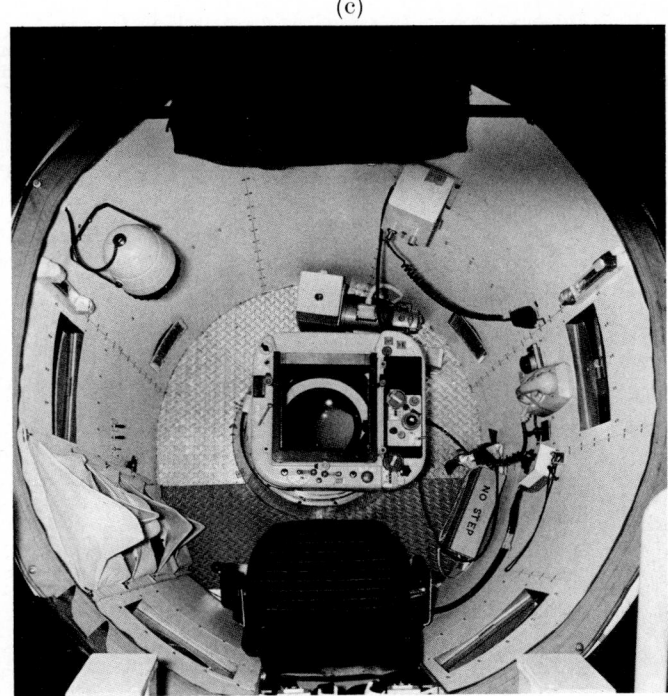

(d)

Interferometers

The largest fully-steerable parabolic telescope is the 100-m radio dish near Bonn, West Germany. At a wavelength of 6 cm it has a resolution of about 2 arc min. To achieve a resolution at radio wavelengths comparable with that set by seeing limitations at optical wavelengths would require a telescope at least fifty times larger. The impossibility of building such a dish, 5 km in diameter, does not mean that high-resolution radio telescopes cannot be built.

To see how this is done, consider what happens when we combine the radio signals from two small telescopes (figure 22.9). Suppose the two telescopes are observing a point source (very small angular size) of radio waves. The radiation incident at each telescope is collected by the dishes separately and then combined together electronically to give an output signal. Notice, however, that the radio waves to one telescope have to travel an extra distance, or extra path length, l, before being picked up by the detector at the focus of the dish. The radio source moves across the sky as the Earth rotates on its axis so that the path-length difference changes continually. At some time the two electromagnetic waves will be in-phase and will give a maximum in the output signal. A little later the path difference will have changed so that the waves will be out of phase: they will then cancel giving zero output signal. Then the signals will come back into phase again. The output signal after a time will look similar to figure 22.10. When the object is above the centre of the interferometer baseline, the output signal will go from maximum to minimum when the path difference changes by half a wavelength $(\lambda/2)$. This will happen once the object has moved through an angle $\beta = \lambda/2D$ where D denotes the separation of the two telescopes. The amplitude of the output signal then goes from maximum to minimum and back to a maximum every time the object moves through an angle λ/D across the sky. These amplitude variations are called INTERFERENCE FRINGES, and they are separated by an angle equal to the resolution of a single, large dish of diameter D. By means of these interference fringes we can locate the position of an object with the accuracy and resolution of a telescope of diameter D, which is now the separation of the two small telescopes and not their individual diameters. This does not mean, however, that INTERFEROMETERS (the name given to this arrangement of small telescopes) can be used simply to replace large single dishes. There are a number of substantial problems associated with their use.

In general, we do not know the exact location of the object we wish to observe. If it is giving a maximum in its output signal at one moment, we know that the path-length difference is a whole number of wavelengths but we do not know how many wavelengths. This means it is not possible to tell at which maximum of the interferometer fringe pattern our object is. We can overcome this problem by observing with a number of different interferometers with different baseline sizes. The various interferometers then give a maximum output signal simultaneously when the object is exactly above the midpoint of all the interferometer base-

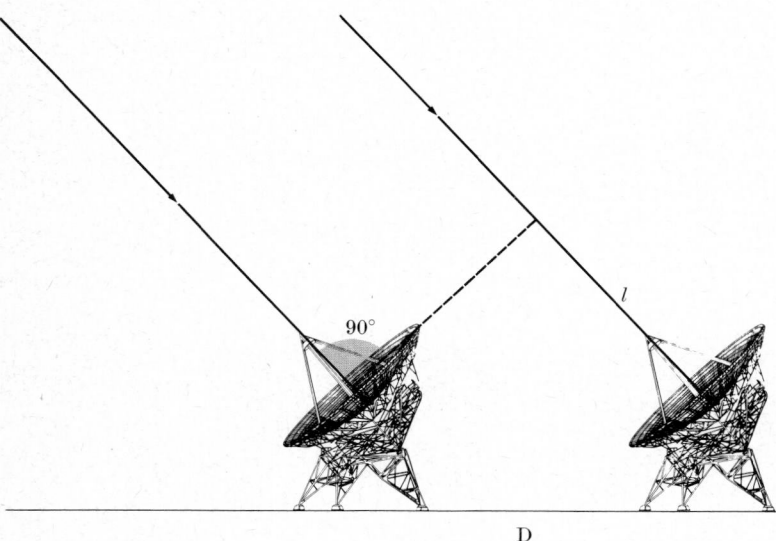

22.9: *Rays from a celestial radio source to two elements of a radio interferometer have path lengths to the receivers differing by l. The value of l depends on the position of the source on the sky and on D, the separation of the receiving elements.*

lines. The other main problem arises when the interferometer is used to observe sources of large angular extent. For a sufficiently large source of radiation, the signals from some parts of the object will be in phase and adding to the total output, while other signals from another part of the same object will be out of phase and therefore subtracting from the total output signal. On average, the output signal will vary by only a small amount, if indeed at all, and we say that the source of the radio signals has been RESOLVED by the interferometer. If we want information about the large-scale structure of a radio source we have to use an interferometer with a smaller baseline, and a correspondingly larger fringe spacing on the sky. Astronomers have found that by a series of baselines from the smallest to the largest possible, they are able to deduce the detailed structure of radio sources of nearly all apparent sizes, as described in the next section.

Much of the interferometry done today is SYNTHESIS INTERFERO-METRY in which a substantial number of different baselines are used. However, the largest baselines are those between telescopes situated on different continents (VERY LONG BASELINE INTERFERO-METRY or VLBI). In this arrangement it is impossible to observe with baselines of intermediate size; astronomers have to accept the ambiguities, mentioned above, that are associated with the simple interferometer. Although the positions of objects are then uncertain in most cases, the enormous resolution (thousandths of a second of arc) possible with intercontinental baselines of many thousands of kilometres has yielded valuable data on the angular sizes of some of the most distant and luminous *radio galaxies* and *quasars* in the Universe.

22.10: *If the elements of an interferometer are left pointing in a fixed direction, interference fringes are recorded as various sources pass through the beam of the telescope. The amplitude and phase of the fringes gives the astronomer valuable clues to the sizes and brightnesses of the sources observed. This trace shows the Sun, Cygnus A and Taurus A. (University of Cambridge, UK)*

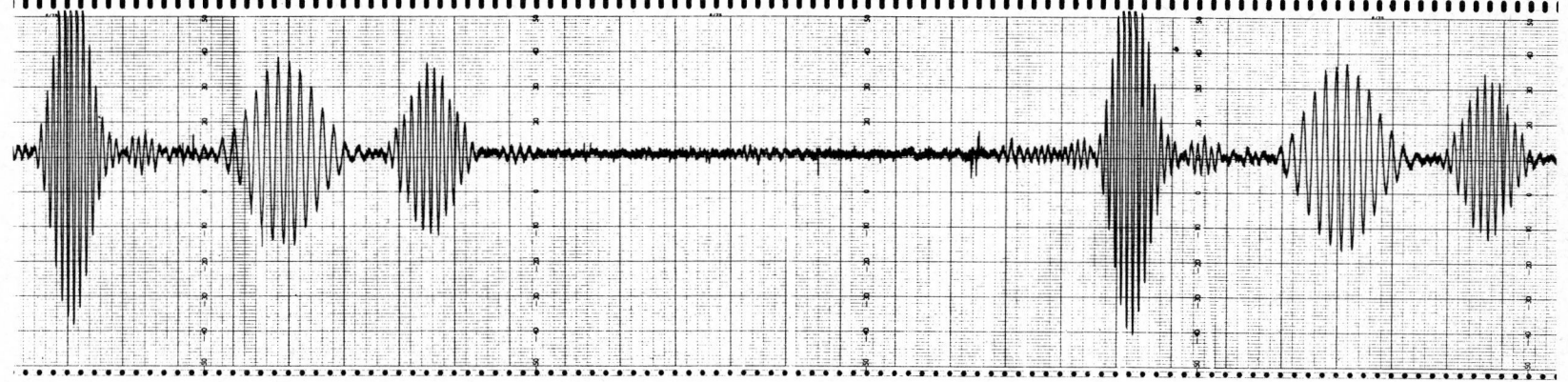

22.11: *Earth-rotation synthesis. In twelve hours the baseline takes all orientations relative to the source on the sky because of the rotations of the Earth. The elements of the interferometer therefore trace out a complete ring about the mid-point of the interferometer baseline. By moving one element of the interferometer, the baseline can be changed to enable the synthesis of several rings.*
This elegant technique was developed at Cambridge by Sir Martin Ryle, who was awarded the Nobel Prize in recognition of its great value to radio astronomy.

Earth-rotation synthesis

The basic purpose of a telescope is to deflect the radiation incident on every part of its surface towards a focus, and to arrange that all the signals reaching this focus are of the same phase. Most astronomical objects only vary their sizes and brightnesses very slowly. If the emitting object remains unchanged for a sufficient time, we can dispose of our large telescope and use instead one which is much smaller. This can be moved so as to sample the signals incident on each part of the area that would have been covered by the large telescope that we want to synthesize. The signals have to be recorded carefully relative to some reference signal before the telescope is moved to the next position. If we consider the waves gathered by one collector of an interferometer, the reference signal is provided by the other collector.

In principle we can move the elements of this interferometer in any direction over the ground, but it is easier to understand an interferometer on an east-west line. Imagine that we are looking down upon it from the north pole as the Earth rotates (figure 22.11). In twelve hours the two elements of the interferometer appear to trace out a complete ring about the mid-point of the interferometer baseline. If the elements of the interferometer are then moved closer together they will trace out the next ring inwards during another twelve-hour period. Eventually, the whole aperture can be filled in this way. The signals recorded throughout the many twelve-hour periods are those that would be simultaneously added together by a single large dish of diameter equal to the largest interferometer spacing. However, in this case we take all the recorded signals, and feed them into a large computer. The computer is asked to synthesize the image we would have obtained with a single large dish. The computer then produces a radio picture of our source with the resolution and sensitivity of a single large dish. This technique is called EARTH-ROTATION SYNTHESIS and was pioneered by the Mullard Radio Astronomy Observatory at Cambridge, England. Their highest resolution instrument has a baseline of nearly 5 km. When operating at a wavelength of 2 cm, it has a resolution of about 1 arc sec, similar to that normally achieved by optical telescopes that are seeing-limited (figure 22.12).

Other important Earth-rotation synthesis instruments have been built at Westerbork, Netherlands, and in West Virginia, USA. A very large array of small telescopes is also being built in New Mexico to provide Earth-rotation synthesis observations of very faint objects.

Stellar interferometers

The angular diameters of stars are much smaller than the limit imposed by seeing conditions in the atmosphere. It may therefore seem that there is no point in building an optical analogue of the radio interferometer in order to improve the resolution of an optical telescope. However, there are moments when the image stabilizes for long enough to give interference fringes. In 1920, an interferometer was assembled on the front of the 2.5-m telescope at Mount Wilson by Michelson and Pease. It had a 6.5-m beam and allowed them to measure the angular size of seven giant stars. They found angular diameters of one-twentieth to one-fiftieth of an arc second.

An alternate approach to the measure of stellar diameters has been developed by R.Hanbury-Brown and R.Q.Twiss in Britain and more recently in Narrabri, Australia. They use two optical telescopes up to 200 m apart. The light from the stars is detected with *photomultipliers* and the intensities of the signals received are cross-correlated and the correlation amplitude measured for a variety of separations of the two optical telescopes. From these data it is possible to deduce information about the angular size of the star being observed. As the correlated signals are very weak, this technique is only applicable to the brightest stars. For these, resolutions down to 5×10^{-4} arc sec have been achieved.

A very different approach called SPECKLE INTERFEROMETRY has been pioneered by A.Labeyrie and colleagues. Although atmospheric fluctuations spread images over their seeing disc, very short exposures (0.1–0.001 seconds) reveal that the images consist of a large number of tiny spots or SPECKLES whose size and shape may be analysed to give structural information on bright stars with a resolution set only by the diffraction limit of the telescopes used (about 0.016 arc sec with the 5-m telescope on Mount Palomar). Stars as faint as 9 mag have been measured with this technique (figure 22.13). For faint stars, large numbers of short exposures have to be processed.

22.12: *The 5-km Earth-rotation synthesis radio telescope at Cambridge, UK. It consists of four fixed and four moveable dishes on an east-west baseline. The dishes are of Cassegrain focus construction. They are steered and the signals are processed under computer control and may be left unattended for several days. (John Stewart, Cambridge, UK)*

22.13: *A computer-based image of the star Betelgeuse obtained by speckle interferometry. The technique shows features on the surface of the star. (Kitt Peak National Observatory, USA)*

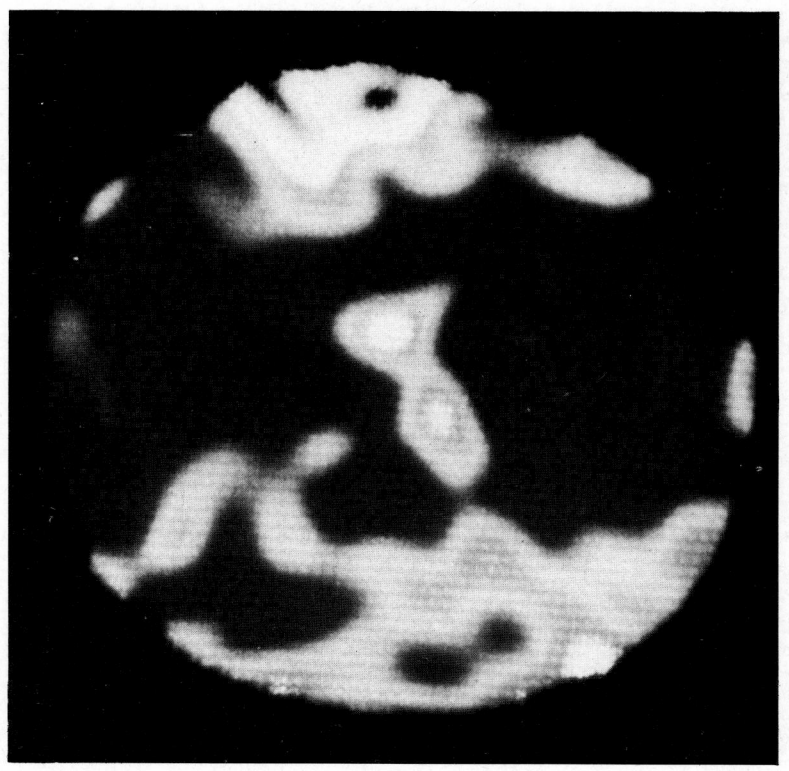

Optical spectroscopy

Instruments that give the spectrum of the radiation from an object are called SPECTROGRAPHS. The most important part of an optical spectrograph is the element that breaks up the light into its constituent colours. This can be done simply by use of a series of colour filters, but such an approach is not an efficient way of using the light from faint objects because scarce photons are absorbed by the filters. However, to examine the two-dimensional colour structure or spectrum of an object it is necessary to make a series of observations in different colour bands using filters. The filters commonly used are of two main types. Coloured glasses or plastic films generally exclude the light above or below a certain wavelength and are used to provide broad-band filtering (e.g. UBV FILTERS) of the light. For work in narrower bands (less than 25 nm wide) INTERFERENCE FILTERS are used. These consist of layers of substances with different *refractive indices*, arranged so that their optical thickness matches the wavelength of the light to be transmitted through the filter. Radiation of different wavelengths is reflected by the many layers (sometimes as many as 17). In this way very narrow bandwidth (<1 nm) filters can be constructed which transmit radiation only within this narrow band.

Spectrographs are usually constructed with either a prism or a diffraction grating to disperse the light and so give its spectrum (figure 22.14). When light crosses an air-glass boundary its path is deflected (refracted) by an amount which depends on the wavelength or colour of the light. Blue light has a shorter wavelength and is refracted more than red light. This dependence of refractivity on wavelengths means that a prism is able to break up white light into a spectrum. This spectrum is visually similar to a rainbow. DIFFRACTION GRATINGS also produce a spectrum although they work in quite a different way. REFLECTION GRATINGS consist of a flat mirror on which are etched a large number of parallel grooves, often as many as several hundred per centimetre. The light is only reflected from the shiny parts between the scratches, as if it had emerged from a series of thin parallel slits. The light waves reflected by these strips of mirror interfere with one another so that in any one direction all the reflected waves cancel out except for a few particular wavelengths. TRANSMISSION DIFFRACTION GRATINGS work in accordance with the same principles as a reflection grating, except that the scratches are marked on a sheet of glass.

When designing a spectrograph we must remember that it is much easier to interpret the spectrum if we make sure that the light is parallel before it enters the prism or hits the diffraction grating. The light from the star or galaxy to be analysed is focused onto the slit of the spectrograph. This ensures that we know exactly from which part of the object the light in the spectrum is coming. After passing through the slit, the light diverges and must be made parallel (COLLIMATED) by a lens before it is DISPERSED by the diffraction grating. After dispersion the light of various wavelengths is in the form of parallel beams each moving in a slightly different direction. All the light of one colour is gathered

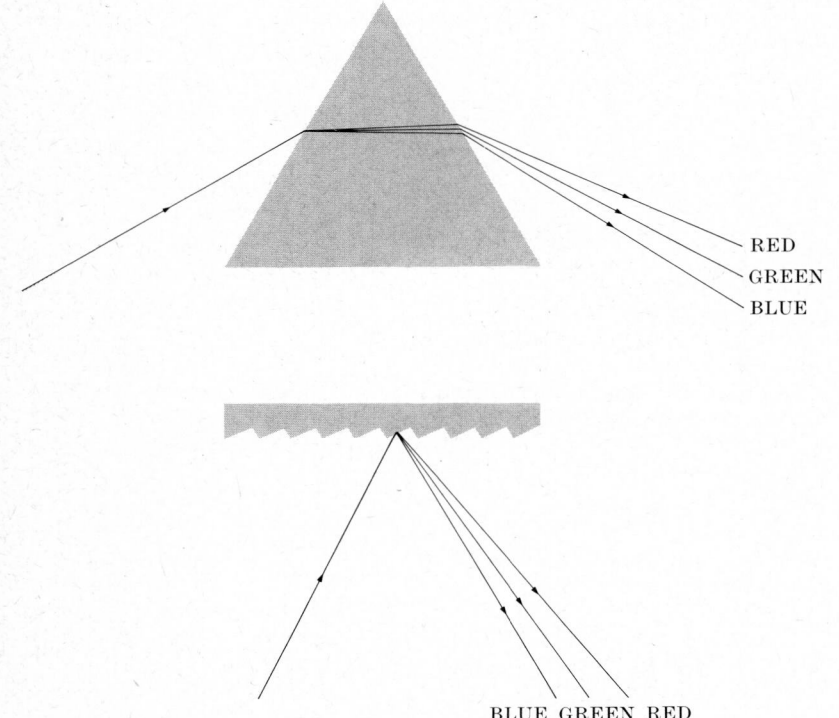

22.14: *The refraction of light through a glass prism (top) and the diffraction of light after reflection by a diffraction grating (bottom), break up the light into its constituent colours.*

RED
GREEN
BLUE

BLUE GREEN RED

and focused by the camera lens to give a clear, focused spectrum of the object.

An objective prism is sometimes placed in front of the primary mirror of a telescope. Objective prisms look rather like thin sheets of glass – which, indeed, they are, but their sides are not quite parallel. Because of this they act like a prism, deflecting the light of a star by an amount dependent on the colour of the light from the star. If we take a direct photograph of a star field through an objective prism, the image of each star is slightly elongated. This is because the light from the stars has been spread out into tiny spectra. These spectra are too small to reveal much detail, but they can help with the crude classifications of stellar or galaxy type. The great advantage of objective prism work is that it is possible to record the spectra of a large number of objects simultaneously, whereas a conventional spectrograph will normally be used to observe only one object at a time. A small portion of a plate taken with an objective prism is shown in figure 2.9.

With bright objects it is possible to use grating spectrographs of much higher dispersion. These spread the light from the object further; consequently we can investigate much finer details of the spectrum of the star. With the highest dispersions, however, the spectrum becomes inconveniently long, requiring massive spectrographs and detectors with a very large sensitive area. One arrangement for producing a high-dispersion spectrum which is still compact is the ECHELLE. We have seen how it is that interference effects produce the dispersed beam with a diffraction grating. In the same way that an interferometer has many interference fringes, a diffraction grating produces many dispersed beams, each in a different direction. By varying the details of the way a diffraction grating is made and is mounted in the spectrograph we can arrange to concentrate much of the light into only a few beams. In conventional grating spectrographs it is usual to concentrate the light into one or two of the first few beams. In the échelle grating configuration, however, the starlight is concentrated into many overlapping higher-order beams. In order to separate the different beams they are all passed to another dispersing element (a prism or a diffraction grating) which has its direction of dispersion nearly perpendicular to the first. The light in overlapping beams is of different wavelength, so that a prism will deflect the light paths differently for each beam. It is possible to arrange that the various beams lie one above the other. The particular format of the échelle spectrum is more convenient than that of conventional high-dispersion spectrographs since it is better suited to the modern detectors described in the next section which usually have sensitive areas that are circular. It is also possible to cover a wider range of wavelengths in a single exposure.

The FOURIER SPECTROGRAPH is used increasingly for measuring the spectra of objects, particularly in the near infrared (700 nm–2 μm wavelength). The way that these work is more difficult to understand. We start by thinking about the basic properties of the light to be analysed. A spectral line has a certain width set by the physical conditions within the object itself. Within that line the light consists of a stream of photons. Two consecutive photons from the line will generally be different, and that difference on average will be greater if the spectral line is wider. If we can find a way of measuring the average difference between two photons we can get information on the width of the spectral line with which they are associated. There is, indeed, a device which can analyse spectral lines in this way; it is called a MICHELSON INTERFEROMETER (named after its inventor, the American physicist, A.E. Michelson). The principle on which it works is identical to the simple radio interferometer. The light from the object is split into two parts that are then directed along paths of different lengths. They are then brought together again in order that the photons can interfere with one another; i.e. add or subtract, depending on their relative phase. As the path-length difference is changed, those photons that are adequately similar will interfere to produce a rapidly fluctuating output signal as their relative phases change. Relatively dissimilar photons will gradually stop interfering with one another as the path-length difference is increased, and will produce a constant output signal. If we record the total output signal from such an interferometer as a function of path-length difference we will find that we have all the information which we need to reconstruct the original spectrum. This is done in a computer using a mathematical function known as the Fourier transform – hence the name of the spectrograph. The big advantages of this method, advantages which justify the considerable complexity of the device are (1) that all the light from the object can be used, since an entrance slit is not needed and (2) that a single detector element is needed rather than a multi-element detector such as a photographic plate. This is of particular importance in the infrared where multi-element detectors are extremely difficult to fabricate.

Radio spectroscopy

Perhaps you are a competent radio spectroscopist, probably without realising it! Every time you turn the tuning knob on a radio or television receiver you are looking for peaks in the radio-frequency spectrum present at the antenna (or aerial) of your receiver. The peaks are radio and television broadcast stations.

The same technique is the essence of simple RADIO ASTRONOMICAL SPECTROSCOPY. In the radio region of the spectrum there are a number of spectral lines produced by clouds of neutral hydrogen (H^0 *regions*) and dusty H^+ *regions* and *molecular clouds*. The observing frequency of a radio telescope may be changed gradually while the astronomer watches the strength of the signal on a meter. In this way he may look for peaks and dips in the spectrum of the object. However, this is a relatively inefficient way of using the signal from a faint object since only one small part of the spectrum is actually being used at any one moment. Much more efficient is a technique using a large number of separate receivers each tuned to a slightly different wavelength. Another valuable method is very similar to that used optically in the *Fourier spectrograph*. In radio astronomy they are known as AUTO-CORRELATION RECEIVERS.

Measuring polarization

Electromagnetic waves consist of rapidly alternating crossed electric and magnetic fields. The radiation from most astronomical objects is such that the direction of the electric or the magnetic fields in the waves varies in a random manner. We say that the radiation from these objects is unpolarized. Some objects, however, emit waves which have these fields preferentially oriented in one direction. We then say that the radiation is partially polarized.

To determine the direction of polarization in an object we need a way of selecting the radiation polarized in one particular direction. At radio wavelengths, the basic antenna which is used at the focus of a radio telescope to pick up the radio signals is a *dipole*. It will only pick up radiation with the electric field parallel (polarized) along the length of the dipole. You may have noticed that in some localities the television antennae on houses are horizontal while in others they are vertical. This is because it is essential for the receiving antennae to be polarized in the same way as the transmitting antennae. Astronomical objects may have their radiation polarized in any direction. The astronomer can determine which direction this is by rotating the receiving dipole until the signal output is at maximum. Then the direction of electric polarization is parallel to the length of the dipole and the magnetic field of the radiation is then perpendicular to this direction.

At optical wavelengths there are a number of substances which respond differently to different radiation polarizations. Only one will be described here – Polaroid sheet. This consists of a plastic material in which are embedded a large number of extremely fine needle-like crystals. The polarized needle crystals are arranged so that they all lie parallel within the plastic substance. Radiation which is polarized parallel to the needles can pass through almost without loss. Radiation polarized perpendicular to the needles is blocked. An analogy can be made with throwing sticks at a fence made out of vertical poles. If the stick is thrown so it is horizontal it will not go through the fence whereas if it is vertical it has a good chance of passing straight through. In this way Polaroid sheet is able to sort out the sense of polarization in the optical radiation incident upon it. You can easily check this with a pair of Polaroid-type sunglasses, especially if you look at light reflected from the surface of a pond of water. Only radiation polarized parallel to the surface of the pond is reflected. Polaroid sunglasses block horizontally polarized light when worn normally. If you rotate the sunglasses by ninety degrees this light will be transmitted. By rotating the Polaroid sheet and noting where the maxima and minima occur, we are able to determine the polarization properties of light. This is essentially what the astronomer does at the telescope when he wishes to measure the polarization of an astronomical object.

Signals from the noisy sky

Before considering the variety of techniques used to detect the radiation collected by telescopes and analysed with spectrographs or polarimeters, we need to establish what we must do to detect radiation. Most astronomical objects are very faint; they are observed in the presence of a considerable amount of unwanted radiation, such as that from the night sky. When we set out to observe a celestial object it is convenient to think of the radiation as having two components. One is the radiation from the object itself; this is called the SIGNAL. The second component is the sum of the radiations from all the other sources, including spurious signals from the detector. This component is what we would detect if the object was not there at all, and is called the NOISE. The quality of any observation can be expressed in terms of the ratio of these two components, that is, the SIGNAL-TO-NOISE RATIO. In order to establish the quality of an observation we must determine the noise level present in the signal.

At any one instant the signal-to-noise ratio of an astronomical observation may be very poor indeed. However if we add up the signal as it comes in (integrate the signal), it builds up in direct proportion to the time, whereas the noise only builds up in proportion to the square-root of the time. This difference occurs because the noise is a sequence of random fluctuations whereas the signal is not. The effect of integrating a signal is, therefore, that the signal-to-noise ratio, and hence the quality of measurement, increases in proportion to the square-root of the time. Another way of improving a signal-to-noise ratio is to increase the bandwidth of the detector (the wavelength range across which the detector is sensitive). This lets through more signal and more noise; but the signal-to-noise ratio is improved by the square-root of the increase in relative bandwidth.

In the above we have assumed that the noise is independent of the signal. However, there are situations in which the noise level is determined primarily by a low signal level. This may happen at wavelengths shorter than 1 μm where detectors can be built which are able to register individual photons, so that the signal simply consists of a stream of photons. The arrival time of successive photons is entirely random. In a series of short identical exposures, the exact number of photons detected varies from exposure to exposure in a way governed by the laws of statistics. These tell us that if we have collected n photons on average, the number we will actually collect in any one exposure will be different from n by an amount $n^{\frac{1}{2}}$ on average. This uncertainty is equivalent to a noise contribution to the signal of $n^{\frac{1}{2}}$ and is known as PHOTON NOISE. This means that any observation which gathers n photons cannot have a signal-to-noise ratio better than $n^{\frac{1}{2}}$. In practice it can also happen that some of the photons detected are themselves not from the object but from other sources which count as noise. This will further reduce the overall signal-to-noise ratio of the observation.

Radiation detectors

The bewildering variety of devices used as radiation detectors could easily give the impression that this is a difficult subject, but this is not so. Electromagnetic radiation can only interact with charged particles. At wavelengths longer than those of X-rays the energy of a single photon is so small that only the lightest charged particles (*electrons*) are significantly affected by the passage of an electromagnetic wave. Consequently all of the radiation detectors discussed below have one essential function: to transfer some or all of the energy in a photon or electromagnetic wave to an electron in a special environment that allows us to detect such an excited electron.

Radio receivers

The basic form of radio-wave detector is the simple dipole or antenna. It consists of two vertical metal rods, one above the other, and a quarter of a wavelength long. If, in the vicinity of the dipole, there is an electromagnetic wave which has its electric field parallel to the length of the dipole then the field causes electrons in the metal rods to move. Although the rods are electrically neutral as a whole, this enforced migration of the electrons produces a small voltage difference between the ends of the rods. Because of this, a small voltage is generated across the terminals of the dipole. The voltage fluctuates in phase with the incident electromagnetic wave.

In practice the voltages generated with radio telescopes are very small ($\sim 0.1\,\mu V$) and the quality of the system is largely set by that of the amplifier connected to the terminals of the dipole rather than by the dipole itself. All amplifiers generate some noise within themselves. Radio astronomers strive to reduce this noise so that the overall signal-to-noise ratio of the system is maximized. In practice there are sometimes other sources of noise which limit performance. For example, at radio wavelengths exceeding 50 cm, background radiation from the Galaxy makes a significant contribution to the system noise level.

Simple dipoles are only sensitive to electromagnetic radiation with a component of their electric field parallel to the line of the rods. This means it is only sensitive to one plane of polarization. The dipole and amplifier combination is very similar to that used for television reception. The main difference is in their sensitivity to very weak signals. It is remarkable that the total amount of radio radiation collected by all the radio telescopes in the world from astronomical sources since the start of radio astronomy is about the same as the energy liberated if a small pin is dropped only one metre. This minute energy gives us some idea of the astonishing sensitivity of radio receivers.

Optical receivers

At optical wavelengths it is convenient to think of the radiation as consisting of a stream of photons. All optical detectors function by transferring some or all of the energy of an incident photon to one or more electrons. The excited electrons are then detected in a wide variety of ways.

A number of basic parameters characterize all detectors. The first is the sensitivity of the device as a function of wavelength (termed the SPECTRAL RESPONSE of the device). Associated with this is a measurement of the QUANTUM EFFICIENCY of the device. No device is totally efficient. Some photons may be reflected away from and others may pass through the device without absorption. In some devices the excited electrons may lose their energy before they are detected, while in others the detection procedure may itself be inefficient. Effects such as these reduce the detector efficiency; the quantum efficiency specifies the relative effectiveness of the detector.

All detectors suffer, to some extent, from what is variously known as FOG LEVEL (in photographs) or DARK CURRENT (with photocathode). This appears as a source of signal even when the detector is completely shielded from all external radiation. To understand this we must remember that the detector is relatively warm (it will normally be at room temperature) and this means that electrons in the detector will have an average energy appropriate to that temperature. When a photon is absorbed, an electron acquires extra energy from the photon. Sometimes, however, two electrons in the material collide so as to give much of their combined energy to one electron which will also be detected in the same way as an electron excited by only one photon. If a detector has appreciable infrared sensitivity, relatively small amounts of photon energy are needed to excite an electron. Therefore it is much more likely that excited electrons will be produced by the random motions within the substance of the detector. Consequently, infrared sensitivity and dark current go hand in hand. The dark current may be reduced by cooling the detector. This happens because the random energy of electrons in the detector material is reduced when the temperature is reduced. This in turn reduces the probability of an excited electron being generated within the detector itself, so reducing the dark current.

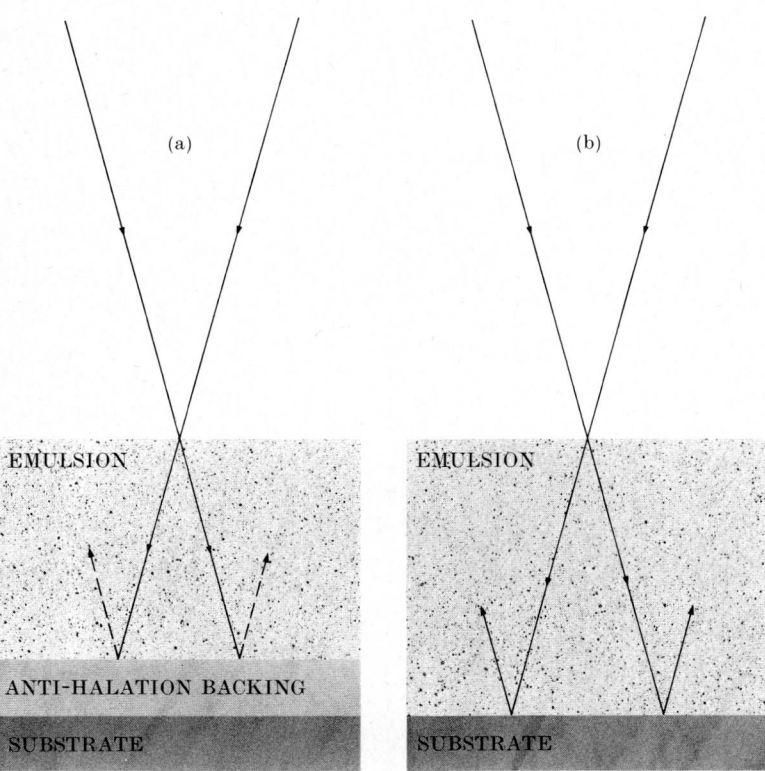

22.15: *A considerable amount of the light striking a photographic emulsion passes through the emulsion. Unless the substrate is coated with a layer which absorbs this light, it is reflected to produce a much more diffuse image. Most modern emulsions have these anti-halation backings.*

EMULSION

ANTI-HALATION BACKING

SUBSTRATE

(a)

EMULSION

SUBSTRATE

(b)

The photographic plate

The most frequently used light detector is still the PHOTOGRAPHIC PLATE. It is easy to get the incorrect impression that the advent of the many modern detectors described below has made the photographic plate obsolete. The quality and simplicity of use of the modern photographic plate ensures that it will be a long time before it is superseded.

The photographic materials used by astronomers are very similar to the black-and-white film used by amateur photographers. Generally astronomers prefer to use photographic plates, rather than film, because of their better resistance to distortion. The EMULSION consists of a large number of tiny GRAINS of silver bromide embedded in a layer of gelatin. This layer is coated very uniformly onto a glass or film base.

Photons incident on the emulsion are scattered by the grains. A few manage to penetrate individual grains, and there the photon gives up much of its energy to an electron inside the grain. The presence of the excited electron is chemically similar to a silver-bromide molecule being broken into silver and bromine atoms. This PHOTOCHEMICAL DISSOCIATION of silver bromide is amplified enormously by the process of development. Developing an emulsion makes the dissociation of the silver and the bromine permanent, so that we see the dark part of the image on a photographic plate. This is simply the dissociated silver. Since the unexposed emulsion is a milky-white colour it helps to remove undeveloped silver bromide molecules, as well as the dissociated bromine atoms, by FIXING the emulsion in, for example, a solution of thiosulphate. Once the plate is dried, the image is permanent and should last for very many years without fading.

Although all emulsions work in the way described above, modern emulsions include a number of features designed to improve the efficiency of the photographic process and the quality of the final image. It is found that grains absorb blue light more efficiently than red light. To improve the spectral response of the emulsion by enhancing the absorption of red light, the grains are coated in chemicals which allow red photons to pass into the grains more easily. This process is known as SENSITIZATION. Various kinds of sensitizations are used to make the emulsion especially responsive at a particular wavelength.

The absorption process is fairly inefficient – the quantum efficiency of a photographic emulsion is between 0.1 and 1 per cent. This is because many photons are scattered and not absorbed. Photons often pass through the emulsion; these are reflected by the surface of the glass plate. Figure 22.15 shows how this reflected light can cause the image to be much larger than it ought to be due to HALATION. To minimize this effect, it is usual to provide a special layer (the ANTI-HALATION BACKING), which absorbs those photons that pass through the emulsion.

In practice, at least two photons must be absorbed by a grain for it to be developable. During long exposures on faint objects (astronomical exposures can be as long as a few hours), there is often a considerable period of time between the absorption of the individual photons by one grain. It then becomes more likely that the first excited electron loses its energy before the second photon arrives to release a second electron. This means that the effect of the first absorption is lost, and clearly this reduces the efficiency of the process. Because of this, emulsions are specially treated to reduce the effect, which is known as RECIPROCITY FAILURE. The name comes from the fact that if the exposure time is doubled, less than twice the number of photons are recorded.

Modern photographic emulsions are very uniform and can be made large enough to allow the recording of images over considerable areas of sky. Plates as big as 35 cm square are used routinely in *Schmidt telescopes*. They are also comparatively cheap and simple to use, requiring very little ancillary equipment at the telescope. Their main disadvantages are associated with their poor sensitivity in comparison with modern electronic detectors. They also suffer from a non-linear variation of their blackening with exposure time.

One of the biggest problems associated with using photographic plates is that of turning them into usable data. Photographic work gives fine pictures which are easy to search for faint objects. They also give a valuable impression of the structure of extended objects such as nebulae and galaxies. However it is relatively difficult to get accurate quantitative data from photographic plates. We start by determining the CHARACTERISTIC CURVE of the emulsion, that is, the relationship between the blackening of the emulsion (or its DENSITY) and the amount of light falling on the emulsion. The plate is then scanned with a MICRODENSITOMETER, a machine which measures the density of the emulsion at a series of points. The measured densities are converted to the corresponding light-flux level and recorded for processing later. In practice, it can take many times longer than the exposure itself to reduce the data on a photographic plate with a microdensitometer. Some modern detectors, such as television cameras, are able to record the data directly, but they suffer from having a relatively small sensitive field size. For wide-field work we have no option but to use photographic plates.

Photoelectric detectors

There is a group of substances that will absorb photons and subsequently emit the electrons excited by them. These materials are said to be PHOTOEMISSIVE and they are used in PHOTOELECTRIC DETECTORS. The emitted electrons are called PHOTOELECTRONS. Materials such as caesium antimonide and gallium arsenide are good photoemitters and can have an efficiency as high as 40 per cent. Photoemissive detectors vary in the way that the photoelectrons are themselves detected and recorded.

In most detectors, the photoemissive substance is deposited as a very thin, semi-transparent layer onto glass. An electric field is applied to attract the photoelectrons away from the sensitive surface, which is known as the PHOTOCATHODE. Without this electric field drawing them away, the photoelectrons would eventually be reabsorbed by the photocathode.

One of the simpler photoelectric devices is the PHOTOMULTIPLIER.

It is impossible or difficult to detect single photoelectrons, and therefore in the photomultiplier it is arranged that the emitted electrons are accelerated to an electrode coated with an electron-emissive material. When the electron hits this material a burst of several SECONDARY ELECTRONS is produced. These electrons are themselves accelerated towards another electrode coated with the same material, so that an even larger burst of secondary electrons is produced in a cascade process. The photomultiplier consists of a series of these electrodes, and it gets its name from the way that the number of electrons in the stream is multiplied at each collision with an electrode. Eventually all the electrons are collected by an electrode called the ANODE. The output current at the anode is then a measure of the number of photoelectrons generated by the photocathode. The whole process from the emission of a photoelectron to the production of the output current takes place in a fraction of a microsecond. If the photons arrive at a rate less than a few million per second, it is possible to detect individual photoelectrons with very fast electronic circuits. In this way we may count individual photons from astronomical objects.

In the same way that glass lenses can focus light from an object to produce an image, it is possible to arrange electric and magnetic fields to produce electron images. We can arrange for all the photoelectrons emitted from any one spot on the photocathode to be accelerated and focused by electromagnetic lenses into another single spot where the electron image is to be formed. If they are focused onto a special material called a PHOSPHOR, a bright spot of light is emitted by the phosphor where the electrons strike. This happens in the same way as in a television tube where electrons are accelerated and focused to produce a bright spot when they hit the phosphor.

Devices known as IMAGE INTENSIFIERS makes use of this phenomenon (figure 22.16). With these, a two-dimensional picture is focused onto the photocathode. The emitted photoelectrons are then accelerated down the tube by an electric field produced by a series of ring electrodes. The electrons are also focused by the magnetic field provided by the focusing coil or SOLENOID. An electron image is formed at the output window, which is coated with a thin layer of phosphor that produces a bright visible image. Because the photoelectrons have been considerably accelerated, the output image can be 10–100 times brighter than the input image. The intensified image can be photographed. The overall efficiency for photons from the astronomical object is set mainly by the efficiency of the photocathode (10–40 per cent) and not by that of the photographic plate (0.1–1 per cent).

Photoconducting detectors

Materials such as silicon and germanium are known as SEMI-CONDUCTORS. The electrons in these materials are fairly tightly bound to the atoms of which they are composed. Because there are few free electrons in these materials, only a little current flows when an electric field is applied across a specimen of the material. However, photons have enough energy to free electrons from their bonds to the atoms of the material. The electrons so created enable an increased electric current to flow in the specimen. For this reason, these materials are called PHOTOCONDUCTORS and they are often used in a device called a PHOTODIODE. By monitoring the current flowing in a photodiode we can measure the intensity of the light that is falling on it. It is possible to construct one-dimensional arrays of photodiodes but the necessity of getting two wires to each photodiode makes it impossible to construct two-dimensional arrays sufficiently compact to have adequate resolution for astronomical applications.

A different approach is used for two-dimensional detectors. Rather than attempt to measure the continuous current flowing through each diode of the array, the number of electrons in each element is allowed to build up during the exposure. At the end of the exposure, the total charge on each diode is passed along from one diode to the next until it reaches the part of the array where the charge is actually measured. Devices of this type are called CHARGE-COUPLED DEVICES and have the advantage that they can be made by conventional integrated circuit manufacturing processes. This means that they are inexpensive. Photoconductors generally have a fairly good detective quantum efficiency – it can be as high as 75 per cent. However charge-coupled devices are less efficient than this because each time the charge packet is passed from diode to diode, some of it is lost or left behind. The charge-coupled devices are applied astronomically to record a two-dimensional image in place of a photographic plate. In this case, however, the image is recorded electronically rather than as the blackening of a photographic plate.

Television camera tubes also work in some cases by using photoconductors. One kind of device uses an array of silicon diodes (called the target), just like that of the charge-coupled device. With these, the charge is allowed to build up on the diode and the total current is established at the end of the exposure by scanning the array, element by element, until all the accumulated charges have been collected. The television camera tube produces a beam of electrons which can be pointed at any part of the target by means of magnetic coils surrounding the camera tube. The electron beam acts like a fine wire which is connected to the diodes at which it points. The current which flows in the electron beam is then a measure of the amount of light that has fallen on the target during the exposure.

22.16: *In an image intensifier, light is focused onto the photocathode which emits photoelectrons. High voltages are applied to the accelerating electrodes and an electric current through a solenoid produces a magnetic field which focuses the photoelectron beam onto a phosphor. The solenoid and the electrodes work together as an electron lens. The light generated by the phosphor is many times brighter than the incident light on the photocathode.*

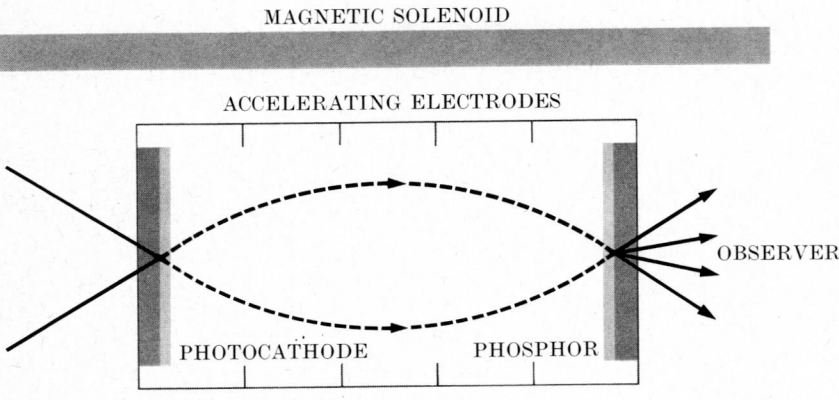

MAGNETIC SOLENOID

ACCELERATING ELECTRODES

OBSERVER

PHOTOCATHODE   PHOSPHOR

Gravitational-wave astronomy

When an electrical charge is accelerated in a straight line or moves around an arc of a circle, the charge radiates an electromagnetic wave. Similarly, when a massive object is accelerated general relativity predicts that it will radiate a GRAVITATIONAL WAVE. Although there is no celestial object we can point to as one that does produce strong gravitational radiation, there is reason to expect that strong gravitational-wave pulses might be produced by binary *neutron stars,* for example. In the hope that gravitational waves might exist and have hitherto gone undetected, a number of workers have built a variety of detectors designed to pick up the waves if they exist. Most are similar to the first one, built by J. Weber of Maryland, USA. Basically they consist of a very large cylinder (often of aluminium), which is squeezed by the incoming gravitational radiation. This causes it to ring like a bell, and sensitive vibration detectors (or PRESSURE TRANSDUCERS) pick up these exceedingly weak vibrations which are then recorded (figure 22.17).

A problem with this detector is that many spurious disturbances can affect the device. For example, earthquakes half the world away are easily detected by seismographs and seismometers and are also easily picked up by a gravitational-wave detector. Even road traffic vibrations can be significant in producing spurious signals. The most promising approach for eliminating 'local' disturbances is to use a number of detectors great distances apart. All pulses from each are recorded, and the recordings are then compared for events that are common to all the detectors. In this way, relatively local disturbances can be filtered out. Seismic disturbances travel much more slowly (sound speed) than gravitational waves (speed of light), so only genuine gravitational-wave disturbances should produce simultaneous signals at all the detectors. However, the extreme difficulty of making these measurements has meant that no gravitational wave or pulse has been unambiguously recorded.

22.17: *The gravitational-wave detector constructed by J. Weber of the University of Maryland, USA.*

Neutrino astronomy

The theory of stellar structure and evolution gives a fairly good account of the observed properties of stars. Part of the theory is concerned with the generation of nuclear energy inside stars, and it appears that during nuclear fusion processes a substantial flux of NEUTRINOS is produced. Neutrinos have no electrical charge and scarcely any interaction with matter. The Sun is thought to produce vast numbers of neutrinos at this moment ($\sim 10^{15}\,\mathrm{m^{-2}\,s^{-1}}$) and these are passing straight through you, this book and the entire Earth without being absorbed or deflected in any way.

One material which does have a weak but significant interaction with the neutrino flux is chlorine–37 ($^{37}\mathrm{Cl}$ an isotope of chlorine with an atomic mass of 37). The absorption of a neutrino by a chlorine–37 atom produces a single argon–37 ($^{37}\mathrm{A}$) atom. R. Davis, Jr. of the Brookhaven National Laboratory, USA, has constructed a vast tank, 6 m in diameter and nearly 15 m long which he fills with nearly 400 000 litres of perchloroethylene ($\mathrm{C_2Cl_4}$) a dry-cleaning fluid. This liquid contains a considerable quantity of chlorine, and Davis has developed equipment for flushing the tank regularly to look for newly-created argon atoms (figure 22.18). In order to ensure that other sources of radiation, such as cosmic rays, do not contribute to the number of argon atoms found, Davis has constructed his experiment at the bottom of the Homestake gold mine near the town of Lead, South Dakota, USA. The tank is about 1500 m underground.

Davis has found significantly fewer argon atoms than would have been expected from the theory, which implies that the details of the nuclear energy production mechanisms in the Sun are not as well understood as astronomers had believed.

22.18: *The large tank of perchloroethylene used to detect solar neutrinos at the bottom of a goldmine in South Dakota, USA.* (*Brookhaven National Laboratory, New York,* USA)

Astronomical coordinate systems

Time

It often happens that an astronomer needs to measure the precise position of an object in the sky. Accurate positions are required for many astronomical investigations. To determine *proper motions*, for example, positions measured over several months or years are needed. It is frequently necessary to compare the position of optically-visible objects with that of nearby radio sources.

All ground-based observations are made from the surface of the rotating Earth. Because of the rotation, the stars appear to move across the sky. It is clear therefore that the measurement of the position of an object requires an accurate record of the precise time at which the position is measured. Man has measured time since antiquity, and has frequently exploited the regular motion of celestial objects (especially the Sun and Moon) in this endeavour. Today several systems of measuring time are used in astronomy.

Although we cannot see the stars close to the Sun because of the bright sky, the apparent position of the Sun slowly moves so that after a year it returns to the same point in the sky relative to the background of stars. The TROPICAL YEAR is defined as the time taken by the Sun to return to its starting point with respect to the distant stars. This starting point is arbitrarily taken to be the *vernal equinox* (defined below). The tropical year gives rise to a system called EPHEMERIS TIME. One second of Ephemeris time is defined as 1/31556925.97474 of the tropical year 1900. The tropical year is 365.24220 mean solar days.

The need for Ephemeris time arose in the early part of the twentieth century, when it was realized by E.W. Brown in the United States and H. Spencer Jones in England that irregularities in the apparent motions of the Sun and Moon were due to the erratic rotation of the Earth. To free astronomical calculations from the vagaries of an irregular clock (Earth), Ephemeris time was introduced, with the second defined relative to the length of the year 1900. Ephemeris time and Greenwich Standard Time (universal time) differ by an amount (currently less than 60 seconds) that is derived by comparing the observed and computed positions of the Moon.

UNIVERSAL TIME is derived from atomic clocks, the fundamental physical standards. It is broadcast throughout the world by station MSF in England, and by station WWV in the USA.

The Sun does not move through the sky uniformly; it moves more rapidly through the background of stars when Earth is at *perihelion* that when it is at *aphelion*. For this reason the Sun is a poor indicator of time, although sundials served man well for millennia. The modern world needs a uniformly-moving fictitious sun, known as the MEAN SUN to regulate daily life; this imaginary sun moves along the equator at a constant rate, and it defines MEAN SOLAR TIME. The difference between mean solar time and APPARENT SOLAR TIME (sundial time) varies throughout the year and is given by the EQUATION OF TIME.

CIVIL TIME is based on the length of mean solar day. It is the same as universal time at Greenwich, England (0° longitude).

The fact that Earth orbits the Sun has an important consequence for the measurement of time. Because of the orbital motion it actually needs to turn slightly more than one complete revolution with respect to the distant stars in order to present the same face to the Sun. This means that the aspect of the stars will slowly change if they are viewed on successive days at a fixed time as registered by a normal (civil time) clock. As the astronomer is more concerned with the time it takes for the Earth to rotate once relative to the background of distant stars and not relative to the Sun, he finds it convenient to work in terms of a SIDEREAL DAY (23 hr 56 min 4.091 sec) rather than a solar day (figure 9.8). As a result of Earth's orbital motion, the sidereal day is about 4 minutes shorter than a solar day; the stars seem to rise about 4 minutes earlier each day as reckoned by civil time. In practice, the sidereal day is defined relative to the *vernal equinox*; since this point moves due to *precession*, a sidereal day is about 8.4 ms less than if it were defined with respect to a fixed point in space.

When long time intervals are involved, it is often more convenient to reckon time entirely in days rather than in terms of days, months and years. The number of days since noon (1200 hours Ephemeris time) of 1 January 4713 BC is called the Julian date. Note that there is no year 0; 1 BC is immediately followed by 1 AD. The Julian date of 1 January 1975 at midnight (the start of the new year) is 2442413.5.

Position

The accurate positions frequently needed in astronomy must be measured relative to a standard reference frame. To understand the coordinate systems used in astronomy, it is helpful to review first the familiar latitude-longitude system. It is convenient to measure positions on Earth in terms of LATITUDE and LONGITUDE. These two coordinates are determined relative to a standard reference frame or COORDINATE SYSTEM that, in this case, is based on the equator of the Earth as the PLANE OF REFERENCE (and the angular distance measured along the equator from the zero point of longitude). The zero point is defined as the longitude of the line perpendicular to the equator passing through Greenwich, England.

It is convenient to use a variety of astronomical coordinate systems depending on the class of object which is being observed. Because coordinate systems are intended to allow the positions of objects to be specified with very great accuracy, it is inevitable that their definitions appear to be pedantic. We will find it helpful to use the concept of a great circle. If we imagine any plane which passes through the centre of the Earth, then the line on the surface of the Earth which this plane makes is called a GREAT CIRCLE. If we now imagine this plane to extend out into space, the imaginary line it marks on the sky (or CELESTIAL SPHERE) is also a great circle. The celestial sphere is an imaginary spherical surface at a great distance from the Earth with the Earth at its centre.

The horizon system of coordinates

In this system the plane of reference is not the horizon but is a plane through the observing point parallel to the horizon. (If the observatory is at the top of a mountain, the horizon and the horizon plane defined here are different.) The line perpendicular to this plane, through the observer, passes through the POLES of the system (figure 22.19). They are called the ZENITH (the direction overhead) and the NADIR (the direction underneath), two words that recall Arabic work in astronomy. The great circle through the zenith and the object is called the OBJECT CIRCLE. The angle between the zenith and the object along the object circle is called the ZENITH ANGLE of the object. The angle from the horizon plane to the object circle is called the ALTITUDE or ELEVATION ANGLE of the object. The other coordinate is measured as the angle (measured from the north point towards the east) of the point where the object circle intersects the horizon plane. This coordinate is called the AZIMUTH of the object. Note that the coordinates of an astronomical object in this frame of reference change continuously as the Earth rotates on its axis.

This is why the equatorial coordinate system, described next, is much more commonly used. The horizon system is commonly used for telescopes that turn on horizontal and vertical axis (ALTAZIMUTH mounting) such as the largest steerable radio telescopes.

22.19: *The horizon coordinate system. Positions are referenced by a measurement of the altitude, or elevation angle, and azimuth.*

22.20: *The equatorial coordinate system. Positions are referenced by a measurement of the right ascension (distance along the equator in hours) and declination (angular distance from the equator).*

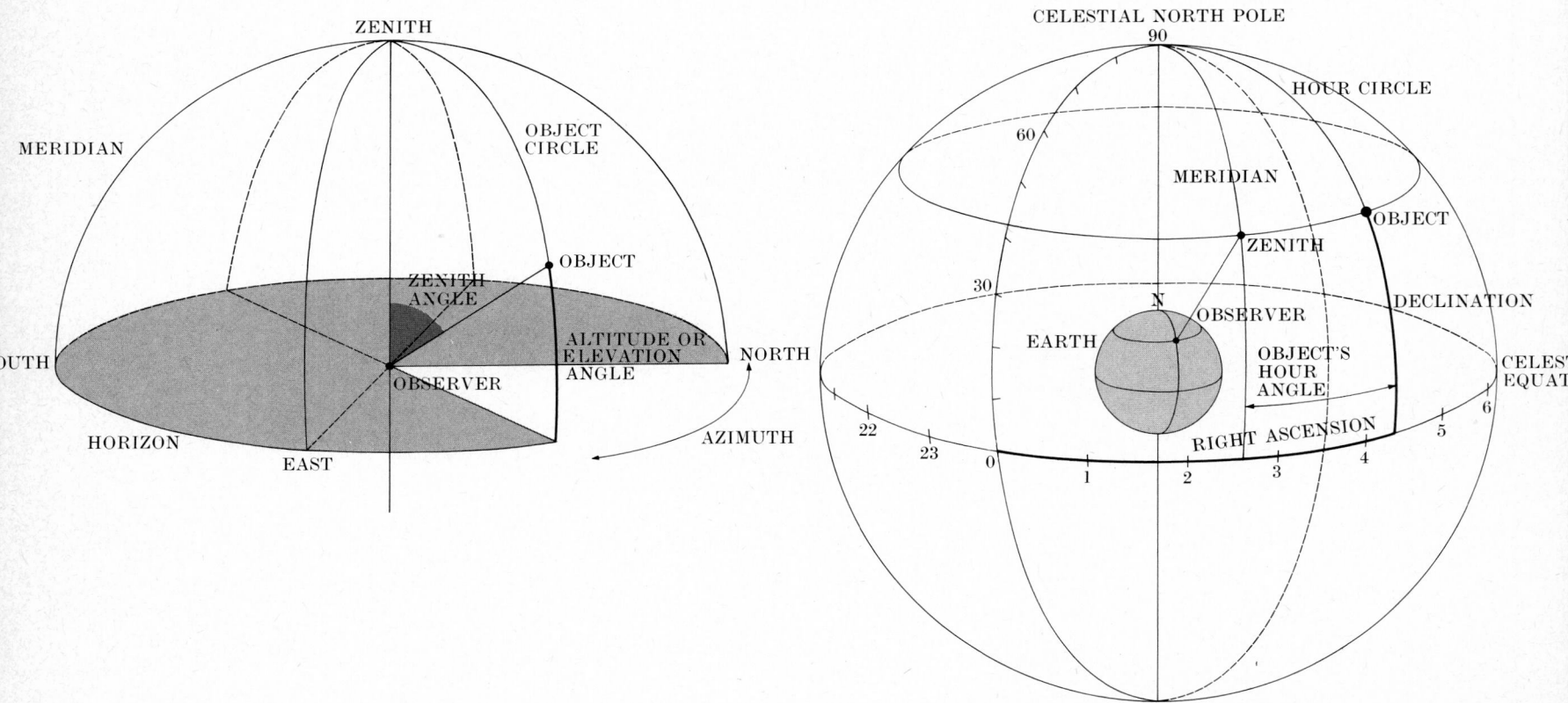

The equatorial coordinate system

The plane of reference of this system is the equator of the Earth and the poles are at the points where the rotation axis of the Earth cuts the celestial sphere (figure 22.20). The poles are called the NORTH AND SOUTH CELESTIAL POLES. The equatorial plane of the Earth cuts the celestial sphere at the CELESTIAL EQUATOR. The great circle that passes through the celestial poles and the zenith is called the MERIDIAN, and the great circle through the poles and the object is called the HOUR CIRCLE of the object. The hour circle and the meridian intersect the celestial equator at two points, the angle between which is called the HOUR ANGLE (HA) of the object. The celestial equator is divided not into degrees but into hours (24), minutes (60) and seconds (60). It is in these units that the hour angle is expressed. The angle between the intercept of the hour circle and the celestial equator, and a reference point (the vernal equinox) is called the RIGHT ASCENSION (RA) of the object. This is also measured in hours, and the direction is such that the right ascensions of objects crossing the meridian increase with time. This also means that if the hour angle of an object starts negative, it becomes zero when it crosses the meridian and thereafter is positive. The other coordinate in this system is the DECLINATION (Dec) of the object, measured in degrees. Declinations are positive when measured from the celestial equator along the hour circle towards the celestial north pole and negative when measured towards the celestial south pole.

The right ascension of the meridian is the same as the local *sidereal time* and it is partly for this reason that right ascension is expressed in time units rather than degrees.

The reference point from which right ascension is measured is the VERNAL EQUINOX. This is one of the two points at which the plane of the Earth's equator and the plane of the Earth's orbit round the Sun (the ecliptic) intersect. The Sun passes through the vernal equinox in the spring (about March 21), and through the opposite point (the autumnal equinox) in the autumn (about September 22). The points on the celestial equator at right ascension of 6 hr and 18 hr are the SUMMER AND WINTER SOLSTICES respectively. Because the equatorial system uses Earth's equator and pole, the system is in motion relative to distant stars because Earth's axis *precesses*. Consequently, the point at which the equator and the ecliptic cross slowly moves through the sky, taking about 26 000 years to make a full circuit. The vernal equinox is now in the constellation Pisces. Many years ago it was in Aries, and so it is sometimes called the first point of Aries.

Precession, nutation and aberration

The right ascension and declination are defined relative to the plane of the Earth's equator and to the vernal equinox. Unfortunately, neither of these is fixed in the sky because of precession. The Earth is not quite spherical but is slightly oblate. Because of this, the gravitational force between the Earth and the Sun produces a couple which causes the axis of rotation of the Earth to PRECESS. The Earth's rotation axis keeps a constant angle to the plane of the ecliptic (the plane of the Earth's orbit round the Sun), but the direction of the rotation axis slowly changes so that it completes one revolution in about 26,000 years. This makes it imperative that a measured position is recorded together with the date or EPOCH of the measurement. The epochs of 1900.0 and 1950.0 have been used extensively: 1950.0 refers to a position on 1 January 1950. The amounts by which right ascension (RA or α) and declination (Dec or δ) change are given approximately by

RA change $= 3.074 + 1.336 \sin \alpha \tan \delta$ seconds of time per year

Dec change $= 20.041 \cos \alpha$ arc seconds per year.

In addition to precession, there are small oscillations of the Earth's axis about its mean position. These are largely due to the influence of the Moon and planets on the orbit of the Earth. The principal component of this nodding motion, called NUTATION, causes objects to be displaced by a maximum of 9 arc seconds with a period of 18.6 years.

The motion of the Earth on its orbit causes small changes in the apparent position of an astronomical object. This change is known as STELLAR ABERRATION and causes a maximum shift of about 20 arc seconds when the direction of motion of the Earth is perpendicular to the direction to the object.

Galactic coordinates

Another coordinate system is sometimes preferred when astronomers are studying the structure of the Galaxy. This system uses the plane of the Galaxy as the reference plane and the centre of the Galaxy as the arbitrary reference point. The coordinates are both expressed in degrees. They are the GALACTIC LONGITUDE (l) and the GALATIC LATTITUDE (b). As the position of the centre of the Galaxy became better established, 'old' galactic coordinates (l^I, b^I) and, much later, 'new' galactic coordinates (l^{II}, b^{II}) came into use. However, only the new galactic coordinates are used now and the superscripts are usually omitted, giving (l, b). The galactic north pole is at right ascension 12 hr 49 min and declination $+27°.4$ (1950.0). Galactic longitude increases from 0° (towards the galactic centre) to 360° in the same direction as increasing right ascension. The galactic latitude is $+90°$ at the galactic north pole, zero on the galactic equator and $-90°$ at the galactic south pole.

The tools of the amateur astronomer

The night sky

Anyone with a keen interest in astronomy may want to acquire their own telescope. There is a large range of good telescopes on sale in most countries, with Europe and North America being particularly well supplied. The amateur astronomer can use a great variety of instruments and techniques, and even build an observatory to professional standards given the money and enthusiasm. In this section our aim is to answer a few of the basic questions on choosing and using an instrument.

The first thing to do before buying any instrument at all is to find your way around the night sky. It is not at all difficult to pick out a few of the brighter constellations and memorize them. The star charts in this book will enable you to recognize the more prominent patterns, and eventually the fainter constellations. If you live in the northern hemisphere learn to recognize Ursa Major (part of which is called the Big Dipper or the Plough), Cassiopeia, Ursa Minor, Cygnus, and Auriga. Southern observers have the glorious constellation Carina, as well as Crux Australis (the Southern Cross), Centaurus, and Scorpius. Orion, the splendid group on the equator, is visible in both hemispheres. Owing to Earth rotation and motion round the Sun, the night sky changes from hour to hour and season to season, so you cannot see all the constellations at one time. It is also useful to remember the names of some of the brighter stars, such as Arcturus, Sirius, Canopus, Betelgeuse and Vega. By identifying one or two constellations and stars each clear night you will soon become familiar with a great many of them; and they become much more interesting once you know where to find them all! A useful aid to elementary star recognition is a small map, not more than 25 cm in size, that can be used easily outside. A torch covered with red paper can be used to examine the map in the dark; without any filter most torches are so bright as to affect the adaptation of the human eye to the darkness of the night sky.

Once the main features of the night sky are well known, it is time to think about an instrument. It is important to appreciate that the very cheapest telescopes are little more than toys and are no good for amateur astronomy. True, they will show the Moon's craters, Jupiter's moons, and the crescent of Venus, after a fashion, but not much more. The cheapest instrument that the amateur astronomer should consider buying is a good pair of binoculars. As these are produced in much greater numbers than astronomical telescopes, economies of scale govern the production costs. Consequently a modest sum of money spent on good binoculars is much better value than a telescope at a similar price.

22.21: *Kitt Peak National Observatory, Arizona, USA is an excellent site, unless there is a thunderstorm! There are numerous telescopes two of which are operated by the University of Arizona. The 4-metre telescope is seen at the highest point of the mountain. Several of the photographs in this book were taken with the 4-metre Mayall Telescope.*
(Gary Ladd, Tucson, Arizona, USA*)*

Binoculars

Binoculars can be used for everyday observing, such as sporting events and nature study, as well as astronomy. They are classified according to their magnification and the diameter of the objective. A 10×50 pair magnifies 10 times (100 areas) and has objective lenses 50 mm in diameter; note, however, that in cheaper binoculars the objective may be stopped down internally in order to improve the sharpness of the image. This reduces the light-gathering power of the binoculars. Remember that larger magnifications give smaller fields of view. Internal reflections on the optical surfaces reduce the amount of light passing through binoculars. Better-quality instruments have bloomed (or coated) lenses, which help to reduce the light-loss. Some cheap instruments may have the outer surface of the objective ostentatiously coated, but this does not imply that all the lenses are bloomed.

Magnifications between 7 and 10 are most suited to celestial work. At higher magnifications it becomes very hard to observe because the unsteadiness of one's hands is magnified as well! For this reason the maximum aperture that is suitable is about 50 mm, because anything larger will be too heavy to hold steadily. Lenses smaller than 30 mm do not gather enough light for worthwhile astronomy. This brackets the range you should consider from 7×30 to 10×50. Of course, if you want to take up comet spotting, or other specialized work, larger binoculars will be needed, perhaps up to 20×80, requiring special mounts for effective use. Our concern here is to get you started for the minimum expenditure.

When choosing binoculars there are a few points to remember. Blooming of the lenses will show up as a blue-purple or yellow colour. Establish, if you can, whether the prisms are held in by adhesive. Prisms mounted in this way tend to come out of alignment relatively easily. A reputable dealer will be able to advise on this matter. Look down through the objectives for chips or blemishes in the lenses or prisms; if there are any defects at all, do not buy. See that all the moving parts function correctly, and assess whether they are robust. The next test is to hold the instrument in outstretched arms and look at the disc of light (exit pupil) visible in each eye-piece. It should be perfectly round and of even brightness. If the instrument passes this test look through it and check for distortion and aberration. In most countries of the world acceptable binoculars will cost you about 1.5 to 4 times the current cost of this book.

Having found suitable binoculars, what phenomena can be observed? First of all, it must be clearly understood that the Sun must not be viewed through binoculars under any circumstances whatever. Even when low on the horizon, and therefore deceptively harmless, it is a potential source of danger. The Moon is a splendid sight. The appearance of its surface changes through the lunar month as the angle of solar illumination alters. At full Moon, brilliant rays may be seen emerging from the brightest craters, although the craters themselves do not stand out sharply at this time, since the Sun is shining on them from overhead. At other phases (crescent, half, three-quarters) the mountains, valleys, and craters near the terminator – that is to say the boundary between the dark and bright sectors of the Moon – show up magnificently. When the Moon is at narrow-crescent phase, it is also possible to see some features on the dark part of the Moon, which is illuminated by reflected light (Earthshine) from Earth.

For planetary observations, binoculars will give a glimpse of the crescent phase of Venus. Mars and Saturn will show no details, although it is often evident that Saturn is more than a simple disc. Jupiter is the most rewarding object, since its four major satellites present an ever-changing aspect from month to month. They look like a set of stars, strung out in a line, in the neighbourhood of Jupiter.

When binoculars are turned onto the stars they will not, of course, resolve any of them into discs. But many observers claim that the colours are more evident for the brighter stars. Some binary pairs can be separated, such as Mizar in Ursa Major, Vega in Lyrae, and, in southern skies, β Tucanae, a superb binary consisting of two 4.5 magnitude stars. Binoculars can be used to great advantage to sweep star fields, because they have a wider field of view (typically $7°–9°$) than a telescope.

The Milky Way is staggeringly beautiful, and is resolved into the myriads of stars first glimpsed by Galileo; the richest star fields are in Sagittarius. Star clusters are also impressive under low power. Northern observers can see dozens of stars in the Pleiades, the Hyades (in Taurus) and Praesepe (Cancer). In the southern hemisphere, M23 (Sagittarius), M6 and M7 (Scorpius) will show a great number of stars. Besides these open clusters, some globular clusters can be found. In this case, southern skies have a decided advantage, being supplied with 47 Tucanae and ω Centauri, two globular clusters making a noble sight under low power.

Gaseous nebulae can be viewed with binoculars. Examples to try are the Orion nebula and 30 Doradus in the Large Magellanic Cloud. The spiral galaxy in Andromeda, M31, is an easy object that will show a soft oval outline, while the Magellanic Clouds are simple extragalactic targets in the south.

From these examples you can see that much can be achieved with good binoculars. A keen observer may consider graduating to a telescope proper. Here the choice is much wider and will be restricted mainly by your personal budget. However, a few general remarks will help you choose the telescope best suited to your interests.

Telescopes

The first decision must be: which type of telescope – reflector or refractor? The advantages and disadvantages can be summarized briefly as follows:

Newtonian reflectors produce images that are free of chromatic aberration (false colour). They are relatively cheap, and it is fairly easy to re-align the optical system. Among the disadvantages are the need to re-surface the mirror with an aluminium coating at regular intervals. In addition they are not so portable or convenient as the smallest aperture (60 mm) refractors. There is little point in considering a reflecting telescope for astronomical use that is smaller than 150 mm diameter, unless the optical components are of the highest quality. If you can afford a medium-priced reflector, then a Maksutov telescope or *Cassegrain* telescope could be considered. These may be harder to maintain if the best optical performance is to be obtained. With a Maksutov structure a compact instrument produces a wide, distortion-free field. Cassegrain telescopes have a short tube length but a long focal length. This permits larger magnifications without needing very short focal-length eye-pieces.

Refracting telescopes should have an aperture of at least 60 mm for attractive views, but 75 mm is the minimum you should consider if you want to do serious observational work. Good refractors often cost rather more than reflectors, because more optical surfaces have to be worked, but the 75-mm refractor is really an ideal beginner's instrument in terms of ease of use. Only simple adjustments to optical components are required, and the eyepieces are not elaborate. We have to offset these advantages against the fact that the tube is longer in the larger-aperture instruments, so heavy mountings are needed. In most practical cases, it is probably cost that will determine choice. However, there are 60-mm instruments which are somewhat cheaper than the cheapest 150-mm reflectors, and are capable of revealing Saturn's rings, the markings on Jupiter, and the brighter galaxies: they are well suited to casual observing.

Whatever telescope is purchased, it is essential to provide a sturdy mount for it. Ideally a permanent mount to which the telescope is clamped or bolted is required. Tripods, preferably of a heavy construction, may be suitable for the smaller instruments, but not if any heavy equipment, such as an electric drive is to be used. The heavier the mount the better, especially when there are slight winds about or inquisitive friends trying to view the wonders of the heavens! Quite frequently, it is better to make a permanent pillar or base to mount one's telescope than to use the tripod supplied by the manufacturer.

Once the telescope is attached to the mount, it should be free to move on two axes that intersect at right angles. The fitting that secures the telescope to its pier or tripod and permits this movement is called a HEAD. Two sorts of head are in widespread use: the altazimuth and the equatorial. An altazimuth mounting is the simpler, it has a long tradition of use for the mounting of terrestrial telescopes: the altitude axis is parallel to the horizontal plane, and the azimuth axis is vertical. It is not easy to undertake serious observing with this arrangement unless you have a special programme in mind, such as comet seeking, because the telescope must be moved along both axes simultaneously in order to compensate for Earth rotation and follow stars across the sky. The equatorial head is much preferable: one axis is parallel to the Earth's rotation axis, so that movement on this axis alone cancels the stellar motion. This type of head makes the telescope slightly more difficult to set up initially, but the advantages outweigh this minor detail. Furthermore, an equatorial head can incorporate engraved scales, known as setting circles, which permit one to set the instrument to a specific hour angle and declination, a considerable help when searching unfamiliar star fields. If celestial photography is intended an equatorial head is essential.

Your choice of telescope and its mounting should also be influenced by a realistic prediction of how much you think your interest will grow. For example, if astronomical photography is of potential interest, a drive, clockwork or electric, will be required at some stage. Therefore it will be essential to acquire an instrument to which a drive can be fitted later. If you are determined to observe faint variable stars or faint galaxies, a larger aperture (upwards of 250 mm) will probably be required.

On the larger refractors and all reflectors, a finder telescope is needed. This gives a wide-angle view of the field; the object of interest is then centred on cross-wires and will, in a correctly adjusted telescope, be in the field of view of the more powerful telescope.

If the telescope does not have a mechanical or electric drive, check to see that it has manual slow motion controls to compensate for the motion of sky. Without these an instrument is absolutely useless for more than a glance at celestial bodies.

When purchasing a telescope, you can seek the advice of reputable dealers, obtain the brochures of manufacturers, and consult your local astronomy club. All these sources of information should help you to narrow the choice.

Finally, it is worth mentioning that you can buy all the materials to grind your own mirrors and construct a home-made telescope. This can be a disheartening procedure for one who is not reasonably skilled at mechanical tasks, or prepared to spend some tens of hours on the grinding and polishing of the mirror. The mirror is made by grinding two circular glass blanks against each other until the correct concave curve is obtained. If you do have a work bench and like constructing things, then this project is worthy of consideration, but no beginner should tackle an instrument with a mirror larger than 200 mm (ideally try 150 mm first), and in any case specialist books on telescope making will have to be consulted. Really skilled, amateur telescope-makers will tackle apertures of up to 400 mm, but this is out of the question for a complete novice.

Observatories

Once the telescope has been acquired, it may well be necessary to construct a simple observatory or telescope housing. Telescopes are not elegant additions to domestic furnishings, and one with an aperture above 150 mm is likely to be awkward to manoeuvre. Local climatic conditions will to some extent dictate the type of observatory to be built. Almost any kind of weatherproof material (treated wood, aluminium, plastics, or fibreglass) may be used. The main consideration is to protect the instrument from damage when it is not in use, and yet allow easy access on clear nights. It is, incidentally, quite absurd to suppose that good observations can be made by pointing the telescope out of the window of a heated building, as local atmospheric turbulence will affect the image seriously.

An example of a simple and cheap observatory is the run-off shed. Such a shed is in two halves, both of which slide away from the instrument on a rail track. Another arrangement would be a rectangular shed with a flat roof that slides off, or hinges open; unless designed carefully, these can restrict the amount of sky that is accessible. Ambitious amateurs occasionally erect an observatory that is basically a miniature version of the professional domes. Constructing the hemispherical dome itself is not hard, given the extensive range of suitable man-made materials available, which make skilled woodworking unnecessary.

A good telescope brings many interesting and rewarding projects within range, but it is usually even more satisfying to undertake them in conjunction with other amateur astronomers. One way to get in contact with other observers is to join a local or national society. In certain areas of study, especially variable stars, the national societies are often well organized for collecting and sifting the data from amateurs, and publishing it in a form that is suitable for professional researchers. Other activities, such as observing particular planets in detail, can produce more comprehensive results if undertaken by a team. Joining a society will also put you in touch with people of experience and thus enable you to become a skilled practitioner more quickly. Contact with other astronomers either directly or through amateur journals provides an essential stream of new ideas, as well as details of interesting new developments in the night sky.

Once an astronomer is reasonably skilled, more speculative programmes can be considered. Examples of this are nova and comet seeking; nova outbursts and new comets are frequently discovered by amateurs; élite corps have found several of each in advance of the professional observatories. This type of work is demanding, but suits people who want to achieve a degree of recognition for their skills. There has not been a supernova visible in the Milky Way since the invention of the telescope. When the next one does occur, the chances are that a dedicated amateur will spot it first.

23. Astronomy in space

23.1: *Drawing of the US Space Telescope, planned for launch into a near-Earth orbit from the Space Shuttle (in background) in about 1985. The 2.4-m Cassegrain mirror will reflect light up to the secondary mirror on the supports visible just inside the tube, and from there down through the centre of the primary mirror to the detector package beyond. Power is drawn from the solar paddles. (NASA, USA)*

Introduction

The science of space astronomy is relatively young, and yet it has given astronomers some of the most exciting findings about our own Solar System and the high-energy Universe beyond. Were it not for the development of a camera that could be operated across 200 million km of interplanetary space we would know hardly anything about the surfaces of planets such as Mercury and Mars. Remote landers have even scratched at the soil of Mars in a fruitless search for life, for some shred of evidence pointing to man's own evolution from the cosmos. After millennia of romance and mythology the Moon finally yielded to the scientific method. The Queen of the Night was reduced to a laboratory specimen after the most fantastic voyage in the whole of human history. The US Apollo exploration program has returned to Earth 380 kg of lunar material for analysis. So far 20 kg has been looked at, and even describing that has filled 30 000 pages of the scientific literature. Within our Galaxy there are many objects that emit infrared and X-radiation, but this cannot reach the ground because our atmosphere is strongly absorbent. Hence high-energy astronomy has to be carried out above the atmosphere, in space. In this chapter we describe in general terms the aims and methods of space astronomy. The scientific achievements are presented in context in the relevant chapters, and this chapter is therefore mainly concerned with hardware, experimental methods, and techniques. There are no detailed discussions of individual missions because these become dated very rapidly, whereas the general principles do not evolve so quickly.

The atmosphere of Earth is a serious impediment to ground-based astronomy. Its absorptive and reflective properties limit satisfactory observing to two wavelength windows: the radio range (including the millimetre region) and optical range (and near infrared). Inhomogeneities in our atmosphere blur the images of cosmic objects and prevent large optical telescopes from imaging as sharply as might otherwise be possible. The gravitational field at the Earth's surface restricts the precision with which instruments can be pointed and moved. The daily rotation of the Earth forces observations of all but the polar regions of the sky to occur at the periodic intervals when the object is above the local horizon. Even in very dark sites, residual atmospheric glow limits sensitivity, and, of course, optical observers can study little apart from the Sun in the daytime. Finally, one of the most devastating effects is that of the weather, particularly for optical observing.

Some of these effects can be overcome. Observatories are built in the best sites, high up and free from contamination by domestic noise (lights, traffic and machinery). *Speckle interferometry* and similar techniques can improve the spatial resolution of optical telescopes to the extent that the discs of a few nearby giant stars are revealed. Computers can take account of the flexure of telescope mounts and instrumentation to some degree. Nothing we can do on the Earth's surface, however, will permit us to receive cosmic X-radiation directly.

This high-energy part of the spectrum is only accessible to us by going above the atmosphere. As many of the chapters in this book reveal, the invisible wavebands are not merely superficial additions to optical astronomy. They actually permit us to see completely new objects and phenomena, the existence of which would have been otherwise unsuspected. If we are to obtain a full understanding of our cosmic environment, we must fully explore the complete spectrum of radiations produced in the Universe.

Space astronomy requires detectors and telescopes to be placed above our atmosphere, where the instruments can search deep space and test cosmological theories, or look back at Earth and allow us to inspect it for what it is: a planet in orbit about a star. We can now make direct studies of other celestial bodies: the Moon, planets, solar wind and planetary magnetospheres, as well as probing parts of interstellar space. All of the planets of the inner Solar System have now been visited and had their soil analysed, or have at least been scrutinized by orbiting spacecraft. Men have driven vehicles on the Moon and there performed tasks similar to those of Earth-bound geologists. Much of this explosion in our knowledge and activities is due to technological progress. The scientific principles of space flight date back to the early years of this century, and from there back to Newton. More romantic ideas of space flight even pre-date that.

The advantages of performing astronomical observations and experiments in space are many, but perhaps the greatest disadvantage is the expense. Even a small satellite carrying, say, 50 kg of scientific experiments costs tens of millions of dollars to manufacture and place in orbit, even though the actual material out of which the satellite or its payload is composed need not be particularly expensive. The design, construction, test, launch, data handling and analysis of such instruments involves much organization and careful work over periods of many years. Even then, satellites have occasionally failed to achieve their desired orbits – some even becoming geostationary on the sea bed! From the development of rockets in the Second World War to present-day space activities, the major thrust to the research and development of spacecraft has come from so-called defence programmes. It is doubtful whether more than a handful of satellites would have been launched by now if it had not been for the enormous quantities of money invested in military projects. For astronomical purposes, though, we now have rocket engines available capable of putting people on the Moon and spacecraft out to Jupiter. This last point is important, for Jupiter is the key to the rest of the Solar System, as far as space travel is concerned.

The United States government, for example, proposes to build and fly the *Space Shuttle*, capable of putting scientists into orbit for weeks or months. These missions are important to astronomers mostly for their relative cheapness, payload-carrying capabilities and their frequency. Furthermore, satellites can be serviced in orbit, thereby prolonging their active lives. This is of note, for most space equipment, left unattended, will either undergo degradation, or fail completely owing to some electrical or mechanical malfunction, after a few years.

23.2: *Launch of the British Skylark sounding rocket from Woomera, South Australia in 1971, carrying detectors to study the cosmic X-ray background. The solid fuel boost and main motors project the payload to an altitude of about 200 km some four minutes after launch. The payload and main motor fall back to Earth, impacting after about a further ten minutes.*

Early space astronomers relied heavily upon SOUNDING ROCKETS (figure 23.2) developed from the V2 rocket in World War II. Small payloads could be exposed to the space environment above most of the atmosphere before plunging back to Earth. Studies carried out in this way revealed the major features of the upper atmosphere and *ionosphere*, and discovered short-wavelength radiation from the Sun. Space astronomy was changed dramatically at the end of the 1950s by the launching of satellites orbiting the Earth and beyond (USSR Sputnik I, 1957; US Explorer I, 1958). This gave way to the numerous space probes that have since explored the Solar System. Series of satellites carrying astronomical experiments, such as the US *Orbiting Solar Observatories* (OSO), *Orbiting Astronomical Observatories* (OAO), *Small Astronomical Satellites* (SAS), the UK *Ariel satellites*, some of the USSR *Cosmos* series and others have opened up the new wavebands only accessible from space. Sounding rockets are still in use, since they are relatively inexpensive. Indeed, the sum total of exposure time to the X-ray sky (excluding the Sun) by detectors world wide from 1962 to late-1970 was only a few hours. *Balloons* are also used to lift instruments to altitudes of 40 km or more, which allows valuable measurements to be made in the infrared, optical, hard X-ray and gamma-ray parts of the electromagnetic spectrum. Flight times of a week or more can sometimes be achieved from transatlantic balloon flights. Certain infrared wavebands can be usefully explored by telescopes carried on high-flying aircraft.

The future of space astronomy depends to a large extent on continued funding by goverments and probably on international cooperation. The United States, for example, have launch vehicles, such as the Titan-Centaur system, capable of putting spacecraft anywhere in the Solar System. The time taken to reach the outer Solar System is, of course, many years, but such remote regions are in principle accessible using the gravitational pull from Jupiter or Saturn. Large Earth-orbiting payloads can be lofted, carrying several square metres of short-wavelength detectors and associated electronics. Programmes proposed for the near future involve the use of reusable launchers, such as the *Space Shuttle*, implying a relatively high degree of space activities. One of the most important proposals is that of the *Space Telescope*: a large diffraction-limited telescope capable of operation over the entire spectrum from the submillimetre infrared down to 90 nm. Such an instrument would have diffraction-limited resolution, approximately 100 times the ultimate sensitivity of ground-based instruments and a lifetime of 15 years or more. The successful launch of the Space Telescope will transform astronomy because it is capable of working down to 29 magnitude. Space-borne instruments will supply many of the expected new results over the next few decades, and hopefully some unexpected results.

Space travel and the space environment

The orbit of an artificial satellite about the Earth, or any other body, can be treated mathematically in exactly the same way as the motion of binary stars, or the planets. The orbit is an ellipse obeying *Kepler's laws*. The period of a satellite grazing the Earth's surface (if it were possible) is 84.3 minutes, and that of a satellite in a 500-km circular orbit is 94.6 minutes. The energy required to put an object from the ground into such an orbit is at least 30 million joules per kilogram; far more is actually expended by the rocket motors on atmospheric drag and so forth. At 500-km altitude, the orbital velocity is 7.73 km s^{-1}, about 0.4 km s^{-1} of which can be obtained from the rotational velocity of the Earth if the satellite is launched in an easterly direction from a site in the tropics. The orbit is then DIRECT or PROGRADE.

The orbit would remain fixed in space with the Earth rotating uniformly under it if there were no perturbing forces acting on the satellite. If the orbit is inclined to the equator however, the bulge of the Earth causes the *nodes* (points where the orbit crosses the equatorial plane) to regress, in a westerly direction for a direct orbit. Under certain conditions, such as an inclination of 80° and altitude of about 1100 km, the period taken for one complete regression cycle is one year. Consequently, it is possible to place a satellite into a near-Earth orbit where it would remain continuously in sunlight. If the orbit is eccentric then the LINE OF APSIDES (joining *perigee* and *apogee*: the points on the orbit nearest and furthest from the Earth, respectively) will rotate completely in several hundreds of orbits. Other perturbing forces are due to drag from the residual atmosphere (which is largely responsible for the finite lifetime of the orbits of near-Earth satellites), solar radiation pressure, magnetic torques from the Earth's magnetic field and the gravitational influences of the Sun and Moon.

At least two impulses must be delivered to a satellite to place it into a suitable orbit that does not intersect with the ground. The first impulse, usually applied in a vertical direction, places the object into a repetitive elliptical orbit with the Earth's centre at one focus. The second impulse, perhaps in a horizontal direction at apogee, is of such a magnitude as to match the requirements of the desired final orbit. In general, the impulses are delivered over periods of several minutes by rocket engines, but the principle is much the same.

Rocket engines operate on the reaction produced when gas escapes through a hole from an otherwise closed container. An untied balloon which is released flies about because of this effect. The force on the motor itself is due to the rate of change of momentum of the gas. This THRUST is just the mass-loss rate of gas multiplied by the gas velocity. The product of a force and the time for which it acts is known as its IMPULSE, and clearly the larger the impulse, the larger will be its effect on the final velocity of the rocket. A useful concept for rocket propellants is that of the SPECIFIC IMPULSE, which is the total impulse on the rocket produced per unit mass of propellant consumed. It is equal to the exhaust velocity of the gases from the rocket engine when operated in a vacuum. Typical specific impulses from chemical propellants lie in the range of $1–5\,km\,s^{-1}$. In order that the rocket may leave the ground, the thrust exerted by its motors must exceed the weight of the rocket and all its fuel. From our definition of thrust, and the above range of exhaust velocities, we see that the launch of a 1000-tonne weight rocket requires a fuel consumption of at least several tonnes per second. If the thrust only just overcomes the weight, as is usually the case, then the rocket acceleration is initially small. This prevents damage to payload components as well as minimizing air drag, which is proportional to the square of the velocity and to the air density.

The final rocket velocity depends upon the MASS RATIO of initial to final rocket mass. This mass ratio exceeds unity because of the amount of propellent consumed and redundant fuel tanks ejected. Owing to the more continuous thrust operating in a rocket, as compared with the firing of a gun, the actual value of the final velocity is given by the product of the exhaust velocity and the natural logarithm of mass ratio. The mass ratio must thus exceed 2.718 if the final velocity is to exceed the exhaust velocity, which as we have outlined, is between 1 and $5\,km\,s^{-1}$. Final velocities of $7\,km\,s^{-1}$ and above are required for Earth launch of satellites and probes; hence a large mass ratio and enormous rockets are necessary. Lift-off from the Moon into lunar orbit requires a final velocity of $2–3\,km\,s^{-1}$; this is achievable with a high specific impulse and low mass ratio such as used in the Apollo lunar excursion module.

The specific impulse of a propellant is roughly equal to the speed of sound in the gas produced. This depends upon the square root of the ratio of gas temperature to mean molecular weight: high temperatures and low molecular weights are therefore necessary. Chemical rockets derive heat from combustion of the propellant, which may be hydrogen or kerosene as a fuel and oxidizer. Liquid propellants (hydrogen and oxygen would be stored as liquids) are the most useful for large rockets, but solid fuel rockets are still in common use. Usually, both a fuel and oxidizer are carried separately and mixed before combining, but some substances such as HYDRAZINE (N_2H_4) decompose in the presence of a catalyst to produce hot gases without combustion. The type of propellant chosen depends upon the conditions applying; solid-fuel motors are often used as boosters, liquid propellants for main engines, and hydrazine for mid-course manoeuvres owing to its ease of storage. Higher specific impulse values are obtained by increasing the exhaust velocity. Monatomic hydrogen recombining to form molecular hydrogen could yield specific impulses of $15\,000\,m\,s^{-1}$, but means have yet to be devised for storing such material. Nuclear reactors could, for example, be used to heat hydrogen to very high temperatures, or charged particles can be electrostatically accelerated in so-called ION MOTORS. The ultimate is the PHOTON ROCKET, the exhaust velocity of which is the speed of light. The energy requirements for such a device are prohibitive at the present. Solar radiation pressure may eventually be used to sail between the planets, but in the following discussion we restrict ourselves to simple ballistic trajec-

tories produced by relatively brief impulses. It is unlikely that anything other than chemical rockets will be used for Earth launches in the near future.

The general technique for sending space probes out to the Moon and planets relies on injection of the probe into a suitable trajectory from an Earth orbit. The magnitude and direction of the impulse are chosen such that the probe follows an elliptical orbit that intersects with that of the desired planet. The timing (LAUNCH WINDOW) is chosen so that the planet and probe arrive simultaneously at the intersection of their orbits. Least energy is required if the probe's orbit is an ellipse of perihelion and aphelion distances equal to the radii of the Earth and planet's orbits. This is the HOHMANN TRANSFER ELLIPSE (figure 23.3) which takes approximately 145 days from Earth to Venus, and 260 days to Mars. Shortening these times by any significant extent enormously increases the energy requirements, and hence size of launch vehicle. Time is not usually the critical quantity in interplanetary missions, and they are usually optimized for maximum payload weight.

A further impulse must be applied to a space probe if it is required to orbit the planet. Such an impulse is usually produced by rocket motors, but a gravitational interaction with a planetary moon (if it has any) may suffice. This may be a very useful technique for orbiters of Jupiter or the other giant planets with relatively massive moons. The spacecraft orbit can be changed by a gravitational encounter with a massive body, even though it need not actually contact the surface – which would produce a dramatic change! Gravitational encounters with the giant planets themselves, or Venus, have been used to fling spacecraft on out to Saturn and beyond, and in to Mercury. Similar perturbations do, of course, change the orbits of comets. The extra energy is taken from the orbital angular momentum of the planet, which is changed by an infinitesimal amount. This technique of GRAVITY ASSIST is the key to extended exploration of the Solar System from quite modest launch vehicles. It is, for example, possible to use an encounter with Jupiter to fling a spacecraft into the Sun or perhaps more usefully into a near approach of a few solar radii. This is not yet possible by directly launching a spacecraft at the Sun, for it would have to lose the $30\,km\,s^{-1}$ orbital velocity of the Earth about the Sun. Present launchers for planetary missions can take probes directly only to Venus, Mars and Jupiter. Such celestial billiards can be used to send spacecraft from one planet to another. As might be expected, the launch windows are short, and the chance to visit most of the outer planets (including Pluto) in one mission starting about 1979 is going to be missed. The occasion will not recur for more than one hundred years, although several separate missions can perform this task at later dates. The end of the century may see spacecraft making repeated and never-ending close approaches within the Jovian satellite system, and Jupiter-flung probes exploring fast-moving comets as they swing near the Sun.

Spacecraft have to be most carefully constructed to withstand the rigours of space. The effects of high vacuum are considerable, although now well known. Any gases absorbed into surfaces leak out, causing movable joints to stick and problems with electronic components. The continual bombardment by cosmic radiation, in number over 10 times more intense (and far more so in the *radiation belts*) than at the Earth's surface, gradually destroys electronic systems, and provides a steady unwelcome background to photon-counting devices. Micrometeoroid dust adheres to surfaces. Temperature control is not trivial and is combatted by the gold-plated foil and painted chequer patterns common on spacecraft. Power may be generated by solar cells, or by radio-isotope generators for missions to the outer planets. Astronomical experiments require some form of stabilization and altitude sensing. The launch itself imposes considerable constraints on spacecraft volume as well as mass, and vibration and stress forces may destroy delicate components designed for a future weightless environment. Data usually has to be returned to Earth, and this necessitates some form of communication system with aerials which may require Earth-pointing. The design is usually the result of trade-offs between scientific payload and necessary spacecraft structure, weight, volume and power requirements.

23.3: *Representation of Pioneer 11's encounter with Jupiter. After receiving an initial impulse in Earth orbit, Pioneer 11 followed an elliptical Keplerian orbit out to Jupiter. The gravitational encounter there then flung the spacecraft back through the Solar System on another Keplerian orbit to intersect with Saturn. The elliptical paths chosen reduce the amount of energy needed to get the probe to Jupiter. Important information was obtained when the satellite passed behind the planet and transmitted radio waves through Jupiter's atmosphere.*

23.4: *The USSR Lunokhod 2 photographed on Earth before being placed on the surface of the Moon in 1973. This automatic vehicle weighed nearly one tonne on Earth and was operated by remote control for several months on the lunar surface. The black rectangular holes house the television cameras, powered by the solar panels revealed when the top hinges back. (Novosti Press Agency, UK)*

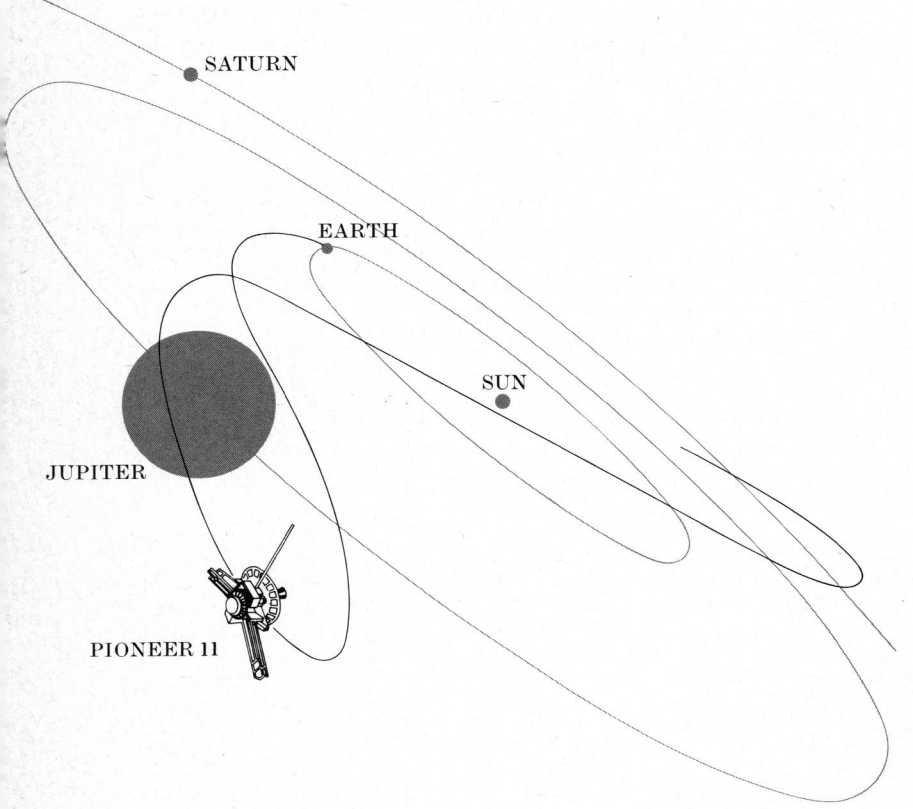

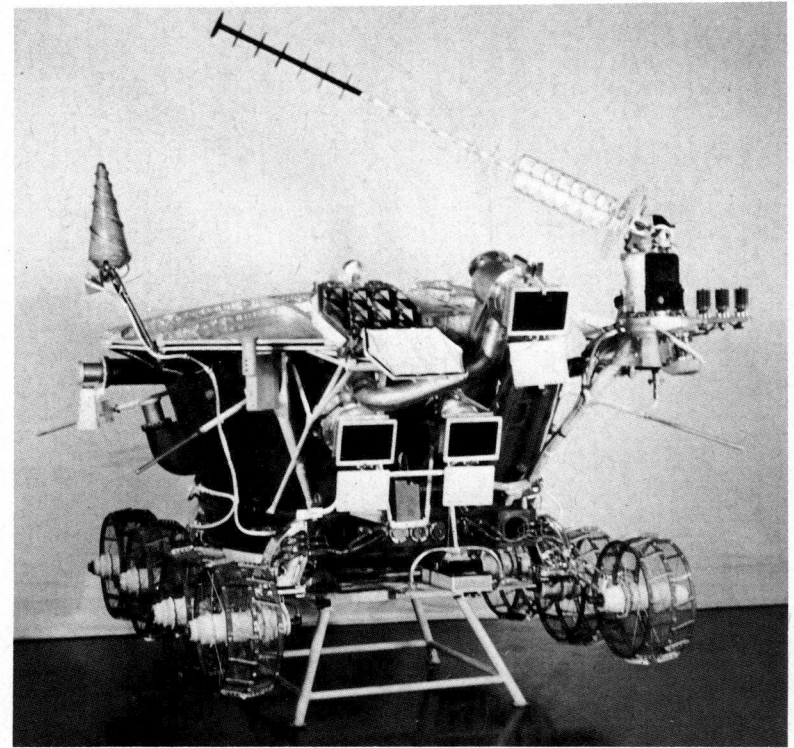

Exploring the Solar System

The results of many of the space missions to the Moon and planets have already been detailed in the chapters on the Solar System. In the present section we outline some of the methods by which these results were obtained. The pattern of study of a planet by subsequent spacecraft generally parallels that applied to the Moon. Initial fly-by missions send back photographs of much higher resolution than obtainable from Earth. Apart from their obvious scientific value, such pictures are also of cultural value, being the results most easily appreciated from such a mission.

Accurate tracking of the spacecraft, usually relying on *Doppler shifts* of narrow-band radio beams retransmitted back to Earth, give its detailed orbit. This usually improves our knowledge of the planet itself and paves the way for orbital missions. Occultation of the spacecraft, due to the planet passing between it and the Earth, is useful in obtaining data on the atmosphere of the planet. The atmosphere acts like a radio lens, deflecting and altering the velocity of the radio beam. Thus, in the few seconds during which the spacecraft enters and exits from occultation, its path inferred from the Doppler tracking appears to waver by a few metres or so (figure 23.3). The precise nature of the changes gives a measure of the refractive index of the atmosphere and thus its mean molecular density. Complete density profiles can be built up, at least above layers which do not severely absorb the radio waves, and from these, relationships between atmospheric pressures and temperatures can be deduced. Independent knowledge of the molecular constitution of the atmosphere allows the pressure and temperature to be separated.

Devices for measuring magnetic fields (magnetometers) and charged particles can reveal details of any planetary magnetosphere. Instruments scanning the planet at selected infrared wavelengths can deduce, for example, the water or carbon dioxide content of the atmosphere and the surface temperature, perhaps down to a fraction of a degree.

The next stage of instrumentation used in the exploration of the planet is usually an orbiter, finally followed by a landing system or, in the case of Jupiter or Saturn, atmospheric probes. ORBITERS are usually designed to take adequate maps for landing craft, which often means a surface resolution of tens of metres or less. This may decide the dimension of the imaging system, which is probably similar to a television camera, having an optical system and vidicon screen. One picture may be composed of about one million picture elements (PIXELS), each of which are coded according to the degree of light or shade. This totals about 10 million bits (binary digits) per picture, which must be temporarily stored on board, for the telemetry bit rate may only be one quarter of a million bits per minute. Repeated occultations allow density profiles of the atmosphere to be constructed for a variety of diurnal and seasonal conditions. Infrared and ultraviolet spectroscopy reveal the nature of cloud cover, and enable some details of the surface composition and temperature etc. to be carefully mapped. Accurate tracking of the spacecraft permits a detailed gravitational model for the planet to be built up. This yields the overall mass distributions within the planet itself.

Landing craft have to be built specifically for each planet, or moon, taking into consideration the atmospheric density and surface conditions. Close-up television pictures may be obtained, as well as the analysis of soil samples. *Seismometers* monitor the internal creaking of the planet and stray meteor hits. Rocket boosters can be deliberately impacted onto the surface, as was done on the Moon, in order to provide valuable seismic information. The atmospheric composition may be measured on the descent, as well as at the landing site, by mass spectrometers. Soil samples can be analysed by the powerful technique of X-ray fluorescence.

The Moon is the only celestial body yet visited by man, and is likely to remain so for a considerable time to come. Automatic roving vehicles, such as implemented by the USSR on the Moon (LUNOKHOD, figure 23.4) are a more realistic means of obtaining samples from extended regions on distant planets. The Lunokhods were controlled by television from Earth, a method which will prove impracticable over the 8 to 46-minute time delay to Mars. Such rovers will need to be sophisticated enough to make their own decisions – by computer of course. It is possible to launch craft to Mars, for example, which can land and then return soil samples to Earth. To simplify the mission and reduce weight, the final package of only a few kilograms may well return to Earth orbit, to await retrieval by the *Space Shuttle*.

Notable planetary spacecraft of the late-1970s included the PIONEER and MARINER series of the US and the VENERA (figure 10.19) and MARS series of the USSR. The Pioneer spacecraft were designed to take approximately 30 kg of scientific payload on extended missions, such as to the outer planets. Stabilization is provided by spinning the whole craft, and solar power may be supplemented by radio-isotope generators. The Mariner series carry about 70 kg of scientific payload and the spacecraft are stablized by gas jets.

An outstanding achievement in 1976 was the safe landing of two Viking craft on Mars. These provided close-up photographs of the rocks on Mars and analysed the soil for traces of life.

Telescopes in space

We have already emphasized, in the introduction to this chapter, the great value of launching telescopes into space. This section concentrates on the infrared, optical and ultraviolet wavebands. It is unlikely that radio telescopes will be placed in orbit in the near future, owing to the enormous size necessary for reasonable angular resolution, but several designs have been proposed which make full use of the weightless environment. Spacecraft carrying radio detectors (other than those necessary for spacecraft performance) may also serve as links in *very-long-baseline interferometers*, or can be designed to explore very long wavelengths.

Early attempts to overcome the atmospheric limit to optical spatial resolution included balloon-borne telescopes. The STRATO-SCOPE missions carried a 90-cm telescope and associated television camera to a height of 20 km. The resolution was degraded to about 0.5 arc second, from the theoretical diffraction limit of 0.1 arc second owing to the convection of residual atmosphere in the tele-scope tube. Several flights were failures. The *Orbiting Astronomical Observatories* were initially conceived in the 1950s and several successful launches have been made. OAO-2 launched in 1968 carried equipment to survey the ultraviolet sky from about 100 to 300 nm. This follows the general pattern for opening new wave-bands: surveys followed by more detailed studies.

OAO-3, renamed COPERNICUS after launch in August 1972, is a good example of precision instrumentation actually in action. The major experiment consisted of a ultraviolet telescope spectro-meter of 80 cm clear aperture. The spectrometer entrance slit is at the *Cassegrain focus* and the spectrometer itself and a fine guidance assembly, (generating signals to maintain spacecraft pointing directions), are situated in front of the primary mirror, partially obscuring it. Two movable carriages containing photo-tubes can be programmed to scan the spectrum from about 71 to 328 nm with a resolution of at best about 0.5 nm. Such a system is ideal for probing the interstellar medium along the line of sight to hot stars, and since it operates in the ultraviolet it can, for example, detect interstellar molecular hydrogen absorption lines. Commands to, and data from, the spacecraft are transmitted when it passes over one of the satellite ground stations, such as the one maintained at Quito in Ecuador. Gas jets and gyroscopes can swing the space-craft around to any selected target. Pointing on that target can then be maintained to better than a tenth of an arc second if the fine guidance system in the telescope is locked onto a bright star. A small package of X-ray telescopes and detectors is also included on Copernicus. Many X-ray sources are not bright enough in the optical or ultraviolet wavebands to operate the fine guidance system. In that case, a bright nearby star would be observed and then the instrument rotated in the required direction to align precisely the X-ray telescopes on the required object. Spacecraft technology is at present capable of producing inertial platforms that point with milliarcsecond accuracy or less, which is much less than the image size on even the most ambitious space telescopes yet proposed.

Infrared observations can be made from the Earth's surface through a number of poor windows at scattered wavelengths. Balloon and aircraft-borne telescopes have extended the range of results, but telescopes have been limited so far to about 2 m diameter, and the residual atmosphere has still severely hampered observations. The rewards of infrared astronomy are enormous; the investigation of star formation, molecular lines, galactic nuclei, the planets and so on. A major difficulty in developing satellite instrumentation is the necessity to cool at least the detectors and possibly the telescope itself. An active refrigeration scheme would use a lot of power, and a more passive approach using liquid helium would limit satellite operations to a relatively short lifetime. Never-theless, survey-type satellites have been proposed, and a large infrared telescope has been proposed as an instrument for some Space Shuttle flights.

The SPACE SHUTTLE is a reusable transportation system designed to carry scientific and application payloads routinely to and from low Earth orbit during and after the early 1980s (figure 23.6). The shuttle can put free-flying spacecraft into orbit, possibly using an additional module called the TUG, to inject these into higher orbits. It can also retrieve and refurbish other satellites already in orbit, and it can take a laboratory, such as the proposed European SPACELAB into low Earth orbit for a period of a week to a month. Spacelab need not entirely fill the space within the shuttle, which would then be available for other instrumentation, perhaps astro-nomical. A 3-m diameter infrared telescope with liquid helium-cooled detectors could be carried on such a mission, yielding vast quantities of important data from even one week's operation.

Perhaps the most significant astronomical instrument so far proposed for a shuttle launch is the US SPACE TELESCOPE (ST) (figure 23.1). This is intended to contain a 2.4 m Cassegrain tele-scope injected into orbit from the Space Shuttle in about 1985. Its design lifetime is at least 15 years; regular maintenance and per-haps retrieval back to Earth for brief periods by the crew of the Shuttle make this realizable. The angular resolution of such a tele-scope would be better than 0.1 arc second. This is in the optical band, although it is designed to operate from 91.2 nm to about 1 mm, thereby spanning ultraviolet, optical and infrared wave-bands. The telescope could be pointed at any desired target with an accuracy of 0.03 arc second and stabilized on that target to 0.005 arc second. The implications for resolving planets round other stars, *binary star systems, astrometry* and extending all the fundamental reference scales are enormous. The focal plane will probably con-tain several detectors on a turret arranged so that any one can be commanded into the observing position. Suggested instrumenta-tion includes cameras, photometers and spectrographs, to cover the different spectral ranges.

The Space Telescope will be able to detect optically objects over 100 times fainter than those detectable on Earth, that is, objects down to magnitude 29. A space telescope similar to that described here would have the capability of detecting extended objects of low surface brightness. This would have a significant impact on our knowledge of the outer parts of galaxies, as well as revealing nebulae and clouds located within our own Galaxy. The giant radio-emitting lobes on either side of most *radio galaxies* may in fact emit more energy in optical wavebands than in the radio. This has been detected by careful ground-based studies, being but a few per cent of the night-sky background. Optical emission at this level would become a relatively easy target for a space telescope.

The use of an occulting disc, similar to that in a *coronagraph*, may reveal planetary systems in orbit about neighbouring stars. Scattering in the Earth's atmosphere renders such a task completely fruitless from the ground. Studies of our own outer planets would allow Uranus, for example, to be resolved to about the same degree as the Pioneer spacecraft photographs of Jupiter. Complete spectra, from the infrared through to the ultraviolet, of a wide range of stars and galaxies will be invaluable for stellar evolution and cosmology.

Other telescope systems can be devised such as very wide-field (60° or so) cameras, deep-sky telescopes and so on that can perform complimentary tasks to a telescope similar to that outlined above. The instrumentation would be similar to that used and designed for ground-based telescopes, excepting that modifications may need to be made to compensate for the space environment and a long unattended life.

23.5: *The European satellite COS-B launched in 1975 to study cosmic gamma radiation of energies 20 MeV to 2 GeV. Gamma rays produce electron-positron pairs in the spark chamber (2) which then create flashes in the scintillators (3 and 4). Cosmic rays are eliminated because they also create flashes in the anti-coincidence scintillators (1) which are transparent to gamma rays. (European Space Agency)*

23.6: *The US Space Shuttle depicted with a scientist operating a proposed ultraviolet telescope. The Space Shuttle should be performing missions on a regular basis in the 1980s. (NASA and Boller & Chivens Division, Perkin-Elmer Corporation, USA)*

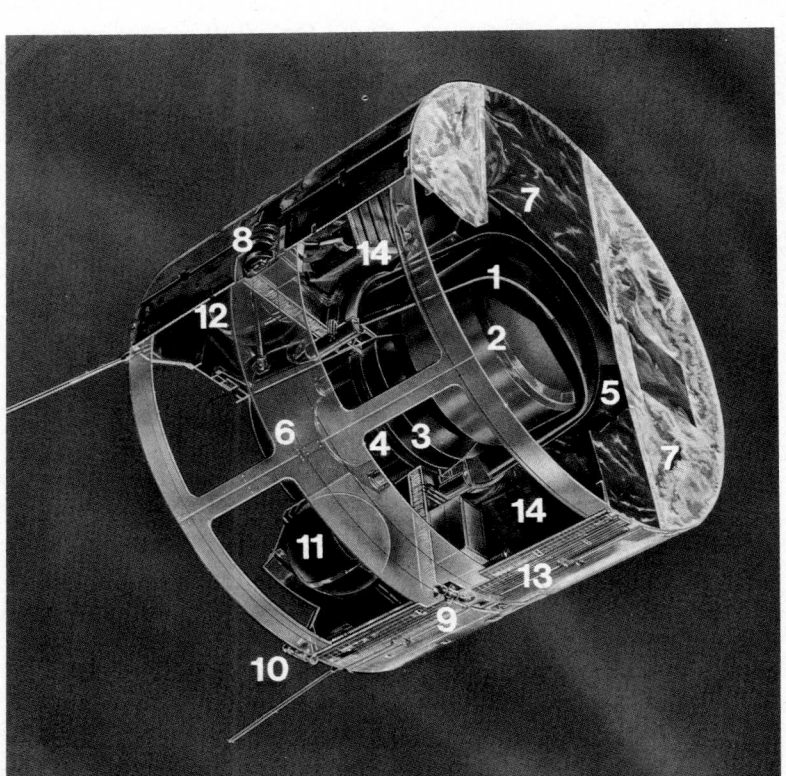

High-energy astronomy

We now discuss the techniques and instruments used by astronomers observing at wavelengths shortward of 91.2 nm. Temperatures in excess of 10^5 K, or non-thermal mechanisms, are required if significant emission is to occur at these wavelengths, and thus we may consider ourselves dealing with high-energy astronomy. Extreme ultraviolet $(100 - 10$ nm$)$, soft X-ray $(10 - 1$ nm$)$, X-ray $(1 - 0.01$ nm$)$, soft gamma-ray $(0.01 - 0.001$ nm$)$ and gamma-ray (below 0.001 nm) radiations can only be directly detected from above the bulk of our atmosphere. High-energy radiations are completely absorbed by even a small depth of air, and indeed it is this ionizing effect of the solar extreme ultraviolet and X-radiation that creates the *ionosphere* around the Earth. A few parsecs of interstellar hydrogen are opaque at wavelengths just shortward of 91.2 nm and so observations even from above the atmosphere are fairly hopeless. The absorption is roughly proportional to the third power of the wavelength, and thus reasonable distances $(\sim 100$ pc$)$ may be probed at wavelengths of 10^2 nm. Even shorter wavelength X-rays and gamma rays can penetrate through most of the Universe unimpeded.

The Sun was the first celestial object detected by its short wavelength radiation, by exposure of a suitably filtered photographic plate on a US-launched V2 rocket in 1947. The first cosmic X-ray source, *Scorpius X-1*, was discovered during a flight intended to detect fluorescent X-rays from the Moon in 1962. Fluorescent X-rays produced from solar X-rays interacting with lunar material were detected from several Apollo command modules when orbiting the Moon, but they are still undetectable from Earth. The *Crab Nebula pulsar* has been observed at all wavelengths up to 10^{-5} nm.

It is convenient in high-energy astronomy to speak in terms of photon energies, and we henceforth use electronvolts (eV) as a measure of these energies. One kiloelectron volt (keV) is equivalent to 1.24 nm, and the photon-energy scales inversely with wavelength. Cosmic X-radiation is thus typically observed between 0.1 and 100 keV, and gamma rays above 100 keV.

To understand the mechanism of detectors of high-energy radiation we must first consider the interaction of such radiation with matter. High-energy photons have sufficient energy to ionize atoms, and thus an important absorption process is that due to *photoelectric ionization*. On encountering an atom, the photon can be absorbed by ejection of an electron, often from the inner shells of the atom. Another electron rapidly fills in the gap left by the ejected electron and fluorescent radiation is emitted. In lighter elements, another electron (Auger electron) can be ejected as the atom de-excites itself, and no fluorescent radiation need be emitted. The net effect is either two electrons, or one electron and a photon, the total energies of which equal that of the initial photon. Photoelectric interactions are most effective at low photon energies and in high atomic weight materials. The photons may also scatter off the electrons in the material, giving them energy by the *Compton effect*. At high energies this is a more important energy loss than photoelectric absorption. If the photon energy exceeds twice that of the rest-mass energy of an electron, electron-positron *pair production* can dominate (in the presence of nuclei). In all these processes, the energy of the incoming photon is converted to kinetic energy of electrons or electrons plus photons (which may themselves be further absorbed).

The fast moving primary electrons (or positrons) produced by the photon-matter interaction can then be detected by means familiar to high-energy physicists in their studies of nuclear particles and *cosmic rays*. The electrons stream through matter leaving a characteristic trail of ionization in their wake. This might further be detected by the light then emitted or by electrostatic means. In both cases the material may be either a solid, liquid or gas, but a solid or gas is preferred for space applications. The capability of any detector to detect radiation in the required range will depend upon how effective it is in stopping the photon. Solids are of course most effective, but lower energy X-rays are stopped very close to their surfaces. This is only useful in SOLID-STATE DETECTORS, which are made out of semi-conductors such as germanium or silicon and are unlikely to be very large. In most other solids, the primary electrons produced by an incoming low-energy photon produce so few ions in being stopped that the capability of determining the incoming photon energy is severely degraded. A primary electron in a gas, on the other hand, produces many ions and the statistical variations in the number of ions finally produced (after the primary electron has created secondary electrons and so on until the individual electron energies are insufficient for further ionization) is proportional to the energy of the incident photon. The scatter in that number then determines the energy resolution of the detector.

Gas-filled detectors are most widely used in X-ray astronomy. The efficiency at high-photon energies is determined by the gas depth, and at low energies by the thickness of the window needed to retain the gas. Such windows are commonly made of thin sheets of organic plastics (perhaps 1 μm or so in thickness). A continuous supply of gas may be required to compensate for that which diffuses through this window. The ionization produced in the chamber is detected by an electric field, usually applied between the body of the chamber, and a thin conducting anode running down the centre. The electric field then rapidly increases close to the anode, and electrons attracted there gain sufficient kinetic energy to produce further ionization. This results in amplification of the initial number of electrons. The ions are swept back out to the chamber walls thereby creating a detectable electronic signal. If the voltage applied is in a certain range, the resulting electrical impulse is directly proportional in amplitude to the initial photon energy, provided that no fluorescent radiation escaped. An ionization chamber operated in this manner is known as a PROPORTIONAL COUNTER. At higher voltages, immediate electrical breakdown occurs whenever a particle ionizes the gas, and the device becomes a GEIGER COUNTER. A proportional counter has an energy resolution 20 per cent of that of a typical X-ray photon, but Geiger counters have no such capability. Resistive anodes, which may be constructed as flat plates, together with some sophisticated electronic circuitry may be used to determine the position at which the incoming photon produced the ionization. This is of great value if placed at the focus of an X-ray telescope.

Inorganic SCINTILLATION COUNTERS rely on detection of the light released when secondary electrons are captured by impurities in the crystals. Materials such as sodium iodide doped with a suitable impurity may be employed. The crystal must be transparent to the light flashes produced, which usually occurs in the visible wavelength; they are detected by conventional photo tubes. Gamma rays may be suitably studied by systems using Compton interactions and high-energy gamma rays can be detected by SPARK CHAMBERS, such as carried on the European satellite COS-B (figure 23.5). Here the photon is energetic enough to interact in a thin lead sheet producing fast electrons which then pass through several parallel layers of thin, electrically charged, conducting plates. The resulting ionization in the intervening gas causes breakdown between these plates. Ionization tracks can then be observed by the light or sound produced, or by electronic means if the plates are composed of fine wire meshes.

The number of cosmic photons incident on any satellite-sized detectors at energies exceeding a few hundred MeV is exceedingly small, and may be as low as a few per day. All known celestial bodies emit fewer and fewer photons as the energy increases. This might mean that the prospects for detecting photons of energies 1GeV and higher is small. However, it then becomes possible to use the atmosphere itself as the detector. The high-energy photons produce very energetic particles at the top of the atmosphere. These move at nearly the speed of light through the air and emit *Cerenkov* radiation in a cone about their direction of motion. This radiation is detectable on the ground. A light collector with a field of view of, say, 5° can view a region 3 km square of the atmosphere at a height of 30 km. Significant results have been derived from such methods.

23.7: *(a) Uhuru, the first satellite devoted to cosmic X-ray astronomy, was launched in 1970 and operated for four years. One of the most successful astronomical satellites, Uhuru was used to discover binary X-ray sources and the extended X-ray emission from clusters of galaxies. The grids on the main body of the satellite are the collimators for the proportional counters used as X-ray detectors in the 2–20 ke V range. The three tubes above these are the star and Sun sensors yielding aspect information. Power was derived from the four paddles covered with solar cells. The first six months' data from Uhuru were used to compile the Third Uhuru Catalogue of some 170 X-ray sources, shown (b) in galactic coordinates. Only about thirty such sources were previously known. (American Science and Engineering, USA)*

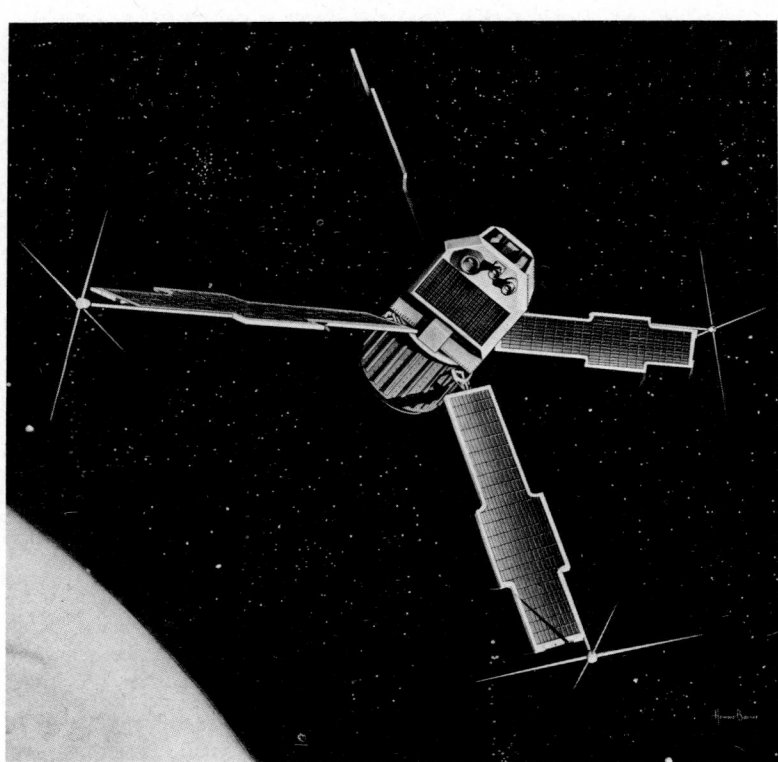

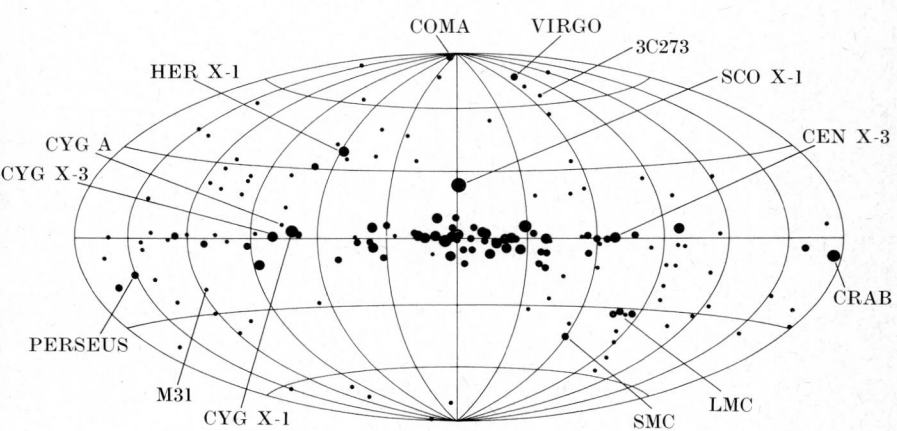

Having discussed the detection of high-energy X-radiation, we must investigate the means for COLLIMATING this radiation. By this we mean a device capable of restricting the field of view of the detector, or better still, forming an image. Simple X-ray proportional counters may make use of thin slats of material placed in front of the window. These MECHANICAL COLLIMATORS can be constructed to give a field of view down to fractions of a degree, but become massive and unwieldy, especially at higher energies, if finer resolution is required over a large detector. The X-ray satellite UHURU made use of such collimators (figure 23.7). MODULATION COLLIMATORS code the spatial information present in the incoming photon directions into a pattern that varies with time. Two wire grids, one above the other may either be rotated at a steady rate (figure 23.7) or oscillated in separation. The moiré fringes formed by these grids will vary regularly and regions in the sky will be alternately visible and then invisible according to a known pattern. This pattern depends upon the source position and becomes impressed in the count rate from a cosmic X-ray source. The data can then be searched for such patterns. Determination of track positions in Compton telescopes or spark chambers yields source positions to a precision of a degree or less.

Conventional imaging telescopes are useless at X-ray or gamma-ray wavelengths owing to the ease with which these radiations are absorbed. Total internal reflection can, however, allow X-ray telescopes to be constructed for use up to a few keV. The refractive index of X-rays in materials is less than unity, and thus X-radiation incident on a metallic surface is totally internally reflected if the angle of incidence exceeds the critical angle (typically 87° or more). Such reflection is referred to as glancing angle or GRAZING-INCI-DENCE REFLECTION. Grazing-incidence telescopes can be constructed to give an image if two reflecting elements are used in any of three standard ways. The paraboloidal elements are essentially made of the outer rim of a very deep ordinary paraboloidal mirror such as might be used in optical astronomy. The centre part is useless owing to the grazing incidence requirement. The total effective collection area is small compared with the total aperture, but nesting of several telescopes inside each other can increase this factor. The reflecting elements may also be assembled in a slat-like manner. Images from grazing-incidence telescopes enable astronomers to map the X-ray sky up to wavelengths of a few keV. Beyond that, collimation systems must be used. FRESNEL ZONE PLATES, making use of the properties of diffraction through masks of alternately opaque and transparent material can be used in the formation of images, but their application is limited by their extremely small size. Only the Sun produces a sufficient quantity of photons to make their use worthwhile.

Grazing-incidence telescopes have been used to observe the Sun from Skylab (figure 8.10) and three small non-imaging X-ray telescopes were carried on *Copernicus* and several later satellites. The second US High-Energy Astronomical Observatory (HEAO-B), will probably carry four nested telescopes with a maximum diameter of 55 cm. The total effective area of these telescopes varies according to the energy of the incident X-rays but is on average several hundred square centimetres below 1keV. The angular resolution of such a telescope would be limited by diffraction to less than a milliarcsecond, but of course this cannot be achieved. Scattering from the surface of the mirrors will limit the resolution to a few arc seconds. The focal length of the telescope will be about 3.4 m. Detectors are thus required to be capable of resolving X-rays incident less than one thirtieth of a millimetre apart. Micro-channel plates producing electron cascades on impact by photons will achieve such resolution. A position-sensitive proportional counter will give one arc minute resolution over a field one degree square.

Spectroscopy of X- and gamma-ray sources is of interest, since atomic lines are expected to occur in the range up to 10 keV or so, and nuclear lines may occur up to a few MeV. Crude spectral resolution is achieved from proportional counters, scintillation detectors and spark chambers. This has been sufficient to resolve a few atomic lines, but much finer resolution is desirable. Diffraction of an X-ray beam by a regularly-spaced array of scattering elements will suffice, and transmission gratings have been constructed with 100 lines per millimetre. The atoms of a crystal also satisfy our requirements. Constructive reflection from the surface of a crystal occurs at specific angles for certain energy ranges. CRYSTAL SPECTROMETERS have been produced and operated on this principle. A major drawback of this sort of spectrometry is its low efficiency. Crystal reflection is polarization dependent and this is made use of in the design of X-RAY POLARIMETERS. Little can be done to improve the resolution of detectors beyond 10 keV or so, and the results rest mostly on the inherent capabilities of the applicable detectors.

With the conclusion of the program to place man on the Moon, the thrust of space astronomy may have appeared to lose direction slightly. This is not true however. Plans are clearly laid down for the continuation of astronomy in space for many years to come. International cooperation is enabling the necessary funding to be raised. What will happen after the Space Telescope? That instrument will definitely find new types of cosmic object – it can scarcely fail since it will see so much more than Earth-based instruments. The long-term aim must be to get a large observatory working as a permanent station on the Moon, probably on the far side. The advantages of such an observatory are so great that it will surely be constructed eventually, probably by many nations pooling their resources.

Star atlas

This star atlas displays the stars visible to the naked eye in both northern and southern hemispheres. Each star is indicated by an eight-point star, and the size of the star symbol is directly proportional to the perceived brightness of the real star in the sky. Also marked on the maps are the boundary of the Milky Way, and the positions of the brighter galaxies and nebulae. The latter will generally only show up in binoculars or a small telescope; the number in the Messier or NGC catalogue is indicated by the numerals next to the symbol. In addition to the static heavenly bodies are marked the coordinate lines of right ascension and declination, certain other imaginary lines such as the ecliptic, and the constellation boundaries approved by the International Astronomical Union.

The star charts on the following pages were produced at the University of Cambridge on an IBM 370/165 computer using a computer tape of the Smithsonian Astrophysical Observatory star atlas. All the information in the SAO atlas and catalog is held on magnetic tape and is therefore easily available for computer processing. Firstly the computer examined the tape and selected only stars brighter than 6.1 magnitude and within the boundary of a particular map. Next the axes of the map were drawn on a graph plotter controlled by the computer. Finally star positions were converted to coordinates on the graph plotter and accurately plotted out. This is, of course, far more accurate than a hand-drawn map could be. For the equatorial charts the computations took just over one minute and the plotting took about 15 minutes for each chart.

The best series of sky charts for many years has been the photographic sky survey made with the Palomar Schmidt telescope. This was made in the 1950s; partly for this reason astronomers have adopted 1950 January 1 as a standard date for the reduction of all astronomical data. The stars on the maps in our Star Atlas have been transformed by the computer for the equinox and epoch of the year 1950. In practice the difference is imperceptible for naked eye observations. The magnitudes of individual stars are represented by a formula which ensures a continuous increase in size of image from the faintest to the brightest star. A key is given on each map in steps of half a magnitude although the individual images are correct to at least one-tenth of a magnitude. The projection used is one that ensures that the angles on the sky are not distorted, this being the most useful compromise for observational astronomers.

If you have not used star maps before some practice will be needed. Although many books give formulae for working out which stars will be on the meridian at any time, it is usually easier for beginners to find the major constellations (Ursa Major, Cassiopeia, Orion, Centaurus, Crux, for example) visible from their latitude and then find their way around using these major reference constellations.

On the six equatorial maps the right ascension is marked in hours along the upper and lower boundary. You can work out which chart is giving the stars on your local meridian in the following simple way. (1) Work out how many whole months have elapsed since September 23, and multiply by 2; (2) work out how many whole days have elapsed since the 23rd of the last month, and multiply by 4. The quantity in (1) gives a number of hours, while that from (2) gives a number of minutes. Add these hours and minutes to Greenwich Mean Time (you need to know the relation between your time zone and Greenwich to do this) at the time you want to observe. Subtract 24 hours if the resultant time exceeds 24 hours. The resulting quantity is approximately your sidereal time. Round it to the nearest number of whole hours and look for the map with that right ascension. The polar projections fill in the high declination parts of the celestial sphere. If you live in the southern hemisphere you will have to hold the equatorial maps upside-down with respect to the orientation of the writing on them in order to get a reasonable representation of the sky.

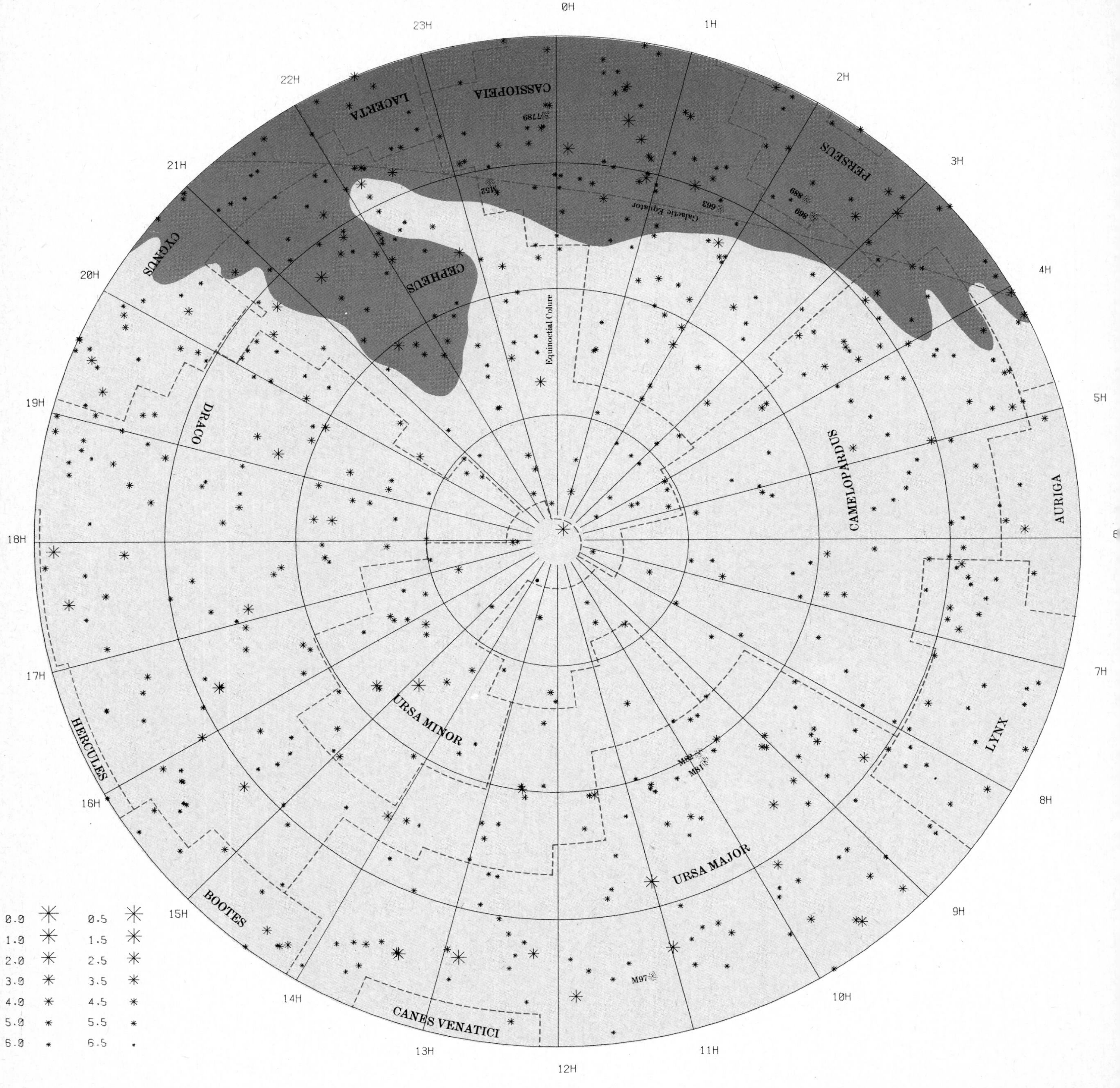

0H

23H   1H

22H   2H

21H   3H

20H   4H

CYGNUS   PERSEUS
                                        5H
19H   DRACO   CAMELOPARDUS
                                            6H
                  CEPHEUS
18H   AURIGA

                    Equinoctial Colure
17H   7H
HERCULES   URSA MINOR   LYNX
16H   8H

            URSA MAJOR
15H   9H
BOOTES
14H   10H
      CANES VENATICI

13H   11H

12H

LACERTA
CASSIOPEIA

M52

603
889
869

M81
M51

M97

Galactic Equator

0.0	✳	0.5	✳
1.0	✳	1.5	✳
2.0	✳	2.5	✳
3.0	✳	3.5	✳
4.0	✳	4.5	*
5.0	*	5.5	*
6.0	.	6.5	.

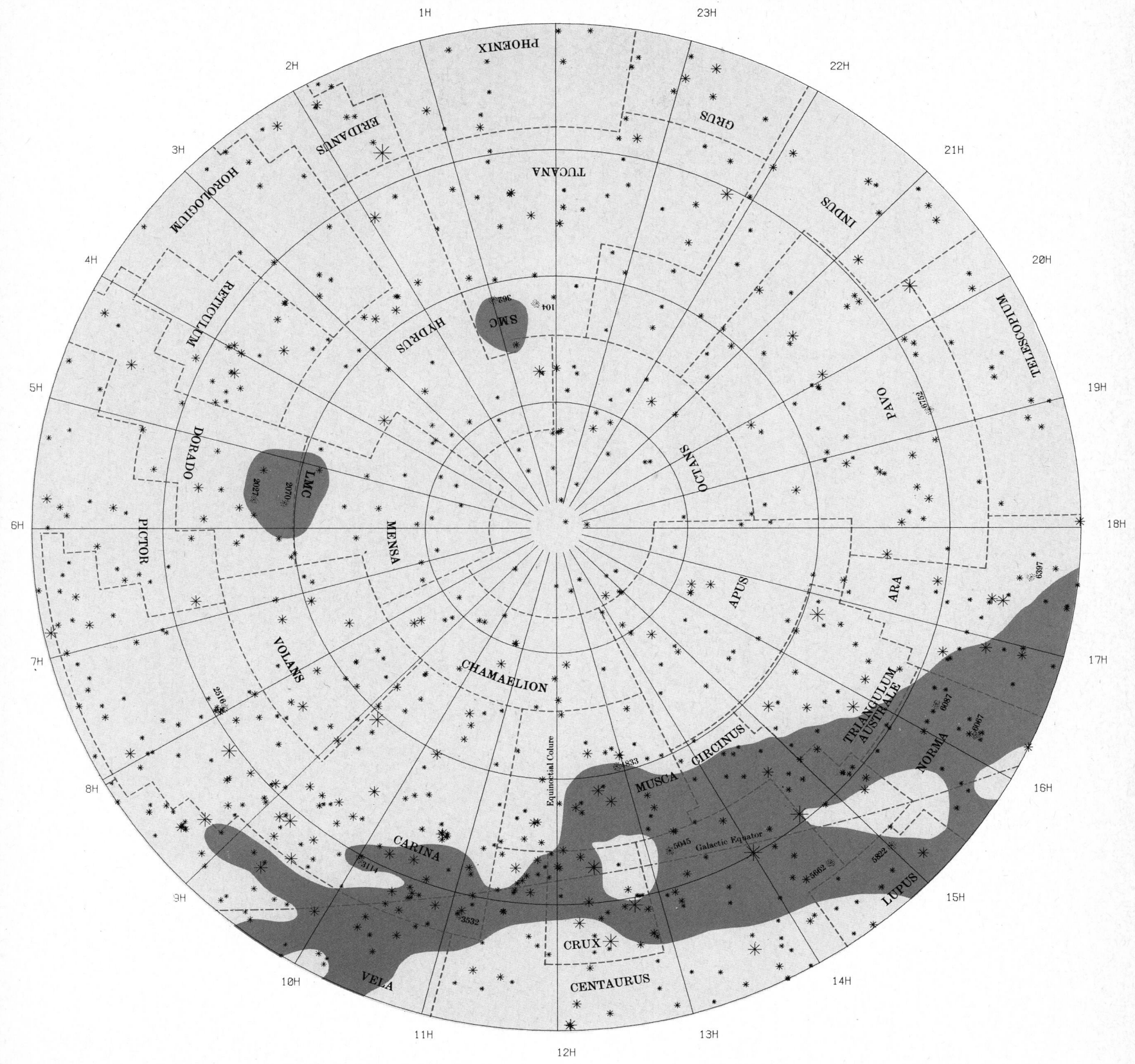

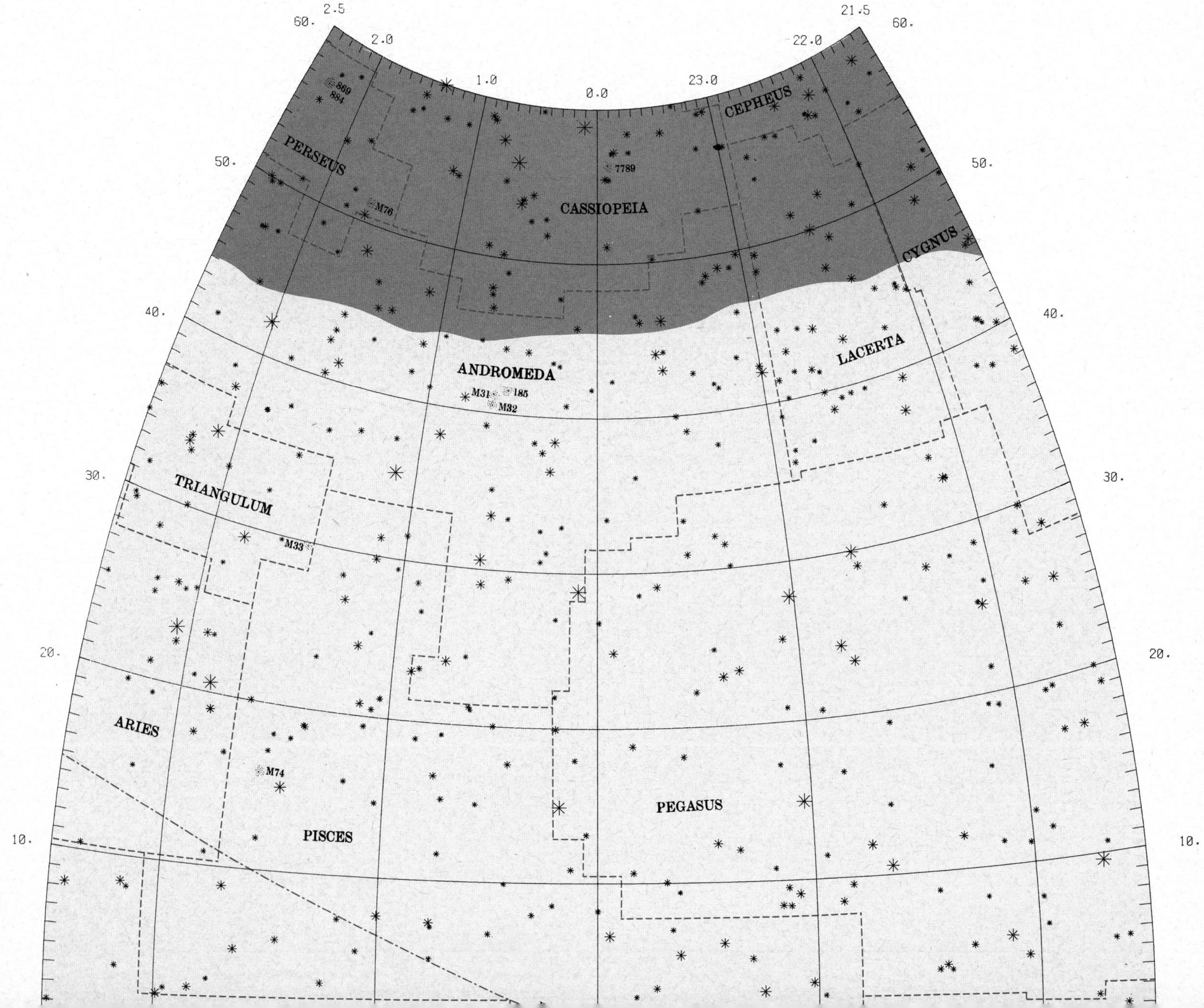
2.5
2.0
1.0
0.0
23.0
22.0
21.5
60.
50.
40.
30.
20.
10.
PERSEUS
869
884
M76
CASSIOPEIA
7789
CEPHEUS
CYGNUS
ANDROMEDA
M31
185
M32
LACERTA
TRIANGULUM
M33
ARIES
M74
PISCES
PEGASUS

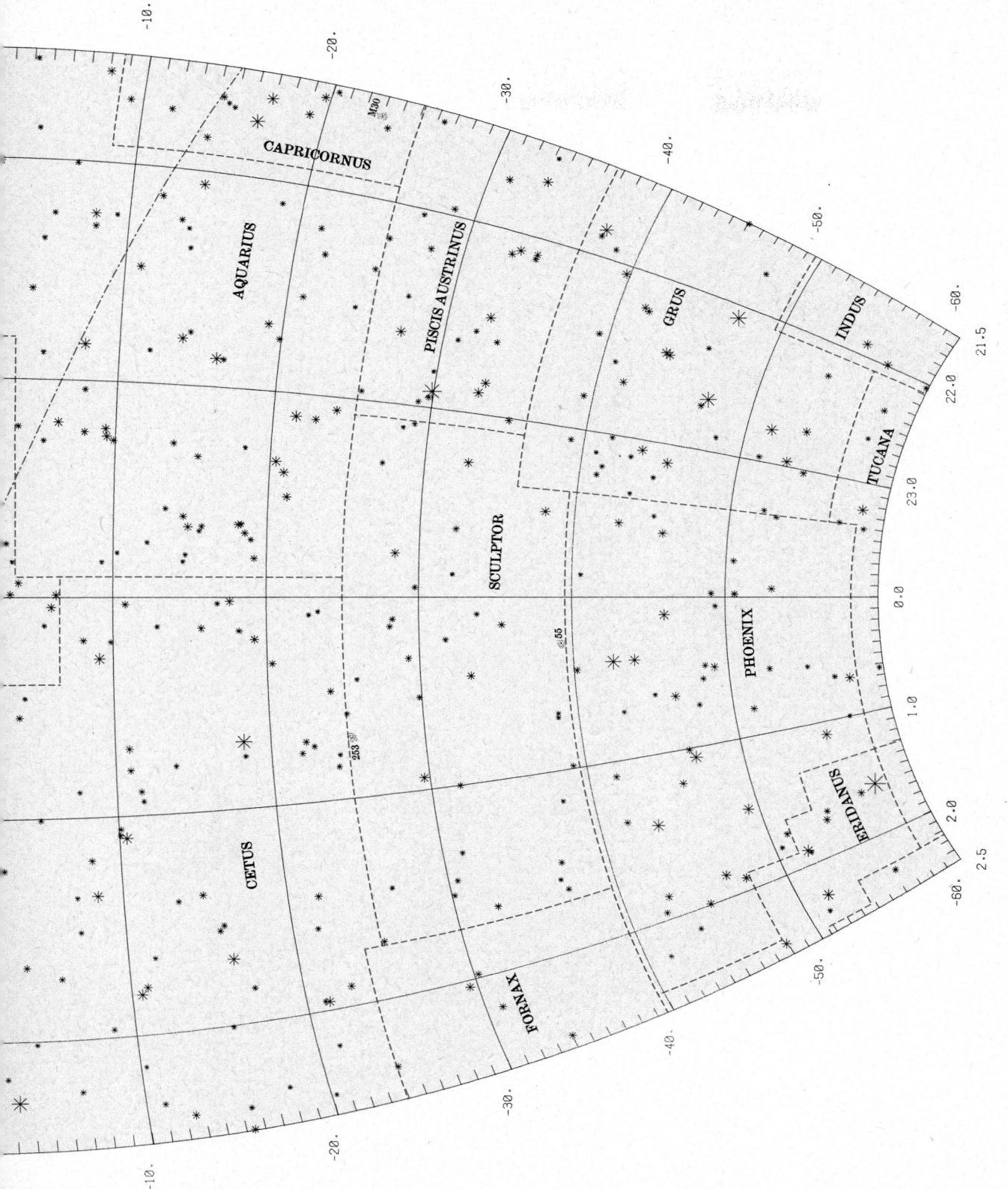

CAPRICORNUS

AQUARIUS

PISCIS AUSTRINUS

GRUS

INDUS

TUCANA

SCULPTOR

PHOENIX

CETUS

FORNAX

ERIDANUS

M30

253

55

−10.
−20.
−30.
−40.
−50.
−60.

21.5
22.0
23.0
0.0
1.0
2.0
2.5

−60.
−50.
−40.
−30.
−20.
−10.

0.0 1.0 2.0 3.0 4.0 5.0 6.0

0.5 1.5 2.5 3.5 4.5 5.5 6.5

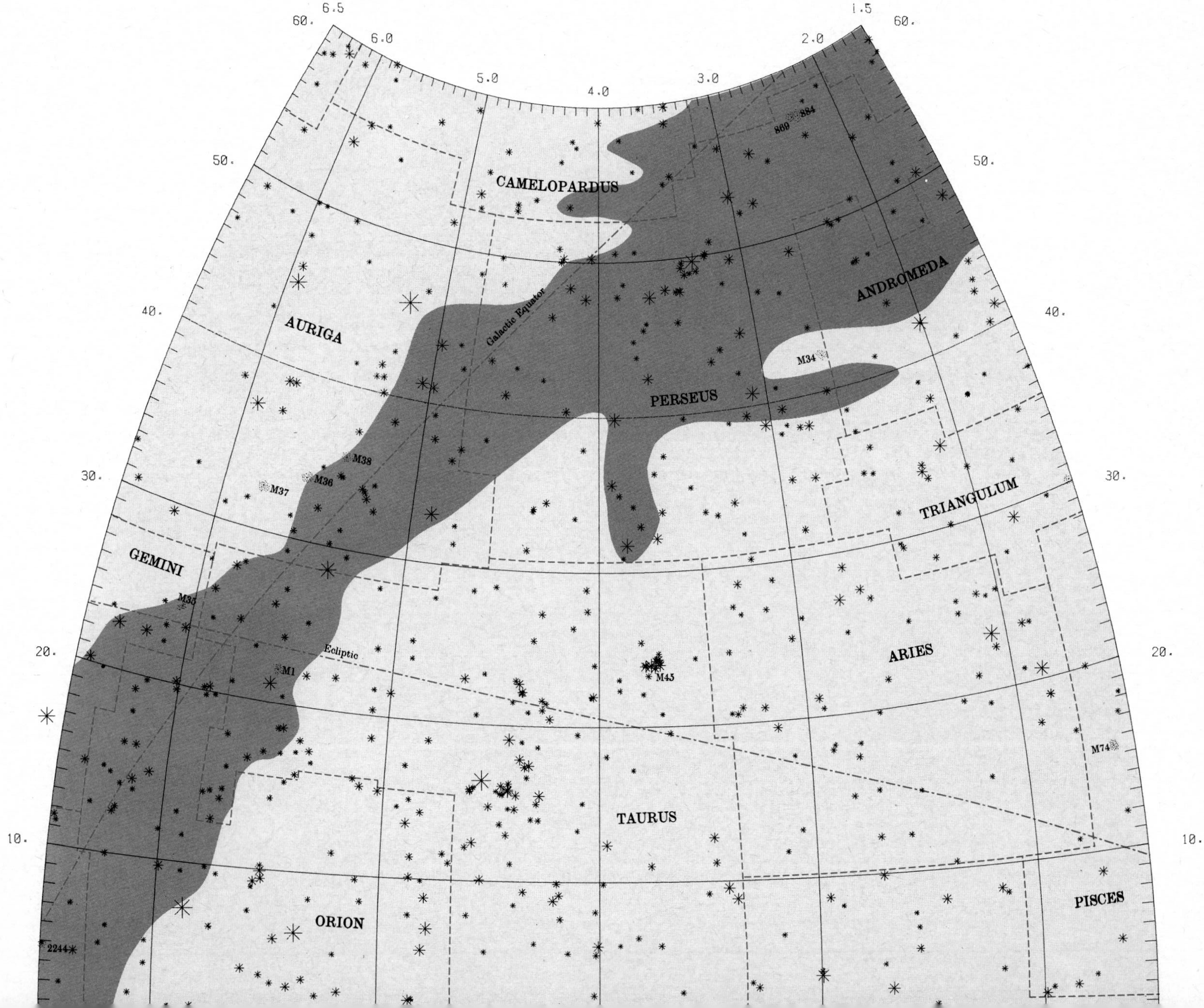

6.5
6.0
5.0
4.0
3.0
2.0
1.5
60.
50.
40.
30.
20.
10.
CAMELOPARDUS
AURIGA
ANDROMEDA
PERSEUS
TRIANGULUM
GEMINI
ARIES
TAURUS
ORION
PISCES
Galactic Equator
Ecliptic
869
884
M34
M38
M36
M37
M35
M1
M45
M74
2244

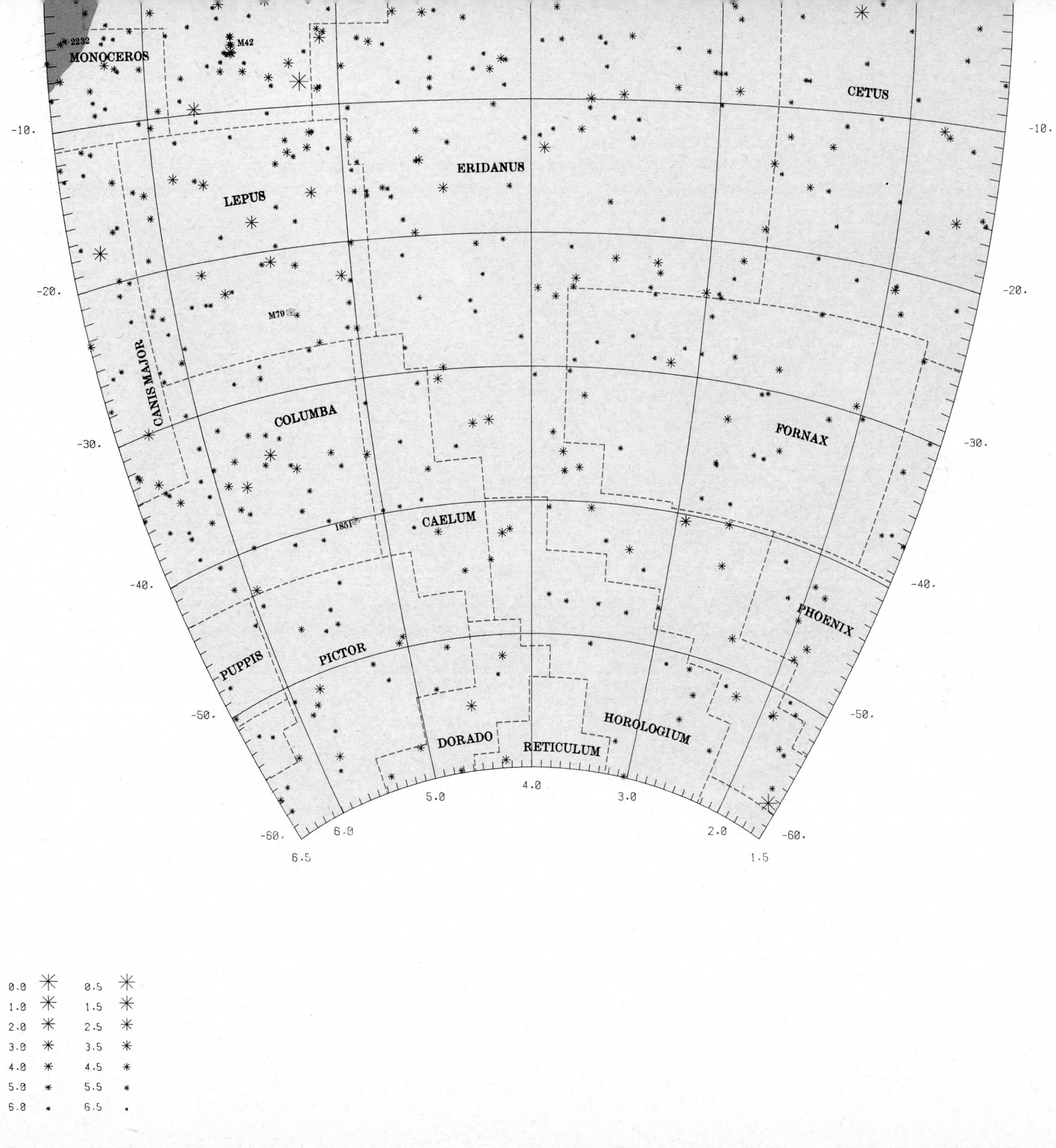

CETUS

MONOCEROS

2232

M42

ERIDANUS

LEPUS

M79

CANIS MAJOR

COLUMBA

CAELUM

1851

PICTOR

PUPPIS

FORNAX

PHOENIX

HOROLOGIUM

RETICULUM

DORADO

-10.

-20.

-30.

-40.

-50.

-60.

-10.

-20.

-30.

-40.

-50.

1.5

2.0

3.0

4.0

5.0

6.0

6.5

	✳	✳	✳	✳	✳	*	·
	0.5	1.5	2.5	3.5	4.5	5.5	6.5
	✳	✳	✳	✳	*	*	
	0.0	1.0	2.0	3.0	4.0	5.0	6.0

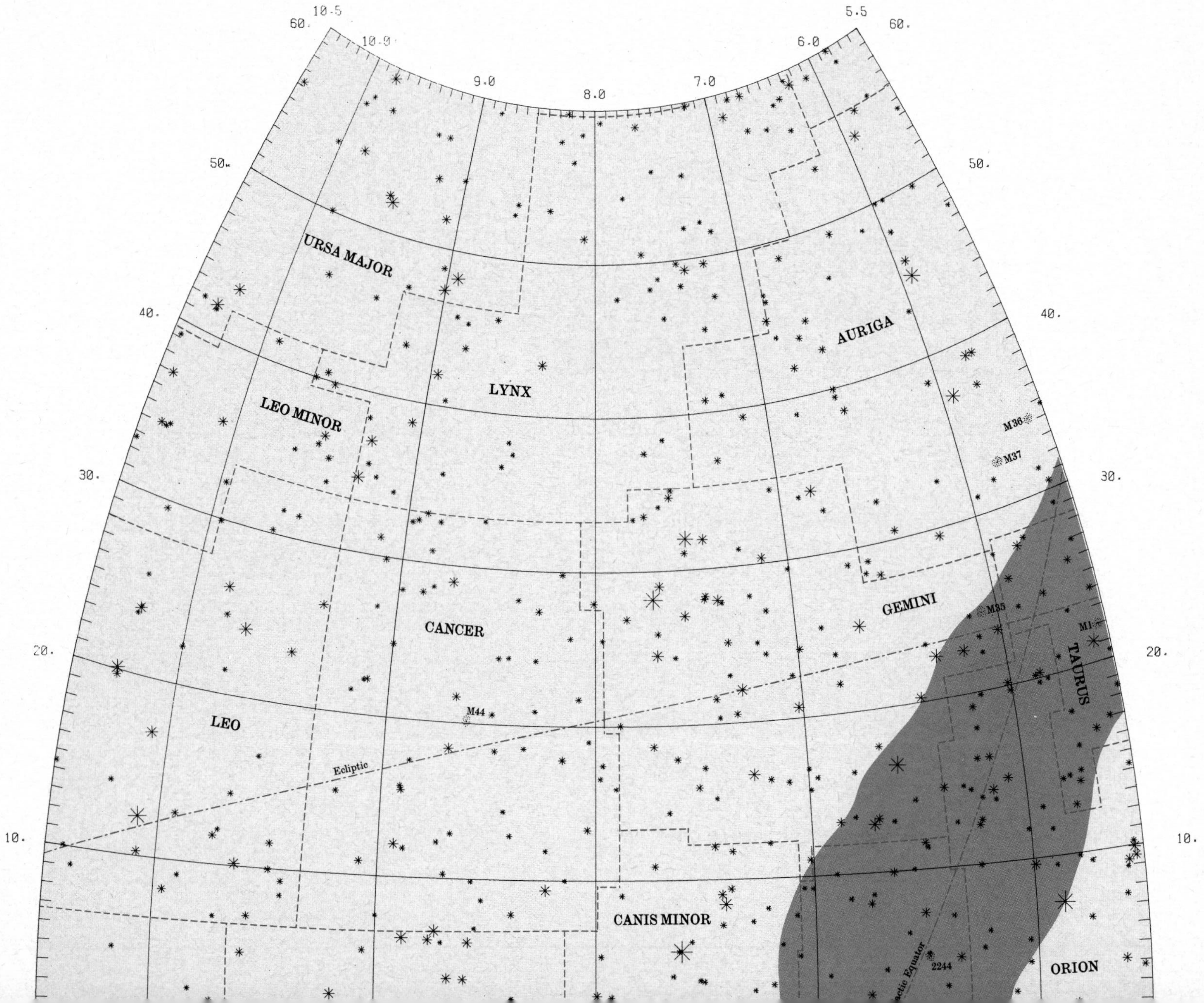

10.5
10.0
9.0
8.0
7.0
6.0
5.5
60.
50.
40.
30.
20.
10.
URSA MAJOR
LYNX
AURIGA
LEO MINOR
M36
M37
CANCER
GEMINI
M35
M1
TAURUS
LEO
M44
Ecliptic
CANIS MINOR
2244
ORION

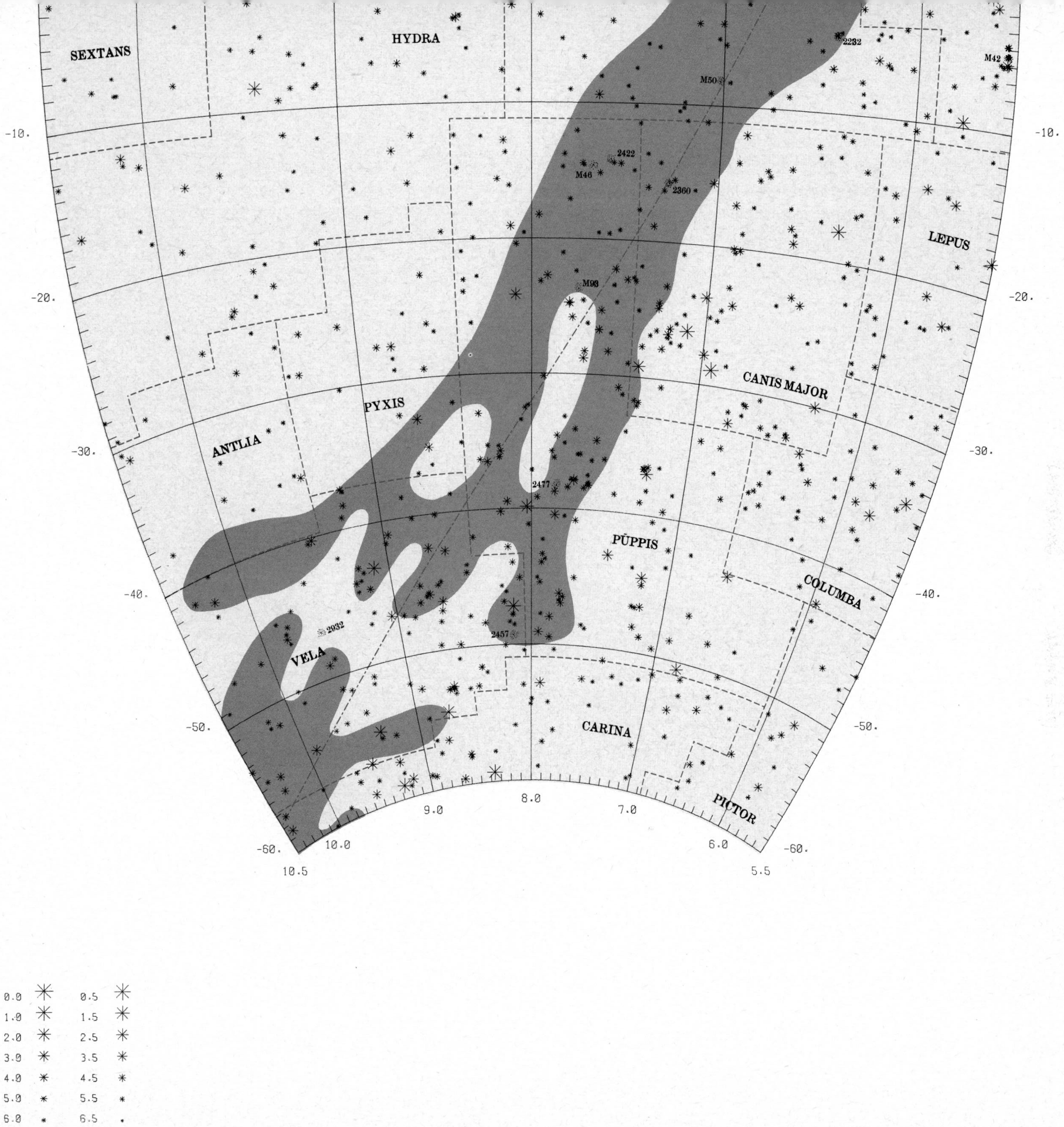
SEXTANS
HYDRA
LEPUS
ANTLIA
PYXIS
CANIS MAJOR
PUPPIS
COLUMBA
VELA
CARINA
PICTOR
M42
M50
2232
2422
M46
2360
M93
2477
2457
2932
-10.
-20.
-30.
-40.
-50.
-60.
10.5
10.0
9.0
8.0
7.0
6.0
5.5
0.0
0.5
1.0
1.5
2.0
2.5
3.0
3.5
4.0
4.5
5.0
5.5
6.0
6.5

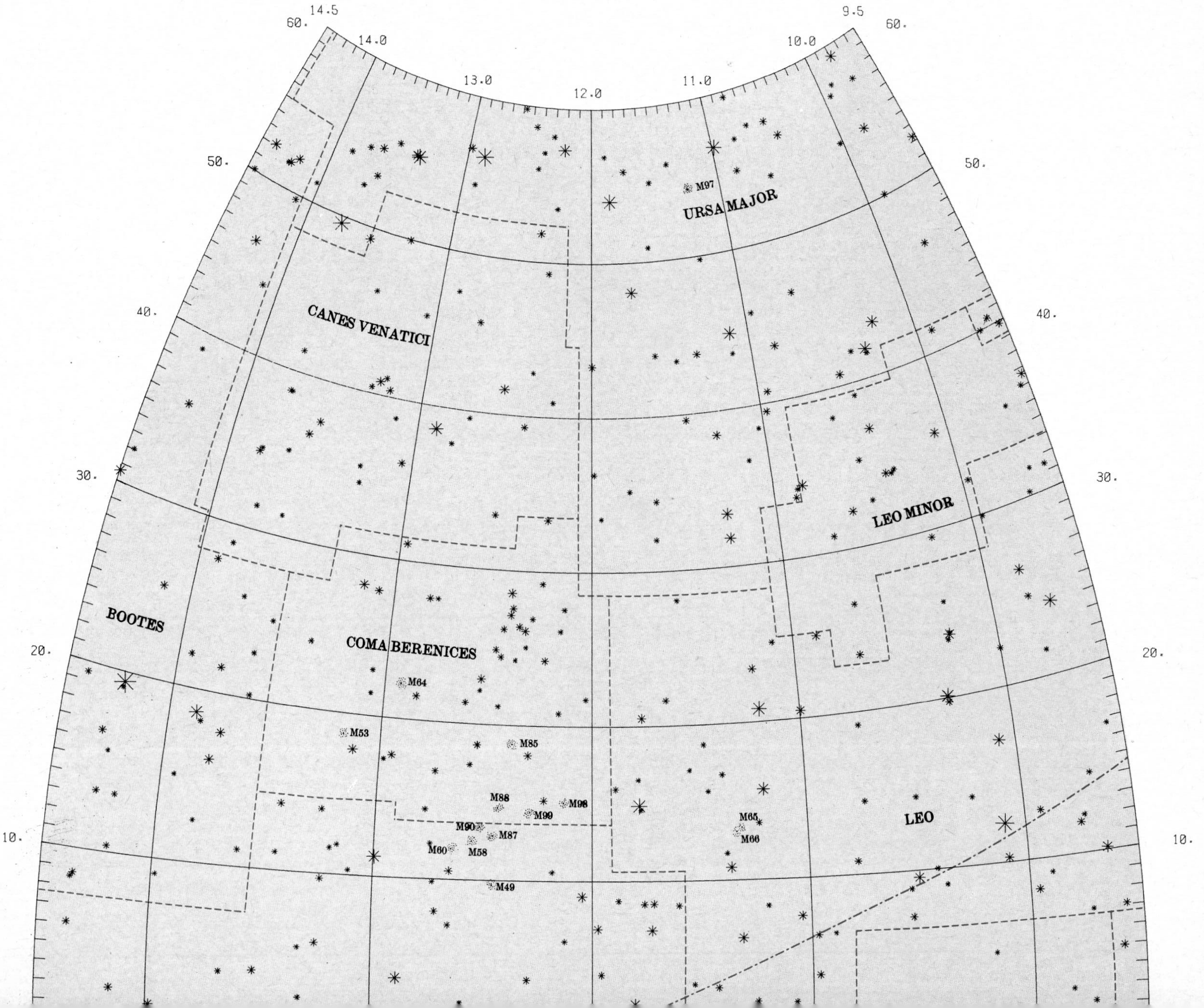
14.5
14.0
13.0
12.0
11.0
10.0
9.5
60.
50.
40.
30.
20.
10.
URSA MAJOR
CANES VENATICI
LEO MINOR
BOOTES
COMA BERENICES
LEO
M97
M64
M53
M85
M88
M98
M99
M90
M87
M60
M58
M49
M65
M66

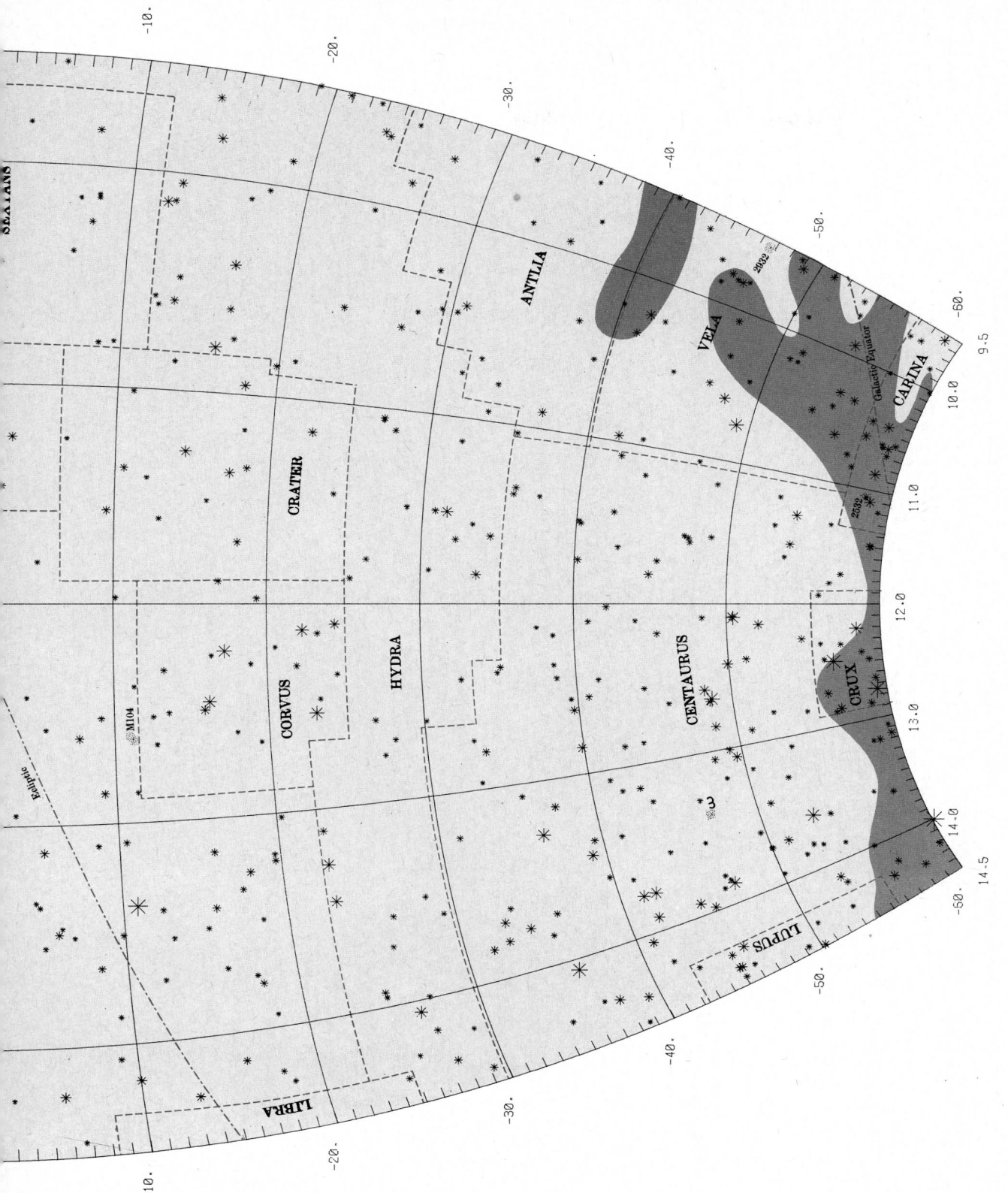

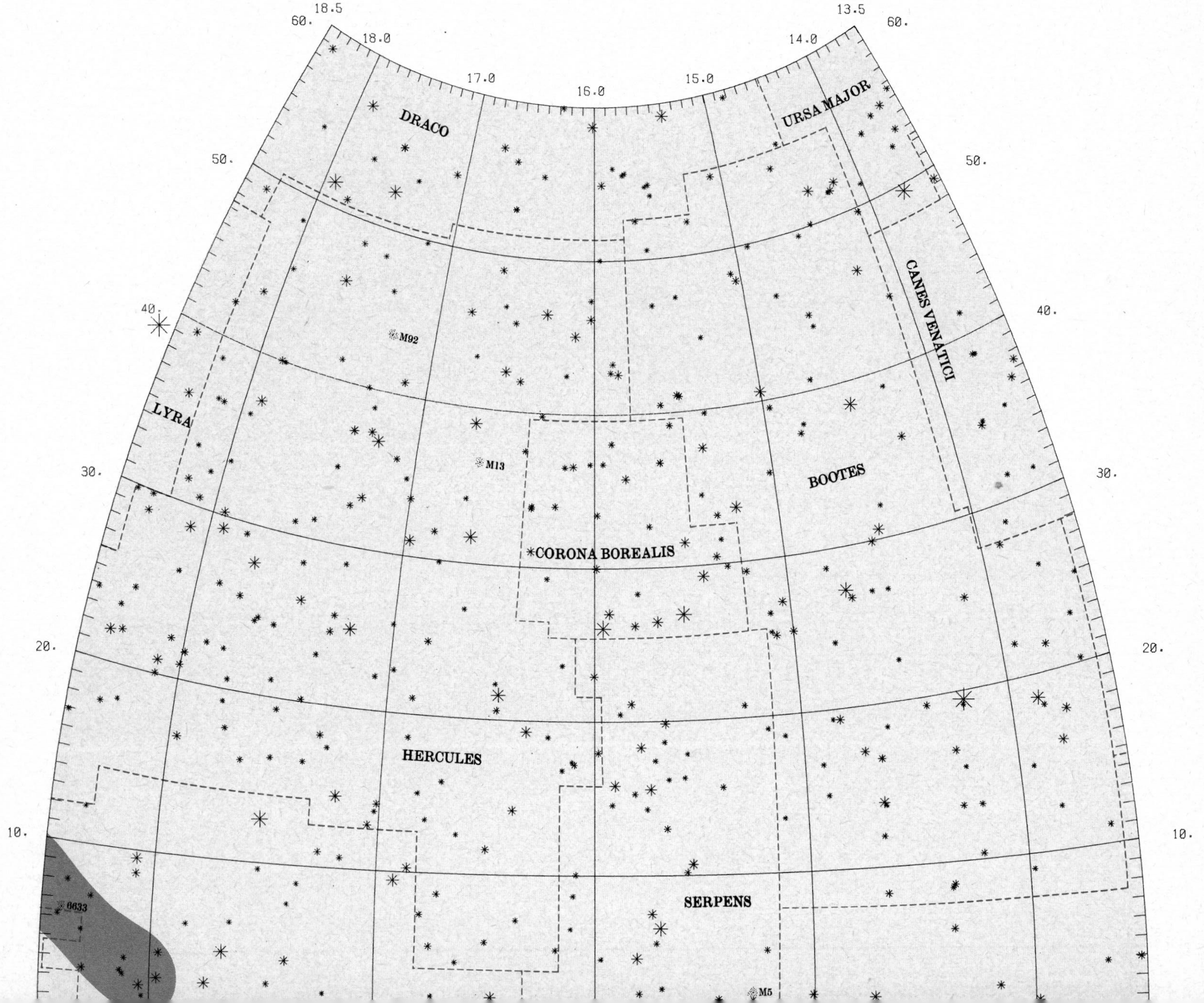

CANES VENATICI

URSA MAJOR

BOÖTES

CORONA BOREALIS

SERPENS

M13

M92

HERCULES

DRACO

LYRA

M5

9433

13.5

14.0

15.0

16.0

17.0

18.0

18.5

60.

50.

40.

30.

20.

10.

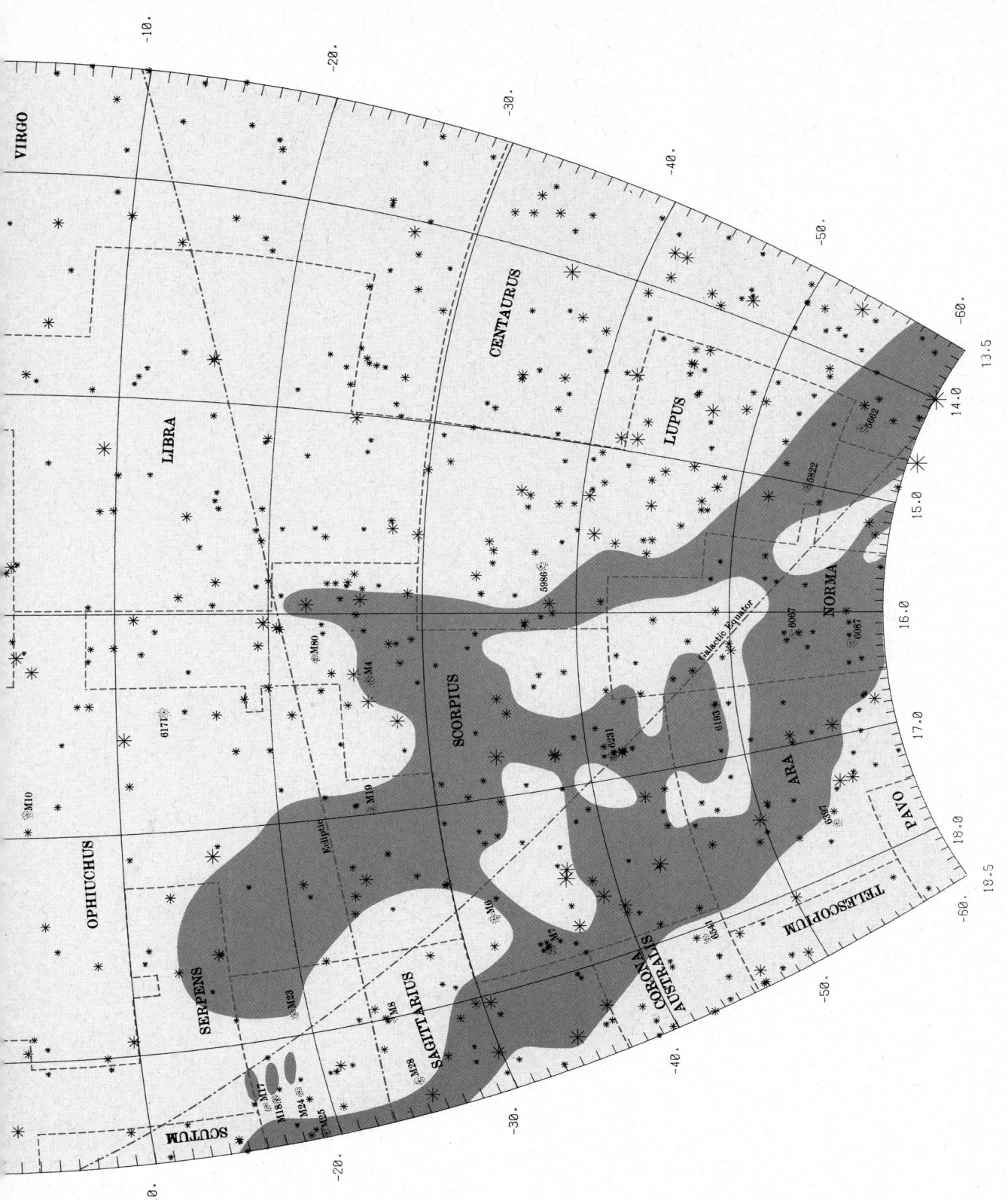

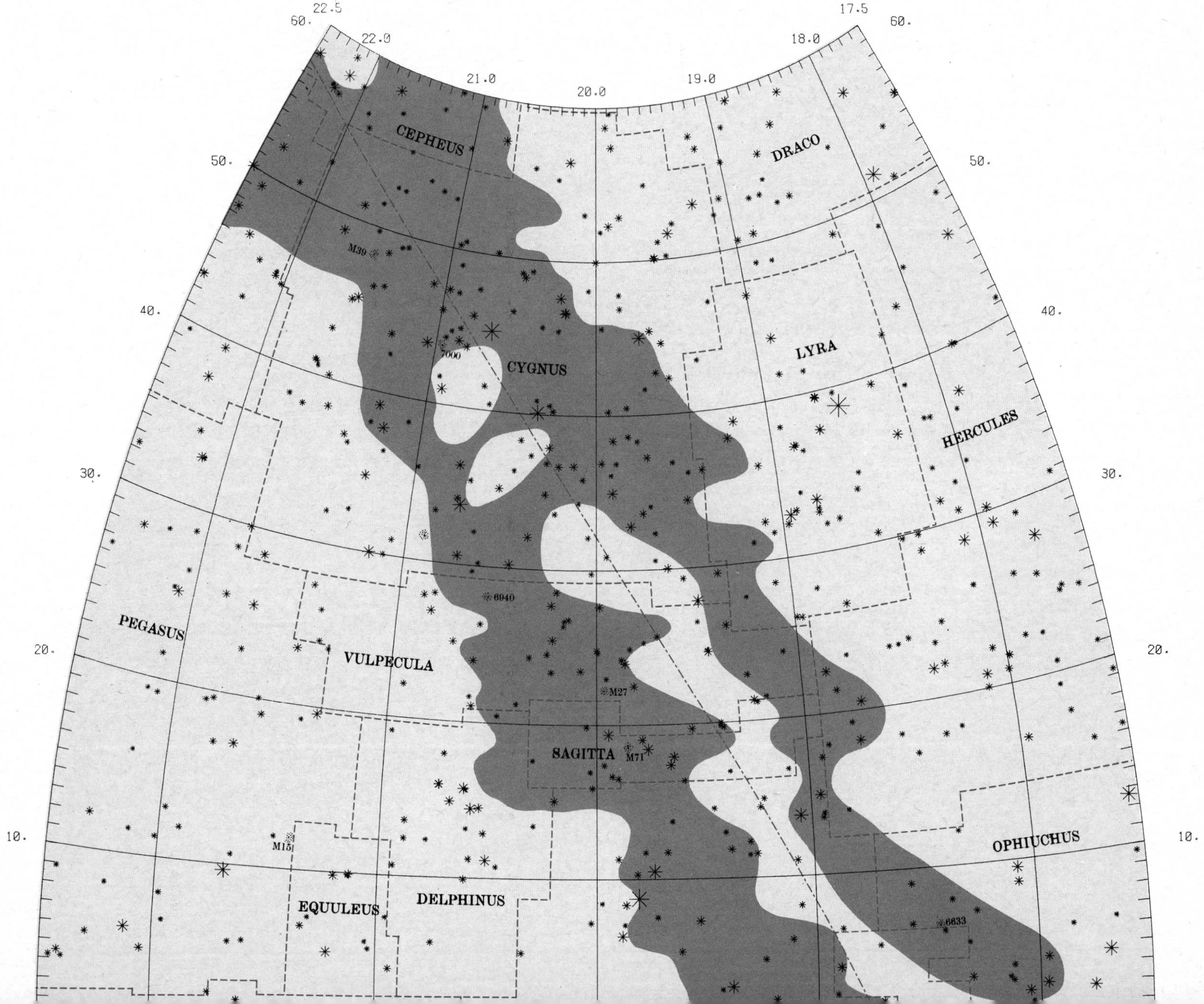
22.5
60.
22.0
21.0
20.0
19.0
18.0
17.5
60.
50.
50.
40.
40.
30.
30.
20.
20.
10.
10.
CEPHEUS
DRACO
M39
7000
CYGNUS
LYRA
HERCULES
6940
PEGASUS
VULPECULA
M27
SAGITTA
M71
M15
OPHIUCHUS
EQUULEUS
DELPHINUS
6633

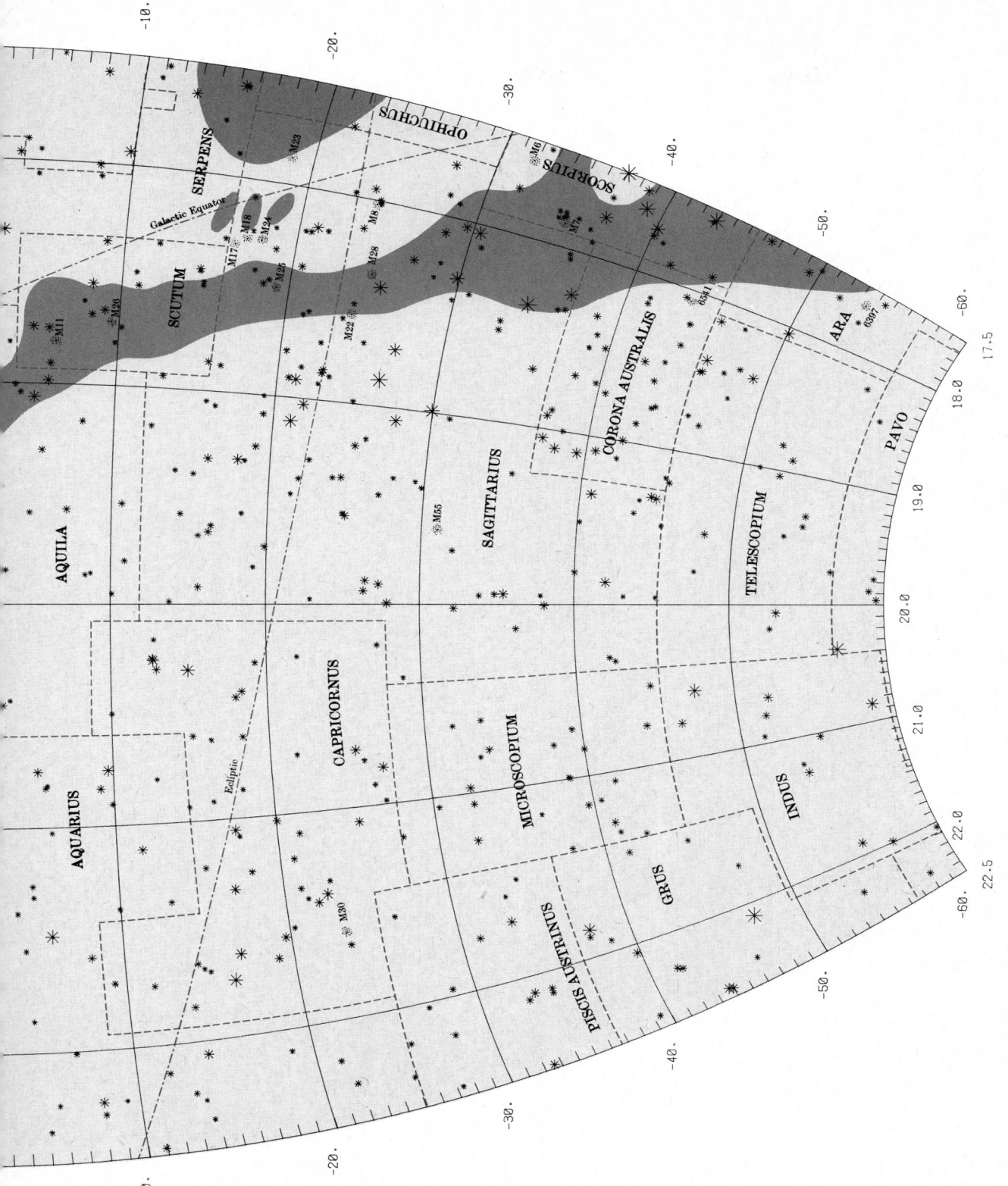

✳	0.0
✳	1.0
✳	2.0
✳	3.0
∗	4.0
∗	5.0
·	6.0

✳	0.5
✳	1.5
✳	2.5
∗	3.5
∗	4.5
·	5.5
·	6.5

List of constellations

Name	Abbreviation	English equivalent	Name	Abbreviation	English equivalent
Andromeda	And	*Daughter of Cepheus*	Lacerta	Lac	*Lizard*
Antlia	Ant	*Air Pump*	Leo	Leo	*Lion*
Apus	Aps	*Bird of Paradise*	Leo Minor	LMi	*Lion Cub*
Aquarius	Aqr	*Water Bearer*	Lepus	Lep	*Hare*
Aquila	Aql	*Eagle*	Libra	Lib	*Scales or Balance*
Ara	Ara	*Altar*	Lupus	Lup	*Wolf*
Aries	Ari	*Ram*	Lynx	Lyn	*Lynx*
Auriga	Aur	*Charioteer*	Lyra	Lyr	*Lyre*
Bootes	Boo	*Bear Driver*	Mensa	Men	*Table Mountain*
Caelum	Cae	*Sculptor's chisel*	Microscopium	Mic	*Microscope*
Camelopardus	Cam	*Giraffe*	Monoceros	Mon	*Unicorn*
Cancer	Cnc	*Crab*	Musca	Mus	*Fly*
Canes Venatici	CVn	*Hunting Dogs*	Norma	Nor	*Carpenter's Square*
Canis Major	CMa	*Greater Dog*	Octans	Oct	*Octant*
Canis Minor	CMi	*Lesser Dog*	Ophiuchus	Oph	*Serpent Holder*
Capricornus	Cap	*Goat*	Orion	Ori	*Great Hunter*
Carina	Car	*Keel*	Pavo	Pav	*Peacock*
Cassiopeia	Cas	*Cassiopeia*	Pegasus	Peg	*Winged Horse*
Centaurus	Cen	*Centaur*	Perseus	Per	*Perseus*
Cepheus	Cep	*Cepheus*	Phoenix	Phe	*Phoenix*
Cetus	Cet	*Sea Monster*	Pictor	Pic	*Painter's Easel*
Chamaelion	Cha	*Chameleon*	Pisces	Psc	*Fishes*
Circinus	Cir	*Compasses*	Piscis Austrinus	PsA	*Southern Fish*
Columba	Col	*Dove*	Puppis	Pup	*Stern*
Coma Berenices	Com	*Berenice's Hair*	Pyxis	Pyx	*Compass Box*
Corona Australis	CrA	*Southern Crown*	Reticulum	Ret	*Net*
Corona Borealis	CrB	*Northern Crown*	Sagitta	Sge	*Arrow*
Corvus	Crv	*Crow or Raven*	Sagittarius	Sgr	*Archer*
Crater	Crt	*Cup*	Scorpius	Sco	*Scorpion*
Crux	Cru	*Southern Cross*	Sculptor	Scl	*Sculptor's Workshop*
Cygnus	Cyg	*Swan*	Scutum	Sct	*Shield*
Delphinus	Del	*Dolphin*	Serpens	Ser	*Serpent*
Dorado	Dor	*Swordfish*	Sextans	Sex	*Sextant*
Draco	Dra	*Dragon*	Taurus	Tau	*Bull*
Equuleus	Equ	*Foal*	Telescopium	Tel	*Telescope*
Eridanus	Eri	*River*	Triangulum	Tri	*Triangle*
Fornax	For	*Furnace*	Triangulum Australe	TrA	*Southern Triangle*
Gemini	Gem	*Twins*	Tucana	Tuc	*Toucan*
Grus	Gru	*Crane*	Ursa Major	UMa	*Greater Bear*
Hercules	Her	*Hercules*	Ursa Minor	UMi	*Lesser Bear*
Horologium	Hor	*Clock*	Vela	Vel	*Sail*
Hydra	Hya	*Water Serpent*	Virgo	Vir	*Virgin*
Hydrus	Hyi	*Water Snake*	Volans	Vol	*Flying Fish*
Indus	Ind	*American Indian*	Vulpecula	Vul	*Fox*

An outline of physics

The purpose of this appendix

Astronomy is a science, and many of its ideas and techniques derive from modern physical theory. This means that in this encyclopaedia it has been necessary to use a certain amount of technical language. We have therefore compiled this appendix of basic physics to explain in a straightforward way certain technical expressions and to indicate how they fit into the broad structure of modern physics. It is not appropriate to supply a textbook on modern physics, so this appendix contains only an outline of the various topics.

Physical processes in astronomy

Astronomy embraces virtually all of the major branches of physics. It includes the more practical aspects, such as electronics and optics needed in the design of telescopes, as well as the topics like nuclear theory and general relativity needed in the study of neutron stars. Indeed, the wide range of physical conditions encountered in the Universe has often placed astronomy in the forefront for new scientific discoveries.

Clearly, to learn all the physics needed for a detailed understanding of astronomy takes years of hard study. Fortunately, however, it is possible to achieve a good grasp of the subject with an elementary knowledge of physics, plus a fair amount of common sense. With this goal in mind, we present a general overview of elementary physics, and follow this with short paragraphs explaining physical processes mentioned in the text. The level of the overview is not to introduce you to physics for the first time; a prior introduction to physics at an elementary (school) level is assumed. Rather, we hope to assist you by reminding you of things previously encountered, and to co-ordinate these diverse facts into a more complete understanding of physics as a whole, and its application to astronomy in particular.

Space, time, matter and energy

Physics is the science of the laws and properties of matter: it is the study of how matter and energy move and change in space and time. At the most fundamental level, we distinguish two entities: on the one hand, there is the SPACE-TIME CONTINUUM: the where and when of the Universe. On the other hand, there is MATTER AND ENERGY: the what of the Universe.

The space-time continuum, as its name implies, is a continuous arena within which all events occur. It has no marks or boundaries intrinsic to it. Commonly, we cover space-time with a hypothetical net called a CO-ORDINATE SYSTEM, in terms of which we measure distances and times. However, this system only has a meaning if we can label the points on it by characteristic events involving matter. Even then, the method of measurement chosen is always arbitrary. There are no absolute distances or times distinguishable in the space-time continuum. All that is important is the relationship between events. This is the essence of the theory of relativity.

Matter and energy on the other hand are a discrete, well-quantified material. One of the most powerful laws of physics, the LAW OF CONSERVATION OF MATTER AND ENERGY, tells us that the total amount of it in the Universe can never change. Matter and energy can neither be created nor destroyed. The truth of this law has been very well tested on Earth, but it is much more difficult to test on the largest scales. One of the most influential modern theories of the Universe, the STEADY-STATE THEORY, assumes that this conservation law is wrong. It states that matter is being continually created throughout the Universe at the rate of about one hydrogen atom per hundred cubic kilometres per year. Such a minute increase could never be detected in the laboratory. However, the Steady-State theory is no longer generally accepted and scientists continue to support the law of conservation of matter and energy.

It was once thought that there were two separate conservation laws, one each for matter and energy. However, the theory of relativity showed that matter and energy were basically the same thing, and that you could convert one into the other, according to the equation:

$$\text{energy} = \text{mass} \times (\text{speed of light})^2$$

Because the speed of light is so large, this means that the conversion of a very little mass will produce an enormous amount of energy. One kilogram of matter would produce 9×10^{16} joules if converted entirely to energy according to this principle.

Continuity and quantum mechanics

One of the most fundamental questions that can be posed in physics is: *what is matter?* Since physics is the study of the laws and properties of matter, the only physical answer that can be given is couched in terms of known experiments and observations that display some aspect of the nature of matter. Any definition of matter that transcends the known data belongs to the realm of metaphysics, and has no place in conventional science.

The nature of matter depends critically upon the way you are looking at it and using it. If you are thinking in terms of billiard balls, and tables and cues, it is perfectly reasonable to regard matter as a rigid body with a clearly defined boundary. This is the so-called CLASSICAL VIEW OF MATTER. If you are trying to understand the properties of gases, it is necessary to think of matter as a collection of atoms, each atom being an independent, irreducible unit. Conjectures about the ATOMIC NATURE OF MATTER date from Greek times, but the modern revival of this idea is attributed to John Dalton. Although other people had been toying with the concept before him, Dalton is accredited with the theory because he was able to show scientifically that the atomic nature of matter is revealed in the behaviour of gases. Thus the definition that matter is a collection of atoms only becomes a scientific definition when a physical experiment can be performed to demonstrate this.

Today, scientists can perform many experiments that together reveal a great diversity of properties in matter. Some of these properties suggest that matter is continuous, with wave-like characteristics. Others suggest that matter is discrete, and exists only as small but finite bundles or quanta. Since a physical definition is of necessity only a reflection of physical observations, it follows that matter is both particulate and wave-like. The real difficulty is therefore to construct a mathematical model that can display both characteristics. The theory that does so is called QUANTUM MECHANICS, and it embraces not only matter, but all forms of energy as well, since these are interchangeable.

There is an important corollary to the fact that matter has a double identity. Once scientists had discovered the dual nature of matter, they tried to devise an experiment that would explicitly demonstrate one or other of its two states, waves or particles. Had they been able to do so, it would have meant that nature is inconsistent: for then matter would indeed be schizophrenic – sometimes one thing, and sometimes the other, rather than a blend of both. In fact they failed in all attempts to make such a distinction, and their failure has been expressed as a physical principle, called the UNCERTAINTY PRINCIPLE.

The Uncertainty Principle states that it is physically impossible to make accurate observations of all the variables needed to describe a physical system exactly. In some ways, it is therefore one of the most empirical laws of physics, that is, a law based explicitly on observation. It lies at the heart of modern quantum mechanics. The Uncertainty Principle means that it is impossible to determine the exact outcome of an experiment, even if all possible initial conditions are known. But are the uncertainties of our observations inherent to matter itself, or are we merely ignorant of the hidden variables that in fact determine the outcome? Since it is not scientifically permissible to give a definition of matter that exceeds our ability to observe it, at the present time we can only accept the dual nature of matter, and the inherent uncertainty that goes with it.

Individuals and groups

There are many situations in physics when the behaviour of the system as a whole is dominated by the behaviour of the individual units acting together as a group. Such processes may be called GROUP PHENOMENA, or sometimes CO-OPERATIVE PHENOMENA. We are all familiar with examples of extreme group phenomena at a human level. These are cases when the action of an individual person is so strongly influenced by the actions of surrounding individuals that the group of people as a whole behaves in a coherent way that may be quite uncharacteristic of the individuals taken in isolation. We see this in mob violence, sports crowds, a coachload of tourists, gangs, armies, and so forth. Society as a whole is a good example of a group phenomenon.

Many processes in physics are of this type, in which the behaviour of the system as a whole depends at least as strongly on the interactions between the individual components, as it does on the properties of the components themselves. Such processes are characterized at the mathematical level by the necessity of using non-linear equations.

An example of a linear system is the STATISTICAL ENSEMBLE. In this case, the system consists of very large numbers of similar individual units, each acting independently of the others. The behaviour of the system as a whole may then be regarded as a statistical average of all the individual units. We meet this kind of situation most commonly in thermodynamics. However, the thermodynamic approach has been applied to many other areas of physics, and science in general. For example, in astronomy we find it applied to the study of stellar systems, and even the properties of black holes.

The simplest kind of group phenomenon to describe mathematically is a WAVE. In a simple wave, the individual units, or carriers act so completely in unison that it is possible to describe the process with linear equations. An example of this is electrodynamics. A simple wave is characterized by being periodic, that is, it returns to the same shape at regular intervals. The entire pattern, repeated over and over again, is called the WAVE TRAIN. The length of each interval is called the PERIOD of the wave. Alternatively, the inverse of this is called the FREQUENCY of the wave, and indicates the number of times the same configuration is repeated in a unit time.

A more complicated wave pattern may be produced by combining linearly two simple waves of different frequencies. This produces the phenomenon known as BEATS. A beat occurs at places where the component carriers are moving in unison so that their contributions to the total wave pattern add together. Elsewhere their contributions do not add together, and at places completely cancel each other.

Still more complicated wave patterns can be produced by combining many waves of different frequencies. Under the most general conditions, these component waves may add together to form a WAVE PACKET. This is a more generalized form of beat pattern that may occur at only one place in the whole wave train. Furthermore, the place at which it occurs in the wave train normally changes. Thus the wave packet moves along the wave train at a certain speed called the GROUP VELOCITY. The group velocity is in general different from the velocity of the component waves.

The existence of wave packets, with their own characteristic group velocities, is of special significance, for they lie at the fuzzy boundary between what are individuals, and what are groups. By construction a wave packet is a group phenomenon. Yet its properties are more akin to those of an individual object. This is the mathematical equivalent to the duality of matter, which behaves sometimes as a particle (or individual) and sometimes as a wave (or group). Quantum mechanics as a whole is concerned with the properties of wave packets.

Four fundamental forces

The behaviour of matter in the Universe is determined by the nature and distribution of its surrounding matter. The influence is exerted via one or more of only four fundamental force fields. These are called the STRONG, ELECTROMAGNETIC, WEAK and GRAVITATIONAL fields. The importance of recognizing these fields is that each has its own characteristic properties, and hence tends to dominate the behaviour of matter under particular circumstances. The properties of principal importance are the strength of the field, that is, how strong a force is exerted via the field, and the range of the field, that is, the distance over which the force is felt.

The strongest field is the strong field, as its name implies. This force holds the nuclei of atoms together. It is therefore important in all nuclear interactions, such as those taking place in the centres of the stars. Over the very short range where the strong field acts, it dominates the effects of the other fields. However, its range is very small, extending only over distances of about the diameter of a nucleus, that is about 10^{-15}m.

The next strongest field is the electromagnetic field. This is the most common everyday field. It is the force which holds atoms and molecules together (as distinct from the nuclei of atoms, which are the domain of the strong field). Thus it is the field which is important in virtually all chemical and biological reactions. It is also important in any process that sends out light or radio signals, for these are electromagnetic waves. Almost all our knowledge of the Universe comes from looking at such waves, so the electromagnetic field is of enormous importance to astronomy. It is more than one hundred times weaker than the strong field. However, its range is infinite, so its effects are felt on all scales.

The third strongest field is the weak field, which is the least familiar to most people. The weak field is about a thousand times less strong than the electromagnetic field, and its range is even smaller than that of the strong field. The weak field is important in radioactive decay processes.

The last of the four fundamental fields, and by far the weakest over very short distances, is the gravitational field. The gravitational field is about 10^{33} times weaker than the weak field. Thus most interactions between matter involving the other three fields take place while completely ignoring gravity. Nevertheless, the gravitational field is the dominant force over astronomical distances, and there are a few contexts, such as in neutron stars and black holes, where its effects dominate the other fields. Gravity is important on macroscopic levels because its range is infinite, and its effects are always additive. This is in contrast to the electromagnetic field, whose range is also infinite, but in which there are both positive and negative charges which cancel each other. There are no negative mass particles; even antimatter is believed to have a normal, positive, mass. Since astronomy is the most macroscopic of all sciences, gravity is more relevant in astronomical contexts than anywhere else. The behaviour of the Universe as a whole is dominated by gravity, as are the motions of the planets.

The physics of astronomy

The Universe, viewed as a laboratory, provides the widest range of physical conditions available for study by scientists. The most striking feature about the Universe is its immense size. By definition, it is the largest physical system that exists. Indeed, the Universe is the totality of all physical things. Not only is it the largest system, but it is also the least dense. The most evacuated vacuum chamber that can be achieved in the laboratory is hardly a vacuum at all by astrophysical standards. It is one thousand billion times more dense than intergalactic space! The range of densities encountered in the Universe ranges up to a neutron star which is 10^{13} times as dense as the densest material on Earth. The Universe also exhibits extremes in temperature, from the very hot, to the very cold. Here, however, we encounter an interesting limitation. The Universe is bathed in a radiation field whose temperature is about $2.7°$ absolute, which is more than $270°$ below freezing. The coldest temperatures in the Universe that we know of, are achieved in terrestrial laboratories (10^{-6}K). Within this vast arena, physical processes take place involving all types of forces and interactions. For convenience, we shall summarize these processes in terms of the nature of the forces involved.

Firstly, the SHORT-RANGE FIELDS (strong and weak) are important when particles come very close together. They do this when the density is very high, and also when the particles are very energetic, so that they can penetrate the atom and reach the nucleus. There are several astrophysical regimes where these conditions apply:

The very early Universe

Stars: (a) normal stars, (b) white dwarfs, (c) neutron stars

Quasars and galactic nuclei.

Secondly, the ELECTROMAGNETIC FIELD is important whenever charged particles are accelerated or change their state. Among other things, this includes all situations where light, radio waves, X-rays and so forth are emitted or absorbed either continuously or in line spectra. There are a great number of astrophysical regimes where these, and other electromagnetic processes, occur:

The early Universe

Ionized regions

Stellar radiation and spectra

X-ray stars

Galactic nuclei.

Thirdly, the GRAVITATIONAL FIELD is important whenever the behaviour of large collections of matter is concerned, that is, at all macroscopic levels. In this context, large means any scale where the total gravitational effects are greater than, or comparable to, the effects of other fields. Thus, in the early Universe, the high densities and temperatures dominate gravitational effects except on the very largest (global) scales. Later, when the Universe has expanded and cooled, gravitational forces are important even down to terrestrial levels and beyond. We list here some of the more familiar contexts:

The expansion of the Universe

Gravitational collapse of galaxies and stars

Binary systems

The motion of planets and satellites.

Other physical processes are relevant within the contexts of the above. For example, quantum mechanical effects are of significance in the very, very early

Universe, or in systems such as neutron stars. Co-operative processes are important in the dynamics of stellar systems, or in astrophysical masers. The conditions required for such processes are often so different from those in the laboratory that the Universe provides the only arena where such phenomena can be studied.

Reflecting on our earlier comments about the nature of physical laws and definitions, we find that this is pertinent in two respects. Firstly, we recall that a physical theory should be both quantifiable and testable. This is exceedingly difficult to satisfy in astronomy. We observe a phenomenon in all of its complexity, but we cannot normally construct an artificially simplified version of it in the laboratory: hence we derive a mathematical model for it as it is observed. Then, having built a model, we cannot test it by performing related experiments in the laboratory.

Secondly, we recall that any theory or definition in physics must be expressible in terms of known experiments and observations. This is of particular importance in those areas that are physically inaccessible to us. We must distinguish a regime which is in principle inaccessible, and one which is only technically inaccessible. An example of the latter is the Sun's interior which we shall never be able to examine directly. However, information from the interior can and does reach us from its effect at the Sun's surface, and also from its neutrino flux. So it is perfectly reasonable to construct a physical theory about its nature.

The most difficult example of a physically inaccessible regime is the epoch before the bang in a Big-Bang Universe. It is an obvious question to ask: what happened before the Big Bang? This is a doubly embarrassing question to most cosmologists. Firstly, we do not know, and secondly, even if we guessed, we could not give an answer that was scientifically meaningful. Some cosmologists attempt to avoid the problem by suggesting that time also began with the Bang, so that there was no time before then. However, the simplest answer is just that the regime before the Bang is physically inaccessible, and hence cannot in principle be discussed scientifically.

Glossary of physical terms

In the following sections, we define terms which are used elsewhere in this encyclopaedia. These terms are all numbered, and listed in sections, in an order which relates to their physical meaning. Thus the term 'electron' is listed after 'fundamental particles', and alongside 'proton', and 'neutron' in the section headed *Atoms and Nuclei*.

Force and motion

1. Mass, weight

Mass is a measure of the quantity of matter in a body. It is to be distinguished from the weight of a body, which depends on the strength of the gravitational field. Thus a person on the Moon weighs less than on Earth, and in space may be completely weightless, but always the person has the same mass.

2. Inertia, moment of inertia

Inertia is the resistance that a body in free space provides against attempts to move it. It is equivalent to mass. Moment of inertia is the resistance that a body provides against attempts to rotate it.

3. Velocity, angular velocity

Velocity is the rate of change of position with time. It is a vector quantity, that is, it defines a direction of travel as well as speed. Angular velocity is the rate of change of angle with time in a rotating system.

4. Momentum

There are two kinds of momentum, linear and angular. They are a measure of how hard it is to stop a body from moving linearly, or rotating, respectively. The linear momentum of a body is its mass times its velocity. Angular momentum is moment of inertia times angular velocity.

5. Force, torque

There are many kinds of force, but the name can be applied to any physical agency that causes (or tries to cause) a body to change its state of motion or internal strain. Its precise definition as a physically measurable quantity comes directly from Newton's second law. It is a vector quantity, having both strength and direction. A torque is the physical agent that causes (or tries to cause) a body to rotate about a given axis. It is equal to the applied force times its (perpendicular) distance to the axis. Torque is also a vector quantity, whose direction is that of the axis of the induced rotation.

6. Newton's laws of motion

Newton enunciated three laws of motion:

(i) every body continues in its state of rest or uniform motion unless acted upon by a force.

(ii) the time rate of change of momentum of a body is proportional to the applied force (both considered as vector quantities).

(iii) to every action there is an equal and opposite reaction.

7. Conservation of momentum and angular momentum

Newton's laws give us two important conservation laws:

(i) conservation of linear momentum: in the absence of any force, the linear momentum of a body does not change.

(ii) conservation of angular momentum : in the absence of any torque, the angular momentum of a body does not change.

8. Inertial frame
A coordinate system in which Newton's laws apply. Newton stated that this frame coincided with the fixed stars. Any reference frame moving uniformly (that is, without acceleration) with respect to the fixed stars is also inertial, as implied by Newton's first law.

9. Inertial force
Newton's laws only are true in inertial frames. If we wish to apply Newton's laws to motion within a non-inertial frame, it is necessary to introduce fictitious forces to compensate for the effects of the acceleration of the frame. These are called inertial forces.

10. Centrifugal force, Coriolis force
Examples of inertial forces. The centrifugal force is the apparent outward force experienced by a body at rest in a rotation frame, as for example, experienced by a passenger in a car turning a sharp corner. A Coriolis force is an additional force experienced by a body moving in a rotation frame. It is commonly encountered in fairgrounds, on some types of apparatus that turn in more than one direction at once.

11. Energy, potential energy, kinetic energy
Energy is the capacity of a body or a system for doing work. It is formally related to the effect of a force acting on a body for a specific distance. Potential energy is the energy a body possesses by virtue of its position or state. An example is a rock perched on top of a cliff, which required a force to have pushed it up the hill ; this energy can potentially be recovered by pushing the rock off the cliff. Kinetic energy is the energy a body possesses by virtue of its motion. An example is a fast-moving rock just before it hits the ground after toppling off a cliff, and which was accelerated by the force of gravity in its downward plunge.

12. Potential well
A position or state of a body where it has less potential energy than it would have in any neighbouring position or state.

13. Gravity, Newton's law of gravity, gravitational constant
Gravity is the force experienced by a body as a result of the positive attraction between masses. Newton's law of gravity states that the gravitational force produced by one body acting on another is in the direction of the body and proportional to the product of the masses divided by the square of the distance between them.

gravitational force =

$$G \times \frac{\text{mass of one body} \times \text{mass of other body}}{(\text{distance between bodies})^2}$$

The two bodies thus exert an equal and opposite force on each other. The constant of proportionality, G, is called the gravitational constant.

14. Gravitational collapse, Kelvin-Helmholtz contraction
Gravitational collapse is the process in which a number of masses come together as a result of their gravitational attraction. Because they are accelerated towards each other by the gravitational force, they gain kinetic energy, which is generally manifested as a pressure. Once this pressure has reached a critical value, it will halt any further collapse unless the system can get rid of some of the excess energy by radiation or some other means. An example of this is the contraction of a cloud in which gas undergoes gravitational collapse, and continually emits its acquired kinetic energy in the form of radiation.

15. Escape velocity, gravitationally bound
The escape velocity is the minimum velocity which one body must have to escape from another's gravitational attraction. This is equal, but in the opposite direction to the velocity it would have acquired if it had been accelerated from rest, starting an infinite distance away. If the body's velocity is less than the escape velocity, it is said to be gravitationally bound. The bigger the product of the masses, and the smaller the distance between them, the larger the escape velocity has to be.

16. Black hole, event horizon
A black hole occurs when a sufficiently big mass is packed into a sufficiently small volume that radiation close to the mass can no longer escape from its gravitational pull. In fact, the quanta do not slow down as they move away from the body, but become less energetic. The farthest distance from the body within which radiation is trapped is called the event horizon.

17. Special theory of relativity
Theory asserting that the laws of physics are identical in all inertial frames. It follows that the speed of light cannot be different in different frames, even if they are in relative motion. Thus the speed of light is a universal constant. Special relativity predicts a number of interesting effects, such as :

(i) Time dilation : identical clocks run at different rates when in relative motion (moving clocks appear to go slower). The exact relation is
$$\tau_1 = \tau_0 / \alpha$$
where τ_0 is the time it takes a stationary clock's hands to go round, and τ_1 is the observed time it would take the clock's hands to go round if the clock were moving. α is the relativistic factor, given by
$$\alpha = \sqrt{(1 - v^2/c^2)}$$
where v is the velocity of the moving clock, and c is the speed of light.

(ii) Length contraction : lengths appear less when moving than they do at rest. The relation is
$$L_1 = \alpha L_0$$
where L_0 is the length when stationary and L_1 is the observed length when in motion.

(iii) Mass increases : the mass of a moving body is greater than it is at rest. The relation is
$$M_1 = M_0 / \alpha$$
where M_0 is the mass at rest, and M_1 is the observed value of the mass if it were moving.

The last effect implies an equivalence of mass and energy, for it tells us that the kinetic energy of the body in one frame can be regarded as a mass increase in another. The well-known relationship is expressed as the law
$$\text{energy} = \text{mass} \times (\text{speed of light})^2$$
Special relativity is a universally accepted theory which has been confirmed by many physical experiments.

18. General theory of relativity
The theory of gravitation obtained by extending the concepts of special relativity to accelerating frames. It asserts that all inertial and gravitational forces are manifestations of the same phenomena. This is suggested by the fact that inertial masses (defined by Newton's laws of motion) and gravitational masses are exactly equivalent. It predicts that Newtonian gravitation theory should be very accurate when the gravitational field is weak, but that differences from Newtonian theory should become apparent when the field is strong. General relativity is the currently accepted gravitation theory, but its verification is much more limited than the special theory. This is because it differs from Newtonian theory only in a few observable situations and by very small amounts, requiring a high accuracy of observation.

Electricity and magnetism

19. Electric charge, static electricity
Many fundamental particles possess a property known as electric charge, which may be positive or negative. Similar charges give rise to a repulsive force whereas opposite charges attract each other. The total overall charge on a body is equal to the difference between positive and negative charges within it. If this is zero, the body is said to be electrically neutral. A familiar example of a charged body is a nylon article taken from a tumble drier, where friction has stripped electric charges from the clothes.

20. Electric current
Current resulting from the motion of charged particles. It takes energy to make these charges move, and this energy can be used to run electrical appliances.

21. Electric conductivity
A measure of how easily a given material will transmit an electric current. A material offering no resistance at all to the passage of electricity is termed a superconductor.

22. Electric field
The field which specifies at each point in space the electric force that would be experienced by a test charge at that point.

23. Magnetism, permanent magnet
Magnetism results when an electric charge moves relative to an observer. Magnetism may be caused by, for example, motion relative to a charge, or from charges themselves moving, as in a current loop or solenoid. The most familiar example of magnetism is that of a permanent magnet, which occurs when the atoms of a material such as iron are aligned. Each atom possesses a magnetic moment, that is, it acts like an individual miniature magnet, essentially because of the presence of spinning charges. When they are aligned, the individual magnetic moments add together to produce a macroscopic magnet.

24. Induced magnetism
Magnetism may be induced in a material such as iron by subjecting it to a strong magnetic field.

25. Lenz's law
Law stating that the force produced as a result of moving a current loop in a magnetic field acts in such a

way as to reduce the motion that produces the force. The simple principle contained in this common-sense law applies to many other situations in physics.

26. *Dynamo*
A mechanism which converts electrical energy into mechanical energy or vice versa.

Waves and wave motion

27. *Oscillation*
A phenomenon which repeats itself over and over again at exactly regular intervals.

28. *Frequency, period*
The frequency of an oscillation is the number of times it repeats itself in a unit time. The period of an oscillation is the time taken for the phenomenon to repeat itself. The period is thus the inverse of the frequency.

29. *Amplitude*
The amplitude of an oscillation is a measure of the maximum amount of change of the regularly varying quantity.

30. *Wave*
A collective phenomenon comprising a continuous spatial array of oscillations (the carriers of the wave) which are everywhere co-ordinated in their motion. This produces an overall wave pattern which changes with time, but repeats itself at the regular intervals characterized by the carrier oscillations.

31. *Node*
The nodes of a wave are the positions at which the amplitudes of the carrier oscillations are zero.

32. *Wavelength*
The wavelength of a wave pattern is the minimum distance in space after which the pattern is repeated.

33. *Phase*
The phase of a wave at a given position in space-time is a measure of how far along its cycle it has gone at that particular point. Phase is generally expressed as an angle with the full pattern occupying $360°$ or 2π radians. Two waves are said to be in phase if their patterns coincide with each other.

34. *Progressive wave, standing wave*
A progressive wave is one in which the overall wave pattern appears to move through space. A standing wave is one in which the positions of the nodes are fixed, and hence the overall wave pattern does not appear to move but merely changes its shape regularly at the same place.

35. *Wave velocity*
The velocity with which the wave pattern moves through space. (Note, however, that it is only the pattern which moves; the carrier oscillations remain fixed in position.) The wave velocity is related to the wavelength and the frequency by the relation

wave velocity = wavelength × frequency

36. *Beats*
Beats occur when waves of similar type but differing frequencies are added together. At certain regular intervals, determined by the values of the differing frequencies, the amplitudes of the component waves add together producing a noticeable peak in the amplitude.

37. *Wave packet*
A generalized kind of beat that occurs when a large number of component waves of different frequencies are added together. The wave packet will be isolated if the number of component waves and frequencies is infinite.

38. *Group velocity*
The velocity at which the beats or wave packets move through space. It is determined by the values of the component frequencies taken together, and is different from the wave velocities of the underlying component waves.

Atoms and nuclei

39. *Fundamental particles*
The simplest kinds of matter known to science, in the sense that they are not themselves composed of more basic particles. They are characterized by certain fundamental properties such as mass, spin, charge, and magnetic moment. It is likely that scientists know all the lower-energy particles, but high-energy particle accelerators continually add to the catalogue of fundamental particles at higher energies. Only a few of these particles are stable on long timescales. However, it is conjectured that in the extreme densities and temperatures of the very early Universe, the more massive fundamental particles existed and survived on timescales greater than the then age of the Universe, and may even have been the dominant form of material.

40. *Proton*
The most massive stable fundamental particle, and one of the major constituents of all matter. It carries a positive charge, and has a rest mass of 1.673×10^{-27} kg.

41. *Electron*
A stable fundamental particle having a negative charge of the same magnitude as the positive charge of the proton. However, it is 1836 times lighter than a proton; its mass is 9.109×10^{-31} kg. Because it is so much smaller than protons or nuclei, it is much more mobile, and this mobility is important in all electrical phenomena.

42. *Neutron*
A neutral fundamental particle, which is unstable and decays into a proton, electron and antineutrino, with a half-life of about 10.6 minutes. It has a mass of 1.675×10^{-27} kg, slightly higher than the proton. It is the other major constituent of atomic nuclei (with protons), and is held there in a stable configuration as a consequence of the strong nuclear force.

43. *Nucleon*
Nucleons are protons or neutrons, the constituents of the atomic nucleus.

44. *Neutrino*
A neutral fundamental particle, which is stable, has no mass, and travels at the speed of light. Neutrinos are a common product of nuclear reactions, and the interior of the Sun is known to be a strong source of them.

45. *Antiparticle*
Every type of fundamental particle occurs as a pair: the particle and its corresponding antiparticle. The antiparticle has the same mass, but opposite charge, spin, and so forth as its corresponding particle.

46. *Antimatter*
Material which is made up entirely of antiparticles, that is, antiprotons, antineutrinos, and anti-electrons (or positrons) etc.

47. *Annihilation*
When a particle interacts with its corresponding antiparticle, the two annihilate each other, releasing energy in the form of radiation and other particles. The amount of energy released is very large since

energy released = mass of both particles × (speed of light)^2

48. *Baryon number, lepton number*
A baryon is a fundamental particle. The known baryons are protons, neutrons, and hyperons, which are each said to have baryon number 1. Their corresponding antiparticles are antibaryons, and have baryon number −1. Non-baryons have baryon number 0. The baryon number of a system is the algebraic sum of all individual baryon numbers. Lepton and lepton number are analogous terms to the above, and apply to the fundamental particles electrons, muons and neutrinos. Their corresponding antiparticles are antileptons. There is no known process which can change the baryon number or lepton number of a system. They are therefore believed to be universally conserved quantities.

49. *Atom, element, atomic number*
An atom is the smallest unit of material which retains its chemical identity. All massive material, which includes liquids and gases, is composed of atoms. Contrary to the original atomic hypothesis, atoms can be further subdivided, but the chemical properties associated with each type of atom, or element, are then lost. All atoms are composed of the same basic building blocks, namely a nucleus of protons and neutrons, surrounded by shells of electrons. The precise number of electrons determines the chemical nature of the element. Specifically, the chemical properties are determined by the number of protons in the nucleus since this determines the number of available sites for electrons. It is the arrangement of the electrons, and the sites available for bonding, that is of principal importance in the chemistry of the element. The number of protons in the nucleus is called the atomic number, and this number ranges from 1 to 92 in nature. Elements of higher atomic number can be manufactured in the laboratory, and there is evidence that some superheavy elements may also exist naturally. Apart from these, there are only 92 naturally occurring elements. Examples are hydrogen (the lightest), carbon, nitrogen, oxygen, sulphur, iron, gold, mercury and uranium (the heaviest, apart from the possible superheavies).

50. *Isotope*
The number of protons in the nucleus of an atom determines which element it is, but for any given element, the number of neutrons may vary. Each type of atom with a particular number of neutrons is called an isotope of the element.

51. *Hydrogen, deuterium, tritium*
Hydrogen is the simplest atom, and consists of a single proton, surrounded by a single electron. It is the major

constituent of the Universe. Deuterium is an isotope of hydrogen, having both a proton and a neutron in the nucleus, surrounded by one electron. Tritium is another isotope of hydrogen, with two neutrons and a proton in the nucleus. These isotopes play an important role in the generation of energy by nuclear reactions in stars. Their relative abundance in the Universe is also of great importance in reconstructing the history of the early Universe.

52. Helium
The second simplest atom, the main isotope having two protons, two neutrons, and two electrons. It also has an isotope, helium-3, with only one neutron. Helium is the second most abundant element in the Universe. It is manufactured in stars, but most helium is believed to have been made in the early Universe.

53. Periodic table
A list of the elements and their isotopes, arranged in such a way as to display their chemical similarities. Groups of elements, occurring at regular intervals by atomic number, display similar chemical properties, due to the similar arrangement of electrons in the outer shell (which are the ones most involved in chemical bonding).

54. Molecule
Under terrestrial conditions, atoms are mostly connected by chemical bonds to form molecules. Molecules may consist of as few as two atoms, linked by a single chemical bond, as in molecular hydrogen, or of many hundreds of thousands of atoms, linked by many complicated bonds, as in the genetic molecule DNA (deoxyribonucleic acid).

55. Ion
An atom or molecule which has gained or lost one or more electrons, and hence carries a nett charge. Ions are therefore strongly influenced by electric and magnetic fields, whereas electrically neutral atoms and molecules are not. The most abundant ion in the Universe is the hydrogen ion, H^+, which is commonly referred to as HII in astrophysics.

56. Ionization, ionization potential
Ionization is the process in which an atom loses an electron to form a positive ion. It may also refer to the process which changes an atom from one ionic form to another, for example, by losing another electron. The ionization potential is the amount of energy required to remove an electron from an atom. It differs from atom to atom, and also depends on the state of the atom, and the number of electrons involved.

57. Radical
A relatively stable ion that interacts as a unit in any chemical reactions. Several kinds of radical have been observed in interstellar space, often associated with interstellar clouds.

58. Alpha particle
A fully ionized helium atom, that is, one which has lost both electrons, leaving a bare nucleus of two protons and two neutrons (^{4}He). Alpha particles are often emitted during nuclear reactions.

59. Cosmic rays
Energetic particles from space. They are usually fully-ionized atomic nuclei, the most common type

being protons or hydrogen ions, and the others being mostly from the lower mass end of the periodic table. However, higher-mass cosmic rays are also seen occasionally.

60. Binding energy
When protons and neutrons are combined in a nucleus, the mass of the nucleus is less than the mass of the individual particles combined. This mass (or energy) difference is called the binding energy of the nucleus, and is a negative quantity. The existence of (negative) binding energy is the reason why neutrons, which are unstable, do not decay when in a nucleus to form protons and electrons: there is not enough energy available to form these free particles.

61. Radioactivity, decay, decay products
A radioactive isotope is one which spontaneously decays or breaks up to form one or more new isotopes of the same or different element, with the emission of energy in some form. The new isotope(s) and the energy released are called the decay products. Radioactive decay occurs when the binding energy of the original isotope is not (negatively) large enough to stabilize the nucleus, so that when a more tightly bound nucleus of lower mass is formed, enough energy is left over to form the necessary decay products. There are restrictions as to what type of decay products may be formed, since charge, baryon number, and so on must all be conserved.

62. Nuclear fission
The break-up of an atomic nucleus into lower mass products. It may be spontaneous, as in radioactive decay, or induced by firing energetic particles, such as neutrons, at a suitable material, as in a nuclear reactor. An atomic bomb is an example of an uncontrolled fission process.

63. Nuclear fusion
The joining of two nuclei, or a nucleus and nucleon, to form a higher mass nucleus, with the release of energy. The total energy released (including the rest mass energy of any particles emitted) is equal to the difference in binding energies of the original and final nuclei. The fusion of hydrogen nuclei to form helium is the dominant source of energy in our Sun and other stars. An example of an uncontrolled fusion process on Earth is the hydrogen bomb. It is likely that the ultimate source of energy harnessed by mankind on Earth will be from a fusion process, which does not depend on the existence of some special fuel, such as oil, coal or uranium.

64. Nuclear reaction, transmutation, nucleosynthesis
A nuclear reaction is any process that changes the nature of an atomic nucleus. Transmutation is a nuclear reaction that changes an element into a different one. All elements in the Universe are believed to have been manufactured as a result of successive nuclear reactions from the simplest element, hydrogen. This process is called nucleosynthesis. Nuclear reactions only occur when very high energies or free neutrons are involved, such as in particle accelerators, the early Universe, or the centres of stars.

Heat and thermodynamics

65. Heat
A form of energy associated with the random motion of the atoms and molecules in a body.

66. States of matter, phase change
Matter may exist in several states, depending on the amount of heat it possesses, and the strength of the bonding forces between the molecules. When matter passes from one state to another, a dramatic change occurs in the properties of the matter. This is called a phase change. The four states are solid, liquid, gas and plasma.

67. Solid
In the solid state, matter exhibits both a definite shape and volume. The bonding forces between the molecules are strong enough for the body to offer resistance against attempts to deform it.

68. Liquid hydrodynamics
Liquids have a fixed volume, but under the influence of gravity a liquid takes the shape of the containing vessel. The bonding forces between the molecules are strong enough for the molecules to prefer to stay together, but not strong enough to preserve any definite shape. As a consequence of this, a liquid will flow under the influence of forces. The science of liquid flows is called hydrodynamics.

69. Gas, gas dynamics
Gases have neither fixed shapes nor a definite volume. A gas fills up the volume in which it is contained. The bonding forces are smaller than the individual kinetic energies of the particles. As a result, the particles try to move apart as far as their energies or the containing vessel permit. The science of gas flows is called gas dynamics.

70. Plasma
A plasma is a state of matter in which the material is so hot that not only have the individual molecules escaped from their bonding forces, but even the electrons of the molecules have escaped. This means that the gas has become ionized. Sometimes, depending on the material and the energy of the particles, the molecules themselves break up. An ionized gas is strongly influenced by electric and magnetic forces, since the individual molecules are no longer electrically neutral. For this reason, a plasma behaves quite differently from a gas. However, the change from an un-ionized gas to an ionized one, or plasma, is not strictly a phase change.

71. Fluid dynamics
The science of fluid flows. It generally embraces both liquid and gas flow.

72. Pressure
The motion of energetic particles against the walls of their containing vessel exerts a force against the vessel walls. This force, averaged over the surface area, is called a pressure.

73. Thermodynamics
The study of the behaviour of matter under the influence of heat energy.

74. Thermodynamic equilibrium
State of a body when all its atoms or molecules have a statistically equal share of the available heat energy. If

the energy is not equally shared, the body is in a non-equilibrium state. Non-equilibrium states are unstable; that is, a body will attempt to reach thermodynamic equilibrium if it can.

75. The laws of thermodynamics
Laws observed to apply to the thermodynamic behaviour of all systems in nature. They may be summarized as follows:
Zeroeth law: when any two systems are in equilibrium with a third, they are in equilibrium with each other.
First law: in any closed system, the total amount of energy of all kinds (including mass) is a constant.
Second law: there can be no net flow of heat energy from a colder system to a hotter system without the help of an external agency.
Third law: absolute zero temperature can never be reached.

76. Temperature
A measure of the degree of hotness of a body. It measures the heat energy possessed by the body. For this reason, the body as a whole only has a definable temperature if all the atoms in the body have on average, the same amount of heat. It is possible to define certain specialized types of temperature appropriate to a particular property of the body (rather than to the body as a whole). In that case, the specialized temperature can be defined only if there is an equal sharing of available energy associated with that particular property (for example, the configuration of electron states in the atoms).

77. Entropy, reversible processes
Entropy is a quantity which is characteristic of the thermodynamic state of a system. It can be regarded as a measure of the amount of disorder in the system. In any closed system, changes of state cause an overall increase in the total entropy. However, for some processes, the increase is small enough to be ignored. Such processes are called reversible.

78. Conduction
A method of heat transfer in which heat energy is transferred through the material by the direct contact of 'hotter' molecules with their 'cooler' neighbours. There is no bulk movement of the material as a whole.

79. Convection
A method of heat transfer in which heat energy is transferred from one region to another by the bulk motion of hotter material into a cooler region. This is a more efficient means of heat transfer than conduction, and occurs in material which can move freely, such as liquids and gases.

80. Radiation
The third common method of heat loss in which energy is emitted in the form of electromagnetic waves. The heat energy in the material excites the electrons in the atoms to a more energetic state, and the electrons then return to a lower energy state by emitting a photon. The heat energy used to excite the electrons is thus lost from the system, provided the photon is not re-absorbed.

81. Opacity
A measure of the fraction of radiation that is absorbed by a body from an incident beam of radiation. It

depends on the density of the material through which the radiation has to pass, the nature of the material, and the frequency of the radiation.

82. Black body, albedo
A black body is a body which is a perfect absorber and emitter of electromagnetic radiation. In practice, all bodies reflect or scatter a certain amount of incident radiation. The fraction of scattered radiation is called the albedo of the body.

83. Black-body radiation
Electromagnetic radiation which is in thermal equilibrium at a particular temperature. It is the radiation which would be emitted by a black body at that temperature.

84. Planck spectrum, Planck curves
The well-defined energy spectrum exhibited by black-body radiation. Planck curves are the set of spectra applicable over a range of temperatures.

85. Planck constant
The universal constant appearing in Planck's formula for the black-body radiation spectrum, which is found to relate the energy of a photon to its frequency.
$$\text{Energy} = \text{Planck constant} \times \text{frequency}$$
Its value is 6.6262×10^{-34} joule seconds.

86. Stefan-Boltzmann law
Law stating that when the temperature of a black body increases, the power radiated increases as the fourth power of the temperature.

87. Colour temperature, UBV bands
As the temperature of a black body is increased, its apparent colour changes. The temperature derived by measuring the colour of an object is called the colour temperature. For a non-perfect emitter, this may differ slightly from temperatures defined by other means. The human eye perceives colour by measuring the relative intensities of the light in the three wavebands corresponding to the three pigments of the eye. Astronomers find it useful to use three wavebands designated U, B and V (ultraviolet, blue and visual) to attribute a colour to an object in a similar fashion.

88. Scattering
Process in which a particle or photon suffers a change in direction due to collision with another particle or photon.

89. Random walk
Name given to the process in which a particle suffers repeated scattering, each resulting in a random change of direction.

90. Mean free path
The average distance travelled by a particle between successive random scatterings. It depends on the density of the medium and the cross section of the scattering particles.

91. Diffusion
Process in which particles migrate through a medium by the successive random scattering of themselves off other particles in the medium. Diffusion therefore causes one type of gas to become mixed with another, or hotter particles to mix with cooler ones. It is to be distinguished from conduction, in which there is no general movement of the particles, although conduction may be regarded as the diffusion of heat energy itself.

Fluid dynamics

92. Equation of state
An equation of state relates the general properties of a fluid to each other. The usual properties related are pressure, volume, temperature, and density, and the equation shows how these will alter in relation to each other.

93. Gas laws, ideal gas
Gas laws are the common equations of state relating the basic properties of an ideal gas. By a circular argument, an ideal gas is one which satisfies these laws. Real gases satisfy the laws closely, over a reasonable range of values of the parameters. The three most familiar gas laws are Boyle's law, Charles' law and the universal gas law.
Boyle's law states that for an ideal gas at a fixed temperature, the pressure P times the volume V is a constant
$$PV = \text{constant}$$
Charles' law states that for an ideal gas at a fixed pressure, the volume V divided by the temperature T is a constant
$$V/T = \text{constant}$$
The universal gas law combines these two results into a single law
$$PV = RT$$
where R is the universal gas constant for one mole of gas, and is equal to
$$8.3143 \text{ joule deg}^{-1} \text{ mole}^{-1}$$

94. Sound wave
A wave that propagates in a fluid by the collective collisions of the fluid particles against each other. It is a longitudinal wave; the fluid particles vibrate in the same direction as the wave. Sound waves cannot travel in a vacuum.

95. Sound speed
The speed at which a sound wave travels in a fluid. It depends on the density of the fluid as well as on the type of fluid.

96. Supersonic speed
Speed that is faster than the sound speed in a given fluid. Since normal disturbances in a fluid are propagated at the speed of sound, a fluid has no way of transmitting advance warning of a particle travelling supersonically.

97. Shock wave
A wave that is characterized by a discontinuity in the state of a fluid (for example, its pressure, density and temperature). It occurs when disturbances in the fluid cannot be dispersed fast enough, and bank up in a shock, as for example, when a disturbing object travels supersonically.

98. Pressure wave
A wave in a fluid carried by oscillations in the fluid pressure at each point along the wave. An example of a pressure wave is a sound wave.

99. Viscosity
The measure of a fluid's resistance to flow.

100. Laminar flow
A fluid flow characterized by the smooth orderly motion of the fluid material, with no macroscopic mixing between adjacent layers.

101. Turbulence

A state in which the agitating forces in a fluid exceed the damping effects of the fluid viscosity. Macroscopic mixing occurs throughout the fluid over a wide range of scales, known as the turbulent scale.

102. Dissipation

The process by which the energy contained in the fluid motion is lost from the system, or converted to another form. A common form of dissipation is due to viscous drag.

103. Magnetohydrodynamics

The science of the flow of fluid that is electronically conductive. A common example in astrophysics is the study of plasma flows.

Light

104. Nature of light, photon

Light is an electromagnetic wave, that is, a wave whose carrier oscillations are fluctuations in the value of the electric and magnetic field strengths at each point along the path of the light ray. These carrier oscillations are perpendicular to the direction of travel of the wave, and hence light is an example of a transverse wave (sound waves are longitudinal waves). The fields themselves possess energy, and a change in the field strength is associated with a transfer of energy; so the progressively changing values of the electric and magnetic fields along the wave are associated with the transport of energy by the light ray. When a light ray interacts with matter, energy is absorbed from the ray in finite bundles or quanta, which are best described in terms of wave packets. These quanta of light are called photons. Since photons can be thought of as particles of light, light is regarded as having a dual nature – particles or waves.

105. Intensity

The intensity of the light is a measure of the rate of energy transfer, and depends on the amplitude of the carrier oscillations. The higher the intensity and the larger the amplitudes, the greater the amount of energy carried per unit time.

106. Colour, monochromatic colour

The appearance of colour in objects is the result of the response of our eyes to light rays of different frequencies. White light contains a uniform mixture of all colours. Pure colours are termed monochromatic, and have the defining property that only one frequency of light wave is present. Most colours we see around us are not monochromatic, but mixtures of many frequencies which the eye combines to give a great variety of different hues and shades.

107. Encounters with matter

When a light ray encounters any material, it is either absorbed, reflected or transmitted. In fact, any given material will do all of these, but in differing amounts.

108. Absorption

Absorption occurs when the light is actually captured or absorbed by the material. The material therefore gains energy, and generally heats up as a result. This energy may subsequently be re-radiated. A dull black object is an example of an absorbing material. It is black because it absorbs light at all frequencies. A red object absorbs light at all frequencies except at red, where some is reflected. That is why it looks red.

109. Reflection

Reflection occurs when the light ray bounces back, like a rubber ball against a wall. The angle at which it strikes the surface is equal to the angle at which it is returned.

110. Transmission, refraction

Transmission is the passage of light through a material. In doing so, the direction of travel may be changed, and this phenomenon is called refraction. The amount of change in direction is measured by the refractive index of the material.

111. Focus, mirror, lens

The reflecting and refracting properties of materials make it possible to focus light rays by the use of optical instruments such as telescopes. When a collection of light rays are focused, the directions of the rays are changed in such a way as to make them all meet at some particular point, called the focus. This may be done by using either the reflecting properties of a mirror or the refracting properties of a lens. A lens consists of refractive material such as glass, shaped in such a way as to produce a well-defined focus. A familiar example of a lens is a magnifying glass. The earliest telescopes were all made with lenses. However, most modern telescopes use a focusing mirror.

112. Dispersion

Dispersion occurs when the refractive index of a material depends on the frequency of the light. When white light is transmitted by such a material, the violet rays are bent more than the red ones. This disperses the colours into the familiar spectrum. A rainbow is a natural example of this effect.

113. Interference

Interference occurs as a result of the combination of two or more waves of differing phases or frequencies. It may be constructive as in beats, when amplitudes add together, or destructive, when amplitudes cancel. The outcome of interference is a change in the observed wave pattern, producing alternate regions of enhanced and reduced intensity.

114. Diffraction

A special case of interference that occurs when an initially coherent wave train becomes out of phase with itself. This may occur for example on a diffraction grating, which reflects or transmits light in such a way that neighbouring waves have travelled slightly different distances, and hence got out of phase with each other.

115. Polarization

Normally, the carrier oscillations of an electromagnetic wave oscillate freely, in any direction in the plane perpendicular to the direction of the wave. If, for some reason, these carrier oscillations are restricted to move along only one axis of the perpendicular plane, the resultant wave is said to be plane polarized. Circular polarization occurs when two perpendicularly polarized waves are combined with a phase difference of $90°$. If the phase differs from $90°$, the result is elliptical polarization. Some materials only transmit light which is polarized in a specific direction. Such a material will reduce the intensity of the transmitted light by eliminating those components of the carrier oscillations which are not aligned to the given direction. An example of this effect is found in certain types of sunglasses.

116. Doppler shift

The change in the observed frequency of a wave as a result of the relative motion of the source and the observer. If, for example, a source emits a wave train at a given frequency ω, that is, it emits ω wave patterns per unit time, and the observer is moving towards the source, then the observer will encounter the wave patterns at a rate faster than ω per unit time because of his motion towards them. Thus relative motion towards the observer produces an increase in frequency, and motion away from the observer produces a decrease in frequency. In the case of light, this implies that the light becomes bluer for motion towards, and redder for motion away. Doppler shift measurements of light spectra are an extremely important tool in astrophysics. They enable us to measure the radial velocities of distant objects with high accuracy. The redshifts of distant galaxies are interpreted as Doppler shifts due to the motions of the galaxies away from us, which implies that the Universe is expanding.

Electromagnetic phenomena

117. Electromagnetic spectrum

Electromagnetic waves (see 104) exist with an infinite range of different frequencies or wavelengths. The entire range is called the electromagnetic spectrum. The velocity of all electromagnetic waves is a universal constant, (designated c, with a value of $299792.5 \, \mathrm{km \, s^{-1}}$). Thus the frequency and the wavelength of the radiation are always related by the equation

$$\text{frequency} \times \text{wavelength} = c$$

Light is just one small part of this range, and is characterized by wavelengths of between $4 \times 10^{-7} \mathrm{m}$ (for violet light) and $7 \times 10^{-7} \mathrm{m}$ (for red light).

118. Radio waves

Radio waves form part of the electromagnetic spectrum. There are several kinds. Long radio waves have wavelengths exceeding $300 \, \mathrm{m}$ in length. Medium radio waves have wavelengths around $100 \, \mathrm{m}$ and short wave radio and UHF (ultra high-frequency) waves have wavelengths between $100 \, \mathrm{m}$ and about $1 \, \mathrm{m}$. Radio waves in most of these wavebands can be received by the usual radio receivers on sale everywhere.

119. Microwave radiation

The Universe as a whole emits electromagnetic waves between $0.1 \, \mathrm{mm}$ and $2 \, \mathrm{cms}$, with a peak at about $1 \, \mathrm{mm}$. This is the microwave background radiation of the Universe and indicates that the Universe has a black-body temperature of $2.7 \, \mathrm{K}$.

120. X-rays

X-rays are in the high-energy part of the electromagnetic spectrum, with wavelengths between $10 \, \mathrm{nm}$ (soft X-rays) and $0.01 \, \mathrm{nm}$ (hard X-rays). Since the energy of the X-rays is universally proportional to the wavelength (see 85 and 117), it follows that X-rays are far more energetic than light photons. This is why they can penetrate materials so easily.

121. Gamma rays, pair production

Gamma rays (γ-rays) are the most energetic type of electromagnetic radiation, with wavelengths less than 10^{-4} nm. They are so energetic that their energy is more than the rest mass energy of electrons and positrons, and for this reason a γ-ray will often pair-produce, that is, spontaneously turn into an electron-positron, pair (thus conserving the necessary quantum properties). Gamma rays are also detected from space in small numbers. Although it is possible in principle for the wavelengths of γ-rays to be arbitarily small, this is in fact not observed since the probability of pair-production becomes very nearly unity as energy increases.

122. Emission, absorption, energy levels

Electromagnetic radiation may be emitted or absorbed by an atom (or molecule) when the energetic arrangement of the electrons in the atom changes. Each electron in the atom is associated with a specific energy, and there is only a discrete set of energies that electrons can have. These are called the electron energy levels of the atom. When an electron changes from a higher energy level to a lower one, it loses energy, and a photon is emitted. Conversely, a photon is absorbed by an electron moving to a higher energy level. The frequency of the radiation depends on the energy difference of the two levels, since

energy = Planck's constant × frequency

123. Emission line, absorption line

When the spectrum of an object (such as a star) is observed, the different colours or frequencies of the radiation received are spread out in a band. Thus one particular frequency is observed as a line in the band. An emission line is a line which appears brighter than the surrounding radiation, and is caused by the object's preferential emission of radiation at that frequency. This is caused by there being many atoms of a particular type whose electrons are making a specific transition from one energy level down to another. An absorption line is a line which appears darker than the neighbouring radiation and is caused by the preferential absorption of radiation in an analogous way.

124. Forbidden transition

The probability that an electron will change from one given state to another depends on the quantum numbers associated with the states, since certain atomic quantities must be conserved. For some changes, it is impossible to conserve the necessary parameters without invoking an improbable process. This significantly reduces the probability of the change, or transition, taking place. Such a change is then called a forbidden transition. Forbidden transitions are frequently observed in nebulae, excited galaxies, and so forth, where the physical conditions are quite different from those normally found on Earth, and favour the occurrence of such transitions.

125. Fluorescence

The emission of radiation which is characteristic of a given substance as a result of exciting that substance energetically. If the radiation is in the form of light, it is called optical fluorescence. Another form at higher energies is X-ray fluorescence.

126. Hyperfine transition

The energy associated with a given electron depends not only on its basic energy state but also on other factors. One such factor is its spin, and an electron may change its energy slightly by shifting, relative to the nucleus, from one spin direction to another. Such a change is called a hyperfine transition. In a hydrogen atom the energy associated with the hyperfine transition in the lowest energy state corresponds to a wavelength of 21 cm.

127. Zeeman splitting

Another factor that affects the energy states of the electrons is their orientation with respect to an external magnetic field. For a given transition this leads to a number of small differences in the frequency of an emitted photon, in the presence of a magnetic field. These differences are called Zeeman splitting and are seen in a number of astrophysical objects, such as some bright stars, white dwarfs and so on. The effect is important because it enables scientists to estimate the strength of the magnetic field in the neighbourhood of the emitting material.

128. Recombination lines

The basic electron energy levels in an atom are determined only by the atomic number. Moreover, there is only a discrete set of energy levels for each element, and hence a discrete set of transitions that an electron can make between them. Thus the radiation emitted by any given element as a result of any of these transitions consists of photons having a discrete set of frequencies. The total spectrum emitted is therefore a set of lines called the recombination lines of the element. Such sets of lines are detected from many astrophysical objects, and at many frequencies. They enable astronomers to estimate the physical conditions existing at the object, as well as the abundances of the elements present.

129. Lyman, Balmer, and Paschen series

The frequencies of many of the lines in an element are often simply related, depending on the nature of the transitions. Thus in a hydrogen atom, the set of all photon frequencies that may be emitted by an electron dropping to the lowest energy level from higher levels in the atom is called the Lyman series. The set emitted by an electron falling to the second lowest energy level is called the Balmer series, to the third lowest energy level, the Paschen series, and so on. The most familiar of these is the Balmer series, since the frequencies of the emitted photon fall in the optical part of the spectrum.

130. Lyman-α

Lyman-α is the name given to photons of the first (lowest) energy level associated with the Lyman series; which is 121.6 nm. Since the Lyman series is the one relating to transitions involving the lowest energy level (or ground state) of the hydrogen atom, it follows that it requires a photon of greater energy than Lyman-α to excite a hydrogen atom out of its ground state, thus when electromagnetic radiation of all frequencies passes through a cloud of neutral hydrogen in its ground state much of the radiation more energetic than Lyman-α will be absorbed, while none below will be.

131. Synchrotron radiation

When a charged particle, such as an electron, travelling at a relativistic velocity, encounters a magnetic field, the magnetic field causes the particle to gyrate (that is accelerate) and hence to emit radiation. This radiation is called synchrotron radiation, and is always polarized on emission. Synchrotron radiation is the usual radiation detected from radio galaxies, but it is thought that optical and even X-ray synchrotron radiation has been detected from highly excited objects such as X-ray stars.

132. Bremsstrahlung

When a moving electric charge decelerates, it loses energy by the emission of radiation. The general name for this radiation is bremsstrahlung. The word is also applied to the radiation emitted by an accelerating charge. It is usually used to refer to radiation emitted from a cloud of moving charges deflecting off each other, and is found in most astrophysical situations where hot gas is present, such as H^+ regions.

133. Thomson scattering

The scattering of incident photons by electrons (or other charged particles) when the energy of the photons is small compared to the rest mass energy of the electron. In this situation there is comparatively little exchange of energy.

134. Compton effect, inverse Compton effect

The Compton effect is the gain of energy by electrons as a result of scattering with photons of very high energy. In this case the energy exchange is significant. The inverse Compton effect is the gain of energy by photons as a result of scattering with electrons of much higher energy.

135. Faraday rotation

The phenomenon in which the plane of polarization of a polarized beam of radiation is rotated as a result of the electrical and magnetic properties of the medium through which the beam is passing. It can be used in astrophysics to determine the nature of interstellar space when a distant source emits polarized radiation. astrophysics to determine the nature of the interstellar medium when a distant source emits polarized radiation.

136. Cerenkov radiation

Electromagnetic radiation caused by a shock wave that arises when a charged particle (eg an electron) passes through a transparent medium at a velocity greater than the velocity of light in that medium.

Index

Page numbers in *italics* refer to illustrations.
Page numbers in **bold type** refer to places in the text where the entry concerned is printed in SMALL CAPITALS, indicating a major description or explanation.